Albania
Australia

Austria Austria
Vienna

Bali, Java and Lombok
Belgium and Luxembourg
Bulgaria

Czech & Slovak Czech & Slovak Republics
Republics Prague

China
Cyprus
Denmark
Egypt

France France
Paris and Versailles
Burgundy
Loire Valley
Midi-Pyrénées
Normandy
Provence
South West France
Corsica

Germany Berlin and eastern Germany

Greece Greece
Athens and environs
Crete
Rhodes and the
    Dodecanese

Hungary Hungary
Budapest

Southern India
Ireland

Italy Northern Italy
Southern Italy
Florence
Rome

Venice
Tuscany
Umbria
Sicily

Jordan
Malaysia and Singapore
Malta and Gozo
Mexico
Morocco

Netherlands Netherlands
Amsterdam

Poland
Portugal

Spain Spain
Barcelona
Madrid

Sweden
Switzerland
Thailand
Tunisia

Turkey Turkey
Istanbul

UK England
Scotland
Wales
Channel Islands
London
Oxford and Cambridge
Country Houses of
    England

USA New York
Museums and Galleries of
    New York
Boston and Cambridge

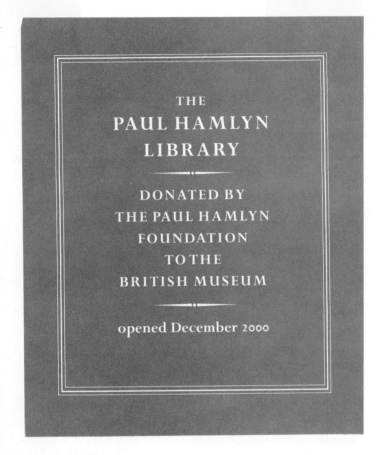

We have done our very best to ensure that this guide is up-to-date and error free. However, things do change between editions. We should be delighted to hear from any of our readers who have comments, suggestions and corrections for the next edition of the Blue Guide. Writers of the most helpful letters will be awarded a free Blue Guide of their choice.

Australia

Erika Esau and George Boeck

BLUE GUIDE

A&C Black • London
WW Norton • New York

1st edition © Erika Esau and George Boeck, September 1999
Published by A & C Black (Publishers) Limited
35 Bedford Row, London WC1R 4JH

Maps and plans ©A &C Black drawn by Robert Smith. Maps of Sydney ferry routes, train network and Melbourne tram system drawn with permission of the transport authorities.

A CIP catalogue record of this book is available from the British Library.

'Blue Guides' is a registered trademark.

ISBN 0–7136–3846–X

Published in the United States of America by
WW Norton and Company, Inc
500 Fifth Avenue, New York, NY 10110

Published simultaneously in Canada by
Penguin Books Canada Limited
10 Alcorn Avenue, Toronto,
Ontario M4V 3B2

ISBN 0–393–31947–4 USA

The authors and the publishers have done their best to ensure the accuracy of all the information in *Blue Guide Australia*; however, they can accept no responsibility for any loss, injury or inconvenience sustained by any traveller as a result of information or advice contained in the guide.

Cover photographs of the Sydney Opera House and the Olgas by Peter Wilson.

Erika Esau was born and raised in California. In 1985 she received a PhD in Art History from Bryn Mawr College, Pennsylvania. In 1990 she was appointed Lecturer in Art History at the Australian National University, Canberra, Australia. She is now an Australian citizen and her most recent publications have focused on the history of Australian photography.

George Boeck grew up in Iowa and Colorado. He first studied Anthropology and English. In 1983 he was awarded a Ph.D in Folklore and Folklife from the University of Pennsylvania, Philadelphia. Since arriving in Australia in 1990, he has worked on ethnographic projects for the National Gallery of Australia and the Australian National University, and in the Research Section of the Australian Institute of Aboriginal and Torres Strait Islander Studies in Canberra.

Printed and bound in Great Britain by Butler and Tanner, Frome and London.

Contents

Maps and plans

Introduction

'A land of contrasts' is a standard phrase that is particularly appropriate when talking about the continent called Australia: it is the world's oldest landmass, but the youngest Western nation; it is inhabited by the world's oldest continuous culture, the Aboriginal culture, alongside a European-based society barely 200 years old. Antipodean nature is famously reversed: trees that shed their bark, but not their leaves; black swans; even mammals that lay eggs. The landscape is for vast expanses unrelievedly harsh and uninhabitable, while the relatively meagre population—fewer people than the state of New York in a land the size of the United States—live in overwhelmingly benign climates along the coasts of the country. The Great Red Centre of Australia is as far removed from the realities of urban Sydney life as it would be if it were on another continent altogether—and yet, the centre's pervasive presence has forged much of what can be called Australianness. Understandably, these contrasts have produced a fascinating culture and people, more complex than usually admitted in tourist brochures.

For the purposes of the Blue Guide, we have tried to illuminate this culture and this land for the visitor interested in more than theme parks and trips to the beach (although the latter is one of the greatest Australian experiences, not to be missed!). We have concentrated most intensely on the Australian cities and Australian material culture, although we have also elected to examine some of the most important aspects of Australia's natural landscape and its famous wonders, as well as some observations about Aboriginal indigenous culture. We have indeed been selective, emphasising what we imagine Blue Guide readers would want to see and know; we fully recognise that we have left out many worthwhile places and even regions, limited as we were by constraints on the book's length. We hope that we have done as comprehensive a job as we could on those regions and places we have covered. We welcome, of course, all suggestions and outcries concerning omissions; we will be most grateful for readers' advice and corrections, and hope we can incorporate as many as possible into a second edition.

Australia changes constantly, an admirable quality and something that we, as New Australians, love about the place; but it leads to predictable errors in all 'time-bound' information when writing a tour guide such as this one! By all means let us know about your experience of Australia, what you found useful and what else you think should be included in such a Blue Guide; we really look forward to hearing from you.

Practical information

 ## Planning your trip

When to go

As an island continent, Australia has a great diversity in climate and geographical variation; but its status as one of the world's oldest landmasses means that there have been no major seismic upheavals for millions of years, making the land relatively flat and the driest continent outside Antarctica. Extremes in temperature run towards the hot end of the scale. Although snow occurs in the mountainous regions, even Tasmania, at the same latitude in the south as New York City in the north, escapes extended periods of frigid weather, while the enormous interior regions experience some of the hottest and driest conditions on earth; all of the major cities can reach temperatures over 40°C in the summer (although rarely in Hobart in Tasmania). While the desert areas will be fiercely hot during the day, at night temperatures can be bitterly cold. Canberra and the nearby Snowy Mountains, New England's upper plateaus, and parts of Tasmania are the only areas that have four weather seasons as visitors from the Northern Hemisphere understand them. The real distinctions, especially in the tropical north, involve rainfall: the northern 'Top End' defines climate as 'The Wet', running from December to March with monsoonal downfalls, and 'The Dry', from May to October when very little rainfall occurs. If you enjoy humidity, go to Queensland and the most northern regions of the country at any time of the year.

Sydney prides itself on its moderate climate, although summers can often be quite rainy; Melbourne, on the other hand, is famous for its changeable but wet weather, although summers can at times be quite hot (as anyone who watches the Australian Open Tennis Tournament in January can attest). The water temperature at beaches in southern New South Wales, Victoria and Tasmania are always bracing and in some places downright frigid.

Overall, the best times to visit Australia are April and September, when most regions will be comfortably warm and clear. The important thing to remember is that the seasons are reversed in the southern hemisphere: Christmas time is at the height of summer, and July is the middle of winter.

Tourist information

As a country increasingly geared towards tourism, Australia's tourist offices will provide the overseas visitor with vast quantities of travel information of all sorts, and the local tourist boards in every city will positively inundate the visitor with local information, including excellent free regional and city maps. Cultural and historical information as provided in this guide is more difficult to find through tourist agencies.

The main offices of the **Australian Tourist Commission** overseas are:
- **United Kingdom**, Gemini House, 10–18 Putney Hill, Putney, London SW15 6AA, ☎ 081 780 2227, toll free 0990 022 000.
- **USA**, 31st Floor, 489 Fifth Avenue, New York, NY 10017, ☎ 212 687 6300,

and Suite 1200, 2121 Avenue of the Stars, Los Angeles, CA 90067;
☎ 310 552 1988, toll free 1 800 433 2877.

• **New Zealand**, Australia Information Centre, Shop 7, Ground Floor, National Bank Centre, Elliot and Victoria Streets (PO Box 1365), Auckland 1,
☎ 09 302 7721.

• **Singapore**, Suite 1703, United Square, 101 Thomson Road, Singapore1130,
☎ 255 4555.

• **Germany**, Neue Mainzerstrasse 22, D6000 Frankfurt/Main 1,
☎ 069 274 00 60.

• **Canadian** travellers should contact the Los Angeles office for information; other European countries contact the London office.

Individual **tourist offices for Australian states** can also be contacted in London:

• **New South Wales**, Tourism Commission, 75 King William St, London EC4N 7HA, ☎ 071 283 2124.

• **Queensland**, Tourist and Travel Corporation, Queensland House, 392/3 Strand, London WC2R 0LZ, ☎ 071 836 7142.

• **Tourism South Australia**, South Australia House, 50 Strand, London WC2N 5LW, ☎ 071 930 7471.

• **Western Australian Tourist Commission**, Western Australia House, 115 Strand, London WC2R 0AJ, ☎ 071 240 2881.

• **Victoria, Tasmania** and **Northern Territory** have regional representatives through the Australian Tourist Commission offices.

Phone numbers and web site addresses for the tourist commissions of the states and territories follow.
Two websites of a general nature are at http://www.austravel.com.au and http://www.aussie.net.au.

• **New South Wales** ☎ 132 077, 02 9331 1111, internet site:
http://www.tourism.nsw.com.au

• **Queensland** ☎ 131 801, 02 6200 1900, internet site:
http://www.qttc.com.au

• **Victoria** ☎ 132 842, no international telephone, internet site:
http://www.tourism.vic.com.au

• **South Australia** ☎ 1300 366 770, 08 8303 0233, internet site:
http://www.tourism.sa.com.au

• **Western Australia** ☎ 1300 361 351, 08 8948 3111, internet site:
http://www.tourism.wa.gov.au

• **Northern Territory** ☎ 08 8999 5184, internet site:
http://www.nttc.com.au

• **Australian Capital Territory** ☎ 02 6205 0666, internet site:
http://www.tourism.act.com.au or http://basil.acr.net.au/tourism.html

Disabled travellers

With the lead-up to the 2000 Olympic and Paralympic Games, Australian tourism services and businesses have become even more aware of the needs of the disabled in terms of access to buildings and other requirements. The 1992 Disability Discrimination Act ensures equal rights to all people with disabilities, and the Building Code of Australia requires that all new hotels and motels incorporate a certain number of rooms which are accessible to those in wheelchairs and with other special requirements. Some legislation is in place to ensure such services, although national laws are not yet enacted, and not all facilities will be equally provided. Most established venues in Australian cities, such as museums, art galleries, and restaurants, and most tourist resorts provide conscientious services for those with special needs, including toilet facilities and accessible lifts.

NICAN, an Australia-wide information service on sport, recreation and tourism for the disabled, has a database on accessible accommodation and tourist attractions around the country; ☎ 1800 806 769/02 6285 3713, fax 02 6285 3714, website: http//www.nican.com.au.

 # The formalities

Visas

Until recently, anyone visiting Australia (except New Zealanders, who are exempt from visa requirements, and need only a valid passport to enter the country) had to apply for a visa through the Australian consulates. Now visas for stays shorter than three months are lodged electronically by the airline or travel agent from whom you purchase a ticket. These short term ETA visas are free and require simply a passport as documentation.

Visas for longer visits must be lodged by post at a consulate and require banking records to demonstrate that the traveller has sufficient funds for their visit, currently about $1000 per month's stay. There is a small application fee for these visas; extensions of visas applied for in Australia, on the other hand, will cost as much as $200. Working holiday visas are available for up to a year for young (18–26 or 26–30 years old), single citizens of the UK, Ireland, the Netherlands, Canada, Malta, Korea and Japan. Other countries' citizens may also apply under more restrictive conditions. Working holiday visas allow young visitors to work at temporary or casual jobs such as fruit-picking or on cattle stations.

Customs

Australia has stringent customs regulations regarding animal products, plants, and many other agricultural items, as well as firearms and prohibited goods such as drugs and poisons. All of these regulations should be explained at the time you purchase a ticket, and will certainly be explained before landing (briefly, you are allowed 1 litre of alcohol, 250 cigarettes and dutiable goods up to $400). Bins for disposal of prohibited items appear the minute you arrive at the airport, and customs dogs will sniff out any forgotten bits of fruit or other vegetative matter; Australian Customs is rightfully proud of the abilities of their sniffer dogs. Be sure to pay attention to restrictions; any goods in violation will be confiscated and if a serious violation, you may be denied entry or be arrested. Do not even consider breaching the regulations with prohibited goods.

Currency

Australian currency is the Australian dollar, divided into 100 cents. Currently, the Australian dollar is worth approximately £0.47 or US$0.75, although this amount can fluctuate significantly. Bank notes are in $100, $50, $20, $10 and $5 denominations. Some money made out of real paper still circulates, but new notes are made of 'forgery-proof' plastic with hologram inserts; they are supposedly more secure, but they look and feel like play money and easily fly out of pockets.

Coins are widely used, including $2 (the smallest but thickest 'gold' coin), $1, 50 cents (largest 'silver' coin), 20, 10 and 5 cents. 1- and 2-cent coins were withdrawn from circulation in 1995; in shops, prices are rounded off to the nearest 5 cents.

Figures commemorated on the most recently released currency are:

• **$5: Queen Elizabeth**, a very controversial choice at this stage, when moves toward a Republic are afoot

• **$10: A B 'Banjo' Paterson** (1864–1941), author of 'Waltzing Matilda' and *The Man from Snowy River*, verso Mary Gilmore (1864–1962), Australian poet and activist, known for her verses on themes of love and courage

• **$20: Mary Reibey** (1777–1855), ex-convict businesswoman, founder of Australia's first financial institutions, verso John Flynn (1880–1951), missionary and founder of the Flying Doctor Services

• **$50: Edith Cowan** (1861–1932), social worker, activist, and first woman member of state parliament (Western Australia), verso David Unaipon (1872–1967), first Aboriginal to have a book published in Australia (*Native Legends*, 1929)

• **$100: Dame Nellie Melba** (1861–1931), opera singer, verso John Monash (1865–1931), army commander and hero at Gallipoli

For visitors, **traveller's cheques** are the most efficient way to carry money. All major brands of travellers' cheques are readily accepted in shops and at banks. **Credit cards** are also quite readily accepted; Mastercard is perhaps less well-known than American Express and Visa. **Automatic bank tellers**, or ATMs, are widely used and are available throughout the country (although not so readily in the country areas). EFTPOS (**Electric Funds Transfer at Point of Sale**) services are also available at many shops, service stations, and supermarkets for those with bank cash cards, and will allow you to receive cash along with a purchase. Bank cards are available to those with accounts at an Australian bank. If staying for more than a short time, it may be worthwhile to set up such an account, which is quite easy to do, as long as you can produce adequate identification (more than a passport in some cases).

 ## Getting there

Let's face it, flying to Australia is really the only efficient and easily available option in the 1990s. The days of the overland 'hippie trail' through Asia are no more, although some adventurous souls may still attempt the trip; and travel by ship is limited to closely scheduled cruise liners that stop briefly in Australian ports. Some cargo ship accommodation does appear occasionally, but it is apparently not encouraged, and requires that people be ready to go at the last minute. However, if you really do want to take a slow boat to Australia, check with cargo shipping concerns in your country's biggest port. The assumption here, however, is that visitors will arrive in Australia by air.

Airlines flying to Australia from the UK

- *Aerolineas Argentinas* (via Buenos Aires and Auckland, NZ), 54 Conduit St, London W1, ☎ 0171 494 1001
- *Air New Zealand* (via North America and New Zealand), 77 Fulham Palace Rd, London W6, ☎ 0181 741 2299
- *Britannia Airways* (charter services from Gatwick and Manchester from November–April), Luton Airport, Luton, Bedfordshire, LU2 9ND, ☎ 01582 424155
- *British Airways* (daily flights from Heathrow), 156 Regent St, London W1, ☎ 0171 434 4700; Heathrow Airport: ☎ 0181 759 5511; Gatwick Airport: ☎ 01293 664239
- *Garuda Airways* (via Jakarta), 35 Duke St, London W1, ☎ 0171 486 3011
- *Malaysia Airlines* (via Kuala Lumpur), 247–9 Cromwell Rd, London SW5, ☎ 0171 354 2020
- *Qantas* (twice-daily flights to all mainland capitals and Cairns, with possible Southeast Asian stopovers and free internal flight arrangements), 395–403 King St, London W6, ☎ 0181 846 0466
- *Singapore Airlines* (twice-daily flights via Singapore), 580–586 Chiswick High Rd, London W4, ☎ 0181 563 6767
- *Thai Airways International* (daily flights via Bangkok, with possible stopovers in India, Nepal and Thailand), 41 Albermarle St, London W1, ☎ 0171 491 7953, 0171 499 9113
- *United Airlines* (via North America, the Pacific and New Zealand), Heathrow Airport, ☎ 0181 750 9699

Specialists in discounted ticket prices

These agencies can also often book accommodation, arrange car and campervan hire, and offer special tours such as wine or adventure trips.

Austravel, ☎ 0171 734 7755	*Bridge the World*, ☎ 0171 911 0900
Flightbookers, ☎ 0171 757 2468	*STA*, ☎ 0171 361 6262
Trailfinders, ☎ 0171 938 3939	*Travelbag*, ☎ 0171 287 5556
Travel bug, ☎ 0171 835 1111	

No matter where the trip begins, whether Europe, America or elsewhere, the flight will be a long one: from Los Angeles direct to Sydney is 13 hours in the air; from Europe, the entire trip will take at least 22 hours and will require a stop somewhere along the way, most likely Bangkok or Singapore.

Unless you have a desire to stop over in Hawaii or New Zealand for several days, try to book a **direct** Los Angeles–Sydney flight if flying via the United States, as the stopovers do nothing but add several wasted hours to an already long flight. However, if you are flying from Europe and have plenty of time, it is worth considering a stopover in Asia or in the Pacific before continuing on to the continent, if the airline ticket allows it.

Aside from package tours, of which there are an abundance on offer from the UK and the USA, the most reasonably-priced ticket to Australia will often be a **round-the-world** (RTW) ticket, which also allows other stopovers, including ones to additional Australian cities. Similar kinds of arrangements as an RTW ticket exist as Circle Pacific fares, combining routes on several airlines around the Pacific.

Airlines flying from North America

- *Air New Zealand* (from Los Angeles with possible stopovers in New Zealand and the Pacific), ☎ 800 262 2468; website:www.airnz.com
- *Canadian Airlines* (from Canadian cities via Vancouver), ☎ 800 665 5554; website:www.cdnair.ca
- *Garuda Airways* (from Los Angeles via Jakarta), ☎ 800 342 7832; website: www.garuda.co.id
- *Malaysia Airlines* (from Los Angeles to Perth via Kuala Lumpur), ☎ 800 552 9264; website: www.malaysiaairlines.com.my
- *Qantas* (daily flights from Los Angeles and San Francisco, with possible internal flight connections), ☎ 800 227 4500; website: www.qantas.com.au
- *Singapore Airlines* (from Los Angeles via Singapore), ☎ 800 742 3333; website: www.singaporeair.com
- *Thai International* (from Los Angeles via Bangkok), ☎ 800 426 5204; website: www.thaiair.com
- *United* (from Los Angeles, San Francisco and Honolulu), ☎ 800 538 2929; website: www.ual.com

As flights within Australia can be quite expensive, the method of tacking on other Australian destinations to your main ticket may be the best arrangement. All of these arrangements should be done in advance of the trip with the airlines or booking agents. Many tourist packages and travel passes are only valid for overseas visitors and cannot be purchased once you reach Australia.

Accommodation

Every possible kind of accommodation is available for the visitor, from backpacker's hostels to pub-hotels to bed-and-breakfasts and five-star hotels. Many of the standard chain hotels have displays on illuminated hotel boards at the major airport terminals, where you can call directly and make a booking and, in most cases, be picked up by an airport shuttle to be taken to the hotel. For a country so avidly involved in motoring trips, motels are of course quite prevalent, and range from entirely seedy to spotlessly new accommodation. All tourist offices can also help with accommodation. The best guides to accommodation are available through the automobile clubs, i.e. the NRMA and the related state branches. For those interested in staying at bed-and-breakfasts, which are burgeoning all over the country, the best sources of information are *The Bed and Breakfast Directory* or *Dawsons Unique Places to Stay*, available in many newsagencies; www.ozemail.com has a list of bed and breakfast directories; www.yha.org.au lists youth hostels and includes maps.

It is **essential** that you make advance bookings if travelling during any of the school holiday periods (as discussed below). High season in the most popular tourist areas will also be busy, and require advance bookings.

This is perhaps the appropriate place to point out the use of the term '**hotel**' in Australia. In many places, and especially in country towns, a hotel is primarily a pub, although some kind of accommodation must by law be made available there. The standard of this accommodation may vary considerably, but will usually be relatively inexpensive and often noisy, if the rooms are placed above a well-attended bar.

A limited number of accommodation possibilities are listed at the beginning of the major city sections of this guide, attempting to offer a variety of categories.

 # Getting around

The enormous distances in Australia certainly make the question of getting around within the country a major consideration. Not only does the traveller have to take into account the time needed to get from place to place, but also the costs involved. Flying is really the only possible solution if time is limited and you want to see several areas of the country. While public transportation is adequate in most urban centres, most country areas are not well-served by bus or train; Australia is very much a land where people depend upon the automobile to get around.

By air

Two airlines control all domestic flights: **Qantas** (☎ 13 13 13; website: www.qantas.com.au), which took over the traditional Australian Airlines domestic links in 1995; and **Ansett** (☎ 13 13 00; website: www.ansett.com.au), which coordinates other smaller air links connecting most of the country. While the airline industry was supposedly deregulated in 1991, attempts to establish other airlines, with more competitive prices, have met with fierce opposition and eventual collapse of the competitor. Consequently, fares for internal flights remain rather high; the current price of a return flight from Sydney to Perth, for example, is as much as a low-season flight from Sydney to Los Angeles. It might be possible to buy discounted passes for several flights if purchased ahead of time and outside the country. Check with travel agents before leaving home. And remember to include internal air flights on your return flight ticket.

By rail

Except for Sydney and Melbourne, and, to a lesser extent, the other capital cities, rail travel is no longer the usual method for long-distance travel. While it is possible to travel by train between major cities, these links are not necessarily convenient or much cheaper than airfares. The situation with railway passenger service in Australia is very much like Amtrak in the United States: trains do run frequently along the eastern coastline, but only along one rail line and to main towns (the service is **Countrylink**, ☎ 132 232; international ☎ 612 9379 3111; website:www.countrylink.nsw.gov.au). Increasingly, the long-distance runs are designed for tourists with lots of time who are looking for an adventure.

Discussion of urban rail systems will be covered under the city and state sections. There are, however, two interstate railway journeys that should be mentioned here: one is the **Ghan**, running from Adelaide to Alice Springs; the other is the legendary **Indian Pacific**, coast-to-coast from Sydney to Perth, taking four days across some of the longest straight track of any railway in the world. Both of these journeys are well worth the effort, with excellent service provided on the trains. An overnight train, **The Overland**, also journeys regularly between Melbourne and Adelaide. The trips are organised by **Countrylink** (☎ 132 232; international ☎ 612 9379 3111); or contact any travel agent.

By bus

Bus services are far more widespread than the rail services, and are certainly a less expensive option than either air or train; the Australian term for a touring 'bus' is usually 'coach'. Touring coachlines exist in abundance and travel everywhere, but with a tour group. The main interstate operators are **Greyhound-Pioneer** (now merged as one company; ☎ 132 030; international ☎ 617 3258 1737; website:www.greyhound.com.au). Other regional companies operate regular services, and are listed in the local phone book under 'Bus and Coach Services'. One of the biggest regional carriers is **McCafferty's** (☎ 131 499; international ☎ 621 746 909 888), based in Brisbane but operating throughout the eastern states.

Special bus passes, such as the **Aussie Pass**, offering unlimited travel up to 90 days, is available from Greyhound-Pioneer, and can be purchased from travel agents, both overseas and in Australia. In the UK and Ireland, check with **Greyhound International**, Sussex House, East Grinstead, West Sussex RH19 1LD, ☎ 0733 51780. In the USA, try **Austravel**, 51 East 42nd Street, New York, New York 10017 (with branches in Chicago, Houston, and San Francisco), ☎ 800 633 3404; website:www.austravel/.net; and in Canada, **Goway Travel Ltd**, Suite 409, 402 West Pender Street, Vancouver, BC V68 1T6 or 2300 Yonge Street, Suite 2001, Toronto, Ontario, M4P 1E4, ☎ 800 387 8850/416 322 1034.

By car

Unless your time is very short or you are travelling on an organised tour, you will want to consider having your own transportation for at least part of your time in Australia. Car hire services are available throughout the country; the major companies, **Hertz**, **Budget**, **Thrifty**, **National** and **Avis**, are all represented here, and offices appear at all airports and in most towns. All reputable car hire companies will include insurance coverage in the rental price. It might be worthwhile checking out the rental prices at home before arriving, since local prices seem rather high; tourist deals may be better for overseas visitors. Many cities also have local firms, most of which are better value than the big companies, and often include 'rent-a-wreck' options for rock-bottom prices. Tasmania is especially geared towards tourist car hire companies, since so many visitors arrive by air or boat without a car; many hire companies are available, and bookings can be made through the Tasmanian tourist offices on the mainland before departing for the island. It is also possible to rent Campervans and motorhomes from reputable agents, although these can be expensive. Look in the local Yellow Pages under 'Campervans & Motor Homes—Hire'.

If you plan to spend more than a month or so in Australia, it really is worth considering purchasing a second-hand vehicle. The local newspapers will be overrun with ads for used motorcars in all price ranges. Sydney also has car markets established especially for visitors, where good car insurance can also be purchased. Try **Backpackers Car Market**, Kings Cross Car Park, Ward Avenue, ☎ 02 9358 2000; or **Flemington Car Market**, opposite Flemington Station, ☎ 1900 921 122, website: www.fscm.com.au. The important thing to remember when making such purchases is to check the vehicle registration sticker; if it is about to expire, you will have to pay for registration as well, which can be expensive. It is strongly recommended to pay the relatively small additional charge to join one of the automobile clubs (**NRMA** in New South Wales,

☎ 132 132; emergency helpline ☎ 132 900), for you are then eligible for the excellent free road service. Membership of other countries' automobile clubs ensures reciprocal arrangements in Australia.

While a foreign driver's licence is valid for those visiting for a short time, each Australian state has different regulations concerning the length of time one can validly use it. (In the ACT, for example, it is only three months.) Consequently, it would be advisable to acquire an International Driving permit before arrival; such a permit is valid everywhere for at least 12 months.

Remember that Australians drive on the **left-hand side of the road**, as they do in Britain. Currently, **fuel** costs about 72 cents a litre, although the prices vary greatly depending on how big the distance is between service stations!

Health

Health standards in Australia are very high, with no major problems with water supply (even when it tastes bad) or infectious diseases. Unless the visitor has travelled to an infected country within 14 days of arrival in Australia, no vaccinations are required for entry. Complacency among the population has led to a decrease in standard immunisations for childhood diseases, a problem that has led to recent outbreaks of whooping cough and measles; but the situation is now being addressed. One of the most prevalent health issues in Australia is allergies and asthma; the country has the highest rates of these afflictions. Many medicines for allergies and hay fever are consequently available over the counter at pharmacies, as are 'puffer' sprays for asthma sufferers.

Drug laws are undergoing some liberalisation, but marijuana is still illegal in most places, as is heroin, although some states are experimenting with services for habitual users. Australia has one of the **lowest rates of AIDS** in the world, because the safe-sex message was spread very early; condoms and, in many places, needles are available free from health agencies and AIDS centres. Condoms can also be purchased in public vending machines and at convenience stores and chemists' shops.

Healthcare services are excellent and readily available, although sparse in the outback, where the **Flying Doctors' Service** still reigns. Malaria has been known in the northern sections of Queensland and the Northern Territory. More significantly, this region is the location for the tropical diseases **Ross River** and **Dengue fever**, also spread by mosquitoes; recently, some outbreaks of the disease have occurred as far south as Sydney. It is relatively rare, but one should **always** use protection, such as the insect repellents *Aeroguard* or *Rid*, against mosquitoes.

The biggest health problem is **skin cancer**. Australia's rate is the highest in the world, caused by the overwhelming amount of fierce sunshine and the country's proximity to the so-called ozone hole near Antarctica. **Sun protection**, in the form of sun-block lotion (promoted by the government's 'Slip, Slap, Slop' campaign advertised everywhere) and the wearing of sun-hats, is essential and should be observed even on cloudy days; these precautions are required for children at school, and any light-skinned European or American can be seriously burned in a very short time. ALWAYS WEAR SUN-BLOCK FOR OUTDOOR ACTIVITIES.

Intense heat may also cause prickly heat, an irritating skin rash, or sunstroke, which can be quite serious. Drink lots of water and avoid over-exposure.

The scaremongering myths concerning the dangers of **Australian wildlife** are highly exaggerated. **Venomous spiders** and **snakes** are usually quite reclusive and if bitten, anti-venom is available (there have been no fatalities for either redback or funnel-web spider bites since the anti-venom was introduced). **Shark attacks** are exceedingly rare; and only a fool would get close enough to a **crocodile** to cause any worry. The only frequently occurring dangers are **box jellyfish**, known as **sea wasps**, that invade the summer waters along the beaches; and the often terrifying **'rips'** or **'dumper' waves** that suddenly occur even at the most benign beach. Just use common sense and heed the signs posted at patrolled beaches. One hundred per cent of **drownings** at Australian beaches in 1996 occurred in areas outside the posted flags. If you see jellyfish in the water, do not get in; this warning will unfortunately apply during much of the summer in Queensland. Do what the locals do when it comes to big waves: **stay within the flags posted by lifeguards**, and get out when the announcement is made to do so. This last tip is very, very important; PLEASE TAKE HEED.

Australia has a national health scheme, **Medicare**, that has reciprocal agreements with the UK, New Zealand, Italy, the Netherlands and Sweden. Citizens of these countries can use public hospitals and casualty centres, and will have a major portion of visits to doctors reimbursed (a doctor's visit costs about $35 at the time of writing). People from these countries staying for a longer period can obtain a Medicare card at any Medicare Centre, which will speed up the processing of treatment. Citizens of Canada and the United States are strongly advised to obtain travel insurance before coming to Australia.

When travelling in the vast expanses of the outback, serious precautions must be taken concerning notification of your movements to authorities along the way. Sometimes there will be no facilities or services for hundreds of kilometres of rugged track. Always carry water and provisions, check with sources concerning the conditions of the track, and do not depend entirely on mobile phones. NOTIFY PEOPLE WHERE YOU ARE.

Crime

In the major cities, all the normal crimes of contemporary city life occur, although the numbers are decidedly lower than most European or American cities, and even notorious locations such as Sydney's King's Cross are relatively tame. Gang- and drug-related crimes are on the increase, but need not be a major impediment for visitors. Take the same precautions as you would in any city, and avoid the few known 'danger zones', especially at night. Alcohol-fuelled violence in the form of the 'blue' or punch-up is a long-standing tradition in some neighbourhoods and bars at the weekends, but usually do not involve anyone but locals. Recent well-publicised incidents of attacks against and even murders of tourists indicate how relatively rare such events still are.

Police throughout the country are strenuous in their crackdown on **drink driving**, with frequent random-breath-test stations along the roads, and **speeding**, so obey the laws when on the road. In most states, the **legal limit** for driving after drinking alcohol is **0.05**, the equivalent of one standard drink in an hour, and penalties for conviction can be severe.

Hitchhiking is not recommended, although it is not illegal, and many people still do it. Take normal precautions if attempting to hitch-hike, particularly by travelling in pairs.

Sexual harassment of women and racial abuse do occur, but stringent anti-discrimination laws are in place, and one can report any incident to each state's Human Rights and Equal Opportunities Commission. To report any crime, contact the local police. In the case of rape—one crime that unfortunately does rate rather highly in the statistics—contact the local Rape Crisis Line before reporting to the police.

Telephone and postal services

Both postal and telephone services are in the process of being priva-tised and 'rationalised', and service has subsequently suffered; many small post offices have been closed recently, and the local GPO now looks more like a gift shop or card dispensary. **Postal delivery** can be rather slow interstate; thus the increase in the use of **express mail services**. For over-seas correspondence, the best option is the **aerogramme** available at post offices; currently, it is a bargain at 70 cents sent anywhere in the world. Other rates are rather high: a post card, or a card sent in an envelope, is 95 cents to the US and Canada, $1.00 to Europe, letters are $1.05 and $1.20 respectively. Package rates are astronomical; you would be advised not to mail books home, as the price for mailing is based on weight, and is truly prohibitive.

In some places, **postal agents** can be found in the news agency or at the general store. Stamps can also be purchased at news agencies and in machines in shopping centres and railway stations. You can receive mail at any post office if sent to 'Poste Restante/GPO' and the name of the place.

The national telephone service, **Telstra**, is now finding competition from services like Optus and other long-distance services. Still, telephone service is quite modern, with all up-to-date telecommunications devices available; Australia is, in fact, a world leader in fibre optics communication systems. Fax machine services are accessible even in the country, and Australians are some of the most enthusiastic users of mobile phones. Telstra's **public telephones** are always available in front of the post office and in most shopping centres, and pay phones can be found in service stations, bars and news agents, as well as along the roadside, although these are sometimes difficult to locate. The cost of a **local call** is currently 40 cents. **International calls** can be made from any phone, either by depositing coins, or, more reasonably, by using a **phone card**, which can be purchased at news agencies. In many places, public phones are specifi-cally geared to take phone cards and credit cards.

International rates are quite reasonable: to Britain or North America, currently about $1.60 per minute, off-peak $1.20; new services seek to drop these rates quite dramatically. Weekend rates for domestic and international long-distance calls also offer special savings. **Reverse charges** are possible by placing the call through the international operator, or for the price of a local call, dialling **Country Direct** to place the call in the country called.

The most important consideration when calling home from Australia is to note the **time differences**. If confused, call the international operator, who can give the correct time. **Emergency phones** in case of accident or breakdown are also provided along great stretches of most major highways.

From 1996, telephone numbers in Australia were changed, with extra digits added in some cities and with new area codes in some locations; all numbers are eventually planned to have eight digits. Be sure to check with directory assistance or in the front of the *White Pages* if the number dialled appears to be incorrect. Even numbers in this guide, although as accurate as possible at the time of writing, may have been changed by the time of publication. The entire directory is now on the Web at http://www.whitepages.com.au.

Telephone numbers come in a variety of forms. The international number for the Sydney Visitor's Centre, for instance, is 612 9255 1788. Dialled within Australia, the international prefix 61 is replaced with an 0, making the number 02 9255 1788. Calls placed from within New South Wales drop the 02. While there are some variations along the borders, basically **02** is the area code for New South Wales; **03** is for Victoria; **07** is for Queensland; and **08** is for South Australia, the Northern Territory and Western Australia.

Toll free numbers work within Australia only. They are generally 6 or 10 figures long and commence with 13. Thus, the Western Australian Tourist Commission toll free number is 1 300 361 351, that for Victoria is 13 2842. 1 800 numbers are also toll free. Charges for local calls are per call regardless of their duration. Long-distance calls are charged by distance and duration. The costs of 190 calls (commercial services such as stock quotations, weather, dating services and psychics) vary from .40 per minute to $30 per call, although most are .75 or $3.00 per minute.

Local Directory Assistance ☎ 013
National Directory Assistance ☎ 0175
International Directory Assistance ☎ 0103
International Operator ☎ 0100
Country Direct:
UK ☎ 0014 881 440   US (AT&T) ☎ 0014 881 011
Canada ☎ 0014 881 150 US (MCI) ☎ 0014 881 100
Ireland ☎ 0014 881 353 US (Sprint) ☎ 0014 881 877

Additional information

Newspapers and mass media

Australia has one **national daily newspaper**, *The Australian* (which also has *The Weekend Australian* edition); it is geared towards the business community, and is also the source for news of and positions listings in education. Sydney's *The Sydney Morning Herald* and Melbourne's *The Age* are also widely available throughout the country in news agencies. Each capital city has its own newspaper, concentrating for the most part on local issues and wire-service reports. Brisbane's *Courier-Mail* is more than reactionary politically, and should be consulted only for entertainment listings; and Adelaide's one newspaper, *The Adelaide Advertiser*, has now gone tabloid (perhaps inevitably, since Rupert Murdoch's media empire began here). The *Financial Review* is the most trustworthy business paper, and also includes thoughtful articles on cultural topics.

International papers are also widely available in the capital cities. Weekly news magazines include Australian editions of *Time* and *Newsweek/Bulletin*. While Europeans may find international news less comprehensive than at home, Australian coverage of international events is superior to that of most American newspapers or television, and the normal person on the street far better informed than the average American. The Australian approach to Asian events is particularly insightful.

Australian **television** consists of **five stations**, three commercial, plus the national broadcaster **ABC** and **SBS**, the last an amazing multi-cultural station which broadcasts news in several languages and offers an abundance of foreign-language films and current events programmes (the latter has commercials, but only between programmes). SBS also has a radio station, broadcasting in over 35 languages. The ABC radio station JJJ (**Triple J**) broadcasts to the more discerning young listener. Other ABC radio stations include a classical music format and an all-news frequency. PNN is the parliamentary network, broadcasting sessions from parliament.

Pay television, after protracted battles and much ambivalence, is now available in some cities. Otherwise, television coverage leans heavily towards sports and imported (British and American) programmes; Australian comedy and current event programmes are worth watching, if only to gain insight into Australian attitudes, and numerous travel and 'infotainment' programmes offer good tips and sights for the tourist.

Opening hours

Public institutions such as town halls and council offices are usually open 09.00 –17.00 weekdays. Banking hours are 09.30–16.00, Monday to Thursday and 09.30–17.00 Friday. In larger cities, some bank branches are open Saturday morning, and country branches at general stores and news agencies may be open longer hours. Museums and galleries are normally open 10.00–17.00 weekdays and weekends, with some having evening hours. Smaller galleries, historic houses, and tourist attractions may have erratic or infrequent opening times; as far as possible, this guide will try to provide accurate times, but these may change according to funding and availability of staff.

Traditionally, shops are open 10.00–17.30. Late-night shopping occurs on Thursdays or Fridays, depending on the state, when the major stores are open until 21.00. Shopping hours on Sunday is the subject of ambivalent debate—although many establishments have resisted, you will now find many shops and stores open for business on Sunday, at least in the cities and larger towns, and in the shopping malls. Most small businesses will be closed on Saturday afternoons, and even the large chain stores will close by 17.00 or 18.00, except during the pre-Christmas shopping season.

Public holidays

Australians revere their days off, so much so that much of the Republican debate centres on the dilemma of losing the **Queen's Birthday** as a national holiday. This holiday, on the first or second weekend in June, involves lots of fireworks, so is a favourite with children. The only days when all public institutions, including museums and tourist venues, are guaranteed to be closed are **Christmas Day** and **Good Friday**.

Public holidays, when public services are closed or on holiday schedule, are as follows:

1 January	New Year's Day	All States
26 January	Australia Day	All States
February	Regatta Day	Tas (south only)
	Launceston Cup	Tas (north only)
March	Labour Day	WA
	Eight Hour Day	Tas
	Labour Day	Vic
19 March	Canberra Day	ACT
March/April	Good Friday	All States
	Easter Monday	All States
	Easter Tuesday	Victoria
25 April	Anzac Day	All States
1 May	May Day	NT
	Labour Day	QLD
	Adelaide Cup Day	SA
June	Foundation Day	WA
	Queen's Birthday	All States but WA
August	Bank Holiday	ACT
	Picnic Day	NT
September	Melbourne Show Day	Vic (Melbourne only)
October	Labour Day	NSW, ACT, SA
	Launceston Show Day	Tas (north only)
November	Melbourne Cup Day	Vic (Melbourne only)
25 December	Christmas Day	All States
26 December	Boxing Day	All States but SA
	Additional Day	NSW, NT
26 December	Proclamation Day	SA

For details of major annual festivals, see p 25.

School holidays vary from state to state, but usually occupy six weeks in the summer, through Christmas holidays and January; two weeks around Easter; two weeks in July; and two weeks in September. During these times, everyone seems to be on the road, and it is **essential** to make advance bookings for accommodation, whether in caravan parks, camping sites, or motels. Be sure to check on school holiday schedules before travelling anywhere.

It is a great Australian holiday tradition, one that apparently is nearly obligatory, to stuff all the children, and probably the pets as well, into the car and drive somewhere other than home for many hours in tremendous traffic jams causing overheated vehicles and frayed nerves. This is especially true on **Boxing Day** (26 December), when traffic can be bumper-to-bumper from Sydney to the Gold Coast, and at the beginning of the Easter holidays, during which time the Hume Highway from Melbourne to Sydney can sometimes be backed up for 10km. January is the month when very little business is accomplished, as everyone goes on holiday. Forget about any kind of transaction between Christmas and New Year, except of the most basic sort.

The other specifically Australian holidays are **Australia Day, 26 January**, which commemorates the arrival of the First Fleet in 1788; and **Anzac Day, 25 April**, the most patriotic celebration, in honour of Australia's soldiers and particularly the war dead of World War I. If possible, try to experience Anzac Day in a country town, with a small parade and a ceremony at the local war monument; the experience offers much insight into the Australian character.

When possible, a holiday will be pinned on to the beginning or end of a weekend, so even non-moveable feasts will sometimes be moved for the sake of a three-day weekend.

Time zones

Australia has three official time zones, plus one small local time zone. **Eastern Standard Time** (EST) operates in Queensland, Australian Capital Territory, New South Wales, Victoria and Tasmania. **Central Standard Time** (CST) encompasses South Australia and the Northern Territory, and is half an hour behind EST. **Western Standard Time** (WST), two hours behind EST, is in Western Australia. The local time zone, **Central Western Time**, operates from 3km east of Caiguna in Western Australia to the South Australian border; it is 45 minutes ahead of WST.

The situation gets more complicated in summer: New South Wales, Victoria, Tasmania, Australian Capital Territory, and South Australia adopt daylight saving time by putting the clock ahead one hour from the end of October to the end of March; but the Northern Territory, Queensland and Western Australia do not. Each of the states adopting daylight saving time may begin the change on different weekends, so it is possible at certain times of the year to have as many as six different times across the continent.

Useful addresses

The embassies and High Commissions are located in Canberra, although many consulates are also available in the other capital cities.
- **USA** Embassy of the United States of America, 21 Moonah Place, Yarralumla, ACT 2600; ☎ 02 6270 5000/02 6270 5914.
- **UK** British High Commission, Commonwealth Avenue, Yarralumla, ACT 2600; ☎ 02 6270 6666/ 1902 941 555.
- **Canada** Canadian High Commission, Commonwealth Avenue, Yarralumla, ACT 2600; ☎ 02 6273 3844.
- **New Zealand** New Zealand High Commission, Commonwealth Avenue, Yarralumla, ACT 2600; ☎ 02 6270 4211.

Religion

While being the most secular of societies, Australia's religious tolerance is an essential aspect of its culture. Traditional British ties see **Anglicanism** as the establishment religion, but it is by no means the only form practised. Except for some early antagonism to Irish Catholicism by the English overseers and some Lutheran sectarianism in the South Australian colony, Australians have never been interested in strenuous religiosity, so people are free to worship as they please as long as they do not impose on others. Virtually all denominations are represented in the population: major Islamic mosques and Hindu shrines exist in the cities, many synagogues are architectural landmarks, and Wollongong is now home to one of the largest Buddhist temples in the world. Forty per cent of the population are nominally **Roman Catholic**, a reminder of the pervasive influence of the Irish in early Australian history; these numbers, of course, also now include those of the many other Catholic groups.

Protestant denominations, faced with dwindling congregations, have carried out a uniquely Australian endeavour. While the dominant Church of England and the relatively strong Baptist Church remain as separate entities, the so-called 'non-Conformist' groups of the Methodists, Congregationalists, and most Presbyterian congregations, merged in the 1970s to become the **Uniting Church**; thus a number of historic churches which used to be one of these denominations are now called a Uniting Church. The fascinating story of this event, and the means by which their separate theological views were merged, can be found in Darcy Wood's *Building on a Solid Basis* (1986) and Bentley and Hughes' *The Uniting Church in Australia* (1996). Church services are listed in the Saturday editions of most newspapers.

Local customs: service
Australian attitudes towards providing service are deeply ingrained and say much about the Australian character. The custom of **tipping**, for example, is not at all required. In restaurants or in taxis, one may give a small tip as acknowledgment of good service, usually rounded off to the nearest dollar, but it is not expected by taxi drivers or other service people, who may actually consider it offensive to be offered such a sign of servitude. Where one sits in a taxi also demonstrates this approach: a single person is usually expected to sit in the front with the driver, otherwise it appears the person is putting on airs (although recent violence against taxi drivers in some cities may be changing this custom).

At best, service in restaurants is informal and friendly, but it does not seem to be part of the Australian character to serve. Perhaps it is best to keep in mind that the Protestant Work Ethic is not an Australian cultural trait; this is not to say that Australians do not accomplish things or work hard, they just do it at their own pace and without the driven intensity of some other cultures. As Ilsa Sharp points out in her book *Culture Shock! Australia: A Guide to Customs and Etiquette* (1992), such an attitude may be a result of the convict past and the extreme sense of egalitarian democracy that permeates all of Australian culture.

Australian columnists frequently remark on the lamentable state of service even in the most popular tourist areas, and the tourism industry is making great efforts to change the situation, with some success. Screaming or demanding service will do no good; just relax, and if you need to return a dinner, or find something really wrong with your meal or hotel room, be friendly and gracious in your requests and carry on conversations with whoever is involved, and you are likely to get something accomplished. Service is not usually surly, just cavalier. Australians are for the most part affable and friendly, and will be more than helpful with any problem, as long as they feel they are on an equal footing with the person asking for help.

Sports

Sports of all kinds are absolutely central to Australian life, whether as spectator or participant; even those who are not sports-minded are affected by its pervasive influence in society. Major moments in Australian history have been defined by sporting achievements. Because of its dominant position in Australian culture and history, the development of individual sports and sporting events are discussed in depth in the relevant touring sections of this book.

Suffice it to say that facilities for the performance of virtually every sport known to man—and that includes hurling, curling, tae kwon do, underwater hockey, netball and darts—can be found throughout the country (indeed, if anyone finds a sport that is not represented in this country at some level, please inform the authors!). Many sports, even ones not normally associated with Australia such as ice hockey, will be played on an organised level of some kind. Every city and town will have at least one sports oval (a playing field) for team play, a golf course, a racetrack, a swimming pool. Canberra was not considered a real community until its Rugby League team won a national championship (in 1989). Children's participation in sports is actively encouraged, and on any weekend afternoon, every oval will be crammed with youngsters and parents involved in some kind of team play. The beaches offer facilities and equipment for all water sports, including the rental of scuba and surfing gear. The ski resorts in the Snowy Mountains and Tasmania offer world-class lifts and equipment hire, even if it seems bizarre to be wedeling among the kangaroos and gum trees.

World-renowned golf courses as well as humble countryside venues attest to golf's status as the premier participatory activity for the average Australian. Melbourne's famous ring of sand-courses rank as among the world's great golfing experiences.

Festivals

Listed below are the major festivals throughout Australia, both those that have international recognition and others that you may want to note if you are in the area. They have been listed chronologically, as they occur throughout the year.

Annual Highland Gathering. Penrith Raceway, Penrith, NSW; New Year's Day.

A revelry of Scottish sport and dance, the festival began in 1869 at the Albert Ground in Redfern. The current event is attended by as many as 10,000 people depending on the weather. Short of a trip to Braemar in Scotland, a more enthusiastic revival of Scottish culture would be hard to find. Activities include tossing the Caber (something like throwing a tree) and the Braemar Stone, shot putt and tug of war. Highland dancing and music and traditional clothing abound as do stalls selling Scottish merchandise and food.

Sydney Festival and Carnival. Sydney, month of January ending on Australia Day weekend.
The city's biggest arts festival, encompassing theatre, opera, art exhibitions, international cultural performances, ferry boat races and children's events. Something to suit everyone's tastes (and pocketbooks), a great summer festival, beginning with the unforgettable fireworks display over the harbour on New Year's Eve and ending with more fireworks on Australia Day.

Schutzenfest (target shooting). Hahndorf, SA, second Saturday in January. In addition to competitions restricted to members of Australian German clubs, an open competition has brought serious target shooters from across Australia.

Tamworth Country Music Awards and Festival. Tamworth, NSW, Australia Day weekend (26 January).
Begun in 1973, this ten-day festival attracts nearly 50,000 stalwart Country and Western (or Bushband) music fans. The Town Hall and the Workman's Club are the main venues, but every sports ground, pub and most sidewalks feature entertainers of varying degrees of professionalism. The televised Country Music Awards are aglitter with national and, increasingly, international performers.

Montsalvat Jazz Festival. Montsalvat, Eltham, VIC, Australia Day weekend. Justus Jorgensen established the Montsalvat Estate as a colony for visiting artists and musicians in the early 1930s. It hosts the premier jazz event in Australia. It presents jazz of variety of styles, but reflects Australia's penchant for mainstream big band and experimental combos. Although the black tie dinner on Friday night is usually sold out a year in advance, the smaller sessions are described as central to understanding the current jazz scene.

Sydney Gay and Lesbian Mardi Gras. Sydney, end of February.
A parade down Oxford Street in a Mardi Gras spirit, now 20 years old. Throngs of every stripe, up to 700,000, pack the street for the world's largest night-time parade. Caricature and camp vie with physique and feathers.

Adelaide Fringe Festival. Adelaide, SA, late February to early March, even-numbered years.
An iconoclastic alternative to the Adelaide Festival, this fête begins with a parade ending at Rundle Street where outdoor stages present contemporary, experimental and novice acts. The shows continue for a month at local venues and are generally either free or quite inexpensive.

Evandale Village Penny Farthing Championships. Evandale, TAS, last weekend in February.
Continuing a hundred-year-old competition as an excuse for a festival, the races include the one-mile championship, 200m sprint, a slow ride (last bicycle across the line wins) and a remarkable slalom. In keeping with the historical theme, Morris dancers, horse and cart rides, and revitalised costume are noteworthy features.

Chinese New Year. Melbourne, usually early February.

Melbourne Music Festival. Melbourne, mid-February for 10 days.
A variety of performances of contemporary music, the Festival opens as a Music Expo at the Melbourne Sports and Entertainment Centre. Here professional musicians and industry leaders shop for the latest equipment and finest instruments. In addition to several dozen performances, master classes and clinics are offered in performance, recording and staging.

Melbourne Grand Prix. Melbourne, February–March.
Recently moved from Adelaide, this is the first Formula One automobile race of the international season.

Festival of Perth. Perth, WA, February.
Organised by the University of Western Australia, the festival is a Western Australian version of the Adelaide Festival directed to the general music listener. It prides itself on introducing new popular bands and classical music to new audiences. Free concerts at the Supreme Court Gardens and alfresco dining in trendy Northbridge are extremely popular. The concert venues include His Majesty's Theatre and modern theatres at the University.

Adelaide Festival. Adelaide, SA, early March in even-numbered years.
Australia's premier arts festival includes music, dance and theatre performances and art exhibits. The purpose-built Festival Centre is the festival's home, but venues include outdoor performances at the Botanic Gardens and along Rundle Street Mall and stages in numerous pubs and clubs. In addition to performance, the festival provides forums for artists and writers to discuss their craft.

Moomba Festival. Melbourne, early March, ending on Victorian Labour Day.
Devoted largely to free entertainment, Moomba (meaning either 'let's get together for some fun' or 'to moon') presents fireworks, concerts, a Labour Day Parade and sporting events.

Corryong High Country Carnival. Corryong, VIC, third week in March for six days.
Remembering Andrew 'Banjo' Patterson's poem "The Man from Snowy River', the festival commemorates Jack Riley's working life as a legendary stockman who rounded up and broke brumbies (wild horses living in the mountains). Events include a four-day trail ride and the thrilling Jack Riley Cup. The latter is a race across broken and hazardous terrain. More sedate events present whip cracking, foot races, a variety of humorous competitions like hat and gum boot throwing and a Drover's Dance.

National Folk Festival. Canberra, ACT, Easter weekend.
The Australian Folk Trust takes pains to attract as diverse an ethnic representation as possible. As a consequence, traditional musicians and dancers from throughout Australia perform. The event is consciously child-friendly and includes Punch and Judy shows, storytelling, sleight of hand and similar entertainments for them.

Blessing of the Fleet. Ulladulla Harbour, NSW, Easter Sunday.
Begun in 1956 when a visiting priest convinced fishermen in the local fleet
to have their boats blessed, the current activities include a parade, yacht
races from Sydney and Bateman's Bay, festooned fishing trawlers and quantities of fresh fish.

Barossa Valley Vintage Festival. Barossa Valley, SA, Easter Monday for
seven days in odd-numbered years.
Naturally, centred around wine tasting, the festival includes a huge parade
along Barossa Valley Way, a Grape Treading Championship in several heats,
a street market, and casual dining.

Melbourne International Comedy Festival. Melbourne, three weeks
starting about April Fools Day.
Humour is a serious business. The festival provides young performers and
writers exposure both at numerous public venues and in the media. Established international performers use the festival as an opportunity to visit
Australia.

On the Beach Carnival. Mindil Beach, Darwin, NT, first Sunday in May.
As the official start of 'the Dry', the festival's activities centre around the
beach culture of the Top End. Sand castles, beach volleyball, take-away food
and, if the box jellyfish are gone, play in the surf. Like much of the Northern
Territory's attitude, participation is the key.

Camel Cup. Todd River's dry bed, Alice Springs, NT, second Saturday in May.
Initiated by a bet between cattleman Noel Fullerton and Keith Mooney-
Smith to race camels down Todd Street (now Todd Mall), the Lions Club has
sponsored the races since the early 1970s. Most entertaining, and a fine
opportunity to put in some bets, the races are diverse and a number of
novelty events are included.

Grenfell Henry Lawson Festival of the Arts. Grenfell, NSW, 376km
west of Sydney, Queen's Birthday weekend (first or second Monday in June).
Henry Lawson, one of Australia's favourite late 19C poets, was born in
Grenfell in 1867. The town commemorates the event in a series of readings
and exhibits with substantial cash prizes. On the Sunday Guinea Pig Races
near town raise a substantial amount of money for local charities.

Barunga Sports Festival. Barunga, NT, early June.
Aboriginal music, dance and crafts frame the events which include both
traditional sports like firelighting and spear throwing and modern sports
including football, softball and athletics. Permits are not necessary during
the festival; bring your own camping gear; alcohol is not allowed.

Sydney Film Festival. Sydney, late May and early June.
The festival premieres feature films, documentaries and shorts. Most of the
documentaries and shorts will not be generally distributed, making the festival
the single best opportunity for young film-makers to display their work.

Cape York Aboriginal Dance Festival. Laura, QLD, north of Cairns, last
weekend in June in odd-numbered years.

Like the Barunga Sports Festival, this is an excellent opportunity to be at ease among Aboriginal people. The dances are traditional with complex body painting and are judged by elders. Arts and crafts, an open air cafeteria and some athletic competitions occur as well. Camping is necessary, no alcohol is allowed.

Melbourne Film Festival. Melbourne, July.
About two weeks of film culture with cash prizes to winners in a number of categories including documentaries, animation, experimental and student films.

Darwin Beer Can Regatta. Mindil Beach, Darwin, NT, late July or early August at the neap tide.
A series of frolicsome events providing an excuse for a good time. The open-bottomed boat races—Henley-on-Mindil—along the beach and the regatta of silly boats made of empty beer cans are the tops of the day.

Birdsville Races. Birdsville, far western NSW, first weekend in September.
Birdsville's 100-plus residents host several thousand horse-racing fans, many of whom fly in for the event in private planes.

Floriade. Canberra, ACT, mid-September to mid-October.
An extensive floral display centred on plants propagated from tubers and bulbs, the festival is organised by the city in Commonwealth Park on Lake Burley Griffin. A number of sculptural works are commissioned as well.

Bathurst 1000. Bathurst, NSW, the last week in September.
Stock-car motor racing on Mount Panorama attracts large crowds.

Australian Bush Music Festival. Glen Innes Railway Station, NSW, Labor Day weekend, first Monday in October.
Bush music is the Australian equivalent of folk music. Generally, it is based on late 19C popular dance music and, in the best of circumstances, one learns the steps in a country woolshed during a local fête. The new ballads are often quite topical. The organisers arrive at the festival in a chartered train which sits behind the main stage throughout event. By late Sunday afternoon whatever tensions the awards ceremony on Saturday night might have fostered are forgotten in a freely flowing session.

Melbourne International Festival of the Arts. Melbourne, end of October until Spring Racing Carnival.
Melbourne's response to the Adelaide and Sydney Festivals, with first-rate theatre, street performances, gourmet food, art exhibitions and displays.

Melbourne Cup. Flemington Racecourse, Melbourne, and by television everywhere, first Tuesday in November.
A large field on a long track, the horses are the season's best. The influence of the event cannot be underestimated. Newspapers publish special supplements, betting is rife, workplaces stop for champagne and office pools of 50 cents to $5, and milliners make a fortune on the day. As a visitor, find a local club or pub an hour before the 3:20 start if you cannot attend the event in person.

Food and drink

One cannot really speak yet of a specific Australian cuisine, although styles of cooking have changed so dramatically in the last twenty years that a true 'food culture' now exists, at least in the cities, and continues to grow with an exciting amalgam of Asian and European methods and ingredients; the term **'Pacific Rim' cuisine** is beginning to be used to describe these new hybrids. Unlike the lamentable state of dining in the recent past, Australia now presents some of the best eating experiences in the world. International gourmet critics regularly rate some Australian restaurants at the top of their lists. Australian agricultural and food products now win international awards.

Traditionally, Australian food followed British customs: eggs and bacon or sausages (called 'snags') for breakfast, 'meat and two veg' for dinner (with potatoes as one of the vegetables), cakes for tea. The only spurts of culinary creativity occurred in the field of desserts, the Australians loving their cakes, slices, and biscuits. Every country-fair cake stall or afternoon tea-tray included the **Lamington**, a yellow sponge cake coated in chocolate and sprinkled in coconut; and **Anzac biscuits**, cookies with brown sugar, coconut and oats. Another favoured sweet has been the **pavlova**; apparently created in New Zealand (although this is the source of heated debate between Australians and New Zealanders) in honour of the Russian ballerina Anna Pavlova when she toured the region in the 1920s, it consists of meringue, whipped cream and fruit.

While beef is eaten in great quantities, **lamb** was, and still is, a very prevalent meat. To the delight of those from countries where lamb is an expensive luxury, it is still tremendously affordable: a whole lamb bought for a barbecue will usually cost less than the price of a leg of lamb in the United States.

As popular imagery suggests, the **barbecue** is indeed an institution in Australia. 'The prawn on the barbie' is rarer than may be expected. Most barbecues involve lamb or beef chump chops, hamburgers, sausages, and the ubiquitous fried onions, the smell of which is a quintessential Australian experience. Many city parks have built-in barbecues for public use.

A brief history of Australian food

Historically, the colonists were dependent on what humorist Sam Orr calls 'the great Australian tradition of living off rations'. Rather than learn from the natives about how to live off the land, the First Fleet nearly starved on a diet of salted pork and dried beans while they waited for supplies to arrive from England. They planted seeds in sandy soil at the wrong time of year, the livestock fled and became the wild game that eventually fed bushrangers. This attitude continued well into the 20C; as late as the 1960s a cookbook discussing Australian food stated that what seafood Australians ate was often imported from Britain or America.

The absurdity of this adherence to the food from 'home' is nowhere more obvious than at **Christmas** time, when tradition demanded the entire English ritual, from stuffed turkey to Yorkshire pudding, despite sweltering temperatures that made the kitchen an inferno and suggested a trip to the beach rather than the burning of a Yule log. Today, many Australians have opted for a more appropriate meal of seafood, oysters, and cold meats; some still cling to the traditional meal, but may choose to cook the turkey on the Weber barbecue in the back yard.

Forty years ago, dining out was not a normal pastime. The only restaurants were in hotels, although every small town, especially in Victoria where Chinese arrived with the 1850s gold rush, seemed to have at least one Chinese restaurant, serving food which had nothing to do with anything ever served in China. Standard fare at hotel restaurants was meat and potatoes, and occasionally battered fish. Pubs also provided (and still do) **'counter lunches'**, consisting largely of sandwiches, eggs, and cheese, and washed down with quantities of beer (not wine).

It was the arrival of continental European immigrants after World War II and, more recently, the influx of a large Asian population, that brought about the dramatic changes in Australian eating habits. The Italians introduced cafes with cappuccino, the Germans delicatessens with a variety of meats and cheeses, the Greeks fish, and the Asians spices and exotic dishes of all sorts.

By the late 1970s, Australia's burgeoning sense of national identity coupled with its multicultural diversity began to pay off in culinary terms. **Restaurant culture** blossomed, with every possible kind of experimentation with new ingredients and a mixing of cuisines. A startling example of how recent an occurrence this is can be seen in Ruth Park's Sydney travel guide of 1973, where not a single Thai restaurant is listed; today there seems to be one on every street. Today Australian cities offer superb dining possibilities, taking advantage of the country's abundant crops of fruits and vegetables, and its incomparable seafood.

International *nouvelle cuisine*, of the meagre portions and expensive prices, made a momentary appearance in the pretentious 1980s, having the positive effect of nurturing a new generation of innovative chefs. If nothing else, this movement emphasised the desirability of fresh produce, a principle now well-established in all good restaurants and shops. In the major capitals, chefs are now lionised the way rock stars used to be.

Cooking in the home has also been affected by this culinary eclecticism. According to Cherry Ripe, author of *Goodbye Culinary Cringe* (1993), a 1991 survey revealed that 65 per cent of Australians cooked stir-fry at least twice a week, an astonishing figure in a country where twenty years ago spaghetti was considered an exotic dish.

Most intriguing is the current attempt to integrate **'bush tucker'**, native ingredients prevalent in Aboriginal diets for millennia, into contemporary dishes. Kangaroo, emu, and crocodile as meats; quandong, wattle seed, and rosella tree as condiments and salsas now appear on the menus of many restaurants, and several speciality shops even sell widgety grub soup and wattle seed coffee.

One culinary institution that continues in a variety of forms is the **takeaway shop**. The traditional takeaways still exist, doling out such truly Anglo-Australian items as the meat pie with tomato sauce (ketchup) and chips (french fries), as well as an inexplicably popular Australianised spring roll known as a Chiko roll (considered surfie fare). A specifically South Australian takeaway speciality is the 'floater', a meat pie swimming in mushy peas. But all manner of other takeaways, from health food to

Mongolian barbecue, are popping up everywhere. Greater awareness of healthy eating habits has also led Australians to exploit their natural abundance of organically-grown produce and herbs, making the country much more amenable to vegetarians and other conscientious eaters. Fast-food outlets of all sorts are also available in abundance, decried as evidence of the Americanisation of Australia.

This healthy-food transformation has not, unfortunately, reached the countryside, where, as one Australian writer put it, the 'great battered food syndrome' of fried and overcooked food prevails. Still there are encouraging signs even in the outback, with some excellent restaurants venturing into the void. Be prepared, however, to survive on greasy fare, canned goods and very few vegetables in the country towns. In the outback itself, it is probably advisable to cook your own food over the campfire.

As far as foods for special occasions is concerned, the most established tradition must be roast chicken, strawberries and champagne on Melbourne Cup Day (both at the race and elsewhere). Other menus are perhaps not as elegant.

Breakfast

Unless you are in the cities where breakfast cafes do exist, the morning meal is not one that Australians regularly eat in restaurants. They do have traditional **British breakfasts** (American-style bacon does not exist), but nowadays simple croissants, cereal or even sandwiches are more common fare. Muffins or scones are not considered breakfast food, although they will probably be available in most cafes that would be open in the morning.

Other interesting items often appearing on breakfast menus include baked beans or spaghetti on toast—and, of course, the ubiquitous **Vegemite**. For British visitors used to such spreads as Marmite, Vegemite will not seem so unusual, but to the rest of the world, this yeast-based, salty brown smear is either something one must be weaned on or it is a decidedly acquired taste. Australians swear by it, and hoard provisions of it when going overseas.

On the road, most motels and hotels offer **breakfast service** to your room. It should be ordered the night before, and usually consists of cornflakes, eggs and toast. In most cases, rooms will be provided with instant coffee and tea bags. Very few will have restaurants open in the early morning; even when restaurants do serve breakfast, it is rare, at least outside the big cities, to find one open before 08.00 or 09.00. There are all-night truck stops along many highways, but the food is either of the fast-food variety or quite grim and to be resorted to only in emergencies.

Lunch and dinner

In restaurants, it is not common to find a separate lunch and dinner menu, although bistros seem to be picking up on the idea. What is served at lunch will usually be the same, with the same price, as what is served for dinner. One cannot assume, then, that lunch will be a less expensive option for dining out. The 'official' lunch hour for office workers is 12.30–13.30, although most restaurants will serve lunch from 12.00–14.00. Dinner in restaurants usually begins service at 18.30 and normally ends by 23.00, perhaps later in the cities.

The use of the term '**tea**' to refer to a meal can lead to some confusion for the uninitiated. While 'afternoon tea' refers to a small meal of biscuits and cakes to accompany a cup of tea, 'tea' itself often refers to the full evening meal. The term is now more likely to be used in the country, although regional usage varies. In the cities, the term for the large meal of the day is normally dinner. If asked to tea, one depends on the time of day to anticipate what is likely to be served.

What in America would be called an 'appetizer' is in Australia the **entree**, or first course. In most restaurants, it is possible to order a main course in a smaller portion as an entree. For the most part, dining out in Australia is a relaxing and casual experience, even in the most elegant places, and in the cities, has become a leading leisure-time activity. Only the fanciest restaurants will require ties and women in dresses. The more common 'dress code' requirement will be that a shirt and shoes must be worn!

Coffee and tea
Coffee, since the arrival of Italians and other migrant groups in the 1950s, is now excellent, with real cappuccino and espresso served in many places. Instant coffee, however, has a pretty strong hold even at some trendier cafes, where they often use the cappuccino machine only to foam the milk, so be sure to ask if they make 'real' coffee before ordering.

Tea is still drunk with great enthusiasm at all times of the day. The so-called 'Devonshire tea', tea with scones and jam and whipped cream, is all the rage and can be found at nearly every kiosk, tourist restaurant, and small cafe. But it does appear that coffee drinking is replacing the 'cuppa' in many places. Fifty years ago, Australians drank ten times as much tea as coffee; today, the figures have reversed, with three times more coffee consumption than tea.

Beer
In terms of drinking habits, the traditional image of the beer-guzzling Australian is changing as well (except in the Northern Territory, where beer consumption per capita is among the highest in the world). **Pub culture** has a completely different tone since the infamous 'six o'clock swill' ended in 1966. Before that time, pubs closed at 6 pm, resulting in the clamour of workmen between 5 o'clock and 6 pm, downing as much beer as was possible before stag-gering home.

Beer is still the main alcoholic refreshment; while most Europeans will find Australian beer surprisingly bland, it is more potent and interesting than Amer-ican beer. '**Boutique beers**' have now become popular and are worth a try at the pub or restaurant where they are made. Some bigger brands to savour are *Cooper's* from South Australia, *Cascade* from Tasmania, and *Redback* from Western Australia. Otherwise, beer brands are tribal: Queenslanders drink *Fourex (XXXX)*, Victorians drink *VB (Victorian Bitter)* or *Carlton*, New South Welshmen drink *Toohey's* or *Resch's*, and Territorians drink it all. *Foster's* appears to be drunk specifically in the more upscale pubs, despite what the overseas advertisements say.

Wine
Serious wine culture has also grown with the food revolution—a recent phenomenon, despite the fact that wine has been cultivated in Australia since

the 1790s, and the major wine-producing regions of the **Hunter Valley** in New South Wales and the **Barossa Valley** in South Australia have been producing world-class vintages for 150 years. Aside from these famous regions, Australia now has wine-producing areas throughout the country, most notably in the **Margaret River** region of Western Australia, **Rutherglen** district of Victoria, in Tasmania, and even very good products from around the ACT (Australian Capital Territory). Indeed for many, tasting the variety of superb Australian wines has become a major preoccupation. The popularity of Australian wine abroad, both in Europe and America, has led to ever-increasing yields and experimentation among the major vintners. Of specific interest is the fact that Australian winemakers have never been afraid of mixing wine types; it is common to see a wine bottle labelled as **'Shiraz-Cabernet-Malbec'**, leading to unusual new tastes. Every wine lover, even the most discriminating, will be impressed with the variety of Australian vintages.

While the **portable wine cask carton** is an Australian invention, and acceptable *vin ordinaire* can be found in these modest containers, reasonably priced wines with well-rounded taste such as **Wolf Blass**'s whites and reds, **Jacob's Creek**, and **Orlando** are perhaps a better suggestion for the discriminating palate on a limited budget. Of course, prestige vineyards produce devastatingly expensive wines as well, most famously **Penfold's Grange Hermitage**, so sought after that their yields disappear almost immediately at enormous prices; the 1991 Grange is now selling for about $500 a bottle, if it can be found. But even Penfold's produces a huge range at all prices, all of which should be tried. One of the most exciting experiences for a wine lover is to sample the smaller vineyards' yields; almost all wineries happily welcome visitors to their tasting rooms, and the experience can be the discovery of surprisingly mature and unusual tastes.

Each major city section in this book is preceded by a short list of restaurants in all price ranges. Given the intense competitiveness of today's food culture, no restaurant is sacrosanct; even the most popular may be closed tomorrow. Every attempt has been made to ensure that this information is up to date, but these few offerings in no way cover the tremendous diversity of dining experiences in Australia. A very good suggestion is to buy the current copy of each city's *Cheap Eats* or *Good Food* guides, available at news agencies and book stores. Other restaurant guides abound, especially in Sydney and Melbourne, and newspapers provide current reviews of restaurants, old and new.

Language

As George Turner states in *The English Language in Australia and New Zealand* (1966), 'The homogeneity of Australian English is remarkable. It would be difficult to find elsewhere a geographical area so large with so little linguistic variation.' While idioms and some words may vary from region to region and urban-rural distinctions exist, the **Australian accent** is essentially the same from Hobart to Perth to Cairns, despite Australians' insistence that they can tell the difference between a South Australian, Victorian and a Sydneysider. The accent and pronunciation, however, is distinctive, and was commented upon in print as early as the 1820s.

Linguists maintain that its development originated in the **Cockney and Irish English** speech patterns of the early convicts and settlers. **Aboriginal**

words have also entered the language, most specifically as place-names and for plants and animals, e.g. 'kangaroo' and 'koala'; Aboriginal speech patterns also provide some variation from 'standard' Australian English.

The use of the Australian accent by comedians such as Barry Humphries and Paul Hogan, while not entirely inaccurate, exaggerates the sound and idiom of contemporary Australian English, which is indeed undergoing lexical change spurred by the arrival of new ethnic groups and Americanisms learned from the mass media. Australians do say 'g'day, mate,' 'no worries' and 'fair dinkum' quite regularly. In some cases, terms are British, e.g., 'nappy' not 'diaper', 'petrol' not 'gas,' and in other cases, American, e.g, 'truck' not 'lorry'; 'cookie' is making inroads, although 'biscuit' is still preferred usage. Pronunciation is equally schizophrenic, e.g., complete variation on whether one says 'CON-troversy' or 'con-TRO-versy'. In the case of place-names, wait until you hear a native pronounce it, since anyone else's choice will invariably be wrong by local custom, and you probably will not have even thought of the 'correct' pronunci-ation. Two major cities, however, are pronounced MEL-burn not Mel-BORN, and BRIZ-bin, not Briz-BANE. The national capital is CAN-berra, not Can-BERra.

Terms for the sizes of beer glasses is very regional, and too complicated to explain here, but a 'tinnie' is universally understood as a can of beer.

An Australian glossary

Below are a few specific usages and phrases that may be unfamiliar to other English speakers; it is interesting to note how many of these unique terms and expressions are irreverent or derogatory.

Arvo afternoon, often meaning afternoon tea. This is one of the more convoluted examples of the Australian penchant for making anything into a diminutive by placing an 'o' or 'ie' on the end, e.g., **'garbo'** for garbageman, **'bikie'** for a motorcycle gang member, **'postie'** for the mailman, **'smoko'** for a coffee or smoke break, **'aggro'** for aggravation.

Aussie pronounced OZie.

Back o' Bourke, Beyond the Black Stump the boondocks, back of beyond, the outback.

BIRs as found in rental ads, it means 'built in robes', that is, closets.

bitumen asphalt, asphalted, or 'sealed', road.

Buckley's as in 'haven't got Buckley's'; haven't got a chance. The term supposedly refers to the most famous of the so-called 'wild white men', William Buckley, an escaped convict who lived among the southeastern Aborigines for 32 years before being discovered in 1835. This popularised origin is disputed by Sidney J. Baker in *The Australian Language* (1966), maintaining instead that the term probably derives from a pun on the name of a Melbourne retail company, Buckley and Nunn; this derivation would explain the phrase, 'there are just two chances, Buckley's and none'.

bugs as in Balmain or Moreton Bay bugs; crawfish.

to cark it to die.

chook chicken, most specifically living, not cooked, ones.

chunder vomit.

cozzie swimming costume, or swimsuit; also called 'bathers'.

dag, daggy nerd, nerdy; unattractive.

drongo a fool, no-hoper; after a horse in the 1920s, who consistently lost every race in the most ignominious fashion. A very derogatory expression.

dunny outdoor toilet.

entree what in America would be called 'appetizer' or first course; what in America is the entree is in Australia the 'main', or main course. In Australia, the word is never accented.

Esky portable ice chest invented in Australia; absolutely essential for any barbecue or event requiring cold beer.

fair dinkum genuine, the real thing; as a question, it has the connotation of 'really?'.

Fritz South Australian for a cold-cut, like the American bologna or English devon.

galah (accent on second syllable) a pink and grey bird found everywhere, but also a noisy person, or, as in 'dumb as a galah'; galahs are supposed to be particularly stupid birds.

grouse far out, cool; most prevalent in Victoria.

hoon a fool; more specifically, a car-based yobbo, a cruiser, frequently seen in groups of threes and fours at events such as Canberra's Summernats, hanging out of car windows and burning rubber.

jelly gelatine dessert, 'Jell-o'; American-style 'jelly' as in 'peanut butter and jelly' does not exist.

Kiwi New Zealanders.

larrikin mischief-maker, frolicsome youth; larrikinism is a much-beloved Australian form of anti-authoritarianism.

lollies candy, sweets.

manchester household linens, sheets; derived apparently from the traditional place of origin for textiles in Australia.

Ocker a redneck; currently used infrequently.

paddock a field, usually for grazing, as in the oft-quoted 'Canberra is a waste of a good sheep paddock'.

perve to take a licentious peek, as a voyeur, e.g. 'look at them perving the women'.

petrol gasoline, as in 'petrol station'.

pissed drunk, *not* angry as in the USA; 'pissed off' is angry.

Pom, as in **whingeing Pom** British, who are widely believed to be complainers.

prawn one throws a prawn on the barbie, *not* a shrimp.

Rego motor vehicle registration.

root vulgarly, to have sex; just remember that one does *not* 'root' for one's team, one '**barracks**'!

Seppo an elaborate example of the survival of Cockney-style 'rhyming slang': Yank = septic tank = septic = seppo, a very derogatory and seldom-used expression for an American. Another example of rhyming slang is 'trouble and strife' = wife.

Squatter originally referring to those free settlers or native-born who moved into newly opened territories and placed themselves upon public lands before any established land policy made such a practice illegal. While in America and England the term usually has pejorative connotations, in

Australia squatters quickly gained status as those who settled and occupied great expanses of land for the purposes of sheep-raising and farming. The '**squattocracy**' describes the old landed money of the country.

station equivalent to the American 'ranch', the latter a term which is *never* applied to Australian property.

tall poppy high achiever; a common Australian pastime is to 'cut down tall poppies', that is, cutting overachievers down to size.

throw a wobbly,'spit the dummy' to have a temper tantrum; a 'dummy' is a baby's pacifier.

Wog derogatory term for migrants, usually of Mediterranean descent; the oft-heard phrase 'to catch a wog' means to be sick, indicating the possible origin of its later definition, as 'wog' initially referred to 'germ'. Many of these New Australians are now so firmly established in the culture that ethnic humorists can themselves make fun of this epithet, as in Greek-Australian comedian Nick Giannopoulos' 'Wogarama' and 'Wogs at Work'.

wowser teetotaller, killjoy; coined in 1889 by John Norton, the notoriously pugnacious and dissipated editor of the newspaper *Truth*. Other variations include **wowserism**, and even 'to wowse'.

ute short for 'utility', a pick-up truck.

yacht ALL sailing vessels are yachts; 'sailboats' is considered American usage.

yakka 'hard yakka' is hard work.

yobbo usually 18- to 24-year-old male, out for general mayhem; also any uncouth person.

Background information

Natural History and Geology

Australia is situated approximately between the 10th and 45th parallels south and between 110 and 160 degrees east. Its total area is 7.68 million sq km (2.96 million sq miles), sufficient to cover Europe to the Urals and include the Mediterranean or nearly to cover the continental USA. Its three principal geological regions are the **Western Plateau** and the **Central Plains** (a Precambrian shield) and the **Eastern Highlands** (the Tasman Geosyncline). The continental base dates from Gondwana at least. Interesting Precambrian troughs run north through South Australia and then to northwestern Western Australia. The Yilgara region of Western Australia is, in fact, Archaean. The Great Artesian Basin, dating from the Mesozoic period, extends from north central South Australia to western Cape York Peninsula and straddles the New South Wales/Queensland border.

> ### Geological eras
> In the Triassic period, about 225 million years ago, Australia was still part of **Gondwanaland**, the supercontinent which combined all present-day continents. About 45 million years ago, the ancient continent of **Sahul**, consisting of mainland Australia, Tasmania and Papua New Guinea, separated from Gondwanaland. During the Oligocene period, about 40 million years ago, the Australian landmass experienced widespread volcanic activity. By the Miocene period, the land bridge with Papua New Guinea was cut, and mammals appeared on the Australian continent. The Pliocene era saw the emergence of primitive people in Africa, and the continued development of marsupials and distinctive bird species.

The Nullarbor Plain of South and Western Australia dates from a sea in the Cainozoic Era, as do the Simpson Desert as far south as Lake Eyre and much of the Murray-Darling River basin. Much of northern Western Australia, the Kimberley and Arnhem Land are Precambrian, the interior northern Great Sandy Desert and central Northern Territory south of the Barkly Tablelands is Palaeozoic.

The land mass was last connected to Antarctica in the early Tertiary Era. Except as island hopping, there has been no access to African or South American biomes for over 150 million years. Even then they were at quite a distance across Gondwana. Australia separated from Antarctica to begin chasing the Southeast Asian Plate at about the same time that North America started separating from Europe about 60 million years ago. Indigenous conifers predate this split. An example of these, touted as the world's oldest still extant tree species, has recently been found in the Wollemi National Park near the Blue Mountains just outside Sydney.

Reduced sea level during the late Pliocene and Quaternary ice ages did facili-

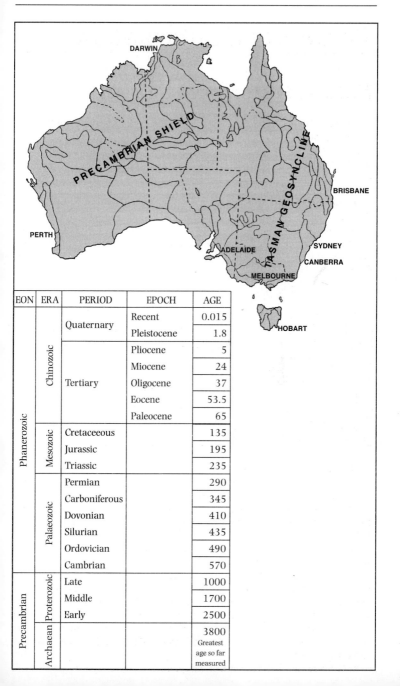

EON	ERA	PERIOD	EPOCH	AGE
Phanerozoic	Chinozoic	Quaternary	Recent	0.015
			Pleistocene	1.8
		Tertiary	Pliocene	5
			Miocene	24
			Oligocene	37
			Eocene	53.5
			Paleocene	65
	Mesozoic	Cretaceeous		135
		Jurassic		195
		Triassic		235
	Palaeozoic	Permian		290
		Carboniferous		345
		Dovonian		410
		Silurian		435
		Ordovician		490
		Cambrian		570
Precambrian	Proterozoic	Late		1000
		Middle		1700
		Early		2500
	Archaean			3800 Greatest age so far measured

tate colonisation of the continent indirectly from southeast Asia. Although there were no land bridges during this time, introductions during this period included palms, humans and, about 5000 years ago, dogs.

The **Western Plateau** covers nearly two thirds of the continent and is comprised of four major deserts rimmed by escarpments. It averages about 300m above sea level and rests on ancient rock shield. The plateau is marked by the Hamersley and Kimberley Ranges in the north west, three east–west oriented mountain ranges (MacDonnell, Musgrave and Petermann) in its centre and the Nullarbor Plain and coastal Bight in the south.

The **Central Plain** extends from the Gulf of Carpentaria to the Nullarbor. It includes the Lake Eyre drainage basin, the Murray-Darling river system, and the Gulf of Carpentaria drainage. Except for the Murray-Darling, the interior river systems in this area generally have seasonally intermittent flow.

The **Eastern Highlands**, locally called the **Great Dividing Range**, extend from Cape York Peninsula to the Bass Strait and include Tasmania. The northern portions are low and broad, the central portion becomes increasingly mountainous. Dating from the Palaeozoic period, these highlands have risen at the same rate as they were eroded.

Climatically, Australia sits across and to the south of the horse latitudes, currently referred to as the Intertropical Convergence Zone (ITCZ). In the north, southeast trade winds descend to well south of the Tropic of Capricorn, bringing the northwest monsoon to the northern regions (Top End). This summer (December to February) pattern causes heavy thunderstorm. To the south, westerly tradewinds push counter clockwise moving fronts formed over the Great Southern Ocean. These bring periodic winter rains once the ITCZ moves north.

The resulting rainfall patterns interact with geology to cause a number of Australia's ecological features. The central desert is possible because the eastern highlands remove water from the South East Trade Winds. Further, these winds limit the southern advance of the monsoon. The monsoon fills the flood plains of Kakadu and Arnhem Land annually. That which falls over the tablelands of western Queensland flows inland, occasionally filling Lake Eyre, but generally simply seeping into the artesian basin.

During 'The Dry', the interior is arid from the west coast well into the central eastern lowlands. Perth, Adelaide and the south coast can be described as Mediterranean in that they receive winter rains.

Because of the prevailing southeasterly trade winds, the eastern coastal mountains have temperate rain forests. Only in the highest and southernmost mountains of the Eastern Highlands does the temperature fall below freezing in winter, although the desert will be quite cool at night in winter. In contrast to the northern hemisphere, low pressure systems circulate clockwise and highs circulate anti-clockwise.

Vegetation and soils are a matter of combining the effects of geology and climate. The **true deserts of the interior**, from eastern Western Australia extending into northwest South Australia and the southwest of the Northern Territory and adjacent central South Australia, are well vegetated relative to the Old World and North American deserts. They tend towards loose stone (called 'gibber'), red and red-brown desert loams. Their sand dunes form extensive longitudinal ridges. Characteristic vegetation is saltbush or, in slightly better soils, hummock grasses like spinifex.

Surrounding the desert is a semi-arid area of grey and brown soils with increasing grass and thinly wooded acacia or eucalypt scrub. The mallee, a low growing, multi-stemmed eucalypt, extends as a band from the coast of Western Australia through the Nullarbor. The name of the plant also refers to the region in which it grows. During the era of sea travel, ships' passengers describe knowing they were nearly to South Australia because they could smell the acacia blossoming in these alkaline soils long before land was sighted. The semi-arid conditions in the central eastern regions often suffer from drought.

The southwestern and southeastern regions are marked by a succession of humid to sub-humid areas of **eucalypt forest and tall woodlands**. In the wettest areas of the eastern coastal mountains and western Tasmania, dense rainforests with trees 30m high dominate, with extensive undergrowth of ferns, orchids and palms in the north. In fact, across the top end of the continent are warm eucalypt forests growing in soils of low fertility and mangroves on the coastal flats.

With the exception of noble efforts to preserve large tracts as national parks and also the establishment of World Heritage sites, there has been little conservation on a local level. Some progress is being made now that it has been recognised that rising salinity in the agricultural soils in the Murray-Darling River Basin in New South Wales and Victoria is an effect of deforestation and erosion. Further, the economic damage of opportunistic forestry (particularly clear cutting for wood-chip export) and the appreciation of the economic benefits of ecological tourism are among the factors leading to the protection of local natural sites.

The **weather** in Australia is remarkably consistent. Across the north of the continent, as mentioned, frequent thundershowers in the monsoonal summer (November and December) alternate with a cooler, dry period (April to August). The region's most uncomfortable period is during the oppressive humidity and heat which eventually results in the monsoonal summer rains.

The southern portions of the continent can expect generally dry and warm summers. During winter (May to July) the South Ocean lows from the 'roaring 40s' latitudes migrate north. These lows bring cool, wet weather across from the southeast. Then a trailing high pressure front brings cooler, drier days. Occasionally, a northwest cloud band from the tropics will cross the continent, bringing rain to the centre and increasing the wet weather already associated with low fronts affecting the southeastern capital cities. In any event, this intermittent wet weather generally lasts a couple of days, to be repeated every five or six days.

The bracing to brisk line of water temperature proceeds from central New South Wales to Victoria from mid-summer to early autumn, but depends, of course, on the sun's heat and ocean currents.

Flora and Fauna

Australia is not particularly interested in the official implementation of emblematic flora and fauna, although the **wattle flower** is the country's official floral emblem. Inexplicably, this beautiful symbol appeared on none of the popularly nominated Republican flag designs recently displayed for future consideration, even though it could be as distinctive an emblem as Canada's maple leaf. The states and other organisations are represented, however, by semi-official emblems of flora and fauna: the ACT Parks and Gardens have a parrot, the gang gang cockatoo; Tasmania has become known for the Tasmanian devil; New South Wales takes the remarkable blossoms of the waratah; Western Australia has the kangaroo paw plant; South Australia's Sturt's desert pea and the rifle bird emblems seem a bit confusing, since the desert pea is more frequently noted in northern Western Australia, and the rifle bird is better known on the extreme northeastern coast of the continent. No one has claimed one of the most prevalent birds, the galah, despite its pleasant pink head and calm grey body.

Flora

The **acacia** (in Australia known as the wattle), casuarina and eucalypts (usually called 'gums') are the most significant indigenous flora. No pines grew here before their introduction by Europeans, although there are a few native conifer species; all deciduous trees are introduced. Acacia comprises some 1000 species of low trees with ball-shaped blossoms tending to be bright yellow to yellow-green with a characteristic scent. Many people claim that wattle cause allergic reactions. However, its pollen is too large to have an effect. It is the grasses which blossom at the same time, i.e. late winter and early spring, which are more likely to be responsible. The brilliant yellow blossoms of many wattle varieties provide a spectacular display of colour along the roadsides and in the parks at the end of August.

Casuarinas, sometimes called she-oaks, occur as stands along river courses. They are quite large trees with a cedar or conifer-like appearance. The seeds provide food for sturdy-beaked parrots.

The **eucalypts** produce 450 distinct species throughout the continent, having adapted to nearly every condition. Approximately 68 per cent of Australia's forest trees and a large portion of woodlands and even tropical trees are eucalypts.

Tea trees, especially the species *Melaleuca alternifolia*, are now widely cultivated for their valuable medicinal oil. Tea trees often resemble forms of eucalypt, although they are more likely to be shrub-like in size.

While the distribution of **native grasses** conforms to the degree of aridity, the area within a couple of hundred kilometres of Cloncurry in western Queensland offers nearly the complete range of habitats and grass types on the continent. Other indigenous and widely distributed floral species include banksias, grevilleas, and bottlebrushes (*Callistemon* spp.).

Mammals

The marsupial mammals, reptiles, and parrots are similarly signal fauna for Australia. Serious naturalists will find numerous descriptions of native species throughout this text, but a summary is provided here for general interest.

The indigenous mammals of Australia include two of the world's three monotremes (of the order Monotremata, native to Australia and New Guinea), most of the marsupials, a few rodents, and bats. Of the monotremes, the **platypus** (*Ornithorhynchus anatinus*), although a mammal with thick brown fur, lays eggs and has webbed feet; the adult male has a poisonous spur that is venomous enough to kill small animals. The other native monotreme is the

echidna (*Tachyglossus aculeatus*), sometimes called erroneously the spiny anteater. The echidna's body is covered in brown hair and has sharp quills on its back, some reaching a length of 6cm.

The **marsupials** gestate outside the womb in a pouch or fold of skin where the infant suckles. Among them, **Kangaroos** and **wallabies** can be found in most natural settings, although the kangaroo is most characteristically associated with fallow pastures and grasslands. They can be quite tame when hand-fed in enclosures. In the wild, the male leader of a 'mob' of kangaroos may attack following a display in which he tilts his head back while scratching his chest. However, this happens very rarely; usually when a mob is disturbed in the wild the leader will simply hop away. Wallabies are more elusive, though frequently encountered on trails in natural settings. There are some 48 different species of kangaroos and wallabies in Australia, some of them quite widespread and others now seriously endangered.

The famed **koala** (*Phascolarctos cinereus*) is a quiet tree dweller with a strong characteristic odour. Like most marsupials, koalas are nocturnal animals. Spotting them in the wild in the daytime is not impossible for someone with a trained eye as they sleep curled in the crotches of tree limbs about 15m off the ground. Since becoming a protected species in the 1920s, koala numbers have reached stable proportions, although in some areas disease and environmental changes pose a continuing threat to their population.

The **wombat** will not be widely recognised outside Australia. Its shape and weight is something like a badger with a blunt nose. It sleeps in a burrow, eats grasses and roots at night. Tales abound about its sole survival tactic which is to squash its pursuer between the flat base of its spine and the roof of its burrow.

One of the most easily seen marsupials is probably one of the many species of **possum**. The name was given to this family of marsupials by Captain Cook's sailors, who thought they resembled the North American opossum. The most widely distributed species is the common brushtail possum (*Trichosurus vulpecula*), who often nest in suburban backyards or in city parks. Possums can be a real nuisance if they manage to establish themselves inside the eaves of houses or office buildings. Other possums include the wonderful sugar glider (*Pteraurus breviceps*), which can glide as far as 50m from tree to tree, and lives off nectar, sap and insects; and the tiny eastern pygmy possum (*Cercartetus nanus*) in eastern Australia, also a nectar eater.

Australian **bats**, which are placental mammals, include a number of fruit bats ranging from flying foxes to blossom bats as small as moths. The grey-headed fruit bat is known for its southerly migration from central Queensland to Victoria following the orchard crop's ripening. A 20,000-strong colony of these flying foxes exists in the Sydney suburb of Gordon, and fly across the city at dusk.

Birds
The birds of Australia are for the most part strikingly social: flocks of parrots, generations of kookaburras, families of magpie and fairy wren; even the more solitary bowerbird courts his mate most elaborately. The eastern coast and mountain range, as well as the northern tropical forests, offer an overwhelming variety of species peculiar to Australia. Opportunities are increasing for bird-watchers due to the trend towards native gardens and parklands and a more protective attitude towards wilderness areas.

The birdlife of urban areas is surprisingly varied, and an unending delight for bird lovers unaccustomed to such brilliant plumage and diversity of bird calls in the neighbourhood garden. Several varieties of black-and-white birds and also parrots are among those which the visitor is most likely to see.

Of the **black-and-white varieties**, locally plentiful species include the mudlark, commonly called the peewee; a dapper flycatcher with twitching tail called a Willie Wagtail; and larger birds like the mellifluous magpie; the yellow-eyed currawong; and the native raven with a call of mocking plaintive crying.

Among **parrots**, the ubiquitous grey-and-pink galah (*Cacatua roseicapilla*), pronounced 'gul-AHH', has a reputation for being stupid, hence the expression 'dumb as galahs'. The sulphur-crested cockatoos are very raucous and will certainly awaken those unaccustomed to their early morning sing-alongs. Parrots and their relatives are non-Passerines, i.e. not northern hemisphere songbirds. Rather they are mostly of the order Psittaciformes. They routinely show green, yellow, red and blue for accent. Smaller parrots and lorikeets are about 20cm long, rosellas 30cm, corellas 40cm and the varieties of cockatoos 40cm and more.

Birds with noteworthy songs include **bowerbirds**, **lyrebirds** and **ground-wrens** for the imitative capacity of their elaborate songs. A variety of **whip** and **bell birds**, the **kookaburra**, with its staccato laugh, and its **kingfisher** relatives are commmon sounds in the bush, as well as in some urban areas.

Some of the surprising varieties prevalent in Queensland and the Northern Territory do have relatives in function or structure in other regions. The **cassowary** (*Casuarius casuarius*) and **emu** (*Dromaius novaehollandiae*) are a case in point. Cassowarys are ostrich-like omnivorous browsers, important or essential to the seed dispersal of about 100 fruiting or seed-bearing species. Up to two metres tall, with a distinctive helmet, a blue head, red nape and wattle and black body, they frequent stream beds and clearings on Cape York's western rain forests. They are reputedly dangerous, attacking if cornered or harassed. Emu are ostrich-shaped birds. Although they look shaggy and charred or smutty, their feathers are delicate. Common throughout Australian grasslands and deserts, they are omnivores and surprisingly opportunistic feeders in picnic areas, and to leave a laden table or grilling meat unattended where emu are about is tantamount to feeding the wildlife. Unlike the cassowary, they are not dangerous to chase off, though it is wise to be careful when approaching creatures kept in enclosures.

Australia's equivalent to a crane is the **brolga** (*Grus rubicundus*), prevalent only in the northeastern corner of the continent. Standing nearly 1.5m tall, it has a reddish mask and a nondescript grey body. Cranes are noted for their social displays and for soaring on air thermals. In somewhat drier grassy habitats, the male Australian or Kori bustard has a remarkable courtship display. The normally quiet bird roars and extends a white throat sack to the ground while stepping from side to side.

Among those birds making unusual nests are the mound-building Australian **brush turkey** (*Alectura lathami*), **scrubfowl** (*Megapodius reinwardt*) and **mallee fowl** (*Leipoa ocellata*). All mate for life and build mounds of vegetation in which they incubate their eggs. Frequenting rainforests and wetter open forests along the northern and eastern coast, the brush turkey's head is bare of feathers and is red with a yellow ruffled collar. The mallee fowl inhabits the dry inland scrub along the southern portion of the continent. The scrubfowl is native to the rainforests and monsoon forests of the north. The **lyrebird** (*Meura ssp.*) builds a small domed nest on the ground but broods rather than buries its eggs in it.

Other nest-builders of note are the **paradise rifle-bird** (*Ptiloris paraliseus*) and bower birds (*Ptilorhynchis* spp.). The former builds a cup-shaped nest, often draping cast-off snake skins around their nest's rim. Their courtship display, like that of the related paradise birds in New Guinea, involves opening their wings and sometimes bobbing or waving their heads. Because their primary feathers have adapted to this display, the birds can frequently be spotted due to the rustling sound they make during flight. **Bowerbirds** are quite common. They build elaborate nests or clear courtyards and decorate either with items of bright colour, often preferring blue. They are known to steal blue clothes-pegs off the line, as well as backyard blue containers or straws. The males spend much of their time calling for mates from their decorated nest. They generally mate in early to mid-summer, but their bowers remain throughout the year.

Australian birds have associated geological regions. The central desert spinifex regions host the spinifex pigeon and a variety of grass wrens; the shrub-lands host chats and pipits; the semi-arid mallee support ringneck parrots and mound-building mallee fowl. The eucalypt woodlands and the mulga regions of Queensland offer a diverse range of both parrots and passerine birds, notably the crimson rosella, lyrebird and scarlet robin. The interspersed wetland areas, especially in the Murray-Darling River Basin, will attract pelicans and the famous **black swans** (*Cygnus atratus*), faunal emblem of Western Australia. Mount Kosciuszko, along with the Torres Strait Islands, are credited with the largest concentration of bird species.

Reptiles

Lizards play a prominent role in the Australian imagination despite a modest representation of species (450 of the world's 4000) and families. Geckoes, dragons, skinks, goannas and legless lizards are frequently encountered.

The small, shiny lizards found in gardens are usually skinks. A much larger skink, the **blue-tongued lizard** (*Tiliqua multifasciata*) also frequents gardens. Prized for eating snails and other garden pests, they are easily injured by handling.

Geckoes are more likely to be encountered in the ground litter and bark of forested areas, or hanging from the ceilings of hotel-rooms in tropical areas. The largest gecko grows to c 25cm in length. Forests are also the habitat of **goannas**, which routinely grow to more than a metre in length. Gould's goanna is frequently seen in dry forests. Surprisingly large at as much as 1.5m, it will lie still if discovered but can run at speed, even charging at those who disturb it. Some goannas can be spotted climbing trees, and they often make a barking sound like a dog.

The **dragons** (a number of whose representatives take up residence at the botanic garden in Canberra each summer) include the desert-dwelling frilly-necked lizard (*Chlamydisaurus kingii*) often featured in wildlife documentaries because of its defensive posture and hind-legged run.

Crocodiles are of two sorts, fresh and salt water. Both are encountered in tropical regions, salt water crocodiles being by far the more dangerous.

Snakes are common in rural and natural areas. Many have striking beauty;

all deserve respect and protection. Except for the large carpet python and the diamond snake (*Morelia spilotes*), one can assume that any snake is venomous. The degree of danger they may present varies. The handsome green tree snake (*Dendrelophia punctulatus*) or the yellow bellied sea snake (*Pelamis platurus*), for instance, are not likely to bite humans unless provoked by rough handling. The red bellied black snake (*Pseudechis porphyriacus*), while venomous and common, is not particularly dangerous. On the other hand, a number of frequently seen brown snake species (*Pseudonaja spp.*) and the tiger snake (*Demansia carinata*) have dangerous bites. The fabled death adder (*Acanthophis antarcticus*) and taipan (*Oxyuranus scutellatus*) are deadly but not frequently encountered and rarely bite humans. All cases of snake bite should be attended to. Antivenins are held at hospitals for such emergencies.

Insects

Despite the mosquitoes, insects offer considerable entertainment in Australia. The awakening of the **ants** in the cooler regions signals the end of winter's wet weather. Australia has over 1500 species of ant, or 10 per cent of the world's total. The bull-dog ant can be as long as 3cm. These red or black beasts are aggressive and have a powerful and unforgettable sting. (The sting starts wearing off in minutes, subsiding much like extreme chills.) Popular belief insists that these feisty creatures will actually go after anyone disturbing their turf.

Most of the other stinging ants are brightly coloured with an iridescent violet sheen. Certainly, most of Australia's ants are innocuous. Some are comical. Disturbed 'silly ants', a favourite of school-age children, will spin rapidly in place with their thorax held aloft. Other species are interesting because of their biology or habits. The honey ants store nectar in their abdomen. Meat ants are reddish black, swarm when their large pebbly nests are disturbed and measure about 5mm in length. Birds are seen rubbing these stingless ants against their feathers. According to experts such as David Attenborough, no one knows why brids do this

Travellers notice **termites** due to those species which build above ground nests. These mounds will be found on nearly every ramble in the bush. Curiously devoid of vegetation, they often appear to be a fresh pile of dirt until closer inspection reveals the mound to be nearly rock hard. The **magnetic termites** build tall, narrow mounds with ends pointing north and south.

Poisonous fauna

The majority of noxious and poisonous fauna are snakes, but, fortunately, they tend to be shy. A few species of jelly fish and spined fish are to be avoided. Well-known to fishing or bathing residents they include a blue-ringed octopus, red-backed and funnel-web spiders (both reclusive) and the spur of an enraged male platypus. Some of the ants will give a hurtful sting.

As frequently mentioned throughout this book, beware mosquito bites, especially in the tropical north where they may carry Ross River Fever. Any number of repellents are widely available. These preparations also work against leeches, which are prevalent in the warmer rainforests and inflict similarly itchy symptoms.

Virtually none of the deadly Australian species, except perhaps the salt water crocodile, are frequent killers. In reality, some circumspection and prompt treatment results in few serious problems. The saying in Australia is 'Swim between the flags'. This dictum applies to supervised bush walking as well as to supervised ocean swimming. A particularly good example is the stinging tree of tropical Queensland. Touching it is painful and results in swelling. The reaction is similar to stinging nettles, hence the name. It is well known, readily identifiable and is routinely disposed of in frequented areas. Get someone to point the tree out to you if you are walking in Queensland, and be sure to stay on marked paths.

The night sky

For many visitors, the night sky in the southern hemisphere is a revelation. Unlike the northern hemisphere, Polaris is missing as are the Big and Little Dippers, Ursa Major and Ursa Minor. Instead, the predominant celestial features are the clearly visible Milky Way, with a stark, black hole near its centre, and our neighbouring galaxy the Large Magellanic Cloud. Find the Southern Cross (Crux) and its two pointers Alpha and Beta Centauri and you should be able to locate the Large Magellanic Cloud (the LMC in astromonical circles). If the Cross is at 12:00, the cloud will be at about 3:30. (There is a Small MC at about 5:30.) Alpha Centauri, our nearest neighbour, is the third most brilliant star in the heavens and is, in fact, a binary star with a third star orbiting the pair at some distance.

Another star not seen in the farther reaches of the northern hemisphere but visible here is Canopus. The second most brilliant star, it sits at the end of Argo's prophetic keel. The star Canopus was mentioned by Babylonian astronomers as well.

Of course, the most astonishing celestial sight is the unfamiliar geography of the moon and the related upside down orientation of the constellations shared with the northern hemisphere. The bull Taurus is going in the opposite direction down under, and 'the man in the moon' is upside down.

Aboriginal and Torres Strait Islander Australians

I want people to change their attitudes to Aboriginal people. I want Australians to have pride in a culture which is practically the oldest culture in the world. Australians need to get out there. Seek and ye shall find! I want them to go out to Fitzroy Crossing and places and just hang a bit. People think blackfellas are unapproachable. It's not true.

The popular newspaper magazine *Good Weekend* presents this call for reconciliation by Ninjali Josie Lawford, a storyteller of increasing recognition. Her mother was a Wangkatjungka and her father was taken from his tribe as a child and, like Lawford, raised on a Kimberley district cattle station. Of course her instructions for Australians suits any traveller in a novel situation. Anyone who wishes to meet and get to know someone from Australia's Aboriginal or Torres Strait Island communities must simply make the effort.

Although Australia's indigenous population has suffered much since European colonisation, systematic land confiscation, murder, confinement, starvation, rape and child kidnapping and enslavement are no longer routinely practised in Australia. This situation is relatively new, however. The removal of children from their families and placement in an institution or foster home was practised until the early 1970s; the Aboriginal population was fully enfranchised to vote in 1962; the High Court ruling on land rights (referred to as the Mabo Decision, 1992) allows access to government owned pastoral land for traditional practices as long as this access does not interfere with the current use of the land. Although Aboriginal deaths in custody continue to be frequent, some pressure is being exerted by political bodies and activist groups to change this situation; Amnesty International has identified this situation as a significant example of human rights violation. Similarly, the general dearth of health services in Aboriginal communities is under attack from the Australian Medical Association and some branches of government. Most importantly, the indigenous groups in Australia have uniformly called on the general population for reconciliation.

One important consideration when discussing contemporary Aboriginal culture is that there is no such thing as a single Aboriginal culture, language or world-view. At present, the indigenous population stands at approximately 303,000, or 1.7 per cent of the Australian population. There are an estimated 1385 indigenous communities in the country, with 81 per cent in remote areas. New South Wales has the largest Aboriginal population, with 80,400 people of indigenous descent living here. At the time of first contact in 1788, estimates indicate about 600 to 700 Aboriginal 'groups' speaking some 250 distinct languages. Today, only about 30 languages are still spoken. In the northern regions of Australia, Aboriginal groups have also developed Kriol, a mixture of English and native language which in some cases is becoming a 'lingua franca' among Aborigines themselves.

The visitor might best begin an understanding of the lives of Aborigines with a description cast in religious terms. The people to whom they are related are recognised first as family members but with religious affiliations. Their art, their property, their stories are set in theology. Tourists are generally surprised by the extent to which religion, art, social relations, and property are integrated.

As with any religion, aboriginal theology is described in myth and enacted in ritual. Unlike European religion, however, not all of the content of this theological structure is freely available to everyone. Some aspects can be revealed openly, others are sacred and may only be revealed to the initiated, those who share participation in the realm of the particular sacred knowledge. Straightforward rules govern initiation into age/experience-related groups in the local community. Levels of understanding and, more importantly, interpretations associated with events portrayed in myth are provided to the initiates. Familiarity with mythic, totemic or ritual knowledge beyond one's station or capacity can be considered spiritually or even physically dangerous.

The myths are accounts of the 'Dreamtime', or more properly '**the Dreaming**', which is primarily the mythic era before the present world took shape: spirit beings moved about the world shaping the land and creating people, arranging totemic affiliations, and instituting rituals. But the Dreaming is also current. Prior to conception and following death, an individual resides in

Dreamtime. Celebrants of the most secret and sacred of rituals re-enact events which occurred in Dreamtime and are themselves in Dreamtime. In fact, creation continues because these participants are involved in Dreaming it.

The songs, dances and stories for their ceremonies and art are attributed to the performers' ancestors or to spirits with whom the performers have some affinity. Rather than being authored, they are conveyed to the artist during sleep, periods of isolation or illness. Should someone deserve the right to use a song or motif, the living owner can pass it on. Upon death, the performer continues this process, conveying the art work to members of the subsequent generation. This often occurs after a period of mourning and a mortuary ritual which releases the spirit to travel to the place of other ancestral spirits. Prior to this ritual and often for a considerable time afterwards, the names of the deceased are not spoken. This observance must be kept in mind by the larger community when an Aboriginal artist dies whose work appears in national or international collections. Depending on the traditions and feelings of the artist's tribe and family, it may be necessary to remove photographs and identifying labels naming the deceased person.

The Aboriginal people have struggled to arrive at a safe and appropriate means of presenting to outsiders their myths and associated art, music, dance and property rights. Some traditional art, whether painting or ceremonial, is inherently more secular. The most well-known of Aboriginal rituals are commonly referred to as **corroborees**. Those which are performed for the benefit of tourists are quite like religious rites in that body painting, dance movements and music describe mythic affiliations and dreamtime events. Musical instruments are extremely simple and likely to include didgeridoos—a painted wooden tube played like a trumpet but without caesura for breath—percussive sticks or rocks, and a folded leaf which acts as a double reed when held between the first knuckle and pad of the thumbs. The dance movements are evocative of animals associated with the myths. The body painting will relate to the associated animals through ornament identifying totemic clan affiliations. In some instances this information is considered sacred and a variation on the decoration is presented instead.

The first Western **music** performed by Aboriginal and Torres Strait Island people came from Christian missionaries. The London Missionary Society introduced this form of worship to Torres Strait Islanders and Cape York Aboriginal communities late in the 19C following its success in the Pacific Islands. Christian musical performances are often marked by traditional instrumentation (clapping, striking boomerang tips or clapsticks) and dancing, but not body painting.

Rock and reggae styles of music are also performed by some Aboriginal people. Again, the northern regions have been the origin for acceptance and dissemination of modern popular music within the Aboriginal community. Music by the Aboriginal band Knuckles from Broome was the basis for Jimmy Chi's reggae opera *Bran Nue Dae* which premiered at the Perth Festival in 1990. The first truly Aboriginal international rock band is arguably Yothu Yindi from northeast Arnhem Land, the creation of Yolngu tribal members of the Yunupingu family. Lead singer Mandawuy Yunupingu was named Australian of the Year in 1993.

Aboriginal Art

When talking to an Aboriginal painter about a particular work, he or she will first of all tell the visitor (as far as the constraints of religious secrecy allow) about the tjukurrpa (Dreaming), which is the painting's source. He or she will describe the specific interpretation which the symbols assume in this story. The artist will point to the tract of country in which the story takes place, often naming the sites in great detail, and he will talk about the custodianship of the area where the story is centred, naming both specific contemporary custodians and the particular subsection of the kin system through whom ownership is generally passed down. For the artists, this is the essential background information to the proper understanding and appreciation of their work. A painting not informed by a Dreaming (if such a thing were seriously possible) would be nothing more than frivolous decoration; simply not art.

Ian Green, 'Make 'em flash, poor bugger'—talking about men's paintings in Papunya in Margaret West, ed., *The Inspired Dream—Life as Art in Aboriginal Australia* (1988).

Aboriginal art is first and foremost representational. Many of its conventions are recognisable to the viewer. Several fish of diverse species are shown caught in a large fish trap or a kangaroo is presented in x-ray style, showing its major organs and skeleton. With a bit of assistance the viewer recognises the half doughnut shapes and bisected angles in dot paintings as camp sites and emu tracks. Warmun community artist Rover Thomas's depiction of Cyclone Tracy, a black path through coloured landscape, is easily recognised once its significance is explained.

Beyond shared conventions, Aboriginal art in every region continues to be representational in its ornament. In many areas the **cross-hatch designs and colours** represent totemic or kin groups associated with stewardship of a particular site. They can represent special relationships with the species or event depicted. Just as one learns representational conventions in order to interpret a painting, there are associated stories and observations learned by Aboriginal initiates. The extent of esoteric knowledge conveyed by the art, a painting for instance, depends upon the status of the observers. Still, a considerable amount of information about a painting is secular. We recognise the fish as a barramundi, for instance, and are told about the fishing techniques. The meaning of the cross-hatches, on the other hand, is not explained; they seem simply decorative to the uninitiated observer, while to the initiated and those skilled in looking, these signs take on additional representational and symbolic significance.

The **rock art** of the **Kakadu region** provides an interesting insight into the process in which the convention of artistic styles develop. Prior to the end of the last ice age, rock art in Kakadu presented human and animal figures in animated poses. At the same time as these depictions became stylised and abstracted, mythic figures of the yam and Rainbow Snake Being are represented. By the time the sea levels rose to what they are now and the monsoonal climatic pattern became established about 1500 years ago, Namarrgon, the lightning man figure, appears, as do **x-ray style** depictions. The depictions are still realistic but have changed in both subject and style to portray new ideas about how the world works.

While the relative permanence of rock art makes it an important means of dating the introduction of motifs and styles, it was not the most frequently used medium. Painting the bodies of celebrants in initiation and similar rites, desert sand paintings not unlike horizontal frescos and painted slabs of bark for the interior of dwellings were from early days the most favoured media. Most of the motifs found in bark and canvas paintings are secular variations on the motifs in the consciously ephemeral body and sand paintings.

The cross-hatching and x-ray style of the Arnhem Land region of the Northern Territory is quite distinct from the styles of the Central Desert. In the **desert communities**, dot paintings and stark in-fill are more likely. Until quite recently, these were generally religious and ephemeral, the work being done as ground (sand) paintings, body decoration or constructions. Public awareness of the forms in the desert depended upon photographs by ethnographers, which were first taken in the early 20C, or rock art and more transportable decorations on implements seen by visitors to the region willing to brave difficult travel. Although some small carved and decorated pieces were produced for sale, little of the art was publicly available until the 1960s and later.

The introduction of **acrylic paints** to replace ground ochres and other naturally occurring materials began in the early 1970s at the **Papunya School** in central Australia. Geoffrey Bardon, a teacher at the school, asked senior Aboriginal men in the community for permission and advice on the Honey Ant Dreaming for a mural at the school. Following considerable discussion about the propriety of depicting sacred knowledge in a secular setting, Papunya elder Old Tom Onion Tjapangati, who owned Honey Ant Dreaming, gave permission to a number of local men to paint the mural. At about the same time, Bardon provided artist board and paints and with the help of Kaapa Tjampitjinpa, one of the mural painters who had used modern materials, the Papunya men began painting in acrylic on board. Initially, respect for ceremonial proprieties caused more naturalistic depictions to replace the sacred iconography. Eventually, recognition that conventional motifs could be described without revealing sacred secrets allowed a return to traditional style. Art board was quickly replaced by the more portable unstretched canvas.

A similar series of events brought the art of the **Warlpiri artists** of the Northern Territory to the public arena. In this instance, Terry Davis, principal of the Yuendumu school asked senior men to paint the doors of the community's school in 1983. The Warlpiri were quite aware of the issues at hand. In fact, the women of the area had been producing decorated implements for a couple of decades for anthropologists. The work would be public, and would be the basis for subsequent, saleable art which would not be ephemeral but would be purchased and would permanently leave the community. In 1985, arrangements for the secularisation of the art were made in Yuendumu through the Warlukurlangu Artists Association, one of the first Aboriginal-run organisations to benefit from commercial sales of traditional artworks. In 1989, six Yuendumu artists installed a Yam Dreaming painting in the exhibition 'Magiciens de la terre' at the Centre Georges Pompidou in Paris. This exhibition marked a significant point in the recognition of Aboriginal art abroad, and in a 'high art' context rather than as ethnographic artefact.

Bark painting began to be sold in the early 1960s. However, in this case the impetus was from outstation missionaries who attempted unsuccessfully to introduce watercolours. While the watercolours were somewhat similar to the charcoal, ochre and other naturally occurring substances, acrylic paints and sized canvas or canvas board were preferred by the artists.

So, in effect, Aboriginal art has been available to the wider public since the 1960s. Of course, a number of anthropological and gallery exhibits pre-date this by a century and more; German and Swiss anthropological collections, such as the ethnographic museum in Basle, were important archives of early Aboriginal artefacts in Europe. The most important inaugural exhibition in Australia was arguably the 1929 National Museum of Victoria's 'Primitive Art' show, which included an anthropologist display of director Baldwin Spencer's collection of bark paintings acquired in 1912. Not until 1959 did an Australian art gallery begin to collect Aboriginal work as art rather than ethnographic artefacts, when the Art Gallery of New South Wales under artist and curator Tony Tuckson began to display works by artists from Tiwi and Arnhem Land cultures.

The state and national galleries now have collections on continuous display. Their material tends to date from this post-1950s period. A number of private galleries and Aboriginal artists' cooperatives provide the opportunity both to see and purchase art. In the best circumstances, the artist may be available to describe the painting's details. This information is routinely provided by the agent as well.

The most frequently mentioned Aboriginal community-based arts organisations include
- Utopia, NT
- Buku Larrngay Arts, Yirrkala, NT
- Bula'Bula Arts, Ramingining, NT
- Maningrida Arts and Culture Centre, Maningrida, NT
- Maruku Arts, Uluru, NT
- Mimi Arts and Crafts Gallery, Katherine, NT
- Papunya Tula Artists, Alice Springs, NT
- Tiwi Designs, Bathurst Island, NT
- Warlukurlangu Artists, Yuendumu, NT
- Waringarri Arts, Kununurra, WA
- Warlayirti Artists Aboriginal Corporation, Halls Creek, WA
- Ernabella Arts, Ernabella, SA
- Yalata Roadhouse, Yalata, SA

Brief descriptions of several of these community-based organisations reveal a consistent pattern. European techniques or material are adopted by local people, often following success in selling crafts to tourists. The success of modest early sales leads to greater community involvement and eventual control. International recognition, based on sales through local galleries and exhibition at national and international exhibitions, follows shortly thereafter.

The **Ernabella Arts group** began in 1949 as handicrafts produced by women on this mission cattle station. Initially, they spun and wove station-grown wool, but the women soon found batik to their liking as well. Similarly, the **Maningrida Arts and Culture Centre** began as production of a variety of artefacts made for tourists in the 1950s. It was established as a community-based enterprise in 1968.

Warlukurlangu Artists was formed in 1985 after senior Yuendumu women purchased a four-wheel drive vehicle with money they had saved from the sale of painted artefacts and canvas board. Their international recognition came upon the production of a 10 x 5m ground painting at the 'Magiciens de la Terre' exhibition in 1989 at the Pompidou Centre in Paris.

Papunya Tula Artists began after the introduction of mural painting at the Papunya community school by teacher Geoffrey Bardon. International recognition increased following the 1988 Dreaming exhibition at the Asia Society Galleries in New York City.

Tiwi Designs was established in 1969 by Melville Island artists Bede Tungutalum and Giovanni Tipungwuti who initially applied screen and block printing techniques to cotton fabric.

Aboriginal political history

The colonial period marked the seizure of most of the arable land in Australia by British pastoralists. Although the indigenous population had been decimated by European illnesses, sufficient numbers remained to mount some opposition to this dispossession. Not surprisingly, prompt retribution from colonial authorities followed each instance of violent resistance.

Named **massacres** include the Risdon Massacre (1804, Tasmania, slaughter), the Battle of Pinjarra (1834, Western Australia, punitive), Murdering Gully Massacre (1839, Victoria, punitive), Fighting Hills Massacre (1840, Victoria, slaughter), Fighting Waterholes Massacre (1840, Victoria, slaughter), Lubra Creek Massacre (1842, Victoria, murders), Hornet Bank Massacre (1857, Queensland, vigilante), the Coppermine Murders (1884, Northern Territory, vigilante), Forrest River Massacre (1926, Western Australia, punitive), Coniston Massacre (1928, Northern Territory, punitive).

Government protection boards eradicated Aborigines in the 19C and 20C more effectively than the armed groups had earlier. Ironically, these protectors were installed in response to public concern for the conditions in which Aboriginal people were living. The efforts of these protectors were marked by paternalism, segregation and sometimes enslavement in the name of assimilation, or, as one contemporary phrase put it, 'to soothe the dying pillow'. In most cases among colonial officials, Aborigines were seen as an inevitably 'dying race', with assimilation the only logical and desirable solution.

Initially able to suppress calls for equitable treatment of their wards, their powers were curtailed once the public came to recognise these state entities as detrimental. Beginning in the 1920s, Independent Progressive Leagues controlled by politically engaged Aboriginal people used high levels of publicity and well-planned events to present the plight of Aboriginal people to the Australian public. The result of this 50-year-long process has been a thorough re-evaluation of the place indigenous people might have in society and their worth to the nation. This re-evaluation has taken the term 'reconciliation' as its banner cry, although, as poet Judith Wright asserts, such a term implies that the two groups were at some time friends.

The modern social ethic is so far removed from that of the 19C and early 20C that we have a temptation to dismiss the missionaries, settlers and government functionaries as inhuman brutes. A more productive approach may be to concentrate on the efforts of the humane participants to establish an attitude of acceptance and assistance.

During the 19C, a number of settlers lamented the plight of the Aboriginal population. At the time social welfare efforts were largely organised by the churches. They established missions to instil Christian beliefs and provide basic sustenance. Although most of these missions were simply gulags, some did offer training in basic literacy and rural job skills. The missions at New Norcia, Western Australia (Benedictine Catholic), Poonindie, South Australia (Anglican), Hermannsburg, Northern Territory (Lutheran) and several later in Arnhem Land (Methodist) were noteworthy successes.

The earliest of these Christian societies was the **British Aborigines Protection Society** formed by Quaker anatomist Thomas Hodgkin. Not to be confused with the odious subsequent 'government protectors' of Aborigines, the society sought to prevent oppression of indigenous people in the British colonies. Their greatest success in Australia was the formation of an Aboriginal reserve, the Port Phillip Protectorate, which kept the area's settlers at bay and left the Aborigines largely to their own devices during the 1840s.

Later in the century Daniel Matthews formed a similar civil society in 1878, the **Aborigines Protection Association**. In addition to furthering the Maloga and Warangesda Missions and criticising the New South Wales protector of Aborigines, the association advocated compensation for dispossessed land and acceptance of Aborigines in responsible positions.

Real political and social advances for Australia's indigenous population began in the late 1920s and 1930s when Aborigines began forming their own political associations. Aboriginal activist **Fred Maynard** (1879–1944), in a letter to the Aboriginal Protection Boards, eloquently stated the politically engaged concern of reconciliation:

> *I wish to make perfectly clear on behalf of our people, that we wish to accept no condition of inferiority as compared with European people. Two distinct civilisations are represented by the respective races... That the European people by the arts of war destroyed our more ancient civilisation is freely admitted and that by their vices and diseases our people have been decimated is also patent, but neither of these facts are evidence of superiority. Quite the contrary is the case.*

Fred Maynard formed the **Australian Aboriginal Progressive Association** in 1926. In Melbourne, William Cooper and Bill Onus formed the **Australian Aborigines League** in 1932. William Ferguson and John Patten formed the **Aboriginal Progressive Association** in Dubbo in 1937. The two latter associations cooperated to stage 'A Day of Mourning' in Sydney on Australia's sesquicentenary (150th anniversary), 26 January 1938, and presented the Prime Minister at that time with a list of ten objectives. The central concerns advocated federal control of Aboriginal affairs and granting Aborigines citizenship.

This theme re-emerged in 1958 upon the establishment of the Federal Council for the Advancement of Aborigines and Torres Strait Islanders following a meeting in Adelaide of representatives from Aboriginal advancement organisations, church bodies, trade unions and social welfare groups. Among a variety of social measures, constitutional issues became their central effort. In 1967 they presented the issues as a constitutional referendum, to be voted on by the Australian people. The referendum amended the constitution so that it could no longer disallow the federal parliament from enacting laws which would apply to

Aboriginal people or from counting them in the national census enumeration. Of 42 referenda presented to Australian voters since Federation in 1901, this was one of nine which have been passed; it received a 90 per cent 'yes' vote.

Contrary to the popular impression that the referendum gave Aboriginal people the right to vote in federal elections, they had actually had this right since 1962. The central effect of the referendum was recognition of traditional law regarding ownership of land; the results of this recognition culminated in the *Aboriginal Land Rights (NT) Act 1976*. Following this recognition, regional land councils came to the fore as cooperative managers of a variety of land rights ceded to them. Shortly, these councils will have increased power over intellectual property as well. Tourists apply to these land councils for permission to enter Aboriginal or Torres Strait Island land.

Of greatest significance for Aboriginal rights in recent years has been the so-called Mabo decision and the Native Title Act of 1993. Eddie Mabo was a Murray Island native who in 1982 began proceedings against the state of Queensland, seeking recognition of the rights of the Island's traditional land. Mabo's case eventually came to the Australian High Court, where the vexed issue of *terra nullius*—the colonial assertion that Australia was uninhabited and unowned, and therefore land could be taken for the Crown or by any settler who wanted it—was ruled invalid. This recognition of traditional ownership of the land, that indigenous people had indeed occupied the continent at the time of white settlement, led to the historic High Court decision resulting in the Native Title Act 1993, ensuring clarification of all land titles throughout Australia and ensuring equality before the law. The conservative government under John Howard, together with pastoral and mining interests, is seeking to extinguish native title in relation to a related High Court decision concerning the Wik people of Queensland. This effort is leading to increased divisiveness and setbacks to the cause of reconciliation.

Not unexpectedly, as the Aboriginal and Torres Strait Islanders have taken control of their social and legal resources, their lot has begun to improve. Further, they have begun calling for rapprochement between Indigenous and newer arrivals. The reconciliation process formally began in 1991 upon the investiture of the Council for Aboriginal Reconciliation. While the council itself has an honour roll membership, its best work has been due to the optimistic, community-based efforts of those espousing its intentions.

A brief history of Australia

Discovery and habitation of Australia dates to at least **60,000 years ago**, the period established for the earliest remains found of an **Aboriginal population**. Recent evidence, in rock art, suggests that Aborigines may have been on the continent much earlier. Like the late-coming Europeans, these people appear to have come by sea after island-hopping along the northern coast. Evidence of the earliest occupation in the central areas of the country dates to **22,000 years ago**. The **dingo** probably accompanied Aboriginal settlers about **12,000 years ago**, well after ocean levels separated Tasmania from the mainland for the last time. Mega-fauna (giant marsupials) became extinct perhaps due to Aboriginal hunting in the late Pleistocene Era; brush burning as a hunting strategy established the predominance of open sclerophyll woodlands and steppe grass-land at about this same time. On this isolated continent the Aborigines remained undisturbed, living a nomadic existence, developing an elaborate kinship system and a complex aesthetic and theological world view. Their relatively small numbers and the fact that the harsh landscape necessitated movement over long distances prevented the development of any substantial settlements or elaborate material culture.

Early explorers

In more recent history, legends about '**Terra Australis Incognita**', the Great South Land, have existed both in Europe and Asia since ancient times. In 350 BC the Greek **Theopompus** wrote of a Utopia in the south, 'a continent or parcel of dry land which in greatness is infinite...'; the Indians of the sub-continent spoke of a Golden City under a banyan-tree found by sailing south; and the Chinese explorer **Ch'eng Ho** may have reached Australian shores as early as 1405, although no substantiated evidence remains.

Malay fishermen are known to have camped seasonally from at least the 16C on the Australian northern coast while harvesting sea slugs (*beche de mer* or trepang) for Chinese trade; and Islamic merchants who entered Java in the 11C seemed to have had some knowledge that a great land, wildly fantastical, existed in the south. Similarly, the **Portuguese** probably knew something of Australia shortly after they colonised East Timor in 1516; **Spanish** documents seem to indicate some knowledge of the existence of a southern land, following their settlement of the Philippines in 1565. By the time of the great era of European naval exploration, from the 16C to 18C, the fabled southern continent was a firmly entrenched myth, as demonstrated by its appearance on Ortelius's map of 1577, where it covers the entire southern end of the globe.

In reality, scientific exploration yielded piecemeal disclosures of the real nature of the Australian landmass; it was not until 1803 that the continent was fully circumnavigated and its true dimensions established. Spanish and Portuguese exploration in the region was frustrated due to the seasonally strong westerly winds and the maze of reefs among the islands to the north, where they, along with the Dutch, claimed land and established colonies for the purposes of commercial trade in the late 16C. It seems likely that the Portuguese landed at Cape York as early as the 1530s, but found little to encourage further investiga-tion. In the 1590s, Spaniards Pedro Fernandez de Quiros and Luis Vaez de Torres discovered the New Hebrides and, believing it to be The Great South Land, named it 'Australia del Espiritu Santo'; Torres' name lives on in the Strait through which the adventurers passed.

Early navigators who did land on Australian soil found it so wanting in any commodities for trade that they simply ignored it for many years. In the early 1600s the **Dutch** discovered and began charting Australia's western coasts; in 1616, Dirck Hartog in the *Eendracht* left a tin plate on the island given his name. They had taken an eastward route to the south seas, striking directly from the Cape of Good Hope at a southern latitude. While the Dutch explorations were sufficient to name the continent '**New Holland**', the Dutch captain's assess-ment of the country and its inhabitants prompted no interest in settlement. Carstensz' description of Cape York Peninsula in 1623 will suffice as an example:

We have not seen a fruit-bearing tree, nor anything that man could make use of;
there are no mountains or even hills... this is the most arid and barren region that
could be found anywhere on earth; the inhabitants, too, are the most wretched and
poorest creatures that I have seen.

In the early 1640s, as preparation to subvert Spanish interests in Chile and Peru, the Dutch captain **Abel Tasman** proceeded farther into southern latitudes than his predecessors. He discovered Tasmania, which he named Van Diemen's Land, after the Batavian governor-general who proposed the expedition. Tasman did not know whether the place was an island or part of a large mainland. Failing to find his way expeditiously to the Solomon Islands, the Netherlands' hoped-for equivalent to the Spanish Philippines, Tasman was ordered to take a more northern route. This voyage completed the Dutch map of the continent from the tip of the Carpentaria Peninsula to central South Australia in 1644, but without any knowledge of the eastern coastline.

The Dutch were not alone in describing the continent and its inhabitants negatively. The English pirate William Dampier visited the northeast and western coasts in 1688 and 1699–1700 respectively. He described the land and inhabitants so critically (the overwhelming number of flies seems to have been the biggest deterrent) that 'terra australis incognita' was left alone even by the British until **Captain James Cook**'s voyages in the 1770s. Dampier's most enduring contribution was as a source for Jonathan Swift's *Gulliver's Travels* (1726), in which he places Lilliput 'within the confines of modern Australia and its adjoining seas.'

The **French** also made forays into this part of the South Seas from the 17C. Indeed, it was fear of French expansion in the Pacific that partially prompted Cook's voyage so far south.

Cook's first voyage was ostensibly undertaken to examine the transit of Venus in the Southern Hemisphere; but Cook was also commanded to chart unknown territory and claim new discoveries in the name of the Crown. Cook's immense navigational achievements were enhanced by the fact that all three of his voyages carried first-rate scientists and artists to record and collect. Most significant was the presence on the first voyage of the great naturalist **Joseph Banks**, who would play an important part in Australia's subsequent settlement. Cook's first voyage on the *Endeavour* resulted in the discovery, in April 1770, of Cape Everard and, further north, Botany Bay, named by Banks because of the number of botanical specimens he was able to find there.

Despite shipwreck at present-day Cape Tribulation in Queensland, Cook successfully navigated the entire coastline; on 21 August of that year, at Possession Island, he formally claimed the eastern coast of New Holland for Britain, naming the land **New South Wales**.

These voyagers established the European vision of Australia as an inverted world in which all natural phenomena, flora and fauna, were contrary to scientific expectations. As Banks wrote, 'All things in this land seemed quaint and opposite', and Cook's flabbergasted descriptions of a kangaroo ('It was unlike any European Animal I ever saw') set the standard for considering Australia a scientific and geographic anomaly. At least Cook was kinder in his descriptions of the Aborigines, countering Dampier's 'miserablest people in the world... who have no houses and skin garments' with a more romanticised idea of the 'noble savage':

They may appear to some to be the most wretched people on Earth, but in reality they are far happier than Europeans; being wholly unacquainted not only with the superfluous but the necessary conveniences so much sought after in Europe.

After Cook's and Banks' return to England and their enthusiastic accounts of the wonders of the continent, much of the myth of *Australia incognita* was put to rest, although great geographical gaps remained until **Matthew Flinders'** explorations at the end of the 18C. In his leaky boat *Investigator*, in 1801–03, Flinders circumnavigated Australia. At this stage and upon Flinders' suggestion in his book of 1814, Australia became the preferred name rather than New Holland. Flinders had established that the continent was a single landmass.

The British inclination to settle Australia has been variously ascribed to hopes to open trade with Asian markets, to find a source of masts and similar naval stores, to prevent French colonisation or even to further understanding of natural history. In fact, the initial means of settlement was through the transport of criminals, burgeoning numbers of whom had been housed on floating hulks in the Thames and along the coast of England. In 1786, the Secretary of State for Home Affairs, Lord Sydney, entrusted the first fleet of ships bearing prisoners to **Captain Arthur Phillip**, a heretofore lacklustre naval officer of German-English parentage. The '**First Fleet**' departed England in May 1787, consisting of 11 ships transporting 750 convicts, about a quarter of them women, and about 250 marine guards. Due to Phillip's care, the passengers arrived after the eight-month journey in relatively good health, and very few deaths had occurred on the voyage, an unprecedented feat in naval history. Rather than establish the colony at Botany Bay, as Banks had suggested, its poor soil, inadequate water and poor anchorage prompted Phillip to search further north. He entered Port Jackson, a brilliant natural harbour, named though not explored by Cook.

Back at Botany Bay, the awaiting crew and passengers were astonished to encounter French ships commanded by Comte La Perouse, who had landed to make repairs, further motivation for the British to establish territorial rights. On **26 January 1788**, Sydney Cove became the site of the new penal settlement, a day still celebrated as Australia's founding (and, for Aborigines, the day of invasion).

The difficulties Governor Phillip faced included refusal of the marine garrison to take responsibility for guarding the convicts, a dearth of useful skills among the convicts, uncertain supplies from Britain and relatively poor soil and fresh water. The first years were ones of isolation and tremendous hardship, with starvation a constant threat, as the colonists confronted a hostile and unfamiliar environment. The Second Fleet, with another 750 convicts, did not arrive until 1790; more appeared the next year, by which time arable land had been found at **Parramatta**, and the crude beginnings of a British colony gained some solidity.

Once the colony was established, transported criminals found colonial life less harsh than it might have been. Convicts were employed by the government or assigned to land owners, and for the most part were not incarcerated at night. Once crops and livestock were well-established, convicts and workers ate better here than they would have back in England. Tickets of leave and pardons were often granted to those who proved useful to the government, and as early as 1793 **free settlers** began arriving. By the turn of the century, the first church, theatre, printing press and brewery had been established in Sydney.

Indeed, the French expedition under **Baudin**, upon visiting Sydney in 1800, reported: 'Europeans whom events at sea or particular reasons bring to Port Jackson cannot help but be surprised at the state of ease and prosperity to which this colony has risen since the time of its establishment.' Baudin's crew member Peron was even more insightful: 'The population of the colony amazed us. Settled there were frightful brigands who had long lost the terror of the government. Most of them, obliged to interest themselves in the maintenance of law and justice, had re-entered the ranks of honest citizens. The same revolutionary change had taken place among the women... Wretched prostitutes are today intelligent and hardworking mothers of families.' Within 14 years, the colony was fairly settled and civilised; just as Australian flora and fauna had upset the Linnean system of scientific order, the phenomenon of early Australian society was a refutation of commonly-held notions about the criminal classes. The peculiar circumstances surrounding the establishment of such a colony, and the common experience of a new land, led to a levelling of classes, a distrust of authority, and a democratic sense of giving everyone a '**fair go**' that still marks the Australian character.

The early economy was based largely on imported rum and other provisions, establishing Australia's long-standing habit of looking to Britain as 'home' and the source of all material goods. By the turn of the century, the New South Wales Corps through the rum trade controlled the labour force of the colony. This situation led to the Rum Rebellion of 1808, when **Governor William Bligh** (1754–1817), previously of *Bounty* fame, tried to thwart the military monopoly. **John Macarthur** (1766–1834), the most powerful officer of the Corps, managed to depose Bligh, but was himself finally arrested and banished from the colony. Macarthur, however, had already brought **Merino sheep** to the colony, establishing Australia's wool industry at Camden Park, where he would return in 1817. He and his extraordinary wife Elizabeth (1769–1850) remained powerful figures in Australian life, as its first traders and agricultural pioneers. In the meantime, Bligh was recalled and the Home Office, recognising the anarchic state of the colony, appointed a new Governor, the Scotsman and experienced career officer Lachlan Macquarie (1762–1824), to bring order to the situation.

The confrontation of white man with indigenous Australians was from the beginning fraught with the tension of two conflicting sets of values and expectations. As the First Fleet chroniclers David Collins and Watkin Tench make clear in their accounts, the new settlers' desire to make order out of the new landscape came into immediate conflict with the 'hard primitivism' of the Aborigines who, seemingly without a sense of ownership or material values, were seen by the whites to have no claim to the land they inhabited, and, in the worst of attitudes, to be hardly human at all. This idea led to the lamentable concept of Australia as a *terra nullius*, an uninhabited land, a misconception that has forever tainted interactions with the native people and has had sweeping consequences to the present day.

Governor Lachlan Macquarie

The arrival of the ambitious Macquarie and his wife Elizabeth in December 1809 saw a move away from the idea of Australia as solely a penal colony.

Governor Lachlan Macquarie

Macquarie supported emancipists, encouraged the rehabilitation of convicts, and subdued the power of the military establishment. He set out to give the colony all the trappings of British civilisation, through massive public works programmes and the implementation of banking and cultural institutions. With the convict-architect **Francis Greenway** (1777–1837), Macquarie created substantial public monuments and churches, and established new towns along the newly discovered Hawkesbury River. He set up the first school for Aborigines, officially recognised Roman Catholicism, and established Sydney's Botanic Gardens. He travelled to Van Diemen's Land, laying out the town of Hobart, and bestowing his name on places throughout the country. During his administration, the Blue Mountains were finally crossed in 1813, allowing expansion into the fertile parts of the inland and establishing a more positive vision of Australia as a livable country.

Macquarie's ambitions were too grandiose for the Home Office, and his encouragement of emancipist settlement brought him into conflict with the burgeoning numbers of free settlers. In 1819, **Commissioner J. Bigge** was sent out to Sydney to report on Macquarie's activities and the state of the colony, which by this time had been transformed from a place of punishment to one of civilised prosperity, eliminating the threat of transportation to Australia as a supposed deterrent to criminals in England. Bigge's negative assessment of public spending and political organisation led to Macquarie's resignation in 1821, as England vacillated in its opinion of Australia's value to the Empire. Further penal settlements were seen as necessary to instil fear, leading in the late 1820s to the establishment of Macquarie Harbour, Port Arthur, Port Macquarie, and Moreton Bay on the Brisbane River.

The establishment of colonies

Free settlement nonetheless continued to grow, leading to the declaration of colonies throughout the continent: in 1825 Van Diemen's Land became a separate colony, in 1826 Western Australia was founded, followed by Melbourne in 1835 and South Australia, proud of having no convict taint, in 1836. These all became self-governing colonies within the British Empire.

By the 1840s, exploration of the continent's vast expanses by Charles Sturt, E.J. Eyre, Ludwig Leichhardt, Burke and Wills, and others completed the Australian map, dashing hopes of a fertile inland as the extent of its dry and barren centre was substantiated. The settlements by the sea flourished, establishing the still-persistent custom by the populace of clinging to the coastline; today over 80 per cent of Australians live in six coastal cities, and nearly 90 per cent can be classified as urban dwellers. Convict transportation ended in New

Early explorers Charles Sturt (left) and E.J. Eyre (right)

South Wales in 1840, and throughout Australia by 1853. Opportunistic adventurers, in most cases British men of means, took up huge tracts of land at the edges of the explored regions, claiming ownership by virtue of settlement and developing a 'squattocracy' that would dominate as Australia's landed gentry to the present day. The population remained overwhelmingly Anglo-Celtic in composition and values, while the increase in native-born Australians led to a growing sense of national identity, especially among the working class.

The gold rush

It was the gold rush of the 1850s, both in New South Wales and the newly-proclaimed colony of Victoria, that significantly transformed the demographic structure of the country, as vast numbers of middle-class migrants and skilled artisans from all over the world joined the ranks of those locals who clambered to the gold fields. For the first time Australia became the focus of international attention. The results of so much immigration and the subsequent development of an industrial and cultural infrastructure to support them led to a more complex and self-conscious Australian society. The phenomenon of **'Marvellous Melbourne'**, developing in one decade to a cosmopolitan city of stature and for a time the wealthiest place within the British Empire, is the most startling example of the rapid transformation made possible by mineral wealth.

In the 1880s, while Melbourne grandiosely expanded its cultural institutions and architectural monuments, development of Australian heavy industry accompanied the discovery of enormous mineral lodes at **Broken Hill** in western New South Wales. These discoveries were an important step, leading to an industrial ethos within Australian society. Still, vigorous trade-unionism in the country grew initially out of the activities of shearers and pastoral workers, leading by the 1850s to the first **eight-hour-working-day** legislation in the world.

Rise of Australian nationalism

By the 1890s, as gold-engendered prosperity collapsed and economic depression permeated society, the strength of the trade unions encouraged nationalistic sentiments among Australian workers. Similarly, in art and literature, ambitious attempts were made to hone a specifically Australian world-view and cultural contribution. Artists of the **Heidelberg School** and writers such as Joseph Furphy, with his novel *Such is Life* (written 1895), forged a style using themes of the Australian landscape and the Australian vernacular idiom. The nationalist sentiment of Banjo Paterson's *Man From Snowy River* (1890) is unmistakable. The establishment of John Archibald's newspaper *The Bulletin* in 1880 promoted national issues and an Australian style of writing and humour.

The move towards federation of the separate Australian colonies into a single nation gained its strongest impetus after a speech by venerable politician **Sir Henry Parkes** at Tenterfield, New South Wales, in 1889. Popular opinion for federation was led by the Australian Natives' Association (native-born white settlers) and the Federal League, and by the end of the century a popular referendum accepted a constitution, which was enacted as a statute by the British Parliament. Australia was officially proclaimed a nation within the British Commonwealth on 1 January 1901, making the six colonies six states.

The period from Federation until the First World War saw a coalescence of national outlook, including the selection in 1913 of a new national capital, removed from inter-state rivalries, to be built at **Canberra**. The seat of government was Melbourne until 1927, when Canberra's Parliament House was finally opened. Australia remained overwhelmingly British in cultural and political attitudes. The government established consisted of a two-tier parliamentary system, presided over by a Prime Minister; each state had a premier and its own governor-general, and the entire system was overseen by a Governor-General nominally appointed by the British Monarch.

One of the first acts of the infant government was the **Immigration Act**, establishing the **White Australia policy** in an attempt to ensure a European, preferably British, population. While directed at the fear of the 'Asian hordes' to the north, the policy also effectively marginalised indigenous Australians, who were for the most part confined to mission stations.

The opening of the **Commonwealth Bank** in 1912 and the coining of separate currency in 1910 established an economy not entirely dependent on Britain's. Progressive measures adopted included universal suffrage in 1902, and, with the rise of the **Australian Labor Party**, an acceptance of a minimum wage law by 1907. Culturally, the 'Mother Country' was still the destination of all home-grown talent, whether in medicine, the arts, or higher learning. Only in the field of sports, especially cricket, rugby, and swimming, did Australia begin to nurture local teams and individual ability; it is one of the few countries to be represented at every modern Olympics Games. Exploits in aviation and exploration, especially **Mawson**'s expedition to Antarctica 1911–14 and **Kingsford Smith**'s trans-Pacific flight of 1928, produced local heroes and major achievements that were hailed as Australian, not British, accomplishments.

First World War

The First World War brought Australia on to the international stage as a separate nation. While conscription was defeated by popular vote at home, despite the efforts of xenophobic Prime Minister **Billy Hughes** (1864–1952), thousands of Australians signed up to fight with the British forces, both in the Middle East and in Europe. Australia also took over the governing of German New

Guinea, its first foray into extraterritorial administration. The disastrous events in 1915 at **Gallipoli** in Turkey, in which the troops of the Australian and New Zealand Army Corps (**ANZAC**s) sustained enormous losses, served as a 'crucible of nationhood', establishing a sense of national pride and a questioning of total dependence on British power. **ANZAC Day**, on 25 April, remains the most patriotic and Australian of occasions throughout the country.

In 1918, Australia's population reached five million. Returning soldiers found Australia in the 1920s increasingly divided between the growing urban population and the concerns of farmers and pastoralists. Immigration from other European countries grew as the United States closed its doors to most migrants in 1921. Labor Party versus anti-Labor battles determined government policies at all levels, becoming a persistent feature of Australian political life.

Modern technology brought Australia into the 20C by decreasing the geographical and social distances on the continent and increased the country's connections to the outside world. Significant developments include the establishment in 1920 of **QANTAS** (The Queensland and Northern Territory Air Services) and The Flying Doctors' Service in the Outback, the arrival of telegraph, telephone and radio services, and improved shipping.

The building of **Sydney's Harbour Bridge** between 1923 and 1932 was hailed as a major engineering feat as well as an emblem of Australia's modernity. The **Australian Broadcasting Commission** (ABC) was formed in 1932, offering a venue for local production and support of Australian artists. Artists by the 1930s still overwhelmingly went abroad to pursue culture, but literature and art created at home became more vigorous, with efforts such as the **Angry Penguins** movement in Melbourne and the arrival of European-trained immigrants in all the capital cities.

The **Great Depression** of the 1930s had as devastating a social impact on Australia as elsewhere; here economic collapse led to a restructuring of the banks, with increased tensions caused by the continued dependence on British financial policy and institutions. Nowhere is Australian obsession with and domination of sport against the 'Mother Country' more symbolically demonstrated than in the infamous **'Bodyline'** controversy of 1932. Indefatigable cricketer Don Bradman (b. 1908), the pride of all Australia, was deliberately abused by British bowlers in a test match; Australia at the time was desperately seeking a loan from the Bank of England, a loan that was made contingent upon Australian authorities dropping their protests against the British cricket team. On the playing field, allegiance to England was eschewed in favour of loyalty to the nation long before any political distancing occurred.

Second World War

The Second World War again brought Australia into global affairs, this time with more recognition of the country's place in the Pacific realm: primary attention was given to the defence of Australia against Asian forces, although Australians still fought under British command. Australian troops were particularly effective in the early North African desert campaigns such as **Tobruk** and **El Alamein**. With the fall of **Singapore** in 1942, during which Australian troops were seen to be abandoned by the British, and with the entry of the United States into the war after Pearl Harbour, the Prime Minister, Labor stalwart **John Curtin** (1885–1945), shifted Australian efforts to the Pacific and established closer political alliance with the United States. General Douglas Macarthur used Australia as a base for coordinating Pacific operations, bringing large numbers of American troops to Australian shores for the first time.

In 1942, the **Japanese** bombed Darwin, a Japanese submarine entered Sydney Harbour, and Japanese troops invaded New Guinea. On every front, Australian troops were present, playing a decisive role along with the US Navy in the **Battle of the Coral Sea** and halting Japanese advances in New Guinea. Australia also played a leading role in the post-war establishment of the United Nations; Dr H.V. Evatt was the organisation's first President of the General Assembly.

1945 onwards

After the war, Australia, acutely aware of its isolated position as an underpopulated European nation at the southern end of Asia, responded with massive assisted-immigration programmes, initiated by Labor leaders **Ben Chifley** (1885–1951) and **Arthur Calwell** (1896–1973). These programmes saw the arrival in Australia not only of British migrants, but for the first time large numbers from non-English-speaking countries. These **'New Australians'** began the transformation of the country into the multicultural society it is today. Asians were still effectively banned from immigration well into the 1970s. The need for a more independent and vigorous economy also led to the implementation of large-scale engineering projects, most notably the **Snowy Mountains Hydro-Electric Scheme**, an unprecedented technological programme to harness water for irrigation and supply electricity to New South Wales. The 'Snowy's' work force was comprised of people from 35 countries, many of whom remained to become Australian citizens.

The 1950s brought to power the newly organised Liberal Party, conservative in policy, under **Robert Menzies** (1894–1978), who would dominate Australian politics into the 1960s. Menzies oversaw the period of post-war prosperity of full employment and material growth, maintaining a staunchly pro-British view while involving the country in prevalent Cold War policies. The visit of Queen Elizabeth II in 1954, the first visit by Australia's monarch, generated overwhelming excitement; over 70 per cent of Australia's population made an effort to see her in person. Australian troops were sent to Korea in 1950. Communism was seen as a threat at home and abroad, and the British were allowed to test atomic bombs in the desert regions of Maralinga and Emu Junction. Under Menzies, literary censorship still banned books such as James Joyce's *Ulysses* and schoolchildren used textbooks that referred to their near-northern neighbours as 'The Far East'. Aboriginal children were still removed from their families, and they were not granted citizenship until 1967. Television was first introduced in 1956, not coincidentally the year of Australia's international debut as the host of the Melbourne Olympic Games.

Menzies sent advisors to Vietnam as early as 1962 and introduced conscription. His successor **Harold Holt** (1908–67) continued the commitment to Vietnam, coining the phrase 'all the way with LBJ' after the visit by US President Lyndon Johnson in 1966. By 1971, public sentiment against Australian involvement in an Asian-American conflict was so strong that most troops were recalled; in all, 500 Australians died in Vietnam and 2400 were wounded. Culturally, the period was still one of expatriation, both to Europe and America, but the so-called **'cultural cringe'** (a term coined in 1950 by writer A.A. Phillips) began to diminish, as new galleries and learned institutions opened, and writers and artists began to explore the peculiarities of the Australian cultural condition.

Prime Minister Holt's death by drowning in 1967 paved the way for Labor's win in 1972 led by a visionary **Gough Whitlam** (b. 1916). The time was right for change, and Whitlam set about implementing these changes. He ended conscription and recalled troops in Vietnam even before he was sworn in. He granted independence to Papua New Guinea, and initiated free higher education and health care. He strongly supported the arts, abandoning stringent censorship laws and subsidising the Australian film industry. Whitlam was instrumental in the purchase in 1973 of the controversial Jackson Pollock painting *Blue Poles* for an enormous sum, Australia's first venture into the world of art politics. In the same year, Queen Elizabeth II opened the Sydney Opera House; her trip generated far less fanfare than the first one. Whitlam also extended Aboriginal rights and returned land to them, infuriating pastoralists and mining interests.

Burdened with a conservative Senate, which refused to approve Labor's budget, and an unfriendly Governor-General, Whitlam's government was doomed. **Governor-General John Kerr** dismissed the government on 11 November 1975; while such powers were theoretically at the Governor-General's disposal, no representative of the Crown had previously taken such a step. The move effectively began a viable **Republican movement** which questioned Australia's continued allegiance to the British Crown, a debate that continues in earnest today.

The 1970s also saw the official end of the 'White Australia' policy, and **Asian immigration** began. The first Vietnamese boat people arrived in 1976, adding another dimension to the country's growing ethnic communities. Australian literature gained international attention: in 1971, Germaine Greer, while resident in London, published *The Female Eunuch* and in 1973, Patrick White became the first Australian to win the Nobel Prize for literature. The environmental movement came into being, and remains a powerful if beleaguered force today.

The 1980s saw the election of popular Labor Prime Minister **Bob Hawke** (b. 1929), who would serve until 1991, when his power was usurped by his former treasurer **Paul Keating** (b. 1944). Labor, however, lost the support of its traditional unionist and working-class constituency, as it became increasingly right-wing in policy.

The 1980s is already being termed the **'decade of greed'**, as entrepreneurs took advantage of world-wide economic conditions to create lavish financial empires, only to see them collapse by the end of the decade. Figures such as **Alan Bond** and Christopher Skase became international celebrities; indeed, it was Bond's *Australia II* that won the **America's Cup** in 1983, an event that caused national celebration. Australian domination in international sports such as cricket and rugby, and media successes such as *Crocodile Dundee* in 1985 increased the country's international standing; indeed, the media paved the way for global moguls such as Rupert Murdoch and Kerry Packer. The Bicentennial celebrations of 1988 symbolised the country's status, as major public events such as the Tall Ships Parade highlighted white Australian achievement, and Aboriginal demonstrations spoke to the continuing inequality of indigenous people.

Australia today

Today, Australia is a multicultural society with a global outlook. Advanced communications has finally allowed the continent to overcome its **'tyranny of distance'**, with major cultural and scientific achievements created locally. Australia produced the first successful frozen embryo fertilisation in 1984, and Australian scientists made the most significant breakthroughs in the process of gene-shearing. Australian **Peter Doherty** won the 1997 Nobel Prize for Medicine, for research initially carried out at the John Curtin School of Medicine in Canberra. Culturally, the arts, architecture, and cinema are as sophisticated and complex as anywhere in the world; the 'cultural cringe' has been put to rest, although international recognition still seems necessary for public approbation. While xenophobic racism occasionally rears its head, and the continued neglect of Aborigines causes world-wide concern, multicultural integration is admirably successful, and is perhaps Australia's greatest contribution to contemporary society.

The most significant event of the 1990s has been the **Mabo decision**, by which the High Court in 1992 legally overturned the concept of *terra nullius*, leading to Native Title legislation to ensure Aboriginal land rights; the decision has world-wide implications and will be a major test of Australian democratic institutions.

A new Liberal-National Party coalition government (that is, conservative) led by **John Howard**, elected in 1996, seems intent on economic rationalisation in step with Thatcher-Reagan policies, decimating many of the social programmes of the last twenty years. The government was nonetheless instrumental in introducing stringent gun controls precipitated by the Port Arthur tragedy of April 1996. The Republican debate continues, and the public recognises the symbolic significance of the upcoming Sydney Olympics in 2000, when Australia will again be the centre of world attention.

Australian art

The history of Western art in Australia began with the navigational records and drawings by those accompanying the first explorations of the South Pacific. The brilliant naturalist **Joseph Banks** (1743–1820) saw to it that Captain Cook's voyages included excellent naturalists and draughtsmen: Daniel Solander (1736–82) and **Sydney Parkinson** (c 1745–71) on the first voyage in the *Endeavour*; William Hodges (1744–97) and German-born George Forster (1754–94) on the second; and John Webber (1752–93) on the third. All of them collected natural specimens and eventually published numerous images of natural wonders, geographical settings, and native peoples that would determine the European vision of the Pacific for many years. Equally significant were the depictions from the French voyages of the late 18C and early 19C: the fascinating prints of Tasmanian Aborigines made on Baudin's 1800 voyage by François Peron (1775–1846) and Nicolas Petit (1777–1804), and the elegant interpretations of sea-life and native fauna completed by Charles-Alexandre Lesueur (1778–1846). Lesueur's enchanting depiction of a wombat, one of the first published in Europe, is still widely reproduced.

Period of settlement

The earliest depictions after colonial settlement exhibit the amateurs' fascination with antipodean difference, and style of draughtsmanship learned by naval officers of the day. They are most interesting for their attitude to the natives they encountered. The **Port Jackson Painter** (fl. 1790s) portrays them in *The 'Hunted Rushcutter'* (1790) as playfully aggressive, while his *Wounded native* (c 1790), in a pose like the Roman sculpture of *Dying Gaul*, embodies connotations of the 'noble savage'. **Governor Hunter**'s (1737–1821) delightful notebook of native flora and fauna, produced during his tenure as governor in the 1790s, expresses the simple joy of discovery of new birds and plants (Hunter's entire journal has been reprinted by the National Library of Australia, 1989). The Austrian **Ferdinand Bauer** (1760–1826) accompanied Flinder's circumnavigation of the continent in 1802–03, and produced the most exquisite natural illustrations ever created, some of them published by the artist in 1813 as *Illustrationes Florae Novae Hollandiae*. In contrast, Flinders' landscape artist, **William Westall** (1781–1850), was disappointed by the lack of the sublime or exotic in the Australian countryside; despite some insightful renditions of Aborigines, most of his landscapes demonstrate the prevailing early perception of Australia as a barren and uninteresting place.

In most cases, these early works mimicked modes of 18C British painting. Convict **Thomas Watling**'s (b. c 1762) views of Sydney in 1800 are exemplary, in which his dismay about the 'otherness' of the Australian landscape led to a combination of picturesque motifs learned at home, and emphasised the civilising effect of the British presence on the land itself. The first panoramic views of the new colony by **John Eyre** (b. 1777) and others appealed to the home audience when exhibited there, and began the rage for 'traveller's views' of the Australian landscape and native life that led to substantial production of prints and illustrated books for London society.

Naturalist-artist **John Lewin** (1770–1819), accompanying Governor Macquarie on his crossing of the Blue Mountains in 1815, created watercolours that successfully depicted the Australian bush, correctly delineating eucalyptus trees that defied rendering through standard pictorial technique. Lewin made the first known drawing of a koala, and his painting of fish done in 1813 is considered to be the first oil painting completed in the colony. It is Lewin's image of the kangaroo that provided the iconographic prototype of the animal that became a metaphor of antipodean oddity. In the 1820s, **Joseph Lycett**'s (c 1775–1828) prints in his *Views of Australia* (1824) presented the Aborigines in Arcadian landscapes, practising their traditional way of life and in possession of their land.

By the 1830s, Australia had become a destination for settlers, as well as adventurer-explorers. The artist **Augustus Earle** (1793– 1838) represented the latter, visiting the continent while travelling the world, then returning to England to produce sympathetic depictions of Aborigines already marginalised by European settlement, as well as adventurous narrative works such as *Wentworth Falls* (1830) and the picaresque rendering of a night-time camp in newly explored territory, *A Bivouac of Travellers in a Cabbage-Tree Forest* (c 1838). In contrast, **John Glover** (1767–1849), already a well-known landscape artist in England, settled in Tasmania permanently at the age of 64 in 1831. While he created some fanciful images of Aborigines in the bush, Glover's main concentration in works such as *My Harvest Home* (1835) and *A View of the Artist's House and Garden, in Mills Plains, Van Diemen's Land* (1835) emphasises the creation of familiar Englishness in this fertile new country. Glover nonetheless made great efforts to depict the Australian bush with accuracy, one of the defining characteristics of early colonial art being the correct rendering of a gum tree.

Australia's coming of age as an independent settler colony is mirrored in the more ambitious paintings of the 1840s and 1850s. **Conrad Martens**' (1801–78) romantic views of Sydney continued a British painterly tradition influenced by Turner, with a concentration on the harbour's water and atmosphere and more grandiose renderings of the virgin landscape. Even Martens' late work of the Zig Zag Railway near Lithgow (1872), a wonder of engineering, stressed the majesty of the landscape rather than technology's scarring of the land.

In Melbourne, the gold rush of the 1850s saw the arrival of several Europeans who brought German and French landscape traditions to the fore. **Louis Buvelot** (1814–88), a Swiss painter, domesticated the Australian landscape, with his *plein-air* technique learned from the French Barbizon School. As Christopher Allen states in his *Art in Australia* (1997), Buvelot's great contribution was as an influence on local artistic practices. Similarly, the Austrian **Eugen von Guerard** (1811–1901) applied elements of the Germanic landscape style in his sublime views of the Victorian countryside and, most notably, in his *North-East View from the Northern Top of Mount Kosciuszko* (1863), a fine combination of geographical accuracy and romantic sentiment.

Landscape painting and national identity

Increasing cultural aspirations accompanied the growth of the cosmopolitan centres of Melbourne and Sydney at the end of the century. Most ambitious young artists travelled to Europe for training and acquired stylistic self-consciousness. As Australia began to formulate a distinct national identity in the 1880s, several artists who began painting together outdoors in the Melbourne countryside around Heidelberg (thus known as the Heidelberg School) sought to create a national style, focussing on depictions of Australian sunlight and images of the bush. The central figures of the groups were **Tom Roberts** (1856–1931), **Charles Conder** (1868–1909), **Arthur Streeton** (1867–1943), and **Frederick McCubbin** (1855–1917). Paintings such as Roberts' *Shearing the Rams* (1890), Streeton's *Golden Summer, Eaglemont* (1889), and McCubbin's *The Pioneer* (1904) still stand as aesthetic icons and have become some of the most reproduced images in Australian art. These artists' approach to the landscape and Australian life represent the greatest artistic achievements of the 19C; their interpretations determined the directions Australian art would take into the 20C. Landscape painting of the bush became the most accessible mode for portraying Australianness, as the works of popular painter **Hans Heysen** (1877–1968) and **Arthur Streeton**'s later *Land of the Golden Fleece* (1926) attest.

By the turn of the century, most Australian artists still needed to become expatriates to be taken seriously. Some stayed in Europe so long that it is difficult to consider them Australian painters: **Rupert Bunny** (1864–1947) gained an international reputation for his large-scale paintings of elegant women in a decorative French style, while **John Russell** (1858–1931) emulated the work of his friend Vincent Van Gogh. **George Lambert** (1873–1930) also established himself as a successful English society painter before the First World War led to his appointment as an official Australian war artist.

It is significant that some of the greatest artistic achievements in these formative years were in the field of **illustration**. The most ambitious publishing achievement of the time was the massive *Picturesque Atlas of Australasia* (1885), coordinated by Sydney artist **Julian Ashton** (1851–1942) and including lithographs and engravings by the colony's best artists. The illustrators of *The Bulletin* of the 1880s and 1890s, initially editorial cartoonists, developed 'The Black and White School', creating memorable images that became part of the national psyche. **Norman Lindsay** (1879–1969), the most well-known member of the prolifically artistic Lindsay family, caused a scandal with his many prints and paintings of voluptuous nudes, but is perhaps most famous for his delightful children's book, *The Magic Pudding* (1918), with his characters Bunyip Bluegum and Uncle Wattleberry. Similarly, **May Gibbs** (1877–1969) created the most enduring and beloved childhood creatures in her *Gum-Nut Babies* (1916) and *Snugglepot and Cuddlepie* (1918). In **design**, the period immediately following Federation in 1901 saw the application of Arts-and-Crafts ideas and Art Nouveau style to every medium, most notably using Australian flora and fauna as motifs in stained glass, furniture, and tilework.

Twentieth century

The First World War marked a real watershed in cultural areas. Many Australian artists worked for the war effort; some returned from Europe, some stayed in England indefinitely. After the war, the battle lines concerning modern art were firmly entrenched. In Melbourne, **Max Meldrum**'s (1875–1955) tonal school fought vehemently against the most modern intrusions, while in Sydney, the most advanced efforts were being made by women artists, many gaining knowledge of modernist ideas and stylistic methods through reproductions, design and graphic arts. Adelaide-born **Margaret Preston** (1875–1963) produced stunningly modern examples of colour and form, and was one of the first artists to incorporate Aboriginal elements and themes into her paintings and prints; **Thea Proctor**'s (1879–1966) graphics epitomised 1920s fashionable modernism; and **Grace Cossington Smith** (1892–1984) created Post-Impressionist masterpieces often focussing on urban scenes and the Sydney Harbour Bridge. Post-Impressionist colour theory was introduced by artists **Roland Wakelin** (1887–1971) and **Roy de Maistre** (1894–1968), further examples of designers who made the first breakthroughs into modern modes. The efforts of Sydney publisher **Sydney Ure Smith** (1887–1949) encouraged in his publications more contemporary aesthetic modes and the development of an art-literate public.

The 1930s saw the arrival of European émigrés, many of whom brought an understanding of the most advanced cultural ideas and artistic styles. In Melbourne, the Russian-born painter **Danila Vassilief** (1897–1958) was influential, both as a painter and as a disseminator of modern aesthetic philosophy. Increased awareness of modernist ideas coincided with the appearance of several ambitious young artists encouraged by the patronage of **John and Sunday Reed** and centred around their home, Heide, in suburban Melbourne. Certainly Heide has a legitimate claim as being the real birthplace of Australian modernism. Aligned with the ideas expressed in John Reed and Max Harris' literary magazine *Angry Penguins*, artists such as **Sidney Nolan** (1917–92), **Albert Tucker** (b. 1914), **John Perceval** (b. 1923), **Joy Hester** (1920–60), and **Arthur Boyd** (b. 1920) began to create distinctly Australian brands of Expressionism and Surrealism. Social Realist directions also became an important trend, with figures such as **Noel Counihan** (1913–86), **Josl Bergner** (b. 1920) and **Russell Drysdale** (1912–81) concentrating on grim images of real people in difficult conditions, an art with a social conscience. A truly original contribution to Surrealist art appeared in the work of **James Gleeson** (b. 1915), who also published some of the period's best art criticism.

Photography

In the 1930s, art photography also gained status, with figures such as the Sydney photographers **Max Dupain** (1911–92) and **Olive Cotton** (b. 1911), inspired by German photography that they discovered in contemporary art journals and books. Dupain's most famous work, *Sunbaker* (1937), was actually taken at this time, but did not become a national icon until its reproduction in the 1960s. The Second World War brought to prominence **Damien Parer** (1912–44), probably Australia's best-known photographer; his film *Jungle Warfare on the Kokoda Front* (1942), a documentary on the Australian fighting in New Guinea, won an Oscar in 1942. The next generation of photographers, most notably **David Moore** (b. 1927), were particularly influenced by documentary modes promulgated by British filmmaker John Grierson and the American photographer Walker Evans. Significantly, Moore, along with **Laurence LeGuay**, were the only Australian contributors to Edward Steichen's famous photographic exhibition, *The Family of Man* (1955).

Conservatism versus Modernism

The first modern art exhibition—that is, one in which works of Impressionism, Post-Impressionism and Cubism were seen in Australia—was the **Sydney Herald exhibition** of 1939, still staunchly opposed by the academic artists and institutions that dominated art politics. The Menzies government in 1937 even organised an Australian Academy of Art in an attempt to control artistic directions. But many young artists were already taking up the modernist call. Along with those of the Reed circle in Melbourne, figures such as **George Bell** (1876–1966) vigorously opposed government intrusion into the realm of artistic expression, implementing The Contemporary Art Society as a response to the 'official' Academy. The absurdity of such attempts to limit the acceptable boundaries of artistic expression was dramatically highlighted in 1944, when portrait painter **William Dobell**'s (1899–1970) Archibald Prize-winning portrait of Joshua Smith was declared by conservative artists to be a caricature and therefore not eligible for the prize. The debate reached the Supreme Court, prompting the first legal consideration of any artistic topic in Australia; Dobell won. Intriguingly, Australia at this time had the greatest number of lucrative **art prizes** in the world, albeit for quite conservative modes of artistic expression. The art-prize trend continues today.

In the 1950s, most artists continued to travel abroad for study and inspiration. But several Australian artists made distinctly Australian contributions: **Sidney Nolan** began in the 1940s his famous series of paintings of that quintessentially Australian hero, *Ned Kelly,* and continued to produce interpretations of Australian lore and landscape. **Albert Tucker**'s *Images of Modern Evil* series (1943–46) used Surrealist forms to comment on the degradation of human relations in wartime. Arthur Boyd continued his mythological and Biblical visions, at times incorporating Aboriginal themes, and devising splendid renderings of the Australian landscape.

The tragic figure of **Albert Namatjira** (1902–59) came to prominence in the mid-1950s. An Arrente Aborigine raised near a mission school in the Central Desert, Namatjira learned watercolour painting from South Australian Rex Batterbee and painted complex landscapes in a Western style that initially brought him fame and some fortune; he was the first full-blood Aborigine to be granted citizenship, in 1957. Eventually he was imprisoned for providing alcohol to his Aboriginal relatives, and died in obscurity soon after he was released.

The battle of abstraction versus figurative art was especially prolonged in Australia. By 1959, a group of Melbourne artists, including **Charles Blackman** (b. 1928), **Arthur Boyd**, and **John Brack** (b. 1920), formed The Antipodeans, a group opposed to non-figurative art; their *Antipodean Manifesto,* written by art historian **Bernard Smith** (b. 1916), focussed on the necessity of the image and the concentration on social realities in art. At the same time, many painters took up the abstract cause, evident most notably in **Fred Williams'** (1927–82) brilliant interpretations of Australian hillsides; **John Olsen**'s (b. 1928) abstraction inspired by the European CoBrA movement; **Ian Fairweather**'s (1891–74) zen-like calligraphic canvases; and **Tony Tuckson**'s (1921–73) paintings and sculptures, inspired by Aboriginal and Tiwi motifs.

The 1960s in Australia as elsewhere was dominated by abstract expressionism, at least on the art market level. Colour-field painting made a brief splurge after **The Field exhibition** of 1968 in Melbourne, when many artists took up hard-edge and op art styles. A self-conscious construction of art aligned with alternative culture identified the most ambitious achievements of the 1970s. This was the era of the 'hippie trail' through Asia and Europe, the famous *OZ Magazine* trial in London, and anti-Vietnam War demonstrations—all vectors of artistic activity in Australia. The constant interchange with European and American youth culture and artistic events led to further integration of Australian art into international directions. **Mike Parr** (b. 1945) carried out Dadaist performances and installation pieces, while the Bulgarian-French artist Christo came to Australia to wrap the rocks of Little Bay in Sydney in 1969. **Martin Sharp** (b. 1942), who had been part of the *Oz Magazine* group, set up the Pop Art-inspired Yellow House in Sydney in 1970–72; **Richard Larter** (b. 1929) produced sexually provocative canvases; and **Jeffrey Smart** (b. 1921) ventured into hip Super Realism. The Sydney painter **Brett Whiteley** (1939–92) embodied the tortured 'artist-genius', first coming to prominence while living in London in the late 1960s. His early works were quite masterful abstract paintings, while he later moved into a mixture of mediums, both figurative and decorative. His alternative and drug-induced lifestyle epitomised 70s cultural attitudes, gaining for him more aesthetic status than his later art-works warranted.

The establishment of the Australian Centre for Photography in Sydney in 1974 indicates the growing recognition of photography as a major form of artistic expression in the 1970s. Indeed, many of the most exciting directions of the period, especially the vibrant contributions of feminist artists such as **Carol Jerrems** (1949–80), **Mickey Allen** (b. 1944), **Sue Ford** (b. 1943), and Aboriginal artist **Tracey Moffatt** (b. 1960), involved photographic experimentation.

In the last two decades, the 'discovery' of **Aboriginal art**, along with Australia's increasing interaction with international trends, has led to an explosion of post-modern and 'post-colonial' considerations in all artistic fields. The most exemplary painter of the 1980s was **Peter Booth** (b. 1940), who early in his career experimented with colour-field abstraction, but finally developed an allegorical style that stands on the cusp of modernist and post-modernist concerns, with some mythic and apocalyptic overtones.

Art today

Contemporary Australian art has lost all vestiges of provincialism, as it participates equally on a global scene. Of singular importance has been the recognition and encouragement of the production on canvas in acrylic paint by traditional Aboriginal artists of the Utopia group, most notably **Emily Kame Kngwarreye** (since her death in 1996, called out of respect to her family the substitute name of Kwementyai, or 'no name,' and her skin name, Kngwarreye). Kngwarreye's works have entered major collections around the world, and her paintings were selected to represent Australia at the 47th Venice Biennale in 1997. Both contemporary Aboriginal artists, such as **Sally Morgan** (b. 1951), **Robert Campbell Jr**, **Tracey Moffatt**, **Judy Watson**, **Lin Onus** (1948–96) and **Gordon Bennett** (b. 1955), and non-Aboriginal artists such as **Imants Tillers** (b. 1950) have now begun to incorporate traditional Aboriginal motifs and iconic elements of colonial painting into their canvases and multi-media presentations as a means of exploring Australian cultural and racial attitudes.

Finally, photography and video, in a variety of manipulations, continues to offer creative possibilities for interpretations of post-modernist society, exemplified by the romantic and disturbing tableaux of **Bill Henson** (b. 1955) and the feminist explorations of **Anne Ferran** (b. 1949). On a popular level, one cannot dismiss the immense iconographic power of the images of artist **Reg Mombassa** (b. 1951), with his surfie-culture 'Mambo'-philosophy t-shirts and books; and the poignant sentiments expressed by cartoonist **Michael Leunig** (b. 1945), printed in many newspapers and as books. It would be nearly impossible to miss the decorative designs and paintings of **Ken Done** (b. 1940), whose bright and cheerful scenes of Sydney and the sea adorn everything from murals to tea-towels and placemats. Done is actually a serious painter as well, who has no qualms about putting his artistic talents to the most profitable use, to the great enjoyment of tourists to the continent.

Australian cinema

No doubt many visitors to Australia gained their first idea of Australia and Australians, whether fanciful or not, from images appearing in the recent spate of internationally-acclaimed Australian films. Indeed, cinema has played a major role in defining Australian cultural life since the invention of the medium. In 1894, the Edison 'Kinetoscope' was introduced in Sydney. The enthusiastic reception that greeted this new entertainment was a portent of things to come;

by the 1930s, Australians were the most frequent moviegoers in the world. Certainly film has contributed more than any other factor to the disappearance of Australia's isolation from the rest of the world. In August 1896, the French film pioneers, the **Lumière Brothers**, had already sent their agent, Marius Sestier, to the country. Sestier shot several local scenes and events, including, quite appropriately, footage of the 1896 Melbourne Cup, which survives today as Australia's oldest film.

Australia's film industry originated in a seemingly unlikely source. The **Salvation Army**, recognising film's great persuasive power, established in Melbourne in August 1897 its Limelight Department, intent on producing morally uplifting moving pictures. Its *Soldier of the Cross* of 1900, interspersed with lantern slides and live evangelical sermons, can be considered one of the world's first 'story' films.

Most early filmmakers had less lofty moral intentions; they looked instead to Australia's recent past, and especially to the legendary accounts of its bushrangers and outlaws, for stories easily translated into cinematic entertainment. In 1906, Melbourne's **Tait Brothers** chose the most popular legend of all for their film *The Story of the Kelly Gang*, shooting it on location throughout Victoria where the Kelly Gang had actually operated only thirty years before. At 4000 feet of film and more than an hour long (five reels), the *Kelly Gang* can make legitimate claim to being the world's first full-length feature film. (The still existing parts have been conserved and can be viewed at the National Film and Sound Archive in Canberra.)

Indeed, between 1906 and 1911, Australia produced more feature-length films than any country; in 1907, versions of *Eureka Stockade* and 'Rolf Boldrewood's popular tale *Robbery Under Arms* appeared, and by 1908 the first of many film versions of Marcus Clarke's novel *For the Term of His Natural Life* was produced. In terms of audiences, Melbourne in 1910 had a purpose-built cinema that would seat 5000, mostly catered to by local production. This period before the First World War is generally considered the golden age of Australian film, although very few of these productions survive today in their entirety.

Raymond Longford (1878–1959) was Australia's first great film director. Beginning as a film actor, Longford directed his first film, *The Fatal Wedding*, in 1911. Longford was associated throughout his life with actress and co-director **Lottie Lyell** (1890–1925), who starred in his greatest work, *The Sentimental Bloke* (1919), the definitive film version of C.J. Dennis's beloved vernacular poem. Filmed in Sydney and mostly outdoors, the *Bloke* is still hugely entertaining and a remarkable document of Australian popular culture. Of Longford's many productions, only this film and his version of another Australian standard, *On Our Selection* (1920), have survived. The Australian film industry that Longford helped establish was essentially overwhelmed by the appearance of Hollywood films; by the end of the 1920s, Longford was forced to abandon film directing, ending his days as a night watchman.

Australians were also among the first to produce serious **documentary film**, known as 'actuality filmmaking'. The pioneer in this field was **Frank Hurley** (1885–1962), also a famous still photographer. Hurley accompanied Mawson and Shackleton on their Antarctic expeditions of 1911–13 and 1914–16, producing extraordinary documentation of this unknown continent. During the First World War, he was an official war photographer, filming battles in Europe and the Middle East. After the war, he produced a full-length documentary on *The Ross Smith Flight* (1920), the record-breaking aeroplane flight from England to Australia. During the 1930s, Hurley was cinematographer on such films as *The Squatter's Daughter* (1933), a remarkable example of ideological filmmaking, glorifying the established 'squattocracy' and British imperial values. Hurley was a tremendous inspiration for later documentary filmmakers, including Damien Parer (1912–44), whose filming along with the Australian troops during the Second World War in New Guinea, *Kokoda Front Line* (1942), received Australia's first US Academy Award.

Grand movie houses

The 1920s were in Australia as elsewhere the era of grand movie houses, and those built in most Australian cities were as elaborate as the Hollywood palaces; Sydney's extravagant State Theatre, built in 1929, was hailed as 'the Empire's greatest theatre', and the Capital Theatre in Melbourne was completed by American architect Walter Burley Griffin. One of the most original architects of this period was Western Australian William Thomas Leighton (1905–90), who specialised in theatres and cinemas with streamlined design.

Australians became the most frequent moviegoers in the world; in a nation with a population of six million in 1927, there were at least 2.25 million movie admissions a week. But most of the films shown were American or British; the local industry found it difficult to compete with overseas products, particularly after sound films became standard. Australian Talkies Ltd. was established in 1930, but full-scale sound production did not occur until entrepreneur and theatre owner Frank W. Thring put his own money into the sound venture. Soon another company, Cinesound, would also commence sound production. In both cases, emphasis was first on shorts and, most significantly, the production of newsreels for the movie-houses: Cinesound produced news footage from 1932 until 1956, the year of television's arrival.

Most of the locally-produced films of the 1930s attempted to appeal to home-grown audiences with rehashes of standard Australian stories and films featuring popular comedians and vaudeville performers. Thring's company, Efftee, brought to the screen the popular stage comedian George Wallace in such lightweight farces as *His Royal Highness* (1932). Cinesound produced the only film featuring the stage and radio character **Roy Rene** (1891–1954) in his comic role as **'Mo'** in *Strike Me Lucky* (1934), a peculiar mixture of Jewish humour and Australian stereotypes. Cinesound was also responsible for the continuing sagas of the **'Dad and Dave'** characters from Steele Rudd's beloved tales, which had become popularised even further in radio drama. The 1932 version of *On Our Selection* was most notable for its 'Bushland Symphony', one of the first attempts in a film to emphasise the sounds of native birds accompanying scenes of Australian countryside.

Despite the paucity of opportunities for serious local filmmaking during this period, some distinctly Australian successes did occur, all of them the work of **Charles Chauvel** (1897–1959) and his wife **Elsa** (1898–1983). Chauvel's first film as a director, *In the Wake of the Bounty* (1933), was actually filmed on Pitcairn Island in a semi-documentary style; evidence of Chauvel's understanding of the Hollywood movie business, this work became the first Australian sound feature to have an American release. The film also launched the career of Tasmanian actor **Errol Flynn**—the first of many Australian film stars to journey on to international fame in Hollywood. The Chauvels were responsible for producing the most important Australian films of the 1940s: *Forty Thousand Horsemen* (1940), with Chips Rafferty, a rousing war story of ANZAC triumph; and *The Rats of Tobruk* (1944), another near-documentary account of Australians in battle, again starring Chips Rafferty, and a very young Peter Finch. The Chauvels' most extraordinary film, however, was Charles's last: *Jedda*, produced on location in 1955, presents a tragic story of contemporary Aboriginal culture, centring on the torments of an Aboriginal girl torn between her 'traditional' life and white civilisation. Although the film now appears ludicrously dated and uncomfortably stereotyped, it was in the 1950s quite ahead of its time and indicative of Chauvel's heartfelt desire to confront distinctly Australian issues and characters. *Jedda* stands as one of the only truly Australian films made in the 1950s.

Post-war ~ foreign productions

The period after the Second World War and into the 1960s represents the nadir of local Australian filmmaking; most of the films produced during the 1950s involved overseas companies choosing Australia as an exotic location. In 1946, the British documentary filmmaker Harry Watt scored an international success with *The Overlanders* (1946), a dramatic re-enactment of outback cattle drovers' adventures, filmed on location in the Northern Territory; once again, Chips Rafferty had the central role, this time as the typical Australian bushman. Watts' success convinced England's Ealing Studios to become the first overseas company to produce films regularly in Australia; such foreign productions became the norm. No government support of the film industry was forthcoming during the Menzies era, and the Prime Minister's cultural attachment to all things British made any alliance with American film companies difficult. Some visiting American productions, using local technicians and some actors, were nonetheless successful: *On The Beach* in 1959, directed by Stanley Kramer, was filmed in Victoria; and Fred Zinneman's *The Sundowners* (1960), with Robert Mitchum, Deborah Kerr and Peter Ustinov, was shot on locations throughout New South Wales.

Rebirth of Australian cinema

The 'rebirth' of Australian cinema began with *They're a Weird Mob* (1966), financed by a British company, but based on the best-selling comedy novel by 'Nino Culotta' (John O'Grady) about an Italian immigrant's adjustments to Australian life. The movie was an immense success, especially in Sydney, proving that there was indeed an enthusiastic audience for locally produced films with local talent and in Australian locations. Still, visiting productions, such as Tony Richardson's *Ned Kelly* (1971) with Mick Jagger, and Nicholas Roeg's infinitely more satisfying *Walkabout* (1971), set in central Australia and including Aboriginal actor David Gulpilil, continued to be the only serious films made in Australia. A more riveting example of co-production was *Wake in Fright* (1971; also known as *Outback*), financed by US, Canadian and Australian money, directed by Canadian Ted Kotcheff, and with stunning performances by Jack Thompson and Chips Rafferty. A dark tale of one man's personal disintegration in the aggressive and violent atmosphere of an isolated outback town, this grimly realistic slice of life received rave reviews abroad (it was Australia's official entry for the Cannes Film Festival), but could not draw Australian audiences, still unprepared for 'serious' Australian film efforts.

The 1970s saw great change, with a resurgence of Australian-produced films, largely the result of government support, especially under Gough Whitlam, of Australian filmmakers and all the arts. The Australian Film Development Corporation (AFDC) was established in 1971 to find investors for locally produced films, and in 1973, the **Australian Film School** (actually, the Australian Film, Television, and Radio School) opened, nurturing a generation of filmmakers to the highest standards. This resurgence coincided with the emergence of a youth counterculture; consequently, some of the first efforts to come out of this era were created primarily to challenge conservative censorship laws. Tim Burstall's sexual romps *Stork* (1971) and *Alvin Purple* (1973) are noteworthy only for their unabashed male cheekiness and as proof that enough local talent and technical skills existed to sustain a national cinema. Similarly, one of the best-known productions of the early AFDC days was **Bruce Beresford**'s *The Adventures of Barry McKenzie* (1972), a broadly drawn and anarchic caricature of Australian ockerdom in Britain that introduced Barry Humphries' Edna Everage to an international audience. Significantly, the film marked the first big break for director Beresford, who would, like Philip Noyce, Fred Schepisi and Peter Weir, go on to Hollywood and international acclaim. This situation, of acquiring local training and support, then moving 'offshore' to greater fame and larger film budgets, became a familiar pattern in Australia, especially for directors and cinematographers.

Australian cinema in the last 20 years has produced a significant number of films acclaimed internationally, while at the same time revealing distinctly Australian stories and specifically Australian characters. The themes chosen by Australian directors and writers most often deal with concepts of national identity, whether through setting or historical reference. On another level, however, their topics take on broader issues that say much about the Australian psyche: 'coming of age' dilemmas (John Duigan's *The Year My Voice Broke* [1987], Gillian Armstrong's *My Brilliant Career* [1979]); perseverance in the face of adversity (Henri Safran's *Storm Boy* [1976], Stephen Elliott's *The Adventures of Priscilla, Queen of the Desert* [1994]); stoicism despite human brutality (George Miller's *Mad Max* series, 1979–85); decidedly black humour (Jane Campion's *Sweetie* [1989], P.J. Hogan's *Muriel's Wedding* [1994]); and confrontations with strange landscapes and the 'other' (Fred Schepisi's *The Chant of Jimmy Blacksmith* [1978], Peter Weir's *Picnic at Hanging Rock* [1975]).

Of greatest significance is the number of **women directors** who have made major contributions in Australian film, not pigeon-holed into any genre, and certainly eschewing the predictably 'feminine' topics of light romantic comedies (a theme that Australians do not film well). One need only consider the work of these leading directors to recognise a distinctly Australian approach to film, evident even when these same directors gain recognition abroad and begin to make films in Hollywood. Consider the following international names:

● **Peter Weir** (b. 1944) began his career with *The Cars That Ate Paris* (1974), a black comedy about an Australian town that makes money from car accidents; his next work, the one that brought him international fame, was the hauntingly imagistic *Picnic at Hanging Rock* (1975). *The Last Wave* (1978) dealt with the confrontation of Aboriginal spirituality and Western materialism, while *Gallipoli* (1981) was a powerful indictment of war's futility through the enactment of Australia's most important historical event (the latter greatly aided by play-wright David Williamson's script). Such recognised achievements brought Weir to America, where his films included *Witness* (1985), *Dead Poets Society* (1989), and *Fearless* (1993), all of them dealing in some way with people outside main-stream culture and surviving in unusual circumstances.

● Similarly, **Bruce Beresford** (b. 1940) made such Australian classics as *The Getting of Wisdom* (1977) and *Breaker Morant* (1980), before making it 'big' in Hollywood with *Tender Mercies* (1983) and *Driving Miss Daisy* (1989).

● In Australia, **Fred Schepisi** (b. 1939) directed *The Devil's Playground* (1976), a grim depiction of life in a Catholic boys college, and a brilliantly radical version of Thomas Keneally's *The Chant of Jimmy Blacksmith* (1978), before making the American-financed production based on Australia's famous Lindy Chamberlain trial, *Evil Angels* (in the US, *A Cry in the Dark*; 1988).

● **Philip Noyce**'s nostalgic rendition of competition between Australian movie newsreel companies, *Newsfront* (1978), was made just before he went to America and directed Tom Clancy thrillers to international box-office success.

● **Gillian Armstrong** (b. 1950), the best known of Australia's many women directors, made as her first feature film the distinctly Australian *My Brilliant Career* (1979), and has since gone on to direct such international hits as *Little Women* (1994) and *Oscar and Lucinda* (1997). All of these directors now work and live primarily in America.

● On an even more popular level is the success of **George Miller** (often referred to as Dr George Miller, to distinguish him from George Miller, director of the immensely popular *The Man from Snowy River* [1982]) and his *Mad Max* trilogy (1979–85), the films that brought Australian-American Mel Gibson international recognition and a ticket out of Australia. Miller has subsequently produced such 'Australian' films as *The Year My Voice Broke* (1987) and Philip Noyce's *Dead Calm* (1989), while directing in Hollywood *Witches of Eastwick* (1987) and *Lorenzo's Oil* (1992). Miller's backing of the smash hit *Babe* (1995) is a good example of the current situation in the Australian film industry: while filmed in Australia with some Australian actors and technicians, the financing was international, and every attempt was made to make the film appear 'universal'. The phenomenon of Paul Hogan's *Crocodile Dundee* (1985), the first 'blockbuster' Australian hit, remains an isolated incident (Hogan, too, has gone on to Hollywood).

Australian cinema today

A more substantial and varied industry exists today, one that is really part of 'global' cinema. The question now is what constitutes 'Australian' cinema: does it include only films made here, or can films made by Australians else-where be gathered into the nationalistic fold? One need only consider two recent examples to see how complicated this question has become. New Zealand-born **Jane Campion**, who began her film work at the Australian Film School and completed her dark tragicomedy *Sweetie* (1989) in Sydney, went on to win the Academy Award for original screenplay for *The Piano* in 1994. The film was touted as an Australian film by many, although it had a New

Zealand director, an Australian producer, New Zealand locations, American cast, French co-production, and American distribution.

The case of **Baz Luhrmann** is even more telling. His first film, *Strictly Ballroom* (1992), told a lighthearted story of Australian multiculturalism and became an international success. On the basis of that film, Luhrmann went to Hollywood to produce the overwhelmingly popular modern-day phantasmagoria of *Romeo + Juliet* (1996). He now commutes between Australia and America, creating innovative productions in both places.

Global filmmaking seems to be the direction determining Australia's vigorous industry today; most of the best work will be snatched up for international distribution, although you can still see some good films here that may never make it elsewhere. A film such as first-time director Scott Hicks' *Shine* (1996), gained attention, and an Oscar for actor Geoffrey Rush, because it was first shown and lauded at the Sundance Film Festival in the US. Other local gems, such as the hilarious *The Castle* (1997) by Rob Sitch, Jane Kennedy, and Santo Cilauro, and such earlier films as Nadia Tass's *Malcolm* (1985), **Paul Cox**'s *Lonely Hearts* (1981) and Gillian Armstrong's *Last Days at Chez Nous* (1991) are worth seeking out in art cinemas or on video.

Australian literature

Australia's dependence on English cultural precedents is particularly evident in the style and production of literature during its colonial period; most books and journals were sent from 'home', and from 1788 to 1830, only 28 works of literature of any kind other than newspapers were published in Australia itself. Imported British works stood as the main source of literature throughout the century. Still, an Australian literary voice, grounded in the stylistic richness of English prose and poetry, began to develop almost immediately; by the end of the 19C, Australian writers had become instrumental in establishing a national idiom and were well on the way to defining a specific cultural identity. In style and theme, Australian writers today, in a vibrant literary culture supported by a strong publishing industry and an enthusiastic reading public, continue to explore those ideas of national identity and the complexities of the Australian psyche.

As with the beginnings of Australian art, literature about Australia originated in the official reports and accounts of exploration and early British settlement. Most notable among these records are the published works of two members of the First Fleet, **Marine Lieutenant David Collins**' *An Account of the English Colony in New South Wales* (1798, 1802) and **Marine Watkin Tench**'s *A Narrative of the Expedition to Botany Bay* (1789) and *A Complete Account of the Settlement at Port Jackson in New South Wales* (1793). Tench's account, recently republished, is particularly lively, and fascinating for its sympathetic portrayal of the indigenous people encountered.

The first book of general literature published in Australia appeared in Hobart in 1818: **Thomas Wells**'s *Michael Howe, the Last and Worst of the Bushrangers of Van Diemen's Land*, dealt with the popular themes of adventure and lawlessness, ideas that would engage Australian writers of all stripes for the next 150 years. Convict **Henry Savery**'s *Quintus Servinton* (1831), also published in Hobart and generally considered to be the first Australian novel, also presents an enduring theme in colonial literature: the moral effects of crime and punishment.

Aspirations towards loftier romantic sentiment, drawing on the experience of life in this new country, appeared at about the same time. Judge **Barron Field** (1786–1846) produced the first book of poetry, *First Fruits of Australian Poetry*, in 1819, filled with whimsical and at times critical reflections on Australian flora and fauna, such as 'The Kangaroo' (much ironic criticism of Field's writing has centred on his apt yet unfortunate name). The first novel printed in Sydney appeared in 1838, published anonymously with the mysterious title of *The Guardian: A Tale, By An Australian*. Intriguingly, the author was later revealed to be a woman, a genteel pastoralist's widow—early evidence of the importance of women authors in Australian literary life.

Charles Harpur (1813–68) most eloquently epitomises the struggle faced by early native-born writers who longed to forge a true Australian literary style. He was the son of emancipists, a 'currency lad', and completely committed to Australia as his own country. Writing often under the pseudonym 'A Hawkesbury Lad', Harpur applied traditional poetic techniques of the era, ornate and ponderous, to themes and settings based on local conditions and experience. His nature and narrative poems, such as 'Genius Lost' (c 1845) and 'The Creek of the Four Graves' (1853), about the murder of settlers by Aborigines in the Hawkesbury region, demonstrate the best of colonial stylistic efforts. Despite his patriotic attempts to be acknowledged as the first 'Muse of Australia', Harpur's works gained little audience in his lifetime; only in recent times has his originality and talent been recognised.

Native-born writers emerge

The growth of a native-born population in the 1830s–1840s and the societal upheavals caused by the gold rushes of the 1850s–1860s led to an increasing self-awareness and conscious consideration of Australia as place. Transient visitors wrote about Australia from a variety of perspectives, from travellers' tales to social commentary; but those who were born here or chose to stay permanently made the greatest literary contribution in attempting to define the country's geographical and human peculiarities. **Henry Kingsley** (1830–76) exemplifies the former; brother of English novelist Charles Kingsley, he arrived in Australia in 1853 and experienced the Victorian goldrush, then returned to England in 1859, where he wrote *The Recollections of Geoffrey Hamlyn* (1859), along with other novels and stories incorporating Australian themes and descriptions of the landscape. As a romantic tale of pastoral Australia before the gold rushes, *Recollections* is considered the first significant novel to capture some of the vernacular speech and to include vivid descriptions of the character of the Australian 'bush'. While later criticised as unrealistic in its views of bush life, the book established a colonial romantic idiom that would influence many subsequent Australian writers.

The concept of **'the bush'**, examined metaphorically in poetic and prose form, became the most powerful and identifiably Australian literary device for those writers who gained prominence on the local scene in the second half of the 19C. The Australian landscape and outback life provided a central focus for writers' ambivalent attitudes about the country itself, from **Marcus Clarke**'s description of its 'weird melancholy' in 1876, to **Rosa Praed**'s reminiscence in her *My Australian Girlhood: Sketches and Impressions of Bushlife* (1902): 'I never smell the pungent aromatic scent [of gum trees]...without falling again under the grim spell of the bush'.

Such ruminations determined in various modes the work of those authors who found favour with a new audience for Australian writing, both at home and abroad. The tremendous popularity of the poems of **Adam Lindsay Gordon** (1833–70) rests largely on his narrative celebrations of bushlife, despite the fact that the majority of his works were conventional verses having more to do with his educated English background. Gordon's fame was certainly enhanced by the romantic saga of his reckless life; he committed suicide the day after the publication of his most popular collection, *Bush Ballads and Galloping Rhymes* (1870). The volume included his most famous poem, 'The Sick Stockrider', considered by many to have established the distinctively Australian ballad form, championing the idea of mateship and the acceptance of bushlife's harsh challenges. Gordon's posthumous fame was so great that his bust was added to the Poets' Corner of Westminster Abbey in 1934, the only Australian so honoured.

A more lyrical ideal of the Australian landscape appeared in the poems of another tragic figure of the period, **Henry Kendall** (1839–82). His *Leaves from Australian Forests* (1869) included his most famous landscape poems, 'Bell-Birds' (1867), 'September in Australia', and 'Araluen' (1870), melodic evocations of the lush and cool fern-gullies of his native Illawarra district. His life ended at the age of 43, a victim of alcoholism and physical neglect. Unlike Gordon, Kendall's work was well-received in his lifetime and largely forgotten afterwards, except as favoured recitation pieces in Australian school-books.

Despite the conscious efforts of mid-century Australians to distance themselves from the country's penal origins, the convict experience inevitably provided obvious themes for literary exploration. It is not surprising that the first Australian novel to gain enduring stature was **Marcus Clarke**'s melodramatic consideration of the convict 'System', *For the Term of his Natural Life* (1874) (originally titled simply *His Natural Life*). Clarke (1846–81), of good English family, arrived in Melbourne at 17 and began his career as a journalist. He soon established himself as an influential cultural figure in the colony. His *Old Tales of a Young Country* (1871) compiled studies of old Australian characters and contributed to a romantic image of the young country's past. On a trip to Tasmania to research convict history for a Melbourne journal, Clarke gained documentary material that would contribute to his sensational masterpiece. *His Natural Life* is a pessimistic and detailed condemnation of the horrific penal system supported by convict transportation, upholding a popular view that convicts were more 'sinn'd against than sinning'. On a more fundamental level, the book is an examination of human capacity for evil. The melodramatic twists of the plot contributed greatly to its continuing popularity; his main character, Rufus Dawes, became Australia's first literary 'hero'.

Despite the growth of cosmopolitan urban centres in the second half of the 19C, Australia's population was still too small to sustain abundant literary patronage or any vigorous publishing industry of its own. In such a society, it is not surprising that literary achievement was often dependent on publication in local newspapers and journals rather than books. Many important writers began their careers in journalism, and major contributions to Australian literature first occurred through serialisation of stories in popular magazines, of which many long-standing and short-lived ones were established in the 1850s and 60s. Such was the case with '**Rolf Boldrewood**' (Thomas Alexander Browne; 1826–1915), son of English-born 'squatters', who arrived in Australia as a child in 1831. Browne led an adventurous life, establishing pastoral properties in Victoria, breeding livestock, serving as a police magistrate on the goldfields, and retiring as a gentleman farmer in Melbourne. Throughout, as 'Rolf Boldrewood' (a name taken from his favourite author, Sir Walter Scott), he published stories in Sydney and Melbourne journals based on his experiences of pastoralist life and the adventures of bushrangers in the Victorian countryside. His immensely popular *Robbery Under Arms* (1888) first appeared as a serial in the *Sydney Mail* in 1882 and was published by Macmillan as a book in 1889. Described by some as the 'first Australian Western', the story is a still-readable adventure yarn, with lively and diverse characters, and, most significantly, a sense of place and vernacular language which would become defining characteristics of the literary achievements of the end of the century.

Nationalist writing

The last two decades of the 19C were ones of growing cultural consciousness, tied firmly to nationalistic sentiment. Nowhere are the ideals and incipient mythology of 'Australianness' more accurately articulated and, indeed, formulated than in the pages of *The Bulletin*, a weekly periodical founded in 1885 in Sydney by **J.F. Archibald** and W.H. Traill. While chiefly a journal of political and editorial commentary, nurturing vehemently Republican, pro-Federation, and anti-Asian views, *The Bulletin*'s greatest accomplishment was its support, especially in the 1890s, of local literary talent; the journal promoted the writers who would become the most popular voices of the bush ethos and the Australian idiom. As cultural critic Geoffrey Serle states, the journal became 'the forum for outbackery'.

The decade's main literary battle of romanticism versus realism was most characteristically defined by two of *The Bulletin*'s most famous contributors, **A.B. 'Banjo' Paterson** (1864–1941) and **Henry Lawson** (1867–1922). Universally described as the 'chief folk poet of Australia', Paterson grew up on the land and personally experienced bush life. He was educated in Sydney in law and was an accomplished horseman and gentleman athlete. He took the nickname of 'Banjo' when he began to write for *The Bulletin* in 1889, with his characteristic long verse, 'Clancy of the Overflow'. Paterson gained rapturous celebrity with the publication of his most famous bush-ballad *The Man from Snowy River* in 1895. The first printing sold out in a week, and it instantly became the most recognisable example of the Australian ballad form; to this day, nearly every Australian knows the opening lines of the poem, 'There was movement at the station/ for the word had got around/ that the colt from Old Regret had got away.' He extended the popularity of his vision with other narrative poems, such as 'The Man from Ironbark' (1892) and 'Mulga Bill' (1902). Paterson achieved international fame as the author (in 1896) of the lyrics to 'Waltzing Matilda', Australia's most famous song. His lyrical evocations of an Australian Arcadia, filled with horses and colourful bush characters, established the legend of the Australian folk, separate from the realities of the society's increasingly urbanised existence.

Henry Lawson, whom historian Manning Clark dramatically described as 'Australia writ large', epitomised all the radical nationalistic fervour of the period and maintained that his version of the bush and Australian life was a more realistic, less mythologised, one than Paterson's popular image; at one point, he and Paterson engaged in a lengthy debate on this topic, in verse form, in *The Bulletin*. Lawson came from radical goldfield background, the son of a Norwegian miner and a politically engaged mother; he maintained his fervent Republican and socialist attitudes throughout his life and in his political writings. He was in Sydney by 1885, and began to publish verse, both character studies of the bush and such politically motivated works as 'A Song to the Republic' (1887), first published in *The Bulletin*. While Lawson occupies nearly legendary status today as Australia's great literary figure, his verse especially was uneven, degenerating eventually into near-doggerel as he himself deteriorated through alcoholism and mental illness. His short stories, however, are enduring embodiments of the concepts of mateship, larrikinism (hooliganism), and stoic acceptance of the hardships of bush life. His 'Drover's Wife' (1892), a ruthless portrayal of a pioneer woman of the outback, is a model of stylistic realism; and 'The Loaded Dog' (1900) is a comic classic by any standard. So great was his popular status in his lifetime that upon his death in 1922, he was the first Australian writer granted a state funeral.

The publishing activities of *The Bulletin* at the turn of the century under the editorship of the learned **A.G. Stephens** (1865–1933) continued to nurture local writers and extend a particular vision of Australian life. In 1899, the journal saw to the first publication in book form of **Steele Rudd**'s memorable stories of a Queensland pioneer farmer family, *On Our Selection*. 'Rudd' was the pseudonym of **Arthur Hoey Davis** (1868–1935); the Rudd family in his many character sketches were based on semi-autobiographical reminiscences of his own childhood on a small pastoral 'selection'. His well-developed characters, especially the increasingly caricatured figures of 'Dad and Dave', appeared throughout the 20C in stories, plays, radio series, and film, epitomising the battlers of Australian rural life.

Twentieth-century developments

Stephens' greatest achievement as an editor was the recognition and publication in 1903 of the novel, *Such is Life*, an immensely idiosyncratic tome by **Joseph Furphy** (1843–1912), alias 'Tom Collins'. Furphy was a self-taught labourer from Shepparton, Victoria, who set out in grandiose fashion to write a realistic tale of rural life, 'temper, democratic; bias, offensively Australian'. The opening line of this extraordinary book is 'Unemployed at last!'—a good indication of its anti-authoritarian stance. Episodic yet ambitiously philosophical in tone, the book displays Furphy's complicated considerations of free will, fate, and class struggle, couched in very Australian story-lines about 'squatters' and toilers on the land. Largely ignored for years, *Such is Life* was rediscovered by literary critics in the 1940s as representing an important turning-point in Australian fiction, and remains today a widely-unread but highly-touted masterpiece.

Australia's masculinist ethos is belied by the emergence in the early 20C of major literary achievements by women, most of them autobiographical in tone and noticeably ambivalent about Australian society. 'Henry Handel Richardson', pseudonym of **Ethel Florence Lindesay Robertson** (1870–1946), produced the most accomplished and thoughtful literature of the period, all of it written after she had moved to Europe, never to return to

Australia. In *The Getting of Wisdom* (1910), she relied on her own experiences as a boarder at Presbyterian Ladies College in Melbourne to present a popular 'coming of age' novel. Richardson's greatest work was her dramatic trilogy, *The Fortunes of Richard Mahony* (1917–29), based emotionally on the trials of her family's life in Victoria, as her physician father, model for the novel's protagonist, descended into madness; cultural alienation is the real theme of the books. Rich in details of the Victorian landscape and societal conditions, Richardson's volumes were, significantly, hailed in England as stylistically sophisticated while remaining relatively unknown in Australia. The author, like so many Australian writers after her, faced the dilemma of all 'cultural *émigrés*', becoming more correctly an English-language writer using Australian experience as themes for her novels.

More clearly Australian and feminist in outlook were the popular writings of **Miles Franklin** (1879–1954), whose stunning début novel was the auto-biographical *My Brilliant Career* (1901), a forthright assertion of a woman's right to self-fulfilment. She, too, spent much time abroad, mostly in the United States. She returned permanently to Sydney in the 1930s, where she was fêted as an influential cultural figure and published many affectionate recollections of her early life on the Monaro Plains of New South Wales.

The period after Federation in 1901 until the 1920s saw little production of serious literature. Surprisingly, the events of the First World War itself, so devastating to the Australian psyche, offered little inspiration to local writers, and the ideal of the bush had lost its impetus in a more cosmopolitan society.

The only significant work engendered by the war was **C.E.W. Bean**'s *The Official History of Australia in the War of 1914–1918*, which began publication of its eventual twelve volumes in 1921. Lauded as an excellent example of analytical military history, the work was also one of the first substantial efforts devoted to Australian history itself; Bean was largely responsible for cultivating the legend of the ANZAC 'digger'. Popularly, the most enthusiastic contribution of the time was *Songs of a Sentimental Bloke* (1915) by **C.J. Dennis** (1876–1938). Beloved among the ANZAC soldiers during the war, the vernacular poem tells the story of a city larrikin transformed by love, and the escapades of his mate Ginger Mick. While criticised for its over-exaggerated use of street idiom, *Sentimental Bloke* was the source for Australia's best silent film in 1919 and caused Dennis to be proclaimed unofficial poet laureate in the 1920s.

In a similarly popular direction, Australians made endearing contributions in the field of children's literature. **Ethel Turner**'s (1870–1958) *Seven Little Australians*, first published in 1894, became an international success, translated into several languages. While the bacchanalian figure of artist-writer **Norman Lindsay** (1879–1969) wrote amatory novels that were long banned in his own country (*Redheap* [1930]), his greatest audience as a writer resulted from his delightful illustrated children's book, *The Magic Pudding* (1918). **May Gibbs** (1877–1969) also contributed at this time to books for young readers with her near-iconic stories of *Snugglepot & Cuddlepie* (1918).

While expatriation, mainly to England, continued to be the usual choice for those with serious cultural aspirations, Australia in the 1920s and 30s began to develop a home-grown cosmopolitanism which could sustain some significant literary life. **Vance Palmer** (1885–1959) was probably the most intellectual figure of the period, worldly and stylistically rigorous. Along with his wife

Nettie (1885–1964), an important cultural commentator in her own right, Palmer as a journalist and later author firmly promoted a literature that embodied an 'Australia of the Spirit'. While he published essays, short stories, novels and plays from the 1920s—his collected stories *Sea and Spinifex* (1934) and his panoramic trilogy *Golconda* (1948) are exemplary—his most significant contribution was *The Legend of the Nineties* (1954), a critical examination of that pivotal decade in the development of an Australian 'inner life'.

Two poets of distinction emerge during this period, both linked in divergent ways to Bohemian Sydney. **Mary Gilmore** (1862–1962) was from the beginning tied to radical causes, even participating in the utopian Australian settlement in Paraguay under socialist William Lane in the 1890s. Her poetry was lyrical and short, her best work appearing in her last book, *Fourteen Men* (1954), when she was nearly ninety. **Kenneth Slessor** (1901–71) was initially inspired by the pantheistic Romanticism of the Norman Lindsay circle, but his finest poem, 'Five Bells' (1939), commemorating the drowning of his friend Joe Lynch, presents a very modernist contemplation of art, life and death.

A radicalised sense of the 'spirit of the people' also informs the work of **Katharine Susannah Prichard** (1883–1969). A founding member of the Communist Party in Western Australia, Prichard's politics informed most of her novels: *Black Opal* (1921) was a story of the opal-mining communities' struggle with mining companies; her most controversial work, *Coonardoo* (1929), is considered the first novel to give a realistic depiction of a contemporary Aborigine and black-white relations.

The most ambitious novel completed in this period was the work of another Western Australian, **Xavier Herbert** (1901–84). His *Capricornia* (1938) is a sprawling story of settlement in the Northern Territory, covering some 50 years and including some 100 characters. Radical in outlook, Anglophobic in tone, it is a savage indictment of the treatment of Aborigines by white settlers, and a love song to the beauty of the Australian frontier. Herbert expanded on these themes in his enormous *Poor Fellow My Country* (1975), at 850,000 words the longest novel ever published in Australia. The story culminates with the Japanese bombing of Darwin in 1942, the flight of white settlers, and a prophetically pessimistic appraisal of continued destruction of Aboriginal society. On a less grandiose scale but with similar concerns is the work of **Eleanor Dark** (1901–85), whose psychological portrayals were both serious and widely read. She was best known for her trilogy *The Timeless Land* (1941), historical fiction about the early years of white settlement. Dark, too, is sympathetic to the Aboriginal plight and presents a heartfelt examination of their spiritual attachment to the land.

The problems facing expatriate authors and their subsequent recognition in Australia is most clearly seen in the case of **Christina Stead** (1902–83), one of the most stylistically original novelists of her time. Raised in Sydney, Stead left for England in 1928, married Marxist and writer William Blake, eked out a meagre existence in Europe and America, and only returned to live in Australia in old age. She crafted exquisite and unconventional prose throughout. Her *Seven Poor Men of Sydney* (1934) was firmly set in Australia, but, more meditative in presentation of characters than narrative, it was considered outside the mainstream of Australian literary concerns. Her most recognised masterpiece was *The Man Who Loved Children* (1941), supposedly placed in America, but drawing on her own childhood for inspiration. Essentially a ruthless exploration of a dysfunctional family, the book was praised by American writer Randall Jarrell as one of the greatest works of 20C fiction. As with Stead's other novels, *The Man Who Loved Children* was not published in Australia until 1965, by which time there were still debates about whether Stead could be considered an Australian writer at all, since she had been away so long and because she wrote about larger themes than the Australian experience. Recent reprints and comprehensive critical studies have now reclaimed Stead for the Australian canon.

Arrival of modernist ideas

Greater literary self-consciousness and the arrival of modernist ideas led in the 1930s and 40s to the establishment of many literary journals that supported local writers and cultural discourse. *Meanjin*, founded in Brisbane in 1940 by **Clem Christesen** as a poetry review, evolved into the most important liberal-humanist organ; it is still published at the University of Melbourne. In 1950, the more right-wing, avowedly anti-Communist *Quadrant* began publication.

One-time *Quadrant* editor, poet **James McAuley** (1917–76), played a major part in the greatest literary scandal in Australian history, the famous 'Ern Malley' hoax carried out in the modernist journal *Angry Penguins*. This quarterly publication was founded in 1940 in Adelaide by **John Reed** (1901–81) and **Max Harris** (1921–96) and quickly became the focus for avant-garde cultural interests in the country. McAuley and his fellow poet **Harold Stewart** (b. 1916), as traditionalist lyricists, decided to expose what they saw as the decadence and lack of craftsmanship of modernist writing by concocting verses from a variety of incongruous sources. They submitted these poems, created in an afternoon, to *Angry Penguins*, presenting them as the posthumous works of a mechanic/salesman 'Ern Malley'. The poems were published in the journal in 1944, and acclaimed by many for their stylistic vigour. When McAuley and Stewart identified themselves as the authors, the ensuing debates, which gained world-wide attention, signalled the end of *Angry Penguins* and its championing of modernism, although the movement in its artistic form continued to resonate in the circle around John Reed and his wife at their home in Melbourne. Many today still consider the 'Ern Malley' poems to be among the authors' best works; the supposedly absurd phrase from one of the poems, 'The Black Swan of Trespass', served as the title for Humphrey McQueen's examination of Australian modernism in 1979.

Popular literature

In terms of popular literature, the period from the Depression to the end of the Second World War saw the emergence of several significant writers whose works combined personal experience with historical characters and an admirable depiction of the Australian landscape. **Ion Idriess** (1889–1979) drew upon his own adventures in the outback and 'Up North' to produce such wildly popular adventure stories as *Lasseter's Last Ride* (1931), an account of the ill-fated gold-mining expedition of Harold Lasseter to Central Australia; and *Flynn of the Inland* (1932), based on the story of John Flynn, founder of the Royal Flying Doctor Service.

Frank Clune (1893–1971) was from the 1940s one of Australia's best-selling authors, with adventurous works of historical fiction, adventure, autobiography and travel (respectively, *Dig* [1937] about Burke and Wills, *The Red Heart* [1944], *Try Anything Once* [1933] and *Tobruk to Turkey* [1943]). Clune popularised through his writings and radio broadcasts the legends of Australia's bushrangers and other heroes.

Another adventurer who became a best-selling author was '**Nevil Shute**' (1899–1960), pseudonym of Nevil Shute Norway, a British pilot who settled in Australia in 1950. His fast-paced narrative novels *A Town Like Alice* (1950) and *On the Beach* (1959) became international favourites; the latter, about the survivors of a nuclear holocaust, was made into a big-budget Hollywood film.

One of the most enduring and internationally recognised Australian writers of the time was **Arthur Upfield** (1892–1964), who in 1929 introduced his famous character, the half-Aboriginal Queensland detective, Napoleon Bonaparte, in *The Barrakee Mystery*. His immensely readable 'Bony' mysteries, including *Death of a Lake* (1954), *Murder Must Wait* (1953), and *The Man of Two Tribes* (1956), combined bush-lore, outback characters, and brilliant depictions of the Australian landscape with the intriguing presence of his main protagonist; most of his novels are still in print and many have been made into less-than-successful television series. Upfield's works were particularly popular in the US, where the author became the first foreign writer admitted to the Mystery Writers' Guild of America.

Post-war literature

The stultifyingly conservative atmosphere of 1950s Australia, with literary censorship and suppression of political opposition by the Menzies government, was nonetheless a fruitful period for local writers. A strand of political dissension is most clearly apparent in writings by members of Australia's then still-vigorous Communist Party, most notably **Frank Hardy** (1917–94), and **Judah Waten** (1911–85). Hardy's immense tome, *Power Without Glory* (1950), a thinly-disguised 'fictionalisation' of the corrupt life of Melbourne millionaire John Wren (1871–1953), caused explosive controversy when it was published. The book led to a famous libel trial against Hardy, which had more to do with his political beliefs than anything he wrote. Waten's works also expressed his left-wing political views—his *Shares in Murder* (1957) deals with human corruption and the power of the police—but his most memorable writing appears in his autobiographical short stories about a European Jewish migrant family; these were collected under the title *Alien Son* (1952).

The towering figure of the post-War years in Australia, at least in hindsight, was **Patrick White** (1912–90), who in 1973 became the first (and so far, the only) Australian writer to be awarded the Nobel Prize for Literature. White represents in many ways the conquest of Australia's 'cultural cringe', or at least an honest confrontation of the ambivalent feelings of those Australians who wanted to create a cultural life on Australian soil in a less than encouraging society. Born in London, he was brought to Australia as an infant, then was sent to English boarding school at 13. He returned to Australia briefly in 1929, then went to Cambridge and remained in London throughout the 1930s, publishing his first novel, *Happy Valley*, set in Australia, in 1939. After war service with the RAF, he decided to return home, 'to the stimulus of time remembered'. On the voyage back, he wrote *The Aunt's Story* (1948), the first example of his unpredictable and original style, a tale of visionary individualism and perceptions of madness. When his novel *The Tree of Man* (1955) gained international acclaim, White began to receive critical if still ambivalent attention at home. Of his complex imagery and characters, he stated that he wanted 'to discover the extraordinary behind the ordinary, the mystery and poetry which could alone make bearable the lives of such people.' He became increasingly reclusive, appearing occasionally to criticise national policies on the Vietnam War, environmental issues, and treatment of the Aborigines. Indeed, he became a kind of cantankerous moral conscience within Australian society. His novel *Voss* (1957) is arguably his most ambitious and best-known work. Based loosely on the 1840s desert expedition of the German Ludwig Leichhardt, the book is a philosophical exploration of spiritual journeys, tied to details of the unforgiving landscape and the ambiguities of physical existence. White received the Nobel Prize specifically for *The Eye of the Storm* (1973), a rumination on spiritual being and memory as explored through the eyes of a dying Sydney socialite.

Several women authors made enduring contributions to the literature of the period, extending the range of acceptable subject matter and focussing specifically on their own experiences of aspects of Australian culture as inspiration. New Zealand-born **Ruth Park** (b. 1922) married the writer **D'Arcy Niland** (1919–67; he wrote the popular *The Shiralee* [1955] and *The Big Smoke* [1959] and lived in working-class Sydney. Her memories of this time among the Irish poor inspired her to write *The Harp in the South* (1948), an evocative rendering of the slum-dwellers of the city and their sometimes tragic situations. At the time it was published, many were shocked at Park's choice of topics, which included abortion; today, *The Harp in the South* and its sequel *Poor Man's Orange* (1949) are considered classics of the genre. Park has written several fascinating volumes of autobiography, the most interesting of which, *Fishing in the Styx* (1993), deals with her life with Niland in Surry Hills.

Dymphna Cusack (1902–81), author of several novels, made the biggest splash with her *Come in Spinner* (1951), a gritty story of the arrival of American servicemen in Sydney during the Second World War and their impact on a varied group of women. The title derives from an Australian idiom used in the popular game of two-up.

A vast outback station in the Kimberleys served as the setting for **Mary Durack**'s (b. 1913) *Keep Him My Country* (1950), a metaphorical tale of the relationship of a white pastoralist and an Aboriginal girl. Larger questions of good and evil, corruption and power, inform the psychological dramas of **Elizabeth Harrower** (b. 1928). Her settings in such works as *Down in the City* (1957) and *The Watch Tower* (1966) were industrial and suburban, demonstrating the increasing recognition of the real living conditions of most Australians.

Despite the increased concentration on decidedly Australian subjects and attitudes in much of the literature of the post-War period, the dualities of Australian allegiance to European, especially English, culture continued to determine the achievements of many of the country's best writers. **Martin Boyd** (1893–1972), son of the distinguished Boyd family of artists and writers, explored in graceful historical fiction the effects of inherited tradition on Australian characters; his semi-autobiographical saga of the Langton family, presented in five novels, is a finely detailed study of aristocratic ideals and social conflicts in Victorian Melbourne. The middle volumes of these novels, *A Difficult Young Man* (1955) and *An Outbreak of Love* (1957), are perhaps the most complex and representative of Boyd's style.

Hal Porter (1911–84) also developed a rather self-conscious style, eloquently used in his well-crafted short stories and novels. His most evocative works were his autobiographical novels, *The Watcher on the Cast-Iron Balcony* (1963), a re-creation of his childhood and youth, and *The Paper Chase* (1966), covering the years 1929–49.

The vexing problems of expatriation can be seen in the case of **George Johnston** (1912–70), a Melbourne-born writer who worked first as a journalist and war correspondent. The traumatic experiences of the war and his disillusionment with life back in Australia led him, with his wife, author Charmian Clift, to leave first for London and then to the Greek Islands, where they tried to support themselves and their family entirely by writing; they did not return to Australia until 1964. While many of his novels were historical and travel 'potboilers', Johnston's great achievement was *My Brother Jack* (1964), a semi-autobiographical account of life in Melbourne between the wars. This successful exploration of mood and the texture of the city was followed by *Clean Straw for Nothing* (1969), a continuation of his own journey, through life abroad and a returning home.

That all of these authors felt the need to use a personal voice to define the Australian experience speaks to the increasing self-consciousness of Australia as a separate nation and culture. The decades of the 1950s and 60s saw many writers seeking to explain the specific nature of Australian identity. **Donald Horne**'s (b. 1921) *Lucky Country* (1964) and **Geoffrey Blainey**'s (b. 1930) *Tyranny of Distance* (1966) were milestones of cultural critique that are still quoted today; the titles of their books, in fact, have become part of the Australian idiom. Even the humorous best-seller, *They're a Weird Mob* (1957) by 'Nino Culotta', was a perceptive consideration of Australian customs and language. 'Culotta', supposedly an Italian immigrant bewildered by the mores of his adopted country, was actually **John O'Grady** (1907–81), a Sydney writer. Australia's fraught relationship with its British roots even affected the writing of history; when **Manning Clark** (1915–91) began to publish his seminal *History of Australia* (1962–87), he was roundly criticised for emphasising the country's development as distinct from British imperialist achievements. That Australia could have its own intellectual life, separate from English academe, was still a controversial consideration.

Australian drama also came to maturity in this period. One of the first landmarks was the 1948 production of *Rusty Bugles* (1948), a comic denunciation of war rich in vernacular language, written by **Sumner Locke Elliott** (1917–91). By the time it was produced, Elliott had already moved to the USA, where he became a successful television playwright, with such classics as 'The Grey Nurse Said Nothing' (1959); he did not return to Australia until 1974, by which time his other plays, such as *Careful He Might Hear You* (1963), had gained international recognition.

The play that is still considered as the 'beginning of the Australian national theatre' was *Summer of the Seventeenth Doll* by **Ray Lawler** (b. 1921), first produced in Melbourne in 1955. A complex examination of such cultural myths as mateship and outback stereotypes, the play was immensely popular for its ability to capture Australian vernacular speech. It was produced successfully overseas, was restaged many times, and has been made into a film and, most recently, an opera by Richard Mills.

The 1960s saw an explosion of dramatic endeavours, encouraged by the emergence of alternative 'street theatre' and new venues such as La Mama and the Pram Factory in Melbourne. Out of this environment came some enduring talents, most notably **Jack Hibberd** (b. 1940) and the most popular playwright of the last few decades, **David Williamson** (b. 1942). Hibberd's *Dimboola* (1969), a comic send-up of country life and customs, was the most popular production of all, and has become the most performed Australian play. Williamson's many satirical portrayals of Australian society have become theatrical standards: *Don's Party* (1971), an hilarious commentary on The Sixties Generation and Labor voters; *The Club* (1977), about the politics of 'footy'; *Emerald City* (1987), a satirical story of Melbourne-Sydney rivalries and the film industry; and *Brilliant Lies* (1993), an insightful study of sexual harassment. Williamson has also scripted several films, including Peter Weir's *Gallipoli* (1981). One of the leading theatrical voices today is **Louis Nowra** (b. 1950), writing such black comedies as *Così* (1992), about an opera production in a mental institution, and *Black Rock* (1995), based on the murder of a Newcastle teenager.

Poetry since the war

Somewhat surprisingly, Australian poets have continued to sustain a sizeable following and have produced significant contributions to literary culture. One of the most admired figures is **Judith Wright** (b. 1915), whose first volume *The Moving Image* (1946) was greeted with great excitement by the literary world. Her poems of nature, the transience of time, and the quest for self-knowledge are prolific, enhanced by her active support of Aboriginal and environmental causes. Wright beautifully summarises the current desire for 'reconciliation' in a statement made in 1981: 'Those two strands—the love of the land we have invaded and the guilt of the invasion—have become part of me. We owe it repentance and such amends as we can...'

Christopher Wallace-Crabbe (b. 1934) is a poet firmly based in Melbourne academic and suburban life, with reflections both joyous and sombre on the state of modern existence; such amusing titles as *The Amorous Cannibal* (1985) give an indication of his free-ranging wit and romantic concerns.

A.D. Hope (b. 1907) was also an academic, writing verse rich in mythological and Biblical allusions (see 'Death of a Bird' and 'Meditation on a Bone'). The most popular poet of the last few decades has been **Les Murray** (b. 1938), described by Wallace-Crabbe as 'Oscar Wilde in moleskins [Australian working trousers]', for his lyrical championing of the old bush imagery and exuberant Australianness. In such collections as *The Vernacular Republic* (1976) and *The Daylight Moon* (1987), Murray writes accessible verse about the wonders of the Australian landscape and its people.

Aboriginal writers

Aboriginal writers also began to gain recognition from the 1960s. The first Aborigine to publish a literary work was **David Unaipon** (1872–1967), whose *Native Legends* appeared in 1929; Unaipon now features on the Australian $50 note. Significantly, the first novel by an Aborigine did not appear until 1965, when the-then **Colin Johnson** (b. 1939) published *Wild Cat Falling*; Johnson is now known by his Aboriginal name, **Mudrooroo**. Mudrooroo suffered the typical fate of many indigenous people: raised in an orphanage, incarcerated for minor offences, he struggled to gain some foothold in the white world. Eventually Mudrooroo continued his studies, travelled widely and even lived in a Buddhist monastery in India. His first book is a ruthlessly honest depiction of this struggle. His later *Doctor Wooreddy's Prescription for Enduring the Ending of the World* (1983) takes as its central theme the story of G.A. Robinson and the Tasmanian Aborigines; the tone, however, demonstrates Mudrooroo's own spiritual and philosophical vision, imbued with Aboriginal and Eastern cosmology.

Protest poet **Kath Walker** (1920–93) also became better known by her Aboriginal name, **Oodgeroo Noonuccal**, which she adopted in 1988 in opposition to the Bicentenary celebrations of white settlement. Her first volume of poetry, *We Are Going* (1964), was a warning to whites that Aboriginal people would endure. Her delightful *Stradbroke Dreamtime* (1972) is a collection of traditional Aboriginal stories based on her childhood memories on an island near Brisbane.

Kevin Gilbert (1933–93) was an extraordinary figure in the Aboriginal protest movement; while in prison, he learned to read, and developed a great talent not only for writing, but for painting and photography. Gilbert was instrumental in the founding of the Aboriginal Tent Embassy in Canberra in 1972, while producing poetry and, in 1988, the important anthology, *Inside Black Australia*. In 1988, he received the Human Rights Award for literature, which he declined until his people were granted such rights.

Particularly poignant and significant for contemporary Australians was the publication of *My Place* (1987) by **Sally Morgan** (b. 1951), a Western Australian whose Aboriginal heritage was hidden from her until she was an adult; the book documents her coming to terms with her sense of belonging and her desire to gain an understanding of her people's cultural traditions and art.

Roberta 'Bobbi' Sykes (b. 1943), sometimes called 'Australia's own Angela Davis', is a black activist and academic, born in Queensland and deceived by her own mother about her mixed parentage (she is probably part African-American). She was the first 'black Australian' to graduate from Harvard University. She has just published the first of a projected three-volume autobiography, *Snake Cradle* (1997), a harrowing and at times painful story of racist violence and personal endurance.

The last twenty years

While many ambitious artists and writers still felt compelled as late as the 1960s to emigrate—most notably, of course, **Germaine Greer** (b. 1939; *The Female Eunuch* [1971]), **Clive James** (b. 1939; *Unreliable Memoirs* [1980]), and **Barry Humphries** (b. 1934; *My Gorgeous Life* [1989])—many more decided to stay to be part of Australia's multicultural transformation of the last 20 years. Literary themes broadened substantially beyond the confines of strictly Australian experience, and increased interactions with global cultural events determined the directions that literature, both serious and popular, would take.

Thomas Keneally (b. 1935) is a good example of a novelist who straddles the line between popular and serious fiction, and who has gained as much international as domestic success. His first well-received work was *Bring Larks and Heroes* (1967), based on Watkin Tench's accounts of early Sydney; and his *Chant of Jimmy Blacksmith* (1972), a grimly humorous re-creation of a true story of Aboriginal-White conflict, gained him an international reputation, especially after its successful filming in 1978. But Keneally's subject-matter extends beyond Australian history, most notably in *Schindler's Ark* (1982), the story of Holocaust survivors and their rescuer, Oskar Schindler; the book was the source for Stephen Spielberg's renowned film, *Schindler's List* (1993).

A more journalistic voice, in the spirit of the American Tom Wolfe, is **Frank Moorhouse** (b. 1938), widely associated in the 1960s and 70s with the intellectual atmosphere of Sydney's Balmain. His collection of stories, *The Americans, Baby* (1972) and *The Coca Cola Kid* (1985), offer humorous insights into the Americanisation of Australian urban life.

Helen Garner (b. 1942) continues to write austere considerations of the moral dilemmas of everyday life, such as her first novel *Monkey Grip* (1977) and the screenplay for the film, *Last Days at Chez Nous* (1992). Her most recent book, *The First Stone* (1994), was a controversial editorial on the issues arising from a case of sexual harassment at the University of Melbourne, infuriating feminists and conservatives alike. Feminist convictions certainly inform the fiction of **Kate Grenville** (b. 1950) in intriguing books such as *Lilian's Story* (1985), based on the life of Sydney eccentric Bea Miles, and *Joan Makes History* (1988), an alternative history centred on an Australian everywoman.

Perhaps the most diverse author of the present period is **David Malouf** (b. 1934), a Queenslander of Lebanese background who divides his time between Australia and Tuscany. Firmly grounded in European tradition, Malouf ranges across a broad spectrum of themes, from autobiographical reminiscences of wartime Brisbane in *Johnno* (1975) to the more epic events of early Queensland settlement in *Remembering Babylon* (1993) and short stories and poems about place and childhood experience. Malouf presented the 1998 Boyer Lecturers for ABC Radio, in which he considered 'the nature of Australians'; these have been published as *A Spirit of Play* (1998).

Peter Carey (b. 1943) is another Australian who, while living in the USA, still draws most of his inspiration from Australian history and characters. Described as a fabulist in the spirit of Garcia Marquez and Donald Bartheleme, Carey's works appeal to a broad public. His most popular novels, imagistic and historical at the same time, include *Bliss* (1981), based on Mark Twain's assertion that Australian history is 'like the most beautiful lies'; the picaresque *Illywhacker* (1985); and *Oscar and Lucinda* (1988), which won the prestigious Booker Prize and has been made into a film.

An enduring presence in Australian literary life today is **Elizabeth Jolley** (b. 1923), British-born who migrated to Western Australia with her husband in 1959. The characters in her many novels and short stories are invariably life's misfits, lonely, eccentric and often deviant; as she states, 'no one comes out on top in my fiction...' Her novels are especially favoured in the USA, especially *Mr Scobie's Riddle* (1983) and *Miss Peabody's Inheritance* (1983). Jolley's *Milk and Honey* (1984) is her most poetic and metaphysical novel, combining everyday characters with grand literary allusions. She continues to extend her dark vision of the world with delicate, sometimes disturbing, examinations of societal losers and 'others'.

The most extraordinary event in recent years was the publication in 1981 of *A Fortunate Life* by **Albert Facey** (1894–1982). A simple man with no formal education, Facey wrote his life's story with no ambition at publication; it was submitted to a publisher by his son, who simply wanted a few copies for the family. Its unpretentious and matter-of-fact presentation of the unbelievable hardships of one man's life gained an immediate world-wide audience. Anyone who wants to understand the roots of a distinctly Australian world-view should read *A Fortunate Life*, the purest form of autobiography.

That many of the best writers of the last 30 years have had their fiction turned into film and television series simply indicates the media-driven directions of contemporary culture. Reaching a broader audience through film has certainly been the experience of Australia's most popular writers, in many cases making them international celebrities. **Morris West** (b. 1916) is probably the biggest-selling author born in Australia. His novels *The Devil's Advocate* (1959) and *The Shoes of the Fisherman* (1963), dealt with religious themes and were produced as major Hollywood films.

Colleen McCullough (b. 1937) also gained enormous international recognition after the televised version of her book *The Thorn Birds* (1977), a family saga of religion, sex and violence. McCullough has gone on to tackle the historical blockbuster, creating so far three volumes of a proposed six about Ancient Rome (*The First Man in Rome* [1990]). She now lives on Norfolk Island and is still famous as Australia's wealthiest author.

Film versions have also played a role in the success of **Peter Corris**'s (b. 1942) Cliff Hardy series of crime stories, and, more indirectly, his hilarious re-creations of 1940s Hollywood through the Errol Flynn-inspired character of Richard 'Box Office' Browning. Corris's mysteries are probably the best example of the crime fiction genre in contemporary Australia, a field that has grown enormously in the last decade.

Another popular phenomenon was the publication in 1979 of *Puberty Blues* by **Gabrielle Carey** (b. 1959) and **Kathy Lette** (b. 1958). Carey and Lette had performed a screamingly popular cabaret act as 'The Salami Sisters'. Their co-authored book was a startling semi-autobiographical account of Cronulla 'surfie culture' from the girls' point of view. While enormously touted as a comic masterpiece and made into a popular film in 1981, the book has a nasty-edged bite that says much about the anxiety-ridden war of the sexes, beach-style.

Writing for children

The Australian authors who seem to have gained the most praise and produced the most original work recently have been writers of fiction for children. While children's literature is not a new phenomenon in Australia, the level and standard of production in recent years seems particularly stellar. **Colin Thiele** (b. 1920), of course, produced the children's classics *Storm Boy* (1963) and *Blue Fin* (1969) in the 1960s, and gained an international audience when these stories of the sea and lonely children were filmed in the 1970s.

Currently, **Paul Jennings** (b. 1943) is Australia's most prolific and successful author; his quirky, magical short stories, both in the series *Round the Twist* and in books with titles such as *Unbelievable!* and *Uncanny!* appeal especially to children between six and 12. Most significant are the ambitious, thoughtful and complex productions of two authors for older children: **Victor Kelleher** (b. 1939) and **John Marsden** (b. 1950). Kelleher, who also writes adult fiction, specialises in tales of adventure-fantasy and sinister events, such as *The Hunting of Shadroth* (1981), *The Red King* (1989) and *Parkland* (1994). Marsden's immensely suspenseful series, centred on a group of children's response to foreign invasion and nuclear war, began with *Tomorrow, When the World Began* (1993), and will culminate after seven adventurous volumes, in October 1999. If these admirable contributions to intelligent and complex fiction for young people are not known abroad, then be sure to buy them here.

Current trends
Current literary trends in Australia represent all the cutting-edge concerns of global culture: post-modernism, gay culture, feminist performance art, computer-generated poetry, television-inspired comedy, punk and grunge. Many critics maintain that Sydney especially is the quintessential post-modernist city, the voice of the twenty-first century; the alternative literary scene, with poetry readings in pubs, internet journals, and multi-media presentations, tends to support this claim. In a recent ABC television production about 'Bohemian Australia,' a grunge-poet named **Edward Berridge** (he created a poetry volume called *Lives of the Saints*) asserts, as a proclamation against the supposed dominance of Sixties-generated ideas, that he and his ilk 'will be determining the intellectual agenda of Australia for the next twenty-five years, so you better get used to it.' Go for it, Edward!

Recommended reading

Guidebooks
General guide books are often convenient for their local maps and listings of popular entertainments. The better ones for Australia are *Explore Australia*, Claremont Penguin; Australia, *Rough Guides*; and the numerous *Lonely Planet* guides.

Andrews, Graeme. *Ferries of Sydney*. Sydney, Oxford University Press, 1994.

Barker, Sue et al. *Explore the Barossa*. Netland, SA, South Australia State, 1991.

Blair's guide: travel guide to Victoria & Melbourne. Hawthorne, Victoria, Universal, 6th ed. 1994.

Cronin, Leonard. *Key guide to Australia's national parks*. Carlton, Victoria, Reed New Holland, 1998.

Coasting: Dirk Flinthart's real guide to the east coast of Australia. Potts Point, NSW, Duffy & Snellgrove, 1996.

Emmett, E.T. *Tasmania by road and track*. Parkville, Melbourne University, 1962.

Gunter, John. *Sydney by ferry & foot* (a Heritage Field Guide). Kenthurst, NSW, Kangaroo Press, 1983.

Huié, Jacqueline. *Untourist Sydney*. Balmain, UnTourist, 1995.

Lawrence, Joan. *Sydney good walks guide*. Crows Nest, NSW, Kingsclear Books, 1991.

Odgers, Sally Farrell. *Tasmania—a guide* (Heritage Field Guide). Kenthurst, NSW, Kangaroo Press, 1991.

Park, Ruth. *The companion guide to Sydney*. Sydney, Collins, 1973, revised ed. 1999.

Rennie, Chris. *The surfer's travel guide*. Doncaster, Victoria, Liquid Addictions, 1998.

Starling, Steve. *Fishing hot spots*. Mills Point, New South Wales, Random House, 1998.

Natural history

Numerous field guides and key guides will be familiar to professional scientists. Unfortunately, the best popular books on Australian flora and fauna, the *Encyclopedia of Australian wildlife* and the *Complete book of Australian birds*, both by Reader's Digest, are too heavy to travel with easily.

Davey, Keith. *A photographic guide to seashore life of Australia*. Sydney, New Holland, 1998.

Haddon, Frank. *Australia's outback: environmental field guide to flora and fauna*. Roseville, NSW, Simon & Schuster, 1992.

Laseron, Charles Francis. *The face of Australia: the shaping of a continent*. Sydney, Angus & Robertson, 1953.

Pizzey, Graham. *Field guide to the birds of Australia*. Sydney, Angus and Robertson, 1997.

Puffin book of Australian spiders. Ringwood, Victoria, Penguin, 1989. (Note: One of an informative series for children.)

Simpson, Ken and Day, Nicolas. *Field guide to the birds of Australia*. Ringwood, Victoria, Penguin, 1989.

von Hügel, Charles. *New Holland Journal, November 1833–October 1834*. (Dymphna Clark, trans.) Carlton, Victoria, Melbourne University, 1994.

Watts, Peter, et al. *An exquisite eye: the Australian flora & fauna drawings of Ferdinand Bauer, 1801–1820*. Glebe, NSW, Historic Houses, 1998.

White, Mary E. *The greening of Gondwana: the 400 million year story of Australian plants*. East Roseville, New South Wales, Simon & Schuster, 1998.

Aboriginal culture

Caruana, Wally. *Aboriginal art*. London, Thames & Hudson, 1993.

Edwards, W.H., ed. *Traditional Aboriginal society*. South Yarra, Victoria, Macmillan, 1998.

Horton, David, ed. *The encyclopaedia of Aboriginal Australia*. 2 vols. Canberra, Australian Institute of Aboriginal and Torres Strait Islander Studies, 1994.

Morphy, Howard. *Aboriginal art*. London, Phaidon, 1998.

Ryan, Judith. *Spirit in land: bark paintings from Arnhem Land*. Melbourne, National Gallery.

West, Margaret. *The inspired dream: life as art in Aboriginal Australia*. South Brisbane, Queensland Art Gallery, 1988.

Art, architecture and cinema

Freeland, J.M. *Architecture in Australia*. Ringwood, Victoria, Penguin, 1968.

Jahn, Graham. *Sydney architecture*. Sydney, Watermark Press, 1997.

Kerr, Joan. *The dictionary of Australian artists: painters, sketchers, photographers and engravers to 1870*. Melbourne, Oxford University Press, 1992.

Maitland, Barry and Stafford, David. *Architecture Newcastle: a guide*. RAIA, Newcastle, 1987. (Note: There are a number of Royal Australian Institute of Architects publications in this city specific series.)

Marsden, Susan. *Heritage of the city of Adelaide: an illustrated guide*. Adelaide, City, 1990.

Sabine, James. *A century of Australian cinema*. Port Melbourne, Reed, 1995.

Shirley, Graham and Adams, Brian. *Australian cinema: the first eighty years*. Sydney, Currency Press, revised ed., 1989.

Smith, Bernard, ed. *Documents on art and taste in Australia, 1770–1914*. Melbourne, Oxford, 1975.

Smith, Bernard. *European vision and the South Pacific*. Melbourne, Oxford, 1989.

Smith, Bernard and Smith, Terry. *Australian painting, 1788–1990*. Melbourne, University of Melbourne, 1991.

Language and literature

Baker, Sidney. *The Australian language*. Sydney, Currawong, 1966.

Bassett, Jan, ed. *Great Southern landings: an anthology of antipodean travel*. Melbourne, Oxford University Press, 1995.

Harman, Kaye. *Australia brought to book: responses to Australia by visiting writers, 1836–1939*. Balgowlah, NSW, BooBook, 1985.

Hergenhan, Laurie. *New literary history of Australia*. Ringwood, Victoria, Penguin, 1988.

Pierce, Peter, ed. *The Oxford literary guide to Australia*. Melbourne, Oxford University Press, 1987.

Wilde, William, et al. *The Oxford companion to Australian literature*. Melbourne, Oxford University Press, 2d ed., 1994.

Wilson, Barbara. *The illustrated treasury of Australian stories & verse for children*. Melbourne, Nelson, 1987.

Cultural history

Clune, Frank. *Saga of Sydney: the birth, growth, and maturity of the mother city of Australia*. Sydney, 1961.

Davidson, Graeme. *The Oxford companion to Australian History*. Melbourne, Oxford University Press, 1998.

Flannery, Tim, ed. *Watkin Tench: 1788*. Melbourne, Text, 1996.

Haskell, Arnold L. *Waltzing Matilda: a background to Australia*. London, A & C Black, 2nd ed., 1941.

Hughes, Robert. *The fatal shore*. New York, Knopf, 1987.

Karskens, Grace. *The Rocks: life in early Sydney*. Melbourne University, 1997.

Luck, Peter. *A time to remember*. Port Melbourne, Mandarin, 1988.

Morris, Jan. *Sydney*. London, Viking, 1992.

Palmer, Vance. *The legend of the nineties*. Melbourne, Melbourne University, 1963.

Ripe, Cherry. *Goodbye, Culinary Cringe!* St Leonard's, NSW, Allen & Unwin, 1993.

Serle, Geoffrey. *The Creative spirit in Australia: A cultural history*. Richmond, Victoria, William Heinemann, 1987.

Sharp, Ilsa. *Culture shock!: a guide to customs and etiquette*. Singapore, Times, 1992.

Statham, Pamela, ed. *The origins of Australia's capital cities*. Cambridge, Cambridge, 1989.

Venturini, V.G., ed. *Australia: a survey*. (Schriften des Instituts für Asienkunde in Hamburg; vol. 27) Wiesbaden, O. Harrassowitz, 1970.

New South Wales

New South Wales is situated on the southeast corner of Australia between Victoria to the south, Queensland to the north and South Australia to the west. East to west, it is marked by a narrow coastal plain, the Great Dividing Range and the Murray Darling Plain. Its population is concentrated along the sea coast, principally around **Sydney**, the state's capital. It is the country's most populous state, with a population  in 1996 of 6,130,200, more than a third of Australia's total population.

The major ports are at Newcastle, Wollongong and Sydney. The highway system is fairly simple. Highway 1, the **Pacific Highway**, extends north from Sydney along the coast through Newcastle eventually to Brisbane. Highway 31, the **Southwestern Highway** then **Hume Highway**, proceeds south through the Murray Darling Plain to Melbourne with a side route to Canberra. An alternative route to Melbourne along the coast, the **Princes Highway**, is considerably slower, but much more interesting. Inland highways include the **New England Highway** (route 15, to the interior from Newcastle to Brisbane); the **Newell Highway** (route 39, through the interior from Melbourne to west of Brisbane); and the **Sturt Highway** (route 20, crossing southern New South Wales to Adelaide).

Geologically the metamorphic rocks and granites of the southern Tasman Geosyncline extend from south of the New South Wales–Victoria border in an arch more or less from Echuca, Victoria, to Hay to Ivanhoe to Broken Hill in the western part of the state. The Palaeozoic sediments extend eastward to the Queensland border northeast of Bourke where younger Mesozoic formations extending southeast to Sydney interrupt. Like the Cainozoic basin in the west and southwest, this formation is relatively flat and dry in the interior. The northeast corner of the state above Newcastle to the Queensland border is again Palaeozoic with igneous intrusions forming the mountains. Sydney, in other words, is part of the Mesozoic formation encompassing most of northern New South Wales and central Queensland. This intrudes on the Palaeozoic coastal highlands which extend from Cape York nearly to Mount Gambier in Victoria.

The physical features most attractive to the visitor include fine surf beaches (thirty-four in Sydney alone and hundreds more along the entire coastline), Sydney Harbour, the Blue Mountains (a day trip west of Sydney), limestone caves at Jenolan and Wombeyan, the Australian Alps or Snowy Mountains in Kosciuszko National Park, the Hawkesbury River, and 'Back 'o Bourke', that is, the outback, in the state's arid northwest.

Sydney

Sydney (population four million) has always been the premier city of Australia. The capital of the state of New South Wales, it encompasses a vast area around Port Jackson Harbour and as far west as the Blue Mountains; officially, it is listed at 33°55' south, 151°17' east. With a population of four million, the Sydney region now comprises almost a quarter of the country's entire population.

Administratively, **Sydney City** refers to a very small segment of this metropolitan area, but the many municipalities and surrounding suburbs around this central district are generally considered part of Sydney. In the last forty years, Sydney has been transformed from a provincial British colonial outpost to a world-class multicultural city, a central player, as David Dale states in *The 100 Things Everyone Needs to Know About Australia* (1996), in Australia's change from 'one of the dullest nations on earth to one of the most interesting'. Jan Morris, in her book on Sydney (1992), mirrors these sentiments, amazed at its transformation since her first visit in 1962; she declares it the '*shiniest*' city of the old British Empire.

Sydneysiders, as residents are called, while notoriously disinterested in self-reflection, would certainly agree with this description. They are immensely proud of their robust and vibrant city, and all the glitzy glamour of its most recent decades, and not very interested in dwelling on its history.

■ Practical information

Tourist information. The **Sydney Visitor Centre**, 106 George Street, The Rocks, ☎ 02 9255 1788/13 20 77 (throughout Australia for cost of local call); **Airport centre**, International Terminal, ☎ 9667 6050. Open every day 09.00–18.00. Hotel bookings made on site and for single nights only. Both centres include hotel phone board from which main chain hotels can be reached for bookings and transportation.

Getting from the airport. Kingsford Smith Airport is located in Mascot on Botany Bay, about 8km from the centre of Sydney. The airport's two terminals, domestic and international, are linked by free shuttle buses. These **Airport Express buses** also travel into the city, running every 20 minutes ☎ 131 500. No. 300 runs to Circular Quay via Central Station and King's Cross; no. 350 runs to Central Station and King's Cross. Currently the cost is $5 single, $8 return. There is also a private bus line, **Kingsford Smith Transport**, that will drop you at most places in the city for the same price as the city bus; ☎ 02 9667 3221. Taxi fare is about $20 into central Sydney.

Trains. All interstate and local trains arrive at **Central Railway Station**, Eddy Avenue, immediately south of city centre. All major bus and city train routes leave from here as well. For information on state and interstate services, ☎ 02 9217 8812 or in New South Wales freecall ☎ 008 04 3126; a **Countrylink Travel Centre** is also available at Circular Quay Station, which is the other centre for rail information. City rail information is open until 22.00; ☎ 131 500.

Bus. The main coach terminal is at the side of Central Station (☎ 02 9212 1500), although the Greyhound-Pioneer buses most regularly arrive at the depot on Oxford and Riley Streets, in Paddington-Darlinghurst; ☎ 13 2323; website: www.greyhound.com.au. From here, local buses nos 280 and 389 go down Oxford Street to Circular Quay; bus no. 378 arrives at Central Station.

Local transport. Sydney has relatively good public transportation, with an extensive and fairly efficient train network from the Blue Mountains to Liverpool and along the coast both north and south. Within the city, buses are the most convenient and cheapest way to travel. Automobile traffic in the entire Sydney region causes some of the worst and most frustrating congestion in the world; travel by public transportation is strongly recommended when at all possible. Bus, train, and ferry information is available at travel offices at Circular Quay and Central Station; ☎ 02 9954 4422/131 500. Weekly **Travelpasses** are available, with colour-coded zone fares; for the buses, a **Metroten ticket** offers the biggest savings, if you are using the buses for several trips. For tourists, the **Sydney Explorer Pass** allows unlimited travel on the many Explorer buses to popular destinations around the city; it is available through the New South Wales Travel Centre, 19 Castlereagh Street, ☎ 02 9231 4444.

Ferries. Do not forget that the harbour's ferries are not just tourist rides, but serve as the major, and certainly the most enjoyable, form of public transportation from the North Shore and to most venues around the harbour as far as Parramatta. They travel frequently and conveniently.

The **Ferries Information Centre** is located opposite Jetty 4 at Circular Quay; information about ferry service is through the State Transit Public Transport Information Line, ☎ 131 1500.

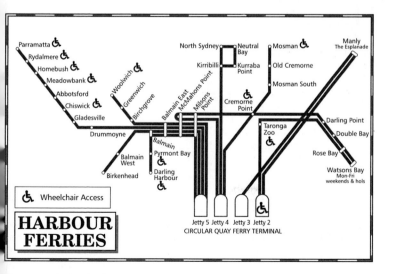

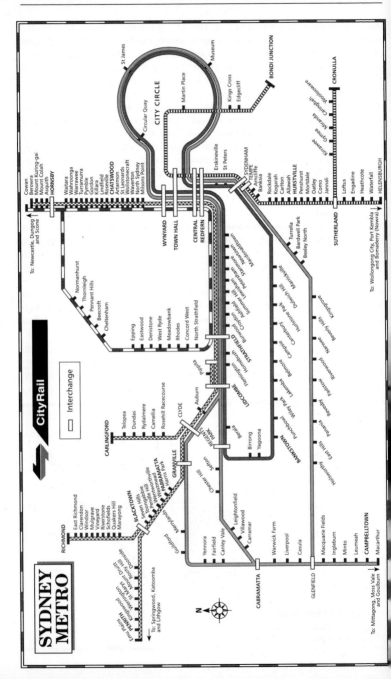

Water taxis are also available 24 hours a day, a bit pricey, but a truly exciting way to get to any place near the water. Telephone **Taxis Afloat**, ☎ 1 300 300 925, website: www.watertaxis.com.au. **Harbour Taxi Boats**, ☎ 9555 1155; or Beach Hooper Water Taxis, ☎ 0412 400 990

Taxis. Taxi fares in Sydney are relatively expensive, and, as in all major cities, the drivers have a reputation for either verbosity or cantankerousness; they represent the multicultural nature of contemporary Australia, and are for the most part excellent drivers. Tipping is appreciated, but certainly not mandatory and is usually only a rounding off to the nearest dollar. Taxis can be located at taxi ranks around the city; one can also try to hail a cab on the street, although this is not as standard a practice as in New York City. Book a cab from **Legion**, tel. 9289 9000; **Premier Radio Cabs**, 02 13 10 17; **RSL**, 02 9581 1111.

Useful addresses

Consulates: *British Consulate General*, Level 16, Gateway Building, 1 Macquarie Street, ☎ 02 9247 7521; *US Consulate*, 59th floor, MLC Centre, 19–29 Martin Place, ☎ 02 9373 9200.

Police: *Emergency*, ☎ 000; *police switchboard*, 151–241 Goulburn Street, Surry Hills, ☎ 02 9281 0000; *city stations*: 192 Day Street, ☎ 02 9265 6499; The Rocks, George and Argyle Street, ☎ 02 9265 6366.

Hospitals: *Sydney Hospital Emergency*, Macquarie Street, ☎ 02 9228 2111; *Royal North Shore Hospital*, Pacific Highway, St Leonards, ☎ 02 9438 7111.

Hotels

$$$$ Hotel Inter-Continental, 117 Macquarie Street, City, ☎ 02 9230 0200/1800 221 828; fax 02 9240 1240. A truly grand hotel, part of which is the old treasury building; cultivated elegance, walking distance to Opera House and Botanic Gardens. Superb restaurant.

$$$$ Park Hyatt, 7 Hickson Road, The Rocks, ☎ 02 9241 1234/131 234, fax 02 9256 1555. In USA: ☎ 1800 233 1234; London: ☎ 0171 580 8197. Architecturally impressive, blending beautifully with Rocks and Quay buildings; balcony rooms directly on harbour.

$$$$ Ritz-Carlton, 93 Macquarie Street, City, ☎ 02 9252 4600/1800 252 888, fax 02 9252 4286. Fine hotel near Sydney's financial district and opposite Botanic Gardens, in 1899 sandstone building; thoughtful service.

$$$ Carlton Crest, 169–179 Thomas Street, City, ☎ 02 9281 6888/1800 252 588; fax 02 9281 6888. A four-star hotel near Darling Harbour, excellent location, rooftop pool. Has special packages in combination with Sydney Festival, and on summer weekends.

$$$ Observatory Hotel, 89–113 Kent Street, The Rocks, ☎ 02 9256 2222/1800 806 245, fax 02 9256 2233. Famed for its 'drawing room' atmosphere—antiques, library, fireplace, as well as canopied pool. On one of the most delightful and calming streets in inner Sydney, across from Observatory Hill.

$$$ Ritz-Carlton Double Bay, 33 Cross Street, Double Bay, ☎ 02 9362 4455/1800 252 888, fax 02 9362 4744. A popular 'celebrity hotel' in the 'village' of Double Bay, 10 minutes from centre city. Impeccable service, famous buffet lunch in the lobby restaurant.

$$$ The Sebel of Sydney, 25 Elizabeth Bay Road, Elizabeth Bay, ☎ 02 9358

3244. 'Boutique' hotel, where Princess Diana and film stars stayed. Small and friendly, personalised service.

$$$ Woolloomooloo Waters Apartment Hotel, 88 Dowling Street, Woolloomooloo Bay, ☎ 02 9358 3100/1800 267 949; fax 02 9356 4839; e-mail: woolres@woolwater.aust.com. Self-contained apartments (studio, one- and two-bedroom), flexible packages for all levels of amenities, good for longer stays, ideal for families.

$$ Hughenden Boutique Hotel, 14 Queen Street, Woollahra, ☎ 9363 4863, fax 02 9362 0398. Small (36 rooms), in renovated historic (1876) house and stables; stylish and popular breakfast room.

$$ McLaren Hotel, 25 McLaren Street, North Sydney, ☎ 9954 4622, fax 02 9922 1868. Boutique hotel (25 rooms) in centre of North Sydney; front building part of National Trust; room cost includes breakfast.

$$ Periwinkle Guesthouse, 18–19 East Esplanade, Manly, ☎ 9977 4668, fax 02 9977 6308. Great location, a 'fun' guesthouse, with a variety of rooms, resulting from the joining of two Victorian houses near the beach.

$$ Ravesi's, On the corner of Campbell Parade and Hall Street, Bondi Beach, ☎ 9365 4422, fax 02 9365 1481. The best place to stay on Bondi Beach: new and comfortable, ocean views, next to Hall Street and Jewish eateries.

$$ Sullivans, 21 Oxford Street, Paddington, ☎ 02 9361 0211, fax 02 9360 3735. Perfect inner-city location, off-street parking, comfortable rooms; great breakfast cafe. Very homey place, family-owned; bicycles available to guests.

$ The Grand Hotel, 30 Hunter Street, City, ☎ 02 232 3755, fax 02 9232 1073. One of Sydney's oldest hotels (only 19 rooms), built over the Tank Stream and opposite Wynyard Station. Excellent value, central location, some shared facilities.

$ "Y" on the Park (YWCA), 5 Wentworth Avenue, City, ☎ 02 9264 2451, fax 02 9283 2485. Next to Hyde Park, spare but clean, upbeat, and reasonably priced.

Restaurants

$$$ Bennelong, Sydney Opera House, City, ☎ 02 9250 7578. Fabulous views, serious dining experience, the creation of well-known chefs Gay Bilson and Janni Kyritsis; Director of Food is now Michael Moore, ex of Terence Conran's Bluebird in London.

$$$ Darley Street Thai, 28–30 Bayswater Road, Potts Pint, ☎ 02 9358 6530. World-class Thai cuisine, complex and elegant, the result of years of serious culinary research by chef David Thompson.

$$$ Rockpool, 107 George Street, The Rocks, ☎ 02 9252 1888. The creation of Australia's most famous chef, Neil Perry, the food here defines elegant 'Modern Australian' cuisine, with emphasis on Asian flavours and seafood. Astronomical prices.

$$$ Tetsuya's, 729 Darling Street, Rozelle, ☎ 02 9555 1017. One of the most highly-acclaimed restaurants in Australia, chef Tetsuya Wakuda mixes Japanese and Continental cuisine, using the best Australian ingredients. Absolutely essential stop for food-lovers; bookings needed well in advance.

$$$ Unkai Dining Room and Sushi Bar, ANA Hotel, Cumberland Street, The Rocks, ☎ 02 9250 6123. High-class Japanese, with overwhelming views from Harbour to mountains; highly recommended by Japanese themselves.

$$$ Wockpool, 155 Victoria Street, Potts Point, ☎ 02 9368 1771. Often voted best Asian restaurant in Sydney, another of Neil Perry's creations; for dinner only. Now Chinese-Australian chef Kylie Kwong runs another **Wockpool**, also superb, at the Imax Theatre in Darling Harbour, ☎ 02 9211 9888, open for lunch and dinner.

$$ The Balkan Continental, 209 Oxford Street, ☎ 02 9360 4970 and **$$ The Balkan Seafood**, 215 Oxford Street, ☎ 02 9331 7670. Run by the same Croatian family, these restaurants a few doors apart have been an Oxford Street landmark for years. Very homey, excellent value, at both the 'meat' and the 'fish' restaurants. Great cevapcici and grilled fish platters.

$$ Buon Ricordo, 108 Boundary Street, Paddington, ☎ 02 9360 6729. Considered by Sydney's Lord Mayor Frank Sartor the best Italian restaurant in town; Tuscan delicacies in generous portions, famous for antipasto and figs.

$$ Edna's Table, Lobby Level, MLC Centre, Martin Place, City, ☎ 02 9231 1400. Authentic 'bush tucker' ingredients in contemporary cuisine; comfortable setting for a highly-touted and original restaurant run with flair by Edna herself.

$$ Edosei, 22 Rockwall Crescent, Potts Point, ☎ 02 9326 9108. Some of best sushi in town.

$$ MCA Cafe, Museum of Contemporary Art, 140 George Street, The Rocks, ☎ 02 9241 4253. Another Neil Perry effort, less pricey, wonderful setting in and out front of Museum building on Circular Quay. Good choice for pleasant lunch.

$$ The Pig & the Olive, 71A Macleay Street, Potts Point, ☎ 02 9357 3745. Advertised as Mediterranean with 'PostModern Pizza'; great meat dishes as well.

$$ Radio Cairo, Military Road and Spofforth Street, Cremorne, ☎ 02 9953 0822. One of the most adventurous of places along North Shore's Military Road strip; spicy African/Caribbean/Sri Lankan. Across the street is **$$ Radio Cairo Cafe** for lunch, ☎ 02 9908 2649.

$ Bac Lieu, 302 Illawarra Road, Marrickville, ☎ 02 9558 5755. Family-run Vietnamese and Chinese, authentic, excellent value.

$ Chinese Noodle Restaurant, LG7, 8 Quay Street, Haymarket, ☎ 02 9281 9051. Tiny space, hand-made noodles on site, North-western Chinese specialities, chef also entertains with Chinese music when noodles are done.

$ Pho 54, 254 Park Road, Freedom Plaza, Cabramatta, ☎ 02 9726 1992. The best of Cabramatta's many Vietnamese 'pho' (beef-noodle) shops; addictive flavours, lots of garlic.

History of Sydney

The development of Australia as a Western nation began on **26 January 1788**, when Captain Arthur Phillip and his shipment of 736 convicts and four companies of marines landed, first at Watson's Bay and, finally, at Sydney Cove; these were the members of **The First Fleet**, so frequently referred to in Australian literature and popular culture. Their trip had taken eight months from Portsmouth and had covered more than 22,000km (14,000 miles). When their proposed site of settlement at Botany Bay proved unsuitable, they sailed on to find what is today **Sydney Harbour**. The penal colony of New South Wales was established as soon as the prisoners and marines disembarked.

This strange event came about as a result of the draconian legal codes and harsh social conditions of 18C England, leading to an enormous prison population which could no longer be housed. Once England lost the

American colonies as a convenient dumping ground for convicts, it had to look elsewhere to find a solution to the prison problem.

The continent that became known as Australia had been discovered and claimed for England in 1770 by **Captain James Cook**; upon the suggestion of Cook's naturalist **Sir Joseph Banks**, this continent on the other side of the world was seen as the ideal place to transport a large portion of the law-breakers. Not only would the horrendous overcrowding in prison be allevi-ated, but British imperialist ambitions in the Pacific would be furthered by the establishment of a colony in this land about which Cook and Banks had so romantically enthused. In his 1771 report, Cook wrote 'it can never be doubted but what most sorts of Grain, Fruits, Roots etc of every kind would flourish' and 'here are Provender for more Cattle at all seasons of the year than can be brought to this Country.'

While the first years of settlement were anything but flourishing, with deprivation and isolation exacerbated by failure of crops and livestock, inadequate housing, lack of building materials and skilled labour, Captain Phillip undertook the venture with ambitious conscientiousness and fortitude. He bestowed the name Sydney in honour of Thomas Towns-hend, 1st Viscount Sydney, who was then Home Secretary in the British Cabinet.

David Collins, marine captain and Judge-Advocate arriving with the First Fleet, provides one of the most valuable early accounts of the settlement:

The spot chosen [at Circular Quay]*...was at the head of the cove, near the run of fresh water* [the Tank Stream]*, which stole silently along through a very thick wood, the stillness of which had then, for the first time since the creation, been interrupted by the rude sound of the labourer's axe... The confusion that ensued will not be wondered at, when it is considered that every man stepped from the boat literally into a wood...the spot which had so lately been the abode of silence and tranquillity was now changed to that of noise, clamour,and confusion... As the woods were opened and the ground cleared, the encampments were extended, and all wore the appearance of regularity.*

On viewing the cosmopolitan congestion of present-day Sydney, it is hard to envision this as a description of the area around Circular Quay.

The Tank Stream, as the freshwater source was called, very quickly proved insufficient for the needs of the colony. Three sandstone tanks were built almost immediately in which to preserve its supply, but by the 1810s the stream was severely depleted and polluted. By 1827, a project was begun to dig a tunnel to the swamps of present-day Centennial Park 4km away. Known as 'Busby's Bore' after its engineer John Busby, it was Sydney's first major engineering feat when completed in 1837. The old Tank Stream is now channelled underneath Pitt Street.

When the First Fleet landed, the cove where Circular Quay is today was a salt-water estuary, and at low tide a mudflat covered the area of present-day Bridge Street, Lower Pitt and Alfred Streets, as well as a part of Loftus and Young Streets. This area was gradually filled in and reclaimed to become the central city itself. Frank Clune, in his *Saga of Sydney* (1961) boasts that 'no water frontage in the world has been so transformed by reclamation of tidal flats as Sydney's Circular Quay'.

The earliest streets were laid out parallel to the course of the Tank Stream, beginning with High Street, today's **George Street**. While the settlement did originally have a town plan—**Baron Alt**, a German surveyor on the First Fleet, laid out the initial settlement—it is obvious to the visitor that any systematic town planning was not enforced in the early days. In the 1810s, **Governor Macquarie** attempted to regulate the growth of the town and the standard of building, decreeing that streets must be at least 50 feet wide and houses set back 20 feet from the road. His efforts did not go unheeded, as one can see in the number of substantial structures from his time by convict architect **Francis Greenway** and others; haphazard development continued nonetheless.

The oldest area around the Circular Quay is a chaotic mishmash of diagonal streets and pathways that developed from short cuts used by pedestrians, a confusion exacerbated today by the overhead gash of the Cahill Expressway, built in the 1950s, which runs directly across the quay from the bridge.

Sydney Harbour

All considerations of Sydney must begin with and centre on the harbour, which Joseph Conrad described in his autobiography *The Mirror of the Sea* (1906) as '...one of the finest, most beautiful, vast and safe bays the sun ever shone upon.' The harbour provides one of the most stunning locations of any city in the world. The harbour dominates Sydney life, and any visitor to the city will undoubtedly begin explorations at the ferry terminus in the heart of the city, **THE CIRCULAR QUAY**. The quay vibrates with activity, intermingling a variety of regular buskers and vendors with a multitude of tourist attractions and excursion opportunities; tens of thousands of Sydneysiders take the ferry into the quay every day. Several organised **walking tours** commence from the quay, leading into the thick of the central city itself. For details of these walks, enquire at the Sydney Visitor Centre, ☎ 132 077.

Harbour trips

You can choose from any number of **harbour excursions**, from individual taxi-boats, sometimes cheaper and faster than a land-taxi, to cruises on a replica of the *Bounty*. But one of the most enjoyable ways to explore the harbour and the city itself is to take the **regular service ferries** to their various destinations.

The most extensive and enjoyable sightseeing experience is the **ferry to Manly**, which leaves the quay regularly to cross the entire bay, culminating at **Manly Beach**, next to the Heads which mark the entrance to the harbour itself. Many writers and regular travellers maintain that this trip is the one thing that all visitors to Sydney should do.

Other ferries travel from Circular Quay to **Balmain**, the **North Shore, Hunter Hill** and **Parramatta**. One of the most popular services is the **ferry to Taronga Park Zoo**, at the end of which visitors walk up to the zoo or, if in operation, ascend above the harbour in a cable car.

The harbour is the true heart of Sydney; explore the city from its shores, and take advantage of transportation on the water.

Walk 1 • Circular Quay and Macquarie Street

Starting at the railway station, follow the pedestrian tunnel at Circular Quay to emerge at the entrance to central Sydney on Alfred Street. Here turn left (east).

Customs House

About 300m down Loftus Street is the **Customs House** (☎ 02 9320 6393; **open** daily 09.30–17.00), now an isolated example of Victorian architecture among the glass and steel skyscrapers. Nearby is a small flagpole, marking the spot where Governor Phillip raised the Union Jack on 26 January 1788.

The original customs house was erected on this site to the Georgian design of Mortimer Lewis in 1844. When additions were necessary, structural difficulties required that this building be demolished. As it stands today it is a conglomerate of government architects' styles, the first floor completed in 1887 by James Barnet and the other floors added by Walter Vernon between 1887 and 1917. The floor in the entryway includes swastikas, traditionally symbols of good fortune.

Architects for the City of Sydney have recently carried out a renovation of the building, creating spaces for galleries and corporate reception areas. The renovation is certainly controversial, demonstrating little sympathy for the colonial character of the structure and adding an incongruously proportioned glass-and-steel upper deck; but the interior levels offer airy public spaces. **Level 2** houses **djamu gallery** (always written in lower case), which will house exhibitions of Aboriginal art ('djamu' is an Eora word meaning 'I am here'), as well as travelling exhibitions of the art of other indigenous people. This gallery is described as a 'project of the Australian Museum', so further information should be available on that museum's website, www.austmus.gov.au. **Level 3** presents a variety of exhibitions organised by the **Centre for Contemporary Craft** (☎ 02 947 9126), whose offices are also located here. Other floors will house restaurants and reception rooms.

Continue east on Alfred Street to Albert Street. Between Young and Phillip Streets along this stretch is the **AMP Building**, which for many years after its opening in 1962 was the highest building in Sydney at 114m (380 ft). Its appearance, along with the opening of the Cahill Expressway in the same year, signalled the end of the old accessible Circular Quay.

At present, construction between the quay and Macquarie Street, along with the rumbling of cars on the expressway overhead, combine to present an unfortunately uninspiring view towards the harbour and the Opera House. Recently mobilised Sydneysiders have begun protesting against the monstrous building blocks being constructed here, on arguably the most valuable real estate in the world, but so far the demonstrations appear to have come too late to save any vestige of the harbour's skyline on the south side.

On the corner of Albert and Phillip Streets is the **NSW Justice and Police Museum** (☎ 02 9252 1144; open Jan 10.00–17.00 Sun–Thurs; Feb–Dec 10.00–17.00 Sun), identified by the kitschy mannequins of police officer and convict on the front of the building. Now a complex of Classic Revival buildings, the first section facing Albert Street was designed by Edmund Blacket (see box, p 108) in 1854 in a Palladian style with an open portico and Doric columns. It originally served as the Water Police Court. Around the corner on

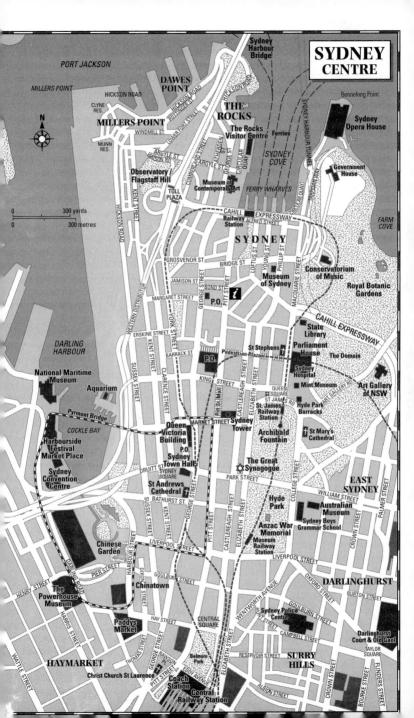

> ### Edmund Blacket
> Edmund Blacket (1817–83) was New South Wales's most prolific ecclesias-
> tical architect, sometimes referred to as the 'Christopher Wren of Australia'.
> He arrived from England in 1842, having escaped a father opposed to his
> dream of being an architect. Intending to settle in New Zealand, he was
> persuaded by Sydney acquaintances to stay in the city and became inspector
> of Church of England buildings. In 1845 he began practice as an architect,
> appointed colonial architect in 1849; in 1854 he set up private practice. His
> first impressive building was the main building for the new University of
> Sydney, completed in 1860. In all, Blacket completed some 58 churches,
> most of them in Sydney and almost all in Gothic Revival style.

Phillip the additions, also in sandstone, were probably designed by Mortimer
Lewis (1870) and James Barnet (1885).

Proceed south up Phillip to Bridge Street; on the corner was the site of the **first
Government House**. Governor Phillip's first headquarters consisted of a canvas
tent placed at Loftus Street near Macquarie Place, but by July 1788, a permanent
residence was begun on this site by convict bricklayer James Bloodworth.
Consisting initially of six rooms, the house was completed in time for King George
III's birthday in June 1789. Although the house continued as the official residence until 1845, every early governor complained of its dilapidated condition; it
was officially declared unfit for occupation in 1825, yet continued as the residence until Governor Gipps finally moved to New Government House. At that
time, the old house simply disintegrated. In 1984, archaeological excavation
uncovered the remains of the foundations, and plans were made to commemorate the site. It is now the location of the controversial **Museum of Sydney**
(MOS) (☎ 02 9251 5988; **open** daily 10.00–17.00), which, its detractors say,
does not emphasise enough the history of the original Government House.

The MOS is part of the Historic Houses Trust of New South Wales, and is
certainly the most post-modern museum in the city; such state-of-the-art exhibition techniques have been employed that it is sometimes difficult to know what
artefacts you are supposed to be seeing. The changing exhibitions are varied and
eclectic, and always innovatively presented. The plaza includes a 'talking poles'
sculptural monument, *Edge of Trees* by Janet Laurence, and Fiona Foley, evoking
through objects and voices the history of Sydney's people. Its exhibitions emphasise early Sydney history, with special displays concerning **the Eora**, the Aboriginal peoples of the Sydney region, and it has one of the most exciting bookshops
in the city, emphasising architecture and design, as well as the requisite chic
restaurant on the plaza.

Rising enormously behind the museum is **Governor Phillip Tower**
(1989–94), one of the newest post-modern skyscrapers in the central business
district, touted for its impressive integration of contemporary elements with the
needs of a historical site.

The Opera House
To reach the Opera House, walk over one block and north down Macquarie
Street to the Opera House at Bennelong Point (c 500m).
No landmark more readily identifies Sydney today than its Opera House,

placed on **Bennelong Point** overlooking the harbour. Its silhouette is so well-known internationally that it is hard to believe that it was only begun in 1959 and was not completed until 1973.

History of the Opera House

The saga of the construction of the Opera House can itself be described as operatic. Indeed, its story has served as the basis for an opera, *The Eighth Wonder*, by Alan John and Dennis Watkins, which premiered here in 1995.

The location at Bennelong Point was an inspired choice. This jutting bit of land to the east of Circular Quay was named in honour of the **Aboriginal Bennelong**, the first 'domesticated' native, whom Governor Phillip took to England as a specimen of the 'civilising experiment.' When he returned he lived in a small hut at this point. He remained a familiar character in early Sydney until his death in 1815 in Ryde.

Until 1902, Bennelong Point was the site of **Fort Macquarie**, designed by convict architect Francis Greenway in 1817; it served as a sentinel post to warn of approaching ships. It was demolished in the early 1900s to make way for, of all things, an elaborately castellated tram shed, built by W.L. Vernon. It still served as a tram terminus when it was torn down to make way for the construction of the Opera House in 1959.

The initial impetus for the building of the Opera House came in 1947, when the English composer **Eugene Goossens**—ironically, a direct descendent of Captain Cook—was appointed Conductor of the Sydney Symphony Orchestra. Goossens persuaded the government that the city should have its own opera house and found an unlikely supporter in the Labor Premier, J.J. Cahill.

In 1956, Cahill announced a £5000 international design competition, for which 216 entries arrived from 36 countries. The winning design, selected by a four-man jury, came from a young Danish architect, **Joern Utzon**. A disciple of Le Corbusier and Frank Lloyd Wright, Utzon conceived of a structure with a dramatically soaring roof line, 'the fine lines defining the form of the curve like the seams in a billowing sail'. (Utzon has described his idea as 'wedges of an orange'.) The jury was impressed with the concept. They also believed that the estimated price—£3.5 million—made the design the cheapest to build. They announced that the entire building would be completed in three years.

Controversy surrounded the project from the beginning on nearly every front. First of all, the project's greatest supporter, Eugene Goossens, was forced to resign his post as conductor and left Australia in 1956, after he was found guilty of importing 'indecent material' in his luggage after a trip abroad. More horrifically, a public lottery organised to fund the project ended in tragedy when the eight-year-old son of the winner of the £100,000 prize was kidnapped and murdered.

Then there was the problem of the building itself. It became apparent that neither Utzon nor anyone else had an idea of how his magnificent sails could actually be constructed. The task of solving complex engineering problems led to endless delays and ever-increasing costs, exacerbated by political infighting and mismanagement. Utzon also confronted bureaucratic resistance and political battles, which increased when a new director of public works, Davis Hughes, was appointed in 1965 after the Liberal Party came to power. When Hughes tried to downgrade Utzon's position from controlling architect to design consultant, Utzon resigned, asking that his name no longer be associated with the Opera House. He left Australia, never to see the building finished. It was finally completed by a team of Australian architects headed by Peter Hall.

The building was opened by Queen Elizabeth on 20 October 1973, fifteen years after construction began. The original cost of $7 million had increased to $102 million.

Despite his rejection of the finished product, Utzon's original vision prevailed, at least in modified form, and the Opera House, with its soaring roof, stands as a work of sculpture. (Utzon's original models and plans have been donated to the State Library of NSW.) Not everyone enjoys its presence; the writer Blanche d'Alpuget wrote that it looks like 'an albino tropical plant rootbound from too small a pot', and Jan Morris considered it 'unguent', making the visitor feel like an 'insect in an ice-cream'.

The surface of the roof is covered in **1,056,000 ceramic tiles** covering an area of 4 acres (1.6 hectares), bonded to 4228 tile panels which had to be constructed on the ground and slotted onto the skeletal shells. Acoustically, the concert hall rates as one of the best in the world; over 2900 events take place annually in its five theatres.

The Sydney Opera House contains more than 1000 rooms, some of curious shape due to the angular exterior. The entrance is up the southern steps off the forecourt to the ticket box and information desk. The major halls are the **Opera Theatre** on the northeast and the **Concert Hall** on the northwest. The northern foyers offer panoramic views of the harbour. The *Possum Dreaming* mural in the Opera Theatre foyer is by Michael Nelson Tjakamarra who also designed the mural at Parliament House in Canberra. The theatre seats 1547 and has a 12 metre wide proscenium. The Concert Hall seats 2690. Despite its size, the wood panelling and acoustic vaults give it an intimate feeling. Ronald Sharp designed and built the Grand Organ (10,500 pipes).

Smaller theatrical venues are accessible along the western boardwalk. These are the **Playhouse** at the boardwalk's northwest corner, the recently opened **Drama Theatre**, and the **Studio**.

Macquarie Street

From here, walk back to **Macquarie Street**. Named by Governor Macquarie (see box) in October 1810, in honour of himself, the street was to be a grand avenue of impressive public buildings; at the time, it was only a rough ridge of sandstone between the valleys of the Tank Stream and Woolloomooloo Bay. Eventually it was to become the most fashionable residential street in the city. The street extends from the Opera House to Hyde Park; on the eastern side it is flanked by the Botanic Gardens and Government Domain.

At **East Circular Quay**, you come to **Moore's Stairs** which lead onto Macquarie Street itself. Moore's Stairs were named for Charles Moore, mayor of Sydney who dedicated them in 1868. From here one can look out over the Quay and into The Rocks.

At the same point is **Tarpeian Way**, at the end of which is the **Sudan Memorial**,

Governor Macquarie

Lachlan Macquarie (1761–1824) was born in the Hebrides and took up a military career at an early age. He fought in the American War of Independence, then went to India in 1788. His first wife died of tuberculosis in 1796, which caused him immense suffering, as recorded in his voluminous writings. In 1807, he married Elizabeth Campbell, who became an active participant with her husband in the development of the new colony of New South Wales. They arrived in Sydney on 1 January 1810; Macquarie remained in his post as governor until 1821, the longest tenure of any Governor until the 20C.

As he wrote about New South Wales when he arrived:

I found the colony barely emerging from infantile imbecility and suffering from various privations and disabilities; the country impenetrable beyond 40 miles from Sydney; agriculture in a yet languishing state; commerce in its early dawn; revenue unknown; threatened by famine; distracted by faction; the public buildings in a state of dilapidation and mouldering to decay; the few roads and bridges formerly constructed, rendered almost impassable; the population depressed by poverty; no public credit nor private confidence; the morals of the great mass of the population in the lowest state of debasement and religious worship almost totally neglected.

This lamentable situation Macquarie set out to rectify. As architectural historian J.M. Freeland eloquently states, 'What William the Conqueror was in English history Lachlan Macquarie was in Australia.' The ambitiousness of his vision for the colony is evident in the scale of buildings that he planned for this promenade: in his 12 years as governor, he saw completed in the city 200 public buildings, the establishment of the city's two cathedrals, the setting aside of Hyde Park, the founding of the Botanical Gardens (1816), the implementation of the colony's first coinage and the opening of its first bank. He founded new settlements along the Hawkesbury River, in which he introduced building regulations, aimed at creating uniform standards and well-ordered living conditions.

Eventually his vision of a self-sufficient, civilised colony, comprised of egalitarian mixing of all classes and surrounded by grand structures and all the trappings of European culture, would be Macquarie's undoing. His support of emancipated convicts as full citizens with equal rights to property and privilege brought him into conflict with free settlers and the military, who were horrified by his stance. The government in England was itself ambivalent in its attitude to this far-away colony established as a penal colony. In response to a list of accusations against him sent by his enemies, the government sent J.T. Bigge in 1819 to carry out an inquiry on the circumstances of the colony. The results of his report tended to support the view that Macquarie was overly ambitious in his endeavours, with particular criticism directed towards his public building campaigns, which were viewed as too grandiose and opulent for the needs of the colony. Greatly offended by this attack on his administration and integrity, Macquarie left the colony in 1821, and died three years later at home in Scotland.

a plaque in Tarpeian Rock, commemorating the first Australian expeditionary force to participate in a military engagement. A New South Wales contingent was dispersed on 3 March 1885 to support the British in the Sudan. Political debate about the constitutionality of this action led to a return of the troops only three months later with three wounded and six dead of fever, but Australia's commitment to fight in British wars was established.

Continue south on Macquarie Street about 200m to see to the east at Bridge Street the **Conservatorium of Music** (☎ 02 9230 1222). The location was the original site of the windmill of John Palmer, purser with the First Fleet; early prints of Sydney clearly show this prominent structure, which has long since been demolished. The current conservatorium was designed by Francis Greenway (see box), Macquarie's emancipated convict architect, and was intended initially as the stables for the governor's proposed new Government House. It was begun in 1817 and completed in 1821. When one views this elaborately 'castellated' structure, meant to house horses behind an even more palatial Government House, one can understand why Commissioner Bigge, arriving in Sydney in 1819 to investigate charges of mismanagement, would criticise Macquarie's extravagant and unnecessary expenditure of public moneys. To make matters worse, Macquarie had not informed the home government of this project for two years. It was this building more than any other which led to Bigge's negative report; Macquarie's new government house was never built.

Between 1908 and 1915, the stables building was converted into the State Conservatorium of Music by W.L. Vernon, amidst protests at such a public expenditure during the First World War. The Premier of New South Wales, W.A. Holman, supported the project which culminated in an inaugural concert held in the new hall on 6 May 1915. The first director was Henri Verbrugghen, appointed in 1914 and responsible for establishing a first-rate conservatory training programme. When Holman's government lost power in 1920, funds ceased and Verbrugghen left for America. Other directors have included Arundel

Francis Greenway

Francis Greenway (1777–1837) was the first fully-qualified architect in Australia. He was trained as an architect and painter in England, and had exhibited works at the Royal Academy in 1800. Greenway was transported to New South Wales for forgery in 1813, following the bankruptcy of his family's company; he carried with him a letter of recommendation from Governor Phillip to Governor Macquarie. By the end of 1814, Greenway had a ticket of leave and had established a practice. Macquarie was so impressed with his skills, and so in need of a real architect to carry out his amibitious plans, that he granted him a full pardon in 1819, and commissioned him for most of his major public buildings. These schemes were considered by Commissioner Bigge as too grandiose for the colony; such condemnation, coupled with Greenway's difficult nature, led to his decline. By the time of Macquarie's departure, Greenway was exiled in poverty to his farm near Newcastle. On his death, he is believed to have been buried in the East Maitland cemetery, in an unmarked grave. While many of his structures have been destroyed, his elegant style can still be appreciated in such important monuments as Hyde Park Barracks and St James's in Sydney, St Luke's in Liverpool, and St Matthew's in Windsor.

Orchard and Sir Eugene Goossens in 1946–56 (see Opera House). The first Australian-born director, Sir Bernhard Heinz, succeeded Goossens. During term time, free recitals are held by Conservatorium students in the Concert Hall.

Along Macquarie Street, near Bridge Street, an information sign commemorates the site of **Exhibition Building**, built in 1879 to house the Sydney International Exhibition. Covering almost two hectares, it was designed in four days and erected in eight months to showcase Australian design, art and technology. On the morning of 22 September 1882, the structure burnt to the ground. In the blaze 300 paintings were lost, as well as relics of the Eora, Sydney's Aboriginal tribe and records of early convicts; legend has it that the fire was deliberately lit by descendants of these convicts wanting to erase their history. All that survived were the **gates**, still standing near Mitchell Library.

On the corner of Bridge Street is the **Treasury Building and Colonial Secretary's Office** (now the *Inter-Continental Hotel*), built 1849–51. The Treasury was designed by Colonial Architect Mortimer Lewis, with additions by W.L. Vernon in 1896. Built of sandstone, these two are quintessential examples of colonial Classical Revival style. The Gold Room in the Treasury, now the hotel's restaurant, was used during the 1850s gold rush to receive gold from the New South Wales goldfields.

On the south side of Bridge Street is the Colonial Secretary's Office, now the **Chief Secretary's Department**, designed in 1878–80 by Colonial Architect James Barnet. Influenced by the French Second Empire style, Barnet covered the building with stone figures, copper towers and cupolas. The three foyers are open to the public on weekdays; at the entrances one can view three statues by Italian sculptor Giovanni Fontana. They represent Queen Victoria and the Prince of Wales, as well as a young girl symbolising the spirit of New South Wales.

History House, at no. 133, is the headquarters of the **Royal Australian Historical Society**. Built in 1872, the building had many owners, including the surgeon William Bland, who had been transported in 1814 for duelling. Bland was pardoned in 1815, and became one of the most eminent doctors in the colony. Macquarie Street was long associated with the medical profession, as many doctors established practices in its buildings. The Historical Society acquired the building in 1969; it now houses their library. Several historical tours originate from the building.

BMA House, nos 135–137, was built in 1929, and is one of the few skyscraper examples of the adaptation of Australian motifs to Art Deco design; its façade includes wonderful renditions of koalas (the only examples on a façade

History House, Sydney

in Australia), as well as the traditional symbol of snake and staff. It is now part of the Australian Medical Association's quarters, despite the entryway's statement to the contrary.

Royal Australasian College of Physicians, no. 145, was once the residence of John Fairfax, founder of the *Sydney Morning Herald*; today's media corporation, the Fairfax Corporation, is an outgrowth of this family's contribution to Sydney's publishing history. The building is described in Joseph Fowles' *Sydney in 1848*, an invaluable source on the architectural history of the city. One of the last Georgian buildings of its type, it is notable for the four-storey timber verandah with box-frame windows on the ground floor and French casements on the upper floors.

Outside the Mitchell Library across the street at **SHAKESPEARE PLACE** is a monument to Governor Richard Bourke, governor of New South Wales 1831–37, and responsible for enlightened reform measures concerning emancipated convicts and education.

State Library of New South Wales ~ the Mitchell Library

At this point you will find the entrance to the **State Library of New South Wales**, often referred to as **Mitchell Library**, although the Mitchell Library only occupies one wing of the building. The library itself was founded in 1845 by members of the Australian Subscription Library, who erected a building on the corner of Macquarie and Bent Streets. The organisation was taken over by the State Government in 1869 to become the New South Wales Public Library. In 1899, the library incorporated the collection of David Scott Mitchell (see box) in order to receive an unprecedented bequest of Australiana.

Another collection, containing even rarer items pertaining to the South Pacific and Australia, was accumulated by William Dixson (1870–1952), a Sydney bachelor who offered his works to the library in 1919. To accommodate the collection, the **Dixson Wing** of the library was built adjacent to the Mitchell

---

David Scott Mitchell

David Scott Mitchell (1836–1907) was born in Sydney, the son of the Chief Surgeon of Sydney Hospital. One of the first graduates of the University of Sydney, Mitchell devoted his life and his considerable inheritance to the collection of anything relating to the history of Australia. Legend has it that he became a recluse when he was spurned in love; by all accounts he was an eccentric figure, dressed entirely in black and with an ever-present bowler hat. Mitchell's initial bequest to the Library consisted of 10,000 volumes and fifty pictures, donated to make room for more of his collection. In order to house the rest of his donation, Mitchell wanted a separate building to be constructed; the Mitchell Wing began to be built in 1906, and was not completed until after Mitchell's death. At that time the Library received the entire bequest of some 61,000 volumes, papers, manuscripts, and paintings, along with an endowment of £20,000. The collection was stored in bank vaults until the Mitchell Wing was opened in 1910. The Library has continued to grow by purchase from this endowment.

Recently, Mitchell's excellent collection of 19C erotica has finally been opened for public view.

Wing. Upon his death in 1952, Dixson bequeathed the rest of his rarities, along with an endowment of £100,000 for additional purchases, and for the publication of manuscripts and reprinting rare books.

The **Mitchell Wing** is an architectural delight; on the floor of the foyer is a mosaic rendering of the **Tasman map**, a copy of the original 17C hand-drawn map from the voyages of Abel Tasman in 1642 (the map itself was given to the Mitchell Library in 1933 by Prince George of Greece). The mosaic was completed by the Melocco Brothers in 1941; they are also responsible for the mosaic in the crypt of Sydney's St Mary's Cathedral. The interior of the Library itself includes a stained-glass dome. While the entire holdings of the Mitchell library are not open to the general public, anyone with a serious scholarly purpose may obtain permission to use the collection. The Dixson Wing also holds regular exhibitions pertaining to Australian history and culture. For information on exhibitions, call the State Library, ☎ 02 9230 1414.

The **State Library** itself is housed in a 1960s building connected to the Mitchell and Dixson wings. It contains a two-level reference library and collection of books and serials. Film screenings and poetry readings are regular events. An excellent shop containing items relating to Australian history and literature is located on the ground floor.

On the Macquarie Street side of the Mitchell Library stands a memorial statue to the explorer **Matthew Flinders** and his cat, **'Trim'** (see box, p 116).

Across Macquarie Street in this block is **St Stephen's Church**, built in 1935 on the site of **Burdekin House**, reputedly the most significant Regency-style building in Australia. The Presbyterian Church purchased the site in 1933 for £50,000; the present structure, now a part of the Uniting Church, houses a congregation of over 600 and offers special services and musical recitals during the week. From 1952 to 1965, the church was the domain of Reverend Gordon Powell, the first Australian-born minister of the church who gained international renown as a preacher, writer, and supporter of Billy Graham Crusades.

The now demolished **Burdekin House** was built in 1841 for Thomas Burdekin, an ironmonger from England who came to Sydney in 1826. Built by architect James Hume, also responsible for the National Trust property Lindesay on Darling Point, the three-storeyed mansion included colonnades and fretted stonework on the façade and offered some of the most richly and elegantly appointed interiors in the colony. It was inherited by Thomas' son, Sydney Burdekin, born in the city; he became a Member of Parliament and Mayor of Sydney. From the 1860s to the 1890s, Burdekin House was the centre of élite social life in the city, as well as a meeting place for politicians from Parliament House across the street.

State Parliament House is still located in one of the wings of the famous 'Rum Hospital', so called because it was paid for by giving the rum monopoly to the builders ('rum' referring to all alcoholic spirits). The hospital was built from 1811 to 1816, allegedly to a design by Mrs Macquarie herself. This wing has served as Parliament House for the State of New South Wales since 1829, making it the oldest Parliament House in the world. In 1843 the Legislative Assembly Chamber, designed by Mortimer Lewis, was added on to the wing; the Legislative Council Chamber is made of a pre-fabricated cast-iron building, which had been shipped from England to serve as a church on the Victorian

Matthew Flinders

Matthew Flinders (1774–1814) is one of the most intriguing naval explorers associated with the early Australian expeditions. Born in Lincolnshire, England, into a family of surgeons, he took to sea after reading *Robinson Crusoe*. He joined the Royal Navy in 1789 and sailed with Captain Bligh's second voyage in 1791. He sailed to Sydney with Captain Hunter aboard the *Reliance* in 1795; it was on this voyage that he met **George Bass**, the ship's surgeon. They struck up an alliance that led to their joint explorations of the Georges River and the south coast of Sydney. In 1798, the pair, in command of the *Norfolk*, circumnavigated Tasmania by passing through the Bass Strait, which Bass had explored in 1797. They returned to Sydney in January 1799, having made some of the first detailed surveys of the Tasmanian coast and establishing Flinders' reputation as a superb cartographer. After a return trip to England in 1800 where he married, Flinders received command of the *Investigator* with instructions to explore the entire coast of New Holland, as it was still called. He completed this circumnavigation on 6 December 1803, completing records so accurate that they are still used by the Royal Australian Navy. He was the first person on record to apply the term 'Australia' regularly to the continent.

Remarkable also on this voyage was the botanical and biological work carried out by the expedition's appointed draughtsman, the Viennese **Ferdinand Bauer** (1760–1826). Bauer made over 1000 drawings, meticulously rendered and later hand-coloured according to an elaborate colour gradation system devised by the artist. His publication in 1815, *Illustrationes Florae Novae Hollandiae*, was not a financial success but his works are now recognised as the most precise and aesthetically pleasing examples of natural history painting ever produced. Flinders named Cape Bauer on the South Australian coast in his honour, and his name is perpetuated in several Australian plants.

Upon his return to England in 1803, and unaware that war had broken out between England and France, Flinders called in at Mauritius (then known as Ile de France) to make repairs on his ship, only to be imprisoned for almost seven years. He finally returned to London in 1810, where he completed his remarkable *A Voyage to Terra Australis* at the end of 1813. His health had been ruined in captivity, and he died on 18 July 1814, only 40 years old, before he saw the first copy of his beloved book.

The inclusion of Flinders' cat in the memorial is an appropriately affecting one. **Trim** was born a seafaring feline in 1799 aboard the *Reliance*, when Flinders commanded a supply ship to South Africa. He accompanied his master on the voyages of the *Norfolk* and the *Investigator*, thus circumnavigating the world. In 1809, Flinders wrote an affectionate and delightfully informative 'Tribute to Trim', describing his unique qualities as a feline sailor. During Flinders' detention on the Ile de France, Trim disappeared without a trace; Flinders wrote, 'My sorrow may be better conceived than described.'

gold-fields. In 1856, it was dismantled and sent to Sydney when the state legislature expanded.

Parliament House is open to the public on weekdays 09.00–16.30 when not in session, and until 19.00 when in session. If Parliament is in session, visitors can view the proceedings from the upper galleries. The sessions are often quite raucous and pugnacious affairs, for Australian politicians love a good shouting match. Excellent exhibitions and historical displays are housed throughout the building, and informative brochures are available. Bookings for viewing of sessions can be made on ☎ 02 9230 2111.

Next to the Parliament House, on the site of the original Rum Hospital, is **Sydney Hospital** (☎ 02 9382 7111), built in 1894. The **Rum Hospital** itself had been structurally unsound since it was built; the builders had been eager to get the rum monopoly, and were not necessarily competent workers. Early stories of the horrors of the hospital itself were rife: unsanitary surgical conditions (operations often occurred on the kitchen table), no facilities or adequate food, inadequate and untrained staff. By the 1860s, improvements had been made, including the beginnings of a nurses' training school approved by Florence Nightingale. By 1879, the structure was considered so dangerous that it was demolished; the new hospital's design, attributed to architect Thomas Rowe, dates from that time, but was not finished for 15 years. The entrance hall stands as an elegant example of late Victorian style, with a grand staircase and stained glass windows. Frequent attempts have been made to close the facility, so far without success. Outside the hospital is a replica of *Il Porcellino*, the famous fountain statue of Florence. The boar collects money for the hospital, as all wishing coins thrown into the fountain benefit their activities.

Next to the present-day hospital is the **Mint Museum** (☎ 02 9217 0311; **open** daily 10.00–17.00), originally the southern wing of the Rum Hospital. In response to the discoveries on the goldfields, the building served as a branch of the Royal Mint from 1854 until 1926, when a new mint was opened in Perth. It served a variety of governmental functions until 1982, when it was salvaged from further dereliction and opened as a **Museum of Colonial Decorative Art**. The displays reveal a remarkable array of Australian-made furniture, clocks, pottery and other artefacts, as well as historical exhibitions of Australian currency. Most interesting is the **'Holey Dollar'**, an example of coinage created during Macquarie's term when legal tenure was scarce; a circle was stamped out of the middle of Spanish coins, counterstamped as New South Wales coinage as fifteen pence for the circle and five shillings for the Holey Dollar. These remained in circulation until 1829.

Continue south on Macquarie Street; next to the Mint is **Hyde Park Barracks** (☎ 02 9223 8922; open daily 10.00–17.00). Designed for Governor Macquarie by Francis Greenway between 1817 and 1819, the barracks provided the first permanent lodging for convicts, who until this point were allowed to roam free. Described by architectural critic J.M. Freeland as 'just a barn—but a very handsome barn', this three-storey sandstone construction could sleep 600 convicts; it is considered one of Greenway's most successful and elegant buildings. After transportation ended, it was used for a variety of purposes, until it was restored as a museum in 1984. The museum shop is an excellent source for books on Australian history and culture. Tours include one that allows the visitor to spend the night in the barracks as a convict would.

Walk 2 • Hyde Park and surroundings

At Hyde Park Barracks, cross Macquarie Street at Queen's Square. In the centre of the Square is a statue of Queen Victoria, the work of English sculptor Sir Joseph Edgar Boehm. It was originally presented to Australia for its centenary in 1888 and has experienced a number of locations throughout Sydney.

Now proceed to **St James Church**, another of Greenway's achievements, built 1819–22. Originally designed as a courtroom, the plans underwent a change when Macquarie requested a church instead. Built of characteristically red-brown local brick, the building's design is admired for its simplicity and balanced proportions. The only exterior ornamentation is the inclusion of pilasters of a different colour. The current building includes numerous additions and alterations, including the spire, probably added in 1824 by Greenway's successor, and eastern porches by John Verge. The opulent interior furnishings were created in the Edwardian era by Anglican Diocesan Architect, J.H. Buck-eridge. The basement houses church offices, as well as a delightful **Children's Chapel**, decorated in the 1930s by a group of women artists known as the Turramurra Painters, led by Ethel Anderson and Grace Cossington Smith. The frescoes depict biblical stories transposed to a Sydney setting, a rare example of what art historian Joan Kerr calls 'Early Christian Australian Nationalism'.

Hyde Park

Cross St James Road to enter Hyde Park itself, a cosmopolitan oasis of greenery that also houses several architectural monuments and is surrounded by some of the most elegant buildings in town. Situated in the park between Elizabeth and College Streets is the **Archibald Memorial Fountain**, erected in 1933 at a cost of £12,000 from the bequest of Jules François Archibald (see box). The fountain commemorates Franco-Australian cooperation in the First World War. In keeping with Archibald's wishes, it was designed by a French sculptor, François Sicard, and represents mythological personifications of the Arts, Beauty and Light.

Also in Hyde Park is the **Anzac War Memorial**, an impressive Art Deco struc-

Jules François Archibald

Jules François Archibald (1856–1919) was an important figure in Australian cultural life. Christened John Feltham by his Irish-Australian parents, his romantic flair for all things French led him to adopt a French name. He was in 1880 one of the founders of the Sydney *Bulletin*, a weekly newspaper which helped to define a national Australian character. Appealing to the native-born Australian, the *Bulletin* conveyed a distinctive mixture of idealism, republicanism, racism, and vulgar humour; it was particularly well-known for its editorial cartoons, the artists of which contributed to an illustrative style known as 'The Black and White School'. Archibald was responsible for the cultural aspects of the paper, and it was in this capacity that he supported and encouraged a group of young Australian writers and artists, including Henry Lawson, A.B. 'Banjo' Paterson, and Norman Lindsay. Upon his death in 1919, his will specified not only the Memorial Fountain, but an amount for an annual prize of £156 for the best portrait painted by an Australian; today, the Archibald Prize has grown to $20,000, making it one of the most lucrative art prizes in the world.

ture designed in 1934 by a local artist, C. Bruce Dellit, with sculpture by Rayner Hoff (1894–1937). At a height of 33m (100 feet), the memorial contains a circular **Hall of Memory** above a circular **Hall of Silence** which incorporates a group of statuary symbolising Sacrifice. The walls of the Hall of Memory include the names of those who fell in the Great War.

Recently, some Sydney politicos have sought to turn much of Hyde Park into an aquatic centre, to the dismay of heritage activists and environmentalists. At the time of writing, final plans were still being debated, although renovations appear to have won out; the section next to St Mary's Cathedral is to become an aquatic centre.

On the College Street side of Hyde Park is **St Mary's Catholic Cathedral**, designed in 1865 by William Wilkinson Wardell, who had earlier designed St Patrick's Cathedral in Melbourne. Modelled on Lincoln Cathedral, St Mary's is probably the largest church erected in the British colonies and appears, according to Jan Morris, as a 'kind of standard Gothic cathedral, such as you might order from an ecclesiastical catalogue'. The interior is rich in dark stained-glass windows, and also includes a majestic mosaic floor in the crypt by Peter Melocco, who also produced the Tasman map mosaic at the Mitchell Library. Currently the cathedral is carrying out a massive fund-raising campaign, high-lighted by concerts and operas performed on site.

At the corner of William and College Streets, south of the Cathedral, is **The Australian Museum** (☎ 02 9320 6000; open daily 09.30–17.00); the street façade is of Neo-Palladian design, constructed by James Barnet's office between 1861 and 1866.

The original museum building, evident in the first rooms of the interior, was built by Mortimer Lewis between 1846 and 1852; it was opened to the public in 1857. The museum was founded in 1836, and supported by Alexander Macleay (1767–1848), then Colonial Secretary and an enthusi-astic scientist. The original specimens were from his own collection; subse-quently government funding allowed the museum to grow into one of the most important collections of Australian zoology, mineralogy, palaeon-tology and ethnology. The institution has an illustrious history, with many famous scientists and cultural figures serving as directors and curators. The present museum has expanded in a variety of directions, allowing for numerous exhibition spaces, as well as the display of the original 19C hold-ings. The museum also houses a large reference library and publishes several scientific and popular journals. Regular lectures and gallery talks are scheduled, and the museum is one of the most popular venues for Sydney school children, particularly drawn to the dinosaur collection.

Next door to the museum on College Street is **Sydney Grammar School**, now a conglomeration of many buildings in various styles. The school itself has great historical significance, as one of the oldest educational institutions in the colony and as the focal point of many public meetings in Sydney's formative years. The earliest buildings here were erected between 1831 and 1835 by Robert Cooper as part of a neo-Classical block of the old Sydney College (from which College Street derives its name). The college closed in 1847. The buildings were next to the University of Sydney which was inaugurated in 1850. After years of financial vicissitudes, the school became Sydney Grammar, founded by an Act of Parliament in 1854 and opened in 1857. While the buildings of the school are of modest sandstone, the school's status as the longest continuous home of an Australian educational institution gives them a special significance.

On the other side of Hyde Park is **ELIZABETH STREET**, named for Governor Macquarie's wife; it is the longest and straightest street in central Sydney, beginning at Hunter Street and extending to the Central Railway Station. At the head of the park is the **Old Supreme Court Building** group, originally designed by Francis Greenway, but substantially altered by the addition of a stone colonnade in 1868 by Colonial Architect James Barnet. The interior, with its cedar staircase, gives some indication of Greenway's gracious design, although additional elements appeared in the 1890s, giving a more opulent Edwardian atmosphere to the chambers.

Further south on Elizabeth Street is the **Great Synagogue**. Opened in 1878, the building was designed by Thomas Rowe and constructed of Pyrmont sandstone. Intended to accommodate two previous Jewish (see box) congregations, the ground floor seats 1600 people. Considered one of the major monuments to Australian Jewry, it still holds services, although larger congregations exist in Bondi and elsewhere in the city. Special admission and tours can be arranged through the synagogue's offices; regular tours occur at noon on Tuesdays and Thursdays (☎ 02 9267 2477).

The first Jews in Australia

Jews arrived in Australia with the First Fleet; at least one, James Larra, eventually became an innkeeper in Parramatta. By 1817, 20 Jews formed a burial society in the colony and from 1828 prayers were held regularly at the home of P.J. Cohen in Jamison Street. By 1835, the Jewish population in Sydney was 345. The first minister, M.E. Rose, arrived in this year. By 1862, under the leadership of senior minister Alexander Davis, Jewish education and philanthropy became organised; Davis presided over the community for 40 years, and was instrumental in the merger of the two congregations that culminated in the erection of The Great Synagogue. The **Sydney Jewish Museum**, which holds regular exhibitions and illustrates the entire history of Australian Jewry, is located at 148 Darlinghurst Road and very near to Kings Cross (☎ 02 9360 7999, open Mon–Thurs 10.00–16.00, Fri 10.00–14.00, Sun 11.00–17.00).

Walk 3 • The Domain, Botanic Gardens, and the Art Gallery of New South Wales

The central park area known as the **Domain** is integral to Sydney city life. It was part of the original government reserve set aside by Governor Phillip. Under Macquarie it acquired the official title 'Government Domain' and was enclosed by stone walls, but it seems to have been accessible to all sorts of citizens from the beginning. By the 1860s, the Domain Gates were opened to the public, and by the 1890s it had become the site for public speakers and political demonstrations. Huge crowds demonstrated against conscription in 1917, and protests here accompanied the dismissal of Premier Lang in 1931 and Prime Minister

Gough Whitlam's sacking in 1975. Today the Domain is still a site for public gatherings, including concerts during the Festival of Sydney in January and carols at Christmas time, as well as what appears to be regular lunch-hour cricket games.

Woolloomooloo

From the Domain one looks out over **Woolloomooloo** (yes, eight 'o's!), once the busiest industrial dock area, now occupied by the navy. Still in operation as a popular public swimming pool and accessible from the Domain is the **Andrew (Boy) Charlton Pool**, which juts into Woolloomooloo Bay; it is named after a great Australian swimmer of the 1920s. The pool is now the site of the annual Gay Swimming Carnival.

The district itself long held a reputation as a tough tenement for sailors and dock-workers; today it has lost some of that image, housing great pubs and entertainment venues. At the time of writing, **Harry's Cafe de Wheels**, a Sydney institution since 1945, was still stationed on the wharf of Wool-loomooloo; you go there for late-night 'pies and peas', as you would for a cheese-steak in Philadelphia—definitely not haute cuisine, but a fun stop for visitors. The van has photographs of celebrity customers pinned on its walls.

The Royal Botanic Gardens

The **Royal Botanic Gardens** (☎ 02 9231 8111, daily sunrise until sunset) are accessible through several entrances on each side of the Domain. The 1889 entrance across from the Shakespeare monument in front of the State Library is often considered the main entrance, although the 'official' entrance is across the street from the Art Gallery of New South Wales.

The gardens were originally the site of **Government Farm**, established by the First Fleet from seeds brought with them; the settlers were able to raise nine acres of corn at what is now called Farm Cove. When barren soil caused the main farm to be moved to Parramatta, Phillip declared this area for the government; hence its earlier name of Phillip Domain.

The Botanic Gardens proper date from 1816, when **Mrs Macquarie's Road** was completed. This road in the Gardens and along the harbour marks the favoured excursion route of Elizabeth Macquarie, culminating in **Mrs Macquarie's Chair**, a stone bench where she allegedly sat to enjoy the view.

From here one can look out into the harbour to **Fort Denison**, more popularly known as **'Pinchgut' Island**, supposedly referring to the fact that in the early days repeat offenders were sentenced to stay here on a diet of bread and water; a more likely reason is that it is at this point that the harbour narrows around it. The island still bears guns and defence towers, evidence of early attempts to defend the harbour from invasion. In 1942, when a Japanese midget submarine entered the harbour, an American cruiser attacked, hitting the fort's tower; the submarine was hit, and its remains can be seen today outside Canberra's Australian War Memorial.

You can also see across to **Garden Island** (see box, p 122), now the site of the Royal Australian Naval base. Here First Fleet sailors grew vegetables. It is also the site of Australia's first known graffiti, and the oldest evidence of white settlement: carved in rocks on the former island are the initials 'F.M.' for Frederick Meredith, a steward on the *Sirius*.

Sydney Harbour islands

Sydney Harbour originally contained 13 small islands, some of them, like Pinchgut, now accessible to the public for tours or just picnicking; some of them, like Garden and Bennelong, were filled in and are now part of the mainland. Some of the most delightful islands are on the 'other side' of the Harbour Bridge, and can be seen when taking the ferries upriver. In most cases, individual transport (with harbour taxis or private boats) must be arranged. Most fascinating is **Goat Island**, seen on the ferry en route to Balmain. It was the site of one of the most bizarre examples of colonial punishment: in the 1830s, a recalcitrant convict named **'Bony' Anderson** was chained to a rock on the island for two years, and fed like an animal; he regularly swore at passing ships, and became such a moral embarassment to decent colonists that he was eventually released and sent to Norfolk Island. Goat Island still has a quarry and remnants of a convict-built village. Other islands worth visiting include: **Shark**, once the quarantine station; **Clarke**; **Rodd**, terminal of the Sydney Rowing Club's river course, and site of the laboratory where Pasteur experiments were carried out; and **Spectacle**, including a Naval depot with a small museum. Tours of the islands are provided by Banks Marine, Island Events, 81 Grove Street, Balmain, ☎ 02 9555 1222.

Governor Macquarie appointed the first Colonial Botanist, Charles Fraser, in 1816; by 1825 some 3000 specimens were growing in the garden. Continuous expansion and botanical accumulation continued under a series of innovative directors, most notably Charles Moore, who ran the gardens for nearly 50 years, from 1848 to 1896. His successor, Joseph Henry Maiden, founded a National Herbarium with a collection of botanical specimens and a substantial botanical library.

The gardens themselves offer a number of delightful walks, incorporating native and introduced species. **Fruit bats** hang in abundance in the palm groves. Ornate statues of all sorts, including replicas of Canova's *Boxers* on the **Main Walk**, dot the gardens. In the middle of the gardens is a refreshment kiosk, including a highly-touted restaurant above and a cafeteria-style facility below; a visitor's centre also provides brochures and books on natural history and gardening.

Most spectacular is the walk along the Harbour around Farm Cove which ultimately leads out of the gardens and to the Opera House. Of special interest is the **Pyramid Glasshouse** near the Macquarie Street entrance, containing rare and endangered species and other tropical plants.

In the middle of the gardens, near Farm Cove Crescent, you can see **Government House** (☎ 02 9931 5222; open Fri–Sun 10.00–15.00). It was designed by Edward Blore, an English architect who had designed Sir Walter Scott's estate, Abbottsford. The foundation stone was laid in 1837, and Mortimer Lewis became supervising architect. It was officially opened on 26 June 1845. The design, with its crenellated turrets and *porte-cochère* entrance, complements Greenway's earlier stables, and marks the rise of the popularity of Gothic Revival style in the colony. Built of Australian cedar, Pyrmont stone and native marble, the structure included cloisters that form a covered verandah comprised of Gothic arches. First occupied by Governor Gipps, the colonial chronicler

Joseph Fowles described it in 1848 as: 'an elegant stone edifice in Tudor Gothic... It is one of the most imposing buildings we have; and whether viewed from the adjacent Domain, the Harbour, or the City, its tall chimneys of elaborately carved stone, white turrets, and numerous windows, render it a conspicuous ornament to our metropolis'. It now houses a collection of 19C and 20C decorative art and furniture.

The Art Gallery of New South Wales

To get to the art gallery of New South Wales, enter the Domain after Hyde Park Barracks on Macquarie Street and you come to Art Gallery Road. Three hundred metres from here is the art gallery.

The gallery dates from 1871, when the New South Wales Academy of Art was formed; it was formally initiated in 1874, when the directors of the Academy formed a Board of Trustees entrusted with the task of purchasing artworks in London. Several temporary locations existed before the gallery moved to its present site. In 1883 it officially became the National Art Gallery of New South Wales, although the 'National' was dropped in 1958. (Note that Melbourne's gallery is still called the National Gallery of Victoria, despite the fact that *the* National Gallery of Australia is now in Canberra—evidence of the continuing cultural competition between the two states.)

■ Open daily 10.00–17.00. ☎ 02 9225 1744; the gallery also includes two restaurants, a coffee shop on Level 3 with a delightful terrace and interesting view into the naval base at Woolloomooloo Bay, and a more elegant restaurant on level 5 which overlooks the entrance lobby.

The original building of 1885 was designed by John Horbury Hunt. Always considered a temporary building, it was concealed in 1895 by the classically designed façade of Colonial Architect W.L. Vernon. It is Vernon's plan that still constitutes the main floor galleries, including the Roman-style entrance completed in 1909, and the grand oval lobby of 1902. Vernon envisioned large bronze reliefs on the exterior walls, only four of which were completed. The building had fallen into disrepair by the 1960s, when the government agreed to rebuild the site as part of the Captain Cook Bicentenary projects. Architect Andrew Andersons completed the new building in 1972, demolishing the original Hunt structure at the rear and doubling exhibition space. Andersons was also responsible for the newest extension at the east end, which opened for the Bicentenary in 1988.

By far the most impressive part of the gallery's collections is its holdings in **Australian art**. As early as 1875, the gallery committed itself to the purchase of local artists' work, an admirable decision at a time when culture was widely believed to originate in Europe alone. The collection, then, is strongest in works after 1875, with earlier works acquired at a much later date.

On entering the gallery's foyer, you step through the oval lobby and into the central hall, where the information desk is located to the left; admission is free except to special travelling exhibitions, which are charged separately.

On the right are the **European galleries**. The current design of these exhibition spaces consciously alludes to 19C academic practices, with richly-coloured walls and paintings hung densely on the walls. Fittingly, the two middle galleries on this side, including the large central gallery, concentrate on **19C Australian paintings**; the small holdings of early European art are in the first gallery off to the left of the first of the Australian rooms, and **18C century and 19C European works** in the gallery behind them.

The first gallery of Australian art includes works painted before 1875, including John Glover's *Natives on the Ouse River, Van Diemen's Land*, one of the artist's interesting depictions of Tasmanian Aboriginals; several works by Conrad Martens, often considered the 'Turner of Australia' for his wispy seascapes; and a characteristic landscape by Victorian artist Eugène von Guerard.

In the central gallery the most famous works appear: those of the so-called **Australian Impressionists**, the artists of the late 19C, whose works are now known as near icons of national identity, popularly accepted as having created a distinctly Australian style. Ironically, many of these artists were either foreign-born or lived extensively as expatriates abroad. Included here are Charles Conder's atmospheric *Departure of the S.S. Orient-Circular Quay*, painted in 1888 and purchased by the gallery in the same year; Arthur Streeton's *'Fire's on!' (Lapstone Tunnel)* (1891), probably his most famous narrative landscape; Frederick McCubbin's *On the Wallaby Track* (1896), redolent of the plein-air techniques of Belgian painter Bastien-Lepage; and Tom Roberts's *Shearing at Newstead (The Golden Fleece)* (1894), establishing the iconography of the Australian shearer.

Dominating the room's walls, however, are the enormous canvases of Rupert Bunny (1864–1947) and George Lambert (1873–1930), two expatriate Australians who concentrated on figurative painting in the grandest and most elegant European tradition.

The galleries to the rear and at the far side, painted in the original deep red, house a considerable number of late Victorian and Edwardian British painting, including Frederic Leighton's voluptuous *Cymon and Iphigenia* (1884) and Ford Madox Brown's *Chaucer at the Court of Edward III*. Other works by the Pre-Raphaelite School demonstrate the strong British concentration of the gallery's early acquisitions.

To the left of the central hall on the main floor are the works of **20C Australian art**, intelligently arranged to present an overview of the country's more recent aesthetic development. Of special interest are the works of the Early Moderns, most particularly the progressive paintings of the women painters Margaret Preston (1875–1963), Thea Proctor (1879–1966) and Grace Cossington Smith (1892–1984), who are now seen as the most accomplished modern painters of the 1920s and 1930s.

The contribution of **Melbourne artists** to Australian modernism is also recognised with works by the social-realists Josl Bergner and Noel Counihan. Works by Sydney artists Russell Drysdale (1912–81) and William Dobell (1899–1970) are especially well-represented, indicative of the Australian directions in portraiture and landscape in the 1930s and 1940s.

No Australian collection would be complete without examples by **Sidney Nolan** (1917–92), probably the most internationally recognised Australian artist; his *Burke* (c 1962) and *Pretty Polly Mine* (1948) are representative of his mythologising of Australian history.

Abstraction enters Australian art in the 1950s and 1960s, in the works of painters such as **John Olsen**, **Peter Upward**, and **Fred Williams**. Williams' *You Yangs* landscape (1963) is exemplary of his abstracted approach to the Australian landscape.

Next to these galleries is one of the spaces for travelling and/or project exhibitions, of which the gallery has had many of international stature. The 'blockbuster' mentality has invaded the Australian art world as it has in every other country, and great competition arises among the leading galleries for the shows that will bring in the largest crowds. Important regular shows occurring here are **Perspecta**, held in February to March of odd-numbered years, and the **Sydney Biennale**, held in July to August of even-numbered years. Both exhibitions focus on Australian and international contemporary art.

Take the escalator to LEVEL 3, which has space for temporary exhibitions as well as housing the permanent collections of **Asian, Aboriginal** and **Melanesian art**. The gallery began collecting Aboriginal art in the late 1950s under the enlightened curatorship of Tony Tuckson, himself an artist who believed that such works belonged in art galleries rather than ethnographic collections. Its new Aboriginal gallery, called Yiribana, brings together these holdings for the first time; changing exhibitions include video displays about the artists and Aboriginal culture. Central to the collection is a set of seventeen grave posts from Snake Bay, Melville Island, which form a sculptural grouping that inspired Tuckson's own work.

Asian art holdings have grown substantially in the last decade, as increased recognition of Australia's presence in an Asian context leads to greater awareness of these cultures. The holdings are varied and eclectic, although concerted effort is being made to enhance the collections of South East Asian art.

LEVEL 2 includes rooms concentrating on the gallery's substantial holdings of **prints and drawings**, as well as contemporary art and a small collection of 20C European works. Descending ever further, LEVEL 1 provides a space for photography exhibitions.

Walk 4 • The Rocks

Immediately below the Harbour Bridge to the west of Circular Quay is the area known as The Rocks, today the most frequented tourist destination in Sydney, and historically the most significant. The name 'The Rocks' was applied to the quarter as early as 1803, when newspaper articles complained of its lack of proper streets. Here you will find more than 100 of Sydney's oldest buildings, all carefully preserved and serving as shops, galleries, and restaurants. As recently as the 1970s plans were afoot to demolish the area to replace it with skyscrapers—confirmation of its lingering reputation as an impossible slum. It was only through the efforts of the Sydney Cove Redevelopment Authority, aided by the 'Green Bans' of the Builders Labourers Union led by Jack Mundey, that the area survived, standing as an architectural reminder of Sydney's historic mixing of the genteel and the disreputable. Today the 'renovation' is so complete—even feisty union man Mundey has been thanked by the government!—that The Rocks' earlier character can only be described, not experienced, as it becomes the city's leading tourist attraction.

History of The Rocks

Amidst the boulders and cliffs of this sandstone outcropping the first convicts built their huts, and eventually created in the section closest to the harbour one of the Pacific's toughest seaports, where whalers and sailors filled the narrow alleyways to carry out every form of vice and mayhem. As many as 20 pubs existed here by 1813 (along with the illegal 'sly-grog' shops and brothels), with 37 by 1855; two pubs, *The Lord Nelson* on Argyle Street (1834) and *The Hero of Waterloo* on Lower Fort Street (1843), survive from the era.

In the 1850s the area also filled with Chinese who had arrived during the gold rush; they established opium parlours, fantan gambling shops, and vegetable hawkers, creating a Chinatown that added to the general cacophony of The Rocks. Chinatown moved to the Haymarket district, near Darling Harbour, in the 1890s.

Long after the penal system ended, this section of The Rocks continued as a filthy, overcrowded slum; sailors' anecdotes maintained that you could hear the noise from The Rocks a mile out to sea and smell it for two miles. In the 1890s, **The Rocks 'Pushes'** were notorious for their gang-style street-fighting; these are brilliantly described by Henry Lawson in his poem 'The Captain of the Push'. 'Then his whistle, loud and piercing, woke the echoes of "The rocks",/And a dozen ghouls came sloping round the corners of the blocks.' As late as 1900, a major epidemic of bubonic plague broke out here, leading to the first systematic 'cleansing' through demolition. Further destruction occurred in 1927 when the most elegant of the upper streets of The Rocks, **Princes Street**, disappeared as the Harbour Bridge was built, and again in 1957, to make way for the Cahill Expressway.

While housing such seamy elements of life, The Rocks also became the site of reputable establishments and genteel neighbourhoods: the first hospital and cemetery were here, and it was the home of the earliest wharves and commercial warehouses. The neighbourhood along the ridge at present-day **Argyle Place** became by the 1850s the location of neat bourgeois houses, with pleasant greens and elegant terraces. This area was known as **'Bunker's Hill'**, reputedly in honour of American sea captain Eber Bunker, who arrived in Sydney in 1791 with a convict ship and subsequently became one of the first whalers in the colony. Bunker participated in the arrest of Governor Bligh and was given 1500 acres at Liverpool by Governor Macquarie.

■ Tours of The Rocks and a self-guided tour map are available from **The Rocks Visitor Centre**, no. 106–108 George Street (☎ 02 9255 1788).

On the west side of Circular Quay, just below The Rocks proper, is the **Museum of Contemporary Art** (☎ 02 9241 5892; 9252 4033, open daily 10.00–18.00), which opened in 1993 in the former Maritime Services Board Building. The structure itself, built in 1949, appears almost Stalinesque in its solidity and functional severity, but the interiors include elegant marble fittings. The transformation of the rooms has created appropriately expansive spaces for the presentation of contemporary art. Along with travelling exhibitions, the museum also houses the Power Collection, a bequest of John Power, and some of

the first modern art collected in Australia. By the time this collection was transferred from its old home at the University of Sydney in 1991, it contained works
by Warhol, Lichtenstein, Christo and Hockney. Along with displays of the
permanent collection, the musem mounts exhibitions of the most contemporary
art, including video, holography, and multi-media presentations.

As seems to be required of all Sydney facilities these days, the museum has
an excellent **restaurant** (one of Neil Perry's creations) and the hippest **art-
bookshop** in town—a welcome change from the duty-free tourist shops
littering the rest of The Rocks.

On the GEORGE STREET side of the museum at no. 119 was the **Julian Ashton
Art School**. Ashton (1851–1942) was a significant figure in Sydney's art life,
gaining fame as one of the 'Black and White' illustrators of *The Bulletin* and in
the production of the immense *Picturesque Atlas of Australasia* (1888). His
school was one of the most progressive in the city, and many of the early modern
artists of Sydney began their careers here.

Now walk north up LOWER GEORGE STREET. The first street in Sydney, it origi-
nated as a track from the Tank Stream's spring at present-day Martin Place.
Originally called Spring Street, it was renamed in honour of King George III by
Governor Macquarie in 1810.

Orient Hotel, no. 89 Argyle Street, was built in the 1850s as a sailor hotel,
with a rounded corner façade typical of colonial Georgian style. Across the
street, at no. 91, is the **Rocks Police Station**, formerly the Victorian ASN Hotel,
a three-storey structure in an elaborate Italianate style noted for its unusual
garland decoration below the parapet.

From here look across towards Circular Quay c 200m to see **Cadman's
Cottage**, 110 George Street off Circular Quay West. Sydney's oldest extant
building, it was built in 1815–16 for John Cadman, pardoned convict and official government coxswain for Governors Macquarie, Brisbane, Darling, Bourke
and Gipps; he was Superintendent of Boats 1827–45. Cadman lived in the
cottage until 1845; his diminutive size explains the height of the doorway. It was
subsequently the headquarters of the Sydney Water Police and, until 1965, part
of the Sailors' Home. It was rebuilt and renovated in 1972 and is now the information centre for the New South Wales National Parks & Wildlife Service (☎ 02
9247 8861; open Mon 10.00–15.00, Tues–Fri 11.00–16.30, Sat and Sun
11.00–16.00).

No. 106–108 George Street, now the **Rocks Visitors Centre** (☎ 02 9255
1788), was originally **The Sailors Home** (the name still appears in blue letters
on the façade facing the harbour). The home, which dates from the 1860s,
provided room and board for sailors as a more comfortable alternative to the
rowdy inns of The Rocks. One can still look up to three floors of cubicle-rooms
and see the pressed-tin roofs. A permanent exhibition on the history of The
Rocks is on the second floor. Tours of The Rocks begin here, and self-guided tour
brochures are available.

The **Australian Steam Navigation Company Building**, 1 Hickson Road,
was designed by William Wardell in 1884; it clearly mimics Flemish mercantile
buildings. It stands on the site of Robert Campbell's (see box, see p 128) first
home and overlooks his warehouses. It is now occupied by the *Ken Done Galleries*.
Now take Customs Officers' Stairs down to the warehouses.

Robert Campbell

Robert Campbell (1769–1846) built a wharf here in 1800–03, becoming the first private import-export merchant in the colony; he is quaintly referred to as the 'Father of Australian Commerce', or 'Merchant Campbell', renowned for his part in breaking the Rum monopoly. He later settled at Duntroon, today the Australian Military Academy in present-day Canberra, where he died in 1846. The warehouses were expanded in the 1840s and again in the 1890s, when the third floor and slate roofs were added.

Campbell's Stores occupy 7–27 Circular Quay West/11–31 Hickson Road. Now a row of restaurants with marvellous views of the harbour at **Campbell's Cove**, these sandstone warehouses include remnants of the original 1820s Campbell's Stores.

You might now decide to go back south to Upper George Street, to examine several restored terraces and sandstone hotels, including the interesting houses on ATHERDEN STREET, Sydney's shortest street. For a longer walk, you can continue down Hickson towards Harbour Bridge to **Miller's Point**. You will pass the entrance to the new *Hyatt Hotel*, which faces out onto Campbell's Cove. The hotel was built in the booming 1980s, in attractive sandstone to blend with the other buildings. Under the bridge is **Dawes Point**, which has a marvellous view of **Luna Park** and **Lavender Bay** on the North Shore.

Miller's Point

Walking under the Harbour Bridge, you enter the original wharf district of Miller's Point. The first wharves have now become restaurants and shops. Further on, the old passenger terminal is now home to the **Sydney Dance Company** (☎ 02 9221 4811) and the **Sydney Theatre Company** (☎ 02 9250 1700), two of the city's premier cultural institutions with active and innovative programmes throughout the year.

At POTTINGER ROAD, walk up the steep incline to reach **The Upper Rocks**. At the top, turn left on WINDMILL STREET towards Lower Fort Street. At no. 73 Windmill Street is the **Stephens Building**. Built for J.M Stephens, a well-known musician and publican, at a cost of £4000, it opened in 1900 as Sydney's first walk-up block of flats. It represents, along with the other terrace houses on the streets, a typical housing form of the early 20C.

At the corner of Windmill and Lower Fort Streets is the **Hero of Waterloo**, (☎ 02 9252 4553) licensed in 1845. A simple three-storey stone building, the inn must have been one of the toughest of The Rocks' pubs—its cellar was used to store drunks until press gangs could shanghai them for ship's crews. It still maintains an air of rowdiness—it has not been entirely gentrified for tourists.

Continue down LOWER FORT STREET to **Holy Trinity Church** (The Garrison Church) on the corner of Argyle and Lower Fort Streets. Built in 1840–44 to the design of Henry Ginn, the building was enlarged between 1855 and 1874 by prominent Gothic Revival architect Edmund Blacket. Still known as Garrison Church, it served as the chapel for the British Regiment stationed at Dawes Point Battery until 1880. The east window of the church was donated by Dr James Mitchell, father of David Mitchell of the Mitchell Library. Next to the church is the old church school, dating from the 1850s, and last used as a school in 1942; it is now the parish hall.

Miller's Point

William Dawes (c 1758–1836) was the son of an admiralty official at Portsmouth. He joined the Royal Marines in 1779, and distinguished himself as a scientific observer and astronomer. He volunteered to sail with the First Fleet to New South Wales, and was put in charge of astronomical observations. He built the first observatory at this site, which was then known as Point Maskelyne in honour of the Astronomer Royal. He also worked as a surveyor, laying out many of the streets of Sydney and Paramatta. A man of great intellectual energy, Dawes came into conflict with Governor Phillip when he refused to join a party sent to track down an Aborigine who had wounded his convict 'master'. He returned to England in 1791, and eventually became Governor of Sierra Leone. He spent the last years of his life in Antigua, West Indies.

Across from the church to the west is **ARGYLE PLACE**, a village green surrounded by houses dating as early as 1830. The name Argyle refers to the Scottish birthplace of Governor Lachlan Macquarie, that inveterate bestower of place-names. The houses here are perfect examples of the colonial style of architecture, with stone walls, wooden columns, and iron lace work. At 50 Argyle Place is **Undercliff Cottage**, built in 1840; it was the home of James Merriam, who was Lord Mayor of Sydney in the mid-1840s.

Continue west up Argyle Street to **KENT STREET**; on the northwest corner is the **Lord Nelson**. Built in 1834, it is the oldest operating hotel in Sydney. Originally a private home for ex-convict William Wells, it became a licensed pub in 1842, and now serves its own brand of beer.

Return along Argyle Street, continuing east to the **Argyle Cut**; above, on the south side, is **Observatory Park**.

Argyle Cut itself was the work of convicts from Hyde Park Barracks, who, in 1843, began to hack through solid rock using nothing but pick and hammer. Since transportation had ended in 1842, work had to be completed in 1859 under the direction of the Municipal Council using free labourers. The Cut provided quick access from Sydney Cove to Miller's Point and the wharves of Watson's Bay. The tons of rock excavated was used to form a sea wall at Semicircular Quay. Old photographs, most notably by Harold Cazneaux, make the Cut appear like a scene from the Old World. In the middle of the Cut, a plaque states simply 'Charles Moore Mayor 1867–1868'.

At the top of Argyle Stairs entering into The Rocks by the Cut, you will find the entrance to the **Pylon Lookout**, at the top of the southeast pylon of the **Harbour Bridge**. Climb the 200 stairs for a spectacular view of the harbour and the surrounding area. At this point it is also possible to reach the pedestrian footpath which leads across the bridge to North Sydney, about a 20 minute walk one way.

After the Cut to the north is **Argyle Arts Centre**, 18–20 Argyle Street at Playfair Street. Formerly **Mary Reibey's** (see box, p 130) **Argyle Bond Stores**, this conglomeration of shops represents a variety of architectural periods, most prominently the 1880s, but with some sections dating from as early as 1828. It is now the home of crafts shops aimed at the tourist market.

Mary Reibey

Mary Reibey (1777–1855) was one of the most remarkable figures in early Australian history; she is currently immortalised on the $20 note. Transported in 1792 for horse theft (she maintained she had only borrowed it), she was only 15 when she arrived in the colony. In 1794 she married Thomas Reibey, a ship's officer. They settled on a farm on the Hawkesbury River, and began to purchase schooners; by 1803, Thomas owned several vessels and ran a coastal trade. In 1809 he received an appointment as a ship's pilot and sailed to China and India, where he died of heat stroke in 1811, aged 42. Mary, now with seven children, had already established businesses and acquired properties in The Rocks, among them the Argyle Bond. She continued to act as a merchant and to manage her late husband's shipping concerns. She increased her land holdings through judicious investments and government grants, and soon established her sons on property in Tasmania, where her grandson Thomas would become Premier. In 1820, she visited England with her daughters, and was greeted as a celebrity; she further solidified her business interests with London firms. She was instrumental in the establishment of banking concerns in the new colony. She worked tirelessly to expand her investments and property, which included a house at Hunter's Hill and many substantial buildings in the centre of town around Macquarie Place; the Bank of New South Wales was one of her tenants. She was a well-known figure in Sydney, accompanied by her enormous Fijian woman bodyguard, Feefoo.

At 13–15 and 17–31 Playfair Street is **Argyle Terrace**, originally a row of workers' cottages dating from the 1870s; they now house more shops and cafés. At George Street, between the Argyle Tavern (built 1830) and the Argyle Cut, are the **Argyle Stairs**, leading to Cumberland Street. These stairs were cut by convicts to a height of 9 metres (30 ft) to provide access to Bunker's Hill and Miller's Point.

At **Nurses Walk** and Globe Street is the **New South Wales State Archives**, a good source of information on early settlement and family history.

Observatory Hill

From **YORK STREET**, walk through the pedestrian walkways to Kent Street and the Bradfield Highway. From Argyle Place in The Rocks use the steps to **WATSON ROAD**, or climb the steep Argyle Stairs to Gloucester Street, then take **Bridge Stairs** to Observatory Road. The area near Bridge Stairs is one of the most pleasant and calmest parts of Old Sydney, evoking some sense of the old neighbourhoods here near the harbour.

At the base of the Hill, at 120 Kent Street, is the **Richmond Villa**, now home of the Australian Society of Genealogists. Originally located in The Domain on Hospital Street, the villa was the home of Colonial Architect Mortimer Lewis, who designed it in 1849. An elegant example of 'Carpenter's Gothic', with pointed parapets and bay windows, Richmond Villa remained in a row of villas behind the State Parliament and served a variety of uses until it was moved, stone by stone, to its present site in 1975.

Next to Richmond Villa is **Glover's Cottage**, the only remaining house of those built in 1820 on the original land grant by stonemason Thomas Glover.

Observatory Hill stands 44 metres (144 feet) above the harbour; since settlement, it has been a major landmark, and was originally the site of the colony's first windmill (hence its earlier name of Windmill Hill). In 1804, Governor King began construction of a citadel to be named Fort Phillip; it was never completed, but remnants of the original stone wall surround the Observatory. The hill was also known as **Flagstaff Hill**, since Governor Phillip erected a flagpole here in 1788, and a later Signal Station (1825) served the same purpose for incoming ships. In 1848, Colonial Architect Mortimer Lewis built a second Signal Station, which remains as the hill's oldest building.

The **Observatory** (☎ 02 9217 0485, open daily 10.00–17.00, 2-hour evening sessions include a lecture and view through the telescope but must be booked about two weeks in advance) itself was designed by Colonial Architect Alexander Dawson and built between 1857 and 1859. From 1858, a time ball on the weather vane dropped daily at 13.00 to signal that a gun be fired at Fort Denison in the Harbour to indicate the correct time; the practice ceased during the Second World War, but was revived in 1987. The copper-domed observation chambers with telescopes were added in 1877, and served as the **official astronomical observatory** until the 1980s; it is now a marvellously informative museum, offering many hands-on displays and evening observation times.

Immediately to the south of the observatory is the **National Trust Centre**, headquarters of the New South Wales Branch of the National Trust of Australia (☎ 02 9258 0123). Part of the present building includes the remains of the original **Military Hospital**, built in 1815 for Governor Macquarie by John Watts; the hospital was moved to Victoria Barracks in 1848, and the structure was significantly altered in 1849 by Mortimer Lewis, who replaced the elegant Doric columns around the verandahs with the heavier Corinthian columns of the Classic Revival Style. From 1850 until 1974 the building was the home of **Fort Street School**, one of the most prestigious schools in the colony; when the boys were moved in 1916, it became

Fort Street School, Sydney

Fort Street Girls' School. The first kindergarten in New South Wales was opened here in 1856; many of Sydney's most prominent citizens were graduates of the school.

Along with the offices of the National Trust, the building's brick extension now houses the **S.H. Ervin Gallery** (☎ 02 9258 0173, open Tues–Fri 11.00–17.00, Sat and Sun 12.00–17.00), named for the businessman who donated his collection of Australian paintings and established the gallery; changing exhibitions are usually devoted to retrospective exhibitions of contemporary Australian artists.

A pleasant way to descend from Observatory Hill is down Watson Road into **LOWER FORT STREET**, proceeding north down the street itself from Argyle Place. The entire length of the street is known as **Regency Row**, and contains a variety of restored houses from all periods of the 19C. This was considered Sydney's most fashionable neighbourhood by the mid-19C, an indication of how closely housed were the most divergent elements of society, with squalid settlements only a few blocks below.

At no. 53 Lower Fort Street is the **Colonial House Museum**, maintained as a typical Victorian terrace house. The Regency townhouses at nos 39–41 are some of the only remaining examples of the elegant work of architect John Verge (1782–1861). **Bligh House** at no. 43 (closed to the public) was the mansion of Robert Campbell Jr, son of the merchant Robert Campbell, and a leading campaigner for the end of convict transportation. Constructed of local sandstone bricks, the mansion has a verandah supported by Doric columns and beautiful cedar joinery in the interior.

To enter back into The Rocks at George Street, continue down to the end of Lower Fort Street, known as **Milton Terrace**, site of some of the best examples of High Victorian domestic architecture in Sydney. At the end of Hickson Terrace are the **Hickson Steps** leading down to Hickson Road and a return to The Rocks under the Harbour Bridge.

The Harbour Bridge

From the earliest days of settlement, contemplation of a bridge from Dawes Point on the South Shore to Milson's Point on the North Shore was on the minds of Sydneysiders. The first serious proposal was made to Governor Macquarie by Francis Greenway in 1815, although there is no record of its actual plan. Many proposed schemes followed throughout the 19C, but no practicable solution could be found, because the depth of the water and the need to maintain access to upstream wharfage for large ships necessitated a high bridge. Finally, in 1912, Dr J.J.C. Bradfield (the Bradfield Highway is named in his honour), Chief Engineer of the Public Works Department, designed a single-arch steel bridge which was accepted. The First World War delayed action, but construction was finally implemented with the selection of architect Sir Ralph Freeman of Dorman Long & Co., England, who received the contract in 1921. Estimated cost was £4,217,721; the final cost was £6,250,000, paid off in 1988.

Work began 28 April 1923, with the excavation of sandstone beds 12m deep, filled with concrete. The bridge took nine years to build, employing some 1400 workers during the worst years of the Depression. Sixteen workers were killed; one wrote on seeing the first die: 'I remember I was standing there with one hand on the wire rope, and I had to prise my fingers off it with my other hand. I was quite safe where I was. But it was the shock—it was just seeing him go down, I knew he'd be killed.'

Constructed as two halves on both shores, the bridge was finally joined in the middle, as cantilevered arches held in place by cables connected to tunnels in the subterranean granite were stretched over the water.

The height at the top of the arch is 134m (439ft) above water level, at the deck 59m (194ft); the entire span is 503m (1650ft). Clearance for shipping is 53m (172ft). The bridge's weight is 65,000 tonnes, all pivoted on six small pins and held together by 6 million rivets.

Its construction generated unprecedented excitement, as a symbol of Australia's modernity and sophistication, and a linking of the north and south. It has served as a source of inspiration for artists, writers, and photographers. Grace Cossington Smith's painting *The Bridge in Curve* (1930) in the Art Gallery of New South Wales is a stunning example; she called the Bridge 'Te Deum in progress'. Max Dupain, David Moore and Harold Cazneaux all made photographic studies during and after construction.

Opening ceremonies were planned for 19 March 1932, and thousands lined the harbour shores to witness the event. As New South Wales Premier Jack Lang began the official opening speech, a Captain Francis de Groot, member of the extreme right-wing New Guard opposed to Lang's socialist policies, rode up on a horse and cut the ribbon before he was dragged away by the police. The ribbon was restored and Lang officially opened the bridge. The scissors used for the 'real' opening are now on display at the State Parliament House on Macquarie Street.

The bridge is part of Australian folklore, known affectionately as **The Coathanger**. On a sombre note, it has been the site of at least 200 suicides, despite extensive security; 60 jumps occurred in the first seven months, until protective barriers were erected, which, unfortunately, block the harbour view for passing motorists or train passengers. Automobiles crossing the bridge from north to south pay a $2 toll. Walking across the bridge takes about 20 minutes and offers exhilarating views.

Darling Harbour

For generations, Darling Harbour (first called **Cockle Bay**, as it still is at its southern end) was the leading cargo facility of the port, the centre of dockside activity. There were berths for 40 deep-sea vessels, with additional wharves for smaller ships. In 1815, the harbour was the site of the assembling of the first steam engine in Australia, brought from England by engineer John Dickson and used to crush grain. Governor Macquarie was so impressed with Dickson's enterprise that he gave him 16 acres of land around Darling Harbour as far as George Street; Dickson eventually became a prosperous brewer and miller, with substantial land holdings throughout the country. Dickson sold his brewery in the 1840s to the Toohey Brothers, who established the most enduring of Sydney beers, Toohey's.

The bay acquired the name of Darling Harbour in honour of Governor Darling (1825–31), who, despite the plethora of places named after him, was the most detested of all colonial governors. By the 1890s, the harbour had an enormous iron wharf with six cargo cranes and a goods yard that covered some 56 acres (22 ha).

Such a thriving industrial port brought with it the inevitable problems of pollution and filth: abattoirs were blamed for luring the rats which led to the outbreak of bubonic plague in The Rocks. During the Depression of the 1930s, the wharves were known as **The Hungry Mile**, as desperate men queued in their thousands for the few jobs available. As maritime industry dwindled in significance, the harbour became more derelict; by the 1970s, the old wooden wharves were filled in with sterile concrete ones to accommodate container shipping.

In 1984, Premier Neville Wran spearheaded a reclamation programme for the harbour, conceived as a Bicentennial gift to the city. The current entertainment extravaganza is the result of this enormous project. The Harbour is now home to the **National Maritime Museum**, the **National Aquarium**, the **Sydney Entertainment Centre**, and a **Chinese Garden** which links Chinatown to the harbour.

Cockle Bay Wharf, at the southern end of the harbour, has now been restored and is filled with sparkling restaurants and al fresco cafes, including **Ampersand**, chef Tony Bilson's latest extravagana. The building, designed by award-winning architect George Freedman, seats enormous numbers inside and out.

> ## Pyrmont Bridge
>
> While today the Pyrmont Bridge seems an inconspicuous span across a bit of the Darling Harbour entertainment complex, its initial construction was heralded as a major engineering achievement. Completed by bridge designer Percy Allan and opened in 1902, it is today the world's oldest electrically operated swingspan bridge; the central gates, which open for ships going up to Cockle Bay, are still driven by the original motor. At the time of its construction, as the second Pyrmont Bridge, the harbour was a bustling industrial area, filled with warehouses and shipping terminals; the first bridge had already provided the thoroughfare enabling industrial expansion to the other side of the bay. The bridge is 1200 feet (369m) long, with 14 spans, the middle ones made of steel and the rest of Australian ironbark. Allan's great innovation was the use of electricity for the bridge's opening mechanism—this accomplished at a time before Sydney streets were fully electrified, and made possible by power generated from the Ultimo station, now the site of the Powerhouse Museum.

A **monorail** loop from the city crosses Pyrmont Bridge (see box), stops near the Powerhouse Museum, and ends at the harbour. The monorail system, costing more than $60 million, was vehemently criticised at the time, as evidence of the government's desire to turn Sydney into 'Sydneyland', and it is easy to agree with those critics. The monorail serves little public purpose except to bring tourists to the harbour without the necessity of looking at many of the historic buildings and streets of the city; it does not run from Circular Quay, which would be the most logical starting-point if it were really meant to provide convenient transportation. But children like it, and it does prepare the visitor for the carnival-like atmosphere that permeates Darling Harbour's activities. **Tickets** are purchased from machines at the stations, the main one being on Pitt Street. Darling Harbour can also be reached by the ferry leaving from Circular Quay Wharf 5.

This is not to denigrate any of the Darling Harbour venues, which are all well worth a visit; both the Maritime Museum and the National Aquarium receive top honours for presentation and educational effort. The **Sydney Aquarium** (☎ 02 9262 2300, **open** daily 09.30–22.00) allows visitors to walk through an acrylic tube to view the sea life above (no performing seals here). The **National Maritime Museum** (☎ 02 9552 7705, **open** daily 09.30–17.00) houses, along with fascinating displays of historical artefacts, actual ships, from the famed America's Cup winner *Australia II* to the sad little Vietnamese refugee boat

Tu Do. The museum's design, by leading contemporary architect Philip Cox, consists of a steel-roofed structure that sets the architectural tone of Darling Harbour.

Powerhouse Museum

One of the stops on the monorail is the **Powerhouse Museum**, Harris Street, Ultimo (☎ 02 9217 0111, **open** daily 10.00–17.00). The largest museum in Australia, the Powerhouse is one of the best museums of its kind in the world. Covering more than 35,000 square metres (376,750 sq ft), the comprehensive nature of its collections is reminiscent of The Smithsonian Institution in Washington. Situated in a converted power station (hence the name) with a tasteful addition of barrel-vaulted glass designed by Lionel Glendenning (the addition is named in honour of former New South Wales Premier Neville Wran), the museum contains exhibitions on everything to do with Australian culture, as well as substantive displays on science and technology, and decorative arts. The exhibitions are state of the art, using computers and videos and other 'hands on' methods to enlighten and entertain; locomotives and aeroplanes can often be climbed on, and scientific apparatus sampled. Changing exhibitions range widely, from the history of television commercials to Australian furniture designers. A favourite permanent display presents the history of the **Australian pub and brewing**, with films describing the infamous days of the 'pub-push', or 'the swill', when all drinking establishments were frantically full before they had to close at 6pm. The **restaurant** in the museum has murals designed by Ken Done.

Set aside a good amount of time to take in all the museum's floors; it is an absolute must for any Sydney visitor, especially those with children.

The lovely **Chinese Gardens** (open daily 09.30–17.00) sit on the northern side of Pier Street, c 250m from the Powerhouse Museum. Known as the Garden of Friendship, the design was a gift of Sydney's Chinese sister city, Guangdong, in 1987. The gardens offer a tranquil spot in the middle of the area's bustle, with a small lake, Chinese pavilion, and tea house. Appropriately, the gardens lead into Sydney's Chinatown.

Chinatown

While not as colourful as the Melbourne version, this Chinatown is certainly thriving, with restaurants, Asian food markets and shops, as well as legitimate practitioners of traditional Chinese medicine. Chinatown is definitely the place to go for authentic and reasonably priced Chinese (see box, p 136) food. Originally, the centre of Chinatown was the area around Dixon and Hay Streets; it is now expanding into the Haymarket District, west to Harris Street, south to Broadway, and east to Castlereagh Street. Dixon Street is still its main thoroughfare.

Haymarket

From Chinatown, to the south of Hay Street, is the area known as the Haymarket, for it was traditionally the home of the grain and hay trade and businesses. Into the early 1900s, the area was the main working-class shopping district; Ruth Park describes a Saturday night here at **Paddy's Market** in her book, *The Harp in the South* (1948). Paddy's Market, which opened as early as 1869, lives on today, a bit smarter, but still a good place for bargain-hunting, good produce, and some atmosphere. The markets are open on weekends, and are now located on the corner of Thamos and Hay Streets.

At 13 Campbell Street is Capitol Theatre (☎ 02 9320 5000), in the 1920s a grand movie house. The theatre has recently been reopened as a venue for musical theatre.

The Chinese in Australia

Large numbers of Chinese first came to Australia after the cessation of transportation in the 1840s, when they were imported as cheap labour. The discovery of gold in the early 1850s resulted in a mass exodus to the gold fields in Victoria and New South Wales. In Melbourne, many of the Chinese remained to establish a still-thriving community (see Melbourne). In New South Wales, the situation was a bit different. Lambing Flat near the town of Young was the site in 1860 of one of the worst aggressive actions against Chinese miners, when 3000 whites stormed their camps and demanded that they leave. In all, some 1200 Chinese fled and hid in the countryside, saved from starvation only by the aid of a station-owner, James Robert, who fed them. In the end, the Lambing Flat incident saw the curtailing of Chinese immigration; indeed, the incident is considered the impetus for the infamous White Australia policy.

On the other hand, individual Chinese gained influence and prosperity in colonial Australia. The most noted figure was **Quong Tart** (1850–1903), a Cantonese who came to New South Wales in 1859. He managed to acquire an interest in a gold mine in Braidwood, and eventually became a wealthy man. He acted as an interpreter and mediator among the white and Chinese communities. Quong Tart was quite fond of Scottish culture, learning to recite in correct accent the poems of Robert Burns. He acted as the first Chinese member of the Oddfellows' Lodge in Australia. In 1874, he moved to Sydney and became a tea and silk merchant with headquarters eventually in the Queen Victoria Building. He married a Scottish woman, and became the unofficial Chinese Consul-General of the colony. In 1902, he was attacked by a robber in his shop. The citizens of Sydney gave him a testimonial at the Town Hall and presented him with a cheque for 300 guineas. He did not fully recover from his injuries and died in 1903, at which time some 1500 people attended his funeral.

Sydney Fish Market

About 15 minutes' walk from Darling Harbour to **Blackwattle Bay** one finds the **Sydney Fish Markets**; access to the markets by water taxi is a more exciting way to get there. The markets provide a fascinating, very Sydney, experience, and also some of the best seafood restaurants in the city (of the buy-and-cook-on-the-spot sort).

Walk 5 • Pitt Street and George Street

From Circular Quay, walk south on Pitt Street. Past Reiby Place, c 150m, is BULLETIN PLACE. In one of the commercial warehouses here, Sydney's most important early literary journal, the *Bulletin*, was first published in the 1890s (see entry on Jules Archibald above). Contributors included Henry Lawson, 'Banjo' Paterson, and a host of cartoonists and 'Black and White' artists.

Walk another 100m to **BRIDGE STREET**, the main east-west link in central Sydney. At the corner of Bridge and Loftus Streets (west) is **MACQUARIE PLACE**, still a delightful little patch of green with great **Moreton Bay fig trees**. It first served as Governor Phillip's vegetable garden. Governor Macquarie, with his ever grandiose visions, planned it as the centre of Sydney at the time when it was much closer to the waterfront. Located here are two monuments of interest: the gun and anchor from the *Sirius*, Governor Phillip's ship in the First Fleet; and **Macquarie's Obelisk**, designed by Greenway in 1816, and intended to serve as the measuring point for all roads leading out of Sydney.

At **BOND STREET**, 100m south, between George and Pitt Streets is **AUSTRALIA SQUARE**, completed in 1967 by Harry Seidler (see box), controversial Bauhaus-trained architect credited with bringing International Style architecture to Australia. At the time of its construction, it was the first substantial skyscraper in Sydney, with 50 floors reaching a height of 171m (560ft) and a diameter of 41m (135ft). Of greatest interest was the building's surrounding **plaza**, similar to those created in New York City by Phillip Johnson and Mies van der Rohe; it created an open space amidst the cramped quarters of lower George Street. While in the 1960s its pre-cast concrete construction was revolutionary by Sydney standards, today its emphatic rendering of International Style modernism is dated and predictable. Its limited ornamentation and severe forms places it firmly in the context of its time; its influence on subsequent building in the city is apparent in the many other 'glass and steel' constructions that followed. Housed in the Australia Tower are numerous shops, as well as restaurants and other tourist venues.

Harry Seidler

When Harry Seidler (b. 1923) arrived in Sydney in 1947, via his native Vienna and after training with Walter Gropius in the US, 'International Style' architecture had made no appearance on the Australian landscape. His first construction here, a house for his mother completed in 1951, caused immediate controversy as being 'too European'; it is still referred to as 'the white box' by many who object to its incongruous placement in the Australian bush. Uncompromisingly Bauhausian with glass walls, flat roof, open planning and minimal colouring, the **Rose Seidler House**, 71 Clissold Road in Wahroonga at the edge of the Ku-ring-gai Chase National Park, is now a property of the Historic Houses Trust and is open to the public (Sundays 10.00–16.30). Seidler remains an important figure in Sydney, still fighting the modernist fight against the onslaught of post-modernism and any architectural ornamentation.

Martin Place

Continue south on Pitt Street, c 300m to **MARTIN PLACE**. Jan Morris describes the square as 'Sydney's substitute for a truly ceremonial centre', and it still serves this purpose in a town not overburdened with public plazas. While it now includes a public fountain, train station, and theatre ticket booth, it is also surrounded by substantial commercial buildings dating primarily from the beginning of the century.

Of most significance architecturally is the **General Post Office**. As in all Australian cities, and particularly in the major city of the country, the post office was constructed as a monumental landmark, symbolising civilisation and commerce. This fact is certainly evident in the history of the Australian postal service, *The City's Centre-piece: The History of the Sydney GPO*, available at the post office shops. Built between 1865 and 1874 by James Barnet, it still exudes an elegant charm, enhanced by colonnades and beautiful brass letter-boxes.

When Australia Post became a private enterprise in 1989, it acquired this landmark. Lamentably, not only has there been no effort to renovate its impressive public spaces, but the exterior has been boarded with unattractive temporary materials for several years, presenting an uninviting and confusing façade. Recently, some construction activity is afoot, which may restore the building to its former glory. In the **clock tower** is, according to rumour, the last surviving chalked 'Eternity' of Sydney legend Arthur Stace (see Sydney Square, p 140).

Martin Place is also the site of the **Cenotaph**. Designed by sculptor Bertram MacKennal (1863–1931), a ceremonial guard and band pay honour to Australia's war dead every Thursday at 12.30. On Anzac Day (25 April), a dawn vigil begins memorial services here.

From Martin Place cross George Street to **BARRACK STREET**, now a pedestrian mall, and on to York Street; looking south up York Street, you will see the **1930s Grace Building** on the corner of King Street. Modelled on the Chicago Tribune Building, it housed the administrative offices of Grace Bros. department store until the Second World War, when it became the headquarters of General Douglas MacArthur.

Turning north down YORK STREET, you see the Art Deco **AWA Building** (Amalgamated Wireless [Australasia]), built in 1939. Site of Sydney's early radio broadcasts, its radio tower was the highest structure in the city until the 1960s. This area was the site of the colony's first military barracks and ancillary structures; the present-day **Wynyard Park** comprised part of the barracks' parade grounds. In Wynyard Park is a statue to John Dunmore Lang, first Presbyterian minister in Australia, who founded the **Scots Kirk** nearby in 1826. The present Scots Kirk at Jamison, York and Margaret Street was built on the site in the 1930s after the original church was demolished.

Across York Street at Jamison Street is **Church Hill**, site of Sydney's oldest church, **St Philip's**; originally it was spelled with two 'l's', in honour of Governor Phillip. The current church dates from the 1840s, when it was designed by Sydney's greatest ecclesiastic architect, Edmund Blacket. The church bells, which were donated in 1858 and 1888, still ring to announce services on Sunday.

The next block on York Street intersects with Grosvenor Street. Turn into this street to reach another church complex, **St Patrick's**, the oldest Catholic church in the city. The 1844 Gothic Revival building was built where early Irish convicts worshipped illegally, having smuggled in a priest.

If you continue south on Pitt Street from Martin Place, the next block at **KING STREET** becomes a pedestrian mall. On the west side of the block is the **Strand Arcade**, 193–95 Pitt Street through to 408–410 George Street. The only remaining arcade of several built in the 1880s and 1890s, it has been faithfully restored to its High Victorian splendour after a fire gutted it in 1976. This arcade connects with the pedestrian mall of George Street.

In the centre of the mall on the east side is the entrance to the **Imperial**

Arcade. From here, you can also enter **Centrepoint**. Underneath the prominent **Sydney Tower**, with predictable revolving restaurant on top, Centrepoint consists of four floors of shops and restaurants. Sydney Tower, rising 304.8m (1000ft), was considered an architectural wonder when it was completed in 1981. The observation decks offer spectacular views of the city and surroundings.

David Jones

Walk through Imperial Arcade and you come to the original branch of the department store David Jones, which straddles Castlereagh, Market and Elizabeth Streets. Considered in Australia and elsewhere as one of the best department stores in the world, **'DJ's'** grew out of the business founded in 1828 by David Jones, an emigrant from Wales. The company grew quickly, and passed through several generations of the Jones family. The current Sydney store, with its impressive interiors, elegant lifts, and excellent service, was built in 1927 at a cost of £1 million. The store has played an important role in Sydney cultural life; it was in the David Jones gallery on the top floor that the first exhibitions of modern art were held in the 1920s and 1930s, and they still have occasional exhibitions. The separate men's store is directly across the street, at Market and Castlereagh Streets. The after-Christmas sales here, beginning on Boxing Day, present a traditional scene of unmitigated mayhem, as shoppers try to find real bargains.

Exit David Jones on Market Street and return west to George Street. Between Pitt and George Streets, at 49 Market Street, is the **State Theatre**. The theatre was designed by Henry E. White and New Yorker John Eberson in 1929 as a moving picture palace in the grandest, most sumptuous cinematic style. Interiors include crystal chandeliers, marble statues, moulded plasterwork, and a high domed ceiling; the **Grand Assembly Room** was supposedly modelled on rooms at Versailles, containing sculptured busts, carved furniture and original paintings. The effect today, after an unfortunate alteration in the 1980s, is a bit overwhelming, but well worth the visit as a monument to the old days of cinema. The annual Sydney Film Festival, an exciting occasion, is appropriately held here in mid-June.

Queen Victoria Building

At George Street is the **Queen Victoria Building**. Built in 1898 by Scottish architect George McRae as a market in a style described as 'Late Victorian American Romanesque', it fell into decline after the city markets were moved in 1910. Its spaces were hideously transformed into temporary city offices, and by 1959 it was considered a white elephant threatened with demolition for a car

The Queen Victoria Building, Sydney

park. Noted modernist Harry Seidler considered it a 'monstrosity' that should be destroyed. Only a vigorous campaign by admirers, including Barry Humphries, saved this phantasmagoric piece of Victoriana. It has now been renovated, at a cost of $72 million, to be, as designer Pierre Cardin has said, 'the most beautiful shopping centre in the world'. It is architecturally delightful, with tile work, filigree, stained glass domes, cantilevered iron staircases, and beautiful wood-work joinery. Its length is 201m (660ft), all covered with an enormous barrel-vaulted glass ceiling, along with 20 smaller metal domes. A **hanging clock** in the centre hourly displays a series of mechanical scenes of British kings and queens, including the beheading of King Charles I.

The Town Hall

Exit the Queen Victoria at its south end, on Druitt/Park Street, to confront the Town Hall Group, considered the best grouping of Victorian buildings in the city.

Referred to by author Ruth Park as **'Bondi Renaissance'**, the Town Hall itself is a conglomeration of architectural styles, with layers of arches, domes, porti-coes, columns and finally, the ubiquitous clock-tower.

On the site of the city's original burial ground, the land was chosen for the Town Hall in 1868; cemetery remains were then sent to Rookwood Cemetery. Designed mainly by J.H. Wilson and Albert Bond, the main structure is predom-inantly of load-bearing brick and concrete with sandstone facing; its lengthy construction period accounts for the diversity of styles. It was finally completed in 1889, at a cost of £620,000. The main feature of the building is **Centennial Hall**, which can seat 2500, and is famous for its organ; its Christmas concerts are a popular Sydney event.

Between the Town Hall and St Andrew's to the south is SYDNEY SQUARE, a small paved area which includes a **Wall of Water Fountain**, completed in 1976.

> The architect Ridley Smith also included here a plaque with the single word **'Eternity'**, a memorial to **Arthur Stace** (1884–1967), a revered Sydney character, who after having a spiritual revelation was saved from 'demon rum' and for 40 years wrote in a fine, flowing script the word 'Eternity' in chalk on Sydney's sidewalks every night; at the time of his death, it was esti-mated he had written the word 500,000 times. Rumour has it that one of his inscriptions still exists, inside the bell of the GPO Clock Tower.

St Andrew's Cathedral, on the corner of George and Bathurst Streets, is a small Gothic Revival building constructed between 1837 and 1886. The latter work was done by Edmund Blacket; the ashes of Blacket and his wife are buried under the floor of the southwest corner. The original entrance at the west was altered, so that the present entrance is where the altar was meant to be. The inte-rior contains 26 windows created in 1860 by a Birmingham company at a cost of £5000.

Central Station area

South of the Town Hall group and St Andrew's Cathedral, George Street passes by Chinatown and the Haymarket on the west side. At RAWSON STREET, turn left to come to the front entrance of the grand **Central Station**, the main railway terminal for the city. All local and long-distance trains depart from here. The station itself is a fine old structure, built by W.L. Vernon between 1901 and 1906, redolent of the glory days of steam trains and rail travel. The main floor of the terminal demonstrates one of the first uses of reinforced concrete in Australia. You can also still see the Mortuary Terminal, the departure terminal of the old 'funeral train' that used to take the dead and the grieving out to Rookwood Cemetery (the terminal that originally stood at the other end has been rebuilt as a church in Canberra). It was built in 1869 to designs by James Barnet, of sandstone in Gothic Revival style. Intriguingly, one of Sydney's original burial grounds had to be moved to build the Central Station.

Back on George Street, at the point near the Central Station, where George and Pitt Streets intersect, is a much-neglected architectural gem, Edmund Blacket's **Christ Church St Laurance**. The design of the church and its ancillary buildings is attributed to Henry Robertson, but was constructed 1843–45 under the supervision of Blacket. The interior of the sandstone Gothic Revival church, on George Street, has cedar joinery, hand-carved 'poppyhead' pews, and a ceiling supported on octagonal timber beams. Blacket's rectory and school were demolished when the railway terminal was built; the current buildings, designed by J. Burcham Clamp, were erected in 1905.

Surry Hills

To the south of Hyde Park and east of Central Station is the traditionally working-class suburb of **Surry Hills**. The best way to get there is to take a train to Central Station, then walk into the neighbourhood; **bus nos 302, 303** and **304** also travel from Elizabeth Street down Bourke Street through Surry Hills, and **bus nos 372, 393** and **395** traverse Elizabeth Street to Cleveland Street at the edge of the suburb. This area was the location for Ruth Park's vivid depictions of desperate slum-dwellers in her brilliant novels, *Harp in the South* (1948) and *Poor Man's Orange* (1949). While some gentrification is currently taking place, Surry Hills is still pretty grotty in places, but there are good cheap restaurants here, mainly Turkish and Lebanese, around Elizabeth and Cleveland Streets. Once the city's garment district, the area also has some good factory outlets and alternative fashion shops at the Oxford Street end of Crown Street.

Of most interest here are two 'cultural' sites: the excellent **Belvoir Theatre**, 25 Belvoir Street (☎ 02 9699 3444), home of Company B, Sydney's hottest and most creative theatre company, with plays regularly featuring the best actors in Australia (Nicole Kidman chooses to appear here when she can, and Geoffrey Rush, Ruth Cracknell, and Hugo Weaving make regular appearances); and the **Brett Whiteley Studio**, 2 Raper Street (☎ 02 9225 1881; open Sat and Sun 10.00–16.00), the late artist's studio that is now a public gallery and museum.

Walk 6 • Darlinghurst and Paddington

Starting from ELIZABETH STREET, walk past Hyde Park to Liverpool Street and turn left (east)—**buses no. 380 and 381** proceed along Oxford Street from here. At the end of the Park, Liverpool veers right to become **OXFORD STREET**, now a lively centre of **gay culture** (see box, p 142). It is also a well-known place for bistros, bars and restaurants. Some parts of it have become decidedly seedy of late, although the area is still worth a visit for shopping, bookstore browsing, and dining. The main interstate bus depot is located around the corner from **Taylor Square**, so for many visitors, this is their first view of Sydney.

Mardi Gras

The Sydney Gay and Lesbian Mardi Gras is held on the first weekend in March. In 1978, when homosexuality was still illegal in New South Wales, a group of some 1000 gays marched from Oxford Street to King's Cross in protest against hostile police. This event marked Sydney's first homosexual Mardi Gras, which is now an enormously successful international event, drawing crowds of more than 500,000 to watch what has become one of the world's most outlandish parades. The event is now televised and even the police force sends a contingent of officers to join the gay marchers. The post-parade all-night party at the Royal Agricultural Showgrounds is by ticket only. They sell out two months in advance. Foreign visitors with passport identification can purchase them from the Mardi Gras offices, although it is becoming increasingly difficult to obtain them.

Darlinghurst

Proceed along Oxford Street past the five-street hub, TAYLOR SQUARE (600m). Continue on Oxford Street; on the left at Darlinghurst Road (200m) behind Darlinghurst Court House is East Sydney Technical College, whose imposing sandstone walls betray its earlier function as **Darlinghurst Gaol**, Sydney's main prison from 1841 until 1914. Some of the walls date from as early as 1822, and architects included Francis Greenway and Mortimer Lewis. The grass outside the main gates was once the public gallows, where many of Sydney's most notorious criminals were hanged before large crowds.

Back on Oxford Street, proceed southeast to Glenmore Road, about 500m from Taylor Square. On the right is the entrance to **Victoria Barracks** (☎ 02 9339 3170, open Thurs 10.00–13.30 with guided tours featuring the Australian Army Band, Sydney), once the centre of Paddington and home to the British garrison regiments in Sydney from 1848 until 1870. Designed by Lt-Col George Barney of the Royal Engineers, this enormous building was constructed between 1841 and 1848 by convicts and free stonemasons. At 220m (740ft), the main building is one of the longest buildings in Australia and is considered to be one of the finest British imperial barracks in the world.

When it was built, Paddington was a backwater, described as 'the saddest heath, the most melancholy swamps', surrounded by desolate sand dunes. Soldiers' pay was so poor that for many years, soldiers' wives sold cabbage tree hats made of cabbage tree fronds outside the gates. Guided tours are available regularly, including the **Changing of the Guard** ceremony (the barracks is now the permanent headquarters of the Eastern Command); a view of a museum examining Australia's military history; and a visit to **Busby's Bore**, the famous water-tunnel that brought water from present-day Centennial Park to Hyde Park.

Immediately south of Victoria Barracks at MOORE PARK ROAD is the **Royal Agricultural Society Show Grounds**. Home of the annual Royal Easter Show for more than 100 years, the grounds are also home to the **Sydney Football Stadium** and the **Sydney Cricket Ground**, both hallowed shrines to Sydneysiders' obsession with sports. The notorious entrepreneur and ex-

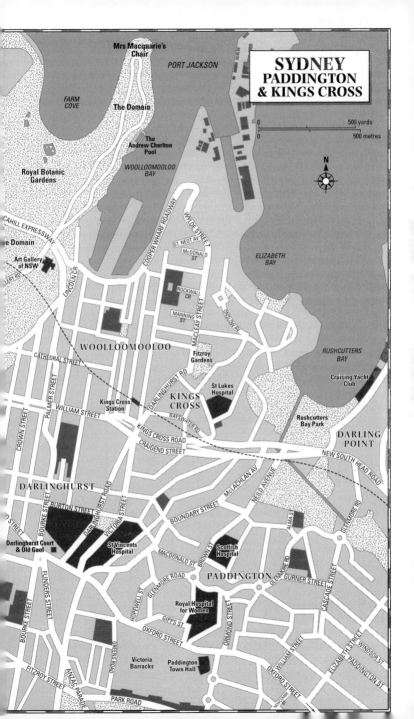

SYDNEY
PADDINGTON
& KINGS CROSS

N

0   500 yards
0   500 metres

Mrs Macquarie's Chair

PORT JACKSON

FARM COVE

The Domain

The Andrew Charlton Pool

WOOLLOOMOOLOO BAY

Royal Botanic Gardens

ELIZABETH BAY

CAHILL EXPRESSWAY

e Domain

Art Gallery of NSW

ERY RD

LINCOLN CR

COOPER WHARF ROADWAY

WYLDE STREET

ST. NEOT AV

McDONALD ST

ROCKWALL CR

MANNING ST

MACLEAY STREET

DIXON WAY

CATHEDRAL STREET

WOOLLOOMOOLOO

Fitzroy Gardens

RUSHCUTTERS BAY

Cruising Yacht Club

PALMER STREET

DARLINGHURST RD

St Lukes Hospital

KINGS CROSS

Kings Cross Station

CROWN STREET

WILLIAM STREET

BAYSWATER RD

KINGS CROSS ROAD

CRAIGEND STREET

Rushcutters Bay Park

DARLING POINT

NEW SOUTH HEAD ROAD

DARLINGHURST

BURTON STREET

BOURKE STREET

DARLINGHURST ROAD

VICTORIA STREET

McLACHLAN AV

NEILD AVENUE

ALMA ST

GLENMORE RD

Darlinghurst Court & Old Gaol

St Vincents Hospital

BOUNDARY STREET

MACDONALD ST

BROWN ST

Scottish Hospital

FLINDERS STREET

BOURKE STREET

GLENMORE ROAD

PADDINGTON

GLENMORE RD

GURNER STREET

CASCADE STREET

HOPEWELL ST

Royal Hospital for Women

GIPPS ST

ORMOND STREET

GREENS ROAD

OXFORD STREET

Victoria Barracks

Paddington Town Hall

ELIZABETH STREET

WINDSOR ST

OXFORD STREET

WILLIAM STREET

PADDINGTON ST

FITZROY STREET

ANZAC PARADE

PARK ROAD

Australian Rupert Murdoch has turned the grounds into a movie production lot, making Sydney a down-under Hollywood (George Lucas is filming his *Star Wars* sequels here). The Royal Easter Show, after 120 years on the site, was moved to the new **Homebush Stadium** in 1998.

Centennial Park

About 1km east at the junction of Moore Park Road and Oxford Street is the entrance to **Centennial Park**. Opened in Australia's centennial year, 1888, the park comprises some 220 ha and includes 12 lakes. It is Sydney's only English-style park, and its popularity with city dwellers is comparable to Central Park in New York City. In the centre is **Lachlan Swamp**, origin of Busby's Bore, the tunnel which provided water for the city in the 1820s. The swamp remains essentially untouched, with prolific birdlife and numerous native species. At **Hamilton Drive**, where the road turns into Grand Drive and overlooking the playing fields, is a wonderful sculpture honouring Rugby League football; called '**We Won**', it was designed in 1893 by Tommaso Sani.

Immediately south of Centennial Park on Alison Road is **Randwick Race-course**, site since 1833 of some of Australia's most exciting **horse races**.

Horse-racing

As the *Australian Encyclopedia* wrote in 1956, horse-racing 'might almost be called the Australian national sport'. While today's Australians are less devoted to the sport than past generations, it is still true that any town of any size has a racecourse, and betting on the horses is a major business, aided by an Australian invention, the automatic totalisator. Racing began in the earliest days of the colony, although the first recorded event dates from 1810, when officers held three days of races at Hyde Park. As early as 1802 Robert Campbell brought from Calcutta **Arab Hector**, who remained the most important sire until 1823. Horse-breeding has been given serious attention since that time, and today's Australian horses rank among the healthiest and most beautiful in the world.

The **Australian Jockey Club** was founded in 1842, and the *Australian Stud Book* appeared in 1878. In the 1880s it was agreed that all racehorses in Australasia would take their ages from 1 August, thus marking the beginning of the racing season. Many trainers and owners will have a **Horses' Birthday Party** on that day, when the public can visit the horses in their quarters at the race-tracks. Legendary trainer Gai Waterhouse has her stables at Randwick.

The degree to which horse-racing is part of the Australian psyche is indicated by the significance placed on the annual **Melbourne Cup** in Melbourne. First held in 1860, the Cup is held on the first Tuesday of November at **Flemington Racecourse**; the entire country virtually stops for its running, with factories and businesses halting for its three minutes' run. The event regularly attracts 80,000 viewers to the track, and includes traditional accoutrements, such as elaborate hats and formal dress, roasted chicken, strawberries, and champagne (see Melbourne). In 1998, more than $80 million in bets were placed on that single race.

Paddington

To the north of Moore Park Road and Oxford Street is the suburb of **Paddington**. In the 1950s, 'New Australians', as post-war immigrants were called, moved into Paddington as a place for cheap rent, bringing an ethnic dimension to the area. In the late 1960s, gentrification began, as it became fashionable again to live in inner-city areas. Oxford Street in Paddington is now the heart of gay culture, with many of the most famous bars and clubs in this stretch of the road.

In 1973 the author Ruth Park, in her guide to Sydney, observed that the area had become 'so picturesque that it makes me feel as though I've been belted over the head with a teddybear'. Its current state is somewhat self-congratulatory, although grimy spots remain.

Return to Oxford Street and continue to **OATLEY ROAD/ORMOND STREET**. On the southwest corner is the **Paddington Town Hall**, the epitome of Victorian Classic Revival style, built in 1891 at tremendous cost and on what was then a grandiose scale for the area; particularly impressive is its colonnaded balcony rounding the corner of the street. Its tower, at one time a major landmark in the area, houses a clock with an inscription to King Edward VII in place of the numerals. The building is now the location of Chauvel Cinema, run by the Australian Film Insitute, as well as the Paddington Library.

Directly across the street on the northwest corner is the **Paddington Post Office**, a great example of Late Victorian design. Opposite, on Ormond Street, is **Juniper Hall** (☎ 02 9258 0123), the most important historical structure in Paddington. Built in 1824 as the residence of ex-convict and gin distiller Robert Cooper, another of Sydney's fascinating early characters, its generous proportions were no doubt necessary because Cooper had 23 children. For years the house served as an institution for children, including an orphanage and a children's court. In the 1920s it was turned into flats, but was finally purchased by the National Trust, which restored it to its present state. For a while, a Museum of Childhood occupied the space; that museum is now housed at another National Trust property, Merchant House, in George Street. Despite much local protestation and political wrangling, it is now in the hands of Sydney's most zealous breed, real estate agents, and is currently used for office spaces. Tours occur about twice a year at various times; check with National Trust office for times.

Walk north on Ormond Street for excellent examples of Paddington's terrace houses, with their impressive cast iron work of Australian motifs, decorative balconies and varying entrance levels depending on the topography. Views to **Rushcutters Bay** appear occasionally, especially at nos 32 and 34.

Down the hill to Olive Street is **Olive Bank Villa**, mansion of Alderman John Ely Begg, built in 1869. The last of the great Paddington mansions, the property's acreage was quickly subdivided in the 1870s along with the rest of the large properties.

GLENMORE ROAD developed from the bullock tracks determined by the carts carrying Robert Cooper's gin from Rushcutters Bay to what is now Oxford Street. The consequent street arrangements were haphazard, leading to the present-day web of narrow alleys and hilly lanes. On these streets are examples of a variety of architectural styles, from the blue-brick 1920s flats near Ormond

Street, to the Victorian villas at Cooper Street a few blocks west on Glenmore and down a short Paddington laneway.

At Cooper Street walk west past the **Scottish Hospital**, original site of **The Terraces**, one of Paddington's finest mansions. Parts of the original buildings have been incorporated into the hospital, and special care was taken to preserve a remnant of The Terrace's magnificent **gardens**. At the entrance, at Cooper and Brown Streets, you can still see a near rainforest landscape amidst the urban surroundings.

Turn left (south) on Brown Street to **MACDONALD STREET**, noting on the left four Edwardian terrace houses, some of the last of their type built in Paddington about 1910. At Macdonald continue west c 200m to **Cutler Footway**, and walk down towards Campbell Avenue, getting a remarkable 'backyard' view of terrace house chimneys, parapets, and rooftops.

On the corner of Campbell and Hopewell Streets note a **Paddington corner shop**, exemplary of the establishments that were so essential in Paddington's early 'commuter suburb' days. The second-storey balcony would have originally been part of the shopkeeper's living quarters.

Continue to Glenmore Road, turn right (south) to Gipps Street, turn left at the **Rose and Crown**, a traditional Victorian hotel. At Gipps and Prospect Streets are Paddington's earliest cottages, sandstone single-storey buildings from the 1840s. These would have been constructed for the stonemasons and carpenters working on the nearby Victoria Barracks.

Meander north again to Glenmore Road, past the **Royal Hospital for Women** and continue east to **FIVEWAYS**, Paddington's major intersection. The hospital served as the main hospital for women for 100 years, until it was closed in 1997 and moved to the outer suburbs. At Fiveways is the **Royal Hotel**, a beautiful corner hotel from the 1880s, complete with ironwork balconies and decorative moulding. At this point, you can continue northeast down Gurner Street to **CASCADE STREET** (c 300m), admiring the harbour views and fine terrace houses. (At the corner of Windsor and Cascade Streets is **'Warwick'**, a castellated wonder built in 1860 in what is affectionately referred to as 'King Arthur' style.) Alternatively, continue south on Heeley Street from Glenmore Road and return to Oxford Street and its many alluring shops.

From Cascade Street (the original stream for Cooper's distillery was located here), turn right (south) to Paddington Street, then left (east) past Victorian and Edwardian terraces, many of which are now art galleries and boutiques. Some of these terrace houses are as little as 4.5m (15ft) wide. At Elizabeth Street, turn right (south) and return to Oxford Street. Proceed left (southeast) down Oxford Street c 300m to **St Matthias Anglican Church**, a Gothic Revival church designed in 1859 by Edward Bell that long served as the Victoria Barracks' garrison church.

Paddington Markets

Proceed back up Oxford Street (northwest) to Newcombe Street, where the **Paddington Markets** take place every weekend, with some 250 stalls selling clothing, books, antiques, jewellery and great take-away food. It is one of the oldest Sydney open-air merchandise markets, and quite beloved by locals.

Kings Cross area

At Queen Street, Paddington merges into the suburb of **Woollahra**, a very upscale neighbourhood marking the beginning of the exclusive eastern suburbs. QUEEN STREET itself is filled with genuine antique shops, exclusive galleries, and fashionable boutiques.

From Queen Street, you can connect with Edgecliff Road, which leads into OLD SOUTH HEAD ROAD, the route across the eastern suburbs to Vaucluse and Watsons Bay. Alternatively take Old South Head Road along the Royal Sydney Golf Course to Newcastle Street, and connect with New South Head Road to travel to Watsons Bay on the 'bays side' of the harbour.

From the city, the main bus route from Circular Quay along New South Road to Watsons Bay is **no. 324**, with connections to **no. 325**; a **ferry** also leaves Wharf 4 that stops at Darling Point, Double Bay, Rose Bay and Watsons Bay.

Kings Cross

At the top of WILLIAM STREET, where DARLINGHURST ROAD, Victoria Street and Bayswater Road intersect, is Kings Cross. Named **Queen's Cross** in 1897 in honour of Queen Victoria's Diamond Jubilee, it was renamed when Edward VII took the throne in 1904. Touted rather proudly as Sydney's **red-light district**, it will appear rather tame to most seasoned travellers.

'The Cross' has been the centre of bohemian Sydney since the beginning of the century, and it was the home of many authors, actors and writers, including the poet Dame Mary Gilmore, now on the $10 note, and Kenneth Slessor, who in 1965 wrote *Life at the Cross*. London-based film producer Robin Dalton, née Eakin, has written a delightful account of growing up in the genteel era of 'the Cross' surrounded by eccentric Jewish relatives in *Aunts Up the Cross* (1965, 1997).

Dulcie Deamer, 'Queen of Bohemia' in the 1920s, wrote of its 'impulse towards Lawsonian mateyness [referring to poet Henry Lawson's famous larrikinism], but rather more sophisticated'. By 1946, the writer George Johnson, who lived here with his wife, author Charmian Clift, described it as 'a coarse, tougher city, poised on the edge of violence. A cocky, callous place'.

It gained its sleaziest reputation after the invasion by American troops on leave during the Second World War and especially those on 'R and R' (rest and recreation) during the Vietnam War. At night the area does fill with street life, taking in strip shows, nightclubs, and many fine restaurants, and drug dealers are apparent. In the daytime, however, it appears as a pleasant village, with cheap tourist hotels and backpacker hostels, good coffee shops, and even some interesting architecture on the side streets.

At the end of the Darlinghurst Road strip in **Fitzroy Gardens** is **El Alamein Fountain**. Installed in 1961 as a memorial to the Australian soldiers who fought in North Africa during the Second World War, the design of the fountain has prompted such nicknames as the Dandelion Fountain or, more rudely, the 'elephant douche'. The fountain's designer was Robert Woodward, who was also responsible for The Tidal Cascades fountain in front of the Convention Centre at Darling Harbour.

At Fitzroy Gardens, Darlinghurst Road becomes MACLEAY STREET, which leads into **Potts Point** and **Elizabeth Bay**, an area recently rated in the *Sydney Morning Herald* as containing one of the most pleasing streetscapes in the city, especially the stretch from Macleay Street to St Neot Avenue. This was originally the land grant of that remarkable scientist and politician Alexander Macleay. Indeed, here are three of the best remaining Georgian Regency houses by John Verge.

> ### John Verge
> John Verge (1782–1861) came from a family of Hampshire stonemasons and worked in London as a builder during the Regency period. In 1828 he left his wife to settle in Australia, bringing along sheep and salt to sell; he was given a large land grant on the Williams River. His agricultural pursuits failed, and he returned to Sydney to set up as an architect. Along with many shops and dwellings in the city, now destroyed, Verge designed mansions for the city's wealthiest landowners. His graceful renderings of Greek Revival and Regency ideas, and his attention to elegant interior details make his works the most beautiful of Colonial architectural monuments.

At Macleay and Manning Streets is Verge's **Tusculum**, now administered by the New South Wales Chapter of the Royal Australian Institute of Architects. Built as an investment property for the banker Alexander Brodie Spark (Verge also designed Spark's mansion Tempe), the first tenant was the Bishop of Australia, William Grant Broughton, who lived here from 1836 to 1851. Later owners, after Spark's bankruptcy, included Sir William Manning, Lord Mayor of Sydney. The building is of stuccoed brick and includes a colonnaded two-storey verandah on three sides, added in 1870. Fittings include cedar from Lebanon and marble from Tusculum in Italy. Its history is a typical one: a private residence until 1927, it then went through several institutional hands, falling eventually into total dereliction until it was taken over by the state government in 1983.

Further down Macleay Street at Rockwall Crescent (c 200m) is **Rockwall**, designed by Verge in 1830 for John Busby, engineer of 'Busby's Bore', Sydney's source of water. Over the years, quite glaring alterations were made, and it was in great disrepair when the site was purchased by an Asian company for a shopping complex. They were required to repair the villa as part of the agreement for purchase.

Elizabeth Bay House
At Onslow Avenue, across Macleay Street, is the most stunning of the area's 19C mansions, **Elizabeth Bay House** (☎ 02 9356 3022, open Tues–Sun 10.00–16.30). Described at the time of its construction as 'the finest house in the Colony', Elizabeth Bay House was designed in 1838 by John Verge for Colonial Secretary and renowned scientist Alexander Macleay and his large family. Fortunately for posterity, one of John Macarthur's granddaughters married a grandson of Macleay; the house thus remained in the family which owned the other great Verge masterpiece, Camden Park.

Now a property of the Historic Houses Trust, the house's crowning glory is its stair hall, with a cantilevered winding staircase and domed oval ceiling. The rooms are superbly restored with Regency period furniture (1835–50). Understandably, for one so interested in science and botany, Macleay's original property of 23 ha (56 acres) included magnificent gardens of rare and native plants which stretched to the harbour's edge; the grounds were the talk of colonial society. Unbelievably, the house itself was subdivided into flats during the 1940s; the artist Donald Friend lived in what was the morning room, and from here watched in 1942 the Japanese torpedo bombing of the ferry *Kuttabul*. The house fortunately came into the hands of the Historic Houses Trust in the 1970s, and was opened to the public in 1977. Along with providing regular tours, the Historic Houses Trust also mounts occasional exhibitions here on architectural themes.

The novelist C.J. Koch, who lived in Elizabeth Bay in the 1950s, described its scenery in *The Doubleman* (1985) as 'inviting as a dream of pre-war Hollywood, from which it took its style, with its white Spanish villas, gardens on the harbour, and apartment towers'. Koch may have been referring here to apartment build-ings such as **Del Rio**, on Billyard Avenue just across the road from Elizabeth Bay House. Built in the 1910s, the building demonstrates the influence of Spanish Mission style architecture that had by this time filtered over from California.

Eastern suburbs

Returning to Kings Cross Road, continue east c 1.5km, when the road becomes NEW SOUTH HEAD ROAD at Darling Point. At this point, take New Beach Road north around **Rushcutters Bay Park** to the **Cruising Yacht Club**, where the magnificent sailing boats that participate in the Boxing Day Sydney-to-Hobart Race converge before the start at 13.00.

To the south side of New South Head Road at Glenmore Road and Alma Street, nominally in Rushcutters Bay Park and Paddington, is the famous **'White City'**, the city's beloved monument to Australia's golden era of tennis. Founded in the 1920s on the site of an amusement park, the courts now have grass courts next to Ace Rebound ones. White City's greatest moment of glory was the 1954 final of the Davis Cup between Australia and the United States, when some 25,578 spectators showed up to cram the stands of the centre court; the US players Victor Seixas and Anthony Trabert defeated the Australians Lew Hoad and Ken Rosewall. The Garden Enclosure, the second 'stadium' court seating 1500, is considered by many to be the best place to watch tournament play in Australia.

Back on New South Head Road heading east, you now enter the Eastern suburbs, or in typical Sydney real-estate talk, 'the status suburbs'.

At **Darling Point**, take a detour by turning left (north) onto Darling Point Road, passing **Ashcam Girls School**, traditionally the most exclusive girls' school in the city. At the end of the road is **McKell Park**, a lovely spot directly on the harbour; a small pier makes it possible to reach the water and take a swim if feeling daring.

Immediately above the park you can glimpse **'Lindesay'**, 1 Carthona Avenue, a Gothic Revival mansion built in 1834 and home of many famous figures of the colonial era. The house's design is attributed to Edward Hallen and James Hume, with sympathetic additions in the 1910s by Robertson and Marks. Owned by the National Trust, the house is currently available only for special events.

One of the most delightful views of this urbane neighbourhood and out to the harbour and beyond can be had by returning on Darling Point Road to

Marathon Avenue; walk down the beautiful Marathon Steps all the way to Double Bay itself.

Return to New South Head Road, and drive past **Double Bay**, **Point Piper**, and **Rose Bay**, the most upmarket neighbourhoods for shopping and dining; properties here are among the most valuable in Sydney (and that makes them very valuable indeed), and many elegant historic mansions can be glimpsed on the side streets. Rose Bay was also the site of Sydney's first airport, and seaplanes still land here regularly.

The **Royal Sydney Golf Course** is also located on Rose Bay, in what was a scallop-shaped swamp. The club first played at Concord in the western suburbs, then moved to the dunes and scrubland at Bondi in what had been mixed pasturage between Ben Buckler Fort and the Ostridge Farm on South Head. These moves all occurred between founding in 1893 and the building of the current clubhouse just after the turn of the century, giving an indication of the contemporary nature of Sydney's social establishment.

Vaucluse

Continue on New South Head Road, to reach Vaucluse, c 3km. **Vaucluse House** (☎ 02 9388 7922; open Tues–Sun 10.00–16.30) is the largest property administered by the Historic Houses Trust.

> Vaucluse was first built and named by Sir Henry Brown Hayes (1762–1832), an eccentric Irish 'Gentleman Convict' transported for kidnapping an heiress and subsequently involved in all kinds of mayhem and political intrigue. He named it Vaucluse because it reminded him of Fontaine-de-Vaucluse in France. He bought 100 acres on this site in 1803 for £100, and built a stone cottage. In the belief that Irish soil would deter snakes, Hayes imported barrels of it and had a trench dug around the house by convicts, in which the soil was placed. His original cottage provided the walls of the living room for present Vaucluse, so in part this structure is the oldest house in Sydney.
>
> The house was acquired by the notorious John Piper in 1822, he who made and lost a fortune through the Sydney rum trade and other activities. Piper sold it in 1827 to William Charles Wentworth (1790–1872, see box, p 151), a remarkable man and important early figure in Australian history.

The house and grounds are extraordinarily well done, presented as a 'living house' rather than a museum. Some of the furniture is original, dating from the 1840s, and donated by the Wentworth family, who remain an eminent Sydney name. The house is impressive in its rusticated 'Georgian Romantic' style. It includes one of the best verandahs in Australia. Especially fine are the meticulously restored wallpapers and floor coverings.

Immediately west of Vaucluse House is **Nielsen Park**, originally part of Wentworth's estate and now part of the Sydney Harbour National Park (☎ 02 9977 6522). The park is frequently voted the most popular beach and picnic spot in Sydney. The views are spectacular, the swimming tranquil, and you can picnic in the shade of trees—a rarity at Sydney beaches. In the middle is **Greycliffe House**, built in the 1840s by Wentworth as a wedding present for his daughter. The house was gutted by fire in the 1890s, and has been completely restored. It now serves as a national park information centre.

William Charles Wentworth

William Charles Wentworth was the son of D'Arcy Wentworth (1764–1827), Assistant Surgeon with the Second Fleet and Catherine Crawley, a convict on the ship transported for stealing clothes. Wentworth, always filled with bitterness at the scorning of his father by Sydney 'society', determined to become a significant and prosperous pillar of society. A solicitor and statesman, he married Sarah Cox, herself the child of two convicts. Despite this 'mismatch', they were apparently quite happy and had ten children on whom he doted. Wentworth was with the first group to cross the Blue Mountains in 1813 and was instrumental in the establishment of New South Wales self-government in 1854; he is often referred to as the 'Father of the Constitution'.

Wentworth lived at Vaucluse from 1827 to 1853, and in brief periods thereafter. Upon his death in 1872, the house was inherited by his wife and children, but had several other tenants. The house fell into disrepair until it was taken over by the New South Wales government in 1910.

Watsons Bay

Drive or take **bus no 324** or **325** from Circular Quay, **no. 387** from Bondi Junction to Watsons Bay. The bay is named after Robert Watson, who came as quartermaster of the *Sirius* with the First Fleet, and was harbour master in 1811. Along the way, on Old South Head Road, is **St Peter's Church of England**, designed by Edmund Blacket, completed in 1864. The church houses an organ, which, according to a plaque on the church, purportedly belonged to Napoleon, and was built by Robert and William Grey in London 1796.

Watsons Bay has always been a fishing harbour, as well as a base for pilot boats, which it still is. It is also the home of the original **Doyle's Restaurant**, a seafood restaurant, established over 100 years ago and situated directly on the water with a stunning view of the harbour and city skyline. The walk around the town gives evidence of its earlier origins in the many small cottages which are now, of course, entirely gentrified and outrageously valuable on the real estate market.

Walk along the beach to reach the small stretch of sand called **Camp Cove**. This was where Captain Phillip first stopped with the First Fleet on 21 January 1788 before landing at Sydney Cove; a marker commemorates the fact. However, because the land was swampy, they went on to Port Jackson.

A walk along the cliffs, part of the **Sydney Harbour National Park**, leads past Lady Bay with **Lady Jane Beach** below, one of two or three official nude beaches (today largely gay), and on to the South Head and **Hornby Lighthouse**.

The lighthouse was completed in 1858 after the tragic wreck of the *Dunbar* (see below). The lighthouse is named after Sir Phipps Hornby, Commander in Chief of the British Pacific Fleet at that time. Evident around the point, along with stupendous views of the harbour entrance (it is a great place for watching sailboat racing), are several old fortifications spanning the 1870s to the Second World War.

Further along from the lighthouse is the **Gap Park**, where 50m cliffs have made it the traditional site for suicide jumps. Nearby is a monument to the wreck of the *Dunbar*, an immigrant ship which crashed onto the rocks here on 20 August 1857, with all but one of the 122 passengers lost; a remarkable photo of

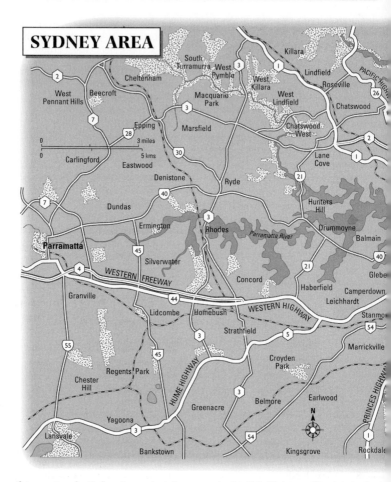

SYDNEY AREA

this survivor by Sydney's greatest daguerreotypist, T.S. Glaister, still exists in the Mitchell Library collection.

Along the descending path in the Gap Park you find the anchor of the *Dunbar*, set in concrete as a monument. At the southern end of the park is a dangerous break in the cliffs called Jacob's Ladder, whence the Dunbar survivor was hauled to safety. From here you can keep walking along the cliffs c 300m to the **Signal Station**, built in 1848, on the site, Dunbar Head, where a flagstaff had been manned since 1790. Whenever a ship was sighted, a flag was raised to warn the colony. Another 300m south along the cliffs brings you to **Macquarie Lighthouse**, an 1883 replica (by James Barnet) of the colony's first lighthouse, built in 1818 by Francis Greenway. Legend has it that Governor Macquarie was so pleased with Greenway's 'noble magnificent edifice' that upon seeing it for the first time, he granted Greenway his pardon on the spot. Robert Watson, for whom Watsons Bay is named, was the first lightkeeper. From the Lighthouse

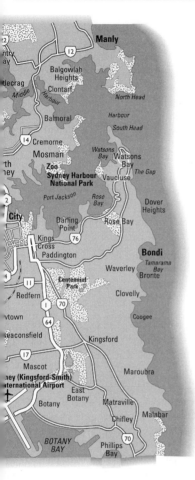

Reserve, it is possible to catch **bus no. 324** back into central Sydney.

Bondi to Bronte

While no train currently reaches Bondi, plans are afoot to extend the links to the beach, but are vigorously opposed by some locals; the well-known bus lines from the city are **nos 380, 382, 389**, and **321**.

A right turn (south) on Ocean Street to Oxford/Einfeld Drive, which becomes Bondi Road, leads to Sydney's most famous beach, **Bondi** (pronounced BOND-eye; purported to mean in Aboriginal 'water breaking over the rocks'). From the central business district (CBD), a most popular drive is the **'Bays to Bondi'**, taking New South Head Road through Double Bay, Rose Bay, and Watsons Bay, then back turning on Old South Head Road to Military Road, through Dover Heights and into Bondi.

Sydney is justly known for its many accessible beaches, and despite the fact that Bondi is no longer the cleanest or most inviting among the many along the shoreline, it is still worth a visit. Here you will find that most Australian of institutions, the **Bondi Lifesaving Association**, as well as the **Bondi Icebergs**, a group of older stalwarts who swim daily, even in winter. Also of interest are the **Esplanade** and **Bondi Pavilion**, where jazz concerts and exhibitions entertain the throngs of sunbathers. The cafes and bars on the streets near the beach have now become a real haven for the trendy and cosmopolitan, especially for breakfasts and brunches. During Christmas/New Year's holidays, the beach and surrounding pubs swarm with foreign tourists, celebrating the warmth of the season. Recent outbreaks of violence and pandemonium have made the New Year's event less enjoyable of late, with police crackdowns on rowdiness and drunken behaviour. Visitors are advised to investigate the current situation and alcohol regulations before venturing forth.

Waverley

Bondi is in the municipality of **Waverley**, which itself contains several locations of historical interest. The name itself comes from the area's first (now demolished) estate, so named by the original landowner Barnett Levey. Levey was the colony's first theatrical entrepreneur, operating the Theatre Royal in the 1830s; he named his estate in honour of Sir Walter Scott's novels.

Directly south of Bondi Beach is **Tamarama**, site of a turn-of-the-century **amusement park** mentioned in Ethel Turner's famous *Seven Little Australians* (1894). It is now a patrolled beach, with good surf. Continuing around Tamarama Bay, you come to **Bronte Park**, site (at 470 Bronte Road) of **Bronte House**, one of the colony's oldest surviving homes. Begun in 1836–38 by Colonial Architect Mortimer Lewis as his home, it was soon sold to famous barrister Robert Lowe, who named it Bronte in honour of Admiral Nelson's title (he was named the Duke of Bronte by the king of Naples). The house was originally so isolated it required shuttered windows for protection from bushrangers. Recently the house has been completely restored and is occasionally opened for public viewing by heritage activist and cultural guru Leo Scofield (he has a regular column on things cultural in the *Sydney Morning Herald*, and has run both the Sydney and Melbourne Festivals).

If you continue south on Bronte Road, **Waverley Cemetery** appears on a bluff looking out to the sea. Described in 1973 by Ruth Park as 'ugly as sin', the cemetery has been restored somewhat, and contains the graves of many important figures in the country's history, including the poets Henry Lawson and Henry Kendall; Dorothy Mackellar, author of the poem 'My Country' ('I love a sunburnt country...'); and a monument to US Civil War Veterans. Also buried here are Fannie Durack, first woman Olympic champion in swimming in 1912, and the first to swim the Australian crawl; and Lawrence Hargraves, pioneering aviator.

Manly

An old saying claims that **Manly** is 'seven miles from Sydney and a thousand miles from care'. This beach suburb, located on the inner harbour side of the North Head, is most easily (and happily) reached by ferry, from Wharf 3 (Jet Cat from Wharf 2), Travelling by car involves a tortuous drive through North Sydney and over the Spit Bridge (often closed to traffic as it opens to allow boats through). Manly has a great **Visitor's Centre** on North Steyne, providing information on North Shore walks and tours (☎ 02 9977 0078).

The most famous Sydney beach after Bondi, Manly was named by Governor Phillip, in honour of the local Aborigines: 'their confidence and manly behaviour,' he wrote, 'made me give the name of Manly Cove to the place'. It is a sad irony that one of these same Aborigines, Wil-ee-ma-rin, speared Governor Phillip after a misunderstanding, an event graphically described in Watkin Tench's account of the early colony.

Despite its famed long beach, it may disappoint, as it is a bit polluted and the famous line of Norfolk Pines along the beach wall is dying. But the **ferry trip** from Circular Quay across the harbour to Manly is certainly worth the trip; unless you are in a great hurry, take the old-fashioned ferry rather than the JetCat. The ferry lands in the same place where it has been landing since 1855.

Manly became famous because of its Victorian gentility, and one can almost imagine the old bathing houses. In 1852, English entrepreneur Henry Gilbert Smith envisioned here a resort such as that in Brighton; the location quickly became the elegant, if chaste, place to holiday. Indeed, it was here in 1902 that newspaper editor William Gocher challenged the laws that until that time forbade daylight swimming in New South Wales; he won, and Sydneysiders have been swimming ever since.

Along the **Corso** at Manly, where the ferry and Jet Cat dock, is a small **aquarium**, quite fun for children, as well as the **Datillo Rubbo Art Gallery and Museum** (it is usually called simply Manly Art Gallery and Museum).

Rubbo (1871–1955) was an Italian artist who arrived in Sydney in 1897; he was an influential teacher of new art methods for decades, introducing Australian artists to Post-Impressionism. The museum contains works by him and some of his students, as well as small exhibitions on cultural history, such as the development of the bathing costume and other events in Manly's history.

Balmain

Take the **ferry from Bay 5** (Circular Quay) to **Balmain**; this is by far the most appropriate way to visit this harbourside suburb, which is about 2km west of the centre of the city. Comprehensive walking tours are available through the Balmain Association at the **Watch House**, 179 Darling Street (☎ 02 9818 4954), and in such publications as Joan Lawrence's *Exploring the Suburbs* series.

No Sydney suburb has experienced as profound a demographic transforma-tion in the last few decades as Balmain. The suburb derives its name from William Balmain, surgeon of the First Fleet who was granted the land in 1800. Long the centre of marine industry, Balmain was traditionally the home of sea-captains, as well as a distinctively 'larrikin' working class. Now its crooked streets and cramped little houses, as well as its ostentatious homes, have become gentrified, many of them owned by well-known artists and writers. For many years, Peter Carey, author of *Oscar and Lucinda* (much of which is set in Balmain), lived here, as did the playwright David Williamson.

The most poignant indication of this gentrified change is that in 1994, the **Balmain Rugby League team**, once the pride of the suburb's dockies and wharfies, moved to Parramatta (it has since returned to its old home at Leichardt Oval). Balmain High School, which had historically produced several of the game's scrappiest and most revered players, could no longer man a team.

Neville Wran, Premier in the 1980s and the quintessential Balmain Boy, made a famous remark in a case concerning the Rugby League chairman, Kevin Humphreys: 'Balmain boys don't cry. We're too vulgar and too common for that and probably vote Labor anyway.' The New South Wales Labor Electoral League, forerunner of today's Australian Labor Party, was founded here in 1891. Sydney policemen, who traditionally came from Balmain, were purported to say 'there are only two kinds of people—those born in Balmain and those who wish they were'. The loyalty of Balmain locals is evident in the naming of the suburb's swimming pool near Elkington Park after Balmain girl and swimming great Dawn Fraser, whose larrikin behaviour endeared her to the hearts of her hometown fans.

With its long history of mercantile development, shipbuilding, and cheek-by-jowl living, the area has numerous sites of architectural and cultural interest, the most remarkable being its amazing variety of domestic dwellings. The best way to arrive at the suburb is, predictably, by sea; the ferry to Balmain goes under the Harbour Bridge, past **Ball's Head** and **Goat Island**; it then lands at **Darling Street Wharf**, the base of the main street.

Ferry wharf, Balmain

Immediately to the right of the landing is **Thornton Park**, once owned by the Russell family, foundry owners; the expatriate painter and friend of Van Gogh John Peter Russell (1858–1930) owed his fortune to the family's business.

At 12 Darling Street is **Waterman's Cottage**. Built in 1841 by John Cavill, it was home from 1880 to 1907 of the waterman Henry McKenzie who rowed passengers after ferry hours to Miller's Point.

The entire street, as well as the closest side streets, contain stone cottages and Victorian terrace houses built between the 1840s and 1900.

At Darling and Duke Streets is **St Mary's Anglican Church**, the first Anglican church in Balmain. It was also one of Edmund Blacket's first buildings, begun in 1845; Blacket himself lived in Balmain, at 393 Darling Street, at the end of his life. While the original minister, a Mr Wilkinson, wanted a Norman church, Blacket, predictably, based his design on 13C Gothic.

Turn north (right) at THE AVENUE and walk down to **Mort Bay**. Named for the great wool magnate and Balmain resident, Thomas Sutcliffe Mort, the bay was the site of some of the earliest docks, and also the most militant workers' strikes of the 19C.

Return to Darling Street, and proceed to Ewenton Street, on the south. At no. 6 is **Ewenton** house. Begun in 1854 by Robert Blake, it was consequently named Blake Vale. In 1856 the house was bought by Major Ewen Wallace Cameron, a partner of Thomas Sutcliffe Mort. Cameron added an extra storey, a porch, and, in 1872, an additional wing with views of Sydney; at this time, it acquired its name of Ewenton. Despite numerous vicissitudes and threats of demolition, the property survived and was tastefully restored in the 1990s. The many additions to the original structure make it a showcase of various eclectic styles, not always harmoniously coordinated.

Return to Darling Street and proceed to no. 179. This is the **Watch House**, built in 1854 by Edmund Blacket. The structure served as the suburb's **police headquarters** until 1887, after which time it fell into disrepair. It narrowly escaped demolition in the 1950s, but managed to be salvaged by the Balmain

Association in 1970, which is now using it as their headquarters. It is rumoured to be haunted.

Balmain Market

St Andrew's Congregational Church at the corner of Darling and Curtis Road, is a Gothic Revival sandstone church built in 1855, reminiscent of an English village church. On Saturdays, the church's yard is the location of the **Balmain Market**, considered by many to be the best market in the city, specialising in antiques, arts and crafts and jewellery. Further along Darling Street are the remains of the many famed pubs of the suburb (in the 1880s, there were 41 pubs, or one for every 360 Balmain citizens). Local historian Kath Hamey organises 'pub crawl' tours, as well as more historic walks around Balmain; ☎ 02 9818 4954.

Hunter's Hill

Take the **ferry from Bay 5** Circular Quay to Hunter's Hill. **Hunter's Hill Peninsula** lies across the harbour to the northwest of Balmain. The Aborigines called it **'Moocooboola'**, or 'meeting of the waters' (note: many translations of Aboriginal names may be viewed with some scepticism, since many of the true meanings have been lost; the majority of them seem to be translated as having something to do with water, when it is just as likely that they originally meant 'white man, go away!').

First settled in the 1830s, the peninsula is one of the few on the harbour that runs west to east. Mary Reibey (see p 130) settled here near the present-day Fig Tree Bridge, living in a house with sheet-iron shutters to protect against bushranger attacks. In 1838, the artist and writer Joseph Fowles, who wrote the invaluable illustrated history *Sydney in 1848*, leased this property.

In 1847, this undesirable area was transformed when two wealthy French brothers, Jules and Didier Joubert, purchased land here. Dubbed 'the first large-scale speculative builders in Sydney' by writer Ruth Park, the Joubert brothers began in 1848 the first of 200 elegant stone houses, complete with European tiles and fittings and finished by French and Italian masons. By 1860, the Jouberts operated a ferry, and when the municipality was incorporated in 1861, Jules was the first chairman of council; Didier became mayor in 1867.

In recent times, Hunter's Hill has been the residence of many authors and playwrights. Author Kylie Tennant lived here for twenty years, and her novel *Tantavallon* (1983) alludes to the peninsula in her descriptions of the fictitious 'Balm Point'.

The remaining houses and streetscapes offer charming sights for strollers. Many of the original stone cottages appear surprisingly French on narrow streets with lovely gardens. Of special interest are **Passy**, off Passy Avenue, built by Joubert in 1854 for the French Consul and later occupied by Sir George Dibbs, Premier of New South Wales; the **Garibaldi Inn**, on Alexandra Street, built in 1861 by the same Italians who built many of the neighbouring stone cottages; and **Carey Cottage**, 18 Ferry Street. On Yerton Street is the only survivor of four

German prefabricated houses brought from Hamburg in 1854, and assembled by German workers. Also of note are the 1866 **Town Hall** at Alexandra and Ellsmere Street, which houses an historical museum, and **Vienna Cottage**, built in 1871 and now a National Trust property open to the public (open on the second and fourth Sunday of each month). Detailed brochures for walking tours are available from the Town Hall museum.

Glebe and the southern suburbs

South of Darling Harbour and west of Central Railway Station at the point where Broadway turns into Parramatta Road is the historic neighbourhood of Glebe. The University of Sydney is immediately south of Glebe on Parramatta Road. Glebe can be reached from central Sydney on **bus nos 431** and **433**.

The word 'glebe' traditionally referred to land given to the church and its officials. Sydney's Glebe was the area allotted by Governor Phillip to the colony's first chaplain, Richard Johnson; a piece was also laid out for a schoolmaster, although none existed at the time of the First Fleet. By 1828, this land was subdivided into estates by the Anglican diocese to raise money for the church, and prosperous merchants began to build substantial residences on the most elevated sites to avoid the noxious odours of nearby Blackwattle Bay. Edmund Blacket lived here as early as the 1850s, when the area was still remote enough to be the haunt of bushrangers in the thick forests. By the 1890s the suburb had been further developed to accommodate growing numbers of immigrants; thus, the plethora of Victorian rowhouses, with minuscule gardens, tile-work, and stained-glass windows.

The suburb's ethnic diversity dates from this period, although now gentrification is again transforming this colourful mix. Old Glebe nearly fell entirely to the wrecking ball in the 1960s, when it was planned to extend the expressway through the district. Fortunately, preservation efforts were successful and in 1976, with the support of Premier Neville Wran's Labor Government, the entire suburb was declared a conservation area by the National Trust and National Estate.

GLEBE POINT ROAD is now filled with trendy restaurants, health food stores, and excellent **bookshops** catering to the nearby university crowd. Weekends bring a colourful **market** to the yard of the **Glebe Point School**, Glebe Point Road at Derby Street, which rivals the more famous one at Paddington.

One example of the district's cultural diversity is the presence here, off Victoria Road on Edward Street, of the **Sze Yup Temple**, a Chinese joss house. Glebe was an early residence of the Chinese vegetable gardeners who arrived in Sydney as early as the 1840s. It is estimated that half of the city's market gardeners before the 1940s were Chinese, many of whom had been in Australia for generations. The current temple dates only from 1955, but replaced a joss house that had been on the same site since 1893. The temple is still actively attended, and visitors are able to view its incense-filled interior.

At the intersection of Glebe Point Road and Parramatta Road is a **monument to Dave Sands**, Aboriginal boxer of the 1940s, who was killed in a car crash in 1952.

Along Glebe Point Road and on the side streets, especially Toxteth and Avenue

Roads and Allen Street, are lovely examples of Victorian cottages with cast-iron lacework and decorative plaques using native species as motifs.

At the corner of Avenue and Victoria Roads is **St Scholastica's College**, the main building of which was **Toxteth House**, built by John Verge 1829–31 for George Allen, the first Australian-trained solicitor. Toxteth refers to the home in England of the Allens' benefactor, Sir Robert Wigram. An elegant Regency stone house, a third storey of Italianate style was added in 1877–81 by architect George Mansfield for Allen's son, George Wigram Allen, also a prominent civic leader. The home was purchased in 1904 by the Roman Catholic Church.

The grounds of the original Toxteth estate, which included a cricket ground and acres of orchards, extended to the area now occupied by the **Harold Park Raceway**; at Avenue and Arcadia Streets, turn right into Arcadia, then left at Maxwell to see the Raceway. Named after Childe Harold—not Byron's hero, but a famous American racehorse—it has had a trotting course since 1902 and a greyhound track since 1927.

Walk back to Toxteth Road, turn left, noting the iron work and decorative plaster of the terrace houses; at The Avenue is **The Lodge**, originally the gate-keeper's house for the Toxteth Estate. It was built in a Gothic Revival style in 1877 by George Mansfield, who subsequently lived here. Note the asymmetrical house at no. 27 Mansfield, with wooden verandah and stone and iron fence.

From Mansfield Street, walk to Wigram Road, turn left (north) and return to Glebe Point Road; turn right (south) and proceed to Hereford Street. The street is named for the original **Hereford House**, an elegant early mansion that stood at the corner of Glebe Point Road and Bridge Road; it was demolished in the 1960s. At no. 53 is another Hereford House, built in 1874, and now part of the New South Wales College of Nursing. Glebe's most famous son, tennis star Lew Hoad, learned to play on the now demolished courts behind this building.

'Kerribee', no. 55, built 1889 by James Fitzpatrick, is one of the last of the large houses on impressive grounds built in the Glebe.

Proceed south to Bridge Street, turning east past Glebe Point Road to Bridge Street (c 600m) to reach **'Lyndhurst'** at 61 Darghan Street. Along with Toxeth, which has been extensively altered, this is the only surviving Regency building in Glebe, built at the centre of Lyndhurst Estate in 1833–36 by John Verge. The owner was John Bowman, John Macarthur's son-in-law and Prin-cipal Surgeon at Sydney Hospital. Overlooking Blackwattle Bay and with lavish fittings, the home's design greatly resembled Verge's work at Camden Park for the Macarthur family. By 1842, financial hardship forced the Bowmans to leave Lyndhurst, and it passed through several hands. In the 1850s and 1860s it housed St Mary's College; run by English Benedictines, the school was renowned for its rigorous classical education. By 1877, the school had lost favour, and the college was closed, the land subdivided and the estate sold. At this time, its verandah and additional wings were demolished. After serving various functions, from a lying-in hospital to a laundry and broom factory, the house was by the 1970s nearly declared uninhabitable. A campaign spear-headed by the National Trust and supported by Premier Wran saved the building, which has now been fully restored to its original form. It serves as the headquarters of the **Historic Houses Trust of New South Wales** (☎ 02 9692 8366, open Mon–Fri 09.00–17.00; no tours), and includes a resource centre for the conservation of historic houses. In many ways, this house is the most enjoyable reminder of Verge's great designs.

University of Sydney

At the beginning of Glebe Point Road and across Broadway to the south are the gates to the grounds of the **University of Sydney** (☎ 02 9351 2222). Founded in 1850 and opened in 1852, it is Australia's oldest university; today it boasts some 30,000 students. The older buildings of the main quadrangle, designed by Edmund Blacket and completed in 1857, certainly mimic Victorian Gothic 'Oxbridge' style, while the additional structures over the years have created a mishmash of institutional architecture. The Chancellor's Committee souvenir shop under the clock-tower is manned by volunteer guides who can answer questions and provide a free map of the campus (☎ 02 9351 4002).

Of interest on campus are the **Nicholson Museum** and the **Macleay Museum** (☎ 02 9351 2274). The Nicholson contains archaeological artefacts collected by the university faculty on digs all over the world. These include the Jericho Head, a rare skull from Joshua; Egyptian sculpture; and glass and sculpture from Roman times.

The Macleay is a biological collection displayed in cluttered profusion in a delightful 19C room with cast-iron stairs and arches. The museum includes a stuffed example of a Tasmanian tiger and the best collection of foreign insects in Australia. Its Aboriginal bark paintings are believed to be the oldest known specimens, and its collection of photographs of pioneer Australia numbers 700,000.

In Clive James's *Unreliable Memoirs*, he describes his days at Sydney University in the late 1950s: 'the place where all the half-worlds met was the Royal George Hotel, down in Pyrmont. The Royal George was the headquarters of the **Downtown Push**, usually known as just the Push. The Push was composed of several different elements. The most prominent component was, or were, the Libertarians—a university free-thought society consisting mainly of people who, like the aesthetes, failed Arts I on a career basis, but in this case as a form of political protest against the state...Here was Bohemia.' The Push also included Germaine Greer and Margaret Fink.

Newtown

To the southwest of the campus, on the other side of MISSENDEN ROAD (the site of The Royal Prince Alfred and King George V Hospitals), is **Camperdown** and **Newtown**, two of the oldest inner-city suburbs and still filled with tiny 19C rowhouses now eagerly gobbled up by gentrifying buyers. In the middle of the district, at Church Street, is **St Stephen's Church** and cemetery. Designed and built by Blacket in 1871–74, the church is an excellent example of Gothic Revival style, and the cemetery contains the graves of some of Sydney's earliest settlers.

Immediately south of the church is KING STREET, a bustling and grimy thoroughfare serving the nearby university community, as well as a decidedly multicultural and gay population. An enormous number of good, inexpensive restaurants of all ethnic stripes line the street, along with great bookstores and second-hand shops. Continuing west, King Street turns into Enmore Road, then into Stanmore Road, and finally Canterbury Road, which leads to the western suburbs and also the M5 Tollway to Canberra. On ENMORE ROAD, just off King

Street, is the **Enmore Theatre**, a good venue for new plays, musicals and alternative comedy shows.

Despite the congestion which often makes for slow going, Enmore to Stanmore Road is a fantastic reminder of Sydney's ethnic diversity. One sees—along with one of Sydney's most exclusive schools, **Newington College**—Portuguese butchers, Lebanese funeral parlours, Korean furniture stores, and even a Greek doctors' roller-skating rink! You pass through **Marrickville**, the suburb most affected by the aeroplane noise from Sydney Airport's new runway. The neighbourhood has coalesced into massive demonstrations to force the government to do something about the situation; at the time of writing, some compensation has been considered, but nothing substantive has yet been accomplished.

Redfern

To the south of King Street is the suburb of **Redfern**, locally considered one of Sydney's roughest neighbourhoods, primarily because the city's largest population of Aborigines live here in neglected poverty. As a centre for the Aboriginal community, Redfern houses some excellent Aboriginal community centres and performance venues. In the 1960s the dispersed Aboriginal people living in urban centres of New South Wales and Victoria began calling themselves 'Koori', a term meaning 'people' in a number of related languages in the area. ('Murri' is the equivalent word in Queensland, 'Nunga' in South Australia and 'Nyungar' in Western Australia.) While anyone with an Aboriginal affiliation can identify themselves as a Koori, a degree of political engagement accompanies the term.

Redfern is also the first train stop out of Central Station, and consequently has a large rail interchange. Immediately south of the Redfern station is the **Eveleigh Railway Workshops**, an enormous 19C complex where trains were built and serviced. Ambitious efforts are now being made by the **Australian Technology Park**, a consortium of university interests along with the National Trust, to conserve a portion of this extraordinary site as a monument to early technology. The US Smithsonian Institution has declared Eveleigh 'the most important historic railway workshops remaining in the world', with its unparalleled collection of 19C equipment and machinery. Sydney photographer David Moore has completed a spectacular photo-essay of the buildings and machinery, instrumental in the drive to preserve this unique piece of Australian history.

Leichhardt and Haberfield

Leichhardt can still be described as an inner-city suburb, although it is off the Parramatta Road that leads to the unending western suburbs. It is the traditional **'Little Italy'** section of town, where Italian migrants first settled and mingled in the 1950s, bringing cappuccino, focaccia and soccer to the city. Leichhardt also refers to the municipality which administers this district of the city, as anyone who saw the fascinating 1996 documentary film, *Rats in the Ranks*, will know.

A visit to Leichhardt must involve food: restaurants, bakeries, and classic Italian cafes. the **Leichhardt Hotel**, on Balmain Road and Short Street, also demonstrates the suburb's new face as a centre for artists, as well as an active lesbian community. It is from here that the Dykes on Bikes take off for their ride in the Gay and Lesbian Mardi Gras each March. The Leichhardt Festival in May is a real old-fashioned block party, when the length of **NORTON STREET** is filled with food stalls and cultural activities.

Some of these suburb communities did not just grow like topsy, but were planned as a whole, and many offer interesting examples of experimentation with planned residential living. **Haberfield** exemplifies this trend. Described by Jan Morris as 'the Sydney suburb *in excelsis*... one of the most truly Sydneyesque places in Sydney', it was created by developer Richard Stanton and architect J. Spencer-Stanfield in the early 1900s as the ideal urban environment. 'Slumless, Lane-less, Pub-less', every house had a bathroom and every home was owned. It is a town of bungalows, most of them designed on 200 acres, by Spencer-Stanfield, in what is known as the 'Federation Style', a reference to their appearance at the time of Australia's Federation in 1901. Morris's description of this style is perfect:

> *It has a touch of Prairieism from the United States, and a hefty dose of Arts and Crafts from England...It is a Queen-Anne-ish Tudory, semi-countrified, sometimes whimsical sort of style, with eaves often, and fancy chimneys, and ornamental ridge cappings, and much woodwork. Stained-glass windows goes well with the Federation style, and tiled floors, and bargeboarding, and a verandah is almost essential.*

Still referred to as the Federation Suburb, it is now largely inhabited by Italian immigrants. Every single house is different, with lots of stained-glass and tiles of Australian natives; there are no back alleys, no slums and still no pubs.

Other good examples of such suburban planning can be seen in **Croydon**, **Burwood**, and elsewhere.

The western suburbs

Sydney is, perhaps more than any other city outside Los Angeles, a city of suburbs. These residential neighbourhoods extend for astonishing distances; the area loosely labelled as 'Sydney' certainly rivals that of Los Angeles in size, covering some 12,500 sq km, twice the size of Beijing and six times the size of Rome. It continues, chock-a-block, in a seemingly unending and for the most part monotonous expanse of small lots with brick and fibro houses in all directions. ('Fibro' is a fibrous-plaster sheeting material much favoured in Australia for quick and inexpensive construction, as was needed in the 1950s housing boom.) **'The West'** encompasses the entire region from about Strathfield all the way to the Blue Mountains, north to Richmond and Windsor, and south as far as Liverpool and Campbelltown. In truth, this *is* Sydney, since 80 per cent of the population lives in these municipalities.

While the planning for the **2000 Olympics** in Homebush includes massive attempts to improve traffic patterns leading to the Games site, travelling on the **Great Western Highway**, which is the Old Parramatta Road, still remains nightmarish at times, crowded and unattractive. One constantly thinks there *must* be a better driving route to take; so far, there isn't, at least not in this direction. Taking the train is probably the best bet as it provides a service all the way to Penrith and on to the Blue Mountains, is quicker and relatively inexpensive. Check at Central Station or the Circular Quay exchange for schedules and ticket prices.

The **Glebe Island Bridge**, opened in December 1995 at a cost of $170 million, is set to become a Sydney landmark. It crosses the mostly industrialised areas of old shipping docks and warehouses, to lead to the Western suburbs through Rozelle, Drummoyne, and over the **Gladesville Bridge** towards Gladesville and Ryde, the real multicultural heart of 'Westie' land. A **'Westie'** is stereotyped as a car-loving larrikin of any of a variety of ethnicities, loyal to the Wests (or Penrith) Rugby League team and prone to playing the 'pokies' and drinking beer at the casino-like RSL (Returned Servicemen's League) Clubs that dot the western landscape. The **Rooty Hill RSL** (☎ 02 9625 5500), in one of the area's least desirable suburbs, is a stunning example of Westie suburban culture: an eight-storey hotel with Las Vegas-style entertainment, near the **Eastern Creek Grand Prix Raceway**, site of regular motor-racing events, and **Australia's Wonderland** amusement park. Take the Rooty Hill Road exit off the M4.

If driving from the city, you can also follow the old route along Parramatta Road. Take George Street to Broadway, which becomes Parramatta Road, now marked as M4, the **Great Western Highway**.

It was possible to walk from Parramatta to Sydney in eight hours along this 25km length of bad road which opened in about 1790. By 1835 the trip took two hours by coach. In the old days, carriages and wagons were required to stop at Brickfield Hill brickworks for a load of broken bricks to fill in potholes along the route from Sydney westward. The ferry service to Parramatta was a week-long round trip. By the end of the 1790s, Parramatta was the real centre of the settlement, while Sydney itself was simply a port with a few governmental buildings. The next section of the road was from Parramatta to the farming area around Windsor and eventually to Wiseman's Ferry across the Hawkesbury River. A public ferry still crosses the Hawkesbury at Wiseman's Ferry (established in the early 1820s) and Peat's Crossing (established in 1844 as part of the infrequently used Sydney-to-Newcastle road); a small ferry also crosses the Berowra at Berowra Waters. The first train out of Sydney went to Parramatta in 1855.

At **Strathfield**, you join the Western Motorway (still M4), which is a real freeway. From Strathfield or Burwood Train Stations, you can at the moment take an Explorer Bus (**nos 401, 402, 403, or 404**) for a tour of the **Homebush Olympic site**.

Homebush

As sports commentators and comedians Roy Slaven and H.G. Nelson are quick to point out, **Homebush** was originally the site of an abattoir in an industrial part of town. Much of the Olympic village is being built near **Bicentennial Park**, initiated in 1988 as a study centre for the area's ecological environment. The Bell Frog has been identified as indigenous to the area, and will no doubt be highlighted in Olympic coverage.

Still, residential areas here were part of the sprawling western suburbs from the beginning of the 1900s. Writer Thomas Keneally, author of *The Chant of Jimmy Blacksmith* (1972) and *Schindler's Ark* (1982) (source for Stephen Spielberg's *Schindler's List*), grew up here and writes about its Roman Catholic insularity, its great remove from cosmopolitan Sydney, in *Homebush Boy: A Memoir* (1995).

Parramatta

About 20km west of the centre of Sydney, **Parramatta** has a population of 140,000. Its **tourist information office** is on the corner of Church and Market Streets, ☎ 02 9630 3703. The spot where the First Fleet finally found arable soil, Parramatta's history goes back to the earliest days of white settlement. While many of the most historical structures have been tragically lost to mindless development, recent efforts have led to the permanent preservation of those few remnants of the colonial days.

By far the most enjoyable and convenient way to reach Parramatta is by taking the **River Cat ferry from Wharf 5** at Circular Quay, a delightful ride up the 'other side' of the Harbour Bridge onto the Parramatta River. The trip takes about an hour to **Parramatta Wharf**. From here, you can take an **Explorer Bus** to visit all the historic sites of the town, or can walk into Parramatta's centre.

You can also take the **train** from Central Station to **Parramatta/Harris Park Station**. From the station, walk south on Station Street, turn left (east) on Bridge Street to Wigram Street; turn left (north) and walk (700m) to Una Street. Turn right (east) and walk (500m) to Experiment Farm Cottage.

If driving on the Western Motorway, exit at James Ruse Drive (route 55); drive past the **Rose Hill Racecourse**, on the site of Rose Hill, where swarms of parrots, subsequently named rosellas, were first seen by colonialists. Turn left at Hassall Street (1.5km), then left on Alfred Street (400m). At Alice Street (300m), turn left to find **Elizabeth Farm** (☎ 02 9635 9488, open Tues–Sun 10.00–16.30).

Elizabeth Farm

Elizabeth Farm was the original homestead of John and Elizabeth Macarthur, established in 1793, although its main period of habitation was in the 1820s–30s. The original site consisted of 250 acres (100 ha), set on the first arable land discovered by the First Fleeters in 1789. Using all his famous manipulative skill, John Macarthur was able to have as many convicts as he wanted sent up to work the land; Greek pirates even arrived to make the first wine in the colony, and later Germans were employed.

The remarkable Elizabeth Macarthur lived here for 50 years, including the period of her husband's exile to England and finally during the years of her husband's madness. Before being sent to his property at Camden Park, he was confined to Elizabeth Farm's library, alienated from his family and convinced of innumerable conspiracies against him.

Miraculously, six acres of the original homestead have survived intact due to the foresight of the purchasers in 1904, William Swann and his family, who lived in the house until 1968. When originally purchased, Swann paid only the price of the land because the house was deemed uninhabitable; it had at one time been used as a glue factory. Fortunately, the Swanns recognised the structure's historical importance.

The buildings were also lucky to survive the wreckers' ball which was so enthusiastically utilised in the 1960s throughout Sydney. When restoration began in the 1970s, the structure itself was remarkably intact, and so provides an excellent example of colonial architectural techniques. Run by the Historic Houses Trust, every attempt has been made at authenticity. The furniture, as an example of the restorers' craft, was reproduced to include the 'mistakes' made

Elizabeth Farm, Parramatta, Sydney

making Macarthur's. One bed, for example, is made with three mattresses: the first of straw, the second of horse-hair, and the top of feathers; as the mercurial John shot 300 wild duck at an outing, they were not without materials. The rooms include kangaroo rugs and lovely oil-cloth floor coverings. Excellent models depict the progressions of the house's development, showing for example that no verandah existed until 1826.

The volunteers and guides who work here are particularly dedicated; the farm even has school groups come to perform 'convict' tasks. A 10-minute video presentation tells the history of the Macarthurs, rightly giving most of the credit for the farm's success to Elizabeth.

The **gardens** include some of Macarthur's original exotic plants, such as olive trees; the banana plants are not original, although bananas were grown from the early days.

The farm is now completely encompassed by the suburban sprawl of multi-cultural Sydney; a wonderful example of this new diversity can be seen immediately across the street on **ALICE STREET**, where there are some extremely garish houses. At the time of writing, most of this neighbourhood appeared to be Lebanese, as is evidenced in **Our Lady of Lebanon Church** also in Alice Street, the church of the Diocese of St Maroun, Lebanese Christian Church.

From Alice Street, follow the road down the hill towards Hassell Street and **Hambledon Cottage** (☎ 9635 6924; open Wed–Thurs, Sat–Sun 11.00–16.00), an easy walk to the flatlands of the Parramatta River. Built in 1824, it was originally occupied by Miss Penelope Lucas, the governess who became Mrs Macarthur's dearest friend and confidant. Described by Ruth Park as a 'charmer', with its lovely courtyard and iron roof, the cottage has been lovingly restored.

Now turn left (west) into Harris Street and left again (south) into Ruse Street, to find at no. 9 **Experiment Farm Cottage** (☎ 02 9635 5655, Tues–Thurs 10.00–16.00, Sun 11.00–16.00). This property is under the auspices of the National Trust. The cottage was restored in the 1970s to emulate the period 1798–1840.

Governor Phillip, impressed by the character of convict James Ruse, provided him the land and some basic implements as an experiment to determine how long it would take a hard-working man to become self-supporting. Remarkably, it took him only about two and a half years to become thoroughly independent; in his account of the early settlement, Watkin Tench meticulously describes Ruse's efforts.

Before moving to a farm in the Hawkesbury river district, Ruse sold the land to surgeon John Harris who in 1798 built the house which is supposed to be the second oldest building in the country. Purchased in 1960 by the Trust for £9000, the restoration focuses not only on the history of the house itself, but on the remarkable story of James Ruse and his agricultural achievements.

City of Parramatta

To explore Parramatta itself will take a whole day. If coming from the centre, take the train from Central Station to Parramatta Station to begin this exploration of the city. A detailed walking guide can be obtained from the **Tourist Bureau** on the corner of Macquarie Street and Church Street Mall.

From Harris Street at Experimental Farm Cottage (described above) walk north c 100m to Macquarie Street and turn left (west). At Smith Street, turn left (south) c 100m to **Lancer Barracks**, across from the train station, a Macquarie-era building still used by the army; a military museum is open to the public at odd hours. Back to Macquarie Street, continue west; at Church Street, now a pedestrian mall, note the **Town Hall**, built in 1883. Across the Church Street Mall at this point stands **St John's Church**, site of an Anglican Church since 1803; here the first colonial chaplain, Sam Marsden, preached for 40 years. The current structure theoretically dates from 1855, when the dilapidated old church began to be rebuilt, but it is essentially a hodgepodge of styles and subsequent renovations; the twin steeples are said to have been donated by Mrs Macquarie, modelled on a church in Kent.

Of greatest interest in connection with the church is **St John's Cemetery**; from the church itself, walk west on Macquarie Street to O'Connell Street and one block south to Aird Street. Many of the most famous early colonists are buried here: Australia's first farmer Henry Dodd, who died in 1791; Baron von Alt, Governor Phillip's surveyor; D'Arcy Wentworth, father of William Charles Wentworth (see Vaucluse, Sydney); Reverend Marsden; and Robert 'Merchant' Campbell.

Government Domain

From O'Connell Street walk north to Macquarie Street, turn left to enter Parramatta Park, the original government domain. **Old Government House** (☎ 02 9635 8149; open Tues–Fri 10.00–16.00, Sat–Sun 11.00–16.00), built in 1799, is the oldest public building in Australia, and always filled with visitors. Operated by the National Trust, the building has been beautifully restored, with guided tours and extensive historical material available on site.

Exit through the **Tudor Gatehouse**; the present structure replaced the original Macquarie gatehouse, and was erected in 1885 to a design of a local architect, Gordon MacKinnon. Just before leaving the park is the **Fitzroy Tree** with a memorial obelisk alongside, commemorating the spot where, in 1847, Governor Fitzroy's wife was killed when her carriage overturned against the oak.

On exiting the park, you will find yourself on George Street; walk east one block to Marsden Street; on the corner is the **Medical Museum**, in one of the oldest Parramatta houses. It was built in 1821 for emancipated convict John Hodges; a diamond design in the back wall commemorates Hodges' winnings at euchre (a card game) with an eight of diamonds. Formerly known as Brislington, it was for nearly 100 years the 'doctor's house', owned by the Brown medical family.

Across the street where the **Courthouse** now stands, was the **Woolpack Inn**, dating from 1821 (and the location for Hodges' game of euchre); earlier on this site, First Fleet convict James Larra had a hotel. Larra is often referred to as Australia's first Jewish landowner. Across George Street is the **Woolpack Hotel**, built in 1890 when the licence was transferred from the old inn, making the hotel that with the oldest renewed licence in Australia.

Walk north on Marsden Street to Marist Place and **St Patrick's Church** and **Presbytery**, the site of some of the first Catholic services in the colony in 1803; there was an uncompleted church structure here in 1828, a few years before the arrival of the first bishop, Bishop Polding. A second church built in 1834 was declared unsound by 1853, and a larger building, designed by James Houison, was erected in 1854–59, with the spires added in 1878–83. An arsonist's fire gutted the historic structure in 1996; parishioners and city officials have begun to rebuild it.

Around the corner west on O'Connell Street is **Roseneath Cottage**, a simple Georgian structure, built in 1837 for Janet Templeton, a Scottish widow who arrived in the colony with eight children and a flock of merino sheep. As evidence of the kind of dwellings that once characterised Parramatta, it is a relief that it has survived the town's modern transformations.

One has to search hard now to find these reminders of Parramatta's colonial history. As the shopping centre of the western suburbs, this is perhaps to be expected, but urban sprawl has overwhelmed it almost entirely.

Towards Penrith

From Parramatta, you might continue on the **M4 motorway**, zooming past the fibro-and-brick houses of many suburbs en route to Penrith and then the Blue Mountains. Or, at Hawkesbury Road west of Parramatta, you can transfer back to the **old Great Western Highway** (route 44) to travel more sedately through the suburbs themselves. It is also possible to take the train all the way from Central Station to Penrith (and indeed into the Blue Mountains) with frequent stops.

If driving, when you reach **St Mary's**, turn off at Mamre Road to the south to come to **'Mamre' homestead** (☎ 02 9670 6178), the original farmhouse of Rev. Samuel Marsden, early Sydney's 'flogging preacher'. Despite his fearsome temper, Marsden was apparently an efficient farmer, and developed this area, explored by Watkin Tench in 1789, into good farming and grazing land; Marsden sent the first shipment of Australian wool to England. The homestead is now open to the public, run by the Sisters of Mercy, with a craft shop and tea room and historical displays. The name apparently refers to the biblical 'Oak of Mamre' under which Abraham lived. The house is a two-storey Georgian structure with verandahs, constructed of sandstone c 1830.

Off the Great Western Highway c 1.5km from Mamre Road, turn north on

Werrington Road; c 3km, near the Werrington train station, is **'Werrington House'**, built in 1829–32 of local stone for the Lethbridge family. The house's design is based on the family's Cornish home. The land on which the house was built was originally granted to Mary Putland in the early 1800s; Putland was Governor Bligh's 'arrogant' daughter, who had so vigorously defended him when he was deposed as Governor.

Near the Werrington train station is a campus of the sprawling **University of Western Sydney**, a product of the amalgamation of several polytechnic colleges. The university, with campuses throughout Western Sydney, is now concentrating on the arts, and is quickly growing into one of the state's most innovative educational institutions.

Penrith

Another 5km west is **Penrith** (population 150,000), founded in 1789 when Watkin Tench and his party explored the region and discovered the Nepean River, which was named after the Secretary of the Admiralty. A flat, broad river that tumbles into the spectacular **Nepean Gorge** some 20km upstream, the river is actually a tributary of the Hawkesbury River. The *Nepean Belle*, a paddlesteamer boat, takes tourists on trips from Penrith up to the gorge. The river at Penrith is also to be the site of the rowing competitions during the Olympic Games. The rowing sprint course begins at Victoria Bridge, originally built in the 1860s to bring the railway to the Blue Mountains. Today, Penrith is quite suburbanised, with the **Penrith Panthers League Club** on Mulgoa Road a glitzy centre of entertainment. Still, historic bits remain and Penrith's agrarian roots are evident in the landscape around it, with the sense that the Blue Mountains are very near. The **tourist information office** is on Mulgoa Road, ☎ 02 4732 7671. For information on Nepean Heritage Tours, ☎ 02 4777 4459.

Local heritage is well-presented at the **Arms of Australia Inn History Museum**, on the corner of Gardenia Avenue and the Great Western Highway in Emu Plains (across the Victoria Bridge; ☎ 02 4735 4394); the museum is open to the public on weekends, and the Archives Room, run by the Nepean District Historical Society, is available through appointment for students and interested citizens. The inn itself was built in 1840 by John Mortimer.

North Sydney and the north shore

Crossing the **Harbour Bridge** by foot or train, or taking one of several ferries, brings you to Sydney's North Shore. A harbour tunnel now also travels under the harbour itself. The city of North Sydney has become a high-rise commercial enclave of its own, and the suburbs on this side have a distinct character. Many Sydneysiders would maintain that 'North Shore' types are a breed apart, entirely removed from the more down-to-earth concerns of those on the south side. The suburbs closest to the harbour are indeed some of the most exclusive in the city, and the views across to the Opera and Circular Quay are stunning. The North Shore is also the site of several inner harbour beaches, including the quite popular Little Sirius Cove in Mosman.

North Shore's earliest development was as a residential settlement. A township site was laid out in 1838, to be known as St Leonards, but it never materialised as planned, although St Leonards is today one of the many suburbs along the Pacific Highway north.

One of the first permanent settlers on the shoreline was the artist Conrad Martens, who in 1844 lived in what is present-day St Leonards. Here he produced an abundant number of watercolours depicting the harbour and the town itself. Other pioneers, especially loggers, had already penetrated the woodlands beyond the bay's shore, and whalers established an industry in the area of present-day Mosman. By the 1850s, vast tracts of land were in the hands of a few landholders whose names have now been given to the suburbs created out of their original estates. The first white settler was William Henry, who received a land grant here of 1000 acres (400 ha) from Governor Bligh, to whom he remained loyal, even after the governor's ousting in 1808.

The first train stop, and the endpoint after walking across the bridge, is **Milson's Point**. James Milson was one of the area's first free settlers, who ran a dairy here and was one of the founding members of the **Royal Sydney Yacht Squadron**.

Kirribilli

At this point, you can either walk east into the commercial centre of North Sydney itself, or west into the pleasantly undulating streets of **Kirribilli** (an Aboriginal word allegedly meaning 'place for fishing'). From the shoreline at Kirribilli, there is the most spectacular view of the Harbour Bridge, the harbour, and across to Circular Quay and the Opera House at Bennelong Point. The small winding streets of the suburb also present structures of every architectural style, from elegant apartment houses to Federation cottages. Many of these houses are now private hotels, most of them quite inexpensive (and some a bit spooky; check out the clientele before booking).

Kirribilli Point is the site of **Admiralty House**, built in 1845 by the Collector of Customs J.G.N. Gibbes. From the 1880s the house served as the residence of admirals of the British Fleet; it is now the Sydney residence of the New South Wales Governor-General. Next door on Kirribilli Avenue, and joined by extensive gardens, is **Kirribilli House**, built in the 1850s in Gothic Revival style for merchant Adolf Frederick Fez. It now serves as the residence of the Prime Minister when he is not in Canberra. The current Prime Minister, John Howard, quite controversially, has chosen to use this as his permanent residence rather than move to the national capital's official residence, The Lodge.

Blue's Point

At the very tip of **McMahons Point** on the other side of the bridge is **Blue's Point**, named for a fascinating early Sydney character, a black Jamaican named Billy Blue who was transported in 1801. Dubbed the Old Commodore by Governor Macquarie, Blue ran the ferry service from this point to the other side of the harbour for many years. It is said that he often had his passengers do the rowing and sometimes changed the price of the trip in midstream. He fathered a family after he was 70, two of his daughters marrying other prominent North Shore pioneers, George Lavender, for whom Lavender Bay is named, and James French of French's Forest.

Blue's Point is now the site of **Blue's Point Tower**, one of Harry Seidler's early 'skyscraper' apartments (1961–62), considered by some a modernist eyesore along the shoreline. Blue's Point Road, running into **MILLER STREET** in the congested centre of town, is one of the major thoroughfares of lower North Sydney.

McMahons Point

The little neighbourhood of McMahons Point is now a tremendously gentrified location, filled with tastefully renovated period townhouses. To have a Mc Mahons Point address is to have arrived, an ironic transformation from its early working-class status. Poet Henry Lawson lived here with his aunt in 1892, near the present-day approach of the bridge. He lived in the area again in the early 1900s; a plaque at 23 Euroka Street, commemorates his residence in 1914.

Lavender Bay and Luna Park

One of the best ways to get to MacMahons Point and Lavender Bay is to take the **Hegarty's ferry**, a private ferry company, from Bay 6 in Circular Quay; the ride gives a spectacular view under the bridge and into this unpretentious little bay. **Lavender Bay** was the site of the artist Brett Whiteley's studio in the 1960s and 1970s, when the area was still rather down-at-the-heels and genuine. From here, you can stroll along the foreshore with great views of the harbour and Sydney city with the high-rise buildings of North Sydney behind.

Right under the bridge at Milson's Point on Lavender Bay is **Luna Park**. This amusement park has been a much-loved part of Sydney since the 1930s, when it was built on the construction site headquarters of the Harbour Bridge, prime harbourfront real estate at any time. It has always been a favoured spot for migrants and American G.I.s on shore leave. Closed down after a disastrously fatal fire in the 1970s, it was lovingly restored and reopened with great fanfare, and much state funding, in 1993. While local residents continually protest about the Big Dipper's noise, and threats of funding loss continue, so far it has managed to remain open. Even if you are not a fan of carnival rides and greasy food, Luna Park is worth a visit to see the vintage decorations and billboard paintings.

Just below Luna Park is the **North Sydney Olympic Pool** (weekdays 06.00–21.00, weekends 07.00–19.00), beautifully situated next to the waters of the harbour, with lovely Art Deco ornaments on its walls (see box).

City of North Sydney

North Sydney itself contains some interesting historical sites amidst all the new skyscrapers. At Lavender Street and Blue's Point Road, turn left into William Street to see **Sydney Church of England Grammar School**, known locally as SCEGGS or 'Shore', and very prestigious indeed. Given its current status as a leading institution for the rich and famous, it is surprising to find that the school was not established here until 1889.

At Mount Street, turn back towards Miller Street; this small triangle is known as **Victoria Cross**, and, as the **North Sydney Post Office** is here, it is the centre of town. Designed by James Barnet in 1886, it also houses the **Court House**. At the intersection is **Greenwood Plaza**. The original building was an Art Deco 1930s structure; a new post-modernist skyscraper has now been added behind. The Plaza has become a whole complex, connected to **Old School**

Sydney swimming pools

Life in Sydney, especially in summer, understandably revolves around water; North Sydney Pool is only one of many splendid pools and ocean baths in and around the city, each with their own atmosphere and aesthetic. North Sydney, for example, is known for its intimidating lane-swimmers; if you are in the Very Fast Lane, watch out. Some others to consider:

Andrew ('Boy') Charlton Pool, Mrs Macquarie Drive, The Domain, ☎ 9358 6686. A beautiful setting if an unattractive pool (chlorinated salt water, solar heated only); some serious swimming, but given its location, it's not surprising that this is the place for gays. Admission $2.50.

Bronte Baths, south end, Bronte Beach. One of the best of the sea baths, carved into the cliff face of the beach and flushed by sea waves that come crashing over the walls. Always open and free. Ever-changing, totally democratic mixing of swimmers.

Gunnamatta Baths, Nicholson Parade, Cronulla. A netted area in Gunnamatta Bay surrounded by parkland. Lots of shallow water and shaded picnic areas, so favoured by families. Sometimes polluted, check Beachwatch information. ☎ 02 9544 3805.

Heffron Park Pool, Robey Street, Maroubra. A whole complex of pools, including kids' waders. Very clean, good for lap swimmers of all levels, also mums with kids. Admission $2.50, open 06.00–20.30, closes 18.00 Fri and weekends.

MacCallum Park Pool, Milson Road, Cremorne Point. Fantastic views of Sydney Harbour, beautiful people clientele, not for kids. Water filtered from harbour. Free and always open.

Mona Vale Pool, Surfview Avenue, Mona Vale. 25m rock baths, wonderful vistas, camaraderie among the regulars. Free, always open.

Northbridge Baths, Widgiewa Road, Northbridge. In Sailors Bay of Middle Harbour, tranquil, next to small marina; great for families, with grassy area. Admission $2; open until dusk.

Sydney International Aquatic Centre, Olympic Boulevard, Homebush Bay, ☎ 02 9752 3666. The pool for the Sydney 2000 Olympic Games. Already overrun with children, despite steep entrance fee ($4.50!). Open 05.00–21.45 weekdays, 06.00–19.45 weekends.

Wylie's Baths, Neptune Street, Coogee. Built in 1907 as an ocean pool, but recently renovated; it is still like swimming in an aquarium, with lichen on the walls and small schools of fish swimming by. No lanes, just recreational; closed when waves are too high. In December, Wylie's is the site of Flickerfest short film festival, when you can watch the movies and swim at the same time. Admission $2.

Ladies Baths of Coogee, Grant Reserve, Coogee. Next door to Wylie's, women and children only for over 70 years; sand floor, seaweed and fish, too. Sheltered area for nude bathing. Admission 20 cents.

House (1883), and is now a series of elegant bars, shops and cafes.

Continue north on MILLER STREET 200m; on the left (west) is **Monte Sant' Angelo College**. Originally named Ma-Sa-Lou, it was the home of Francis Lord, son of the Jewish ex-convict Simeon Lord; Francis was at one time Mayor of St Leonard's.

On Miller Street, between McLaren and Ridge Streets are the attractive **North Sydney Council Chambers**; all kinds of enlightened social services are available here, from the Baby Health Clinic, to holiday care and the **Stanton Library**, an excellent public facility. The council building itself includes mural-size copies of the harbour panoramas originally created in 1875 by Bernard Holtermann (1838–85), discoverer at Hill End, New South Wales, of the largest deposits of gold, quartz and slate ever mined. In order to create these panoramas, Holtermann constructed an enormous tower overlooking the harbour and had photographs made of all angles. The chambers' photograph is placed next to one made in 1975 of the same view.

Behind the Council Chambers, at McLaren and Church Streets, is **St Thomas's Church**, CHURCH STREET. This was the last substantial structure designed by Edmund Blacket; the final construction was carried out by his sons, and completed in 1884. An older St Thomas's was on the site from 1843, and it is in this church's cemetery that the painter Conrad Martens and family are buried. The cemetery includes a pyramidal monument, commemorating Edward Wollstonecraft (1783–1832) and his sister Elizabeth Wollstonecraft Berry, cousins of writer and the poet Shelley's wife, Mary Wollstonecraft. The monument was erected by Alexander Berry, Edward's business partner and founder of the New South Wales town of Berry (see p 224). Wollstonecraft also established a 500-acre landgrant at Crow's Nest in North Sydney, and the nearby suburb of Wollstonecraft was named for him. St Thomas's first rector in the 1840s was William Branwhite Clarke (1798–1878), a well-known geologist who is often called the father of Australian science.

At Ridge and Miller Streets to the east is the entrance to St Leonard's Park and the site of **North Sydney Oval**, a lovely old ground complete with Victorian stands. It was the home of the North Sydney Bears Rugby League football team, which, sadly, moved to Gosford in 1999.

St Francis Xavier's, on McKenzie Street, was built in 1881. The church contains a massive stained-glass wall, and charming wood-carvings of the Stations of the Cross, completed by German carver Josef Dettlinger in the 1880s.

North shore suburbs

MILITARY ROAD, on the east side of the bridge, is the main thoroughfare from the Harbour Bridge to **The Spit**. The road is almost always congested, filled with shops and an unbelievable range of good restaurants. Any drive to Manly requires traversing its full length to Spit Road. Note also that the **Spit Bridge** has specific opening times; be sure to check before setting out, so that you can avoid delays (☎ 02 9194 1018).

The first suburb along Military Road is **Neutral Bay**, so named by Governor Phillip, because it was designated as the anchorage for all foreign ships entering the harbour. In Neutral Bay, at no. 5 Wallaringa Avenue, is **Nutcote**, home in the 1920s of illustrator and children's author May Gibbs, creator of the enormously popular Snugglepot and Cuddlepie stories and *The Gumnut Babies*. The house is open Wed–Sun 11.00–15.00 (☎ 02 9953 4453).

On Military Road, Neutral Bay blends into the suburb of **Cremorne**. At no. 380 Military Road is the **Hayden Orpheum Theatre**, a marvellous old picture house, built in the 1930s; admission to the cinema includes, before the film, performances on the grand old Wurlitzer organ, mounted on a hydraulic stage that rises majestically in front of the screen. It was built by Italian immigrant Angelo Vergona, whose son, Bob, in the 1940s, greeted every guest in the foyer, and sometimes drove home the last patrons after late-night screenings.

Cremorne leads east into **Mosman**, named for Archibald Mosman, who in the 1820s established a whaling industry here. Today Mosman is one of the prestige suburbs. The area along the harbour boasts some of the most ornate Edwardian houses, complete with copper cupolas and gabled roofs. The Mosman strip of Military Road is also one of the best places in the city for upmarket fashion shopping.

Taronga Park Zoo

Mosman is also the site of **Taronga Park Zoo** (☎ 02 9969 2777, open daily 09.00–17.00, some evenings 17.30–23.30, but telephone first for details), undisputably the most beautifully situated zoo in the world. As already mentioned, a ferry from Circular Quay arrives at the base of the zoo and a lift (when operating) brings you to the top of the hill, from which the views of the harbour and Sydney are breathtaking. The city's first zoo was in Moore Park. When Taronga opened in 1916, all the animals were conveyed by ferry to the new site, including the much beloved elephant Jessie, who lived until 1939 and provided Sydneysiders with the expression 'a hide like Jessie's'.

Great attempts have been made in the last few years to upgrade the animals' facilities, so that the exhibits are more comfortable for the enclosed wildlife. The zoo is active in worldwide breeding campaigns of endangered species, and Australia's native species receive particular attention. As the facility is excessively popular with school groups and other visitors, it is almost always crowded. Admission is relatively expensive (the zoo depends entirely on private funding), although family packages are also available.

To the south of the zoo—and, indeed, around nearly every point along this part of the North Shore, all the way to Manly—segments of the **Sydney Harbour National Park** have preserved bushland for walking and recreation. At the end of Bradley's Head Road is **Bradley's Head**, named for First Fleet cartographer William Bradley; you can see here remnants of fortifications installed around the harbour in the 1870s. Bradley's Head is a superb spot from which to view the start of the Sydney-to-Hobart Yacht Race on Boxing Day (26 December). The sight of the yachts lining up in the harbour for the starting gun is one of the most exquisite visions imaginable, not to be missed by any visitor.

Balmoral

Take Bradley's Head Road back up to Raglan Street and turn west to come to **Balmoral Beach**, a lovely inner-harbour spot on Middle Harbour. On the Esplanade is the beautiful 1930s **Bathers Pavilion**, considered by *The Sydney Morning Herald* to be one of the 'best places in Sydney for a lunch or coffee'. The architecture is that of a quasi-Moorish palace. During the **Sydney Festival** in January, Balmoral hosts performances, 'Shakespeare by the Sea', by the Sydney Theatre Company, and concerts take place in the Rotunda.

North of North Sydney

If you continue out of North Sydney on Miller Street, it turns into Strathallen Avenue; when this street ends, turn left (west) to EASTERN VALLEY WAY, and enter Northbridge. This now thoroughly urbanised part of town is entered through an elaborately crenellated bridge that appears as if it is part of a medieval castle. It was built in the 1890s by the area's land developer as a ploy to lure potential buyers.

At Edinburgh Road, turn right (east) to enter **Castlecrag**, a residential community planned by Walter Burley Griffin, designer of Canberra. Several of his houses, all bearing the mark of his teacher Frank Lloyd Wright, still exist, set back and blending into the craggy cliffs and twisting roads above Middle Harbour.

Back on Eastern Valley Way, continue north through the suburban sprawl of **Chatswood**. This area is named in honour of the wife of Richard Hayes Harnett, an early settler of land from Willoughby to Mosman. Charlotte, or 'Chat', loved to sketch the wildlife in the forests of the area, which thus became known as 'Chat's wood'.

Northern beaches

Eastern Valley Way will become WARRINGAH ROAD (Route 29) at Roseville; continue east to Wakehurst Parkway (Route 22) to Pittwater Road (Route 14), turning east into BARRENJOEY ROAD. This route will pass the beautiful northern beaches of **Bilgola**, **Avalon**, **Palm Beach** and **Whale Beach**, ending finally at Barrenjoey Head, part of the vast **Ku-ring-gai Chase National Park**. The **no. 12 bus** from Manly Wharf also travels along this coastline to **Pittwater**, including the popular beaches of **Curl Curl**, **Dee Why** and **Collaroy**.

At **Barrenjoey Head**, the view across the Bay and out into the Tasman Sea is worth the trip. As novelist C.J. Koch describes the Barrenjoey Peninsula in *The Doubleman* (1985), 'the latitude is the South Seas; and the time, for the Peninsula's cargo of beachside suburbs, is always holiday.'

Ku-ring-gai Chase National Park

Encompassing the entire end of West Head Road and across Pittwater at Barrenjoey Headland, Ku-ring-gai Chase National Park consists of 14,712 ha of bushland only 24km from the city itself. It was set aside in 1894, and is one of Sydney's most popular recreational sites; the name derives from the Guringai people, the local Aboriginal clan. Damage from the 1994 bushfires was extensive, but regrowth of natural bush has been speedy.

To enter the main part of the national park, return via Barrenjoey Road, turn north into Pittwater Road, and follow around Church Point to the toll booth at West Head Road; there is an entrance fee.

The park's main visitor centre is the **Kalkari Visitor's Centre** (☎ 02 9457 9322, open daily 09.00–17.00), where brochures and guided tours are available; this centre can be reached by taking Ku-Ring-Gai Chase Road off the Pacific Highway in Mt Colah. The railway also stops at Mt Colah near the park's entrance. **Shorelink bus no. 577** also leaves from the Turramurra Station to the Bobbin Head Road entrance of the park.

Perhaps the most enjoyable way to come to the park is via ferry. The ferry from **Palm Beach Wharf** will stop at The Basin Entrance to the park, and provides a marvellous tour of **Broken Bay** itself.

The park is the site of several Aboriginal carvings which can be visited, especially along the **Basin Trail** off West Head Road on the Lambert Peninsula. This part of the park also offers spectacular views of Pittwater, Palm Beach, and Warringah Peninsula. A community project in the park and the rest of the Pittwater region is attempting to ensure the future of the long-nosed bandicoot, a small native marsupial once abundant in number and now decimated by feral and domestic animals.

Pittwater

Governor Phillip explored the Pittwater region in 1788, describing it as 'the finest piece of water which I ever saw... it would contain all the Navy of Great Britain'. He named the region after British Prime Minister William Pitt.

As mentioned above on access to Ku-ring-gai Chase National Park, exploration of Broken Bay is most enjoyable on the Palm Beach Ferries, leaving from Palm Beach Wharf. Several boat hire options are also available from Palm Beach, to explore the bay and on into the Hawkesbury River. Another exciting possibility is to take the regular commuter flight of the **Sydney Harbour Seaplanes**, flying from Rose Bay along the coastline to Palm Beach.

Palm Beach

That a regular commuter flight is available to Palm Beach gives some indication of the privileged status of the place. It is home for many people in the arts and wealthy businessmen. The place has also been associated in the public eye with shady political doings, as the site of some famous weekend party deals; writer Peter Corris plays on this image in his story *Heroin Annie* (1984), in which his investigator Cliff Hardy comes here to bust a drug ring and refers to Palm Beach as 'the biggest playspot of them all...all chicken fat and pinballs and the popping of cold, cold cans.' Recent attempts by beachside landowners to privatise the beach itself has been greeted with horror; the idea of owning a beach is seen as completely un-Australian, no matter how exclusive the area might be.

The 'Macquarie towns' ~ Richmond and Windsor

From Penrith, you can take Parker Street/Richmond Road (route 69), which becomes the Great Northern Road to the twin Macquarie towns of **Windsor** and **Richmond** along the Hawkesbury River, some 55km from Sydney. From the city, you can take the M2 Motorway. The train also travels all the way to Richmond, with a stop at Windsor. Many tours to the towns are organised by the Tourist Information Bureau as well; check at any of the city offices, particularly at the services at the Circular Quay.

The **M2 MOTORWAY** is now a completely concealed freeway from Lane Cove on the north side of Sydney Harbour, zipping past the countryside northwest to Windsor Road; the old road closely follows the original Windsor Road of 1794. The **Old Windsor Road route** will take you through **Ryde**, location of the first hops-grower and brewer in the colony, James Squire. Squire also befriended the famous Aborigine Bennelong after his return from England in 1794; Bennelong's grave is believed to be in the Ryde district.

The Ryde district's other great claim to fame is as the site where Maria Ann Smith, better known as 'Granny Smith', first cultivated her famous apples in the 1860s. A small park to her memory exists in nearby Eastwood, off

Abuklea Road on Threlfall Street, the location of her original orchard.

Today it is hard to imagine that the area along the M2 at Pennant Hills was in the 19C teeming with bushrangers where the suburban homes are now thick on the hills looking over the city. Drive through **Castle Hill**, site of one of the two armed uprisings in Australia, the Battle of Vinegar Hill, brought about in 1804 by Irish political prisoners attempting to escape. The 'battle' was quickly quelled by authorities, leaving 15 dead; nine of the 'conspirators' were hanged for their attempts at insurrection.

Continue along the Windsor Road (route 40 and 2) to **Rouse Hill**. The area was named for Richard Rouse, free settler and Superintendant of Public Works in 1806. In 1813–18, Rouse built **Rouse Hill House**, now part of the National Estate. Despite many additions to the original dwelling, the house still survives intact, as one of the earliest private country dwellings in the country and with many of the original furnishings. Of special interest are its outbuildings and the gardens, still extant in its original design. For 162 years, until taken over by the New South Wales government in 1979, descendants of Richard Rouse occupied the property. Access to the public is by appointment and requires a fee (PO Box 123, Rouse Hill, New South Wales 2155; ☎ 02 9627 5108).

The **Hawkesbury region** was explored by Governor Phillip in his desperate attempt to find farmland for the colony. By 1794, 22 pioneers had settled along the river, and by 1796, some 1000 acres (400 ha) were under cultivation here. Of most importance to the colony was the success of grain farming in the region, but soon all kinds of produce flourished and reached the Sydney markets via the river. The river itself, then, became a centre of great activity, including a vigorous boat building industry. (See the Hawkesbury River section, p 183.)

Windsor

Although it was named Green Hill by the original settlers, **Windsor** (population 13,500) was the name given by Governor Macquarie in 1810 when he established the 'Five Macquarie Towns'; these were Windsor, Richmond, Wilberforce, Pitt Town and Castlereagh. Macquarie selected these sites on high land to avoid the river floods which habitually plagued early settlements, and along with the inveterate architect Francis Greenway, indulged his passion for town planning and architectural ambition. The towns today still retain evidence of this planning and the original buildings—even the street curbs and guttering are those built by convicts—are still home to the descendants of the first settlers. Tourist information can be obtained from **Hawkesbury Visitor Centre**, Ham Common Bicentary Park, Richmond Road, Clarendon, ☎ 02 4588 5895; open Mon–Fri 09.00–17.00, Sat 10.00–15.00, Sun 09.00–13.00.

Entering Windsor from the M2 at Macquarie Street leads to THOMPSON SQUARE, the centre of the town. The train stops at Church Street south of the Richmond Road; walk north on George Street to come to Thompson Square. Substantially restored as part of a Bicentennial project, Thompson Square's numerous colonial buildings now remain as a monument to the Hawkesbury pioneers. The square owes its name to the first landowner Andrew Thompson, an emancipist whom Macquarie so admired for his diligence and ambition that he made him magistrate. Thompson died heroically in 1810, after valiant efforts to save lives and property during one of the Hawkesbury's many floods.

On the southeast corner of the square is the **Macquarie Arms**, built to the order of Governor Macquarie in 1811–15. The inn was built and operated from 1815 to 1840 by ex-convict Robert Fitzgerald, who became the richest man in the town. The building includes excellent cedar joinery and stone verandahs. Next door to the Macquarie Arms is the **Hawkesbury Museum** (☎ 02 4577 2310; open daily 10.00–16.00), housed in an 1820s building that was originally an inn. Along with historical displays, the museum is also the Tourist Information Centre. The next structure on the square is a small cottage from the 1850s, privately owned; next to the cottage towards the river is the **Doctor's House**, so named because doctors have lived here since the 1870s. The structure itself dates from 1844 and is a great example of a colonial terrace building, with fanlights above the doors and columns flanking the doorways.

Continue to walk towards the river, cross over The Terrace and turn right onto a walkway, which will lead under a bridge to the river. From here you can see **Windsor Wharf**. Walk up the hill and return to Thompson Square. Houses on this side date from the 1850s and 1860s. Cross George Street to the site of the **School of Arts**, built in 1861 in an Italianate style; it is now a boot factory. Turn north onto George Street and walk one block to Arndell Street; on the left side of the street is a plaque commemorating the site of **Old Government House**, built here in the 1790s. Turn into Arndell Street; on the left at North Street are a series of cottages built 1840–60, some of the only examples of this period remaining. On the corner is the **Swallows Inn**, so named because of the fairy martin nests under the eaves; the building also served as the surgery in the television series 'A Country Practice'.

Walk down NORTH STREET for a view of the farmland near the town; turn right into Palmer Street and continue to a set of buildings called the **John Tebbutt F.R.A.S. Observatories** (☎ 02 4587 7388). Here the famous amateur astronomer John Tebbutt (1834–1916) first set up his observatory in 1863; the building now on the site was built in 1879. Here Tebbutt established local mean time, discovered the Comet Tebbutt of 1881, and published some 370 accounts of meteorological observations. Tebbutt was such an important figure in astronomical circles that he appeared on the Australian $100 note in the 1980s. The observatories are still owned by the Tebbutt family; they are now open to the public and contain scientific displays.

Return via Palmer Street to Pitt Street; turn left and walk to the corner of COURT STREET. Here is the **Windsor Courthouse**, built in 1822 by William Cox (of Blue Mountain exploration fame) to the design of Francis Greenway. It is considered by many as Greenway's most harmonious building and one of the best preserved, built of sandstone bricks with worked stone lintels and sills. The interior includes rough cedar beams; it still serves as the town's courthouse. In the public gallery is a controversial portrait, believed by many to be of Governor Macquarie, although debate about its authenticity continues.

Off Court Street, turn left onto a footpath leading to the **Tollhouse**, a reminder of the old toll system on the roadways. The current building dates from the 1880s; its unrestored condition points to the continuation of flooding along the river. Return to Bridge Street and proceed into Thompson Square and then right (west) onto Baker Street; turn left (south) onto THE TERRACE along the river. Between Kable and Fitzgerald Streets is **Sunnybrae**, built in 1875 and still owned by the same family. Continue on The Terrace, cross the small park by the

water tower, built in 1889. At New Street are two cottages from 1830; continue down the Terrace to Catherine Street and turn left to Little Church Street, on the corner of which is the **Bell Inn**, built c 1845 with an interesting barrelled corner. Walk down Little Church Street and note **St Matthew's Catholic Church**, built in 1840.

At Tebbutt Street turn right and return to The Terrace; on the left, on what is now MOSES STREET, is the **Rectory** and **St Matthew's Anglican Church**, Francis Greenway's most memorable building. The site was chosen by Macquarie expressly for building a church; its elevated position led it to become the district's most famous landmark, as it could be seen throughout the Hawkesbury region. The church is built of bricks produced by William Cox; its most stunning feature is the sculptural square tower with octagonal cupola. When the foundation stone was laid in 1817, Governor Macquarie placed a Spanish dollar under the stone; it was stolen that night. After another ceremony led to the same result, the stone was quickly laid without the coin and built over. Halfway through the building, Greenway, angry at the building contractor's shoddy workmanship, demolished the entire structure and rebuilt it. It was consecrated in 1822 by the fiery colonial chaplain Samuel Marsden. Marsden in fact died here, at the rectory, while visiting a friend in 1858. In the church's portico is the Bible, along with the clock and bell tower, presented to the congregation by King George IV.

The **rectory** was built in 1825 by William Cox; the architect is unknown, but its Georgian design complements Greenway's church. The church's **cemetery** contains the graves of Andrew Thompson, for whom Thompson Square was named, and explorer William Cox, as well as the Tebbutt family vault.

Past the cemetery is Claremont Crescent; **Claremont Cottage** was built in 1822 out of stuccoed brick either by John Jones or William Cox.

Return to Moses Street, turn right and cross Richmond Road into Cox Street; turn right onto FAIRFIELD AVENUE to reach the High Victorian mansion of **Fairfield House**. The first part was built as early as 1833, again for William Cox. In 1866, it was acquired by the McQuade family, who added the two-storey northern wing in the 1880s. William McQuade was the manager of Her Majesty's Theatre in Sydney and lived in opulent style; he even had a private race track here.

From Fairfield, head back to Barbyn Street; turn left into GEORGE STREET. No. 394 was built in 1897 as a **general store** by George Robertson; the façade includes interesting carved stonework. Further along George Street past the Richmond Street crossing is **Oxalis Cottage**, between the city council chambers and the library. It was built in the 1850s by Wesleyan missionary Peter Turner. At no. 312 is **Mrs Cope's House**, a large five-bay Georgian structure with 15-pane windows; it was once home to one Maria Cope, who apparently owned extensive grounds here in the 1830s. At no. 266 is the old **Royal Theatre**, now the **Windsor Antique Markets**. George Street soon becomes a pedestrian mall and ends back at Thompson Square.

Richmond

Author Ruth Park, in her 1973 guide to Sydney, considered **Richmond** the prettiest of the Five Macquarie Towns. Only 8km from Windsor, at the end of the train run, the town used to be the busiest in the area, as it was at the convergence of the main trading roads. The railway line was opened in 1864, linking Richmond directly with Sydney. The Richmond RAAF Base now dominates the road linking Windsor and Richmond, and a major campus of the **University of Western Sydney**, emphasising agriculture and animal sciences, occupies a large expanse of land to the south of town.

From the train station, you enter Richmond at **Richmond Park**, once the town's market square. To the west of the park is the **Post Office**, built in 1875, with a second storey added in 1888. Further west on WEST MARKET STREET is **St Andrew's Uniting Church**, built in 1845 as a Presbyterian Church by George Bowman, Richmond's leading philanthropist. A memorial to Dr Andrew Cameron in front of the church demonstrates the significance of the Cameron family to the Richmond area; James Cameron was the minister of the Presbyterian church in the 1860s, and was married to Bowman's daughter. Across West Market Street is the **Masonic Lodge**, built as the Presbyterian School in the 1860s. Next door, on the corner of MARCH STREET, is the old **School of Arts building**, opened in 1866 by politician Henry Parkes. George Bowman was again involved in the organisation of this public institution. Further west on March Street are interesting early houses, and in the middle of the block, the offices of Shaddick Baker and Paul, with fine iron lacework and a bull-nose verandah; the original structure was built in 1868, with sympathetic additions made in the 1980s.

On the corner of March and Bosworth Streets, turn right and walk to Windsor Street. On the southeast corner is the site of the **Black Horse Inn**—now only the roof line is visible—once the most famous hotel in the region. The inn opened in 1819 and for years was known for its sign of a black horse in full gallop (now in the Hawkesbury Museum in Windsor). At one time the inn marked the centre of town, and was the finishing post for horse races down the main street. The inn served as the polling place in Australia's first election in 1843; it was also a popular honeymoon destination until it closed in the 1920s.

Turn left into WINDSOR STREET, the oldest residential section of the town. No. 315, now the **Richmond Restaurant**, was built in 1865 by the Cornwell family, and was known as 'the **Cottage**'; both no. 315 and '**Eltham**' next door are managed by the National Trust. Across the street is **Bowman Cottage**, built 1815–17 by free settler James Blackman; it was acquired by George Bowman in 1820, and was run as the Royal Arrow Inn. Bowman lived here until his death in 1878. Today it is the local headquarters of the National Parks and Wildlife Service (☎ 02 4588 5247; open Mon–Fri 09.00–17.00).

Towards the end of Windsor Street past Chapel Street is **St Peter's Church of England**, a rectangular brick church built between 1837 and 1841 to a design by Francis Clarke, a prominent architect; this is only one of two surviving works by him. The interior is intact, with beautiful cedar work and stained glass windows added in the 1890s. In the **churchyard**, a small obelisk was made out of the bricks of the 1810 school-church once on the site. William Cox was also involved with the early construction of the church. From the churchyard you have a panoramic view of the Blue Mountains to the northwest, with **Pughs Lagoon** in the foreground. The church's cemetery was first laid out in 1811 under Governor Macquarie's direction, and bears the graves of several prominent pioneers, including the remarkable ex-convict Margaret Catchpole (1762–1819), who served as a midwife in her Richmond years. Catchpole became something of a legend in her native Suffolk (England), with a highly fictionalised account of her adventures made popular through Richard Cobbold's *The History of Margaret Catchpole: A Suffolk Girl* (1845). Other graves include those of the Bowman family, and William Cox, Sr.

Back along Windsor Street, turn left at CHAPEL STREET. On the corner of Chapel and Francis Streets is **'Josieville'**, built in the 1830s for Joseph Onus, a convict who arrived in Australia in 1803 and went on to become one of the most prosperous farmers in the Hawkesbury region. The additional storey was added in the 1870s, creating a great two-storey verandah. Also on Francis Street is **Clear Oaks Homestead**, also owned by the Onus family; the two-storey brick farmhouse dates from the 1820s.

Far at the end of Chapel Street is **'Hobartville'**, a fine sandstock brick mansion built for William Cox Jr, possibly from a design by Greenway. The property is still in private hands, but you can view the house with its three-sided verandah bay in beautiful grounds.

Proceed along Windsor Street back into town. On the other side of Richmond Park, at East Market Street, is **Toxana**, residence of William Bowman, George Bowman's younger brother. It was built in the 1840s and stood in magnificent grounds. The Cameron family lived here in the 1880s, but by the 1890s, the building had a variety of owners and lamentable incarnations. It was restored in 1978, and is now used by the **Macquarie Towns Arts Society**.

Continue along Windsor Street, turning left into Toxana Street. On the right at Francis Street is **Benson House**, built in the 1840s by the shipwright Benson's. The upper floor was added in 1900, but the bottom storey and servants' quarters are original. Continue along Francis Street c 1km and turn right into Jersey Street; here is the **Presbyterian Cemetery**, which dates from the 1860s and includes the graves of the Camerons and the Bowman family vault.

Going back to Windsor Street, at the corner is a modern Catholic church on the site of St Monica's, first consecrated in 1854. Turn right into Windsor Street; the first cottage on the southern side was the shop and residence of Bob Eggleton, prominent Richmond wheelwright in the 1860s. The building is typical of the kind of **tradesman shops** that existed here in the mid-19C.

No. 89 Windsor Street is the **Manse**, an 1890s Presbyterian school. In the grounds are the incongruous **Kamilaroi Gates**, all that remain of a grand house built in the 1890s by Benjamin Richards, one of Richmond's wealthiest citizens. The house was used as a school from the 1920s until 1956, when it was demolished.

At the corner of Windsor and Paget Streets is **Andrew Town's House**. It was from this point that the old horse races to the Black Horse Inn began. Appropriately, Andrew Town was one of Australia's most famous horse breeders and racing figures; in the 1880s, he had the largest pedigreed stock in the world, until the 1890s depression saw him lose his properties.

Finally, at no. 126 is **'Heritage Cottage'**, which displays three period rooms from the 1850s, along with the ever-present tea-room that occupy nearly every historical venue in the country.

Windsor to Wiseman's Ferry

To the west of the Hawkesbury River at Windsor, route 69 travels north to WILBERFORCE, another of the Macquarie Towns, and now best known as the site of **Australian Pioneer Village**, Rose Street (☎ 02 4575 1457; open Thurs–Sun 10.00–17.00), a rather successful 'historic village' initiated in the 1970s by Bill McLachlan, who introduced water-skiing to the Hawkesbury. Appropriately, Wilberforce is now home to one of the world's leading **water-ski speed races**, 50km from Brooklyn up to this point. The town of Wilberforce still has a few old buildings, including a **'Macquarie' schoolhouse**, built in 1819 by John Brabyn; it was here that the famous bushranger Thunderbolt (Fred Ward) went to school. Edmund Blacket also built a church here, **St John's**, in 1856. Nearby to the west in Freeman's Reach is **'Reibycroft'**, one of the district's oldest farmhouses, built for the ever-acquisitive Reibey family in the 1820s.

From Wilberforce, the Sackville road continues north to a ferry crossing on the river; at **Ebenezer**, c 5km, is a rectangular stone Presbyterian church, built by Scottish farmers between 1807 and 1817 overlooking the Hawkesbury River; it is the oldest extant church in Australia.

Further north on route 69 is **Colo** and the **Wollemi National Park** (☎ 045 885 247, or 047 878 877). Only 100km northwest of Sydney, the park of 487,648 ha is the state's largest and most unpolluted wilderness, with spectacular canyons and gorges. There is an old railway tunnel near the ruins of the old settlement of Newnes that is filled with glow-worms. The park is also the location of the recently discovered **Wollemi Pine**, the world's oldest species of tree. These trees are in completely inaccessible locations. Their whereabouts are carefully guarded from any human intrusion by the Parks and Wildlife Service, whose rangers discovered them (as reported in *The Sydney Morning Herald*, 7 June 1997). The Colo River, reached by following Bob Turner's Track, provides swimming possibilities and scenic beaches.

On the eastern side of Windsor, route 65, the PITT TOWN-CATTAI ROAD travels through the other Macquarie Town of **Pitt Town**, a very small village; 6km north is **Cattai National Park**, a small area which is great for picnics and walks; it surrounds the **'Cad-Die'** homestead, built in 1821 for Thomas Arndell.

Another 30km brings you to **Wiseman's Ferry**, the most historic of the Hawkesbury ferry crossings. Solomon Wiseman (1778–1838) was transported to New South Wales in 1806 for the crime of stealing wood; he was pardoned in 1812 and in 1817 took up 200 acres of land at this site on the Hawkesbury River. He ran an inn here from the 1820s, and had his finger in every sort of industry, legal and otherwise; a contemporary clergyman wrote that Wiseman was 'deeply read in the corruption of human nature'. He built the imposing **Cobham Hall**, still standing, and the remains of his inn are still part of the present-day hotel, said to be haunted by his first wife, whom he supposedly tossed down the steps, and perhaps by old Wiseman himself.

Wiseman became a wealthy man once the road from his ferry was continued across the river to the Hunter Valley in 1827; this convict-built GREAT NORTHERN ROAD still exists, and was for half a century the main road leading north. Today it continues to the old settlement of **St Alban's**, with its church ruins and historic cemetery (the oldest grave dates from 1837); and to **Dharug National Park** (☎ 02 4324 4911), named for the local Aboriginal people. This park has many Aboriginal rock engravings believed to be more than 8000 years old.

NORTH COAST
NEW SOUTH WALES

Sydney to the Queensland border

From the north side of the Sydney Harbour, the Pacific Highway (route 1) proceeds north through the suburbs along the railway line, until the outskirts of Hornsby, where it becomes the sleek **SYDNEY–NEWCASTLE FREEWAY** just as the Ku-Ring-Gai Chase National Park begins (see North Sydney section for more on the park). The city **rail lines**, heading all the way to Newcastle, and then into Queensland, follow the road until the waters of the Hawkesbury River at **Brooklyn**, at which point the train diverges to pass through spectacular scenery inaccessible to those in an automobile. This stretch of the railway, which is fast, inexpensive and frequent enough to be used by commuters as far north as Gosford, is definitely recommended for the visitor. The Old Pacific Highway continues north as routes 83 and 111 at a more leisurely pace through Gosford and around Lake Macquarie all the way to Newcastle.

The Hawkesbury River

As already discussed in the section on the Western Suburbs and the towns of Windsor and Richmond, the discovery of the Hawkesbury River by Governor Phillip in 1789, on his third exploration of **Broken Bay**, was greeted with rejoicing by the fledgling colony, as the land surrounding the river promised fertile ground to plant desperately needed crops. Phillip named the river for Baron Hawkesbury, Earl of Liverpool.

The river originates in the Wollondilly River, which begins near Crookwell in central New South Wales some 300km west of Sydney, and winds romantically through the countryside, most picturesque, with many inlets, in the 20km before it reaches Broken Bay and the sea. The Aborigines called it Deerubbin. Intrepid Watkin Tench, First Fleet chronicler who discovered the Nepean River, realised when he revisited the area in 1791 that the Nepean and the Hawkesbury were the same river. In his famous *Journal of an Excursion Across the Blue Mountains of New South Wales* (1822), Barron Field, who usually found Australian landscape unpicturesque, called the river 'the Nile of Botany Bay', and British author Anthony Trollope, on his famous visit in 1871, was so taken by the river's charms that he remarked, 'in my opinion, the Hawkesbury beats the Mississippi'. It is indeed one of the most grandiose of Australian rivers, which are often quite sinuous and turgid.

Along with the establishment of prosperous farms and ship-building industry along its banks, the river inevitably became the haunt of smugglers in colonial times, when spirits (that is, rum) were still a form of currency. The many inlets, coves and caves, now seemingly so picturesque, were the ideal hideaways for the most opportunistic pirates. Early poet Charles Harpur (1813–68), born in Windsor, used the pseudonym 'A Hawkesbury Lad' and wrote of the river's beauties in poems such as 'A Storm in the Mountains'; contemporary poet Robert Adamson also grew up in the district and set many of his poems here.

If you do not have time to travel extensively along the river, it is worth a detour to visit the river inlet of **Berowra Waters**. Berowra is 13km north of Hornsby on the freeway, and Berowra Waters is c 7km west of there. A delightful little car ferry goes across the water of this little gorge, leading to a serenely situated restaurant directly on the water itself.

The first stop on the river off the main freeway is **Brooklyn**, so named because the company that built the first Hawkesbury River railway bridge was the Union Bridge Company of Brooklyn, New York. It is easier to reach Brooklyn by continuing from Hornsby on the Old Pacific Highway rather than the freeway itself. From Brooklyn, you can take the **Brooklyn Ferries** cruises up the river, as well as the daily ferry service to **Patonga** across Broken Bay (☎ 02 9985 7566); Patonga has some of the best oysters in the region.

One of the most interesting ways to see the Hawkesbury River is to take the **River Boat Mail Run**, leaving every weekday morning from Brooklyn. The boat provides postal services for those who live along the river, but they allow tourists to come along for the ride (about four hours) for a very reasonable rate. The 08.15 train from Sydney and the 08.17 from Gosford are scheduled to link with the postal ferry at Brooklyn, and offer combined tickets for both rides.

The freeway continues north over the river at **Mooney Mooney**; the bridge itself is awe-inspiring, and it is worth the stop at the scenic lookout on the northern side to view the bridge and the extraordinary scenery below. The freeway now skirts the coastline, with frequent turn-offs to reach the more interesting lakes and beachside sites.

Gosford

At 85km north of Sydney, **Gosford** (population 38,210) is within commuting distance from the city (the commuter train from Sydney runs regularly from Central Station), and has recently experienced a residential boom that has spoiled whatever small-town charm it may have had. But it sits at the northern edge of the **Brisbane Water National Park**, an enormous (7870 ha) and varied reserve that encompasses sub-tropical rainforest, estuarine mudflats and beaches; the popular beachside communities of **Woy Woy** and **Umina** on Brisbane Waters are nearby, as is the chic **Pearl Beach**, an inlet beach with 'pearl-like' wave formations, noted by Captain Cook on his 1770 voyage. Pearl Beach is a popular holiday spot for the Sydney artistic scene, and has a community jazz festival over the Queen's Birthday weekend. **Tourist information**: 200 Mann Street; ☎ 02 4325 2835.

Gosford itself has little of historical interest, aside from the stone cottage where poet Henry Kendall lived from 1873 to 1875, recovering from alcoholism in the care of local timber merchants, the Fagans. The cottage dates from 1838, and is now used as a local history museum. To the west of town is **Old Sydney Town**, one of Australia's oldest 'theme parks', a historical village that attempts to recreate events and activities from Macquarie's era. It is open Wednesday to Sunday, and daily during school holidays.

19km southeast of Gosford is the **Bouddi National Park**, a series of small beaches with great opportunities for bushwalking. Directly east of Gosford is **Terrigal**, a very popular holiday resort with excellent surfing. The area from here north to **The Entrance** on **Tuggerah Lake**, c 20km, is filled with caravan parks and holiday camps taking advantage of the clean beaches and lakeside views (the **tourist information office** is at the Tuggerah Lakes Tourist Association, Memorial Park, Marine Parade; ☎ 02 4332 9282). This is really family holiday country, and is best avoided during school holidays.

Wyong, 22km north of Gosford on the Pacific Highway, has an interesting District Museum depicting the history of the ferries and logging activities in the area. On the northeast side of Lake Tuggerah, in **Norahville** on Elizabeth Street, is a timber house of the same name built in 1860 for Edward Hammond Hargraves, of gold-fields fame—Hargraves' discoveries at Ophir began the gold rush in New South Wales. The house, on the cliffs of Norah Head near a lighthouse, has a commanding view of the Pacific Ocean. It is possible from this point to travel north on the coastal road as far as **Elizabeth Bay** to rejoin the Pacific Highway around the eastern side of Lake Macquarie.

Lake Macquarie

The largest seaboard lake in Australia and the largest saltwater lake in New South Wales, **Lake Macquarie** has no town centre, but its population (c 158,300) is comprised of tiny settlements around the lake itself. **Tourism Lake Macquarie**, Council Chambers, Main Road, Speers Point; ☎ 02 049 21 0221.

In the 1820s, one of Australia's first missionary anthropologists, Lancelot Threlkeld (1788–1859), established an Aboriginal mission at Belmont and later at Toronto; while they closed in the 1840s, Threlkeld was able to produce some of the first systematic studies of Aboriginal languages. In 1841 Threlkeld opened a coal mine on his property at Toronto, the first in the Lake Macquarie region. The region is still home to many poets, including Donald Moore and Roland Robinson. Moore's poem 'No Mark for Lake Macquarie' (1980) captures the confusion of geographical beauty and modern holiday-makers' noise that marks the area: 'There is for a while/ a suspicion of haloes/ as the sun goes down/ but no son walks/the unquiet waters/ among the Saturday/ Sunday crowds/ of herons cats and outboards/ inboards and followers on skis.'

William Dobell

William Dobell lived in this house from 1942 until his death in 1970, and became known as one of the area's leading 'identities'. He was born in Newcastle, where his father was a builder (Robert Dobell built this house). William demonstrated artistic talents at an early age, and in the 1920s he studied at Julian Ashton's school in Sydney. In the 1930s he studied in England and travelled throughout Europe, developing a style inspired by the Dutch Masters, as well as the English artist Walter Sickert and the French modernist Chaim Soutine. He returned to Sydney in 1939, where he acquired a circle of admirers and honed his skills both as a satirical artist and portrait painter; his work was always within the social realist direction and never abstract.

Satire and portraiture were at the centre of the controversy that erupted when Dobell received the Archibald Prize in 1944 for his portrait of his friend Joshua Smith. The prize is awarded by the Trustees of the Gallery of New South Wales. Conservative artists, still fighting the anti-modernist battle, argued that the painting was a caricature of Smith rather than a 'likeness', and therefore did not qualify for the portrait prize; the Archibald Prize was, and still is, lucrative and highly coveted. The arguments reached the Supreme Court of New South Wales, becoming Australia's first legal consideration of artistic values, in many ways mirroring a similar modernist-conservative debate between Whistler and John Ruskin in England nearly a century before. The case was eventually dismissed, after much popular debate about the issue; the verdict was greeted as a victory for the modern movement, although Dobell was never really a modernist painter. Dobell continued to paint his portraits until his death, was knighted, and became a venerable figure in Australian art; many of his idiosyncratic works can be seen at his Wangi Wangi house, and in nearly every gallery in Australia.

The main occupation here today is fishing, water-skiing, and cruising the lake on such ships as the *Wangi Queen* and the *Macquarie Lady*, which leave from the wharves at Toronto and Belmont. From the Morisset exit off the freeway, travel on route 133 c 20km to **Wangi Wangi**, at the tip of a western inlet of the lake. At 47 Dobell Drive is the home of famous and controversial Australian portrait painter, Sir William Dobell (1899–1970; see box, pp 185–6). The house contains a collection of his work and memorabilia (open Sun and holidays 14.00–16.00, Thurs–Sat 09.30–11.30, ☎ 02 4975 4115.)

From Lake Macquarie you can proceed north back on route 133 and travel along the lake into Newcastle; or travel around the lake to catch the Pacific Highway again (route 111). The Sydney–Newcastle Freeway, no. 1, can also be joined again west of Toronto, for the quickest route into Newcastle, after which the Freeway connects again to the Old Pacific Highway.

Newcastle

As Australia's largest industrial city and New South Wales's second largest city (and with a population of 255,800, the sixth largest in the country), Newcastle has a dubious reputation in the public's imagination. While once reviled as a dirty and polluted factory town—writer Donald Horne called it 'Australia's Pittsburgh'—the city has gained international recognition in the last two decades for its efforts to clean up industrial waste and grime and to emphasise its magnificent geographical setting. Located on a huge harbour, Newcastle is also surrounded by fantastic surf beaches, and sits most salubriously at the edge of Australia's premier wine-growing region, the Hunter Valley.

The area was the traditional home of the Awabakal and Worimi Aboriginal groups. While its real development stemmed from the discovery of huge coal deposits in the region, similarities with its English namesake end there. Newcastle came to world attention in December 1989, when the area experienced one of Australia's only major earthquakes, which killed 13 people;

community spirit has led to rebuilding of those areas that were damaged. A bigger blow has recently struck the region: in 1997, the town's main industry, the great BHP steel plant which has been the town's mainstay since 1913, announced that the factory would close in 1999, leading most to lament the end of Newcastle's traditional working-class culture and causing widespread predictions of economic disaster. But the town has such a splendid physical location that it seems unlikely that the tourism industry could ever bypass Newcastle entirely. Like citizens of working-class towns the world over, the Novocastrians, as they call themselves, are intensely proud of their city.

Tourist information: Queens Wharf; ☎ 02 4929 9299.

Festivals in Newcastle include 'Mattara' in the spring; the name is Aboriginal for 'Hand of Friendship'. The Newcastle Agricultural Show is held annually in February/March, and the Conservatorium of Music sponsors a prestigious Keyboard Festival each year.

History

Captain Cook described present-day Nobbys Island at the entrance to present-day Newcastle Harbour as he passed by in 1770; the harbour itself was first discovered in 1797, when Governor Hunter ordered a group of marines to search for four convicts who had escaped by boat and headed north. While the convicts and the boat were never found, Lieutenant John Shortland in the *Reliance* explored the coastline upon his return to Sydney and found the Newcastle harbour. He also identified coal in the rocks along the nearby river, thus naming it the 'Coal' River, now the Hunter; by 1798 a mining operation began there.

The settlement at present-day Newcastle was not established until 1804, when New South Wales Governor King decreed that a new penal colony, for recidivists and recalcitrants both male and female, should be founded at the mouth of the Hunter River. Charles Throsby became the first Commandant with only 20 soldiers and 20 convicts in the first year. By 1816 Captain Wallis had 1000 convicts under his control here, 400 of whom began to build the breakwater in the harbour, connecting Nobbys Island to the mainland. In the early 1820s the settlement gained its most fearsome reputation, when Major Morisset, popularly known as 'King Lash' (later to become the notorious Commandant of Norfolk Island), imposed his rigorous system of flogging, and forced convicts to construct the bathing pool known as Bogey's Hole, along with the backbreaking task of building the breakwater. By 1823, Morisset left, and under the term of Captain Gillman, the place became a free settlement and was named Newcastle. Land grants were quickly taken up in the region, particularly in the Hunter Valley, which soon became the breadbasket for the entire colony and, most importantly, a major source of red cedar (see box), the colony's prime timber.

Once Newcastle was declared a free town, the surveyor Henry Dangar was commissioned to devise a town plan. Dangar's solution, a simple grid of three east–west and seven north–south streets with a central north–south public axis, still forms the basis for Newcastle's inner city. Dangar also established city blocks of only 90m width, unlike the larger scale of Melbourne and Adelaide; this scale accounts for the unusually intimate and compact dimensions of central Newcastle today. While the 1820s saw the area become a primary agricultural centre with the founding of the Australian Agricultural Company, the town's real industry and reason for being was coal-mining. The first pit opened in 1831; by 1848, the convict gaol closed and the last remnants of penal settlement were removed. In the late 1840s, the opening of the immense coal deposit, the Borehole Seam, in the present suburb of Hamilton, led to new miners' encampments outside central Newcastle. This situation caused Newcastle to develop as a series of separate villages and townships that were not amalgamated as Greater Newcastle until the early 20C although Newcastle itself had become a municipality in 1859.

The area grew rapidly in the 1850s and 1860s, prompted by the arrival of the railway. Many of the early historical buildings date from this period. The great number of elaborate commercial buildings, many of them built by an immigrant architect from North Germany, Frederick Menkens (1855–1910), arose in the High Victorian era from 1880 to 1910, when Newcastle's coal-mining still sustained a thriving economy based on coal and shipping. By the time of Federation in 1901, however, the coal began to run out, and the city faced hard times. The decision by the New South Wales government to build a state dockyard in Newcastle Harbour coincided with the most significant event in Newcastle's development: the arrival of the Broken Hill Proprietary Ltd (BHP) steelworks in 1913, and the subsequent attraction of additional heavy-industry factories. By the 1920s, one-third of Newcastle's workers were employed in either the steelworks or the docks, and their factories came to dominate Novocastrian skyline and the citizens' lives; as novelist Elizabeth Harrower, who was born in the suburb of Mayfield in 1928, wrote, the city 'had been—you might say on principle—low-lying, single-storeyed in everything, that is, but steelworks and factories'.

Newcastle's sprawling suburban development did not augur well for inner-city living and architecture; still, the city did see the appearance of some interesting modernist architecture in the 1960s and 1970s. Particularly interesting is the work carried out at the University of Newcastle, especially those buildings completed under the direction of the German-Swiss-born architect Frederick Romberg (1913–92), the university's first Professor of Architecture. Romberg's presence at the university, after many successful years in Melbourne, inspired other leading architectural groups to build in the area. The university campus itself is an important architectural and cultural centre in the area; physically, it is set in bushland and is considered the most 'arboreal' of Australian campuses. Literary activities here are strong; the campus is the location for Nimrod Publications, which specialises in local writing, and the English department sponsors important poetry competitions and writers-in-residence programmes.

Visitors staying for any length of time in the Newcastle area might want to get a copy of the excellent *Architecture Newcastle: A Guide* by Barry Maitland and David Stafford for the University of Newcastle and the RAIA; it is a thorough examination of buildings and sites of historical and architectural interest.

Red cedar

The use of the common name of 'cedar' for various types of wood in Australia is a good example of the early settlers' practice of giving familiar Northern Hemisphere names to newly discovered flora which in some way resembled the tree or plant they knew at home. When Australians speak of red cedar, they mean *Cedrela australis*, a large tree of the family Meliaceae, the only species of the genus indigenous to Australia; these trees are not members of the genus *cedrus*, the 'real' cedar known to Europeans and Americans. Australians also talk of white cedar, *Melia dubia*, and even Mackay cedar, which is actually *Albizzia toona*. But red cedar was the timber at the heart of the colonial industry; the tree was once a familiar feature of most eastern coastal forests, and recognised immediately for its durability and flexibility—a feature missing from most other Australian woods. As early as 1795, Australian cedar was exported to India, and cedar felling was an important early industry, especially in the Hawkesbury and Northern coastal regions of New South Wales; the culture of the cedar-getters became legendary, as a rough and ready group. An American, writing about them in 1851, stated 'They labour very hard but they are certain the most improvident set of men in the world, often eclipsing in recklessness, mystery and peculiarity of character the wood-cutters of Campeachy and the lumberers of the Ohio and Mississippi.' Most of the beautiful interior floors and woodwork of the Macquarie-era buildings were of red cedar. By the 1890s, these once majestic trees had been almost entirely logged out; today, red cedar is one of the rarest and most prized woods for furniture-makers, and house salvagers still make enormous profits if they can find old house-fittings of cedar to recycle.

Newcastle City

The Pacific Highway leads directly into Newcastle City, becoming the main shopping thoroughfare, Hunter Street, which ends at the harbour and near Nobbys Island. The foreshore at this point stretches along the harbour, which is comprised of the mouth of the Hunter River where it enters the ocean through an opening between the Nobbys Island breakwater and the land-spit of Stockton on the northern bank. **Queen's Wharf**, a project of the Newcastle Foreshore development scheme completed for the Bicentenary in 1988, is the location of the main **tourist centre**, and is linked to Hunter Street by a pedestrian bridge; the redevelopment continues into the Foreshore Park heading up towards Nobbys Island. The design of the wharf could be labelled 'post-modern' in its use of varying shapes and sizes, and won many awards at the time it first opened. It already appears dated architecturally, but is a valuable addition to the cityscape for its reclamation of previously inaccessible land. You can climb a tower here for magnificent views of the harbour and the city. A replica of *William IV*, the first Australian-built steam/sailing ship, is also moored along this reclaimed foreshore, and harbour cruises, as well as the ferry over to Stockton on the other side of the river, originate from the pier. The tourist centre is an excellent one, and provides a comprehensive heritage walk map.

Return to HUNTER STREET, which at this point is City Mall, and then becomes SCOTT STREET heading east. Past the Railway Station, now a rather neglected

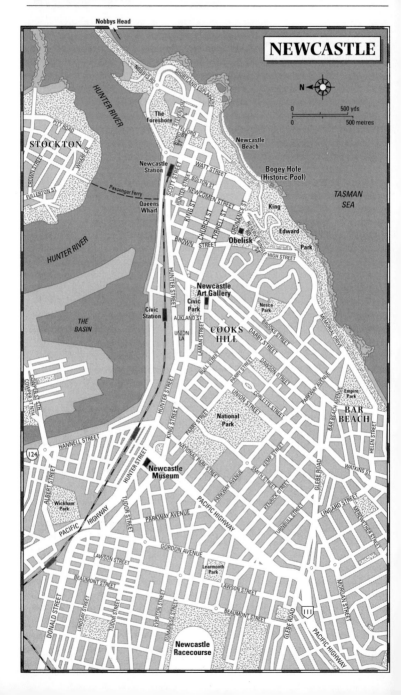

NEWCASTLE

Nobbys Head

HUNTER RIVER

STOCKTON

PITT ROAD

WHARF CR.

CROWN STREET

FULLERTON ST.

HUNTER RIVER

THE BASIN

COMPED. HILL STREET

124

ALBERT STREET

Wickham Park

DONALD STREET

LINDSAY STREET

TUDOR STREET

PACIFIC HIGHWAY

NOBBYS RD.

SHORTLAND ESPLANADE

The Foreshore

STEVENSON

TELFORD

Newcastle Station

Passenger Ferry

Queens Wharf

SCOTT STREET

HUNTER STREET

WATT STREET

BOLTON ST.

NEWCOMEN STREET

KING ST.

CHURCH ST.

TYRELL ST.

BROWN STREET

ORDNANCE ST.

RESERVE RIDGE ROAD

Obelisk

Newcastle Beach

Bogey Hole (Historic Pool)

King

Edward Park

HIGH STREET

TASMAN SEA

Newcastle Art Gallery

Civic Park

Civic Station

AUKLAND ST.

UNION LA.

LAMAN STREET

COOKS HILL

Nesca Park

DARBY STREET

BROOKS STREET

MEMORIAL DRIVE

BULL STREET

PARRY STREET

DAWSON STREET

CORLETTE STREET

PARKWAY AVENUE

BAR BEACH AVENUE

Empire Park

BAR BEACH

HELEN STREET

HUNTER STREET

KING STREET

National Park

UNION STREET

NATIONAL PARK STREET

SMITH STREET

KEMP STREET

KENRICK STREET

TURNBULL STREET

GLEBE ROAD

WATKINS ST.

LINGARD STREET

MEREWETHER STREET

HANNELL STREET

Newcastle Museum

PARKWAY AVENUE

PACIFIC HIGHWAY

PARKWAY AVENUE

GORDON AVENUE

LAWSON STREET

Learmonth Park

LAWSON STREET

MORGAN STREET

PACIFIC HIGHWAY

BEAUMONT STREET

EVERTON STREET

DUMARESQ STREET

BEAUMONT STREET

GLEBE ROAD

111

Newcastle Racecourse

N

0   500 yds
0   500 metres

Victorian structure, is the Convict Stockade, an unassuming area between Scott and Bond Streets of great historical significance for its archaeological record of early Australian convictism. Nearby, on the corner of Watt and Scott Streets, is the striking **Customs House** with Italianate tower, built in 1877 by Colonial Architect James Barnet, with 1900 additions by Government Architect W.L. Vernon. Situated on a plaza overlooking the harbour, this graceful building has a commanding presence in this early part of town; its architecture is complemented by the **Earp Gilliam Building** on the corner of Bond and Telford Street immediately to the east of Customs House. This former bond store and produce market was one of the many works of Newcastle's greatest early architect, Frederick Menkens, who completed this polychromatic brick structure in 1888. Its restoration was completed by Brian Suters' architectural practice, responsible for much of the conservation work carried out in the city in the 1980s.

From Customs House Plaza, travel c 1km towards Nobbys Head and Flagstaff Hill (also known as Beacon Hill). At Stevenson Place and Nobbys Road are **'Boatman's Row' terraces**, a group of houses built in 1892 and associated with the lifeboat men responsible for rescue after shipwrecks. Travel up NOBBYS ROAD to **Fort Scratchley**, now the site of the Military & Maritime Historical Museums (☎ 02 4929 2588, open daily in cooperation with a number of other sites). The hill was the site of the town's first coal mine, probably the first mine in Australia. In 1876, in response to fears of Russian invasion, Major-General William Jervois and Lieutenant Colonel Peter Scratchley recommended that fortifications be built at the entrance to Newcastle Harbour. The gun emplacements here, surrounded by concrete walls, were erected between 1881 and 1886. These guns, kept fully operational throughout the 20C, were finally used against a Japanese submarine during the Second World War. The museum on this site houses a collection on nautical history in the region and includes the relics of the French Barque *Adolphe*, wrecked on the infamous Oyster Bank in 1904; the hull of the ship can be seen against the Stockton Breakwall.

Continue up Nobby Road to **Nobbys Head**.

In 1816, the then Nobbys Island, still separated from the mainland, became the location of a prison for recalcitrant female convicts. At about the same time, Captain Wallis ordered the building of the breakwater to link the island. Under brutal Major Morisset, work continued in the 1820s, until suspended by Governor Brisbane. The breakwater was finally completed in 1846. In 1854, a certain Colonel Barney of the Royal Engineers, convinced that the island was an obstruction to navigation, attempted to blow it up with two tonnes of gunpowder. Novocastrians protested and the demolition was halted, although 30 feet from the top were cut away. The present lighthouse was erected in 1857, when the coal fire previously used for navigation on Beacon Hill was extinguished. The lighthouse, built by Colonial Architect Alexander Dawson, is the oldest lighthouse in New South Wales installed with modern 'Trinity House' codes.

Return to town via the SHORTLAND ESPLANADE, travelling past the old **Rock Baths**, built in 1883 and known as Soldiers Baths because of their use by the garrison at Fort Scratchley. These baths fell into disrepair with the opening in 1922 of the Ocean Baths to the south by Newcastle Beach. Shortland Esplanade continues along the beach past the Royal Newcastle Hospital, situated nearly on the beach with amazing views of the Pacific Ocean. At Fletcher Park along the beach near Watt Street is a statue to James Fletcher (1834–91), an important friend of the miners and union organiser. Continue south c 500m to the **Bogey Hole**, the infamous Commandant's Pool built by convict labour for Major Morisset between 1819 and 1822. 'Bogey' derives from an Aboriginal word for bathing. The pool was opened for public use in 1863; it is now the earliest reminder of Newcastle's convict past.

Bogey Hole sits at the edge of **King Edward Park**, one of the many attractive public parks throughout the city. This one includes sunken gardens, an iron-

work rotunda from 1898, and a garden named in honour of Newcastle's American 'sister city', Arcadia, California.

At the top of the park off Reserve Road is the **Obelisk**, on the site of the settlement's first flour mill, the windmill of which was an important navigational marker from the 1820s until its demolition in 1847. In response to the demand for another marker on the site, the Obelisk was built in 1850. From here, citizens in 1866 watched one of the worst maritime disasters in Australian history, when on a single day five ships were blown onto the notorious Oyster Bank sandspit on the northern side of the harbour.

Detail of the iron-work bandstand at King Edward Park, Newcastle

The Obelisk is also at the edge of the area known as **The Hill**, from the early days the location of the best houses and public buildings. Across the street from the Obelisk on ORDNANCE STREET is Jesmond House, one of the grandest Victorian villas in Newcastle, built in 1875 and long associated with the brewer John Wood. The tower was added in the 1880s, to allow the son John Robert Wood to pursue his hobby of landscape and ocean photography. When the younger Wood married a popular Shakespearian actress, the house became the venue for the city's most fashionable social events. It was in the process of building the rear wings of the house that Frederick Menkens accused the electrical sub-contractor of shoddy work, was sued by the contractor, refused to pay, and was sent to gaol for 12 months.

The Hill is now dominated by the Newcastle **Court House** on CHURCH STREET near Bolton Street. Built in 1890 by Colonial Architect James Barnet and completed by W.L. Vernon, the building is a well-proportioned example of High Victorian Classical architecture. It is located on what was originally the army parade ground and then the first cricket ground in Newcastle. Around the corner on Newcomen Street, within the walls of the present James Fletcher Hospital, the Medical Superintendent's Residence is an excellent example of an early garrison house with verandah; it was built in 1841 to serve as officers' quarters for the barracks. Diagonally across the street from the Court House on the corner of Church and Bolton Streets is the **former Newcastle East Public School**, home of the oldest continuously existing school in Australia until its closure in 1980. A school was on the site from 1816. The present structure is an example of a rather loosely defined Federation Style applied to public buildings, completed in 1912 by W.L. Vernon, with Arts and Crafts-style proportions; the alternating brick-and-stone bands are referred to as a 'blood and bandages' or 'bacon-rind' façade.

This block of Bolton Street, between Church and King Streets, contains two other exemplary buildings. **Cohen's Bond Store**, a five-storey warehouse, was one of the most significant commercial works of Frederick Menkens, built in 1901 of monochromatic dark brick. Only the elegant façade remains, with its dramatic arches and detailed cornice; behind is now a car park. In contrast, the corner building on King Street is the **Court Chambers**, a whimsical two-storey High Victorian office building designed by E.C. Yeomans in 1898. Almost every window and gable includes a different form of decoration, and the corner entrance is topped by the bust of a judge.

Further along Bolton Street, on the corner of Hunter Street is the sober **ANZ Bank building**, built by Scott and Green in 1914 in what is called an 'Inter-War Commercial Palazzo style'; while around the corner at nos 127–131 Scott Street between Bolton and Newcomen Streets is Frederick Menkens' most exuberant building, now the **Air Force Club**. Originally built in 1892 to house the offices and auction rooms of wine merchant Joseph Wood, it became the Longworth Institute, with art gallery and recital hall, in 1907. The elaborate decorative façade is the most fanciful indication of Menken's North German origins.

Turn south on Newcomen Street to return to The Hill. At KING STREET is **Claremont House**, unique in Newcastle as an intact Victorian residence in Georgian style. It was built in the 1840s and was at one time the home of artist Richard Read, who sold it to mining boss Alexander Brown in 1843. It is a charming example of a two-storey timber house with impressive verandah and ironwork balustrade.

This part of The Hill is also the site of **Christ Church Cathedral**, certainly the most significant structure in Newcastle. The entire city centre was planned around its axial location, and its initial design was the largest work of the important early church architect, the Canadian-born John Horbury Hunt (1838–1904). The saga of the church's construction is, as one source states 'of medieval duration'. Commissioned to replace the dilapidated church that had occupied this prominent site since 1817, Hunt began the design in 1868, but many disputes between Hunt and the Dean of the Cathedral, Arthur Selwyn, delayed construction until 1883. By 1895, more feuds led to the sacking of Hunt, at which time only the external walls to the level of the nave were completed. Further variations were made in the next few years, although the present form of the cathedral was not carried out until the appointment of Frederick Menkens' partner F.G. Castleden in 1912. Castleden worked on the church over the next 20 years and added the castellated parapet to Hunt's original design. The tower was not raised until 1979, 110 years after the commencement of the cathedral. The 1989 earthquake caused substantial structural damage, leading to its reinforcement with 4km of concealed steel rods through the fabric of the building.

About 300m further west on CHURCH STREET is **St Mary's Star of the Sea Church**, built in 1866 as the first Roman Catholic Church in the town. Around the corner on Brown and Tyrrell Streets is the historic Navigation Beacon Tower, erected in 1865 as one of a pair of navigational aids. One tower had a red light, and the other a white light, by which ships could steer a course through the heads into the harbour. Another project of Colonial Architect James Barnet, the towers were used until 1918, when they were made obsolete by other devices.

Tyrrell Street proceeds west to Darby Street and Civic Park, where it becomes Laman Street, in the area known as **Cooks Hill**. This area is elevated from the main centre of town, offering good views of the area to the ocean.

At no. 1 LAMAN STREET is the **Newcastle Regional Art Gallery** (Tues–Sun, 10.00–17.00; ☎ 02 4929 3263), a rather uninspiring contemporary building, opened by the Queen in 1977. The gallery houses the city's art collection, largely Australian works with many examples by Novocastrian native William Dobell (see p 186), and has regularly changing exhibitions. Next door is the Newcastle Regional Library, formerly the War Memorial Culture Centre, which opened in 1957 with the art gallery and conservatorium of music.

At the corner of Laman and Dawson Streets, an astonishingly Classical **Baptist Tabernacle**, built in 1890, stands as testimony to architect Frederick Menkens' German training in a variety of stylistic modes. One need only compare this church, with its Corinthian columns, with another of Menkens' designs, **St Andrew's Presbyterian Church**, across the street on the other corner of Civic Park. For this church, built in the same year as the tabernacle, Menkens selected a more predictable Gothic style, facing the entrance away from the park rather than facing in and with a highly vertical spire.

In spacious Civic Park is the **Captain James Cook Fountain**, the result of a sculptural competition in 1966. The sculptor Margel Hinder has attempted to incorporate water and non-water elements to signify, according to one critic, 'the energy, vigour and metallic strength of Newcastle'.

Across Auckland Street from St Andrew's is an exciting new addition to Newcastle's architectural and cultural life, the **University of Newcastle Conservatorium**. Built as a Bicentennial project in 1988 under the auspices of Government Architect J.W. Thomson, the post-modernist exterior, with its evocation of Art Deco motifs, envelops one of the best acoustic spaces in the world, designed specifically for music performances with state-of-the-art recording facilities.

The **Cooks Hill area** was in the early Victorian era a working-class residential neighbourhood, and some examples of these domestic structures remain, most of them now used as galleries or offices. Just as with the campaign to save The Rocks in Sydney, however, these buildings only barely escaped the wreckers' ball of the 1970s. The **von Bertouch Galleries**, 1–7 Hanniford's Lane off Laman Street, represents one of the first 'rescues' of these buildings from demolition. In 1969, the campaign was able to save these four terrace houses from the 1870s, and turned them into the first commercial art gallery in Australia outside the main cities. Also of historical interest in the area is **'Leslieville'**, at no. 63 Union Street. Now the headquarters of the Workers' Educational Association, this lovely Victorian residence with two-storey iron lace balcony was built by William Arnott (1827–1901), founder of Arnott's Biscuits, still one of Australia's best-known companies. Arnott migrated from Scotland, first setting up a successful bakery in Maitland. He moved to Newcastle in 1864, and established his famous biscuit factory on a site adjoining this house, named Leslieville after his first son. While the Arnott family moved to Mayfield in 1888, this building served as the main company offices until Arnott closed the Newcastle works in 1914 and moved to Sydney.

On the Pacific Highway heading west, where the Old Pacific Highway intersects with Hunter Street, is the **Newcastle Regional Museum** (☎ 02 4962 2001; Tues–Sun 10.00–17.00), housed in the old Castlemaine and Wood Bros Brewery complex. The brewery buildings date from 1876, with many alterations and additions before the brewery closed in 1931. Used as an open-air market for many years, its successful recycled renovation was the work of Brian Suters' firm in 1988. The museum concentrates on industrial and social history of the Newcastle area, and includes Supernova, a fun technology centre.

Newcastle suburbs

Many of Newcastle's older suburbs, those that were developed originally as mining villages, are well worth a stroll, both for examples of 19C architecture and to visit the Victorian-era parks, such as Lambton Park in **Lambton**, created by ambitious local residents out of swamp and scrubland. Other mining-village suburbs worth a visit are **Wallsend**, established in 1859; **Mayfield**, in the 1880s the location of fashionable homes and now the most working-class neighbourhood; and **Waratah**, dating from the 1860s, now a students' neighbourhood.

Of particular interest is the very old suburb of **Hamilton**, site of Newcastle Racecourse and Learmonth Park, an Edwardian 'garden suburb'. Hamilton is now the most multicultural community in Newcastle, with Beaumont Street as its heart; the street is a good place to find ethnic eateries and markets.

University of Newcastle

Continue west on the Pacific Highway and follow the turn-off signs to University Drive in Callaghan, location of the University of Newcastle. Established as a university in 1965 from the amalgamation of an earlier college, the bushland setting of the campus provided ample opportunity for many important works of contemporary architecture. The first of these was the Student Union, completed in 1969 by Archer Mortlock Murray and Woolley. Described poetically by architectural critic Robin Boyd as 'tamed Australian romantic...brutalism', the building was one of the most important in the region in the 1960s, for introducing this organic style. Similarly, the Architecture Building, completed by the firm of Romberg and Boyd in 1970, at the time Romberg was Professor of Architecture here, blends well into the landscape and begins to define what would be called a Sydney Regional style. Similar low-scale modernism determines the look of the Great Hall, completed in 1973 by the Archer Mortlock group, while later buildings, such as the 1992 BSC Building by renowned British architect Michael Wilford with Suters Architects, and the 1994 high-tech Advanced Technology Centre by Jackson Teese and Associates, represent Australian architecture's coming of age. Finally, the Design Building of 1994, designed by Stutchbury and Pape, EJE Architecture, demonstrates the best of contemporary design sensitive to environmental needs and economic stringencies.

The Hunter Valley

Only 50km west of Newcastle and 200km north of Sydney, **Cessnock** (population 17,500) marks the beginning of the Hunter Valley, Australia's first centre
for viticulture and still one of the leading wine-producing areas in the country.
The region extends from Cessnock in the south to the area near the Upper
Hunter River in the north, around the town of Scone. Dotted throughout are
some of the oldest and still the best known Australian wineries.

History of the Hunter Valley vineyards

The Hunter Valley was not settled until the 1820s when explorer and pioneer
John Howe blazed a trail from Windsor through Singleton to Maitland on the
Hunter River. Wine-growing, bizarrely juxtaposed in the region with coal-
mining, was established here almost immediately upon settlement. While
vines accompanied the First Fleet and early figures such as John Macarthur
and Gregory Blaxland had already established vineyards on their properties
from the earliest days of the colony, wine became a viable Australian product
only after the initiation of the Hunter Valley vineyards.

James Busby (1810–71) was instrumental in the establishment of the
region for wine-growing. A remarkable Scottish immigrant (son of the
engineer of 'Busby's Bore' fame in Sydney) with no previous knowledge of
wine-making, Busby decided before arriving in the country that Australia
held great promise for wine-producing. He set out to learn all he could
about viticulture, publishing in 1825, at the age of 24, *A Treatise on the
Culture of the Vine*, followed in 1830 by *A Manual of Plain Directions for
Planting and Cultivating Vineyards and for Making Wine in New South Wales*.
Busby was granted 2000 acres near the Hunter River, and on a trip to
Europe in 1831, he assembled some 400 vine cuttings, both French and
Spanish, to be planted in the Sydney Botanic Gardens upon his return in
1832, and distributed to suitable growers throughout the colony. He left
Australia in 1833 for New Zealand, where he was instrumental in the
development of that colony. At that time, he turned over the mantle of wine
developer to **Dr Henry Lindeman**, founder of the Lindeman label still in
operation today, and George Wyndham, founder of Wyndham Estates. In
1842, Lindeman, an ex-navy doctor, purchased the property Cawarra, near
Paterson; by 1861, this estate produced some 5000 gallons from his own
vineyard and 30,000 gallons from grapes purchased from neighbouring
growers. The **Cawarra Estate**, listed by the National Trust, with buildings
from the 1880s and a wine cellar used from 1853 to 1918, still stands in
the Paterson River Valley, 3km north of Gresford. (The property is a private
residence, not open to the public.)

The second half of the 19C was the golden era of Hunter Valley wines,
with an increase in yields for their white table wines and recognition at
international exhibitions. By the turn of the century, however, South
Australian wines came to dominate the market, as Australian tastes tended
towards sweet and fortified wines, a situation that continued until the
1970s. Hunter Valley whites, especially Semillon varieties, continued to be
produced, but much of the land was turned back into grazing pasture, and
vineyards were consolidated under a few labels. In the last twenty years, of
course, all this has changed, as Australian drinking habits have been trans-

formed. An enthusiastic wine culture, both at home and abroad, has nurtured new vineyards as well as the expansion of the established names. Along with *Lindeman* and *Wyndham*, these names include *Tyrell's*, *Drayton's*, and *Rothbury Estate*.

Any tour of the region should begin in **Cessnock**. The **tourist information centre** (☎ 02 4990 4477), on the corner of Wollombi and Mount View Roads, will provide maps and brochures of all the wineries and restaurants (dining opportunities in the area are excellent), and can help with the arrangement of tours, should you wish to partake of the grape and not be worried about driving after drinking (the state's strict .05 limitations are enforced here as well!).

Although wineries (and dining) are the real reason to visit the Hunter Valley, a few other points of interest can be found in the region. 30km southwest of Cessnock is the historic village of **Wollombi** (an Aboriginal word for 'Meeting of the Waters'), filled with sandstone buildings dating from the 1840s and the Endeavour Museum, located in the 1866 Wollombi Courthouse.

On the road northeast of Cessnock (route 132) is **Kurri Kurri** (18km), which has an architecturally curious three-storey turn-of-the-century pub, *The Kurri Kurri Hotel*, on the corner of Land and Hampden Streets. Such large verandah-and-ironwork hotels in quaint country villages dot the Hunter Valley landscape, many dating from the prosperous period before the country-wide economic depression of the 1890s.

Maitland

Maitland, with a population of 46,000, is on the Hunter River, 28km west of Newcastle. There is a regular train service from Newcastle.

Settled in 1818 when convicts were brought up the river to chop cedar trees, Maitland was a flourishing town by the 1840s; until the early 20C, Newcastle students had to travel to Maitland to attend high school. The *Maitland Mercury and Hunter River General Advertiser* was established in 1843 and is the oldest surviving country newspaper in the state. Its greatest claim to fame in the 20C was as the birthplace of the legendary boxer Les Darcy, who died tragically in America at 21 in 1917; and as the site of devastating floods in 1955.

The **tourist information office** is at Hew Cottage, New England Highway, ☎ 02 4933 2611. The entire inner city around High Street, as well as several buildings on Church Street, are listed as National Trust properties. Of note are 'Brough House' and Grossman House, on Church Street, built as mirror images adjoining each other by merchants Samuel Owen and Isaac Becket in 1860–62. **Brough House** is now the Maitland City Art Gallery (☎ 02 4933 165; Mon–Fri, 13.00–16.00, Sat 13.30–17.00, Sun 10.30–17.00) and **Grossman House** is a history museum (☎ 02 4933 6452; Sat and Sun 13.30–16.30).

Other outstanding structures include **'Aberglasslyn'**, a two-storey stone Regency house dating from the 1840s and situated on the banks of the river; and **'Cintra'**, Regent Street, an elegant homestead of the 1880s now open as a bed and breakfast. At 1 High Street in East Maitland is **Fosters Farm**, a small brick and stone farmhouse built in 1829 by ex-convict Samuel Clift.

Only 5km northeast of Maitland is the historic village of **Morpeth**, at one time the major port on the Hunter River and the seat of the bishops of Newcastle. Established as a river port from 1831–41, it developed on the property of Edward Close. The opening of the Great Northern Railway in 1857 bypassed Morpeth and caused Newcastle's emergence as the regional centre. The town consists of a surprising number of intact buildings from the 1850s, including Close's Georgian-style house 'Closebourne' and a charming courthouse (now a public library) dating from the 1860s as well as numerous shopfronts and verandahs.

From Maitland, the New England Highway (route 15) continues through historic coal-mining towns such as **Singleton**, home of the Australian Infantry Corps Museum, and **Muswellbrook** and **Scone**, one of the largest horse-breeding centres in the world.

20km north of Scone is **Burning Mountain Nature Reserve**, site of an underground burning coal seam that has been smouldering for a thousand years. Early settlers believed it was a volcano.

Barrington Tops National Park

From Scone, you can take a largely unsealed road 80km east towards Gloucester to reach this stunning mountain park. More conveniently, you can travel from Maitland north towards Gloucester, through the historic village of **Scone**, famed for its convict-built Anglican Church of St John, constructed of local clay bricks in 1833.

At Gloucester, turn west and proceed 38km on dirt roads to the park's entrance. Rightly considered a 'must-see' by most travel writers, **Barrington Tops National Park** (☎ 02 4987 3108) has been World Heritage listed since 1969 and is the catchment area for six rivers feeding into the Manning and Hunter Rivers. The most extraordinary feature of this 39,000 ha park is the abrupt altitude changes, from subtropical rainforest at the base of the peaks (highest point is 1555m) to windswept plateaus with snow gums and occasional snow. Tremendous walking trails, including a riverside walk suitable for wheelchairs, make the journey to reach the park more than worthwhile. The mountains served as inspiration for popular poet Les Murray's 'The Bulahdelah-Taree Holiday Song Cycle' (1984).

New England region

The New England Highway (route 15) northwest from Newcastle leads inland through the region along the Great Dividing Range designated since 1836 as **New England**. First crossed by explorer John Oxley in 1818 on his way into Queensland, this farming region sits on a high plateau which leads to seasonal weather changes unlike those on the warm northern coast of the state; the region extends as far north as Warwick in Queensland. As a way to avoid the most touristy parts of the coast, this route offers an interesting alternative. Because of its escarpment and its geological formation, the region is famous for its fossicking possibilities. Jaspers, serpentine, quartz, crystal and chalcedony are found throughout the countryside, and the area around the town of Glen Innes contains major deposits of sapphires, as well as tin. Some diamond and gold-mining are also still in operation.

Driving through New England offers picturesque scenery, with mountains, streams, and deep gorges on one side, and black-soil plains planted with wheat and cotton on the other. River fishing is also excellent. Tourist information for the entire region is available through **New England Tourism Development Authority**, 215 Beardy Street, Armidale; ☎ 02 6772 8155. The rail from Sydney travels daily along this route, ending at Armidale (with bus connections to Inverell).

Major towns in New England include **Tamworth** (population 35,000), world-famous to country-music fans as the Down-Under Nashville. Major recording studios for Australia's thriving country music scene are established here, and the week-long Country Festival occurs here every year, ending on Australia Day weekend (end of January), when the country music awards are presented. On a historical note, Tamworth calls itself the 'city of light', as it was the first city in the southern hemisphere to be totally electrified, in 1888. The **tourist information office** is on Kable Avenue, ☎ 02 6768 4462. The office can provide information on possible visits to country-music recording studios in the city.

Armidale

A further 110km north on the New England Highway is **Armidale** (population 20,000), a convenient and pleasant place to stop over on the Sydney to Brisbane drive. **Tourist information**: Marsh and Dumaresq Streets, ☎ 02 6773 8527. The University of New England, formed as an amalgamation of two university colleges in 1954, is located 5km northwest of the city, and provides an academic atmosphere in much of the town. The campus has a number of impressive buildings, including 'Booloominbah', a large three-storey residence built by J. Horbury Hunt in 1883. Author Thomas Keneally once taught here, as did the detective novelist Robert Barnard. Native daughters include the great poet Judith Wright, who was born at nearby Thalgarrah Station; and contemporary poet Kaye Mill, who wrote in one poem, 'Armidale flatly denies time'. The town sits at 1000m high, and so has true autumn, with attending colour changes of the area's many trees.

In town, the **New England Regional Art Museum**, on Kentucky Street, contains the Hinton Collection, a substantial and significant collection of Australian art. Also in Kentucky Street is the **Aboriginal Centre and Keeping Place** (☎ 02 6771 1249, weekdays 09.00–17.00, weekends 10.00–16.00), which has regular exhibitions. In the centre of Armidale, at Dangar and Tingcombe Streets, is the Cathedral Church of St Peter Apostle and Martyr, a veritable extravaganza of brick in Gothic Revival style by J. Horbury Hunt (1871–78).

About 6km west from Armidale, near the airport, is **Saumarez Homestead**, the 1830s property of pastoralist F.J. White. The main house dates from the 1890s, with cast-iron roof and cedar joinery. Run by the National Trust, the property is open to the public; hours vary, so check before visiting (☎ 02 6772 3616).

Route 78 east from Armidale leads to two national parks of interest. 42km east is **Oxley Wild Rivers National Park** (☎ 02 6773 7211), a vast (90,276 ha) expanse of gorges, valleys, and stunning waterfalls, including Australia's highest (457m), **Wollomombi Falls**. The park contains some 750 species of plants. A further 40km east is **New England National Park** (☎ 02 6657 2309), part of the World Heritage listed rainforest parks of the northeast section of the state. The park includes great views and bushwalks, and provides some interesting cabin accommodation in the grounds itself.

Another 38km north on the highway leads to the small town of **Guyra** (population 2,000), which is an Aboriginal word for 'fish may be caught'; indeed, the many local streams provide excellent fishing opportunities. **Tourist information**: Crystal Trout Caravan Park, New England Highway, ☎ 02 6779 1241. The town is situated on the highest part of the Great Dividing Range (at 1320m), so rivers east of the railway line flow towards the Pacific Ocean, those on the west flow west to the Murray River and ultimately the Southern Ocean. The area was first settled in 1838, when several families took up large tracts for sheep and other livestock; the area is also famous for its potatoes (commemorated in a lamb and potato festival in January). Ollera station is still owned by the original settlers, the Everetts, and is now classified by the National Trust; the lovely brick and timber house dates from the 1870s (not open to the public). Also in town is the **Guyra & District Historical Museum** (☎ 02 6779 1621; open Sun afternoons), run by an active historical society, and St Bartholomew's Church of England (1876), one of the most dramatic of Newcastle architect John Horbury Hunt's small rural churches.

From Guyra, the highway proceeds north 60km to the dairying and mining town of **Glen Innes** (population 6000), a centre for sapphire fossicking. The town includes many fine examples of country-town hotels, defining the corners of the street and including two-storey colonnaded verandahs; the *William's Club Hotel*, on the corner of Wentworth and Grey Streets, is a good example of this vernacular style. The town also has **Land of the Beardies History House**, an amusing folk museum with period rooms housed in the town's first hospital. The **tourist information office** is on Church Street, ☎ 02 6732 2397.

As with so many other areas in Australia, Glen Innes is immensely proud of its Scottish heritage, hence a number of Celtic monuments and events: street signs in Gaelic, the Australian Standing Stones monument on a hill above town, Celtic Festivals in early May, and an Australian Bush Music Festival in early October.

West of Glen Innes on route 38 some 67km is **Inverell** (population 10,800), centre for sapphire mining. Industrial diamonds, zircons, and tin are also mined in the area. **Tourist information**: Water Towers Complex, Campbell Street, ☎ 02 6722 1693. A self-guided walk brochure is available from the information centre, and sapphire fossicking trips can also be arranged there.

Further west c75km is the small town of **Bingara** (population 1,250), also a centre for mining, especially gold and tourmalines. An interesting way to travel from Inverell to Bingara is along the small road around Copeton Dam (a section of the road is unsealed) to the road west towards Keera along the Gwydir River; the area is filled with small creeks and rivers and old mines.

Immediately northeast of Bingara is the **Myall Creek area**, site of one of the most significant massacres of Aborigines. In May 1838, a group of 40 Aborigines had set up camp near a stockman's hut on the Myall Creek station, only recently settled. While the group had established friendly relations with the stockmen, on the night of 9 June, 12 armed men arrived and without any provocation murdered 28 men, women and children; they later returned to burn the bodies. When the station manager returned to Myall Creek and learned of the incident, he informed the police, who in turn informed the Governor of New South Wales, Sir George Gipps. Gipps demanded an investigation; the murderers were arrested and tried on 11 counts of murder. While the prisoners freely admitted the killings, they were astonished that they would be charged with murder, considering Aborigines less than human. Despite protests from many colonists, seven of the men were executed—the first time white offenders were tried and convicted for crimes against Aborigines. At the time of writing, efforts are underway by the Uniting Church and others to place some kind of memorial at the site of the massacre, believed to be some 23km northeast from Bingara along the road to Delungra, at Whitlow Road. For more information, contact Paulette Smith, ☎ 02 6724 1626.

The last town of any size in New South Wales on the New England Highway is **Tenterfield** (population 3300), well-known as the birthplace of entertainer Peter Allen, whose song 'Tenterfield Saddler' was an international hit in the 1970s. The town's more serious claim to fame is as the birthplace of Australian Federation. Here, on 24 October 1889, Sir Henry Parkes (1815–96) gave a famous speech that led to the move towards a national convention and drafting of an Australian constitution. These efforts culminated in federation of the Australian states in 1901. A museum at Centenary Cottage commemorates this event, as well as displays at the Sir Henry Parkes Memorial School of Arts, corner Manners and Rouse Streets, ☎ 02 6736 1454. On the Woodenbong Road 29km northeast of Tenterfield is **Bald Rock National Park** (☎ 02 6732 5133), with its enormous domed granite rock 213m high. Also on this road is Boonoo Boonoo National Park, with river, waterfall, and beautiful spring flowers. **Tourist information:** Rouse Street, ☎ 02 6736 1082,

The North Coast

The Pacific Highway continues north from Newcastle through the state's most popular resorts and holidaymakers' beach towns. The **railway** from Sydney and Newcastle continues along the coastline, with a dip inland at Wauchope (the closest station to Port Macquarie), all the way to Brisbane.

The great attraction along this stretch is indeed the extravagant number of beautiful beaches and inlets, as well as the transformation to tropical terrain as one nears the Queensland border. The towns, while having some remnants of historical interest, are now largely geared towards tourism and suburban living, and will be a disappointment if not viewed in light of the heavenly ocean and tropical landscapes surrounding most of them.

Only 50km from Newcastle, **Port Stephens** is one of the most unspoiled and calming spots along the North Coast. Take either routes 121 and 122 northeast to the small settlement of Nelson Bay, or continue north on the Pacific Highway to Tea Gardens Road to reach **Tea Gardens** and **Hawks Nest** on the northern shore of Port Stephens at the mouth of the Myall River.

Port Stephens is actually the water inlet around which these small communities are situated. This is an ideal place to enjoy the charms of the Australian coast, without the overwhelming hype of the more touristy places. At **Nelson Bay** (population 9500), boat hire and cruises are available, and one can visit the historic lighthouse at Nelson Head. **Tourist information,** Victoria Parade, ☎ 02 4981 1579. Nude bathing is also allowed at Samurai Beach. Nelson Bay is a great place to see dolphins, and there are even dolphin watch cruises from the harbour.

From Hawks Nest, travel north c 30km on a dirt road to **Myall Lakes National Park** (☎ 02 4987 3108); or turn off east of Bulahdelah on the Pacific Highway. These lakes, the largest coastal lake system in the state, are popular with campers and bushwalkers but not at all overdeveloped. The park includes ocean beaches with headlands as well, and is a superb waterbird habitat.

From Bulahdelah, continue north on the Pacific Highway, past Alum Mountain, known not only for its enormous alum deposits, but for an abundance of rock orchids. About 5km north of here is the turnoff to see **The Grandis**, the state's biggest tree, a *eucalyptus grandis*, 76m high and 2.7m wide. You can also travel from Myall Lakes along the coastal route to the twin towns of Forster-Tuncurry, on either side of the sea entrance of Wallis Lake; tours by Aboriginal rangers are available here (☎ 02 6555 5274).

Taree (population 5000) is the next community en route north, located on the Manning River. The town is 72km from Bulahdelah and 340km from Sydney. Popular poet Les Murray is from this area, where his ancestors were timber-cutters in the rich forests up the river. Murray's 'The Bulahdelah-Taree Holiday Song Cycle' speaks of 'Taree of the Lebanese shops'. Today the most noticeable sight in town is one of those roadside grotesques so beloved by Australians, in this case The Giant Oyster. Tourist information at **Manning Valley Tourist Information Centre**, Pacific Highway, ☎ 02 6552 1900. About 10km west of Taree is **Wingham**, oldest town in the Manning River Valley, established as a centre for timber in 1836. Near the middle of town is the Wingham Brush, one of the few remaining sub-tropical rainforests in the state. The small roads in this valley are filled with lush vegetation, flying foxes and 100 species of birds.

Port Macquarie

Port Macquarie (population 30,000) is typical of the tourist-geared towns along the coast. **Tourist information**: Horton Street; ☎ 02 6583 1293. While it was founded in 1821 as a penal colony for repeat offenders and recalcitrants, it became such a desirable location for free settlers that the convicts were soon moved on to terrifying Norfolk Island or the Moreton Bay settlement.

Very few reminders of 'The Port's' early history remain, only **St Thomas the Apostle Church** (1824–28), a **Court House** (1869), and the **Historic Museum** on Clarence Street. The town remained for much of the 20C a sleepy little fishing village with a harbour too unreliable for real commercial development. Tourists and retirees seeking warmer climes in the 1970s caused the first real boom for the region. The beaches in the area, especially Crowdy Bay to the south, and Hat Head to the north, are what attract visitors; from Port Macquarie north, the coast becomes increasingly lush and tropical. While tourism means that some of the tackier holiday 'attractions' begin to make an appearance here, a few of the more serious venues are worth a visit.

Kooloonbung Creek Nature Park (free admission), near the centre of town, is a lovely patch of rainforest in the midst of suburbia. The **Sea Acres Rainforest Centre** (☎ 02 6582 3355, daily 09.00–16.30), on the Pacific Highway, is a serious display of information about the coastal rainforest regions, including a 1.3km-long boardwalk (easy wheelchair access) through the adjacent rainforest floor and canopy. Port Macquarie is also home to Australia's only **Koala Hospital** (☎ 02 6584 1522, first feeding 07.30, second 15.30),

The Akubra

The Akubra hat holds a place in Australian life comparable to that of the Stetson in America; it is an icon of the bush, an essential element of Australian dress, at least among the 'jackeroos' and other men of the countryside. The famous slouch hat of the Australian soldier is also made by the Akubra company. Known as 'the twelve-rabbit hat', because most of them are made from rabbit-fur felt, the style that would eventually become known as the Akubra was developed in the early 1870s by Benjamin Dunkerley, first in Tasmania and then in Sydney. The Dunkerley Hat Mills was joined by Stephen Keir, who in 1918 began branding the hat 'Akubra', an Aboriginal word for headdress. In the early 1950s, the company obtained a coveted manufacturing agreement with Stetson in the United States, at a time when most Australian men still wore a hat daily, even in the city. In the 1970s, as hat-wearing fell out of favour with urban folk, the company moved to Kempsey, where it still produces a variety of Akubra headgear, the most prevalent ones readily identifiable as 'The Man from Snowy River' or mounted stockman look.

housed on the grounds of a 19C homestead, **Roto**, which can also be visited. Another 48km north is **Kempsey** (population 9000), a commercial centre on the Macleay River, noted as the home of the famous Akubra hat factory (see box). The **tourist information office** is on the Pacific Highway, ☎ 02 6562 5444. Also in town is an excellent history museum, the **Macleay River Museum and Settlers Cottage** (☎ 02 6562 7572, daily 10.00–16.00), housed in an award-winning building designed by architect Glenn Murcutt.

47km northwest along the road up the Macleay River is **Bellbrook**, a National Trust village with a famous old pub.

> The area around Bellbrook includes an initiation ground of the Thungutti Aboriginal group, still highly sacred and inaccessible to the public. Another Aboriginal site is at **Mount Anderson**, northeast of the village; the mountain is a clearly visible landmark of the area, over 850m high. The Aboriginal name for the mountain is 'burrelbulai', or 'cooking-grill mountain', referring to a myth involving a green-twig frame used to grill a large eel from the mountain stream.

Returning to the coast, a small road northeast from Kempsey (route 12) leads to the beachside community of **South West Rocks** (population 3800), on the stunningly beautiful Trial Bay. The area is surrounded by world-class surfing beaches. On the headlands 3km east of the town is Trial Bay Gaol and Arakoon State Recreation Area. The gaol was built in 1886, and is now a small museum; it stands dramatically as a ruin on a peninsula looking out to sea. It was a prison for German internees during the First World War, and a monument to these prisoners is also on site. **Tourist information**: Ocean Drive, ☎ 02 6566 7099.

Return to the highway, and continue north through Macksville and on to **Nambucca Heads** (population 6000), one of the first places along the coast to develop as a holiday retreat. Tourist information at the **Nambucca Valley Visitor Information Centre**, Ridge Street, ☎ 02 6568 6954. In the 1920s it became a popular honeymoon destination. The name comes from the local Aboriginal group, the Gumbaynggirr, meaning 'entrance to the waters' or 'crooked river', referring to the Nambucca River which exits into the ocean here. The river was an important centre for the cedar-timber industry, and in the 1870s supported some shipbuilding concerns as well; 26km up the river from Macksville is **Bowraville**, location of *Taylor Arms*, the 'Pub with No Beer' made famous by country singer Slim Dusty's song.

Nambucca Heads houses a history museum at **The Headland** (open Tues–Sat and Sun 14.00–16.00 ☎ 02 6568 6380) with Aboriginal artefacts; and **Gordon Park Arboretum** on Wellington Drive, a small rainforest with boardwalks in the heart of town. Local lookouts, most especially Yarrahapinni Lookout, provide spectacular views of the area, and pleasant river cruises aboard the *Nambucca Princess* can be booked from the information centre. The area's beaches are some of the best surfing spots in the state.

Some 25km further north turn west onto **The Waterfall Way** (route 78); pass through the pleasant village of **Bellingen**, with its historical streetscape and an important artsy-craftsy market the third Saturday of each month, to reach, 41km west, **Dorrigo National Park** (☎ 02 6657 2309), another of the World-Heritage-listed rainforests of the region.

The village of Dorrigo itself contains a wonderful old hotel with tiled façade and other interesting buildings. But the real attraction is the park 4km south-east of the village, situated on the Dorrigo Plateau (the name means 'stringy-bark'). Boardwalks allow views of the canopy of the forest; and picnic areas attract local brush turkeys (*Alectura lathami*), fascinating creatures that build enormous mounds of brush in which to lay and incubate their eggs. Several walking tracks of varying lengths and difficulty begin in the picnic area, and lead to some exquisite waterfalls. The park is also famous for its variety of wild orchids. The entire area around Dorrigo and Bellingen is full of small roads, flying fox colonies, beautiful countryside, and even a memorial red-cedar forest, the Tallow-wood Grove, on Cedar Road out of Dorrigo.

To the west of Dorrigo c 60km is a rugged and remote area, **Guy Fawkes River National Park** (☎ 02 6657 2309), a great place for spectacular views, camping and hard bush-walks. (Alternatively, you can reach the park via Armidale, 100km southwest). At Ebor Falls, on the edge of the park, the Guy Fawkes River plunges spectacularly off the tablelands.

Coffs Harbour

Return to the Pacific Highway and continue north c 25km to **Coffs Harbour** (population 20,300). **Coffs Harbour Tourist Centre**, Urara Park, Grafton Street, ☎ 02 6652 1522. Coffs Harbour airport has direct flights from Sydney and Brisbane. At this point, the Great Dividing Range reaches the sea for the only time. Like Port Macquarie, Coffs Harbour's current reason for being is as a family tourist resort and a centre of sun worshippers' housing developments. The appearance, on the highway itself, of the Big Banana Leisure Park, highlighting the dominance of banana growing in the region, should give some indication of the general level of entertainment here outside the glorious surf beaches; the town marks the beginning of serious 'tourist attraction' country, mostly theme parks of one sort or another and most of which will not be mentioned here. Still, the older area of town near the harbour is picturesque and accessible, even when the summer holidays pack the place with sun-seekers.

The settlement's name is a corruption of Korff's Harbour, a reference to John Korff, a sailor who sheltered near here in 1847. The original settlers in the 1860s and 1870s depended upon the cedar industry and shipping from the town's harbour. The township was laid out in 1887, and the wharf, which shipped timber and other products around the world, was built in 1892. The railway arrived in 1915, marking the end of the port's importance. The town's resort status dates from the early days of the century; in *They're a Weird Mob* (1957), the main character 'Nino Culotta' spends his honeymoon here, learning to 'crack a wave'. The real tourist boom began in the 1970s, and does not appear to be abating.

The nicest place to visit in town, aside from the surrounding surf-beaches, is the **North Coast Regional Botanic Garden**, on Hardacre Street. Located near the centre of town, the park has great displays and walks through the sub-tropical vegetation of the coast. North of the harbour, one can visit Muttonbird Island, where thousands of these birds breed (see the Great Ocean Road, Victoria for more on muttonbirds).

The next 84km north along the highway travels inland to Grafton, while superb and usually isolated surfing beaches can be reached by small side roads. 26km north of Coff's Harbour, the village of **Woolgoolga** includes a gleaming Sikh Temple, the Guru Nanak Temple (not to be confused with the touristy Raj Mahal Indian Centre also in town), evidence of a large Indian population that accounts for the excellent Indian food available here.

Grafton

Grafton (population 17,000) lies on the Clarence River at the junction of the Pacific and Gwydir Highways; the river, in fact, divides the suburb of South Grafton from the centre of town, and was an obstacle to the completion of the railway until 1932, when a double-deck bridge was completed connecting the two sides. The town is 663km north of Sydney. **Clarence River Tourist Centre**, Pacific Highway, ☎ 02 6642 4677.

The river provided the means for early settlement in the area; in the 1830s, exploration began as timber-getters arrived, and soon cattle stations were established. The town was proclaimed in 1849, named after then-Governor Fitzroy's grandfather, the Duke of Grafton. Poet Henry Kendall lived here as a child in the 1850s, as did adventure writer Ion Idriess in the 1890s. Writer Edwin James Brady ran a newspaper here in the 1900s with the wonderful name of the *Grafton Grip*.

Now Grafton is considered a nice country town, filled with substantial (if predictable) 19C architecture, and famed for its glorious jacaranda and flame-trees lining the streets. In late October, the Jacaranda Festival takes place when the brilliantly coloured trees are in bloom. Of the historical buildings, the most interesting are the **Grafton Gaol**, designed in 1893 by H.A. Wiltshire, an elaborate fortress of more imposing proportions than most country gaols; **Schaeffer House** (open Tues–Thurs and Sun 13.00–16.00; ☎ 02 6642

5212), 192 Fitzroy Street, run by the National Trust as a small regional museum; and **Prentice House** (open Tues–Sun 10.00–16.00; ☎ 02 6642 3177), 158 Fitzroy Street, which houses a fine provincial art collection.

On Victoria Street is **Christ Church Cathedral**, designed in the 1880s by John Horbury Hunt, the Canadian architect responsible for the cathedral in Newcastle; the interior of this cathedral is particularly pleasant, with louvred aisle windows as a concession to the area's tropical climate. Also in this block of buildings are three civic buildings designed by Colonial Architect James Barnet: the Courthouse, 1877–80, of apricot brick; the former Police Station; and the elegant Post Office, built in 1874 with clock and bell tower. The notable aspect of the buildings in this historical precinct is that they are remarkably intact and well-preserved examples of this period.

In the middle of the Clarence River is **Susan Island**, which is home to a huge colony of fruit bats, or **Flying Foxes**. These extraordinary creatures are quite common along the coast, and even in Sydney; with a wing-span of nearly a metre and with their screeching cry, they can make a rather terrifying sight when they take off at night, but they are harmless, although devastating to fruit orchards.

The highway north now heads back towards the coastline, through **Maclean** (population 3000), still on the Clarence River, and home of a large fishing and prawning fleet. These fishermen, along with those in **Iluka** and **Yamba**, 21km east, provide about 20 per cent of the state's seafood. The town plays up its Scottish heritage, hosting a Highland Gathering at Easter time. Near Iluka is Woombah Coffee Plantation, the world's southernmost coffee plantation. From Yamba, the little town of **Angourie** is 5km south; here is a fascinating freshwater pool of unknown depth, only 50m from the ocean, as well as a surf beach with quite enormous waves and conditions for experienced surfers only.

To the north of Iluka, the **Bundjalung National Park** (☎ 02 6642 0613 south; ☎ 02 6628 1177 north) stretches along the coast for 38km of stupendous beaches. The park also preserves one of the last wild coastal rivers, the Esk, as well as mangrove flats, cypress swamps and, at Woody Head, an exceedingly rare coastal rainforest. This region also had a relatively substantial Aboriginal population; evidence of indigenous habitation can be found in many forms, some of them accessible to the public and some not. Consult the park's information centre to determine if Aboriginal sites are available to the public.

At **Woodburn**, 98km north of Grafton, the highway diverges west to Lismore, and east 10km to **Evans Head**, another holiday and fishing resort with a great seafood restaurant run by the trawler fishermen's co-operative; it is also known for its safe surf beaches and riverflats. Woodburn was the site of the settlement of **New Italy**, established in the 1880s by a group of Italians from Treviso who had embarked on the abortive scheme to form a colony in New Ireland (New Guinea). After much travail, these travellers were rescued by the New South Wales government and allowed to select land here on the Richmond River. While the colony lasted intact for several years, by the 1930s most of the new generation had moved on to other parts of Australia.

Just north of Evans Head and east of Woodburn is **Broadwater National Park** (☎ 02 6628 1177), with 8km of beach and a walking track around Salty Lagoon, a swamp forest. Unusual rock formations and small caves have been created by wave erosion.

At this point, you can continue north on the Pacific Highway 36km to **Ballina** (population 13,000) past some excellent surf beaches; the town itself, on the Richmond River, is a quiet fishing village with a Maritime Museum/Tourist Office (☎ 02 6681 1002) housing *Aztlan*, a small raft that sailed from South America as part of the Las Balsas expedition. The Ballina Transit Centre on the Pacific Highway (☎ 02 6686 0086) has another roadside grotesque, The Big Prawn; and the **Thursday Tea Tree Oil Plantation** (tours on Mon–Thur at 11.00 and 14.00 and Fri 11.00; ☎ 02 6686 7273), also on the Pacific Highway, extracts oil from over one million trees. From here, take the Bruxner Highway west 31km to Lismore. Or from Woodburn, travel 40km on a small road through beautiful country to this inland town surrounded by rainforest and abundant evidence of people seeking 'alternative lifestyles'.

Lismore

Lismore (population 30,000) is the commercial centre of this exquisitely fertile rural region known incomprehensibly as 'The Big Scrub', apparently because of geological oddities engendered by prehistoric volcanic activities here. Tourist information is at the **Wilson's River Heritage Centre**, on the corner of Ballina and Molesworth Streets, ☎ 02 6622 0122.

Situated on Wilson's River, the town grew in the 1870s as a centre for the timber industry, and then to accommodate dairy and fruit farming. It continued as a thriving rural community until the 1970s, when the original 'hippies' and serious commune-dwellers discovered the tranquillity and fecundity of the tropical surroundings. These alternative New Age sorts, some now converted even more primitively into 'Ferals', have somewhat transformed the community style; they have now been joined by an active and committed environmentalist contingent, intent on saving the rainforests and other wilderness areas.

Given its current status at the more cultivated end of 'hippie culture', with all the attendant paraphernalia of arts and crafts and remnants of psychedelia, it seems incongruous to find in Lismore itself some well-preserved examples of 19C rectitude and prosperity: a Classical Revival **courthouse** from 1888; **St Carthage's Catholic Cathedral**, believed to be designed by Wardell and Denning with a spacious Victorian interior; and an imposing brick Post Office from 1879, complete with clock tower. The **Regional Art Gallery**, 131 Molesworth Street (☎ 02 6622 2209), regularly showcases substantial local talent; next door is a small Historical Museum, predictably haphazard with photographic displays and artefacts, but also featuring a walk-through rainforest display, and situated in a beautiful park. Local artistic achievements are also highlighted at the annual **Arts and Crafts Expo**, held every October, and a professional theatre group, Theatre North, provides an active production programme.

As will be evident from a regional map, the area around Lismore is filled with a maze of small roads traversing the wilds of this hilly hippie heaven, all of which are worthwhile exploring. While the train from Sydney stops in Lismore, any exploration of the adjacent area requires a car. The best drive to consider is directly north; head first to **The Channon**, a little town on the road towards Nimbin and home of one of the best and most characteristic weekend hippie markets, held on the showgrounds on the second Sunday of every month. The area's many markets are legendary and a great way to experience the cosmic lifestyle of the local inhabitants. You can even find waterfalls nearby in which to swim.

That **Nimbin**, 30km north of Lismore, is officially the sister city of Woodstock, New York, should give a good indication of its public character. In 1973, Nimbin held an Aquarius Festival that established its near-mythological stature as the Woodstock of Australia. Indeed, the place does appear to be stuck in a Seventies time warp, with psychedelic shopfronts and herbal tearooms. Even the local Aboriginal legends seem to enhance this cosmic atmosphere: at nearby **Nimbin Rocks**, an outcropping of giant stones surrounding a forest, the local Bundjalung group believe that a little man named Nyimbunje, possessor of supernatural powers, is buried, thereby imbuing the place with a magical aura.

From Ballina, the Pacific Highway continues north 36km into Byron Bay; or take the coastal route, 35km, along another stretch of beautiful surf beaches through the relaxed village of **Lennox Head**. From Lismore, take the road through Bangalow and into **Byron Bay** (population 5000). **Tourist information office**, 69 Jonson Street, ☎ 02 6685 8050. Novelist Craig McGregor, who lived here for many years, provides a great description of this well-known spot:

> *Byron Bay—an enormous, limitless, crescent-shaped sweep of seawater, fringed with white sand, culminating in a high rocky cape and the virginal white phallus of the lighthouse. The township is a mess of galvanised iron roofs fractured by Norfolk Island pines. Looking north across the bay...past the trails of Brunswick Heads prawn trawlers heading for home, a jagged backdrop of mountains dwindles away into Queensland.*

Cape Byron, 3km southeast, is the site of the lighthouse, the most powerful on the eastern coast, built in 1901 in the then-new method of concrete block. The cape itself—the most easterly point on the Australian continent—was named by Captain Cook as he sailed by on 15 May 1770, in honour of the navigator John Byron, Lord Byron's grandfather. Byron Bay is renowned world-wide to surfers, and has recently become the summer resort of the rich and famous from 'down South' in Sydney; people such as *Crocodile Dundee*'s Paul Hogan now have homes here.

It is conveniently accessible by train and bus from both north and south. Given this glitzy reincarnation, it is hard to imagine that the township used to be considered an ugly working-class community, known primarily for its abattoir and as the end of a camel track. While the high-rises of Queensland's Surfer's Paradise can actually be seen from the hills in town, and the stunning beaches can hold their own with any along the coast, Byron Bay citizens have made an effort to prevent total commercialisation à la the Gold Coast. Consequently it remains a relaxed and low-scale beach town, free of fast-food outlets and theme parks. The holidays can get exceedingly crowded, especially during the Easter weekend Blues Festival, which has become overwhelmingly popular with 'southerners'.

En route to the Queensland border from Byron Bay, the village of **Mullumbimby** (population 3000) is 3km west of the highway, about 15km further north. Best known for its semi-reconstructed hippie residents, the town has an admirable art gallery worth a visit, as well as a carefully restored house, Cedar House, on Dalley Street. The Brunswick Valley Historical Museum (☎ 02 6688 4356) is in the 1907 post office building. Sakura Farm in the nearby hills provides a Buddhist retreat run by a monk. Back on the highway, **Brunswick Heads** is a further 5km north. The alluvial sands of the Brunswick Heads Nature Reserve, at the mouth of the Brunswick River, support a sub-tropical rainforest unlike any other in the state. The location represents the southernmost distribution of several plant species, creating a habitat different from any further south. Mangrove swamps sit adjacent to rainforest, providing unique opportunities to view waterbirds of many species.

Another 32km north is **Murwillumbah** (population 8000). The town sits on the Tweed River, 10km south of the Queensland border, and 882km north of Sydney. The name derives from an Aboriginal word meaning either 'place of many possums' or 'people's campground'. Bob Ellis (b. 1942), journalist and screenwriter of *The Year My Voice Broke* and *The Nostradamus Kid*, was born here and grew up in nearby Lismore. The most prominent building in town is the **Australian Hotel**, on the corner of Wharf and Commercial Road. It is one of the few remaining timber weatherboard hotels in the area, built in 1912, with a verandah colonnade extending to the street kerb. The **Tweed River Regional Art Gallery** (open Wed–Sun, 10.00–17.00, ☎ 02 6672 0409) on Queensland Road has a surprisingly good collection of regional and international art and craft and hosts the Douglas Moran Portrait Prize. **Tourist information office** on the corner of the Pacific Highway and Alma Street, ☎ 02 6672 1340.

Of greatest interest in the area is **Mount Warning National Park** (☎ 02 6673 7211), 12km southwest of Murwillumbah off the Murwillumbah–Kyogle Road. The top of this volcanic mountain is the first place to see the sun rise in Australia. The name was given to it by Captain Cook, who nearly ran aground at Point Danger, on the state border, from where this prominent mountain could be seen to warn later navigators. Now only half of its original height, Mount Warning is one of the earth's most ancient volcanoes; the many walking tracks in the park provide fantastic views of rainforest and the surrounding countryside.

From Murwillumbah, it is about 30km via the Pacific Highway to **Tweed Heads** (population 55,000). **Tourist information** on the Pacific Highway, ☎ 07 5536 4244. While this is the last settlement in New South Wales, the town is actually a twin city of Coolangatta in Queensland, and is for all intents and purposes a part of the Gold Coast. The appearance of a Big Thing, in this case a Giant Avocado at **Avocado Adventureland**, 15km south of town, is a good sign that tourist entrapment is beginning. The town is filled with gambling clubs and casinos.

One interesting place to visit is the **Minjungbal Aboriginal Cultural Museum** (open daily 10.00–16.00, ☎ 07 5524 2109), Kirkwood Road in South Tweed Heads. It is run by the local Aboriginal Council, and includes displays and videos about pre-Contact Aboriginal life in the region. In the bushland nearby is a bora ring, a sacred initiation site.

Straddling the state line at Point Danger is the Captain Cook Memorial, erected in 1970 to commemorate the bicentenary of Cook's first voyage. The monument is topped by a lighthouse containing a laser-beam light visible 35km out to sea. A replica of the capstan of Captain Cook's ship *Endeavour* is here as well, made from the ballast Cook dumped when the ship ran aground further up the coast on the Great Barrier Reef; this ballast was recovered along with the ship's cannons in 1968.

Western interior ~ Blue Mountains to Broken Hill

The Western Suburbs of Sydney have already been discussed in the main Sydney section. From Penrith, the M4 road continues west across the Nepean River and joins at Glenbrook with the Great Western Highway (route 32) again. This road now leads into the Blue Mountains and onto the plains at Bathurst.

The Sydney trains also travel as far as the Blue Mountains, a delightful way to venture into this region, Sydney's favoured holiday spot for 150 years, offering cooler temperatures in the summer and wintry weather in July.

> The Great Dividing range formed as the Kosciuszko Uplift in the Pliocene Epoch. The geological event affected Australia from Cape York (in fact from Papua New Guinea south) in an arch along the eastern seaboard to the Victoria–South Australia border. The Dividing Range's highland regions are generally about 800 to 1000m above sea level. The mountainous areas were formed by granite intrusion beneath the sedimentary rocks and often reach elevations of 2000m.

Blue Mountains

Access to the Blue Mountains for the tourist is by train, tour bus from Circular Quay or car. The mountains are actually a part of the 245,929 ha of the **Blue Mountains National Park** (☎ 02 4787 8877 or 02 4588 5247), with headquarters in Glenbrook, although there are many entry points off the Great Western Highway between Glenbrook and Mount Victoria and at the railway stations along the route. **Blue Mountains Information Centre**, Great Western Highway, Glenbrook; ☎ 02 4739 6266. The centre can provide detailed self-guide brochures delineating the many bush-walks in the region, as well as information on rock-climbing schools.

> The remarkable valleys and lookouts of the Blue Mountains were caused as the sandstone surface eroded to expose Permian shale and coal beneath. These softer materials eroded more quickly, undercutting the sandstone to produce cavities, overhangs and vertical faces. The currency of advances in geological science can be noted here. Charles Darwin visited the area in 1836. Unable to conceive of the extreme geological time frame in which erosion could work, he assumed that the land was formed as a coastline. The gradual action of erosion has allowed archaic species of pine and fern to persist here.
>
> The eroded plateau takes its name from the observed blue tint of both distant objects and haze. The volatile oils of the eucalypt and tee tree

suspended in the air refracts light more in the low wave-lengths, causing the marked blue appearance, an effect called Rayleigh Scattering.

While forays into these ranges began with Watkin Tench and his exploratory party in 1789, the mountains were first crossed by Gregory Blaxland, surveyor William Lawson, the young William Charles Wentworth and four convicts in 1813. As with several earlier attempts, the need for new pasture land prompted the effort. Unlike these early explorations, which sought passage along the water courses, Blaxland and Lawson suggested that the party travel along the ridges. The current road and rail lines follow their passage, ascending near Glenbrook to the tableland around Wentworth Falls. To this point the ridge is never very wide. Shortly beyond the falls are sheer sandstone walls dropping 300m to the Jamison Valley.

The Blaxland, Lawson and Wentworth party continued as far as the meadows below Mount York. George W. Evans followed their course later in the same year, eventually reaching Lithgow and the plains at Bathurst.

Governor Macquarie then commissioned William Cox to construct a road following this route through the mountains. Incredibly, Cox completed the road within six months. The Governor travelled the route shortly thereafter, heading a vice-regal party in 1815 which included artist **John William Lewin** (1770–1819). Of the 20 or so watercolours Lewin painted, 15 survived in Captain Henry Antill's journal. These are now at the Mitchell Library in Sydney and are occasionally on display. In addition to his work on birds, butterflies and sporting events, Lewin is mentioned as the first artist to depict Australian scenes without many of the encumbering conventions of British painting, so his eucalypts look like gum trees in an Australian landscape rather than oaks in composed British scenery.

An artist of a thoroughly different era, **Norman Lindsay** (1879–1969), had his studio near **Springwood** (the address is now Faulconbridge, the next settlement along the Great Western Highway). As the **Norman Lindsay Gallery and Museum** (14 Norman Lindsay Crescent, open daily 10.00–16.00, ☎ 02 4751 1067), it is now open to the public, showing Lindsay's sculpture as well as the bacchanalian illustrations so easily recognised as Lindsay's. Many British visitors will recall more readily his children's story, *The Magic Pudding*.

The railway stops at **Wentworth Falls**, a good starting-point for the day visitor wanting to take in some of the scenery. The falls area was first known as Weatherboard Hut, after William Cox's slab huts built here in 1814. Also here is **Yester Grange** (☎ 02 4757 1110), a historic homestead built in 1888, now an art gallery and tea room with excellent gardens. It is a pleasant and simple walk to the falls themselves. Be warned, however: if you decide to climb down the precipitous cliffside steps for a further bushwalk, the route back to the top is long and arduous! It is definitely worth it for the exquisite views, but be prepared for a good 7–10km hike.

Katoomba

For those coming by train, the logical stopping point is **Katoomba** (population 15,000). The name derives from the Aboriginal word 'Kedumba', for 'shiny, falling water'. From this hamlet the Katoomba Skyway, built in 1958 over the mountain gorge above Cooks Crossing, and the Scenic Railway (it has been a tourist attraction since the 1880s), descend into the valley. The 45-degree angle makes this a hair-raising trip! **Tourist information**: Echo Point, ☎ 02 4782 0756.

Katoomba is filled with tea rooms, restaurants and guest houses, some of them dating from the Victorian era of holiday travel. One of the loveliest experiences at many of these houses is the **Blue Mountains Yulefest**, held in July— that is, in the winter—when a Northern Hemisphere Christmas feast makes sense. Such an event makes for a nice winter outing, especially if the area has some snow (a not uncommon occurrence in July).

Numerous lookouts and walking trails allow access to the Blue Mountains scenery. A pleasant walk into the **Jamison Valley** allows one to catch the train for a ride back up. Check the current timetable but the last departure is at 16.55.

Katoomba Falls, **Echo Point**, the **Three Sisters** and **Witches Leap Falls** are all beautiful. The Three Sisters, the most famous of the region's characteristic rock formations, is floodlit at night. Maps of the numerous trails are available at the Information Centre at Echo Point.

A less heavily visited area is just beyond Katoomba at **Blackheath**, also a rail stop on the Sydney route. Starting at the **National Parks and Wildlife Services Blue Mountains Heritage Centre** on Govett's Leap Road (☎ 02 4787 8877), the Fairfax Heritage Track has wheelchair access to Grose Valley and Bridal Veil Falls.

Charles Darwin's walk in this area was from Blackheath to **Govett's Leap**. Govett, by the way, was not as legend sometimes has it a bushranger who rode his horse over the cliff to die rather than be captured. Rather, Govett was a surveyor with a Scottish ear, a leap being a waterfall in that language. In any event, Govett's Leap, sometimes called Bridal Veil Falls, is a spectacular view.

Govett's Leap as depicted in the Picturesque Atlas of Australia

Artists such as the early adventurer Augustus Earle (1793–1838) have made magnificent paintings of the place, and early photographers often depicted genteel tourists standing at this location. Walking farther to the picnic area at Evans Lookout provides more or less continuous views.

The **Open Garden Scheme** flourishes in the area, particularly in the spring. **Lindfield Park Garden** (☎ 02 4756 2148) on Mount Irvine road at Mount Wilson is a first-class private garden open daily. The **Mount Tomah Botanic Garden** (☎ 02 4567 2154, open 10.00–16.00 March–Sept; 10.00–17.00 Oct–Feb), on Bells Line Road, is one of the Sydney Botanic Garden outposts. It is open daily. Both gardens are across the Grose Valley via the Darling causeway between Mount Victoria and Bell or on Bells Line Road from Lithgow.

Except for winter (June through August), the area is well travelled. Fellow bushwalkers and trekkers can be depended upon for suggested walks, eateries, routes and directions. Brochures and assistance can be had through the **Blue Mountains Visitor Information Centre** (☎ 02 4739 6266).

The road past Katoomba and Blackheath passes through Hartley on its way to Lithgow, 40km west. **Hartley** was the first settlement (1832) west of the Blue Mountains. Many of its older buildings date from the 1840s. Near here the forest gives way to low scrub, grasses and intermittent eucalypts.

Lithgow

Lithgow (population 12,370) is at the westernmost edge of the Blue Mountains proper. The town came into being as an important centre of coal-mining in the mid-19C, and was renowned as Australia's first producer of steel. **Tourist information**: 285 Main Street, ☎ 02 6351 2307.

A sudden drop in elevation revealed a coal bed below the Hawkesbury sandstone and Narrabeen shales which characterise the Blue Mountains plateau. This drop necessitated a Zig-Zag Railway to open the mines; this technological wonder opened in the 1870s, and was the subject of a famous series of watercolours by Sydney painter Conrad Martens (1801–78). Industrial growth during the 1870s saw the opening of four coal mines, a blast furnace iron works and copper smelting plants. The iron works passed through a number of ownerships, having been founded by Bathurst resident James Rutherford who also partially owned the coach firm Cobb and Co. By 1928 Broken Hill Proprietary (BHP) had moved its operations to Newcastle, local ore resources having been largely exhausted.

The coal seam, which is still in production, was discovered in 1841 by Thomas Brown who built **Eskbank House** (☎ 02 6351 3557; open Thurs–Mon 10.00–16.00). The house is a simple four rooms with a surrounding verandah and courtyards, hexagonal garden house and stables.

In keeping with the origins of the town, a number of industrial displays are open to visitors as well. The **Zig-Zag steam railway**, 10km east of town, in Clarence (☎ 02 6353 1795; weekends and holidays 10.30, 12.15, 14.00 and 15.30; weekdays 11.00, 13.00 and 15.00) has been restored by local rail buffs. Designed by Chief of Railways John Whitton, it was an acclaimed feat of engineering when it opened in 1869. The ride offers wonderful scenic views and crosses three viaducts. The ironworks blast furnace site is near Eskbank House. The pottery kiln on Hassan Street is well preserved. It fired some glazed pottery but terracotta pipe and bricks were its primary products. Established in 1875, the plant was closed in 1908.

To the southeast of Lithgow, c 56km, is **Jenolan Caves**, probably the best known of the many cave systems in this region. Discovered in the 1830s, the caves were systematically explored after a bushranger named McKeown who had hidden here was tracked down by the Whalan brothers. The Whalans then explored the caves; Charles Whalan and his sons acted as honorary guides for the throngs of visitors who came to the caves until the 1860s.

Formed of limestone and slate in the upper Silurian period, the caves feature remarkable stalactites and stalagmites and fantastic arches and chambers. The Grand Arch is over 130m long, between 12 and 20m high and equally wide. The larger Devil's Coachhouse is more than 80m high, 120m long and 35m across.

In 1866 the Jenolan Caves Reserve was established in an attempt to protect the caves' environment, but they remained one of the most popular tourist destinations. Electric lighting and as many as 2000 visitors a day seriously eroded the caves's natural formations. Still the area remains a popular site, with walking tracks and roads in the region, as well as good educational displays about the caves themselves. Guest houses and restaurants are also prevalent around the site. Guided cave inspections operate daily 09.00–17.00, at half-hourly intervals; for more information ☎ 02 6359 3311.

Bathurst

The next town beyond Lithgow is **Bathurst** (population 25,000). On the Macquarie River, it is near the site from which G.W. Evans elected to end his exploration and where William Cox's road terminated. The town was Australia's first inland settlement in 1815, named for Lord Bathurst, Secretary for War and the Colonies. Despite having a coach service from 1824 (it was a 24-hour journey in 12- to 15-mile intervals), the town's population was meagre until gold was discovered in the 1850s by an Aboriginal employed on a property near the Turon River immediately north of the city. **Tourist information office**, Courthouse Building, Russell Street; ☎ 02 6333 6288.

Except for the sandstone of **Government House** (built c 1820), red brick from Lithgow predominates. The Courthouse was built by David Jones whose style is recognisably consistent in his design for the Goulburn Courthouse. A National Trust house at 321 Russell Street, **Miss Traill's House** (☎ 02 6332 4232; open hours vary) is a picturesque Georgian cottage (c 1845) with gardens. Abercrombie House on Ophir Road (☎ 02 6331 4929), about 8km from town, was built as a mansion for J.H. Stewart in the 1870s; it now houses a quaint Museum and Archive of Australian Monarchy, with 'guided lecture tours' on Sundays.

St Stanislaw College is the oldest Catholic boarding school in the country, built in 1873 and enlarged occasionally since. Of the other areas of particular note here, the entrance to town has lovely poplars lining the road. The showground's brick gatehouse and timber pavilions are from the 1880s.

The town also has a particularly good **regional art gallery**, at 70–78 Keppel Street (☎ 02 6331 6066; open weekdays 10.00–16.00; Sat 11.00–15.00, Sun 13.00–16.00), with an emphasis on 20C Australian art, especially the paintings of Lloyd Rees (1895–1987). The Bathurst and District Historical Museum, Russell Street (☎ 02 6332 4755; open weekdays 09.00–16.30, Sat 09.30–16.30, Sun 10.00–16.00) contains predictable displays of the town's history, including the discovery of gold. Bathurst was also the birthplace of Ben Chifley (1885–1951), Labor Prime Minister 1945–49. It was during Chifley's term that the great Snowy Mountains Hydro-Electric Scheme was initiated, and 'Australia's own automobile', the Holden, first came off the assembly line. **Chifley's Cottage** (☎ 02 6332 4755; open Mon–Sat 14.00–16.00, Sun 10.00–12.00) at 10 Busby Street, was his lifelong home, and contains artefacts from his life and career.

Currently, Bathurst's fame results from **car races on Mount Panorama** each October, considered in motor-racing circles as one of the great annual events in the world. The Sir Joseph Banks Nature Reserve on the Mount in McPhillamy Park provides an idyllic contrast to zooming engines, with 41 ha of bush and parkland; open daily 09.00–16.00 (☎ 02 6333 6285).

To the south of Bathurst, 72km along the small Bathurst–Goulbourn Road, you find **Abercrombie River National Park and Caves** (☎ 02 6368 8603), well worth the trip for cave lovers. The caves are set in 2200 ha of wildlife sanctuary; some 80 other caves are scattered throughout the park, discovered in the 1820s by European settlers. The main caves contain the Arch, the biggest natural limestone arch in the Southern hemisphere. Cave tours are scheduled regularly and camping facilities are available.

At Bathurst the main road divides, south to Cowra, Young, Cootamundra, Wagga Wagga and eventually Albury/Wodonga; north to Orange, Dubbo and Bourke or Broken Hill.

South from Bathurst

The southern route crosses largely sheep pasturage. At **Cowra** (population 8500) you may be surprised to find the **Japanese Garden and Cultural Centre** (open daily 08.30–17.00). The centre, which commemorates the losses of the Second World War, is the result of Cowra having had a Japanese prisoner of war camp here. On 5 August 1944, 1000 Japanese prisoners broke out of the camp; in the ensuing response, 231 Japanese prisoners were killed. Opened in 1979 as a memorial to peace and cultural cooperation, the centre includes Japanese gardens with lakes, waterfalls and plants, and a good Japanese restaurant. **Tourist information**: Mid-Western Highway; ☎ 02 6342 4333.

56km west of Cowra on the Mid-Western Highway is **Grenfell** (population 2100), birthplace of national literary icon Henry Lawson. Every year in June (Lawson was born on 17 June 1867), this tiny town hosts the Henry Lawson Festival of Arts, attracting some of the best Australian writers and literary figures for readings and performances. The event is capped by the Guinea Pig Races on the final day of the festival. Grenfell loves these races so much, the town also hosts the guinea pigs for a run on Easter Sunday.

Further south c 70km is **Young** (population 6900), yet another gold-mining town. Now a centre of cherry and prune orchards, its railway station is quaint and sits in a pleasant park. **Tourist information office**, Olympic Way, ☎ 02 6382 3394. Every year, the first case of cherries from Young (in December) is auctioned off for charity, often raising $10,000 or more. Young cherries are a special Christmas treat throughout the state.

Cootamundra (population 6800), some 50km south of Young, is Sir Donald Bradman's birthplace, making his house at 89 Adams Street a stop for cricket enthusiasts. It is open daily 09.00–17.00. The town is also famous for the Cootamundra wattle (*Acacia baileyana*), one of the most spectacular of the many yellow-blooming wattle that appear at the end of winter. **Tourist information office**, Railway Station, Hovell Street ☎ 02 6942 4212.

North from Bathurst

The Mitchell Highway from Bathurst continues west and after c 56km passes through the prosperous old town of **Orange** (population 30,000). The area was named by explorer General T.L. Mitchell, in honour of the Prince of

Orange, later King of the Netherlands. An obelisk in honour of Orange's most famous native son, A.B. 'Banjo' Paterson (see also p 81), has been erected in the town, and every year his birthday, 17 February, is celebrated with artistic and cultural activities. The poet Kenneth Slessor was also born here in 1901. **Tourist information:** Civic Gardens, Byng Street; ☎ 02 6361 5226.

The early gold discoveries at nearby Ophir and Hill End made Orange a wealthy town in the 1850s, evident in the number of substantial and elegant houses and public structures in the area. Of special interest are **Bowen Terrace**, 3–25 Bathurst Road on the southern approach to town, a rare example of a country town terrace, built in 1872 with stuccoed brick and a continuous roof of corrugated iron. Beautiful examples of fancy ironwork occur at **'Kangaroobie'**, Molong Road, with encircling verandahs and carved interior woodwork; and at **'Ammerdown'**, off Molong Road, built in 1906 with polychrome brickwork and cast-iron grates; these are both private residences, not open to the public. In the city centre are excellent Victorian public buildings, including a James Barnet **Courthouse** (1882) and two notable brickwork churches, **St Joseph's** (1870) by Edward Gell, and **Holy Trinity** by Thomas Rowe (1879). On Byng Street near the information centre is another of the state's good regional art galleries (☎ 02 6361 5136; open Tues–Sat 11.00–17.00, Sun 14.00–17.00), including the Mary Turner Collection of Australian paintings.

Today, Orange is a centre of the district's **wine-growing** interests; the Visitors' Centre provides information on winery and food tours to the surrounding region. In April, the 'Food of Orange District' (FOOD) festival takes place.

From Orange, travel northwest on the Mitchell Highway (route 32) through agricultural country. The small town of **Wellington** (population 6000) has an interesting curved main street, with many early shopfronts. **Tourist information:** Cameron Park, ☎ 02 6845 2001. Nine kilometres from town are **Wellington Caves**, with very large stalactite formations and rare cave coral.

Another 50km northwest is **Dubbo** (population 26,300). **Tourist information:** 232 Macquarie Street, ☎ 02 6882 5359. An agricultural service centre, Dubbo is rightly known for the **Western Plains Zoo** (☎ 02 6884 1722; open daily). In keeping with current zoo practice, animals from around the world are kept in very large enclosures and fed as nearly as possible their natural diet. The zoo's staff attribute its successful breeding programme to both these factors. The zoo is the one and only reason to come to Dubbo, but it is definitely worth the trip for anyone interested in the preservation of rare and endangered species. The Dubbo XPT train from Sydney arrives in Dubbo daily in the early afternoon.

Beyond Dubbo the land becomes quite arid, the scrub giving way to tufted grasses and occasional acacias. The Macquarie River ends in a marsh north of Nyngan. **Bourke**, 350km to the northwest of Dubbo, is a wool processing centre on the Darling River. **Tourist information:** Old Railway Station, 45 Anson Street, ☎ 02 6872 2280. The area was explored by Charles Sturt via the river in 1829 and again by T.L. Mitchell in 1835. The stockade Mitchell built on Eight Mile Lagoon is about 10km southwest of Bourke. The phrase 'Back o' Bourke' means something like beyond civilisation. Past Bourke the outback, the great red centre of the continent, begins, sparsely watered with scrubby trees and virtually no ground cover. 260km north is Cunnamulla in Queensland. Bourke is the site of Fred Hollows' grave and memorial, in the cemetery on Cobar Street. Fred

Hollows (1929–93) was a great Australian character and world-famous opthamologist who established eye clinics in Third World countries and in Aboriginal communities. His affinity for, and assistance to, oppressed people led to the admiration of many Aboriginal groups, especially those around Bourke. Hollows' work continues through the Fred Hollows Foundation.

To the west of Nyngan another 600km lies **Broken Hill** (population 25,600). **Tourist information office**, on the corner of Blende and Bromide Streets, ☎ 08 8087 6077. Broken Hill actually looks more towards the nearer ports of South Australia than New South Wales; it is 50km from the South Australian border, and it operates on Central Standard Time, one-half hour behind Sydney. The Broken Hill train leaves Sydney every Tuesday afternoon, arriving in Broken Hill on Wednesday night; the Indian Pacific also stops here, on Tuesdays and Fridays en route to Western Australia.

A mining community depending on the silver-lead-zinc deposits in the Barrier Range, this surprisingly cultivated town boasts two dozen art galleries and was home to artists Pro Hart and Jack Absalom, the 'Bushmen of the Bush'. Canberra sculptor Ingo Kleinert praises the tip, that is the dump, in the area, from which he gleaned the corrugated and galvanised roofing necessary to make his 200-dingo piece, as one of the best in the country.

> Serious mining in the area began in the 1880s, BHP being floated in 1885 as 2000 shares at £20 each. BHP, of course, stands for Broken Hill Proprietary Company, an indication of the enormous mineral wealth that has been derived from this region. The ore body in question turned out to be over 5km in extent. Strikes by miners in 1892, 1908, 1916 and 1919 were disgraceful affairs, the vicious methods used by the company against miners affecting the reputation of both BHP and the town itself. The settlement in 1920 was a landmark since which reasonable relations have largely prevailed.

The vast outback surrounding Broken Hill is like no other place on earth. It is not surprising to learn that the region has served as the location for such films as *Wake in Fright* and *Mad Max 2*. It also figured, of course, in the recent high-camp spoof, *The Adventures of Priscilla, Queen of the Desert*.

Author Arthur Upfield, in one of his best-known 'Bony' mysteries, *The Bachelors of Broken Hill* (1958), describes its atmosphere:

> *There is nothing parochial or bucolic about Broken Hill. There is no city in all Australia remotely like it except perhaps the golden city of Kalgoorlie. There is nothing of the snobocracy of Melbourne, or the dog-eat-dog taint of Sydney, in the community of Broken Hill, and there is no thoroughfare in Australia quite like Argent Street, Broken Hill's main shopping centre...You may pause before a building erected at a section of mining camp of the 1870s; stay at a hotel the exact replica of those from which emerged the American Deadwood Dicks; eat at ultra-modern cafes run by smart Greeks and Italians; hire a gleaming automobile and shop at lush emporiums.*

While some of this ambience has altered in the intervening 40 years, the attitude remains the same.

Although the paved highways in this area are well enough travelled to ensure the safety of tourists, you must inform the local authorities if you plan to take secondary roads. They will give instructions regarding safe travel, the conditions of routes, and necessary subsequent reporting. **TAKE HEED OF ALL INSTRUCTIONS WHEN DRIVING IN THE OUTBACK.**

To the southeast of Broken Hill, 111km, near the small settlement of Menindee (where the ill-fated Burke and Wills expedition stopped on their way north in 1860), is **Kinchega National Park** (☎ 08 8088 5933), a magnificent surprise in the middle of this vast, dry landscape.

On the banks of the Darling River and filled with glittering lakes in an area of 44,180 ha, the park is filled with Aboriginal sites and European relics such as a restored woolshed. The region teems with extraordinary birdlife and massive red river gums along the river. Lake Menindee provides water for Broken Hill; Lake Cawndilla is suitable for swimming. Camping facilities are available on the river and near Lake Cawndilla; it is also possible to book accommodation in the old shearers' quarters.

About 200km southeast of Kinchega National Park, and more readily accessible (over dirt roads) from Mildura, Victoria (110km to the southwest) and Balranald, New South Wales (150km southeast), is **Mungo National Park** (Mildura office, ☎ 03 5023 1278), a World Heritage-listed site, part of the Willandra Lakes World Heritage Area.

Now a dry lake, Lake Mungo was once a large freshwater lake, the shores of which hold a continuous record of Aboriginal life dating back to 60,000 years ago. Other skeletal finds in the area suggest that the Australian continent may have been inhabited by two different groups of early humans. The park of 27,847ha contains remarkable geological features, especially the Walls of China, a 30km crescent of orange and white dunes stretching across the eastern shore of the lake bed. Camping facilities exist here, as well as accommodation in shearers' quarters, which must be booked well in advance from the park office.

South of Sydney

South Sydney to the Royal National Park

Getting to the south of Sydney by road leads to one of the most confusing bottle-necks in the city's transportation network. Recent efforts to upgrade access to the Kingsford-Smith International Airport at Mascot have been bogged down in political battles, so travel is still tangled. To get to Botany Bay and points south from the city, take Dowling Street, which is marked as both route 64 and Highway 1; it will become Southern Cross Drive, then General Holmes Drive at the airport, finally becoming the Grand Parade along Botany Bay itself.

At **Kirrawee**, this road joins with the **Princes Highway**, which is route 66 from the city, and then becomes Highway 1, to continue along the entire southern coastline of the state and into Victoria. Following the signs to the airport will take you in the right direction. For day outings, the **train** from Central Station runs all the way to Cronulla and beyond to Wollongong.

La Perouse

The park site of La Perouse (see box) sits on the opposite side of Botany Bay from Captain Cook's landing point at Kurnell. To reach this interesting fort and memorial site, take **Anzac Parade** (route 70) south from the city to the end.

La Perouse

The place is named for **Comte Jean François de Galaup La Perouse** (1741–88), the gentleman captain of a French expedition to the South Pacific in 1785–88. In his ships *Boussoule* and *L'Astrolabe*, La Perouse and his crew landed at this spot on Botany Bay only six days after the First Fleet's arrival in 1788. Relations between these two camps, astonished to find each other serendipitously in a new land, were cordial. La Perouse assured Captain Phillip that his voyage was one of scientific exploration rather than conquest; he even concurred with Phillip's decision to move the fleet to a site more suitable than Botany Bay. La Perouse's men camped on this point until 10 March, then set sail for the north, never to be heard from again. Forty years later, other explorers determined that La Perouse had been shipwrecked near the New Hebrides.

At the very tip of La Perouse is the **La Perouse Memorial Group**, now part of **Botany Bay National Park** (☎ 02 9311 2765); the site includes a memorial to the French navigator and a tomb to Père La Receveur, a priest and naturalist who died on La Perouse's voyage. These structures were built by early Colonial Architect George Cookney in 1825; they are some of the few remaining works by Cookney. Also on the site is a two-storey octagonal watchtower, built in 1811 and believed to be the oldest customs house in Australia, and the oldest building on the New South coast. In the nearby cable station, built in 1882, is the **Laperouse Museum** (the organisers prefer this spelling of the captain's name) (☎ 02 9311 3379; open daily), with historical displays. A long-standing **Aboriginal community** is also located here; on Sundays, they have been giving boomerang demonstrations, along with a snake show, for decades.

From this site, you can cross a causeway to **Bare Island Fort**, one of the many military fortresses built in the 1880s in response to fears of Russian invasion. The construction out of concrete was considered exceptionally advanced by military experts of the day. The fort includes a museum, open on the weekends.

Botany Bay

Much of Botany Bay has been given over to the airport, oil refineries, and industrial sites, but immediately south of the airport beginning at **Brighton-Le-Sands**, THE GRAND PARADE presents a pleasant view of the bay, with tourist hotels and beachside cafes along the entire stretch. It is hard to imagine that Captain Cook and Joseph Banks would have chosen this flat, sandy spot as the ideal location for a new settlement; Governor Phillip was wise to look elsewhere for fertile ground.

To the south of the bay in **Rockdale** is **Lydham Hall**, 18 Lydham Avenue (☎ 02 9567 4259); it was built in the 1860s on a high point of land overlooking Botany Bay. Architecturally, the house demonstrates a transitional style from simple Georgian to ornate Victorian; historically, it is of interest as the childhood home of Christina Stead, author of *Seven Poor Men of Sydney* (1934) and *The Man Who Loved Children* (1941). Stead's father was a famous naturalist who named the nearby suburb of Banksia. Lydham House is open to the public on weekends and public holidays, 14.00–16.00. It is most easily reached by taking the train to Rockdale Station, then walking west on Herbert Street to Lydham Avenue, c 1km.

Directly south of Rockdale is the suburb of **Kogarah**, where writer and expatriate raconteur Clive James spent his childhood; in his *Unreliable Memoirs* (1980), he paints an amusing picture of Sydney suburban life, including the intriguing fact that most of these neighbourhoods still had outhouses, or 'dunnies', into the 1950s.

Back on THE GRAND PARADE (route 64) along the bay, continue south. At **Sans Souci Wharf** on the **Georges River**, you can book cruises to explore the upper regions of the river. The **oyster farms** of Georges River are reputedly the source of Sydney's best oysters, which means they are very good indeed. The cruises will travel past **Sylvania Waters**, the overstated residential development, filled with canals and *nouveau riches* residents, made famous through the 1991 BBC programme of the same name.

Cross the Georges River at Captain Cook Bridge at Taren Point. To the west of here in **Kareela** is the **Joseph Banks Native Plants Reserve**, a lovely botanical display including a 'scented' garden of native plants and a rainforest environment. The reserve is located on Manooka Place; turn off the Princes Highway at Bates Drive, left onto Alpita Street and left again on Garnet Road. It is open weekdays 07.00–15.30, weekends 10.00–17.00. Nearby on Bates Drive is the Kareela Golf Club (☎ 9521 5555), reputedly one of the best places to find Georges River oysters.

Further west from here on Carina Bay is **Como**, accessible by the Illawarra line train; on Cremona Road near Scylla Bay is the **Como Hotel**, built in 1880–82 for the workers on the railway construction project. A three-storeyed brick structure, the building has delightful timber verandahs with cast-iron filigree balustrading and a decorative roof. The hotel is a quintessential example of an Australian adaptation of the Victorian 'pleasure palace'.

Captain Cook's Landing Place

Off Taren Point Road, turn east on Captain Cook Drive to **Kurnell**, c 13km, and Captain Cook's Landing Place Historic Site. **Bus 987** from the city travels here. Some 436 ha have been set aside here as part of Botany Bay National Park for recreational purposes. On the spot where Cook landed on 29 April 1770 in the *Endeavour*, a **memorial obelisk** was erected in 1870. Other monuments commemorate Midshipman Isaac Smith, Mrs Cook's cousin, and the first white man to set foot on the shore; and Daniel Solander, the Swedish naturalist who accompanied the voyage (his name has been given to the boxes that hold botanical specimens).

The **Discovery Centre** (☎ 02 9668 9111) in the park presents excellent exhibitions about Cook's exploration of the region, and also focuses on the natural history of the Botany Bay wetlands; most of the vegetation here remains as it would have been at the time of Cook's landing. Aboriginal rock engravings and axe-grinding grooves are also in evidence on the site. Entrance to the park is free; the Discovery Centre is open weekdays 11.00–15.00, weekends 10.00–14.00.

Cronulla

Travel west back to Captain Cook Drive and turn south on Elouera Road to come to Cronulla, rightfully famous for its glorious surf beaches on Bate Bay. Cronulla is the administrative centre for the Sutherland Shire, which includes the Royal National Park. The Cronulla beaches were the location for the outrageous adolescent activities recounted in Kathy Lette and Gabrielle Carey's controversial book, *Puberty Blues* (1979); director Bruce Beresford made the book into a film in 1981. Cronulla is also the only one of Sydney's beaches **accessible by train**; take the Illawarra line to the Cronulla Station directly on Gunnamatta Bay for a short walk to the beach.

Cronulla is also located on **Port Hacking** and the picturesque **Hacking River**. Cruises from the Cronulla Marina (☎ 02 9523 6919) provide lovely old-fashioned tours of the many inlets and bays up the river, blessedly unspoiled by development because the Royal National Park borders the river to the south.

From Cronulla, head back west to the Princes Highway (route 1) at Kirrawee; travel south to **Loftus**, c 2km, to the **Sydney Tramway Museum** (☎ 02 9542 3646); this can also be reached by train on the **Waterfall Line**, and the

Australian Trams

Sydney had one of the largest **tram networks** in the world until 1961, when the entire system was dismantled, victim of the Sydneysiders' obsession with the motor-car and with being 'modern'. For 100 years, Sydney rivalled Melbourne in tram service, first with horse-drawn cars, then, in 1879, with steam. By the turn of the century, Sydney trams were all electrified, the envy of their southern neighbour. During the 1920s, the phrase 'shooting through like a Bondi tram' demonstrated the domination of this form of transport in the public mind. During the Royal Easter show, the trams could move 50,000 people efficiently and in record time. While very few lamented their disappearance at the time, many Sydneysiders now regret their passing. Indeed, the recent installation of the **light-rail lines** in the inner city are an attempt to bring back some kind of tram system, but certainly without the character that still prevails on Melbourne's old green-and-yellow boxes. The Tramway Museum provides a 'hands-on' experience, with actual rides on vintage cars.

Parkline tram from the museum enters the Royal National Park.

The Royal National Park

The 15,014 ha of the Royal National Park can make a legitimate claim to being the first national park in the world. While Yellowstone National Park in the USA was established in 1872, it was not designated in legislation as a national park until 1883. Sydney's National Park was gazetted in 1879, the first time this designation was applied to a public reserve.

The Royal National Park came to world attention during the devastating bushfires of January 1994, when 98 per cent of the park, more than 14,500 ha, were entirely burned. Scenes of its devastation prompted assistance from around the world, particularly from Sutherland Shire's Japanese sister city Chuo. Today, the park is a remarkable example of natural regeneration of Australian vegetation; it is almost entirely regrown.

The park offers a marvellous conglomeration of coastal walks, beaches and woodlands, with opportunities to view some 700 species of flowering native plants, as well as waterfalls and rockpools. The **Visitor's Centre** is located at the Audley entrance from Loftus and is open daily; it is administered by the New South Wales National Parks and Wildlife Service, South Metropolitan District

(☎ 02 9542 0648). As the land of the **Dharawal people**, Aboriginal sites are present here, but are stringently protected by the parks service. The park's coastal trail, 26km long, travels by a variety of beaches, some of them patrolled, others secluded and usually uninhabited.

South New South Wales

Wollongong

Wollongong (population 206,800) is an industrial city and port. It lies north of Lake Illawarra and Port Kembla, and 84km south of Sydney. The Sydney train regularly travels here from Circular Quay and Central Station, and some continue on to Bomaderry, with stops at Kiama, Gerringong and Berry.

The third largest city in New South Wales, it is at the entrance to the Illawarra region, one of the most scenic parts of the Australian southern landscape. First mapped by sea when Bass and Flinders explored the coast in 1796 and first approached by land when Charles Throsby drove cattle there in 1815, Wollongong's origin rests in coal-mining in the 1850s. Its Aboriginal name means either 'five clouds' or 'hard ground near the water'. **Tourist information**: 93 Crown Street, ☎ 02 4228 0300.

The place is dismissed by most as a 'coal town' and is therefore thought too unattractive to be considered worth visiting. But it is situated amidst wonderful scenery, with a dramatic descent from Sydney over **Bulli Pass** into town, fern-gully mountains to the west, and fantastic beaches along its shores. At the beach town of **Thirroul**, just off Bulli Pass, the writer D.H. Lawrence, en route to America, stayed for two months in 1922, and began writing his Australian-based novel, *Kangaroo* (1923). The **Wollongong City Gallery**, on the corner of Kembla and Burelli Streets (☎ 02 4228 7500; open Tues–Fri 10.00–17.00, weekends 12.00–16.00) is Australia's largest regional art museum. It has a good selection of works by Australian artists, as well as artefacts of Wollongong's exciting history; admission is free. The **Port Kembla industrial area** to the south of town has now been tagged as **'Australia's Industry World'**, as if it were a theme park; indeed, the area now does provide interesting guided tours of the BHP Steelworks, the coal terminals, and the port operations.

After the Second World War, thousands of new migrants from Europe and the Middle East arrived to work in the Wollongong factories, creating an ethnic diversity described in Mary Rose Liverani's wonderful novel *Winter Sparrows* (1975). This diversity is also celebrated annually in June at the city's **Folklorika Festival**, a most enjoyable event with food, dancing and entertainment. The **University of Wollongong** is a dynamic institution, organising among other things the Science Centre and Planetarium (☎ 02 4221 5591; open Fri 19.00–21.00, weekends 13.00–17.00), a good hands-on exhibit 'to encourage scientific literacy'. The centre is located on Cowper Street in the Fairy Meadow section to the north of the central business district.

South of Wollongong in the suburb of **Berkeley** is the **Nan Tien Temple** (☎ 02 4272 0601), the largest Buddhist temple in the Southern hemisphere, opened in 1995. The complex includes a museum, pagoda, main shrine, many meditation rooms, and conference facilities that are used for international gatherings. The temple's Pilgrim Lodge provides accommodation for those interested in a Buddhist retreat. Take Berkeley Road off the Southern Freeway to reach the temple.

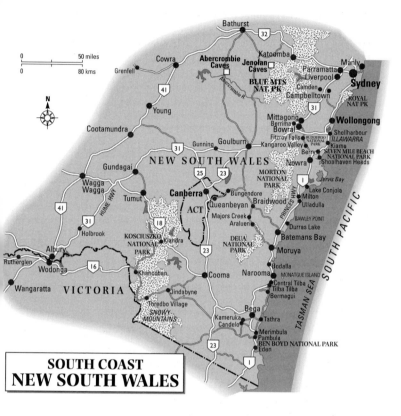

**SOUTH COAST
NEW SOUTH WALES**

The Illawarra

Immediately south of town is **Lake Illawarra**, known for its superb fishing and prawns; on its south is **Shellharbour**, a popular seaside resort. At **Bass Point**, 3km southeast of Shellharbour itself, Aboriginal kitchen middens have been excavated and establish that Aborigines inhabited the site 17,000 years ago.

Back west on the Princes Highway at this point, you can take the **ILLAWARRA HIGHWAY** west over **Macquarie Pass** and onto Moss Vale in the Southern Tablelands and the Hume Highway to Canberra. (The state rail line also takes this route, leaving the coast at the Wollongong suburb of Dapto.)

Just before Robertson, 28km west of Albion, is a small park, Macquarie Pass National Park. It features some of Australia's most southerly sub-tropical rainforests; the 2km Cascades Walk from the car park offers spectacular views.

31km along the Illawarra Highway is **Robertson**, in a potato-growing district and with spectacular views of the coast. Robertson recently gained fame as the location for the filming of George Miller's 1995 talking-pig epic *Babe*; the area will surprise any visitor to Australia who envisaged a country without green meadows or rolling verdant hills.

PRINCES HIGHWAY, route 1, continues south from Wollongong along the entire New South Wales coast and into Victoria and Melbourne. The region from Wollongong as far south as Bateman's Bay is known as the **Illawarra**, appropriately enough an Aboriginal word for 'high and pleasant place by the sea'.

Continuing on the Princes Highway south and then to the west, on route 80, is **Jamberoo** (population 480), surrounded by enormous escarpments and with lush green pastures attesting to its status as a prime dairy region. Jamberoo is a real bush town, famed for the **Jamberoo Valley Folk Festival**, which takes place each February.

West of Jamberoo c 3km is the **Minnamurra Rainforest** in **Budderoo National Park** (09.00–17.00, though the walks close slightly earlier, ☎ 02 4236 0469), a beautifully organised park that includes rainforest walks up the lush hills, where you can often see elusive **lyrebirds** with their resplendent tail-feathers and mimicking calls. Tours can be arranged, and a first-rate **visitor's centre** provides information on rainforest environments. The Minnamurra is definitely worth a detour.

Back on the coast from Jamberoo is **Kiama** (population 9200), an attractive coastal town most famous for its astounding **Blowhole**, which at times shoots water up to 60m high. It is no surprise to learn that 'Kiama' means 'where the sea makes a noise' in the local Aboriginal (Dharawal) language. From the Blowhole site, you can often spot whales off the coast during the migratory season in September. In October, the **Kiama Seaside Festival**, with all kinds of entertainment and food, takes place. **Tourist information** is at Blowhole Point; ☎ 02 4232 3322.

At Omega, 8km south of Kiama, you can turn off to a small coastal road to Gerringong (population 2500), and from there to **Seven Mile Beach** (now famous for wind-surfing). At the northern end of the beach, a memorial to Sir Charles Kingsford-Smith commemorates the site where the aviator took off for his historic flight to New Zealand in 1933. Bushwalking in the rainforests around the white-sand beaches is excellent.

Continuing south on the Princes Highway, you pass through **Berry**, one of the area's earliest settlements. In 1822, Alexander Berry (1781–1873), in partnership with Edward Wollstonecraft, received a grant here of 4047 ha, with government assurances that convict labour would be made available to them to improve the land. While the convicts were not forthcoming, the pair nonetheless were able to find workers and eventually claimed more than 260,000 ha, creating a virtual private fiefdom (see p 172). Industry, most notably the production of timber from the once-abundant cedar forests, brought the area great prosperity. The region also became known for its dairy farms, as it still is today.

In town are several substantial Victorian buildings on the National Trust, most of them originally built as banks and now restaurants and cafes; Berry is a convenient place to stop for tea.

10km south of here on the Shoalhaven Heads Road is **Coolangatta Estate**, the village that grew up around Berry's original homestead. Most of the historical buildings, which date from the 1820s and 1830s, are now part of a tourist resort, although tours are available. From here, you can also see **Mount Coolangatta**, which offers beautiful views of the Shoalhaven River and the coastline.

1 The Rocks, Sydney
2 Paddington, Sydney

3 *Above; Hunter Valley,*
  New South Wales
4 *Left; The Blue Mountains,*
  New South Wales
5 *The Snowy Mountains from*
  the west, New South Wales

6 Right; New Parliament
   House, Canberra
7 Aboriginal Memorial,
   Ramingining Artists,
   National Gallery of
   Australia, Canberra

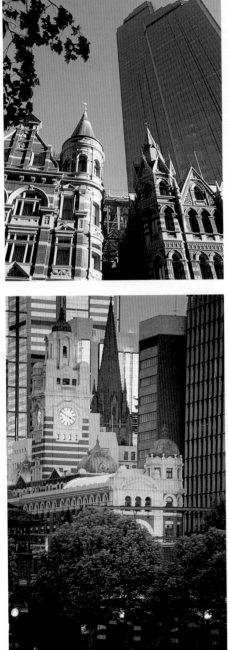

8 *Gang gang cockatoo*
9 *Left; Collins Street, Melbourne*
10 *Below left; Flinders Street Station, Melbourne*
11 *Right; St Kilda Pier Kiosk, Melbourne*
12 *Below; The Twelve Apostles, Victoria*

13 Constitution Dock, Hobart, Tasmania
14 Uniting Church, Penguin, Tasmania

15 Glenelg, South Australia
16 Padthaway Estate, South Australia

17 *Frilly-necked lizard*
18 *Sturt Desert Pea*
19 *Great Australian Bight, South*
    Australia

Kangaroo Valley

From Berry, a scenic 19km drive west leads to route 79 and into **Kangaroo Valley**; or drive from Coolangatta to **Bomaderry** and take route 79 north c 20km. A daily train service from Sydney Central Station travels to Bomaderry. The journey offers stupendous views, with steep ascents and descents into the valley. Nearby in **Morton National Park**, (☎ 02 4887 7270) but still on route 79, is spectacular **Fitzroy Falls**, which plunges precipitously over the plateau. In the village of Kangaroo Valley itself is **Hampden Suspension Bridge**, spanning the Kangaroo River; the bridge was built in 1898 and has castellated arches on each side. The valley is known for its pub, the Friendly Inn, and Sharply Vale Fruit World, with 80 ha (200 acres) of orchard.

Shoalhaven District

From **Bomaderry's Shoalhaven Tourist Information Centre**, 254 Princes Highway (☎ 02 4421 0778), you can purchase tickets to visit **Bundanon**, the exquisite property on the Shoalhaven River given in 1993 as a 'gift to Australia' by the artist Arthur Boyd and his wife Yvonne.

> Bundanon is located 21km west from the tourist centre, 8km of which is dirt road. Bundanon was established as a land grant in 1837; four years later it was purchased by Scottish Dr Kenneth Mackenzie, who built the first timber buildings in the 1840s and in 1866 the sandstone house at the centre of the homestead. Mackenzie's son Hugh continued to work Bundanon and purchased the nearby Terrara Estate, building the Terrara House at the beginning of the 20C. In the 1970s, Arthur and Yvonne Boyd purchased the property; in the 1980s, in joint ownership with their friend, the artist Sidney Nolan, they added nearby Eearie Park to the estate's holdings. Here Boyd produced some of his most stunning series of landscapes, capturing the beauty of the Shoalhaven River and its rocky vegetation. In the 1990s, while still resident at Bundanon, the Boyds announced their intention of leaving the property to the Australian Government, to be used as a cultural centre and artists' retreat. In 1993, the gift was officially accepted by Prime Minister Paul Keating on behalf of the Australian people.

Along with the property itself, the Bundanon bequest includes a significant collection of artworks by the Boyd artistic dynasty, from Emma Minnie Boyd (1858–1936) and Arthur Merric Boyd (1862–1940) to Arthur's own children and grandchildren. Other paintings by Sidney Nolan, Charles Blackman, Brett Whiteley and other notable Australian artists are part of the collection, as well as furniture, books, and photographs. Bundanon is open to the public on the first Sunday of each month, with guided tours of the buildings and Arthur Boyd's studio, and bush walks along the river. Bookings for the Bundanon Trust are through the Shoalhaven Tourist Centre for visits on the first Sunday of the month between 10.00 and 16.00.

Take route 79 south back through Bomaderry and into **Nowra** (population 20,000), now the administrative hub of the Shoalhaven District; the region is known as the Shoalhaven, after the long, meandering Shoalhaven River, which winds through town. As the centre for the region's tourist trade, Nowra has recently become suburbanised, with fast-food strips and tourist shops everywhere. **Shoalhaven Tourist Centre**, 254 Princes Highway, Bomaderry; ☎ 02 4421 0778. The region around Nowra is filled with holiday homes, caravan parks and water-related tours and cruises. Every type of beach, and accompanying water sports, can be found within the Nowra area.

Nowra's life in quieter times can be experienced at **Meroogal** (☎ 02 4421 8150, Sat 13.00–17.00, Sun 10.00–17.00), on the corner of West and Worrigee Streets, administered by Sydney's Historic Houses Trust. Built in 1885, this charming timber house with iron lace-work balcony belonged to four generations of the Thorburn family and exhibits a rich collection of domestic artefacts, particularly highlighting women's life and activities in the early 20C century.

Jervis Bay

Jervis Bay is c 40km south of Nowra, an extensive inlet that is now a popular holiday resort. The bay was first explored in 1791 by Lieutenant Bowen on the *Atlantic*, and named in honour of Bowen's commanding officer Sir John Jervis. First Fleet chronicler Watkin Tench speaks of the excitement surrounding its discovery in his wonderful memoirs (see p 78).

When the government established the Australian Capital Territory (ACT) in 1908, it was decided that the Commonwealth required access to the sea; 28 square miles of Jervis Bay were selected to be the port of the federal government administered by the ACT. Today the **HMAS Creswell Naval College** is located here; the rest of the inlet, with its beautiful beaches and dark green water, has developed into prime holiday property amidst nature reserves. To the south of Jervis Bay itself is a **botanical garden** emphasising native plants and filled with birds who are happy to be hand-fed.

Also to the south on Summerland Bay is **Wreck Bay**, an Aboriginal community accessible only by permission of the residents.

Nearby **Sussex Inlet** provides access to **St Georges Basin**, as well as a canal leading to the coast itself; the area is known for its good fishing, and a variety of beaches.

The Princes Highway continues south through state forests with no views of the coastline; **Conola Lake** is a popular fishing spot. The coastal plain from here to Bateman's Bay is now dotted with lagoons, inlets and lakes, along with ocean beaches. **Milton**, 65km south of Nowra, is the birthplace of 'bush poet' Henry Kendall (1839–82) at Kirmington Farm; the site is marked by a stone cairn near the present homestead.

Four kilometres further south is **Ulladulla** (7500 population), where the highway again reaches the sea. While 'Ulladulla' sounds Aboriginal, one tribal leader maintains that the town fathers actually 'Aboriginalised' the town's original name of 'Holey Dollar', after the early Australian coinage, to make it sound more authentic. The town is a true fishing port, with a fleet in the harbour; at Easter time, the town holds a colourful 'blessing of the fleet' ceremony. **Shoalhaven Tourist Information Centre**, Princes Highway; ☎ 02 4455 1269.

The Princes Highway south is now surrounded by forests on both sides, with occasional side roads leading to numerous beaches and caravan parks; popular turn-offs are **Bawley Point**, 21km from Ulladulla, and **Durras**, another 22km south and 5km east to a windswept beach with pounding surf. **Pebbly Beach**,

5km north of Durras off the highway, is also well-known for its beach-wandering kangaroos, but requires a rather rough ride along a boulder-strewn road to get there.

Batemans Bay (6500 population), an attractively situated beach town on the Clyde River, marks the end of the Shoalhaven district; it is the major centre for Eurobodalla Shire (although Moruya to the south is its headquarters), which extends west up the Kings Highway (route 52) leading to Braidwood and Canberra. The bay itself appeared on Captain Cook's chart, discovered by his expedition on 21 April 1770; Cook named it after Nathaniel Bateman, Captain of the *Northumberland*, on which Cook had sailed as Master. As the most accessible coastal town from the ACT, and with the upgrade of the Kings Highway road, Batemans Bay is overrun with holiday-makers in the summer and on school holidays, and has consequently lost much of its earlier fishing-port charm. **Eurobodalla Coast Visitor's Centre**, Princes Highway; ☎ 02 4472 6900.

Still, it is a great place to find fish restaurants and Clyde River oysters; you can also hire houseboats here to travel up the picturesque Clyde River to **Nelligen**, site of a homey country-music festival in December.

Kings Highway to Canberra

The road to Canberra from Bateman's Bay is 150km and takes two hours to drive, ascending through the fern gullies of the **Budawang Range** to the 'cattle country' region at Braidwood and the beginning of the Monaro Plains region. **Braidwood**, 60km west of Bateman's Bay, is filled with pleasant 19C buildings, a remnant of its days as the administrative centre of surrounding goldfields, making it a popular site for filmmakers. Tony Richardson's version of *Ned Kelly* (1970) starring Mick Jagger was filmed here, as was the 1995 version of *On Our Selection* with Leo McKern, Joan Sutherland, and Geoffrey Rush. From Braidwood, take the road east 20km for the easiest entry into Budawang National Park (☎ 02 4887 7270), 16,102 ha of wild sandstone country and rugged peaks; very hardy bushwalking for the very fit. From Braidwood, you can also take a rugged road to Pigeon House Mountain in Morton National Park (☎ 02 4887 7270), offering spectacular views to the south.

South of Braidwood c 30km is the gorgeous **Araluen Valley**, in the 1850s the location of a bustling gold-fields community; the poet Charles Harpur was a gold commissioner here, and poet Henry Kendall named his daughter Araluen, which means 'place of waterlilies' (the waterlilies are gone, dug up by greedy miners). The valley is now famous for peaches, which one can buy from roadside stands in January.

A rugged unsealed road from Araluen travels east all the way to the coast at **Moruya**; the trip provides glimpses of the unspoiled Deua River, which is now part of the **Deua National Park** (☎ 02 4476 2888).

Also in the region is the old gold-mining village of **Major's Creek**, which holds a homey old-fashioned folk festival in September, with lots of bush ballads and improvised music.

Continue on Kings Highway 48km to **Bungendore**, another historic township that has lately become a bedroom community of Canberra. Bungendore is an ideal place to celebrate **Anzac Day** (25 April), with an old-fashioned parade and a ceremonial service at the War Memorial in the town park.

Queanbeyan (population 27,000) is one of the oldest settlements on the Southern Tablelands, now 10km east of Canberra and the Australian Capital Territory. The Southern Highlands train from Sydney to Canberra makes a stop in Queanbeyan, but there is no local train service between the cities. Deane's Bus Service makes regular and frequent runs from Central Canberra to downtown Queanbeyan.

The area was first explored in 1820, and by 1828, an ex-convict squatter named Timothy Beard had named a property here along the Molonglo River 'Quinbean', supposedly Aboriginal for 'clear waters'. The Aborigines of the region belong to the Ngunnawal group. By 1838, Queanbeyan was declared a township, although it was still largely a sheep station. By the 1850s, gold discoveries in the area led to growth as a regional centre, and in the 1880s, James Farrer's success with rust-free wheat in the surrounds established the town as a leading agricultural area.

The most significant event in Queanbeyan's history was the establishment in 1911 of Canberra as the national capital. Not only did Queanbeyan grow as a result of the project, but its borders were strangely cut with the establishment of the territorial boundaries to the south of town; the residents of the neighbour-hood Oaks Estate are officially in the ACT (Australian Central Territory), although they walk across the street to do shopping in New South Wales. While Canberra remained a 'dry' town, Queanbeyan established its reputation as the capital's watering hole—a reputation it has never quite lost.

Today it is known as a poor cousin of its supposedly élitist neighbour; it is one of the fastest-growing areas in the state, it has great rugby teams, and an envi-able theatrical venue in the **School of Arts Cafe**, located on Monaro Street (☎ 02 6297 6857), the main drag. Queanbeyan also has one of the best second-hand bookshops in the region, *Queanbeyan Books and Prints*, housed in an historic building on Collett Street near the Queanbeyan River park; the shop specialises in fishing books.

Snowy Mountains

From Canberra, the Monaro Highway heads south 110km to **Cooma**, gateway to the Snowy Mountains and Kosciuszko National Park. The Snowy Mountains encompass the highest mountains in Australia, and Kosciuszko National Park (see p 230) is, at 690,000 ha, the state's largest national park. Mount Kosciuszko, at 2228m, is the continent's highest mountain—its rather piddling elevation an indication of how flat and old the land is. While you cannot expect grandiose peaks, this mountainous region is fascinating to explore, not only for its ski resorts and alpine meadows, but because the High Country is also the source of two of Australia's most important rivers, the Snowy River of 'Banjo' Paterson fame and the Murrumbidgee River.

The region is the habitat of several indigenous species, including the exquisite Snow Gum (*Eucalyptus pauciflora*) and the endangered Mountain pygmy-possum (*Burramys parvus*), the only Australian mammal limited to the alpine region and the only marsupial known to hibernate for long periods. The Snowys are also the destination in summer of thousands of bogong moths, flying some 1000km from Queensland to rest among the boulders of the High Country. The region is especially beautiful in the summer, when the skiers have left and the countryside is full of wildflowers. Ski season runs from late June until October; snow levels are always unpredictable, although one can expect some ground cover at least in July and August.

Except for some rugged areas in Victoria, the Australian Alps generally appear more like occasionally broken high plains than mountains. Their climate and elevation, however, cause the familiar succession of alpine plant communities. The open pastures of the Goulburn and Monaro tablelands are broken by abruptly rising granite mountains. As the elevations rise the dry eucalypt forests become wetter and cooler; Stringy Barks are replaced by Blue Gum and its associates. Eventually the conditions favour Snow Gums and fairly dense subalpine scrublands. In the ravines ash, beech and ferns thrive. At the highest elevations, over 1800m, above timberline herbfields, ferns, bogs and grasslands typify the alpine plant communities. Glacial effects are evident at the highest elevations, particularly in the Kosciuszko area.

The snow country was first described by Hume and Hovell during their trip to the upper Murray catchment, but early squatters brought sheep to the highlands by the 1830s. In 1834 Polish explorer Lhotsky described the southern aspects of the Snowy Mountains. His countryman Count Paul Strzelecki described the area coming from its western side, naming its highest peak after patriot and democrat Tadeusz Kosciuszko in 1840. The first comprehensive survey was by Thomas Townsend between 1846 and 1850. Perhaps the most famous descriptions of these mountains were by German naturalist and artist Ferdinand Mueller in the 1850s and by English botanist Joseph Hooker in 1860. Mueller was the Governmental Botanist of Victoria; his collections are in Melbourne. Hooker wrote the Introductory Essay to *Flora Tasmanie*, which correlates Australian flora to that of geologically related areas of prehistoric Antarctica and South America. This work can be read in conjunction with Darwin's to understand the radical changes in 19C natural science.

Cooma

Cooma (population 8300) is the starting-point for any trip to the High Country. The name comes from the Aboriginal word meaning either 'big lake' or 'open country'. Captain Mark Currie, Brigadier Major John Ovens and veteran explorer Joseph Wild first explored the area in 1823 during a trip on which they found Lake George and charted the upper Murrumbidgee.

Cooma itself was settled as early as 1826, but was not surveyed and gazetted until 1849. It grew rapidly for a few years after 1860 when gold was found at Kiandra, in the mountains between Cooma and Tumut.

Its present population is due to Merino sheep raising, the Snowy Mountains Scheme and tourism to the snowfields and Australian Alps.

Among its architectural sites is **St Paul's Church** on Commission Street overlooking the town. Built in 1865, its alpine ash joinery, roof framing and floors are original. The spire and roof shingles are from 1891. The rectory is in Edwardian style and was built in 1906.

The first inn in the district, the former Lord Raglan Hotel at 11 Lambie Street, is now a gallery. Like most of the town's commercial buildings, its verandah makes pleasant what might otherwise seem plain.

The **Royal Hotel** on Cambie and Sharp Streets remains one of Cooma's important social centres. Constructed in 1858, it has a substantial iron verandah and 12-pane windows. Local residents will describe rough times at the hotel on weekends when the workers on the Snowy Mountain Hydro-Electric Scheme (see box, p 231) came to town.

Cooma's tourist centre is open all year and includes fairly extensive information about the region. It is located on the town's main street, next to Centennial Park. (**Tourist information:** 119 Sharp Street; ☎ 02 6452 1108.) This is a good place to find out about accommodation in the ski resorts, but it is probably best to arrange this ahead of time in the many tourist agencies in Sydney, Melbourne or Canberra who specialise in skiing holidays (the Jolimont Centre in Canberra (see Canberra) is a good example). The park's **International Avenue of Flags**, with its flags from 27 nations, was erected in 1959 in recognition of the many nationalities who worked on Australia's greatest technological project, the Snowy Mountain Hydro-Electric Scheme, for which Cooma was the headquarters during construction from 1949 to 1972.

From Cooma, travel 60km to **Jindabyne** (population 1750), another town that as a village was moved in 1962 to make way for Jindabyne Dam. As is immediately apparent, the township is geared for tourists, both winter sports fans and all year round fishermen. Across from the information centre is a monument to Kosciuszko, and the Polish explorer who named Mt Kosciuszko, Paul Strzelecki (see box in Victoria, p 395). **Snowy River Information Centre**, Petamin Plaza; ☎ 02 6456 2444.

20km west of Jindabyne is the entrance to **Kosciuszko National Park**, on Sawpit Creek Road (☎ 02 6456 1700; entrance fee). The entrance fee, which is a rather steep daily fee, is currently being contested by the ski resorts within the park, but at the moment the fee still stands. The **information centre,** a bit further on from the entrance gate, provides excellent walking-trail maps and other park information. From here the road continues through the ski resorts of Smiggin Holes and Perisher and onto Charlotte Pass at the base of Mt Kosciuszko.

At Charlotte Pass, site of the coldest recorded temperatures in Australia (the record is a mere -22°C!), is a Swiss-style chalet, built as the *Hotel Kosciuszko* in 1909. It has twice been rebuilt after fires. From here, you can walk to the footpaths which lead to the top of Mt Kosciuszko, a 16km hike. It is more of a cross-country hike than a mountain climb. En route is Seaman's Hut, a stone cottage built to commemorate Laurie Seaman, an American skier who, along with Australian Evan Hayes, perished in a blizzard in 1928. It is a good reminder that weather conditions here are variable at all times—there have even been blizzards on Christmas Day. Be prepared for inclement weather when travelling anywhere in the Snowy Mountains.

From the entrance to the park, the Alpine Way travels some 20km to **Thredbo Village**, the most well known of the ski resorts. In 1997, the village suffered a disastrous land-slide, which killed 18 people (one survivor was found, miraculously, after being buried for three days). The community is still recovering from this blow to tourism. The region is certainly the most pleasant place to visit in the summer, with excellent walks and the possibility of a chair-lift ride without skiers (see box, p 232).

The Alpine Highway from Thredbo continues north c 75km to **Khancoban**, another township built by the Snowy Scheme and site of the Murray 1 Power

The Snowy Mountains Hydro-Electric Authority

On 17 October 1949, the Snowy Mountains Hydro-Electric Scheme was officially opened by Australian Prime Minister Ben Chifley at a ceremony in Cooma, New South Wales. The project, intended to harness the waters of the Snowy Mountains to generate power for the entire country as well as irrigation for the inland, was the largest and most ambitious engineering project ever undertaken in Australia: at a cost of $800,000,000, the scheme would ultimately comprise 16 large dams and several small ones spread over 2000 square kilometres of the Snowy Mountains, 80 kilometres of aqueducts with more than 145 kilometres of tunnels, a pumping station, and seven surface and underground power stations. Lake Eucumbene, created when Eucumbene Dam was completed in the late 1950s, caused the entire town of Adaminaby to be moved; the resultant lake holds nine times as much water as Sydney Harbour.

The entire Snowy scheme was completed in 1972, under budget and on time. In 1967 the Scheme was listed as one of the Seven World Engineering Wonders by the American Society of Civil Engineers, and the same organisation recently declared it an International Civil Engineering Landmark, along with the Panama Canal and the Statue of Liberty.

By any standards the Snowy Scheme was a monumental task, and one that would require an enormous and committed workforce, a workforce that Australia did not possess. At the end of the Second World War, Australia's population stood at 7.5 million in a landmass the size of the United States. With a predominantly Anglo-Celtic population in a continent at the edge of Asia, Australia at the time was intensely concerned about its survival as a Western culture; and recognising that population growth was necessary and desirable, the one way to ensure this survival was to actively recruit migration by Europeans (not Asians). Immigration, then, was taken on as an essential task, one that both government and business were to encourage and support through federal policies and job programmes. The Snowy scheme at its height employed 100,000 people from 33 countries, many of whom stayed on to become the New Australians of the 1950s and 1960s. These 'Snowy People', then, were instrumental in the transformation of Australia into the multicultural, ethnically diverse country it is today.

The Snowys' authorities did make some effort to consider environmental questions at the time of construction, but certainly such considerations would have prevented such a massive project being constructed today. Indeed, current residents of the region lament the fact that the once-mighty Snowy River is now a mere trickle because of the dams; strong grass-roots movements are afoot to release more water. Still, the achievements of the scheme are notable and impressive, and visitors may enjoy a closer look at the workings of the dams and tunnels. The Snowy Mountain Hydro-Electric Authority's headquarters are on the outskirts of Cooma, with an impressive information centre (☎ 02 6453 2004). At **Cabramurra**, Australia's highest township and one of the permanent townships created by the scheme, a photographic display concentrates on the 'Snowy People'. A view of the nearby Tumut Pond Reservoir gives the most awe-inspiring impression of the gruelling conditions under which these people worked.

Skiing in Australia

Skiing as a sport, not as transport, was actually practised in Australia well before it became popular in the European Alps. In the 1860s, Norwegian gold-miners at the snow-bound goldfields in nearby Kiandra introduced the long-pointed ski then used in Scandinavia. By 1862, ski races were well established here, and even the Chinese diggers participated. Kiandra's gold quickly disappeared and so did the settlement; skiing then became limited to those few High Country graziers who stayed in the area.

By the beginning of the 20C, tourists began to take an interest in the sport, and the 'Alpine Club of New South Wales' was founded. This led to the construction of chalets at Mt Kosciuszko and at Mt Buffalo in Victoria. During the 1920s, Australians travelling overseas brought back news of well-established skiing resorts, which prompted the importation of Austrian ski instructors and the development of more modern courses in the Australian Alps. Further impetus occurred with the arrival of so many winter-country immigrants during the construction of the Snowy Mountains Scheme. The construction of the Snowy's present ski-resorts date from that time. Australians have competed in the Winter Olympics since 1952; so far, the combined winter-sport teams have only won two bronze medals.

Skiing in Australia is an interesting experience, if for no other reason than to come down a hill of gum-trees and view kangaroos in the snow. While the ski resorts are geared for downhill skiing, with many chair-lifts, none of the hills are spectacularly high; the land seems much more suited for cross-country skiing, an activity that is growing in popularity. Because of the short season, the ski resorts charge astronomical prices for lift tickets and accommodation in season. Still, enthusiasts from as far away as Sydney fill the slopes and the highways every winter weekend. Be sure to make bookings ahead of time if you plan to hit the slopes, and remember that many roads in the region may be impassable. Authorities also require snow chains on cars driving in substantial snow.

Another interesting feature of the Snowy Mountains region is the series of Alpine huts dotted throughout the mountains to provide shelter for those skiing or walking through the most rugged parts of the region; one can even stay overnight in these simple dwellings. These huts were first erected at the beginning of the century, and are maintained by a devoted group of bushwalkers. Information on the huts can be obtained from the Cooma Information Centre, and in any of several books by Klaus Hueneke, an avid Snowy mountaineer.

Skiing in the Snowys centres on Jindabyne and Thredbo. It is more expensive in Australia than it generally is in the United States or Europe. Ski holidays are bookable as packages or in part at any tourist office or travel agent. The Jindabyne Reservation Centre (1800 026 356) will make arrangements for accommodation. Reservations for accommodation are at a premium during the season; take care to book several weeks in advance. During ski season, regularly scheduled flights depart from Sydney. Most visitors either drive their own cars or take the bus, either one of the many charter coaches or regular services through Greyhound-Pioneer, Murrays, or Countrylink.

Station. The drive provides spectacular mountain views; in the area are opportunities for trout fishing and whitewater rafting. From Khancoban, continue on
to the old gold-town of **Kiandra**, now a ghost town, on the main Snowy Mountains Highway between Tumut and Cooma, or proceed west into Corryong over
the Victorian border.

Back at **Cooma**, the MONARO HIGHWAY continues south across the tussock-grass
plains, then splits into two routes. As route 23, the road proceeds south through
Bombala and into Victoria; at Cann River, it joins the Princes Highway along the
Victorian coast. Route 18 jogs east and becomes a road of lush fern gullies with
great views down to the ocean at Bega.

South of Batemans Bay

From Batemans Bay to Bermagui, the Princes Highway traverses the **Eurobodalla Coast**. Murrays, Countrylink and Greyhound-Pioneer have a bus
service along the coast, but there is no local public bus service to speak of; you
really need a car to explore the region. At **Mogo**, c 8km from Bateman's Bay, a
road travels east to Tomakin and the popular beaches of **Mossy Point** and
Broulee, and passes the surprising **Mogo Zoo**—one part of the zoo is a taxi-
dermy display, while the other presents significant wildlife displays, including a
rare pair of red pandas and a TV-star cougar.

Mogo itself is all craft-and-tea shops; the highway continues south into
Moruya (population 2400). In the 1850s and 1860s, Moruya was an impor-
tant stopover on the way to the goldfields of Araluen; the old road to the Araluen
Valley along the Deua River still enters the town. **Tourist information**: Princes
Highway, ☎ 02 4472 1111.

History
Captain Cook sited and named nearby Mt Dromedary when passing by the
coast in 1770, and in 1797 a group of shipwrecked survivors walked
through the area on their way from Gippsland to Sydney. The first white
settler was Irishman Francis Flanagan in 1829. By the end of the 19C,
Moruya's isolation was eased by the regular appearance of the steamship
ferries plying the coast between Sydney and Melbourne (see Tathra below).
In the 1920s, Moruya boomed when the contractors for the Sydney
Harbour Bridge chose its quarry on the Moruya River for the granite pylons
needed to build the bridge. Hundreds of immigrant stonemasons, most from
Scotland and Italy, poured into 'Granite Town', and the wharf became a
loading zone for the stone. By the end of the decade, this boom had passed,
and Moruya fell back on timber and agricultural industries. The
surrounding landscape gives evidence of its position as a leading dairying
district. Today it is a leading holiday destination for Canberrans.

A further 20km south is **Bodalla**, now a major cheese-making centre. In the
1850s, the area was part of the 15,000 ha (38,000 acre) holdings of entrepreneur Thomas Sutcliffe Mort (see box, p 234) and evidence of his cultivated ambitions remain in the town's All Saints Anglican Church, built by leading ecclesiastical architect Edmund Blacket in Gothic Revival style in 1880 as a memorial to the
town's founder; the castellated tower was added by Blacket's son Cyril in 1901.

Thomas Sutcliffe Mort

Thomas Sutcliffe Mort (1816–78) was one of the most successful and visionary businessmen in colonial Australia. He arrived from Lancashire in Sydney in 1838 as an agent of a brokerage firm that quickly collapsed; Mort then went into business for himself as a wool auctioneer. His firm Mort & Co. became the most important wool-selling agency in Australia, eventually amalgamating with R. Goldsborough & Co. to become Goldsborough & Mort. The company's enormous wool warehouses still stand near Darling Harbour in Sydney, now turned into a car museum and car park. Mort also became involved with steamship companies and mining concerns, both of which made him enormously prosperous. In 1856 he acquired vast land holdings at Bodalla and developed the area into a model dairy farm. He also established some of the first dry docks at Balmain, building ships as well as locomotives, and established the first employee profit-sharing scheme in Australia. He invested immense sums to develop a system of refrigerating meat on ships, the first successful refrigeration endeavour, although he died before the first shipment reached Europe in 1879.

Continue south 20km to **Narooma**, a popular fishing resort. 9km off the coast, and accessible by boat from Narooma's wharf, is **Montague Island (Narooma Tourist information ☎ 02 4476 2881)**, site of a well-known granite lighthouse built in 1881 to a design by prolific Colonial Architect James Barnet. The island is known popularly as an important landmark along the Sydney-to-Hobart yacht race on Boxing Day. Most enjoyably, the island provides excellent venues to view waterfowl, fur seals, and **fairy penguin colonies** without the tourist spectacle so prevalent on Victoria's more famous Phillip Island. While weather is often inclement, with very rugged seas, Montague Island is a splendid day-trip destination; its tour operators have won a recent Excellence in Tourism Award.

Nearby, among the verdant hills are the twin towns of **Central Tilba** and **Tilba Tilba**, the latter classified by the National Trust as an 'unusual mountain village'. Founded in the 1890s, virtually all of the buildings, made of timber, date from this period; the village is surrounded by spectacular mountainous terrain. A great favourite with tourists and film crews alike, the residents carry out crafts, cheese production, and shoe-making, and give the strong impression of a village-life commune. From Tilba Tilba, it is possible to take a walking track up Mt Dromedary.

Bermagui

From Tilba, you could make a short journey southeast to the fishing port of **Bermagui**. Big-game fishing in Australia was virtually invented here, or at least most actively promoted, after the arrival of American Wild-West author Zane Grey (1872–1939). Grey came here in 1935, and was so impressed with the marlin fishing that he stayed for months; his book *An American Angler in Australia* (1937) recounts his fishing experiences along the eastern coast. He also promoted the glories of Australia:

> I was hardly prepared for this land of staggering contrasts, of unbelievable beasts, of the loveliest and strangest birds, of great modern English cities, of vast ranges that rivalled my beloved Arizona, and of endless forestland, or bush, as they call

it, never adequately described, no doubt because of beauty and wildness beyond the power of any pen to delineate.

Bermagui lives up to Grey's praises still. Fishing in all forms dominates, although the coastline also provides beautiful rugged beaches with splendid rock-pools, and opportunities for bushwalking. Montague Island, 23km north (see p 234), is still an international mecca for big-game fishermen. The ocean here can be quite cold but still enjoyable—do not expect Queensland-style bathing experiences anywhere along the south coast.

The Sapphire Coast

The coastline from Bermagui to the Victorian border has acquired the label of the **Sapphire Coast**, an invention of the tourist industry rather than an historic appellation. The unofficial centre of the region is **Bega** (population 4300), 80km south from Narooma. **Tourist information**, Gipps Street; ☎ 02 6492 2045. Bega itself is not a particularly attractive town, but it is ideally situated to experience this part of the country. From here the SNOWY MOUNTAINS HIGHWAY climbs up into the mountains, offering breathtaking views, and eventually reaching **Cooma** (c 127km; see p 229), gateway to the Snowy Mountains ski resorts; indeed, Begans boast it is possible to ski and swim on the same day when staying here.

Bega is known especially for cheese, and the **Bega Cheese Heritage Centre** offers tours and tastings, and wonderful historical displays about the dairy industry in Australia; the centre won the 1997 NSW Heritage and Cultural Tourism Award. **Grevillea Winery** (☎ 02 6492 3006; open Mon–Fri and Sun 09.00–17.00, Sat 10.00–15.00), just to the south of town, also offers tours.

28km east of Bega is the small fishing village of **Tathra**, at one time an important stop for the steamship ferries between Sydney and Melbourne. The **Tathra Wharf** is still intact, parts of it dating from the 1860s; it now houses a Wharf museum, which tells the story of the old steamship trading links (☎ 02 6494 1483).

From Bega, the Princes Highway heads south to a side road west to the 19C village of **Candelo**, and the **Kameruka Estate**, an important remnant of the early dairying industry; its homestead dates from 1845, with interesting examples of 19C dairying buildings and equipment. Kameruka is open daily. Candelo has a popular market on the first Sunday of the month.

Travelling back to the Princes Highway, you enter **Merimbula**, now a flashy tourist town, filled with new condominiums, which takes advantage of its stunning peninsula location, with lakes, inlets, and sparkling beaches (**Merimbula Tourist Information**, Beach Street, ☎ 02 6495 1129). The region was the land of the **Dyirringan** people; Merimbula means 'place of the big snake'. Of historic note is the **Munn Tower House** on Monaro Street. Built in the 1870s by Matthew Munn, founder of Merimbula, the building is a large stone cottage with an added two-storey timber tower that could be seen for great distances. Munn developed the area agriculturally, most notably in the production of 'maizena', a cornflour. Also in town is the School Museum, between the Anglican and Roman Catholic churches on Main Street. The museum is run by the Merimbula-Imlay Historical Society, and includes local history displays, as well as memorabilia as of the Munn family and a description of shipping on this part of the south coast.

Pambula and Eden

The Princes Highway continues 6km south to **Pambula**, an 'historic village' centred on **The Grange**, the grand mansion of a 19C sea-captain. Also in the village is a small stone house that served as a post office and store; it was built by Syms Covington, who had assisted Charles Darwin on his *Beagle* voyage, after which he settled in Australia and bought land here in 1853.

Directly east of here is the northern section of **Ben Boyd National Park** (☎ 02 6496 1434) (see box), which runs to Twofold Bay and Eden; the park continues to the south of Eden and on to Disaster Bay. The **Wonboyn Dune System** of 26 parallel coastal dunes are in the park, as are nesting grounds for an endangered species, the Ground Parrot.

Eden (population 3300) on Twofold Bay is a real fishing port with a fishing fleet and opportunities to undertake deep-sea fishing cruises. **Tourist information:** Princes Highway; ☎ 02 6496 1953.

Ben Boyd

Ben Boyd (c 1796–1851) was one of the more colourful figures in Australia's early history. He was a Scotsman, working as a stockbroker in London, where he acquired ships for the purpose of trade with Australia. He devised an elaborate scheme of floating investments whereby he could acquire land in several locations throughout Australia. In 1842, he arrived in Sydney in his yacht the *Wanderer*, along with his brother and the water-colourist Oswald Brierly (1817–94). By 1843, he had established a bank, and, using the bank's money, had acquired enormous properties in the Monaro district, along the Murray River and at Port Phillip. His most ambitious venture involved the purchase of several steamships, which would aid in the founding of the twin townships of Boyd Town and East Boyd on Twofold Bay. Boyd built here a jetty and lighthouse, as well as a Gothic church, a hotel and several houses. By this time, he had nine whalers working for him from this port. In 1847, Boyd tried to ship natives from the South Pacific to the area to provide cheap labour, but the scheme failed.

His grandiose commercial dynasty, certainly too ambitious for the circumstances of mid-19C Australia, began to collapse, and by 1849, he was removed from control of his bank. He set sail in the *Wanderer* for the California gold rush in 1849, where he had no success; in 1851 he began a voyage around the Pacific Islands. In October of that year, he landed in the Solomon Islands, and was apparently killed. Boyd's name lives on in North Sydney's Ben Boyd Avenue, in the Ben Boyd National Park, and in the ruins of his beloved Boydtown.

The town's name commemorates not paradise, but the family name of Baron Auckland, Secretary of the Colonies when the town was laid out in 1842. As the excellent **Eden Killer Whale Museum** (182 Imlay Street; ☎ 02 6496 2094) demonstrates, Twofold Bay was an important whalers' station from the early 19C. As early as the 1790s, American and British whalers plied these waters, carrying out the less laborious practice of 'bay whaling'. The Whale Museum includes the skeleton of 'Old Tom', a legendary leader of a killer whale pack which allegedly guided the whalers to their prey. The museum is open Mon–Sat 09.15–15.45, Sun 11.15–15.45.

8km south of Eden on the Princes Highway is the **Seahorse Inn** (☎ 02 6496 1361), built around the remnants of Ben Boyd's original house. After Boyd's departure and disappearance, the house became a thriving hotel, used by local whalers and travellers en route by ship from Sydney to Melbourne. The inn had fallen into disrepair until it was rebuilt in the 1930s; it has recently been renovated again. While there is little evidence of Ben Boyd's original structure, the inn is still a major landmark in the area, and provides wonderful views to the beach and Twofold Bay.

Sydney to Melbourne

The **HUME HIGHWAY** is the main road to the south and inland between Sydney and Melbourne, a total of 870km or 1020km via Canberra. You can also take the Hume Highway as a tour loop south of Sydney to the Illawarra Highway at Moss Vale just south of Bowral across Macquarie Pass to the ocean and back to Sydney (240km). The main Sydney to Melbourne train route (the Melbourne XPT, travelling daily) follows much of the same route.

> The highway, which actually bypasses virtually every town in New South Wales and Victoria, was named for explorer **Hamilton Hume** (1797–1873). Born in Parramatta, the son of Andrew Hume, the superintendent of convicts, Hume began exploring the country south of his family home in Appin, New South Wales in 1814, when he was seventeen. Three years later, Governor Macquarie arranged for Hume to guide pastoralist-explorers Charles Throsby and James Meehan through the area. They eventually reached the Goulburn Plains and Lake Bathurst. In 1830 Surveyor-General Major Mitchell planned a road and followed Hume's track, which traversed an easier route than the existing route over the Mittagong Range to Bong Bong. By 1832 the road reached Goulburn and by the late 1830s, Albury. Nonetheless, today's hour by car to Berrima took nearly a week by bullock dray.

The highway, which takes Hume's name, passes tortuously through Sydney's entangled suburbs to leave the urban area at about Campbelltown (much of this part of the route is circumvented now by the M5 Tollroad to the far edge of Liverpool). Just beyond Campbelltown, the hills fringing Sydney become rougher and eucalypt forests replace the grassland scrub. Beyond these low mountains, the land is relatively flat sheep and cattle paddocks to a point between Yass and Gundagai where gentle hills break the monotony. (Mind the speed limit in this valley; on one holiday weekend the New South Wales patrol issued more than 1500 citations for speeding near Goulburn—nearly double the amount in the rest of the Southern Tablelands region.) Again, past these hills, farmland extends with a few variations all the way to the outskirts of Melbourne.

While **Liverpool**, 31km from the heart of Sydney, was initially a separate town, it is now part of the most congested districts of suburban development.

But since the inception of the M5 Tollway, the agonising drive through these streets can be avoided, and Liverpool is thought of largely as a place to avoid. Still, there are many places of historical note in the town. The train travels most expeditiously to Liverpool and on to Campbelltown from central Sydney. The train also travels to Casula, where the exciting **Casula Powerhouse Arts Centre** is located at 1 Casula Road, next door to the Casula Railway Station (☎ 02 9824 1121; open daily 10.00–16.00). The 1994 design of the building, a renovation of a 1950s power station, won the RAIA President's Award for recycled buildings. The open spaces in two galleries provide great opportunities for some of the most innovative art shows and performances in the Sydney region.

In the Liverpool area, two early **bridges** still in use and worth comment were constructed under Scottish stonemason David Lennox, one at Lapstone (built in 1833 using local stone by a gang of 20 convicts) and the other (1836) an elegant solution to a difficult crossing of Prospect Creek on the Hume Highway more or less between Bankstown and Cabramatta. The latter design harkens back to Lennox's training under the great English engineer Telford, particularly the crossing of the Severn at Over.

Campbelltown

Campbelltown (population 38,250), named for Elizabeth Campbell, wife of Governor Lachlan Macquarie, is famous for the Fisher's ghost story centred here. Frederick Fisher, a convict who arrived in 1816, secured a ticket of leave and established a farm in the town. Some time after his disappearance in 1826, a local resident was directed by Fisher's ghost (or having seen it on a fence rail convinced the authorities) to search the area. His body was discovered in a nearby creek. George Worrall, who rented a nearby farm (or who shared Fisher's hut with him), was convicted of manslaughter and executed for the murder. This basic story has been elaborated to heroically gruesome proportions. The legend is commemorated every year at the Campbelltown City Festival of Fisher's Ghost, beginning in early February, and continuing for two to three weeks, with Highland Games and raft races on the Nepean River. **Macarthur Country Tourist Association**, on the corner of Hume Highway and Congressional Drive, Liverpool; ☎ 02 9821 2311.

Noteworthy architecture includes the old Campbelltown **Post Office**, an Italianate design by James Barnet who was the Colonial Architect from 1865 to 1890 during Australia's period of strongest expansion. **St John's Church** (1825) may be the oldest Catholic church in Australia. James Ruse, the pioneer farmer associated with the Experimental Farm Cottage in Parramatta, and his wife Elizabeth are buried here.

In nearby **Camden**, the Macarthur family had their second residence. Although the bulk of Macarthur's interests were engaged at Elizabeth Farm in Parramatta (see p 164), **Camden Park** supported, among other enterprises, his winery. The First Fleet had brought vines to Sydney (planted in what is now the Botanic Gardens and later at Government House in Parramatta), but when Macarthur returned from England and France in 1817, he brought a number of plants for cultivation here. By 1827, he was producing 90,000 litres per year and in 1839 he brought out six German wine-makers to tend the plants. His son William improved the process to the extent that the wines and brandies were recognised in Europe.

The Macarthur house was designed by John Verge and built in 1835. It features a classical stone parapet, a large two-storey wing (added in c 1880), and single storey symmetrical wings. In addition to the family mausoleums, the well-maintained grounds and award-winning gardens are attractions. The farm is in private hands and, except on rare occasions like the Open Garden Scheme days, is closed to the public.

Along with Bowral and Moss Vale nearby in what is called the Southern Table-lands, **Mittagong** (population 4830) owes its existence to the railway rather than the road. The name is from an Aboriginal word meaning either 'little mountain' (a reference to Mount Gibraltar) or 'plenty of native dogs'. The area was referred to by Governor Macquarie as early as 1816, but was not settled until William Charker began raising cattle here in 1821; George Cutler ran the area's first licensed inn, known for its breakfasts. Once a renowned bottleneck between Canberra and Sydney, a new bypass now circumvents the town, offering splendid views of rocky escarpments heretofore unseen. **Tourist information**: Winifred West Park, Hume Highway; ☎ 02 4871 2888. The town has some very good antique stores.

The **Wombeyan Caves** can be reached by taking the Wombeyan turn-off from the Hume Highway, then travelling 60km northwest of Mittagong. These caves are fully developed for visitors, with railings and steps, and walking tracks around the area; spectacular mountain scenery abounds. ☎ 02 4843 5976.

Bowral (population 7400) is where cricket legend Sir Donald Bradman spent his childhood; his house is now part of the Bradman Museum on St Jude Street (☎ 02 4862 1247; open daily, 10.00–16.00). Arthur Upfield, creator of the Napoleon Bonaparte detective series, retired here. He describes the area in his *Bony and the Kelly Gang* (1960): 'the autumnal tints; the soft blues of the shadows and the jet black gaping jaws of the surrounding mountain slopes and cliffs'. **Wingecarribee House**, the homestead of the founding Oxley family, was imported as a kit from England in 1857. The Bowral area, along with the other towns of the Southern Highlands, is a popular destination for garden tours, with many nurseries and private gardens open for inspection in the spring. Especially popular is the Tulip Time festival in late September and early October. For tourist information, see Mittagong.

Travellers wishing to return to Sydney at this point can take the ILLAWARRA HIGHWAY. It proceeds east from here through some spectacular scenery, crossing the coastal range at Macquarie Pass. Intrepid motorists will be rewarded in good weather by taking the unsealed road from just beyond Robertson to Jamberoo.

For Wollongong on the coast, see New South Wales South Coast section, p 222.

Those motorists continuing south to Canberra or Melbourne on the Hume Highway will next pass **Berrima** (**tourist information** at Mittagong; or at Berrima Courthouse Museum, Wilshire Street, ☎ 02 4871 2888). From the Aboriginal word meaning 'to the south', Berrima was named by Surveyor-General Major Mitchell and established at the easily bridged crossing of the Wingecarribee River on the Great Southern Road opening the Southern High-lands of New South Wales. It replaced the first town in the region, Bong Bong, which lacked adequate water, but did offer the Argyle Inn. The *Sydney Gazette* (17 March 1832) mentioned that the inn 'with its dashing hostess, forms an agreeable insipidity for the dullest of dull settlements.'

Berrima's architectural highlights include the surrounding wall and gate-house (1866) of the Berrima Training Centre (the current incarnation of the Department of Corrective Services' former gaol), the country's oldest continu-ously licensed hotel (the **Surveyor-General Inn**, erected using sandstone blocks and bricks by William Harper for his son James in 1834) and the two-storey sandstone residence, **Harper's Mansion**, corner Hume Highway and Wilkinson Street, ☎ 02 4877 1501 (considerably restored by the National Trust of New South Wales). The oldest section of the town is pleasantly laid out and the architecture includes a number of buildings dating to the 1830s. It is a favoured spot for travellers to stop, either for a picnic lunch on the town green or to dine in one of the centre's ambitious inns. Several shops also cater to antique browsers.

Goulburn

From Berrima to Goulburn is c 80km on the highway. Advertised as the 'first inland city', **Goulburn** (population 23,000) was gazetted by March 1833, and was already settled in the late 1820s. Originally a garrison to supervise the convicts impressed to build the road and to attempt to control the flagrant bushrangers who operated in the district until the 1870s, the town's character is now essentially that of a rural service centre. The main street's design is a particularly good example of late 19C style. Note the **Post Office** which was designed by Colonial Architect James Barnet in 1880. It features a central clock tower flanked by a two-storey colonnade of offices. The arches of the ground floor colonnade have moulded keystones and Doric pilasters. **St Saviour's Cathedral**, designed by Edmund Blacket in 1874, offers interesting interior furnishings and an organ built by Forster & Andrews (Hull) in 1884. **Tourist information**: 2 Montague Street; ☎ 02 4821 5343.

In addition, two of the town's three historic houses are maintained for public inspection. These are **Riversdale**, Maud Street (☎ 02 4821 4741; open Mon–Thurs 10.00–12.00, weekends 10.00–16.30), a stone barn built in 1840 on the Sydney side of town near the gaol, and the only structure surviving from the town's Macquarie era. It has been restored by the National Trust. The more modest **St Clair**, at 318 Sloane Street, one block off the business district, was built in 1843 and has been restored by the Goulburn Historical Society. **Garroorigang** (1857) on the Braidwood Road is currently lived in, but the persistent fan of local histories stands a good chance of being welcomed in the late morning or early afternoon. Also in town near the railway station is the Goulbourn Brewery, including a flour mill (1836) and brewery (1840); it is one of the only surviving examples of 19C industrial buildings.

The FEDERAL HIGHWAY to Canberra begins c 13km south of Goulburn. It skirts **Lake George**'s western edge. Like its companion, Lake Bathurst c 20km due east, the lake is quite shallow and occasionally empties if the water table drops. This and the conviction that fisherman too frequently disappear on the lake provoke lively superstitions. In fact, the lake is considerably less dangerous than the 20-minute ride along the two-lane road beside it; the recent upgrading of the road was prompted by the disproportionate number of fatalities occurring along this short stretch. Both lakes were popular tourist attractions in the late 19C, when the water level was very high, but little evidence of the lodges or piers remains.

Further west on the HUME HIGHWAY is the **Hume Homestead** at **Frankfield**, 8km south of Gunning. It was granted to Francis Hume in 1836 for the capture of Patrick Bourke, a bushranger. The current house with a verandah on three sides and French windows was built in about 1870. In fact the Hume family was sprinkled throughout the area, with Hamilton's brother's residence at Collingwood (late 1830s) in Gunning. Hamilton Hume squatted in the area, buying grazier Cornelius O'Brien's bungalow in 1839. This homestead, called *Cooma Cottage*, is now a pleasant museum and gallery about 5km north of Yass near the entrance of the Barton Highway from Canberra. The home is open six days (closed Tues) 10.00–16.00; ☎ 02 6226 1470.

YASS (population 5300) was formally laid out by Thomas Townsend in 1832 and first settled in the 1840s. **Tourist information**: Coronation Park, ☎ 02 6226 2557. The town's entire **Main Street** is listed by the National Trust. Miraculously, the town fathers elected to maintain the verandahs and supporting posts, so wrought-iron lacework designs are abundant. The **Court House** and **Post Office** (1882) are of a Classical Revival design by James Barnet. The **railway station**, though a bit hard to find on the outskirts of town, is a gem largely due to the delicate hand evident in the gardening. Other buildings of this period are the Bank of New South Wales, 1885, by Blackman & Sulman and the Rural Bank, 1886, by Smedley.

Although a new bypass on the highway detours around this notorious old bottleneck on the route to Melbourne, Yass is still worth a stop, for its excellent information centre, and for some good tea rooms. Anyone travelling from Canberra by train to Melbourne must depart from the Yass Station (a bus brings passengers from Canberra).

Gundagai

Gundagai (population 2125) may be small in population, but its name looms large in Australian folklore, having inspired several popular poems and songs. On the approach to town is a tourist feature commemorating the **Dog on the Tucker Box** tale. (The centre itself is now a quintessential tacky tourist conglomeration.) While authorities debate the details of the story, a popular version describes a wandering swagman who commanded his loyal dog to guard his tuckerbox (basically a small portable kitchen cupboard holding provisions). The poor creature's master never returned and the dog held his post until death. A version more revealing of the Aussie character describes a bullock driver having a difficult day at the crossing of the nearby creek. When he failed to return to camp promptly, the dog shat on the tuckerbox. This version was passed from the bullock driver to a wine salesman, Jack Moses, who made the poem famous. The dog was sculpted by local Frank Rusconi and the monument unveiled by Prime Minister Joe Lyons in 1932. The most famous song about the town was written by Jack O'Hagan, who had never been there. In 1922, his nostalgic melody 'Along the Road to Gundagai' became an international success and was the theme song for the 'Dad and Dave' radio programme.

Gundagai itself is a pleasant country town which offers an excellent Art Deco style **theatre** (built in 1929 as the Masonic Lodge) with intact interiors. Frank Rusconi's idiosyncratic **Marble Masterpiece**, an ornate model cathedral, is on display at Rusconi's Place. **Tourist information**: Sheridan Street; ☎ 02 6944 1341.

The **Prince Alfred Bridge**, made of three spans of iron and wooden approaches, was constructed in 1863–65. It crosses the Murrumbidgee River. Tragically, the town was first built on the river's flood plain. Ignoring the advice of the local Aborigines, 80 of the town's 250 inhabitants drowned and 71 buildings were destroyed by flood in 1852. The present bridge is now for pedestrian use only.

48km off the Hume Highway east on the Snowy Mountains Highway is **Tumut** (population 6140). The name is supposedly Aboriginal for 'a quiet resting place by the river'. Hamilton Hume and William Hovell, during their inland journey to Port Phillip, discovered Tumut valley and river in 1824. Part of the Hume and Hovell Walking Trail is accessible in town. (This trail extends from Gunning to Albury but has various access points throughout for shorter walks; more information from Department of Lands, Wagga Wagga, ☎ 02 6921 2503.) Today, the town is known not only for its mountain scenery, but as the site of one of the great dams of the Snowy Mountain Hydro-Electric Scheme, the Talbingo; group tours can be arranged through the **tourist information office**: Snowy Mountains Highway; ☎ 02 6947 1849.

Wagga Wagga

48km in the other direction off the Hume Highway is **Wagga Wagga** (population 40,800), usually referred to only as Wagga. From the Aboriginal phrase meaning 'place of many crows', the area was first described by Charles Sturt in 1829 as a 'rich and lightly timbered valley ... parts of the [Murrumbidgee] river were visible through the dark masses of swamp-oak ... or glittered among the flooded gum trees'. Originally part of the Wiradjuri tribal grounds, it was settled by squatters, became a village in 1847 and a city as late as 1946.

Mark Twain visited the town in 1895 due to its fame as the home of the Tichborne Claimant, a notorious English legal case growing out of a satirical mystery written by the local newspaper editor which featured a local butcher. More to its credit, the town has a School of Arts (1859), associated Literary Association (1873) and Shakespearian Club (longest running in the southern hemisphere) and offers an annual dramatic festival. In town is a lovely **Botanic Gardens**, Tom Wood Drive, that includes a small zoo and model trains; a **city art gallery** on Baylis Street (☎ 02 6926 9660; open Tues–Sat 10.00–17.00, Sun 12.00–16.000), with an excellent glass collection, as well as changing print shows; and Charles Sturt University. Wagga Wagga considers itself the cultural centre of the **Riverina district**, which begins here. The region is also known for its excellent new wineries—many of which offer tastings (check at tourist information); it has also begun to produce olive oil. **Tourist information**: Tarcutta Street; ☎ 02 6923 5402. The office has brochures for self-guided walks.

From Wagga, you can continue on the Olympic Way for another 100km to Albury, or return to the Hume Highway, passing through the little town of **Holbrook**, with its amusing town slogan, 'Where the Hell is Holbrook?'

Albury/Wodonga

Our only experiences in **Albury** (population 38,000) involved fines for parking violations and non-existent cafes. This impression seems to be substantiated by the experiences of such writers as Robert G. Barrett, whose character Les Norton in the story *St Kilda Kooler* (1990) presents a similar interpretation of the city's charms. Just be *sure* to park according to the well-concealed traffic signs, and do not jaywalk. Situated on the Murray River, the town does indeed have many sites of historic interest. **Crossing Place Visitor's Centre**, Hume Highway; ☎ 02 6041 3875/1800 800 743.

Albury/Wodonga marks the border between New South Wales and Victoria. Travelling by train from Sydney to Melbourne, the 19C American humorist Mark Twain was prompted at this juncture to observe a singular thing:

> ... the oddest thing, the strangest thing, the most baffling and unaccountable marvel that Australasia can show. At the frontier between New South Wales and Victoria our multitude of passengers were routed out of their snug beds by lantern-light in the morning in the biting cold of a high altitude to change cars on a road that has no break in it from Sydney to Melbourne! Think of the paralysis of intellect that gave that idea birth ... It is a narrow-gauge road to the frontier, and a broader gauge thence to Melbourne.

This situation arose through miscommunication as well as state rivalries, but during the era of train travel, it was the subject of much derision and, indeed, inconvenience. It has always served as a metaphor for the lunacy of New South Wales-Victoria competition (see Wodonga below). The **Albury Railway Station**, built in 1881 after designs by New South Wales Government Railways chief engineer John Whitton, is an imposing structure with an extremely long platform and stuccoed decorative elements on the exterior. Its interior contains most of the original cedar joinery and a domed booking hall.

Wodonga (population 22,000) is Albury's twin city on the Victorian side of the border. The tourist information office is the same as for Albury.

History

The town began as a squatters' station built by Charles Huon and called Belvoir from the 1830s until it reverted to a form of its original name in 1874. The Victorian rail line reached Wodonga in 1873, eight years before its mate from Sydney reached Albury and ten years before a bridge over the Murray allowed passengers to continue to the Albury station. The absurd controversy regarding the rail gauge was compounded at this break in the journey. Neither government would allow the other to disembark at the end of its territory. Rather, the bridge was built double width, enabling the northbound train a terminus in Albury and the southbound train a terminus in Wodonga. After some acrimony about the Melbourne-bound trains' breakfast break prior to crossing the river, Albury was selected in 1886 as the station at which travellers changed trains.

The ethnic diversity of this inland area is due to **Bonegilla Camp**, a processing centre for immigrants which functioned between 1947 and 1971. A number of the 315,000 people passing through the camp settled locally.

Because of the proximity to the Murray River, this region presents many possibilities for water activities, and bushwalking tracks dot the landscape. Check with the information centre for details.

En route to Melbourne

Outside Wodonga, the Hume Highway begins its long and utterly boring drive into Melbourne. If you have the time and are driving, it is worthwhile to make some detours off to the towns along the road.

The **wine district** of northeast Victoria is west of here, centred around **Rutherglen** on the Murray Valley Highway. The winery at **All Saints** was established in 1864 by G.S. Smith and J. Banks. The present building dates from about 1880 and is operated by Smith's descendants. The **Mount Ophir Winery** was built by Eisemann & Gleeson during the last decade of the 19C for the English family Burgoyne. The Victoria Hotel dates from 1868 and features a cast-iron verandah and parapet with prominent stables in the back. Nearly all of the many wineries in the region are open daily for tastings; tours, as well as maps highlighting all wineries and opening times, are available from the **Tourist Information Centre**, Drummond Street, Rutherglen, ☎ 02 6032 9166/1 800 62 2871.

Wangaratta (population 16,600) is a pleasant little town at the juncture of the Ovens Highway heading north to Bright and the Victorian Alps. **Tourist information**; Hume Highway, Wangaratta South, ☎ 03 5721 5711.

History

The first settler in the area was George Faithful who took up land at the junction of the Ovens and King Rivers in 1838. William Clarke is regarded as the father of the settlement. He opened an inn and operated a punt and stock crossing. The town was largely deserted during the 1851–52 gold rush, but came to prosper as a staging point en route to the diggings. Like Glenrowan (see below), Wangaratta had its own bushranger, Dan 'Mad Dog' Morgan, a vicious murdering brute so appalling in his crimes that his head was cut off and sent to the University of Melbourne for analysis. He was thought to have the brains of a gorilla (rather a chauvinistic slight for those creatures), but public sentiment about the dismemberment led to the reprimand of the local superintendent of police.

The most famous of bushrangers (see box, p245) met his end in the small village of **Glenrowan**, between Wangaratta and Benalla. **Ned Kelly** was finally arrested here in 1880, and his gang members were killed by the police.

The village of Glenrowan today, of course, plays up to the legend; the **Glenrowan Tourist Centre** (☎ 03 5766 2367) is essentially a re-enactment through animation of Kelly's Last Stand.

Benalla (population 9300) is an otherwise modest town known for its **regional art gallery** (☎ 03 5762 3027) containing the Ledger Collection of Colonial and Heidelberg School Paintings (see pp 68 and 345). Located on Bridge Street, the gallery is open normal business hours. The Old Court House (1864, design by G. Joacimi) on Arundel Street is evidence of the change to Victoria's architectural styles. The façade is from 1888. In October, the town has a Rose Festival. Joe Byrne, of the Kelly Gang, is buried in the cemetery here. **Tourist information**: 14 Mair Street, ☎ 03 5762 1749.

Situated 18km north of Benalla on the old Hume Highway is **Seymour**

Bushrangers

The Australian fascination with bushrangers results from the exploits of a relatively small number of outlaws active in the 1860s and of the Ned Kelly gang in the late 1870s. In fact, highway robbery and preying upon isolated settlements had its first phase during the colonial era when convicts who had escaped into the bush stole sheep and generally operated as bandits. The surprisingly civil Matthew Brady—he would tolerate no improprieties against women or children—and his associates in Tasmania and Bold Jack Donahue in the Hawkesbury River area of New South Wales are examples of these sorts. During the gold rush era, shipments of gold were the focus of the criminal imagination. Still, the tendency to bail up (that is to rob) passers-by of any description was central to the outlaw, many of whom were ex-convicts from Tasmania.

The free-born bushrangers of the 1860s were a little more complicated. In one sense they were the result of the social inequities pitting the land-rich squatters against the land-purchasing selectors. The bushrangers were supported by these latter, poorer rural relations and, as such, attained something of a Robin Hood status in the press and among the locals. The police were generally disliked as representatives of the socially powerful, while the rangers were reported as daring and romantic and their exploits sensationalised.

That Ned Kelly rather than his predecessor and exemplar Ben Hall, also active in both New South Wales and Victoria, continues to receive the attention he does seems unwarranted. While it is nearly sacrilegious to slight the Kelly legend, in fact the man was a petty criminal from an unseemly family. Jailed several times and indeed unfairly harassed by the police, Kelly and his three associates (his brother Dan, Steve Hart and Joe Byrne) goaded the police into misuse of their power under the Felons' Apprehension Act.

In fact, more horses were commandeered by the police than stolen by the bushrangers, more provisions and weapons taken, more people held without recourse. Public sentiment naturally rested with the outlaws who boasted of never harming a woman or robbing a poor man, who joked about offering rewards for the capture of police chiefs, who took the entire town of Glenrowan captive, then donned armour, both helmet and chest plate, made of the mouldboards of ploughs to fight their last battle in 1879. It is this particularly bizarre iron mask that gained public attention, leading to the establishment of Ned Kelly in his armour as a recognisable Australian icon which appears in a plethora of visual forms, from Sidney Nolan's famous series of paintings to garden sculptures.

At the end of the Glenrowan siege, Joe Byrne was shot dead, and Dan Kelly and Steve Hart probably took poison to avoid being burned to death during their siege. The police shot, tried and finally, after a famous trial in Melbourne, hanged Ned Kelly on 11 November 1880. Earlier in the year, his mother's last words to him had been 'Mind you die like a Kelly, Ned.' His last words were, at least in legend, 'Such is life!'

Bridge, set in a park-like setting and also known as the Old Goulburn Bridge or the Hughes Creek Bridge. Built in 1859 by Hugh Dalrymple, it is comprised of six arches supported on piers with string courses.

Australian Capital Territory

The Australian Capital Territory, always referred to as 'the ACT', sits in a mountainous area immediately south of the Goulburn Plains, a small portion of hilly country of what would otherwise be New South Wales. Canberra proper and some pastoral holdings are in the northern portion of the ACT. **Namadgi National Park** is the alpine remainder. Its mountains include the Tidbinbilla

Range, the eastern edge of the Brindabella Range and the Billy and Booth Ranges directly south. (A range of mountains in Australia can refer to quite small sections of mountainous areas.)

Canberra's nearly alpine setting can produce cool weather all year round. The region's arid summer makes for pleasant nights even during the warmest weather; temperatures can be fierce in January and February. Morning frosts and fogs occur from late April through October. Fogs occasionally interfere with air travel: the pre-dawn flight out nearly always leaves, but subsequent departures are sometimes delayed until mid-morning. Except in the mountains south of town, snow rarely falls. Rainy periods seem slightly more frequent in winter.

Geologically part of the lower Palaeozoic Tasman Geosyncline, the surface soils are hard setting and of limited fertility. Eucalypt forests thrive here, numerous acacia species occur as well. The former give lush, gentle green hues to the hills, especially in the low angles of evening or morning light. The native species contrast with the stark green of the hillside pine plantations immediately outside Canberra. Acacia trees blossom in late winter until nearly mid-summer. Delicate pea species and orchids are common in the forests.

The Murrumbidgee River flows across the territory from southeast to northwest immediately south of Canberra. The Molonglo River flows through Canberra and into the Murrumbidgee west of town. Lake Burley Griffith is the result of some sensible engineering along the Molonglo and was finally filled in 1964. The Gudgenby and Cotter Rivers empty into the Murrumbidgee as it flows along the face of the Tidbinbilla Range.

History

The Australian Capital Territory encompasses an area of 2368 sq km surrounded by New South Wales and includes vast expanses of national park and bush, as well as its federal port at Jervis Bay on the southern coast. For all practical purposes, the ACT is identified with the city of Canberra, and Canberra is unfortunately equated with the federal government in the minds of most Australians, although only about 50 per cent of the working population of the city are employed directly by the public service.

The Ngunnawal and Ngarigo people occupied the Canberra and Monaro region for some 20,000 years; evidence of their early presence exists in several rock sites throughout the territory, and in charcoal deposits uncov-

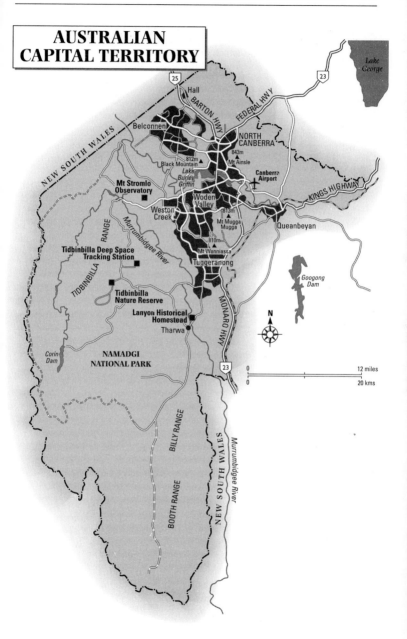

AUSTRALIAN CAPITAL TERRITORY

Lake George

NEW SOUTH WALES

Hall

BARTON HWY

FEDERAL HWY

Belconnen

NORTH CANBERRA

812m
Black Mountain

843m
Mt Ainsle

Canberra
Airport

Mt Stromlo
Observatory

Lake
Burley
Griffin

KINGS HIGHWAY

Woden
Valley

Weston
Creek

813m
Mt Mugga
Mugga

Queanbeyan

RANGE

Murrumbidgee River

TIDBINBILLA

810m
Mt Wanniassa

Tidbinbilla Deep Space
Tracking Station

Googong
Dam

Tidbinbilla
Nature Reserve

Tuggeranong

Lanyon Historical
Homestead

MONARO HWY

Tharwa

N

Corin
Dam

NAMADGI
NATIONAL PARK

0   12 miles
0   20 kms

BILLY RANGE

NEW SOUTH WALES

Murrumbidgee River

BOOTH RANGE

ered at nearby Lake George. Present-day Canberra was the site of annual summer gatherings of Aboriginal groups, who came to capture and eat the migrating bogong moths, which still arrive in their millions from Queensland on their way to the cool rocks of the Snowy Mountains. The Ngunnawal people today are establishing an Aboriginal 'keeping place' in the capital, and are actively involved in plans for the new Canberra Cultural Centre.

The area was first explored by white men in the 1820s, when Charles Throsby, James Vaughan and Joseph Wild came looking for the Murrumbidgee River, which they failed to find. A later expedition in 1823 with botanist Allan Cunningham found the river near Lanyon, and settlement began on what was called the Limestone Plains. Joshua John Moore took up the first land grant in 1824 on what is today the Acton Peninsula. He named the property 'Canberry', after hearing local Aborigines refer to the spot as 'Kamberra', thought to mean 'meeting place', or, alternatively, 'women's breasts'. In 1825, successful businessman Robert 'Merchant' Campbell was granted 4000 acres here in compensation for a wrecked ship; he established the estate of Duntroon as a near fiefdom of graziers and farmers, and donated moneys for a church and school. By the time Duntroon was purchased by the government for the establishment of the Royal Military College in 1911, the original land grant had grown to 30,451 acres (12,323 ha).

By the 1830s, several other homesteads were established throughout the region: George Palmer's **'Palmerville'** at Ginninderra Creek, which later became the location for Gungahlin Homestead; Terence Murray's **'Yarralumla'**; **Tuggeranong Homestead** in the valley now filled with suburbia; squatter James Wright's **Lanyon**, now preserved as an historic site; and further out on the edges of present-day Namadgi National Park, William Farrer and George de Salis' **Lambrigg** and **Cuppacumbalong**, now a craft centre. Miles Franklin, author of *My Brilliant Career* (1901), grew up on a homestead in the Brindabella Mountains, a time she fondly recalls in her *Childhood at Brindabella* (published 1963). The region remained prosperously rural until its selection to become the national capital in the early 1900s.

Canberra

As a completely planned federal capital, the city of Canberra has very few structures pre-dating 1910; it is a city of many important public monuments, as well as a sprawling conglomeration of many suburbs. Currently, with a population of 300,000, Canberra has far more to offer than its (many) critics would espouse. The natural setting is glorious, and cultural events abound.

Canberra comes honestly by its claims to being 'the Bush Capital'. The surrounding countryside is magnificent, with superb national parks within 30 minutes of Civic Centre, and it is one of the only cities in Australia where one can easily experience native species in the wild—kangaroos do appear in residents' back yards.

Birds to watch for include the **sulphur-crested cockatoo**, a large, white bird with raucous call; **king parrot**, a fairly large parrot, crimson below green; crimson and **eastern rosellas**, brilliant everywhere; willie wagtail, unmistakably dapper in black and white and with its chattering song; and superb fairy wren, very tiny with brilliant blue heads on the males and stick-straight tails. (The latter are particularly plentiful on the Australian National University campus.)

At twilight, possums and grey kangaroos appear in the trees and shrubs of many suburbs. A **platypus** is rumoured to live in Sullivans Creek, which flows through the centre of the Australian National University's campus. The local bird watching group, however, closely guards the secret of its whereabouts.

The flora includes numerous species of **wattle**, producing glorious yellow blossoms at the end of winter and in spring, pink-flowering fruit trees that line many streets, and eucalypts mixed in with European and North American species. It is said that Canberra contains more trees per capita than any other Australian city—some eight million. The most notorious of the imported trees are the **cottonwoods** that are abundant on the Australian National University campus; tradition among students has it that if you have not begun studying for exams by the time the cotton fluff begins to cover the ground like snow in October, it is too late to have a successful pass.

Conscious efforts in the early years by the government saw the establishment by Thomas Weston of an experimental nursery at Yarralumla which still provides residents with appropriate trees and shrubs, free of charge to owners of new homes.

■ Practical information

Tourist information. Canberra Tourist Information Centre, Jolimont Centre, 67 Northbourne Avenue; ☎ 6205 0044/008 02 6166; and Visitor's Information Centre, Northbourne Avenue, Dickson; ☎ 6249 7577.

Airport. The Canberra airport is located near Pialligo, on the road to Queanbeyan. A mini-bus service provides shuttle service from the airport for about $5.00 (☎ 6287 1676; mobile ☎ 018 62 57 219). No. 80 city bus service runs from the airport to the centre of town and on to Belconnen. Given the relatively short distance into the Civic Centre, a taxi ride costs only about $12.00 to any of the major hotels.

Rail service. Run by *Countrylink* (☎ 13 22 32) it provides reasonable connections from Sydney, with stops in nearby Bungendore and Queanbeyan; the trip is quite scenic, passing through the Southern Tablelands region and stopping in Goulburn, Bowral and Mittagong, but it currently takes about 5 hours to travel. Plans for a Very Fast Train link, which would substantially reduce travelling time, have been debated for years, and may soon be implemented. Rail travel between Canberra and Victoria requires a bus trip first to the **Yass train station** to link up with the Melbourne service. The Canberra train station is on Wentworth Avenue, from which one can get a **city bus** (routes 39, 50, 84) into town.

Coach service: most specifically *Greyhound Pioneer Australia* (☎ 13 20 30), runs out of the Jolimont Centre, the main travel centre on Northbourne Avenue (☎ 6257 4424). Service to Sydney runs hourly most of the time, and connections to Victoria and beyond are also frequent.

City bus service. Called ACTION, it is reliable and extensive, if at times infrequent.

FareGo ticket books offer discount prices for books of 10. A *Family Day Ticket*, for two adults and three concessionary passengers, allows for unlimited travel. ACTION also runs a free inner-city loop called the '*Downtowner*' and sightseeing services (routes 901 and 904) that stop at all the major attractions.

The main bus interchange is on East Row in the centre of Civic Centre, where tickets can be purchased; tickets are also available on the bus, and from news agencies, as is the ACTION Bus Book. Timetable enquiries can be answered on ☎ 13 17 10. NOTE: the entire bus service is currently being revised; bus numbers may have changed, along with timetables and fares. Call first! No city bus services run on Good Friday, Christmas Day, and New Year's Day.

Bicycles are available for hire at the kiosk by Lake Burley Griffin at the Commonwealth Bridge exit. An extensive network of bicycle trails throughout the ACT make cycling a magnificent way to explore the region; a map of cycle trails is available from the tourist centres.

Useful addresses

Consulates. All the embassies and high commissions are located in Canberra, most of them in the suburb of Yarralumla; see p 23 for further details.

Police. *Emergencies*, ☎ 000; *Police attendance*, ☎ 11 444; *City Station*, London Circuit, ☎ 6245 7208. *Australian Federal Police National Headquarters*, 68 Northbourne, ☎ 6256 7777.

Hospital. *Canberra Hospital*, Yamba Drive, Garran, ☎ 6244 2611; *Calvary Hospital*, Hayden Drive, Bruce, ☎ 6201 6111.

Rape Crisis Line. ☎ 6247 2525.

Hotels

$$$ Hyatt Hotel, Commonwealth Avenue, Yarralumla, ☎ 02 6270 1234. Canberra's most historic hotel, ambitious renovation enhances Prairie School-style architecture; beautiful spaces, good service, ideal location.

$$$ Parkroyal Canberra, 1 Binara, ☎ 02 6247 8999. Canberra's continental-style hotel, in the city near the Casino; 290 rooms, good restaurants.

$$$ Rydges Lakeside, London Circuit, ☎ 02 6247 6244/1 800 026 169; fax 02 6257 3071. As the name implies, near Lake Burley Griffin; a high-rise hotel, a convention/conference venue.

$$$ Rydges Capital Hill, corner Canberra Avenue and National Circuit, Forrest, ☎ 02 6295 3144/1 800 020 011. Popular with politicians, near Parliament House.

$$ Brassey Hotel, Belmore Gardens, Barton, ☎ 02 6273 3766/1800 659 191. Historic, idiosyncratic, within walking distance of Parliamentary Triangle.

$$ Forrest Motor Inn, 20 National Circuit, Forrest, ☎ 02 6295 3433/1 800 676 372; fax 02 6295 2119. Quiet inner 'garden suburb' location, good value, walking distance of Parliament House.

$$ Hotel Kurrajong, National Circuit, Barton, ☎ 02 6234 4444; fax 02 6234 4466; e-mail: hotel.kurrajong@aihs.edu.au. Operated by the Australian International Hotel School, public spaces restored to 1930s decor.

$$ James Court Apartment Hotel, 74 Northbourne Avenue, ☎ 02 6240 1234/1 800 655 187. Serviced apartments, attempt to bring luxurious inner-city living to Canberra.

$$ Olims Canberra Hotel, corner Ainslie & Limestone Avenues, ☎ 02 6248 5511/1 800 020 016; fax 02 6247 0864. Another historic hotel, across from War Memorial; pleasant grounds, comfortable rooms.

$$ University House, Balmain Crescent, Acton, ☎ 02 6249 5275; fax 02 6249 5252. Charming 1950s self-contained units, on university campus; good eating facilities, beer garden; discounts for Automobile Club and international University Club members.

$ Telopea Inn on the Park (formerly *Telopea Park Motel*), 16 New South Wales Crescent, Forrest, ☎ 02 6295 3722; fax 02 6239 6373. Lovely location, across from Telopea Park School, leafy street, good family situation.

$ YHA Youth Hostel, Dryandra, O'Connor, ☎ 02 6248 9155. Voted 2nd Place in World's Best Youth Hostels competition; beautiful location.

Restaurants

$$$ Atlantic, 20 Palmerston Lane, Manuka, ☎ 02 6232 7888. The latest hot spot, an elegantly appointed space with divinely prepared seafood; chef James Mussillon brings fresh fish to Canberra.

$$$ Chifley's at the Kurrajong, Hotel Kurrajong, National Circuit, Barton, ☎ 02 6234 4444; fax. 02 6234 4466. Part of the Hotel School's training programme, the restaurant serves innovative 'Pacific Rim' dishes; attentive service.

$$$ Fringe Benefits, 54 Marcus Clarke Street, ☎ 02 6247 4042. In the city, classy and slick, famed wine cellar; a new chef, trained with Neil Perry of Sydney's Rockpool, does not disappoint.

$$$ Ottoman, corner Franklin St and Flinders Way, Manuka, ☎ 02 6239 6754. Turkish/Continental cuisine, superb seafood, one of the best restaurants in the region; chef Serif Kaya is largely responsible for the improvement in Canberra's dining scene in the last decade.

$$$ Tang Dynasty, 27 Kennedy Street, Kingston, ☎ 02 6295 0102. Elegant, pricey Chinese fare.

$$ Boffins, University House, Balmain Crescent, Acton, ☎ 02 6249 5285; fax 02 6249 5256. On Australian National University campus, elegant dining.

$$ Chez Moustache, corner Iluka Street & Boolinba Crescent, Narrabundah, ☎ 02 6295 7283 (also fax). A real Belgian restaurant in an unlikely location, excellent value, uses kangaroo meat in traditional game dishes.

$$ Jewel of India, Manuka Court, Bougainville Street, Manuka, ☎ 02 6295 7037. Freshly made curries, elegant Indian.

$$ The Lobby, King George Terrace, Parkes, ☎ 02 6273 1563; fax 02 6273 2627. Located in Parliamentary Triangle, a hang-out for politicians, lovely views of Rose Garden.

$ Canberra Institute of Technology (CIT) Restaurants, Constitution Avenue, Reid, ☎ 02 6207 3196. The teaching branch of the CIT's School of Tourism and Hospitality, these facilities are wildly popular for excellent food (with Central European flair) and budget prices; bookings essential, both lunch and dinner.

$ Charcoal Restaurant, 61 London Circuit, city, ☎ 02 6248 8015. A real steakhouse, in central Canberra since 1962.

$ Dickson Asian Noodle House, 29 Woolley Street, Dickson, ☎ 02 6247 6380. Unpretentious, authentic Thai noodles and other Southeast Asian fresh dishes, located in what passes as Canberra's Chinatown; no credit cards.

$ Rasa Sayang, 49 Woolley Street, Dickson, ☎ 02 6249 7284; fax 02 6249

7265. Malaysian and other Asian, in Chinatown; great spicy dishes.

$ **Santa Lucia Trattoria**, 21 Kennedy Street, Kingston, ☎ 02 6295 1813. Canberra's oldest Italian restaurant, family-owned, home-made pasta and sausage; outdoor tables in fine weather.

$ **Timmy's Kitchen**, Furneaux Street, Manuka, ☎ 02 6295 6537. Chinese-Malaysian, reasonable prices, best for take-away, immensely popular.

History

Canberra's early history commences with an acrimonious debate about the location for a new national capital, which began with Australia's Federation in 1901. Sydney and Melbourne were felt to be too caught up in interstate rivalry. After examining several other possible locations, and basing their decision on the report of surveyor Charles Scrivener, the officials finally chose the site of Canberra in 1909. They maintained that the area's physical situation would enable the development of a 'beautiful city, occupying a commanding position, with extensive views...' At the time, Canberra consisted mainly of the estate of Duntroon, founded by the Campbell family in the 1830s, and several substantial sheep stations.

Upon its founding, officially in 1911, the capital was shackled with an American-born fanatic named King O'Malley, who had somehow gained the position of Minister of Home Affairs; he designated the territory as alcohol free. Fortunately Queanbeyan was merely eight miles (13km) away and any sensible civil servant could get the train to Sydney for the weekend. The city grew as a series of overstated monuments surrounded by ill-designed houses in unimaginative suburbs despite, or rather instead of, the elegant designs of American architect Walter Burley Griffin (see box), who had in 1911 won the international competition to design the new national capital.

Despite the supposed failure of Griffin's Canberra design, his basic ideas remain the foundation of the city's layout, in which the surrounding hills act as focal points for the main streets of a 'garden city', with a central lake surrounded by triangles of avenues. Thus at the centre is Capital Hill, the site of the permanent Parliament building; from here one looks across to the main ceremonial route, Anzac Parade, at the end of which is the War Memorial. Other ceremonial buildings are placed in a 'governmental triangle' below the Parliament and along the main lake basin. Griffin also envisioned the self-contained suburbs, each with its own shops and school, with no front fences to the houses and no buildings constructed above a certain point on the hills. Initially, suburbs were designated by class of public servant to occupy them, and the houses were built accordingly; while these distinctions have dwindled as the suburbs have expanded, the 'garden' suburbs of the inner north near the Parliament Building and around Civic Centre still retain traces of these elitist designations.

The capital was officially named Canberra (with accent on the first syllable) by Lady Denman, wife of the Governor-General, on 12 March 1913; the day is still celebrated as Canberra Day. As photographs (and cartoons) of the day indicate, the ceremony took place in a dry dusty field with little sign of habitation. Initially conditions here were primitive, with inadequate housing for the early government officials, and very few additional facilities; even the Vice Regent had to spend the night in a tent in

Walter Burley Griffin

Walter Burley Griffin (1876–1937) was born and raised in Chicago. He studied architecture at the University of Illinois and worked in the office of Frank Lloyd Wright, where he met his wife Marion Lucy Mahoney, an architect in her own right. Wright's stylistic principles of organic design, in keeping with the natural surroundings, are quite evident in Griffin's own designs. Legend has it that it was the skill of Marion's drawings which influenced the Australian judges to accept his proposal for the design of Canberra. He came to Australia in 1913 to oversee the construction of his plans. Although appointed as Federal Capital Director, he constantly faced bureaucratic opposition and political difficulties which made it impossible to carry out his original vision. By 1921 he was replaced by a committee, which he refused to join; he left Canberra with bitterness, although he remained in Australia to design the towns of Griffith and Leeton, as well as some works in Sydney and Melbourne. His greatest practical achievement was the design and construction of the Sydney suburb of Castlecrag; many of his original houses are still standing there. In 1935 he left Australia to carry out a commission in Lucknow, India, where he died in 1937 (according to Marion, under suspicious circumstances).

Acton. By the time the 'temporary' Parliament House was completed in 1927 (it served its purpose for 60 years), a few public buildings existed, and some public servants had been transferred from Melbourne to the city, where they were housed either in hotels or government-built boarding houses.

Development of the new capital was hampered first by the Depression, then Second World War; only in the 1960s did the city take off, with the final implementation of the outer suburb centres as had been envisioned from the beginning.

The greatest and most persistent complaint was—and continues to be—about the cold weather, a climactic feature unusual for Australians and one not adequately considered in the design of housing. Anyone still occupying one of the many extant 'ex-govies' (government houses) built here between the 1930s and 1960s can attest to the heating problems during Canberra's winter months, when temperatures often reach -5°C. As late as 1969, the novelist Christina Stead wrote of Canberra as 'beautiful, desolate, inspiriting Erewhon', but envisioned it as a city of the future.

It is only in recent years that Canberra has lost some of its negative reputation (in the words of one early parliamentarian, 'a waste of a good sheep paddock'). The number of official cultural institutions has increased and the population has reached a substantial size, already much larger than Burley Griffin's plan had ever envisioned. Historian Keith Hancock describes the city in an equivocal manner recognisable to many Australians:

Canberra, now that I saw it again, both irritated and charmed me, as it has always done. Charles Hawker used to say that it was a good sheep station spoilt. It is meticulously planned, yet it sprawls. Its elaborate geometry is lost in verdure. It lacks vertical lines. Its domestic architecture is bijou. Its red roofs are clamorously at war with the Australian blue and umber. But its gardens are glorious in leaf and flower. Its encircling hills are enchanting. Its early-morning light is so liquid and mellow that I fancied myself drinking it out of a bowl.

The addition of Lake Burley Griffin, which was filled in 1964, and the increasing popularity of native species for gardens since Hancock wrote would have heightened his appreciation. The amoebic extension of its suburbs would have offended him further. All the same, there are a number of pleasant buildings and some terrific day trips from what must be one of the rare national capitals without international air flights and with direct rail service to only one of its country's major cities (Sydney). Passengers to Melbourne must travel first to Yass, an inconvenience that was particularly exasperating in the early days, when horse-drawn coaches were the only way to make the bumpy ride.

A tour of Canberra

Because of the distances between attractions, Canberra's sites of interest are not easily accessible on foot if you set out from the Civic Centre—the middle of town, which you could easily miss if you were not informed that it is such. Directions for excursions will begin here, but in most cases, you must expect a substantial walk, or take a bus or car to your destination. Despite its relatively small size, Canberra's circular plan and the sprawl of the suburbs often makes it difficult to get oriented in terms of directions; even visiting Australians complain of getting lost. Use the flagpole of the New Parliament building on Capital Hill and Telstra Tower on Black Mountain as landmarks to establish directions.

Australian National University

From Civic, it is possible to walk to the campus of the Australian National University (ANU), at the foot of Black Mountain to the west of downtown, c 15-minute walk, about 1.5km. Although the university was not established until after the Second World War, a number of earlier structures on its campus and exhibits mounted by its departments make for an entertaining walking tour.

Occupying the site Walter Burley Griffin planned for a university in his original design of the national capital, ANU was established as Canberra University College of the University of Melbourne in 1929. Parliament established the university as presently constituted in 1946. Initially, it occupied rooms in the old Canberra Hospital and Acton area residences. The university is comprised today of both research schools and a teaching faculty. Undergraduates were first admitted as late as 1960.

On an approach to the campus from Civic along GORDON STREET is **Ian Potter House**, formerly Beauchamp House. This two-storey I-shaped building with balconies and wisteria arbours on either side was built in 1927. A neo-Colonial design by Anketel and Kingsley Henderson, it originally housed female government workers who had been transferred to the new seat of government from Melbourne (see also Gorman House). It was converted to office space in 1972 and refurbished to its current use in 1987 by the Australian Academy of Science. While the central reception and banquet areas and the exterior remain pleasant, most of the refurbishment is of a utilitarian nature.

The **Academy of Science** (1958) also uses the interesting bowl-shaped building with scalloped arches and moat located across the way to the west. The design is by Grounds Romberg, and architect Robin Boyd, author of the

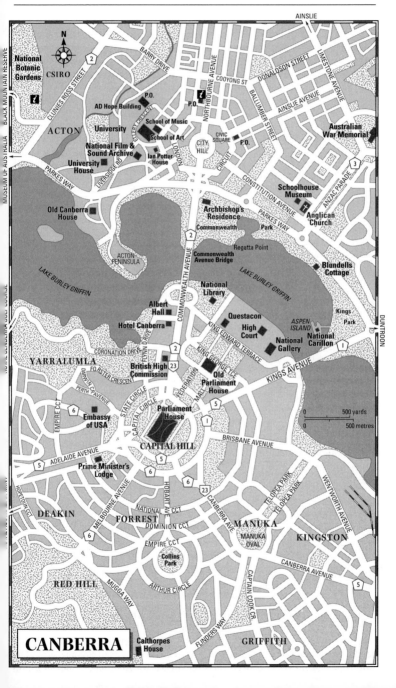

AINSLIE

National Botanic Gardens

CSIRO

BLACK MOUNTAIN RESERVE

MUSEUM OF AUSTRALIA

N

BARRY DRIVE

CLUNIES ROSS STREET

COOYONG ST

NORTHBOURNE AVENUE

BALLUMBIR STREET

DONALDSON STREET

LIMESTONE AVENUE

AINSLIE AVENUE

P.O.

AD Hope Building

University

ACTON

National Film & Sound Archive

University House

School of Music

School of Art

Ian Potter House

EXETER CRESCENT

LONDON CIRCUIT

P.O.

CIVIC SQUARE

CITY HILL

CIRCUIT

P.O.

ANZAC PARADE

Australian War Memorial

3

CONSTITUTION AVENUE

Schoolhouse Museum

Anglican Church

Old Canberra House

PARKES WAY

LIVERSIDGE RD

ACTON PENINSULA

Archbishop's Residence

Commonwealth

2

COMMONWEALTH AVENUE

Commonwealth Avenue Bridge

Regatta Point

PARKES WAY

Park

LAKE BURLEY GRIFFIN

Blundells Cottage

LAKE BURLEY GRIFFIN

National Library

Albert Hall

Hotel Canberra

FLYNN DRIVE

Questacon

KING EDWARD TERRACE

High Court

ASPEN ISLAND

National Gallery

Kings Park

National Carillon

DUNTROON

1

YARRALUMLA

CORONATION DRIVE

FORSTER CRESCENT

DARWIN AVENUE

PERTH AVENUE

British High Commission

2

23

FEDERATION MALL

KING GEORGE TCE

Old Parliament House

KINGS AVENUE

5

EMPIRE CCT

STATE CIRCLE

CAPITAL CIRCLE

Embassy of USA

6

Parliament House

CAPITAL HILL

1

5

BRISBANE AVENUE

500 yards

0

500 metres

0

ADELAIDE AVENUE

5

Prime Minister's Lodge

6

6

HOBART AV CCT

CANBERRA AVE

23

TELOPEA PARK

TELOPEA PARK

WENTWORTH AVENUE

HOPETOUN CCT

DEAKIN

MELBOURNE AVENUE

FORREST

NATIONAL CCT

DOMINION CCT

MANUKA

MANUKA OVAL

KINGSTON

6

EMPIRE CCT

Collins Park

CANBERRA AVENUE

RED HILL

MUGGA WAY

ARTHUR CIRCLE

CAPTAIN COOK CR

5

CANBERRA

Calthorpes House

FLINDERS WAY

GRIFFITH

influential book, *The Australian Ugliness* (1960), which bemoans Australian suburban architecture.

Across the street from the Academy of Science on McCoy Circuit is the **National Film and Sound Archive** (☎ 02 6209 3111, open daily 09.00–18.00), the main building of which was formerly the Anatomy Building. Designed by W. Hayward Morris and built in 1929–30, the ornament includes Art-Deco-incised concrete and large wooden doors at the entrance. The faunal motifs include a stained glass platypus in the foyer ceiling and koala friezes on the plaques in the courtyard. The marble floor continues the geometric motif of the doors. Recent expansion has been complementary to the original structure.

The Film and Sound Archive's exhibit documents Australia's entertainment industry. Several small viewing rooms present silent and early spoken films and radio dramas, and regular exhibitions focus on aspects of Australia's prolific film, radio and recording history. The archive is a great place to bring the children. The tiny gift shop offers a number of tapes and videos on similar themes.

On LIVERSIDGE STREET to the north of the archive is **University House**, designed by Brian Lewis in 1952. The house serves as a centre for university life, providing conference spaces, accommodation for visiting scholars, and eating facilities. Architecturally it is a delightful example of 1950s integrated design, with lovely grounds and built-in furniture in the apartments. The courtyard includes a calming fish pond from which kookaburras often catch fish, and a large beer garden offers a pleasant environment for lunch or drinks. It recently received an award for enduring architectural design in the ACT.

Leaving University House from the main entrance, walk north down Liversidge Street to ELLERY CRESCENT and cross to enter the **Canberra School of Art** (☎ 02 6249 5811). Part of the ANU since 1992 as the Canberra Institute of the Arts, the school is housed in Canberra's first secondary school (1938–68). Architect Daryl Jackson's extension to the original school building succeeds admirably. The Art School's gallery features contemporary and student artist exhibits. The school is also involved in the operation of the Drill Hall Gallery on the northern edge of the campus (follow Childers Street from the front of the school, then right on Hutton Street), which presents an extensive number of art exhibitions throughout the year (☎ 02 6249 5810).

The other school of the Canberra Institute of the Arts is the **School of Music**, housed down the hill from the School of Art (its progressive Jazz Department lives in the suburb of Manuka, where recitals and performances are also held). The school carries out an active performance schedule, with major concerts and operas staged as well as first-rate recitals by students in the school's auditorium, Llewellyn Hall. Almost all of these are open to the public, many of them free (☎ 02 6249 5700).

From the Music School, walk across the car park and down to Ellery Crescent again, at the end of which is the **A.D. Hope Building**, named in honour of Australian poet Alec Derwent Hope (b. 1907), who was for many years ANU's Professor of English.

In this nondescript building the **Classics and Archaeology and Anthropology Departments** have mounted exhibits. The displays include a large scale model of 4C AD Rome, a replica of a large Aztec Calendar Sun Stone, and an ambitious presentation of artefacts and coins from Greco-Roman sites. The anthropological exhibit concentrates on Australian Aboriginal foods, hunting and gathering implements, and representative decorative artefacts. The displays are all in the public spaces of the building, open every weekday.

Acton era buildings

On the south end of campus, walking the other direction on LIVERSIDGE STREET from University House, a number of buildings from the earliest period of Canberra's federal history are still in use. These include **Old Canberra House**, which is now a cafe and pub with an open billiard table. Although substantially remodelled, the interior rooms and woodwork remain attractive in what was originally the residence of David Miller, the city's first planning authority supervisor. Directly across the street are the endangered buildings that were originally the single men's quarters for the officers of departments supervising the planning of Canberra. Built in 1913, these single-storey, weatherboard residences have housed students and staff child care services. For some reason they are the bane of the university's administration and have been imperilled for a considerable time. Further down this road is **Acton Peninsula** on the lake. Once the site of the Royal Canberra Hospital, an unfortunate demolition in 1997 was carried out to make room for other buildings on this valuable piece of real estate. The site is proposed to become the home of Australia's National Museum, now housed at Yarramundi near Scrivener Dam on the lake.

The ANU campus also houses several excellent library collections. **Menzies Library** has internationally recognised collections of Asian literature and culture, as well as holdings on Aboriginal culture. **Chifley Library** is the main undergraduate library, while **Hancock Library** houses science and technology. All library collections are accessible through state-of-the-art computer catalogues.

Australian Botanic Gardens

Directly north of the Australian National University campus, on Clunies Ross Street at the base of Black Mountain, is the entrance to the **Australian National Botanic Gardens** (☎ 02 6250 9540, daily 09.00–17.00, later in summer). The tourist bus route starting at Civic, reaches the gardens among its numerous stops, as well as travelling to Black Mountain and Telstra Tower.

As early as 1935, plans were underway for the establishment of a national botanic gardens in Canberra. Planting for the gardens began in the 1950s, under the direction of botany professor Lindsay Pryor to landscaping designs by Otto Ruzicka, but the grounds were not officially opened until 1970. From the beginning, the gardens were at the forefront of horticultural experimentation, at a time when little was known about the propagation of native species. They now present a glorious survey of Australia's indigenous species and representative plant life, from authentically constructed rainforests of the northern region, scrupulously maintained with climate and humidity control, to a display of plants from the more hardy climactic conditions of Tasmania.

Ambitious public programmes serve to enlighten the public concerning conservation, native habitats, the dangers of introduced species of flora and fauna, and the delights of Australian wildlife and bushlife. Events include activities surrounding Wattle Day on 1 September, and other reminders of Australia's unique natural resources. Regular guided tours are available, as well as bird-watching walks.

The visitor's centre includes an excellent bookshop, as well as a small exhibition space, a theatre, and a plant library for serious researchers. The grounds also contain an education centre, where workshops and classes are conducted, and a popular cafe on a picnic green, where cheeky kookaburras, wattle birds, and magpies come to share in your lunch. Lizards and the larger dragons can be seen sunning themselves on the rocks of the nearby pond.

CSIRO

Clunies Ross Street is also the location of the main offices of the Commonwealth Scientific and Industrial Research Organisation, or CSIRO. Established in 1926, the organisation is the country's premier research facility in all branches of science, and has made internationally significant discoveries, especially in plant technology, entomology, forestry and mineralogy. The process of gene-shearing, first formulated in the laboratories of Plant Industry, was first carried out on this site in the early 1990s. In 1999, CSIRO will open a $5-million Discovery Centre here, with hands-on displays and exhibitions from all divisions of the organisation's interests. ☎ 1 300 363 400 (or fax 03 9545 2175) for updated information.

Black Mountain

First climbed and surveyed in 1832 by explorers Charles Throsby and James Vaughan, Black Mountain was probably so named because of the thick eucalyptus vegetation that covered the hill; it is only 812m high. Significantly, the composition of the mountain is Silurian sedimentary rock, while most others in the region are igneous; sandstone impregnated with quartz covers the rock itself. The entire mountain is now a nature reserve, and has several well-marked walking trails, which allow the visitor to discover its intriguing vegetation, including several orchid species and many varieties of acacia and eucalypt. Guides to these walks are available from the Visitor's Centre at Telstra Tower. The tower at the top of Black Mountain has been a Canberra landmark since it opened in 1979, and it can be seen throughout the region. The structure itself is a truly hideous radio tower, but the views from the observation deck are stunning. The tower also includes the predictable revolving restaurant, coffee lounge, and viewing galleries. It is open daily 09.00–20.00 ☎ 02 6248 1911.

Parliamentary Triangle

From Civic, you can take one of several buses across the lake at Commonwealth Bridge to the site of the most important public buildings, what is now known as the Parliamentary Triangle. A walk across the **Commonwealth Bridge** is also possible, and will take about 20 minutes, affording some pretty views of the lake towards the Brindabella mountain range. On the left, after City Hill and onto the bridge, you will see the **Archbishop's Residence**, built in 1938 (a private residence). Further on, you may enter **Commonwealth Park** at Regatta Point, where the Regatta Point Lookout and Exhibition Centre provide a display on Canberra's history. This is also the site of **Floriade**, the floral festival in September and celebrations during Canberra Day in March. On the lake here is the Captain Cook Memorial Globe and Jet Fountain, which rises up to 135 metres at set times each day, and has given rise to comparisons of Canberra with Geneva, Switzerland, and its similar water fountain.

After crossing the bridge, on the left to the west are two important early buildings, first the Albert Hall and then Hotel Canberra. **Albert Hall** was completed in 1928 and was the site of much of the capital's early social life; a young Joan Sutherland sang here in 1950, and in 1954, the Royal Commission into the infamous Petrov affair, concerning the defection of a supposed Russian spy, was housed on the site.

Hotel Canberra (now the Hyatt) is an important monument in the capital's political history. J.S. Murdoch, chief architect for the Department of Works and Railways, was directed to design 'on garden pavilion lines'. The resulting hotel, built in 1922–25, was intended to appear home-like, and provide privacy for those civil servants and particularly elected politicians (most particularly Liberal, i.e., conservative, politicians) staying for longer periods. It is one of the rare examples in Australia of Beaux-Arts planning influenced by American Prairie-style architecture. The gardens and lawns, like many public places in the city, are famed for roses. These were encouraged by A.E. Bruce, successor of Thomas Weston as ACT gardener, who planted 155 varieties along Commonwealth and Kings Avenues.

The hotel was closed in the 1970s and, to the horror of right-thinking citizens, was in danger of being demolished. Fortunately, the Hyatt Hotel renovated and enlarged the building and grounds, reopening the hotel in 1988. The visitor should notice the paintings in the lobby which are conscious imitations in the style of identifiable Australian artists, such as Rupert Bunny and George Lambert.

As the Commonwealth Bridge ends, turn left (east); the road is officially labelled as KING EDWARD TERRACE, although it is rarely called that. It is here along the lakefront that most of the 'national' buildings are located. First on the left is the **National Library of Australia** (☎ 02 6262 1699, open Mon–Thurs 09.00–23.00, Fri and Sat 09.00–17.00, Sun 13.30–17.00).

Built in 1968, the building's design is in a diluted neo-classical modernist style, similar to the LBJ Library in Texas, or any other number of public buildings erected in the 1960s and 70s. The entrance lobby contains stained-glass windows by the artist Leonard French; these are now visible in the lobby's restaurant. The library, aside from being the national book repository, also contains extensive pictorial, audio-visual, manuscript and oral history collections. Many of these resources are now available on state-of-the-art computer programmes. The Reading Room has generous opening hours, during which time the general public has access to the collections. The library also presents impressive exhibitions based on its collections, and (at the time of writing) free movies on Thursday nights. The library's bookshop provides a particularly good selection of books and cards on Australian themes.

Next in line along this promenade is **Questacon**, the National Science and Technology Centre (☎ 02 6270 2800, daily 10.00–17.00). The building was partially a gift of the Japanese government to honour Australia's bicentennial in 1988. The building houses some 150 'hands-on' exhibits in six different galleries designed around a 27m-high drum around which a spiral walkway leads to all levels. Children are especially impressed with the simulation of an earthquake and the lightning chamber.

Walk south across the Parliamentary Lawns by the Treasury Building to reach KING GEORGE TERRACE and the **Old Parliament House** (☎ 02 6270 8222, daily 09.00–16.00). The lawns themselves have been the site of several demonstrations, and still house an Aboriginal Embassy, reopened in commemoration of the first embassy of protest established here in 1972; it still serves as the rallying point for Aboriginal demonstrations concerning land rights and other causes, and is usually occupied by members of Aboriginal groups.

> The Old Parliament House was opened by the Duke of York in 1927 and designed by J.S. Murdoch at a cost of £174,000. The opening ceremony included singing by the famous Australian soprano Dame Nellie Melba, as well as an ill-planned reception that saw thousands of meat pies wasted and buried in the back paddock. Many more visitors had been expected, but failed to show because the day was not a public holiday and transportation to Canberra was still primitive. This supposed 'temporary' building was finally vacated in 1988 with the opening of the New Parliament House; it is still fondly remembered as the site of much of Australia's political history. Stories circulate that the place is haunted by as many as three ghosts, perhaps disgruntled politicians. For years in the 1950s, Mr Bainbridge, the parliamentary barber, was also the parliamentary bookie and privy to years of political secrets. It was on the steps of this building on 11 November 1975, that the proclamation dissolving Gough Whitlam's government was read, and it was here that subsequent protesters jeered the Governor-General John Kerr for his actions.

Fortunately, recent renovation and the installation of several exhibitions and museum spaces assure its continued use and care. Its architecture is a pleasant example of a modified Australian Federation design, with loggias and simple open spaces, although several wings and extensions were 'added on' over the years. The visitor can take advantage of well-informed tours by volunteer guides, or simply look around independently, which allow views of the House of Representatives and the Senate.

The Old Parliament House is now the home of the **National Portrait Gallery**, which presents regular exhibitions based on official collections. Other exhibitions, staged by the National Library, the National Museum, and other institutions, present a variety of topics dealing with Australian life. The bookstore presents an excellent range of books and other sources of information on Australian politics and history. The old parliamentary dining room is now a public restaurant.

Hotel Kurrajong

Exiting Old Parliament House, turn right on King George Terrace, proceed right into Walpole Crescent to National Circuit; turn left to find Hotel Kurrajong one block south after Kings Avenue.

> This hotel was also designed by J.S. Murdoch in 1925 and built by Colonel Walker. It lacks the aesthetic extent of Prairie School style of the Canberra Hotel and features central courts enclosed by two-storey pavilions and central communal blocks which gives it a less domestic and more institutional feeling. This was the hotel where most members of Parliament stayed when they were in town without their families. Labor Party MPs and workers preferred this hotel because they could walk to Parliament from it. Those MPs who early

resided in Canberra with their families bought homes in the nearby 'garden' suburbs Red Hill or Telopea Park. It was here that Ben Chifley, former Labor Prime Minister and head of the Opposition, died on 13 June 1951. The hotel has recently had a major facelift, which restored the lobby to its original Art Deco style; it is now an International School of Hotel Management.

New Parliament House

From National Circuit, walk back to Federation Mall and up the hill to the New Parliament House (☎ 6277 7111, daily 09.00–17.00, extended when Parliament in session). This imposing edifice is one of the most ambitiously symbolic buildings in the world: every stone, piece of wood, and colour is representative of some aspect of Australia and its democratic government, with conscious metaphorical considerations of power and geography.

Designed by the architects Mitchell, Giurgola and Thorp, the building was finally completed at a cost of $1.1 billion. Amazingly, the building opened on time, in the Bicentennial year, on 9 May 1988. The architects' aim was to emphasise the hill ('for centuries ... occupied with structures as signs of possession and power') as well as the building's profile and the land axis, which mean to affirm Burley Griffin's original scheme. The building is actually placed into the hill, and citizens can—again, with great symbolic intention, intimations of the relationship of government to the people—walk down from the impressively imposing flagpole (at 81m, the highest flagpole in the country) onto the grass slopes surrounding it. The view of the city from this point is impressive, and the circular design of the capital's road system and monumental buildings is most obvious. The profile of the flagpole, which can be seen from anywhere in Canberra, has become a near-iconic landmark.

The **main entrance** includes a ceremonial pool with a huge rock mural designed by Aboriginal artist Michael Nelson Tjakamarra and completed out of granite; the architects maintain some reference to Aboriginal Australia 'outside', while European/Western references dominate 'inside'. Entrance into the grandiose foyer emphasises the building's post-modernist elements, with the elaborate blend of coloured marble columns; art-historical references to monuments of power, such as the Pantheon and Persepolis; and inlaid panels out of Australian woods.

The **Great Hall**, the main ceremonial space, includes an enormous tapestry designed by prominent Australian artist Arthur Boyd. The side galleries, off the foyer and up the staircases, include changing displays of art from the substantial parliamentary art collections. From this level, one can then proceed to view chambers of both the House of Representatives and the Senate; of interest here is to see how the traditional colours of green for Representatives and red for Senate have been turned into post-modernist pastels. Visitors may attend sessions when Parliament is sitting. The Parliament House, given its ambitious sense of ceremony and symbolism, has become the most popular destination for tourists in the capital; consequently, tours are thorough and frequent, with well-informed guides (tours in other languages are readily available).

High Court of Australia

On the other side of the Parliamentary Lawns, back on KING EDWARD CRESCENT, is the High Court of Australia. Designed by the architectural firm of Edwards, Madigan, Torzillo and Briggs (the design leader was Chris Kringas), the building was not completed until 1980. Along with the impressive waterworks at the front of the building, the structure's central foyer has been described as 'one of the most dramatic spaces in Australia'.

Lindy Chamberlain

The case of Lindy Chamberlain preoccupied Australians for much of the 1980s. In August 1980 Azaria Chamberlain, the nine-week-old daughter of Seventh-Day Adventists Lindy and Michael Chamberlain, disappeared from a tent near Uluru (Ayers Rock) where the family was camping. Lindy was convinced a dingo had taken her baby; the body was never found. The subsequent trial first ruled in the family's favour, then decided that Lindy was guilty of murder. This verdict, based largely on innuendo, the belief that dingoes would not take babies, and the assertion that the Chamberlains were acting bizarrely, saw Lindy sentenced to life imprisonment in 1982. Appeals to the High Court were unsuccessful in overturning the verdict. In February 1986, a baby's jacket, believed to be Azaria's, was found near Uluru, leading to Lindy's release and a judicial inquiry, which found that the dingo story was probably true. In 1988 both Chamberlains were fully exonerated. The trial formed the basis for the 1988 film *Evil Angels* (*A Cry in the Dark*), directed by Fred Schepisi and starring Meryl Streep.

On the north wall of the Great Hall, known as Constitution Wall, is a mural by the Australian artist Jan Senbergs that depicts the functions and ideals of the High Court. On the south wall, another Senbergs mural presents a symbolic depiction of the Australian states. The Great Hall often houses art exhibitions and other displays. Visitors may also view the three courtrooms, where questions concerning the constitutionality of an issue, most of them having come as appeals from state and federal jurisdictions, are considered. The most famous appeals presented here were, in 1982, the constitutionality of the federal government's intervention to block the building of Tasmania's Franklin River dam; and in 1983–84, the notorious Chamberlain case, in which appeals were made to drop the murder charge against Lindy Chamberlain (see box). Most recently, the court has ruled in favour of Aboriginal Native Title claims, in the famous Mabo case and the Wik decision (see Aboriginal political history, p 55). Both of these rulings were major breakthroughs in the battle for Aboriginal land rights.

National Gallery of Australia

Next to the High Court is the **National Gallery of Australia** (☎ 02 6240 6411, daily 10.00–17.00), another product of Edwards, Madigan, Torzillo, and Briggs (credited to architect Colin Madigan). Completed in 1982 and opened by Queen Elizabeth II, the severe 'art brut' concrete structure in many ways overwhelms the art inside; a recent renovation of interior spaces has somewhat alleviated this problem (and was greeted with great anger by the architect himself), although the floor plan still makes it difficult to know which galleries are where. A recent addition at the rear of the first floor (Level 4), along with a wonderfully symbolic garden space by artist Fiona Foley, creates more pleasing spaces.

The collection, intended to be considered as the national collection, is a fascinating manifestation of the intrigues of museum and collecting politics faced by galleries attempting to acquire a representative art collection from scratch in the 1970s and 1980s. The most famous example of this interweaving of the political and artistic was the purchase in 1973 of the American painter Jackson Pollock's *Blue Poles* (1952) for the then unprecedented sum of $1.2 million. The ensuing controversy preoccupied all Australians for months, since the work was purchased with government funds approved by Gough Whitlam. That such an amount should be paid for a non-Australian painting done by 'drunkards', as the newspaper headlines reported, led to parliamentary battles and endless letters to the editor, both pro and con. The painting's arrival and subsequent exhibition in every Australian city saw record crowds come to see the 'million-dollar painting'. In many ways, the *Blue Poles* incident marks Australia's cultural coming of age. Now, of course, the 'investment' is deemed good 'value for money', as *Blue Poles*' latest evaluation is $30 million.

Despite the political wrangling, the resultant collections are impressive, and the gallery is worth the trip to Canberra in itself. Currently, the general arrangement of the gallery is as follows, although curators here are wont to rearrange frequently, especially during the run of one of the many 'blockbuster' exhibitions for which the gallery has become famous.

Entrance ~ Level 4

The entrance level is actually Level 4; the **first gallery** is named after Melbourne art patrons and donors the Smorgons. Currently it is devoted to the display of one of the gallery's most significant collections, **Aboriginal art**. The central focus of this display had been the set of Memorial Poles, created by several Aboriginal artists and communities as a Bicentennial 'gift' to the nation. (This work has now been moved to the gallery behind the bookstore on the same floor.) Traditionally such poles were created as memorials to the dead, in which an individual's bones would eventually be placed. Here are 200 poles from different regions, one for each year of white settlement and black displacement. As the organiser of the project explained, the aim was to 'present Aboriginal culture without celebrating—to make a true statement' about the effects of white-black conflict. Significantly, the poles were originally placed in the gallery's lower level; it is only since the recent growing popularity of Aboriginal art that it has been given pride of place in the first gallery to greet the public.

The walls in the Smorgon Gallery display examples of the enormous variety of Aboriginal art, both traditional and contemporary. Note especially the paintings of Rover Thomas and Emily Kame Kngwarreye, and Lin Onus' witty political sculpture, *Dingoes* (1989).

Gallery 2 presents, in fairly chronological fashion, **modern Western painting**, highlighting the gallery's first focus for major acquisitions. This gallery has now been partitioned into three sections, which focuses the works more specifically. Most notable are an early Courbet study for *Young ladies on the banks of the Seine* (1857); Cézanne's *An afternoon in Naples* (1877); and two exemplary works by Claude Monet, one of his *Haystacks* series of 1890, and *Waterlilies*, painted at Giverny c 1910. Also of note is a delightful painting by the Russian Natalia Goncharova, *Peasants dancing* (1910–11).

Around the corner from the Monets is the **'wall of Surrealism'**, focusing on Magical Realist and Surrealist works, most notably Magritte's *The Lovers* (1928), and Miro's *Landscape* (1927). Also displayed are reproductions of Duchamp's *Bicycle Wheel* (1913) and, illuminated on the wall, his *Hat rack* (1917). Opposite this wall is a case filled with objects of Dada and Surrealism, including Man Ray's *The enigma of Isidore Ducasse* (1920).

The partitioned space across from this section focuses on the gallery's important works of **Abstract Expressionism**, with one wall given over to Pollock's *Blue Poles* (1952). Surrounding works complement and illuminate this aesthetic direction: Pollock's earlier *Totem lesson 2* (1945), and the work of his wife Lee Krasner, *Cool white* (1959). Also displayed are Willem de Kooning's *Woman V* (1952–53) and Mark Rothko's *Brown, black on maroon* (1957).

Gallery 3 presents **contemporary art**, always in rotation. Most likely to be on view is the massive work by the German Anselm Kiefer, *Twilight of the West* (1989), Chuck Close's *Bob* (1970), and Francis Bacon's *Triptych* (1970).

Tucked up next to the stairs is a small gallery which at the moment displays Pre-Columbian and/or African art.

Before proceeding upstairs to Australian art, one must note that Level 4 also houses, at the other end of the building, **Nomura Court**, evidence of the gallery's recent efforts to establish an important collection of Asian art. Permanent acquisitions are especially strong in Southeast Asian textiles and sculpture.

Level 6

Proceed up the stairs from Gallery 3 to Level 6, or from the Nomura Court side, take the lift and enter the **Australian art collection** from the other end, which will lead through the galleries backwards chronologically. Australian art is the real strength of the gallery's collection. Throughout the intention has been to integrate all the arts of a period, including crafts and photography, to give a sense of historical context; appropriately, the first galleries devoted to the Colonial period are painted 'Colonial' green. Stellar works here include Augustus Earle's portraits of John Piper and Mrs Piper, c 1826; John Glover's romanticised views of Tasmania from the 1830s; and the artistically crude but historically important work by Benjamin Duterrau, *Mr Robinson's first interview with Timmy* (1840), championing the efforts of Robinson with the Tasmanian Aborigines. The section also includes superb examples of early Colonial furniture and decorative arts.

The middle gallery concentrates on landscape painting, most notably the various attempts by Europeans to depict Australian vegetation; Eugen von Guerard's *View from Mt Kosciuszko* (1864), Louis Buvelot's *View near Heidelberg* (1866), and Nicholas Chevalier's *Mt Arapiles and the Mitre Rock* (1863), demonstrate distinct applications of European modes.

The next gallery represents the solidification of the Australian 'national' school with the works of the **Heidelberg painters**, so named for the Melbourne suburb where the artists painted outdoors. Exemplary works of this landscape direction include Roberts' *In a corner of the Macintyre* (1895), supposedly depicting a bushranger shootout, but more about Australian light and rock; and Arthur Streeton's iconic *The selector's hut: Whelan on the log* (1890).

You can tell that you have entered the modern era when the gallery walls turn to white; again, the gallery's holdings in **20C Australian art** are substantial, with notable examples by George Lambert (*Station at Michelago*, 1923), Rupert Bunny (*Pastoral*, 1892), Margaret Preston (*Aboriginal design*, 1941 and *Portrait of a Flapper*, 1917) and Grace Cossington Smith (*Four panels for a screen*, 1929). The most impressive works are those by the artists of the 1930s and 1940s, especially John Perceval's Expressionistic pieces, Albert Tucker's Surrealist series *Victory girls* (1943), Russell Drysdale's *The rabbiter and his family* (1938) and Arthur Boyd's many portraits and mythological scenes. An entire wall is devoted to Sidney Nolan's famous series of *Ned Kelly* paintings, 1946–47. Nolan's works present a narrative well-known to all Australians, while visitors will find the accompanying quotations enlightening about this folk hero, including the explanation of the square black head, which is not, as a *New York Times* reviewer assumed, meant to represent a television! For more information on Ned Kelly, see the entry under Glen Rowan, Victoria, on the Hume Highway (p 237).

Other galleries continue the progression into Australian contemporary art, including works by John Brack, Ian Fairweather, Fred Williams and John Olsen. This floor also has galleries devoted to displays of the gallery's substantial holdings in graphic arts, photography, decorative arts, and travelling exhibitions.

One of the most enjoyable aspects of the gallery is the **Sculpture Garden**, located between the gallery and the lake and situated amidst native gardens. Exit into the garden from the entrance level. At varying intervals one finds, among others, Rodin's *Burghers of Calais* (1884; cast 1974), Bourdelle's *Penelope* (1912), and Bert Flugelman's wonderfully reflective *Cones* (1982), popular with children. Further on towards the **Mirrabook restaurant** is the fascinating *Fog sculpture* by Fujiko Nakaya (1983), which at periodic intervals creates a steamy mist across the ponds.

The north side of Lake Burley Griffin

From the National Gallery, drivers may cross the KINGS AVENUE BRIDGE to explore venues along the lake and up Anzac Parade to the Australian War Memorial. If coming from Civic, reverse the process along Parkes Way from Commonwealth Park. The city sightseeing bus travels here. After crossing the bridge, you will see directly ahead the **Australian-American War Memorial**, unveiled by Queen Elizabeth in 1954. Although the aluminium shaft is supposed to be topped by a majestic eagle, the odd angle of its wings has led to its nickname of 'Bugs Bunny'.

Surrounding this monument are the offices of the defence forces, regularly voted the ugliest public buildings in Australia (they are currently undergoing major renovation and demolition). Turn left at Morshead Drive, and proceed c 1km to the **Royal Military College** of Duntroon, on the site of the home of the area's first substantial settler, Robert 'Merchant' Campbell. On the grounds is the original **Duntroon House**, built by Campbell in 1833 and extended by his son George in 1862. Today it houses the Officer's Mess and Commandant's Office; guided tours are available weekdays from April to October.

Blundells Cottage and Carillon

Return to Morshead Drive and travel west to Russell Drive, c 1km; turn left and continue past the Defence Forces complex, where the road becomes CONSTITUTION AVENUE; a small road to the right leads to **Kings Park** on the lake's foreshore at **Blundells Cottage** (☎ 02 6273 2667, daily 09.30–16.00). Built in 1858 for one of Duntroon Estate's foremen, this stone cottage is the last example of the many houses built by Campbell for his employees. It was occupied for 50 years, from 1888 to 1933, by George Blundell, along with his wife and eight children. In 1964 it was restored and is now maintained as a museum by the Canberra and District Historical Society.

From here, you can walk along the lakefront southeast to Aspen Island, site of the Carillon. Before walking to the island is the HMAS *Canberra* memorial, in honour of the Australian cruiser sunk by the Japanese during the battle of Savo Island on 9 August 1942.

The **Carillon**, which stands on an artificially-built island at the edge of the lake, was a gift of the British government on Canberra's 50th anniversary in 1970. The bronze bells were cast in Leicestershire and range in size from 6 tonnes to 7kg. The interior of the Carillon is lined with English oak. Regular recitals occur at 14.45 on Sundays, and 12.45 on Wednesdays, and other concerts are performed throughout the summer months. The building itself is open for inspection on weekends.

Anzac Parade and Australian War Memorial

Return to Constitution Avenue and proceed west one block to **ANZAC PARADE**. This long ceremonial avenue, culminating in the War Memorial and Mount Ainslie behind, is the central axis of Walter Burley Griffin's original plan; from the Memorial itself, you look directly down the Parade to see across the lake the two parliament houses in perfect alignment. Griffin envisioned this route as a recreational and entertainment area, but would not have objected to its current form as the rather sombre location of the national monuments to Australia's fighting forces. Anzac Parade also serves as the route for the solemn commemorative services and parades held on Anzac Day in April, and on other patriotic occasions.

Church of St John the Baptist and Schoolhouse Museum

Cross Anzac Parade on Constitution Avenue and turn in to the car park of St John's Schoolhouse Museum. The Anglican church of **St John's** was established here by Robert Campbell of Duntroon on 12 March 1845 as St John Canberry— on the same date in 1913, Lady Denman officially named Canberra. The original church walls were made of local bluestone, quarried in nearby Campbell. The sandstone chancel was added in 1872; the tower and spire, designed by Edmund Blacket, was added in 1878. The slightly asymmetrical appearance of the spire was caused by timber shortages during construction, leading to a shortfall between the ribs when pulled together. The interior is small but impressive, with early Australian stained glass windows and an Australian cedar hammerbeam roof. The adjoining cemetery contains the graves of early Canberra pioneers, including George Blundell, the Guise family, and Robert Garran, Commonwealth Solicitor-General 1916–32 (the Canberra suburb of Garran is named for this important figure). The gravestones often include the ceramic roses that seem so favoured in many Australian cemeteries.

Next to the church is **St John's Schoolhouse Museum** (☎ 02 6249 5839), in the settlement's first school building, in use from the 1840s until the 1900s. Taken over by the National Capital Development Commission in 1969, the museum offers interesting artefacts and displays about the history of the school, the church, and Canberra in general. Open Wed 10.00–12.00, weekends 14.00–16.00, and holidays 10.00–16.00 with admission fee.

Anzac Parade monuments

As with all heartfelt patriotic monuments, these memorial sculptures are rife with symbolic content, and aesthetically range from the impressive to the over-stated. First in line on the west side is the **Desert Mounted Corps Memorial**, in honour of the Australian Light Horse Brigade, as well as other Australian and New Zealand troops who fought in the Middle East during the First World War. Arguably the most aesthetically traditional and sophisticated monument on the Parade, this equestrian sculpture was originally created by Webb Gilbert (1867–1925), and completed by Paul Mountford and Australia's leading sculptor Bertram Mackennal (1863–1931). The original monument stood from 1932 at Port Said, Egypt, until it was blown up during the Suez Crisis in 1956. This replica was installed in 1968, while another one stands in Albany, Western Australia, from which the troops had embarked.

Immediately across the Parade is the **Rats of Tobruk Memorial**, commemorating the famous Australian forces who held the German Afrika Corps in Tobruk, Libya in 1941. An obelisk monument at the Tobruk War Cemetery, designed by soldier R.L. Sands, was meant to serve as the basis for this design, although the present sculpture, designed by Marc Clark and unveiled in 1983, differs from the original in its inclusion of the bronze 'Eternal Flame' in the centre. An original marble inscription stone and steps from the Tobruk Post Office appear beneath the flame.

Next in line on the west side of the Parade is the **Vietnam Veterans' Memorial**, the most recently completed monument, dedicated in 1992. In keeping with the wishes of the Vietnam veterans themselves, sculptor Ken Unsworth sought to incorporate 'a feeling of time and place' and to refrain from 'abstract design'. The resulting work includes photographic images, a 'graffiti wall' with soldiers' own words, and a black halo containing the names of all those Australians who died in the conflict (520 of them).

The **Royal Australian Air Force Memorial** is immediately across the Parade. The second monument erected after the Desert Mounted Corps Memorial, it is the most abstract and therefore caused the most controversy. Designed by German-born Inge King (b. 1918), the sweeping stainless-steel forms symbolise flight. The inscription, *per adua ad astra*, 'through adversity to the stars', is the motto of the RAAF. It was dedicated in 1971.

The site for the proposed **Korean War Memorial** is next in line. Dedicated in 1996 with the support of the Korean Government, the interim design, five carefully placed boulders from the Kapyong region of Korea, is most affecting. A more ambitious monument is currently being planned.

The **Australian Army's Memorial**, further north on this side, was erected in 1989. The army gave explicit instructions that the monument was to be 'unmistakably representational' of the Australian soldier, without abstract symbolism, and this requirement is certainly manifest in the final product. Designed by Joan Walsh-Smith (b. 1946), it consists of two oversized sculptures of the characteristic 'Aussie digger' surrounded by seven pillars representing the seven army campaigns. Some symbolism crept in with a simulated rock platform representing the land base of the army's operations.

Across the street is the **Royal Australian Navy Memorial**, an odd conglomerate of the representational and the geometric, complete with water fountains. Designed by Croatian-born sculptor Ante Dabro (b. 1938) in 1986, the aesthetic integration of the figures and forms were almost overwhelmed by the hydraulic considerations that the flowing water required. In the end, water took on a more subordinate role than initially planned.

Two of the most intriguing monuments are at the top of the Parade. The first is the **Hellenic-Australian Memorial** completed in 1988 in honour of the Anzac troops who died in the 1941 Greek campaign. Designed by Ken Woolley (b. 1933), the form of the monument is decidedly post-modern, with its inclusion of Doric columns, a Greek amphitheatre shape, a Greek Orthodox cross, and mosaic pavement. The strength of the Greek-born community in Australia and the subsequent close ties between Greece and Australia made this monument possible.

The **Kemal Ataturk Memorial** is similarly the result of Turkish-Australian relations. Indeed, the proposal for this monument came from the Turkish government, which in 1985 renamed a portion of the Gallipoli coast Anzac Cove. Gallipoli, of course, is the most famous and historically resonant battle in which Australian troops were involved during the First World War. The modest design, created by Turkish artist Huseyin Gezer (b. 1920), incorporates the crescent symbol of the Turkish flag with a mask-like head of Kemal Ataturk, father of modern Turkey, above a moving quotation from the leader about the Australian soldiers who died on Turkish soil. Soil from Anzac Cove is enshrined beneath a plaque in the centre of the memorial.

Australian War Memorial

In the 1920s, proposals for a national Australian War Memorial to be located in Canberra gained momentum. The major impetus for the project came from C.E.W. Bean, official historian of the Australian participation in the First World War, and John Linton Treloar, an official who devoted his life to the memorial (☎ 02 6243 4238, daily 10.00–17.00).

The War Memorial is one of the most visited institutions in the country. The volunteer staff, most of them ex-servicemen, provide excellent free tours and will help with any research questions presented to them. During holidays, the facilities can be crowded, so try to go early.

In 1926, two Australian architects were chosen as a compromise after an international competition. Emil Sodersten (1901–61), best known for his Art Deco buildings, and John Crust (1884–1964), a more traditionally trained architect, presented joint designs for the structure, but aesthetic differences and political intrusions led to inevitable conflicts, and by 1938, Sodersten was forced to withdraw from the project. The building, an odd mixture of classical restraint and Art Deco touches yet appropriately solemn, was finally opened in 1941. The Hall of Memory was not completed, with its impressive stained glass windows and Byzantine-inspired mosaic decorations by Napier Waller, until 195 9. Major extensions were made to the original structure in the 1970s to accommodate the ever-expanding collection. The Tomb of the Unknown Soldier, at the heart of the Hall of Memory, was not dedicated until 1993, when a soldier buried at the Australian Imperial Force cemetery in France was returned here and interred on Remembrance Day.

EMBASSY DISTRICT • 269

As with any national patriotic monument, the main focus of the memorial is a commemoration of the 102,601 Australians who have died in military conflicts. Australians are proud that every one of their war dead is included in the Memorial's Roll of Honour on panels along the cloisters' walls. The court-yard walls also include 26 delightful gargoyles of Aborigines and native fauna.

The galleries include informative exhibitions detailing Australia's involvement in foreign wars, using artefacts, oral history recordings, and video displays; these galleries, arranged chronologically by conflict, are located on the ground floor. The **lower ground floor** consists of special exhibitions on aspects of war, as well as surprisingly rich displays from the Memorial's substantial collections of art. These include not only paintings and drawings created by Australia's offi-cial war artists, most of them leading painters and illustrators (Australia continued to employ such artists even in the Vietnam War), but also an odd assortment of Byzantine mosaics, European sculptures, and Middle Eastern artefacts. The main entrance of the Memorial is flanked by the Menin Gate lions, which originally stood at the entrance to the Belgian town of Ypres, site of Australia's most costly battle in the Great War (38,000 Australians were killed or wounded here in 1917). Ypres gave them to the Australian nation as a commemorative gift. The Memorial also houses an active research centre and library.

Most recently, the **Treloar Technology Centre**, housing wartime vehicles and artillery, has been opened in an enormous facility in the Canberra suburb of Mitchell; open Wed and Sun 11.00–16.00, small admission fee (☎ 6241 8949).

Inner South ~ Yarralumla

Yarralumla is the site of Government House, the Governor-General's residence, and as such is the 'first' suburb of the capital. In the 1920s it was known as Westridge, and was one of the town's slums; the area where embassies are now located is where the toughest workers lived. This reputation has changed dramatically, especially since the lake was filled in, making Yarralumla one of the most desirable of residential neighbourhoods.

Sir Albert V. Jennings (1897–1993) was a builder who in 1951 and 1952 contracted 150 German carpenters to come to Canberra to build government-designed houses. The group were dubbed 'Jennings' Germans'; they built some 1800 houses in O'Connor, Ainslie, Turner and Yarralumla (then Westridge). The old 'guvvies' still remaining are their legacy.

Embassy district, Yarralumla

As the seat of the Federal government and national capital, Canberra is home to most foreign embassies, although many countries also have consulates in Sydney and Melbourne, where often more business occurs. The majority of these embassies are in Yarralumla, just off COMMONWEALTH AVENUE and near Lake Burley Griffin, although several smaller ones are in rather large but ordi-nary-looking suburban residences in places such as O'Malley and Red Hill.

While the Yarralumla embassy area is popular with tourist bus tours, many of the embassy buildings are undistinguished representatives of Canberra's adher-ence to the diluted modernism of the 1950s and 1960s: cinder block, glass and steel in various formulations. See, for example, the dreary British, Canadian and New Zealand High Commissions in a row on Commonwealth Avenue itself, just below the new Parliament building. The **British High Commission** was built in 1953 by the British Ministry of Public Building and reflects all of the austere attitudes of the time; a recent renovation has enhanced the entrance, but has changed little else externally. Several embassies have more recently been constructed in suitably 'ethnic' styles meant to represent the country's native architectural character. In a few cases, such as the Indian and the Japanese embassies, these architectural attempts are moderately successful in evoking regional flavour, but in many other cases, the results border on kitsch.

Turn west off Commonwealth Avenue on to CORONATION DRIVE; on the left is the British High Commission, on the right the Hyatt Hotel. On the left behind the British High Commission on FORSTER STREET stands the enormous embassy of the **Republic of China**. This much-touted complex, completed in 1990, looks as though it was taken directly from the back lot of a movie company, and could just as easily have been constructed for Disneyland, fulfilling Jean Baudrillard's famous statement that Disneyland has become the reality. When it was opened to the public during one of the annual Embassy Open Days, the queues extended for blocks, and every day bus loads of tourists arrive early in the morning to have their pictures taken in front of the edifice, ignoring the fact that traffic does continue to pass on the road. One rarely ever sees anyone enter or leave the place, which only exacerbates the sense that it is a stage set.

Proceed left up Forster Street past the New Zealand and Canadian High Commissions. On the left is the **High Commission of Papua New Guinea**. A replica of an authentic *haus tamburan*, or ceremonial house, the embassy is one of the most interesting and inviting—you can actually visit the house any time during the day, to view examples of indigenous art.

Continue on Forster Street past the Embassy of Brazil and the High Commission of Singapore; at DARWIN AVENUE, turn left and proceed to the **Indonesian Embassy**, which includes a sculpture pavilion housing statues of Hindu deities, as well as *gamelan* instruments and handicrafts from every Indonesian province. The pavilion is open to the public on most working days. Across the street from the embassy is a protest site, where demonstrators regularly converge to agitate against Indonesia's 'occupation' of East Timor and Australia's involvement in this event in the 1970s.

Continue up Darwin Avenue past the French Embassy, recently the site of enormous protests against French nuclear testing in the Pacific. On the right are the imposing walls surrounding the **American Embassy**.

This embassy, which was the first one constructed in Yarralumla, in 1941–43, imitates the Georgian architecture of Williamsburg, with substantial quantities of brick and even a gilded bust of George Washington above the main door and an eagle weathervane. As with all US embassies these days, the place is an armed fortress, nearly impossible to gain access; even those who need to conduct business must do so through a slit in a bullet-proof window at a side entrance.

If you walk around to Perth Avenue and on to RHODES PLACE, you will find the **Embassy of South Africa**. According to Graeme Barrow, author of *Embassies of Canberra* (1978), 'Canberra is fortunate to possess such an example of graceful architecture as the South African Embassy because normally South Africa does not build overseas.' Apparently South African diplomats are happy in Canberra, because it is very much like the 'easy-going' atmosphere of their own capital, Pretoria. The building, designed by Malcolm Moir, is a great example of Cape-Dutch-style residential architecture.

Return to Perth Avenue. Opposite the American Embassy and down the hill is the **High Commission of India**, rather successfully imitating Northern India's Mogul architecture.

From here continue on TURRANA AVENUE past the heavily guarded Israeli Embassy on the right, and the heavily forested and secluded Swedish Embassy on the left. Next in line is the diplomatic mission of Poland, and on the corner that of Greece. The building of the **Greek Embassy** is one of the better examples of pre-post-modern eclecticism, with its art-historical references to Classical architecture. As it was built at a time when architectural dogma required a building within modernist purist constraints, these classical elements are only eclectic touches; the structure itself is essentially modernist, just as the **German Embassy** across the street is.

Turn left on to EMPIRE CIRCUIT, and walk past the **Japanese Embassy** on the right, and further on, the **Embassy of Thailand**, both of them in regional style. The Thai Embassy regularly stages cultural days, in which local Thai restaurants participate to present the cuisine of their country.

Return to Empire Circuit and walk back (west) past the German Embassy on the right and the Dutch Embassy on the left. At ARKANA STREET, turn right. On the west side is the **Embassy of Spain**, one of the nicest and most effective examples of contemporary Spanish architectural design, although the architect was an Australian, Robert Warren. It opened in 1980.

Opposite the Spanish Embassy is that of **Ireland**, designed by Sydney architect Philip Cox as if it were a country cottage with a contemporary function. Next on the corner is the **Embassy of the Republic of Myanamar** (formerly Burma), its lovely violet shades in contrast to the starkness of neighbouring Israel.

Walk back to Empire Circuit; turn right. On the left is the **Canberra Mosque**, which serves the city's Muslim community; appropriately, the **Malaysian High Commission** is opposite on the right on the corner of Empire Circuit and Perth Avenue. Its design, completed in 1983, is reminiscent of typical Malaysian architecture, and is decorated with 14 hibiscus flowers representing the states of the Malay Peninsula.

Across the street is the **Embassy of Mexico**. Designed by Terrazas de la Pena in 1982, it is reminiscent of Luis Barragan's work, with diagonal slashes of walls, and a replica of an enormous stone Aztec calendar embedded in the wall at the entrance.

Yarralumla Nursery and Sri Chinmoy Peace Walk

From Empire Circuit, head south back to Schlich Street, turn right and travel to Novar Street. From the Yarralumla shops on Novar Street, proceed north to Lake Burley Griffin; turn left on Brown Street and right on Banks Street to enter **Weston Park**, which occupies a pleasant peninsula on the lake. This is a popular picnic spot, with children's playground, maze and miniature train ride, usually quite crowded on summer holidays. The city **bus routes** stop at the corner of Novar and Schlich Streets, requiring a bit of a walk to the park.

Weston Park Road also turns into **Yarralumla Nursery**, the original government-run facility founded in 1915 by Thomas Weston. From here, most of Canberra's eight million trees were grown and provided to new homeowners.

Weston also planted experimental stands of trees on this peninsula, many of which can still be seen along the **bike trail and walking path** that leads to the Sri Chinmoy Peace Walk and Government House.

The entrance to this lovely trail is on Banks Street immediately before entering Weston Park; the walk to the entrance of Government House is c 1.5km with pleasant views to the lake at Yarramundi Reach, where the Olympic Rowing Course is established for rowers in training. The trail also passes the side of the Royal Canberra Golf Course.

Royal Canberra Golf Club

Founded in 1926 along the Molonglo River, the club moved to its present site upon the filling of Lake Burley Griffin in the 1960s. As might befit the capital, John Harris designed the course with no hidden hazards, but with a call for accuracy down the tree-lined fairways and concentration putting on the large greens. The kangaroos which lounge everywhere on the course shy from people without clubs but take no notice of golfers. The government has attempted methods of sterilisation to control the population, which continues to multiply nonetheless.

Government House

This house has been the residence since 1927 of the Australian Governor-General, the Queen's representative and nominal head of state. The first Governor-General to live here was Sir Isaac Isaacs (1855–1948), first native-born Australian to hold this post; he moved in 1931. The house itself was built in 1891 by Frederick Campbell, grandson of Robert Campbell of Duntroon. By the time the house was purchased by the government, the property consisted of 40,000 acres (16,200 ha), mainly used for sheep grazing; the nearby Yarralumla Woolshed, still used for bush-dances and community events, attests to the property's heritage. The name Yarralumla apparently derives from the Aboriginal word 'Arralumna', which is believed to relate to the surrounding hills. Government House is only open on special open days during the year. The best view of the house itself is from a special viewing point off Lady Denman Drive, from the Cotter Road exit off Adelaide Avenue.

Australian Royal Mint

From Adelaide Avenue, take the Kent Street exit and continue across to Denison Avenue to find the Australian Royal Mint. Action buses from Civic also travel here. The Mint manufactures all of Australia's coinage as well as some for foreign countries, from preparation of raw material to final distribution; currency is still produced in Melbourne. Visitors are able to take a tour that exhibits all stages of production. A small shop emphasises, naturally, coins, where proof sets can be purchased. ☎ 02 6202 6999, weekdays 09.00–16.00, weekends and holidays 10.00–15.00.

Mount Stromlo Observatory

From Adelaide Avenue, take the Cotter Road turn-off and turn at the sign for Mount Stromlo Observatory, c 8km from Canberra's Civic Centre. The drive passes by the acres of pine forests planted originally by T.C. Weston, and now harvested as lumber; the forests seem at odds with the surrounding Australian vegetation, but provide interesting spots for bush-walking and picnics.

Astronomy in Australia

The earliest interest in astronomy in Australia involved determining geographic positions for navigators. Marine Lt. Dawes erected the first observatory in 1788 at Dawes Point as part of his work for the British Board of Longitude. By 1791 it was equipped with a transit sent by the Astronomer Royal. Explorer Matthew Flinders calculated the Point's latitude and longitude in the late 1790s. In keeping with his excellent cartographic skills, his calculations were a mere two seconds in error.

Governor Thomas Brisbane erected the first telescopic observatory at Parramatta in 1822 at his own cost. The equipment included a transit instrument (Troughton, 3.75 inch aperture and 64 inch focal length), a 16 inch repeating circle (Reichenbach), and a 46 inch achromatic telescope (Banks). Several of these instruments are still in the Sydney Observatory's collection. Assisted by German astronomer Carl Rümker (1788–1862) and particularly James Dunlop, Governor Brisbane compiled sufficient observations to result in William Richardson's Parramatta Catalogue of 7385 stars for the equinox in 1825.

Having established longitude and latitude and catalogued the significant celestial bodies, astronomy in the colony languished in New South Wales until the appointment of W.E. Cooke in 1912 as Government Astronomer and Professor of Astronomy.

In Victoria, initial efforts to provide accurate time to ships' captains commenced in the 1850s. The observatory at Williamstown was moved to the Domain in 1863. By that time the principle interest was completion of a geodetic survey begun in 1858. By 1866 the observatory was working on its portion of the sky (60° to 80° south declination) for a southern version of the *Durchmusterung* (a survey catalogue of stars). The observatory began a 20-year-long systematic revision of South African John Herschel's work on the southern nebulae using a Cassegrain reflector (Grubb, primary aperture 48 inches and focal length 360 inches, secondary aperture 8 inches and focal length 74.7 inches). Solar observations formed a part of the observatory's work in the 1870s, but the routine work continued to be meridian observations of star positions. The Victorian government discontinued its support for the observatory in 1943. Its time work was transferred eventually to Mount Stromlo.

While the preoccupation with latitude, longitude, meridian and time continued among governmental observers, independent astronomers tended to find planetary observations more engaging. Charles Todd mapped Jupiter and its satellites; Francis Abbott specialised in comets in the 1860s; W.J. MacDonnell, G.D. Hirst (well known for his planetary drawings) and Walter Frederick Gale all concentrated on planets, particularly Mars and Jupiter.

In 1910 James Oddie, an amateur astronomer from Ballarat, donated a Grubb equatorial refracting telescope (9-inch aperture, 135-inch focal length) to the Commonwealth as the basis for an observatory in the new capital territory. Mount Stromlo, at 782m height, was selected as the site for the building to house the telescope. This effort was furthered by Dr W.G. Duffield with the support of the British Association for the Advancement of Science and the Australian Solar Physics Committee in 1914.

The First World War interrupted work at the complex. The observatory's first reflecting telescope was a 76cm instrument, again donated by an amateur astronomer, J.H. Reynolds of Britain. Work in the 1930s continued to give prominence to solar observations, while atmospheric observations were given increasing prominence.

After the Second World War the solar observations were taken over by CSIRO and Canberra's city lights began affecting observations in the visible spectrum. The current work concentrates on the Magellanic clouds, the process of star formation and the structure and evolution of galaxies.

The Great Melbourne Telescope, built in 1868, was sold as scrap to the observatory in 1945 and re-erected. By the 1990s, 100 years of wear to its bearings and gears finally necessitated it be rebuilt as an infra-red telescope.

A visitor's gallery in the dome of the 1.9m telescope is open to the public daily during regular business hours; and occasionally, there are special night-time viewings. ☎ 02 6249 0230, daily 09.30–16.30. The observatory has recently expanded its public spaces, providing some nice exhibitions, as well as a good cafe. Touring amateur astronomers will find active societies in the major cities. Frequently, they offer introductory evenings for the general public, as they do at Mt Stromlo.

Lady Denman Drive
From Civic, take Parkes Way west, exit on to Lady Denman Drive at Clunies Ross Street for a pleasant drive along **Lake Burley Griffin** past Black Mountain Peninsula, a popular picnic spot. Travel another 1.5km along the lake to Yarramundi Reach next to Scrivener Dam. Alternatively, take the Cotter Road exit off Adelaide Avenue and follow Lady Denman Drive across Scrivener Dam to reach the centre. Currently, the Yarramundi Visitor's Centre and the National Aquarium occupy the site.

National Museum, National Aquarium and Australian Wildlife Sanctuary
The **Yarramundi Visitor's Centre** ☎ 02 6256 1126; (open daily, 10.00–16.00) currently houses a portion of the proposed National Museum's collections of Aboriginal artefacts and objects related to Australia's history. Plans are now afoot to build a comprehensive National Museum on Acton Peninsula; this centre will probably become an environmental centre offering walking tours of the Yarramundi grasslands.

Next to the Visitor's Centre is a modest aquarium and wildlife exhibition park, with interesting aquatic displays and exhibitions of koalas, fur seal, penguins, and a Tasmanian Devil. The complex will soon expand with more touristy accoutrements, including a ski slope and hotel. The grounds are a nice place for a picnic (☎ 6287 1211; open daily, 09.30–17.30).

Forrest, Deakin, Red Hill, Manuka
Immediately south of the Parliament House on Capital Hill are the 1930s 'garden city' suburbs of Forrest, Deakin, and Red Hill. These contain some of the oldest, as well as the most prestigious, homes in the capital. Australian-born media baron Rupert Murdoch has a residence in Red Hill, along with former Prime Minister Keating.

The Lodge

Off Adelaide Avenue on National Circuit, just below New Parliament House, is the prime minister's official residence, the Lodge. The first Prime Minister to occupy the building was Stanley Melbourne Bruce, who lived there in 1927. Over the years, some prime ministers have chosen to live in nearby hotels instead, but Robert Menzies, long-serving conservative Prime Minister and champion of Canberra development, resided there throughout his 17-year reign in the 1950s. Various controversies concerning subsequent redecoration of the Lodge's interiors have reached the political arena, most notably that done by Harold Holt's flamboyant wife Zara and Prime Minister Paul Keating's notorious penchant for teak tables and antique clocks. The current Prime Minister John Howard has flagrantly refused to set up permanent residence in Canberra, although the Lodge is still at his disposal. The Lodge is open to viewers only occasionally, usually during a heritage week in early April.

To the east of the Lodge, the suburb of **Forrest** includes many diplomatic residences, as well as the Jewish Memorial Centre and the Italian-Australian Club and, on **CANBERRA AVENUE**, one of the many Australian monuments to the Scottish poet Robert Burns. Take Melbourne Avenue south, past Canberra Church of England Girls' Grammar School, and turn left on to MUGGA WAY, arguably the most prestigious address in the capital. The huge properties here sit at the base of **Red Hill**, a nature reserve. The road up to Red Hill Lookout offers spectacular views of the city, and is a popular spot from which to enjoy the city's frequent fireworks displays; from here it was also possible to observe the recent appearance of the Hale-Bopp Comet.

Calthorpe's

At 24 Mugga Way is **Calthorpe's**, a preserved example of the 1920s middle-class residences built for Canberra's first public servants. The architectural firm of Oakley and Parkes designed the house in 1927 in a Spanish Mission style prevalent in other structures throughout this suburb; at the time, much of the area was given the unfortunate name of Blandfordia, mercifully changed later on. The original owners were the J.H. Calthorpe family; Mr Calthorpe was one of Canberra's first real estate agents. The family lived in the house until 1979, leaving the furnishings and fittings virtually intact as they had been since the 1930s. The ACT government acquired the house and has opened it to the public as a fascinating exhibition of early Canberra domestic life. The gardens are particularly attractive, and the back yard even includes the remains of an air-raid shelter and children's 'cubby' house. Open Tues–Thurs 09.00–17.00 with brief guided tours at 09.30, 11.00 and 13.30, weekends 13.30–16.30; ☎ 02 6295 1945.

Manuka

From Civic, several **bus routes** travel to Manuka, one of the earliest shopping centres in the city; it is a short ride down CANBERRA AVENUE from the New Parliament House. Today, **Manuka** is still the most popular place for cafes, restaurants, some nightlife, and boutique shopping. Remnants of its original design, shop-fronts with stained-glass windows and tiled façades, can still be seen in the courtyard.

Across Canberra Avenue from the shopping centre on Manuka Oval, behind the Retired Servicemen's Club, is the **Canberra Institute of Art's Jazz**

Department, which regularly gives concerts during the school term (☎ 6249 5754). Next to the school is the Manuka Swimming Pool, built in the 1930s in a delightful Art Deco style.

Northbourne Avenue to Barton Highway and Hall

NORTHBOURNE AVENUE is the main thoroughfare into central Canberra from Sydney. It is lined with office buildings, housing projects, and hotels, and is thoroughly uninteresting. However, it does lead to some interesting suburban attractions. From Northbourne heading north, turn right into Ipima Street, which becomes Cowper Street at Limestone Avenue; at Cowper and Bonney Streets is **All Saints Anglican Church** in the suburb of **Ainslie** (a city bus also travels here).

The church is notable because the structure was originally built in the 1860s by Colonial Architect James Barnet as the cemetery station at Sydney's famous Rookwood Cemetery, where trains would bring the funeral processions and coffin. By the 1950s, the church station had fallen into disrepair; in 1957, All Saints' minister Ted Buckle, purchased the lot for £100. Each stone was numbered and transported in 83 semi-trailer trucks, then faithfully reassembled on this site. The interior, with 52 arches, 365 different carvings and beautiful woodwork, testifies to the wisdom of the reconstruction; oddly, the church can also be considered as one of Canberra's oldest structures.

Back on Northbourne Avenue, continue north 1.5km to Antill Street; turn right to Dickson Street, and Canberra's **mini-Chinatown** on WOOLLEY STREET. It is really only a block of excellent restaurants, mostly Asian, and a few old-fashioned Asian grocery stores; plans are afoot to make it more flashy and self-consciously geared to tourists, but at the moment, it is still pleasantly authentic.

Barton Highway

Another 1.5km north along Northbourne Avenue is the turn-off to the Barton Highway towards Yass. Immediately north of this intersection is the **Canberra Racecourse**, with regular horse races, and the **National Exhibition Park**, site not only of the Royal Canberra Show in February, but also home to **Summernats**, the biggest 'revheads' event held every year between Christmas and New Year. At that time, Northbourne Avenue swarms with customised cars and their adoring fans.

The Barton Highway leads to the **Federation Square Shopping Complex** (c 3km), with assorted tourist attractions. The attractions are on the site of the old Ginninderra homestead, and a few 1880s buildings remain. The site also includes Cockington Green, a scale-model village of the English countryside, and an English pub. Across Gold Creek Road is the **National Dinosaur Museum**, containing Australia's largest collection of dinosaur artefacts (some replicas) and fossils (☎ 02 6230 2655).

Another 2km along the Highway leads to **Hall**, the ACT's only other 'town' aside from Canberra. It is a pleasant little village, with antique shops and a market on the first Sunday of the month on the showgrounds. The annual Australian **sheep-dog trials** take place here in March, presenting a wonderful experience of traditional rural culture and outstanding working-dog skills.

Lanyon

The Tuggeranong Parkway, off Parkes Way from Civic, leads around Lake Burley Griffin and through the suburb-filled Tuggeranong Valley to **Lanyon Homestead**, just before Tharwa on the edge of Namadgi National Park. Lanyon is c 35km south of the centre of Canberra, beautifully located near the Murrumbidgee River. Open Tues–Sun, 10.00–16.00; ☎ 02 6237 5136.

Established in 1834 by pastoralist James Wright and John Lanyon and worked by convict and free labour, Lanyon remains as the only fully-preserved homestead station in the region. The original land holdings by Wright extended to 3540 acres (1432 ha) and were soon a self-sufficient community, ruled by Wright with an iron hand (he is said to have used the lash liberally on his workers, and was certainly instrumental in the systematic decimation of local Aborigines). Financial difficulties led Wright to sell the property to Andrew Cunningham in 1848; the Cunningham family occupied Lanyon until 1926, extending their holdings to some 10,000 acres (4500 ha) and 60,000 sheep. Under the Cunninghams, the station became one of the most prosperous in the region. The Field family owned Lanyon from the 1930s until 1971, when the Commonwealth Government took over the land; in 1980, it was opened to the public as an historic house and museum.

The grounds of Lanyon offer a most pleasant and informative excursion from the city. You can tour the homestead itself, built by the Cunninghams in 1859, with its marvellous verandah; great effort has been made to preserve the interior furnishings as they appeared in the Victorian era, and tours of the building allow detailed inspection. The out-

Lanyon Homestead

buildings are especially interesting, with well-presented information panels, and even taped oral histories by former Lanyon workers. The old barracks and store now operate as a cafe. Most stunning are the gardens and surrounding grounds, including some of the original plantings. Musical evenings and food festivals are frequent events at Lanyon, especially in the summer.

Also in the grounds is the **Nolan Gallery**, built originally to house a collection of paintings donated by Sidney Nolan to the Commonwealth Government in 1974. The gallery, which normally displays these important Nolan paintings, opened in 1980 and now carries out an active exhibition programme focusing on contemporary Australian art. Open Tues–Sun, 10.00–16.00; ☎ 02 6237 5192.

Namadgi National Park

From Lanyon, return to Tharwa Road and continue south, crossing the Murrumbidgee River on the **Tharwa Bridge**, opened with great fanfare in 1895 and now the oldest bridge in the region and one of the only remaining Allan Truss bridges in the country. Turn left after the river following the

Namadgi National Park signs. About 1km along this road is the turn-off to **Cuppacumbalong**, a homestead site originally established in the 1840s by the Wright family of Lanyon. The present house was built in 1932 and now houses an excellent craft centre and cafe, as well as sculpture exhibitions amidst the beautiful gardens. You can also walk from here down to the Murrumbidgee River for picnics.

Return to the road and continue south c 5km to the **Namadgi National Park Visitor's Centre** (☎ 6237 5222). 'Namadgi' was the name given to the park's mountain ranges by the original Aboriginal inhabitants. The region, which at 105,900 ha comprises 50 per cent of the ACT's land, was declared a national park in 1984. The area is one of rugged beauty with stupendous Alpine valley views as well as remote wilderness, walking trails to suit all levels of bush-walkers, and comfortable campgrounds set in the bushland. At Honeysuckle Creek, an area often covered in snow in winter, are the remains of an early satellite tracking station. Several Aboriginal sites, with rock paintings at **Yankee Hat**, are also accessible to visitors in the park.

The Visitor's Centre provides excellent free maps and information about conditions on the walking trails and wilderness hiking routes; be sure to notice the flocks of swallows that regularly nest around the centre building. The south-west portion of the park joins the Kosciuszko National Park (see p 231). While the Boboyan Road through the park does travel all the way to Adaminaby in the Snowy Mountains (see p 228) some 80km away, the road conditions from the region around Brandy Flat are extremely rough and should really only be undertaken with a four-wheel drive vehicle.

Tidbinbilla Nature Reserve

From Tharwa, you can take the Tidbinbilla Road west c 5km, or from the city, take the Cotter Road c 35km to **Tidbinbilla Nature Reserve**. Traditionally one of the most popular excursions for locals and visitors, recent implementation of admission fees ($8 day pass) may see fewer regular visitors dropping by casually. The name 'Tidbinbilla' derives, at least in local tradition, from the Aboriginal 'Jedbinbilla', meaning 'place of initiation.' Open daily, 09.00–18.00; some tours available through the visitor's information centre at the front gate; ☎ 02 6237 5120.

While only 5510 ha in the reserve, the place has wonderful wildlife attractions, including enclosures for the viewing of kangaroos, koalas, and native birds, all of them in the wild; visitors must sometimes do a bit of searching to find the animals, especially when trying to spot the koalas in the trees. Intrepid and patient animal watchers may even be able to see a platypus in the creeks near the enclosures, and those in the know can also find bowerbird nests, with their collections of blue objects, hidden among the bushes. Picnic areas in the reserve are also great spots to view kangaroos and emus, who actually make pests of themselves and will steal any food left on the tables. Tidbinbilla's walking trails are also adventurous and varied, including a very short one to Hanging Rock, an impressive granite outcrop that seems to balance precipitously on one end and certainly served as an Aboriginal shelter. These trails are where naturalist David Attenborough found the lyrebird that could mimic camera shutters and chainsaws (seen in his programme, *The Life of Birds*).

Canberra Deep Space Communication Complex

From Tidbinbilla Nature Reserve, travel 4km north on Cotter Road to reach the entrance to the Canberra **Deep Space Communication Complex** (☎ 02 6201 7800, open daily 09.00–17.00, and from Oct–March until 20.00) space centre, established in 1965 as the Tidbinbilla Space Tracking Station to support the US National Aeronautics and Space Administration's deep space programme. The centre acts as the primary headquarters in the Southern Hemisphere for the tracking of satellites and space launchings, including the Apollo missions and lunar landings. The recent photographs produced by the Mars exploratory vehicle were first broadcast from this station through its link-up to NASA headquarters, and the public were allowed to view them here as they were beamed directly from the planet. The focal point of the centre's activities are its enormous dish antennas, the largest 70m in diameter; the visitor can watch them move automatically at regular intervals. The centre has fascinating displays of spacecraft and information about their tracking programmes, as well as a space-related gift shop and cafe.

Victoria

Victoria is on the southeast corner of the continent, with Melbourne as its capital and around which most of the population of the state is congregated. Its ports are within Port Phillip Bay at Port Melbourne and Geelong. The highways radiate from Melbourne. Highway 1, **Princes Highway**, follows the coast-line. The **Western** and **Dukes Highway**, route no. 8, is a more direct route

east to Adelaide. The **Calder**, route no. 79, proceeds northwest to Mildura where it meets the **Sturt Highway**. The **Newell**, no. 39, runs directly north, across New South Wales to Queensland. The **Hume**, no. 31, is the most direct route to Sydney or Canberra.

The physical features most frequently visited by tourists are the mountainous regions, the Great Ocean Road, the mining towns of Ballarat and Bendigo and the southwest coastal areas. The mountain ranges include the **Grampians** (variously coloured sandstone and shale with grey granite intrusions noted for their wildflowers in spring lying in the state's central west), the **Dandenongs** (fairly moist with fertile volcanic soil a mere hour northwest of Melbourne), and the **Victorian Alps** (the southern extension of the rugged alpine granite forma-tions of the Kosciuszko Uplift 250km northwest of Melbourne).

Geologically, Victoria is at the southern end of the Tasman Geosyncline, a Palaeozoic formation. The surface of the western portion of the state is sedi-mentary and metamorphic rocks of the Cainozoic era. This area is a corridor of fairly flat land extending from the central north near Wagga Wagga in New South Wales to the west and south to beyond the South Australian border. Part of the Darling River basin, this border area is marked by the Mallee region to the north and the Little Desert, an area which gives way to Palaeozoic granites in the Grampian Mountains.

Igneous intrusions are abundant on the volcanic plains west and northwest of Geelong, this activity being the basis of the mining deposits at Ballarat, Bendigo and elsewhere. Similar intrusions are revealed by erosion in the high relief hills and mountains in the Australian Alps in the west of the state. The **Murray**, **Murrumbidgee** and **Lachlan Rivers** form the Murray floodplain to the inte-rior of these highlands.

The natural vegetation is predominantly eucalypt forest, becoming quite tall and interspersed with ferns in the Dandenong Mountains to the east of Melbourne. The soil in Victoria is routinely fertile, mostly supporting sheep and cattle with some grains planted in the north and west and vineyards around Rutherglen. Irrigation on the sedimentary plains allows some vegetable and fruit production, particularly to Melbourne's southwest.

Climatically moderate, the winters (May through September) receive rela-tively more rain than the summers, although the Dandenongs and the southeast coast receive relatively uniform precipitation during the year. The summer temperatures are rarely uncomfortably hot (average maximum 26°C, minimum 14°C), and heatwaves infrequently last longer than a few days. Winter is cool (in Melbourne, average minimum 7°C), rather than cold, though snow falls frequently in the mountain ski fields of the northern section of the state. Melbourne itself is famous for its fluctuations in climate, with rain and sunshine intermingling throughout many days.

Melbourne is situated on Port Phillip Bay, a large inlet bounded by the **Mornington** and **Bellarine Peninsulas**. The prevailing southwesterlies have created sandy eastern beaches. Speaking of Port Phillip Bay's narrow entrance, known as the **Rip**, the Australian Encyclopedia mentions 'in some conditions of weather and tide vessels encounter very heavy seas when negotiating the Rip, which has cleared many dining salons in its day'. The tidal flow through the Rip can attain speeds up to eight knots. Four natural channels cut through shoals and sandbars within the bay.

The coastline west of Melbourne faces Bass Strait, and includes some of the most rugged and tempestuous waters of the entire Australian continent. The **Great Ocean Road** (Princes Highway west of Melbourne) hugs this coastline, with its many enormous rock formations near the coast giving evidence of the immense power of the waves to erode the sandstone cliffs. Although a small state by Australian standards, Victoria encompasses great geographical diversity and spectacular scenery. Victorians are rightfully proud of their 34 national parks and 40 state parks, all of them carefully tended and enjoyable for the visitor.

Melbourne

Geographically, **Melbourne** (population 3,230,000) has nothing to compete with Sydney's harbour, the Yarra River being a muddy stream that supposedly runs 'upside down', with the mud on top. The flatness of the town and unpredictable weather lead to acrimonious comparisons with its more glamorous northern neighbour. The Melburnian psyche has been described by many writers as introverted, more political and community-based (Melbourne has traditionally been the centre of unionism and left-wing politics) than Sydney's individualistic hedonism.

Despite such generalised and oft-stated opinions, the visitor to Melbourne can easily be charmed by the cultivated atmosphere of the place, an interesting blend of the patrician and the multicultural, in many ways more comfortable and intriguing than Sydney's flashy façade; it has often been voted one of the world's 'most livable cities' in international polls, and it is certainly the most 'European' city in Australia. As Melbourne has been a centre for immigration since the 1850s, its **ethnic diversity** is significant and deeply entrenched. It is said to have the largest Greek community in the world outside Greece, and its Italian, Lebanese, Turkish and Maltese populations are of long standing; a thriving Chinatown has existed here since last century. Between 1947 and 1968, some 800,000 non-British European immigrants came to Australia, a large percentage of them settling in Melbourne. In the 1970s, Asian immigration expanded the multicultural communities even further. Consequently, restaurants of all types present superb dining opportunities, and ethnic festivals abound.

Cafe culture is an essential part of the city's street life; Carlton's Italian residents of the 1950s can make a valid claim of having introduced Australia to the concept of espresso coffee at small tables accompanied by music and art-journals, as well as ethnic eating experiences. The city also has some of the country's best bookshops, and art galleries present both the well established and the contemporary. Of most significance is Melbourne's place in the country's theatrical life, from grand and revered venues for the established repertoire to its long tradition of alternative and street theatre; it is the host of the annual Comedy Festival, as well as numerous theatrical events, comedy television and outdoor performances. Melbourne is undisputedly the fashion capital of Australia, with prominent designers, elegant boutiques and the best shopping opportunities in the country. The city also boasts a plethora of carefully considered parks and green areas, which provide pleasant places to cycle, walk and relax. Unlike Sydney, which dismantled its tramways in the 1950s, Melbourne's green and yellow trams are not only the most pleasant way to get around the city, but add considerably to Melbourne's character.

Despite Melbourne's reputation for staidness, the city does nurture some alternative or subversive strands, both of the intellectual street theatre and New Age sort, and, more explicitly, the Gothic and skinhead sort (the controversial film *Romper Stomper* took place in Melbourne). The city is also the location of Moonee Ponds, fabled home of Edna Everage, comedian Barry Humphries' alter ego, and a place that has come to epitomise the sprawling sterile suburbs of 1950s Melbourne.

In *Road to Gundagai* (1965), author Graham McInnes commented on Melbourne's suburban sprawl, 'these immense deserts of brick and terracotta, or wood and galvanised iron induce a sense of overpowering dullness, a stupefying sameness, a worthy, plodding, pedestrian, middle-class, low-church conformity'. Today this suburban phenomenon does not seem so unusual, and Melbourne proper can still be an interesting place to visit.

▪ Practical information

Tourist information. Victorian Visitor Centre, 230 Collins Street; ☎ 132 842. Central tourist information centres also include the **Royal Automobile Club of Victoria** (RACV, ☎ 03 131 955) at Bourke and Elizabeth Streets. This serves as the Victorian Tourism Centre, but is more of a travel agency than a source of detailed information on Melbourne itself. **Information Victoria**, 318 Little Bourke Street, provides free maps and brochures, and many books and tour maps for sale. There are also **visitor information booths** at City Square and Bourke Street Mall, as well as **tourist information video screens** at the train stations and in front of the Town Hall on Swanston Street. The Town Hall's City Experience Centre offers a greeting service which arranges personal city tours. '*Hello Melbourne*', the free brochure produced by the Australian Tourist Commission, is available at all tourist centres and at hotels, and is especially valuable for providing the tram and train maps.

Airport. Melbourne's international airport, **Tullamarine**, is located 22km northwest of the city centre, near the suburb of Essendon. Despite its rather downtrodden appearance, many overseas flights will land or depart from this airport. Melbourne is also the main centre for flights to Tasmania. *Kendell*

Airlines (booked through Ansett, ☎ 13 13 00) is the largest regional operator for flights within the state. *Skybus* (☎ 9335 3066) operates a bus service (every 30 minutes) from the airport into town, dropping passengers at the Spencer Street Station. A taxi ride from the airport will cost about $20.00 into the city centre.

Rail. The interstate trains of *Countrylink* and the national rail system arrive from New South Wales and Adelaide at Spencer Street Station (☎ 13 22 32; or 9619 5000); the Melbourne–Adelaide *Overlander* also departs from here.

Trams and buses. Melbourne is famous for its wonderful system of trams (see plan, p 284). They are much more than decorative tourist attractions, but are part of an excellent and efficient public transport system combining trams, buses and trains. More information can be obtained at the Met Transport Information Centre (103 Elizabeth Street) or by ☎ 131 638. Services for passengers with disabilities can be obtained by calling Flinders Station, ☎ 9610 7482 or Spencer Street Station, ☎ 9619 2300. The Met runs on a zone system, which extends in Zone 3 to a very wide radius outside the city. Day tickets, weekly and short trip cards are all available at very reasonable prices; day tickets are an especially good buy, as they enable one to go anywhere within Zone 1 (almost all of the metropolitan area) all day on either tram, train or bus.

All tourist brochures and the free guides contain tram maps; *Melways* street directories also include comprehensive information on tram and bus schedules.

Driving. Caution must be taken in driving around tram intersections, and overtake only on the left of a tram. A very peculiar rule for drivers here involves getting into the far left-hand lane when making right-hand turns and waiting until the light turns yellow. Watch the other drivers before attempting these turns!

Taxis. Many companies operate throughout the city with regular cab ranks especially in centre city: *Arrow*, ☎ 9417 1111; *Black Cabs*, ☎ 13 22 27; *Embassy*, ☎ 13 17 55; *Silver Top*, ☎ 13 10 08.

Bicycles can be rented at Princes Bridge, next to the Boat Sheds on the Yarra River, South Side (☎ 9801 2156); or at Bicycle Now, Chapel Street and Alexandra Avenue, South Yarra (☎ 9826 8877). Cycling paths around the city are excellent, especially the Yarra River cycle path (11km) and the bayside path. Maps of cycling paths are available from the tourist information centres, cycling shops and some bookshops.

Useful addresses
British Consulate-General, 17th floor, 90 Collins Street, ☎ 9650 4155.
Canadian Consulate-General, 1st floor, 123 Camberwell Road, Hawthorn, ☎ 9811 9999.
US Consulate-General, 553 St Kilda Road, ☎ 9526 5900.
Police. *Emergency* 000; *City*, 637 Flinders Street, ☎ 9247 6666.
Hospitals. *Alfred Hospital*, Commercial Road, Prahran, ☎ 9276 2000; *Royal Melbourne*, Parkville, ☎ 9342 7000; *St Vincent's*, Fitzroy, ☎ 9807 2211.
Rape Crisis. *Royal Women's Hospital*, ☎ 9344 2210.

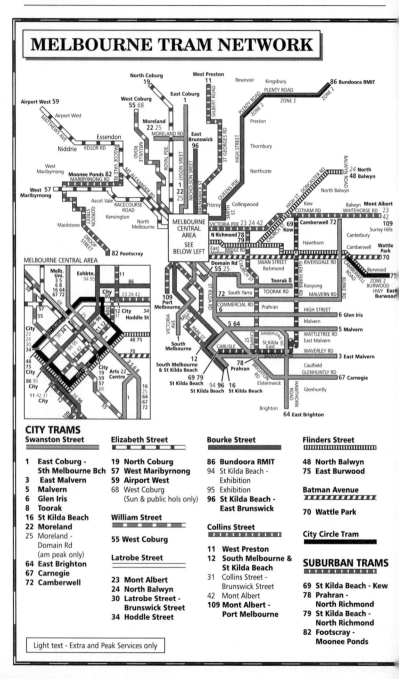

MELBOURNE TRAM NETWORK

CITY TRAMS

Swanston Street

1	East Coburg - Sth Melbourne Bch
3	East Malvern
5	Malvern
6	Glen Iris
8	Toorak
16	St Kilda Beach
22	Moreland
25	Moreland - Domain Rd (am peak only)
64	East Brighton
67	Carnegie
72	Camberwell

Elizabeth Street

19	North Coburg
57	West Maribyrnong
59	Airport West
68	West Coburg (Sun & public hols only)

William Street

55	West Coburg

Latrobe Street

23	Mont Albert
24	North Balwyn
30	Latrobe Street - Brunswick Street
34	Hoddle Street

Bourke Street

86	Bundoora RMIT
94	St Kilda Beach - Exhibition
95	Exhibition
96	St Kilda Beach - East Brunswick

Collins Street

11	West Preston
12	South Melbourne & St Kilda Beach
31	Collins Street - Brunswick Street
42	Mont Albert
109	Mont Albert - Port Melbourne

Flinders Street

48	North Balwyn
75	East Burwood

Batman Avenue

70	Wattle Park

City Circle Tram

SUBURBAN TRAMS

69	St Kilda Beach - Kew
78	Prahran - North Richmond
79	St Kilda Beach - North Richmond
82	Footscray - Moonee Ponds

Light text - Extra and Peak Services only

Cruises. Yarra River Cruises (☎ 03 9614 1215) depart every half hour midday from Princes Walk and Southgate. About an hour in duration, they proceed either up river to Herring Island and back or down river towards Port Melbourne and back.

Hotels

$$$$ Le Meridien at Rialto, 495 Collins, ☎ 03 9620 9111/1800 331 330. European-style hotel in historic building in Melbourne's centre.

$$$$ The Windsor, corner Spring and Bourke Streets, ☎ 03 9633 6000. The *grande dame* of all Australian hotels, central to Melbourne's cultural life since 1883.

$$$ Country Comfort Old Melbourne, 5 Flemington Road, North Melbourne, ☎ 03 9329 9344/1800 065 064. Nice location, variety of room sizes, undercover parking.

$$$ Grand Mercure Hotel, 321 Flinders Lane, Melbourne, ☎ 03 9629 4088; fax 03 9629 4066. Formerly the Sebel of Melbourne. In the heart of the city, small and intimate; spacious suites. A favourite with businessmen; includes corporate health club, secretarial services, suites for disabled.

$$$ The Prince St Kilda, 2 Acland Street, St Kilda, ☎ 03 9536 1111; fax 03 9536 1114. Newly renovated boutique hotel in formerly grungy art-deco building; extremely chic, well-decorated interiors (40 rooms). On St Kilda's food street, surrounded by exciting night life.

$$$ South Yarra Hill Suites Hotel, 14 Murphy Street, South Yarra, ☎ 03 9868 8222; fax 03 9820 1724. Five-star swank, one- & two-bedroom self-contained apartments with all the amenities (even stretch-limousine service). Near Toorak shopping streets. Has some special weekend packages.

$$ Boutique Hotel Tolarno, 42 Fitzroy Street, St. Kilda, ☎ 03 9537 0200; fax 03 9534 7800. Another cosmopolitan gem, in 1960s decor; once a grand Victorian mansion, with links of Melbourne's alternative art scene.

$$ East Melbourne Apartment Hotel, 25 Hotham Street, East Melbourne, ☎ 03 9412 2555/1800 335 786; fax 03 9412 2567. Lovely location near MCG and Fitzroy Gardens; good value, pleasant staff.

$$ Hotel Ibis, 15 Therry Street, ☎ 03 9639 2399. Great location on the edge of Central Business District (known as the CBD); geared to business travellers.

$$ Lygon Quest Lodgings, 700 Lygon Street, Carlton, ☎ 03 9345 3888/1800 621 654; fax 03 9349 1250. Serviced apartments on famous restaurant/cafe street near University of Melbourne.

$ Victoria Vista Hotel, 215 Little Collins, ☎ 03 9653 0441/1800 331 147. Great fun, an old rabbit's warren of a city hotel (500+ rooms of all sizes and shapes!) in an ideal location. Great bargain; apply governmental rates for those qualified.

$ YHA Queensberry Hill, 78 Howard Street, North Melbourne, ☎ 03 9329 8599. Award winner for budget accommodation; all types of rooms, including family suites. Has bistro, free parking, travel agency on site.

Restaurants

$$$$ Jacques Reymond's Restaurant, 78 Williams Road, Windsor, ☎ 03 9525 2178. For many Melburnians, a once-in-a-lifetime experience is to eat at Reymond's; winner of every gourmet award imaginable. Owner-chef Reymond has created a modern Australian cuisine, with French techniques and Asian flavours. Exquisite service in beautiful, historic mansion. Menu always includes special vegetarian five-course dinner.

$$$ 111 Spring Street, the Windsor Hotel, 111 Spring Street, ☎ 03 9633 6004. The traditional Windsor roast of the day joins excellent ethnic fare with a middle-eastern touch. Windsor's Grand Lunch served Fridays.

$$$ B.coz, 403 Riversdale Road, Hawthorn East, ☎ 03 9882 7889. A mix of Cajun and Asian flavours in recently expanded quarters; excellent wine list.

$$$ Circa, The Prince, 2 Acland Street, St Kilda, ☎ 03 9536 1122. Ultra-chic restaurant in the Prince Hotel, with British chef Michael Lambie, ex of Marco Pierre White's kitchen. Stunning classical French food, exceptional wine list.

$$$ Da Noi, 95 Toorak Road, South Yarra, ☎ 03 9866 5975. Sardinian specialties, such as pig's trotters with saffron; rustic and intimate.

$$$ Flower Drum, 17 Market Lane, ☎ 03 9662 3655. At the top of everyone's list for Cantonese food and impeccable service; daily specials can be overwhelmingly luxurious.

$$ Akita, 34 Courtney Street, North Melbourne, ☎ 03 9326 5766. Innovative Japanese food in old corner pub; renowned for changing 'daily specials'; lots of seafood.

$$ Becco, 11–25 Crossley Street, ☎ 03 9663 3000. Great value, with produce store, bar, and Mediterranean food; great favourite with Melbourne gourmets.

$$ Shark Fin House, 131 Little Bourke Street, ☎ 03 9663 1555. In the heart of Chinatown, unbelievable array of yum cha (about 150 different kinds). This is where the Chinese eat.

$ Pellegrini's, 66 Bourke Street, ☎ 03 9662 1885. A Melbourne institution, one of the first European-style cafes in the city. Real, old-fashioned pasta and, of course, coffee to get nostalgic about.

$ Old Salonika, 325 Smith Street, Fitzroy, ☎ 03 9419 5260. As genuine a village-style Greek taverna as you can find outside of Greece; only six tables, simple grilled fish and a few other dishes each night.

$ Eshel Deli and Takeaway, 57–59 Glen Eira Road, Ripponlea, ☎ 03 9532 8309. Jewish kosher meals and outstanding desserts.

Theatre tickets. All bookings for theatre, concerts and other entertainment events can be made through Ticketek.

History

The area around Port Phillip had been surveyed as early as 1803 during Flinders' circumnavigation of the continent (see p 58). In that same year, **Lieutenant David Collins**, Judge-Advocate with the First Fleet, was sent from Sydney to found a settlement here, but having attempted to settle on the eastern side of the bay, at present-day Sorrento, found the area unsuitable and continued on to Tasmania. The site for the settlement of today's Melbourne was not chosen until the 1830s, when two groups of explorers out of Launceston embarked for that purpose. One group was headed by John Pascoe Fawkner in 1835. The other group, headed by John Batman, was the first to find an appropriate location, acquiring some 600,000 acres (240,000 ha) through a 'treaty' with the indigenous Aborigines in exchange for blankets and tomahawks. From 1836 to 1850, the so-called

Black War saw nearly continuous battles with tribes who fought to keep their land and deter settlers. By 1850, great decimation of the Aborigines through disease and the increasing pressure of white settlement caused their numbers to dwindle from about 16,000 to 2500.

In September 1835, at the site of the present-day Spencer Street railway yards, an advance party established a camp named Batman's Hill on the banks of the **Yarra River**, where it begins to be fresh water (Yarra is an Aboriginal word meaning 'flowing water'). It was here that Batman established a permanent home in 1836; as the writer Barry Oakley concludes, 'if Batman pioneered the district, Fawkner founded the town'. (See box.) While the settlement was not considered legal by the authorities in Sydney, settlers continued to arrive until acknowledgment of its existence could not be

---

John Pascoe Fawkner

John Pascoe Fawkner (1792–1869) epitomises the colourful characters that define much of early Australian history. Born in London, Fawkner as a young boy accompanied his family when his father was transported to Australia for receiving stolen goods. In 1803, the Fawkners were part of David Collins' unsuccessful settlement at Port Phillip, travelling eventually to Hobart, where his father received a land allotment for good behaviour and the family took up various occupations. In 1814, the younger Fawkner assisted some convicts in building a boat with which to escape and was consequently sentenced to prison in Newcastle, an experience which strengthened his lifelong fight against oppression and authority. He returned to Hobart in 1817, and moved on to Launceston in 1819, where he worked as a baker, a butcher, a bookseller and an entertainment promoter, before marrying in 1822 and establishing the Cornwall Hotel in 1824. His battle against authoritarian rule gained impetus when he founded the *Launceston Advertiser* in 1829, a newspaper that became a leading advocate for governmental reform and an end to convict transportation.

In 1835, Fawkner took advantage of reports of opportunities for settlement across the Bass Strait in the Port Phillip District. He purchased the schooner *Enterprise* and prepared it for exploration and the transportation of settlers to the region. While Fawkner himself was prevented from making the first voyage because of seasickness, his party sailed up the Yarra River in August 1835, and established a camp near present-day Spencer Street. Fawkner and his family arrived here in October and set up a store and hotel in a framed cottage he had brought along. By 1838, he established a hotel on the corner of Collins and Market Streets, as well as the colony's first newspaper. By 1840, he owned three newspapers and a large plot of farming land, and had leased the hotel to the early Melbourne club. By 1841, he began his long career as a prominent public servant in the rapidly growing colony. His pugnacious temperament made him a popular champion of the people's causes, and he was a central figure in the tumultuous events during the period of the gold rush; he was a member of the Melbourne Legislative Council from 1851 to 1869 and most significantly on the Commission for the gold-fields from 1851 to 1856. By the time of his death in 1869, Fawkner's status as Melbourne's founder and elder statesman was well established.

ignored. Governor of New South Wales Richard Bourke appointed William Lonsdale as Police Commissioner of the region, and in 1837 visited the town and named it Melbourne after the then British Prime Minister.

A town was first laid out in 1837 by surveyor **Robert Hoddle** and his assistant Robert Russell on a grid plan; Hoddle's enlightened vision led to the creation of wide streets (originally 99 feet), with narrower city lanes in between (the present-day 'Little' streets). The original area was defined by Flinders, Spencer, Lonsdale and Spring Streets. At the time known more generally as the Port Phillip District, the town's streets were renowned for their poor drainage, and habitation was primitive. As late as the 1850s horses and riders were being drowned in Elizabeth Street, and many town dwellings were no better than 'piggeries', to quote one contemporary.

With the discovery of gold near Ballarat in 1851, Melbourne's haphazard growth was immediately altered, as 250 immigrants a day arrived heading for the **goldfields**. In one decade, from 1851 to 1861, the colony grew from 77,000 to 540,000, although by the 1880s this number stabilised at about 500,000 with the official population of the Port Phillip region at about 250,000. In 1857, some 160,000 settlers were still living in tents or 'humpies' within the city limits. In July 1851, only days before gold was discovered, **Victoria** gained separation as a self-governing colony from New South Wales, a rivalrous division that, as the states of Victoria and New South Wales, is still vociferously (and, many would say, almost childishly) maintained.

Comparisons between Melbourne and Sydney (a curiously unconsidered slight to the remainder of the country) are still a national obsession. Playwright David Williamson, who has lived in both places, offered in 1980 the following assessment: 'Melbourne is a much more belligerent city [than Sydney]. Its dinner parties are more violent. The trouble with Melbourne is that it's made up of Scots stockbrokers and Irish publicans.' Historians corroborate this assertion: Scottish and Irish settlement in the region was especially pronounced from the 1840s.

The period between the 1860s and 1880s, until the precipitous economic crash of the 1890s, saw the rise of **'Marvellous Melbourne'**, a term coined by journalist George Sala in the newspaper *Argus* in 1885. The frontier town was transformed into a bustling cosmopolitan city, described in its ambition and modernity as 'Yankee' compared to Sydney's 'English' sleepiness—quite the opposite of the notion today. Not only did it become the largest city on the continent, but also one of the wealthiest in the world. Evidence of what one critic called its 'confident palladianism' can be seen in the lofty goals of its early leaders: the judge Sir Redmond Barry (see box), who saw that the new public library contained every work mentioned in Gibbons' *Roman Empire*, but no fiction; Governor Charles La Trobe (see box), who laid out English-style parks in the surrounding bush; and those citizens who founded a university in 1853, when the town was less than 30 years old. It can be said that Melbourne is the only city in the world to develop into a metropolis entirely during the Victorian era, and the era's architecture and institutions today make it seem more Old World than Sydney.

By the time of the crash and depression of the 1890s, Melbourne was known as the financial capital of Australia, as well as a major manufacturing centre. At the time of Federation in 1901, Melbourne became the national

Redmond Barry

Redmond Barry (1813–80), an important figure in the development of Melbourne, arrived in Australia in 1839. Having already studied law at Trinity College, Dublin, he immediately set up practice in the fledgling community of Melbourne. By 1842 he was commissioner of the Court of Requests. Barry was instrumental in the establishment of most of Melbourne's first cultural institutions. Before a library could be established, he allowed people to use his personal collection at his home in Bourke Street. The first president of the Mechanics' Institute and a founder of the Melbourne Hospital, Barry was appointed Solicitor-General in 1851 when Victoria became a separate colony. In 1853 he became a Supreme Court Justice (one of his greatest claims to fame was as the judge who sentenced Ned Kelly to hang). He was the university's first chancellor, a position he held until his death, and remained personally involved in the development of the public library and the National Gallery. The epitome of the Victorian gentleman, Barry nonetheless refused to marry his mistress of many years, the mother of his four children—a bewildering situation for 19C moralists.

Charles Joseph La Trobe

C.J. La Trobe (1801–75) was born into an intellectual family of the Moravian religion in London; his father, a minister, was a personal friend of the composer Franz Haydn. Many years of travel throughout Europe and America in the 1820s and 1830s led Charles to consider himself a 'citizen of the world'. Washington Irving, his travel companion in America, called him a 'complete virtuoso'. He wrote several books about his travels which brought him to the attention of the British Colonial Office. After submitting a report on the question of negro education in the West Indies, he was appointed as Superintendent to the Port Phillip District in 1839. His tenure spanned the most tumultuous period in Victorian history. As La Trobe himself commented on the period after the discovery of gold in 1851, just as an independent Victorian government was being established, 'it was a matter of wonder...that the government was in any way enabled to stand its ground and perform its manifold functions.'

La Trobe was greatly hampered by the fact that, administratively, he was still considered subordinate to the Governor of New South Wales, a situation that caused confusion and unease throughout his administration. Despite his immense achievements—the establishment of Melbourne's many gardens, the founding of the Royal Melbourne Hospital, the University and the Public Library—La Trobe's administration was criticised for indecisiveness, certainly an unfair claim given the unprecedented circumstances during his tenure. While he personally objected to the goldfields taxes which ultimately led to the famous Eureka Stockade Rebellion in 1854 (see p 370), he was unable to convince his legislative council of the taxes' inequity. La Trobe resigned his office in 1854 and retired to England.

capital until Canberra was established in 1927. Despite its heady days in the 19C, Melbourne has not since been able to surpass Sydney as the premier city of the continent, a fact that has often led to a defensive snobbishness among its citizens.

The cultural character of Melbourne can be exemplified with the story behind its biggest public festival, **Moomba**, which takes place each year in March. Originally the event was conceived as a Labor Festival to celebrate the unions' victory in the 8-hour day campaign. With the coming of the 1956 Olympics to the city, an event which precipitated the introduction of television to the country, Melbourne wanted to present a more elaborate festival with a conscious national theme. The planners asked Bill Onus, Koorie leader and artist, to suggest a name for the festival; he gave them 'Moomba'. There is still great debate about what it means; usually it is translated as 'let's have a good time,' but others maintain it is an Aboriginal word for 'back side': hence, an insider's joke on the part of Aboriginal people.

The festival originally revolved around floats parading down Swanston Street, but it has now developed to include a variety of street events, loosely joined together under the Moomba banner. The city is also the location for the **Melbourne Festival of the Arts** in September, a more cultural event combining music, theatre, and art exhibitions.

Finding your way around

As Melbourne's **central streets** were originally laid out as a grid, the town is easy to negotiate on foot. The main thoroughfare is Swanston Street, running northwest through the centre of the original town grid. Since 1992 Swanston Street between Flinders and Latrobe Streets has been a pedestrian walk and increasingly a showcase for modern sculpture—Petrus Spronk's *Architectural Fragment*, a diagonal slice of a pediment, and Pamela Irving's *Larry Latrobe*, a bronze cast dog being particularly light hearted.

To the west of Swanston Street are Spencer, King, Queen, and Elizabeth Streets; to the east Russell, Exhibition, and Spring Streets. The main cross streets are, from the south, Flinders, Collins, Bourke, Lonsdale and Latrobe Streets, with the narrower 'Little' streets in between. This grid still marks the Central Business District, the 'CBD' in local parlance.

Walk 1 • Southgate to the Arts Centre

This walk begins at **Flinders Street Station**. In many ways, this grandiose railway station is the real landmark of Melbourne's cityscape; 'under the clocks' of Flinders Station is the Melburnian's traditional point of rendezvous. The site was the centre of the city's railway system from 1854, and the rail-lines themselves were well-established before the building was completed in 1910. The architects, J.W. Fawcett and H.P.C. Ashworth, were winners of a design competition. The architectural style seems supremely imperial, with hints of colonial India in its cupolas and arched entrance.

Across the street from Flinders Station is **Young and Jackson's Hotel**, a famous watering hole, now pretty seedy, but best known as the residence of the daring painting *Chloe* which hung behind the bar for years.

The hotel stands on land purchased by John Batman in 1837 for £100; built in 1860, the hotel was purchased by Henry Young and Thomas Jackson in 1875. Their business sense saw the establishment become one of the first hotels to feature Foster's new lager beer in 1888. The painting of the standing nude, by Jules Le Febvre, had won the gold medal at the 1880 International Exhibition, and caused a scandal when exhibited at the National Gallery. It was eventually purchased by the bar in 1908, where it remained until moving to the restaurant upstairs.

From Flinders Street Station, you can walk south one block and turn right on to Flinders Walk, which leads in about 250m to a footbridge to SOUTHGATE PROMENADE, the site of **SOUTHGATE PLAZA**. For many years an industrial site and a major eyesore on the edge of the business district, this area has now been redeveloped as an activities centre in conjunction with the nearby Victorian Arts Centre. Much of the Southgate complex is dedicated to fashionable franchise shopping venues and restaurants, but the ground floor includes an interesting aquarium suspended from the ceiling, housing over 100 species of fish.

Continuing west along the promenade, you come to Queens Bridge, on the other side of which is one of the earliest areas of settlement in Melbourne. At 400 FLINDERS STREET is **Old Customs House**, built in two stages, in 1856 and 1876. The building is typical of the simplified 'Classical' style of many Victorian buildings; on this site were earlier buildings, of which the foundations still exist. This area was originally the landing of Queen's Wharf, with the Customs House at the top of the busy port on the Yarra, now occupied by the railway yards. The building was the subject of a major preservation battle when it was threatened with demolition in the 1970s. Old Customs House (☎ 03 9927 2727) currently houses the Immigration Museum on its first floor and the Hellenic Antiquities Museum on its second floor. The former presents a thematic display of the immigrant experience recounting for a number of periods why people left their birth places, how they travelled, and what conditions they met upon arrival. The Hellenic Antiquities Museum is supported by the Greek government and presents changing exhibits designed and mounted in Greece.

On the corner of William and Flinders Streets in front of the Customs House is a plaque commemorating the site where John Batman declared, 'this is the place for a village' (see History). The point on the river across the street was where a waterfall marked the beginning of fresh water, the only source of drinking water for the early settlement; it was here that Batman's only son drowned at the age of nine.

Back on the Southgate Promenade, you come to the **Crown Entertainment Complex** and Casino (☎ 03 9292 8888; casino always open), filled with shops, restaurants and cinemas. This centre, which opened with unprecedented and extravagant fanfare in 1997, represents Premier Jeff Kennett's ambitious bid to turn Melbourne into 'Las Vegas on the Yarra'. The casino in the complex is the largest in the southern hemisphere, with something like 1km of poker machines! The architectural design of the complex is predictably extravagant, and the casino has, so far, been far from the money spinner envisioned by the planners; but the restaurants include some of the showiest in town, and the shops are of the Gucci-Christian Dior range. It is not Las Vegas, but it beats the industrial wasteland that used to be here.

Further along, on the western side of Spencer Street, is the Melbourne Exhibition Centre, then along Yarra River Board Walk about 300m, the **Polly Woodside Maritime Museum** (☎ 03 9699 9760; open daily 10.00–16.00); vehicle access is also from the west, at Lorimer Street off the Charles Grimes Bridge, Footscray Road. The centrepiece of the museum is the commercial sailing ship *Polly Woodside*, built in 1885, now restored as one of the last functional windjammers in the world. The museum includes other artefacts of Melbourne's

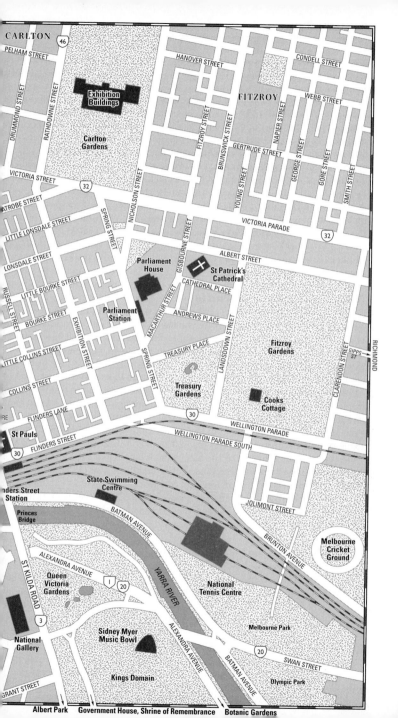

CARLTON

PELHAM STREET

HANOVER STREET

CONDELL STREET

FITZROY

WEBB STREET

DRUMMOND STREET

RATHDOWNE STREET

FITZROY STREET

BRUNSWICK STREET

NAPIER STREET

GEORGE STREET

GORE STREET

SMITH STREET

Exhibition
Buildings

Carlton
Gardens

GERTRUDE STREET

YOUNG STREET

VICTORIA STREET

NICHOLSON STREET

VICTORIA PARADE

LATROBE STREET

LITTLE LONSDALE STREET

SPRING STREET

GISBOURNE STREET

ALBERT STREET

LONSDALE STREET

Parliament
House

St Patrick's
Cathedral

CATHEDRAL PLACE

LITTLE BOURKE STREET

MACARTHUR STREET

ANDREWS PLACE

RUSSELL STREET

EXHIBITION STREET

BOURKE STREET

Parliament
Station

LANDSDOWN STREET

CLARENDON STREET

RICHMOND

GIPPS ST

LITTLE COLLINS STREET

TREASURY PLACE

Fitzroy
Gardens

COLLINS STREET

Treasury
Gardens

Cooks
Cottage

FLINDERS LANE

St Pauls

WELLINGTON PARADE

FLINDERS STREET

WELLINGTON PARADE SOUTH

State Swimming
Centre

nders Street
Station

JOLIMONT STREET

Princes
Bridge

BATMAN AVENUE

BRUNTON AVENUE

Melbourne
Cricket
Ground

ALEXANDRA AVENUE

ST KILDA ROAD

Queen
Victoria
Gardens

YARRA RIVER

National
Tennis Centre

Sidney Myer
Music Bowl

ALEXANDRA AVENUE

Melbourne Park

National
Gallery

BATMAN AVENUE

SWAN STREET

Kings Domain

Olympic Park

GRANT STREET

Albert Park   Government House, Shrine of Remembrance   Botanic Gardens maritime history. On the north side of the Spencer Street Bridge is the World Trade Centre and behind it, the thriving Crown Casino, Melbourne's plush gambling venue.

Back at Southgate Plaza, it is an easy walk south along St Kilda Road to the **Victorian Arts Centre** (☎ 03 9281 8000), comprised of three buildings, the Concert Hall, Theatres Building, and the National Gallery of Victoria. The centre is topped by an appallingly ugly tower. When it was first built in the 1860s, a promotional campaign had children donate a penny to be hammered into a copper dome; this was never accomplished, although thousands of children donated their pennies. The Concert Hall is said to have better acoustics than the Sydney Opera House (hence the saying that Australia has one great concert hall, the exterior in Sydney and the interior in Melbourne). The Theatres Building includes what is said to be one of the biggest stages in the world and also houses the enjoyable **Performing Arts Museum** (open weekdays 11.00–17.00, weekends 12.00–17.00), with changing exhibitions and audio-visual displays. If you can, try to see a theatrical performance here in the Theatres Building, to appreciate the ambience of the venue.

National Gallery of Victoria

The National Gallery of Victoria (☎ 03 9208 0202; open daily 10.00–17.00, Wed till 20.30), despite its impressive waterfall wall at the entrance, must be one of the ugliest exteriors of an art gallery. J.M. Freeland, writing in 1968 in *Architecture in Australia*, found Roy Grounds' solution to be particularly pleasing, expressing modernist tastes of that time when the building had just been completed. Its use of bluestone perhaps contributes to its penitentiary appearance. The interior spaces, however, are quite functional and effective in displaying the gallery's significant collections, considered the most comprehensive in Australia. At the time of writing, however, plans were afoot for a major new building project to transform the gallery completely. At this point no new exhibitions are planned until the year 2001, and only a small segment of the collections will be exhibited at the old museum building at the State Library of Victoria on Russell Street. (The museum, of course, is also closed until 2000, when the Carlton Gardens buildings are completed.) This description, then, will simply describe what these collections have to offer. The Great Hall includes a stunning stained-glass ceiling designed by prominent Melbourne artist Leonard French, who also created the stained-glass for Canberra's National Library.

The history of the National Gallery

The history of the National Gallery begins with the noble ambitions of Melbourne's early benefactors, who in the 1860s sought to provide the new colony with all the cultural attributes of home. Under the auspices of people such as Redmond Barry, funds were established to purchase in London a set of casts of classical sculpture and reproductions of great paintings; these were the first collections of the colony's 'National' Gallery, in emulation of the National Gallery in London. (When the National Gallery was opened in Canberra in 1982, Victoria chose to retain the 'national' title for their gallery as well.) In the first years, the gallery also established a school of art. By 1863, further funds were provided for the purchase of paintings—again in England. The resultant pieces, still in the collection, reflect popular tastes of the time for sentimental genre works such as *A Fern Gatherer* by R. Herdman and Thomas Faed's *Mitherless Bairn* (1855). By the 1870s, more ambitious British paintings, such as a duplicate of Alma-Tadema's *Vintage Festival* (1871) were acquired.

Under the directorship of artist Bernard Hall, who from 1891 became the gallery's driving force for 40 years, major acquisitions of a more substantial nature occurred. These included historical works of the British school, such as John Waterhouse's *Ulysses and the Siren* (1891), and graphic works by Rembrandt, Max Klinger and Whistler. The gallery's collection of Australian art started slowly and with some ambivalence; art by local artists began to trickle into the collection in the late 1860s. In 1868, a competition awarded Nicholas Chevalier's painting *The Buffalo Ranges* the honour of first Australian work in the gallery. Soon other Australian paintings entered the collection. The artists included the popular Swiss-born Melburnian Louis Buvelot (*Waterpool at Coleraine* [1869]) and Eugen von Guerard (*Valley of the Mitta Mitta* [1866], presented to the gallery in 1871). These came to be the basis for the collection's greatest strength.

Of special significance to the gallery, and the reason it was able to become the foremost art collection in the country, was the bequest in 1904 by Melbourne merchant Alfred Felton of a portion of his estate for the purchase of art works of quality. The story of those works accepted and rejected is a fascinating study in artistic politics and aesthetic tastes. The gallery acquired through the **Felton Bequest** such paintings as Pissarro's *Boulevard Montmartre* (1897), Van Dyck's *The Countess of Southampton* (1640) and Turner's watercolour *Oakhampton*. The Felton Bequest has subsequently allowed the acquisition of major European paintings, such as Tiepolo's *Banquet of Cleopatra* (1743–45), purchased in 1934 from the Soviet government and paid for in London with a suitcase full of hard cash; and in 1938 Cézanne's *La Route Montante*. Australian icons were also acquired through the Felton Bequest, including Tom Roberts' *Shearing the Rams* (1890), not purchased until 1932; and Frederick McCubbin's *The Pioneer* (1904), purchased in 1906. The bequest also enabled the development of major collections in Chinese and Indian art, an area of substantial recent growth.

Despite the gallery's early ambivalence concerning **Australian art**, the collections are now substantial. Along with Roberts's and McCubbin's famous works, the gallery also owns Arthur Streeton's famous *Purple Noon's Transparent Might*, purchased by Hall in 1896, and numerous works by lesser-known members of the Heidelberg School and the Melbourne art scene, such as Aby Alston, John Longstaff and Emmanuel Phillips Fox. It was only in the 1950s and 1960s that any serious collecting of early Australian art took place, with the acquisition of paintings by John Glover, William Westall, and Conrad Martens.

Of special interest for the viewer is the great selection of paintings by that group of Australian artists loosely associated with the **Angry Penguins** movement and the circle of art patrons John and Sunday Reed: Sidney Nolan (1917–95) (*Luna Park in the Moonlight* [1945] and one of the Ned Kelly series, *Sergeant Fitzpatrick and Kate Kelly* [1946]), Arthur Boyd (b. 1920) (the Chagall-like *Shearers Playing for a Bride* [1957] and *Burning Off*

[1958]), Albert Tucker (b. 1914) (*Night Image no. 28* [1946]), John Perceval (b. 1923) (an Expressionistic *Survival* [1942]) and the Russian-born Danila Vassilieff (1897–1958) (a sculptural piece, *Expressive Female Nude* [1950]). More contemporary holdings include exemplary works by Melbourne artists Roger Kemp (b. 1908) and John Brack (1920–99), as well as representative paintings by Fred Williams, Brett Whiteley, and Peter Booth.

Recently, the gallery has also assembled an excellent collection of Aboriginal art, with active acquisition programmes now keeping the holdings up to date and contemporary.

The gallery also established the country's first department of **photography**, which now contains its own collection and mounts important international exhibitions. A popular **restaurant** adorns the back of the gallery, looking on to a soothing enclosed garden.

Behind the gallery on Sturt Street is the headquarters of **Alcock's**, maker of fine billiard tables since 1853.

Billiards and snooker

Henry Upton Alcock came to Melbourne in the 1850s as a furniture-maker, and established himself as the colony's sole maker of billiard tables. Finding appropriate materials was at first difficult, with slate taken from prefabricated houses and wood in short supply. Alcock stimulated sales by arranging tours by British players, establishing the popularity of the game in Australia. The game of snooker was introduced into Australia in the 1880s by members of the Indian army, and was also taken up enthusiastically. The world's greatest champion billiards player, Walter Lindrum, was born into a billiards family in Melbourne. Master of the 'nursery cannon', Lindrum's prowess was so great that rules had to be changed to limit his phenomenal scores. At his death in 1960, Lindrum, who had retired in 1950, still held 47 world records. His residence at 26 Flinders Street is now the Lindrum Hotel which maintains a billiard room for its guests.

Back on ST KILDA ROAD, you can walk back into the **Central Business District** (CBD), crossing the Yarra River on Princes Bridge, a major monument dedicated in 1853 by Governor La Trobe to open up the southern regions for urban expansion; the present bridge is a replacement of the earlier timber bridge. St Kilda Road is still the major thoroughfare into the southern suburbs.

Walk 2 • Collins Street

Traditionally, a stroll down Collins Street began at Spring Street, as this walk does. If you are walking up from Flinders Street Station, to Collins Street from Swanston Street to Spring Street, reverse the order of buildings.

In the 1880s, the eastern end of Collins Street at Spring Street became known as 'the Paris end' because the planting of trees along the footpath and the construction of elegant office buildings provided an air of cosmopolitan European style. As early as the 1850s, the street became the site for medical practices and residences and subsequently the location for banks and financial institutions in smart and substantial buildings. This area was early known as Howitt's Corner, after Dr Godfrey Howitt and his family, who arrived in 1840 and immediately acquired considerable properties from Collins to Flinders Streets. Dr Howitt was not only a leading medical practitioner, but was famed for his work as a botanist and naturalist; he established magnificent gardens at his house here. By the 1860s, Howitt's properties had been completely subdivided and his family had moved to the suburb of Caulfield.

No. 1 Collins Street was an example of the neighbourhood's stately buildings in the late 19C. It was designed by Leonard Terry in 1870 as a town house for pastoralist William Campbell; the adjoining terrace houses were constructed in the 1880s. During the First World War Australia's war cabinet met there. The current building, constructed in 1984, incorporates elements of the original building in the façade. Across the street at no. 2 is **Alcaston House**, a 1920s example of a multi-storey apartment and office building in a Renaissance Revival style. Next door at nos 4–6 is **Anzac House**, built in 1938 of reinforced concrete as offices for the Returned Sailors and Soldiers Imperial League of Australia. **Portland House**, at 8–10 Collins Street, dating from 1872, was also designed as a town house and surgery as a wedding present for the daughter of Henry 'Money' Miller, a well-known land speculator, financier and politician who was instrumental in the founding of the Bank of Victoria and several insurance companies.

Melbourne Club, no. 36, was established in 1838, making it Victoria's oldest institution; the club purchased this land from Melbourne founder John Pascoe Fawkner. The present building was erected in 1858 by Leonard Terry, with later additions from the 1880s. In a Classical style, the building also features an enclosed rear garden known for its plane trees, one of the only private gardens left in the central city. **Melville House**, at nos 52–54, dates from 1881.

Across the street is **Collins Place**, a shopping plaza originally designed in the 1970s by American architect I.M. Pei. Its construction was plagued by industrial disputes; it was eventually completed in 1981 by E.A. Watts. Its vast interior plaza offers musical performances and other activities, and an arts and crafts market takes place here on Sundays.

A sterling example of the street's medical-commercial reputation is **Harley House** at numbers 71–73. Designed by Sydney Smith Ogg and Serpell in 1923 as a building for medical practitioners, it was owned by Dr Gengoult Smith, Lord Mayor of Melbourne from 1931 to 1934. The building's decorative motifs indicate the Art Deco interest in Greek, Roman and Egyptian elements.

The **Athenaeum Club**, nos 83–87, was originally founded in 1868 on the site of what is now the Athenaeum Theatre further down Collins Street. This building dates from 1929 and was designed by Cecil Ballantyne with an elaborate Spanish-style interior.

The **C.B.A. Bank** at 70 Collins Street was built in 1867 for surgeon John Wilkins, and operated as a surgery until 1911. Next door, nos 72–74 is one of the only surviving Georgian style town houses in the city, dating from 1855.

Nauru House, the 1972 precast concrete skyscraper further along on the north side of the street, represents the kind of modernist office block which began to appear all over town in the 1960s and 1970s, leading to the demolition of many old Melbourne buildings and the subsequent, if belated, establishment of active preservation organisations. It seems somehow appropriate that this building is named for a South Pacific island so rich in phosphate that most of the land has been mined to retrieve it.

The two surviving terrace houses at nos 86–88 were designed in 1873 as medical offices for Dr Robert Martin by architect James Gall; shops have occupied the ground floor since the 1920s. The building's pleasant proportions, with arched windows and ironwork balconies, is representative of the prevalent streetscape during the city's boom years. The Professional Chambers at nos 110–114 were designed by architect Beverley Ussher in 1908. The design represents a blending of Gothic-medieval elements with Australian 'Federation style' characteristic of office buildings for the period.

The rather theatrical façade of the **Austral Building**, at nos 115–119, is the product of architect Nahum Barnet, who was commissioned to design this commercial building by Alex McKinley & Co., publishers of *Melbourne Punch*. Described as 'Queen Anne Revival' in style and completed in 1891, the building was home to the Lyric Club, the Austral Dramatic Club, and the studio of the German-Australian photographer J.W. Lindt.

Evidence of the optimistic extravagances of 'marvellous Melbourne' is the Former Alexandra Club, at nos 133–39, commissioned by one of the city's most colourful characters, the surgeon Dr J.G. 'Champagne Jimmy' Beaney (see box). In 1887 Beaney held a competition for the design of his house and surgery; the result was a 23-room structure designed by William Salway and known as Cromwell House. In 1916, the building was purchased by the Alexandra Club, which added the top floor.

James George Beaney

James George Beaney (1826–91) arrived in Melbourne from England in 1852, and established himself as a high-profile surgeon, despite his unkempt and grossly bejewelled appearance and the suspicion by many that he was a charlatan; as the *Australian Encyclopedia* describes him, 'self-advertisement was an art in which he may be said to have specialised'. Even in the 1880s, Beaney disdained the germ theory, operating in filthy blood-soaked clothing while wearing diamond rings and prescribing champagne as anaesthetic. Even after his trial in 1866 for the performance of an 'illegal operation' resulting in a girl's death, Beaney somehow retained his reputation and died a wealthy man, bequeathing £3900 to the medical school.

His gravesite in Melbourne's General Cemetery is marked by an enormous monument.

Uniting Church (formerly the Independent Church), on the northeast corner of COLLINS and RUSSELL STREETS, is the site of Melbourne's earliest permanent church. The present building, with its campanile tower and unusual polychrome brick, was designed by Reed & Barnes in 1866 for the Independent Congregational Church. The interior, in the shape of an amphitheatre, includes superb stained-glass windows.

Across Russell Street from the Independent Church is **Scots Church**. This church was built in the 1870s as a rather austere Gothic Revival structure by Joseph Reed. Parishioners made rich by gold eventually donated more elaborate interior decorations. It is associated with many famous churchmen, including the educationist and temperance leader Reverend James Forbes, who was instrumental in the founding of Melbourne's Scotch College, one of the country's greatest public schools. The famous opera singer Nellie Melba and David Mitchell both sang in the church choir. The adjoining Assembly Hall was added in 1914; designed by H.H. Kemp, it blends well with the original church. The grounds are defined by the fountain which was donated by Georges Ltd in 1981, and designed by the architect Peter Staughton.

Having gained an awareness of the American penchant for skyscrapers, the architects of the offices of the **Temperance and Life Assurance Society** across the street from the Scots Church (now the T & G Buildings) designed in 1928 a modified version of Chicago-style high-rise buildings. In 1930, the *Herald* newspaper voted it 'Melbourne's most beautiful building'. The entrance hall includes a mural painted by M. Napier Waller.

The **Former Auditorium Building**, nos 167–173, has had a colourful past, belying its current incarnation as yet another shopping complex. Designed in 1913 by Nahum Barnet for a theatrical firm, it was redesigned as a cinema in the 1930s by C.N. Hollinshed.

Another Barnet building was erected in 1884 at nos 162–68 as a warehouse for entrepreneur Benjamin Fink. In 1888 it was converted to **Georges Store** by Albert Purchas; for years it was the most exclusive retail shop in Melbourne. Sadly, Georges Store closed in 1995. In 1998, it reopened, completely redesigned by British designer Terence Conran, with an entirely different style of product and a glitzier kind of fashionable clientele.

The **Baptist Church** on the north side of Collins Street at nos 170–174 is the oldest Baptist church in Victoria. The original brick building was erected in 1854; the present façade, with its beautiful Corinthian portico, was added in 1861–62 by Reed & Barnes when the church was expanded to seat 1000 people. The colony's first Baptist minister, Reverend John Ham, arrived in 1842 with his three sons; his son Thomas engraved the brass plate that served as this building's foundation stone. Ham's engravings of Melbourne views are important historical documents and collector's items today.

Further along, the **Athenaeum Theatre** at 184–92 Collins Street was formerly the Mechanics' Institute. As in all colonial towns, the Mechanics' Institute was an important social and educational centre in the early days of settlement; its building was on this site as early as 1840. The present structure dates from the 1880s, and includes a theatre with verandah completed in 1924. The classical façade includes a statue of Athena.

Across the street, the **Regent Theatre** (bookings through Ticketek, ☎ 132 849) was designed by Cedric H. Ballantyne for Thring's Hoyts Theatres, and was meant to rival the State Theatre on Flinders Street. After a fire in 1947, the interior was remodelled as a true Hollywood-style cinema, which along with the adjacent Plaza Theatre could seat more than 3000. In 1969, the theatre fell into disrepair and stood derelict for 27 years, before it was lovingly and expensively ($35 million) restored in 1996. It is now the city's main venue for musical theatre and other productions.

On the corner of Swanston and Collins Streets is the **MELBOURNE CITY SQUARE**, an attempt at an urban plaza that had long been a consideration among

Melbourne's town planners. Work on the present site began in 1961, and by 1968 acquisition of this site saw the demolition of the Queen Victoria Buildings although an approved design for the square was not in place until 1976. The winning firm was Denton Corker Marshall, with a design incorporating waterfalls, shops and a pedestrian plaza. A famous statue commemorating the explorers Burke and Wills (see box), designed in 1865 by Charles Sumner, was moved from Collins and Russell Streets to the square. This original conception never functioned successfully, the pedestrian intentions hampered by the fact that the city trams continued to intersect the area, and in 1989 the square was redesigned to mixed reviews. Public events including street theatre and afternoon concerts are presented here amid the clamour of inner-city traffic and congestion.

Burke and Wills

The Burke and Wills Expedition is, like Gallipoli, another example of a disastrous event that has become an important part of Australian lore. In 1860, the Royal Society of Victoria organised an expedition to explore unknown Central Australia to the Gulf of Carpentaria and back. Chosen to lead the expedition was Robert O'Hara Burke (1821–61), a temperamental Irishman who had served as a policeman on the Victorian goldfields. Selected as astronomer and surveyor of the expedition was William John Wills (1834–61).

Leaving in August 1860 amidst great fanfare with camels and several other men, including the German naturalist and artist Ludwig Becker (c 1808–61), the group headed north, well equipped but with little knowledge of the bush. Through Burke's impetuousness, incompetent blunders, and inability to learn survival skills from the Aborigines encountered, both he and Wills perished near Cooper Creek in June 1861, trying to return after reaching the mouth of Flinders River. Becker had already perished south of Cooper Creek in April of that year; his illustrated journals of the ill-fated trip survived, and provide fascinating images of the hardships encountered. One member of the expedition, King, survived by seeking aid from the Aborigines. Despite the complete failure of the explorers and the fact that it was the rescue parties sent to find them that actually accomplished the task of traversing the region, Burke and Wills were championed as heroes, with statues and commemorative artworks produced throughout the colony. Tim Bonyhady's book *Burke & Wills: from Melbourne to Myth* (1991) analyses the endurance of the Burke and Wills iconography in the Australian national psyche.

St Paul's Cathedral, on the corner of FLINDERS and SWANSTON STREETS, is considered Melbourne's most significant ecclesiastical structure. It was designed by William Butterfield and building commenced in 1880. On this site the first church service in Melbourne was held in 1836. As with so many other public projects in Australia, the architect had great difficulties with the authorities concerning his choice of materials and the extent of his supervision of the building. After much haggling over choice of stone and certain design aspects, Butterfield resigned, and the work was completed by J. Reed in 1891. While still Gothic in style, the original plans were substantially altered. The interior retains the best of Revival ornamentation and colouring. The church spires were not completed until 1931. Beside St Paul's is a statue commemorating Matthew Flinders (see p 116).

Melbourne Town Hall, 90–130 Swanston Street, is another design of the firm of Reed & Barnes. Built between 1867 and 1870, its foundation stone was laid by Prince Alfred, Duke of Edinburgh, during his royal visit. The portico dates from 1887. The clock tower, named after Prince Alfred, was added in 1869. The main hall includes interesting murals, chandeliers, and an impressive organ.

The **Westpac Bank** on the southwest corner of Collins and Swanston Streets was originally the Manchester Unity Building. Designed by Marcus Barlow in a 'Commercial Gothic' style in 1932, it was at the time the tallest building in Melbourne, and included the city's first escalator and a ventilation system using tons of ice. Manchester Unity was an Order of Odd Fellows organisation established in Melbourne in 1840 by Dr Augustus Greeves, a pioneer politician instrumental in the separation of Victoria from New South Wales and founder of the Mechanics' Institute.

Capitol House, 109–117 Swanston Street, is one of the only remaining examples in Melbourne of the work of American architect Walter Burley Griffin; the building vaguely imitates a Chicago-style commercial building. The Capitol Theatre inside the building contains remnants of Griffin's auditorium design, including a crystalline ceiling created by his wife Marion Mahony.

At 241–245 COLLINS STREET, the **Fourth Victorian Building Society** building has one of the city's only examples of an Art Nouveau façade. Designed in 1911 by Robert Haddon, the façade incorporates terracotta decorations with Aztec and Egyptian motifs.

Next door is **Newspaper House** (now Tasmanian Tourist Bureau), which was occupied from the 1930s by the *Herald* and *Weekly Times*. At that time, the publishers conducted an architectural competition for renovation of the existing building; the winners were Stephenson and Meldrum, who created an interior around a glass mosaic by Napier Waller based on the newspaper's motto 'I'll put a girdle around the earth.'

Next to Newspaper House, a small walkway leads one block south to Flinders Lane, where two buildings of unusual design are worth seeing. **Royston House**, 247–51 FLINDERS LANE, is the only remnant of a massive commercial warehouse that originally extended to Flinders Street. It was built in 1898 by Sydney architects Sulman & Power and represents the kind of large warehouses that surrounded this area at the turn of the century.

Majorca Building, 258–60 Flinders Lane, designed by Harry Norris in 1928, is so called because of its coloured terracotta façade, meant to be reminiscent of the Spanish island's decor. The façade, with its delicate pilasters and arches at the cornice placed in front of recessed windows, is reminiscent of Louis Sullivan's Chicago commercial buildings.

Walk back through Centre Place to Collins Street. **Block Arcade**, 282–4 COLLINS STREET and 96–102 ELIZABETH STREET, is Melbourne's earliest fashionable shopping mall. In the 1880s and 1890s, all of fashionable Melbourne knew that the place to be seen was 'the Block'. Between 2.30 and 4.30 pm, one would 'do the Block', a promenade around Elizabeth and Collins Streets (the phrase and the practice may have been in existence as early as the 1850s). At the centre of this promenade, architect David Askew, with the backing of financier B.J. Fink, built the Block Arcade in the early 1890s, a six-storey L-shaped commercial building in a style based loosely on Milan's Galleria Vittoria. It is still one of Melbourne's most chic shopping complexes.

In colonial days, Elizabeth Street was known locally as River Townend, as a small creek ran along this roadway down to the Yarra River; thus the early problems with flooding. Even today basements on this street can be flooded in torrential weather.

333 Collins Street dates originally from 1891 to a design chosen in competition by the architects Lloyd Tayler and Alfred Dunn. A new façade was added in 1939 which incorporated the original foyer and its great domed interior; renovation in 1990 retained this last feature, which was considered the most splendid Victorian-era interior in the city.

Former Mercantile Bank, nos 345–349, was designed by William Salway in 1888 in an elegantly flamboyant style representing the rise of the 'land banks' during the great boom of the 1880s; by 1892, the bank had been liquidated.

ANZ Bank Ltd, formerly the **English, Scottish and Australian Bank** (386–388 on the corner of Collins and Queen Streets) was built in 1883 by the English-born architect William Wardell. In a style reminiscent of the Doges Palace in Venice, the three-storey bank is now combined with the **Stock Exchange**, a six-storey structure designed by William Pitt in 1888. They remained separate buildings until the 1920s when they were extended and joined. Historically, the Stock Exchange is associated with B.J. Fink, its founder and great boom speculator, while the 'Gothic Bank' was the inspiration of its General Manager, Sir George Verdon, well-known as a connoisseur of the arts. The interior of the bank is well worth a visit, to inspect the carefully restored ceiling stencils and Gothicised pillars. This complex houses (at 380 Collins Street) the **ANZ Banking Museum** (☎ 03 9662 2688; open weekdays 09.30–16.30). The museum depicts the history of Australian banking and financial services.

On the opposite corner is the **ANZ Bank Building**, an example of standard commercial style, with storeys added between the 1870s and 1920s. On this site the first Methodist church was established; by 1857, this land had become so valuable for commercial ventures, that the church sold it for a handsome sum and built several churches with the proceeds.

A truly fanciful structure, an example of 19C historicist symbolism, is the former **Melbourne Safe Deposit Building** around the corner from the 'Gothic Bank' on Queen Street; it is now part of the large bank complex. Designed in 1890 by William Pitt, its neo-Gothic façade seems to mimic an elaborate storage chest of the era, and even appears to be slightly crooked.

Another Gothic Revival office building is down Collins Street at nos 389–90; now called the A.C. Goode House, it was originally built for an insurance company in 1891 by Adelaide architects Wright Reed and Beaver; the vestibule is in original form with elegant mouldings and freestone. The former AMP Building, nos 419–29, is an example of a steel-framed construction, clad in a Renaissance Revival style of freestone and granite; built in 1929, it won a medal for 'street architecture' in 1932. At this time, Melbourne still imposed a 132-foot (20m) height limit to all buildings, a mandate maintained until the 1960s.

Midway through this block of Collins Street is a small lane called **BANK PLACE**, accessible on Collins Street by steps; street entry is on Little Collins Street. You will find two buildings of historical interest here. The **Mitre Tavern** has been a popular meeting place for artists and businessmen since it was built in 1868; its present medieval decor dates from the 1920s. Further along is the **Savage Club**, a portion of a large townhouse built in 1884 for Australia's only baronet, Sir William Clarke. The club has owned its structure since 1923, altering its interior in 1927; the dining room includes giant palm fans for cooling.

Continue on to **LITTLE COLLINS STREET**; on the corner of Bank Place is **Stalbridge Chambers**, one of the only examples in the city of a multi-storeyed building built in the Victorian period. Designed in 1895 by architect David Askew, it curves around the street corner, defining the entire block in the best modernist fashion. Continue west on Little Collins Street to WILLIAMS STREET; on the corner is the **Australian Club**, the most elegant of the Victorian clubs in Australia. It was built in three stages between 1879 and 1893; the principal architect was Lloyd Tayler. The interior still maintains a sense of Victorian opulence.

Continue south to William Street nos 90–98, **Scottish House**. Erected in 1907 as the headquarters of the shipping firm McIlwraith McEachern Ltd, the name comes from the Scottish Line of Sailing Ships founded by this firm in 1875. One of the founders, Malcolm McEachern, was Mayor of Melbourne, as well as Lord Mayor in 1903–04.

Squeezed next door to Scottish House is the six-storey **Queensland Building**, a delightfully whimsical structure with an ornate façade incorporating Australian motifs, as became fashionable in the 1910s.

At the corner of Collins and Williams Streets are a number of noteworthy buildings. At the southeast corner is **National Mutual Plaza**, which was originally the site of Western Market, Melbourne's first market laid out by Robert Hoddle in 1837. In the 1860s, a covered market was constructed of bluestone with colonnades. This remained until 1960, when it was demolished for the construction of the present building and plaza. In the forecourt of the building are statues in honour of Melbourne's two founders, John Batman and John Pascoe Fawkner.

The **Olderfleet Building** at 477 Collins Street consists of three Gothic façades of what was originally a complex extending to Flinders Lane. It was designed by William Pitt in 1888 for businessman Patrick McCaughlan; the brick façade is decorated with tiled surfaces and festooned with arches, half columns, and pinnacles and topped with the ever-popular clock tower. It was on this site that Peter Bodecin's cottage served as the first gathering place for Catholic settlers at the time of settlement.

On the southwest corner of William and Collins Streets, where the Capita Centre now stands, John Batman built what is believed to be the first brick house in the settlement in 1837. When Governor La Trobe arrived in 1839, he was formally greeted here, during a land sale interrupted by the Collector of Customs to read La Trobe's Commission. The governor then adjourned to Fawkner's Hotel at Market and Collins Streets.

At 497 Collins Street is the **Rialto Building**, built in 1890 as one of the last great buildings of the 'Marvellous Melbourne' boom. In profuse Venetian Gothic, with gargoyles and arches in polychrome brickwork designed by William

Pitt, it once housed the offices of T. Fink and his Wool Exchange, one of the most prominent of the boomers. It has now been transformed into a luxury hotel, **Le Meridien** (☎ 03 9620 9111/1800 331 330). Next door, facing Flinders Lane, is **Rialto Towers** (☎ 03 9629 8222; open weekdays 11.00–23.30, weekends 10.00–23.30), touted as one of the tallest building in the Southern hemisphere. It was built in the mid-1980s and has the requisite observation deck on the 55th level that gives a view of Melbourne and Port Phillip Bay. Across Collins Street on the northwest corner of King Street is the present-day *Stock Exchange*, open to the public on weekdays (☎ 03 9617 8611), with a market display centre, bookshop and investor centre.

Walk 3 · Bourke Street and Chinatown

The top end of **Bourke Street** is dominated by the **Parliament House**, which sits on a rise which is at this point called either Bourke Hill or Eastern Hill (see Eastern Hill walk, p 313). The street itself has retained some of its earlier residential character, with most buildings being only two or three storeys high.

This area was also the centre of the city's theatre life, with many of the most prominent venues nearby. One of the most beloved of the Spring Street theatres is **Princess Theatre** on the north side of Bourke Street. While a theatre has been on this spot since the 1850s, the present structure dates from 1887, when it was redesigned by William Pitt to celebrate Queen Victoria's Jubilee. He transformed it into the largest theatre in the country, and added such extravagant touches as a roof that could be opened on warm nights. The building's style could be called Renaissance; its imaginative figures and decorations symbolising the arts certainly emphasise its historicist leanings. It backs on to the former Palace Theatre on Bourke Street; the two were at one time managed by the same firm and were joined by a covered walk. When the Princess was remodelled in the 1920s by Henry White, so was the Palace. Its most recent refurbishment brought the theatre up to standard for live, modern performances. One of the first was *Phantom of the Opera* which ran for two years after opening here in 1990. Next door to the Palace is the Metro Theatre, quite a contrast with its Art Deco façade.

Facing Parliament House on Spring Street between Collins and Bourke Streets is the **Windsor Hotel**, Melbourne's most historic hotel; it is locally called 'the Windsor' (☎ 03 9633 6000). Designed by Charles Webb and built in 1883 as the Grand Hotel, it was a temperance hotel from 1886 until 1920. Upon obtaining its licence, it was renamed the Windsor. Situated near the theatre district, it has been the favoured hotel of visiting celebrities such as the Oliviers in 1948, Robert Helpmann, Katherine Hepburn, Robert Morley and Rudolf Nureyev. In 1961, the hotel was extended to the corner, replacing the famous White Hart Inn, a well-known theatrical haunt. Chrysopher Spicer has written a book chronicling the hotel's history, *Duchess: The Story of The Windsor* (1993).

On the corner of Spring and Bourke Streets is the **Imperial Hotel**, dating back to the 1850s, taking the corner from an early theatre 'Salle de Valentino'. The hotel began trade in 1864, when the upper storeys were added to the ground floor section: it still operates as a pub-style of hotel. A sign of the times is the presence across the street of the *Hard Rock Cafe*.

Next to the Hard Rock Cafe is the **Society Restaurant**, nos 23–29 Bourke Street, which has been a restaurant, first known as the Italian Society, since

1910. In the 1950s and 1960s it was a popular meeting place for Melbourne's literary set, and was the venue for the raucous annual dinners of the Fellowship of Australian Writers.

Less boisterous activities took place at the neighbouring shop at nos 35–37. Built in the 1870s as a glass and china shop, it served as a local post office until 1969. Its façade is one of the only remaining traditional shopfronts in the city.

Crossley's Building, across the street at nos 54–62, is one of Melbourne's oldest surviving buildings, erected in 1848 by William Crossley as a butcher shop and slaughter yard, before the goldrush boom. The artist Eugen von Guerard had a studio here in 1857–58.

At 65–73 Bourke Street is the **Salvation Army Citadel**, headquarters in Australia for the organisation. The building originally housed the YMCA in the early 1890s, but was purchased by the Salvation Army in 1895. Described as 'decorative Boom Style' in design, the building saw the production in 1900 of *Soldier of the Cross*, widely believed to be the first full-length motion picture in the world.

Florentino Restaurant, at 78–82 Bourke Street (☎ 03 9662 1811), encompasses remnants of buildings dating from 1853 to 1860. From 1900 to 1928, it housed a wine shop, which in that year became Cafe Florentino, one of the city's first 'cosmopolitan' restaurants. The upstairs dining room has wall murals painted by Napier Waller and his students in 1934. As described in *The Age's Good Food Guide 1999*, 'Influence, power and achievement are the subtext of this most traditional of restaurants. Everything suggests permanence...'

Across the street, on the southwest corner is the **Southern Cross Hotel**. It was on this site that the Eastern Market was established as the city's vegetable market in 1859. It was in operation until the 1950s; the present hotel was built in 1962.

Chinatown

One block north from here is LITTLE BOURKE STREET; from here to Swanston Street is Melbourne's **Chinatown**.

Melbourne's Chinatown became the most important locus for Chinese culture and protection during the gold rush years. Businesses and restaurants, as well as residences, shot up, most of them in buildings of Victorian, not Chinese, design. The warehouse structure at 112–114 Little Bourke Street is one of the most substantial of these buildings, built in 1888 for Lowe Kong Meng, a wealthy merchant and leader of the community. On the many side alleys warehouses and small businesses appeared, such as those at 15–17 Celestial Lane, which was built as lodgings in 1883; next door is housing constructed by the See-Yup Society, a fraternal benevolent association. One of the only early restaurant buildings to survive, from 1891, is the former Wing Ching Restaurant, 11 Heffernan Lane; while its name changed over the years, it remained as a restaurant.

Nam Poon Soon Chinese Club, at 200–202 Little Bourke Street, is in the heart of Chinatown. This two-storey structure dates from 1861 and is believed to have been designed by Peter Kerr for another benevolent society, the **Sam-Yup Society**, which supported migrants from the districts of Nanhai, Punyu and Shute. It has been a significant centre for Chinese-Australian life since its erection.

At nos 107–109 the **Chinese National Club** was established in 1903, in a building designed by Nahum Barnet for the merchant C.H. Cheong. It was this building that Walter Burley Griffin redesigned in the 1920s; much of his façade was for some reason removed in 1978.

Another important part of Chinese life in Australia centred on the mission churches, such as the **Methodist Mission Church**, no. 196, the oldest of these churches, opened in 1872 and designed by Crouch and Wilson in an incongruous Gothic style. An Anglican training centre and hall was commissioned by missionary Cheong Cheok Hong at 108–110 and built by Charles Webb in 1894. After this church was given to the Church Missionary Association in 1897, Cheong Cheok Hong built the Church of England Mission at 119–125, another Nahum Barnet design.

A fascinating and informative description of the Chinese contribution to Australian society is available at the **Museum of Chinese Australian History** (☎ 03 9662 2888; open Sun–Fri, 10.00–16.30, Sat 12.00–17.00), opened in 1985 at 22–24 Cohen Place in an 1890s warehouse building. The entrance is through a replica of the Ling Xing Gate which faced the Heaven Palace in Nanjing. Exhibitions include the Dai Loong dragon used in New Year's festivities, and an excellent audio-visual presentation chronicling Chinese life in Australia. Tours of Chinatown are available through the museum.

Little Bourke Street still bustles with life, food shops and restaurants, bookstores and shops of many Asian varieties. Dining in one of Chinatown's many authentic restaurants is an essential Melbourne experience.

Chinese immigration

Chinese immigrants first entered Australia in the 1840s, when the end of convict transportation led to a lack of cheap labour and employers looked to China as a new source. This practice ended when gold was discovered, as the Chinese flocked to the fields. In 1854, there were 2300 Chinese in Victoria; by 1858, that number had risen to 42,000. Their presence almost immediately led to racial hostilities with other miners, and by 1855 restrictions on Chinese immigration were enacted. In every goldfield town, the Chinese presence was significant. In some places, such as Ballarat's Sovereign Hill and Bendigo's Chinese Museum, their contribution is positively commemorated; in others, their presence is indicated only in the graveyards and perhaps through descendants who still run Chinese restaurants in these country towns.

Back on **BOURKE STREET**, the blocks from Exhibition Street to the General Post Office on Elizabeth Street are dominated by modern cinema houses and, from Swanston to Elizabeth Streets, a pedestrian mall. Here are the major department stores, **David Jones** and, that very Melbourne establishment, **Myers** (see box).

The pedestrian mall followed years of debate about the desirability of such a mall in the inner city; it was officially opened by the Prince and Princess of Wales in 1983. Next to the Myer Building is another Melbourne institution, the **Buckley and Nunn Menswear Store**; the building, designed by Bates, Smart & McCutcheon, won the Royal Victorian Institute of Architects Street Architecture Medal in 1934. The company's name has entered Australian folk etymology as the origin of the term 'haven't got Buckley's'; the first usage was as 'you have two chances: Buckley's and none (Nunn)'.

Myers

The Myers store was founded by Sidney Baerski Myer (1878–1934), a Polish immigrant who arrived in Australia in 1897. He first established businesses in Bendigo and Ballarat, and then moved to this site in the 1920s, constructing a 'Cathedral of Commerce' after acquiring several other companies. By 1928 the business was enormous, employing in the 1930s some 5000 workers, and providing them with rest homes and holidays at the seaside. At Sidney Myer's death in 1934, his will was valued at £920,000. The Myer family continued his charitable activities, providing unemployment relief during the Depression, promotion of the Melbourne Symphony Orchestra, and contributions to the University of Melbourne (the Chair of Commerce was named in honour of Sidney Myer). The Myer name continues to be associated with business and philanthropy throughout Australia. This main store of the Myer empire is part of Melbourne life; everyone awaits Myer's Christmas windows, and the best buskers are located outside its doors.

Royal Arcade, 331–337 Bourke Street to Little Collins Street, was erected in 1869 and designed by Charles Webb in Classical style. The arcade contains the seven-foot wooden sculptures of the mythological giants Gog and Magog who serve as strikers of the giant clock, designed by Mortimer Godfrey in 1870. It is the oldest arcade in Melbourne. The rest of the mall block of Bourke Street contains some delightful commercial structures from the early 1900s, including, at no 310, an Art Deco gem with a decorative glass façade, and at 315, a little gothicised pink skyscraper.

At the corner of Bourke and Elizabeth Streets is the **General Post Office**. A post office was on this site from 1841. The present structure was begun in 1859, and was not completed until 1909; during its construction Bourke Street became the commercial centre of the city, and it served as a focal point for Melbourne activities. Evidence of its significance to the colony was its final cost of £140,000. When its main structure was completed in 1867, all of Melbourne turned out to inspect this most important building. In the early days, the arrival of mail from England was an enormous event, and flags were flown from the GPO to announce the sighting of the mail boat; the post office then became a hive of activity, with more than 10 tons of mail sorted. Designed by A.E. Johnson, this building incorporates ideas from as many as 65 architects. An architectural heritage guide gives the following description of its style: 'It is the finest example in Victoria of an arcuated structure in the Classical style with a superimposed trabeated system of Doric, Ionic, and Corinthian pilasters rising up the façade.' In any case, the building demonstrates the central role the post office played in the civic life of 19C Melbourne. Available inside is a *History of Postal Services in Victoria*, a quite substantial publication.

Early skyscrapers

On the southwest and southeast corners of WILLIAM and BOURKE STREETS are two contemporary buildings: the Australian Mutual Provident Building and BHP House. When erected in the 1970s, they caused great controversy for their height (certainly above the traditional 132 feet prescribed for earlier Melbourne buildings) and for their modernist functionalism which contrasted with the rest of the streetscape. Both were designed in association with the American firm Skidmore Owings and Merrill: the epitome of a corporate architectural group. This block was also the original site of St James Cathedral, which had been moved in 1913; somehow these new skyscrapers seemed a sacrilegious assault on such hallowed ground. The award to the BHP House of an architectural medal in 1975 fanned the flames of public outrage. The Menzies Hotel, an important early focal point for Melbourne's social life, stood on this spot until it was demolished for this building. Anthony Trollope, when visiting Australia in the 1870s, stayed at the Menzies and praised its hospitality.

Several other historically significant buildings were lost to these skyscrapers and other building projects in the 1970s. At no. 472 Bourke Street was the city's first public hospital, on the site of Fawkner's brick residence. It remained in operation until 1848, when Queen Victoria Hospital was opened. Across the street was the first Synagogue, established in 1847 and furnished through the donations of the community. In 1852, James Webb built a permanent structure here. To the right of the synagogue was St Patrick's Hall, purchased by the St Patrick's Society (with the proceeds from the Queen's Theatre performance, described below, that caused Irish patriotic riots). It was the setting for a grand ball to celebrate separation from New South Wales in 1851, and also the location for the first meeting of the state's legislative council.

If one compares these contemporary buildings to the **Abrahams Building** down Bourke Street, the reason for outrage about the modern skyscrapers is apparent. This extravagant Queen Anne-style warehouse and office building, built in 1901 by architect Charles D'Ebro, epitomises the colourful Victorianism that was characteristic of 19C Melbourne architecture.

Further along, past King Street, is **St Augustine's** Roman Catholic church, a Gothic design in bluestone designed by T.A. Kelly and built by Reid and Stewart in 1869–70 to replace a timber church which was on the site from 1853. The hall used to house St Augustine's School, a leading parochial institution in the early 20C. The church has traditionally been the mission church for seamen; the Stella Maris Seafarers Centre is located behind the church.

On the same side of the street, the **Tramways Building** was designed in 1891 by Twentyman & Askew for the offices of the Melbourne Tramway & Omnibus Co. The company itself was founded in 1868 by an American businessman, F.B. Clapp, who operated horse-drawn cabs to the suburbs. He convinced the government to install a cable tramway system, considered the largest in the world. Clapp ran the company as a monopoly until 1916.

Robert Hoddle, Melbourne's first surveyor

The southeast corner of Bourke and Spencer Streets (where the Savoy Tavern is today) was purchased in 1840 by Robert Hoddle, Surveyor-General of central Melbourne. He established a home here with a garden of native plants. Along with laying out the city's streets, Hoddle also served as the colony's first land auctioneer, in payment for which he was given the block of land now occupied by the State Bank Centre on the southwest corner of Bourke and Elizabeth Streets.

Hoddle's Corner, extending from Bourke to Little Collins Street along Spencer Street, was early known as **Government Block**, as at the Little Collins Street intersection, the first police magistrate William Lonsdale built his cottage in 1836 and erected barracks for soldiers and policemen. Further barracks were erected in the 1850s between Little Collins and Collins Streets; in the middle of this block towards King Street, the first permanent gaol was established in 1839. The execution ground was located at Melbourne Gaol, near the present site of the Royal Melbourne Institute of Technology.

The area on SPENCER STREET near Collins Street and Flinders Lane, is the site of the original **Batman's Hill** (now levelled and indistinguishable). The hill was a source of great contention between rivals Batman and Fawkner. Fawkner spent all his life fighting Batman's claim as founder of the settlement and eventually settled elsewhere. Batman's Cottage was no doubt a humble affair, although it is known to have had a chimney constructed by William Buckley, the famous escaped convict who had lived with the Aborigines for 20 years when discovered. When Batman died, having never legally acquired the hill, his family were evicted from the farm.

Walk 4 • Upper Business District

The block between Lonsdale and Little Bourke Streets at **WILLIAM STREET** houses the **Law Courts** and **Supreme Court Library**, built 1874–84 by Smith & Johnson and J.J. Clark & P. Kerr of the Public Works Department around a courtyard. With its bluestone footings, Tasmanian freestone façade, and Doric pilasters, these courts are among the finest public buildings in Australia. The Library on William Street side includes a dome modelled on one in the Four Courts of Dublin, a reminder of the Dublin men prominent in the early legal life of Melbourne. The interior includes domed rotundas at each corner of the building, each one fenced by cast-iron balustrades. The courts are still open to the public when in session.

North on William Street to LITTLE LONSDALE STREET is the site of the former Royal Mint, now the **Royal Historical Society** of Victoria (☎ 03 9670 1219). In 1854, an Exhibition Building modelled on the Crystal Palace was built here, but quickly fell into disrepair. In the early 1870s, the Mint was erected to a design by J.J. Clark, in a style more reminiscent of a private mansion than a Public Works structure. It operated as a mint until 1968. The royal coat of arms still adorns the front iron gates.

One block east is **300 Queen Street**, now the Australian Institute of Family Studies, built as the residence of John Thomas Smith, early businessman, long-standing mayor of Melbourne and member of the State Legislature 1859 and 1879. In 1845, Smith was successful enough as a publican to build the colony's first real theatre, Queen's Theatre, on the southwest corner of Queen and Little Bourke Streets, next to his hotel. The theatre saw a riot in 1846 between Orangemen and Southern Irish at a St Patrick's Day benefit, and another in 1855. The Irish tragedian Gustavus Brooke, the first well-known British actor to visit the continent, performed *Othello* here to packed houses. Smith's success soon allowed him to build this Georgian townhouse as his residence. Built between 1849 and 1856, to a design by Charles Laing, a third storey was added 1858 by David Ross. In the late 1850s, it was leased as a gold store by the state government, and it was subsequently used for other government functions; at one point it was a jam factory, then served as a boarding house and nurses' home for the nearby Queen Victoria Hospital.

Walk north to Latrobe Street and west to William Street; here is the entrance to **Flagstaff Gardens**. Located to the southwest of Queen Victoria Markets, the gardens stand on the site of the town's original burial grounds. The first burial here was a child, James Goodman, in 1836. Formerly a prominent hill, in 1840 it was chosen as the location for a signal station, hence the name flagstaff. It became the most popular meeting place for early settlers, as they could gain news of incoming ships and the arrival of mail. From here, one could see the Williamstown Time Ball Tower; the ball dropped every day at 1 pm for ships to set their chronometers. In the middle of the gardens is the Pioneers' Monument, commemorating the resting place of the earliest settlers.

On the King Street side of Flagstaff Gardens, at BATMAN STREET, is **St James Cathedral**. Built in 1842–51 on a site at the corner of Collins and William Streets, it was for many years the most prominent landmark in the city. It was moved, stone by stone, to its present location in 1913. Designed by Melbourne's first architect, the London-born Robert Russell, its foundation stone was laid by Governor Charles La Trobe in 1839. As Melbourne's oldest surviving building the cathedral is closely associated with its founding families: John Batman donated £50 for its erection, and William Lonsdale, first Police Magistrate of the district and a lay preacher himself, was instrumental in its construction. It remains as Russell's only surviving work, although disagreements during construction led to his dismissal in 1841. Upon its opening in 1842, it was far from complete, with later stages being built by Charles Laing. Construction is of sandstone, both locally quarried and imported from Tasmania.

The tower still contains the original bells, which were cast in London and hung in 1853, when the building was consecrated as a cathedral. They are rung by hand during Sunday services and practice is on Friday evenings at 19.30. The interior includes an 800-year-old baptismal font, brought from **St Katherine's Abbey** in London, a church demolished in 1837. Other features include an elaborate Bishop's Throne and solid walnut pulpit; the windows are those originally installed.

Queen Victoria Markets

Exit Flagstaff Park at William Street, where it turns into Peel Street at the entrance to the **Queen Victoria Markets** (☎ 03 9320 5822; open Tues and Thurs 06.00–14.00, Fri 06.00–18.00, Sat 06.00–15.00, Sun 09.00–16.00). This is a world-class inner-city open market, wonderful to visit on Saturday morning, with hawkers, buskers, divine sausage sandwiches, and an invigorating cosmopolitan atmosphere. Spanning two city blocks, the market is now listed by the National Trust, not only because of its historical buildings, but for the significant place it has held in the hearts of Victorians for more than 100 years.

Locally the area is described as the Upper and Lower Markets, with the Lower Market being the oldest. In 1857, area market gardeners petitioned Parliament for a permanent vegetable market to be set up at the corner of Swanston and Victoria Streets; this area was used mainly as an animal market until 1867, when it reverted to fruit and vegetables. Eventually the markets expanded and areas for produce, meat, dairy and retail goods were specifically delineated in the 1880s, when the present buildings were erected, with their arched halls and appropriately decorated façades.

Now the markets include stalls for leather goods, clothing, and housewares. One section of the markets between Peel and Queen Streets at Victoria Street was the site of the town's original cemetery; many of the graves were removed and reinterred at the Fawkner Cemetery in Coburg, where some of their 'red-gum' headstones can still be seen, along with a memorial to John Batman, who was believed to have been buried in the original cemetery. As one of the last inner-city open markets, Queen Victoria is a must for any Melbourne visitor.

From the markets return towards the city via Elizabeth Street. At LATROBE STREET, turn east (left) to enter Melbourne's glitziest new shopping mall, **Melbourne Central** (300 Lonsdale Street; ☎ 03 9665 0000; open daily). Along with the most upscale shops in town, the complex includes a Marionette clock, Butterfly Vivarium, and, most astonishingly, a glass cone over the historic Shot Tower. **Coop's Shot Tower**, built in 1889–90, is one of two surviving shot towers in Australia (the other is outside Hobart). It retains much of the original shot-making equipment.

Around the corner on ELIZABETH and LITTLE LONSDALE STREETS is **St Francis's Church** (☎ 03 9663 1425). The foundation stone for this church was laid in 1841 and dedicated in 1845, making it one of the earliest churches built in Melbourne and its first Roman Catholic church. Melbourne's first priest, Reverend Patrick Geoghegan, arrived in 1839; his congregation was so impoverished that it was unable to raise enough money to qualify for a land grant, but Captain Lonsdale allowed them to take possession of this site until the funds could be raised. The structure now standing was meant to be a temporary one, but has managed to survive and has recently undergone major renovation. It was designed by Samuel Jackson in a modified Gothic style; the interior includes a cedar panelled ceiling added in 1850, which creates a soothing atmosphere in the middle of the city. It was in this church that Ned Kelly's parents were married, and Dame Nellie Melba gave recitals here.

State Library and museum complex

Continuing east on Little Lonsdale Street, you come to the **State Library** (☎ 03 9669 9888; open Mon 13.00–21.00, Tues, Thurs and Sun 10.00–18.00, Sat 10.00–21.00) and **museum** complex facing Swanston Street. On the front lawns stands a statue of Sir Redmond Barry, the driving force behind the establishment of so many of Melbourne's cultural institutions. The foundation stone for the Public Library was laid in 1854, on the same day as that for the university. Among Joseph Reed's earliest large-scale works, the central portion was completed in 1870; the long façade was not completed until 1961. The original interior design is now only apparent in the first-floor reading rooms; the dome, added in 1911, is one of the largest concrete domes in the world. In Glen Tomasetti's novel *Thoroughly Decent People* (1976), main character Bert Pater marvels at the reading room, with its eight sides and 'three tiers of balconies adorned with plastic laurel leaves linked by swags of fruit'. The library also contains enormous collections of artworks and the largest photography collection in Australia. Until 1968, the accompanying galleries contained the art collections of the State of Victoria, now housed at the National Gallery of Victoria.

The museum (☎ 03 9651 6777) will be closed until the end of 2000 at which time the collections and exhibits will re-open in new premises in Carlton Gardens on Rathdown Street. It will include a Children's Museum and inter-active cultural heritage displays. This museum has been the most beloved excur-sion for decades of Melbourne children, for it contains the stuffed remains of **Phar Lap**, Australia's most famous racing horse, winner of 37 of his 41 races. After his mysterious death in America in 1932, his body was returned to Melbourne; his heart now resides at Canberra's National Film and Sound Archive, and his body is a major exhibition here, albeit the source of much cynical amusement among locals.

The museum, in conjunction with the University of Melbourne's history department, has recently undertaken a fascinating archaeological excavation of the **Little Lonsdale area**, known in the early days as the 'heart of slumdom', most specifically the location of the town's brothels, gambling schools and opium dens. The site of the present Telstra Exchange buildings, near Spring Street, once housed the properties of the notorious **Madame Brussels**, reputed to have entertained the Duke of Edinburgh when he visited Melbourne in 1867 and the owner of several 'Little Lons' brothels. It was in one of these houses of ill-repute that the Parliamentary ceremonial mace supposedly appeared after going missing in 1891. As a working-class inner-city neighbourhood, 'Little Lons' figures prominently in C.J. Dennis's classic story *Songs of a Sentimental Bloke* (1915). (For an example of the *Sentimental Bloke*'s prose, see Kalgoorlie, Western Australia, and the discussion of 'two-up').

Back on LONSDALE STREET and to the south are two institutions closely associated with this once-poor neighbourhood. The **Wesley Church** (now Uniting Church) was built in the 1850s during the ministry of Daniel Draper. It was highly criticised by Methodists for its Gothic design (by the seemingly ubiquitous Joseph Reed), a style too closely linked to Catholicism. For many years, it was referred to as 'a blunder in bluestone'. In the entrance is a well-known statue of John Wesley. For many years located in the most deprived section of town, the church gained a reputation for social welfare and reform.

Further along Lonsdale Street is the **former Melbourne Hospital** (Queen Victoria Hospital). The foundation stone for the city's third hospital was laid in 1846; most of the buildings still extant date from the 1910s. In 1896, the site became the home of the Queen Victoria Hospital, staffed by women for women; it operated as such until 1946, when the new Royal Melbourne Hospital was established. Closed in 1987, the site is currently occupied by a weekend market.

The other side of the block is a small **Greek Quarter** in the inner city, worth visiting for its great cafes, bakeries and restaurants.

Old Melbourne Gaol

Turn north on to Russell Street; continue past Latrobe Street to **Old Melbourne Gaol** (☎ 03 9663 7228; open daily 09.30–16.30), probably the most popular tourist site in the city, due largely to the fact that **Ned Kelly**, the famous bushranger and Australian legend (see p 245), was hanged here in 1880. The exhibitions include Kelly's suit of armour, as well as his wax death mask, along with those of the many colourful outlaws who also met their end here. In the 19C many people held the belief that moral character could be determined by physiognomic features; just as now we feel that something of the character of Ned Kelly can be understood by seeing the impression of his face. To the physiognomist, however, these death masks were made to use as case studies.

Architecturally, the gaol is a fascinating example of colonial penal design. The first section was opened in 1845, with constant expansions, especially during the goldrush days, until the massive bluestone structure occupied the entire block (most of it has now been taken over by the Royal Melbourne Institute of Technology). One of the most intriguing features is the elaborate corrugated iron ceiling above the execution chamber—an extravagant, nearly medieval, example of the Australian mastery of this building material.

City Baths, Melbourne

To the west of the gaol on Victoria Street is the marvellous **City Baths** (weekdays 06.00–12.00, weekends 08.00–1800). Since 1858, public baths have been available on this site. This ornate Orientalist structure dates from 1903, designed by J.J. Clark, with separate swimming pools for men and women, as well as actual baths. The building was restored in 1980, and is now a 1990s gym, with aerobics classes, spas and saunas.

Royal Melbourne Institute of Technology

At this point, the buildings of the Royal Melbourne Institute of Technology, more popularly known as **RMIT**, straddle both sides of VICTORIA STREET. The City Campus fills the block behind the baths to Latrobe Street, and on the other side of Victoria Street, runs over to Lygon Street and north to Queensberry Street. The institute is one of Australia's largest and oldest campuses, renowned for its training in architecture, art and technical studies. At 360 Swanston Street is **RMIT BUILDING no. 8**, a smashing new structure that dominates the streetscape, looking like a colourful, jewel-encrusted crown. The polychromatic façade, added in 1993, covers a severe 1980s structure which houses the Kaleide Theatre and the student union and, in the new additions, the library and several faculties; one critic described it as a 'feral vision'. The renovation was designed by architects Peter Corrigan and Maggie Edmond; it has won numerous architectural awards, including the Royal Australian Institute of Architects' Walter Burley Griffin Award for Urban Design in 1995.

From 1908 to 1962, the RMIT area at **350–352 Swanston Street** was the premises of the *Australian Journal*, one of the most significant literary journals in the colony's history. It began as a weekly in 1865; its editor in 1870 was Marcus Clarke, whose pioneering book *For the Term of His Natural Life* (1874) originally appeared as a serial in the *Journal* in 1870–72. Other writers who published in its pages were Charles Harpur, Ada Cambridge, and 'Rolf Boldrewood' (Thomas Alexander Browne).

Walk 5 • Parliament House and Eastern Hill

At the top of SPRING STREET, on what was known as Eastern Hill, the new colony of Victoria built its grand **Parliament House** (☎ 03 9651 8568; tours weekdays on the hour until 16.00). Begun in 1856 but not completed until 1930, this building and the other public structures surrounding it more than any other epitomise Victoria's grand efforts to be considered as a seat of government and civic responsibility. Evidence of the success of this effort, after Federation in 1901, the Commonwealth Parliament sat here until Canberra was opened in 1927. The Parliament dominates and defines the East Melbourne area. Designed by Peter Kerr and J.C. McKnight, the original plan included an enormous dome which, once the economic boom waned, was never built. The Doric façade with its massive colonnade presents one of the most architecturally complex designs in Australia. The interiors are equally impressive, with stone and gilded columns and ornate carvings representing industry, government and other symbolic references to the strength of Victoria. Queen's Hall, added in 1879, includes a sombre statue of Queen Victoria. Tours are available when the houses are not in session, and include a view of the jewel-like library.

Next to the Parliament is **Gordon Reserve**, named after statues in the l-block park of General Gordon, at the south corner, and poet Adam Lindsay Gordon. In 1890 the Eight-Hour-Day Memorial was installed at its northern corner; this has since been moved to the intersection of Russell and Victoria Streets, near the Trades Hall from whence the eight-hour day campaign was waged. In 1932, a statue to the poet Gordon was erected on the northern spot. The reserve also includes a fountain, sculpted by convict William Stanford while in prison in the 1860s; upon his release he returned to his masonry business in St Kilda.

Adjacent to the reserve is the **Old Treasury Building** (☎ 03 9651 2277 or 03 9651 2233; open weekdays 09.00–17.00, weekends 10.00–16.00), terminating at Collins Street. Designed by J.J. Clark in 1862, its Italianate style mimics Florentine palazzi in mass and fenestration. The groups of cast-iron lamps are an integral part of the architectural complex. Tours of the gold vaults take place daily at 13.00 and 15.00. Nearby are the State Government Offices, designed by M. Egan in 1874, which continue the historicist references with a well-proportioned Doric loggia, surmounted by a royal coat of arms.

At this point on Spring Street you can enter **Treasury Gardens**, laid out by Clement Hodgkinson in 1867. The lake in the middle, which now includes a memorial to John F. Kennedy, was first created to help drain the swampy land. Also in the gardens is one of the hundreds of statues in Australia to Robert Burns; this one was erected by the Royal Caledonian Association in 1904.

At **PARLIAMENT PLACE** behind the Old Treasury Building and State Government Offices is **Tasma Terrace**, a lovely block of six terrace houses constructed between 1878 and 1887 to a design by Charles Webb. The use of ironwork decoration is particularly pleasing. The offices of the National Trust are located here.

Continue along GISBORNE STREET to **St Patrick's Cathedral** (☎ 03 9662 2332; open daily 07.00–17.50, later for evening services). This splendid Gothic Revival church dominates the Eastern Hill skyline; the third church on the site, its foundation stone was laid in 1850. Building began in 1857 to the design of W.W. Wardell. It stands as his masterpiece, although the rapid expansion of the town during the gold rush required constant additions, and the building itself was not completed until 1897. The three spires, part of Wardell's original plans, were not added until 1939; the marble altars are also credited to Wardell. It is now the largest cathedral in Australia, and the 103m spire is the tallest in Melbourne.

Across the street on ALBERT STREET is the **Victorian Artists' Society** (☎ 03 9662 1484; open weekdays 10.00–16.30; weekends 13.30–16.30), first founded here in 1874. The present building, which still houses the society and a gallery, was completed in 1893, and was probably modelled on the 'American Romanesque' style of H.H. Richardson.

On the other side of the cathedral, on the corner of ALBERT and GISBORNE STREETS, is **St Peter's Eastern Hill**. Building began here in 1848, to a design by Charles Laing; the first walls were built of English brick, imported as ballast, which were plastered to give a lighter appearance among all the bluestone edifices of the area. The accompanying vicarage and school were designed by William Pitt in 1886. In 1848, Melbourne was proclaimed a city on the steps of St Peter's.

Across Albert Street in this block, squashed next to the imposing ICI Building skyscraper, are several ecclesiastical structures. The **Baptist Church**, designed to seat 700 and built between 1855 and 1865, has a fine classical façade. Next door is the **Synagogue** of the East Melbourne Hebrew Congregation. This group split in 1857 from the Bourke Street synagogue. The building dates from 1877, and is Melbourne's oldest existing synagogue. The design by Crouch and Wilson includes a classical façade with two eight-sided domes.

On Albert Street is also the Salvation Army Printing Works, home since 1901 of the army's paper *War Cry* (it has been printed in Melbourne since 1883). Around the corner, on Gisborne and Victoria Streets, is the former **Eastern Hill Fire Station**, built in 1891; its imposing tower offered great views over Melbourne. The building now houses the **Fire Services Museum** (☎ 03 9662 2907; open Fri 09.00–15.00; Sun 10.00–16.00).

To the east of Treasury Gardens are **Fitzroy Gardens** (☎ 03 9658 8713), originally planned as subdivided blocks, but set aside in 1848 in honour of Governor Fitzroy. Perhaps appropriately for a site named for this 'immoral' governor, the place was first used as a refuse tip. Formal designs for a garden were first drawn in 1857 by Governor La Trobe's nephew, Edward La Trobe Bateman, a plan greatly modified by the gardens' first curator, James Sinclair. He had been responsible for the planting of Czar Nicholas' Royal Gardens in the Crimea. Sinclair intended to create here an English plan with woodlands and fern gullies; he designed the pathways roughly in the shape of the Union Jack. In 1929 a conservatory was erected, and in 1934, to celebrate Melbourne's centenary, the Yorkshire **cottage of Captain Cook's parents** was disassembled, transported and re-erected here (open daily, 09.00–17.00). In the 1930s, Ola Cohn sculpted a **faerie tree** here, which she describes in her book *The Fairies' Tree* (1932); the tree, with its possums and wombats, is still a popular attraction for children. The author Jack Lindsay wrote that he was conceived in the Fitzroy Gardens.

Melbourne Cricket Grounds (The MCG)

Across Wellington Parade from the southeast corner of Fitzroy Gardens is **Jolimont**, original site of Governor La Trobe's cottage (it supposedly received its name, meaning 'pleasant hill', from La Trobe's French-Swiss wife). The portion of Jolimont known as Yarra Park is the home of the **Melbourne Cricket Grounds** (known throughout Australia as the MCG) (☎ 03 9657 8879; open daily, 10.00–16.00, tours hourly). The site has been the home of the Melbourne Cricket Club since 1853, though only the historic Members' Stand survives from the early days of competition. The MCG is the hallowed playing fields of not only cricket, but Victoria's own beloved sport, Australian Rules Football, also known as AFL, for the Australian Football League (see box). The stadium as it appears today was built for the 1956 Olympics, with the Southern Stand added in the 1980s; it can easily seat 100,000. The tours of the grounds and facilities are

Australian Rules Football

Nothing can compare to the Victorians' near religious devotion to Australian Rules Football; except for very early matches, the game has traditionally been played only in Victoria. It has now spread at first-grade level to most parts of Australia, in what is seen as near sacrilege by some Victorians, especially when these 'outsider' teams make it into the national play-offs. Crowds of over 80,000 are not uncommon for an ordinary Saturday afternoon game, and championship games at one time drew as much as five per cent of the total population of the city. First codified in the 1850s, the game's 'invention' is credited to Thomas Wentworth Wills (1835–80), a pastoralist's son from western Victoria who captained Victoria's first Rugby XI and was also a champion cricketer. Experts consider it to be a conglomeration of rugby, soccer and Gaelic football, although there is also strong support for the belief that a similar game was played by the Aborigines of the region; currently, great Aboriginal players are leading figures on many teams.

The traditional teams were established in the largely Irish working-class suburbs of Melbourne, where they were recruited locally and where loyalties to the local team were fiercely maintained. Sadly, these traditional neighbourhoods have now changed demographically, and many of the famous teams are being amalgamated or moved; the once-proud Fitzroy Lions are now the Brisbane Lions. The first recorded game occurred in 1858 between Scotch College and Melbourne Grammar School; the Australian Rules Football League was established in 1896.

Consisting of teams of 20 players, the game involves tremendous amounts of running and kicking on an enormous field towards a double goal. Played at its best, the performances are truly balletic, with tremendous jumps up an opposing player's back to catch the kicked or punched ball, known as 'taking a mark'. Players need to be tall, lithe and sinewy. It is more enjoyable to watch in person than on television, where it is difficult to follow its frenetic pace. It is almost as much fun to watch the white-coated referees, with their elaborate hand signals, as the players, and the crowds are tremendously entertaining. Tradition requires the players to wear extremely short shorts and singlets, a fact that supposedly explains the game's large number of female fans. During the season from March to September, Melbourne is filled with fans carrying banners, shawls and emblems in the colours of their teams, and singing team songs.

essential for 'footy' fans, who make special pilgrimages to Melbourne for this purpose. The grounds also house the **Australian Gallery of Sport**, filled with the most precious of cricket memorabilia as well as artefacts of all other sports, and the **Olympic Museum**, dedicated to all the 20C Games, with special attention to the 1956 Melbourne event. Next door, across the railway yards in Flinders Park is the National Tennis Centre, home every January of the Australian Open; it has 21 courts, a 15,000-seat capacity on centre court, and a 700-tonne retractable roof.

South of the river

Cross the Princes Bridge and take ST KILDA ROAD south. On the right you will pass the Victorian Arts Centre (see p 291). On the left are gardenlands along the Yarra. First is **Queen Victoria Gardens** (☎ 03 9658 8713), with its monuments to Queen Victoria (1907) and Edward VII. The annual Moomba festival in March has been held here since 1957. On the other side of Linlithgow Avenue are the Kings Domain and then the Royal Botanic Gardens. Immediately south of Linlithgow Avenue is Sidney Myer Music Bowl (☎ 03 9281 8360), site of popular outdoor concerts seating up to 70,000. The **Kings Domain** includes **Jolimont (La Trobe's Cottage)** (☎ 03 9654 5528; open Mon, Wed and weekends 11.00–16.00), the original residence of Governor Charles La Trobe. When La Trobe was appointed administrator of Port Phillip, he contacted H. Manning of Holborn, a London manufacturer renowned for his prefabricated wooden houses designed especially for colonial outposts. Manning had already provided such structures for the Swan River settlement in Western Australia and for Governor Hindmarsh in South Australia. While La Trobe ordered two structures, one more substantial than the other and certainly intended to be his Melbourne residence, he was forced to sell the larger one on his arrival in order to afford the purchase of the land on which he was to establish his governmental headquarters! (New South Wales was notoriously parsimonious in its dealings with its southern subordinate.)

The present cottage is a restored and expanded version of the smaller structure which served as 'government house' during La Trobe's tenure. Originally located near present-day Charles and Agnes Streets where it at one time served as the caretaker's cottage for a shoe factory, it was moved in 1963 to its present more appropriately landscaped position near the entrance to the Royal Botanic Gardens. Its restoration prompted the return of many original items of furniture and paintings, while other objects date from the same period.

Also in the King's Domain, off Alexandra Avenue between the Yarra River and Government House, is the Pioneer Women's Memorial Gardens (☎ 03 9658 8713), a lovely sunken garden, built in 1934 by sculptor Charles Web Gilbert to commemorate the achievements of Victoria's early women settlers.

Royal Botanic Gardens

The Royal Botanic Gardens on Birdwood Avenue (☎ 03 9252 2300; open daily, 07.30–20.30 Nov–Mar, 07.30–18.00 April, Sept–Oct, 07.30–17.30 May and Aug) are considered by many to be one of the finest botanic gardens in the world; Arthur Conan Doyle said that it was 'the most beautiful place that I have ever seen'. German historian J.A. Froude comments on Australian gardens in his *Oceana*, a description of his visit to the country in 1885:

> *Whether it be the genius of the country, or some development of the sense of beauty from the general easiness of life, or the readiness of soil and climate to respond to exertion, certain it is that the public gardens in Australian towns are the loveliest in the world, and that no cost is spared in securing the services of the most eminent horticulturalists.*

Certainly Melbourne's gardens evoke a quite genteel atmosphere, situated on the banks of the Yarra River, bounded by Government House to the west and the King's Domain to the south, and filled with ornamental lakes, winding paths, and magnificent flowerbeds. Although only 35.4 hectares in area, careful design gives the impression of infinite space. The grounds were chosen in 1845, but real development began when the great botanist and explorer Ferdinand von Mueller was appointed director in 1857. In keeping with his tenacious interest in Australian flora of all sorts, he immediately established the **National Herbarium**, an invaluable collection which is still part of the gardens. The herbarium is now an administrative and research centre, and contains an extensive botanical library. Guided walks of the gardens leave from the herbarium Tues–Fri 11.00 and 14.00, and Sun 11.00. The oldest part of the gardens is **Tennyson Lawn**, which includes Arthur's Elms, four English elm trees some 120 years old. Near the ornamental lake is **Separation Tree**, memorialising Victoria's separation from New South Wales in 1851. The real landscaping of the gardens occurred under Mueller's successor, William Guilfoyle, who, from 1873 to 1909, took advantage of Mueller's collections, both native and imported, and used them in the topographical designs of the beds and lawns.

Government House

Behind the gardens, following DALLAS BROOKS DRIVE, is **Government House** (☎ 03 9654 5528 or 03 9654 4711). The present majestic structure is the fourth official residence, the earlier ones extending from a wattle-and-daub hut in 1837, to a prefabricated wooden structure for Governor La Trobe (see above) in 1840, and finally the rental of the substantial 'Toorak House' in 1854.

> By the 1870s, Victoria's growth and prosperity within the empire was such that a more dignified and grandiose house was deemed necessary. Certainly Victorians were also quite consciously stressing their progressive ambitions in relation to New South Wales when they constructed this lavish structure for their own governmental leader. The Inspector-General William Wardell (1823–99) was assigned the task of designing an appropriately ostentatious building. Unlike his more common Gothic Revival plans, Wardell drew heavily on Queen Victoria's Italianate Osborne House on the Isle of Wight for the design of Government House.

Situated in 11 hectares of beautiful grounds, the stuccoed-brick building includes an impressive tower which dominates the exterior view. The stunning State Ball Room occupies the entire south wing of the building. It is 46 metres long, 18 metres wide, and 15 metres high—surpassing in size the ballroom in Buckingham Palace—a fact that did not please Queen Victoria. The walls have been painted with stencilled patterns and adorned with highly crafted plaster- and woodwork; the room is illuminated by three massive chandeliers. The State rooms are just as sumptuous, with detailed columns and iron works around the staircases and balustrades. The outer buildings, especially the stables, are architecturally significant in their own right. The current residents are kind enough to allow the National Trust to conduct regular tours of the residence. These generally occur on Monday, Wednesday and Saturday mornings, but bookings are essential.

Back on to St Kilda Road and heading south you come to the **Shrine of Remembrance** (☎ 03 9654 8415; open daily 10.00–17.00) which is also in the King's Domain (you could also walk there directly from Government House, about 1km). In 1934, only 16 years after the end of the Great War in which Australia experienced appalling losses, this massive war memorial was opened by the Duke of Gloucester in front of a crowd of some 300,000. The monument's design incorporated heroic elements of the Parthenon and the Temple of Halicarnassus, with a pyramidal dome some 26m high. The Shrine is laden with symbolic inscriptions and sculptures; the central effect is a ray of light which dramatically strikes a marble plaque at the moment of armistice, in the eleventh month on the eleventh day at the eleventh hour. Sombre ceremonies also occur on Anzac Day, 25 April (see p 63). On its opening, one critic described the structure as 'old-fashioned, over-cautious, and, as usual, excessively obsessed with getting a landmark by invoking the great Australian hobby of gilding the lily'. A cenotaph in the forecourt, with eternal flame, commemorates the victims of the Second World War. The Shrine's upper balcony offers spectacular views of south Melbourne.

Back on St Kilda Road, south of the Botanic Gardens, is **Melbourne Church of England Grammar School**, one of the city's oldest private schools. The foundation stone was laid in 1856, and the building designed by Charles Webb and Thomas Taylor in a style that could be called Elizabethan School style. Building materials include bluestone with sandstone dressings, and white painted woodwork. The Witherby Tower was added in 1876, and the grounds retain a sense of the school's traditions and links to English public school ideas.

Albert Park

About 500m south is the beginning of Albert Park (☎ 03 9816 6938), a lovely and enormous city greenland with a lake big enough for sailing, a golf course and other sporting facilities. It is now also the site of the Australian Grand Prix racing event each year, despite tremendous controversy and protest by local residents and environmentalists, concerned about the inevitable destruction of Albert Park itself (especially its venerable trees) and the ensuing noise. The Grand Prix was happily ensconced in Adelaide until 1995, when the present Victorian premier, Jeff Kennett, ever ambitious to increase Melbourne's tourist dollar and its cultural status, managed to whisk it away from South Australia and plonk it in the middle of Albert Park. So far, the event seems successful, although at the time of writing resident protests continue. The park is still a superb place to go cycling, sailing and walking.

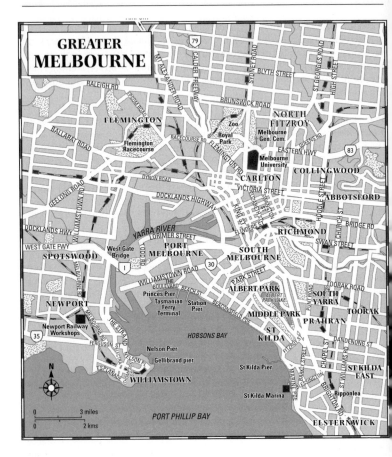

GREATER
MELBOURNE

North Melbourne

To the north of the inner city, on the other side of Victoria Street bordered by
Rathdowne, Carlton and Nicholson Streets, is **Carlton Gardens**. From
Nicholson Street to the east past Hoddle Street are the historically working-class
suburbs of Melbourne. Today, the suburbs of Abbotsford, Alphington, Burnley,
Clifton Hill, Collingwood, Fairfield, Fitzroy, North Carlton, North Fitzroy and
Richmond are administered as the **City of Yarra**. While these traditional neighbourhoods have seen tremendous demographic change, the old divisions
remain, and Melburnians have strong emotional and historical ties to the old
neighbourhoods. All of these suburbs are well served by public transport, with
trams, trains, and buses travelling to them from the centre of Melbourne and
from Spencer Street Station.

The **Richmond Council Offices** and **Town Hall**, on Bridge Street at Church
Street, offer several brochures, including *Discover Yarra* and a guide to The Yarra
Trail.

Carlton Gardens

Today Carlton Gardens (☎ 03 9658 8713) appear to be two separate spaces, with the great complex of the Royal Exhibition Buildings in the middle. While designated a park area as early as 1852, plans for the design of the gardens did not begin until 1858, when paths were laid out. The area continued to be the haunt of vandals and feral goats until the 1860s, until careful surveillance allowed the planted trees to grow. In 1880, one of the most significant cultural events in Australian history took place with the inauguration of the International Exhibition, a time for 'Marvellous Melbourne' to present itself to an international audience. The Carlton Gardens exhibition grounds covered 20 acres (8 ha) during the event. The remaining buildings, built by Reed & Barnes in 1879–80, were part of the main complex at the exhibition. The dome was modelled on that of Florence Cathedral. The buildings served as the home of the Victorian Parliament from 1901 to 1927, while the Parliament buildings were used by the Federal Parliament. Now the buildings house exhibitions and trade fairs, and provide an elegant backdrop for pleasant garden strolls. Carlton Gardens will house the Museum of Victoria when it reopens in 2000.

Fitzroy and Collingwood

On the eastern side of Nicholson Street begins the suburb of **Fitzroy**, and, at Smith Street to Hoddle Street is Collingwood. Together they originally formed the neighbourhood of Newtown. By the 1850s, their constituencies had developed competitive rivalries, evident not only in football, but also in the grandiosity of their town halls. Built in the 1880s, both town halls are vastly overscaled amidst the modest terrace houses of the area.

> Fitzroy was the birthplace of Alfred Deakin, prime minister and would-be novelist. Also born here was novelist 'Henry Handel Richardson' (Ethel Florence Lindesay Richardson), author of *The Getting of Wisdom* (1910). Edmund Finn, better known as 'Garryowen', early chronicler of Melbourne life, lived here for 38 years; he is commemorated with a park on the site of his house in Leicester Street. In 1966, Peter Mather in his novel *Trap*, ruminated on Fitzroy's fate: 'and one day soon … this area will be discovered by the suburb-haters and wrested from the natives and hoisted level with Carlton and Parkville. And probably made twee and chi-chi—unless enough of the present locals can hang on'.

Always a working-class area, at times quite rough, Fitzroy became bohemian in the 1960s and 1970s, when students and artistic types moved in. Brunswick Street is still the arty centre, with alternative and women's bookshops, second-hand clothing stores, ethnic cafes, and a strong gay presence. Intriguingly, Brunswick Street no. 11 is also the location of the Mary McKillop Pilgrimage Centre (☎ 03 9419 9273; open weekdays 09.30–16.30, and Sun 14.00–16.30) with displays about the life of Australia's first saint. Most of the Aboriginal community centres are located in Fitzroy, and Johnston Street is also the location for Melbourne's Spanish-speaking community. Also here, at 211 Johnston Street, is the **Erwin Rado Theatre**, site since 1994 of previews for the Melbourne International Film Festival, and seating only 60. Gertrude Street has recently become a centre for avant-garde art galleries and craft centres;

200 Gertrude Street houses a complex of studio spaces and contemporary galleries (☎ 03 9419 3406). **Craft Victoria**, 114 Gertrude Street (☎ 03 9417 3111), sponsors exhibition programmes and provides information on Victorian crafts people.

At the time of writing, the immense **Town Hall**, on Napier Street, was only partially used for the public library, in a lovely wood-lined room. Across the street on King William Street, next to blocks of housing project apartments, is an adventure playground, where children are allowed to build cubbies and express themselves creatively. The Fitzroy Swimming Pool on Alexandra Parade one block east of Brunswick Street is still an old-fashioned neighbourhood playground.

Collingwood remains a bit more rugged, less trendy. SMITH STREET, its main thoroughfare, is unpretentious, with budget clothing places and modest ethnic eateries. Also located here, at 174 Smith Street, is the **Australian Toy Museum** (☎ 03 9419 4138; open daily, 10.00–18.00), which includes in the garden an operative miniature railway. Named for one of the admirals at the Battle of Trafalgar, Collingwood was a bucolic place in the 1840s, and as late as the 1900s, farmers here still herded their cows down to the Yarra River.

The area's greatest claim to fame is as the location, under the name of Carringbush, for Frank Hardy's epic novel, *Power Without Glory* (1950), a barely fictionalised account of the rise of notorious bookmaker and criminal entrepreneur John Wren (in the novel, John West) spanning the 1890s to the 1950s. Hardy, a leader in left-wing politics of the period, was sued by Wren in a famous legal battle of the early 1950s that coincided with government attempts to ban the Communist party in Australia. Many of the locales in Collingwood where Wren began his career are only thinly disguised in the book, including Cullins Tea Shop, 146 Johnston Street, the site in the 1890s of Wren's original tote (gambling operation). The Carringbush Regional Library, 415 Church Street, Richmond, also commemorates Hardy's great literary achievement.

The southeast corner of Gipps and Hoddle Streets was actually the site of a goldmine, opened in 1862 and quickly closed. Following HODDLE STREET north past Johnston Street, you come to the Victoria Park Football Ground, across the street from the Victoria Park railway station. The Collingwood Magpies, often AFL champions, have been playing football here since 1892.

Abbotsford

On the eastern side of Hoddle Street, the suburb is actually called **Abbotsford**, filled along Victoria Parade with grim reminders of the industrial factories that were the source of employment for Collingwood's poor, and the cause of hardship during times of depression. It is no coincidence that many of the factories were involved in activities that utilised the quickly polluted waters of the nearby Yarra River: breweries, wool scouring and tanning.

Two venues marking this industrial period are of interest: the former **Alma Wool Scouring Factory**, 663 Victoria Street, Abbotsford; and the **Carlton Brew House Visitor's Centre** (☎ 03 9420 6800, two-hour-long tours at 10.00, 11.30, 14.30 weekdays), on the corner of South Audley and Nelson

Streets, Abbotsford, presenting a history of beer. The Yarra had, of course, been the home of the Wurundjeri people for thousands of years. By the early 1900s, the river was so ruined by industrial waste that it was unusable as a water source.

To the south of Johnston Street Bridge (c 300m) and on the Yarra River is the **Collingwood Children's Farm**, St Heliers Street (☎ 03 9205 5469 or 03 9417 5808; open daily 09.00–17.30), a fun petting farm on a nicely reclaimed stretch of riverbank at one of the many bends in the river. The site was farmed for 100 years by the Sisters of the Good Shepherd to feel 1000 residents of the convent here (the historic convent buildings are visible from the farm).

Along the Yarra

On the east side of Johnston Street Bridge, the road becomes Studley Park Road, and you enter **Yarra Bend Park** (☎ 03 9482 2344), 223ha of natural bushland amidst the many bends of the upper Yarra River—a delightful amount of open space nearly in the heart of Melbourne. This area of the Yarra was understandably popular with early Melbourne artists, and Yarra Bend scenery figures in many paintings by Eugen von Guerard, S.T. Gill, and Tom Roberts. These parklands are beloved by runners, picnickers, rowers and cyclists; a variety of walking trails and excellent cycling paths meander throughout the area, all of them discussed and mapped in a number of brochures available at the tourist offices or from the Yarra City Council offices in the Richmond Town Hall on Bridge Street (☎ 03 9205 5063). The **Yarra Bend Public Golf Course**, on the gentle slopes down to the river, is considered one of the most picturesque courses in Australia.

The best way to explore the park is either by car, along the many scenic drives, or by bicycle. Public transport entrance will involve quite a bit of walking. Take the **no. 42 tram** from Collins Street east along Victoria Street, get off at stop no. 28 and walk up Walmer Street and over the footbridge into the park at Dickinson Reserve; or take **bus nos 201** or **203** from Flinders Street Station, which travel up Studley Park Road with stops in the park near the public golf course and several picnic areas along the river at Boathouse Road.

At the boathouse (☎ 03 9853 8707), you can rent rowing boats, and nearby is Kanes suspension bridge, which takes you to the other side of the river. From here it is about a 20-minute walk to **Dights Falls**, now a picnic area at the confluence of the Yarra River and Merri Creek (the falls can be reached by car from Trennery Crescent, off Johnston Street in Abbotsford, on the western side of the Johnston Street Bridge). The walk goes by **Deep Rock Picnic Area**, where a foundation stone commemorates the Deep Rock Swimming Club, a popular recreation spot here until the 1940s. In 1918, a member of the club, Alec Wickham (who also invented the Australian crawl), dived 62.7 metres from the cliffs on the opposite bank into the Yarra River with 70,000 people looking on; he lost his swimming togs, but survived the attempt. Near these cliffs on the southern side of the river is also the **Pioneer Memorial Cairn**, honouring Charles Grimes, an early settler considered the first European to discover the Yarra River in 1803, and who brought cattle from Sydney to Melbourne in 1836.

Until recently, Merri Creek was thoroughly neglected and largely polluted (although its volcanic soil has long been used for the Melbourne Cricket Ground pitch). Since 1976, efforts by the local councils and government agencies have seen the area impressively revegetated, with native flora and fauna returning. The area around Dights Falls was an important ceremonial site for the Wurundjeri tribe, one of the five groups belonging to the Woiworong clan within the Kulin nation that occupied the Port Phillip region. In the 1840s an Aboriginal mission was established here.

Today, the walk along the Yarra River at Victoria Street Bridge, about 2km from Hoddle Street on Victoria Street, is part of a 29km trail around the city known as the **Capital City Trail**. This part of the walk takes about 1.5 hours, and passes many important sites, including an Aboriginal sacred Corroboree Tree, and at Yarra Bend itself, the Burnley School of Horticulture, since the 1860s an experimental garden on the river's banks. The trail continues all the way along the river to Barkly Avenue in Richmond. You can also get to Richmond from Victoria Street, south on Hoddle or Church Streets. There are train stops at North, West, and East Richmond.

Richmond

Most Melburnians come to **Richmond** to shop, especially at the clothing outlets along BRIDGE STREET (east on Wellington Parade). Richmond is also the centre of Melbourne's enormous Greek population, with the best Greek restaurants and bakeries here. A sign of the changing face of Melbourne culture can be seen on VICTORIA STREET, now filled with the city's best Vietnamese restaurants, evidence of the area's latest wave of immigrants. In January, Victoria Street hosts the Lunar Festival, to celebrate the city's Asian culture.

Richmond's mercantile past is represented by **Martin's Hardware**, 38 Victoria Street, run by the same family for more than 100 years, and, on Swan Street, the suburb's other major shopping strip, **Dimmeys Department Store**, with its 80-year-old dome and clock tower. This discount department store has been there since 1853, and is a wonderfully old-fashioned bazaar of wares.

The walk north along CHURCH STREET from Swan Street to Bridge Street includes several structures of interest in Melbourne's history. The area was known as Richmond Hill, and was quickly subdivided into elegant residential blocks. The site of the **Carringbush Regional Library**, at no. 415 (☎ 03 9429 3644), used to be the Globe Picture Theatre, a classic old cinema palace with a sliding roof. **'Ivanhoe'**, at 383 Church Street, was the home of Joseph Bosisto, first manufacturer of Parrot Brand eucalyptus oil (still available) and twice Mayor of Richmond. 'Helenvale', no. 377, was built by Johannes Koch in 1884; he too was Mayor of Richmond and a noted architect. No. 293 was Lalor House, built in 1888 for Dr Joseph Lalor, son of Eureka Stockade hero Peter Lalor (see p 370), who died here in 1889.

St Ignatius Roman Catholic Church was built by William Wardell in 1870, with a 213-foot spire that dominated the skyline. St Stephen's Anglican Church, built in the 1850s, was the first bluestone church in Gothic style in the colony, although little of the original structure remains.

Turn into **Vaucluse** at St Ignatius Church; this was from the 1870s one of the most exclusive neighbourhoods in the city. Most of the area became the property of the Jesuit Order in 1882, where Vaucluse College is now. Amid the clothing shops and cafes on Bridge Street is **the Bookshelf**, at no. 116, containing what is probably the best collection of books by and about Aborigines in the world.

Carlton

To the north of Carlton Gardens is the famous suburb of Carlton, which borders and surrounds the campus of the University of Melbourne and continues, on Lygon Street, alongside the Melbourne General Cemetery. Several tram lines from the city travel up Royal Parade, Lygon Street, and Nicholson Street. Rathdowne Street, along Carlton Gardens, was the site of one of the earliest tram lines out of the city. Elizabeth Street north from the city turns into **ROYAL PARADE**, a wide tree-lined boulevard leading past the university and, to the west, the architecturally elegant district of **Parkville**, next to the Royal Park. Royal Parade turns into Sydney Road and the ethnically diverse suburb of **Brunswick** at Brunswick Road, leading out to the Hume Highway towards Canberra.

University of Melbourne

While today Melbourne and vicinity boasts several prominent institutes of higher learning, for at least a half century the **University of Melbourne** stood alone. Founded by an Act of Parliament in 1853, it opened in 1855 with three professors and 16 students; in 1995, it had 16,000 students. The current campus comprises the 19 hectares originally set aside for the purpose; in the early days, much of this land served as a public park with lake and walking paths. Those areas are now occupied thickly by academic buildings. Women were first admitted to the university in the late 1870s, some 40 years before their counterparts in England.

The campus now is a blend of predictably Oxbridge-style Tudor buildings of the 1870s and multi-storeyed contemporary facilities built since the Second World War, when enrolment soared. As one description of the campus states, '...no logical course exists by which one might easily comprehend the university entire'. Indeed, there is a cosiness about the campus, aided by well-planned landscaping and public sculpture, but it is difficult to orientate oneself, as the older buildings radiate from the northern edge with pathways leading towards other centres. Noted historian Geoffrey Blainey wrote a centenary history of the university in the 1950s, which is still a good source for historical information. The university is currently home to two of Australia's most important literary magazines, *Meanjin* and *Scripsi*. The campus also includes some interesting collections: the **Sir Ian Potter Gallery** in the Physics Building (☎ 03 9344 7153; open Wed–Sat 12.00–17.00; closed Jan) has changing exhibitions; the University Gallery contains some important works of Australian art; and the **Percy Grainger Museum** (☎ 03 9344 5270; open Mon 10.00–13.00, Tues 10.00–16.00, Wed–Fri 10.00–17.00) commemorates the life and work of the eccentric Australian composer Percy Grainger (1882–1961), including his significant collection of world folk music.

Directly to the north of the university is the **Melbourne General Cemetery**; it is the country's first landscaped garden cemetery, and was opened in 1852. The cemetery follows the Scotsman John Claudius Loudon's (1783–1843) directive that 'churchyards and cemeteries are scenes not only calculated to improve the morals and taste, and by their botanical riches to cultivate the intellect, but they serve as historical records'. The principle architect was Albert Purchas; the Melbourne Botanic Gardens supplied much of the plantings, and it is indeed a pleasant place to walk and study historical gravestones—monuments to singer

Nellie Stewart and physician Emma Stone, to bookman E.W. Cole of the Cole's Book Arcade and artist Louis Buvelot. The cemetery also houses a memorial to Elvis Presley, maintained by the local fan club. (The most impressive funereal monument in the city is the Springthorpe Memorial, built by Dr John Springthorpe after the death of his young wife in the early 1900s; it is in Boroondara Cemetery in Kew High Street, a little west of the central city.)

The suburb of Carlton was Melbourne's most dynamic ethnic enclave from the early days of the arrival of New Australians after the First World War until the waning of European immigration in the late 1970s. Before the Italians and Greeks arrived, Carlton was principally Jewish. Yiddish author Pinkus Goldhar, who lived in Melbourne from 1926 until 1947, set many of his short stories in Jewish Carlton.

Traditionally, LYGON STREET, leading from the central district into Carlton, was the domain of Italian migrants who early on established restaurants along this stretch. In the 1950s, Lygon Street, with its espresso bars and pizza stands (the restaurant **Toto's**, still operating, claims to have introduced pizza to Australia), was positively exotic in staid Melbourne, and the area became the hip place to be. Today, it caters to a much more upscale market, with glitzy fashion boutiques and yuppie bars, the bohemians having moved elsewhere (although student life from the nearby university still keeps the neighbourhood lively).

In Carlton one will still find **La Mama** on Faraday Street (☎ 03 9347 6142). Founded in 1967 by Betty Burstall, La Mama is one of the oldest of Melbourne's excellent experimental theatre venues. Today, 'po-mo culture' ('post-modern', alternative and hip) thrives at Rumbarella's and the Black Cat Cafe, but the four-day Lygon Street Festa in November still presents fantastic Italian food and fun.

DRUMMOND STREET, from Victoria to Palmerston Streets, is filled with Victorian townhouses and shopfronts, appearing spruce with cast-iron verandahs and tree-lined verges. RATHDOWNE STREET along Carlton Gardens was one of the first cable tram routes from the central city and consequently saw early commercial development. At no. 357 Rathdowne Street is **Our Lady of Lebanon Church**, originally designed in 1878 by Reed & Barnes as the Carlton Independent Church. In 1958 it became the first Lebanese Catholic Church in Victoria: further evidence of the area's ethnic diversity.

Royal Park and Melbourne Zoo

To the west of the university and Royal Parade is the huge expanse of Royal Park. The residential area between Royal Parade and the park itself is known as **Parkville**, and contains terrace-houses adorned with one of the greatest concentrations of wrought-iron work in the country. Strolls through Parkville's streets are recommended for all fans of such architecture; several books have been written discussing these works from the late 19C, many of which may be available from local bookshops or in the tourism centres. Royal Parade from Grattan Street to Gatehouse Street, then along the Avenue are particularly good venues for an architectural stroll. In the park itself is the **Royal Melbourne Zoological Gardens** (☎ 03 9285 9300; open daily 09.00–17.00, until 21.30 on some summer nights), established in 1861, making it the oldest zoo in Australia and the third oldest in the world. It is a pleasant, visitor-friendly spot, and the **Butterfly House**, with many varieties of Australia's impressive lepidoptera population fluttering everywhere, is definitely worth a visit. Public transport from the city stops directly in front of the zoo's main entrance; take the **Upfield-line train** to Royal Park Station, or **tram nos 55** or **56** from William Street.

Back south on ROYAL PARADE towards the city, turn into Peel Street, then take Queensberry Street west to Howard Street, turn north on Howard Street to Courtney Street and the **Meat Market Craft Centre** (☎ 03 9329 9966; open Tues–Sun and holidays 10.00–17.00). Built in 1880 by G.R. Johnson as a private market hall, it was designated in 1979 by the Victorian Government as a centre for the promotion and implementation of crafts. Today craftspeople of all sorts work on site, and there are demonstrations, displays and salesrooms. The quality and standard is very high, and the setting particularly attractive.

Flemington Racecourse

About 4km along Flemington Road at the end of appropriately named Racecourse Road is Flemington Racecourse, the most famous horse-track in Australia (see the Sydney section for a history of Australian horse-racing). **Tram no. 57** goes up Epsom Road from Flinders Street Station to the racecourse, and the Broadmeadows train has a Flemington Racecourse Station.

The Melbourne Cup

Melbourne is perhaps best known internationally as the home of the **Melbourne Cup**, the race that brings the nation to a halt for three minutes each first Tuesday of November. The race has run every year since 1861, and is the biggest all-age handicap in the world. The city's obsession with The Melbourne Cup and horse-racing in general was remarked upon by Mark Twain when he visited in 1897: 'It has one specialty ... It is the mitred Metropolitan of the Horse-Racing Cult. Its raceground is the Mecca of Australia.' The Melbourne Cup is the pinnacle of weeks of racing and cultural activities, which also serve as a showcase for Australian fashion and, especially, millinery (everyone wears a hat to the Melbourne Cup). Even non-gamblers usually place a bet on the Melbourne Cup, and millions of dollars change hands. During the day's festivities, thousands of race-goers pack the stands and lawns, and Melbourne Cup parties take place across the country. If you are in Melbourne in November, you must go to the Melbourne Cup, or at least take in some of the events of the Spring Racing Festival. Other racecourses in Melbourne include Caulfield, Moonee Valley and Sandown Park; the Caulfield track includes the **Victorian Racing Museum** (☎ 03 9257 7279; open Tues and Thurs, 10.00–16.00, race days 11.00–16.30), opened by the Queen in 1981 and filled with racing memorabilia.

South Melbourne

From **Albert Park**, take Clarendon Street north into **South Melbourne**. The **no. 1 tram** from Swanston Street travels down Sturt Street to South Melbourne, Albert Park and South Melbourne Beach; the **no. 12 tram** leaves Collins Street to South Melbourne, Albert Park, Middle Park and St Kilda. A pleasant residential area centred on the early settlement of Emerald Hill, the area is bounded by

Clarendon, Park, Cecil and Dorcas Streets. The Town Hall provides a heritage trail brochure with a well-marked bicycle ride. The site was originally surrounded by swamps and was a corroboree spot for Aborigines. Off Clarendon Street on Raglan Street is a **Chinese Joss House**, built in 1856 by the Sze-Yup Society, and one of the best in Australia. As with other churches and temples, please keep in mind that while it is open to the public, it is a place of worship.

Continue on Clarendon Street to PARK STREET, where a former knitting mill has been converted into the Victorian Tapestry Workshop, now producing large-scale tapestries and weavings by contemporary artists. One block further north is Bank Street, where the grandiose **South Melbourne Town Hall** looms enormously on the summit of a hill; erected in 1880, it is another Classical edifice by Charles Webb. In contrast, the adjacent police station and courthouse were constructed in 1927 in Spanish Mission style.

At Cecil Street, continue two blocks north to the ever-popular **South Melbourne Market** (☎ 03 9695 8295). Operating since 1867, it is open on Wednesdays, Fridays and weekends, offering fish, fruit, delicatessen products, as well as clothing and jewellery.

At **399 Coventry Street** are three prefabricated iron houses, erected in the 1850s, some of the few surviving iron cottages. These sites are open on Sunday afternoons, with displays illustrating the history of portable housing in Australia (☎ 03 9822 4369). The **Clarendon Street** shopping district at Emerald Hill still retains its Victorian shopfronts. Further south on Ferrars Street, on the border with the neighbourhood of Albert Park, is ST VINCENT PLACE, a remarkably well-preserved residential square, laid out in 1875 and reminiscent of London squares. Ferrars Street leads south into Kerferd Road, then west to the neighbourhoods of **Albert Park** on one side, **Middle Park** on the other side and the bay beaches at the end of the road (tramroutes 1 and 2 end here). The **Kerferd Road Pier**, erected in 1881, sets the tone for this lovely city beach area, most popular with the locals. Running parallel to the stretch of sand is a walled promenade that extends from **Port Melbourne** to the northwest and **St Kilda** to the southeast, about 5km. Albert Park feels like a village, with tiny beach-cottage-like houses, and a cosy shopping block on Bridport Road at Dundas Place, filled with great cafes and clothes shops.

Port Melbourne

Port Melbourne, locally known simply as The Port, is still dominated by rugged industrial docks for the largest container port in the Southern hemisphere. Tram route 109 from Collins Street ends at the Station Pier. The neighbourhood still hints at its working class origins, having fought to escape total gentrification. Sometimes these battles to preserve the character of The Port have been unsuccessful. In 1991, the Centenary Bridge, built in Art Deco style in 1934 as the only road link over the rail lines, was needlessly demolished by 'eager developers'. In the same year, the 140-year-old Swallow & Ariell bakery complex on Beach Street, a major port employer and significant architectural monument, closed its doors to be replaced by condominiums.

History

Initially named Sandridge, the port's first settlers were Wilbraham Liardet and his large family, who landed here in 1839, and quickly built a jetty, watchtower and a hotel (now the *Cafe Amphlett*, Beach Street), then established a ferry service between this point and Williamstown. Liardet's jetty stood on the site of today's Port Melbourne Yacht Club. At the time of settlement, the area now noted only by Lagoon Pier was a verdant swamp, which was completely polluted by the 1870s; once it was dredged and filled in, the road to St Kilda could be built. The lagoon marked the eastern boundary of the port town. With the gold rush, the port swelled in population; in 1854, Australia's first passenger railway service was opened between the port and Melbourne, and soon the Railway Pier (now Station Pier) allowed ships to be unloaded directly onto trains going into Flinders Street Station. Some of the Victorian workers' cottages and storefronts on Bay Street have been restored, and there are great neighbourhood pubs.

At one time, the port maintained its reputation of having a **pub** on every corner, although in the 1880s a religious temperance group called The Rechabites made a concerted effort to close as many as possible, installing drinking fountains near the hotels. By 1919, only 19 pubs remained, and the other hotels took on different functions. Some of those still operating are grand old structures, such as **The Rex**, on Bay and Graham Streets, formerly The Victoria or 'Squares', opened in 1859; the 1869 **Hibernian**, at Graham and Evans Streets, a true working man's local pub; and, next door to the Town Hall on Bay and Spring Streets, the **Prince Alfred Hotel**, named in 1868 in honour of the visit of Queen Victoria's son. At Bay Street between Graham and Liardet Streets is the **Rose & Crown**, with an Art Deco façade and original 1875 interior. At Bay and Rouse Streets is the former Post Office and Mail Exchange, opened in 1860 and at one time the colony's busiest; it is now the headquarters for the innovative troupe Circus Oz.

Further west along BEACH STREET is **Station Pier**, the main passenger terminal and the point of departure for the ferries travelling to Tasmania. The current pier was completed in 1930 and is the largest timber structure in Australia. The **light-rail tram 109** from the city ends here, on the same route that the first rail service travelled in the 1850s.

To the west of Station Pier is **Bayside**, now the most ambitious housing development in the region, a sign of the port's new popularity as a place to live. The Boulevard continues past Princes Pier to **Garden City**, a planned estate built in the 1920s in emulation of Britain's Garden City movement. The original intention was to provide low-cost housing and to eliminate the squalid conditions existing on this side of the tracks. These 'bank houses' were built on small streets to discourage traffic, with green spaces in between. The district between the Boulevard and Howe Parade was erected in the 1940s, and known locally as 'Baghdad' for it supposedly attracted 'forty thieves'. Ironically, the 'bank houses' constructed north of Howe Parade required a deposit of £50 to buy, beyond the reach of most workers. The architectural experiment is nonetheless interesting to view today, despite its enormously increased value as real estate. The beach here is on the migration route of thousands of birds each spring.

Williamstown

From Todd Road in Port Melbourne, you can enter the West Gate Freeway heading west over the towering West Gate Bridge and exit at Melbourne Road (route 37) into the historic maritime district of Williamstown. The area is also accessible by **train** from the centre of Melbourne (the Williamstown line), the **no. 472 bus**, and by **ferry** from St Kilda on weekends; the **tourist boat** along the Yarra River from the World Trade Centre also travels here on Sundays. For Bay & River cruises information and timetables, ☎ 03 9397 2255.

History

Williamstown was established as the settlement's main port in 1837 by Governor Bourke. It bustled with maritime activity until the Yarra River was dredged and the Port of Melbourne was expanded in the 1880s; then this little peninsula was forgotten, allowing it to remain a well-preserved community of 19C buildings and working-class neighbourhoods. Locals affectionately refer to the place as 'Willy'. It is one of the only places in Australia named after King William IV, whose reign ended the year it was settled. From 1893 to 1912, novelist Ada Cambridge lived here with her Anglican vicar husband G.F. Cross; it is the setting for her novel *Fidelis* (1895), in which she describes it as 'quiet and homely, and unpretentious! Not overrun with summer lodgers, like St Kilda'. Author Hal Porter also lived and taught school here during the 1930s Depression, a period he recounts in his autobiographical novel, *The Paper Chase* (1966). More recently, Williamstown has gained some recognition as the hometown of young tennis phenomenon, Mark Philippousis.

Take Melbourne Road to Ferguson Street and east towards the bay and **NELSON PLACE**, the most significant historical area, named appropriately enough after Admiral Horatio Nelson (since it is a maritime centre and was founded at the time of Nelson's greatest fame in the British Colonies). To the north of Nelson Place, the road along the bay is **The Strand**, where wealthy homes have the most outstanding view of the port and the skyline of Melbourne. At Nelson Place, old-fashioned hotels amongst the historic public buildings offer ambience and good cheap food; at Nelson Place and Kanowna Street is the **Prince of Wales**, one of the most historic hotels from the 1850s. A short distance from here, at the end of Nelson Place at Gellibrand Point, is the **Lighthouse** and **Time Ball Tower**; in the 19C it was topped by a copper-plated ball that dropped every day at 13.00 and could be seen from Flagstaff Gardens in the city. Of particular note on Nelson Place near the elegant Yacht Club are the **Customs House**, built in 1873 by Peter Kerr in subdued classical style; and the **Tide Gauge House**, erected in 1860 at the head of Breakwater Pier, one of the only surviving automatic tide gauges, and now in Commonwealth Reserve.

The **Commonwealth Reserve** is also the location for a craft market (☎ 03 9391 7584), held on every first and third Sunday of the month, and, over Australia Day weekend in January, the Williamstown Summer Festival. At Gem Pier is HMAS *Castlemaine*, a Second World War mine sweeper built in Williamstown and now converted to a **maritime museum** (☎ 03 9853 0823; open weekends, 12.00–17.00).

From Commonwealth Reserve walk up Parker Street to ELECTRA STREET to find the **Williamstown Historical Society Museum** (☎ 03 9397 5423), in the former Mechanics' Institute, filled with maritime memorabilia and artefacts; it is only open on Sunday afternoons. About 300m north on Electra Street at

Ferguson Street is the Town Hall with its memorial plaque to novelist Ada Cambridge. To the right on Ferguson Street, is **Cox's Gardens**, which contains one of the only surviving examples of a 19C worker's cottage, built in the 1850s and still inhabited. Thompson Street south from Nelson Place leads to The Esplanade and a cosy beach with the Anglers Club and the Williamstown Life Saving Club.

At North Williamstown, next to the train station and in the **Newport Railway Workshops** is a Railway Museum (☎ 03 9397 7412; open 12.00–17.00 on weekends and public holidays). Steam-train rides and locomotive displays make this a popular destination for children.

Spotswood

Just north of Williamstown, off Douglas Parade on Booker Street in Spotswood, is the excellent museum **Scienceworks** (☎ 03 9392 4800, open daily 10.00–16.30), the science and technology campus of the Museum of Victoria. Built on the site of Melbourne's earliest sewage plant on the banks of the Yarra River, the museum incorporates the old industrial buildings along with its contemporary structure, with hands-on displays and interactive exhibitions. The section on the science of sport is especially innovative. The museum is a 15-minute walk from the Spotswood train station.

St Kilda

At the other end of the beach is the atmospheric area of St Kilda; from Swanston Street in central Melbourne, take **trams 15** or **16**; from Collins Street, **trams 10** or **12**; from Bourke and Spencer Streets, the **light-rail tram 96**. According to Melbourne historian Garryowen, this seaside suburb acquired its name from a passing clipper ship that happened to be there when Governor La Trobe attended a picnic. Until the 1920s it was a fashionable and exclusive neighbourhood; the publisher George Robertson built his mansion in East St Kilda in 1865. After the 1890s crash, the rich began to move to Toorak, and the area declined into a seedy area of strip-tease joints and carnival rides, cheap lodging and bohemian hangouts.

Before and after the Second World War, European migrants settled here in large numbers. Today the suburb has been rejuvenated, with a mixture of beach-town attractions, great Jewish and Continental (European) bakeries, elegant dining and boating venues. The main thoroughfare into St Kilda is **FITZROY STREET**. It retains hints of its reputation as the city's red-light district, although it is now more noticeable for its cafes and entertaining shops. **ACLAND STREET** between Carlisle and Barkly Streets is a foody's heaven, with Central European cake shops and real delicatessens.

The upper end of Acland Street is residential, including, at no. 26, **'Linden'** (☎ 03 9209 6560, Tues–Sun 13.00–18.00), an 1870 mansion built by Alfred Kursteiner for German entrepreneur Moritz Michaelis; the building is now operated by the National Trust and houses a contemporary art gallery. In February, Acland Street is the site of the St Kilda Festival, known for its tremendous displays of food. The Town Hall, corner of St Kilda Road and Carlisle Streets (☎ 03 9209 6209), serves as an information centre and can provide a *St Kilda Heritage Walk* brochure.

At Barkly Street at the end of Acland Street, turn on to BLESSINGTON STREET to reach the lovely, quiet **St Kilda Botanical Gardens** (☎ 03 9536 1333), first planted in 1859 and now with a conservatory and rose garden.

About 500m down Blessington Street west is the **St Kilda Beach** and **Marine Parade**. Walking towards St Kilda Pier, at Cavell Street, is the site of Melbourne's **Luna Park** (☎ 03 9534 0654; open Fri 19.00–23.00, Sat 13.00–17.00 and 19.00–23.00, Sun and school holidays 13.00–17.00), a nostalgic fun-park landmark since 1912, with its gaping-mouth entrance and tacky old-fashioned rides said to be modelled on those at New York's Coney Island. It was opened by the American cinema entrepreneurs J.D. Williams and the Phillips Brothers. Walk up to THE ESPLANADE, the main beachside centre and promenade. At the corner are two of the traditional entertainment venues, the Palais Theatre and the Palace. **The Palais** was built in 1927 by Harry E. White as a grand picture palace, seating 3000. It is now used for live shows. The Palace was a dance-hall opened in 1913 and used during the Second World War as a postal office; it burnt down in 1968, to be replaced by the present building. Down on the beach on Jacka Boulevard near the pier is **St Kilda Baths**, one of the only remaining hot sea baths in Australia. At one time, there were four sea baths along this beach, with separate facilities for men and women. At the time of writing, this delightful Moorish spa was undergoing renovation.

The Upper Esplanade continues as an entertainment centre, focusing especially on **The Esplanade Hotel** (☎ 03 9534 0211), still a place for live bands and comedy, and famous because Sarah Bernhardt stayed here in 1891 (it was built in 1880). Recently, local residents and lovers of live music have begun a campaign to save The Esplanade from possible closure; so far, the campaign has been a success, and the venue has even featured in an ABC-TV Variety programme, *'Hessie's Shed'*.

Directly east is ALFRED SQUARE, site of the first building erected in St Kilda in 1840. The square now contains two interesting war memorials and the remnants of two very early cottages. On Sundays, the Upper Esplanade is the location of a long-standing art and craft market (☎ 03 9536 1333). A walk out along the **St Kilda Pier** has become something of a local weekend ritual—to have coffee at the historic Edwardian kiosk and to watch the sailing activities. It is also one of the most interesting places to experience the sudden transformations of Melbourne's infamous weather, as sea breezes bring in clouds and rain and as swiftly blow them out to the bay again. The breakwater rocks on the end of the pier are now a wildlife sanctuary for Little (Fairy) Penguins (see box p 343), who can occasionally be seen here at sunset. On Sundays, ferries depart from here to Williamstown. On the other side of the pier is **Catani Gardens**, named in honour of Carlo Catani, Chief Engineer of the Public Works Department at the time of its construction in the 1910s. Judging by the other edifices named in his honour—a Memorial Clock Tower on The Esplanade and the Catani Arch on the foreshore—Catani was quite successful in having things named after him.

Take The Esplanade east to Barkly Street and north to Alma Road to enter St Kilda East. The **Jewish Museum of Australia** (also known as the Gandel Centre of Judaica, ☎ 03 9534 0083, open Tues–Thurs 10.00–16.00, Sun 11.00–17.00) is at 26 Alma Road, fittingly in the middle of Melbourne's traditional Jewish neighbourhood, next to the St Kilda Synagogue, in itself a historical structure, built by Joseph Plottel in 1927. The museum includes permanent and temporary exhibitions, focusing on Australian Jewish history and culture.

Prahran suburbs and South Yarra

To the east and north of St Kilda are the city's most fashionable suburbs. The Prahran Council area covers the upscale suburbs **'south of the Yarra'**, these being, South Yarra, Prahran, Toorak and Armadale. The **no. 8 tram** goes through these suburbs along Toorak Road, **tram no. 6** travels along High Street to Glen Iris, and **tram no. 72** is on Commercial Road, Malvern Road, and on to Burke Road to Camberwell.

The Pakenham train line travels via Toorak, Armadale, and Caulfield; the Sandringham Line stops at Prahran, Ripponlea, and Elsternwick.

South Yarra is one of the earliest suburbs to be established, and was traditionally working class. The novelist 'Rolf Boldrewood' (Thomas Alexander Browne) remembers his childhood here in the 1840s as 'the sandy forest of South Yarra'; by the 1920s, according to Martin Boyd, it had become the 'Mayfair of Melbourne'. As well as remaining the residence of Melbourne's most established gentry, these suburbs are now known for upscale shopping.

Toorak has the most exclusive designers' shops, art galleries, luxury car dealers and antique stores, on TOORAK ROAD. CHAPEL STREET, from Dandenong Road in Windsor, to Toorak Road in South Yarra, is less exclusive, but chock-a-block with trendy clothing shops and multicultural boutiques, unique if still pricey. It used to be a real inner-city shopping street for local business, but is now geared to the rich and fashionable. GREVILLE STREET, a side street off Chapel Street between High and Commercial Streets, is an old hippy hangout that now has New Age shops and antiquarian bookdealers. Further east on High Street, **Armadale** has the best art stores, antique furniture dealers, and accompanying bookshops.

As an area that was early developed as a place for prestigious residence, South Yarra and Toorak are littered with elegant homes and estates. The stellar example of these mansions is **Como House** (☎ 03 9827 2500, daily 10.00–17.00), at Williams Road and Lachlade Avenue, South Yarra. To get there take Toorak Road to Williams Road, and follow the signs, or take the no. 8 tram from Swanston Street.

In the 1840s and 1850s, prosperous merchants began buying property and building on estates to the south of Yarra River, with its views towards the city but still in bucolic settings. Como was one of the first of these estates. The property was developed by lawyer Edward Eyre Williams in 1846; the earliest parts of the house date from this period. During the gold rush, the house changed hands twice before being transferred to the architect John Brown in 1854. It was Brown—who came to be known as 'Como Brown'—who gave the property its pretentious proportions, with an elegant Georgian-style mansion and superb gardens; the characteristic wrought-iron railings and gates were imported from Scotland.

The property became the centre for extravagant social life, until Brown's fortunes were reversed and Como sought a new owner. In 1864, pastoralist Charles Henry Armytage purchased the house. He made substantial additions and changes to the house, most notably a two-storey ballroom completed by Arthur Ebden Johnson (architect of Melbourne's General Post Office and the Law Courts). Armytage also developed the splendid gardens, with the aid of the famous curator of the Botanic Gardens, Baron von Mueller. The house was turned over to the National Trust in 1959.

Como House, South Yarra, Melbourne

Next door is **Como Park**, originally part of the Como grounds and now a public park, directly on the banks of the Yarra itself. It is one of the few remaining suburban gardens in Melbourne, and still contains examples of trees and shrubs planted in the 1850s.

Elsternwick

From Prahran, follow Williams Street directly south past Dandenong Road where it becomes Hotham Street. At the point where the suburb of Balaclava becomes **Elsternwick**—now the most Jewish suburb in Melbourne, with consequent delis and bakeries—you will find another great publicly accessible mansion, **Rippon Lea** (☎ 03 9523 6095; open Tues–Sun 10.00–17.00). Get there by the **Sandringham train line** to Rippon Lea and a short walk, by **bus nos 216** or **219** from Bourke and Queen Streets or by **tram no. 67** from Swanston Street. Once there, you can view the house on 30-minute tours.

A lavish Romanesque-style brick estate, Rippon Lea was the brainchild of Frederick Thomas Sargood (1834–1903), a leading Melbourne merchant and politician. A product of Melbourne's most extravagant boom period, Sargood set out to create a stunningly impressive estate worthy of his stature and his times. Built by the firm of Reed & Barnes, Rippon Lea was named for Sargood's mother. The original house consisted of 15 rooms in the 1860s, and grew to 33 rooms by the 1880s.

By the time of Sargood's death in 1903, his property included 43 acres (30 ha), complete with elaborate gardens, a 1.6 ha lake, aviary, conservatories, carriage houses, archery range, shade house and a lookout tower with a view of Melbourne and Port Phillip. After many changing of hands, mercenary subdivisions, and a tenacious battle to preserve its main features, Rippon Lea remains on 9.5 ha.

The house is relatively intact. Elegant features include a cast-iron *porte-cochère*, and stunning Renaissance motifs in the interiors. The gardens are a reminder of the grand manner of 19C private urban gardens.

The third of these fine suburban mansions is **Labassa**, 2 Manor Grove, Caulfield North (☎ 03 9527 6295; open last Sun of the month 10.30–16.30). Take Hotham Street north to Balaclava Road, turn east and travel c 1km to Orrong Road, turn north directly to Manor Grove. **Tram no. 3** from Swanston Street travels down Balaclava Street one block south, and Balaclava Station of the train line is c 1km west. Originally known as 'Ontario', it was built by J.A.B. Koch for pastoralist William Alexander Robertson; when it was purchased in 1905 by mining baron John Watson, it was renamed 'Labassa'. The building is noteworthy in that its design is more European Baroque than English in style, and the interiors include elaborate stencilling, still intact.

Mornington Peninsula to Phillip Island

Travelling on ST KILDA ROAD, at St Kilda Town Hall, the route becomes Brighton Road and then, at Elsternwick, joins the Nepean Highway (route 3) to travel south along the east side of Port Phillip Bay and around the **Mornington Peninsula**. The peninsula is also easily accessible by public transport from the city, using a Zone 3 ticket on both train and bus.

The suburbs closest to town were, naturally, the first areas to develop as beach neighbourhoods, emulating British seaside towns with names like **Brighton** and **Sandringham**, and, further along, the loftier-sounding **Beaumaris** (pronounced 'bow-maris') and **Mentone**. At the Brighton foreshore near the Marine Hotel is a plaque in memory of poet Adam Lindsay Gordon, who shot himself here in 1870. Mentone was one of the favoured spots for painters Charles Conder and Arthur Streeton in the 1880s, site of Conder's elegant painting, *A Holiday in Mentone* (1888), now in the Art Gallery of South Australia.

Golf in Australia

While there is some controversy about the date of the establishment of the first golf club in Australia, the first course was probably that laid out in 1847 at Flagstaff Gardens in Melbourne. At about the same time a club was formed in Geelong, Victoria; the **Melbourne Golf Club** was formed later at Caulfield in 1891. The first course in Sydney was established in 1855, but the first Sydney course of long standing was the **Australian Golf Club** which opened in 1882. After a pause in the early 1890s, this club was revived and became the Royal Sydney Golf Club. Its Cadogan Cup dates from 1883. What was to become the **Royal Brisbane Club** was established in the 1890s as well. The Royal Brisbane, the Royal Queensland at Hamilton (1920) and the Indooroopilly were the first full-length courses in Queensland until the 1930s.

The first women's Open, The Lady's Championship of Victoria, dates to 1894. Another early women's competition was held at the Botany Links of the Australian Golf Club under the auspices of the New South Wales Ladies' Golf Union. The cup is still played for. The first juniors competition was a boys' championship in 1930 in Victoria.

Early golf greats of Australia include professionals Jim Ferrier, Norman von Nida and Peter Thomson. Ferrier was strongest in the 1930s, von Nida in the late 1930s and again after the war and Thomson in the early 1950s. The finest amateur was probably Ivo Whitton of the Melbourne Metropolitan Club. He won five Australian Opens between 1912 and 1931 and dominated in the early 1920s. Today, golf continues to be the most widely-played game in Australia, made possible by the accessibility of great public courses as well as more privileged members' clubs. Queensland especially has seen the rise of 'boutique' golf courses attached to sprawling resorts, built especially for Asian tourists. The many Melbourne courses, with their famous sandy courses and limited water features, are the genuine article from which many of Australia's recent spate of great golfers have arisen. (Greg Norman, of course, is a Queenslander!)

In his autobiography *A Man's Childhood* (1997), author and artist Robin Wallace-Crabbe describes the gradual transformation of **Black Rock**, the suburb between Sandringham and Beaumaris: 'the suburb mutated from a sleepy retreat beyond the end of the Sandringham train line ... to a place for the upwardly mobile with leased motor cars, who wanted to raise children close to sandy beaches. By degrees, the timber cottages ... gave way to solid middle-class, brick and tile residential investments. The housewives became slimmer, better dressed and more worldly. Children who went off to school from there wore the uniforms of Melbourne's private schools rather than that of the local High.' The area, then, quickly became a playground for the upwardly mobile.

Indeed, one of the district's greatest claims to fame is as the location of a series of famous 'sandy' golf courses. In Sandringham is the grandest of all, the **Royal Melbourne Golf Club**. The club, founded in 1891 and initially limited to 100 members, moved from Caulfield to Sandringham in 1901. Alister Mackenzie, renowned for the design of Augusta and Cypress Point in the US, laid the West course in 1926. Alex Russell, his local partner, built the East course.

The Mornington Peninsula

The Mornington Peninsula proper extends from **Frankston**, now a commuter suburb of Melbourne, all the way around the eastern side of Port Phillip Bay to Portsea and Point Nepean National Park at the entrance to the bay. Frankston and the nearby beach of Canadian Bay in Mt Eliza gained some fame in the 1950s as the location for the film of Neville Shute's book *On the Beach*. (It was at this time, of course, that Ava Gardner, starring in the film, made her famous comment about Melbourne: 'It's a story about the end of the world, and Melbourne sure is the right place to film it.'

An **information centre** for the peninsula is on the Nepean Highway at **Dromana** (☎ 03 5987 3078). It has been the most popular excursion destination for Melburnians since the 1870s and before that was the site of pastoral settlement. It still retains its mixture of resort towns and rural industry. The bayside or 'front beaches' provide sheltered locations good for family outings, while the 'back beaches' along the ocean coastline have rugged open-surf stretches with stunning views. It was on this side of the bay that Lieutenant David Collins unsuccessfully attempted to establish a colony in 1803, at present-day Sorrento (see p 286).

At **Seaford**, you can take SEAFORD ROAD from the Nepean Highway, join with the Frankston Highway (route 11) and travel south to Skye Road (officially in the suburb of Langwarrin). Here, connect with McClelland Drive south to find **McClelland Art Gallery** (☎ 03 9789 1671; open Tues–Fri, 10.00–17.00, weekends and holidays, 12.00–17.00), surrounded by bushland with sculptural displays. The collection was donated by the McClelland family and specialises in Australian 20C art, primarily watercolours and sculptures. From here, you can continue south on MCCLELLAND ROAD past the **Langwarrin Flora and Fauna Reserve** (☎ 03 9705 5200; open daylight hours) (2km); the reserve is on the site of a colonial military installation once used for German prisoners of war and as a hospital for the treatment of venereal disease. All evidence of its former usage is gone, and the area has returned to its natural state. The reserve offers walking tracks into native heathlands with great displays of wildflowers in the spring.

Continue on McClelland Road a further 3km to GOLF LINKS ROAD in Baxter to reach **Mulberry Hill** (☎ 03 5971 4138; open by appointment; tours Sun 13.30, 14.15, 15.00. Closed July), a National Trust property, home from the 1920s until the 1980s of Sir Daryl and Joan Lindsay. Yet another member of the artistic Lindsay clan, Daryl was best known as the director of the National Gallery of Victoria and as an art critic. His wife Joan is most famous for her book *Picnic at Hanging Rock* (1967), the basis for Peter Weir's 1975 film of the same name (the *Hanging Rock* in question is located 80km north of Melbourne, near the town of Woodend; Lindsay's direct inspiration may have been a painting of the site by William Ford, completed in 1875. Contrary to widely-held belief, the story is not based on a specific historical incident). The property has been left as it was at the time of Joan Lindsay's death in 1984, including hand-painted murals by Daryl in the writing rooms. It is open to the public on Sundays, and the Trust often holds musical and artistic events in the grounds.

From Golf Links Road, turn south on to Fultons Road, travel c 1.5km to Baxter-Tooradin Road (site of **Baxter train station**), turn west towards the bay and continue on to Sages Road. Near the intersection to the Moorooduc Highway is **Sages Cottage** (☎ 03 5971 1337; open Wed–Sun and holidays, 11.00–16.00), a pastoral property built by John Edward Sage in the 1840s; he became well known for the development of stations in the area. Now the cottage is best known for its restaurant, which uses fresh herbs and vegetables from its own gardens.

Return to the bay via the Moorooduc Highway (route 11) and the MORNINGTON– TYABB ROAD (route 62) into **Mornington**, the shire headquarters of the peninsula. To the north of here on Nepean Highway is Mount Eliza. Off Kunyung Road towards Moondah Beach is the property **'Moondah'**, now the Australian Management College, the gatehouse of which is a castellated Gothic Revival structure built for James Grice in 1888 as his 'castle by the sea'; the grounds offer superb views of the bay. Off Nepean Highway at Mt Eliza Way is the Anglican church **St James the Less**, a small brick Gothic Revival structure built in 1865 and noted for its sanctuary murals painted by local artist Violet Teague (1872–1951) in 1931.

Mornington

Back on MORNINGTON–TYABB ROAD, you come to Civic Reserve, at Dunns Road before entering the main street of Mornington. At Civic Reserve is the **Mornington Peninsula Arts Centre** (☎ 03 5975 4395; open Tues–Fri, 10.00–16.30, weekends 12.00–16.30), one of the Victorian regional art galleries, concentrating on the collection of Australian drawings; the contemporary sandstone building is located next to a small lake in a bushland setting. Earlier known as Schnapper Point, Mornington includes some fascinating examples of 19C architecture, including the **courthouse** and **police station** from the early 1860s, and the **old post office**, now a museum (☎ 03 5975 3613; open Sun 14.00–17.00), at MAIN STREET and the beachfront Esplanade. From here, you can walk to **Schnapper Point** with its wonderful views of the bay and down the peninsula.

At Queen Street is **St Peter's Church** of England, one of Leonard Terry's Gothic Revival designs, built in the early 1860s. At the northern end of The Esplanade, at Frontage Way, is **'Southdean'**, a delightful wooden structure, in a

Gothic Revival style; its elaborately detailed tower is a local landmark. It was built in the 1870s for Judge George Henry Webb, possibly to a design by Edward La Trobe Bateman, Governor La Trobe's nephew. Further north on The Esplanade at 42–4 Kalimna Drive is **'Beleura'**, a private home, but well worth a view. Built in 1863 for James Butchart, it is an extraordinary example of Italianate design, with its verandah-like colonnade of Corinthian columns and extensive balustraded parapet.

From Mornington, you might take THE ESPLANADE south to enjoy views of the bay to **Mount Martha**, a pleasant beach community; the mountain behind the town was named in honour of the wife of Captain Lonsdale, the colony's first lieutenant-general. Alternatively, you could return to the NEPEAN HIGHWAY (route 3) and continue south c 5km to **'The Briars'** (☎ 03 5974 3686; open daily, 11.00–17.00) in Mount Martha. A National Trust property, this pastoral holding was established in 1843 by Alexander Balcombe, who named it after his birthplace on the island of St Helena; Balcombe was supposedly a friend of Napoleon, and one room of the homestead includes Balcombe's furniture, with a table said to have been used by Napoleon to write his memoirs. The homestead, dating from 1863, now houses the Dame Mabel Brooks Napoleonic Collection in conjunction with Balcombe's artefacts. The grounds are particularly interesting, with marked walks through the wetlands where many varieties of birds can be viewed from enclosures. The site also houses a Wine Centre, with tastings from the Briars Vineyard, as well as other wines from the area.

Arthurs Seat and Dromana

The Nepean Highway south c 5km connects with the MORNINGTON PENINSULA FREEWAY (route 11), which leads directly to Dromana at the base of the panoramic rise of **Arthurs Seat** (☎ 03 5987 2565); exit at Arthurs Seat Road to enter the public and state park, with a chairlift to the top of the 305m promontory (the chairlift is open daily from 11.00 Sept–June, and on weekends and school holidays in winter). The mountain received its name from Lieutenant John Murray, on Flinders' expedition in 1802–03, inspired by a place of that name in Scotland. Matthew Flinders himself climbed the peak at that time. A winding road also leads to the summit, offering spectacular views of Port Phillip Bay and Melbourne. The park (☎ 03 5981 8888) includes several walking and driving trails, with bistros and tearooms dotted throughout. **Simon's Creek** in the park is named for Simon the Frenchman, a 19C eccentric who lived here in a tree and survived on goannas (monitor lizard).

On Purves Road, 500m south but still in Arthurs Seat State Park, is **Seawinds**, enormous formal gardens first established by surgeon Sir Thomas Travers in 1946. A number of walks meander through the grounds, which include fountains and sculptures by William Ricketts, creator of the William Ricketts Sanctuary in the Dandenongs (see Dandenongs section). Seawinds is definitely worth a visit for an inspiring stroll in a natural setting with views to the sea.

At **Dromana**, the real tourist beaches begin, and the foreshore is filled with camping sites, caravan parks, boat landings and picnic areas. Traffic in this area is quite overwhelming in the summer.

At Latrobe Parade, just south of the main **tourist information centre**, is

'Heronswood', another National Trust property, built of bluestone in 1871 as a retreat for academic and politician William Edward Hearn. An unusual Gothic Revival design, the house is believed to have been built by Edward La Trobe Bateman. Today it is best known for the surrounding cottage gardens with original 1870s plantings, best viewed between October and April; the house is not open to the public.

Further along the coast is **McCrae Homestead** (☎ 03 5981 2866; open daily, 12.00–16.30), located off the Nepean Highway near Eastern Lighthouse; turn on to Beverley Road, and then left into Burrell Street.

> The story of pioneers Andrew and Georgiana McCrae epitomises the extraordinary adventures of Victoria's early settlers; Georgiana's story is especially powerful, for she was an accomplished artist, musician and writer, and her diary serves as a vivid account of a talented woman's struggle for recognition while living a difficult life in a new land. Lawyer Andrew arrived in Australia from England in 1838; he was an abolitionist, fighting against the slave system that had brought wealth to his father through Jamaican sugar plantations. His wife Georgiana, the acknowledged illegitimate daughter of the Duke of Gordon, joined him with their four children in 1841. They moved to this house in 1844 on 12,800 acres of land; it was the first homestead in the region. Four more children were born here, before the family returned to Melbourne in 1851. As upper-class people with little practical skills on the land, the McCraes depended on servants, including the tutor John McLure, and the local Bunurong tribe of Aborigines for help and support in farming and hunting. Georgiana, who had studied painting with the English watercolourist John Varley, continued to paint miniatures and landscapes, and to record her impressions in her illustrated diaries; she has recently been championed as a stellar example of a pioneer woman of strength and cultivation, and her artworks are now eagerly sought. Examples of her work are exhibited at the homestead, along with original furniture. The McCraes did not succeed as graziers; when they left, the property went through a succession of owners until it was purchased in 1961 by George Gordon McCrae, a great-grandson of the original owners. In 1969, his son sold the homestead to the National Trust.

Sorrento

About 11km along the coast from Dromana, in **Rye**, is Whitecliffs, on Point Nepean Road. From the 1840s, this was the site of a limekiln for the Melbourne building trade; it has now been re-created as an historic exhibit.

Sorrento, site of Victoria's first, albeit brief, settlement, begins c 15km from Rye Limekilns. The site of the Collins camp at Sullivan Bay (3km southeast of Sorrento proper), established in 1803, is marked by a small historic display (☎ 131 963). The site includes gardens incorporating four graves from the 1803 settlement.

> The purpose of this settlement was to establish an English presence here to prevent French occupation of the coastline, and to explore this unknown part of the continent. Collins led a group of some 310 convicts and marines and families; after several months, the site was abandoned, as water was

scarce, and the group moved on to Tasmania. Before leaving, Collins also discovered the 'wild white man' William Buckley, who had lived with the Aborigines here for decades.

It was not until 1872, when entrepreneur George Coppin established the Sorrento Ocean Ampitheatre Company and formed a steam ferry operation between here and Queenscliff, that the region developed as a fashionable resort. The great paddle-steamers *Ozona*, *Hygeia*, and *Weeroona* plied the waters of the bay into the 1910s.

Sorrento has a **tourist information centre** at 3183 Nepean Road (☎ 03 5984 5678). Sorrento still has an air of wealth, as the playground of Melbourne's old money, who often own holiday houses here and come for the 'season', from Boxing Day to Easter. Just as in Coppin's day, Sorrento is the landing point for the ferries from Queenscliff crossing the entrance to Port Phillip Bay. The foreshore here has beautiful rock pools and **Sorrento Back Beach**, at the end of Ocean Beach Road on the ocean side of the peninsula, is a great surf beach. **Sullivan Bay** is now a popular place for snorkelling, and cavorting dolphins can often be seen swimming here. **Sorrento Park** on the breakwater is a popular picnicking spot, with stunning views of the entire bay. Remains of the town's 19C elegance can be seen in **Continental Hotel**, built in 1875 on Ocean Beach Road, as well as **St John's** Church of England of 1874 on Point Nepean Road. Also on Nepean Highway is **'Hindson House'**, built in the 1870s from local limestone as the summer home of Judge George Briscoe Kerferd, Premier of Victoria and Supreme Court Justice in the 1870s. At the corner of Melbourne and Ocean Beach Roads is the **Nepean Historical Museum** (☎ 03 5984 4424; open Thurs–Sun and holidays, 10.00–17.00), in the former Mechanics' Institute, built in 1876, with limestone additions from 1895. The museum has an interesting display of historical artefacts, and sits next to a lovely formal garden surrounded by limestone walls, a project in the 1980s of the Flinders Shire.

Continue on POINT NEPEAN ROAD, past the Sorrento Golf Club—one of the many famous 'sand courses' along the peninsula—to **Portsea**, an even swankier resort town at the entrance to **Mornington Peninsula National Park/Point Nepean National Park** (☎ 131 963). The passenger ferry to and from Queenscliff also stops at Portsea Pier. Of greatest interest here, aside from the opulent summer mansions of the rich, are the splendid surfing back beaches, which are actually part of the National Park (no dogs allowed). Diving and snorkelling facilities abound for the seasoned and beginning diver. Follow London Bridge Road to the natural rock formation and walking beach.

At the end of Point Nepean Road is the **Orientation Centre** for the National Park. No vehicles are permitted into the 2200 ha park, which includes 28km around the coastline to Cape Schanck. Because of the fragile ecology of the point, only 600 people are allowed into the park at a time, so it may be necessary to make bookings during the busy seasons; call the Orientation Centre (☎ 03 5984 4276). The centre also provides an informative brochure to guide the visitor through the park. From the Orientation Centre, you can also take a tractor-drawn transporter into the park, if you do not fancy a 14km walk around the point. On the first weekend of each month, when the transporter does not run, the park is also opened to cyclists. The **Peninsula Coastal Walk**, well marked and with a brochure obtainable from the Orientation Centre, extends from London Bridge to Portsea Back Beach, Cape Schanck and Bushrangers Bay.

As a former military site, the park has many areas marked on maps as 'unexploded ordnance', making them inaccessible to the public and allowing a return to natural vegetation; it is important, therefore, to remain on the roads and tracks. You can, however, visit the former **Quarantine Station** and the **cemetery**, where many immigrants, victims of illness or shipwreck, were buried before they reached Melbourne. The Quarantine Station, now the School of Army Health, was established in 1852 as a result of a typhus outbreak on board the immigrant ship *Ticonderoga*. The cemetery also contains the remains of some early settlers, including James Ford, a convict transported for 'machine breaking' in 1841 who was pardoned and settled on the peninsula; he named Portsea after the town near Portsmouth in England.

About 1km along the road from the cemetery is **Cheviot Hill**, with **Cheviot Beach** below it; the name commemorates a ship that crashed here in 1887. It was at Cheviot Beach that Prime Minister Harold Holt went missing in December 1967. Many conspiracy theories arose, including that he was whisked away by a Chinese submarine or that the American CIA had a hand in the disappearance, but it is most likely that he simply drowned while diving into dangerous surf; his body was never found. The coastline from Point Nepean to London Bridge is now known as the Harold Holt Marine Reserve. From Cheviot Hill there are terrific views across The Rip and to Queenscliff on the other side. It is no surprise that swimming at the beach is not permitted, since the currents are strong and unpredictable.

From the hill you can continue along the **Walter Pisterman Heritage Walk** to Point Nepean itself, visiting **Fort Pearce** and finally **Fort Nepean**, built at the same time as Fort Queenscliff, in response to the fear of Russian invasion after the Crimean War. Major construction occurred in the 1880s; the complex cost over £1 million to construct, and was one of the largest engineering projects undertaken in the colony. The fort was used as a military installation throughout the Second World War, when there was fear of Japanese submarine invasion into Port Phillip Bay. You can tour the remains of the fort, with its many tunnels and gun emplacements. The brochure available from the Orientation Centre gives detailed descriptions of the site.

Somers

Exiting the National Park, several small roads lead down to various ocean beaches. Alternatively, return to Boneo Road in Rosebud (route 67) and travel south to **Cape Schanck** and its **lighthouse station**, built in 1859 as a landmark on the eastern side of Port Phillip Bay and still functioning. The area has several picnic areas and majestic views to Bass Strait. From here, return to route 67 and travel east to **Flinders**, a small fishing village at the beginning of Western Port; a plaque here commemorates George Bass's discovery of the port in 1798.

Continue along the Flinders–Frankston Road (route 67) 18km, turn on to Sandy Point Road at Balnarring and travel 2km to **Coolart Reserve** and **Homestead** (☎ 131 963; open daily, 10.00–17.00) on Lord Somers Road in **Somers**. This mansion is part of one of the most prosperous of the early peninsula properties. First settled in 1840 by Alfred Meyrick, the main mansion was built in 1897 by Frederick S. Grimwade, founder of a famous pharmaceutical firm. Subsequent owner Tom Luxton, owner of the hardware chain McEwans, developed the elegant gardens and created the nearby lagoon. Today some 15 ha of wetland provide an important bird sanctuary, carefully maintained by the state government. Excellent **walking trails** allow visitors to observe the many birds in their natural habitat.

From here, take the SOUTH BEACH ROAD back to route 67 and on to **Stony Point**, to catch the **passenger ferry** to French Island and Phillip Island. It is also possible to cross a bridge to Phillip Island (see below) by travelling all the way around Western Port and crossing over at San Remo, a trip of about 90km from the other side of Western Port.

French Island

From Stony Point, a passenger ferry travels daily to Tankerton, the only settlement on French Island; no cars can arrive on the island, so sightseeing is either by a 4-hour coach tour, conducted by an islander family, or by bicycle rental or walking. More than 50 per cent of the island is state park, and only 75 inhabitants live on the island. **Tortoise Head French Island Lodge** (☎ 03 5980 1234) provides the only accommodation, aside from four camping sites; the lodge is also the only place for meals. With 144km of relatively undisturbed coastline, the island makes for a fascinating day trip, with abundant examples of Australian flora and fauna. It is home to the **potoroo**, a small member of the kangaroo family, decimated on the mainland by feral foxes, but thriving here. Also plentiful are koala and a variety of waterbirds. The shoreline includes salt marshes, mudflats, and mangrove forests.

History

French Island was actually named by French explorers; two ships on a scientific expedition, *Le Geographe*, captained by Nicolas Baudin, and *Le Naturaliste*, were in these waters in 1802, when Matthew Flinders was exploring the same region. The French made the most complete charting of this port. Earlier, in 1801, Lt James Grant on the *Lady Nelson* had explored the area, building a cottage on Churchill Island off Phillip Island and planting crops. French Island saw the establishment of several processing industries, including a salt works, and a few pastoral runs, and in 1893 the Victorian government subsidised six settlements with lofty names such as Energy and Star of Hope. The main activity at this time was chicory production, which continued into the 1960s. Remains of these settlements' homesteads can still be seen. For most of the late 19C and into the 1970s, the island was a prison centre, considered a country club farm because of its sports facilities and lenient conditions. The prison was closed in 1975 and used as a youth camp; visitors can take a tour of the complex.

Passengers can travel from here on the ferry to Cowes on Phillip Island, the more developed and tourist-oriented island in the port.

Phillip Island

Phillip Island is one of the most popular tourist destinations in Australia, because of the appearance every night in enormous numbers of **Little (Fairy)**

Penguins. These wonderful birds are the smallest of the penguins and inhabit the southern coast of Australia, extending as far north as the New South Wales–Queensland border. While they occasionally establish colonies on the mainland, they prefer to nest on islands; the Phillip Island colony has been a popular attraction since the 19C. The viewing area is well controlled to prevent people disturbing the birds. Every hotel in Melbourne will have brochures advertising tours to the island that include a visit to the **Penguin Parade**. Access via the bridge at San Remo has been possible since 1940, when a suspension bridge was completed. The current concrete bridge was opened in 1969, and carries almost four million day trippers a year.

There is no public transport on the island, but it can be reached by taking the train to Dandenong and transferring to a bus to Cowes, the island's main town; on Fridays a direct service runs from Melbourne, and on weekends tours by ferry are available from St Kilda Pier. From the island, it is possible to arrange inexpensive flights to Tasmania.

History

In the early 19C, French exploration of the port led the British to establish a military presence here; in 1826, a Captain Wright built on Phillip Island near Rhyll a small post, named ironically Fort Dumaresque. Later this settlement was moved to Corinella on the mainland. Permanent settlers did not arrive until the 1840s, when dairy farming and grazing were established. A sign of the island's success as a dairy producer can be seen at the Australian Dairy Centre (☎ 03 5956 7583; open daily), across from the Information Centre, with its small museum. Phillip Island was also a major centre for chicory production, and the island still has many of the old chicory kilns.

The **tourist information centre** at Newhaven is built in the form of an old-fashioned kiln. This centre, 1km from the bridge from San Remo, is the best place to begin a visit to the island; and you can make bookings here for the Penguin Parade (☎ 03 5956 7447). It is a good idea to book for the Penguin Parade (see below), especially in the summer, when the crowds at the event are enormous.

Off the coast at Newhaven is **Churchill Island**, until recently the only privately owned island in the state. Because James Grant landed here in 1801 on the *Lady Nelson* and planted wheat and corn on the island, it is sometimes considered the first European settlement in Victoria; but Grant did not stay for long. A small bridge gives access to the island, where you can visit the historic homestead and gardens, as well as enjoy the natural setting and birdlife.

About 5km south of Phillip Island's information centre is **Cape Woolamai**; the name is an Aboriginal word for 'snapper', given by George Bass who thought the point appeared like the shape of this fish. The cape has a famous surf beach, and is now a fauna reserve, particularly for the shearwater, or mutton-bird, who have a rookery here between September and May.

Rhyll, about 14km from Newhaven, is the site where George Bass landed in 1798 and where Fort Dumaresque was established by Captain Wright to guard against any possible French invasion. It is a quietly beautiful spot with cliffside walks and places to explore the salt marshes and view the birds.

The main settlement on the island is **Cowes**, 8km west. It is a picturesque village, aptly named after the holiday town on the Isle of Wight. The ferries from

Stony Point and French Island land here, and cruises depart from here to **Seal Rocks**, off Summerland on the southwest tip of the island. As many as **6000 fur seals** arrive here in November to begin the breeding season—this is the best place to see these animals along the whole of the Australian coast. Early sealers came to these waters to hunt the seals; by 1891 their numbers had been so drastically reduced that they had to be protected, which they have been ever since. The Seal Rocks Sea Life Centre (☎ 03 9793 6767) has recently opened on Cowes–Nobbies Road, and provides a boat trip to see the seals close up. Cowes also houses the **Phillip Island Heritage Centre** (☎ 03 5956 9214; open daily Dec–Jan; Feb–April, Sun, Tues and Thurs 14.00–16.30 & Sat 10.00–12.00; weekends in winter), with displays on the island's natural history and geology. Another tourist attraction is Mini Europe, an incongruous miniature village of famous European buildings!

Along Phillip Island Road is a **Koala Reserve** and the **Koala Conservation Centre** (☎ 03 5956 8691; open daily, 10.00–17.00), established to protect and preserve the dwindling number of koalas on the island. The centre includes an excellent interpretative centre and informative displays; fondling of koalas, however, is not allowed in the State of Victoria.

From Cowes, it is another 10km to **Summerland** and the **Penguin Parade** (☎ 03 5956 8300; fax 03 5956 8394), the major tourist attraction. Be sure to bring warm weather gear at all times; it is most enjoyable to visit here in the off season when there is less of a tourist mob. The authorities are to be commended for controlling the crowds who come to see this delightful natural phenomenon and protecting the penguins and their environment at the same time. The beach is illuminated for about an hour every night at dusk as the penguins arrive; more muted lighting later allows visitors to enjoy the penguin antics after the main show. Be mindful of the walkways and obey the guidelines for viewing.

Between Summerland and Sunderland Bay is the **Phillip Island Racing Circuit**, site of Grand Prix motorcycle racing and stock-car races which often bring some 60,000 fans to the island for a very noisy event.

Back at **San Remo**, a pleasant fishing village with a 50-boat fishing fleet, you can explore the cemetery, which includes the graves of early pioneer families such as the Anderson family, who took up graziers' leases in the 1840s. The coastline south of here is called the Anderson Peninsula, and from Punchbowl, 3km south of San Remo, the **George Bass Coastal Walk** follows the shore on a 10km round-trip to Kilcunda. The walk traverses the grounds of the Bunurong Aboriginal group, and evidence of kitchen middens can be found near the beaches. The Punchbowl itself is an impressive blowhole. George Bass explored the area by sea in 1798, while William Howell covered it on foot in 1826.

Outer suburbs ~ Heidelberg, Eltham and Warrandyte

To reach the famous **Heidelberg** area, in the northeast of Melbourne, begin at Princes/Alexandra Parade in Carlton/Fitzroy. The Hurstbridge Line of the train network travels through all of these suburbs, and several bus routes also go to the area. At Brunswick Street, turn into Queens Parade (route 46) which becomes HEIDELBERG ROAD, or continue into the Eastern Freeway (route 83) to Bulleen Road and on to Templestowe Road. Heidelberg Road is the older route, although it is no longer the bucolic stretch into the country as it was in the 1880s, when Heidelberg and Eaglemont were the favoured destinations for a group of young artists intent on depicting the Australian landscape and creating a national style in painting.

> Heidelberg's name, along with that of Coburg to the west, indicates the prevalence of German settlers in this region in the 1870s, when it was a farming village. The artists Tom Roberts, Arthur Streeton, Charles Conder, and Frederick McCubbin travelled here to set up camps where they could experience 'the bush' (city boys that they were) and paint *en plein air* in emulation of the painters of Barbizon. Significantly, Heidelberg was only 15km from central Melbourne, and by the time the artists were travelling here, a train deposited them easily into the landscape; today the area is entirely suburban, and it is difficult to envision it as open bushland. In nearby Eaglemont, Arthur Streeton set up house in the mid-1880s where the group that came to be known as The Heidelberg School coalesced. Frederick McCubbin late in life fondly recalled the area as 'not the suburban Heidelberg of today, but the remote sleepy Heidelberg of years ago, with its winding country roads, its wooded hills and quiet village life'. In his poem 'That Last Summer at Eaglemont', Christopher Wallace-Crabbe evokes the brilliant landscapes of the Heidelberg paintings:

> *In the beginning it was much to do with light*
> *Feeling at brushtip the afternoon's full glare,*
> *Pale paddocks and streaky stalks of grass*
> *Crushed only where an easel had briefly stood...*

Today, you can take part of the Yarra Trail through the area, on foot or by bicycle, where reproductions of the artists' paintings are strategically placed near the relevant views.

Museum of Modern Art, Heide

Significantly, for an area so identified with artistic creativity, the **Museum of Modern Art** at Heide (☎ 03 9850 1500, open Tues–Fri 10.00–17.00, weekends 12.00–17.00) is near to the centre of Heidelberg. From the Heidelberg **train station**, take Banksia Street east c 2.5km across the Yarra Flats by Banksia Park (or catch **bus no. 291** from the station); turn north on Bulleen Road to enter Heide Park; from the Central Business District every second or third **Yarra Valley Views bus** from Russell and Lonsdale Street will stop here.

As the current director maintains, it is no exaggeration to consider 'Heide' as the birthplace of modernism in Australia, for it was here that wealthy patrons John and Sunday Reed purchased a dairy farm in 1934 and converted it into the most significant meeting place for artists, writers, and poets. They named the place 'Heide' in the 1940s. It was here that Sidney Nolan painted his famous Ned Kelly series, where Joy Hester and Albert Tucker created, and where the Reeds nurtured avant-garde ideas in all the arts. In the 1950s, the Reeds even established a museum of modern art in central Melbourne, using their own collection as the basis for exhibitions—quite a feat in a city that still considered Impressionism as too 'modern'. In the 1960s, they built a modernist house on the Heide site; the present museum incorporates this house along with a gallery added in 1993. The gardens are equally important, as homage to Sunday's inspired gardening; additionally, a 5 ha Sculpture Park provides an ideal setting for Australian and international sculpture.

Recently a number of books and television productions have appeared documenting the lives of this fascinating couple and their unconventional lifestyle; this museum is a fitting legacy to their nearly single-handed commitment to the modernist cause. One architect has described the museum building as 'International Style set down amongst the Melaleucas [ti-trees]', and that assessment certainly sets the tone for the display of modernist artworks, most notably but not exclusively those who worked at Heide. Not to be missed are the delightfully expressionist early paintings by **Sidney Nolan**, before he became a famous expatriate in England. The museum also mounts original exhibitions, predominantly focusing on contemporary Australian art.

Montsalvat and Eltham

To get to Montsalvat from Heide, continue east on Templestowe Road about 5km to Fitzsimmons Road; turn north and travel about 4.5km to Mount Pleasant Road. Turn east and travel past the cemetery about 1.5km, turn south on to Hillcrest Road to Montsalvat in Eltham. The **train service** is on the Hurstbridge Line.

Montsalvat (☎ 03 9439 7712; open daily 09.00–17.00) was an artists' colony founded in 1934 by Justus Jorgensen, a visionary artist who died in 1975. Eclectic artists' houses are dotted aesthetically throughout the hills in a variety of styles on some 8 ha of gardens; the main aim was to appear as if it were a French provincial village. Members of the community included Mervyn Skipper, correspondent for the *Bulletin* and author of *The White Man's Garden* (1930); and Robert Close, who in the early 1940s lived in a Montsalvat hut and wrote the novel *Love Me Sailor* (1945), for which he was jailed for obscenity. Betty Roland wrote a fascinating depiction of the community, *The Eye of the Beholder* (1984). Montsalvat now hosts an annual poetry festival, as well as a well-known **jazz festival** at the end of January. At the centre of the community is the Great Hall, which includes Gothic windows which were taken from the Royal Insurance Building in Collins Street before it was demolished. The Great Hall is open to the public and contains some of Jorgensen's paintings.

Eltham itself, about 2km north back on MAIN ROAD, has also been the home of many writers and artists, including C.B. Cristensen, who moved here in 1945 to establish the literary journal *Meanjin*; his house Stanhope on Peter Street became a literary meeting-place. The poet Chris Wallace-Crabbe lived here from 1976 to 1983, in one of the pisé houses (pisé means mud bricks) built in the suburb by the novelist J.M. Harcourt. The town also houses the **Eltham Library** and **Shillinglaw Cottage**. The cottage dates from 1878 and is now a fine restaurant; the library is a stunningly modern building, designed in a style reminiscent of Frank Lloyd Wright's Marin County Civic Center in California.

Warrandyte

From Eltham, you can continue northeast on Main Road (route 44) c 4km to Research Warrandyte Road; or back south on Fitzsimmons Lane to Porter Street/Warrandyte Road (route 42, tourist route 2) to the village of **Warrandyte** near the winding Yarra River. Take Harris Gully Road south to Gold Memorial Road; along Andersons Creek, only 30km from central Melbourne, the very first Victorian **gold** was found on 5 July 1851, marked now by a memorial cairn. This discovery began the gold rush, but was quickly abandoned when the larger strike was found at Clunes soon after. The area has been a popular getaway for artists and writers since the 1870s. Most notable were the artist Clara Southern, a pupil of Frederick McCubbin; the painter Penleigh Boyd, brother of writer Martin Boyd (Boyd's novel *Outbreak of Love* [1957] was set here); the great potter Reg Preston; and painter and writer Adrian Lawlor, who built a Bauhaus-style house on Research Road after his first home was destroyed in the 1939 Black Friday fires. The Warrandyte Historical Society on Warrandyte Road contains artefacts and photographs from the area's gold-mining era; it is open on weekends. The Warrandyte State Park, with entry gates at Jumping Creek Road and Pound Bend, has excellent walking and cycling paths along the many bends of the upper Yarra River. The area is great for picnicking, bird watching, and canoeing. The gates to the park close every evening at dusk, so be mindful of closing time signs.

Southwest of Melbourne

Taking Princes Highway (route 1) south out of Melbourne towards the Bellarine Peninsula and Geelong, you come to **Werribee Park** (☎ 03 9741 2444, open daily 10.00–17.00), 34km from the CBD. The train's Werribee Line ends in the town of Werribee, about 2km from the park.

Standing grandly alone in the sandy flatlands west of the city, the elaborate estate of Werribee Park was built in the 1870s for pastoralists Thomas and Andrew Chirnside, who at one point owned an enormous empire of sheep. In the 1880s they were even able to purchase a castle in their native Scotland. The mansion here is Italianate in style, made of bluestone with a freestone facing, with opulent use of Corinthian columns, gold leaf, and classical ornamentation. Tradition maintains that one brother had it built to convince a countrywoman to marry him; indeed, Andrew did marry and occupied the house with his family. The original house had some 50 rooms, but extensive additions by the Chirnside sons included a tower and other incongruous details.

The building is noteworthy as an ugly heap; obviously, the two bachelors, with very little aesthetic sense but a lot of money, were responsible for this oddity in the middle of nowhere. At various times in the early 20C, the estate was used as a research farm, airforce base, and Jesuit seminary, all of which made additions and some unfortunate modifications; it has also served as the location for several Australian films, including *Libido* (1973). It is now owned by the Victorian government, and open to the public. Attendants in 19C costume can provide some history and comment for self-guiding tours. The gardens have also been restored to their original state, including one of the few remaining Lake Grottoes (recently closed because of vandalism), greenhouses and lodge, as well as a unique ha-ha, a bluestone wall set in a trench to create a moat. The outbuildings and well-kept gardens are really the most interesting things to see.

Also in Werribee Park, on K Road, is Werribee Zoo (☎ 03 9731 1311; open 09.00–17.00), an open range zoo with African, Asian and Australian wildlife.

A further 8km south on the Princes Highway is Little River Road, which leads to You Yangs Regional Park (☎ 131 963), some 2000 ha with an interesting range of volcanic hills, discovered and climbed in 1802 by Matthew Flinders himself. Climb Flinders Peak in the park for great views to Geelong and the coast, or enjoy the walking tracks with abundant birds and native animals.

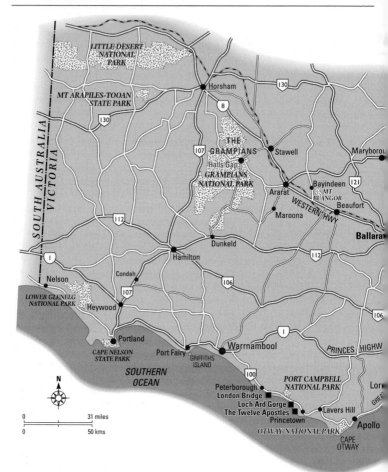

Western Victoria

The construction of the **GREAT OCEAN ROAD**, which begins in Geelong, began in 1919 and was completed in 1932, during the Great Depression. Initially conceived as both a memorial to and an employment project for the servicemen of the First World War, the initiative in many ways mirrors the construction of California's Pacific Coast Highway. The similarities between the two are great, with spectacular scenery along its windy route on the edge of seaside cliffs and through gentle, forested slopes. The region is popularly known as '**Shipwreck Coast**', its jagged rocks leading to the demise of some 100 ships over the last two centuries, and the subsequent construction of lighthouses crucial to safe navigation. During his circumnavigation of Australia in 1803, the explorer Matthew Flinders wrote of the area around Cape Otway, 'I have seldom seen a more fearful section of coastline'. Visitors have ample opportunity at the many scenic

WESTERN VICTORIA

overviews to gain an appreciation of the efforts of those sailors and passengers who made the dangerous journey through Bass Strait on their way to the new settlements of the continent.

The journey along the Great Ocean Road from east to west begins on the **Bellarine Peninsula** (see below). The peninsula itself has several points of interest, and is easily accessible from Melbourne.

Transport

Trains run frequently from Melbourne to Geelong every day; there are also daily V/Line trains running between Melbourne and Warrnambool (about a 3-hour trip). Along with many organised tour buses (check with tourist offices in Melbourne or Geelong), a regular V/Line bus service leaves daily from Geelong railway station for Apollo Bay, with a weekly service (on Fridays) to Port Campbell and Warrnambool. Bellarine Transit (☎ 03 5223 2111) provides a regular bus service between Geelong, the Bellarine Peninsula, Point Lonsdale and Torquay.

Geelong

The most logical place to begin a tour of the peninsula is in the industrial town of **Geelong** (population 128,300), 72km south of the city. Geelong itself is popularly known for two things: **Geelong Grammar School**, probably the most exclusive boarding school in the country, founded in 1857 (Prince Charles attended here in the 1970s); and the **Geelong Cats**, the town's fiercely loved Aussie Rules Football team. The location of the school is a telling commentary on the development of the town, for it now sits on the edge of the enormous Shell Oil Refinery and next to a fertiliser factory. The Cats are sponsored by Ford Motor Company, which has major plants in town. **Tourist information**: Great Ocean Tourism, National Wool Centre, Moorabool St; ☎ 03 5222 2900. Despite the overwhelming presence of such industrial sites, Geelong as one of the oldest cities in Victoria, contains many historical buildings and areas of interest.

History

When overland explorers Hume and Hovell reached the tip of Corio Bay in 1824, the local Aborigines, the Wathaurong tribe, told them the bay was called Jillong, hence the town's name. Settlers began to arrive in 1836, at first taking up enormous runs around the bay; land blocks went up for sale in 1839, and by the time of the gold rush in the 1850s, Geelong's population of 8000 supported the wool and grazing industries developing inland. The influx of immigrants during the 1850s saw the population treble, with Geelong seriously rivalling Melbourne for position of premier city, as goldseekers arrived and travelled the flatter route from here to the goldfields. Those made wealthy in this period constructed mansions and public buildings around Western and Eastern Beaches along the bay itself.

By the 1860s, the frenetic pace eased, and Geelong settled into a period of increasing mercantile activity. Indeed, a popular saying asserts that 'wool is to Geelong what gold was to Ballarat'; enormous quantities of this most important Australian product were shipped around the world via the port of Geelong, a fact demonstrated in the National Wool Museum.

The **National Wool Museum** (☎ 03 5227 0701; open daily 10.00–17.00), one block from the waterfront on the corner of BROUGHAM and MOORABOOL STREETS is in the heart of the city's wool trading district. The museum is housed in the old bluestone Dennys Lascelles Wool Store, originally constructed in 1872 by Jacob Pitman and considered the model for all future wool stores because of its window design; subsequent buildings were added on until 1930. The museum is tastefully designed and includes oral history displays in re-created shearers' quarters, and a functioning Jacquard textile loom. Geelong's main tourist information centre—a very thorough and well-staffed one—is also located here.

Turning right into BROUGHAM STREET from Moorabool Street, you will find the sandstone **Customs House**, built in 1856 by W.G. Cornish from a design by Colonial Architect James Balmain as Geelong's third customs house. It is considered one of the finest Victorian public buildings in this region, and still serves its original purpose. Walk one block up Moorabool Street and turn west on Malop Street to reach Johnson Park and Little Malop Street, location of the **Geelong Memorial Art Gallery** (☎ 03 5229 3645; open weekdays 10.00–17.00, weekends and holidays 13.00–17.00). The collection includes several excellent regional paintings, most notably Frederick McCubbin's famous *Bush Burial* (1890).

One block west of Johnson Park is **Latrobe Terrace**, a six-block stretch of historic houses from different eras, most of them originally owned by doctors. They include **'Sarina'**, nos 266–8, double-storey brick houses built c 1854, and **'Ingliston'**, a single-storey villa with wooden verandah built in 1871 by Joseph Watts and owned by well-known doctor Robert Pincott.

Back at Corio Bay, the most interesting route is off Princes Highway on to the **Esplanade** around Western and Eastern Beaches. In Osborne Park at Swinburne Street is **Osborne House**, now the **Maritime Museum** (☎ 03 5277 2260; open Mon, Wed, Fri–Sun 10.00–16.00), presenting the shipping history of both Corio and Port Phillip Bays. Built in 1857 for pastoralist squatter Robert Muirhead, the building has a colonnaded verandah and views to Corio Bay. It served as the First Australian Naval College in 1913 and as a submarine base in the early 1920s.

Go back to Princes Highway and turn at Bell Parade into the Esplanade; on the west is **Lunan House**, a spacious two-storey mansion built in 1850 for James Strahan, early wool broker and member of Victoria's first Legislative Council. The design by Charles Laing included a Doric portico and elaborate iron gates that are now at the entrance to Geelong Grammar School.

If you have transport, you might drive around Western Beach to look at **Cunningham Pier** and **Steampacket Gardens**; the gardens are on land reclaimed from the sea, and originally used for industrial purposes. (A small walking tour brochure of this area is available at the Tourist Information Centre in the Wool Centre.) Further along at Eastern Beach is **The Royal Geelong Yacht Club**, established in 1859; the first sailing regatta here was in 1844. In the early days, Eastern and Western Beaches had six bathing complexes, segregated for men and women.

One of the most fasci-
nating structures in
Australia—probably the
most famous domestic
building in the country—
is **Corio Villa**, 56 Eastern
Beach; it is still a private
residence, so visitors can
only view the exterior.
The villa is a single-storey
prefabricated iron house
designed by the Edin-
burgh firm of Bell & Miller
and cast in Scotland

Corio Villa, Geelong

before being shipped to Australia in 1855. Soon after, the factory and its moulds burned to the ground, making this villa the only known extant example of this unusual building process. Upon arrival in Geelong, the original consignee (believed now to be Land Commissioner William Gray, who died in 1854) did not claim the order and the crates of bulky 13mm thick plates were discarded, even-tually to be purchased by magistrate and banker Alfred Douglass, and assembled without any detailed specifications. The overall impression of the house is one of delicacy and lightness, despite the nature of the material; iron lacework abounds, its interiors include English cedar and oak linings, and throughout are decorative motifs of rose and thistle.

At the end of Eastern Beach at Garden Street is another important mansion, still in private hands: **Merchiston Hall**, designed and built by Backhouse and Reynolds in 1856 for businessman and politician James Cowie. From its balcony there would originally have been sweeping views of Corio Bay, but these are now obscured.

At the end of Eastern Beach Road there are the **Geelong Botanical Gardens** (☎ 03 5227 0387), one of the oldest in Victoria, with 'notable trees' surviving from the first plantings in 1857. The original designs, laid out by Daniel Bunce, are no longer distinguishable. In the gardens is Geelong's **first Customs House**, prefabricated in Sydney in 1838 and moved to this site in 1938; a small wooden building, it also served as the settlement's first telegraph office. The gardens sit on what was originally called **Limeburner's Point**; a cairn at the point recounts the story of the supposed discovery here of a set of keys (now lost), believed to have come from a Portuguese ship in these waters in 1522—one of many mysterious legends throughout Australia alluding to explorers here before Captain Cook or Abel Tasman.

Another National Trust property open to the public is **The Heights** (☎ 03 5221 3510; open Wed–Sun and holidays 11.00–16.30), on Aphrasia Street in Newtown; take Ryrie Street, the Hamilton Highway, west past Princes Highway to Shannon Avenue, turn south to Aphrasia. The original part of the house was prefabricated in Germany, and erected on the site in 1854. Home to three generations of the Ibbotson family, the home was extensively 'modernised' in the 1930s, although the 1850s outbuildings still remain.

Also in Newtown, on Fernleigh Street off Fyans Street, is **Barwon Grange** (☎ 03 5221 3906; open Sept–April, Wed and weekends, 11.00–16.30), another National Trust property located on the banks of the Barwon River. Built in 1856 for merchant and shipowner Jonathan Porter O'Brien, this house is distinguished for its decorative roofline and elegant rooms. The homestead is in original condition, with beautiful gardens.

Wineries
In the 1840s and 1850s, the Geelong region became the most important **wine-producing area** in Victoria. By the 1870s there were over 100 vineyards here, propagated by German, Swiss and French settlers. Unfortunately, Geelong was also the point of entry of the phylloxera virus, which destroyed all the vines by 1880. In 1966, **Idyll Vineyards** (☎ 03 5276 1280) (Ballan Road) began the renewal of wine-making in the district, and now several others have followed suit in the immediate vicinity. All are well signposted on the major roads and offer tours and 'cellar-door' sales.

Bellarine Peninsula
Still in Geelong, Garden Street heads south to Ormond Street, which leads to BELLARINE HIGHWAY (route 91) and the resort villages of the Bellarine Peninsula. At Wallington, an area known for strawberries, turn south to **Barwon Heads**, where limestone reefs led to numerous shipwrecks; several surf beaches now lure bathers. The town was recently the location for the popular ABC series, *Sea Change*. Nearby **Ocean Grove** acquired its name from American Methodist missionaries who attempted in the 1880s to establish a temperance resort here similar to Ocean Grove, New Jersey (it did not succeed).

Grubb Road leads north to **Drysdale**, a picturesque village known for its natural springs. Its name derives from Anne Drysdale who, along with Caroline Newcomb, settled here in 1849 and established the **Coryule homestead**, still in existence today. From Drysdale, you can take a **tourist steam train** (☎ 03 5227 0270) to Queenscliff, the furthest point on the peninsula.

History of the peninsula
It was here, between present-day Point Lonsdale and Point Nepean (on Mornington Peninsula), that Matthew Flinders entered Port Phillip Bay in 1802, navigating the treacherous Rip; from Point Lonsdale, at Rip View, you can still witness the danger of the passage, as ships negotiate the heads on their way to Port Melbourne. Flinders sailed on and named Indented Head for the notch of land jutting out of the peninsula. David Collins came

here with a surveying party on an expedition from New South Wales in 1803 to form a settlement; finding no adequate water supply, they went on to Tasmania.

At Indented Head in 1835, John Batman's party landed here, and encountered the extraordinary figure of William Buckley, a convict who had escaped from Collins' party 32 years before and had lived with the Aborigines all that time. Buckley subsequently became a go-between with the natives and his seemingly romantic story became the stuff of legend (in reality his limited intelligence led him to be less than the heroic figure presented along with other stories of 'wild white men'); his name lives on in Buckley's Cave below the Point Lonsdale Lighthouse.

To the northwest of Indented Head is **Portarlington**, a lovely fishing village, and the site of the **Portarlington Mill** (☎ 03 5259 3048; open summer months, Sun 14.00–17.00), a flour mill opened in 1857; the building is now part of the National Trust, which conduct tours of the preserved steam-driven mill.

Queenscliff

Queenscliff rapidly developed as a pilot station and customs point for entering ships. In 1861 **The Black Lighthouse** was erected here; along with the nearby **White Lighthouse**, it provides a line bearing for navigation of the Rip waters.

By the 1880s, Queenscliff had become Melbourne's most popular weekend seaside resort; while initially smart, it quickly became the holiday destination for all stratas of society. In Frank Hardy's *Power Without Glory* (1950), the poor of Carringbush in the 1900s dreamed of weekends at Queenscliff, and rides on its giant paddlesteamers; in Graham McInnes' *The Road to Gundagai* (1965), Queenscliff is 'pedestrian, respectable and family'.

Remnants of its more elegant days are the Victorian era hotels, *The Grand* (now the Vue Grand), *The Ozone*, and the *Queenscliff*, still open for visitors. The **Queenscliff Hotel** is architecturally the grandest of all; the Grand Dining Room here should not be missed.

Queenscliff was also a garrison town; during the Crimean War (1853–56), fear of Russian invasion led Australians to build fortresses everywhere, particularly around Port Phillip Heads. **Fort Queenscliff** (☎ 03 5258 0730; open daily) is a fascinating reminder of this period, built to withstand assault from land or sea; a tour of the facility includes a museum in the underground powder rooms. The town also houses the **Queenscliff Maritime Centre** (☎ 03 5258 3440; open holidays, 10.30–16.30, weekends 13.30–16.30), on Weeroona Parade, with changing displays relating to the seagoing history of the peninsula, and the **Marine Studies Centre** next door; and the **Queenscliff Historical Centre** (☎ 03 5258 2511; open daily, 14.00–16.00), on Hesse Street, which presents the history of the region, including relics from shipwrecks.

Queenscliff is also important as the point of departure of the **Sorrento-Portsea-Queenscliff ferry** (☎ 03 5258 3244), including the car ferry linking the Bellarine and Mornington Peninsulas. The route is a great way to avoid Melbourne for those travelling the Princes Highway between the Ocean Road and Gippsland.

Along surf coast ~ the Great Ocean Road

The GREAT OCEAN ROAD proper begins at **Torquay**, on the Bellarine Peninsula, some 106km south of Melbourne. Torquay has a nicely protected town beach, around **Point Danger** which faces the Bass Strait; this point was the site of the wreck of the three-master clipper, *Joseph H. Scammell*, in 1891. **Tourist information:** The Esplanade ☎ 03 5261 4127.

Torquay is most famous for the big **surfing beaches** nearby. **Rip Curl**, makers of surfboards and surfing paraphernalia, have been here since the 1960s. First to the west along the Ocean Road is **Jan Juc Beach**; then, most famous of all, is **Bell's Beach** (☎ 03 5261 4202), location of some of the toughest, meanest surf, revered by the most skilled surfers in the world. Waves as big as 3m with exceedingly long swells are standard fare, and 6m waves are not unknown. The area is named after the Bell family, original settlers in the 1840s. There is a lookout above the beach where viewers can watch surfers in action and admire the spectacular view along this rugged coast of the Bass Strait; the lookout includes a memorial plaque to a young surfer drowned in waves in 1984. At Easter time, the **Bell's Beach Surfing Carnival** attracts participants from around the world, and the beach has been the site of the World Surfing Championships. A splendid **Surf Coast Walk** begins at Jan Juc Beach and continues all the way to Airey's Inlet.

The Ocean Road continues 15km to **Anglesea**, the tranquillity of which is somewhat blighted by the presence on the edge of town of a coal mine and power station. The town itself has a lovely beach; on New Year's Day, an annual regatta of the town's 100-year-old boats sails on the Anglesea River, and in September the Angair Festival presents displays of wildflowers and excursions into the bushland. The area also displays charred reminders of the **Ash Wednesday Fire**, the devastating bushfires of 1983 that spread across much of Victoria and all the way to the coastline.

10km along the road is **Airey's Inlet**, named for settler J. Eyrie in 1846. Of most interest here is the **Split Point Lighthouse** (☎ 03 5289 6306), built in 1891 after the wreck of the *Joseph Scammell* at Torquay. Still in operation, the lighthouse can be climbed by visitors, to provide stunning, if vertigo-inducing, views of the cliffs and sea. Its location figures in detective writer Arthur Upfield's *The New Shoe* (1952).

Lorne and Apollo Bay

From here the road continues 21km to **Lorne** (population 930), a traditional old summer resort, initially established as such by the local grazier family the Mountjoys at the temperance hotel **Erskine House** in 1868. While Erskine House still remains, the town is now thoroughly overrun by hordes of tourists (at least in summer), making it difficult to appreciate any bucolic charm it may have had. Arthur Upfield, in *The New Shoe* (1952) nicely sums up the atmosphere:

> *Once upon a time Lorne was charmingly beautiful. Situated above a wide, sandy and safe bathing beach, its doom was inevitable. Crowded hotels and a fun fair, souvenir shops and crude cafes attracted the flash elements from the city. When Bony saw Lorne, he shuddered.*

In the 1960s, this scenario was overlaid with a hippie-surfer attitude; now it is a bit more yuppified, with oversize holiday condos on the main street, but the overall impression is the same. **Tourist information:** 144 Mountjoy Parade, ☎ 03 5289 1152.

Nearby is **Teddy's Lookout**, with magnificent views of the coastline, and the **Angahook-Lorne State Park** stretching 50km along the coast, with pleasant walking trails through the hills and to the beautiful **Erskine Falls** (☎ 131 963).

45km further west on the Ocean Road is **Apollo Bay** (population 880), still a quiet, lovely spot, with gorgeous, soft hills in the background where hang-gliders fly (there is even a hang-gliding school here), and which provide open views of relatively **calm surf**, and a long, friendly stretch of beach. **Tourist information:** 155 Great Ocean Road, ☎ 03 5237 6529.

Founded in the 1860s as a timber town, the area is also home to the **Old Cable Station Museum**, marking the site where in 1936 telephone cable was laid across the Bass Strait to Tasmania; it now contains a local history collection. In March, Apollo Bay hosts a popular music festival. On Noel Street is a shell museum (☎ 03 5237 6395; open daily), including some very rare seashells.

Be sure to take a trip up into the meadows and hills north of Apollo Bay to **Paradise**, c 6km. Enchanting fern forests along the Barham River offer a beautifully cool respite, especially on hot days.

West of Apollo Bay on the Ocean Road, you enter the **Otway National Park** (☎ 03 5237 6889), site of treacherous **Cape Otway**; about 7km into the park is a turn-off to the cape, some 14km south. After numerous early shipwrecks along these reefs, the sandstone **lighthouse** here was erected in 1848, making it the oldest along the Bass Strait coast; the second lighthouse keeper, Henry Bayles Ford, lived here with his family for 30 years. The lighthouse can be climbed, offering a terrifying glimpse of this dangerous coastline; nearby is a cemetery with the graves of lighthouse families and shipwreck victims.

The **Otway Ranges** receive some 200 days of rainfall a year, making this one of the wettest spots in Victoria. The park is also home to the **Otways Black Snail**, a rare carnivorous snail that retards its prey through an injected secretion. One can also spot **koalas** in the wild here, along with a vast number of other native species. **Bimbi Park** provides camping accommodation within the park, and nearby are excellent **walking trails** with views of the coast.

'Shipwreck Trail'

Back on the Ocean Road, it is c 50km to **Lavers Hill**, and 3km further west to **Melba Gully State Park** (☎ 03 5237 3243; open daily), a 48 ha preserve donated to the state by the local Madsen family and named for the famous opera singer Dame Nellie Melba. The park is known for its fern gullies, myrtle beech trees, and **blue glow worms**.

From this point, continue west some 20km to **Port Campbell National Park** (☎ 03 5598 6382 or 131 963), the starting point of the **Historic Shipwreck Trail**, 100km of steep cliffs and world-renowned rock formations within sight of land. All of these landmarks have well-marked turnoffs from the Ocean Road.

15km from the beginning of the national park is **Princetown**, site of the **Glenample Station** (☎ 03 5598 8209; open Sept–July and school holidays, Fri–Mon, 10.30–17.00), owned in the 1860s by Scottish immigrant Hugh

Hamilton Gibson. Gibson built his own homestead in 1868, on the Simpson Road nearby. Gibson built the **Gibson's Steps** to reach the nearby beach; these still provide access to the sand. It was also at Gibson's homestead that, in 1878, the only two survivors of the shipwreck *Loch Ard*, Tom Pearce and Eva Carmichael, were rescued and recuperated (see below).

A bit further west is the turn-off to the **Twelve Apostles**, the most famous of the limestone rock formations, now some 65m out to sea, having eroded from the cliffs over time. The rocks vary in height from 10m to 50m; as the plaques at the well-maintained overviews explain, one cannot always see all twelve formations at once, but at any time the view is impressive. From here you can take helicopter rides to view from the air this stretch of coastline.

Further on is the turn-off for **Loch Ard Gorge**, so named because it was near here that the above-named *Loch Ard* crashed in June 1878, killing all but two of its 53 passengers; only four bodies were recovered, and the story of survivors Tom Pearce and Eva Carmichael provided numerous romanticised stories. The cave on the beach here where Eva sought refuge is named in her honour.

The gorge area reveals some fascinating examples of the interaction of sea and rock, including a blowhole and caves; it is also the nesting site for **mutton birds**, the short-tailed shearwaters that annually make an extraordinary 15000km migration around the Pacific Ocean. Recently the gorge has provided the backdrop for delightful Shakespearian performances in the summer (information from Apollo Bay or Port Campbell tourist office).

The road from here to the town of **Port Campbell**, c 7km, is dotted with more scenic views of the rough coast; the town itself (population 250) is named for a Captain Campbell who sheltered here in the inlet in 1843. Indeed, the turn into this small port leads to one of the only **calm beaches** along this rugged coast, where swimming is a cold prospect at most times. **Tourist information**: Morris Street, ☎ 03 5598 6382.

7km west of Port Campbell is another interesting set of ocean rock formations. Originally called **London Bridge** because a bridge linked what are today two separate rocks, the formation's central section broke off on 15 January 1990, stranding two people on the outer rock; they were quickly airlifted to safety.

From here, the next town is **Peterborough**, believed to have been settled by people who had come to see the shipwreck *Schomberg* in 1855. As with so many other shipwrecks here, the timbers and fittings were salvaged and reused. The *Schomberg* was captained by flamboyant 'Bully' Forbes, who had in 1852 made the Liverpool–Melbourne run in the unprecedented time of 68 days. In his haste to make the run in 60 days with the *Schomberg*, he ran aground here to the east of Curdies Inlet, today known as Schomberg Rock.

About 6km west of Peterborough is **Massacre Bay**. Its scenic turn-off includes information plaques about the *Mahogany Ship* (see below), one of the most romantic and mysterious legends along the coast, and thought to be located somewhere nearby. See Flagstaff Maritime Museum, Warrnambool, for a more detailed description.

Warrnambool

The coastal road now turns inland through grazing land and dairy farms. **Allansford**, just outside Warrnambool, has a large **cheese factory** (☎ 03

5563 2127; open weekdays, 08.30–16.30, Sat 09.00–12.00). It is 66km from Port Campbell to Warrnambool.

Warrnambool

At **Warrnambool** (population 28,000), the GREAT OCEAN ROAD meets PRINCES HIGHWAY. The town seems much larger than it is, perhaps because it is decentralised in layout and because its natural port, although unsuitable for large-scale maritime activity, enabled the early growth of a thriving industrial economy. Fletcher Jones, a leading clothes manufacturer, and Nestlé, both have headquarters here. **Tourist information**: 600 Raglan Parade, ☎ 03 5564 7837. The V/Line trains from Melbourne via Geelong arrive daily.

History

Settled in the 1840s by squatters, the town's name, originally Warnimble, derives from an Aboriginal word meaning either 'running swamps' or 'place of plenty'. In 1842, the writer 'Rolf Boldrewood' (Thomas Alexander Browne) arrived here before settling on his nearby property Squattlesea Mere; he fondly remembered his joyous time in that 'kingdom by the sea'.

By 1847, the settlement was big enough to host a horse race, an event that has continued as the **Warrnambool Grand Annual Steeple Chase**; the race is a major event on the racing calendar, and brings thousands of visitors to the beautiful Warrnambool Racecourse during the first week of May.

From Princes Highway, proceed to Spence Street and Raglan Parade, where a substantial **tourist information centre** offers excellent material about the region's features, including a small brochure of the town's **Heritage Trail**.

The blocks bounded by Timor, Liebig, Koroit and Fairy Streets still contain many fine examples of buildings from Warrnambool's 19C boom period, many of them built by local architects Andrew Kerr, George Jobbins, and James McLeod. A **mural** on the corner of Liebig and Koroit Streets depicts much of Warrnambool's history, including the contribution of Chinese immigrants and the amusing images of deep-sea divers playing cards underwater, homage to those who helped dredge the harbour in the 1880s.

The most grandiose structure of this period, **The Grand Ozone Coffee Palace** (1890), was on the corner of KEPLER STREET, where the Hotel Warrnambool now stands; the palace burned to the ground in 1929.

On the corner of LIEBIG and TIMOR STREETS (locally pronounced LAI-big and TAI-mor) is the **Warrnambool Regional Art Gallery** (☎ 03 5564 7832; open daily, 12.00–17.00), in a modern blue building tastefully designed to complement its 19C neighbours. Its excellent collection of Australian paintings includes Eugen von Guerard's brilliant *Tower Hill* (1855, the painting has been used as the model for recent reforestation of the Tower Hill site) and Robert Dowling's *Minjah in the Old Time* (c 1858). Also on display is a model of the demolished Grand Ozone Coffee Palace.

Other interesting sites are the lovely **Botanic Gardens** (☎ 03 5564 7800), c 2km north on Fairy Street. Laid out in 1877 by William Guilfoyle, Director of the Melbourne Botanic Gardens, the gardens retain their original design.

At the south end of Banyan Street, on MERRI STREET, is **Flagstaff Hill Maritime Museum Complex** (☎ 03 5564 7841; open daily, 09.00–17.00), an excellent 'open-air museum' re-creating the history of this part of the Australian coast. The museum is built around the remains of an old fort built after the Crimean War (fear of that Russian invasion again!). Other buildings include two original **lighthouses** from the 1870s and various artisan shops where such activities as shipbuilding and blacksmithing are demonstrated.

On the water the passenger steamer *Rowitta* (1909) and a trading ketch *Reginald M* are on view. In the **Shipwreck Museum** are many artefacts and treasures retrieved from the coast's many shipwrecks. Of greatest interest is the **Loch Ard Peacock**, a magnificent life-size piece of Minton pottery, designed by Italian Paul Comolera and on its way to Melbourne for the International Exhibition of 1880 when it was salvaged from the *Loch Ard* disaster in 1878. The museum complex's restaurant, The Mahogany Ship (see box), alludes to the area's most enduring legend.

The Mahogany Ship

Between 1836 and 1880, several reliable sources maintained that they had seen in the drifting sandhills outside of Warrnambool the remains of an ancient wreck, consistently described as built of dark wood and with enormous timbers. Aborigines of the region agreed that the remains had been there for centuries, and even, in some stories, spoke of 'yellow men' coming from a big ship. As the *Australian Encyclopedia* (1956) summarises, 'it poses a problem of the first magnitude in the controversial history of the discovery of Australia by European navigators'.

Alas, none of the witnesses at the time established an accurate location for the relic. By the 1850s the timbers had been removed and burned by whalers, and by 1880, the remains disappeared entirely from view beneath the dunes. The wreck figures romantically in Henry Kingsley's novel *Geoffrey Hamlyn* (1859) and in Vernon Williams' historical romance *The Mahogany Ship* (1923). Poet George Gordon McCrae made an intensive investigation of the subject, presenting a paper on his findings to the Royal Geographical Society in 1910. As late as 1992, the Victorian government offered a prize of $250,000 for the rediscovery of the ship. To date, the only remnants found are a few iron bolts and latches, now being carbon-dated.

Some 15km west on the Princes Highway is **Tower Hill State Game Reserve** (☎ 03 5565 9202). The site provides fascinating evidence of Victoria's largest volcano. Geologically, the site is described as a nested maar with a flooded crater and deposits of volcanic tuff creating fertile soil. The lake contains three small islands, produced when eruptions produced scoria cones (scoria is lava with steam holes). The region was cleared for farming and quarried in the mid-19C, leaving barren hills; recent reforestation has depended on the 1855 oil painting by Eugen von Guerard, now in the Warrnambool Regional Art Gallery. A loop drive around the lake is well worth the detour. The Natural History Centre in the reserve is open daily, 09.30–16.30.

Port Fairy

29km west of Warrnambool is the historic village of **Port Fairy** (population 2500). Today the town is internationally famous for its **Labour Day folk festival** in March, which brings up to 20,000 visitors to hear formal and impromptu performances by folk bands and music groups of all stripes; tickets for the formal events are sold out months in advance (contact tourist information for details). In January, the town also hosts the **Moyneyama Festival**, with outdoor events and boat races along the Moyne River. During the rest of the year, the town remains a charming fishing village with an interesting maritime history. **Tourist information**: Borough Chambers, Bank Street; ☎ 03 5568 2682. V/Line buses run here daily from Warrnambool and Mount Gambier.

History

The area was first visited by whalers and sealers at the beginning of the 19C. Indeed, the town's name is in honour of the cutter *Fairy*, the boat of early sealer and explorer Captain James Wishart who sheltered here in the 1820s. By 1835 a whaling station was established on **Griffiths Island**, a spit of land at the southeastern end of town and now site of the largest mutton bird rookery on the mainland. Viewing platforms here make it possible to watch the birds' arrival at twilight during the months of September through April, when they take off again on their 15,000km migration. The island also has a lighthouse built in 1859 of local bluestone and now solar-powered. At Griffiths Island, you can also get a great view of Port Fairy Bay and East Beach, usually windswept and choppy, although enjoyable for picnicking on a sunny day.

In 1844, Irishman and New South Wales solicitor James Atkinson obtained thousands of hectares of land here and renamed the area Belfast after his native town. He subdivided the area, created a harbour, and established the township, controlling all properties until land sales in the 1880s; at that time, the town was renamed Port Fairy. In the 1840s and 1850s, the town prospered along with the business enterprises of Atkinson and William Rutledge & Co., a commercial concern controlling an international firm headquartered here; most of the substantial buildings of the settlement date from this period. When Rutledge crashed in 1862, the town was paralysed and development ground to a halt. Consequently most of the old buildings have been retained, with minimal additions since the turn of the century. Today there is a small fishing fleet, and it is a centre for the abalone industry (but do not expect abalone on the town's menus; most of it is exported).

Entering on Princes Highway, turn on to BANK STREET to reach the centre of town. Here you will find several historic buildings, including, on the left, the **Drill Hall**, built c 1896 and now an antiques barn; and on the right, the **Caledonian Hotel**, believed to be, since 1844, Victoria's oldest continuously licensed hotel. In the hallway of the hotel you can see original hand-adzed timber, plus a section left unfinished when workers dropped their tools when word of the Ballarat gold discovery reached them. In the hotel's yard, author 'Rolf Boldrewood' sold horses bred from his nearby station. A little further on Bank Street, on the east side at Barkly Street, is **St John's Church** and Hall, designed by Nathaniel Billing and erected in the late 1850s at a cost of £7000, an extravagant sum at the time. The tower was completed in 1956 by Maltese stonemasons.

Back on Bank Street, in what was once the second post office building of

1881, is *'Lunch'*, a pleasant restaurant; next door is the **tourist information centre**, which provides an excellent historical walking tour brochure, as well as a 'Shipwreck tour'. Next to the centre is the **Star of the West Hotel**, on the corner of Sackville and Bank Streets. The hotel was built in 1856 by John Walwyn Taylor, a West Indian who made money on the goldfields and dreamed of building a chain of 'Star' hotels throughout Victoria. This was the only one to be built, and was at one time a staging post for the Cobb & Co. coaches (see p 368).

SACKVILLE STREET has always been the main public street, and still includes many 19C structures, such as the **Lecture Hall**, completed in 1884; the **Corangamite Regional Library** next door, which was once the Mechanics Institute; the **Cafe Gazette** in the building which was the home of the *Port Fairy Gazette* from 1849 to 1989; the bluestone **ANZ Bank**, designed in 1857 by Nathaniel Billing, a well-known architect in Western Victoria, and considered by famous educator and historian James Bonwick in his description of 1858, 'the handsomest house in the town'; and the opulent **post office**, opened in 1881 at a cost of £4200.

On the corner of Sackville and Cox Streets is **Seacombe House**, begun in 1847 and in the 1850s the social centre of the town. In 1873, it became a boys' school and later a guest house. Walk south down Cox Street to GIPPS STREET and the lovely **Moyne River canal**; the two blocks here between Campbell and Bank Streets contain some of the most historic buildings from the town's early days, including **'Emoh'**, 8 Cox Street, now a youth hostel and originally the residence of William Rutledge, 'the King of Port Fairy' (see above).

On the corner of Cox and Gipps Streets is a bluestone wall, the only remnants of **Rutledge's warehouses**. The early structures have been tastefully preserved, with later buildings complementing their architectural styles. East on Gipps Street is **Mill House**, originally a flour mill constructed in 1866, and now a bed and breakfast; the stone house across Gipps Street belonged to the miller Joseph Goble. West from Cox Street on Gipps Street is **Mills Cottage**, incorporating the 1841 wooden hut that was the original home of Charles Mill, Harbour Master from 1853 to 1871.

Further along Gipps Street is the former **Court House**, now the headquarters of the **Port Fairy Historical Society** (☎ 03 5568 2263; open Wed & weekends, daily during holidays 14.00–17.00) and a local museum. The building, begun in 1859, was unusually large as it was designed to seat the **Supreme Court** as well as the county and magistrates' court; a sign of Port Fairy's early importance in this rather isolated location. At Gipps Street and Campbell Streets is the old 1861 **customs house**, now a private residence; at the time of its construction, Port Fairy was an important point of entry into Victoria. Also at this corner is the **Merrijig Inn**, built in 1841 and, opposite the **Old Moyne Mill**, a five-storeyed wind-driven mill that operated until 1883.

Back on Sackville Street is **Mott's Cottage** (☎ 03 5568 1038; open Wed–Sun 13.00–16.00), a typical 1850s cottage now owned and operated by the National Trust; Sam Mott had been a member of Captain Wishart's whaling crew. Along Campbell Street are fine examples of stone cottages of the 1850s and 1860s. Further north at Cox and College Streets is **St Patrick's Church**, the town's second Roman Catholic church built in 1859 and another example of architect Nathaniel Billing's design.

From Port Fairy, you can also take a four-hour boat tour out to **Lady Julia Percy Island**, a volcanic island that is now home to some **4000 fur seals**, the animals that were nearly decimated by sealers in the 19C.

Portland

From Port Fairy, the Princes Highway continues west 71km to **Portland** (population 11,000), the westernmost Victorian coastal town and the only deepwater port between Melbourne and Adelaide. **Tourist information:** Cliff Street, ☎ 03 5523 2671.

History

Now an industrial town with aluminium factories and huge commercial docks, including berths for 8-tiered sheep ships, the area was the land of the Gunditjmara Aborigines who called it **Pulumbete**, or 'little lake' for the swampy region now known as Fawthrop's Lagoon. French navigator Baudin passed by here in 1802, and Matthew Flinders charted the bay's waters in 1803.

Permanent white settlement here began in 1833, with the arrival of the whaler William Dutton and then the Henty family (see box), although whalers and sealers had been processing oil in the area from the early 1800s. The region was one of the best whaling areas in the world, until stocks were nearly depleted by the end of the century. In recent years, whale numbers have increased and migrating groups can be seen around Portland from June to September.

The Henty family

The Henty family epitomise the history of squatters in Australia: opportunistic adventurers who laid claim to large runs in 'uninhabited' and unexplored regions of the new country, developing pastoralism and gaining wealth and prominence by tenacious occupation of the land. Thomas Henty (1775–1839) was a Sussex farmer and breeder of Merino sheep. One of his six sons was the first Henty to arrive in Australia; he joined the Swan River settlement in Western Australia in 1829. Other members of the family moved to Tasmania in 1832 and took up large tracts of land there. In 1834, another son, Edward (1810–78), sailed into Portland Bay in the *Thistle* to establish the first permanent white settlement in Victoria. By 1835, sheep and cattle were grazing here, and Henty began a whaling operation, joined by his brothers. On the basis of this venture, Portland is considered 'Victoria's Birthplace by the Sea'.

When explorer Thomas Mitchell arrived from overland at the bay in 1836, he was astonished to discover the Henty settlement. By 1842, the Hentys claimed some 110,000 acres around the bay and inland as far as Wannon near Hamilton. After some reversals of fortune, the Hentys settled on these large inland properties, developing lavish estates and becoming prosperous graziers and ultimately politicians.

In the Portland region, as in every other part of Australia, the arrival of white settlers provoked inevitable conflict with the indigenous inhabitants, who as supposedly nomadic people appeared to the whites to have no real claim to land at all. Ironically, in this region, many of the Aborigines were not nomadic at all. Aborigines for the most part were viewed as little more than pesky obstructions in the way of civilised settlement. Whalers were the first to 'punish' these inhabitants, through outright slaughter, for their 'theft' of whale catches on the beach.

Resistance by Aborigines to the invasion of their tribal lands was fierce once they recognised their total displacement by these new arrivals. The **Eumeralla Wars** of this region raged until the mid-1840s, when the remaining Aborigines were defeated and eventually removed to mission settlements such as the one at **Lake Condah** north of Portland. Officially operating as an Aboriginal mission for 'assimilation' from 1867 until 1919, Lake Condah remained an Aboriginal settlement into the 1950s. It was from this base that the Gunditjmara people successfully fought for compensation for their traditional land in a famous legal battle of the 1980s, being awarded $1.5 million from the Alcoa company who built an aluminium smelter on a sacred site near Portland. The award included 4000 acres (1600 ha) at Lake Condah, now operated by the Gunditjmara as a **Koori-owned tourist resort**. A trip to the site is a worthwhile experience for anyone interested in Aboriginal culture and the current political battles which these people are fighting. Contact the resort (☎ 03 5578 4257) for more information. The Gunditjmara Aboriginal Co-operative at Warrnambool (☎ 03 5562 9729) would also be worth contacting.

Portland itself maintains a strong consciousness of its historical past as a pioneering settlement. The **information centre**, on CLIFF STREET at Henty Park, provides excellent material on the region and friendly service; the centre also organises several walking tours, and natural history day-tours around Portland.

The information centre is in an 1850 bluestone **watchtower**; this historic area of town contains many substantial bluestone buildings that are well preserved. Nearby on Bentinck Street is the former **Steam Packet Hotel** (☎ 03 5521 7496; open Thurs, Sun 14.00–16.00), one of Victoria's oldest timber buildings, erected in 1842 from pieces prefabricated in Van Diemen's Land (Tasmania). Of special note is the hotel's steep staircase and attic roof with dormers. The hotel is now managed by the National Trust.

The Town Hall on CHARLES STREET, built in 1864 to a Classical design by Alexander Ross, now houses the **History House** (☎ 03 5522 2266; open daily 10.00–12.00, 13.00–16.00), which displays relics and artefacts of the pioneer period. Next door is the tiny **Rocket Shed** of 1887, which stored rockets and ship rescue equipment; today it displays memorabilia of the town's 150th anniversary celebrations which took place in 1984.

The basalt ashlar **Court House** on Cliff Street next to the town hall was completed in 1853 from designs by Colonial Clerk of Works Henry Ginn; it is still used as the court house and stands as Ginn's most significant work. For many decades the judge would arrive in Portland for court from Melbourne by sea; once sentenced, a prisoner would be sent to the gaol next door. When excavations were made for Beach Road from here to the bay, builders uncovered a tunnel underneath the gaol, apparently dug by a convict who left it unfinished a few metres from the beach cliff.

On Gawler Street next to the information centre is another fine building by Henry Ginn, the **Customs House** (☎ 03 5523 2399; open weekdays 09.00–16.00) completed in 1850 and reminiscent of Tasmanian structures of the period; it is still used for its original purpose, and is open for tours.

One of the loveliest spots in Portland is the **Botanical Gardens** (☎ 03 5523 2671) on the corner of Glenelg and Cliff Streets. One of the oldest public gardens in Victoria, the site was first developed in 1857 by William Allitt, using Chinese convict labour. Allitt was a protégé of the famous Ferdinand von Mueller, curator of the Melbourne Botanical Gardens. As official curator of the gardens in the 1860s, Allitt planted some 2000 species, only a quarter of which still survive. The gardens' area has decreased substantially since Allitt's day, although several unusual plants remain, including the state's largest known New Zealand cabbage tree, registered on the National Trust's list of 'Notable Trees'. The grounds also include the 1858 **Curator's Cottage**, restored and maintained by the Historical Society.

Also of interest in Portland are its many gracious homes, most notably **Burswood**, 15 Cape Nelson Road, now operating as a bed and breakfast. The splendid gardens (☎ 03 5523 4686) are still open to the public in the summer, but views of the interior are limited to guests. This was the third home of Edward Henty (see box, p 361), designed by James Barrow in 1853 in a Regency style reminiscent of the Hentys' Sussex home.

Burwood House, Portland

It has a glazed verandah and superbly decorated interior walls.

On Battery Hill at Bancroft Street is **Kingsley**, a charmingly fanciful structure built in 1893 for William Thomas Pile, an eccentric businessman who made money on the Castlemaine goldfields and in the wattlebark industry. Kingsley is now home to the state's southernmost **vineyard** (☎ 03 5123 1864; open daily, 13.00–16.00) and winery.

Around Portland

The area around Portland provides some stunning coastal views and opportunities for picnicking and serious bushwalking. **Cape Nelson** (☎ 03 5523 1308), 11km south of Portland, is now a state park with a 3km self-guided **cliff walk** around its 24m-high lighthouse and through the **soap mallee**, a unique kind of bush fauna. **Cape Bridgewater**, 21km southwest of the town, now the site of a convention centre, provides stunning coastal views, as well as tours of its **petrified forest** and **blowhole**. It is also the site of a **seal colony**, which can be reached after a 90-minute bushwalk. The National Trust also runs a lodge here, on Cape Bridgewater Road (☎ 03 5526 7271), that provides accommodation for up to six people.

For the truly adventurous, the **Great South West Walk** begins at the Portland Information Centre and encompasses 250km of track through the **Lower Glenelg National Park** and the seaside village of **Nelson**. **The National Park** and **Information Centre** (☎ 03 8738 4051) is located on North Nelson Road. Campsites with limited facilities are well marked along the trail. Shorter walks along the track can be reached by following the **emu-logo markers**.

On the Henty Highway north towards Hamilton, you can turn off towards Homerton and travel c 50km to **Mount Eccles National Park** (☎ 03 5576 1014 or 131 963) with fascinating walks through volcanic scenery (long extinct), lava caves, and Lake Surprise, a crater lake. The visitor's centre has great displays about Aboriginal life in the region, and the park is filled with birdlife.

The Wimmera and the Grampians

From Portland, you can reach the gold country and Ballarat by travelling north on the HENTY HIGHWAY (Highway 1 to Heywood; route 107 to Hamilton). V/Line bus service extends from Melbourne via Ballarat to Hamilton and on to the Mt Gambier in South Australia, and a daily train to Dimboola via Ballarat, Stawell and Horsham. A more direct train travels weekdays from Melbourne to Stawell, stopping only in Ballarat. A 'Grampians link' is a daily train-and-coach service to Halls Gap. To the northwest are the wheat-growing flatlands of the **Wimmera**, an area reminiscent of grasslands America in its vastness. This region was that explored by Major Thomas Mitchell in the 1830s. Commemoration of his expedition appears in plaques and monuments throughout the district, and a 1700km tourist route through the region retracing his wanderings is called the Major Mitchell Trail. Mitchell's *Three Expeditions into the Interior of Eastern Australia* (1838) gives an exciting picture of these early days. Mitchell was so impressed by the green landscape on the eastern side of the Grampians that he labelled it 'Australia Felix', encouraging pastoralists to settle here.

To the north is **Grampians National Park**, one of the state's largest parks, filled with bizarre rock formations and voluptuous bush. It is one of the best places in the state to view Aboriginal art, especially at those sites run by the Aboriginal communities themselves.

Hamilton

From Portland drive 27km north to **Heywood**, where you can turn off to the Aboriginal community of **Lake Condah**, 12km east (see Portland section). Continue 58km north on the Henty Highway to Hamilton. **Hamilton** (population 11,000) proudly proclaims itself as the 'Wool Capital of the World', a fact reinforced by the Big Woolbales Centre on the outskirts of town—one of the 'big things' tourist attractions, a more subdued example of the 'roadside grotesques' so popular throughout Australia. The area was founded by Scottish pastoralists and German settlers arriving from South Australia; it remains an important centre for the rural community. Of most interest for the visitor are the Hamilton Art Gallery, the Ansett Transport Museum, and the Aboriginal Keeping Place. **Tourist information centre**: Lonsdale Street, ☎ 03 5572 3746.

The **art gallery** (☎ 03 5573 0460; open daily), on Brown Street, is an impressive regional gallery, emphasising an excellent collection of Mediterranean pottery and antique porcelain, donated by local grazier Herbert Buchanan Shaw, as well as a superb collection of paintings and watercolours by the 18C English artist Paul Sandby purchased from local resident C.C.L. Gaussen.

The **transport museum** (☎ 03 5571 2767) on Ballarat Road commemorates Sir Reginald Ansett, who began his airline service in Hamilton in the

1930s; Ansett Airlines is now one of the leading services within Australia. The museum includes a replica of Ansett's first plane, a Fokker Universal.

In the former Mechanics Institute on Gray Street is the **Aboriginal Keeping Place** (open Wed–Fri, 13.00–16.00), an exhibition depicting Aboriginal culture in western Victoria. Also in the area there are several private gardens that are part of the Open Garden Scheme, and are open to the public at different times throughout the year.

Grampians National Park

From Hamilton, take the GLENELG HIGHWAY (route 112) 29km to Dunkeld, and proceed north 65km on route 111 to **Halls Gap**, entrance to Grampians National Park. An excellent **visitor's centre** (☎ 03 5356 4381) here provides displays, audio-visual presentations, detailed walking guides and books, and tours into the ranges. The Aborigines—first the Buandig and later the Jardwa tribe—called the land Gariwerd or Nambun Nambun. When Major Mitchell passed through the mountains, he named them the Grampians because they reminded him of that Scottish range. One of Arthur Upfield's best Napoleon Bonaparte mystery novels, *The Mountains Have a Secret* (1952), is set in the Grampians.

The 167,100 ha of national park was officially proclaimed as protected in 1984. The chain of mountains is actually the westernmost end of the Great Dividing Range, separating the fertile coastal plains from the dry interior.

Some 65km on the western side of the park is the pastoral town of **Horsham** (population 12,300; **tourist information**: Wimmera Tourism, 20 O'Callaghan's Pde, ☎ 03 5382 3778).

36km northwest of Horsham, the **Little Desert National Park** (information in the town of Nhill, ☎ 03 5391 1714) exemplifies the scrubby woodland of the Mallee, indicating the beginnings of the arid desert land of the interior.

33km southwest of Horsham is **Mt Arapiles-Tooan State Park** (☎ 03 5837 1260 or 131 963), widely regarded as the best rock-climbing location in Australia. Local climbing schools offer instruction for the neophyte and the advanced climber.

The **Grampians** display all the vegetation and geology of their transitional situation: the dramatic rock formations are filled with abundant displays of wildflowers (especially brilliant in the spring and autumn), waterfalls, shady picnic grounds and prolific numbers of native birds and animals.

The main reason to come to the Grampians is to go bushwalking and rock-climbing; trails and climbs exist for every level of skill and endurance. The **visitor centre** at Halls Gap (see above) can give detailed information on the best sites and directions to take. The most popular—because it is the most accessible—section is the **Wonderland** area immediately west of the centre.

A lovely spot for a simple picnic is **Zumsteins**, 5km into the park, named for pioneer Walter Zumstein, who came here in the early 1900s and established a bee farm. By the 1910s, he had planted orchards and attracted kangaroos that he hand fed. He built a few tourist cottages and a swimming pool, and the area has been the most popular picnic spot in the park since 1920. The kangaroos are unbelievably brazen, despite strict warnings not to feed them. Be warned that during the summer and school holidays, all campgrounds and facilities are quickly booked out; be sure to check about accommodation before planning an excursion here.

Since Aboriginal habitation of the area dates back thousands of years, it is not surprising that the Grampians are the site of numerous examples of **Aboriginal art**. Rock art at least 2000 years old has been substantiated, and more than 4000 different motifs have been recorded. Next to the Halls Gap visitor centre is **Brambuk Living Cultural Centre** (☎ 03 5356 4452; open daily, 10.00–17.00), organised and operated by the Aboriginal communities of this region. (**Note:** Contemporary Aborigines in this part of the country are known as Koories; the term is also sometimes applied to urban Aborigines in other areas of Australia, although not so readily used by the people of the Central Desert, Western Australia, or the Northern Territory.)

Along with permanent exhibitions of Aboriginal art and artefacts, the centre also provides the best introduction to the rock art of the park and surrounding area; the community makes every attempt to protect sacred sites and to preserve the fragile art from too much tourist intrusion. The Brambuk Centre has also been instrumental in returning Aboriginal names to the park's topographical features. Of the 60 known rock sites in the park, only about six are advertised as available for public view, among them **Billimina** and **Wab Manja**, near the Buandig camping site.

Outside the park, on the Pomonal Road, 11km south of Stawell, is **Bunjils Shelter**, a major Aboriginal site. Bunjil is the creator-spirit of the Aborigines of this region. The trail to the shelter is well marked with explanatory signs that describe the Bunjil story.

Gold Country

Travel on to **Stawell**, a pleasant country town (population 6700). **Tourist information:** 54 Western Highway, ☎ 03 5358 2314. At this point you are entering the **gold country** proper. By the end of the 1850s, more than 60,000 diggers had descended upon the fields between Stawell and Ararat; by the 1860s, alluvial gold was gone, but Stawell sustained its prosperity until the end of the century through newly opened quartz reef mines such as Deep Lead to the north of town. Radical miner John Wood, whose socialist ideas about ownership of property and division of church and state found great favour with the newly arrived diggers, began his career here.

Memorials to gold now exist, both at the alluvial fields of the Mount Pleasant Diggings to the west of the Western Highway; and at the **Reefs Gold Memorial** in Stawell itself, on the site of the first quartz mining in 1856. But Stawell's greatest claim to fame is the **Stawell Easter Gift**, one of the most lucrative foot races in the world; the prize money for the 120m race is currently about $100,000. The first race was run here in 1877, when a group of prominent citizens organised the Stawell Athletic Club and offered a prize of $200. Now the event attracts some 20,000 visitors and many participants from all over the world. The event traditionally begins in Central Park, site also of the Stawell Gift Hall of Fame (☎ 03 5358 1326; open by appointment only), commemorating those athletes who have been involved in the event.

Along the Western Highway

Travel south on the WESTERN HIGHWAY 14km to the little town of **Great**

Western, site of the oldest vineyards in the district and today home of **Seppelt's Great Western** (☎ 03 5361 2239; open daily 10.00–17.00, tours Mon–Sat, 10.30, 13.30 & 15.00), makers of champagne-method wine. Winemaking was first introduced in this region in 1863 by Frenchmen, the Blampieds and Jean Pierre Trouette.

Western vineyards

A **Western Vineyards Tour** covering 110km and several wineries begins here. (For information and maps of this tour, contact the **visitor's information centre** in Melbourne, or the tourist office in Ararat, ☎ 03 5352 2096). The **Seppelt's tour** is especially interesting as it includes a tour of the underground cellars built by gold-miners over 60 years; they were begun in 1868 by the founding vintner Joseph Best and continued under Hans Irvine in the 1880s and 90s. Irvine really established the area as a champagne-producing region. The cellars provide over 6km of rack space. Also in the area is **Best's Concongella Vineyard** (☎ 03 5356 2250; open weekdays, 10.00–17.00; Sat and holidays, 10.00–16.00, Sun 12.00–16.00), another winery founded by Henry Best in 1868 and continued by his son Charles into the 1920s, when it was purchased by the great wine-maker Frederick P. Thomson. Tastings and sales are, of course, available here, as at all the other wineries in the region.

Continue 17km into ARARAT (population 8200), so named in 1841 by the first settler Horatio S. Wills, 'for like the Ark, we rested here'. Wills holds the dubious honour of being the first squatter to use strychnine to kill dingoes. Gold was discovered here in 1857 by Chinese prospectors, hence the name of the find, the Canton Lead. On the site of this lead is a life-size sculpture by Dorothea Saaghy of a Chinese miner. However, the gold here quickly dwindled, and by the 1860s, Ararat returned to sheep-farming as its major occupation. **Tourist information**: Barkly Street; ☎ 03 5352 2096.

The town has several bluestone municipal buildings of note from the late 1800s. The **Ararat Gallery** (☎ 03 5352 2836; open weekdays, 11.00–16.00, Sun & holidays, 12.00–16.00), on Vincent Street, houses an excellent collection of fabric and fashion, centred on the Collection of Lady Barbara Grimwade, a Melbourne socialite who donated her own gowns of the 1950s–80s in 1991. Also included is a collection of Japanese packaging and paperworks. On the corner of Barkly and Queen Streets is a funny little collection of Aboriginal arte-facts, household appliances, and photographic equipment in the **Langi Morgala Museum** (☎ 03 5352 4858; open weekends, 14.00–16.00).

One of the weirdest tourist attractions in Ararat is **J Ward**, on Girdlestone Street (☎ 03 5352 3357; open Sun and holidays, 11.00–15.00), formerly the institution for the criminally insane; it now gives tours that display all those gruesome implements of psychiatric treatment over the last 100 years.

On Golf Links Road in town is **One Tree Hill Lookout**, which offers a tremendous view towards the Grampians and of Mt Langi Ghiran (an Aborig-inal word for the Yellow-tailed Black Cockatoo).

At **Maroona**, 19km south of here, was the property of radical politician and poet J.K. McDougall, Labor member of parliament 1906–12, during which time the National Party leader Billy Hughes deliberately distorted McDougall's poem

'The White-Man's Burden' to discredit his socialist politics. The shabby tactic by Hughes so inflamed public opinion that McDougall was tarred and feathered by some war veterans.

Continue on the Western Highway, passing through the tiny mining town of **Buangor**, which consists only of a general store and a Cobb & Co. staging station.

Cobb & Co.

Established in 1853 by Americans Freeman Cobb, John Peck, James Wanton and John Lamber and purchased in 1859 by James Rutherford, the company dominated Australian inland transport for 70 years and provided horse-drawn carriage service until 1924. The company used American coaches in contrast to the prevalent English imports because the Australian road conditions required the leather-sprung, cradled design for stability and comfort. Similarly distinct from the English black body, the Concord-manu-factured bodies were bright red with gold and floral ornament.

The company passed into Australian hands relatively quickly. After the Victorian goldfields had access to railways, the company moved to New South Wales where it again first served the goldfields, then the rural settlers. As the railways were extended, Cobb & Co. moved its routes farther inland. In the 1870s, the firm harnessed 6000 horses daily and travelled nearly 45,000km per week. The country's affection for the firm was furthered by its generous treatment of its drivers who were themselves often near legends. Legendary driver Cabbage-tree Ned (Edward Devine), who drove the English cricketers during their famous 1862 tour, was buried in a Ballarat pauper's grave before a public subscription caused the erection of a suitable tombstone.

Restored coaches can be seen at the Queensland Museum, Vaucluse House in Sydney, and the National Museum in Melbourne, and other smaller venues in Victoria and New South Wales.

A further 21km south along the Western Highway is **Beaufort**, birthplace of another radical poet, Bernard O'Dowd in 1866. At **Lake Goldsmith**, 15km south of here is the twice-yearly Lake Goldsmith Steam Rally, one of the biggest meetings of steam-powered machines in the country (usually about 300 of them).

Travel another 48km to reach the grand Victorian town of Ballarat.

Ballarat

Ballarat (population 63,500) holds a special place in the hearts of most Australians, not only because it became the grandest city in Victoria's goldfields, but also because it was the site of the **Eureka Stockade Rebellion**, Australia's only significant civil uprising and a symbol of democratic resistance to govern-mental authority. **Tourist information**: 39 Sturt Street, ☎ 03 5332 2694. Regular and frequent V/Line trains and buses leave Melbourne for Ballarat, Bendigo, and other towns in the goldfields region; local bus services to smaller towns from the main centres such as Ballarat are also quite good. Ballarat itself has a very good bus service to all parts of town (☎ 03 5331 7777).

History

Balla-arat, from the Aboriginal word meaning 'camping or resting-place', lies on a rich alluvial plain much favoured for hunting by the indigenous people; evidence suggests that Aborigines occupied this area 26,000 years ago. In the 1830s the Scottish squatters Yuille and Anderson established sheep runs here.

This bucolic existence ended when, in 1851, Edward Hargraves, fresh from the goldfields of California and convinced that Australia's landscape was similar geologically, discovered gold in New South Wales. Victoria had just achieved separation from its northern neighbour. In the euphoria of independence and with the knowledge of Hargraves' discovery, the new colony at Melbourne encouraged the search for goldfields nearby.

In 1850–51, considerable deposits were found at Clunes, 40km north of Ballarat by James Esmond and then in the Buninyong Ranges to the south. The rush was on, and by the end of 1851, full mining production was in swing, with hordes of people arriving daily in unprecedented numbers from all over the world. Subsequent finds appeared throughout the undulating hills of the region. By 1853, more than 20,000 miners were digging here; by the end of the 1850s, 2,500,000 ounces of alluvial gold had been found, including, at Bakery Hill in 1858, the **Welcome Nugget**, at 2195 ounces (63,000 grams) one of the largest intact nuggets ever found.

As old fields were exhausted, new ones were begun, until the alluvial resources were depleted. By the 1860s, quartz mining shafts into the deeper reefs enabled further finds, producing gold into the 1920s. By the 1860s, Ballarat had developed such a thriving economy that it was able to establish a strong industrial base, producing mining equipment and locomotives, and becoming the hub of the region's agricultural cultivation. This diversity enabled it to prosper even when the gold ran out.

The social and cultural transformation of Australia caused by gold fever cannot be overestimated. Victoria became the focus of world attention, and for a time, the wealthiest and most socially diverse spot on earth. As Mark Twain wrote in *Following the Equator* (1897), 'A celebrity so prompt and universal has hardly been paralleled in history.' Diggers direct from the California goldfields arrived by ship in Melbourne and Geelong, along with thousands of other hopefuls of all nationalities, making the inland journey on bush tracks to Ballarat by whatever means possible. Australians everywhere fled to the fields, leaving jobs in the cities and abandoning farms. The state's population quadrupled in four years, while the rest of the country was brought to an economic standstill.

Ballarat and the surrounding area took on all the chaotic trappings of any frontier boom town. Stories of tragedy, opportunism, opulent indulgence, and social injustice all played a part in these vigorous days. The renowned artiste Lola Montez caused a sensation when she performed her exotic dances here in 1855, and came to blows with the newspaper editor on a public street; the editor had dared to criticise her performance and impugn her morality. *Australia Felix*, the first volume of the semi-autobiographical trilogy *The Fortunes of Richard Mahony* (1917) by 'Henry Handel' (Ethel) Richardson, is set here and gives vivid descriptions of the physical discomfort of dusty roads, oppressive heat, and substandard housing.

No event came to symbolise more forcefully the unjust conditions that greeted the hopeful arrivals than the **Eureka Rebellion**, a fifteen-minute armed conflict that occurred on 3 December 1854 during which 30 men, both miners and government troops, died. The 'spirit of the Eureka Stockade' has a romantic resonance that far outweighs the event itself, and the design of the **Eureka Flag**, carried by the miners, is still flown as a sign of protest against governmental power; in many quarters, there is today strong sentiment to make the flag Australia's national emblem.

The conflict stemmed from the miners' discontent at the imposition of stiff licensing fees for the right to dig; the payment of these fees was brutally enforced by thuggish and corrupt officials, and little democratic representation was offered in return. The situation led several miners, including J.B. Humffray, Peter Lalor, Frederic Vern and Raffaello Carboni, to form the Ballarat Reform League. Inherent in the organisation's aims were larger issues of democratic rights along with reforms in the administration of the goldfields. The leaders were branded as dangerous radicals, fuelled by the fact that the protesters were seen as non-British and, most especially, Irish discontents continuing in Australia the conflicts of 'home'. A confrontation with the forces of Crown authority was inevitable. Ironically, the process of licensing reform had already been proposed by Governor La Trobe when the rebellion itself took place, but the wilder elements among the miners led to a breakdown of negotiations and consequent bloodshed. The insurrection became a symbol of a revolutionary spirit, and the leaders, particularly Peter Lalor who lost an arm in the conflict, were long championed as the first Australian democrats. Even Karl Marx described Eureka as 'a symptom, a concrete manifestation of the general revolutionary movement in Victoria'.

In reality, the Eureka Rebellion saw the establishment of a more equitable system of licensing and more civilised conditions for the region. Peter Lalor went on to become a politician in the Victorian Parliament, espousing for the most part conservative views.

By far the best chronicler of social conditions of this period was the artist **S.T. Gill** (1818–80). His anecdotal lithographs of life on the diggings, with his witty renditions of the nouveau riches as well as the pathetic failures, embodied, as art historian Bernard Smith describes, 'a distinctly Australian attitude to life; the sardonic humour, the nonchalance and the irreverent attitude to all forms of authority.' Gill's work popularised the image of the Australian bush for the world, an image that endured long after frontier life had disappeared in places like Ballarat, where the urge for civic improvement and the trappings of civilised society quickly overtook the haphazard squalor of the miners' settlements.

Indeed, 'civic pride' and 'grand' are the terms most frequently used to describe Ballarat's public character by the 1870s. From the 1850s, while the east side of town continued as a place of tents, 'sly grog shops' and rough shanty dwellings, the west side developed broad tree-lined streets and elegant public buildings. East and West Ballarat remained separate municipalities for decades.

When Anthony Trollope visited the city in 1871, he was astonished at its opulence and the quality of its civic amenities. By that time, Ballarat boasted a mechanics' institute, a town hall, several large banks and a mining exchange, a substantial library, an elegant theatre, a synagogue and prominent churches, and distinguished hotels. Architecturally, the city today retains outstanding representatives of the Australian adaptation of late 19C British municipal styles.

Ballarat's **information centre** is located at 39 **STURT STREET**, one of the city's main thoroughfares, three chains wide and tree-lined. From here you can walk through the historic commercial area of West Ballarat; you can also join **heritage walking tours** which start here on Saturdays and Sundays. In front of the tourist centre is an informative monument, commemorating some of the greatest gold discoveries and highlighting the area's mineral wealth.

Directly opposite in Sturt Street's median strip (the landscaped dividing area between the traffic lanes of the street) is the delightful **Titanic Memorial Bandstand**, erected in 1915 with an elaborate hipped roof and Titanic weather-vane. The bandstand is an indication of the street's pleasure building programme and its aspirations as the city's centre for social festivities. Three blocks west on Sturt Street in the median strip is the **Queen Alexandra Bandstand**, constructed in 1908 with iron filigree decorations and a more delicate appearance. This median strip also includes a number of memorial statues, including the inevitable monument to the Scottish poet Robert Burns (Australia is said to have more Burns monuments than Scotland). The statue's sculptor John Udny came from Italy and sculpted the piece from Carrara marble.

To the east of the information centre at 11 Sturt Street is the **Union Hotel**, erected in 1863 and in relatively original condition, making it an important example of gold rush period building. Its first-floor French doors once opened into an iron balustraded verandah. Further along is an 1891 shop, designed in a Flemish style and covered with decorative blue glazed tiles, a distinctly Australian Art Nouveau element.

On the north side of the street, the equally

Speculators on 'the corner' in Ballarat, from the Picturesque Atlas of Australia

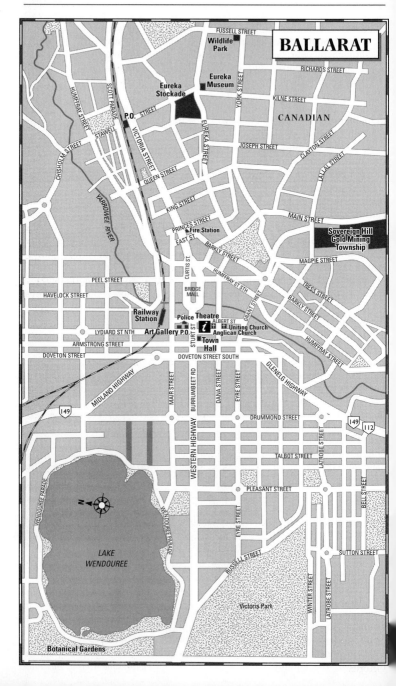

BALLARAT

FUSSELL STREET

Wildlife Park

RICHARDS STREET

Eureka Museum

KILNE STREET

Eureka Stockade

CANADIAN

P.O.

JOSEPH STREET

CLAYTON STREET

LALAL STREET

HUMFFRAY STREET

SCOTT PARADE

STAWELL

VICTORIA STREET

YORK STREET

EUREKA STREET

QUEEN STREET

CHISHOLM STREET

YARROWEE RIVER

KING STREET

MAIN STREET

PRINCESS STREET

Fire Station

EAST ST.

Sovereign Hill Gold Mining Township

BARKLY STREET

MAGPIE STREET

CURTIS ST.

HUMFFRAY ST STH

TRESS STREET

PEEL STREET

BRIDGE MALL

GRANT STREET

BARKLY STREET

HAVELOCK STREET

Railway Station

Police

Theatre

ALBERT ST.

Uniting Church

HUMFFRAY STREET

LYDIARD ST NTH

Art Gallery P.O.

STURT ST.

Anglican Church

Town Hall

ARMSTRONG STREET

DOVETON STREET

DOVETON STREET SOUTH

MIDLAND HIGHWAY

MAIR STREET

BURRUMBEET RD

DANA STREET

EYRE STREET

GLENELG HIGHWAY

149

WESTERN HIGHWAY

DRUMMOND STREET

149 112

LATROBE STREET

TALBOT STREET

BELL STREET

WENDOUREE PARADE

PLEASANT STREET

N

WENDOUREE PARADE

EYRE STREET

SUTTON STREET

LAKE WENDOUREE

RUSSELL STREET

WINTER STREET

LATROBE STREET

Victoria Park

Botanical Gardens

colourful **Camp Hotel**, built in 1907, is covered in green tiles.

To the east of the centre, at 115–119 Sturt Street, is the **Mechanics' Institute**, the foundation stone of which was laid in 1869; the present façade was added in 1878. The interior includes a fine staircase. The institute's Library still functions as such, while the rest of the building is now occupied by a cinema. Next door is the former **Unicorn Hotel**, parts of which were erected as early as 1856, making it one of the town's oldest hotels. The building is now considerably altered, but its two-storeyed verandah with ironwork is one of the only remaining examples in the state.

The intersection of LYDIARD STREET SOUTH and Sturt Street was known as **'the Corner'**, for it was here that the most frenzied trading took place during the boom days in the offices of the share brokers, and where major gold discoveries were announced. The National Mutual Insurance Company Offices of 1905, on the western side of the corner, demonstrates the ostentatious ambition of the Ballarat town fathers. While the proportions of the building have been ruined by first-floor modernisation, the Venetian Gothic design of architects J.J. and E.J. Clark can be seen in the trefoil arches of the upper floors. These same architects designed Melbourne's City Baths, and had originally included here a huge ceiling dome similar to their work in Melbourne.

In the same block on Sturt Street is **Ballarat Town Hall**. As in so many other Australian towns with grandiose aspirations, this public structure became the focus of much architectural and civic wrangling. Initially conceived as a plain utilitarian building in the 1860s, by 1868 the City Council decided to conduct a design competition, then promptly rejected the judge's choice and settled for separate architects for exterior and interior. The resultant building is an amalgamation of the designs of J.T. Lorenz, H.R. Caselli, and Percy Oakden. It was completed in 1872 at a cost of £18,000; the four-storey tower was added in 1912. The town fathers were immensely proud of this awkward conglomeration when it opened and were disappointed when visiting English dignitaries were unimpressed. Of greatest interest are the preponderance of giant Corinthian columns, its Palladian form, and its rectangular interior stairway.

From here, it is easy to walk back to LYDIARD STREET NORTH, the location of the most substantial early commercial buildings. The entire length of Lydiard Street was first surveyed in 1851 and named after a police officer on the Mt Alexander diggings. The northern end's importance grew with the establishment of the railway station above Mair Street in 1862, thus prompting the erection of several hotels and commercial warehouses in this section.

On the northwest corner of Sturt and Lydiard Streets are a cluster of banks' buildings, all designed in the 1860s by prominent architect Leonard Terry. They are considered to be the most important group of buildings in Ballarat, speaking to the confident commercial prosperity of the town's early days. While Terry used a variety of styles and a mixture of Tuscan and Corinthian orders, the group presents a unified integration of rustication and arched fenestration.

Further north on this block is **The George Hotel** (☎ 03 5333 4866), still operating as a hotel. A hotel occupied this site from 1853 and was an important social centre, with some of the only fashionable dining in town. The present building was erected in 1902; its three-storey ironwork verandah is unique in Victoria.

Immediately across the street are the most significant 19C public buildings. At no. 6 Lydiard Street is the former **Mining Exchange**, built in 1887 to replace the exchange that had been on 'the Corner'. In keeping with its pivotal role in Ballarat's economy, the building was a formidable construction by architect C.D. Figgis, featuring a grand main hall with Tuscan arcading and elegant natural lighting, and an elliptical entrance arch. The building now houses antiques and collectables, but the architecture is relatively intact.

Next door is **Old Colonists' Hall**, built in 1887 on the site of the early gold escort stables; it is now owned by R.F. Scott & Co., leading suppliers of fishing and shooting equipment. Its elegant upper-storey iron balustrade complements the adjoining verandah of the Alexandria Tea Rooms, with its unusual iron panels with a radiating pattern. The tea rooms were originally the club rooms of the Commercial Club.

At 40 Lydiard Street is the **Ballarat Fine Art Gallery** (☎ 03 5331 5622; open Mon–Fri, 10.30–16.30, weekends and holidays, 12.30–16.30), the first provincial art gallery in Australia, designed for this purpose in 1887 (with renovations in 1927 and 1967). Leading parliamentarian Alfred Deakin officially opened the building on 13 June 1890 amidst great fanfare. Initially the main galleries were upstairs, reached by ascending an impressive stone stairway. The important historic paintings are still on the first floor, while the ground floor galleries are used for changing exhibitions.

The gallery's collection is an important one, emphasising the full spectrum of Australian art. One section on the ground floor is dedicated to artworks associated with the Eureka Stockade, the centrepiece of which is the **Eureka Flag** itself. Surrounding it are the only known eyewitness drawings of the rebellion by Swiss digger Charles Doudiet, recently purchased from Canada. The gallery also has a long affiliation with the Lindsay family, renowned Australian artists, who originally hailed from nearby Creswick (the Lindsay Gallery includes the family's Creswick sitting room); the collection of drawings and prints by the Lindsay artists is extensive.

Upstairs the rooms include some of the early monuments of Australian painting, not only Eugen von Guerard's view of *Old Ballarat* in 1853 and Walter Withers' *Last Summer* (1898), but also J.C.F. Johnstone's delightful *Euchre in the Bush* (c 1867), a folk-art depiction highlighting the ethnic diversity on the goldfields, and, of course, many of S.T. Gill's famous watercolours from the gold rush era. As part of Victoria's regional gallery scheme, in which these institutions concentrate on specific special collections, the Ballarat collection also contains a small but impressive number of medieval manuscripts.

Heading north to MAIR STREET and one block east is the crooked Camp Street, so named because the first Government Camp was installed here in 1851. Here are some splendid old buildings: **Pratt's Warehouse** on the corner of Mair Street, the Greek Revival **Freemason's Hall** (now Electra Hall) of 1872, the 1887 **Trades Hall**, and the bluestone **Old Ballarat Police Station**, also from the 1880s. These are now somewhat overshadowed by the imposing State Government Offices built in 1941.

From the corner of Lydiard and Mair Streets and along the next block north are several early **commercial warehouses**, evidence of the mercantile activity engendered by the railway. Most intact is J.J. Goller & Co. Warehouse, erected in 1861–62, its rusticated façade and window quoinings reminiscent of early Chicago warehouses. At the end of this block opposite Market Street is **Reid's Coffee Palace**, built in the 1880s at the height

Reid's Coffee Palace, Ballarat

of the Coffee Palace vogue. While much of its exterior has been lamentably renovated, the interior still includes the original hand-painted ceiling.

Across the street on the corner of Mair Street is the former **Ballarat Palace Hotel** of 1887 (now an insurance company), notable for its original exterior with crisp details and proportions. In marked contrast on this side of the street, further north at Ararat Street, is the flamboyant **Provincial Hotel**, built in 1909 by P.S. Richards, on the site of an earlier hotel of the same name. It is a remarkable if clumsy example of eclectic Edwardian design, with its orientalist towers and Romanesque arched balconies.

At this point the railyards begin. The **railway station** itself represents the central position played by Ballarat in the growth of Victoria's provincial rail system. The main building was constructed in 1862, when an indirect line from Melbourne reached the city. The platform shed covered three railway tracks and extended sixteen bays along the platform. By 1889, when the link between Ballan and Bacchus Marsh finally created a direct route to Melbourne, the southern entrance building, with its impressive clock tower—devoid of clocks!—was completed. Trains from Melbourne and other parts of Victoria still arrive at this station.

LYDIARD STREET SOUTH properly begins at the junction of Eyre and Armstrong Streets and continues to Sturt Street. Interestingly, this corner is the site of **Ebenezer Presbyterian Church**, with the former Gaol and Supreme Court next door. The church is a Classical Revival structure, erected in 1862 to a design by H.R. Caselli; the ornate iron fence which surrounds the church, manse and hall was added in 1892. The remnants of the **gaol** next door on Lydiard Street South, as well as the former Supreme Court Building, are now part of the **Ballarat School of Mines** grounds.

When the gaol was built in 1857, it was one of several gaols constructed in the Victorian countryside in response to the need for prison accommodation once the hideous prison hulks (in Port Phillip Bay) were removed. As with the other prison buildings in the state, the design was based on the Pentonville system, with a central hall and radiating wings. Now only the gateway, flanking buildings and guard tower remain.

The adjoining **Supreme Court building**, from 1868, consists of a public room and a central court room with flanking offices. Its façade is similar to any number of Commonwealth country courthouses of the era. Further north is the original building of the **School of Mines and Industries**, a central institution in Ballarat's social history since 1870. Founded by members of the Mining Board to provide all-rounded practical education of use to the mining industry, the school soon gained a reputation for the excellence of its training in engineering, metallurgy, chemistry and geology.

To the right at DANA STREET is the **Ballarat Club**, representative of the town's ambitious striving for English sophistication. Formed in 1872 and in this building since 1888, the purpose of the club was to uphold upper-class English values. Historians of the social life of the era point out that the club did not allow membership to tradesmen, women, Jews, or Catholics. The predominant entertainment in the club, after eating, drinking, playing cards and smoking, was betting. The building, by C.D. Figgis, is one of appropriately restrained elegance.

On the opposite corner of Dana Street is further evidence of genteel society, in the cluster of churches, most notably the former **Wesleyan Church** by architects Terry and Oakden (Terry seems to have specialised in the ecclesiastical buildings of the non-conformist denominations, while Oakden served the needs of the Anglicans and Catholics). Thus begins the most public block of the street up to Sturt Street and 'the Corner', dominated by two of the most historical structures in the city.

On the east side is the former **Academy of Music**, now the Royal South Street Memorial Theatre, and the scene of some of the most boisterous events in Ballarat's social history. Here was an annual music competition for which Ballarat was well known in the late 19C. Opening in 1875 with an operatic production of *La Fille de Madame Angot*, the building also saw performances by Dame Nellie Melba, Gladys Moncrieff, and Harry Lauder; future prime minister James Scullin won a debating championship here when a young man.

Architecturally, the building has been substantially renovated, first in 1898 by the famous theatre architect William Pitt. This remodelling extended the seating capacity to 2000 and saw the addition of the Art Nouveau interior decorations and a double balcony, which still survive.

Across the street is the grandest hotel associated with the gold rush era, **Craig's Royal Hotel** (☎ 03 5331 1377). The building stands on the site of the town's first licensed hotel, opened in 1853 by Thomas Bath. In 1857 this modest timber building was purchased by Walter Craig, and by 1862 he had built the grandiose southern wing, in an Italianate style. Over the next 40 years the hotel expanded, incorporating a variety of architectural styles and culminating in the ostentatious corner tower in 1890. Many original features remain, especially the elegant stairway, the dining room pilasters, and a fantastic bar surrounded by painted stuccowork. The entrance is still flanked by original gas lamps.

Historically, Craig's has many important associations. The poet Adam Lindsay Gordon ran the livery stables here in 1867; the cottage in which he lived behind the hotel has been re-erected in the Ballarat Botanic Gardens. Famous guests included Queen Victoria's sons, Prince Alfred, the Duke of Edinburgh, and the Prince of Wales, and Mark Twain. At the end of the American Civil War in 1865, officers of the Confederate ship, the *Shenandoah*, were fêted here, while they supposedly recruited men for their cause (although it appears more likely that they were just having a rip-roaring good time). In 1911, Dame Nellie Melba began a tradition of singing operatic arias from the Grand Victorian Balcony for the people in the street below.

East Ballarat

Sturt Street travelling east from Lydiard Street makes a loop around a shopping mall to become Victoria Street or the Melbourne Road. This is now East Ballarat, where the diggers lived and where construction was far less organised and stolid than in West Ballarat. The roads are less regulated, with small streets that simply emerged from the growing settlements.

Turn south on East Street to BARKLY STREET, and turn left into Barkly Street (named for Sir Henry Barkly, Governor of Victoria 1856–63). At this juncture on both sides of the street are major brick structures of the early period. On the right is the **East Ballarat Library** (now a branch of the School of Mines), erected in 1867 by J.T. Lorenz and C.H. Ohlfsen-Bagge, an innovative engineer-architect much taken with polychrome brickwork. Across the street is the **East Ballarat Fire Station**, the brick tower of which was constructed first in 1864 to house the fire bell.

At the corner of Barkly and Princes Streets is the elegant **Synagogue**, built as early as 1861 by T.B. Cameron—evidence of a sizeable Jewish population in early Ballarat; Jewish author Pinkus Goldhar, in fact, wrote a story, 'The Last Minyan' (1939), set among the community here. The building follows the pattern of European Orthodox synagogues, although the exterior is a Classical design with Tuscan columns. It is one of the only 19C synagogues remaining in Victoria.

Gold-mining in Ballarat ~ Eureka Street

Turn south on Princes Street to **EUREKA STREET**, location of many historical attractions. Here were the actual goldfields and the miners' settlements, and here the Eureka Rebellion took place. This section was strongly identified with the Irish community, and a Catholic chapel was erected as early as 1854.

West towards Main Street is **Montrose Cottage** (☎ 03 5332 2554, open daily 09.30–17.00), the oldest stone cottage in Ballarat, built in 1856 of bluestone by Scottish stonemason John Alexander. It has been restored with as many original furnishings as could be found, and is now a public museum.

Continue east on Eureka Street and turn left at Queen Street to no. 7, the **Old Curiosity Shop** (☎ 03 5332 1854, open daily 10.00–17.00), proudly described as 'the queerest house in Australia', a marvellously idiosyncratic structure. The builder James Warwick came to Ballarat from Cornwall in 1855 and found ample opportunity to ply his trade as a chimneymaker. He began to collect bottles, bits of crockery, and shells which he plastered on to the sides of his house with a mortar he made from African shells. His wife contributed to this eclectic collection with objects such as a fan made from the feathers of her pet cockatoo. In 1897, they opened the house to an eager public, becoming Australia's first roadside tourist attraction. As one book says, the house epitomises the 'shell and glass ethos' of so many Australian vernacular displays. While still privately owned, the house is open to the public.

Back on Eureka Street heading east, you now come to the supposed site of the **Eureka Stockade** (☎ 03 5331 2281). At the time of writing, this spot was being reconstructed, although all indications are that the site itself will consist only of a small commemorative obelisk. Across the street is **The Eureka Exhibition**, telling the story of the rebellion through a series of computer screens (it used to be life-size figures in tableaux).

At Fussell Street, turn south to the **Ballarat Wildlife Park** (☎ 03 5333 5933; open daily, 09.30–17.30), 16 ha, replete with all the expectable Australian fauna.

Turn west on York Street, then follow the signs south on Main Street to **Sovereign Hill Gold-Mining Township** (☎ 03 5331 1944, open daily 10.00–17.00). As an open-air museum re-creating an 'authentic' 1850s gold-mining town, Sovereign Hill does as good a job as any of these kinds of endeavours, with everyone dressed in 19C costumes and using original machines and equipment. You can pan for gold, walk down a re-created main street, and visit a mining museum with actual tunnel tours. There is even a Chinese village, although at last count no Chinese were included amongst the historically dressed guides. Overnight accommodation is even offered in a re-created Government Camp.

At night a sound-and-light production, 'Blood on the Southern Cross', recounts the Eureka story (it requires separate booking and an additional fee). The entry fee is (as with so many other tourist venues in Australia) rather steep, but Sovereign Hill makes a good attempt to give one value for money. Opposite the venue itself is the **Gold Museum** (open weekdays 09.30–17.20, Sat 12.00–17.20); admission here is included in the township's entry fee. A thoughtfully designed building allows a view of the hills and gullies of Ballarat where the gold was found. The exhibitions themselves are quite spectacular in terms of actual minerals displayed, and include a good history of gold and minting, as well as a social documentation of Ballarat and Eureka.

Western Ballarat

If you enter Ballarat from the west on the BALLARAT–BURRUMBEET ROAD, you pass by a 23km **Avenue of Honour**, containing 4000 trees commemorating the soldiers of the First World War. It ends at an **Arch of Victory** (☎ 03 5320 5500), erected through the fund-raising efforts of the women employees of E. Lucas & Co., makers of women's underwear. The arch was opened in 1920 by the Prince of Wales. From this point, it is a short distance further to **Lake Wendouree** and the **Botanic Gardens** on Wendouree Parade (☎ 03 5331 3277). Turn north on Gillies Street to reach the gardens and its conservatory. The lake is on the site of what was Yuille's Swamp; by the 1850s it had been consolidated into this lake, and by the 1860s boating clubs and other amusement centres began to develop. At the same time, the adjacent police horse paddock was converted into the botanic gardens.

The real heyday of the area was the 1880s, when genteel ideas of leisure activity led to the establishment of picturesque walks, the installation of paddle steamers, and the erection of picnic pavilions. Elegant Victorian villas surround the lake. The gardens contain a **Statuary Pavilion**, erected in 1887 and filled with sculptures imported from Italy (Ballarat is known as Victoria's 'city of statues'). These had been donated by wealthy Ballarat bachelor Thomas Stoddart, one of several prominent citizens who sought to elevate Ballarat's self-image. Also in the gardens is the **Begonia House**, centre of the city's annual Begonia Festival each February/March. The house is now the **Robert Clark Conservatory** (open daily 09.00–17.00), an elegant new greenhouse that recently won a design award from the Royal Australian Institute of Architects. The grounds also display several trees that are now on the National Trust's Register of Significant Trees. Most striking are the California redwoods, difficult to grow in Australia; they commemorate the historical ties between the Californian and Victorian gold rushes, and the number of American diggers who arrived here in the 1850s. It should be noted that, conversely, Australian diggers brought eucalyptus trees—now ubiquitous in the US state—to California in 1856.

The **Ballarat Vintage Tramway** (☎ 03 5334 1580; open weekends and holidays) also operates at the botanic gardens, the last vestige of the city's previously extensive tram system. The lake was the venue for the rowing events at the 1956 Melbourne Olympics, and one still finds Olympic athletes training here.

Imposing churches

As a city with grand Victorian-era aspirations, Ballarat of course set aside prime land for the construction of imposing churches. To the west of Doveton Street (Glenelg Highway) on STURT STREET are several: on the southern corner of Sturt and Dawson Streets is **St Patrick's Cathedral**, for which construction began as early as 1857, but work halts delayed its completion until 1891. In the 1860s, the main design was conceived by J.B. Denny, local architect in thrall of Puginesque Gothic Revival; elements of Pugin's ideas are evident throughout the cathedral complex, a characteristic that makes it unique in Victorian ecclesiastical design.

Opposite the cathedral on Dawson Street is the former **Baptist Church** of 1867 (now Church of Christ), a marvellously intact example of classical Roman revival design, quite similar to the Collins Street Baptist Church in Melbourne. Across Sturt Street on the northwestern corner is **St Andrew's Kirk**, another formidable structure that took more than 30 years and several architects to complete, from 1862–89. Overall, the impression is of Norman detailing and Presbyterian sobriety (it is now a Uniting Church).

A block north on the corner of Dawson and Mair Streets is the former **Congregational Church**, an 'eclectic Gothic' monument of the 1880s. Finally, it is interesting to see at Neill and McCarther Streets, in an area of residential buildings, a set of three churches of the same congregation, built at twenty-year intervals as the congregation outgrew the last building.

Ballarat to Bendigo

From Ballarat, you might decide to travel north on the **MIDLAND HIGHWAY** (route 149) to the other great gold-town, **Bendigo**; there are also **train connections** between Ballarat and Bendigo, and from Melbourne. En route, the rolling countryside is dotted with small towns that owe their existence to the presence of gold in the nearby rivers and hills, and each is rich in historic buildings, tourist attractions, and has information centres which provide walking tours and detailed descriptions.

18km from Ballarat is **Creswick**, home of the famous Lindsay family. The author and artist Norman Lindsay based the descriptions in his *Redheap* novels on the town, referring to it as 'one of those eruptions of human lunacy called a mining centre'. The books were banned in the town for their unsympathetic portrayal of recognisable residents. Lindsay's father, the town doctor, was present at the birth here in 1885 of **John Curtin**, the famous Labor Prime Minister during the Second World War. A granite monument commemorates Curtin as a native son. The present **Creswick Historical Museum** (open Sun and holidays), in the 1876 Town Hall, displays many artworks by the Lindsays and other regional artists, and provides historical background on the area.

Daylesford and Hepburn Springs

A further 27km north are the twin 'spa towns' of **Daylesford** and **Hepburn Springs**. In the region are numerous mineral springs; 50 per cent of Australia's mineral water sources are located here, and the residents have been bottling water since 1850. **Tourist information**: 49 Vincent Street, ☎ 03 5348 3707. A daily bus/train service runs from Melbourne, and also has weekday buses to Ballarat, Castlemaine and Bendigo. A shuttle bus between Daylesford and Hepburn Springs runs eight times a day, weekdays only. The area developed quickly as a fashionable health resort, only an hour's drive from Melbourne. Initially, gold discoveries here encouraged the arrival of European diggers: at Daylesford Swiss-Italian tunnellers, and at Hepburn Springs some 20,000 Italians by the 1860s. Consequently, much of the early architecture bears a resemblance to Northern Italian and Tyrolean models.

By the 1890s, the region had the elegant air of a European spa, evident in the **Hepburn Springs Spa Complex** (☎ 03 5348 2034), originally constructed in 1895 and renovated in 1991. Today renewed interest in natural health therapy has made the area a centre for alternative lifestyles and New Age crafts (and excellent bookshops!). Each April since 1987, the Daylesford Spa Festival is held. In Daylesford is also the **Convent Gallery**, corner of Daly and Hill Streets (☎ 03 5348 3211), a lovely arts-and-crafts centre in a restored 1892 convent which is also known for its restaurant. The town has the requisite Historical Society Museum and botanic gardens (at Wombat Hill).

Daylesford is also the site of the **Scottish Highland Gathering** in the first week of December, purported to be the largest Scottish gathering outside of Scotland. In July, the region's Swiss-Italian heritage is celebrated at the Mid-Winter Festival.

Castlemaine

From Daylesford, continue north 40km to **Castlemaine** (population 7450), one of the major centres for gold-mining. The Mt Alexander Goldfields were here, whose gullies produced some of the richest alluvial yields in the world. Castlemaine was initially the administrative centre for all of the goldfields and site of the government camp. **Tourist information centre**: Duke Street; ☎ 03 5472 2480. Daily trains operate from Melbourne to Castlemaine and on to Bendigo and Swan Hill.

Today Castlemaine is known for its substantial number of **gold-era buildings**, and most especially the **Market Hall** (☎ 03 5472 2679) on Mostyn Street, designed as if it were a Roman basilica, complete with Tuscan portico and a statue of Ceres, Roman goddess of the harvest, on top of the entrance. It was used as a market until 1967, and is now a museum.

The **Castlemaine Art Gallery and Historical Museum** (☎ 03 5472 2292; open weekdays 10.00–17.00 and weekends 12.00–17.00) contains some excellent Australian paintings, including Frederick McCubbin's *Golden Sunlight* (c1895) donated by Dame Nellie Melba, and works by Margaret Preston. The **Theatre Royal** (☎ 03 5472 1196) on Hargraves Street is touted as one of the oldest theatres in Victoria, one where the notorious Lola Montez played to rowdy and adoring miners. Today, it serves as a popular cinema and restaurant.

The gallery is also the caretaker for a superb historical house and gardens, **'Buda'**, 42–8 Hunter Street (☎ 03 5472 1032; open daily, 09.00–17.00). The house was originally in the style of a British-Indian bungalow with wide verandahs, built for Colonel John Smith, but it was purchased in 1857 by noted Hungarian silversmith Ernest Leviny, who named it after his native city and extended the rooms considerably to accommodate his large family. While the present exterior appears rather shabby, the house's treasures are the beautiful gardens and the interior rooms, lovingly maintained by Leviny's five daughters with fine examples of their father's silver work. Each spring, an Annual Garden Party continues a Leviny tradition; the gardens are considered among the most important in Victoria.

Castlemaine also has one of the oldest provincial **botanic gardens**, at Downes Road along Barkers Creek (☎ 03 5471 1727), begun in 1856 with many plants provided by Melbourne's famous botanist Ferdinand von Mueller. The town is also famous as the original home of Queensland's **XXXX Beer**; it was first brewed here by Irishman Edward Fitzgerald in 1859. When Fitzgerald moved to Brisbane in 1887, he took the name and the recipe with him; hence the 'Castlemaine' on every Queensland bottle today.

The area around Castlemaine is dotted with picturesque towns and remnants of old diggings, and the countryside boasts an abundance of tranquil country bed and breakfasts. 18km northwest is **Maldon** (population 1110), voted in 1965 by the National Trust as the 'First Notable Town in Australia' for its well-preserved overall streetscape. It has subsequently served as an ideal stage-set for historic films and now is filled with tea-rooms, antique shops and cottage gardens. The buildings are quite 'authentic', offering small storefronts of 1850s and 1860s. **Tourist information centre**: High Street; ☎ 03 5475 2569.

The road to the town travels through hills with a distinct geology, and evidence of mining tailings appear in the landscape everywhere. The **Historical Museum** (☎ 03 5475 1027; open weekdays 13.30–16.00, weekends 13.30–17.00) has quaint and informative displays, and the Castlemaine and Maldon Preservation Society run **steam trains** along an old section of track. Call ☎ 03 5475 2966 for running times.

Gold was discovered here in 1853 by German prospector John Mechosk, who located several other major finds. Once the rich alluvial fields were depleted, enormous quartz reefs were discovered, and continued to produce until the 1930s.

From Castlemaine 48km west on the Pyrenees Highway (route 122) is **Maryborough** (population 7800), another country town growing out of gold diggings. It certainly had delusions of grandeur if the **railway station** is any indication. It is worth visiting just to see this grandiose structure, 400m long with marble dressing-tables in the toilets and oak and walnut panelling. Legend has it that the design was actually produced for Spencer Street Station in Melbourne. On his famous tour of Victoria in 1895, Mark Twain described Maryborough as 'a railway station with a town attached'. **Tourist information**: Tuaggra Street, ☎ 03 5461 2643.

Bendigo

Back at Castlemaine, proceed 40km on the CALDER HIGHWAY (route 149) to **Bendigo** (population 70,000). The train from Melbourne and Castlemaine also travels on to Bendigo. If 'grand' describes Ballarat, 'proudly prosperous' describes Bendigo, more low-key and less touristy than its southern neighbour. **Tourist information**: Charing Cross; ☎ 03 5444 4445; freecall 1 800 813 153.

History
The first gold discovery here occurred in 1851, when **Margaret Kennedy**, the stationmaster's wife, allegedly made a small find. Initial alluvial mining quickly died out, but plentiful reef mining began in the 1860s. Ultimately, over 35 reefs would be discovered in the vicinity. Improved mining methods allowed Bendigo to continue as a gold producer into the 1950s.

The town itself was first called Sandhurst, but popular opinion finally led to the official adoption of the goldfield name Bendigo in the 1890s. The name, popular tradition maintains, was the nickname of a shepherd who had become a local prizefighter and emulated 'Bendigo' Thompson, a famous English fighter of the time. The name itself is a corruption of the Biblical Abednego.

In his humorous novel, *Illywhacker* (1985), Peter Carey's hero Herbert Badgery gives a poetic description of Bendigo which captures the impression it must have given to 19C eyes:

> *I have heard people describe Bendigo as a country town ... These people have never been to Bendigo and don't know what they are talking about ... if there are farmers in the streets, dark cafes with three courses for two and sixpence and, in Hayes street, a Co-op dedicated to Norfield Wire Strainers and Cattle Drench, it does not alter the fact that Bendigo is a town of the Golden Age.*

Early aspirations for Sandhurst to be a grand British provincial town are evident in the naming of streets. The surveyor Richard Larritt called the central square **Charing Cross** and its intersecting street **Pall Mall**; a bit north of here on View Street is the information centre. The park Larritt planned to the north of Pall Mall was later called **Rosalind Park**, after the character in Shakespeare's *As You Like It*.

At **CHARING CROSS SQUARE** is **Alexandra Fountain**, built in 1881 by noted architect W.C. Vahland and named for Alexandra, Princess of Wales. At the time the town was proud of its reputation for polished stonework, and the fountain gave an opportunity to employ local talent. From here you can begin a **Heritage Walk** with accompanying brochure available from the information centre.

This square was originally known as **View Point**, because it overlooked Bendigo Creek. The town's early prestigious banks were located across the street, as can be seen in a row of buildings on the northwest block and leading up View Street itself.

VIEW STREET NORTH is lined with public buildings of the Victorian era, some of them carefully restored and preserved and others in various states of renovation. The elegant **Union Bank** (now ANZ Bank), no. 45, built in 1876 with

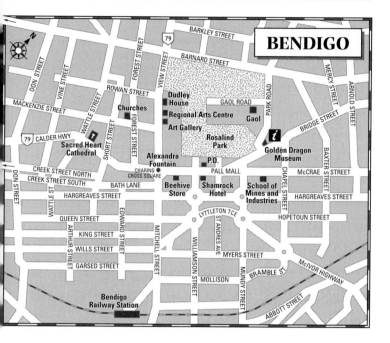

Corinthian columns and bluestone pedestals, has been restored to its original state, to complement the stupendous **Masonic Hall and Temple**, further north on the west side, no. 52. The architects of this impressive structure were Robert Getzschmann and W.C. Vahland (not surprisingly, they were both freemasons and Vahland was Grand Master of this lodge); the majority of prominent early buildings in town were designed by this prolific architectural team. The main building, with its perfectly proportioned Corinthian portico, was completed in 1873. The interior contains ornate plasterwork with Masonic symbols and above every window a depiction of Tubal Cain, the Biblical metal-worker. In 1890, the building became the **Capitol Theatre**; next to the Melbourne Town Hall, it was the largest hall in Victoria. Originally part of the ground floor and the basement were the Masonic Hotel, known as the 'Shades'; a faded sign at the back still bears witness to this establishment, although the hotel was delicensed in 1922. The hall is now the **Bendigo Regional Arts Centre**, which opened in 1991; it has a year-round programme of artistic events and community activities.

Next door is the **Bendigo Art Gallery** (☎ 03 5443 4991; open daily Mon–Sat, 10.00–17.00, Sun and holidays, 14.00–17.00). The original structure was a polychrome brick Orderly Room built for the town's Rifle Brigade, again by Vahland and Getzschmann, in 1867. This building was covered over in the 1950s by the unfortunate façade. Plans are apparently afoot to retrieve the original façade, although this may be wishful thinking on the part of the gallery's curators. The interior gives evidence to the original building's pleasant proportions.

The gallery's collection is a jewel in the crown of Victoria's regional art gallery system. Not only is there a good selection of Australian paintings, but also a substantial number of 19C English and French paintings, especially of the Barbizon School. Most of these works were given to the gallery by Dr Neptune-Scott, a local surgeon, and by some of the gold-wealthy citizens of the community.

On the northern side of the Arts Centre Building is **Dudley House** (☎ 03 5443 4695; open weekends and holidays, 14.00–17.00), Bendigo's oldest government building. It was originally the offices of surveyor Richard Larritt, who moved in 1854, having already laid out Bendigo's street plan. The building now houses the Bendigo Branch of the **Royal Historical Society of Victoria**, and contains period furnishings and historical documents.

At no. 28 View Street is **Temperance Hall**, another Vahland and Getzschmann structure of 1860, now a Chinese waxworks museum. Note to the north of the building an old wall sign indicating the 'Births and Deaths Registrar Office' with finger pointing up the passageway.

Pall Mall

From Charing Cross, travel northeast on Pall Mall, the central business district. At no. 18 is the **Beehive Store**, site of the earliest trading exchanges in the city. After a fire gutted the first structure in 1871, this handsome building was erected by Charles Webb, architect of the Windsor Hotel in Melbourne.

In the next block, on the corner of Williamstown Street and Pall Mall is the **Shamrock Hotel** (☎ 03 5443 0333), centre of Bendigo's social life from the town's earliest days. As early as 1854, a restaurant with entertainment hall was located here; as the Shamrock, it had one of the first liquor licenses in town. The Irish owners, Billy Heffernan and John Crowley, made a fortune presenting first-class entertainment and good dining; the goldfield comic Charles Thatcher, a popular entertainer of the period, appeared here nightly. By 1860, they had built a new hotel and theatre, designed by the ubiquitous team of Vahland and Getzschmann. It was lit by gas throughout and had a bowling alley in the basement. The present building was erected in 1897 for new owners; the architect this time was Philip Kennedy, who had trained in the Vahland offices. No expense was spared in the opulent design, and the hotel boasted electricity and hot water. Every distinguished visitor to Bendigo stayed here.

In 1898 the Australian Natives Association, the most powerful social organisation in the country, met at the Shamrock and agreed to support Federation of the Australian colonies (see p 62). In 1975, the hotel was threatened with demolition, until it was rescued by the State Government to the tune of $2,300,000. It is still a centre of social life, with good restaurants and accommodation.

Across the street from the Shamrock on Pall Mall is the **Post Office**, as ambitiously grandiose as so many other Victorian post offices. The building, designed by G.W. Watson, is identical in external details to the Law Courts next door, also designed by Watson. This one was completed in 1887 at a cost of £50,000. The clock tower contains bells to chime the hour; these have been a source of some civic controversy over the years. Dame Nellie Melba, staying across the street at the Shamrock, apparently complained vehemently about the bells when she visited in the 1900s.

At Pall Mall and Bridge Street along Rosalind Park is the **Conservatory**, an

1898 structure with a cast-iron framework. It was so derelict in 1981 that it was almost demolished. It has now been restored, with elegant woodwork in the interior. In Rosalind Park itself are several interesting buildings. The former **Supreme Court Building**, first erected in 1858, was rebuilt in 1865, and is now the gymnasium for Bendigo High School; the high school, first known as Central School and also in the park, was built in 1877. Next to the old court building is the **Bendigo Gaol**, a grim old 1860s complex still in use.

At the junction of Pall Mall, Bridge and Mundy Streets, Pall Mall becomes McCRAE STREET. In the first block are several old hotel buildings, as well as another Vahland and Getzschman structure, the former **Mechanics Institute and School of Mines** (now part of the TAFE), built between 1864 and 1889. The institute's octagonal library is worth a look; its domed ceiling includes a 'Sunlight' by T.J. Connelly, an American whose lamp store provided such illumination for all of Bendigo's public buildings. The Connelly Store operated from 1860 until 1985, and the business's building still exists on the corner of High and Forest Streets.

BRIDGE STREET was initially the location of Bendigo's substantial Chinese community, and here, at nos 5–9, is the **Golden Dragon Museum** (☎ 03 5441 5044; open daily 09.30–17.00), an excellent tribute to Chinese culture in the goldfields. The central exhibit is the **Sun Loong Dragon**, at 100m long and requiring 52 carriers the longest imperial dragon in the world. Since 1892, the Bendigo Chinese have paraded a Loong dragon in the town's annual **Easter Fair parade**, still a major civic event. The present 'new dragon' was made in Hong Kong and has been paraded since 1970; the older Loong dragon is also on display. Other museum exhibits give a good picture through artefacts and costumes of the daily life of Chinese during the goldfield days. The museum has recently added classical Chinese gardens with arched bridges and temple, and is developing more extensive exhibition halls.

Further out of the centre of town, at Emu Point, site of an early Chinese encampment, is the **Chinese Joss House** (☎ 03 5442 1685; open daily, 10.00–17.00) on Finn Street (the word 'joss' derives indirectly from the Latin 'deus' for god). The **Talking Tram tour** from Central Deborah Mine (see below), which also stops at the Tram Museum en route, ends here.

Built as the Chinese Masonic Hall in the 1860s of hand-made bricks, it is painted a traditional Chinese red and consists of a central main temple flanked by an Ancestral Temple. It is the oldest functioning joss house in Australia and is dedicated to General Kwang Gung (c AD 300), revered for his wisdom. While the house is operated by the National Trust and is open to visitors, one should remember that it is still an active place of worship rather than a tourist attraction.

Belgravia

The area to the southwest of Charing Cross developed into a prosperous residential neighbourhood; in the early days, it was called **Belgravia**, with allusions to fashionable London. Many of the wealthy merchants' and miners' villas still remain here, as well as substantial churches and other public buildings. Pall Mall now becomes HIGH STREET.

The area bordered by View Street, Rawson, Vine, and High Streets contains several good examples of these fashionable buildings from the late 19C, including **All Saints Old Cathedral**, on the corner of Forest and MacKenzie Streets, showing the signs of erratic building phases between 1855 and 1935. On Forest Street towards High Street are exemplary residences. **Bishopscourt**, no. 40, was in the 1870s the home and surgery of Paul MacGillivray, resident surgeon at Bendigo Hospital; it later became the Anglican bishop's quarters, hence the name. Across the street, no. 57 is **'Illira'**, built in 1886 by architects Smith and Johnson for a wine merchant, with lovely cast-iron verandah and balcony. Next door, no. 22 is a more modest residence of 1864, with unusual arches and French windows.

Around the corner on MacKenzie Street is **'Euroma'**, an example of Vahland and Getzschmann's domestic style, built in 1870 for miner-financier William Tipper and purchased in 1874 by George Lansell of 'Fortuna Villa' fame (see below). Its cavity wall construction is a feature adapted by later local architects.

On the corner of Wattle and High Streets is **Sacred Heart Cathedral**. Conceived in the 1890s on land acquired in 1855 by Bendigo's first parish priest, Rev. Henry Backhaus, the cathedral was not completed until 1977, by which time stonemasons had been brought in from England and Italy to finish the work as it was meant to appear in the original plans.

A few streets further west on Don Street, and six blocks north at Webster Street, no. 233 is **'Braeside'**, local architect Robert Getzschmann's own residence, built in 1871 as a timber cottage with decorative iron ornamentation. The area to the west of here around OLD VIOLET STREET was originally a German neighbourhood, evident in the 1866 Violet Street Primary School, another Vahland and Getzschmann project, which for years was known as the German School. Similarly, the **Lutheran Church and School** at Violet and MacKenzie Streets are the earliest-known examples of Vahland's work, from 1857. Services and classes were conducted in German until the First World War.

On High Street at Violet Street is also the **Central Deborah Mine** (☎ 03 5443 8322; open daily 09.00–17.00), one of the latest deep shaft mines to be opened (not until the 1940s). While it closed in 1954, it has been reopened by the Bendigo Trust to serve as a living monument to the town's mining history.

George Lansell ~ Fortuna Villa's first owner

Lansell was the best example of a goldfield success story, arriving from England as a brewery worker in 1853 and striking it rich in the 1860s when after shrewd investments he purchased for £30,000 the claim to New Chum Reef at Victoria Hill, where this villa now stands. Lansell mined here to a depth of 900m and earned over £180,000 from this reef alone. (A 'new chum' was the term given to new arrivals on the goldfields, or inexperienced diggers—like an American greenhorn; the term appears in many guises throughout the Victorian goldfields.)

In the 1870s, Lansell made a trip to Pompeii, and on his return had a replica made of Pompeii's Fortuna fountain. The conservatory contains a set of etched windows of Australian scenes and animals, completed in Italy by artists who had never seen the scenes or animals themselves. As the architectural historian Mike Butcher says, the villa 'could not possibly be described as harmonious', but it shows 'a house which may have lacked an overall plan but not money'. The house is now owned by the Australian Army, but is open to visitors on Sunday afternoons.

There is both an above ground exhibition of mining history, as well as an underground mine tour, with hardhat, mining lights and descent into the second of the mine's seventeen levels. Not a tour for claustrophobics, the experience is fascinating nonetheless.

From here, you can catch the **Talking Tram Tour** to the Chinese Joss House (see above), 8km away in North Bendigo, with several stops along the way.

Between Lily and Booth Streets on ST BARNARD/CHUM STREET is **'Fortuna Villa'** (☎ 03 5442 0222; open most Sundays), an extravagant mansion, begun in 1869 by mining magnate Ballerstedt and extended over the next 40 years as the home of 'Quartz King' mining boss George Lansell.

The district around Victoria Hill is known as **Ironbark**, and still contains architectural remnants of its early history. One of the most pleasant is **Goldmines Hotel**, on Marong Road (Calder Highway, route 79). Another Vahland and Getzschmann structure of 1872, the hotel is still owned by the original family, the Sterrys. David Sterry arrived in Bendigo in 1853, and gained his wealth from the Victoria Reef, a mine across the street from this hotel. He built a hotel on this site as early as 1857. The present owners should be acknowledged for their efforts to preserve the building both internally and externally, allowing no contemporary advertising on the façade.

North of Bendigo on the MIDLAND HIGHWAY in **Epsom** (c 10km) is **Bendigo Pottery**, the most historical of several ceramic factories in the region. It was founded in 1858 by entrepreneur George Duncan Guthrie, who recognised that the superior clay in the soil here would produce exquisite pottery. After his death in 1910, production of sewer pipe and tiles kept the plant going. Today, fine pottery is again produced in the salt kilns, and the distinctive dinnerware, particularly in white and blue, is still stamped with the original label.

Murray River

The Victoria–New South Wales border is largely determined by the Murray River's course. The **Murray River** is Australia's longest river, flowing for some 2600km, mostly towards the west. It was first named the Hume by explorer Hamilton Hume, when he saw it in November 1824, but it was renamed by explorer Charles Sturt in January 1830 after Secretary of State for the Colonies, Sir George Murray.

The river's basin has its catchment on the western slope of the Great Dividing Ranges generally south of Sydney. The source of the Murray itself is in Victoria's Alpine National Park. At Corryong in Victoria, it is only a few metres across in midsummer. By Albury/Wodonga, on the New South Wales–Victoria border, a succession of smaller rivers have joined it, making a river of substance.

The lovely **Murrumbidgee River** rises near Kiandra in the Snowy Mountains and meanders over 2000km to join the Murray near Balranald in Victoria. Its progress is initially southeast, then it makes a giant northward loop through the ACT and then finally westward; it is joined by the Lachlan River from central New South Wales a short distance before its junction with the Murray. The **Darling River** from west-central New South Wales joins at Wentworth near the Victoria–South Australia border. Once in South Australia the Murray flows south to Lake Alexandrina and into Encounter

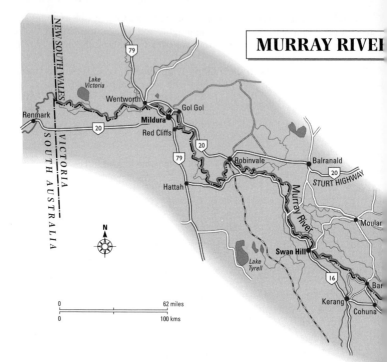

MURRAY RIVEI

Bay on the southwest side of the Fleurieu Peninsula east of Adelaide.

The Murray's initial appearance is like that of the Murrumbidgee: steep inclines, forested gorges and occasional open grassy valleys. Casaurinas thrive along the banks and in the seasonally dry floodplain. Beyond Albury/Wodonga to the west the land around the river becomes quite flat, allowing the river to meander, form billabongs, fill and drain swamps and marshes. Here the river red-gum is the predominant tree. From about Swan Hill to the South Australia border, the Murray passes through mallee scrub. Once past the border its source is marked by limestone cliffs and remarkable twists and turns. At the entrance to Lake Alexandrina these cliffs are 30m high.

River-boat trade on the river from its source reached as far north as Albury but rail lines to the agricultural centres brought this lengthy extension to a halt by the end of the 19C. For a short while in the mid-19C, Echuca in Victoria

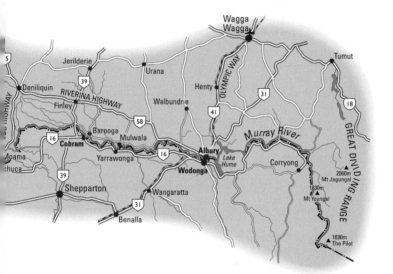

became the second busiest port in the state after Melbourne. Recently, the pleasure of vacationing on a Murray riverboat has been rediscovered. **House boat rentals, day cruises**, and **river trips** are available at Albury, Cobram, Echuca, Swan Hill, Mildura, Wentworth, Renmark, Mannum, Murray Bridge and Goolwa.

Albury/Wodonga (see p 243) has been described in the section on the Hume Highway. **Cobram** (population 3650), 140km west of Albury on the river, is a small town with large, sandy beaches along the river. Its Australian Yabby Farm is the largest in the country. Yabbies, by the way, are freshwater crayfish prevalent throughout Australia. Although richer than their marine cousins, they are easily caught and prepared. The light-coloured *Euastacus armantus* yabby is native to the Murray and may reach 40cm excluding their pinchers. **Tourist information**: Station and Punt Streets; ☎ 03 5872 2132.

Echuca (population 8500) at the junction of the Murray and Goulburn Rivers, was founded by Isaac White, who first operated a punt service across the river, and by eccentric ex-convict Henry Hopwood, who took a greater interest in the settlement by operating a punt, building a pontoon bridge to cross sheep destined for the Victorian goldfields and opening a hotel. **Tourist information**: Old Pumphouse, corner Hagarth and Cobb Highway, ☎ 03 5480 7555.

At one time, Echuca was Australia's largest inland port, leading to its designation as the 'Chicago of Australia'. The **Port of Echuca** and its red-gum wharf, built in 1864 and at one time a mile (1.6km) long, has been restored; a variety of paddle steamer and other boat tours depart from here. Echuca is a great place from which to begin a Murray River Cruise. The **Star Hotel**, now the **Port Visitor's Centre** from which visitors obtain passes to enter the Wharf district, has an underground bar and escape tunnel. The **Dharnya Centre** (☎ 03 5869 3302) in the nearby Barmah Red Gum Forest presents the traditional life of the area's Aboriginal population.

Swan Hill (population 8830) c 157km north of Echuca along the river, was named by explorer Thomas Mitchell when he camped here in 1836. The nearby black swans had disturbed his sleep. This was the farthest point Francis Cadell reached on his pioneering steamer voyage up the Murray in 1853. The local history museum, the **Pioneer Settlement** (☎ 03 5032 1093; open daily, 08.30–17.00), is a reconstruction of a pioneer community, with buildings brought from all over the state; it operates as an 'open air museum' with evening performances and daily tours by costumed guides. **Tourist information**: 306 Campbell Street; ☎ 03 5032 3033.

The town's multi-cultural population—both Italians and Aborigines are here in large numbers—is reflected in the **Swan Hill Regional Contemporary Art Gallery** (☎ 03 5032 1403; open weekdays 10.00–16.00, weekends 14.00–17.00), which specialises in Aboriginal and folk/naive art.

Mildura and Renmark

In the heart of the mallee, **Mildura** (population 22,300) in Victoria and **Renmark** (population 4260) in South Australia owe their establishment to irrigation. Mildura is 558km northwest of Melbourne, at the junction of the Calder and Sturt Highways. **Tourist information**: Langtree Mall, ☎ 03 5023 3619.

History

Following a serious drought in the 1880s, prominent parliamentarian Alfred Deakin visited the United States to study its irrigation systems. While in California he persuaded brothers George and William Chaffey to examine the Murray as a possible source for the first major irrigation system in Australia. Their achievement in the late 1880s and early 1890s saw the region blossom and brought thousands of settlers to the area. The historical significance of this achievement is chronicled in novelist Ernestine Hill's *Water into Gold* (1937) and by Mildura native Alice Lapstone, in *Mildura Calling* (1946).

Mildura is currently a wine grape and citrus centre. The name '**Sunraysia**' for this region and its produce originated in a competition started in the 1920s by writer and newspaperman C.J. de Garis; sultanas and raisins grown here were said to be 'Sunraysed'. De Garis then founded a local newspaper called the *Sunraysia Daily*.

Mildura is a pleasant agricultural town. The **Arts Centre** (☎ 03 5023 3733; open weekdays 09.00–17.00, weekends 14.00–16.30) is located in W.B. Chaffey's 1890s home, '**Rio Visto**' on Cureton Avenue, overlooking the river. The building of red brick had extravagant appointments, with jarrah woodwork, stained-glass windows and Italian tiles. The collection centres around the donations of senator and publisher R.D. Elliott, and contains mostly British and Australian paintings. The ground floor has several murals by Sir Frank Brangwyn. The gallery is especially proud of its Degas pastel (1890) and a 1924 sculpture by Sir Jacob Epstein. Mildura can also be proud of its local tennis courts. In 1998, the Davis Cup competition was played here, to overwhelming praise for its excellent grass surface.

Given the majesty of the Murray at this point, it is no surprise that Mildura's great attraction is a variety of river cruises. A special treat is the opportunity to rent a houseboat, for lazy meanders on the river. Many of the trips on offer can be arranged through the tourist office.

Renmark is 143km west of Mildura, over the South Australian border and at the centre of the Chaffey brothers' irrigation area. Charles Chaffey's wife, M. Ella Chaffey, set a novel, *The Youngsters of Murray Home* (1896), here. Their home, '**Olivewood**' (☎ 08 8586 6175; open Thurs–Mon, 10.00–16.00, Tues 14.00–16.00), built in 1887 of horizontally placed mallee logs, is now a National Trust Museum. **Tourist information:** Murray Avenue; ☎ 08 8586 6704.

The river at Renmark is particularly enchanting. Many of the boat tours on the river end their cruises here. The **Renmark Hotel** (☎ 08 8586 6755) overlooking the river's bend was established in 1897 as a public trust in a successful effort to suppress local bootleg liquor trade. It was the first communally owned hotel in the British Commonwealth. It is still an impressive structure, with three storeys of verandahs in the original section and beautifully situated across from the river's most expansive turn.

Also on the river here is the **PS Industry** (☎ 08 8586 6704; open weekdays 09.00–16.30, Sat 09.00–15.30, Sun 12.00–15.30), a restored paddle steamer now opened as a museum. Still powered by steam, it makes regular river trips.

The **Renmark Rose Festival** held in October centres on **Rustons Rose Garden**, Moorna Street (☎ 08 8586 6191; open Sept–July), filled with more than 50,000 bushes with more than 3000 varieties. The garden also has a large number of flowering trees, iris and day lilies.

Eastern Victoria

The Dandenongs

Directly to the northeast of Melbourne proper c 35km are the **Dandenong Ranges**, a popular and convenient excursion destination for all Victorians. Comprised of volcanic lava and cooled by high rainfall, the area supports not only natural reserves and forests filled with all manner of Australian flora and fauna (most notably the relatively rare lyrebird), it is also the location of many impressive public gardens and ornamental flower farms. Walking trails abound, making the area a great spot for weekend outings and bushwalking. The main tourist offices in Melbourne will have vast amounts of information, maps, and tour options to the Dandenongs.

Access is along MOUNT DANDENONG TOURIST ROAD, from Upper Ferntree Gully to

EASTERN VICTORIA

NEW SOUTH WALES

SNOWY RIVER
NATIONAL PARK

1199

23

Orbost
Cann River
Mt Everard
Mallacoota
CROAJINGOLONG
NATIONAL PARK

N

0 _____ 50 miles
0 _____ 100 kms

Mount Dandenong and Montrose, or from SHERBROOKE ROAD to Kallista. The Belgrave line of the **train** goes through Upper Ferntree Gully and on to Belgrave, where you can take a bus to further destinations. Scores of **tourist coaches** also travel here daily; check with the Melbourne tourist office, or with the Department of Conservation and Natural Resources, 240 Victoria Parade, East Melbourne, ☎ 03 9412 4795.

At **Upper Ferntree Gully**, take Old Monbulk Road 5km to **Belgrave** to take **Puffing Billy** (☎ 03 9754 6800), an antique steam train 13km to Menzies Creek. A few kilometres east of here is **Emerald Lake Park** (☎ 03 5968 4667), part of the original Nobelius Nursery, in the 1900s the largest nursery in the Southern Hemisphere, founded by Carl Alex Nobelius, a relative of Alfred Nobel. The park now consists of several kilometres of walking tracks, interspersed with freestanding plaster murals depicting the region's history.

From Upper Fern Tree Gully, you can take MT DANDENONG TOURIST ROAD north to **Olinda** and Mt Dandenong. Along the route are many popular picnic grounds and forest reserves known as the haunt of lyre birds. Near Olinda is the **National Rhododendron Garden** (☎ 03 9751 1980), with brilliant floral displays and walking trails. Olinda is also the site of the **Edward Henty Cottage**, one of the many properties of Victoria's first settler, see p 361.

At Mount Dandenong, the range's highest point at 633m, is the **William Ricketts Sanctuary** (☎ 03 9751 1300, open daily 10.00–16.30), the legacy of inspirational eccentric artist William Ricketts (d. 1993). From the 1930s, Ricketts began to create an outdoor 'church' dedicated to the spirit of Aboriginal mythology and love of the land. His clay sculptures—most of them based on the real likenesses of Aborigines he knew—are fitted into the ferns and forests, surrounded by grottoes and springs gushing forth from sculpted concentric circles, a sacred symbol among Central Australian Aborigines. Ricketts hoped to encourage harmony and unity among the races, and lamented the lack of understanding of Aboriginal culture. The sanctuary was most prominently featured in comedian Billy Connolly's video tour of Australia.

From here, continue to take the winding Mt Dandenong Tourist Road some 10km to connect to the CANTERBURY ROAD and DORSET ROAD, then to Lilydale on the Maroondah Highway. The **Lilydale Museum**, 39 Castella Street (☎ 03 9735 8221; open Wed–Sat 11.00–16.00, Sun 14.00–17.00), contains the only permanent exhibition to Australia's famed operatic prima donna, Dame Nellie Melba, who lived in the area at the end of her life. Tourist information at Lilydale will have information on winery tours in the Yarra Valley region: corner Victoria Road and Maroondah Highway, ☎ 03 9739 7333.

The MAROONDAH HIGHWAY then leads 22km through beautiful eucalyptus forests to **Healesville**, a popular tourist destination because of its native fauna sanctuary (☎ 03 5962 4022, open daily 09.00–17.00). Originally part of the Coranderrk Aboriginal Reservation, the sanctuary includes excellent facilities to view Australian fauna; it was here, in 1944, that a platypus was bred in captivity for the first time. The centre does significant work towards the preservation and care of Australian native species.

19km northwest of Healesville is **Toolangi**, site of Arden, home of C.J. Dennis. Here Dennis wrote many of his books, including his classic *The Sentimental Bloke* (1915), made into Australia's first great film in 1919. The **C.J. Dennis Singing Garden and Tea Rooms**, 98 Main Road (☎ 03 5962 9282, open Sat–Thurs 10.00–17.00) were developed by Dennis and his wife, with great shows of rhododendrons and semi-formal walks.

Back at Healesville, you can continue on the Maroondah Highway through forest ranges to **Alexandra**, a tidy little country town formerly known as Red Gate Digging. 26km east of here is Eildon, site of **Lake Eildon** (☎ 03 5772 2038), Victoria's largest man-made lake. At this point, you are only 138km northeast of Melbourne.

Continuing northwest on Maroondah Highway it is 69km to **Mansfield**, which is at the edge of the Victorian Alps and location for the 1982 filming of the movie, *The Man from Snowy River*. The road proceeds eastwards 48km to Mt Buller Alpine Village, the most developed ski resort on this side of the Snowy Mountains. The first ski lift here was installed in 1949, and as it is only 250km from Melbourne, it is the most popular spot for weekend skiers. From Mansfield, route 153 continues as the Midland Highway into Benalla and the Hume Highway.

Gippsland to the southeast corner of Victoria

Gippsland is the region in the southeast corner of Victoria, from the eastern edge of Melbourne at Dandenong to the Pacific Coast and north to the beginnings of the Victorian Alps.

History
The area was named in honour of New South Wales Governor Sir George Gipps (1791–1847) by the Polish explorer Paul Strzelecki (see box), who traversed the area in 1840. Strzelecki was heralded as the white discoverer of Gippsland, but in 1839 Scottish explorer and settler Angus McMillan (1810–65) had already entered the region from the north with an Aborigine of the Monaro region, Jimmy Gibber, and eventually, with the help of Aboriginal trackers, managed to cross the country to the sea at present-day Port Albert.

Because of its dense vegetation and teeming wildlife, the region was much favoured by indigenous people; the Aborigines were mostly of the Kurnai tribe, while around Western Port were the Bunurong group of the Kulin tribe. The Kurnai were studied extensively by Lorimer Fison and A.W. Howitt in the 1880s, with many of their legends published in popular editions.

Because of McMillan's early reports about the region, the first European settlers were Highland Scots speaking Gaelic; many Gaelic words persisted in local vernacular, and place-names demonstrate the predominance of Scottish settlement. The development of the region was particularly valuable as a source for rich arable land, and early clearing led to the establishment of flourishing dairy farms, for which much of the region is still known. Indeed, three internal geographical divisions identify the region: the dairy land of South Gippsland, the central plains of East Gippsland, and the mountainous timberland of the northeast. The southern section also was a major coal-producing area (at Wonthaggi, South Gippsland's major town, the State Coal Mine offers guided underground tours) and the coastline, with its many lakes and marshlands, quickly became a holiday destination for all Victorians. The author Hal Porter describes the scenery of the southern forests as 'Pre-Raphaelite stuff', while Anthony Trollope described the region favourably in his *Australia and New Zealand* (1873).

Paul Edmund de Strzelecki

Paul Edmund de Strzelecki (1797–1873) was born in Poland, and had an adventurous life exploring in the Americas and the South Seas before his arrival in Australia in 1839. His use of the title of count was an unsubstantiated affectation, but he was certainly trained as a scientist, a skill he put to work in his exploration of Australia. While exploring New South Wales in 1839, he discovered gold, but was persuaded by Governor Gipps to keep it secret for fear of unrest caused by such an announcement in the penal colony. Years later, when the gold rush began, he felt compelled to verify his early findings to prove that he had successfully carried out his tasks as a geologist.

In 1840 he set out from Sydney to explore the inland territory en route to Port Phillip and Tasmania. On 15 February of that year he ascended the highest peak in the Snowy Mountains, naming it **Mt Kosciuszko** in honour of the great Polish patriot. He then made a treacherous journey through dense scrub to reach Westernport, surviving only by the aid of Aboriginal companions who could provide food. By the end of May he reached Melbourne, where he was hailed as the discoverer of this important territory. He then went on to Tasmania, collecting specimens and exploring unknown regions of the island. His physical descriptions of Tasmania's geology and topography remained the standard reference for 50 years. By 1845, he was back in England, where he worked with relief societies to appease the suffering caused by the Irish famine. Late in life he worked with Caroline Chisholm to assist emigration of poor families to Australia. His name is commemorated in several locations throughout Australia, most notably in the Strzelecki Ranges in western Gippsland.

Wilsons Promontory

From Melbourne, the greatest tourist destination in this region is **Wilsons Promontory** in South Gippsland, 230km from the city. The train from Melbourne goes as far as Fish Creek, some 60km away; it is best to arrange a tour here, or have your own car. To reach this rugged rock, the southernmost tip of the Australian mainland, travel from Melbourne via the South Gippsland Highway (route 180) through Leongatha; at Meeniyan, take route 189 south c 60km into the **Wilsons Promontory National Park** (☎ 03 5680 9555). The Tidal River entrance includes a National Parks Office, with excellent displays and tourist information. The park also offers a variety of overnight accommodation, from camping to bunk houses and holiday flats; most facilities centre around the Tidal River area, and all are booked out well in advance of school holidays. Call ☎ 03 5680 9500 to make bookings. The 'Prom', as it is locally called, was named by Bass and Flinders after Flinders' friend, London merchant Thomas Wilson; it had originally been known as Furneaux's Land, for Tobias Furneaux, explorer of this region and captain of one of the ships on Captain Cook's second voyage. The area became a national park in 1908, now one of the most popular sites for bushwalkers and holiday-makers.

The dominant features of the region are the enormous granite crags, the highest of which, Mt La Trobe, rises to 754m. The park contains more than 80km of **walking-tracks** of varying lengths and over all kinds of terrain. The beaches here are of white sand with rugged mountains in the background. At the southern tip of the park is a lighthouse, built in 1859 as one of the most important markers for ships around the coast between Sydney and Melbourne. In Nathan Spielvogel's 1913 novel *The Gumsucker at Home*, the rock dominates: 'Looking south I saw Wilson's Promontory, like a crouching lion, far more imposing than Gibraltar.'

Gippsland Lakes

Return to the South Gippsland Highway at Foster and head east into the **Gippsland Lakes** district which begins at Sale, about 160km from Foster. From the 1860s, the Gippsland Lakes, centred around **Port Albert**, served as an important shipping centre, allowing for the opening of the interior as far as present-day Sale. The railway link (which extends to Bairnsdale) from Melbourne to Sale opened in 1879 and led to the demise of the water shipping trade.

From **Sale** today you can easily reach the **Gippsland Lakes Coastal Park** (☎ 03 5144 1108) and the start of the amazing **Ninety Mile Beach**, a stretch of sand between the lakes and the ocean that provides a great location for seaside holidays. The dominant activity around the lakes is fishing, fishing, fishing—both along the coast on the beach, and in deep-sea fishing boats out to sea. **Tourist information**: Central Gippsland Tourism, 8 Princes Highway, Sale, ☎ 03 5144 1108.

On Princes Highway (Highway 1) c 22km east of Bairnsdale en route to Lakes Entrance is the turn-off to **Metung** (population 425), a charming village built on a narrow strip of land next to Lake King on Reeve Channel, one of the primary entrances to the inland waterways. Naturally, this location makes Metung an ideal spot from which to begin boating cruises; many companies here offer all types of boat hire. The major industry in the village is Bull's Marine Industries, begun in the 1870s by pioneer Captain James Bull, who in his paddle steamer *Tanjil* explored the waterways before the entrance was cut.

51km from Sale is **Bairnsdale** (accessible by train), the agricultural centre of East Gippsland. Settled by Archibald McLeod in the 1840s, the name supposedly derives from the fact that the settlement was soon teeming with children or 'bairns'; but the name of his property was originally 'Bernisdale', after a place on the Isle of Skye.

In town is **St Mary's Roman Catholic Cathedral** (☎ 03 5152 6444), built in 1913. In the 1930s, an Italian labourer, Francesco Floreani, who had studied art in Turin, painted *trompe l'oeil* murals and ceilings throughout the church. Also of interest is the **court house** on Nicholson Street (☎ 03 5153 1000; open daily), dating from 1894, with gables and towers reminiscent of Loire châteaux; the stonework, however, depicts Australian flora and fauna.

At **Lakes Entrance**, 34km from Bairnsdale, the Ninety Mile Beach ends; a small footbridge here allows visitors to walk over to the surf beach. Lakes Entrance has one of the most active and productive fishing fleets in the state. In the summer, the town and surrounding area is overrun with holiday-makers, and consequently quantities of tourist activities, including numerous **cruises** that take the visitor to destinations throughout the fascinating inland waterway system, one of the biggest and most interesting in Australia. From Lakes Entrance it is also possible to arrange for all varieties of fishing trips. **Tourist information**: corner Marine Parade and The Esplanade, ☎ 03 5155 1966.

Nyermilang Park (☎ 03 5156 3253; open daily, 09.00–16.00), 10km northwest of Lakes Entrance, was originally a homestead taken up in 1884. The present house, set in formal gardens, was built in 1892 by Frank Stuart; it is open to the public. Nyermilang derives from an Aboriginal word meaning 'chain of lakes'; the Aborigines here were Tatungolung, part of the Kurnai group. The park offers spectacular views of the channel and neighbouring islands.

10km east of Lakes Entrance is **Lake Tyers**, part of which is an Aboriginal settlement. Founded as a mission in the 1860s by John Bulmer and his wife, who stayed for 50 years, the 1600 ha settlement was the first area in Australia to be returned to the resident Aborigines under the groundbreaking Aboriginal Lands Act of 1970, precursor of the current Native Title Act.

From Lakes Entrance the PRINCES HIGHWAY continues east through the central plains of Gippsland, much of which is now industrialised in places around Orbost. **Orbost** itself has a rainforest centre on Lochiel Street (☎ 03 5161 1375; open weekdays, 09.00–17.00, school holidays 10.00–17.00), with good displays on the kinds of rainforest environments in Victoria. **Tourist information**: Nicholson Street, ☎ 03 5154 2424.

From Orbost, you can travel 58km north to the little town of **Buchan**, noted for its limestone caves and at the foot of the **Snowy River National Park** (see p 230). The **caves** are covered in stalactites and stalagmites, evidence of the fact that the land was covered by sea 400 million years ago. Regular tours of the caves are given year round, with more frequent trips offered in the peak season (☎ 03 5155 9264; open daily, 08.30–16.30).

The road north from Buchan travels along the **Snowy River**, through landscape made famous in Banjo Paterson's *Man From Snowy River*; it offers an adventurous route all the way to Jindabyne in the heart of the Snowy

Mountains of New South Wales. The scenery at places such as the lookout at Little River Gorge, about 65km from Buchan, is stunning. As much of this road is unsealed, and many parts impassable in winter, be sure to check conditions before setting out.

At Orbost, the PRINCES HIGHWAY continues east through forests on each side. **Cann River** has long been a favoured fishing resort. Strong local Koori associations are expressed at Nulluak Gundji Cultural Centre (☎ 03 5158 6261) immediately west of town. The Cann Valley Highway continues north to the New South Wales border, where it becomes the MONARO HIGHWAY (route 23). The road offers a lovely forest-and-mountain-meadow alternative route to Cooma and on to Canberra in the ACT.

If you continue on the Princes Highway from Cann River to the New South Wales border, a nice side trip is to take the 8km road to **Mallacoota Inlet**, the last stop in Victoria before crossing into New South Wales. The inlet village is surrounded by 86,000 ha of **Croajingalong National Park** (☎ 03 5158 0263). As the last stop in Victoria, Mallacoota is tremendously popular as a holiday retreat for people from both states, and can be quite crowded during summer and school holidays. The inlet provides some stunning scenery, with calm beaches on one side and the wild surf of Bass Strait on the other. You can also take **boat trips** out to the small islands off the inlet, now nature reserves.

Omeo and the Australian Alps

From Bairnsdale, you can take the OMEO HIGHWAY (route 195) 120km north to **Omeo** (population 285), in the heart of the mountain-cattle country. **Tourist information**: Octagon Bookshop, Day Avenue; ☎ 03 5159 1411.

History

In 1834, the explorer John Lhotsky wrote of viewing from the Snowy Mountains a vast plain to the south that the Aborigines called Omeo, believed to mean 'mountains'. The region was settled as early as 1835, when James McFarlane took up a pastoral run, pre-dating McMillan's explorations. More squatters arrived in the 1840s, and gold discoveries in the 1850s and 1860s caused Omeo to become one of the roughest frontier towns in the country. 'Rolf Boldrewood', author of *Robbery Under Arms* (1881), was believed to be a magistrate here in the 1860s; in his novel *Nevermore* (1892) he recalls the district as lawless where 'the worst villains in Australia are gathered together'. In *The Recollections of Geoffrey Hamlyn* (1859), author Henry Kingsley incorporates real bushrangers and thieves of the region, such as the infamous 'Bogong Jack'. Members of the Kelly family and horse thieves such as Thomas Toke also operated in the mountains around Omeo. The cattlemen of this High Country were of course heroicised in the 'Man from Snowy River' legend and stories made popular by author 'Banjo' Paterson.

Today, the town is still a centre of Victoria's 'high country' cattle industry; the **Omeo Calf Sales** every March are a major event, bringing buyers from all over the world. The area also marks the beginning of 'brumby' territory: wild horses, some of which are rounded up each year (see Longford, Tasmania, p 435, for an explanation of brumbies). Annual rodeos attracting national audiences are also held throughout the area. In the centre of Omeo is **A.M. Pearson Historical Park** (☎ 03 5159 1232), which includes an 1892 Romanesque-style court house which is now a museum. It was designed by A.J. MacDonald, who also built the Bairnsdale court house and the post office at South Yarra in Melbourne.

A 100km scenic drive south of Omeo through **Cassilis**, **Swifts Creek** and **Ensay** passes through the old gold-mining areas, dotted with old mine tailings and timber and weatherboard cottages. Alternatively, you could continue north into the **Bowen Mountains**; 29km northwest is **Anglers Rest**, a great fishing retreat and site of *The Blue Duck Inn* (☎ 03 5159 7220), dating from the 1890s and an important roadhouse along the gold-fields. The area has abundant **walking trails** with some breathtaking mountain scenery.

Route 195 continues north from here 128km, some of it unsealed road, through **Mitta Mitta** in a picturesque river valley near Dartmouth Dam and on to Tallangatta (pronounced Tal-LAN-gatta, while nearby Wangaratta emphasises the first syllable!) on Lake Hume.

Route 156 from Omeo to Ovens Valley

Another route from Omeo is to take the Tourist Road west (route 156) towards Mt Hotham in the **Dargo High Plains**; 56km along is the **Mount Hotham Alpine Resort**, surrounded by the **Alpine National Park** (☎ 03 5755 1577 or 03 5761 1611). The resort provides some of the best downhill skiing in the country. **Tourist information**: Alpine Resorts Commission, Hotham Heights, ☎ 03 5759 3550. The area is also the home of the rare mountain pygmy possum, Australia's only alpine mammal; many walking trails provide opportunities to appreciate the park's flora and fauna. Be sure to check on road conditions before venturing on any of these roads in the winter; many will be closed.

Continue on route 156 10km west, where the road continues north as the ALPINE HIGHWAY, 41km to the old-fashioned town of **BRIGHT** (population 1675) in the Ovens Valley. **Tourist information centre**: Delaney Avenue; ☎ 03 5756 2062.

Originally a pastoral settlement explored by Hume and Hovell in 1824, Bright became the centre of alluvial gold-mining in this region in the 1860s. This popular holiday destination is known for its impressive displays of autumnal foliage, the result of the planting of thousands of deciduous trees along its avenues in the 1930s. Walnuts and chestnuts are also grown and harvested here. Every April, the **Bright Autumn Festival** brings thousands of visitors to the town. The **historical museum** (☎ 03 5755 1356; open Sept–May, Sun 14.00–16.00, school holidays Tues, Thurs and Sun 14.00–16.00) in the former railway station highlights district history, and the **Bright Art Gallery** on Mountbatten Avenue (☎ 03 5750 1660; open Wed and school holidays, 14.00–16.00) sponsors a prized art competition to coincide with the Autumn Festival.

The town is the starting point for many excellent walks, all signposted with triangular markers. One of the nicest is the 5km **Wandiligong Walk**, beginning 2.5km south of town and ending at the tiny village of **Wandiligong**, registered on the National Trust for its landscape features and picturesque buildings. It is also the location of Wandiligong Apple Orchard, said to be the largest in the Southern hemisphere.

6km further west on route 156 is **Porepunkah**, a pretty settlement known for fishing and hiking. It is also associated with Pearson William Tewkesbury (see box), who made his fortune in gold here in the early 1900s, when alluvial gold was still present.

Pearson William Tewkesbury

Pearson William Tewkesbury was born in nearby Yackandandah in 1867. After working as a watchmaker in Sydney, he came to the Ovens River and made £1 million by dredging for gold. He then went on to establish in Sydney and Melbourne motor hire services in the 1910s, and in the 1920s the famous Yellow Cab Co. In 1920 he also produced the first film version of *Robbery Under Arms* by 'Rolf Boldrewood'. He was a great entrepreneur, raising more than £20,000 for disabled servicemen during the First World War by raffling the 'Kitchener Flag' bearing signatures that he had collected of Allied war leaders and other famous men. He bought the Oriental Hotel in Melbourne, where he lived until his death in 1953.

At the junction of Porepunkah, another road travels south 21km to **Buckland**, site of a notoriously gloomy gold-mining valley. In 1857, the Buckland Riot directed against Chinese miners took place here; the event is commemorated in the Australian-Chinese Museum in Melbourne (see p 306).

Back on route 156, you can enter **Mount Buffalo National Park** (☎ 03 5755 1466), site of Australia's first ski lift in the 1930s. *Mount Buffalo Chalet* (☎ 03 5755 1500) is an old-fashioned timber guest house built in 1910, still calling guests to dinner by bell (and now known for its excellent cuisine). The park also has well-organised **walking tracks**, over 140km of them, with brochures available at the **Visitor's Information Centre** (☎ 03 5155 1500). It is also one of the summer homes of the **bogong moth**, an incredible creature that migrates thousands of miles from Queensland every year to spend the warm months in the rocks of the Alpine valleys; they arrive in the thousands in October. The moth was considered a great delicacy by the Aborigines, who would visit this area and other parts of the Snowy Mountains to have bogong feasts in the summer.

From Porepunkah, travel 23km on the OVENS HIGHWAY (still route 156) to **Myrtleford** (population 2850), the major town in the Ovens Valley and a centre for the growing of hops, tobacco, and walnuts. One of the most prosperous growers in the region was William Pan Look, a Chinese businessman whose store was razed during the Buckland Riot; by the 1890s, he and his sons had cultivated over 600 ha of tobacco and hops. The town has some lovely picnic spots, and on the highway just north of town is *The Phoenix Tree*, an enormous sculpture created out of a red gum tree by local sculptor Hans Knorr. Knorr also was one-time owner of **Merriang Homestead**, a beautiful old property 6km southwest of town with wrought-iron verandah and hand-made bricks. At the time of writing, it was closed to the public.

Beechworth

It is always a surprise to find such a tidy and well-preserved town as Beechworth (population 3250), with its many imposing 19C honey-coloured granite buildings, tucked away at 550m altitude and seemingly removed from civilisation. **Tourist information centre**: the Rock Cavern, corner of Ford and Camp Streets; ☎ 03 5728 1374. V/Line has bus service to Beechworth from Wangaratta and Bright; the closest train connection is Wangaratta, with runs to Albury, Adelaide, and Melbourne. A local bus also travels daily to Albury/Wodonga.

The twisting road from the Ovens Highway is itself quite charming, with views into the fields and valleys that make it clear this was an area where gold was found. Indeed, gold was discovered at nearby Spring Creek in 1852; by 1857, some 400kg of gold left Beechworth for Melbourne every fortnight, and in 14 years, a total of 1,122,000 ounces (31,800 kg) of gold were mined here. At its height, Beechworth had a population of 42,000 and boasted 61 hotels and a theatre. The writer Henry Kingsley was here in 1854; part of his novel *The Hillyars and the Burtons* (1865) was set in the area. Most significantly, Robert O'Hara Burke, leader of the ill-fated Burke and Wills expedition in the 1860s, was Beechworth's officer-in-charge of police from 1856 to 1859, a fact commemorated in the **Library** and **Burke Museum** (☎ 03 5728 1420; open daily, 10.30–15.30) on LOCH STREET, which includes Burke memorabilia, along with gold-rush artefacts. The **Tourist Centre** can provide a detailed brochure of walking tours.

The Ovens Highway from Wangaratta to Wodonga is known as **'The Kelly Way'**, demonstrating that this region is Ned Kelly country (see also p 245). Beechworth's other great claim to fame is that both Ned Kelly and his mother were jailed here in the 1880s, in the **Beechworth Gaol**, built in 1859 and still used as a prison (mostly for prisoners involved in reforestation projects). The gaol is part of a group of public buildings constructed 1857–59 at the northern end of FORD STREET; hence the uniform appearance. The group includes the **Courthouse** (☎ 03 5728 2721; open daily, 10.00–16.00), Police Station, Survey Office, and Forest Office along with the gaol.

Other significant public buildings along Ford Street include banks; the **Rock Cavern**, where the **information centre** is located, used to be the Bank of Victoria. Further along is the Bank of New South Wales, designed by Robertson and Hale in 1856, which includes an elaborate coat of arms at the corner entrance.

For goldminers, of course, the most important buildings in town were the hotels, a number of which still survive. The most impressive is **Tanswell's**, privately restored with lovely ironwork, dating originally from 1873. It still operates as a hotel and restaurant, as do the historical **Hibernian Hotel** (☎ 03 5728 1070) on Loch Street and the **Nicholas Hotel** on Camp Street. Regular visitors also make the *Beechworth Bakery* on Albert Street a regular stop for its hundreds of cakes and breads.

From Ford Street, take CAMP STREET west to Last Street and **Murray Breweries** (☎ 03 5728 1304; open daily, 10.00–16.00). Begun in the 1860s by George Bilson, the brewery produced beer until the 1950s; but it was also known for its cordials and aerated waters. It still produced them from nearby spring water. The cellars are now a museum, with a fascinating history of the aeration process.

Going out of town towards **Wodonga**, you will pass through the **Golden Horseshoes Monument**, a reference to a famous event during the gold-rush days. At that time, the miners were divided between the 'punchers', the dry diggers, dressed in moleskins, and the 'monkeys', wet miners, dressed in black woollen trousers. The rivalry between them was so intense that they fielded different candidates for parliaments. In 1855 the Monkeys' candidate, Cameron, paraded into town on a horse shod with golden horseshoes. They have been a symbol of the town ever since.

Also leaving town, on the right of the Golden Horseshoes Monument is the **cemetery**, including two Chinese Burning Towers, evidence of the number of Chinese miners here in the 1860s; as many as 500 Chinese graves are found in the cemetery behind the towers.

To the Murray Valley Highway and Corryong

From **Beechworth**, you can take several routes towards Wodonga; one takes you through **Yackandandah**, a National Trust classified gold town, with attractive verandahed streets (population 480). **Tourist information**: Court House, William Street, ☎ 02 6027 1222. Known locally as 'Yack', it was the childhood home of Australia's first native-born Governor-General Sir Isaac Isaacs, and the birthplace of Pearson William Tewkesbury, founder of the Yellow Cab Co. (see box, p 400).

From here, or by another route reaching Wodonga, take the KIEWA VALLEY HIGHWAY (route 191) south and join the MURRAY VALLEY HIGHWAY (route 16) east to find Corryong on the border of New South Wales and at the foot of the Snowy Mountains and Kosciuszko National Park. The road passes by, at Tallangatta, **Lake Hume**, which, if the water is low, looks spookily like a Surrealist painting, with lots of dead tree stumps sticking out of the surface water and with yellow hills behind.

Corryong (population 1274) is 77km from Tallangatta and is towered over by the boulders and granite ridges that mark the beginning of the Snowy Mountains (for detailed coverage of this area, see p 230). The area is true bushman's and cattleman's country, and indeed, **'The Man from Snowy River' Folk Museum**, 105 Hanson Street (☎ 02 6076 1363; open Sept–May, daily 10.00–16.00) in the centre of town commemorates the life and resting place of Jack Riley, widely believed to be the inspiration for 'Banjo' Patterson's famous poem (see p 81). **Tourist information**: 43–49 Hanson Street, ☎ 02 6076 1381.

In December, a folk music festival, celebrating the Australian folk ballad and other forms, takes place at nearby **Nariel Creek**, and in March the **Annual Corryong High Country Festival** offers a first-hand look at the life of the high-plains cattlemen.

From here, you can take a breathtaking drive into **Kosciuszko National Park** (see p 230), past the most impressive construction of the Snowy Mountains Hydro-Electric Scheme, Tumut Ponds Dam, and on to Cabramurra, the highest township in Australia. See Snowy Mountains section (p 230), New South Wales for more detail.

Tasmania

One of the most significant aspects for the development of Tasmania is the island's geographical location. **Hobart**, the capital city, lies at latitude 42°53' south, longitude 147°21' east, making it one of the southernmost cities in the world. The only land further south is the southern section of New Zealand, a bit of South America, and Antarctica. This extreme isolation allowed the develop-

ment of unique flora and fauna. The **Tasmanian tiger**, the thylacine, occurred only here, and was last seen alive in 1935 (although myths persist about sightings in the wild). The Tasmanian Aborigines appear to be an indigenous group distinct from those on the mainland.

Most strikingly, present-day Tasmania, despite its accessible size, is a land of stark contrasts, with the settled eastern portion more 'English' than the mainland and the wild western portion containing primeval forests and some of the most untrammelled terrain remaining in the world. Today, the apples and potatoes for which the island was famed have dwindled in number as orchards disappear, but the state can now provide visitors with some of the most exquisite dining experiences in the country, with its unparalleled dairy products and seafood, especially shellfish.

Tasmania's **geology** is as complex as any in Australia. Its basic form proceeds from older Proterozoic rock on the northwest tip and as a tongue from the South West Cape extending inland to an area east and north of Queenstown. Sedimentary formation from the Palaeozoic era surround this tongue and are found in the northeast as well. The most arable land is found in the east and central basins between Hobart and Launceston along the island's northern coast and consists of weathered igneous deposits from the Mesozoic period. Many of the peaks, including Ben Lomond and Mount Wellington, are of dolerite extruded at this time.

Tasmania was joined with the mainland until the Tertiary Period when the Bass Strait, a rift valley, subsided. The Kosciuszko Uplift raised the island, tilting it to the south. During the three ice ages of the Pleistocene, glaciers covered as much as half of the island. Evidence of these glacial periods can be seen in the island's southwestern highlands in erosion of rock, deeply cut watercourses, and moraines. In each of these periods marine water levels were low enough to provide a landbridge to Victoria. As far as Aboriginal populations are concerned, the Yolande (100,000 to 50,000 years ago) and Margaret (20,000 to 10,000 years ago) glaciations allowed cultural and genetic introductions between the mainland and Tasmania.

The physical features most attractive to tourists include the **Mount Wellington** and **Ben Lomond** areas, the agricultural and pastoral plain from Hobart to Launceston and east along the northern coast, and the highland camping and bushwalking areas in the west and south. Ben Lomond, Mount Barrow and Mount Arthur are situated in a relatively accessible mountainous area in the northeast.

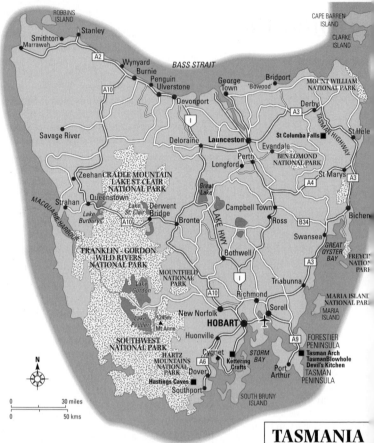

TASMANIA

The Tasman Highway east from Launceston passes through relatively tall eucalypt forest to as far as Scottsdale. At this higher elevation herbaceous groundcover and grasses predominate until the road turns south, returning to eucalypt as it drops into the George River Valley toward St Helens.

The agricultural areas to the east of Launceston are bordered to the south by the **Great Western Tiers**. This remarkable escarpment rises virtually from sea level to over 1000m. About 50km west of Launceston, then south an hour out of Deloraine is a tableland with numerous lakes, the **Great Lake** being the largest and **Lake St Clair** described as the most beautiful. Lake St Clair is on the eastern edge of a series of **national parks** extending from the southern coast nearly to the Bass Strait. These parks contain two World Heritage Areas and some areas which have been protected since 1863. The six day, **76km trek** between Waldheim Chalet in Cradle Valley and Lake St Clair is a favourite with campers. Details, maps and gear are available at well-stocked campers' stores in Hobart and Launceston. Much of the equipment for camping can be rented.

Mount Field National Park, an easy drive 80km west of Hobart, is noted for its waterfalls. Russell Falls cascades in two steps into forested gorges. The walking and camping in this area varies from sedate to strenuous. Many of the best views of Russell Falls are easily accessible.

The **beech trees** of Tasmania, like many of the plants in the rainforest reserves in western and southern parts of the island, date from the Cretaceous period. They vary depending upon the niches in which they grow from scrub-like in the highlands to huge in sheltered areas. Similar species are found in the rainforests of Lamington National Park in the Mcpherson Range on the New South Wales–Queensland border and at Barrington Tops.

History

Tasmania, initially called **Van Diemen's Land** after the Dutch East India company's progressive administrator who sent Abel Tasman to explore the area in the 1640s, became an independent colony in 1825, making it the second Australian colony. Soon after the settlement of New South Wales, the authorities realised Tasmania's strategic importance and decided it should be settled before another maritime power conquered it. As the frequency of French place names throughout and around the island attest, French vessels had explored the region extensively in the years immediately following the Revolution. First scouted by Lieutenant James Bowen in 1803, Van Diemen's Land as a colony began actively in 1804 with the arrival of **Lieutenant Governor David Collins**. Collins is remembered in his famous First Fleet narrative for having attempted a settlement first in Victoria. Once in Van Diemen's Land, he moved the location of the colony from that first sited by Bowen to a more advantageous spot at what was called Sullivan's Cove, present-day Hobart.

In keeping with the home government's accepted philosophy that these colonies were established as an antipodean prison, the island became the place for the most recalcitrant convicts, thus establishing its popular reputation as an even greater hell on earth than Sydney. Port Arthur in the east, and the notorious Macquarie Harbour in the west certainly lived up to this reputation. The island was not named Tasmania until 1855, by which time convict transportation had ended, and free settlement took priority. The new name was introduced to suggest that a moral renovation had occurred, and this consideration of moral outlook is an underlying thread in all discussions about Tasmanian culture.

Another bleak chapter in Tasmania's history concerns the confrontation of settlers and **Aboriginal natives**. From the beginning of white settlement, the Tasmanian natives, who probably numbered about 4000 when Collins arrived, were seen as an impediment to economic and cultural growth. Initially few attempts were made at any kind of peaceful coexistence. In 1824, Lieutenant Governor George Arthur (1784–1854) arrived and, with the declaration of Tasmania's status as a separate colony, established a despotic administration intent on 'civilising' the island according to Arthur's own ideas about moral good and civilised institutions. By this time, many free settlers had arrived in the colony, and their interests were foremost in Arthur's plan.

Hostilities with the Aborigines, or at least the fear of black aggression from those natives who had resisted, were so intense that the government devised one of the most notoriously farcical campaigns in history, the so-called **Black Line**. The purpose of this effort was to round up those remaining blacks (probably less than 2000 by 1830) and to confine them to a single reserve away from white settlement. The offensive took the form, as Robert Hughes says, 'of an immense pheasant drive', in which every white man in Van Diemen's Land participated, walking across the bush to 'flush out' the natives. In the end, only two blacks were caught, but the natives' days were numbered.

The next, seemingly more benign, approach to the problem involved a well-meaning Methodist house-builder, George Augustus Robinson (1788–1866) who earned the title of 'The Great Conciliator'. Instead of force, Robinson, with the help of the natives Woureddy and Truganini, used persuasion to convince the remaining natives to 'give themselves up' and to enter a camp set up for them at Flinders Island, and later at Oyster Cove. Thus another form of transportation was imposed upon another group of unfortunates. By 1855, only three 'full-blooded' natives survived, while others, taken as wives and slaves of American whalers, persevered on the Bass Strait Islands (see Truganini, p 418) and as small groups in Victoria. Despite the belief, then, that all traces of Tasmanian Aboriginals were vanquished, Aboriginal awareness today has led to a reassertion of Aboriginality among those who identify themselves as such. For instance, Tasmanian Aboriginals have sole rights to the hunting of mutton birds on Flinders Island. Conscious efforts to voice their presence and their sense of pride are evident in a number of Aboriginal centres on the island.

Sharing with Western Australia the distinction of having been a separate colony, Tasmania presents a character unlike the rest of Australia. Affected by its extreme southerly position and the surrounding seas, the climate as well as the geography differ markedly from that of the mainland, giving the island a more 'English' atmosphere, an attitude quite consciously nurtured by popular sentiment and the Tasmanian tourist industry. In *Following the Equator* (1895), Mark Twain wrote:

How beautiful is the whole region, for form, and grouping, and opulence, and freshness of foliage, and variety of colour, and grace and shapeliness of the hills, the capes, the promontories... And it was in this paradise that the yellow-liveried convicts were landed, and the Corps-bandits quartered, and the wanton slaughter of the kangaroo-chasing black innocents consummated on that autumn day in May, in the brutish old time. It was all out of keeping with the place, a sort of bringing of heaven and hell together.

More recently, Tasmanian native Christopher Koch, author of *The Year of Living Dangerously* (1978), describes the ambivalence associated with Tasmania's history:

The convict past is like a wound, scarring the whole inner life of Tasmanians. It is taken lightly nowadays; but Tasmanians of my generation well remember when the suspicion of convict ancestry was a matter of real shame and anguish.

One of Tasmania's greatest talking points, at least by Australian standards, is its **weather**. 'Changeable' would be the best way to describe it. In the space of a few hours, especially on the Mount Wellington side of Hobart, temperature and winds can change dramatically and quickly, from scorching heat to blasting breezes and blustery conditions. On the whole, Tasmania is usually cooler than the rest of Australia. Planning of any outing must include provisions for any type of weather, from rain to heat. Patrick White, in *A Fringe of Leaves* (1976), states the situation poetically:

> ... *buffeted by wind, threatened by a great cumulus of cloud, between the mountain which presided over man's presumptuous attempt at a town, and the shirred waters of the grey river rushing towards its fate, the sea.*

Hobart

■ Practical information

Visitor Information Centre: at 20 Davey Street, on the corner of Davey and Elizabeth Streets, ☎ 03 6230 8233. They can book accommodation, travel and wilderness trekking. Arrangements for camping and hiking expeditions can be made at the Wilderness Society (☎ 03 6234 9370) in the Galleria at 33 Salamanca Place.

Airport. Flights arrive from the mainland mainly at the Hobart airport, but also into Launceston, Wynyard (Burnie Airport) and Devonport. The only international flights to Tasmania are from New Zealand. **Kendell Airlines** (via Ansett, ☎ 13 13 00) offers discount fares to international ticket-holders through Melbourne to King Island, Flinders Island, Devonport and Burnie. **Airlines of Tasmania** (☎ 03 6248 5030; 1 800 030 550) operates flights within the island.

Hobart **airport** is 26km northeast of the city in Cambridge. A shuttle bus (about $6) drops passengers at hotels in town and at the Redline depot. A taxi ride will cost at least $20.

Ferry. Traditionally, people have travelled to Tasmania via the TT Line Bass Strait ferry from Melbourne to Devonport (in Port Melbourne, ☎ 03 9644 5233). This is an overnight trip, with suite, private cabin, or hostel accommodation. The crossing can be rough. It used to be quite pricey as well, but in an attempt to lure tourists to the island, the car freight on the *Spirit of Tasmania* is for the moment subsidised. A high-speed Sea Cat also runs across the strait from November to April, taking only five hours for the crossing; this trip continues to be quite expensive.

Bus. The island has three bus companies, **Tasmanian Redline Coaches** (☎ 03 6231 3233), **Hobart Coaches** and **Tasmanian Wilderness Travel** (both at ☎ 03 6234 4077). They do not accept mainline passes, and service is rather limited. Within Hobart, **Metro Tasmania** provides adequate local service to most of the outlying parts of the city. The Metro Shop is located at the City Bus Station, 18 Elizabeth Street, ☎ 6233 4223. You can purchase a bus timetable and special bus passes from the bus station or at the main office on 212 Main Road, Moonah. Except for a new line between Launceston and Devonport, there are no trains.

Driving. Because of the expense of taking your own car on the ferry, Hobart (and all of Tasmania) has more reasonable car rental companies and weekly packages than the mainland; this really seems the best way to sightsee on the island. During the heavy holiday periods, you should consider booking such rentals before you arrive (consider fly-drive options). Tasmanian travel centres on the mainland can provide addresses and telephone numbers and make reservations.

Bicycling. Bicycle rentals are available in both Hobart and Launceston for short- or long-term trips. Check with the tourist offices for arrangements. While the flat road from Hobart along the coast and through the midlands to Launceston is well-suited to cycling, you would have to be a very fit cyclist to take on Mt Wellington or Ben Lomond or the Great Western Wilderness!

Useful addresses
Consulates. **British Consulate-General**, 39 Murray Street, Hobart, ☎ 6230 3568.
Hospitals. *Royal Hobart*, 48 Liverpool, ☎ 6222 8308.
Police. ☎ 6230 2111.

Hotels
$$$$ Hotel Grand Chancellor (formerly Sheraton Hotel), 1 Davey Street, Constitution Dock, Hobart, ☎ 03 6235 4535; fax 03 6223 8175. Excellent location opposite Constitution Dock, with views of Derwent Estuary; predictable hotel decor.
$$$ Salamanca Inn, 10 Gladstone Street, Hobart, ☎ 03 6223 3300; fax 03 6223 7167. Self-contained suites, cooking facilities available; central location.
$$$ Wrest Point Hotel Casino, 410 Sandy Bay Road, Sandy Bay, Hobart, ☎ 03 6225 0112. As glitzy as Hobart gets; a great waterfront location, all casino-style conveniences.
$$ Alice's Cottages, 17 York Street/129 Balfour Street, Launceston, ☎ 03 6331 4533; fax 03 6334 2696. A series of historic cottages in the centre of Launceston, self-contained units.
$$ Colonial Battery Point Manor, 13 Cromwell Street, Battery Point, Hobart, ☎ 03 6224 0888; fax 03 6231 0972. Lovely National Trust property (c 1834), only 8 rooms; five-star rating by NRMA.
$$ Colville Cottage Bed & Breakfast, 32 Mona Street, Battery Point, Hobart, ☎ 03 6224 6968; fax 03 6224 0500. Historic building (1877), with cottage garden and excellent breakfast, only six rooms.
$$ Freycinet Lodge, Freycinet National Park, ☎ 03 6257 0101; fax 03 6257 0278. Timber cabins in the national park, spectacular views of Oyster Bay, breakfast included, good value for 'wilderness' accommodation.
$$ Franklin Manor, The Esplanade, Strahan, ☎ 03 6471 7311; fax 03 6471 7267. Bed & breakfast retreat, beautifully restored, excellent restaurant, only 14 rooms.
$$ Innkeepers Penny Royal Watermill, 147 Paterson Street, Launceston, ☎ 03 6331 6699. Next to historic Penny Royal Watermill and park.
$$ The Islington Private Hotel, 321 Davey Street, Hobart, ☎ 03 6223 3900/03 6223 7911. National Trust property (1842), cultivated atmosphere, with swimming pool and lovely garden; no children.

$$ Lenna of Hobart, 20 Runnymede Street, Hobart, ☎ 03 6223 2911; fax 03 6224 0112. Historic old mansion in Battery Point, with some modern additions; geared to tourists.

$$ The Lodge on Elizabeth, 249 Elizabeth Street, ☎ 03 6231 3830; fax 03 6234 2566. Comfortable, charming bed & breakfast in National Trust building; delightful breakfasts.

$$ Prospect House Bed & Breakfast, 1384 Richmond Road, Richmond, ☎ 03 6262 2207; fax 03 6262 2551. National Trust building (1830), renowned restaurant, 11 rooms.

$ Jane Franklin Hall, 6 Elboden Street, ☎ 03 6223 2000. Residential college of University of Tasmania, available for accommodation during holidays, very good value, lovely neighbourhood & views to the harbour, some self-contained units.

Restaurants

$$$ Kabuki by the Sea, 12km south of Swansea, ☎/fax 03 6257 8588. Superb Japanese food in an unbelievable setting overlooking Oyster Bay, Freycinet Peninsula and Schouten Island.

$$$ Mure's Upper Deck, Mure's Fish Centre, Victoria Dock, Hobart, ☎ 03 6231 1999. Most well-known fish restaurant in the midst of fishing boats on the docks. Better food than most tourist places.

$$$ Prospect House, 1384 Richmond Road, Richmond, ☎ 03 6262 2207. Historic house, long known for its restaurant, specialising in Tasmanian fare.

$$ Battery Point Brasserie, 59 Hampden Road, Battery Point, Hobart, ☎ 03 6223 3186. Recently expanded bistro, which hopefully will not affect the excellent Continental menu; specialities offal and game.

$$ Dear Friends, 8 Brooke Street, Hobart, ☎ 03 6223 2646. Finest Tasmanian produce, from seafood to game and dairy products.

$$ Fee and Me, 36 The Kingsway, Launceston, ☎ 03 6331 3195. Light Australian fare in historic building in central Launceston, excellent service.

$$ Mit Zitrone, 333 Elizabeth Street, North Hobart, ☎ 03 6234 8113. Innovative food, unpretentious surroundings.

$$ Panache, 89 Salamanca Place, ☎ 03 6224 2929. Elegant Southern French cuisine using Tasmanian produce, reasonably priced.

$$ Prosser's on the Beach, Sandy Bay Regatta Pavilion, Beach Road, Sandy Bay, Hobart, ☎ 03 6225 2276. Unpretentious seafood restaurant overlooking Derwent estuary; considered by some the best fish restaurant in Hobart.

$ Squid Roe, 210 Liverpool Street, Hobart, ☎ 03 6234 7978. Very small, very reasonable, run by ex-abalone fisherman, great for takeaway.

Elizabeth Street, North Hobart: the entire street is filled with restaurants of all stripes, including Middle Eastern, European, and Asian.

History

The second oldest city in Australia, and with a population of 184,000, Hobart is situated on both the eastern and western shores of the Derwent River. The river was named in 1793 by John Hayes, a naval officer who explored the region independently and without knowledge of previous explorations; most of the names he gave places were not acknowledged, but the Derwent and Risdon Cove remain. Hobart was established in February 1804 by Lieutenant Governor David Collins, when he left Victoria and decided Van Diemen's Land was a more appropriate location for a second settlement separate of New South Wales. He had moved settlement across the river from Risdon Cove, where Lieutenant John Bowen had initially established a headquarters. Collins wrote: 'In respect to situation, I am as well placed as I could wish. I have land immediately about me...sufficient for extensive agricultural purposes.' Collins named the settlement after Robert Hobart, Earl of Buckinghamshire and secretary of state for war and the colonies; it was actually called Hobart Town until 1881.

Governor Macquarie, ever the intrepid organiser, visited in 1811, and immediately drew up a town plan consisting of a main square and seven streets, which he also named. He also formulated regulations for future development. By the time of his second visit in 1821, buildings had trebled and faced regular street fronts.

Even today Hobart's 'Englishness' both in town planning and architecture is particularly striking. The town's gardens contain very little evidence of native flora, preferring 'cottage garden' arrangements, the plants of which do well in this climate. Houses are varied in design, and the grander ones often look like British country homes, with classical columns and Georgian proportions, constructed of sandstone or, later on, red brick.

Despite being located so far south, Hobart's latitude is comparable to that of New York City or Rome. In fact, the town's blustery weather and harbour setting, with its strong seafaring tradition, are somewhat reminiscent of American New England, although the weather is never as rugged as the American upper Eastern Seaboard. This atmosphere is not surprising, when you consider that from the 1830s onwards, Hobart was a great port of call for American whalers, who were active in Tasmanian waters until the American Civil War. The French whalers were also drawn to Hobart; Alexandre Dumas gives vivid descriptions of the town in *Les Baleiniers*, based on the diary of a surgeon on a French whaling ship.

The plethora of substantial buildings from Hobart's early period of settlement is so unlike anything to be seen in New South Wales that you begin to wonder why this should be. Historically, it seems that Tasmania by the 1830s, despite its grimly effective convict system, actively sought ambitious free settlers who would develop an agricultural economy. Colonists were enticed with promises of large land grants, the use of convict labour, and, as one settler approvingly wrote home in 1834, 'the scarcity of the Black Natives'.

While free settlers also began arriving in New South Wales at this time, the colonial government did not as actively encourage the development of the land and its resources. Consequently, rural agriculture was at least initially more modest on the mainland, and with less conscious emphasis on the cultivation of the trappings of English culture.

Writer Hal Porter, in his novel *The Tilted Cross* (1961), calls it 'a town of the dispossessed...a foundling London', which it seemed to be in its early days. Cultural aspirations were more readily pursued in Van Diemen's Land than in early New South Wales. Indeed, the first book of general literature in Australia was published here in 1818: *Michael Howe, the Last and Worst of the Bushrangers of Van Diemen's Land* by Thomas H. Wells. At present only three copies are known to exist, making it one of the rarest colonial books in the English language. That the modest publication concerned bushrangers is appropriate, as Tasmania was tyrannised by outlaws well into the 19C. Michael Howe was by no means the last one!

Today, Hobart is a delightful place to visit, quite unlike any other city in Australia. The sense of tradition is strong with less ethnic mix in the population, making islanders more conservative and predictably insular; but tourists will find the residents friendly, the facilities and attractions accessible and enjoyable. Currently the greatest attraction in Hobart is the availability of Tasmanian food-products; restaurant culture here is thriving, taking advantage of the superb resources available both on the island and from the surrounding sea and its islands.

Exploring Hobart

Hobart is a pleasant town for walking, although its position at the foot of Mount Wellington means that some streets proceed steeply uphill. All of the following walks begin at the Visitor Information Centre, conveniently located north of Salamanca Place on the corner of Davey and Elizabeth Streets by the wharves on Sullivans Cove.

For more distant tours, you will need a car, or public transport, details of which are given, although it is not always plentiful.

Walk 1 • Constitution Dock and Battery Point

On leaving the tourist bureau, turn left, and walk two blocks to Constitution Dock. **Constitution Dock** is at the centre of the wharf area, where you can find a variety of harbour tours, famous seafood restaurants, and fish markets. Harbour cruises depart from the Brooke Street Pier, about 100m east of Constitution Dock. Of greatest significance is that Constitution Dock is the terminus of the Sydney to Hobart Yacht Races.

Sydney to Hobart Yacht Race

Begun in 1945 with nine entrants, the race now attracts over 200 entrants and is considered to be one of the most exciting and treacherous of blue water yacht races. It is worth a trip to the continent just to experience the thrilling start of the race from Sydney Harbour on Boxing Day (26 December) . The yachts must brave Bass Strait, which even in summer can present dangerous seas. A recent example of its unpredictability occurred in the 1993 race when off Flinders Island, the lead boat's skipper was lost overboard; he was miraculously found after six hours by tanker ship. Many of the other favoured boats were damaged and forced to drop out. Following the 1998 race, which was also affected by rough weather and loss of life, the race organisers reaffirmed that the yachts' skippers are ultimately responsible for deciding whether to continue or not under the conditions at sea. The end of the yacht race marks Hobart's biggest party and most exciting event of the year. Anyone visiting at this time should be sure to book accommodation well in advance, and expect to get caught up in the excitement.

Just above the docks is a raised plaza where placards describe the wharf buildings and point to Parliament Square, which is past Elizabeth Pier further south

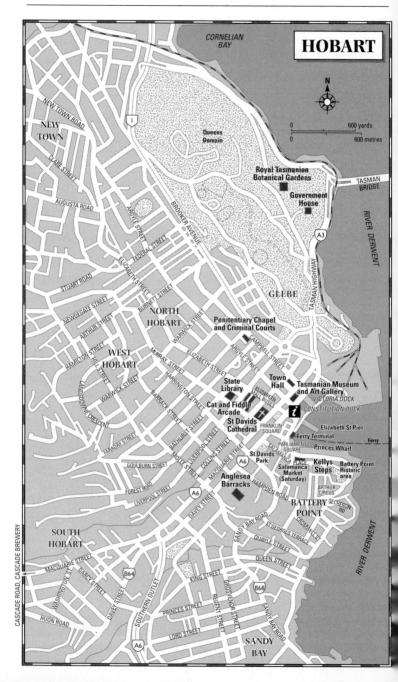

HOBART

CORNELIAN BAY

NEW TOWN ROAD

NEW TOWN

CLARE STREET

AUGUSTA ROAD

Queens Domain

Royal Tasmanian Botanical Gardens

Government House

TASMAN BRIDGE

A3

RIVER DERWENT

STUART ROAD

NEWDEGATE STREET

ARTHUR STREET

HAMILTON STREET

FEDERAL STREET

ELIZABETH STREET

BURNETT STREET

BROOKER AVENUE

ARGYLE STREET

NORTH HOBART

GLEBE

WEST HOBART

WARWICK STREET

LANDSDOWNE CRESCENT

WARWICK STREET

MURRAY STREET

HARRINGTON STREET

BARRACK STREET

ELIZABETH STREET

ARGYLE STREET

CAMPBELL STREET

Penitentiary Chapel and Criminal Courts

State Library

Town Hall

Tasmanian Museum and Art Gallery

ELIZABETH MALL BUSES

Cat and Fiddle Arcade

St Davids Cathedral

VICTORIA DOCK

CONSTITUTION DOCK

FRANKLIN SQUARE

FARADAY STREET

BATHURST STREET

LIVERPOOL STREET

MOLLE STREET

COLLINS STREET

MACQUARIE STREET

GOULBURN STREET

FOREST ROAD

LIVERPOOL STREET

A6

St Davids Park

PARLIAMENT SQUARE

Elizabeth St Pier

Ferry Terminal

Princes Wharf

Ferry

SALAMANCA PLACE

Salamanca Market (Saturday)

Kellys Steps

Battery Point Historic area

Anglesea Barracks

HAMPDEN ROAD

ARTHUR CIRCUS

SECHERON RD

DAVEY STREET

A6

SOUTH HOBART

SANDY BAY ROAD

ST GEORGES TERRACE

CROMWELL ST

BATTERY POINT

RIVER DERWENT

CASCADE ROAD, CASCADE BREWERY

MACQUARIE STREET

WASHINGTON ST

D'ARCY STREET

DAVEY STREET

B64

SOUTHERN OUTLET

KING STREET

PRINCES STREET

REGENT STREET

GROSVENOR STREET

SANDY BAY ROAD

B68

QUAYLE STREET

QUEEN STREET

HUON ROAD

LORD STREET

A6

SANDY BAY

N

0   600 yards
0   600 metres

on Morrison Street at the corner of Murray Street. Originally Customs House, **Parliament House** was built between 1836 and 1841, by Colonial Architect John Lee Archer. Other alterations were made in 1856, and with the introduction of responsible government, it became Parliament House. The exterior presents a rusticated first floor, ashlar work on the second floor. Fine interior chambers remain intact and can be visited; the tiny Legislative Council Chamber, which remains exactly as it was in 1856, can also be viewed.

Across the street from Parliament Square is **Customs House Hotel**, built in 1846 for Charles Gaylor. Still in business, this was the hotel where many politicians resided while in town for parliamentary sessions.

Circle around Parliament Square to the left to come to **Salamanca Place**. The place runs in front of a series of seafront buildings dating from 1835–60. Originally fronting on to 'New Wharf', these buildings were the centre of trade in Hobart, and still represent the best-surviving examples of Georgian warehouses in Australia. The New Wharf in front of Salamanca Place is now called **Prince's Wharf** in honour of Prince Alfred, Duke of Edinburgh, who visited here in 1868. The wharf is still the passenger terminal, and you can sometimes see in port such cruise ships as the P & O's *Sea Princess*.

As with so many other place-names in Australia, Salamanca Place was named in honour of a battle in the Napoleonic Wars (hence the proliferation of Wellington place-names throughout the country). The façades of the Salamanca Place warehouse buildings are virtually unchanged, except now they are shops, galleries, and cafes. Each Saturday (08.00–15.00) since 1972 the Salamanca Markets have been held here, essentially a more upscale 'trash and treasure', with arts and crafts, Tasmanian products, produce, and all the other kinds of stalls seen at flea markets. It is a delightful setting, exuding an old-world atmosphere.

Battery Point

To the east and above the cliffs behind Salamanca Place is **Battery Point**, the most historic area of Hobart. Its significance is in its preservation of continually occupied buildings which were built from the 1820s through to the early 1900s. Many of these structures are unequalled in Australia in terms of historical and architectural significance. The area's name stems from the battery of guns originally placed here in 1818. By 1828 they had been supplanted by a signal station (see box), which now stands in Prince's Park, at the northern end of Salamanca Place. At this end of the plaza is also the Australian Postal Museum.

The Signal Station

The Signal Station became an important element in the elaborate semaphore telegraph system devised in the 1830s by the Commandant at Port Arthur, Captain Charles O'Hara Booth. By 1840, Booth had established a series of eleven stations between Port Arthur and Hobart Town which enabled messages to be relayed within 15 minutes. At its height, the coded system, using a three-tiered six-armed semaphore mast, could relay as many as 3000 phrases. By the 1850s the system was abandoned as too costly and by the 1860s the telegraph replaced this inventive device.

History of Battery Point

The area of Battery Point was first occupied by **Reverend Robert 'Bobby' Knopwood** (1761–1838), first clergyman in Tasmania and a notoriously colourful character in the island's early history. Taking up the ministry only when he had squandered his own considerable fortune and was in need of employment, Knopwood was fond of the bottle and loose with money. The *Australian Encyclopedia* describes him delicately, 'It was a brutal, hard-drinking, hard-swearing age, and Knopwood does not appear to have been in advance of his time.' He arrived in Hobart in 1804 and was granted 30 acres near Sullivans Cove by Lieutenant Governor Collins. Financial difficulties, however, compelled Knopwood to sell off plots by the end of the 1810s. Concerned about Knopwood's failing health and general dissipation, Governor Macquarie pensioned him in 1821 to land at Rokeby, in the Clarence area near Risdon Cove. Here he continued to minister unofficially until his death in 1838. His diaries, kept for 30 years, are a remarkable, if at times nearly incomprehensible (his spelling and penmanship were idiosyncratic at best), account of the early days of Hobart.

William Sorell, third Lieutenant Governor, acquired the remaining 90 acres (36.5 ha) of Battery Point, but eventually sold it to William Kermode, who developed the property, transforming the area from a rural expanse to a residential district. By the 1830s, this transformation was well under way and many buildings constructed in this era still survive.

Governor Arthur (see box), upon his arrival in the colony in 1824, decided that the waterfront road, initially a part of Knopwood's grant, should be turned over to the government for access to the wharves. This decree caused great outrage among those who had purchased the land from the original grantee. Nonetheless, Arthur was able to effect the usurpation when he found that Sorell had never signed an earlier agreement with Knopwood. This disputed strip is now the site of Salamanca Place.

George Arthur

George Arthur (1784–1854) was a career soldier who had already established his reputation as a colonial administrator in British Honduras before arriving in Hobart to take on the duties of Lieutenant Governor. Implacably stern and morally self-righteous by nature, Arthur imposed on the colony what to his detractors was a despotic rule. His rigid system of punishment and rewards for convicts affected not only the convicted but their overseers as well. His establishment of Port Arthur was to his mind a crowning achievement, as it made possible the implementation of his supposedly foolproof system for penal administration. Ultimately it would remain as his infamous legacy to Australian history. During his tenure, he attempted to rout the notorious bushrangers who plagued the countryside and sought to appease the growing number of free settlers by attempting to round up the Aborigines in the infamous 'Black Line' campaign. Constantly criticised by the press and even at odds with the home government, Arthur was recalled in 1837, serving further in Canada and as Governor of Bombay in 1842.

From Salamanca Place, you can enter Battery Point at several spots. Climb up **Kelly's Steps** between the warehouses at Kelly Street. These steps were built in

1839 by James Kelly, Hobart's first harbourmaster. Walk down Kelly Street one block, turn right on Hampden Road and walk two blocks to the corner of Hampden and James Street, the site of Narynna. Alternatively, at the south end of Salamanca Place, turn left up Montpelier Retreat; walk two blocks to Hampden Road, and turn left. On the left corner is **Narynna**, now **Van Diemen's Land Folk Museum** (☎ 6234 2791; open Tues–Fri 10.30–17.00, weekends 14.00–17.00, except July, Christmas Day, Good Friday, and Anzac Day).

Narynna was originally built as a house for a Scotsman, Captain Andrew Haig, on two acres bought from Knopwood in 1824. Haig constructed the first stone warehouse on Salamanca Square, then left Hobart for nine years. He returned with his wife and family in 1833 and began to build this house with the help of convict architect Edward Winch. At the time of its completion in 1836, only three other houses existed in Battery Point. Financial difficulties compelled Captain Haig to sell the house in 1842. Owned privately until 1946, it was then sold to the Government which allowed the hospital across the street to use it as a home for the elderly.

In 1957, through the efforts of several prominent Tasmanians, Narryna was established as a museum depicting 19C colonial living. It contains a large collection of artefacts representing comfortable living in a seafaring community, among them, for some reason, Reverend Knopwood's death mask. Narryna provides an excellent reconstruction of everyday living, highlighting dress, kitchenware, leisure activities, including lantern slides and children's games, most of which were donated by Hobart families. Especially noteworthy is a collection of early Tasmanian daguerreotypes, some of them most certainly by Albert Bock, son of the artist Thomas Bock. Interesting stables and back rooms are reminiscent of a European open-air museum.

Walking down HAMPDEN ROAD, you will see on both sides of the street, rows of small cottages dating from the 1840s and 50s. On the corner of Stowell Avenue is a chocolate shop and milk bar, still selling old-fashioned 'penny candies' from the jar, even if they are no longer a penny each. It has been a candy shop since 1886, an indication of the traditional pace of Battery Point.

After crossing South Street, walk half a block, turn left into **Arthur's Circus**, a fascinating residential circle with modest if historically significant houses. The land was divided into 16 plots by Governor Arthur himself, and sold at auction in March 1847. A children's playground now stands in the central oval.

Cross Colville Street, veering right into SECHERON ROAD, which will lead you to the **Maritime Museum** (☎ 6223 5082; open daily 13.00–16.30). Originally Secheron House, it was built by George Frankland (1797–1838), surveyor-general of Van Diemen's Land 1828–1838. Arriving in Hobart with his family in 1827, Frankland's first task was to improve the harbour and waterfront. He also assisted Governor Arthur in the design of the Presbyterian church at Bothwell. He was responsible for naming the Hobart suburb of Bellerive, taking its name—as well as that of Secheron—from places he knew on Lake Geneva. The Frankland Range near Lake Pedder is named in his honour (see p 453).

He received a grant of 8 acres (3 ha) at Battery Point at this time, and began to build this impressive residence. Constructed of Australian cedar, it offers a spectacular view of the Derwent River. The house became the Maritime Museum in 1974. Displays centre on Hobart's maritime history: sailing and steamships, passenger ferries and yachts, and artefacts of the state's long history of whaling and sealing.

Return to walk along COLVILLE STREET towards Sandy Bay for an admirable view of a variety of historic houses and cottages; indeed, each house in the entire neighbourhood is an architectural entity. The street itself was named after Lord Colville, whose grandson was the same George Frankland who built Secheron. No. 57 at the end of the street is thought to be the oldest building on the street, part of the original Gleeson's Farm which occupied the site in the 1830s.

Turn right on Cromwell Street, to find on the left **St George's** Anglican Church, often called 'the mariner's church'. Designed by John Lee Archer (nave) and James Blackburn (tower) between 1836 and 1847, it is one of Australia's finest examples of Greek Revival style. The church includes a nave of five bays divided by pilasters and with 50-pane windows. Next door is **St George's School**, in a simple Georgian style of stone blockwork. A very early school building, it preceded the first state school, Trinity School.

Continue to De Witt Street, turn left; on the other side of the street is a row of cottages built in the early 1850s by Robert Logan. At St George's Terrace you have a good view down to the bay and up to the hillside residential areas.

Return to ELIZABETH STREET by returning to De Witt Street and walking back to Hampden Road; a turn in either direction leads to Sandy Bay Road, a busy street. At Sandy Bay Road and Harrington Street, continue along the diagonal plaza of houses into Harrington Street (one block) and enter on your right into St David's Park.

St David's Park was Hobart's original burial grounds and because it was on a raised hill with views of the sea, it also quickly became a popular picnic spot. Included here are the tombs of Lieutenant Governor David Collins, designed by John Lee Archer in 1838, and a Gothic Revival memorial to Governor Wilmot dating from 1850. When it was decided to change the place into a public park in 1926, some of the headstones were removed to Anglesea Barracks; others have been preserved in two walls leading out of the park up to Harrington Street (the graves themselves remain at rest beneath the grass). The park also includes a charming bandstand and the Salamanca Place entry way has a delightful gate with carved lions' heads.

Leave the park at the Harrington and Davey Street gateway. Across Davey Street on your left is an old stone building which stands in front of the **Royal Tennis Court**. In 1875, S. Smith Travers purchased this building (originally part of a brewery built in 1860) to introduce royal tennis (or real tennis, as known here) to Australia. Smith's house next door became the Hobart Trades Hall and is now part of the Commonwealth Law Courts buildings. Unlike tennis as we know it today, royal tennis relies on angled shots off sloping surfaces. Regular sessions occur on the courts, and visitors may attend. There are now courts for Royal Tennis in Melbourne and Ballarat, with plans for one in Sydney.

From here proceed down Davey Street, some two blocks, back to the Visitor Information Centre to visit the Art Gallery.

Walk 2 • The Tasmanian Art Gallery

At the Visitor Centre, turn right on Macquarie Street, one block to Argyle Street. On the corner is the **Tasmanian Museum and Art Gallery** (☎ 6235 0777; open daily 10.00–17.00). The building is an interesting conglomeration of styles. The central part dates from 1808 and is Hobart's oldest surviving building. The main edifice dates from 1902, and an addition was made in 1966, in a predictably diluted 'urban renewal' modernism. The separate wings are now joined by a complementary post-modernist entryway.

The museum originated in the activities of the Tasmanian Society for the Study of Natural Science, founded by Sir John Franklin when he was Lieutenant Governor of the colony. This organisation eventually became the Royal Society. By the 1850s, the group was conducting monthly meetings, often presenting original scientific research. The museum's collections are quite impressive, beginning in the right wing with natural history displays which include the sad story of the **Tasmanian tiger**, the thylacine. The last Tasmanian tiger died in a Hobart zoo in 1936. After years in which a bounty was placed on their heads, they were ambitiously hunted and killed, despite early warnings by naturalists of the possibility of extinction. Rumours abound that tigers still exist in the wilds of the southwest, but no substantiated sightings have been documented.

The collection of **colonial art** exhibited on the first floor is especially significant for its representation of the Tasmanian landscape. The most impressive

John Glover

John Glover (1767–1849), born near Leicester, had an established reputation as a watercolourist and oil painter in the Claudean Romantic landscape tradition. His views in the early 1800s, especially those done in the Lake District and in Italy, made him so fashionable that at one time he was seen as a serious rival to J.M.W. Turner. In 1820 Glover was wealthy enough to open his own gallery in London. By the end of the decade, however, interest in his style of painting—he had devised a characteristically meticulous 'stippling' method for depicting foliage—was waning. In 1830, at the age of 64, Glover sold everything and joined his sons, already immigrated to Van Diemen's Land. He received a land grant in Deddington, near Ben Lomond, where he established a farm, 'Patterdale', in memory of the Lake District.

The paintings Glover produced in Tasmania, art historians claim, are markedly different from his works completed in England. The argument concludes that, confronted with a wholly new environment, Glover was compelled to adapt his technique to different atmospheric conditions and to the unique elements of the antipodean landscape. Many experts maintain that Glover was the first to depict accurately the Australian gum-tree, one of the major points of contention when discussing Australian painting of the 19C.

His *My Harvest Home* on view here is a delightful piece of propaganda, emphasising his new country's fecundity, in its abundant harvest of wheat, and symbolising the presence of British culture in the appearance of a typically lush garden filled with northern flowers. Glover is buried in the churchyard of Deddington, next to the church he supposedly helped to design. When the artist Tom Roberts honeymooned near here in the 1880s, he spearheaded a campaign to restore Glover's neglected grave.

works are by William Piguenit (1836–1914), one of the first Australian-born landscape artists of note, and by John Glover (see box, p 417), probably the most famous immigrant artist of the period.

Several works in the gallery concentrate on the depiction of Tasmanian Aboriginals. Intriguingly, the earliest white settlers, unlike those in New South Wales, seem not to have had an artistic interest in the island's native population. No images exist until the late 1820s and 1830s, by which time native 'containment' was nearly complete. Of greatest importance are **Benjamin Duterrau**'s

George Augustus Robinson and Truganini

George Augustus Robinson (1788–1866), a Methodist bricklayer and builder, had been appointed in 1829 to take charge of the Aborigines on Bruny Island immediately prior to Lieutenant Governor Arthur's failed 'Black Line' round up of Aborigines. Robinson suggested that he take a number of the Bruny Island people with him on an attempt to talk the Aboriginal people around Hobart into accepting relocation. After a number of trips into the interior with Truganini as his guide and protector, he had convinced nearly all of the local people to accept transport to Flinders Island. As the *Encyclopedia of Australia* describes the Aborigines' situation, 'removed from their regular hunting grounds, they pined away and died'.'Robinson was subsequently made Chief Protector of Aborigines and stationed near Port Phillip, a position he held between 1839 and 1849 when administration became more important than contact with the indigenous people in the region.

Truganini (1803–1876) was the daughter of Mangana, an elder in the group of Aborigines living on Bruny Island. She had witnessed her mother's death, stabbed by a white settler in a night raid, and her sisters' abduction by whalers. She was living as a prostitute in Hobart when Robinson and his guide Woorrady convinced her to accompany them on the 'conciliation' trip. Truganini is credited with saving Robinson's life by floating him across a river while under attack by hostile Aborigines during his early ventures at concilliation in Tasmania. Efforts by Robinson to 'Europeanise' the Aborigines at Flinders Island were unsuccessful. The efforts of his successors to demoralise them further succeeded in reducing the population to 54 in 1843. In 1856 Truganini was among the surviving Aborigines moved to Oyster Cove near Hobart. She died in 1876 in Hobart, seven years after her husband William Lanne (or Lanney)'s corpse had been mutilated in a gruesome conflict between the Royal College of Surgeons in London and the Royal Society in Tasmania. Her dying wish was to have a decent burial 'behind the mountains'; it was not to be, as her bones were displayed for years in the Tasmanian Museum. Her wish was finally honoured a century later when her ashes were scattered in D'Entrecasteaux Channel.

In his essay *The Spectre of Truganini*, art historian Bernard Smith elucidates the cultural significance of depictions of Truganini, the 'last Tasmanian Aboriginal', and Robert Hughes writes movingly of Truganini's gruesome plight in *The Fatal Shore*. Indeed, in the recent ABC-TV (Australian Broadcasting Corporation) series, *Frontier* (1997), Truganini's story symbolises the worst of white–black conflict in 19C Australia.

historically significant if artistically lamentable depictions of the Tasmanian Aborigines and **George Augustus Robinson** ('The Conciliator')'s attempts to bring them into settlements. Duterrau (1767–1851), who revered his fellow Methodist Robinson, wanted to create an epic historical painting of such an attempt; his *The Conciliation* (c 1840), is indeed the first history painting created in Australia. While earlier examples of Duterrau's work, including his self-portrait on the other side of the room, indicate that he had some painterly skills, the deterioration in ability evident in his Tasmanian paintings may be the result of age, or perhaps over-ambition.

Portrait of Truganini, from the Picturesque Atlas of Australia

There is some evidence that this version of the Conciliation was a smaller one than that Duterrau eventually planned to make. Also on display here are casts of Benjamin Law's brooding busts of Truganini (see box, p 418) and Woureddy, presented appropriately in classic pose, as the last representatives of their race.

The most poignant portrait in this gallery is **Thomas Bock**'s small watercolour of *Mathinna* (1842, see box), commissioned from Bock by Lady Jane Franklin. This picture offers an appropriate focus to consider two important figures in the cultural life of colonial Tasmania. Thomas Bock (c 1790–1855) had been a painter and engraver before being sentenced to 14 years' transportation for administering a drug to cause abortion. Upon arrival in Hobart in 1824, his skills as an engraver were quickly put to use in the design of banknotes and illustrations. By 1832 he gained a full pardon and had already established himself as a portrait painter. His portraits in pastels, watercolour and oil include those of prominent citizens, as well as condemned prisoners and bushrangers. He even made a post-mortem likeness of the cannibal Alexander Pearce. It is no surprise that he would have been commissioned for portraits by Lady Jane Franklin (1791–1875), wife of the Lieutenant Governor John

Mathinna

One of Lady Jane's 'projects' was Mathinna, an Aboriginal girl brought to Government House when she was seven. Franklin's aim, it seems, was to show the 'degree of civilisation' that natives under guidance could acquire. The red dress in which Bock depicts her was her prized possession, and she wrote of it proudly in a letter to her real stepfather. As with so many of her other charitable projects, Lady Jane eventually moved on to other concerns and, when the Franklins left the island in 1843, Mathinna was abandoned. She was sent to the Queen's Orphan School and eventually joined the remaining Aboriginals at Oyster Cove. She was found dead at 21, 'intoxicated...in mud and water on the road...choked, suffocated and stifled'. The small mining town near Fingal in northeastern Tasmania is named in her honour.

Franklin (1786–1847). When they arrived in Hobart in 1837, Sir John was already famous as an Arctic explorer (he would perish in an attempted exploration of Antarctic waters). Lady Jane was an intelligent, ambitious philanthropist. She was the first woman to climb Mount Wellington and the first to travel overland from Melbourne to Sydney. She involved herself in a number of projects to improve the lot of prisoners and to advance education and cultural pursuits in the colony (see Lady Jane Franklin Museum, p 425).

Further galleries on the first floor house changing exhibitions on Australian 20C art, Aboriginal art, and photography.

Leaving the museum on MACQUARIE STREET, you can see across the street on the corner of Argyle Street a red-brick Classical Revival style building which is now used by the Hobart City Council. It was built in 1907 as the city's public library, funded largely by the American philanthropist Andrew Carnegie, who donated £7500 for its establishment.

Immediately across Macquarie Street on the opposite corner is Hobart's **General Post Office**, a two-storey building with, predictably, a corner clock tower; it was designed by A.C. Walker and built in 1905.

Turn right at the museum's exit and continue up Macquarie Street one block to the **Town Hall** on the corner of Elizabeth Street. The Town Hall was completed in 1866 by Henry Hunter, one of the colony's best architects. With its three-bay Corinthian entry porch, rich interior and grand staircase it reflects the confident ambitions of a prosperous city in the middle of the Victorian period.

Across Elizabeth Street is **Franklin Square**, a lovely park with a famous Wishing Well fountain. From here **Walking Tours** of Battery Point, conducted by the National Trust, commence every Saturday at 09.30.

Next to Franklin Square on the same block is a complex of buildings, often referred to simply as the Treasury, although it actually has had several functions and today houses a variety of public offices that have integrated previous structures on the site. The central façade on Macquarie Street was designed by W.P. Kay and built between 1860 and 1914. The impressive scale of this three-storey building presents a fine example of the Victorian Classical Revival style that dominated public buildings in Australia during this period. The right-hand side of the building was originally the 1830 courthouse, an important cultural centre for the early colony; the left-hand side was the 1858 courthouse.

Across the street is **St David's Cathedral**, a stone Gothic Revival building begun in 1868 to a design by the English architect G.F. Bradley; it was not finished until 1936. The entryway includes a west window with tracery. The tower, made of stone quarried in Oatlands, has a castellated parapet. To the south is a lovely small close with many old trees.

At 130 Macquarie Street is the J. Walch & Sons Building, dating from 1860, and housing Walch's Stationery, the oldest surviving stationers in Australia. **St Joseph's Catholic Church**, at 165 Macquarie Street, dating from 1841–43, was designed by J. Thomson and is the oldest surviving Roman Catholic church in Hobart.

Anglesea Barracks

At Barrack Street, turn left, walk across Davey Street to the entrance to **Anglesea Barracks** (☎ 03 6237 7100; open daily 09.00–16.00). The barracks were built between 1814 and 1879, making it the oldest occupied military facility in Australia. They were named after the Duke of Anglesea, hero of the Battle of Waterloo. Devised by Governor Macquarie on his first Tasmanian visit in 1811, the first building was the hospital, constructed in 1814. It is now the Commandant's residence. At the same time work began on the Officer's Quarters and Mess, but these were not completed until 1829. These were designed by Lieutenant John Watts and John Lee Archer and consist of three single-storey buildings with verandahs, cement-rendered bricks and slate roofs. The Officers' Married Quarters and the Old Drill Hall were completed in 1824, and contain interesting architectural details, such as the pilasters placed between each set of windows.

The military gaol, finished in 1846, is built out of local sandstone. The Garrison Tap Room from 1834 includes an interesting stuccoed brick entrance portico. Set in the most imposing location of the complex is the Soldiers' Barracks, built in the 1850s and facing the Lower Parade Ground.

Tours of the complex are available with a detailed brochure describing the barracks' history. Enquire at the barrack's museum or at the Visitors' Information Centre at Davey and Elizabeth Streets.

After touring the barracks, you may want to return to the centre of the city by catching a bus on Macquarie Street.

Walk 3 • Cat and Fiddle Arcade

From the Visitor Centre walk up Elizabeth Street two blocks to Collins Street, where Elizabeth Street becomes a pedestrian mall known as **'Restaurant Row'**. The restaurants here, as well as others throughout Hobart, demonstrate how Tasmanian produce is being used to create some of the best dining experiences in the world. Halfway up the mall is the CAT AND FIDDLE ARCADE, an intriguing complex of shops. Enter the arcade on the left, and walk through to Murray Street. Outside turn right and walk 150m across Liverpool Street to the State Library on the corner of Bathurst Street.

The **State Library** building is a hideous early 1960s glass and metal five-storey structure, but housed inside (along with a lending library, research library, archives, and the **W.C. Crowther Tasmaniana** Library) is the **Allport Museum and Library** (☎ 6233 7011; open weekdays, 09.30–17.00). On the library's ground floor is a small collection, a bequest from Henry Allport, heir to the Allport family, one of the earliest free settlers in Tasmania. The original generation included **Mary Morton Allport** (1806–95), a gifted artist and musician, who left some of the earliest artistic and literary accounts of the colony. The Allports remained one of Tasmania's leading families, producing many significant artists. The collection, based on Allport's own bequest, plus purchases through his endowment, consists of decorative arts, period rooms, as well as an impressive library of rare books and items of Tasmaniana. While the holdings are rather eclectic, and at times it is difficult to determine the collection's aim, within the atmosphere of the library it seems a sweet attempt at cultural loftiness. The library itself includes some of the most important works concerning Tasmania, Australia, and the South Pacific. The presentation of the significance of the Allport family in Tasmanian history is appropriate and warranted. The Allports' estate 'Aldridge' (c 1830) on Elboden Street stayed in the family until 1968.

After leaving the library, make a right on to Bathurst Street. At 106 Bathurst Street is the **Playhouse**, originally the Union Chapel. It was built in 1863 by H.R. Bastow in an unusual 'Romanesque' Revival style that incorporated a colonnade and Roman-arched windows.

Two blocks along Bathurst Street is ARGYLE STREET; turn left to see midway down the block at no. 59, Australia's oldest existing **synagogue**. Before its construction, the Jewish community met at the home of Judah Solomon, who eventually donated this site in his garden for the synagogue. It was built in 1845 by James Thomson in a delightful Egyptian Revival style, a popular style for synagogues of the 1840s. At one time, the Jewish population of Hobart rivalled that of Sydney, but the population dwindled significantly by the 1870s. Services, both Liberal and Orthodox, are held on Fridays. Contact the Hebrew Congregation of Hobart for tours of the building.

Return to Bathurst Street and proceed right to **Scots Church**. Built in 1834–36 by J.E. Addison as St Andrew's Presbyterian Church, it was one of the first attempts in the colony at an historically accurate Gothic Revival style. The building complex includes a hall with a simple sandstone chapel of undressed block; this edifice seems to have been designed by W. Wilson in 1834. The church is the oldest surviving Presbyterian church in Australia.

After leaving the church, turn left to CAMPBELL STREET, then left again for two blocks to Penitentiary Chapel and **Criminal Courts**, on the corner of Brisbane Street. An extensive site, it is the remaining portion of the original military complex, much of which is now occupied by the Royal Hobart Hospital. The chapel was commissioned after the free citizens of the city complained about the convicts attending services at St David's Church. Building commenced in 1831, again from a design by Colonial Architect John Lee Archer. As well as being the convicts' church, it was also the original church for the Holy Trinity Parish. By 1857 the addition of law courts made the entire site part of the Hobart Town Gaol. It remains the only surviving example of Georgian ecclesiastical architecture in the Commonwealth. The chapel was used until 1961, the courts until 1983. Tours of the site, including subterranean tunnels, and solitary cells, are conducted daily by the National Trust (☎ 03 6231 0911).

Leave the complex on Brisbane Street, turn right back to Campbell Street, and proceed right five blocks to the **Theatre Royal** (☎ 03 6233 2299/1 800 650 277). Opened in 1837 as the Royal Victoria Theatre, it is the oldest continuously working theatre in Australia. It was designed and financed by Peter Degraves, owner of the Cascade Brewery. Originally a plain Georgian structure, it was remodelled in 1857 by the new owner John Davies. Many of the world's greatest actors and musicians, from Ellen Tree and Sarah Siddons to Dame Sybil Thorndike, have performed here. Laurence Olivier, who acted here in the late 1940s with his wife Vivien Leigh, called it 'the best little theatre in the world'.

Threatened with demolition in the early 1950s, the theatre was saved largely through the efforts of novelist Hal Porter, who physically barred the bulldozers at the door. The interior is a gem of early Victorian decoration, with a domed ceiling including painted portrait roundels of the great composers; in a disastrous fire in 1984, all of these (save Wagner!) were destroyed, but they, as well as the entire interior, have been lovingly restored.

Queen's Domain and Botanical Gardens

Take the bus from the Elizabeth Street Bus Station to the **Royal Tasmanian Botanical Gardens** (☎ 6234 6299; open daily 08.00–16.45). The gardens are located in **Queen's Domain**, the largest park in Hobart, which also includes the cricket grounds, Olympic swimming pool, and Rose Garden. These facilities are located near the Domain entrance off the Tasman Highway. At this same junction on the other side of the highway is the **Memorial Cenotaph**, an obelisk honouring Tasmania's war dead.

The bus into the Domain ends its route a short and pleasant walk from the entrance to the Botanical Gardens. The gardens are adjacent to the **Government House**, residence of the Tasmanian Governor-General. Built in 1857, its elaborate castellation and grand appearance caused it to be considered an extravagant waste of colonial funds. From here, you have a grand view of the Derwent River as it is crossed by the **Tasman Bridge**. This bridge was opened with much ceremony in 1965. In 1975, the bulk ore carrier *Lake Illawarra* struck the bridge, demolishing several spans and sinking the vessel. Remnants of the spans can still be seen. The bridge was repaired and reopened.

Huon Pine

As every tourist will be bombarded with examples of Tasmania's unique wood Huon Pine, a description of its appearance is perhaps not necessary, but its significance cannot be overlooked in an antipodean setting where workable hardwoods were so hard to come by. Huon Pine, moreover, holds a singular place in Australian history, as it contributed greatly to the rise of shipbuilding and the viability of seafaring enterprise. First discovered in the Huon River district by Robert Brown (the river and region were named after the French explorer Huon de Kermandec, who explored the region in 1792), the wood was the economic excuse for the establishment of the penal colony by Governor Sorell at Macquarie Harbour in the southwest corner of the colony. From 1821 until its abandonment in 1832, **Macquarie Harbour** was by far the grimmest and most isolated penal settlement of the English-speaking world, not least of all because of the treacherous efforts necessary to lumber the pine trees growing there. While slow-growing and long-lived—one tree was ringed in 1974 as being 2200 years old—Huon Pine is considered to be the best shipbuilding timber in the world. It is so durable that a sea-going vessel of its timber can remain unaffected by rot for more than 100 years.

As you can see in many of the museums and historic houses, the wood's beautiful colour and texture also made it ideal for furniture and framing. Such an economic goldmine in the days of wooden vessels necessarily led to the rapid decimation of many of the Huon forests. As early as 1879, legislation was introduced to limit the felling—beginning what remains today an ongoing and emotionally fraught battle between conservationists and the timber industry in Tasmania. Current accounts seem to indicate that at present the tree is not in danger of extinction, as it will propagate easily. Examples of the tree and an informative brochure are available at the Botanical Gardens.

Botanical Gardens

The **Botanical Gardens** are quite a hidden treasure, being probably the best-kept and most advantageously situated small public garden in Australia. The gardens were established in 1818, initially as a government garden to provide food for the colony. As early as 1826, Governor Arthur had planned construction of Government House nearby, but this early project was abandoned because of costs. Arthur then set himself to the task of establishing a proper botanical gardens. In 1828, William Davidson, a young horticulturist from England arrived to become the first Superintendent. Not only did he import plants and trees from England, but he collected native plants from the Hobart area. His house in the grounds is now the Museum and Education Centre.

One interesting early feature is the heated wall, commissioned by General Arthur, to warm experimental fruit trees. The wall was not in operation for very long, as Tasmania's relatively mild climate made it unnecessary; it is now in some disrepair.

The gardens are beautifully laid out, with a walk along Derwent River on one side, and stunning views up to Mount Wellington behind. The grounds also include an elegant Conservatory, filled with blooming plants and lovely fountains. The Japanese Gardens were created in honour of Hobart's sister city Yaizu, Japan. A nice **restaurant** with views to the river serves teas and lunch. Near to the restaurant, examples of Tasmania's most famous wood, the Huon Pine, are on view.

Upper Hobart and Mount Wellington

Travelling up Davey Street, at Southern Outlet Road turn right to Macquarie Street which now becomes CASCADE ROAD, leading to the **Cascade Brewery** (☎ 6224 1144; open Mon–Fri, 09.30–13.00; the Davey Street bus from Elizabeth Street opposite the post office will pass the brewery). The brewery itself is a delightful structure, with a seven-storey façade that is reminiscent of a German castle or a Victorian 'wedding cake' style (the interior was gutted in the 1967 bushfires). The brewery, founded in 1824 by the Degraves family, is the oldest operating brewery in the country. Cascade Beer still enjoys a well-deserved reputation as one of Australia's purest and best beers.

Peter Degraves was granted 2500 acres on the side of Mount Wellington by Governor Sorell. Here he established a sawmill, which prospered; in the next decade he initiated the brewery, which Degraves designed himself. Degraves was also responsible for the design and financing of the Theatre Royal. Today you can tour **Woodstock**, Degraves' original home. Immediately below the brewery are the **Cascade Gardens**, owned and operated by the company. Nestled in a cool gully, the gardens offer a soothing atmosphere in its well-kept grounds which include some of the plants originally brought by Degraves.

If you return to Davey Street and continue west, the winding road becomes HUON ROAD and eventually travels to the top of **Mount Wellington** (the M runs buses from Macquarie Street opposite the post office). At 1271m high, it one of Tasmania's highest peaks. In his novel *A Fringe of Leaves* (1976), Patrick White describes the peak as a 'shrouded mountain looming over all', and the native Tasmanian writer Peter Conrad in *Down Home* declared that 'Hobart belongs to Mount Wellington'. Along the road to the top there is an interesting picnic stop at the point where the earliest inn opened in the 1860s; it was destroyed in the bush fire of 1967, also chronicled in the placards here. At The Pinnacle, you can experience an impressive display of Tasmanian weather at its most whimsical. A well-organised enclosure presents spectacular views of Hobart and the entire Derwent River area; placards describe views and give an account of some of the intrepid early explorers to this wind-swept site. A small path allows visitors to venture into the craggy rocks and low bush that make up this barren landscape.

Runnymede and Lady Franklin Gallery

Drive north out of central Hobart on Highway 1, Brooker Highway. Turn left at Risdon Road, follow signs to Runnymede at 61 Bay Road, or take **Bus Route 20**.

Runnymede (☎ 6278 1269; open daily 10.00–16.30) was built c 1836 for Robert Pitcairn, Tasmania's first lawyer and anti-transportation advocate. In 1850 Pitcairn sold the property to the first Anglican bishop, Rev. Francis Russell Nixon, who made additions to the house. Finally it was acquired in 1864 by Captain Charles Bayley, who named it Runnymede after his favourite ship. Now run by the National Trust, the house has been furnished in period style, and the beautiful cottage gardens are a popular wedding spot.

Upon leaving Runnymede, turn north on Risdon Street; continue to Augusta Street and turn right. Augusta Street becomes Lenah Valley Road. Continue c 1.5km to **Lady Franklin Gallery** (☎ 03 6228 0076; open weekends 13.30–16.30). This incongruous location for a Doric temple is another result of Lady Franklin's ambitious philanthropic activities. In this case, she had acquired 410 country acres (166 ha) with the intention of establishing a cultural and educational centre. Designed in 1843 by James Blackburn, it is a skilful example of the Greek Revival style. As the *Heritage of Australia* guide describes it, 'the values of convict-based society were inimical to its use as a cultural centre and it was abandoned for many years, then used as an apple shed'. It is now owned by the Art Society of Tasmania, who hold weekend exhibitions there.

Return to Highway 1, proceed north c 5.5km to Elwick Street. The Elwick Racecourse is on the right. Turn left, then right on to Grove Street to Anfield (100m); here is the **Tasmanian Transport Museum**, Glenorchy (☎ 03 6272 7721; open weekends and holidays, 13.00–16.30), with an exhibition of the history of trains in Tasmania, including train rides, both diesel and steam.

Return to Highway 1, and continue north to Claremont, 5km. Signs lead to **Cadbury's Schweppes Factory** (☎ 03 6249 0111/1 800 627 367; tours 09.00, 09.30, 10.30, 13.00, bookings essential), a very popular Hobart attraction. The plant covers some 100 ha on a peninsula jutting into the Derwent River; indeed, boat tours to the factory are available from Franklin Wharf. The factory is the largest confectionery plant in Australia. Tours include a video history of Cadbury's and chocolate sampling. Be sure to make bookings in advance!

University of Tasmania

From the centre of town, take Davey Street to Harrington, turn left; the road will become Sandy Bay Road. At Grace Street (c 2km), turn right to the **University of Tasmania**. The university is the fourth oldest university in Australia, founded in 1890. Beginning with three lecturers and six students, classes were originally held in a former high school in Queen's Domain; it moved to its present site after the Second World War. Errol Flynn, who was born in Hobart, was the son of Thomas Flynn, professor of biology at the university. In 1961, Peter Loftus and Paul Fenton revived the university magazine *Diogenes* with this scathing editorial:

> *Can Tasmania ever be anything but an intellectual backwater? Will Tasmanians ever progress from their present stage—a collection of passive natives ogling at coloured beads—the ships in the dock, the snow on the mountains, the ANZ Bank, the castration of Georgian charm, pyjama-pants, television towers, and the university's soulless shiver of squares? ... Culture? There's no such animal—maybe that's why Hobart needs a zoo.*

The university was also the site of Australia's most notorious sexual harassment case, that of Professor Sydney Sparkes Orr in the 1950s; Orr's case has been the subject of much study, including Michael Boddy's story 'A Matter of Mourning', W.H.C. Eddy's *Orr* (1961) and the more recent explorations of the topic such as the 1993 film *Orr* by George Miller of *Mad Max* fame. Today the university magazine *Island* is a widely-respected journal of literary and cultural review.

The university's architecture is for the most part undistinguished, dating primarily from the functionalist 1960s; one interesting attraction is the **John Elliott Classics Museum** (☎ 03 6220 2235; open afternoons, Feb–Nov) on Churchill Avenue. It contains examples of art and artefacts of the ancient world, from Mesopotamia to Early Christian.

From Churchill Road, turn left into Nelson Street; cross Sandy Bay Road and continue on Drysdale Place to the **Wrest Point Casino** (☎ 03 6225 0112), the site of Hobart's claim to glamorous nightlife. When it opened in 1973, it was the first legal casino in Australia and was touted as a tourist goldmine. Designed by one of Australia's most prolific 'modernists' Roy Grounds, the tall tower of the building—yes, complete with revolving restaurant at the top—is endearingly known by locals as the Salt Shaker. From the casino, Heritage Walks by the Sandy Bay Historical Society (☎ 03 6223 6703) commence tours on Saturday afternoons; bookings are essential.

South of Hobart

On the road out of Lower Sandy Bay to Snug and Kettering, 11km south outside of Hobart, is the **Shot Tower** (☎ 03 6227 8885; open daily, 09.00–17.30). The tower was built in 1870 by Scottish immigrant Joseph Moir. Standing 48m high, it contains 31 landings and some 300 steps to the top, where you have a tremendous, vertigo-inducing view of Derwent River and out to Storm Bay. A small museum and video presentation gives the history of Moir and his tower and explains the process of making shot, which varies little from modern methods. From all reports, the Moir family, heirs included, were amusingly eccentric, given to inventive practical jokes. The site includes a house with tea room and gift shop.

Bruny Island

Kettering (population 318), 34km from Hobart, is a picturesque fishing village. From here you can catch one of the more or less hourly vehicular ferries to **Bruny Island**, today a leisurely getaway, but historically significant in the early exploration of the South Pacific. It was actually discovered by Abel Tasman, and explored by every other prominent explorer from Cook to Bligh. Its name was bestowed upon it by the French Admiral Antoine Raymond Joseph de Bruni D'Entrecasteaux (1739–93), who made the first extensive survey of the channel now known by the admiral's last name. Only a thin isthmus connects the southern and northern portions of the island; at this point you can often see fairy penguins on shore.

At **Adventure Bay** is the **Bligh Museum** (☎ 03 6293 1117; open daily 10.00–17.00) chronicling the island's early history as a whaling centre; it is said that Bligh himself planted the island's first apple tree here in 1788. The building was made out of 26,000 convict-made bricks that were collected from Variety Bay. The artefacts exhibited include the remains of **Cook's Tree**, a tree on the bay where Captain Cook had carved his name in 1777. The tree was destroyed in a fire in 1905; a monument now marks the spot where it stood.

The Aboriginal name for the island was Lunawanna-Allonah, and these names are still preserved for two towns on the southern end of the island. It was here that Truganini (see box, p 418), known as the last full-blooded Tasmanian Aborigine, was born in 1812. After years in which her skeleton was on display in Hobart's Museum, her wishes were finally granted in 1975, when the remains were cremated and the ashes scattered on the island.

Bruny Island has several places to stay, most of the 'holiday cottage' or caravan park variety. Bookings can be made through any Tasmanian tourist office.

From Kettering, you can continue on the Channel Highway (route B58) south around the edge of D'Entrecasteaux Channel 48km to **Cygnet** (population 924), originally named Port de Cygne by D'Entrecasteaux because of the number of swans here. This region is still the centre of Tasmania's famous apple-producing orchards (Tasmania is still called the **Apple Isle**), although many orchards have fallen to development.

At **Huonville**, 17km north on B58, Huon pine was first discovered by D'Entrecasteaux and named, along with the town and the river, after his colleague Captain Huon de Kermadec. 6km north of Huonville on the road back to Hobart is **Huon Valley Apple and Heritage Museum**, a display and collection of all things apple.

At Huonville, you can also join the HUON HIGHWAY (route A6) and travel south through the timber town of **Franklin**, named for Sir John Franklin, who took up property here on the river before his ill-fated journey to Antarctica in 1845. In town is **Shipwright's Point School of Wooden Boatbuilding** (☎ 03 6266 3586; open weekdays 11.00–11.30, 13.00–13.30, 15.00–15.15), which offers Australia's only accredited course in wooden boatbuilding. Further on is **Geeveston** (population 750), another timber town at the gateway to **Hartz Mountains National Park** (☎ 03 6298 1577), a very popular park for weekend walks; the Arve River and Weld Valleys to the west of town contain 95m tall hardwood trees, said to be the tallest in the world. The road is sealed part of the way, and leads to several lookouts to the Huon Valley and forests. At Port Huon, just outside Geeveston, you can join cruises of the Huon River. Geeveston is also the site of Australian Paper Mills' pulp-mill, one of the largest in Australia.

Continue south through the picturesque fishing village of **Dover**, with three islands in the harbour known as Faith, Hope, and Charity. Finally, 21km south of Dover, you come to **Southport**, the southern end of the roads of Tasmania. The intrepid can continue a further 2km on to route C635 to **Lune River**, which boasts the southernmost post office in Australia, and the site of thermal springs and good walking trails. Nearby are **Hasting Caves**, impressive limestone caves discovered in 1917.

Tasman Peninsula and Port Arthur

Travel from Hobart across Tasman Bridge to Sorell (27km). The **Tasmania Golf Club** (☎ 03 6248 5098) is on **Barilla Bay** near Hobart airport before you cross over to Midway Point and on to Sorel. Set on a rock promontory and surrounded on three sides by water, the physical setting of the course alone might make the game here a treat. Par is hard to beat as well. Originally called Linisfarne, it was only accessible by boat until a bridge was built and the club moved to its present site. Al Howard designed the course and Ian Grimsley constructed the fairways, greens and landscaping.

Proceed east via the *Arthur Highway* to Copping (21km), turn south to Dunalley, c 10km, the site of a monument of Tasman and the location of a spit bridge. You now travel through the Forestier Peninsula to Eaglehawk Neck, 21km, and the Tasman Peninsula. A number of tour buses make this trip and can be booked at the Visitor's Information Centre in Hobart.

Tasman Peninsula is itself a contradiction; today's gorgeous wind-swept beaches must not have seemed so beautiful to those incarcerated at **Port Arthur**, or even those stationed there. Located at the end of the Tasman Peninsula, it was connected to the rest of the island only by a 420m-wide stretch of land, **Eaglehawk Neck**. Today a beautiful beach site with several natural sites worth visiting, at the time of Port Arthur's existence this isthmus was guarded by fierce dogs chained across it, nine to eleven of them, effectively preventing any possibility of escape. It worked, for there were very few escapes. The **Visitor's Centre** (☎ 03 6250 3497) at the beach provides some contemporary descriptions by soldiers and a soldier's wife, describing the intense isolation, loneliness, and boredom endured at this outpost.

Be sure to stop at Eaglehawk Neck to see the natural wonders, especially the **Tessellated Pavements**, a remarkable geological feature at the beach, in which rocks appear almost as a sunken man-made tile floor. The phenomenon is caused by curiously straight fractions in Permian mudstone which, following water erosion, give the appearance of gigantic natural bricks or tiles.

The water at the beach, even in the height of summer, is treacherous and very cold; there is beautifully inviting surf, but a wet suit is recommended at all times if you want to swim.

On the other side of Eaglehawk Neck (c 3km) are other interesting sites: the **Tasman Arch** and the **Devil's Kitchen** are worth a view, again for the bizarre interaction of sea and stone. **The Blowhole** can be a bit of a disappointment, except at the right time of tide. It was here that Marcus Clarke set the climax for his 1872 novel *For the Term of His Natural Life*. Travelling to Tasman Arch, you will pass through **Doo-town**, a holiday resort village in which all the houses have been given a name with 'Doo' in it, as in 'Doo Drop Inn', 'Love Me Doo'.

Port Arthur

Return to the main highway and continue on to Port Arthur (21km). The tragic events of April 1996 at Port Arthur, during which a deranged young man shot and killed 35 innocent visitors, must be mentioned here, if only to commemorate the victims of this senseless slaughter and to commend the attempts by all Tasmanians to persevere and endure. More than any other place, this historic site captures the dichotomy of Tasmanian life, with its romantic ruins belying an horrific past.

Port Arthur Historic Site (☎ 6250 2539; open daily 09.00–17.00), as it is called today, early on became the most notorious penal colony in Australian history. Founded in 1833 by Lieutenant-Governor George Arthur, the prison intended, a contemporary document quite clearly states, 'to inspire terror and to improve the moral character of an offender'. Its main purpose was as a place of incarceration for transportees who committed further crimes while in the colony, or for those convicts deemed incorrigible and incapable of following Arthur's specific rules of behaviour. It continued to operate as a prison until 1877, some 24 years after transportation ended in Tasmania. Port Arthur came to symbolise all that was most hideous about the transportation system, although by contemporary standards the conditions were probably better than in many other prisons.

Robert Hughes, in his book, *The Fatal Shore* and elsewhere, has warned of the temptation to turn the site into a convict Disneyland:

> *Australia has many parking lots but few ruins. When Australians see the ruin of an old building, our impulse is either to finish tearing it down or to bring in the architects and restore it as a cultural centre, if large, or a restaurant, if small. Port Arthur is the only example of an Australian historical ruin appreciated and kept for its own sake (although local entrepreneurs have tried, and so far failed, to refurbish it as Convictland)...Far more than Macquarie Harbour or even Norfolk Island, Port Arthur has always dominated the popular historical imagination in Australia as the emblem of the miseries of transportation, 'the Hell on earth'.*

While it is not quite that blatant, the deference paid to tourists at this most popular Tasmanian attraction does run the risk of such commercialisation. The fascination of the site lies in the incongruity of its current romantic atmosphere with the realities of its true 19C past. Arthur offered the possibility of 'reform' by good behaviour through a rigid system of steps. Convict life was obsessively proscribed, as the book of regulations (reprinted and for sale at the Port Arthur Museum) indicates. Convicts were kept at hard labour from sunrise to sunset, with two brief breaks for meals; those on the chain gangs were forced to wear chains, and to dress in the distinctive yellow and grey costumes with the word 'felon' stamped across them in several places. Conversation was forbidden, with separate cells for each prisoner. Food, while by present standards minimal, was probably more plentiful and reliable than the free poor of England would have had at the time; those in extreme hard labour received as much as a pound of meat a day. Training in trades was possible. Port Arthur was also one of the first institutions to set aside a separate facility for young offenders (Port Puer), where they were provided with training, religious instruction, and some rudimentary education.

A well-devised **pocket-size map** accompanies admission to the complex. The entry fee is a rather hefty sum, but includes the boat ride to the cemetery on the Isle of Dead. The guide indicates walking routes to take on the basis of time available for those who do not want to take an organised tour (of which there are many). Displays and presentations concentrate on archaeological excavation and restoration, with some discussion of social history, although little is said about the women (wives and servants) and children who were part of this bizarre social matrix.

The four-storey Penitentiary building, while badly damaged, still gives enough evidence of its inhospitable purpose. The **Museum**, which at one time was an insane asylum, has an excellent, if limited and eclectic, presentation of actual social conditions of the place. There are examples of stone carving done by convicts, an example of their uniform, excerpts from writings by soldiers and convicts, and displays of physical remnants.

The '**Model Prison**' is a grotesquely ironic name for the building reserved for the most recalcitrant inmates. Based on the ideas of England's Pentonville Prison, punishment took the form of total silence and isolation. The building included 50 cells, two 'dark and dumb' cells for those who refused to obey, exercise yards, and even a chapel in which cubicles made it impossible for prisoners to be in contact with each other. When out of their cells, 'model prisoners' were required to wear a cap over their faces which prevented them from recognising each other.

The **Commandant's House** has meticulous descriptions of its restoration following its many careers. After abandonment of the site, the structure became a tourist resort, the **Hotel Carnarvon**; in the 1880s it apparently acquired the unusual wall murals of exotic scenes, probably completed by the Mason sisters who lived in the hotel.

William O'Brien's cottage commemorates the stay at Port Arthur of its most 'high profile' convict, the Irish political prisoner, who was only there for three months. Leader of the Irish Home Rule movement, O'Brien refused to state that he would not escape, and was consequently sent to Norfolk Island, where he indeed tried to escape. As O'Brien was a highly volatile political prisoner, the government was unable to dole out the normal treatment for him; they could not afford a martyr to the cause. The authorities simply watched his activities, placing him under a kind of house arrest. O'Brien was finally given a ticket-of-leave, whence he made his way to Brussels at the end of the 1850s; in 1856, he was finally allowed to return to Ireland.

Port Arthur's **Church** was central to Governor Arthur's penal system; attendance at religious services was compulsory, in the belief that moral rehabilitation of the convicts might arise (as one of the descriptive plaques points out, very few prisoners were thus reformed). The colony's church, then, was a significant edifice, able to seat as many as 1500 convicts and members of the garrison. Apparently designed by convict architect Henry Laing, the foundation stone was laid in April 1836. The remaining ruins of the church (it was burned in the 1880s) give evidence of an ambitious building campaign. Religious dissent at the prison arose when the many Catholic convicts eventually refused to attend the Anglican religious services. An embarrassed government finally succumbed and allowed a Catholic priest. The Catholic church was built in 1857.

Offshore from the main complex is the **Isle of Dead** where convicts and other Port Arthur figures were buried, many with elaborate tombstones. While the trip to the island is included in the entrance fee, an additional fee is charged to take a longer harbour tour. Some 1769 convicts were buried in unmarked graves, while officers and free person's graves include interesting headstones. Many of them sculpted by convicts, they include the work of Thomas Pickering, recognised by his rope-like borders and penchant for flowers and verse. The grave of Henry Savery, whose *Quintus Servinton* (1831) is considered Australia's first novel, is one of the anonymous graves; he committed suicide here in 1840.

Port Arthur also conducts 'ghost tours' during some evenings. Check at the Davey Street Information Centre for availability, or at the Port Arthur entrance gate. As you can imagine in a place with such a desperate past, legends of lingering ghosts abound. A display in the Commandant's House even includes supposed photographic 'evidence' of their presence.

Hobart to Launceston

The Hobart to Launceston road was completed in 1826. At that time it took 12 hours to complete by coach. By 1872 Anthony Trollope could observe that 'the road from Launceston to Hobart Town is as good as any road in England and is in appearance exactly like an English Road.' While the comment was probably meant as a compliment, the paternal implication offended a number of Tasmanians. **Buses** make the trip between Hobart and Launceston routinely. Tour buses will make some of the stops described here.

From Hobart travel north on Highway 1, the **MIDLAND HIGHWAY**, to **Bridgewater** (19km), which for years was the main north–south crossing of the Derwent River. The original causeway was constructed in the 1830s by convict labour in chains, who brought by wheelbarrow some two million tons of stone and clay. Continuing on 8km, you will come to the twin towns of **Brighton** and **Pontville** (population 908), situated on the Jordan River. Named perhaps facetiously by Macquarie, being nowhere near the sea, Brighton was at one time seriously considered to become the colony's capital. It has always been an important garrison town, and is still the site of the main Tasmanian military base. When passing through Brighton, look left to see Mount Dromedary, famed as the hideout for the legendary 'Robin Hood' of bushrangers, Martin Cash.

Martin Cash

Convicted as an attempted murderer, Cash arrived in the colony in 1837; he was one of the only prisoners to escape from Port Arthur (four times!) by swimming Eaglehawk Bay. As a bushranger, he was famed for his courtesy to women and the poor. After many successful years as an outlaw, Cash was caught and sentenced to death in Hobart, but ended up on Norfolk Island. When that settlement closed, he returned to Tasmania and was for years caretaker of the Government House gardens; he died on his farm in Glenorchy in 1877.

Pontville is known for its lovely Anglican church, St Mark's, designed by James Blackburn and built 1839–41. From the entrance there is a splendid view back to Mount Wellington. The church graveyard contains many interesting grave-stones of the Butlers, a leading Tasmanian family.

The highway now proceeds through **Mangalore** and **Bagdad** (6km and 8km). The proliferation of such exotic place-names, including as well Lakes Tiberias and Jericho, has two conceivable explanations. The more prosaic is that the early soldiers in the region had seen service in Africa and the Levant before arriving in Tasmania; the other, more romantic, story is that the original surveyor Hugh Germain carried with him into the inland the Bible and a copy of *Arabian Nights*, and named sites from them.

Kempton (population 226), 19km from Brighton, was originally named Green Duckholes, and was changed to honour Anthony Fenn Kemp (1773–1867). An early settler, he built Mount Vernon, a rural property named in honour of George Washington whom he had apparently met in America. Mount Vernon was located in Melton Mowbray, 6km further north on the highway. Kempton used to have seven inns, but is now becoming an arts-and-crafts village, known now as Kempton Village (☎ 03 6254 1212). Of architectural interest here is 'Dysart House', built as a hotel in 1842, and St Mary's Church, built in 1844 and attributed to convict-architect James Blackburn.

The LAKE HIGHWAY (route A5) begins at Melton Mowbray and ends in 83km at **Great Lake**, a popular fishing resort which is 40km in length, one of the largest freshwater lakes in Australia. 19km from Melton Mowbray on the A5 is **Bothwell** (population 370), declared a Historic Town and filled with remnants of its 19C past; at least 20 buildings are classified by the National Trust. Particularly striking is the quite formal layout of the town, indicating the civic awareness of the founders. **Tourist information**: Council Offices, Alexander Street, ☎ 03 6259 5503.

Founded in the 1820s by Scottish settlers, Bothwell may be the site of the very first golf course in Australia. While this cannot be entirely substantiated, it is true that the course, located on 'Ratho', the property of early settler Alexander Reid, is still in use and open to anyone holding membership in any golf club. Appropriately, Bothwell also houses the **Australasian Golf Museum** on Market Place (☎ 03 6259 4033; open Sun–Fri, 10.00–16.00, winters 11.00–15.00); it is located in the historic sandstone school house.

Of note in Bothwell itself is **St Luke's Church**, on Alexander Street, one block to the right off the main street, Patrick Street. Designed by John Lee Archer, the church first held services in 1831. The sculptures over the door are believed to have been carved by convict artist Daniel Herbert. The town is also the site of Nant Cottage, home in the 1850s to John Martin and John Mitchell, famous Irish political exiles, known for their 'treasonable' political writings.

Return to route A1 and continue north. 16km further is **Jericho**, outside which is Spring Hill, at 488m the highest point on the Midland Highway. The next Historic Town is **Oatlands** (13km; population 545), so named by the peripatetic Macquarie because the region reminded him of the oat-growing country of Scotland. Established as a garrison town, it still feels like one. The town possesses the largest number of remaining sandstone buildings in all of Australia, some 138 within the town boundary, including a Court House from 1829 and a gaol building from 1835. **Tourist information**: 71 High Street, ☎ 03 6254 0011.

Most impressive, and dominating the landscape, is a delightful white **windmill**, one of only four in Australia. For years derelict, the mill complex has been restored as the Callington Mill Historic Site, with admirably instructive explanatory signs. Included in the complex is a steam-driven mill for times when there was no wind. It operated from 1846 until the early 1900s, when mass-produced flour made it impracticable. While many historical buildings remain in the town, most are extremely small and, in the end, uninteresting in their sameness, even if they give a good picture of a 19C townscape.

When heading north from Oatlands to Tunbridge, look for several amusing examples of **topiary** that local landowner Jack Cashion created from the hawthorn bushes on his property; they have been maintained with regular trimming since his death. The landscape now becomes flatter with growing evidence of the grain crops for which the Midlands are famous.

Ross

37km from Oatlands turn off to the village of **Ross** (population 300). Named in 1821 by Governor Macquarie in honour of the hometown of his friend H.M. Buchanan, Ross marks the dividing line between the original northern and southern counties created in 1804 by Governor King. Described by the Irish exile Thomas Meagher, who lived here in 1849, as a 'little apology of a town', Ross remains a modest village rife in historical monuments. The region possesses a large quantity of freestone, which made it possible to complete substantial structures in a Georgian style. **Tourist information:** Church Street, ☎ 03 6381 5466.

Danish author Jorgen Jorgensen was constable here in 1833, at which time he reported the town had seven pubs, a military and a convict barracks. He was forced to resign when he accused the local magistrate of allowing the theft of materials for the new bridge being built across the river.

Jorgen Jorgenson

The most famous Scandinavian associated with Australia, Jorgen Jorgensen was described by the historian Marcus Clarke as 'one of the most interesting human comets in history'. Born in 1780, he went to sea under the British flag as a boy. In 1800 he was in Australia as part of the crew of the surveying vessel *Lady Nelson*, which landed in Victoria. On this ship he saw the founding of Newcastle, and the establishment of both Hobart and Launceston. In 1804 as captain of the *Alexander*, he was instrumental in the establishment of Tasmanian whaling. After returning to England under ever more adventurous circumstances, Jorgensen ended up in Iceland, where he proclaimed himself king for nine weeks, before the British took him into custody. He then managed to find work as a spy during the Napoleonic Wars; ultimately his penchant for gambling led him into debt, and when he pawned his landlady's furniture, he was arrested and exiled for life to Van Diemen's Land. Here he again managed to wriggle his way out of the sentence, serving instead as an explorer of the inland. After receiving a full pardon in 1835, he preferred to remain in the colony working as a journalist and writer, until his death in 1841.

It is this same disputed **bridge** which today is the best known and most striking architectural feature of the village, and probably the most well-known

Ross River Bridge

monument in Tasmania. Built in 1836, the bridge was designed by Colonial Architect John Lee Archer, but its fame rests on the work of the stonemasons who actually constructed it. They were two convicts, Daniel Herbert, convicted as a highwayman in 1827, and James Colbeck, a thief. Consisting of three symmetrical arches, the bridge has attractively proportioned stone staircases on either side leading down to the river, with chain-linked stone pillars leading to the bridge on each side of the road. In the arches of and underneath the bridge, Herbert carved Celtic symbols along with images of royalty, heads of animals and indecipherable inscriptions; in all, there are 186 panels decorating the arches. For this work he received a full pardon; his headstone, carved by himself, marks his grave in the town's old burial ground. The house where Herbert is believed to have lived still stands in the village on Badajos Street.

The centre of the village, at the intersection of Bridge and Church Streets, is affectionately known as the **Four Corners**. Each corner caters to one of humankind's needs: on the southwest, Temptation: the Man-O-Ross Hotel, established in 1835; the southeast, Salvation: the Roman Catholic Church, originally a store; the northwest, Recreation, in the form of the Town Hall; and the northeast, Damnation, the site of the original gaol, now an elegant colonial home of the Council Clerk.

The entire length of CHURCH STREET, essentially the only street in town, consists of buildings of historic interest. These include the **Scotch Thistle Inn**, built in 1844 as a public house and now a well-known restaurant, and **St John's** Church of England, built in 1868 from the stones of the original 1848 church. The interior of the church is well known for its stained-glass windows, oak lectern, stone pulpit, and hundred-year-old organ.

To the north of the Four Corners on Church Street is the **Uniting Church**, built as a Methodist church in 1885. With pews of blackwood and a ribbed pine ceiling, the church contains a modern tapestry designed by Australian artist John Coburn, which was woven in France.

Walking up the hill to the right of the church and across the street, you can see the foundation stones of one of the two female factories in the state. Here women convicts did sewing and laundry for the town, and were allowed nurseries for their children. A gate leads across the railway to the cemeteries, including the original burial ground where Daniel Herbert and other pioneers are buried.

Campbelltown

Return to the highway and continue north 10km to **Campbelltown** (population 879), an attractive town on the Elizabeth River. Another example of Governor Macquarie's orgy of self-commemoration, the town was named for his wife. The main street is the highway and is here called Bridge Street. Most of the town's major buildings are located along it. Originally another garrison station, the area soon became more important for its agricultural and wool productivity. Each June Campbelltown hosts Australia's longest-running agricultural show, initiated in 1838. The town also has a convict-built bridge, this one of red brick and built in 1836. **Tourist information**: 105 High Street, ☎ 03 6381 1283.

Important buildings include **St Luke's** church, on the corner of Pedder Street, designed by John Lee Archer in 1837; the church's cemetery includes the graves of many early prominent citizens of the area. In the block between William and Queen Streets is **The Grange**, built in the 1840s for Dr William Valentine, a doctor and scientist who even installed an observatory in the house. It now offers tourist accommodation. Further along on the corner of the High Street is **St Andrew's** Presbyterian church. Built in 1857 and considered to be one of the best churches of this period in Australia, the interior includes an organ and desk that belonged to Bishop Nixon, first Anglican Bishop of Tasmania. Before leaving town, you will notice on the left in a small park an odd little memorial to Harold Gatty, native son, who with American Wiley Post first circumnavigated the world by plane in 1931.

After leaving Campbelltown, you enter the region known as the **Norfolk Plains**, covering some 5830 sq km of pastoral land. It takes its name from some of the original settlers who came in 1807 from Norfolk Island where their attempts to establish a viable free settlement had failed.

Passing through evidence of their successful agricultural efforts for 48km, you then turn left on C521 to **Longford** (c 8km; population 2027). Originally named Latour by a member of the Cressy Establishment, a land syndicate that purchased massive tracts here in the 1820s, Longford's history is tied to that of some of the most prominent pastoral families in Tasmania. The many estates in the district, built by pioneering members of these families, bear witness to the agricultural prosperity made possible by the area's rich soil and successful stock-breeding. **Tourist information**: Council Offices, Smith Street, ☎ 03 6391 1303.

Longford has been classified an Historic Town, and here you will find a succession of interesting architectural sites, most dating from after the founding of the township in 1827. Of special note is Christ Church, erected of sandstone between 1839 and 1844. The bell and clock were supposedly donated to the earlier church on this site by King George IV. The church's cemetery contains the vaults of the Archer, Reibey and Brumby families. Special mention should be made of the vault of James Brumby, who died in 1838, for he supposedly lent his name to an Australian legend, the wild horses of the high country. The story goes that when James left New South Wales for Van Diemen's Land, he could not round up his horses and they 'went bush'. When people asked who owned the wild horses, the answer was 'they are Brumby's'. Some experts are sceptical of this derivation and provide other possible sources, but it makes a good local story.

Longford is also the site of the **Tasmanian Folk Festival**, attracting an international crowd during its annual run over the Australia Day weekend in January.

8km southeast of Longford on the banks of the Macquarie River, just past Point Road on your right is **Woolmer's** (☎ 03 6391 2230, open daily 10.00–16.30, except Christmas), the estate of Thomas Archer (1790–1850), one of four brothers who would prosper in the area. Thomas Archer came to Launceston in 1813, and by 1818 began this estate, named after a place in Hertfordshire. One of the least altered historic houses today, Woolmer's is still in the hands of Archer's descendants, who conduct tours of the residence. The original part of the house comprises two wings at the rear which form a courtyard. After Archer retired to the estate in 1821, he began extensive additions, including the Italianate front, completed in the 1840s. The dining room, 'redecorated' in 1859, remains in its original condition; many original artefacts and paintings, including works by Salvator Rosa, are also in situ. Equally impressive are the extensive number of outbuildings on the complex outside the high wall surrounding the main house. At one time, the estate supported fifty families, so several cottages, stables, coach-houses and workman's quarters were necessary. The coachhouse still houses the Archers' original 1913 Wolseley car.

The gardens contain many of the plants Archer imported in the 1820s. The hawthorn hedgerows along Woolmers Lane are also authentic, and are listed on the Register of Significant Trees.

Another Archer property, **Brickendon** (☎ 03 6391 1251; open Wed–Sun 09.30–17.00), on Woolmers Lane 2km from Longford town centre on route C520, is also part of the Archer Family Guided Tour. Built by Thomas's brother William in 1823, the farm complex still contains the area's earliest brick cottage in which he lived while building the estate. Now a museum, the bricks were made on the property and timber was hand-split by convict labour. On view now are the blacksmith's shop, shearing shed, and cookhouse, as well as 6 ha of gardens planted with imported species in the 1830s.

3km northwest of Longford Township is **Perth**, so-named by Governor Macquarie on his visit in 1821. Macquarie stayed there with early settler David Gibson, a native of Perth in Scotland, hence his choice of name. Here was located a dock for the punt-crossing of the river before a bridge was built in 1839. The bridge was washed away in the 1929 floods. A walking tour brochure is available at the Longford Information Centre. An intriguing structure along the tour is the Baptist Tabernacle on Clarence Street. Erected in 1889 by William Gibson, its unusual octagonal shape and the vaguely Indian architectural elements perhaps reflect the fact that Gibson had travelled extensively in the East.

Now travel east, cross Highway 1 and into **Evandale** (13km; population 850). Named after explorer and Deputy Surveyor George William Evans (1780–1852), the village of Evandale is obviously conscious of and nurtures its historic sites. Several of the earliest structures still exist as tea-rooms, bed-and-breakfasts and restaurants. The village was not incorporated until 1866, but settlement dates from 1809; it has been an agricultural centre since 1811.

A township named Morven by Governor Macquarie was laid out 3km to the southeast. When a scheme was initiated to build a water tunnel from the South Esk River to Launceston, it developed instead at its present site. The **Information Centre**, housed in the community's original circulating library on High Street (☎ 03 6391 8128), provides walking tours, a family history library and local history books of all kinds. The history of the town was written by a Karl von Stieglitz, one of the few German names prominently evident in Tasmanian history. Of architectural note are the two St Andrew's churches, across the street from each other on High Street. **St Andrew's** Church of England, in Gothic style, was built in 1879 to replace an earlier structure of 1841. It contains a bishop's chair made of timbers from Australia's first warship, HMS *Nelson*. **St Andrew's** Uniting Church across the street, is a fine early example of Greek Revival architecture, and was built 1839–41 through the efforts of Reverend Robert Russell, the first Presbyterian minister to the district. His grave in the churchyard is marked by an impressive memorial.

Also on High Street on the way to Launceston is the town's unused 'landmark', a Gothic water tower erected in 1896. While no longer in use, it features in logos for the town and is floodlit at night as their 'ruin'. Other historical buildings include, next to the information centre, **Solomon House**, built in 1836 by merchant Joseph Solomon, whose son would be Tasmanian Premier from 1912 to 1914; it is now a bed and breakfast and tea room. Also on High Street is **'Blenheim'** (c 1832), originally Patriot King William IV Hotel, an excellent example of hotel architecture of the period.

Evandale is the site of the annual **Penny-Farthing Cycle Races**, held the last weekend of February. They now attract thousands of participants and spectators, and include a race down the runway of the Launceston airport, which lies immediately out of town.

Outside Evandale to the south on Nile Road (route C416) c 10km is **Clarendon** (☎ 03 6398 6220; open daily 10.00–17.00), now preserved by the National Trust. The Red Line bus from Hobart will stop near here. One of the finest Georgian houses in Australia, Clarendon was built in 1838 as the home of James Cox (1790–1866).

William Cox and the history of Clarendon

Cox was the son of William Cox, the engineer who was a member of the first party to cross the Blue Mountains in New South Wales. After schooling in England, James arrived in Sydney in 1804, and settled in Tasmania in 1814; he was granted 700 acres in 1817. By 1819 he managed to acquire the 6000 acres that would become Clarendon; eventually his estate comprised some 20,000 acres (8000 ha). Cox was instrumental in establishing Merino sheep in Tasmania, bringing Merino stud first from James Macarthur's flock in Camden, New South Wales, and then importing them from England and the Continent. He also established cattle breeding and bred a renowned stable of thoroughbred horses, having imported the stallion Hadji Baba.

Cox became involved in politics, eventually representing his district in the first elective House of Assembly in 1856. He lived the life of an English squire, even establishing the Clarendon Hunt and a deer park, and the village of Lymington nearby (now Nile). The fortune amassed from these activities, and from his work as a merchant in Launceston, enabled Cox to commence work on this estate, completed at a cost of some £30,000. The house remained in family hands until 1917 (James Cox had 19 children by two wives); it was finally donated to the National Trust in 1962 by the owners, W.R. Menzies.

While the architect is not known, it is possible that the plans for Clarendon were purchased from England. The builder was John Richards who worked with convict labour, taking eight years to complete this impressive mansion. Its spacious proportions are most impressive, with a high-columned Ionic portico and large windows, reminiscent, perhaps not coincidentally given the fact that they were built at the same time, of the antebellum plantations of the American South. There are six rooms on the ground floor and ten on the first, with a kitchen and seven other rooms in the basement. A connecting service wing included a dairy, bakehouse, butcher's, laundry and store-rooms. The stables and barns are still in the process of restoration, but the nine-acre grounds have been restored to evoke garden settings of the 1840s.

The house was in need of serious repair when turned over to the National Trust; in fact, it was sinking into the alluvial soil. As 'before and after' photographs reveal, the basement had been filled in and the front portico had been bricked over. Restoration continues, and displays of the work in progress are included in the house. Artefacts of the period have been donated in generous numbers, so that every room appears as it would have in the period. Of special interest are two beautiful period clocks which still chime on the quarter hour. Despite its rather isolated location, it is one of the only public sites that does not include a kiosk or tea room (although tea and biscuits can be purchased by placing money in a tin in the kitchen, an indication of an endearing Australian approach!).

From Evandale you can join the road leading to the entrance to **Ben Lomond National Park** (☎ 03 6390 6279), some 50km east of Launceston and only 30 minutes from Evandale. Ben Lomond is the premier ski resort in Tasmania, located amidst the 16,450 ha of the park. **Legges Tor** at 1572m is the park's highest peak. The park consists of glacial boulders and moorland and alpine flora and fauna. In warmer seasons, the area is ideal for bushwalks, with abundant examples of cold-weather eucalypts, wildflowers, and birdlife.

Launceston

Now return to Evandale and proceed 20km on Highway 1 to Launceston. The second largest city in Tasmania (population 94,000) and the third oldest city in Australia, **Launceston** (pronounced LON-sess-ton) lies on the confluence of the Tamar, North and South Esk Rivers. **Tourist information**: Paterson Street, ☎ 03 6336 3122. Accessible by air from Melbourne, with possible stops on Flinders or King Island, or from Hobart, most visitors will be motoring from Hobart or the ferry stop at Devonport. The Red Line buses depart from the top of George Street for northern and western towns.

History
Launceston's history dates from the discovery of the Tamar River by Flinders and Bass on their 1798 circumnavigation of Van Diemen's Land. They named the harbour at the mouth of the river Port Dalrymple in honour of the Admiralty Hydrographer. Settlement did not begin until Lieutenant Colonel William Paterson was dispatched by Governor King in 1804 with the express purpose of securing the northern part of the island for British settlement. First settling in George Town, Paterson moved to the town's present site in 1806. It was first called Patersonia, but by 1807 the

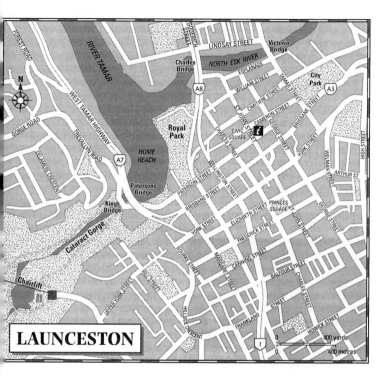

name had changed to Launceston, in honour of Governor King's home-town. By 1824, when it was officially proclaimed a township, it had consolidated as the second city of the island, beginning a long-standing rivalry with Hobart to the south.

Launceston became a centre for anti-transportation efforts in the 1840s, and its non-conformist tradition still sets it apart from Hobart. Ironically, one of Launceston's greatest claims to fame is as the birthplace of Melbourne. John Batman (1801–39) left from Launceston in the scoop *Rebecca* in May 1835 to explore the area which would become the Victorian capital. Melbourne's other founder, John Pascoe Fawkner, moved here in 1819 and established the newspaper the *Launceston Advertiser* in 1829 before sailing for Port Phillip in 1835. Famous novelist Katharine Susannah Prichard lived here as a child in the 1880s when her father was editor of the town's *Daily Telegraph*. She wrote of her time in the town in *The Wild Oats of Han* (1928). Today the centre of Launceston is filled with late Victorian buildings, most dating from 1880–1900.

The most impressive aspect of Launceston is a natural attraction—the spectac-ular **Cataract Gorge and Cliff Grounds**. Only a 15-minute walk from the centre of Launceston, the gorge was described by its discoverer, William Collins in 1804, as a 'strange gully between perpendicular rocks about 15 feet high. The beauty of the scene is probably unsurpassed in the world'. The result of its unusual geology, the area has been successfully incorporated into the town's civic landscape. In typical Australian fashion, several **walks** for all levels of fitness have been created throughout the grounds, and a detailed brochure with maps, including walking time and grade, is available at the Visitor Information Centre. **Tasmanian Chairlifts** (☎ 03 6331 5915) also runs a chairlift ride across the gorge every day, weather permitting.

To walk to the gorge from the Information Centre in town, turn right from St John Street into Paterson Street and proceed west until Paterson Street becomes Bridge Road. Here the Cataract Gorge Reserve begins at Kings Park. Kings Bridge spans the gorge. This graceful open girder iron bridge was built in two sections, the earlier in 1863 designed by W.T. Doyne. Other attractions in the park, aside from the famed Zig Zag Walk to the gorge's First Basin, are the **Penny Royal Watermill**, erected in 1825 and now containing displays of a gunpowder mill and cannon foundry. The Richies Mill Art Centre is near the landing dock of the paddle steamer *Lady Stelfox* which makes daily cruises up the gorge.

Shott's Umbrella Shop, Launceston

An easy walk from the Information Centre on St John Street leads around the corner east to George Street where the National Trust runs the old **Umbrella Shop** (☎ 03 6331 9248, open Mon–Fri 09.00–17.00, Sat 09.00–12.00) on the original premises of a real umbrella shop and factory, opened in the 1860s by the Shott Family. It is lined with beautiful Tasmanian blackwood and retains the shop's original fittings. Further down George Street, turn east or Cameron Street to find **City Park**, site of the original Government House grounds which were laid out in 1820. The elegant iron entrance gates were added in 1903. Inside the park are the **Tasmanian Design Centre** (☎ 03 6331 5506; Mon–Fri 10.00–18.00, Sat 10.00–13.00, Sun 14.00–17.00) supporting local crafts with excellent examples of the island's woodwork **Albert Hall**, containing a unique water-powered organ in a High Victorian exhibition building; and the John Hart Conservatory presenting a variety of ferns and flowers, as well as a monkey island with Japanese macaques.

From the Elizabeth Street car park back in town, turn right on Elizabeth Street and walk to St John Street (50m); on the corner to the left is **St John's Church**. Commissioned by Governor Arthur in 1824, the church's foundation stone was laid by him in January 1825. Legend has it that the original plans, designed by David Lambe, were for a church as large as that in Hobart but that Governor Arthur demanded that it be made smaller. The clock tower was added in 1830, and further additions made by architect Arthur North in 1901–11. The interior of the church contains some amusing carvings which depict Tasmanian animals and plants amidst biblical emblems and coats of arms. These were apparently designed by the architect North himself and carried out by Hugh Cunningham and Gordon Cumming. Note especially the choir stalls which include figures of four pairs of possums.

Turn left into St John Street and enter PRINCE'S SQUARE at the next corner, on Frederick Street. Originally a brick field, it became a military parade ground in the 1840s, and by 1859 was established as a public park designed by Thomas Wade. The square includes a fountain, commemorating the first water supply; the fountain was purchased at the Great Paris Exhibition of 1889.

Continue east on FREDERICK STREET; opposite is **Chalmers Church**, named for Sir Thomas Chalmers and opened in 1860. A good example of Gothic Revival, it now houses the **Launceston Players Theatre**. Further down in the same block is **Milton Hall**. Built in 1842, this simple brick building with Doric portico was originally St John's Square Independent Chapel, the pastorate of noted historian and newspaperman, the Reverend John West. West preached vehemently against transportation and wrote the first account of *The History of Tasmania* (1852). He was instrumental in the establishment of *The Examiner*, Tasmania's oldest newspaper, the Mechanics' Institute, and the City Mission. (The City Mission Chapel, built in 1862, still stands at 46 Frederick Street.) In 1854 West left to become editor of the *Sydney Morning Herald*.

The main **Post Office** is on the corner of St John and Cameron Streets. As in all other Australian cities, distances between towns are measured from the post office, which perhaps explains the grandiose scale of their construction and the ubiquitous presence of a tall clock tower. Launceston is no exception. The building was completed in 1889 without a tower, but public demand led to its addition in 1909, after which time it did indeed dominate the skyline.

On CIVIC SQUARE, bordered by St John, Paterson, Charles and Cimitiere Streets, is **Macquarie House**, built in 1830 as a warehouse for early merchant Henry Reed. It now houses the local history collection of the Queen Victoria Museum.

From Civic Square, exit west on to Charles Street. The block of **CAMERON STREET** between Charles and Wellington Streets is one of the town's oldest, with a remarkably well-preserved 19C streetscape. The buildings include several impressive flour-mills and warehouses, evidence of early river trade nearby, as well as the **Batman Fawkner Hotel**, no. 37. The present hotel is late Victorian, but remnants of the original 1823 building on this site have been preserved at the rear. The original name was the Cornwall Hotel, Fawkner having built it shortly after starting the *Launceston Advertiser*. Also of interest on Charles Street is **Staffordshire House** at no. 56, originally Fergusson's Warehouse. A rare example in Australia of a Regency style building, it was built in 1833 for James Cox, founder of the Clarendon estate.

Queen Victoria Museum and Art Gallery (☎ 03 6331 6777; open Mon–Sat 10.00–17.00, Sun 14.00–17.00) is on Wellington and Patterson Streets in Royal Park. Parking near the museum is nearly impossible, and you must cross busy intersections to reach it, but it is worth the effort. As a museum and gallery for such a small community, the institution is admirably well organised and intent on educational display. Opened in 1891 in honour of Queen Victoria's Golden Jubilee, exhibits are varied, ranging from a complete Chinese Joss House (with an interesting history of the Chinese presence in Tasmania from the time of the gold rush to the present) to artefacts of convict life, and displays of Tasmanian flora and fauna. Tucked away in one dark corner is a fascinating glass case containing the hummingbird collection of the famous naturalist John Gould. The upper galleries are devoted to Australian art, including decorative arts and crafts. The gallery of colonial art, while not as extensive as that in Hobart, contains some important examples by John Glover, Thomas Bock, and William Piguenit.

George Town

50km north of Launceston on the Tamar Highway (A8) is **George Town** (population 5310). Considered by many to be the oldest town in Australia (as distinct from the oldest city), the area was indeed visited by Bass and Flinders in 1798, when it was named Port Dalrymple. Renamed George Town five years later by Colonel William Paterson, it no doubt would have remained the chief northern city if it had a reliable water supply. For this reason, and other more elaborate political intrigues involving Governor Macquarie and Inspector Bigge, the capital was moved to Launceston, up the Tamar River, in 1825.

Because of its age, and its importance as a port in the 1830s and 1840s, George Town today still possesses several historical sites and buildings of interest. Entering the town on route A8, turn left into Macquarie Street. The **information centre** at the corner of Macquarie and Sorell Streets (☎ 03 6382 1700) is in the Old Watchhouse; built in 1843, it used to be the gaol and is now a folk museum.

Walking up MACQUARIE STREET, you come to Anne Street; turn left to **St Mary Magdalene** Anglican Church. Built in 1883 as the third church on this site, the graveyard contains interesting gravestones of early settlers. Further up Macquarie Street you find several early residences; at Windmill Point is a monument to William Paterson, founder of the town in 1804. Continuing the walk, turn right at Cimitiere Street, to no. 25, '**The Grove**'. Situated in an excellent Old World garden, 'The Grove' was built c 1827 for the Port Officer, Matthew Curling Friend. It is a good example of a Georgian building, with Tuscan portico and columns.

Franklin House

6km south of Launceston on the road back to Hobart is **Franklin House** in **Franklin Village** (☎ 03 6344 7824; open daily 09.00–17.00). It is most easily reached by driving east on Bass Highway until this becomes Normanstone Road at an intersection known as Six Ways; here turn left on to Hobart Road, drive through the suburb of Kings Meadow, and in the village of Franklin, the house is on the left.

History

The first house owned by the National Trust in Tasmania, Franklin House was, like Clarendon, built in 1838. Not nearly as grandiose in scale or pretension, Franklin House was built on speculation by brewer and innkeeper Britton Jones on 4 ha across the road from the inn. Jones stated in his initial advertisement for the sale of the property that the house has 'all the appurtenances fit for the reception of a respectable family and are finished without regard to expenses, by the proprietor in a manner not to be surpassed in this colony'.

First owned by George Horne, a keen gardener, its grounds were well established when it was purchased by William Keeler Hawkes (1804–82) in

1842. Hawkes, with his wife and three spinster sisters, arrived in Launceston in April of that year, with the intention of establishing a school. This house served for some 40 years as a boarding school, and became the leading educational institution of the colony. A strict disciplinarian, Hawkes was, in keeping with his time, free with the stick. In 40 years of teaching, according to guides at the house, he only caused the death of one student!

After Hawkes's death (he and his family are buried in the cemetery of St James's Church across the street) the house passed through several hands until it was purchased by the National Trust in 1960. At that time it was renamed Franklin House; the house has no direct connection to Sir John and Lady Jane Franklin (although two rosewood chairs in the dining room supposedly belonged to her).

The informative brochure available at the house gives an elaborate explanation for the choice of furnishings used in the presently restored building. It is argued that, although officially built during Victoria's reign, the house itself is actually Late Georgian, probably built from English plans, and that furniture from earlier eras would be more readily available in the colonies; thus, the furniture selected for display is period rather than Victorian. Some rare early Tasmanian pieces are included, as well as several fine examples of English furniture and clockwork.

Great care has been taken in preserving the original fittings and surfaces. Of particular note are the floors and other wooden fittings of Australian cedar which Jones had imported from New South Wales. This wood was so sought after as one of the best native hardwoods that today no substantive cedar forests survive. Plantation grown cedar, heritage conservators mention, is lighter because it is harvested at a young age. The upstairs reception room is especially noteworthy, and includes the original floor-to-ceiling room partitions which were found languishing in the stables. Another interesting piece is the 18C Welsh bacon cupboard in the kitchen, made of oak and containing the original meat hooks at the back. To the side of the original house is the schoolroom added by Hawkes in 1842.

Hobart to Richmond

An alternative route from Hobart north to Oatlands (see p 432) includes several sites of historical interest. These sites will be included on several of the coach day-tours to the area; check with the Hobart Visitor's Centre for a variety of tour options. If travelling by car, leave Hobart heading north on Highway 1 c 6km to Goodwood Road/Bowen Bridge (route B35); proceed right across the bridge and immediately turn right on to route C324 towards Risdon Vale; at this juncture is the **Risdon Cove Historic Site**, the location of Tasmania's first settlement in 1803. A visitor's centre contains interesting relics and displays. Ironically, Risdon is also the site of Tasmania's only current prison, a pink Victorian structure that you can see from the Historic Site. Risdon Cove itself is now Aboriginal land, having been returned recently to the Tasmanian Aboriginal community. The site will be used for Aboriginal cultural events, and may on occasion be closed to the public. The Aboriginal community are preparing plans for the future use of the site; ☎ 03 6234 8311 for details.

Richmond

Return to route C324 and continue north 12km to the town of **Richmond** (population 587). Richmond is a charming town, laid back, with a mucky little river, imbued with the Tasmanian desire to emulate an English village. Until 1872, when the Sorell Causeway connected Hobart and Port Arthur directly, Richmond was the major crossroads en route to the Tasman Peninsula. Since then, it has become a sleepy rural village, and now a tourist destination, with many substantial buildings dating from the 1830s and 1840s. **Tourist information centre**: 48 Bridge Street, ☎ 03 6260 2132.

Entering the town, **Prospect House** (☎ 03 6260 2207) is on the left. Now a well-known restaurant and a heritage accommodation property, it was built in the 1830s by James Buscombe, a local innkeeper who was responsible for several of the other Georgian-style buildings in the town.

Turn right on to Henry Street, site of the **Richmond Hotel**, then left into Torrens Street. Here is an old sandstone school designed by John Lee Archer in 1834, and the old Congregational burial ground with many gravestones from the last century. Further along the same street, at no. 26, is St Luke's Anglican Church, another of Archer's designs from 1834. Built of local sandstone, the church has a square, three-level tower with a clock; made in England in 1828, it was in Hobart's St David's before being brought here in 1922.

The **bridge** across the Coal River at Richmond is Australia's oldest existing bridge. Completed in 1823 using convict labour, it spans 41.5 metres. Much of its charm springs from its irregularity; the arches are not uniform and one span humps at the corner.

St John's Church, on St John's Circle, is the oldest Roman Catholic church in Australia. The foundation stone was laid in August 1835. Designed by convict architect Frederick Thomas, the nave was built in 1836, the rest in 1839, and the spire in the 1900s. It is famed for its polished brown wood ceilings.

Richmond **gaol** (☎ 03 6260 2127; open daily 09.00–17.00) predates Port Arthur, having been built in 1825 to house both local convicts and convict road gangs. The complex is nearly intact and unaltered. While the earliest elements, the original gaol and gaoler's house, were probably designed by Colonial Architect David Lambe, the additional wings were added by John Lee Archer.

Evidence of Richmond's early prominence is the complex of public buildings, including municipal buildings, court house, watch house and hall situated near the gaol, and a number of fine inns and hotels dating from the early days of settlement. In about 1832 James Buscombe built a group of buildings at 36–8 Bridge Street, now the Old Store and Granary Group. The plethora of granaries and mills in the region indicate the significance of wheat production to its economy in the 19C.

Leave Richmond via route B31 north towards Campania (6km), then proceed 40km to connect at Jericho with the Midland Highway.

Launceston to Devonport and along the northwest coast

From Launceston, head south and connect with BASS HIGHWAY (Highway 1) to travel west. Pass through Hadspen and turn left onto route B52 to come to Entally House (18km). Built in 1819 for Thomas Haydock Reibey, son of Thomas and Mary Reibey (see p 130), **Entally House** (☎ 03 6393 6201; open daily 10.00–16.30; the Launceston city bus from Patterson Street has a stop near the house) is one of the oldest of the Tasmanian houses belonging to the National Trust. Involved in family shipping interests, Reibey arrived in Tasmania in 1816 and received a 2600-acre (1052 ha) land grant where he built this house, named after the family home in Sydney, which had itself been named in honour of a Calcutta suburb. The house and its immediate surrounds reflect his character as an outdoorsman devoted to horses and hounds. Reibey's son Thomas (1821–1912) would become Archdeacon of Launceston and in 1876, premier of Tasmania: an extraordinary example of Australian achievement, given Mary Reibey's convict origins.

Entally, unlike Clarendon or Franklin House, was not built on English Georgian models, but is one of the first examples of the wide-verandahed, sloped-roof single-storey dwellings so identified with Australian rural architecture. Opened to the public in 1950, Entally House contains a fine collection of Regency furniture and is set in well-restored gardens and grounds, with many interesting outbuildings, including a small bluestone chapel and a coach house.

Return to Bass Highway and continue west through Carrick and Hagley (site of a famous experimental school) and **Westbury**, another Historic Town.

49km from Launceston, at the junction of Bass and Lake Highways, is **Deloraine** (population 2100). Astride the Meander River in a valley dominated by Quamby Bluff, Deloraine was considered in the 1950s by Emmett to be the prettiest inland town in Tasmania. The town derived its name from its surveyor Thomas Scott, who was inspired by his kinsman Sir Walter Scott's *The Lay of the Last Minstrel*, in which Sir William Deloraine seeks the hand of the Lady of Branksome Hall. In 1856, it was surveyed to become the terminus for the first railway line from Launceston; the line was not completed until 1871, and was always a source of great political debate. **Tourist information**: 29 West Church Street, ☎ 03 6362 2046. Entering town from the Bass Highway, on the right at 98 Emu Bay Road is the **Folk Museum**, originally the Coaching Inn, 1865; it houses local memorabilia and agricultural artefacts. Continue south, turn left (west) on West Parade. On the left is Bonney's Inn; established in 1831, it is the first brick building and inn in Deloraine. The **Deloraine Racecourse** is the oldest continuously used track in Australia.

Devonport

Continue now north on Bass Highway 50km to **Devonport** (population 22,700). This far northwestern tip of the island is extremely well-watered and heavily timbered in its interior. The wetter areas on the west-facing slopes are dominated by myrtle and sassafras with stringybark and peppermint eucalypts above 600m and gum-topped stringy barks below this line. Where the soil is relatively infertile, scrub and heath plants prevail. The better soils are eroded tertiary basalt flows from the north–south-running Dundas Trough and Pre-Cambrian sedimentary deposits from the coast to the Donaldson River. **Tourist information**: 5 Best Street; ☎ 03 6424 4466.

After agriculture, timber and mining are the prevalent industries in this region. The production of decorative timbers is increasingly replacing the more destructive practices of the recent past. Numerous joineries and furniture manufacturers have showrooms in Burnie, Ulverstone and Devonport, among other locations.

Emmett's comments on Tasmania's northern coastline made during his walking tour of the island in the 1950s still apply:

> *If I attempted to write of each town of the rich northwest that I passed through or stayed at, I should be risking tedium for the reader, for they are, in a sense, made of the same last; though I wish to make it plain that the journey is through perhaps the very sweetest farming country in the whole of Australia.*

Devonport is the landing point of the **ferry from Melbourne**; those arriving in Tasmania by ferry will indeed want to follow this route in reverse order to Launceston. The Devonport Airport, 4km east of town, has regular flights arriving from Melbourne. Located on the Mersey River (called in the 1820s the 'Second Western River'), Devonport is named after the English county. It was originally founded in the 1840s as two towns, Formby on the west bank of the river and Torquay on the east.

Of special interest here is **Tiagarra** (☎ 03 6424 8250; open daily 09.00–17.00), the Tasmanian Aboriginal Culture and Art Centre. The centre's displays describe the life of Tasmanian Aborigines prior to European contact. A map of the locations of adjacent rock art sites allows you to view Aboriginal carvings in rocks of the Bluff. The centre is located on the north edge of town at the top of William Street.

Devonport was also the home of Sir Joseph and Dame Enid Lyons; their residence **'Home Hill'**, 77 Middle Road (☎ 03 6424 3028; open Tues–Thurs, weekends 14.00–16.00), is now open to the public. Joseph Lyons (1879–1939) became in 1931 Australia's only Tasmanian-born Prime Minister. His wife Enid Lyons (1897–1981), became the first woman to hold Federal Cabinet rank, while also raising ten children.

From Devonport head west on Bass Highway 12km to **Ulverstone** (population 14,000); from here turn on to the Old Bass Highway for a scenic drive along the rugged coastline to **Penguin** (population 3000), a further 12km. Along with the roadside Giant Penguin, Penguin abounds in penguin symbols, honouring the Fairy Penguins that come ashore nearby. Several walking tracks along the cliffs are well posted for visitors; maps of the tracks are available from Penguin Council Chambers, Main Street, ☎ 03 6437 1421. South of Ulverstone on road B17 beyond Gunns Plains are caves with limestone formations (open daily 10.00–16.00).

From Penguin travel west along the coastal drive 15km to **Burnie** (population 21,000), the largest town in the northwest of the state. Founded on the deep water port of Emu Bay, Burnie was named in 1841 after William Burnie, a director of the Van Diemen's Land Company. Now an important industrial centre, it is the home of the Associated Pulp and Paper Mills and Lactos Cheese. **Tourist information centre**: Little Alexander Street, ☎ 03 6434 6111.

On entering town, turn right on Alexander Street. Turn left on Jones Street to **Pioneer Village and Museum** (☎ 03 6430 5746; open weekdays 09.00–17.00, weekends & holidays 13.30–16.30), a reconstruction of Burnie's early buildings and shops. Further along Alexander Street, at Wilmot Street is the Civic Centre and **Regional Art Gallery** (☎ 03 6431 5918; open weekdays 09.00–17.00, weekends 13.30–16.30), housing a small collection and occasional travelling exhibitions. Continue north on Alexander Street, turn left at North Terrace. Burnie Park will be on the left at York Street. The park includes extensive rose gardens and Burnie Inn, the town's oldest building, re-erected and restored in the park in 1973.

Continue west on North Terrace, which becomes Bass Highway. At Somerset (7km), route A10 continues south to Tullah and Queenstown. Further west (9km) on route A1 is **Wynyard** (population 4582). Located on the Inglis River, Wynyard was once the principal port of the northwest; its airport has daily flights to Melbourne. It is now the centre of a prosperous farming region, with beautiful gardens and interesting natural surroundings.

7km north of town on route C234 is **Fossil Bluff**, a fascinating geographical formation and for a time the site of the discovery of the oldest marsupial fossil. Continue west on route C234 to Table Cape, a volcanic rock some 170 metres above the sea, offering stunning coastal views. Return to Bass Highway and proceed 31km west to **Rocky Cape National Park** (☎ 03 6458 1415). The cape itself was named by Bass and Flinders who first saw it in 1798. The park consists of 3000 ha of heathland, with several walking trails, a bird sanctuary, and rich Aboriginal sites, in particular a shell midden in the north cave. You can also see from the lighthouse point at the end of the cape the first view of 'The Nut', the famed rock at Stanley.

Stanley

Return to the Bass Highway and continue west 26km; turn north on to route B21 and travel 7km to **Stanley** (population 588). Just before entering the town, turn left into the Scenic Drive, Dove Cote Road and follow signs to **'Highfield'** (☎ 03 6458 1100; open daily 10.00–17.00 Oct–Apr, 10.00–16.00 May–July), the original homestead of the director of the Van Diemen's Land Company. Designed in 1832 by surveyor Henry Hellyer, the house and grounds have now been restored.

Drive into town to the north. Dominated by the volcanic plug 'Circular Head', more popularly known as **'The Nut'**, this small village was settled in 1825 as the headquarters for Van Diemen's Land Company. Recently declared a Historic Town, Stanley has several interesting early structures, including on Alexander Terrace the birthplace of Joseph Lyons, the only Tasmanian Prime Minister, and several houses built by the ubiquitous colonial architect John Lee Archer, who died here in 1852. Alexander Terrace includes several other historic houses and inns. Archer's own home, known as 'Poet's Cottage', sits at the base of The Nut. The Stanley Burial Ground on Browns Road contains Archer's own grave and headstone. On Church Street visit the **Plough Inn**, restored as a craft centre; next door is the **Discovery Centre**, now a folk-museum and gallery (☎ 03 6458 1145; open daily 10.00–16.00, closed June–Aug). Entering The Nut Reserve, you can take a chairlift to the top for a breathtaking, if windswept, panoramic view. Stanley is the site of the Circular Head Arts Festival, held every September.

The Bass Highway continues 22km west to **Smithton** (population 3495), the administrative centre of the far northwest in a rich forestry area. The highway ends a further 51km west at Marrawah, the most westerly town in Tasmania. Author Bernard Cronin ran cattle here at the beginning of the century; the isolated region is well described in his five novels, including *The Coastlanders* (1918) and *Timber Wolves* (1920), referring to the hardwood forests so prized here. This area marks the beginning of the densely forested regions of Tasmania's western coast.

Northeast from Hobart to Swansea

From Hobart, take route A3 across the Tasman Bridge and on to **Sorell**, 27km from the centre of town. Named after Governor Sorell, the town was founded in 1821 and is one of the earliest sites for the cultivation of grain in the state. The main bus companies from Hobart and some local companies have runs between Swansea, Coles Bay, Bicheno, St Marys, St Helens and Derby. Service on weekends is very limited. Cycling along the east coast is a very popular way to travel as well (cycle rental can be arranged in Hobart). Note that banking facilities along the coast are extremely limited, and ATM facilities are (or were at the time of writing) non-existent.

37km further north on route A3 is **Buckland**, known for **St John the Baptist Church**. The church contains a stained-glass window which by local legend is said to date from the 14C, from a church on the field where the Battle of Hastings took place! A local brochure attempts to substantiate this claim on the basis of a *terminus post quem*, arguing that the glass was in place before 1848, before which reproduction of such glass was not possible. Emmett in 1952 maintains that it was actually commissioned by the minister of the church, a Reverend Cox, in the 1850s. Despite any arguments, the church is a lovely example of a small provincial Anglican church, complete with local graveyard which seems to have specialised in ceramic rose arrangements attached to the tombstones.

At **Orford**, 18km further east, you reach the eastern coastline, dominated by a view over to **Maria Island National Park** (☎ 03 6257 1420). From **Triabunna**, 7km further along route A3, you can take a fascinating trip by ferry to the island, which has remnants of an old convict settlement. It is possible to arrange camping on the island overnight, where there is no electricity or facilities. The island is the only national park in Tasmania where all 11 of the state's native bird species are visible, including Cape Barren geese and emus.

From Triabunna, travel 51km north along the coast to Swansea, with outstanding views out to sea and past many beautiful beaches ideal for picnics. Outside Swansea c 8km south is **Spiky Bridge**, built in 1843 by convicts; the spikes are of local crystalline rock. The beach here gives a tremendous view of **Oyster Bay**, down to Maria Island and over to the famous Hazards of Freycinet Peninsula (see below).

Also on the Tasman Highway, 12km south of Swansea, is **Kabuki by the Sea** (☎ 03 6257 8588), a Japanese restaurant revelling in the use of superb Tasmanian seafood and produce.

Swansea

Swansea (population 400) is the centre of Glamorgan, the oldest rural municipality in Australia. The town includes a **local historical museum** (open daily 10.00–16.00) and community centre, housed in an 1850s schoolhouse, which is a marvellous example of a home-grown collection. Along with an eclectic collection of artefacts donated by local residents—some of them connected with the region and others as varied as Fijian baskets and German swords captured in the First World War—are two portraits of members of the Meredith family by Thomas Bock, several books by Louisa Anne Meredith, and local watercolours by 19C artists, very few of which have been identified. The place is a conservator's nightmare and an historian's paradise.

The Merediths of Swansea

Swansea was so named by first settler George Meredith (1778–1856), who came with his servants, John and Adam Amos, in 1821. A son by his first marriage, Charles (1811–80), accompanied him, and would later become a prominent politician in the state. In 1838, Charles returned to England and married his cousin, Louisa Anne Twamley (1812–95); in 1840 the couple settled north of Swansea, at George Meredith's property, Riversdale. Louisa Anne Meredith became a prolific writer and artist; her *My Home in Tasmania* (1852) and *Bush Friends in Tasmania* (1860) with delightful illustrations still provide remarkable insights into 19C Tasmania. Another Meredith property, 'Cambria', built in the late 1820s, still remains, 2km north of Swansea.

The museum also includes an anomalous **billiard table**. Built to order by the premier billiard table makers, Alcock Thomas & Taylor of Melbourne, for the 1879 International Exhibition, the table had to be built larger than standard size, because the half-a-ton slab sent from Italy was too big, and the local craftsmen deemed it too risky to alter; the frame is of a single Tasmanian hardwood. It is still available for play, at $2 a game, although, as the present caretaker states, the only takers are a regular group of elderly men. The table is a splendid example of the skill of Alcock's (see Melbourne, p 296), and the museum is worth a visit.

From Swansea, it is about 10km along Nine Mile Beach to **Freycinet National Park** (☎ 03 6257 0107). This 10,000 ha park begins 2km south of Coles Bay. Its most prominent feature is a huge granite rock known as **The Hazards**. Mount Freycinet is the highest point at 614m. The park contains a wide number of orchid species, as well as other heathland plants and birds. There are secluded sandy beaches, and a variety of excellent walks with views to the sea. Off the coast 1km across Schouten Passage and also part of the park is **Schouten Island**, named by Abel Tasman in 1642 after a member of the Dutch East India Company; the island can be visited by boat.

There is a fee (at the time of writing, $9) and an excellent park brochure at the gate. You will need to supply your own water. The park is named after Louis Freycinet (1779–1842), French naval officer on Baudin's *Le Naturaliste*, who in 1802 explored throughout this region. Freycinet is best remembered for his round-the-world voyage in command of *L'Uranie* in 1818, during which time his wife Rose disguised herself as a man in order to accompany him and kept a lively account of her most extraordinary journey, *Journal de Madame Rose de Saulces de Freycinet* (1927).

Some 42km north of the park is **Bicheno** (pronounced BEE-sh'n-O), a very popular beach resort, known for its fishing and scuba diving. In town is the

Sealife Centre (☎ 03 6375 1082; open daily 09.00–17.00), a quaint little aquarium including an old Tasmanian-built timber boat, *Enterprise* on display. This part of the coast contains some of the best oyster beds in the world, as well as crayfish and abalone fishing; new restaurants cater to this cuisine, making it an ideal destination for seafood-lovers. **Tourist information**: Tasman Highway, ☎ 03 6375 1333. The information centre also arranges nightly penguin tours of about a one-hour duration.

From Launceston northeast to St Marys

This route through northeastern Tasmania has some bus services during the week, but weekend services are very spotty, if they run at all. One road to Scottsdale from Launceston is route B81, which leads 27km north to **Lilydale** (population 357). 7km before the town is **Hollybank Forest Centre**, a lovely reserve of ash trees on the site of an 1855 sawmill; it is now run by the Forestry Commission and is open to the public from October to May. Lilydale itself is best known for **Bridestowe Lavender Farm**, a long-standing and productive source of lavender oil and sachets, considered the purest product in the country. It produces over 2 tonnes of lavender oil annually.

The 41km from Lilydale to Scottsdale is through heavy bush with craft shops and wineries along the way. **Scottsdale** (population 1980), settled in the 1850s by surveyor James Scott, is the centre of the northeast's dairying region. One interesting stop in town is **Anabel's**, 46 King Street (☎ 03 6352 3277), in an 1890 Federation building classified by the National Trust and set in elegant gardens with a 12m wistaria walk and rhododendron trees; it is now a restaurant and four-star hotel.

21km north of Scottsdale on route B84 is **Bridport** (population 980), a popular fishing village on the Bass Strait with excellent picnic beaches and some tremendous views from nearby Waterhouse Point out to the strait and including Waterhouse Island.

An example of the area's early architecture can be seen at **'Bowood'**, c 12km northwest of Bridport on route B82, at the Little Forester River. Built in 1839 for Peter Brewer, the house was constructed by ex-convict carpenter James Edwards and an American sealer Robert Rhodes, who in the 1830s jumped ship to stay in the region; Rhodes' headstone nearby states that he was from Philadelphia and died here in 1863. 'Bowood' is a private residence, but interesting to view in situ, along what used to be the Launceston Road.

From Launceston, the TASMAN HIGHWAY (route A3) also continues north 70km to Scottsdale, then east through dairy and hops country that used to be one of the biggest timber regions of the state until the trees were forested to stoke the fires of the nearby tin mines. The area from **Branxholme**, 25km east of Scottsdale, to Pyengana and east to the coast was from the 1870s to the 1950s a booming tin-mining centre.

The town of **Derby**, 8km east of Branxholme, has a **Tin Mine Museum** (☎ 03 6354 2262), 'Shantytown' historical village, and views to the old Briseis mine face (named after the 1876 Melbourne Cup winner).

Weldborough, c 14km south along route A3, was also a mining centre; its old **Chinese Joss House**, now in Launceston's Queen Victoria Museum, is evidence of the thousands of Chinese miners who came to the region during the tin boom, many of whom stayed on in Tasmania. To the south of Weldborough is **Maa Mon Chin Dam**, named for a leader of the Chinese community who arrived in 1875. At Weldborough Pass, 595m high, is the Weldborough Pass Scenic Reserve (☎ 03 6376 1550), a 20-minute walk through myrtle forests that offers spectacular views of the valley and out to the sea.

Pyengana, 19km south of Weldborough, is known for cheese and as the site, 13km south on route C428, of **St Colombia Falls**, the state's tallest waterfall, cascading 110m on to the rocks below. The falls take their name from the property here of the Quaker family Cotton, who arrived in 1828. In the 1870s, Margaret Cotton set up one of the island's first apple exporting businesses. To the east of here, the near ghost towns of Goshen, Goulds Country, and Lottah hearken back to the days of open tin-mining of the Blue Tier Mountain, now closed.

St Helens (population 1200), 18km southeast of Goshen, is one of the most popular seaside resorts in Tasmania, known for its beaches around Georges Bay and its temperate climate. The town's main thoroughfare is CECILIA STREET; at no. 57 is the **Local History Room** (☎ 03 6376 1329; open Mon–Fri 09.00–16.00, Sat 09.00–13.00), which is also the **information centre** where you can get a detailed brochure about the town's history. The History Room contains a quintessential conglomeration of local artefacts, including a black hat worn by local coach driver George Avery when in the 1880s he drove the Duke of Edinburgh through the region. Cecilia Street and side streets include other 19C buildings, including St Paul's Church of England, built in 1884, the 1874 District High School around the corner on Groom and Circassian Streets, and, at no. 5 Cecilia Street, an 1870 weatherboard house. Surveyor George Frankland, who laid out the town in the 1840s, endowed the streets and places with lofty Greek names, such as Golden Fleet Rivulet and Medeas Cove. Route C851 leads over Golden Fleece Bridge to Jasons Gates and on to **St Helens Point** at the end of Georges Bay, a state recreation ground. This is a great location for bushwalking and, again, this area is one of the best places to sample Tasmania's superb seafood.

Continue south on route A3 along the coast, passing through the resort town of Scamander, known for bream fishing in the Scamander River. At St Marys Pass, 10km south of Scamander, is a turn-off to **Falmouth**, 3km further east; it is an historic village with several convict-built structures, as well as great views both of the coast and of the mountains south through Elephant Pass.

The picturesque village of **St Marys** (population 668) sits at the junction of the Tasman Highway (route A3) and the Esk Main Road (route A4) and is at the headwaters of the South Esk River. Originally known as 'Break O'Day Plains', the town is now at the centre of a coal-mining region and is a major depot for the distribution of hydro-electric power.

Continue on route A4 to Fingal, 21km west of St Marys. Along the road, c 10km, is **'Killymoon'**, built between 1842 and 1848, by Frederick von Stieglitz, with Tuscan portico and substantial brick-walled gardens. The property is a marvellous example of the grandiose homestead mansions so characteristic of Tasmania.

2km north of Fingal is **'Malahide'**, a Georgian stone house built for original settler William Talbot in 1828. With a name like Fingal, it is not surprising that the place was founded by an Irishman, Roderic O'Connor, who arrived in

Tasmania on his own ship the *Ardent* in 1824; his cargo included the first free Irish immigrants to the state. On Talbot Street in town is the Fingal Hotel (also the **tourist information centre**, ☎ 03 6374 2121), formerly the Talbot Arms, built in 1844; true to its Celtic tradition, the hotel has the largest collection of Scotch Whisky in the Southern emisphere, 348 different brands acquired since the Second World War.

Route A4 continues on from here 27km to **Avoca**, at the junction of the South Esk and St Pauls Rivers. The village's St Thomas Church of England of 1842 is a local landmark, attributed because of its Romanesque Revival style to James Blackburn.

From Avoca, you can take route B42 c 11km to the foot of Ben Lomond; walking tracks at Rossarden lead to the top of the mountain. On the same road c 8km a turn-off leads to '**Bona Vista**', a late Georgian style homestead built in 1845 for the famed ex-convict Simeon Lord; at one time, the bushranger Martin Cash was a horse-groom here. Back on the A4, the road continues 26km to connect with the Midland Highway at Conara Junction.

Hobart to Strahan

Leave Hobart on Highway 1 towards Launceston; at Granton/Bridgewater, continue west on route A10 towards **New Norfolk** (38km), another of the towns founded by Governor Macquarie and named Elizabeth Town after his wife. It became New Norfolk after the arrival of settlers from Norfolk Island in the 1820s. Entering town, turn right at signs for **Tynewald** and **Oast House** (☎ 03 6261 1030; open Wed–Sun 09.00–17.00); originally one estate, Tynewald is now a guest house and Oast House, originally the drying kilns for the extensive hop fields of the estate, is now a museum depicting the history of hop-growing in the region.

Returning to the main highway, continue west past Lachlan River. At Bathurst Street on the left, note **St Matthew's Anglican Church**; dating from 1823, it is the oldest Anglican church in Tasmania. Of special interest here is the lovely church garden.

Further west on the main highway to the right are **Old Colony Inn** (☎ 03 6261 2731; open daily, 09.00–17.00; winter 10.00–16.00), c 1835, now a restaurant and museum, and **The Bush Inn** (☎ 03 6261 2011), c 1815, which is reputed to be the oldest continuously licensed inn in Australia, although this seems to be a hotly sought-after title by several old hotels.

From New Norfolk, you can take route B62 to B61, which leads 115km west to Strathgordon and the Gordon River Power Station, where the road ends at Lake Gordon in the wilderness of the **Southwest National Park** (☎ 03 6288 1283). 35km along the road is the entrance to **Mount Field National Park** (☎ 03 6288 1149), Tasmania's oldest national park, preserved since 1863. Only 80km from Hobart, the park is one of the most visited in the state, offering great rock-climbing and bushwalking amidst the waterfalls, Huon pine, and ancient gum trees. About 50km further, immediately after passing through Strathgordon is McPartlan Pass, where a lookout enables you to see both **Lake Gordon** to the north and **Lake Pedder** to the south.

The Southwest National Park is 605,213 ha of rugged, remote wilderness, penetrable only by the fittest and most tenacious of campers and walkers. Its World Heritage status acknowledges it as a 'site of outstanding universal value' under the UNESCO World Heritage Convention. Also included in this World Heritage Area here are the Franklin–Lower Gordon Wild Rivers National Park and the Cradle Mountain–Lake St Clair National Park.

You get some idea of the overwhelming expanse and remoteness of the region when you learn that the Gordon and Serpentine Rivers here were first explored by Lithuanian-born **Olegas Truchanas** as recently as 1958. Truchanas' photographs are world-famous, gracing many a wilderness society calendar.

Lake Pedder

In 1972, the flooding of Lake Pedder by the Hydro-Electric Commission led to the establishment of the **Tasmanian Wilderness Society**, and the beginning of landmark conservationist battles that brought international attention to the region and saw the first coalescence of an effective environmental movement. While the Greens were unable to prevent the destruction of Lake Pedder, their activities now took on the authority that sought to dam the Lower Gordon River, destroying the wilderness of the Franklin River. The controversy led to the Franklin Blockade, spearheaded by the Wilderness Society's Dr Bob Brown, now a Federal senator. Years of campaigns and protests, in which the environmentalists fought not only the authorities but hostile locals who resented the loss of possible employment on the project, finally saw the entire southwest territory declared a World Heritage site in 1981.

In 1983, after the election of the Labor Hawke government, all further incursions into the region by the HEC were stopped by a High Court decision. The fervent sentiments surrounding these events are expressed by novelist James McQueen in his *The Franklin: Not Just a River* (1981) and Bob Connolly's *The Fight for the Franklin* (1981).

One of the best ways to experience this vast area if you do not want rigorous and extended trekking is to take a flight across the region. Two airlines operate flights to Melaleuca from Cambridge, 15km outside Hobart. Check with the tourist information office in Hobart, or ☎ 03 6248 5390 or ☎ 03 6248 5088.

The LYELL HIGHWAY (route A10) to the western coastline proceeds from New Norfolk north towards **Derwent Bridge**. Continue 34km to the village of **Hamilton**, described by Emmett in 1954 as 'change and decay in all I see', but by Odgers in 1989 as 'one of the most charming yet sleepy of the southernmost towns'. Tourism has led to the encouraging restoration of originally derelict buildings, including several 19C cottages now offering bed-and-breakfast accommodation. On the right of the main street is **Glen Clyde House**, a restored inn with craft gallery and tea rooms.

Continue north on the A10 through Ouse (14km) and on to Tarraleah (33km), centre of the **Tarraleah-Tungatinah Hydro-electric Scheme**, which channels water from the Upper Derwent River and Lake St Clair.

Follow the A10 further north towards Bronte Lagoon; c 50m after the turn-off to route C173 is a surveyors' monument marking the geographical centre of Tasmania. From Bronte Park, it is 26km to Derwent Bridge, the final stop before entering the Western Tasmania Wilderness National Parks Area; it also marks the southern end of the **Cradle Mountain/Lake St Clair National Park** (☎ 03 6424 7833), a vast wilderness area famed for its rugged walking trails, including the 85km **Overland Track** known to all serious bushwalkers. **Lake St Clair** itself is over 17km long and 200 metres deep. The **visitor's centre** (☎ 03 6492 1133; daily 08.00–17.00) has a number of maps and pamphlets describing the area. Lake cruises and trekking expeditions can be booked here as well. For those who would like a less arduous walk, several two-hour-long trails start at the Waldheim Chalet and at Lake Dover.

From Derwent Bridge, route A10 now continues west into the forested terrain of Western Tasmania; the 83km road to Queenstown has no shops, service stations or telephones, and can be hazardous in snowy weather. Not completed until 1932, the road now passes through the **Franklin-Lower Gordon Wild Rivers National Park** (☎ 03 6471 7122), the centre of Tasmania's World Heritage Area and known for its wilderness walks and white-water rapids. Short walking trails to spectacular lookouts and through rainforests are also accessible from the highway for less adventurous travellers.

At Lake Burbury, the highway skirts the lake, offering stupendous mountain views before driving down the steep slopes of Mount Owen past the once-thriving mining towns of Gormanston and Linda, and into the bizarre scenery surrounding Queenstown itself.

Queenstown

Queenstown (population 3600) was established as a mining town in 1896. Literally carved out of the mountains, Queenstown came into being when huge mineral resources were discovered at Mount Lyell. The field so far has produced 670,000 tonnes of copper, 510,000 kg of silver and 20,000 kg of gold. Copper Mines of Tasmania employs most of the town's inhabitants. **Tourist information centre**: 1 Driffield Street, ☎ 03 6471 2388.

As one commentator has noted, modern-day visitors to Queenstown will think they have landed on the moon, for the surrounding hills are entirely barren of vegetation and riddled with weirdly coloured craters, a result of defor-estation and the sulphur mining processes of the past. Recent efforts by the mining company to refoliate the hills have, it is rumoured, been thwarted by residents who recognise that their eerie landscape is their greatest claim to fame and the attraction of tourist dollars.

Upon entering the town, the highway becomes Batchelor Street and then turns left into Driffield Street. On the left at the corner of Sticht and Driffield Streets is the **Galley Museum** (☎ 03 6471 1483, open weekdays 10.00–16.30, weekends 13.00–16.30), a delightfully idiosyncratic collection begun by local eccentric Eric Thomas. A conglomeration of old photographs, telephones, beds, and china, the museum offers an appropriately off-beat introduction to the area's history. Across the street from the museum is **Miners' Siding**, an equally eclectic display of mining equipment and ore samples, as well as a set of bronze sculptures by local artist Stephen Walker which were cast in Queenstown. At the corner of Driffield and Ore Streets is the Empire Hotel, one of the only surviving hotels from Queenstown's heyday at the beginning of the century, when the town boasted 14 hotels. Three-and-a-half-hour-long tours of the mine are also available, departing from the Western Arts and Crafts Centre, 1 Driffield Street (☎ 03 6471 2388). The number of people on the tour is limited to six, so book in advance. This is one of the few working mines allowing tours to the working face.

To travel to the coastal town of Strahan, turn left just beyond Miners' Siding where the Murchison Highway begins and west on to route B24; Strahan is at the end of the road, 38km away.

Strahan (population 575), named after Tasmanian governor Sir George Strahan, is picturesquely situated on Macquarie Harbour. Originally the centre of Huon pine milling, it became a booming port during the early mining years and with the establishment of the Strahan–Zeehan railway in 1892. Today tourism is the major industry, as the town is the starting point for the popular **Gordon River cruises**, which circumnavigate **Macquarie Harbour**, passing by **Sarah Island** with its grim reminders of its early days as Tasmania's first and most treacherous penal prison. It was Macquarie Harbour's penal colony that was depicted by Marcus Clarke in his novel *For the Term of His Natural Life* (1874). Its inhumane horrors are most vividly described by Robert Hughes in *The Fatal Shore* (1987). Macquarie Harbour is still notoriously hazardous to navigate, with its narrow entrance and treacherous sandbars and waves that originated in South America.

Along the town's Esplanade is the elegant **Customs House**, one of the town's only substantial buildings; it now houses the **World Heritage Visitor's Centre**, part of the Department of Parks, Wildlife and Heritage (☎ 03 6471 7122; Mon–Fri 09.00–16.00) which offers a variety of tourist information. Strahan's **visitor's centre** (☎ 03 6471 7488, open daily 10.00–20.00, variable in winter) on the Esplanade will help with charter services. Further along the road is **Ormiston**, the residence built in 1902 by Strahan eccentric F.O. Henry, known as the Duke of Avram. The area also includes several spectacular beaches, most impressively Ocean Beach which stretches for 33km. Of particular interest at Strahan to tourists is the availability of **seaplane tours**, which offer exhilarating views of the coastal landscape.

From the town turn left into route B27 towards Zeehan (which can also be reached direct from Queenstown), 47km north. **Zeehan** (population 1200) derives its name from Abel Tasman's ship, which passed by the coast in 1642 and sighted the peak named Mount Zeehan by later explorers Bass and Flinders. At the height of the mining boom in 1901, Zeehan had 26 hotels and a population over 5000; its near demise by the 1950s perhaps accounts for the air of melancholy which still pervades the town, despite it modest resurgence as a tourist destination and with the opening of Renison Bell tin mine. Of interest is the Zeehan School of Mines and Metallurgy, established in 1892 and now housing the **West Coast Pioneers' Memorial Museum** (open daily 08.30–18.00 Oct–Mar, 08.30–17.00 April–Sept). The museum has a characteristically eclectic assortment of mining paraphernalia, a mineral collection, a railway car, photos, stuffed animals and historical objects. Along the same street are many examples of buildings from the pioneer days, including the Gaiety Theatre where Nellie Melba and Lola Montez purportedly gave concerts.

South Australia

The predominant physical features of South Australia include the Great Australian Bight, the Nullarbor Plain and Great Victoria Desert, the Simpson Desert and Lake Eyre and the Sturt Desert. It is the driest state of the driest continent; as writer Geoffrey Dutton muses, 'Fate, it seems, did not want South Australia to have too much... South Australia was granted only one river and

that rising in the eastern states, almost no timber except the tough, twisted mallee, comparatively few minerals, and frontiers of sand or desolate scrub.'

The most densely populated areas are found around Spencer Gulf and Gulf St Vincent which are formed by Eyre Peninsula and Yorke Peninsula and Kangaroo Island. Although there are some modest highlands to the extreme northwest and north of Adelaide, most of the state is remarkably flat. The major river, the Murray, drops only 22m in 642km.

Physical curiosities include a basin of ancient sandstone in the Flinders Range called Wilpena Pound, volcanic craters and peaks near Mount Gambier, the cliffs of the Bight, and the normally dry inland lakes which infrequently fill to become lush and productive. The wet winters in the south allow eucalypt forests as well as the lush agricultural and wine-producing areas of the **Barossa Valley**, the **Clare Valley** and **McLaren Vale**. The wineries of these regions have greatly contributed to Australia's international reputation in the field of wine-making.

Mount Lofty is the highest point in the modest range of hills north of Adelaide. Currently a mere 700m high, it spent the Tertiary Period submerged. East to west lateral folding during the Cambrian Period established the area's basic structure. When the Mount Lofty Range rose as a horst, rift valleys along the north–south faults brought the sea inland along the western edge of the range as far as Lake Torrens. Spencer Gulf and Gulf St Lawrence are, in fact, rift valleys. The Lofty Range continues to run northward, eventually becoming the **Flinders Range**. The Barrier Highway from Adelaide through Gawler to Peterborough passes along this range.

North of the Flinders Range, arid dunes and flood plains become the norm with surface drainage to playas, the interior **salt lakes** named Torrens, Frome and Eyre. Lake Eyre is actually 16m below sea level, and is dry for years at a time. After heavy rains, the area quickly fills with water and generates a profusion of wildflowers, along with huge quantities of birds and native animals. The vegetation is scrub eucalypt mallee to this point. Past the line of annual rainfall below 25mm, the vegetation becomes tussock saltbush and blue bush with low wattle shrubs. The Great Victorian, Simpson and Sturt Stony Deserts mark the northern border from west to east. At the northernmost extent of the Flinders Range is the **Flinders Range National Park** and, after another 150km, **Gammon Ranges National Park**, a vast and rugged wilderness of gorges and geological sites that contain untold numbers of gemstones.

Wilpena Pound, near the Flinders Range National Park's southern entrance, is a geological curiosity. One of several oval basins atop mesas (flat-topped hills), Wilpena Pound is about 8km wide and 20km long. It appears to be a tiered amphitheatre of quartzite. The sole entrance is through a narrow gorge and across Sliding Rock. Nearby are Aboriginal rock carvings at Arkaroola Rock on the southern slope of Rawnsley Bluff and at Sacred Canyon on Hawker Road south and east of the Rawnsley Park Station. The spring wildflowers and verdant flora along small watercourses in the valley floors contrast with the stark desert mountain range. The colours in the strata range from purple to red to white.

The rock art at **Arkaroola Gorge** is accessible by permission at Arkaroola Village. The sinuous gorge is said to have been carved by the serpent from which it takes its name. The Proterozoic quartzite, granite and tillite of the surrounding canyons have eroded to form sheer rock walls and lovely pools. Scrubby eucalypt, acacia and yucca are the predominant flora, but wildflowers sprout after winter rains. The road from Hawker, 100km north of Port Augusta, to Parachilna is well-tended gravel.

The **Panaramitee Rock Art Site**, east of Leigh Creek in Gammon Ranges National Park, is in the Ngadjuri people's region. It dates from the Pleistocene era and may be as much as 30,000 years old. Like other engravings in the area, the motifs include tracks, circles and geometric forms in a style current in the central desert. Because the area is rugged and isolated, only bushwalkers experienced in arid conditions should consider travel here.

2700km long, the **Stuart Highway** crosses Australia from Port Augusta to Alice Springs, Northern Territory, and eventually Darwin. The major stops are **Woomera**, headquarters for the former British nuclear testing site; **Coober Pedy**, the well-known underground opal-mining town; **Alice Springs**, the railhead of the Ghan from Adelaide and gateway to Uluru and other desert Aboriginal areas; **Tennant Creek**, near the round granite rocks called the Devil's Marbles and Devil's Pebbles; and **Katherine**, a cattle station and RAAF airbase near Katherine Gorge rock art and an idyllic natural setting. Broadly, there are two reasons to undertake the drive across country. One is to have driven a long way across desert. The other is to have first-hand experience of Australian **desert-dwelling Aboriginal people** (for more information see p 594 in the Northern Territory section).

The Aboriginal presence, particularly in the desert areas, remains strong. Permits to travel are routinely required, though readily obtainable. The northwest of the state is **Pitjantjatjara land** and includes the Musgrave Ranges. To the south, the Great Victorian Desert is shared with the Maralinga people. Above-ground nuclear testing in the Woomera in the 1950s blighted some of their land. Along the Bight are the Wirangu. To their north and west are a number of desert-dwelling people, the most well known being the Pitjantjatjara in the state's extreme northwest. East of the Pitjantjatjara in the Simpson and Sturt Stony Deserts are the Witjira and Innamincka Reserves. This environment is on the whole extremely dry and hot with unreliable rainfall. Rockholes and dry river soaks provide water.

Indigenous people in the better-watered conditions of the south central regions traditionally included the Adnyamathanha who lived from Port Augusta north to the salt lakes along the windward face of the Flinders Range. Continuing south, the Narangga lived on Yorke Peninsula. Despite wet winters, they shared scant water resources with the other groups mentioned. Their environment consisted of mallee and coastal scrubs with some mangroves along the gulf coast. The Ngadjuri, Narangga and Nukunu living along the coastal wetlands enjoyed the best conditions, water and food being routinely available.

South Australia's **climate** is governed by low pressure fronts which bring colder moist air from the southwest. These usually come every seven to ten days in the summer and every three to five days in the winter. Summer temperatures can be excessive even in the milder southeastern corner and in Adelaide (although Adelaide's average maximum summer temperature is 29°C, it is not uncommon on some summer days for the thermometer to climb above 40°C). The Surveyor-General George Goyder demarcated the areas most likely to be affected by drought (rainfall below 350mm per year). They include all of the state except for the southwest portion of Eyre Peninsula, some of Yorke Peninsula and the far southeast corner of the state.

Colonial history

Although Europeans first sighted the South Australian coastline in 1627, when the Dutch ship *Gulden Zeepaard* reached as far as Nuyts Archipelago, no other white exploration occurred until 1792–93. In that year the French explorer Bruni d'Entrecasteaux discovered the head of the Australian Bight. It was not until Matthew Flinders's famous circumnavigation of Australia in 1802–04 that any detailed exploration of the area was carried out; in his ship *Investigator*, Flinders made a thorough study of the coast from Fowlers Bay to Encounter Bay, naming such sites as Port Lincoln, Spencer Gulf, Kangaroo Island, Gulf St Vincent, Yorke Peninsula, Mount Lofty, and Cape Jervis. Whalers and sealers had certainly already made some settlements along this coastline, particularly at Kangaroo Island, by the beginning of the 19C.

Unlike the history of the eastern states and Tasmania, South Australia owes its development to voluntary and private settlement, a fact of which the state is still quite proud—no convicts were ever transported here. The intention was to induce unemployed, working-class Britons to migrate to Australia where they would work for landowners until they had sufficient funds to buy land of their own. The state's first governor, Captain John Hindmarsh, established the colony upon his arrival in late December 1836. The first 300 settlers had arrived earlier aboard whalers' and surveyors' ships.

The intention to found a colony of free settlers from among the unemployed working class predates South Australia's establishment by six years. As early as 1830, amidst the fervour of Jeremy Bentham's notions of democratic idealism and the movement to reform Parliament, Edward Gibbon Wakefield (see box, p 459), Robert Gouger and a number of Trinity College liberals formed the **National Colonisation Society**. Its aim was to alleviate unemployment by founding a chartered colony under the auspices of the society, as opposed to those of the government. That South Australia was the chosen site was largely due to Charles Sturt's exploration (see box, p 461) and reports from whalers and seal hunters who had been using Kangaroo Island for many years before white settlement here.

The selection of Adelaide as the town site and its design by **Colonel William Light** (see box, p 461), the presentation of land orders and

Edward Wakefield

Edward Wakefield (1796–1862) had a chequered past. Well educated, from a Quaker family, he had worked for a time for the Foreign Service. Wakefield had twice abducted Quaker heiresses, the first time receiving a handsome annual settlement, the second time as a widower receiving a gaol sentence. In Newgate Gaol, Wakefield met his subsequent associates Robert Gouger and Major Anthony Bacon. While in prison he formed a theory of systematic colonisation in keeping with the current theories of self-improvement. At Newgate he also met sea captain Henry Dixon who was familiar with Kangaroo Island and adjacent southern Australia. In 1829, Wakefield published anonymously *Eleven Letters from Sydney*. As if written by a land-owner in New South Wales, it exposed the evils of the convict system and outlined a system whereby land in colonies could be sold, the proceeds assisting free immigrant settlers.

Upon his release in 1830, he formed the National Colonisation Society with Robert Gouger. When the society dissolved after merely a year, Wakefield looked to the Whig banking community and Major Anthony Bacon to form the South Australian Land Company. The Colonial Office rejected the radical notion that the chartered promoters of the enterprise should function as the colony's government. The bankers hesitated due to Bacon's role—he was a direct descendant of impeached Chancellor of the Exchequer Robert Harley.

At this point a group of radicals in Parliament suggested that their South Australian Association should act as trustees. The resulting legislation, the South Australian Act (1834), formed a vague relationship between the Colonial Office and a Board of Colonisation Commissioners. In addition to this novel administrative form, no convicts were to be sent to South Australia. The land was offered at 20 shillings per acre, then, because of poor response, at 12 shillings per acre; the necessary funds were raised for the endeavour by the end of 1835. Only one quarter of the land was purchased by colonists. In fact the largest buyer was the South Australian Company formed by London banker and ship owner **George Fife Angas**. In effect, the colony started with prominent owners and landed families (who would send miscellaneous relatives to manage their holdings in Australia), influencing events in both London and the colony.

auctioning of remaining lots, the reconfiguration of the governing body to allow outstation settlement, and a flurry of land and commodity speculation engaged the colony until September 1839. At this point the number of penniless working-class migrants reached proportions which necessitated that Governor George Gawler begin construction of public buildings and expanded surveys far in excess of the colony's brief. The buildings included a gaol, barracks, hospital, a mansion for himself, and housing for officials. He established **Glenelg** on the nearby coast, building wharves there. The governing commission, bankrupted by their own activities in London as surely as by the needs of the colony, was dissolved in 1842. Governance of the colony then reverted to the Colonial Office.

The first colonial officials included Robert Gouger as secretary, Captain John Hindmarsh as Governor, James Hurtle Fisher as Resident Commissioner

William Light

William Light (c 1786–1839) was born in Malaysia, the son of an English trader who founded the town of Penang and a Malaysian mother. After his education in England, he joined the navy and then, in India in 1808, joined the army, and eventually became an intelligence officer for the Duke of Wellington. He was praised by his superiors for 'the variety of his attainments—an artist, musician, mechanist, seaman and soldier'. After serving in the Spanish army in the 1820s, he married the daughter of the Duke of Richmond, and spent the next ten years travelling through Europe and Egypt, and publishing volumes of his drawings. In 1834, he separated from his wife. After meeting Captain John Hindmarsh in Egypt, and after being bypassed for the post of Governor of South Australia, he became the new colony's Surveyor-General. Light arrived in South Australia in August 1836, with the mandate to determine the most appropriate location for the colony's main settlement. He decided on the present 1042-acre site for Adelaide on the heights of the Torrens River, named for King William IV's queen, despite protestations from the incompetent Governor Hindmarsh and others, who wanted a settlement closer to the sea, or even at the mouth of the Murray River. In deference to Hindmarsh's wishes, Light also surveyed some 300 acres at the harbour, now **Port Adelaide**. He stood firm in his belief that he had chosen the right spot, fighting against constant attempts to sack him. He proceeded with his enlightened plan for a grid layout for the city. After his surveying methods were questioned by the Commissioners back in England, Light resigned, as did his entire loyal crew of surveyors. He continued to carry out surveying expeditions nonetheless, but was plagued by bad luck, including the burning of his work-papers and memoirs, and ill health. When he died of tuberculosis in October 1839, he named his mistress Maria Gandy as his sole beneficiary and executrix, although he left his estranged wife and two sons back in England.

and William Light as Surveyor. Wakefield distanced himself from the venture, maintaining that the land titles were too inexpensive. His theory of settlement required waged labourers who would work for landowners while saving sufficient money to afford their own parcel.

William Light's first task was to survey 1500 miles of coast, and to select and survey the site of the capital, which had to be a port, and secondary towns. To Light's credit, he selected the heights above the Torrens River despite some argument by Governor Hindmarsh that the capital be set at Port Adelaide or at the mouth of the Murray at 'Walker's Harbour', then at Granite Island with a breakwater constructed into Encounter Bay on the Fleurieu Peninsula (now Victor Harbour). Port Adelaide had insufficient water.

'Walker's Harbour' was the alcoholic imaginings of a Kangaroo Island sealer. Flinders had reported that the area at the mouth of the Murray was too dangerous for shipping. Tragically Judge Jeffcott, one of the more able colonial administrators, Captain Blenkinsopp and two sailors drowned here in 1837, confirming this observation. Not long thereafter five ships were lost as Hindmarsh continued the effort to find a suitable port in the vicinity. Light maintained that history would prove him right; in his *Brief Journal*, published in 1839 shortly before his death, he sought to justify his choice of

Charles Sturt

Charles Sturt (1795–1869) was one of the most extraordinary and tenacious of the colonial inland explorers. Born to a judge of the East India Company in Bengal, he was well educated in England and joined the army in 1813. In 1826, his regiment accompanied a transportation of convicts to New South Wales; Sturt was immediately taken with Australia, and determined to explore its unknown regions. He gained the confidence of Governor Darling, and first led an expedition in 1828, along with Hamilton Hume, to discover the source of the Macquarie River. During this trip, they also discovered, in 1829, the Darling River. At the end of that year, Sturt headed the inland expedition to determine the course of the Murrumbidgee River, a journey which is considered one of the greatest in Australian history, for Sturt and his company overcame incredible hardships to discover the continent's largest river-system, the Murray–Darling basin. Of greatest significance was Sturt's sympathetic treatment of and interest in the indigenous people they encountered; no natives were harmed during any of Sturt's many expeditions.

Sturt had expected promotion as a result of his many accomplishments, only to be denied compensation due to the jealousy of fellow explorer T.L. Mitchell. This disappointment, along with his failing health caused by the hardships of his journeys, prompted Sturt to return to England. Here he published *Two Expeditions into the Interior of Southern Australia 1828–31* (1833), which served as inspiration for Edward Wakefield's choice of South Australia for his Utopian settlement (see below). Sturt married and returned to Australia in 1834, to take up property in New South Wales. He was soon anxious to explore further, and in 1838 took on the dangerous assignment of bringing provisions overland to the struggling colony at Adelaide. This strenuous journey allowed him to explore the mouth of the Murray River and much of southeastern South Australia. He settled in Adelaide, where he built a house, the Grange, which still stands. When his hopes of being appointed Governor were dashed in 1841, Sturt continued his services to the colony, and in 1844 mounted his most ambitious expedition, to explore the interior of the region. While Sturt considered this horrendous episode, where temperatures sometimes exceeded 50°C, to be a failure, he succeeded in establishing that no inland sea existed; that he survived this gruelling assignment was victory enough. His efforts were recognised in the naming of Sturt's Stony Desert to that most desolate area between Cooper Creek and the Diamantina; and in that most showy of Australian wild-flowers, Sturt's Desert Pea.

the site of Adelaide, stating that he would 'leave it to posterity to decide whether I am entitled to praise or blame'.

Almost immediately after settlement, free settlers and Governor Hindmarsh pressed to allow selection of land at a distance from Adelaide. Commissioner Fisher held to Wakefield's notion of a concentrated settlement. When Hindmarsh and Fisher resigned in 1838, their administrative positions were combined. Lieutenant Colonel George Gawler, appointed in their stead in 1839, opened settlement in country sections. He also dismissed the bumptious George Strickland Kingston who had replaced

Light in a magnificent proof that incompetent political administration prefers incompetent functionaries.

Arguably Gawler could never have succeeded in establishing a stable settlement. The funds for the colony were depleted; unemployed labourers were placed on a wage to build civic structures; an administrative nightmare was furthered by special interests in both London and Adelaide. Prosperity came to the colony only after Captain George Grey began administering the colony in 1841. During his four-year term, silver-lead was discovered at Glen Osmond (1841) and copper at Kapunda (1842) and Burra (1845). An agricultural surplus began in 1843, although it did little good as an export until the repeal of the Navigation Acts in 1849. By 1850 the population of South Australia was 63,700 people. Some clever exchange arrangements saw the proceeds of the Victorian gold fields passing through Adelaide in the early 1850s.

As the city prospered, its suburbs offered inexpensive land for poorer migrants (Enfield and Salisbury), investment opportunities along trade routes (Hindmarsh, Bowden and Prospect), or small estates for the well-to-do (Walkerville, Kensington, Norwood and, even further afield, Glenelg). Contrary to Wakefield's notion, the working class simply bought where they could afford land and made do until times improved rather than working diligently for someone else while living in the squalid rentals familiar from Europe. By the 1850s the busiest part of town was already the intersection of King William Street and the Huntley Street/Rundle Street axis.

Aboriginal-European relations were more civilised in colonial South Australia than elsewhere in Australia. While thoroughly conforming to a 19C manner, the Europeans here were less likely to shoot or poison indigenous people. As early as 1845, the great explorer and protector of the Aborigines **Edward John Eyre** (1815–1901) wrote a thorough account of Aboriginal manners and customs, treating them as human beings and defending their traditional place on the land. Rather than extermination, the South Australian government consistently planned assimilation. The Waste Lands Act (1842) reserved marginal agricultural land for natives. An Aboriginal settlement at Moorundie (today's Murray Bridge) on the Murray River, the Adelaide Native School and Walkerville Aboriginals School were established in the 1840s as well. A Parliamentary Select Committee of Inquiry into Aborigines in 1860 established the Point McLeay Mission.

Sadly, the modest gains being made in Aboriginal-European relations were spoiled by draconian measures introduced early in the present century. Following the other states, South Australia introduced **protection boards** which segregated, restricted and separated Aborigines from traditional lands, family members and white society. Eventually, South Australians elected to repeal the worst discriminatory measures. By the late 1960s protection was given to sacred sites; segregation of public facilities was outlawed; Aboriginal Studies was introduced at teachers' schools; and communities on the reserves were allowed to incorporate.

Adelaide

....

Central Adelaide (total population 1,081,000), a square-mile grid, is defined by Terraces which comprise the rim of the main civic centre, in the middle of which is Victoria Square and beyond which are parklands. **North Terrace** contains the most historic public buildings, and is one of the most gracious streets in Australia. The adjacent parkland contains many of the city's notable public institutions. Across the Torrens River is **North Adelaide**. Adelaide Airport is west of town, virtually on the Gulf of St Vincent, and the Rail Passenger Terminal is across the West Terrace Cemetery from the city proper.

In 1910 J.F. Fraser observed, 'Adelaide for culture, Melbourne for business, Sydney for having a good time.' Adelaide still evokes a sense of cultivation, enhanced by its fame as the location for the **Adelaide Festival**, Australia's oldest and most successful cultural festival, held since 1960 every two years in February–March. The festival is definitely worth a visit as it includes the best of international theatre, dance, music, literary events, and performances, as well as the most contemporary of Australian productions and artistic efforts.

Adelaide has always been a good centre for bookshops, some of which have contributed substantially to the literary life of the country. **F.W. Preece** opened its bookshop in 1907 on King William Street, from where the owner published many books about South Australia, as well as the first publications of the Jindy-worobak poets and the cultural journal *Desiderata* in the 1930s. **Mary Martin's Bookshop**, 249 Rundle Street (☎ 08 8359 3525), was founded in 1945 by Mary Martin and Max Harris, who were important literary figures in the community. Harris went on to found the modernist journal *Angry Penguins*, and was most famous for his publishing of the Ern Malley hoax (see p 85). The store remains an important cultural institution.

In 1869 Charles Wentworth Dilke, an imperialist author from Britain, called Adelaide 'the farinaceous village', **'the City of Churches'**, 'The Athens of the South', 'the resting place of Australian wowsers', 'a kind of high-rise-pimple surrounded by an ever-extending contusion of villas'. The town's reputation received the comment by others that it was 'beautifully laid out ... like in a morgue'. Its many stone churches are indeed still prominent architectural features, constructed in a variety of stone and in many styles, and speak of Adelaide's rare status in Australia for harbouring a multitude of religious congregations, leading to inevitable early debates over theological distinctions.

More caustic observations are similarly unfair. Dilke continued to describe it as 'One of the most crude and impracticable schemes in reference to a British race population that the brain even of modern practical economists has hatched'; he conceded finally that 'in Adelaide, all the comfort and luxuries of life may be obtained; and an individual who is pining in the cold-catching and uncertain climate of Great Britain—struggling to keep up the necessary appear-ances of fashionable life, and to be a somebody, upon a limited income may, by changing his abode to the genial climate of South Australia, live like a little prince, and become a "somebody", with the same income on which he could barely exist in England.'

Even native son, the writer Geoffrey Dutton, described it in the 1960s as the 'square city, named for a dull dead queen, ...a level-headed city of ornate feuds'.

Adelaide is also known to have the worst drinking water in Australia. While substantial improvements have been made in the last few years, popular belief still maintains that it is one of only two ports where international ships do not take on water, the other being Dubai.

Still, the city is an attractive and comfortable place, with some of the best and most reasonably priced restaurants in the country. The presence from the early days of settlement of Germans has had the positive effect of nurturing a more varied cultural climate; even Dutton must concede that 'the humble *leberwurst* or *mettwurst* has always given South Australia some heritage more varied than boiled mutton and Irish stew'. This early ethnic diversity also accounts for Adelaide's long-standing reputation as the home of good food and, of course, wine.

■ Practical information

Tourist information: South Australian Government Travel Centre, AMP Building, 1 King William Street; ☎ 08 8303 2033/1300 655 276; Rundle Mall Visitor Information Centre, Rundle Mall, ☎ 08 8203 7611. Information on national parks in South Australia is available from the South Australian Department of Environment and Natural Resources Information Centre, 77 Grenfell Street, ☎ 08 8204 1910.

Airport. Adelaide's international airport (flights arrive internationally from Malaysia and Singapore), is located 8km from the centre of the city; the domestic terminal is about 500m south of the international terminal. The airport bus (☎ 08 8381 5311) will take you to most city accommodation; a taxi ride into the city will cost $15–20. **Kendell Airlines** is the main regional operator, booked through Ansett Airlines (☎ 13 1300).

Rail. All three of the main national railway trains, the **Indian-Pacific**, the **Ghan**, and the **Overlander**, travel to Adelaide. They arrive at the interstate railway terminal at Keswick (☎ 08 8231 7699) c 3km south of the Adelaide airport. The airport bus also stops here to take passengers into town or one can catch a suburban train here that also goes into the city centre. The metropolitan train service (☎ 08 8210 1000) runs south to Noarlunga and Belair, west to Grange and north to Outer Harbour and Gawler. South Australia has no other intra-state railway links.

Bus. Interstate coaches of *Pioneer-Greyhound* (☎ 08 8231 1701) arrive at the Central Bus Station, 111 Franklin Street. State services, which are quite extensive, can be booked from the *Bus Booking Centre*, 33 King William Street (☎ 08 8212 5200). Within the city, the State Transit Authority runs a good system of buses, as well suburban trains from Adelaide Train Station, one 30-minute **tram** that travels to the seaside suburb of Glenelg, and a funny little **O-Bahn** fast-track bus running through Torrens Linear Park between the city and Tea Tree Plaza in Modbury. Timetable information and advice on an array of ticketing options are available at the Customer Service Centre, on the corner of King William and Currie Streets, ☎ 08 8210 1000. Bus services also include a free inner-city service, the Bee line and City Loop runs. A **metro guide** to all public transit services in the region is available at this office.

Taxis. The main city cab rank is on the corner of Rundle and Pulteney Streets at Rundle Mall. Companies include *Adelaide Independent* (☎ 13 22 11), *Yellow Cabs* (☎ 13 22 27), and *Suburban Transport* (☎ 13 10 08).

Cycling. Many outlets supply bicycles and cycling maps: *Bicycle SA*, 1 Sturt Street (☎ 08 8213 0637); *Pulteney Street Cycles*, 307–309 Pulteney Street (☎ 08 8223 6678).

Useful addresses
Hospitals. *Royal Adelaide*, North Terrace, ☎ 08 8223 0230.
Police. Emergency, ☎ 11 444; switchboard 08 8207 4550.
Rape Crisis Centre ☎ 08 8293 8666.
Consulates. *British*, 25 Grenfell Street at Hindmarsh Square, ☎ 08 8212 7280; *Indonesian*, Level 1, 45 King William Street, ☎ 08 8217 8288; *Malaysian*, 144 North Terrace, ☎ 08 8212 2236.

Hotels
$$$ Hilton International Adelaide, 233 Victoria Square, city, ☎ 8217 0711. Typically grand Hilton block; 18 storeys, 380 rooms, central location. Includes the city's most renowned restaurant.
$$$–$$ Treacles Row Cottages, 17 Gray Street, ☎ 08 8410 3983; fax 08 8357 8324; internet: http://www.treacles.com.au; e-mail: jandersen@treacles.com.au. Joyce Andersen runs several 'heritage accommodation' sites, most of them, as Treacles is, cottages with all the modern comforts and homey conveniences.
$$ Apartments on the Park, 274 South Terrace, ☎ 08 8232 0555/13 11 22. Self-contained apartments (studio or 2-bedroom), kitchen & laundry facilities. Good value, ideal location; motor club discounts.
$$ Adelaide Paringa Motel, 15 Hindley Street, ☎ 8231 1000/1 800 088 202. Central location near North Terrace and Adelaide Casino.
$$ Buffalo Motor Inn, 766 Anzac Highway, Glenelg, ☎ 08 8294 6244. At popular beachside resort, good family spot.
$$ Corfu Holiday Units, corner Mosley and Kent Streets, Glenelg, ☎ 08 8295 2345, fax 08 8294 5666. Self-catering apartments on the beach; Corfu Accommodation also runs other beachfront locations, at same phone number.
$$ Grosvenor Vista Hotel, 125 North Terrace, ☎ 8407 8888/1800 888 222; fax 8407 8866. Another North Terrace location; 283 rooms, underground parking, discounts for motor club members.
$$ Georgia Mews Cottages, 31 Wakefield Street, Kent Town, ☎ 08 8362 0600, fax 08 8362 1317. 2km east of Adelaide, bed and breakfast as self-contained apartments; historic building, friendly hosts.

Restaurants
$$$ The Grange, Adelaide Hilton, 233 Victoria Square, ☎ 8217 2000. Renowned chef Cheong Liew, famed for his exquisite blending of Asian flavours and Australian ingredients, has led to the Grange's being voted Australia's best restaurant by many international food writers. Truly 'global cuisine', essential Adelaide dining.
$$$ Petaluma's Bridge Mill, Mt Barker Road, Bridgewater, ☎ 08 8339 3422. Towards Adelaide Hills in idyllic setting, long-standing and award-winning

'modern Australian' fare; excellent wines at reasonable prices.

\$\$ Botanic Cafe, 4 East Terrace, ☎ 08 8224 0925. Italian ultra-cool. Great coffee and always packed. Outdoor tables, too.

\$\$ Charlick's Feed Store, Ebenezer Place, East End, ☎ 08 8223 7566. Award-winning chef and foodie celebrity Maggie Beer now directs this inner-city 'Modern Australian' gourmet experience. Only the best produce and ingredients used; extensive wine list, outdoor dining.

\$\$ The Chesser Cellar, 29 Chesser Street, ☎ 08 8223 3791. Traditional and sensible, with food described as 'sort of English buffet'.

\$\$ Landhaus Restaurant, Bethany Road, Bethany, ☎ 08 8563 2191. In the Barossa Valley, very small, using home-grown ingredients along with imported luxuries. Booking essential; also limited accommodation available.

\$\$ Red Ochre Grill, Ebenezer Place (off Rundle Street East), ☎ 8223 7566. Advertised as '40,000 years in the making', internationally recognised for its use of native Australian ingredients: emu and wallaby, quandong and warrigal leaves, bush tomato and wattle seed.

\$ Art Gallery Cafe, Art Gallery of South Australia, North Terrace, ☎ 08 8232 4366. Beautifully situated in gallery's new wing and on courtyard lake. Breezy atmosphere, simple well-cooked fare.

\$ Lemon Grass Bistro, 289 Rundle Street, ☎ 08 8223 6627. Good Thai dishes, in the heart of Rundle Mall.

\$ Paul's, 79 Gouger Street, ☎ 08 8231 9778. Across the street from the market halls, an Adelaide institution for decades. Arguably the best fish and chips in town, unpretentious and inexpensive.

\$ Peaceful Vegetarian Restaurant, 167 Hindley Street. Founded by Buddhist nuns, unusual Asian vegetarian, with pictures of the Dalai Lama everywhere. Tasty and tranquil.

\$ Ying Chow, 114 Gouger Street, ☎ 08 8211 7998. Shanghai Chinese, sublime duck. Open late.

History

Adelaide is quite clearly a 'planned city'. The original site was chosen by Colonel William Light in 1836, Surveyor-General of the newly established colony (see p 460). Named by the new free settlers (upon the suggestion of Governor Hindmarsh) after Queen Adelaide, wife of King William IV, the entire city had been completely planned before any building began. Light's enlightened plan established a grid of the city on the south side of the River Torrens, which would contain the major public buildings and govern-mental structures.

The River Torrens runs through the middle of town, and there are a number of parks and reserves along its flood plain. In 1937 the river was diverted through a series of weirs which drained a section of reed beds at the delta shared with the Port Rivers and this produced a large area of land for suburban development.

The river was named for Sir Robert Richard Torrens (1814–84), who was the 21st Premier of South Australia and an original member of the South Australian Land Co. in 1831. He wrote *Colonization of South Australia* in 1835 and emigrated in 1839. His service to the colony was enhanced when he devised a simplified method of property transfer described in his book,

The South Australian System of Conveyancing by Registration of Title published in 1859. Initially, he was attempting to clarify the transfer of freehold land, an extremely important aspect of the law in a colony so far from the homeland and so fraught with questions of ownership and land distribution. The Torrens system was adopted in Canada and the United States by the 1880s and in England in the 1920s following the Birkenhead legislation.

Walk 1 • Around Victoria Square

Victoria Square lies at the heart of the town. A 3.6 hectare open plaza, it was laid out by Colonel William Light in 1837 'for the use and recreation of the public'. KING WILLIAM STREET cuts through the square to the north and south. The walk described here begins at the General Post Office at the northeast corner and continues clockwise around the square, ending at the courthouses on the southwest.

The **General Post Office** on the corner of King William and Franklin Streets was built in 1867–72 on the site set aside for the post office in the original plan of the city. (It superseded the original 1851 building which continued to serve as the police station until it was demolished in 1891. That building's clock was removed in 1876, and still functions in the tower of Glenside Mental Hospital.) Following a design competition, the architects of the General Post Office were E.W. Wright and E.J. Woods.

Prince Alfred laid the foundation stone during his visit to Adelaide in November 1867. It opened with great fanfare on 6 May 1872, at a cost of £53,258. The building's crowning glory is its **clock tower**. The clock itself was made in England in 1874 by J.B. Joyce of Whitchurch, and the chimes are meant to correspond with those of Great St Mary's in Cambridge, England, as well as those at the Houses of Parliament in London. A great throng appeared to hear the first chimes on 13 December 1875, and despite an initial mistake in striking the correct hour, the clock has served as an Adelaide landmark ever since. The clock is purported to be the most accurate GPO clock in Australia; it is kept within the limits of plus or minus one second from true mean time, and is checked daily with the observatory at Mount Stromlo in the ACT.

The central hall presents arched and deeply coffered ceilings and a gallery with ornamental cast-iron trusses and balustrade. The middle King William entrance was originally used as a carriageway, while an extension to King William façade was added in 1891–93. The interior of the building, with its painted ceiling, is an impressive example of Victorian public space.

Outside the General Post Office on Franklin Street is one of Adelaide's many 'pie carts', an institution in the city since 1915. These carts serve the Adelaide speciality, a 'Pie Floater': a hot meat pie with tomato sauce (ketchup) floating in a bowl of green pea soup. A trip to Adelaide is not complete without a taste of this dish.

North of the post office on King William Street is **Electra House**. The classical detailing and figure brackets framing the entrance make this building an architectural pleasure. It was associated first with the insurance industry then with the Eastern Extension Australasia and China Telegraph Company, which had somewhat earlier established electrical communication between Darwin and Singapore and thereby Europe, as well as service between South Africa and Adelaide.

Like the post office, the Palladian-style **Town Hall** complex, across King William Street on the southeast corner of Pirie Street, was also designed by E.W. Wright (see p 472), and built in 1863–66. The building immediately to the south, built in 1869 by Daniel Garlick (architect) and Charles Farr (builder), was originally the Prince Alfred Hotel. In 1953 it was incorporated into the town hall, its balcony removed and the entrance and vestibule extensively renovated with a covering of marble. Now the building functions as a venue for civic and club meetings and a hall for concerts.

The **Treasury Building** is across King William Street on the northeast corner of Victoria Square. It was designed by E.A. Hamilton, Colonial Architect, and built in several stages beginning in 1858. It took nearly 20 years to complete the block, although its unified style suggests that its design was conceived of by Hamilton as a whole. The construction proceeded in the following order: 1) most northerly King William part of two storeys, built 1858; 2) corner two-storeyed section, 1859; 3) central three storeys, 1860; 4) eastern two-storeyed Victoria Square, 1867; 5) three-storeyed Victoria Square block completed in 1876. The central courtyard gardens were started by James Milton in 1840. The building now houses the **Old Treasury Museum** (☎ 08 8226 4133; open weekdays 10.00–15.00), dedicated to the display of the history of surveying.

Behind the Treasury Building on Flinders Street is **Pilgrim Church**, formerly Stow Memorial Church. Originally named after T.Q. Stow who was important in the establishment of Congregationalism and the Bible Society in South Australia, the church was designed by Robert George Thomas (see his Baptist Church on the opposite side of Flinders Street a block further along), built by Brown and Thompson, and opened in 1867. The design is English neo-Gothic style, and includes carved capitals and sandstone-dressed bluestone walls. The interior has a wide nave and narrow aisles. The Gothic style is softened by the double-porch column and the large windows in the south wall. Behind the church is the former meeting hall, constructed in 1863 of bluestone, also in a Gothic Revival design by E.W. Wright.

The Pilgrim Church manse is now the Ethnic Affairs Commission building. Initially built in the same style as the church, it was given an Italianate colonnade façade just after the turn of the century. At that time it functioned as a sanatorium under Dr T.A. Hynes, an Australian graduate of Edinburgh University who followed the then radical American approach of making mental patients comfortable in cheerful conditions. The renovations undertaken in 1975–76 won an architectural award of merit.

The large **Torrens Building**, across Flinders Street and along Victoria Square to the corner of Wakefield Street, now houses the Public Works and Registrar-General's Department. Built in 1876, the simple style of Melbourne architect Michael Egan's design makes the building something other than an austere block, particularly the lightened effect of the arched windows on the first storey.

The architectural history of **St Francis Xavier's Cathedral**, across Wakefield Street, is a series of building programmes. Plans for the building began in 1848 with a subscription drive. After initial hesitations, the Catholics, uncharacteristically, accepted state aid to defray construction costs. Richard Lambeth was selected as the architect, but construction had not got far beyond the foundations when the Victorian gold rush lured most of the colony's workforce to the gold fields. The cathedral attained its present shape in 1926 based on designs by

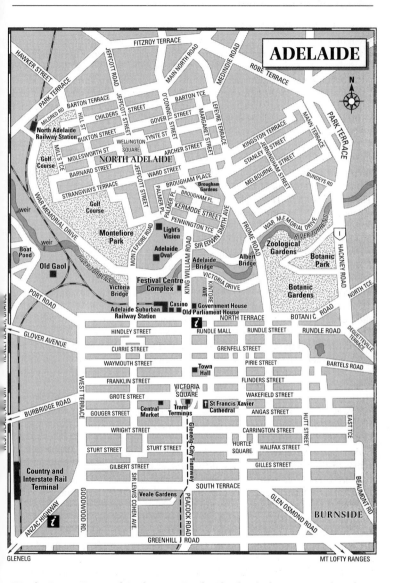

Woods, Bagot, Jory and Laybourne Smith. The firm's designs were based on those of Pugin and Pugin, of London's Houses of Parliament fame, for the 1887 enlargement and included plans for a tower.

Supreme, Magistrate and Local **Court Buildings** are at either side of King William Street at the south end of the square. The **Magistrate's Courthouse** on the southeast corner was originally the Supreme Court. Begun in 1847, this is the only Greek Revival building, with a Doric façade, in Adelaide. The portico is constructed of Finniss River sandstone. Except for the original courtroom's skylight, canopy and public gallery, very little of the original building remains.

Richard Lambeth, who was described as the 'Clerk of Works and Architect' in the Colonial Engineer's Office, designed the structure. Berry and Gilbert report an anecdote related to the building in their *Pioneer Building Techniques in South Australia* (1981): 'Although the new building was eventually completed and occupied on 30th June, 1850 after having taken three years to build, it was not without a struggle, as the builder had barricaded himself in and the authorities had to make a forced entry.'

The building was not completed upon occupancy and the *Adelaide Times* complained that the 'vast height of the hall, the large globular skylight that surmounts it, and the extensive subterranean vault leading to the dock, seem all combined to deprive the voice of any speaker of any particle of distinctiveness'. The judges themselves complained about the placement of the bench, the lack of toilets and robing rooms and about the smoking fireplaces in chambers. The building was used for the Supreme Court until 1873, then as the Local and Insolvency Courts until 1891, and finally as the Police Courts.

Colonial Architect R.G. Thomas and William McMinn designed the **Supreme Court**, across King Street, facing the square. Originally the Local and Insolvency Court, it was built between 1866 and 1869 by Brown and Thompson, who also constructed the post office. The front is Tea Tree Gully sandstone in a Victorian Classical Revival style with balustraded parapet, carved keystones on the arches and Ionic columns. The south and west elevations are of bluestone. It has been used by the Supreme Court since 1873.

The **Local Court House**, across King Street behind the Supreme Court, was built in 1867 as the police court when William Hanson was the Colonial Architect. The building features a Roman Doric portico, cement dressings and what was described at the time as a 'somewhat elegant interior'. In 1891 it became the Local and Insolvency Courts.

Across GOUGER STREET on the southwest corner of the square, the **Local and District Courts**, also known as the Samuel Way Building, were formerly Moore's Department Store. Opened in 1916 and consciously inspired by store owner Charles Moore's trip to the Paris Exhibition of 1878, the building was radical for a number of reasons at the time of its construction. The shell is of reinforced concrete with cast cement and run cement dressings. Its original function as a department store placed it a considerable distance from the retail section of the town which at the time was along the far northern edge of the central business district. Charles Moore hired Garlick and Jackman as the architects and William Lucas from England designed the central staircase. A fire in 1948 required substantial rebuilding of the structure and only the façade and central staircase of the original survive.

The site for the **Central Market** dates from 1870. It is back across Gouger Street to the west, extending through to Grote Street. The present structure was constructed in the mid-1960s, but maintains the original partitioning of space into stalls. The market is a great place to find fresh produce and delicatessen items of the best quality. It is open Tuesdays and Thursdays 07.30–17.30, Fridays 07.00–21.00, and Saturdays 07.00–13.00. Adelaideans are so proud of their market that they have organised entertaining 90-minute tours on the historic premises; for details ☎ 08 8336 8333. **Paul's Cafe** across Grote Street is a traditional fish, chips, coleslaw and beer cafe, but its fish is more than a cut above the average battered fish offering. It has remained the same for decades, and is a beloved Adelaide institution.

Her Majesty's Theatre (☎ 08 8216 8774), on the north side of Grote Street towards Victoria Square, was erected as the Princess Theatre in 1912–13 and was first leased by Harry Rickards, a well-known Vaudevillian who had made his name in Britain and America before becoming a leading 'variety entrepreneur' in Australia. The original stage was 81 x 63 ft with a height of 53 ft, considered quite large by Adelaide standards of the day. It seated more than 2000 and featured a then state-of-the-art ventilation system which pumped 2600 cubic feet of air per minute. After alterations in 1962, it received its current name, although it was called the Opera Theatre in the 1970s, when it was home to the State Opera Company of South Australia until they moved to the Festival Theatre in 1989. It is still one of Adelaide's major venues for musical performances and theatre.

The Central Business District

The Central Business District (CBD) covers three blocks north of the General Post Office on either side of King William Street, up Rundle Street to the market.

The first section of the ANZ Bank, formerly the **Bank of Adelaide**, on the corner of King William and Currie Streets, was built in 1880–81 by Wright, Reed & Beavor at the end of a period of prosperity caused by success in agriculture. While it replicated the Doric ornament of the original, the contrasting sandstone dressings were painted and the interior remodelled.

Behind the ANZ Bank on Currie Street is the Head Office of the **Savings Bank of South Australia**. Designed by Edward Davies and constructed of Pyrmont stone (imported amid much controversy from New South Wales), the turn-of-the-century Classical style building needs a more interesting street in order to look at home.

Across King William Street from the ANZ Building, the **T & G Building** was built during the boom years immediately following the First World War to house the South Australia branch of the T & G Insurance Company. One of Adelaide's first high-rise buildings, its eleven storeys were the maximum allowed in Adelaide at the time of its opening. The design is by K.A. Henderson and the construction was through the McLeod Brothers, a Sydney firm. The building was renovated in 1982.

Edmund Wright House is on King William Street on the left. Formerly the Bank of South Australia, until recently the Registrar of Births, it is now the State History Centre (☎ 08 8226 8555). The Bank of South Australia is the oldest in the state. Founded in 1835 as a department of Angas' South Australian Company, the bank received its royal charter in 1847 and was among the more important colonial banks operating in London at the time. The Union Bank of Australia took over the business and operated out of this building from 1893 until it merged with the Bank of Australasia in 1951 to become the ANZ.

The style is French Renaissance and the main façade is in two orders, ground floor Composite, first floor Corinthian. The Scottish sculptor William Maxwell carved the keystones and Joseph Durham's coat of arms, which refer to the Royal Charter under which the bank was founded. The interior is lavish with Corinthian pilasters, enriched pedestals and entablatures—all in Devonshire marble—a deeply coffered ceiling in the banking chambers and original cedar fittings. During the 1970s, the building was seriously threatened with destruction because of its valuable site. Due to a public outcry, the State Government purchased the structure for $750,000 rather than have it demolished. Musical performances are held here every Wednesday at lunchtime.

Edmund William Wright

The 1878 building was designed by **Edmund William Wright** (1824–88). He had trained in London as a civil engineer and architect. On his way to South Australia, he stopped in Canada, where he constructed a tubular bridge over the St Lawrence River in Montreal. Once in Australia, he proceeded to the gold diggings in Victoria before returning to Adelaide to set up practice in 1860 in partnership with E.J. Woods. He became Mayor in January of 1859, but resigned in December of the same year, for which he was fined £10. Despite this setback, he succeeded in his design for the Town Hall in 1863, and remained an important figure in architectural circles.

Taking a left turn on Hindley Street, you come to the Tattersalls and Princes Berkeley Hotels. The **Tattersalls Hotel** was rebuilt in 1901–02 by the South Australian Brewing Company. Garlick and Jackman were the architects. The original structure on the site was the Blenheim Hotel (1851), which was subsequently known as the Weilands (1879) before taking the current name (1882). In its current form the verandah and balcony ironwork deserve attention.

The **Princes Berkeley Hotel** building dates from 1878 and was erected on the site of the earliest colonial hotel, the Buffalo's Head (1838). The building was designed by Thomas English and constructed by Charles Farr. The balcony was extended to span the building in 1905 and 1923. The present name dates from 1947, though this structure's original name, the Black Bull, is still applied to it occasionally by old-time locals.

At the turn of the century there were 16 hotels along Hindley Street, down from a high of 18 in 1880. The number dropped as restrictions were placed on pub life. Bar maids were abolished in 1908; six o'clock closing was enforced in 1916. Only Tattersalls Hotel and the Royal Oak would be recognised today by their early patrons.

As an aside for **beer aficionados**, John Warren was the first brewer in South Australia, having been licensed by Captain Hindmarsh in 1836. The South Australian Brewing, Malting, Wine and Spirit Co. was formed by the merger of the older West End Brewery and the Kent Brewery. This company now holds a virtual monopoly on brewing in the state. Cooper and Sons, also a mid-19C firm, offers a series of beers, some of them at micro-brewery standards. The Tasmanian firm Cascade Brewery, founded in Hobart in 1824, and Redback and Matilda Bay in Perth are of similar size and quality.

RUNDLE MALL is the main shopping complex in Adelaide, touted as the largest pedestrian mall in the Southern hemisphere; it runs east from King William Street to Pulteney Street, one block south of North Terrace. This strip has been Adelaide's premier shopping district since the 1880s. It contains all of the leading shops, such as Myer Centre and David Jones. It was at the intersection of

Rundle/Hindley Streets and King William Street that Adelaide's first electric street lighting was installed in 1985.

ADELAIDE ARCADE runs from Rundle Mall to Grenfell Street. The arcade was built during the economic boom of the 1880s when Rundle Street was established as a renowned shopping area, distinct from the working class hotels across King William Street on Hindley Street. Withall and Wells' original plan showed ambition in its use of electric light, plate glass, and cast-iron. (Their design of the Adelaide Racing Club Grandstand in Victoria Park off Wakefield Road shows similar structural and ornamental use of cast iron.) The main promenade is nearly 8m wide and features three fountains; its floor is of Carrara marble and white encaustic tiles. Although some alterations of doubtful taste were allowed to the shop fronts on the ground floor in the 1950s and 1960s, the first floor shop fronts are splendid. The pedestrian mall allows a good view of the octagonal tower and dome at the arcade's top floor which also depicts the Australian coat of arms on the entrance side of the tower.

GAYS ARCADE, which joins the Adelaide Arcade at a right angle from Twin Street, was designed by J. Cumming and constructed by N.W. Trudgen at about the same time as the Adelaide Arcade to replace Patrick Gay's fire-damaged furniture showroom.

Walk 2 • North Terrace

If the area around Victoria Square is governmental and the section slightly to the north is a shopping district, then North Terrace and the Park Lands are for public institutions. North Terrace is still the location of the city's most important and impressive cultural monuments. This walking tour begins from the western end of the street.

The **Lion Arts Centre** (☎ 08 8231 7760) at 19 Morphett Street close to the junction with Hindley Street is the original building of the Mumzone jam and pickle factory in the section of town called St Peters. The complex houses bilingual theatre performance spaces, and a variety of experimental exhibitions. The centre also houses the **Jam Factory** (☎ 08 8410 0727), a craft and design centre since 1973, with four training workshops devoted to glass-blowing, leatherwork, silver-smithing and weaving. The centre also houses an impressive gallery and a craft shop, as well as the administrative arm of the **Fringe Festival**, an alternative or experimental variation on the Adelaide Arts Festival, and the **Nexus Cabaret**. The redesign of the structure represents a successful example of creative adaptation of 19C architectural space.

A little further afield is the **Adelaide Gaol** (☎ 08 8231 4062, weekdays 11.00–16.00, and hour-long guided tours on Sundays 11.00–15.30). It is located in the northwest section of the parklands from the corner of North and West Terraces. Built in 1840–41 under the supervision of Sir George Kingston, its eventual cost of £32,002 greatly exceeded the original estimate. Criticism of the cost and design of the gaol was one of the contributing factors in Governor Gawler's replacement by Governor Grey in 1841. It was built to accommodate 140 prisoners, but the conviction rate in the colony at the time was only 24 per year.

The gaol is one of the best examples of Kingston's surviving work and an interesting demonstration of the model prison design of the late 18C and early 19C: a radial layout gave the central guard station a general overview and prisoners were grouped according to the seriousness of their crimes.

The buildings are surrounded by stone walls, designed by E.J. Woods in 1882. The western tower later became the gallows; the second half of the building was built in 1848, with various additions over the next 30 years. The Powder Magazine behind the gaol was also designed by Woods in the same year. These are the only surviving examples of such magazines in South Australia, and remain virtually unchanged from their original days.

Holy Trinity Church, Adelaide, as depicted in the Picturesque Atlas of Australia

Holy Trinity Church, at the corner of North Terrace and Morphett Street, is one of a few churches to be routinely open during the day; its Sunday services commence at 08.00. It was the first Anglican Church in the city and is the state's oldest surviving church. The foundation stone was laid by Governor Hindmarsh on 26 January 1838 and the church was finished in August of that year. The design was by John White. A temporary church, which preceded this structure, had been imported as a prefabricated building, but was partially ruined on the voyage out. To provide a roof for this temporary structure the first vicar, Reverend Charles Beaumont Howard, and the Colonial Treasurer, Osmond Gilles, dragged a ship's sail on foot from Holdfast Bay. Reverend Howard is locally remembered as having refused to visit the dying Colonel Light because Light was living with a woman who was not his wife.

The clock in the tower, intended as the Adelaide town clock, was cast by King William's clockmaker, Vuillamy. The church was rebuilt again in 1888 and now only the lower parts of the nave and tower survive of the original edifice and only a stained-glass window commemorating King William IV remains of the prefabricated church building. Its current appearance was based on architect Edward John Woods's original design.

Adelaide Railway Station, currently the Adelaide **Casino** and Convention Centre (☎ 08 8212 2811; open weekdays 10.00–16.00, weekends 24 hours), comprises the north side of North Terrace. Built under railway commissioner W.A. Webb during the 1920s, the building's size assumed the continued heavy use of rail transport. Webb's aggressive refurbishment of the system nearly bankrupted the state at the beginning of the Depression of the late 1920s. On the other hand, construction of the railway station was continued during these years to give employment to workers who would otherwise have had no likelihood of work. It also contributed to the readiness of South Australia to advance the manufacturing necessitated by the Second World War. The neo-classical station was designed by Garlick and Jackman. Its construction is reinforced concrete. After considerable, largely sympathetic, renovation during the 1980s, it now houses the Adelaide Casino.

Next to the current Parliament House, on the corner of North Terrace and King William Road, the **Old Parliament House** and Legislative Council Chambers building has had a chequered history. The initial design was by W. Bennet Hayes who became Colonial Architect shortly after being awarded the design competition for the building. The competition was held in 1851 to replace a stone cottage where the Legislative Council met. Hayes' winning design was later rejected as too expensive.

The subsequent construction attracted much debate and controversy. Due to labour and materials shortages caused by the gold strike, the initial building contract was based on usual builders' profits rather than a total contract award; it was built in 1854 at a cost of £17,000. Substantial additions were made in 1857 to suit the bicameral system of government instituted at the time. It was used by Parliament until 1889, when Parliament House was completed.

Architecturally, it features an unusual modified Dutch gable form, rusticated brick quoins and semi-circular ground-floor archways. Until 1980 it housed a variety of governmental departments and had been altered and neglected for some time. (It would have been demolished but for the start of the Second World War.) Visitors can only view the interior lobby.

New **Parliament House** (☎ 08 8237 9100) on the northwest corner of North Terrace and King William Streets is open to the public when parliament is sitting (tours occur on non-sitting days at 10.00 and 14.00). It was constructed of Kapunda marble on a base of West Island granite; the original design was by E.W. Wright & Lloyd Taylor of Melbourne. Progress on the building was delayed by financial problems and arguments about whether North Terrace or Victoria Square was the better site. The location was decided in 1883 and the building was begun, using a slightly altered design by then Colonial Architect E.J. Woods. By 1889 only the west section was completed; the remainder was not built until 1936–39 when the state received a centenary gift of £100,000 from Sir Langdon Bonython (1848–1939), editor of the *Adelaide Advertiser* and public benefactor. A planned central dome was abandoned and the number of columns in the portico increased from six to ten. The finished work includes carved portraits on keystones of past governors, presidents and speakers and a sumptuous interior of teak, maple and walnut. The stone lion was a gift from London in 1939.

In response to the hot and stuffy chambers in the Old Parliament House, a complex system of heating and cooling was incorporated in the new building, described in a governmental brochure thus: 'A unique system of evaporative cooling was a feature of the building. Air shafts were incorporated in the walls, terminating in openings under the windows with water trays and deflecting plates to direct the air over the water before it entered the room. The trays had taps and wastes to enable them to be simultaneously emptied and filled with fresh water.'

Adelaide Festival Centre (☎ 08 8216 8600) is located behind the railway station on King William Road. The biennial **Adelaide Festival of Arts**, begun in 1960 as a celebration of the city's commitment to the performing arts, necessitated the construction of the centre. Should you have the good fortune to be in Adelaide during March on an even-numbered year, you will find the city taken over by its festival. Theatre and dance are the central activities, but a variety of musical and alternative performances are presented as well.

Designed by Hassell and Partners and built by A.V. Jennings Industries, the centre was completed in 1973. It features the Hajek sculpture plaza and several theatres in a starkly modern setting. Although subject to much criticism (the stark plaza uncomfortably abuts the northern wall of the Parliament House; the structure of the Festival and Playhouse Theatres is made to look like concrete when it is steel), audiences and artists describe the facilities as versatile and comfortable performance spaces.

Across the river on the way to North Adelaide via King William Road or Montefiore Road is the **Adelaide Oval** (☎ 08 8231 3639), leased to the South Australian Cricket Association in 1872. The first grandstand was erected in 1882 and the inaugural match played between England and South Australia. The present appearance of the park dates from renovations undertaken in the mid- and late-1920s. The scoreboard dates from 1911 and was noteworthy at the time for its novel layout of the tallies, batters and score. Widely considered to be the best and most beautiful cricket oval in the world, it is the site of international test matches as well as state contests. It was on this oval in the 1932–33 season that the infamous 'bodyline' defence, in which several Australian players were actually injured by balls thrown at them by English bowlers, reached its climax, when the Adelaide crowds nearly stormed the field in protest.

The clubhouse for the **Municipal Golf Course** is at the corner of Montefiore Road and War Memorial Drive just across the Victoria Bridge. Said to be Australia's most popular public course, it is certainly within walking distance of North Terrace. The links, encircling the western edge of North Adelaide, offer two courses. That to the north is 69 par and extends as far as the Adelaide Aquatic Centre, that to the south is par 72 and features bunkers. Both have tree-lined fairways.

Facing the Festival Centre is **Government House**, the earliest-surviving building in Adelaide. It is open to the public twice a year, on changeable open days advertised in the newspapers. The oldest section of Government House is the east front, built in 1839–40 to replace the wattle-and-daub slab hut which had been Governor Hindmarsh's residence, on the site of the present-day casino. His successor, Colonel Gawler, preferred to sleep in a tent, using the hut as offices while he arranged for more appropriate accommodations. The Regency style design of Government House was adapted from a London pattern book by Edward O'Brien, but was substantially altered and erected in stone by Sir George Kingston, the colony's first 'Government Architect'.

The central portion of the structure was added in 1855, to a design by W.B. Hayes. At this point it took on the dimensions of an elegant mansion, with ball-room, state dining room, Adelaide room, Governor's study, south hall and entrance portico. In 1873 the Watchhouse—constructed of bluestone with Classical Revival stuccoed detailing—at the entrance was added, as was the west wing, designed by G.T. Light in 1878. Much of Adelaide's public history has taken place in Government House, including the hosting of the Duke of York when he visited Australia to open the first Federal Parliament in 1901. (His visit is commemorated in stained-glass windows installed at the north end of the ballroom.) The grounds include beautiful gardens, tours of which are regularly advertised in the local newspapers.

A **bronze equestrian statue** at the corner of North Terrace and King William Road commemorates the efforts of the South Australian Bushmen's Corps in the Boer War (1899–1902). Sculpted and cast by Adrian Jones of Ludlow, Shropshire, it was paid for by subscription and public fund-raising, and erected on a base of Murray Bridge granite in 1902. Australian soldiers in London for the coronation of Edward VII were asked to visit Jones to give information on regimental regalia; as it turned out, the regimental quartermaster, George Henry Goodall, sat for the sketch of the head of the mounted trooper.

Set in the footpath of the **Jubilee Walk** are 150 commemorative bronze plaques honouring prominent individuals, such as the inventor of the jump stump plough and the founder of Meals on Wheels. Ask at the downtown bookstores for a biographical guide to the walk.

The Migration Museum

The Destitute Asylum, now the site of the **Migration Museum**, is further east along North Terrace and left on Kintore Avenue (☎ 08 8207 7570, open Mon–Fri 10.00–17.00, Sat, Sun and holidays 13.00–17.00). This complex had its origins in the earliest days of the colony: construction began in 1853 and continued for 30 years. While the original social welfare functions of the buildings began to be replaced by the 1880s, many of the original buildings survived in various capacities. The remaining five buildings have now been restored to comprise the Migration Museum, which offers a fascinating and well-planned exhibition of the experience of migrants to South Australia; it is still the only museum in Australia to explore this historical process, through displays of past material culture as well as participation by current ethnic groups living in the state. The museum ranks as one of the most intelligent, in terms of presentation, in Australia.

The complex was originally established with the reasonable acceptance by the South Australian government of some responsibility for those immigrants who found themselves destitute upon their arrival. The museum also presents a moving, if at times grim, description of the building's tragic early history as the 'place where Adelaide hid her poor and homeless'. In the late 1870s, for example, the lying-in hospital for women in childbirth was separated into three areas. One was for women who had only 'fallen' once, another for women who had previous illegitimate children, and a third for prostitutes. Remarkably, once a woman was admitted, she was routinely confined for six months. The Victorian associations of unwed mothers with other forms of socially unacceptable behaviour led to the establishment of a reformatory for women at the same site. Not surprisingly, other refuges for women in the city which opened at about this time proved more popular due to a somewhat more sensible approach to the women's situation. In keeping with this history a recent exhibition displayed, along with descriptive texts, the horrific medical instruments used in childbirth in the 19C.

The remaining buildings include the chapel, the government store (now the museum proper) and the barracks. The chapel and schoolroom was erected in 1865 as a schoolroom for soldiers of the adjacent barracks. After 1870 it was the chapel for the Destitute Asylum. To the left is a building from 1861 which was meant to be a schoolroom for soldiers' children, although it soon became the laundry for the asylum. It is assumed to have been designed by E.A. Hamilton. The Historical Museum was built in 1867 as the Colonial Ordnance Store. It became the State Archives in 1919, after having served as army offices during the First World War. In 1976 it was restored to its original condition.

The Mounted Police Barracks, now the South Australia Police Museum within the Migration Museum complex, was built somewhat earlier, in 1854. Designed by W.B. Hayes as a quadrangle of buildings, only the central armoury, part of the west building and the gateway remain. At one time, the armoury contained up to 2000 arms. Extensive additions and alterations were made to the building between 1860 and 1888. The gateway, now undergoing restoration, was originally described as looking like a dog kennel.

The Institute Building, now the **Mortlock Library of South Australiana** (☎ 08 8207 7200; open Mon–Wed and Fri 09.30–20.00, Thurs 09.30–17.00, weekends 12.00–17.00), can be visited by returning to the northeast corner of North Terrace and Kintore Avenue. Originally a Mechanics' Institute, this was one of the first public buildings on North Terrace. It is a typical example of a Victorian era building in a derivative 'Renaissance' style. Constructed of Angaston white marble, the south front has a porch with Doric columns and is surmounted by a balustrade. The State Library is 'Jervois Wing' and was added from 1879 to 1884. Originally it held the Public Library and the Art Gallery; in 1881, the Princes Albert, Victor and George opened the gallery. A statue of Robert Burns in front of the library was designed by Scottish sculptor W.J. Maxwell and erected in the 1890s.

The 1877 design of the Mortlock Library is attributed to R.G. Thomas but the drawings were prepared in the Colonial Architect's Office by E.J. Woods, who was responsible for governmental buildings at the time. When the post office was being built, Thomas had been the Colonial Architect and Woods the designer. The style is a rich conglomerate of French Renaissance and Victorian Classical Revival. The east wing, which mimics this original style, was added in 1909–11, and lacks some of the earlier wing's historicist detail. Its name commemorates Colonial Governor William Jervois (1821–97) and houses part of the South Australia Museum.

South Australian Museum

The entrance to the **South Australian Museum** is on the windowed side of the Institute Building which reveals an awe-inspiring exhibit of a complete whale skeleton (☎ 08 8207 7500, open daily 10.00–17.00). Special features of the natural history museum include the state's geology and minerals, Aboriginal artefacts (one of the largest collections of its kind), and an array of dioramas presenting South Australian fauna in something like their natural settings. The museum also holds excellent collections of artefacts from the Pacific islands and ancient Egypt.

The North Wing was designed by C.E. Owen Smith during the Depression of the 1890s. Despite an extremely limited budget which required him to use brick rather than stone, the decoration makes a reasonable match with the State Library. It opened in 1895.

Immediately east of the museum is the **Art Gallery of South Australia** which opened in 1898. (☎ 08 8207 7000, open daily 10.00–17.00.) The building, in freestone Classical Revival style, received additions in 1936–39 (the Tuscan portico) and 1963 and a complete restoration in 1979. The most recent renovation, completed in 1998, presents a grand staircase which leads into a series of contemporary galleries.

As with so many other institutions in Adelaide that function successfully without much fuss and fanfare, the gallery has been quietly acquiring an intelligent and thoughtful collection for many years. In the last decade, an aggressive acquisitions programme, under the leadership of director Ron Radford and aided by generous local benefactors (public philanthropy for cultural institutions is more well established in South Australia than in the other Australian states), has transformed the gallery into one of the best and most comprehensive collections in the country.

The North Terrace entrance leads into a vestibule which spans the upper ground floor's two wings. On the left side, the **Melrose Wing** houses the gallery's **European Collection**, the section that contains some of the collection's most surprising treasures, including Claude Lorrain's *Caprice with Ruins of the Roman Forum* (c 1635), Anthony van Dyck's *Portrait of a Seated Couple* (c 1620), Luca Giordano and Giuseppe Recco's *The Riches of the Sea with Neptune* (1684), and a superb Scipione Pulzone portrait from 1580. This section also displays much of the gallery's extensive collection of British art, highlighting an aluminium statue of *Eros* by Albert Gilbert (c 1892) and a portrait of *Madame le Brun* by Thomas Gainsborough (1780). Twenty bronze sculptures by Auguste Rodin are also displayed throughout these rooms.

The **Elder Wing** on the right-hand side of the entrance vestibule exhibits the gallery's excellent collection of Australian art, particularly valued for its major works of the **colonial period**. Paintings include John Lewin, *Fish catch and Dawes Point, Sydney Harbour* (c 1813), one of the first still-lifes painted in Australia; John Glover's *A View of the Artist's House and Garden, Van Diemen's Land* (1835), the English painter's optimistic tribute to his new country; Tom Roberts's *A break away!* (1891), one of the most iconic works of the nationalist school; and Charles Conder's *Holiday at Mentone* (1888), the epitome of the Australian adaptation of Impressionist technique and theme.

Examples of specifically **South Australian painters**, such as Alexander Schramm's paintings from the 1850s and those of George French Angas (1822–86), form an important exhibition in these rooms. Also in this collection are significant examples of **Aboriginal art**, with the finest collection of the desert dot paintings, such as Clifford Possum Tjapaltjarri, *Honey Ant Dreaming* (1980) and Turkey Tolson Tjupurrula, *Straightening Spears at Ilyingaungau* (1990). More contemporary Australian art, of which the gallery is now a major collector, occupies the west wing galleries of this floor, and range from works by Peter Booth to Imants Tillers and performance pieces and installations.

The lower ground floor houses the gallery's growing collection of **Asian art**, especially fine in Southeast Asian ceramics. Also on this floor are the rooms devoted to **decorative and folk arts**, announced by entrance to the galleries through an actual Barossa Valley German stone chapel. These exhibitions include probably the best examples of German craftsmanship, especially woodwork and furniture, produced in the regions around Adelaide; an identifiable 'Barossa style' developed here and is well documented in the gallery's displays.

The **Adelaide Club** at 165 North Terrace on the south side of the street east of King William Street is private. Founded mainly by English and Scottish men of financial substance, the Adelaide Club has been a meeting place for the city's business leaders since its completion in 1864. An example of an early Victorian palazzo style, it was designed by G. & E. Hamilton and built by English & Brown. The materials are Dry Creek stone with shaped brick quoins and window surrounds.

University of Adelaide

The **University of Adelaide** was established in 1874 by a group of philanthropists, among whom was Sir Walter Watson Hughes, commemorated by the statue near the entrance. Nearby is a statue of another city father, Sir Thomas Elder (see box), a Scotsman who rose from modest finances to become the organising force behind the wool-selling firm of Elder Smith Goldsbrough Mort. Adelaide University was the first Australian university to admit women to degrees in 1881; they had admission to classes from the beginning.

The **Mitchell Building**, the nucleus of the university, was constructed between 1879 and 1881 from a design by local architect William McMinn (1844–84), a colourful Irishman who came to South Australia in 1850. He was at one time a surveyor in the Northern Territory, and gained fame for accomplishing a 2000-mile voyage in an open boat from Escape Cliffs to Champion Bay in Western Australia. McMinn set up practice as an architect in Adelaide in 1870, where he worked for the last 14 years of his life. One of the best examples of Gothic Revival in Adelaide, the building's design was apparently contested by Melbourne architect Michael Egan, and it is usually considered to be Egan's design and McMinn's construction. Initially housing administration, class rooms and the library, it now houses a good **Museum of Classical Archaeology** (open weekdays 09.00–17.00) which displays some 500 objects.

Across Goodman Crescent from the Mitchell Building is **Bonython Hall**, designed by Walter Hervey Bagot in 1936. Funded from a bequest by Adelaide's great benefactor Sir Langdon Bonython, its intended use was as a great hall similar to those at the universities in Melbourne and Sydney. Its structure and ornament consciously evoke British university style. The exterior is of Murray Bridge limestone, in a rough finish which shows the stone's texture. The windows

are arcaded to shelter against direct sunlight. The slate roof is from Willunga, near McLaren Vale in the south of the state. Its interior is marked by a sloping floor because Bonython wanted the building to be used for ceremonial purposes rather than frivolous dancing. Other features include steel trusses and reinforced concrete as a decorative ceiling, jarrah and pine floors, and oak joinery.

Elder Hall, Adelaide

Thomas Elder

Thomas Elder (1818–97) was an important pastoralist and partner from 1863 in Elder, Smith & Co., one of the most prosperous wool-brokers, stock and station agents, and general merchants. He owned (with fellow pastoralist and eventual philanthropist to the University of Adelaide, Peter Waite) Paratoo Run and Beltana sheep station behind the Flinders Ranges. He subsequently owned a tract of land larger than Scotland. In 1862 he brought camels to South Australia from India; these became invaluable in the exploration of inland tracts, several expeditions of which were funded and supplied with camels by Elder. He was also a legislator, involved in copper-mining, and an expert horse breeder, bringing valuable blood-stock from England. In 1874 he endowed the University with £20,000; his later gifts amounted to £100,000. He was also a benefactor of the Zoological Gardens.

Elder Hall (☎ 08 8228 5925), the conservatory of music, is the university's second oldest building. Built through a bequest by Sir Thomas Elder (see box) in 1898 as part of a series of bequests, which included the first art gallery and a number of workman's homes, it opened in 1900. The design by F.J. Naish is in Gothic Revival style; built in sandstone, the roof line is ornamented with flèches and corner turrets. It remains one of Australia's finest concert venues with a famous organ built by Casuant Freres, Quebec. The conservatory has regular free concerts at lunchtime; call for details and current times for the concerts.

Barr-Smith Library is behind Elder Hall to the west of the University Club. Robert Barr Smith was a benefactor of the university library during the late 1800s. Upon his death in 1915, his son continued the family's interest, eventually funding the W.H. Bagot-designed library which bears his father's name. It opened in 1932 and features a Mediterranean style façade and interior design. The reading room is particularly pleasant, the colours lightening in hue as they rise to the ceiling.

A bit of a walk through campus to the north, just across Victoria Drive, leads to **River Torrens Footbridge**, a romantic favourite for weekend walks. This cantilever welded steel bridge, built in 1938 by the South Australian Railways, features light ornament and an aesthetically pleasing relationship to the site.

Scots Church, across North Terrace from Bonython Hall, was built in 1851 to a design by Thomas English; the spire was added in 1856 and the gabled addition to the south in 1863–64. Now a Uniting Church, this was the first permanent place of worship for Presbyterians in the city. It is also the second oldest extant church in Adelaide. Constructed of bluestone, with brick quoins, an asymmetrically placed spire and a steeply pitched roof, its stained-glass windows are original.

Ayers House and Botanic Chambers Hotel

Architect Sir George Kingston took nearly 30 years to build **Ayers House** across North Terrace past Frome Road. This beautiful structure is now owned by the National Trust (☎ 08 8223 1234; open Tues–Fri 10.00–16.00, weekends 13.00–16.00). The central one-storeyed section was built in 1846 for William Paxton, a Rundle Street chemist. Sir Henry Ayers, active in South Australia government for 50 years, was intermittently South Australian premier in the 1860s and 1870s and was the namesake of Ayers Rock, now again called Uluru. Ayers bought the property in 1855, and added the downstairs library and second-storey bedrooms in 1858. The western wing, which includes an elegant drawing room, was added in 1874. The building features white-painted shuttered window architraves, stuccoed entry porches, original cedar joinery and flooring and underground excavation for living accommodation during the hot summer months.

The Botanic Chambers Hotel, Adelaide

Next door to Ayers House is **Botanic Chambers Hotel**, an absolute gem of a 19C grand hotel and pub. The hotel is reminiscent of a wedding cake, with stepped-back verandahs culminating in the heavy cornices and Corinthian-capped pilasters, as well as a balustraded parapet and a mansard-roofed short tower. In country areas and other cities, verandahs straddling the footpath were continued through the full height of the building on every floor. Regulations taking effect in the 1920s and 1940s have caused examples of footpath-wide verandahs to be removed in Sydney and Melbourne, and in Perth only one such hotel survives. The same regulation has begun to affect hotels in Adelaide. As a consequence the Botanic Chambers Hotel is now one of the few as well as the finest example of stepped-back verandah construction in Adelaide. The Botanic has served as a centre for social life for over 100 years.

Originally without verandahs and balconies, the hotel now features a spectacular double recession typical of the tiered balconies of Adelaide. The main entrance is emphasised by verandah pediments. The balconies feature paired columns and elaborate spandrels and frieze work, cast-iron hand rails and balustrading. The date of their introduction is uncertain, but Harley's 'Sun' Catalogue, a local publication dated 1914, affirms that they were in place by then; they may, however, have been made in earlier years. The stepping back of the first-floor balcony and the top floor left without façade is a device peculiar to Adelaide and Brisbane.

The hotel was designed by Michael McMullen and built by J. Barry for R. Vaughan in 1876–77. This elaborate survival of the city's original structures was intended as a family, that is, a temperance, hotel. Initially, it had seven residences, each with twelve rooms and a bay window on the ground floor and a balcony above. The hotel contained twenty-five rooms. A liquor licence was granted the hotel in 1883. Most of the modern renovations have been internal.

Tandanya Aboriginal Cultural Institute is at 241–59 GRENFELL STREET, two blocks south of North Terrace, in a building that was formerly the central power station for Rundle Street. (☎ 08 8223 2467, open daily 10.00–17.00.) Tandanya was established in 1989 as Adelaide's premier gallery, cultural centre and artists' cooperative devoted to Aboriginal culture. The multicoloured design in concrete block at the entrance is of the *River Spirit Dreaming* by Bluey Roberts. The institute's performing arts space seats 160 people and is used by the resident drama group, Eastenders. Tandanya is the sole Aboriginal-operated outlet for arts and crafts in Adelaide. Offering work from across Australia, it is arguably the best gallery of Aboriginal art in the state.

The building's original use as a power station is a reminder of Adelaide's once ambitious system of **trams**. Although there is little evidence currently of electrical tramways, they did exist after the government purchased all privately owned horse-drawn tramways in 1906. The electricity was supplied by the new Municipal Tramways Trust. Its power station was erected on East Terrace behind Grenfell Street Power Station. Rebuilt in 1912, it was designed by Alfred Wells and M. Stuart Clarke in a British Baroque style similar to Luytens' style. The electric tramways buildings on Hackney Road were built in 1907–08. Designed as a single project by H.E. Sibley and C.W. Woolridge, they included an administration building, now called Goodman Building after the first electrical tramway engineer.

A nostalgic collection of the tramway cars of this period (the last Adelaide tram system was dismantled in 1958) is preserved at the **Australian Electric Transport Museum** (☎ 08 8261 9110, open Sun and holidays; call for times), located in St Kilda on Barker Inlet, c 25km north of Central Adelaide off Port Wakefield Road, on St Kilda Road.

The Botanic and Zoological Gardens

The main gate of the **Adelaide Botanic Gardens** (☎ 08 8228 2311, open 09.00 until sunset) is on North Terrace; the back entrance is on a road to the left off Hackney Road. Both the Botanic Gardens and the adjacent Zoological Gardens accessible on Frome Road, were established in the 19C spirit of scientific investigation. The gardens were founded in 1855 by G.W. Francis and opened to the public in 1857. Initially they also provided a forum for speakers, similar to Speakers' Corner at Hyde Park, London.

The **Zoological Gardens** (☎ 08 8267 3255, open daily 09.30–17.00) were an outgrowth of the Acclimatization Society. This curiously misguided group sought to import European, especially British, animal and plant species to Australia. Like those people who found the bush forbidding and ominous, these people found it necessary to 'import to our somewhat unmelodious hills and woods the music and harmony of the English country life'. To this rather ambitious aim, they introduced blackbirds, sparrows, and starlings among other now pernicious species. Today, the zoo is a pleasant one, with a famous reptile house and walk-through southeast Asian rainforest. The zoo is also well known for its participation in conservation efforts and research about endangered species. An enjoyable way of travelling to the zoo is by motor launch along the Torrens River; check with the tourist office for details.

Consonant with the spirit of the times, what had been a wilderness area here was groomed into an English garden. It offered public venues for concerts and forums and was the site of the inaugural meeting of the Salvation Army in Australia. The gardens currently contain some 3000–4000 plants from Australasia and Malaysia.

The **Palm House** in the Botanic Gardens was erected during the directorship of Dr Richard Schomburgk (1811–91). Schomburgk's biography is uncommon in Australia. Born in Freiburg and educated in Berlin and Potsdam, his brother was Sir Robert Hermann Schomburgk, who explored British Guiana in 1830s. During the 1848 German Revolution, he migrated to South Australia where he cultivated vineyards on Gawler River on a property named Buchsfelde. In 1865, he somehow succeeded G.W. Francis as director of the Botanic Gardens, a post he held for 26 years. The palm house was one of his best improvements during his tenure. He imported it from Bremen in 1871 and it opened in 1876. After a period of disrepair, the city has renovated it. Since the tropical gardens have been housed in the conservatory, this cute building has recently been given over to a novel display of the cool, dry climate of Madagascar.

The **Museum of Economic Botany** (Herbarium) is a result of Director Schomburgk's notion that crop testing as well as species sampling was a function of the gardens. It displays changing demonstrations in a pedagogical vein. The building was erected from sketches prepared in 1878 for a museum building to house botanical specimens. Originally in Romanesque style, the then Colonial Architect E.J. Woods altered it to a Grecian style. The ceiling decoration is by W.J. Williams.

The **Bicentennial Conservatory**, opened in 1988, is the largest interior rainforest in the Southern hemisphere and includes its own cloud-making system. It holds 15 to 20 medium-sized rainforest trees and associated ground vegetation. The sculpture in front of the conservatory is entitled *Cascade*; made of Pilkington glass it is by Sergio Redegalli, and was installed in the 1980s.

At the north entrance to the Botanic Gardens is North Lodge, now the gardens' shop, with brochures of the gardens and a variety of books on gardening and Australian plant life.

North Adelaide

In Colonel Light's original plan, **North Adelaide**, across the Torrens River, was laid out as a grid of 1042 one-acre lots and associated squares and parks; he envisioned this section as the residential area, close enough to the commerce of the city but removed enough to allow quiet and comfortable living conditions. Permanent development began by the 1840s, with continuous growth throughout the 19C. The area today retains its historical charm, with many of the Victorian mansions and small shops still in evidence.

The main thoroughfare is KING WILLIAM ROAD, crossing the River Torrens and continuing as O'CONNELL STREET, which became the shopping and commercial street of North Adelaide and led into the outer suburbs. You can walk across the bridge at King William Road or the Victoria Bridge at Montefiore Road and reach North Adelaide in 10 minutes. In *Early Adelaide Architecture* (1969), Morgan and Gilbert wrote about the various routes that Light envisioned to reach this section of the city.

North Adelaide is accessible via King William, Montefiore and Frome Roads, across the park district, Torrens River and common lands from the central district. If a more extensive walk through the old neighbourhood is desired, take **bus nos 231–233 and 235–237** on King William Road to JEFFCOTT STREET, where many of the earliest colonial buildings in North Adelaide are located.

Immediately north across Adelaide Bridge on King William Road at **PENNINGTON TERRACE** is **St Peter's Cathedral**, designed by English architect William Butterfield and built by the local firm of Woods and McMinn. The foundation stone was laid in 1869, and construction progressed in stages, with the final Lady Chapel consecrated in 1904. The church is said, by Bishop Reed in the 1960s, to have the 'finest and heaviest ring of bells in the Southern hemisphere'. The interior includes an excellent organ and particularly elegant stained-glass windows, as well as a carved and painted reredos, installed in 1904.

Also in Pennington Terrace is the **Quakers' Meeting House**, a prefabricated timber building brought from England in 1840. It was shipped in 69 separate packages of wooden sections and iron pillars; another ship brought its 3000 roof slates. Behind the cathedral at St Mark's College is **The Cottage**, also built in 1840; it is one of the oldest extant brick buildings in South Australia.

At the western end of Pennington Terrace is Montefiore Hill, site of **Light's Vision**, a rather poignant statue of Adelaide's creator, William Light. The statue originally stood on Victoria Square, where it was unveiled in 1906; it was moved to this location in 1938, where it looks across the parklands and the river to the city and the Adelaide Hills beyond.

The **North Adelaide Railway Station**, north on War Memorial Drive by the intersection with Mildred Road, was opened in 1857, two years after the construction of the Torrens Railway bridge during a period of rapid steam-driven railway development. Benjamin Herschell Babbage (1815–57), in association with Isambard Kingdom Brunel, designed and built railways in England and on the continent for the Great Western Railway Company. The Adelaide to Port Adelaide line was of the same type. The line to the north to Gawler opened the same year as the North Adelaide Station and by 1860 the rail service to Kupunda had commenced. Alterations made in 1878 to the station's doors, windows and verandah altered its appearance relatively little. The signal box was erected shortly thereafter, and remains one of the only original boxes in the city.

On the eastern side of the North Adelaide terrace circuit, **ROBE TERRACE** is an old residential area with large, wealthy homes. Before the expansion of the road it was very close to the parklands. The intersection traffic makes it unlikely that its present functions will be changed.

Settlement of the area was slow, largely due to the flooding of the River Torrens each winter. These floods routinely destroyed bridges until 1856, when the second King William Bridge was built. It stood until replaced in 1931. The Morphett Street bridge, replaced in 1965, had stood since 1870. The 1879 Frome Road bridge, a cast-iron structure with attractive hand rails and scalloped girders, still stands.

The finest house in North Adelaide is arguably **Kumanka House**, still a private residence. Originally called St Margaret's, it can be found on CHILDERS STREET west of Jeffcott Street, on the northern fringe of the district. Henry Hill had it built in 1870 at considerable cost. He and his son John Hill founded a coach and carrying company which bought the failing South Australian branch of Cobb & Co. in 1871. The house has been associated with many prominent Adelaide families, most notably the colourful Charles Valentine Tighe Wells, owner of a New Guinea gold-mine and founder of Guinea Airways, who lived in the house in the 1930s.

Ru Rua Mansions, Maori for 'both equally', is a block north at nos 101–110 Barton Terrace. The place was named by a syndicate of medical doctors who set up practice in the three pairs of houses. The design was by F.W. Dancker, probably influenced by the designs of American architect George Barber, a populariser of Queen Anne style, whose designs were available through catalogues. These houses have since returned to private residences after years as part of a nursing home.

The most socially prestigious area of North Adelaide is perhaps TYNTE STREET west of O'Connell Street. At nos 165–169 is the **North Adelaide Hotel**. Margaret Iben, widow of William, had it built at the outset of the 1880s boom. Its elaborate Italianate design and stuccoed detail alone would have offended the sensibilities of many of the era's more sober civic leaders.

Across the street from this pub are the classical blocks of the North Adelaide Institute and Post Office, the former Rechabite Hall and University College. Their solidity and lack of ornament are a clear indication of the dour attitude at work in the design of the late-19C suburbs.

The **Rechabite Hall**, erected in 1858 for the South Australian Total Abstinence Society, is one of a number of meeting and entertainment venues built by abstemious 19C Australians. The Rechabites took their world-view from the story of Rechab in the Bible, the Book of Jeremiah. Rechab followed his son's insight and told his people not to drink wine or cultivate crops but to live nomadically in tents. The Lord, according to Jeremiah chapter 35, commended the filial loyalty of Rechab's subsequent generations and brought disaster on Jeremiah's Jerusalem for not heeding His prophets. There were established branches of the Rechabites in most Australian cities by the end of the 19C.

The Rechabite building was designed by James William Cole, a Methodist and participating member of the society. Built in 1856–58, it was remodelled in 1883, three years after the Rechabites move to Grote Street.

The Nonconformist aesthetic of the time draws on English sources. It follows John Soane's aesthetic simplicity: no ornament atop the columns or corners, virtually no entry porch, plain horizontal lines. A somewhat later and more ambitious structure of Nonconformist design is a block west at Tynte Street on Wellington Square, the former **Primitive Methodist church**. Designed in the early 1880s by Daniel Garlick, it displays something like a Gothic Revival style allowing more ornament than J.W. Cole might have presented.

At nos 34–38 Wellington Square is the **Wellington Hotel**, first licensed in 1851; it retains its original wooden balcony, although most of the building was substantially altered in 1885. The unusual cantilevered balcony has distinctive verandah brackets, unlike the usual cast-iron embellishment of the time.

The combined **Institute** and **Post Office** to the right of the Rechabite Hall on Tynte Street demonstrates the importance of civic participation in building design. Local donations enabled the building of the hall to the building's rear and the Institute; the Post Office was built with public funds. According to Susan Marsden in *Heritage of the City of Adelaide* (1990), repeated calls for a cultural institute in North Adelaide were successful only when a local post office was constructed in 1882. The eventual construction is unconventional for its classical style, brick façade with cement dressings and asymmetrical frontage.

A final note on North Adelaide's late-19C social fabric on Tynte Street also concerns religious matters. While the German Lutheran schisms in the early century occurred in a relatively agrarian setting, the Baptists of North Adelaide were thoroughly suburban. They had been prominent and divisive since the colony's foundation; David McLaren, manager of the South Australia Company, was father of Alexander McLaren, divine of the English Baptist church.

Church buildings were erected upon each congregation's division. Some of these divisions had theological bases. The appointment of Reverend Silas Mead and the building of his church in Flinders Street in 1863 was meant to effect unity in the North Adelaide Baptist community. **The Manse**, a modest two-storey residence with window seats at 142 Tynte Street, and now a restaurant, was built by James Cumming in 1877. Next to the manse is the **Baptist church**, completed in 1820, also by James Cumming. He attempted to add grandeur to the design by using contrasting colours in the stone. The heavy style is some-what similar to the Flinders Street Baptist church. The interior includes perfo-rated zinc ceiling grates for ventilation and curved pews.

Entering North Adelaide via Frome Road near the zoo leads to the eastern section of the area, bounded by Kingston Terrace on the north, and crossing the river at Albert Bridge. This route leads through the parklands to **MELBOURNE STREET** (or take bus nos 204–209 from King William Road), the chic shopping street of the suburb, filled with good cafes, antique shops and clothing boutiques.

Western Adelaide and Glenelg

From the centre of town, a single vintage tram, the **Bay Tram**, travels the 11km to the popular beach resort of Glenelg; it departs from Victoria Square and ends its run at Moseley Square on the beach.

Glenelg is called the 'Birthplace of South Australia', for it was here, on 28 December 1836, that John Hindmarsh was proclaimed governor of the new colony. The **'Old Gum-Tree'** on McFarlane Street (c 1km east of Glenelg North beach off Tapleys Hill Road), now reinforced with concrete and iron, is still used as the site for Proclamation Day (28 December) ceremonies every year. **Tourist information centre**, Moseley Square, Glenelg, ☎ 08 8294 5833.

To the northeast of Glenelg c 3.5km at the suburb of Novar Gardens is **Cummins House** (☎ 08 8294 1939; open Sun 14.00–16.00, weekdays by appointment), off Saratoga Drive on Sheoak Avenue. This was the property of John Morphett (1809–92), South Australian pioneer and surveyor with Light's expedition. The house includes original furnishings in its Italianate interiors.

The area around the beach at Glenelg includes the usual beachside amuse-ment park and outside eateries, but the adjoining streets also house extravagant Victorian summer homes, where the wealthy used to spend the hot summer days. Also on the foreshore is a replica of the HMS *Buffalo*, Governor Hind-marsh's ship (see p 458). Its interior serves as a museum depicting early settle-ment and life on ship (☎ 08 8294 7000; open daily 10.00–17.00).

8km north along the coastal Military Road and past the other popular beach resort of **Henley Beach**, is the suburb of **Grange**, named for the home that explorer Charles Sturt built here in 1840. The house, on Jetty Street, is an inter-esting place to visit (☎ 08 8356 8185; open Wed–Sun 12.00–17.00). After overlanding cattle to Adelaide from New South Wales, Sturt purchased two 84-acre (34 ha) sections of land here, then called Reedbeds. The house Sturt built here was, according to his friend George MacLeay, 'the most English-looking place in the Province'. Sturt's wife often played her harp for informal summer gatherings on the stone terrace that looks out on to Mount Lofty. When the Sturt family finally left the colony for England in 1853, the Grange passed through many hands and fell into disrepair. In 1956, it was purchased by a trust which set out to restore it. Aided by donations of original furniture from the Sturt family, the house is now a historical museum with many authentic artefacts.

The **Royal Adelaide** (☎ 08 8356 5511) and **Grange Golf Clubs** (☎ 08 8235 1820) are in Seaton, about 2km from Grange and 10km northwest of Adelaide. One of the country's oldest clubs, the Royal Adelaide's founding was the dream of Scotsman Sir James Fergusson, Governor of South Australia from 1869 to 1873. Its location changed several times. The present Seaton location was laid out by Dr Alister Mackenzie in 1926 and its seaside atmosphere has been maintained during more recent upgrades.

The Grange Golf Club was established in 1926 and subsequently enlarged to include the East Course which higher handicapped players sometimes prefer. The West Course was cleared by hand, explaining the effect the rough can have on the game. On a day with wind the 6th hole par 4 is a challenge made more difficult by the rough and scrub flanking it and the traps at the green. Golfers are advised to swing slowly to keep their shots low. On the way back, a wind from behind and a raised tee facing a wide and open fairway make the first two shots look impressive.

Port Adelaide

MILITARY ROAD continues from Grange c 6km north to Bower Road and into **Port Adelaide**, the original area of harbour development that caused such grief for William Light's vision of Adelaide (see p 460). You can also take a train to 'the Port' from Adelaide's central station, or bus nos 258 or 259 from North Terrace. **Black Diamond Visitor Information**, on the corner of Commercial Road and St Vincent Street, ☎ 08 8447 4788.

In Port Adelaide, three vessels offer cruises along the river and around Barker Inlet. These cruises depart from Queens Wharf; check with the tourist office for full details. Queens Wharf is also the site of Sunday markets (08.00–17.00), featuring 'trash and treasure' and ethnic food.

The early authorities, at least the naval men such as Governor Hindmarsh, were furious that Light's settlement was situated so far from the sea; in the early days, transportation from the port to the town was indeed rigorous, as supplies had to be dragged through the mud and scrub. Eventually, of course, Light's persistence proved to be correct, as the port area would have flooded and would not have had enough fresh water to support a large settlement.

The area around the port itself did develop from the 1840s as the principal gateway to the colony for both immigrants and supplies; by the 1880s, Port Adelaide was a thriving hub of industry and shipping, a fact attested to by the many substantial buildings in the historic precinct around the intersection of St Vincent Street and Commercial Road. Particularly noteworthy are the 1861 **Court House and Police Station**, 66 Commercial Road, with its graceful arcades; and next door, at no. 56, the **former Customs House**, ingeniously constructed on a bed of red-gum timbers embedded in lime concrete. The tower of the Customs House was an important landmark for ships coming into port.

Two blocks east of Commercial Road on Lipson Street is the excellent **South**

Australian Maritime Museum (☎ 08 8240 0200; open daily 10.00–17.00), located in an old Bond Store. The museum, now run by the History Trust of South Australia, was originally the Port Adelaide Nautical Museum, the oldest in Australia, with all kinds of artefacts of maritime life along the South Australian coast. Today, the main concentration in this well-presented museum is the story of migration to South Australia, as well as a history of the coastal ketch trade.

Further along Lipson Street is the **Port Dock Station and Semaphore Railway** (☎ 08 8341 1690; open daily 10.00–17.00), filled with the predictable detritus of the era of rail, including miniature steam trains and large numbers of locomotives. Also in the port, at Ocean Steamers Road, is the **South Australian Historical Aviation Museum** (☎ 08 8341 2678; open weekends and holidays, Tues–Sun in school holidays, 10.00–17.00).

On Hart Street, 3km to the west, you pass by **Fort Glanville** at **Semaphore**, open to the public every third Sunday from September to May. This site is the most complete of the many fortress complexes built along the Australian coast after the Crimean War led the colonies to fear the possibility of Russian invasion. Also in Semaphore, on Semaphore Road, is a **Time Ball Tower**, built in 1874 in stone, to enable ships' masters to set their chronometers by reference to a black ball dropped every day at 13.00. It operated until 1932 and is still preserved as a reminder of the importance of the shipping trade in the early days of the colony.

From Semaphore, the Esplanade along the foreshore continues north to the **Outer Harbor**, which is now the location of the Overseas Passenger Terminal. En route, at **Largs Bay**, is **Largs Pier Hotel** (☎ 08 8449 5666), an elaborate three-storey bluestone structure curving around the corner with Classical arcades running around each storey. Ernest Bayer and Latham A. Withall designed this grand structure in 1882. Despite many internal changes, the building still boasts an impressive double-flight staircase, ingeniously connected to the lobby and verandahs. The hotel would have been one of the first buildings seen by newly arrived visitors from overseas in the 19C.

Towards the Adelaide Hills

A trip to the Adelaide Hills is usually discussed as 'taking a tourist drive', but public transport may also be available to some of these locations, and coach tours operate throughout the region. For public buses, check with the bus Customer Service Centre, ☎ 08 8210 1000. For coach tours, contact the tourist office on King William Street, Adelaide, ☎ 08 8303 2033.

Only 15 minutes from the city centre in the suburb of Magill is **Penfold's Magill Estate** (Penfold Road, ☎ 08 8301 5569; open daily 10.30–16.30), a living museum on the site of the first cellars of Australia's most highly regarded wine-making families. Take Wakefield Road east, turn left (north) on Fullarton Road, then east on to The Parade; c 6km is Penfold Road, with the winery on the corner. Tours are given of the historic vintage and maturation cellars, ending with a view of the Still House, from where came the first of Penfold's great vintages. The Still House now operates as a tasting room and offers cellar door sales.

Leave the centre of town heading south on Glen Osmond Road, which becomes Highway 1. 6km southeast of Adelaide, between the suburbs of **Burnside** and

Glen Osmond on the Princes Highway, is **Beaumont House** (631 Glynburn Road, Beaumont; ☎ 08 8379 5301; open first Sun each month, 14.00–16.30). This Classic Revival house with a deep arcade and narrow-arched windows is an early attempt by the Adelaide residents to cope with the heat of the region. Built in 1851 on Samuel Davenport's property for Anglican Bishop Augustus Short, it was donated in 1967 to the National Trust by owners Kenneth and Lilian Brock.

Also in Burnside, at Kurralta Drive off Greenhill Road, is the homestead **'Kurralta'**, built in 1843–46 by the architect of Ayers House, George Strickland Kingston, for Dr William Wyatt (not open to the public). Wyatt was an important figure in the early colony, serving many roles as well as physician. As Protector of Aborigines, he was a staunch advocate of their rights, and became an authority on the tribes of Adelaide and Encounter Bay. He chose to name the house 'Kurralta', an Aboriginal word for 'on the hill'. Wyatt was also a keen botanist, and the gardens at Kurralta rivalled those of the city's Botanic Gardens; despite encroaching development, some of these plants still exist in the gardens around the house. From the balcony of the house, Wyatt had a panoramic view of the town and the Gulf of St Vincent; his telescope here could read the time on the General Post Office clock. The house itself has a decidedly Mediterranean style, with limited ornamentation, large bay windows, and an arched patio.

To the southwest of Burnside c 5km in the suburb of Springfield is **Carrick Hill** (46 Carrick Hill Road, ☎ 08 8379 3886; open Wed–Sun and holidays, 10.00–17.00; tours 11.00, 12.00, 14.00, 15.00), an extravagant property famed for its 39 ha of gardens and spectacular views of the city. From the city, take Fullarton Road south c 7km until it becomes Carrick Hill Road. The creation of leading Adelaide businessman Sir Edward Hayward and his wife Ursula Barr Smith, the house, built in 1939, is in the style of an English manor. The gardens are considered the best English-style gardens in Australia, and include a sculpture, park and a number of beautiful walks.

Immediately north of the Carrick Hill site, also along Fullarton Road, is the **University of Adelaide**, Waite Campus; the postal address here is Netherby, but the area is now referred to as the Mitcham Foothills Tourist Precinct, because of several historic attractions in the district. On the campus at Fullarton Road between Cross Road and Kitchener Street is the **Urrbrae House Historic Precinct** (☎ 08 8303 7497; open weekdays 10.00–16.00). The house itself is a bluestone mansion built in 1891 as the home for prominent South Australia pastoralist Peter Waite (1834–1922), who donated this property to the university for the purposes of establishing an agricultural research centre. During Waite's residence here in 1895, the house became the first in South Australia to have electricity for lighting and refrigeration.

The building now houses a museum about the Waite family, and maintains the original rose gardens, filled with 'heritage plants'. The lower level of Urrbrae House is now the home of the **National Textile Museum** (☎ 08 8303 6728; open Wed–Sun 11.00–16.00), Australia's only museum devoted specifically to the history of textiles. While the permanent collection is small, the museum carries on an active changing exhibition programme, as well as lecture series.

The house's adjacent Coach House and Stables now exhibits the Mawson Antarctic Collection, which includes the famous photographs and films taken by Frank Hurley during Douglas Mawson's 1911–14 exploration of Antarctica.

Also on the Waite campus is the Waite Arboretum (☎ 08 8303 7405; open dawn to dusk, tours 11.00 every first Sunday). Established in 1928 soon after Waite had donated the land to the university, the arboretum contains more than 2500 labelled trees of native and introduced species. The grounds include a watercourse and lake.

Adelaide Hills

Only 30 minutes' drive from the middle of the city, the green hills of the **Mount Lofty Ranges** have always provided Adelaidians with a refreshing getaway. Many people live in the Adelaide Hills, and regular bus and train services run throughout the area. **Tourist information**: 41 Main Street, Hahndorf, ☎ 1 800 353 323/08 8388 1185. The famous **Hans Heysen Trail**, a long-distance bushwalking trail, cuts across these hills, through a variety of terrain. The trail, inaugurated in the 1970s, now covers 1500km from Cape Jervis on the southern tip of Fleurieu Peninsula to the Northern Flinders Ranges. Routes of the Heysen Trail are available as a set of 15 maps with trail notes, obtainable from the Department of the Environment and Natural Resources in Adelaide, 77 Grenfell Street, ☎ 08 8204 1910 (website: www.recsport.sa.gov.au). Opportunities for bushwalking at all levels of skill are rife throughout this district.

From the city, Glen Osmond Road becomes the SOUTH EASTERN FREEWAY, the main route to Melbourne. From here, take the exit at Crafers for Summit Road, which leads past the lovely **Mount Lofty Botanic Gardens** (☎ 08 8228 2311; open daily) to the Mount Lofty lookout, at 727m the highest point in the range. The lookout offers truly splendid views, on one side all of Adelaide and out to the Gulf of St Vincent; on the other side, calming views of the gently rolling green valleys of the hills themselves. On Summit Road is an information centre with a digital camera that provides close-up views of the panoramas; ☎ 08 8370 1054.

To the west of the lookout is **Cleland Conservation Park**, which includes a wildlife park (☎ 08 8339 2444) and picnic areas.

To the south of Mount Lofty is **Belair Recreation Park** (☎ 08 8278 5477), accessible from the city by a delightful train, which begins at the Morphett Street Station in central Adelaide and provides great views of the city and coastline as it climbs up into the park. One half of the park, originally the property of early pioneer Nicholas Foot, is rather elegant, with man-made lake, hedge maze, and a restored Old Government House, which is open on Sunday afternoons. The building was constructed in the early 1860s as a retreat from the summer heat; it was used by many vice-regents until it was replaced in the 1880s by Marble Hill in nearby Ashton. (Today, most of Marble Hill stands as a ruin after it burned to the ground in 1955, the victim of the area's frequent bushfires.) It has been carefully restored, with donations from pioneer families of furniture and artefacts. It has a ballroom and an indoor pool fed by two springs. 6km from Norton Summit on the Ashton Montacute Road, Marble Hill (☎ 08 8390 1884; open Wed, Sat 13.00–17.00, Sun 10.00–17.00) now has a restored tower with excellent views and a reconstructed governor's study.

Hahndorf

Only 28km southeast from the centre of Adelaide, the village of **Hahndorf** (population 1600) is the most immediate reminder of the presence of German settlers and the significance of German culture in the history of the South

Australian colony. From the South Eastern Freeway (Highway 1), exit on to Mount Barker Road (Highway 57), which becomes Main Street in Hahndorf. (It can be reached from central Adelaide by taking the Mount Barker Passenger Service bus from Franklin Street, ☎ 08 8391 2977.) **Tourist information:** 64 Main Street, ☎ 08 8388 1185. Hahndorf is the central location for the **Adelaide Hills Harvest Festival**, held annually in March, when hotels, wineries and restaurants throughout the region join together to present a weekend of food, wines and fun.

History

The village was founded in 1839, when a group of Prussian Lutherans, seeking freedom to worship according to their own beliefs, arrived in South Australia on the ship *Zebra*. Their captain, Dirk Meinertz Hahn, had never even heard of Adelaide when he was commissioned to bring his cargo of pious Prussians to the country. In the course of the trip, Hahn became quite attached to his charges, and, upon arriving in the colony, helped them to negotiate the purchase of the settlement's property from the new English landowner, W.H. Dutton. The grateful settlers, all followers of Reverend Kavel (see Barossa Valley, p 495), named their new village Hahndorf in honour of the captain. The industriousness of these first German settlers led to a thriving community, well established by the turn of the century. Anti-German sentiment during the First World War caused the village's name to be changed to Ambleside in 1917, and its German Lutheran school was closed. The town returned to the name Hahndorf in 1935 as part of the state-wide celebrations of the contribution of German pioneers during a century of settlement.

Haebichs Cottage at Hahndorf

Today, Hahndorf is a State Heritage Area, fully conserved and protected, famous for the beautiful European trees which line its Main Street. This historical status has not, however, stopped it from becoming the tourist-trap to beat all tourist-traps. Essentially one street long with a few side lanes, every one of the historic buildings now houses a tea room, craft gallery or tourist shop of some kind. Every weekend is tremendously crowded with visitors who are catered to by German-style restaurants and delicatessens. Still, the buildings are a fascinating display of German vernacular architecture transplanted to a colonial setting. Every building has a plaque with a full history of its functions. While one is warned not to trespass on private property, it is especially interesting and a more authentic experience to take a look into the side alleys and the back yards of the buildings, where small structures and farming functions remain untouched by tourism's heavy hand.

At the north end of Hahndorf's Main Street, across from the caravan park and tourist facility, is Ambleside Road (route 53); turn on to the road and continue c 1km to Hans Heysen Road, where you will find **'The Cedars'** (☎ 08 8388 7277; open weekdays, tours at 11.00, 13.00, and 15.00), the residence of beloved South Australian painter Hans Heysen.

Hans Heysen

Hans Heysen (1877–1968) became one of the most famous of Australian painters for his many depictions of gum trees in all their varieties and for his admiration for the rugged terrain of South Australia's Flinders Ranges. Heysen came from Hamburg to Adelaide as a child, and studied at the Adelaide School of Design, where he came to the attention of a group of city businessmen, who supported his art studies in Europe. Upon returning to Australia, he applied his technique, both in watercolour and oil, to the Australian landscape. Following some years of struggle, he gained enthusiastic patronage after an exhibition in Melbourne in 1912. He was championed by such celebrities as Dame Nellie Melba. He became the great populariser of Australian landscape painting and was identified entirely with his views of sinuous eucalyptus and the unique colours of the Australian bush. In 1912, he and his wife discovered 'The Cedars', built by a pastoralist in the 1870s, while walking in the Adelaide Hills, and determined to make it their home. As the artist Norman Lindsay wrote about Heysen, the Hahndorf environment 'was to Heysen what the little village of Barbizon was to ...Millet. It made him the intimate of nature and of the life of the farmers.' The property became the centre of Heysen's creative and family life; extensive renovations to the house were carried out in the 1920s by Adelaide architect E. Phillips Dancker, who was sympathetic to the natural setting and to the German-style homesteads of the area. Here Heysen and his wife Sallie raised their eight children, including Nora, also a painter who in 1938 became the first woman to win the Archibald Prize. Any famous visitor to Adelaide was obliged to make the trek to 'The Cedars', including the ballerina Anna Pavlova in 1926, and in the 1940s Laurence Olivier and Vivien Leigh, and Helen Keller. Today the house has been preserved essentially as it was when the Heysen family lived there.

To the north of Hahndorf c 20km via Lobethal and Gumeracha, and still considered part of the Adelaide Hills, is the **Torrens River Gorge**, one of the most beautiful valleys in this scenic area. From the centre of Adelaide, travel east via the NORTH EAST ROAD (route 58), which becomes the Adelaide–Mannum Road. (A coach service is also available to the area through *A.B.M. Coaches*, 101 Franklin Street, ☎ 08 8349 5551, although it will be difficult to explore all the area's small towns and views unless you have your own car or are part of a coach tour that will stop frequently.) Alternatively, take Payneham Road to Lower North East Road or Gorge Road, passing by **Black Hill Conservation Park**, 88 Addison Avenue, Athelstone, and **Morialta Conservation Park**, Stradbroke Road, Rostrevor, both of which offer scenic walking trails and picnic spots; Morialta is well known for its three waterfalls.

Off North East Road, at Perseverance Road in **Tea Tree Gully**, 20km from central Adelaide, is **Highercombe Hotel Folk Museum** (☎ 08 8264 0309; weekends and holidays 14.00–17.00), now a National Trust property. Built in

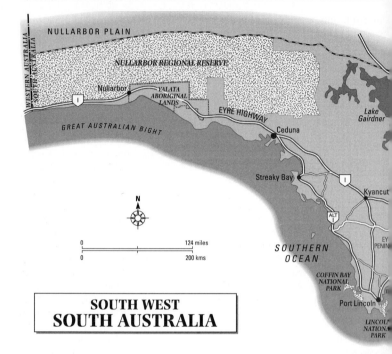

NULLARBOR PLAIN

NULLARBOR REGIONAL RESERVE

WESTERN AUSTRALIA
SOUTH AUSTRALIA

Nullarbor

YALATA
ABORIGINAL
LANDS

EYRE HIGHWAY

GREAT AUSTRALIAN BIGHT

Ceduna

Lake
Gairdner

Streaky Bay

Kyancut

ALT

N

0   124 miles
0   200 kms

SOUTHERN
OCEAN

EY
PENIN

COFFIN BAY
NATIONAL
PARK

Port Lincoln

LINCOLN
NATIONAL
PARK

SOUTH WEST
SOUTH AUSTRALIA

1854, the hotel was an important community centre until the main road bypassed it in 1875; it then became the Tea Tree Gully post office. The hotel now contains historic furniture and memorabilia of the late 19C. From the upper balcony, one can see as far as Port Adelaide.

Lobethal (population 2100), 36km southeast from Adelaide and c 12km northeast of Hahndorf, was settled by Pastor Gotthard Fritzsche in 1841, along with 18 Prussian families; hence the name, which means 'Valley of Praise'. The original 'Hufendorf' plan for the village, that is 'horseshoe village', is typical of German agricultural settlement patterns of the time. In town on Main Street, the **Lobethal Bakery** (☎ 08 8389 6318) is known far and wide as probably the best German bakery in Australia; it is open on weekdays only. Also on Main Street is the **Lobethal Archives and Historical Museum** (☎ 08 8389 6164; open Sun 14.00–17.00), which has interesting displays about the history of German settlement in the area.

From Lobethal, route 58 continues through some of the most impressive of the Torrens Gorge scenery to **Cudlee Creek**, home of Gorge Wildlife Park (☎ 08 8389 2206; open daily 08.00–17.00), Australia's largest privately owned collection of animals and birds, where you can have cuddly experiences with koalas and other creatures, as well as find a children's petting zoo. The other road from Lobethal leads to **Gumeracha** (population 840), one of the oldest settlements in the state, founded in 1839. While the village has a Baptist church and Randell Mill dating from the 1840s, its greatest attraction is an 18.3m tall **rocking horse** in front of a wooden toy factory (☎ 08 8389 1085; open daily);

you can climb to the top of the horse, all six storeys of it.

At Gumeracha, the Torrens Gorge, with its high rock walls, begins to soften into grazing pastures. At **Birdwood**, c 6km further east on the Adelaide–Mannum Road, the surrounding landscape is pastoral. Originally named Blumberg—German for 'hill of flowers'—the name was changed after the First World War in honour of Australian Forces Commander Field Marshall Lord Birdwood. Today, the village is best known for **Birdwood Mill: National Motor Museum** (☎ 08 8568 5006; open daily 09.00–17.00). The mill was built in 1852 by W.B. Randell and his sons; you can still see the massive adze-trimmed red gum columns and beams in the interior, with stone lintels and plinths. The original 18m high round chimney still stands. In 1965, the mill was bought by a motorcycle enthusiast to display his collection of historic motorcycles; it has now become Australia's largest collection of vintage automobiles and motorcycles. In September/October of even-numbered years, the museum is the destination of the participants in the Bay to Birdwood Motorfest, in which pre-1950 vehicles travel from Glenelg on the Adelaide bay to Birdwood. The event attracts participants and spectators from around the country.

The Barossa Valley

There are five major wine-growing districts in South Australia. Here, the Barossa Valley has been outlined as a fairly comprehensive tour. The other districts include some scattered vineyards in the Adelaide Hills; Clare Valley, north of the Barossa Valley; McLaren Vale, less than an hour south of Adelaide; and the justly famous Coonawarra, in the southeast corner of the state.

■ Practical information

Tourist information. The main tourist office for information on Barossa Valley tours, wine guides and accommodation is the **Barossa Wine and Visitor Centre**, 66–68 Murray Street, Tanunda, ☎ 1 800 812 662/08 8563 0600. Other centres are **Gawler Tourist Office**, Lyndoch Road, ☎ 08 8522 6814, and the central Adelaide office on King William Street, which has substantial information on tours and transport to the region. Another interesting source is the **Barossa B&B Booking Service**, ☎ 1 800 244 873, which arranges accommodation at homesteads, heritage cottages, and rural retreats in the valley (email bookings:bookings@dove.net.au).

Transport. As mentioned below, driving from Barossa Valley winery to winery requires a driver who will not partake heavily of the grape. If you cannot arrange for an abstemious driver (or a true wine connoisseur, who tastes but does not swallow), here are some other transport options, all of which, along with many other tour possibilities, can be arranged by calling directly or through the tourist offices:

Adelaide Suburban Rail (☎ 08 8210 1000) has a regular service as far as Gawler.
Barossa-Adelaide Passenger Service (☎ 08 8564 3022) offers a 3-times-a-day bus service between Adelaide and Tanunda. Reasonable fares for regular service; more specialised tour packages also available.
Bluebird Barossa Train (☎ 08 8212 7888; fax 08 8231 5771; e-mail: arto@chariot.net.au) operates a rail journey from the Adelaide Rail Station to the valley, passing through picturesque scenery and historic townships and stopping at many wineries; gourmet meal provided in the fare (currently $85 per adult). Various kinds of tours at various prices available. Advance bookings essential.
Barossa Experience Tours (☎ 08 8563 3248), **Barossa Vintage Tours** (☎ 1 800 244 873), and **Valley Tours** (☎ 08 8563 3587) are among the many agencies offering various personalised tour packages, catering to small groups. **Barossa Daimler Tours** (☎ 08 8524 9047) drive you luxuriously to many wineries in an 8-seat Daimler, with 2-course lunch and wine provided in the fare.
Ecotrek: Bogong Jack Adventures (☎ 08 8383 7198) organise great and easygoing bicycle trips for small groups through the valley, with emphasis on heritage accommodation and gourmet food.
Bicycle hire is also a good form of transportation through the small villages of the valley (although you must remember it is also dangerous to cycle while under the influence!): hire from Barossa Caravan Park, Lyndoch (☎ 08 8524 4262), Tanunda Caravan & Tourist Park (☎ 08 8563 2784).

Barossa Valley

Geologically part of the Flinders and Mount Lofty ranges, the Barossa Valley sits between the Bremer and Stockwell fault zones. Its easternmost edge is the Kaiser Stuhl, an early Palaeozoic injection of granite and gneiss outcropping through the valley's bed of quartzite, schist and marble. Deposits of copper, gold and other minerals in this area led to early mining and prospecting. The western slopes of the Barossa Range are relatively infertile dark brown cracking clays and deep sands which support some orchards, cereal crops and beef cattle. The valley's famous vineyards are grown on the alluvial soils and red-brown earths of the valley's floor.

The naturally occurring vegetation in the valley was first influenced by the Aboriginal hunting method in which fires were set in the undergrowth and scrub to drive game towards hunters or nets. The two dominant species of large eucalypt at the time of settlement can still be readily seen, where the red gums follow the creek beds and the taller blue gums are thinly scattered in paddocks and along roadsides. Other fire resistant species include acacias, peppermint gums and tufts of kangaroo grass and, at higher elevations, stringybarks.

The native populations of Peramangk, Kaurna and Ngadjuri Aborigines suffered much the same fate as the other indigenous people in the southern and eastern regions of Australia. Mobile, successful hunting and gathering groups of about 30 individuals fell victim to European diseases, then were displaced by the parcelling of land to European immigrants. Following continued population decline, those few remaining Aboriginals from the area were moved to Manuka Mission on the Murray River around the beginning of the 20C.

History

European settlement occurred in the 1840s and 1850s. The valley was given its name by William Light who had fought under Baron Thomas Graham Lynedoch (1748–1843) in Barrossa, Spain, against the French in 1811 (both names, for the place and hero, were misspelled when Light used them for his Australian locations). Unlike most of Australia, the area's early history is based on religious sectarian and denominational relations. The initial immigrants were Evangelical Lutheran Prussians settling on land owned by the Angas family. George Fife Angas (1789–1879) controlled the South Australian Company which owned a considerable part of South Australia. Pastor August Kavel of Klemzig, Prussia, approached Angas in 1836, requesting his help to resettle the persecuted sect. They had refused to follow Prussian King Frederick William III's unification of the Calvinist and Lutheran churches in the 1830s. Following an investigation by Charles Flaxman and protracted negotiations with the Prussian government, Angas loaned the group £8000 necessary for transport. Arriving in late 1838 and early 1839, the first shipload leased land from Angas northeast of Adelaide which they called Klemzig, after their native region in Brandenburg. The next group to arrive leased land in the Adelaide Hills from W.H. Dutton which they called Hahndorf after the captain of their ship (see p 492).

The first road into the Barossa Valley was finished by 1841 and Kavel's group established Bethany in 1842. Their land-use pattern was the Prussian *Hufendorf* style in which the Tanunda Creek provided the back of their properties with narrow strips of orchards, then cultivated land running from the creek to houses aligned along the road. The crops were in a three-year rotation (vegetables, cereals, then left fallow). Subsequent English and German settlers coming in the late 1840s and 1850s followed English land-use patterns in which the farm buildings were centred on the property, and the crop rotation proceeded through six years (barley, beans, wheat, clover and rye, oats, and manured fallow). Throughout the valley, these two land-use patterns now intermingle.

The two most noteworthy additions to the population in the Barossa Valley occurred in 1846 and then in 1851. At the annual Lutheran synod in 1846, the district's two Lutheran theologians, Kavel and Gotthard Fritzsche, split the church over doctrine. While the immediate cause of the schism was interpretations of Luther's Small Confession regarding the separation of church and state, chiliasm was the actual basis of the divergence between the two congregations. Plainly stated, Kavel anticipated a thousand-year-long reign of Christ prior to the world's end. Fritzsche considered this an idle hope not supported by Christ's statements that he would return only once on the day of final judgement. The result was adherents of Kavel's stance from Hahndorf followed him to Hain and Gruenberg in the Barossa.

This strident debate was somewhat ameliorated by the arrival of Wendish Catholics from Saxony in 1851 and Cornish Wesleyan Methodists in 1852. Like many of the later arrivals, they settled to the north of the valley. Subsequent movement by the valley's East European Lutheran Germans established settlements in the Murray River basin, near Hamilton in Victoria, and in the Darling Downs of Queensland.

History of wine production

Although now justly famous for its wine, the Barossa valley did not always have a substantial export market. In 1888, while travelling as a nominee of the French Minister of Trade and Industry to the International Centenary Exhibition in Melbourne, Oscar Comettant wrote:

While the wines are still produced on a small scale, they are full of flavour, vinosity and colour, and with a very good taste. On the whole they are incontestably better than the so-called commercial European wines, made from a little grape juice and a lot of mystery ... What Australia needs, if wine-growing is to be seriously encouraged, is some way of producing wine in bulk.

Viniculture did not become important to the valley until the 1890s when the falling fertility of the soil reduced crop yields and Victoria's vineyards were devastated by the Phylloxera (grape louse) blight. Until that time, wine-making for the farmstead's consumption predominated. These wines would have tended to be dark and sweet, the grapes having been left on the vines until late in the season and the skins of the grapes having been left in the must until quite late in the fermentation process.

Nonetheless, modest commercial operations did exist in the late 1840s and early 1850s. Wine-makers Carl Sobels and, somewhat later, Benno and Oscar Seppelt, were instrumental in establishing the character of the export wines. Sobels made dry table wines and introduced hock and verdelho at Pewsey Vale, and shiraz, riesling and muscatel at Evandale. He was marketing his wines in Melbourne and England in the 1850s. Benno and Oscar Seppelt, son and grandson of pioneer settler Joseph Seppelt, introduced important production techniques (particularly pasteurisation and cooling to control wild yeasts) to the region, making Seppeltsfield the region's largest producer in the 1890s. By this time, demand from the English export market, perhaps as a result of South Australia's superb showing at the Colonial and Indian Exhibition in London in 1886, induced the establishment of the second series of Barossa wineries.

Production grew steadily in the first half of the 20C as vintners responded to public taste for wine varieties. Table wines were preferred from the 1800s to the 1920s, then sweet wines and sherry from the 1920s to the 1960s when table wines became quite popular again. The upsurge in wine drinking and the development of an enthusiastic local market in the last 20 years has greatly increased the yield and the quality of Barossa wines today.

During the **Barossa Valley Festival**, in the week following Easter on odd-numbered years, the entire valley celebrates its ethnic and occupational heritage. The climax occurs in Tanunda (see p 501) on the Saturday after Easter. The **Barossa Classic Gourmet Festival** in August also highlights the region's food and wine. In October, the **International Barossa Music Festival** provides 16 days of classical music performances accompanied by gourmet meals and wine tastings.

The Barossa Valley tour described here leads from Adelaide to Gawler then through Tanunda, Seppeltsfield, Greenock, Nuriootpa, and Angaston. While it is certainly possible to accomplish a visit to the Barossa Valley from Adelaide in a day, the experienced tourist will have to be somewhat selective in the choice of walking tours if several wineries are to be visited.

In common with any wine-making region, the valley's most characteristic and interesting wines are often those intended for sale exclusively from the wineries' **cellar doors**. This pleasant institution allows an unobtrusive look at the Barossa Valley's rural buildings, construction techniques and occasionally wine production equipment.

> **Drinking and driving**. Throughout Australia the level of blood alcohol necessary to be arrested, fined and even gaoled is very low. Two drinks in the first hour and one drink an hour thereafter will put you dangerously near the limit. The test is not based on behaviour but on breath tests. These are administered by the police at road blocks. You cannot refuse to take the test. Should you fail the breath test, you will be taken to the local police station where a more sophisticated instrument will administer a second breath test to confirm the first. Should you fail this test, your vehicle may well be impounded; you will have to arrange for a lawyer; pay a hefty fine ... Do not drink and drive in Australia, there is too much at stake.

Head north out of Adelaide on MAIN NORTH ROAD, taking care to follow its jog to the left at Grand Junction Road. The cityscape is rather dreary until you pass Elizabeth and approach Smithfield.

Gawler

The first destination is **Gawler** (population 16,000), about 45 minutes from the journey's start. **Tourist information**: Lyndoch Road, ☎ 08 8522 6814.

South Australia's second oldest town, Gawler was founded in 1839 as a property investment based on city plans drawn by Colonel William Light. It was named in honour of George Gawler (1795–1869), South Australia's second governor (Light had wanted it named after himself). A manufacturing town during the 19C, its smelters supplied equipment for agriculture and mining and ornamental ironwork. The buildings in the central historical district are constructed of locally quarried bluestone, slate, and sandstone. The accent is provided by stucco, brick quoins and openings, and decorative ironwork. Much of this ironwork was manufactured at the Phoenix Foundry built by town patron James Martin.

To the right across Julian Terrace immediately after crossing the bridge is the **Union Mill**. Built in 1915 to replace the original 1855 flour mill destroyed by fire the year before, it now functions as a shopping centre. At 51 Murray Street is the **Old Telegraph Station** (☎ 08 8522 2730; open Sun 13.00–16.00), built in 1859–60, now the oldest surviving public building in town. It now houses a pioneer museum with early musical instruments—perhaps in commemoration of Carl Linger, an early German pioneer and musician who in 1860 wrote in Gawler 'The Song of Australia', which served as an unofficial anthem until anti-German sentiment in the First World War led to a neglect of any German-Australian accomplishment.

Continue on Murray Street to the central business street. To the right are the **South End Hotel** (1859) with an interesting curved iron roof, the Professional Chambers (1859) with a fairly formal and Italianate façade, and, a bit further along, the **Savings Bank of South Australia** (1911), with a balustraded parapet and pediment in an ornate version of Classical Revival style. To the left, set off the street, is the **Baptist church**'s complex (1870–1905) with limestone and contrasting brick.

Down the street on the left is the **Kingsford Hotel** (1858) with noteworthy decorative cast-iron lacework. It was the first home of the Gawler Humbug Society *Chronicle*, a sometimes satirical and libellous newspaper, currently published as the *Bunyip*. At no. 58 Murray Street, the Italianate mood of the post office's Tuscan-style clock tower continues a bit further along in the National Bank (1881), Town Hall (1878), Gawler Institute (1870) and ANZ Bank (1857–59). The simplicity of the latter, along with its locally manufactured fences and gates, offers an interesting contrast to the other more ornate buildings in its proximity.

For those travellers particularly interested in bridge engineering, the sole remaining example of a timber-arch bridge is a few minutes to the west of Gawler in Heaslip Road in Angle Vale. Built in 1876 and redecked in 1940, it has four parallel arch ribs spanning 25.9m.

Lyndoch

Following the BAROSSA VALLEY WAY (also called Lyndoch Road) towards **Lyndoch**, grape arbours begin to replace wheat fields as the soil improves. After about 9km, a sign directs you to the left to the **Chateau Yaldara Estate Winery** (☎ 1 800 08 8300). The castle-like **Charles Cimicky Winery** (☎ 08 8524 4025) is on the right; the elaborately formal gardens and architecture of Chateau Yaldara are offset by the swinging footbridge which crosses the North Para River.

Again on the Barossa Valley Way c 1.5km further east, the **Kies Winery** (☎ 08 8524 4110) on the left in a tidy German-style house of the 1850s, acts as one of the valley's **tourist information centres:** ☎ 08 8524 4511. A stop here provides the opportunity to buy *Explore the Barossa* by Sue Barker, a well-produced booklet. The proprietor's family has been in the Barossa since the 1850s; most of the land in the area originally belonged to the Kies family. The **Burge Family Winemakers** (☎ 08 8524 4644) is on the right.

A little further along, Lyndoch's older buildings date from the 1850s and 1860s and are constructed of ironstone. The town was established in 1839 when Stephen Gower built the Lord Lyndoch Hotel. The current structure, now a hardware store immediately to the right at the town's centre, dates from 1855. Other structures at the crossroads include the Lyndoch Hotel (1869; rebuilt after being gutted by a fire in 1914); the Institute Hall and Public Library (1912; with 1940s Art Deco front) and Post Office (1912).

Now turn left on the Sturt Highway towards Rowland Flat and Tanunda.

The **Orlando Winery** (☎ 08 8521 3140), on the right just beyond **Rowland Flat**, was established by Johann Gramp in 1847. This site was given to his son Gustav as a wedding present in 1877. The winery was sold to international concerns in 1970 and ownership returned to the valley when the Orlando management bought it back in 1988. The wine-tasting centre is in a bluestone and red-brick building from the 1870s which was originally a primary school and teacher's residence. Orlando produces the well-known label Jacob's Creek, plus many other popular brands.

Grant Burge Wines (☎ 08 8563 3700), on the left, is in the restored winery of William Jacob's Moorooroo property (1851). At Krondorf Road, c 700m, turn right to Rockford Wines (☎ 08 8563 2720), one of the best of the small vineyards, set amongst original farm buildings of the 1850s; farm cottages are used for the tasting room and sales cellars. Also on Krondorf Road in historic surroundings is **Charles Melton Wines** (☎ 08 8563 3606), producer of 'Nine Popes' label red wine. On the other side of Krondorf Road on St Hallet Road, off the highway, is **The Keg Factory** (☎ 08 8563 3012), an old-fashioned cooper's shop with barrels and furniture.

Bethany

A right turn on Bethany Road (from the Barossa Valley Way) leads to **Bethany** (1842), the original Barossa Valley settlement. The properties from the 1850s are on the north side of the road. Although most of them are now private residences, the land-use is particularly indicative of the Germanic *Hufendorf* land use pattern. **Bethany Wines** (☎ 08 8563 3666) is in the bluestone quarry which supplied much of the stone for the area's building. Of special interest is the pioneer cemetery which includes a cast-iron statue commemorating H.A.E. Meyer, Bethany's first pastor from 1848 to 1862. The Lutheran church, **Herberge Christi** (Christ the Shelter), was founded by Pastor Gotthard Daniel Fritzsche in 1845. The original simple mud-walled and thatch-roofed church was replaced in 1883. The current church was built by J. Basedow of Tanunda. The adjacent school house and teacher's residence, added in 1888, maintain the church's style.

Tanunda

Return to Barossa Valley Highway and turn right towards **Tanunda**. Entry into the town in spring is charming, with banked beds along the road filled with native plants and flowers. The significance of the many wineries in the area is apparent; you enter the town through the Orlando arch and leave it through the Seppelt arch.

The area around what became the town was settled by Pastor Augustus Kavel and his followers. Tanunda itself was planned around goat square (*der Ziegenmarkt*). The land had been granted to Charles Flaxman who laid out the town in 1848. Central to the nearby villages of Bethany (Bethanien at the time) and Langmeil (now a street running parallel to Murray in the north end of town), Tanunda became a market and gathering place. Goat Square is to the left of Murray Street on John Street.

The oldest buildings date from the late 1850s and 1860s. These include a two-storey winery and several other rust-coloured sandstone buildings on LANGMEIL STREET and some houses on Goat Square itself. Of the latter, **Rieschiek House** is perhaps the most interesting, if more modest than modern taste might admire. It is a single-storey clay, rubble and brick building of five rooms with flanking verandahs. Originally built for the town shoemaker, Johann G. Rieschiek, it was used for church services when Kavel broke from the local synod in 1860. The associated church, St John's, on Jane Place, was built in 1868. The extent of the fractious religious sentiment in these communities should not be underestimated (see p 487). Both the St John's and Langmeil congregations petitioned the colonial government to close the other's cemetery as a danger to public health.

MURRAY STREET has a number of interesting buildings. Starting from the entrance to the town from the south (from the Orlando Arch), the wine cellar at no. 14 was originally Pastor John Auricht's printery. Like the buildings on Goat Square, the walls are of rubble and brick.

Set back from the street, the **Langmeil Lutheran Church** is a Gothic Revival structure of random bluestone built in 1888. Inside, it has an unusual matchboard ceiling which follows the rafters to a cross at the collar ties. The sanctuary is contained by a columned arch and the gallery at the rear features cast-iron columns and balustrade. Pastor Fritzsche (see p 494) is buried in the adjacent cemetery. Several of the tombstones present biographical details in Gothic script.

The **Barossa Valley Tourist Information** (☎ 08 8563 0600, fax 08 8563 0616) is on the corner of Murray and John Streets. This office also serves as the Barossa Wine Centre, and includes a 'wine trail' map; an audio-visual presentation about the Barossa Valley; and taped talks by famous wine-makers, such as John Duval, speaking about the illustrious Penfold's Grange. Originally functioning as a post office, telegraph station and post master's residence, this structure from 1865 is a good example of colonial era public buildings. The **Tanunda Museum** (☎ 08 8563 3295; open daily 11.00–17.00), with local artefacts is at the corner of Mill and Murray Streets. The **Tanunda Hotel** next door was first licensed in 1847. Redecorated and eventually rebuilt in marble in 1945, its lacework and columns come from England. What was the temperance hotel is a fairly nondescript building, now housing a group of shops on the corner across the street from the museum.

The Tabor Lutheran church on the right-hand side of Murray Street just beyond the Tanunda Hotel was rebuilt in 1870 on the site of the Free Evangelical church organised in 1850 by Dr Carl Mielke. Note the fine railing around the graves of the Schroeder family.

The museum in Tanunda

Residences of bluestone or ironstone are scattered along the length of Murray Street. A number of them feature cast-iron fences. That at no. 90 Murray Street has a windmill-driven waterpump and concrete cisterns at the back, and no. 76 Murray Street (now a business) has

Wunderlich-pressed metal sheeting. The monument across Julius Street from this building commemorates E.H. Coombe (1858 –1917), a Member of Parliament from the district who was convicted and fined for his opposition to military conscription during the First World War.

In north Tanunda, still on the Barossa Valley Highway, is the **Kev Rohrlach Technology and Heritage Centre** (☎ 08 8563 3407; open daily 11.00–16.00, Sun till 17.00), an amazing private collection ranging from pioneer memorabilia to aerospace rockets, solar-powered machines and vintage cars. The centre is also the location of the Barossa Markets held every Sunday, with arts and crafts and speciality foods. The main wineries around Tanunda include **Peter Lehmann**, Para Road (☎ 08 8563 2500); **Richmond Grove** (☎ 08 8563 2204); and **Veritas**, Langmeil Road (☎ 08 8563 2330).

Seppeltsfield

Seppeltsfield lies to the north and west of Tanunda. While nearly all of the roads will lead through pleasant rural scenery, the simplest route follows the Barossa Highway (Murray Street in Tanunda) north nearly 8km to Siegersdorf Road. Turn left towards **Marananga**. This area, currently called **Dorrien**, was originally called Siegersdorf (German for Victory Village, a problem during the First World War solved by renaming the area after British General Smith-Dorrien). The palm trees flanking the avenue were planted during the 1920s and 1930s in association with the Seppelt family's Doric-columned mausoleum which stands prominently, and surprisingly, on the north side of the road.

Just beyond Marananga's **St Michael's Gnadenfrei Church** (1873, tower added 1913), the road takes a series of turns to the **Seppelt winery** (☎ 08 8562 8028). The first vines here were planted by Joseph Seppelt in 1852. The main cellars, built of Bethany bluestone with a parapeted front and balcony, were completed in stages between 1867 and 1878. The old offices and columnar chimney on the boiler house are in Roman Revivalist style and date from the late 19C. The gravity-fed wood and iron-stepped winery was designed by Benno Seppelt in 1888. His building programme saw the completion of a dining area for workers and, remarkably for the time, rooms for child care.

Having toured Seppeltsfield, turn right at the entrance to continue towards Greenock. On the right at the first junction is an old-style bush vine vineyard planted in about 20 rows. Modern vineyards are trellised and drip irrigated. In either case, the fields are often interplanted with field beans which control weeds and are turned under as green manure. Turn right, cross the highway, and drive through Greenock. Turn right (east) on Murray Street towards Nuriootpa.

Nuriootpa

Nuriootpa, first a neutral barter centre for Aboriginal groups, grew around a slab hotel built for bullock drivers serving the Kapunda mines. The two most noteworthy domestic buildings in the town are Schaedel House and Coulthard House. Turning left (north) on yet another Murray Street, **Schaedel House** is on the left side of the street a few doors beyond First Street. Built around 1870 by Carl F.J. Schaedel and his wife Maria, the house has clay walls and hand-adzed beams. **Coulthard House** was begun in 1855 by the town's planner, William Coulthard. The house features a pleasant verandah on three sides and timber fretwork decorations. Next to the village's Lutheran church, called 'Strait

Gate' (☎ 08 8562 1057) and built in 1851, is **Luhrs Pioneer German Cottage** (open weekdays 10.00–16.00, weekends 13.00–16.00). Built in 1848 by J.H. Luhrs, the valley's first German school teacher, the building documents German home and school life in 19C Barossa.

The main wineries around Nuriootpa include **Penfolds**, Tanunda Road (☎ 08 8560 9389), the valley's largest and most commercial winery; and, c 4km north of town, **Wolf Blass**, 97 Sturt Highway (☎ 08 8562 1955), run by its eccentric eponymous wine-maker, well known for consistency. This complex includes a small wine museum.

Continue east on Penrice Road towards Penrice and Angaston. At the railroad tracks just past Light Pass Road lies the **Stockwell Fault** zone which forms the Barossa Valley's eastern scarp. At the base of the hills, known for a good light marble, about 500m beyond the Penrice Quarry is a contemporary sculpture by Paul Trappe on the left. The Cornish mining community, Penrice, is another 500m along at Salem Road.

Penrice was established in 1849 by Captain Richard Rodda, a mining agent who subdivided part of his land grant to form the community. Named after an estate near Rodda's native St Austell, Cornwall, it is noted for its Wesleyan Methodist chapel (currently the Salem Lutheran Church) and village Cornish cottages. The stone shed and houses opposite Salem Road were part of the flour mill Rodda established to supply the men going to the gold fields, eventually transported through the Murray River shipping trade.

Angaston

Angaston (population 1950) was named in 1839 after George Fife Angas by his agent Charles Flaxman. Although it was first inhabited by Johann Gottfried Schilling and his family in 1841, the style of the town is English rather than German. The oldest building in town is the remnants of the **Union Church**, established in 1841 by Angas who intended it as the community's sole church. More recently, the building was used as a barn. It stands on the right just at the edge of town before Penrice Road jogs slightly to the left.

Angas built a second, more substantial, church in 1854. It is to the right on Murray Street. Now the **Zion Lutheran Church**, it has bluestone walls with quoins and dressing of pink and cream sandstone. The Congregationalists withdrew from the church in 1861; the Baptists used it until 1929. After a period of disuse, the Lutheran congregation bought it in 1941 and have made a number of improvements to the building, notably the halls on the eastern side.

One of South Australia's more interesting bridges is a bit further along the road. The skew-arched masonry of 1865 bridge is one of two in the state; the other is about 30km to the northwest of the Barossa in Tarlee.

Returning on Murray Road past Penrice Road to take a right on Sturt Street then a short walk on Washington Street to the first left on Fife Street, you will find the **Town Hall**, built in 1911 on a base of bluestone with walls of grey marble; it was initially the second home of the local Institute, then a library and cinema. The former police station and gaolhouse from 1855 and 1864, built largely through Angas's donated land and materials, are also on the street, as are the Uniting Church's buildings. This latter was built by the Congregationalist group in stages. The initial 'colonial bond' brickwork church, now the Sunday

School Hall, was built in 1861. The present Gothic Revival church was designed and built by Adelaide architect D. Garlick in 1878.

Turn left on Sturt Street, then right on Murray Road for a glance at the town proper. Among the most interesting buildings are a number of businesses. The old flour mill (a stone's throw to the left down Tyne Street) was established by Edwin Davey and his son Arnold in 1885 when their mill in Penrice burnt down. On the right beyond Tyne Street is the old blacksmith shop (c 1873), recognised by the galvanised iron front. Established by William Doddridge in 1849, its last proprietor was the founder's grandson, Hardy, who at one time contracted to keep the Angaston to Freeling mail coach teams shod for five shillings a month.

Angaston is flanked by two prominent wineries, **Sal-tram** (☎ 08 8564 3355) to the east on Murray Street and Nuriootpa Road, and **Yalumba** (☎ 08 8561 3200) to the south on Eden Valley Road. Both of these wineries are among the original Barossa vineyards and are still housed in their 1850s buildings, with aesthetically attractive tasting

Collingrove, a National Trust property and B&B

rooms. Beyond Yalumba is **Collingrove**, also on Eden Valley Road (☎ 08 8564 2061; open weekdays 13.00–16.30, weekends 11.00–16.30), a National Trust property serving currently as a bed and breakfast. This large, single-storey house was designed by Henry Evans for John Howard Angas, his brother-in-law, and built about 1854 of blocks of micaceous slate quarried on the property. The quoins, sills and chimneys are of contrasting soapstone. Its verandah and symmetrical wings give the building visual appeal. The property was named for Angas's new bride, Suzanne Collins, and the land and cost of building were a wedding gift from the elder Angas.

To return to Adelaide, either work your way towards the west, through Angaston to the Barossa Valley Highway or the Sturt Highway, or continue on a longer route through Eden Valley and Mount Pleasant.

South of Adelaide

Fleurieu Peninsula, named by French navigators after the scientist Comte de Fleurieu, extends some 115km south of Adelaide, ending at Cape Jervis. From here, the **vehicular ferry** crosses Backstairs Passage to take visitors to **Kangaroo Island**, at 150km long and 55km wide Australia's third-largest island (see p 508). The Adelaide suburban **rail service** (☎ 08 8210 1000) runs as far as Noarlunga. **Bus services** throughout the peninsula can be arranged from the *Bus Booking Centre in Adelaide* (☎ 08 8212 5200); *Premier Coach Service* (☎ 08 8415 5555)

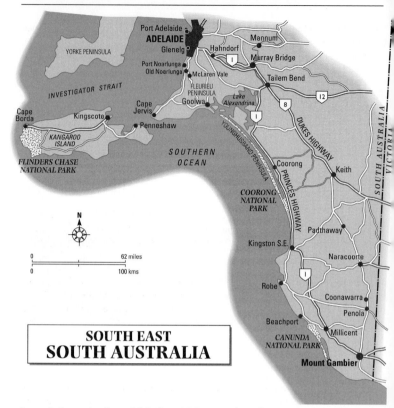

SOUTH EAST SOUTH AUSTRALIA

has a daily service from Adelaide to McLaren Vale and Victor Harbour. The *Victor Harbor Tourist Railway* (☎ 08 8391 1223, fax 08 8391 1933) also operates 'on selected Sundays' some vintage trains: *The Southern Encounter* from Mt Barker railway station in the Adelaide Hills through Strathalbyn and Goolwa to Victor Harbor; and *The Highlander* from Mt Barker to Strathalbyn.

Another form of travel through the Fleurieu Peninsula is along the **Tom Roberts Horse Trail**, a network of trails named after a famous South Australian horseman and instructor of the South Australian Mounted Police. The first section was opened by Roberts's widow in 1993 at Blackwood Reserve, and now traverses most of the peninsula. For more information, contact the *Adelaide Trail Horse Riders Club*, Unley, ☎ 08 8389 3298; or check the website of the Department of Recreation and Sport (☎ 08 8416 6677): http://www.recsport.sa.gov.au.

Fleurieu Peninsula

From Adelaide, take the South Road out of town. At **Reynella**, 20km south of Adelaide city, is **'Reynella House'**, a homestead built in 1845 by pioneering vintner John Reynell (it is a private residence). He constructed elaborate wine cellars in the limestone, using local gum trees as supports. His house here has small-paned French windows and an encircling verandah. The old towns of

Noarlunga—now Port Noarlunga, with good beaches, and Old Noarlunga—to the south contain some interesting pioneer buildings. About 10km south of Old Noarlunga is **Maslin Beach**, famed throughout Australia for being the first legal nude beach. Another 10km east of Maslin Beach is **McLaren Vale** (population 1200), centre of what tourism now calls **'The Wine Coast'**. Indeed, excellent wines have been produced here since 1876, when Thomas Hardy bought Tintara Vineyards; **Hardy's** (☎ 08 8323 9185) is still the main winery in the area, although at least 40 others are clustered here as well. **Tourist information**: Main Road; ☎ 08 8323 9944; here you can get a detailed map of all the wineries that can be visited. The best times to visit if you want elaborate tours of the wineries and accompanying festivities are during McLaren Vale's three annual events: Twilight Tastings in January; From the Sea and the Vines in May/June; and The Continuous Picnic and McLaren Vale Wine Bushing Festival in October.

At the southern end of the Southern Vales is the town of **Willunga** (population 1200). In 1837, the first expedition in the state ended here. In 1840, slate was discovered here and became an important industry in the colony, prompting the arrival of Cornish slate workers. Once the slate industry waned, the town became the centre of almond growing, which it still is; each spring when the almond trees are in bloom, the town holds a festival. The main street of Willunga has many examples of colonial architecture, including the **Willunga Hotel** (1870), with a cantilevered balcony, and the former Police Station and Court House, built in two stages in 1855 and 1864. At **Delabole Quarry**, now operated as a historic site of the National Trust, is evidence of the slate industry that ran here for 60 years, including miners' cottages.

Encounter Bay

From McLaren Vale, it is 42km to the south side of the peninsula, with its old port towns along Encounter Bay. **Goolwa** (population 2400) was an important port during the paddlesteamer days, when bales of wool and produce from inland Australia were shipped down the Murray River and on to overseas ships here. You can still book cruises here to the mouth of the Murray from the Goolwa Wharf. The railway was also important to the region; as early as 1854, a horse-drawn railway operated between Goolwa and Port Elliot, 10km west. One of the most interesting buildings in town, evidence of the difference between South Australian vernacular architecture and other Australian colonies, is the **Old Railway Superintendent's Cottage**, on Government Road, now a National Trust property. Built in 1852 of limestone rubble, it has a distinctive semi-circular vaulted roof covered in galvanised iron. The **National Trust Museum** (☎ 08 8555 2221; open Wed and weekends 14.00–17.00) depicts the heritage of the region and is housed in an 1872 blacksmith's shop.

Port Elliot also has some fine colonial buildings, including **St Jude's** Church of England, built in 1854 out of bluestone, with a turretted tower. The town is located on Horseshoe Bay, with a very pleasant beach. **Tourist information centre**: Signal Point Interpretative Centre, Goolwa Wharf, ☎ 08 8555 3488. This centre offers excellent displays about the Ngarrindjeri people of this region.

The coastline between here and Victor Harbor, 5km south, has good surf beaches. From Goolwa you can also take a vehicular ferry to **Hindmarsh**

Island, a once tranquil spot at the mouth of the river and now the centre of a vexed political dispute between developers and the indigenous owners.

Victor Harbor (population 5300) has been a whaling post since the 1830s, and since the beginning of the 20C a popular holiday resort for South Australians. For reasons unexplained, the town does use the American spelling for 'harbor'. Whales are again the focus of attention here, but now as a tourist attraction. Encounter Bay was the summer breeding ground for Southern Right Whales, making this the most popular spot for the killing of whales in the 19C. By the 1930s, whales had nearly been exterminated here. In recent years, their numbers have begun to increase; in 1991, over 40 were seen in the bay, and thousands of tourists now flock here every year. **Hotel Victor** is now a **Whale Watch Station** (☎ 08 8552 5644; open daily 09.00–17.00), and you can even call a whale information hotline (☎ 0055 31 636) to get information on sightings. **Tourist information:** Torrens Street, ☎ 08 8552 5738/1 800 241 033.

Visitors to Victor Harbor may be interested in two attractions involving transportation. The **horse-drawn tram**, a service begun here in 1894, still travels along a small causeway rail between the mainland and **Granite Island**, the small island which is home to a colony of fairy penguins (the island's Penguin Interpretative Centre has displays about the creatures, and tours can be arranged through the tourist office). Next to the horse tram on Flinders Parade is the **Encounter Coast Discovery Centre** (☎ 08 8552 5388; open Wed–Sun and holidays, 13.00–16.00), a history museum housed in the Old Customs and Stationmaster's Residence (1866). The other transport adventure is **'The Cockle Train'** (☎ 08 8231 1707), another venture of the **Victor Harbor Tourist Railway** service (☎ 08 8391 1223). Considered one of the most scenic train rides in the country, this 'selected Sundays' run travels along the coast past the beaches and historic towns between Victor Harbor and Goolwa; only 40km long, the ride takes about 30 minutes.

South of Victor Harbor around Encounter Bay, take Franklin Parade to the end at **Rosetta Head** (c 3km). This 100m high granite outcrop has good walking trails and magnificent views of the bay. Also here is a tablet dedicated to intrepid explorer Matthew Flinders, who explored and named the many places in the region on his famous circumnavigation of Australia 1801–04.

The **Gulf St Vincent** side of the peninsula also has glorious beaches, most of them a bit calmer than the Southern Ocean side. At the end of the west coast is **Cape Jervis**, with its important lighthouse. From here there are splendid views across Backstairs Passage to Kangaroo Island. It is also here that the famous Hans Heysen Trail (see p 491) begins its 1500km trail to the Flinders Ranges. 11km east of Cape Jervis is **Deep Creek Conservation Park** (☎ 08 8598 0263), 4030 ha of rugged hills, luxurious fern gullies and several varieties of native orchid in the valleys. The walking trails along the cliffs in the park provide spectacular views across to Kangaroo Island.

Kangaroo Island

Lying 13km off the Fleurieu Peninsula south of Adelaide, access to **Kangaroo Island** (known as 'KI' to locals) is by air through *Air Kangaroo* or *Lloyds Aviation* out of Adelaide and by vehicular ferry from Adelaide via Island Seaway or from Cape Jervis (Philanderer III) (☎ 13 13 01). **Tourist information:** Kangaroo Island Tourist Information Centre, Howard Drive, Penneshaw, ☎ 08 8553

1185; National Parks and Wildlife Service, Flinders Chase National Park, PMB 246 via Kingscote, ☎ 08 8559 7235. The latter can provide annual island passes for park entry, camping and guided tours.

Kangaroo Island is largely sea-worn granite with limestone deposits from the Permian Period of the lower Paleozoic. The **Remarkable Rocks**, large rounded boulders on Kirkpatrick Point, are reminiscent of the Giant Marbles of central Australia. The northern coast has higher elevations with limestone arches, cliffs and inlets.

The **Flinders Chase National Park** (☎ 08 8553 7235) comprises the western end of Kangaroo Island. The vegetation here is essentially a mallee thicket alternating with towering eucalypt forest.

Mount Taylor Conservation Park (☎ 08 8552 2381) contains some small limestone caves but is known for the flourishing population of the otherwise endangered Trigger Plant. South and east of Mount Taylor Conservation Park is the **Seal Bay Refuge**, home to sea lions, fur seals and leopard seals as well as koalas and platypus. The **Nepean Bay Park** is also on the island, a short distance south of Kingscote. As well as Tammar Wallabies, it has remnant areas of the original vegetation of this part of the island.

History

The history of habitation on Kangaroo Island is an intriguing one. Archaeological evidence suggests that Aborigines inhabited the place some 11,000 years ago, and at some time later disappeared. Flinders charted and named the island in 1802, but it had also been explored by the French navigator Nicolas Baudin, who left so many French names in the region. In the early 19C, whalers, sealers, and escaped convicts all inhabited the island, establishing rather brutal conditions that included the enslavement of native women captured in Van Diemen's Land and carrying out piracy on passing ships.

The island's relative geographical isolation has allowed the native flora and fauna to flourish without the dangers of introduced species such as rabbits and foxes. Recently, the koala and platypus have actually been introduced here, to promote the survival of these species. So successful has been the koalas' adaptation that they now threaten to decimate the island's stock of gum leaves, and many have had to be removed back to the mainland.

Today, the island is an excellent place to enjoy Australian natural environments. Despite an active tourist campaign over the last decade, the place is still relatively unspoiled and makes for a great getaway. The ferry (in Adelaide, ☎ 08 8553 1233 or 13 13 01 for information) from Cape Jervis lands at **Penneshaw**, along with **Kingscote** and **American River** the island's only towns. A ferry from Port Lincoln and Adelaide also lands at Kingscote. There is no public transportation on the island, so you must either bring a car or rent one (preferably in advance) on the island itself. While the island has more than 1600km of roads, many of them are unsealed and care must be taken when driving.

Penneshaw is located on cliffs filled with fairy penguins, who come into town at night. American River sits on Pelican Lagoon, and is a quiet little beach resort. In winter, the southerlies blow so fiercely on the other side of the island that the roar of the waves can be heard here. One heritage-listed construction here is

First House, built c 1844 by boat-builder John Buick, who made the colony's first boat out of native pine. **Kingscote** (population 1400) is 60km west, on the Cygnet River, and is the island's main town. Located here is an Esplanade, leading to **Reeves Point Historic Site**, the colony of South Australia's first settlement (in 1836); an original mulberry tree here in the old cemetery still produces fruit. On Seaview Road is the **Hope Cottage Folk Museum** (☎ 08 8553 2308; open Sat–Mon, Wed 14.00–16.00), with artefacts and history relating to the house's original occupants from the 1860s.

Just outside Kingscote is an earlier settlement of Cygnet River, near the airport. 28km south of here is **Cape Gantheaume Conservation Park** (☎ 08 8553 8223), an expansive 21,254 ha park extending along the southern coast from Bales Beach near Seal Bay on the west to Cape Linois on the east. Access is largely confined to bushwalkers, who can view carved high cliffs and caves, as well as an amazing variety of wildlife, sheltered in the mallee heath and including bandicoots, possums and marsupial mice. Also in the park is **D'Estrees Bay**, a long sweep of beach, once a whaling station and notorious site for shipwrecks. The tourist centre provides a guide to the island's **Maritime Heritage Trail**, which leads you to the location of the island's many shipwreck disasters.

Also on D'Estrees Bay at Hundred Line Road is **Clifford's Honey Farm** (☎ 08 8553 8224), evidence of KI's status as an official sanctuary for Ligurian honey bees, an important genetic pool untainted by mainland bee diseases. The bees are descendants of 12 hives imported from Liguria, Italy, by August Fiebig in 1881. The island's sanctuary status means that no honey or honey products can be brought to the island.

From the Victorian border to Adelaide

The PRINCES HIGHWAY crosses the Victoria–South Australia border in the state's far southeast corner. Mount Gambier, Millicent, Kingston and Meningie are along the route that traverses the coastline known as the **Coorong**. To the north, the DUKES HIGHWAY parallels the route, passing through Bordertown and Keith before joining the Princes Highway at Tailem Bend and on to Murray Bridge on the Murray River. Between the two, quite near the border north of Mt Gambier, is the famous wine-growing region of **Coonawarra** (see p 512).

Mount Gambier is an agricultural and forestry service centre with a popula-tion of about 20,000. The Hentys, the first white settlers in Victoria (see p 361), built the first house here in 1841. Interstate rivalries, however, were already rife by this stage, and the South Australian colonists evicted them in 1844, giving the land grant to explorer Charles Sturt's brother. Soon a community grew up, and regular postal service between Melbourne and Adelaide made a stop here by 1850. Its most interesting buildings are constructed of locally quarried white stone. The Town Hall and Post Office date from the 1860s. G.T. Light designed the **Old Court House**, built in 1864. Currently, the National Trust uses it as a folk museum (☎ 08 8723 2041; open Sun–Fri 11.00–15.00). **Tourist information**: Lady Nelson Visitor and Discovery Centre, Jubilee Highway East, ☎ 08 8724 9750/1 800 08 7187.

The same limestone formed a number of caves in the area and impart the stark blue to Mount Gambier's four crater lakes. The most impressive of these lakes, appropriately named **Blue Lake**, is 197m deep. Its greatest curiosity is the change from grey to blue in November and back again at the end of summer, a normally occurring, seasonal inversion due to temperature changes. In 1910, poet Mary Gilmore wrote longingly of the lake, 'once more to see the Blue Lake like a sapphire shimmer', while Arthur Upfield's Aboriginal detective Napoleon Bonaparte is told in *Battling Prophet* (1956) that the colour comes from washing blue that the locals dump into the lake every few months (a popular local myth).

Much is made locally of horseman and balladeer Adam Lindsay Gordon's horseback leap to a ledge above the lake in the 1860s. An obelisk commemorating this feat still exists on MacDonnell Bay Road, erected in 1887 at the height of Gordon's posthumous fame.

About 50km west of Mount Gambier through pine plantations, **Millicent** (population 8200) sits on reclaimed land near the **Canunda National Park** (☎ 08 8735 6053). The park is known for its extensive sand dunes and wild grasslands. **Tantanoola Caves Conservation Park** (☎ 08 8734 4153) is south of Millicent. These limestone caves with delicate formations have walking trails and provide wheelchair access.

In Millicent itself, on Mt Gambier Road, the National Trust operates a museum and gallery in the town's first school (☎ 08 8733 3205; open daily 09.30–16.30). Built in 1873, the school's exhibits present a number of period rooms as well as an array of horse-drawn carriages from the late 19C. Also in town is the wonderfully eccentric **Shell Garden** on Williams Road (☎ 08 8733 2072; open daily Dec–Apr 08.00–17.00, Jan 07.00–19.00). The creation of Iris Howe, who began covering things with shells and glass in 1952, the garden is now a whimsical extravaganza of vernacular visionary art.

The coastal road (Princes Highway, route 1) north passes by turn-offs to Beachport and Robe, then travels through Kingston S.E. and Meningie to Adelaide. Again the sand dunes, lagoons and salt lakes are the predominant geological features.

The remarkable sand dunes on **Younghusband Peninsula**, called the Hummocks locally, shelters the **Coorong**, a 140km-long lagoon, now a national park (☎ 08 8575 1200). The name derives from a local Aboriginal word 'Karangh', meaning 'narrow neck'. The entire coast provides habitats for an incredibly diverse shore and water bird population. Nearly 420 species have been logged in the park. Coastal mallee, tea tree and paperbark grow in the reddish, late Pleistocene sand and heaths. At **Camp Coorong** near Meningie (☎ 08 8388 2552; 08 8575 1557) the **Ngarrindjeri** community provides camp sites and bunkhouses and descriptions of their traditional culture.

At **Beachport**, 32km northwest of Millicent, **fairy penguins** can be spotted in the evenings on Penguin Island. These birds come ashore at Robe as well. Colin Thiele's touching novel *Storm Boy* (1963) was set here, and the later film version was also made in the area. The town has one of the longest jetties in Australia, and a fleet of lobster boats. Aboriginal artefacts are displayed at the local museum, a former school on McCourt Street. The drive between Beachport and Robe, c 40km north, is particularly scenic. About 5km north of Beachport is the **Pool of Siloam**, a lake seven times saltier than the ocean and reputed to have therapeutic qualities.

Robe

The lobstering fleet docks at **Robe** (population 950) between October and April. Robe acted as a major wool shipping port in the mid-19C. To avoid the £10 Victorian Poll Tax imposed to profit from the influx of Chinese miners on their way to the Ballarat gold fields, thousands of Chinese (as well as other hopefuls) disembarked here in late 1857. The restored and functioning **Caledonian Inn** on Victoria Street (☎ 08 8768 2029) was built as a result of the port's prosperity. It was here in 1862 that poet Adam Lindsay Gordon met and married the innkeeper's daughter, Margaret Park.

Due to the pleasant sea breezes, a number of prominent South Australians built summer homes at Robe. This tendency continues, the winter resident population increasing from around 1000 to ten times that in summer. Self-guided tours of the town commence from the public library building, also on Victoria Street. **Tourist information**: Robe Library, Victoria Street; ☎ 08 8768 2465.

Kingston S.E. (population 1360) was first named Maria Creek, after the wreck of the *Maria* in 1840. A memorial cairn commemorates the massacre of the ship's survivors by local Aborigines. The town has another 'Big Thing' tourist centre at the entrance to town, in this case, **'Larry Lobster'**. The town's elegant little post office, built in 1867, was chosen for an Australian stamp design in 1982. **Tourist information centre**: the Big Lobster, ☎ 08 8767 2555.

North from Mount Gambier

The highway north from Mount Gambier passes through Penola, Naracoorte and Keith where it joins the DUKES HIGHWAY. The region is on a limestone base on terra rossa soil which provides excellent conditions for growing wine grapes, particularly at **Coonawarra** and **Padthaway**.

Coonawarra wines

John Riddoch began the viniculture at Coonawarra in 1890. He established an orchard and vines on his property. While these were successful and produced excellent wine from the start, the Coonawarra did not gain its current reputation until the 1960s, when awareness of wines expanded in Australia. Today the area packs nearly a dozen wineries into a region only 12km by 2km. Well aware of the current resurgence of interest in Australian wines, a number of wineries are open for cellar door sales and tastings. Probably the best known of these wineries is Wynns Coonawarra Estate (☎ 08 8736 3266), established in 1896 and still producing its great reds. The **Penola tourist information centre** on Arthur Street (☎ 08 737 2855) on the Memorial Park provides maps and directions.

Penola's (population 1300) current reputation depends as much on the beatified **Mary McKillop** as on wine. Australian-born McKillop formed an order of nuns here, the Sisters of Saint Joseph of the Sacred Heart, in 1866. Mother Mary McKillop and Father Julian Woods founded the first Australian school to admit children of lower socio-economic backgrounds in 1867. The school, on the corner of Portland Street and Petticoat Lane (☎ 08 8737 2092; open daily 10.00–16.00), is open to the public with much McKillop memorabilia. As the first Australian to be beatified and on the way to becoming a saint, as

20 Cyclone Tracy by Rover Thomas
21 University of Western Australia, Perth

Opposite: 22 Bungle Bungle National Park, Western Australia;
23 Gum flowers, Western Australia; 24 Quokka, Rottnest Island, Western Australia

25 Above; Exchange Hotel, Kalgoorlie, Western Australia
26 Below left; Cats paw, Western Australia; 27 Wildflowers in Pilbara, Western Australia

28 Left; Magnetic Termite Mound,
   Litchfield National Park,
   Northern Territory
29 Government House, Darwin

30 *Above; Twin Falls, Kakadu National Park, Northern Territory*
31 *Right; Kakadu National Park,*
32 *Uluru (Ayer's Rock), Northern Territory*

33 Katherine Gorge, Northern Territory
34 Kata Tjuta (Olgas), Northern Territory

35 *Above left; Hermannsburg
    Aboriginal Mission,
    Northern Territory*
36 *Above; Stockmans Hall
    of Fame, Longreach,
    Queensland*
37 *Left; Brisbane*

38 *Glasshouse Mountains, Queensland*
39 *Coral, Great Barrier Reef*
40 *Aboriginal rock art, Quinkins,*
   Queensland

announced by the Pope when he visited Australia in 1995, McKillop's residence in Penola has made the town one of three significant McKillop pilgrimage sites.

Adam Lindsay Gordon was stationed here in 1853–54 and married here. In 1868, Gordon stayed at the nearby **Yallum Park** (☎ 08 8737 2435; open by appointment), property of his friend, the vintner John Riddoch; it is believed he wrote his most famous poem, 'The Sick Stockrider', at this time.

North of Penola, the Dukes Highway traverses a fairly arid part of the state which depends on irrigation for agricultural activities. 12km southeast of Naracoorte are three caves of note: the **Victoria Fossil Cave**, the **Blanche Cave** and **Alexandra Cave** (☎ 08 8762 2340). The former has an incredible record of fossilised Ice-Age animals and the latter two have stalagmite and stalactite formations worth seeing; tours of the caves, both guided and self-guided, are available. The bird sanctuary at **Bool Lagoon Game Reserve** (☎ 08 8764 7541) allows views of Cape Barren geese and brolgas among other wetlands species.

Irrigation marks the approach to **Keith** (population 1200) where the low scrub of an arid plain abruptly becomes farmland. The *Oxford Literary Guide to Australia* quotes Keith-born Christine Churches's poem 'My Mother and the Trees', creating an image that is characteristic of much of Australia:

> She shook the doormat free of dogs,
> struck the tank to measure water, as she
> marshalled us with iron buckets
> to carry rations for the trees
>
> From fibres of air, who wove
> us there the hope of leaves,
> and in the flat and tepid dust
> she dreamed a dwelling place of shade.

The journey from Keith, on Dukes Highway, to **Tailem Bend** (population 1540) is 130km. **Tourist information centre**: 51 Railway Terrace, ☎ 08 8572 3537. The town sits at the junction of the Princes and Western Highways, and on the Murray River. Its name is derived either from the Aboriginal 'thelim' meaning 'bend in a river', or from the vernacular 'tail 'em', referring to lambing. Nearby is the Point McLeay Mission, where **David Unaipon**, member of the Ngarintjari group, was born. Unaipon became the first Aborigine to publish his writings in English, and now appears on the Australian $50 note.

Murray Bridge

A further 24km northwest is **Murray Bridge** (population 11,800), South Australia's largest river town. Only 80km from Adelaide, the town is a welcome sight for those who have been travelling the long and arid distances from Victoria. The town has had many names. The local Ngaralta group called the area 'Moop-pol-tha-wong', or 'haven for birds'; white settlers changed this to Mobilong. The first white resident, George Edwards, settled here in the 1850s. At his property, overlanding cattle used to swim across the river; thus the early name of Edwards Crossing. The first bridge over the Murray River—named by Charles Sturt after George Murray, Secretary of State for the Colonies—was constructed between 1873 and 1879. The town was not officially named Murray Bridge until 1924. **Tourist information centre**: Community Information and Tourist Centre, 3 South Terrace; ☎ 08 8532 6660.

The town is a pleasant little place, with a classic old river-town hotel, appropriately enough called the **Murray Bridge Hotel**, on Sixth Street (☎ 08 8532 2024). The hotel has broad upper-storey balcony-verandahs that look out on to the flat river. Also in town on Mannum Road is **St John the Baptist** Anglican cathedral, the oldest church in town (built in 1887) and the smallest cathedral in Australia. The **Murray Bridge** itself, is classified by the National Trust; made of iron, it measures 1980 ft (594m) in length. Until 1925 it carried the rail line as well, during which time toll gates were used at each end.

To the north of Murray Bridge 34km on the river is **Mannum** (population 2000), a picturesque little town, one of the oldest on the river. Mannum is recognised as the place where the *Mary Ann*, the river's first paddle steamer, was launched by W.R. Randell in 1853. It was also the place where the first steam-driven car was built in Australia by David Shearer in 1900. The National Trust operates a museum on the PS *Marion*, built in 1898, and now at Arnold Park. This boat is also the town's tourist office, ☎ 08 8569 1303; open daily 09.00–16.00.

For a full description of places along Murray River, see pp 387–392.

West of Adelaide

Travelling north of Adelaide, HIGHWAY 1 veers west towards Two Wells and continues c 60km to Port Wakefield and the edge of the **Yorke Peninsula** (see p 517), the boot-shaped bit of land that sits between Gulf St Vincent on the east and Spencer Gulf on the north. At the same point that Highway 1 heads west, the STURT HIGHWAY (route 20) heads north to Gawler, then continues as the MAIN NORTH ROAD/BARRIER HIGHWAY (route 32) another 113km to the interesting mining town of **Burra**. At Riverton, only 96km north of Adelaide, the Main North Road becomes ROUTE 83 and heads northwest towards **Clare**, the centre of the wine-growing Clare Valley.

The best—and in some cases, the only—way to explore all of these regions is to have your own car, or to be part of a coach tour, which can be arranged through the Adelaide tourist office. *Greyhound-Pioneer* travels through the Clare Valley on its Adelaide–Broken Hill run; *Stateliner* has a daily service (except Saturday) to some Clare Valley towns; and the Greyhound Adelaide–Sydney route stops at Burra. The Yorke Peninsula has a daily bus service from Adelaide to Moonta with *Premier Roadlines*, and the Yorke Peninsula Bus Service (☎ 08 8823 2375) runs a four-hour trip from Adelaide to Yorketown, alternating daily between east coast stops and those in the centre. There is no public transport to the Innes National Park.

Burra

This former copper-mining town (population 2000) is only 154km north of Adelaide, in the Bald Hills Range, but already in the arid landscape that marks the beginning of the immense South Australian outback. **Tourist information**: 2 Market Square, ☎ 08 8892 2154.

History

The derivation of the town's name, taken from the nearby Burra Burra Creek, is the source of some debate: initially thought to be of Aboriginal origin and meaning 'great', it is now believed to be of Hindi origin, since many Indian shepherds were in the region before the discovery of copper here. In 1845, a shepherd named Pickett discovered copper-ore in the area, and by 1849 smelters operated here, greatly aiding the economy of the fledgeling colony.

For the first ten years of its existence, the Burra mine was the largest mine in Australia. For most of its productive life, the mine was managed by two men: Henry Ayers (1821–97), company secretary and later Premier of South Australia for whom Uluru was given the name of Ayers Rock; and Henry Roach, chief captain of the mine who arrived in South Australia from Cornwall in 1846. The township was divided in two, the present township of Burra (previously Kooringa) with the wealthier owners on the south side, and Burra North (formerly Redruth and Aberdeen) where the miners lived on the other side. In between was 'no man's land', where the mine's smelter was situated. Mining copper here yielded more than £5 million of ore, but was worked out within 32 years. The mine closed in 1877, and many of the miners who had arrived from Cornwall, Wales and Scotland dispersed; the town became a virtual ghost town for a while, although some pastoral activity kept it going as a market town into the 20C.

The current residents of Burra and the surrounding region have been particularly devoted to the preservation of the town's heritage with an eye to tourism. The tourist office has arranged a unique 'Burra passport' system, whereby the visitor can follow a self-guided drive and walking trails to 43 heritage sites, all of which are explained and highlighted in the information found in the passport package. Some of the sites on the tour include the **Burra Mine Site and Powder Magazine**, off Market Street, an enormous archaeological site of the mine itself; the **miners' dugouts** on Blyth Street, a group of mud shacks along the river where as many as 2000 miners lived rather than pay rent in company housing; **Morphett's Engine-house Museum**, also off Market Street, restored to original condition and displaying beam engines and the engine-house itself; and the **Police Lock-Up and Stables**, on the corner of Ludgvan and Tregony Streets, built in 1847. The **Redruth Gaol**, also on Tregony Street, was built in 1856; after 1894, it served for many years as a girls' reformatory. The gaol was the location for the filming of Bruce Beresford's famous film *Breaker Morant* (1979), all of which was shot in the area round Burra. On Bridge Terrace another part of the passport tour is the **Unicorn Brewery Cellars**, the cavernous interior providing cool temperatures for Unicorn Beer, which was brewed in town from 1873 to 1903.

Other town features outside the passport package include the **Bon Accord Mine Complex** (☎ 08 8892 2056; open weekdays 12.30–14.30, weekends and holidays 12.30–15.30), now a museum and interpretative centre with a viewing platform looking down a mine shaft; at the time of the mine's operation in the 1850s, Burra had a population of 5000 when Adelaide only had 18,000 people. **Malowen Lowarth**, on Paxton Square, gives an indication of the cottages built for miners between 1849 and 1852; one of the cottages is now a museum of miners' furniture and artefacts, open Sat, 13.00–15.00 and Sun, 10.30–12.30. Finally, the **Market Square Museum** (☎ 08 8892 2154; open Sat, 14.00–16.00, Sun, 13.00–15.00), on Market Square, re-creates the buildings of the 1870s, including a general store, post office, and family home. It is interesting to explore the region around Burra, for remnants of the 19C industrial landscape in this rather bleak terrain.

Clare Valley

The town of **Clare** (population 4000), only 136km north of Adelaide, is a picturesque place nestled in the green and fertile landscape in the northern Mount Lofty Ranges. The town serves as the centre of the Clare Valley vineyards, one of the lesser-travelled wine-making regions of the state. Wines have been produced here for nearly 150 years, and today over 28 wineries offer tastings and cellar sales. These include such well-known names as *Leasingham* (7 Dominic Street, Clare, ☎ 08 8842 2555), established in 1893; *Sevenhill Cellars* (College Road, Sevenhill, ☎ 08 8843 4222), the first vines of which were planted by Jesuit priests in 1848 and the cellars still housed in the original buildings from the 1850s; and *Tim Knappstein* (2 Pioneer Avenue, ☎ 08 8842 2600), established in 1976 on the site of the Clare Brewery (1878), a structure built of bluestone and with massive timber joints. Tours of many wineries and maps of the district are available through Clare's tourist information office: Town Hall, 229 Main North Road, ☎ 08 8842 2131. The **Clare Valley Gourmet Weekend** is held annually in May over the Adelaide Cup long weekend, and highlights Clare wine-makers, presenting a progressive lunch through the region.

The town of Clare and the surrounding area have several other architectural and historic attractions besides wineries. **Bungaree Station** (☎ 08 8842 2677; open by appointment), 12km north of town off Main North Road, was established as a sheep station in 1841 by the Hawker brothers, famous Australian graziers. George Hawker (1818–95) eventually bought out his brothers and extended his holdings here to almost 80,000 acres (32,376 ha). He entered the South Australian House of Assembly in 1860, retired in 1865 to England, but returned in 1874 and again became a Member of Parliament until his death. This property, which in its heyday operated as a self-sufficient community with shearing complex, workers' cottages, local council chamber and its own church (**St Michael's**, built 1864 in Gothic Revival style by E.A. Hamilton), is still owned by Hawker's descendants. It is still one of Australia's leading merino sheep studs. Most of these historic buildings have been preserved as a living museum.

Also in town is the **Old Clarevale Museum** on Lennon Street (☎ 08 8842 1222; open daily), appropriately a museum of wine-making incorporating the still functional Clarevale Winery and including an arts and crafts gallery and restaurant. Evidence of Clare's age of prosperity for early Irish immigrants can be seen at **Wolta Wolta** on West Terrace (☎ 08 8842 3656; open Sun, 10.00–12.00), home to four generations of the Hope family and featuring a fine collection of antiques. The house was built by pioneer Irish immigrant John Hope between 1846 and 1870; badly damaged in the 1983 bushfires that swept through this district, it has been carefully restored. The **Old Police Station**, now a museum (☎ 08 8842 3656; open Sat 10.00–12.00 and 14.00–16.00, Sun 10.00–12.00), is also on West Terrace; it was Clare's first public building, and demonstrates an interesting vernacular style of architecture. On Old North Road the **Clare Library** (formerly the Mechanics' Institute) is a lovely example of a rural adaptation of Classical Revival style, erected in 1871 with French windows opening on to small balconies enclosed by iron railings and brackets. The interior staircase has radiating steps. The building is one of several Victorian-era structures along Old North Road and Ness Street.

Yorke Peninsula

From Clare and the Clare Valley, it is c 80km southwest (via Main North Road 26km south, then west on the route towards Balaklava) to **Port Wakefield** (population 500) at the northeastern edge of Yorke Peninsula. Port Wakefield is also 99km north of Adelaide.

Yorke Peninsula is often described as 'that funny, leg-shaped bit of land opposite Adelaide across the Gulf St Vincent'. The peninsula has some 800km of coastline, much of it secluded and unspoiled and only two or three hours from Adelaide itself. With little surface water, the peninsula would not have easily sustained any Aboriginal population; to date, no Aboriginal sites have been found in the region. The area first gained some attention when great copper deposits were discovered in 1859 and 1861 at Kadina and Moonta at the north-western edge of the peninsula. The 'Copper Triangle' of Kadina, Moonta and Wallaroo soon attracted thousands of Cornish miners, a heritage still nurtured and recognisable in architecture and festivities: in May of odd-numbered years, the 'Triangle' hosts the **Kernewek Lowender**, said to be the only Cornish festival in the world. By 1923, the copper mines had been worked out, and the area became best known for its wheat and barley, touted as the richest grain yields in Australia. Its status as the 'Granary of Australia' is commemorated in the biennial (odd-numbered) Yorke Peninsula Field Days, held in **Paskeville** (19km southeast of Kadina) in May; this event is the oldest of its kind in Australia, first held in 1895 and featuring farm machinery and agricultural demonstrations. It is now a multi-million-dollar event, with hundreds of exhibitions. The **main tourist office** is now at **Moonta**, 165km northwest of Adelaide, 67km west of Port Wakefield: **Yorke Peninsula Visitor Information Office**, Railway Station, ☎ 08 8825 1981.

The road along the east coast of the peninsula passes through several small settlements all in sight of the sea; because of its long isolation before roads were built, this part of the coast is dotted with long jetties and landing ports where coastal ships could stop to load grain. These areas now provide excellent fishing opportunities, as well as spots for diving and beachcombing.

The first of these settlements, **Ardrossan** (population 1100), is still a thriving port. Proclaimed in 1873, the town's pioneers initially lived in dugouts while they attempted to clear the difficult mallee brush to build houses. These circumstances led to the invention by an ingenious local of the famous 'stump jump' plough which greatly eased the farmers' work; the Smith brothers, Clarence and Richard, developed the machine in the 1870s for world-wide use, and are rightly commemorated at the local Historic Museum, on Fifth Street (☎ 08 8837 3062; open Sun 14.30–16.30).

The area around Ardrossan is also a major source of dolomite in Australia.

The next settlement south is **Port Vincent** (population 400), a sleepy seaside resort with a backdrop of steep tree-covered cliffs; the calm waters here provide good swimming, and water sports of all kinds are available. 17km further south **Stansbury** used to be known as Oyster Bay (no oysters are here now), and promotes its waters as a great place for power boating. The village also has a funny little schoolhouse museum in the town's 1870s schoolroom (☎ 08 8852 4136; open Wed and Sun, 14.00–16.00).

Another 20km south is **Edithburgh** (population 450), a popular site for fishermen and especially for underwater divers; a wonderful rock swimming pool stands at the beach and the area reefs are wonderful for viewing fish. In town, many late 19C buildings remain; the Edithburgh District Museum (☎ 08 8852 6214; open Sun and holidays 14.00–16.00) presents the region's maritime history, and highlights the importance of the salt industry on the peninsula. Just offshore is **Troubridge Island**, a conservation park, great for birdwatchers; the island includes an historic lighthouse, along with 5000 penguins, 3000 nesting terns and 10,000 cormorants as well as other seabird species. Tours of the island and accommodation can be arranged by calling ☎ 08 8852 6290.

The main road now heads inland 15km to **Yorketown** (population 750), the southern peninsula's main shopping centre, surrounded by salt lakes, which were the source of the region's early salt industry; some of the lakes have an unusual pink tinge. The coast road from here to Innes National Park at the tip of the peninsula goes down to a number of bays, ideal for fishing, and surrounded by craggy cliffs.

Innes National Park, c 75km southwest of Yorketown, occupies the 'big toe' of the peninsula; its visitor's centre is at Stenhouse Bay on the eastern side of the peninsular tip (☎ 08 8854 4040). Now encompassing 9100 ha, the park was declared in 1970 in part as an effort to save the rare Great Western Whipbird, which was sighted here, in one of its easternmost locations. Vegetation in the park ranges from cleared land with regenerating mallee scrub to sand dunes and saline lakes. On the western side of the park is a set of high sand-dune barriers leading down to **Pondalowie Beach**, world renowned for its surfing. Some of the most ancient rocks ever discovered—over two billion years old—can be seen in the granite boulders at Rhino Head and Cape Spencer, at the very southern tip next to **Inneston**, once a thriving mining centre and now a ghost town managed by the park authorities; during school holidays, the park rangers organise guided activities here for children.

The western coastline of Yorke Peninsula is particularly rugged with crashing waves and jagged rock formations at the southern end. You now travel a bit inland through **Minlaton** (population 790), birthplace of early aviator Harry Butler, and on to **Port Victoria** (population 350), c 114km from Innes National Park. This port was at one time an international destination for the great wind-jammer clippers from the Northern hemisphere that stopped here to load grain. It was consequently the starting point of the great competitive races to see which ship could get the most grain back to England and America most quickly. Such mad shipping traffic, coupled with Spencer Gulf's turbulent waters accounts for the inordinate number of shipwreck sites in the waters surrounding the entire peninsula. Port Victoria's **Maritime Museum** on Main Street (☎ 08 8834 2057; open Sun and holidays, 14.00–16.00) documents this era with displays of the square-rigged sailing ships; at the jetty next to the museum is a Shipwreck Interpretative Display, as well as the start of an interesting Geology Trail. Most interesting is the **Wardang Island Heritage Diving Trail**, centred around **Wardang Island**, about 10km offshore from the port. The island is surrounded by shipwrecks, eight of which have been located and are identified by underwater plaques. Divers can also purchase waterproof booklets from the museum and other local shops. Trips to the island by groups of divers require permission from the Point Pearce Community Council; for more information call ☎ 08 8207 2378. Other materials about this and other aspects of this Maritime Trail are available from the *South Australian Department of the Environment bookshop* in Adelaide, 77 Grenfell Street, ☎ 08 8204 1910.

Moonta

From Port Victoria, travel north via **Maitland** (population 1200), the peninsula's inland farming hub, c 56km to **Moonta** (population 2500), one of the Cornish 'Copper Triangle' towns. Sitting on Moonta Bay and only 163km from Adelaide, the town is a popular seaside resort with pleasant beaches and excellent fishing; the town's name apparently derives from a corruption of the Aboriginal 'Moonterra', or 'place of impenetrable scrub'. Moonta makes much of its mining and its Cornish heritage, as a trip to the main **tourist information office** in the old Railway Station will attest (☎ 08 8825 1981). **Moonta Mines Museum** on Verran Terrace (☎ 08 8825 1988; open Wed and weekends, 13.30–16.00, holidays 11.00–16.00), a National Trust property, is situated in the Moonta Mines School building, constructed in 1878. At one time, the school had more than a thousand students a year. After it closed in 1968, the building was turned into a tribute to the mine and the Cornish miners who worked there. The complex also houses the Moonta History Resource Centre, a collection of rare documents and microfilm concerning local history; it is open to the public every afternoon except Monday. The Trust also runs as part of the museum the **Moonta Mines Railway**, a narrow-gauge steam train that runs through display yards of mining equipment and ore trucks, and even passes through a tunnel under a copper skimp heap. The train departs hourly on weekends and holidays from the railway station next to the museum. The National Trust also maintains a **Miner's Cottage and Garden** on Vercoe Street (☎ 08 8825 1988; open Wed and weekends, 13.30–16.00, holidays 11.00–16.00), an original wattle-and-daub and mudbrick Cornish cottage built in the 1870s. The garden and picket fence have been re-created, the furnishings are in 'period style'. The town also has an enormous **Methodist Church** on Milne Street, built in 1865; it can seat 1250, is noted for its beautiful cedar fittings and stained glass, and has a 600-pipe organ.

The **Moonta Mines State Heritage Area**, on Arthurton Road 2km southeast of town, is a fascinating glimpse at the remains of the mining industry and its altered landscape.

Kadina

Kadina (population 4000) is the largest town on Yorke Peninsula and its commercial centre. The town also has a tourist railway, which operates on the second Sunday of the month, leaving Wallaroo at 13.00 for Kadina (☎ 08 8821 1356/08 8823 3111). Its citizens actively preserve the town's Cornish architecture, and several heritage trails are worth exploring; guides are available from the information centre in Moonta and from some local shops. **Kadina Heritage Museum** and **Matta House** (☎ 08 8821 1083) on Kadina–Moonta Road is now a complex of buildings (Matta House was built in 1863 for the manager of the Matta Matta copper mine at Wallaroo) that explore all aspects of the region's history. Photographic displays document Kadina's history, emphasising mining and Cornish culture, while the grounds now house one of Australia's most significant collections of dry land farming equipment; Matta House also includes a large museum about printing and printing machines in South Australia. Another intriguing attraction in town is the **Banking and Currency Museum** on Graves Street (☎ 08 8821 2906; open Sun–Thurs 10.00–17.00, closed June), a private museum housed in Kadina's oldest surviving bank building, an elegant Classic Revival Bank of South Australia from 1873. The collection displays used and proof coins, old ledgers and promissory notes, and examples of Australian currency.

The last of the 'Copper Triangle' towns is **Wallaroo** (population 2480), 9km west of Kadina and an important deep-water port on Wallaroo Bay. The origins of the town's name are convoluted: from an Aboriginal word 'wadlu waru', supposedly meaning 'wallaby's urine' (what this would have to do with the town's location is entirely unclear), the squatters of the region came up with Wall Waroo, which was eventually shortened to Wallaroo when the word was stencilled onto wool bales for shipment. During the mining boom, Wallaroo was the location of a smelter, with ore that yielded an amazing copper ratio of 30 per cent. Once the copper was gone, the port's deepwater jetty and bulk-loading capabilities caused it to remain an important shipping and export centre. Now rock phosphate processing is a major industry. The beaches around the bay are calm and pleasant, and the town boasts of its excellent fishing. The **Heritage and Nautical Museum** on Jetty Road (☎ 08 8823 2366; open Wed, weekends and holidays 10.30–16.00) presents a worthwhile exhibition of the region's history, with emphasis on its status as one of the state's busiest ports.

Towards Western Australia

The highways north and west from Adelaide lead to Western Australia via the Eyre Highway (route 1) or to the Northern Territory via the Stuart Highway (route 87). The highways to the north and east lead to New South Wales via the Barrier Highway (route 32) or to Victoria via the Sturt Highway (route 20) through Renmark, the Dukes Highway (route 8) or the Princes Highway (route 1) along the coast. The great transcontinental train, the *Indian Pacific*, also traverses the Nullarbor, completing its four-day journey from Sydney through Adelaide to Perth.

The EYRE HIGHWAY proceeds from Adelaide across the Nullarbor to Western Australia. Travelling north from Adelaide round Spencer Gulf, the first towns of note are **Port Pirie** and **Port Augusta**. The former was established in 1845 as an agricultural centre. Its industrial functions began at the turn of the century when Broken Hill Associated Smelters began treating silver, lead and zinc here for export.

Port Augusta

Port Augusta (population 15,000) itself is an industrial town and junction for the Ghan (north to Alice Springs) and the Indian-Pacific railways (trans-continental to Perth). It is the major commercial centre for the far north as well as the most northerly port in the state. Largely built in the 1880s, the town continues as a supply centre for the outback sheep stations to the north along the Ghan. The waterworks building was originally a troopers' barracks (1860 to 1882); the **Town Hall** (1866 by Black and Hughes) is a two-storey Victorian Revival building; on the town square are a curiously ornamented cast- iron drinking fountain and a handsome rotunda. The **Australian Arid Lands Botanic Garden** (☎ 08 8641 1049; open daily) is at the end of McSporin Cres-cent; it focuses on the fragile ecology of South Australia's northern regions. From the adjacent Red Cliff lookout, the Gulf and Flinders Range can be seen. The railway workshops offer interesting guided tours on Tuesdays. **Tourist infor-mation**: Wadlata Outback Centre, Flinders Terrace, ☎ 08 8641 0793. The Wadlata Centre serves as an interpretative centre about Outback life.

The Eyre Peninsula

The Eyre Peninsula can either be crossed via the Eyre Highway to Ceduna or circumnavigated via the Lincoln and then the Flinders Highway. On its east coast a number of small tourist and fishing villages below Whyalla, the indus-trial hub of the region, have a natural appeal. Among them **Cowell** is noted for jade, including the rare black jade, and **Tumby Bay** (population 1000) for fishing among the off-shore islands. The beaches along the Eyre Peninsula on Spencer Gulf are quite fine, with white sand, excellent fishing, and gentle surf.

Port Lincoln (population 11,500) at the tip of the peninsula sits on a crys-talline Boston Bay, home of a tuna fishing fleet. It was at one time considered as a site for South Australia's capital city. **Tourist information**: Civic Building, 66 Tasman Terrace, ☎ 1 800 629 911/08 8683 3544. Port Lincoln holds South Australia's oldest festival, and the only Australian festival dedicated to fish, the Tunarama Festival, held annually over Australia Day weekend. It includes a variety of processions and concerts and a tuna-tossing contest.

Situated 20km south of Port Lincoln is **Lincoln National Park** (☎ 08 8683 3544), 17,000 ha along the headland of the southeast tip of Eyre Peninsula. The park features cliffs and sheltered beaches and encompasses a number of small islands off the coast. With an average rainfall of 55mm, the area offers a considerable variety of habitats and vegetation types and supports a number of migratory sea birds along the coast, including the Wandering Albatross, the White-Breasted Sea Eagle and the Osprey. The mallee scrub regions of the park are the eastern limit of some western species, including the **Port Lincoln** (Ring-neck) **Parrot** (*Barnardius zonarius*), **Western Yellow Robin**, and the **Western Whip Bird**. At **Stamford Hill** on the northern end of the park and overlooking Spencer Gulf, is the **Flinders Monument**, an obelisk erected in 1844 in honour of that inveterate explorer Matthew Flinders; that it was erected by Flinders' nephew and Governor of Tasmania Sir John Franklin adds to its historic signifi-cance as one of the earliest commemorative monuments in the country. Also in the park is **Memory Cove**, commemorating one of the few places in South Australia where Flinders came ashore during his circumnavigation of the conti-nent. The Flinders Tablet at the cove is in honour of the sailors on Flinders' voyage who drowned here when their boat capsized. Thistle Island off the coast at this point further commemorates one of these sailors, Master John Thistle, who had also accompanied Flinders and Bass on their 1798 exploration of the Bass Strait. Understandably, Flinders christened this point Cape Catastrophe.

At the southernmost tip of Eyre Peninsula, 32km south of Port Lincoln, is an area locally referred to as **Whalers Way**, site of some of the most dramatic coastal scenery in Australia. The area around Sleaford Bay is filled with cliffs, caves, blowholes and beaches with yellow sand. **Cape Carnot** features a lookout, with one of the oldest rocks found in the state, estimated to be more than 200 million years old. Information about this tourist route is available from the Port Lincoln tourist office.

To the northwest of Port Lincoln c 50km is **Coffin Bay**, a beautiful village named by Flinders in honour of his friend Sir Isaac Coffin. The area cultivates Australia's best oysters and scallops, and provides superb fishing. **Coffin Bay National Park** (☎ 08 8683 3544) surrounds the small settlement, and includes several scenic drives, some accessible only by four-wheel drive. Almonta Beach, to the east of Flinders-named Point Avoid, is one of Australia's best surfing beaches. The park's wildlife includes Coffin Bay brumbies, free-ranging horses.

The west coast of the Eyre Peninsula is unprotected and has spectacular coastal scenery and rugged cliffs to **Streaky Bay**, so named by Flinders for the streaks of seaweed in the bay. This is a great spot for beaches and fishing. **Tourist information**: 13–15 Alfred Terrace, ☎ 08 8626 1126.

Crossing the peninsula to the north, the predominant plant species are scrub eucalypt and acacia, the latter becoming dominant between Port Augusta and Kimba.

Coober Pedy

If 'godforsaken' and 'infernal' were meant to be applied to any place on earth, **Coober Pedy** (population 2500) is it. **Tourist information centre**: District Council Offices, Hutchison Street, ☎ 1 800 637 076/08 8672 5298. *Kendell Airlines* (book through Ansett ☎ 13 13 00) flies from Adelaide to Coober Pedy daily and from Coober Pedy to Uluru once a week. The Greyhound bus passes through on the Adelaide–Alice Springs route.

On the STUART HIGHWAY from Port Augusta in the south it is 540km through extremely harsh terrain traversing the Woomera Prohibited Area, site in the 1950s of British atomic bomb testing sites; it is 937km northwest of Adelaide. The town's sole purpose for being is opal-mining, and the landscape around the town is dotted with thousands of deserted mine shafts (the area is indeed one of the largest opal-producing centres in the world, Australia providing 95 per cent of the world's supply of the gem). The name of the settlement derives from an Aboriginal (the Arabana group) term meaning 'white fellows in a hole', referring, of course, to Coober Pedy's one claim to fame, that the extreme temperatures found here compelled them to build houses underground. (These subterranean habitations were also the result of the fact that the surrounding countryside provides no timber for any kind of construction.) Indeed, summer temperatures regularly climb to 50° C (over 130° F) and night temperatures can be very cold. Water is the area's most precious commodity, with reticulated water provided from a bore 23km north of town. This overwhelmingly harsh environment provided the backdrop for the films *Mad Max III* (1985) and Wim

Wenders's *Until the End of the World* (1991). In his novel *The Fire in the Stone* (1973), Colin Thiele describes Coober Pedy's appearance:

> *A flat, bare landscape it was for the most part, with undulations here and there and flat-topped hills and breakaways and wind-swept plains. An old land, eroded and wrinkled, worn down over endless ages...And in the sides of the slopes, cut into very knoll and knob, were doorways and entrances and burrows as if the whole place was inhabited by five-foot-high rabbits walking about on their hind legs.*

Unless you are really fond of opals—you can find interesting ones to purchase in town—or have an overwhelming desire to admire eccentric underground dwellings, there is very little reason to travel here. The town is volatile, filled with 'colourful' characters who can border on the desperate and violent, and the landscape is risky to walk through, with mine shafts a constant danger. One can experience the great Australian Outback, and vast expanses of desert scenery, in better places, too.

Nullarbor

Beyond Kimba, the vegetation becomes increasingly scrubby, and the true outback begins. From Kimba, it is 311km west along the Eyre Highway to Ceduna, the last major settlement on the eastern edge of the Nullarbor.

Ceduna (population 3650), which derives its name from an Aboriginal term for 'resting place', sits on Murat Bay, named by French expolorer Ncholas Baudin in 1802. Denial Bay, on the western side of the inlet, received its name from Matthew Flinders, who was disappointed that this point offered no waterway into the interior. If you follow Jonathan Swift's maps in his *Gulliver's Travels* (1726), the Lilliputian should have lived on **St Peter Island**, offshore from Ceduna. This island is now part of the Nuyts Archipelago Conservation Park. Peter Nuyts sighted these islands in 1627 while exploring aboard the Dutch ship the Gulden Seepard. Nuyts' reports of this voyage no doubt provided Swift with his geographical information. Today, Ceduna is a favoured spot for whale watching and home of the Big Oyster, symbol of the area's thriving industry. All kinds of whale spotting cruises can be arranged through Ceduna's **tourist information office**: 58 Poynton Street, ☎ 08 8625 2780.

200km west of Ceduna, the Yalata Aboriginal community sells artefacts at their roadhouse. The cliffs of the **Great Australian Bight** are near the road about 350km west of Ceduna in the Nullarbor Regional Reserve. Here and at **Eucla** (on the border with Western Australia) are spectacular views of the storeys-deep abrupt drop from the limestone plains to the Southern Ocean. This section of the Nullarbor, all 495km of it, crosses Yalata Aboriginal land.

The extent and austerity of the Nullarbor is difficult to describe. The distance from Ceduna to Norseman (at the end of the Eyre Highway in Western Australia) is 1207km. The towns between have a combined population of less than 100—Eucla (30), Mundabrilla (12), Madura (under 20), Cocklebiddy (12), Caiguna (10) and Balladonia (12). Beyond the view of the Bight and a meditative calm caused by driving across such an incredible expanse of arid bushland, the purpose of the journey is to stop for refreshment and a cordial chat at the roadhouses. The cars and their occupants travelling in the same direction become quite familiar.

Beyond **Balladonia** (towards the end of the Eyre Highway in Western Australia)

Nullarbor Plain's caves

The Nullarbor's caves were formed by surface drainage through limestone deposited during the Tertiary Period. Throughout this period the plain was covered by a shallow sea extending over 250km inland from the present coast. The limestone deposits are the remains of minute marine organisms and have been found to be 300m deep in places. Mechanical erosion rather than the chemical reactions of calcium carbonate and carbon dioxide carved caverns and watercourses. This would have occurred principally at the end of the Tertiary era, for it was during the Pliocene era that this part of Australia last had considerable rainfall.

a series of sand ridges mark the change in geology from the current era to some of the oldest Archaean and Proterozoic material on the continent's Precambrian shield. The soil worsens here, becoming intermittently saline and calcareous. Calcareous soils have high levels of calcium carbonate which reduce the availability of what nutrients may be present. In fact, except for some patches east of Perth around Northam and Narrogin and on the far southwestern tip of the state, the soils of this area are remarkably poor. Despite this, as water becomes more prevalent, the eucalypt and acacia species re-emerge between Balladonia and Norseman, the acacia becoming increasingly rich to the south and west.

Western Australia

The state of Western Australia is aptly named as it includes the entire western section of Australia, 2,525,500 sq km, or 32.87 per cent of the total area of the continent. Its coastline stretches 12,500km along the Indian Ocean and north into the Timor Sea. Its capital is **Perth**, situated in the southwest. Perth's population of 1,262,600 comprises 73 per cent of the state's total. The major

ports are Fremantle, Albany, Bunbury and Geraldton. The principal highway is **Route 1**, a variously named highway which stretches along the coast from the South Australian border to the Northern Territory, except for an inland section from Broome which bypasses the Kimberley region. Other interior routes include **no. 94**, which departs north from Esperance in the south to Coolgardie, then east to Perth; and **no. 95**, which traverses an inland route north from Perth to about Port Hedland, nearly 1400km away.

The **Great Western Plateau** covers most of Western Australia, the Northern Territory, northwest South Australia and the Mount Isa district of Queensland. Western Australia is largely a uniformly flat plateau with shallow valleys becoming deeper as they approach the coast. The plateau is comprised of granite and gneiss in the south and sandstone in the north. The **Darling Range**, visible to the east of Perth and running north and south, is in fact an escarpment marking the western edge of the plateau. The area to the east of the range is known to be among the oldest geological formations in the world, having been formed in the Archaean era and remaining stable for about half of its existence. Exceptions to these ancient formations are the Mesozoic and upper Paleozoic areas along the coast and the eastern sections of the Great Sandy and Gibson Deserts. The occasional low granite and gabbro outcrops on the Nullarbor Plain are 1500 million years old.

The **Nullarbor** is an arid, largely uninhabited plateau lying in South Australia and Western Australia; the name comes from the Latin for 'no trees'. The plain's limestone was deposited during a massive subsidence during the Cretaceous period which also saw much of Victoria and South Australia submerged. The **Great Australian Bight**, sheer cliffs which fall up to 90m to the southern ocean, forms the plain's southern edge. The plain is crossed by the Eyre Highway near the coast (Eucla is the only settlement along the route) and by the Indian-Pacific railway. Remarkably, one section of this famous railway line is straight for 479km. (For more information about the Nullarbor and the Bight, see p 523.)

People speaking the **Nyungar languages** lived in the area from the Nullarbor to the Western Australian coast as far north as Geraldton and inland as far as Kalgoorlie-Boulder and Mount Magnet. Groups living in the cooler, wetter regions in the southwest built temporary weather-proof thatched huts. Those living inland practised male initiation rites similar to the neighbouring desert people, indicating some social relation with these groups.

The first massacre of Aboriginal people in Western Australia occurred south of Perth on the Murray River at **Pinjarra** in October 1834, five years after settlement. At the prompting of settler James Peel, Governor James Stirling sent five mounted police to attack the Aboriginal settlement. One of about ten punitive raids during the decade, this one broke the tribe of the local leader, Calyute, and resulted in an accord.

North of the Nullarbor, the Great Victorian, Gibson and Great Sandy Deserts form the state's inaccessible eastern regions. To their west are the goldfields which seem to crop up here and there through virtually the entire north and western area of the state.

The state's population and major agricultural areas form a triangle on the southwest. Here winter rainfall exceeds 25mm inland and increases as you approach the coast. Perth receives nearly as much rain as Sydney or Brisbane, though this falls generally in the winter months.

The **Pilbara** of northwest Western Australia is a pair of plateaus flanking the Fortescue River valley. The area received some attention for gold and, until the late 1960s, asbestos, but is now best known for the remarkable colours in the walls of the gorges in the **Karijini National Park** area of the Hamersley Mountain Range. At Oxer's Lookout, near the village of **Wittenoom**, three such gorges converge. (Care must be taken, however, to avoid remnant asbestos fibres in Wittenoom itself.)

Above the Hamersley, the **Great Sandy Desert** nearly reaches the Indian Ocean in Western Australia's far northern corner between Port Hedland and Broome.

The **Kimberley** region makes up the far north, east of Broome. It receives summer (December to February) monsoonal rains, but is dry during winter. The predominant flora is scattered eucalypt of low to medium height above hummock grass. Along the coast is an intertidal mixture of mangrove, shrubs and mud flats. In river deltas these features can be extensive. The area is noted for spectacular gorges at Fitzroy Crossing and Wandjina figures in the Aboriginal rock art near Kununurra.

Flora and fauna

Travellers routinely praise the colours in the Perth and Fremantle area. The beaches here have brilliant white sand of calcareous limestone and the ocean is, indeed, India Blue. Locals point out that Leighton and Port Beaches have patches of emerald-coloured water offshore. The Austrian adventurer Charles von Hügel (see box), in his *New Holland Journal* of 1833, rhapsodises about the vegetation: 'The flora in all its splendour do not strike the eye till you are close up. The cheerless grey-green changed to the most varied shades of green, from the lightest and brightest to lush dark hues, mingled with brilliant flowers of every kind, in untold numbers... I roamed around this world of colour as if intoxicated.'

The wildflowers of the Western Australian spring in September still offer unprecedented displays for the visitor. Over 100 species of flowering plants are found only in Western Australia, with thousands of others contributing to the blanketing of the grasslands after rains. The other predominant floral species are eucalypt and acacia, but hakea, dryandra and banksia are also stunning. One of the most spectacular is the royal hakea (*Hakea victoria*), first described in 1847.

Charles von Hügel

Baron Carl Alexander Anselm von Hügel (1795–1870) was an Austrian aristocrat and avid naturalist who, supposedly as a result of a broken heart, determined to visit the new continent of New Holland. In 1831, he set out from Europe for Africa, and eventually arrived in Fremantle in late 1833. He travelled throughout the colonies, collecting natural specimens and making observations in his journal about the landscape and the incipient society that he encountered. When he returned to Europe in 1836, he was fêted everywhere, bringing along vast quantities of seeds and samples of flora, some of them never seen before. His garden in Vienna became renowned throughout Europe, and included a number of Australian plants, such as *Acacia huegelii*, which were named after him or members of his family. His descriptions of Australian vegetation inspired such figures as Ferdinand von Mueller, who would later become the influential director of the Melbourne Botanic Gardens. Hügel's journals, previously unpublished, have recently been translated and brought into print by Dymphna Clark, widow of famous historian Manning Clark; they offer valuable insights into the nature of early Australian life. See *Baron Charles von Hügel: New Holland Journal* (1994).

The **bird** populations of Western Australia include similarly familiar species, but novel sightings can be logged of the smaller rock and elegant parrots, various honeyeaters, ringnecks and gerygones (a small warbler). Miraculously, the vile introduced species of starlings and mynas of the east coast are absent here, as are sparrows. The state takes considerable care to keep these agricultural and aesthetic vermin out. Mammal species include the echidna, local species of wallaroo, kangaroo and possums, but no platypus, wombat or koala.

Perth
....

Visitors to **Perth** (population 1,262,600) remark on its stunning geographical beauty, with the lookout from Mount Eliza across the Swan River a required stop on any tour. Mount Eliza is in the part of the city called **Kings Park**, thankfully gazetted as parkland as early as 1831 and still one of the most attractive urban parks in Australia. From the 1840s, British residents in India travelled to Western Australia to enjoy the Mediterranean climate, the most temperate and consistent of all Australian cities.

The most notable factor determining the development, history, and social conditions of Perth has been its vast distance from anywhere else, most significantly its remove from the rest of developed Australia. Indeed, being 2700km from Adelaide, the city can still be described as the most isolated Western capital in the world. Telegraph communication with the eastern states was established only in the 1870s, and the famous Trans-Australian Railway, now the Indian–Pacific Line, across the enormous and desolate Nullarbor Plain, was not completed until 1917. Perth is substantially closer to Indonesia than to Sydney or Melbourne; recently, with regular airline connections, many Indonesians actually commute between the city and Jakarta.

Still, Perth is distinctly Australian in its attitudes and lifestyle, revelling in its independence and isolation from the 'Eastern States', as Western Australians consider the rest of the country. (In turn other Australians refer to Western Australians as 'sandgropers'.) During the Depression of the 1930s, a strong secessionist movement developed, prompted by the belief that Western Australia could do better on its own than as a state in the Australian Commonwealth.

A booming economy in the 1980s led to Perth's 'discovery' by outsiders, both Australian and international, resulting in population growth and greater communication with the rest of the world—a situation not always welcomed by old-timers. Perth was the base from which such well-known entrepreneurs as Alan Bond, Laurie Connell and Christopher Skase amassed their fortunes in this greedy decade, only to see their paper empires plummet amidst lawsuits, bankruptcy and criminal charges in the more sober atmosphere of the 1990s.

Today, the city is both vibrant and laid-back, with high-rise buildings everywhere, along with the sometimes overwhelming mansions of the *nouveau riche*, but still nurturing its love of the sun and enjoying its magnificent ocean. The city hosts many international sporting events and festivals. In early January, the prestigious Hopman Cup precedes the Australian Open Tennis competition in Melbourne; other events that have taken place here are the Heineken Classic, Australia's richest golf tournament, and the Triathlon World Championship in 1997. Fremantle, of course, is a port of call for many yacht races, most particularly the Whitbread Round the World Race. The **Festival of Perth**, the oldest international arts festival in the Southern hemisphere, is held here in February and March every year, and the **Fremantle Festival** is held annually in November.

■ Practical information

Tourist information: Western Australian Tourist Centre, Albert Facey House, Forrest Place and Wellington Street; ☎ 08 9483 1111; 1300 361 351. Another excellent source for information on Western Australia's national parks and natural wonders is the website of the Conservation and Land Management Office (CALM): www.calm.wa.gov.au

Airport. Perth has an international airport 20km east of the city, and a domestic terminal a few kilometres closer. Shuttle buses run regularly between the city and both terminals (☎ 08 9250 2838/9479 4131). There is a taxi service but as it takes 30 minutes to get into town it is much more expensive than by bus.

International airlines servicing Perth are *British Airways* (☎ 08 9483 7711); *Garuda* (☎ 08 9481 0963); *Malaysian Airlines* (☎ 08 9325 4499); *Qantas* (☎ 08 9225 2222); *Singapore* (☎ 08 9483 5777); *United Airlines* (☎ 08 008 230 322). Domestic airlines are *Ansett WA* (☎ 13 1300); *Rottnest Airlines* (☎ 08 9478 1322); *Skywest* (☎ 08 9334 2288).

Train. The *Indian-Pacific* (☎ 13 22 32), the interstate train, arrives at the **East Perth Railway Terminal**, Summers Street, two stops before the main railway station; India-Pacific trains operate twice a week in each direction. Within the state, *Westrail* (☎ 08 9326 2771), also based at the East Perth Terminal, provides services between Perth and Kalgoorlie, and Perth and Bunbury. There is no train service to the far north.

Transperth (☎ 13 22 13), the city's excellent suburban transport service, runs trains regularly from its central **station on Wellington Street**, including frequent journeys to Fremantle.

Bus. There are two bus stations on Wellington Street next to the central railway station. *Greyhound Pioneer Australia* (☎ 13 20 30) runs services from all state capitals and also connects Perth to many Western Australian locations. *Westrail* (☎ 13 22 32) also provides bus services within the state.

Transperth, the city's public transport service, coordinates the local bus service based on an eight-zone fare system. Individual tickets can be bought on board the bus and also from ticket vending machines at the stations. *Transperth Fast-cards* can be pre-purchased at most newsagents and bus stations, and are much cheaper. Perth's central business district is a **'Free Transit Zone'**, where any *Transperth* service is free. The **Perth Tram** (☎ 08 9367 9204) is a recon-structed old tram that provides sightseeing tours with taped commentary. It can be boarded and reboarded at many stops throughout central Perth.

Ferries. A regular ferry service, also part of *Transperth*'s system, operates from the city at Barrack Street Jetty across the Swan River to South Perth. From September to April the ferry service runs to Coode Street jetty.

Also departing from the Barrack Street Jetty are Fast Ferries to **Rottnest Island**, run by *Boat Torque Cruises* (☎ 1300 368 686; 08 9221 5844), which advertises as the largest privately owned ferry company in Australia. Other boat cruises available on ☎ 08 9325 3341/08 9325 1191.

Taxis. Ring for taxi service on ☎ 08 9333 3333 or 08 9444 4444.

Useful addresses
British Consulate, 77 St George's Terrace, ☎ 08 9221 5400; **US Consulate**, 16 St George's Terrace, ☎ 08 9231 9400; **Canadian Consulate**, 11/111 St George's Terrace, ☎ 08 9322 7930.
Police: *Emergency*, call 000; *city station:* Curtin House, 60 Beaufort Street, ☎ 08 9223 3305; *headquarters*: 2 Adelaide Terrace, East Perth, ☎ 08 9222 1111.
Hospitals: *Royal Perth*, Victoria Square & Wellington Street, ☎ 08 9224 2244; *King Edward Memorial Hospital for Women*, Bagot Road, Subiaco, ☎ 08 9340 2222; *Fremantle*, Alma Street, ☎ 08 9431 3333.

Hotels
$$$$ Burswood Resort Hotel, Great Eastern Highway, Victoria Park, ☎ 08 9362 7777. Perth's swankiest resort 'centre', with every elegance.
$$$$ Esplanade Hotel Fremantle, on the corner of Marine Terrace and Essex Street, Fremantle, ☎ 08 9432 4000. Extravagant prices, Fremantle's great luxury hotel, on the foreshore.
$$$$ Hyatt Regency Perth, 99 Adelaide Terrace, ☎ 08 9225 1234/131 234. Predictably elegant grand hotel, with tennis court, fitness centre, and 25m pool.
$$$ Sebel of Perth Hotel, 37 Pier Street, ☎ 08 9325 7655; fax 08 9325 7383. Elegant and pricey 'boutique' hotel, central location, attractive decor. Nine storeys, 100 rooms, 19 suites.
$$-$$$ Metro Inn Apartments, 22 Nile Street, East Perth, ☎ 08 9325 1866/

☎ 1 800 804 889 (central reservations ☎ 1 800 00 4321). Self-contained units with kitchenettes, overlooking Swan River.

$$ Fothergills of Fremantle, 20–22 Ord Street, Fremantle, ☎ 08 9335 6784; fax 08 9430 7789. Lovely historic limestone guest house, views of harbour and beach; non-smoking.

$$ Miss Maud Swedish Private Hotel, 97 Murray Street, ☎ 08 9325 3900/ ☎ 1 800 998 022; fax 08 9221 3225; e-mail: www.missmaud.com.au. Centrally located, moderately eccentric 'Alpine' decor which varies from room to room; popular smorgasbord in downstairs restaurant.

$$ Sullivans Hotel, 166 Mounts Bay Road, ☎ 08 9321 8022. Cousin to Sydney's hotel of the same name, in a wonderful location. Family run, with pool, and free bikes for guests. Lovely breakfast cafe.

$ Flying Angel Club, 76 Queen Victoria Street, Fremantle, ☎ 08 9335 5000; fax 08 9335 5321. 20-room private hotel, very reasonable prices.

Fremantle Homestays, ☎ 08 9335 7531. This agency organises stays at bed & breakfasts and self-contained units in the Fremantle area.

Restaurants

$$$ Chez Uchino, 120 Wellington Street, Mosman Park, ☎ 08 9385 2202. An exciting mixture of Japanese and French flavours and techniques by chef-owner Osamu Uchino.

$$$ Fraser's, Fraser Avenue, Kings Park, West Perth, ☎ 08 9481 7100. Outstanding views, award-winning menu. Specialities are duck and local fish.

$$$ The Loose Box, 6825 Great Eastern Highway, ☎ 08 9295 1787. Thirty minutes from Perth, this classic French restaurant, winner of every dining award, is worth the drive. Chef Alain Fabregues has built a world-class French restaurant stove, and serves food worthy of the effort. Rooms can be arranged for those who wish to stay overnight.

$$$ Mead's Fish Gallery, 15 Johnson Parade, Mosman Park, ☎ 08 9383 3388. A boat shed on the Swan River, transformed into one of Perth's most opulent dining venues. Excellent fish specialities, near-excessive service; valet parking for car or launch.

$$ Altos, 424 Hay Street, Subiaco, ☎ 08 9382 3292. Described by a local as 'a romantic neighbourhood *boite*', tasteful decor, well-prepared food and impressive wine cellar.

$$ Cafe Bellissimo, 3 Bay View Terrace, Claremont, ☎ 08 9385 3588. One of Perth's most popular eateries, serving traditional Neapolitan fare, some cooked on wood-fired ovens. No reservations, so there is often a queue. Unlicensed.

$$ é cucina, Central Park, 777 Hay Street, Perth, ☎ 08 9481 1020. An Italian open-air 'kitchen', one side of which opens onto one of the only green spaces in Central Perth; popular for lunch. Impeccable service, first-rate menu and wine list.

$$ Genting Palace, Burswood International Resort Casino, Great Eastern Highway, Victoria Park, ☎ 08 9362 7551. Considered Perth's best Chinese restaurant, especially weekend dim sum and Peking duck.

$$ Quattro, 26 Marine Terrace, Fremantle, ☎ 08 9336 4500. Fremantle's most stylish brasserie, two blocks from the busy cappuccino strip. Expansive views, attentive service, freshly prepared entrees, excellent desserts. Good wine list.

$ Annalakshmi, 12 The Esplanade, Perth, ☎ 08 9221 3003. Hindi for 'Goddess of Food and Plenty', this unusual restaurant, with views of the Swan River, is staffed by volunteers serving Indian vegetarian food. Non-smoking and non-alcoholic.

$ Gino's, 1 South Terrace, Fremantle, ☎ 08 9336 1464. The ideal pavement cafe on Fremantle's cappuccino strip. Opens early, closes late, good Italian fare, excellent coffee and desserts.

$ 44 King Street, 44 King Street, Perth, ☎ 08 9321 4476. Very good and inexpensive food, great service, in converted warehouse.

Perth beaches

Perth is justly proud of its many city beaches, acclaimed as the best in Australia (and this is a very large claim indeed). Most of them have stunning white sands and bright blue waters, and most are accessible by bus or train (check with Transperth, ☎ 13 22 13). Some beaches that any visitor should see include:

Cottlesloe: 11km southwest of Perth's city centre, this is the trendiest place to go to 'see and be seen'. Only 4km north of Fremantle, easily accessible from the Fremantle train.

City Beach: the quintessential city beach, broad and spacious, home of the Perth Surf Club. About 10km west of the city centre, with a bus service.

Scarborough Beach: 14km northwest of central Perth, this is probably the best known of Perth beaches, a continuation of the city's coastal run of surf and sand; some very nice ocean view hotels and holiday units are located here.

Sorrento Beach: 19km northwest of town, this is the family beach *par excellence*, the location of Hillarys Boat Harbour, Sorrento Quay, and—of most interest to children—Underwater World (☎ 08 9447 7500; open daily 09.00–17.00), a 'hands-on' aquarium, with a tunnel to view sharks and manta rays, and a touching pool with dolphins.

Leighton Beach, Fremantle: very close to the railway terminal, a world-famous surfing spot, but also good for swimming.

History

Perth is set at the base of Mount Eliza on the banks of the Swan River. Named after the Scottish birthplace of then Secretary of State George Murray, the city is built on a grid plan following the work of Surveyor General John Septimus Roe in 1829. The area of present-day Perth was first sighted by the Dutch under Willem de Vlamingh in 1696, who mapped and named the **Swan River**, after the black swans he saw there. The first instance of European interest in the western edge of the continent was a suggestion by Jean Pieter Purry in 1718 that the Dutch East India Company form a settlement in its southwest section; this suggestion was never taken up, as explorers could find no obvious trade resources in this apparently barren land. In 1801, the French under Nicolas Baudin also explored the area, but considered it unsuitable for anchorage or settlement.

In 1826, Lord Bathurst in London instructed Governor Darling, then in Sydney, to survey Shark Bay on the far northwest in case the French were interested in the area. Bathurst immediately changed his mind, instructing Darling to settle convicts at **King George Sound** on the southern tip of the state. Envisioned as a strategic outpost in line with shipping from England to Port Jackson, this settlement was near present-day Albany. Founded in 1826, it lasted only two years before the personnel were transferred to Swan River, where efforts to establish a settlement had just begun.

The founding of Perth and Fremantle was due to the insistence of **James Stirling**, who led the first British expedition to the Swan River in 1827. About this area he wrote:

We sailed through a rich and romantic country...the bright foliage of the shrubs, the majesty of the surrounding trees, the abrupt and red-coloured banks of the river occasionally seen, and the view of the blue summits of the mountains, from which we were not far distant, made the scenery around the spot as beautiful as anything of the kind I have ever witnessed.

His glowing descriptions of the area and his audacious request to become the settlement's first governor fell on deaf ears. John Barrow, the Secretary of the Admiralty, described Stirling's expedition as quixotic and contradicted his account of the entrance to the Swan River and adjacent country upstream.

Depending instead upon his father-in-law's connections, Stirling sought a combination of private capital and a grant of Crown Land to found the colony. The first attempt to accomplish this venture involved Thomas Peel (1793–1865), the second son of prominent cotton manufacturer Robert Peel, and a few opportunistic investors. They asked for four million acres and first choice of land. The government's counter offer of one million acres and fair apportionment of land resulted in the venture being withdrawn.

Renewed fears of French interest in the area and the flurry of applications from prospective settlers convinced the Colonial Office to proceed with a land grant approach to settlement. The terms required minimal expense for the civil and military presence: that 40 acres be given for each £3 invested and that the holdings be improved within ten years of occupation. The *Challenger*, which carried the civil authorities, and the *Sulphur* (some authorities report this ship to have been the *Parmelia)*, which carried the military personnel, entered the Swan River on 1 June 1829. The first private settlers arrived in August on the *Calista*. The captain of the *Challenger*, Charles Fremantle, was the first to use the word 'Australia' officially when he formally claimed Western Australia for Britain.

Financially, Stirling and Peel looked to emancipist merchant banker Solomon Levey (1794–1833) in Sydney to provide the money in a partnership kept secret to avoid the taint of his being Jewish and a transported convict. Levey's contemporaries attributed his death shortly thereafter to the fiscally ruinous situation at Swan River.

From the first day, when Stirling's enthusiastic attempt to take a short cut through the shoals at the mouth of the Swan River caused the *Parmelia* to run aground, conditions for the settlers were grave. The land was sandy and dry except where it was thick with trees or boggy. While Stirling maintained a sense of gentility, Thomas Peel became increasingly bizarre: taking a shot in the arm in a duel with the captain of the ship carrying settlers for his acreage south of Fremantle, issuing promissory notes which were not honoured to workers he sued for passage money when they insisted they be paid, and riding about his property ill dressed.

By the time Stirling left the colony in 1839, it was only nominally productive and still imported all of its wheat and flour from Hobart. In 1846 some colonists petitioned for help in the form of convicts to work. To the consternation of the Victorian Anti-Transportation League, the first lot of transportees (75 felons and 54 guards) were sent in 1850. By 1868, nearly 10,000 men had been transported to Western Australia, most of them after transportation had been abandoned in the other colonies. In *The Fatal Shore*, Robert Hughes maintains that the population growth and prosperity of South Australia, Victoria, New South Wales and Queensland contrasts with the lagging economies of Western Australia and Tasmania because the latter were 'stuck for decades in their hangover from the malign indulgence of semi-slave labor'. Only the discovery of gold in the Kimberley region (1885) and particularly in Kalgoorlie (1893) brought both money and a sharp increase in population to Perth.

Selecting a site for the colonial capital followed straightforward 19C principles. Fremantle, 19km south of Perth, would serve as the port, but the capital had to have secure defences against foreign attack. Point Heathcote (now Applecross), near Fremantle on the south shore of the Swan, or Point Frazer would also have suited as a settlement site. While Point Heathcote had a slightly better anchorage and much better cooling sea breezes, the Perth location was more picturesque and had access to the agricultural land held by Stirling, Roe and other colonial stalwarts.

Roe is reported to have modelled the town after the 'New Town' section of Edinburgh. The town plan described a three-square-mile rectangular arrangement between the Swan to the south and east, Mount Eliza to the west and some swamps to the north. Streets ran parallel to the Swan beginning with St George's Terrace, Hay Street (its slight elevation made it the most important thoroughfare), Murray Street (after Hay's superior, Colonial Secretary John Murray) and Wellington Street. Sadly, no effort was taken to convert the swamps into a garden district. Worse, Roe sold the reserve land between the Swan and St George Terrace and behind the barracks. Although Stirling repurchased the Government House site, the opportunity for a strong area for governmental buildings was lost.

Development of Perth and the rest of the state proceeded slowly; by 1858, the population of Perth was 3000, and when it was incorporated as a city in 1871, only 5000 citizens had settled here. The gold rushes in Kalgoorlie and elsewhere at the end of the century brought thousands of immigrants, and by the time of Federation in 1901, the metropolitan area, including Fremantle, had increased in population to 44,000.

As well as building mines and bridges and dredging channels for shipping and transport, convict labour between 1850 and 1868 erected a number of public works. They built or improved roads between Fremantle and Perth, east to York, and to Bunbury and Albany to the south. They erected public buildings including Government House, the Town Hall, Perth Gaol, Pensioner Barracks and Causeway. In Fremantle, the equivalent convict-built structures are the Fremantle Gaol and Convict Asylum. The latter is now the site of the Fremantle Arts Centre.

Initially, the area around Barrack Street and St George's Terrace were devoted to administrative, business and upper-class residences; Hay Street contained commercial and shopping venues; and the area to the north around Wellington Street became artisans' workshops and cottages. The elite families built their residences at the west end of St George's Terrace, particularly above where it becomes Mount Street and rises to catch the sea breezes. Australian novelist and teacher J.K. Ewers described the architecture of the older residential areas in *Money Street* (1938):

The houses were closely packed with ornate frontal decorations that were relics of the late-Victorian age of cottage architecture. Here was a wreath of flowers, species unknown, set in masonry. There, a pillared balustrade hid a receding gable. Quaint houses they were, each breathing a definite personality.

Central Perth

Central Perth forms an elongated rectangle at Perth Water on the Swan River. Although oriented on a west-northwest to east-southeast grid, for simplicity, the directions given in the walk below assume that Perth Water is directly south rather than south and a bit west. The highway into the city crosses the Causeway at Heirisson Island. The **major streets** from south to north are Riverside Drive, Adelaide Terrace, which becomes St George's Terrace, Hay (originally Howick), Murray and Wellington Streets. The Perth Railway Station is on Wellington Street. The major cross streets are Plain, Victoria Avenue, Barrack and William Streets. Adelaide/St George's Terrace is the principal road; it leads past the larger hotels, Government House and St George's Cathedral, then over the Mitchell Freeway at Malcolm Street to enter Kings Park Botanic Gardens. The highway leading to the University of Western Australia, some older suburbs and Fremantle skirts Kings Park on the Swan River side of William or Barrack Streets.

A walk around the city centre

This walk follows a route through the city centre in a clockwise direction from the tourist centre to Victoria Square, through the Stirling Gardens on the river, into the centre again and west, returning to end at the Hay Street Mall. On p 540 there is a description of the Western Australian Museum, most of which is situated immediately north of the railway station.

The **West Australia Tourist Centre** (☎ 1300 361 351) is on Forrest Place next to the General Post Office. From here you can book a variety of walking tours and find out about Heritage Walks and other guided tours. At the head of the street is the Perth Railway Station and a pedestrian walkway called the Horseshoe Bridge. The station was built in 1891–94 following a design by G.T. Poole. The flanking bays were added in 1897 to cope with the gold rush traffic. The area immediately in front of the station was used as a plaza for election campaign rallies until recently. The mechanical signal box near the station still functions to control railway traffic. Note the ornate arcade and swans—Western Australia's conspicuous emblematic bird—which decorate the lamp posts on the bridge.

Next to the Tourist Centre is the **General Post Office** (1930s), which has a classical façade and colonnade faced with Mahogany Creek granite and Donnybrook stone. The framework is, in fact, steel encased in concrete. This tendency to construct modern buildings in a style reminiscent of the 19C is also seen in

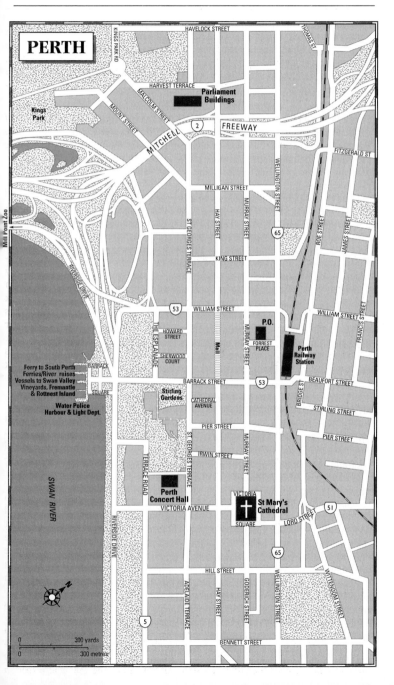

PERTH

Kings Park

Mill Point Zoo

HAVELOCK STREET

THOMAS ST

HARVEST TERRACE

Parliament Buildings

MALCOLM STREET

MOUNT STREET

KINGS PARK RD

(2) FREEWAY

MITCHELL

FITZGERALD ST

WELLINGTON STREET

MILLIGAN STREET

HAY STREET

MURRAY STREET

(65)

ROE STREET

JAMES STREET

ST GEORGES TERRACE

KING STREET

WILLIAM STREET

(53)

WILLIAM STREET

FRANCIS STREET

THE ESPLANADE

HOWARD STREET

Mall

MURRAY STREET

P.O.

FORREST PLACE

Perth Railway Station

SHERWOOD COURT

BEAUFORT STREET

BRIDGE ST

Ferry to South Perth
Ferries/River cruises
Vessels to Swan Valley
Vineyards, Fremantle
& Rottnest Island

BARRACK
SQUARE

BARRACK STREET

(53)

STIRLING STREET

Water Police
Harbour & Light Dept.

Stirling Gardens

CATHEDRAL AVENUE

PIER STREET

PIER STREET

ST GEORGES TERRACE

TERRACE ROAD

IRWIN STREET

SWAN RIVER

RIVERSIDE DRIVE

Perth Concert Hall

VICTORIA AVENUE

VICTORIA SQUARE

✝ **St Mary's Cathedral**

LORD STREET

(51)

MURRAY STREET

(65)

WITTENOOM STREET

HILL STREET

ADELAIDE TERRACE

HAY STREET

GODERICH STREET

WELLINGTON STREET

(5)

N

BENNETT STREET

0   300 yards
0   300 metres

the **Commonwealth Bank** immediately south of the GPO on the northwest corner of Forrest Place and Murray Street. The bank, built in 1930–33, consciously matches the design of the GPO, with cornice lines, pilasters and giant columns. Initially, a second structure nearly identical to the bank was to have been built north of the GPO to further accentuate the symmetry, but the Depression brought an end to such ambitious construction.

Walking east on Murray Street leads past a bookshop at no. 196. William Wolf designed the exuberant bay windows and inset balcony as a hotel in 1924.

The former Government Printing Office is at the corner of Murray and Pier Streets. Designed by G.T. Poole and built on the site of the Poor House in 1879, the building includes additions made in the early 1890s which are readily identified as the mismatched upper floors and as an extension at the building's northern end.

The Fire Brigade Historical Society runs the **City Number 1 Fire Station** (☎ 08 9323 9468) on the corner of Murray and Irwin Streets, across from a well-known Moreton Bay Fig, listed on the National Registry of Trees. A turn-of-the-century brick and rusticated limestone structure, the fire station functions as a museum of firefighting, now called officially the Fire Safety Education Centre and Museum (open weekdays 10.00–15.00).

Another of Poole's designs is again on the north side of Murray Street just past Irwin Street. Now the Administration Building of the Royal Hospital, its Romanesque style derives from the hatchwork on the balconies.

At the end of Murray Street is VICTORIA SQUARE, which dates from plans in 1833 to establish the site as Church Square. When the Church of England decided to build nearer Barrack Street, the Roman Catholic Church was given the land. **St Mary's Cathedral**, on the south side of the square, was built by Benedictine Brothers under the second Roman Catholic Bishop Martin Griver beginning in 1863. These monks built the original Bishop's Palace in 1859 and churches in Fremantle and Guildford as well. Their dawn-to-dusk working hours and daily trudge from their hospice in the suburb of Subiaco are frequently recounted. The Gothic Revival design was drawn by noted English ecclesiastical architect Augustus Pugin shortly before his death in 1852. Considerable remodelling and additions make it difficult to discern the original lines of the church.

Children of Mary Chapel and **Sisters of Mercy Convent** are south of the square on Victoria Avenue to Hay Street. The original buildings are simple cement-rendered brick structures built during the 1840s. The two-storey building on the east side of the convent was completed in 1849 and features triple Gothic windows and fanlights over some doorways. The Mother House of the Convent was built in 1873 based on plans drawn by an Irish political prisoner named McMahon. Its construction is of chequered brickwork, timbered verandahs with cast-iron lace work and three steep gables.

From Victoria Square, walk one block south to HAY STREET again. One block east at Hill Street is the **Perth Mint** (☎ 08 9421 7277; open weekdays 09.00–16.00, weekends 10.00–13.00), open to the public daily to view gold melting and the production of bullion. It also includes some historical displays about refining and mining processes.

If you continue east on Hay Street, then north on Plain Street c 1km, you will come to the **East Perth Cemetery** (☎ 08 9325 3709). This cemetery dates from the colonial period, the first burial having taken place in 1830. Its grounds are divided by denomination. St Bartholomew's Chapel in the cemetery was built in 1871. Some of the city's earliest settlers are buried here.

Return to Pier Street to reach **St George's Cathedral** and its **Deanery**. The first St George's Church was erected between 1841 and 1845 and was a stolid, unimaginative design. The current cathedral was designed by famous Sydney architect Edmund Blacket as an architectural reference to 13C gothicism (successful except for the blockish tower erected in 1902); it was completed in 1882. Notice how your eye is led upward by the shortening stone courses. Another illusionistic device is the miniature bas-relief colonnade with reduced-sized windows which make the building look taller. The interior features a warm rose-coloured brick, vertical windows behind the altar, and jarrah hammerbeams.

The **Deanery** is immediately to the east on St George's Terrace. An Australian version of English cottage style, it was constructed in 1859 for the colony's first dean, George Pownall. Either Pownall or Richard Roach Jewell (see box), the Colonial Clerk of Works, provided the design. Like other buildings of the time, it features light-coloured bricks. The house, one of few from the period, escaped demolition in the early 1950s when the then Dean John Bell accepted public opinion to save it and even stood the cost of restoration.

> ### Richard Roach Jewell
> Richard Roach Jewell (1810–91) was born in Devon, England, and apprenticed there as an architect and builder. For the sake of his wife's delicate health, he migrated to Western Australia in 1852. Here he worked briefly in the Convict Settlement, transferred as foreman to the Department of Public Works in Perth, and was appointed superintendent by Governor Fitzgerald. Initially, his talent for controlling expenditure served him well, his early projects being largely to repair roads and bridges and construct the Perth and Fremantle Boys' Schools. Once the impact of convict labour freed some funds for more ambitious projects, he built the Perth Town Hall, Wesley Church, Public Trust Office, Treasury and Cloisters as well as a number of buildings in surrounding towns.

Across St George's Terrace to the east is **Government House**. It had a predecessor which, by the time the current structure was begun in 1859, was termite-ridden with a leaking roof. Western Australian Governor Kennedy approved its design, but his successor, John Stephen Hampton, found it necessary to insist on extensive revisions, primarily increased room size. Like the other signatory buildings of Perth—the Town Hall, Cloisters and Barracks—Government House is a Colonial Gothic design with Tudor influences. For evidence of the former, note the pointed arches on the verandah; for the latter see the towers. Also in common with the buildings of the period, the coloured bricks are laid in 'Flemish bond' style familiar in Richard Jewell's buildings. While Jewell supervised the construction, the design was by E.Y.W. Henderson. Interior features of note include a jarrah and cast-iron stairway and marble fireplaces. The ballroom was replaced in 1899 with the current room designed by J.M. Grainger. As the official tourist brochures state, 'Government House and its private gardens are 'open to the public from time to time', indicating that 'open days' occur occasionally.

Stirling Gardens, which extend from the corner of Irwin Street and St George's Terrace to Barrack Street, are of some interest. Representing an example of 19C English landscape gardening, they feature 'Royal Trees' planted by each visiting member of the British Royal Family, formal rose beds, and large expanses of lawn. The Norfolk pines were planted in 1867.

The Old Court House, Perth

The **Old Court House** on the southeast corner of Stirling Gardens is a modest building, the oldest in Perth. A primitive colonial structure with stuccoed walls and a later portico, it was designed by Henry Reveley in 1836. He had travelled in Italy and Greece, thus the hint of neo-classicism in the design. It functioned in its early days as a church, boys' school, girls' school and concert hall. As a concert hall, it saw a memorable charity concert in 1846 given by Rosendo Salvado, an impoverished Benedictine monk from Spain who sought support for his order's mission to the Aborigines at New Norcia, north of Perth (see also p 566). The Old Court House now houses the **Francis Burt Law Museum** (☎ 08 9325 4787; open weekdays 10.00–14.00), which offers guided tours and arranges viewing of court proceedings, and even participation in mock trials.

To the west of the Old Court House is the **Supreme Court Building**. Situated on what was once the foreshore embankment, the design of this 1906 building reflects the post-gold rush boom years. The Italianate columns are of Donnybrook white stone. J.M. Grainger, father of famous composer Percy Grainger, was the design architect. These structures are surrounded by pleasant gardens that lead to the Swan River. At Barrack Square are the ferries to the zoo, Rottnest Island, and touring cruises.

Across Barrack Street on the northwest corner of THE ESPLANADE is the **Weld Club**, an award-winning design by J.J. Talbot Hobbs built in 1891–92. The building has especially fine woods in the interior, and is situated in elegant gardens down to the river. The Esplanade Gardens to the south of this row of buildings, leading down to the Swan River, is another pleasant green spot in the city, including the **Allen Green Plant Conservatory** (open Mon–Sat 10.00–16.00, Sun and public holidays 12.00–16.00), a pyramid-shaped glasshouse with tropical plants, and the Alf Curlewis Gardens.

Walk north on Barrack Street to ST GEORGE'S TERRACE to find the **Central Government Offices**. This group of Classic Revival Victorian public buildings were constructed between 1874 and 1905, and served as the General Post Office until 1923. Facing them on Barrack Street, the section to the left of the arched entrance dates from 1874, that to the right is from 1877. Both were designed by R.R. Jewell. The third storey was added in sections between 1896 and 1905. The section linking the two wings was completed by Jewell's successor, G.T. Poole, in 1887 to 1890. The building is an interesting transition between the Gothic Revival and the Italianate styles in that the simpler patterned, coloured brick gives way to projecting pilasters and ornament around the windows and doors. Jewell had arrived in the settlement a mere year before his appointment as Superintendent of Works in 1853; he served for 30 years.

The **Town Hall**, behind the Treasury on the corner of Barrack and Hay Streets, is also believed to have been built by R.R. Jewell. This Scottish Tudor-style structure was erected between 1867 and 1870. Its construction was largely carried out by convict labour and stories recount that the downward pointing arrow-shaped windows in the tower are their memen-toes to the town, as such designs appeared on convicts' uniforms. The hood mouldings above the windows are stone-cut hangman's ropes. Efforts by city councillors in 1924 to demolish the tower were frustrated, but the Tudor style

The Town Hall, Perth

arches on the ground floor did succumb to subsequent renovation when the City Council let the area for commercial use. The city recently razed a hideous bank building to the Town Hall's south and west, revealing façades previously hidden.

Trinity Congregational Church is reached by walking west on Hay Street along the Mall, left on Sherwood Court to St George's Terrace, then west again. (Walking through London Court is a short cut.) The original church on the site was designed by Jewell in the mid-1860s. Like much of his so-called 'Colonial Gothic' work, the ornament is created with patterned brickwork. It can be glimpsed through the garden area beside the later church. This later structure dates from 1893, a period of gold rush prosperity which is given full expression in the design by Henry Trigg in its ornate Romanesque windows, turrets and wrought-iron filials.

The **Palace Hotel** stands on the west side of Trinity Church. This three-storey hotel, now used as a bank, dates from 1895. It was designed by Porter and Thomas and constructed of bricks imported from Melbourne. The timber balconies with cast-iron balustrades are decorative. Internally, the cedar stair-case, marble fireplaces and moulded plaster ceiling in the dining room are evidence of the prosperous era of its construction.

Old Perth Boys' School, west on St George's Terrace and on the left past William Street, has a venerable history. Resembling a church, the school was built in 1852 with wings added in the mid-1860s. Unlike other structures of the period, the builders used local materials including sandstone quarried at Rocky Bay near Fremantle. The Gothic design was by William Ayshford Sanford, an amateur architect responsible for Fremantle Boys' School as well. Sanford was colonial secretary at the time and devoted to the Camden Society, a group fostering Elizabethan interests. This National Trust building currently houses a coffee shop, open weekdays 09.00–17.00.

Continuing west on St George's Terrace, on the right past King Street is the **Cloisters**. Actually built as Bishop Hale's Collegiate School, the name refers to the cloistered verandah on its north side. Built in 1858 from R.R. Jewell's design, the Tudor-influenced Colonial Gothic style is immediately recognisable. Again,

Flemish bond chequered brickwork provides the ornament; that on the east side of the building is particularly pleasant. Hale intended the school to be an alternative to education in England, but it closed for want of pupils in 1872. Subsequently used as a girls' school, a seminary and a dormitory, it currently houses professional offices and businesses.

The west end of St George's Terrace was once occupied by the **Barracks**. Along with the Cloisters and the Town Hall, the Barracks have been strongly associated with the history of the city. Sadly, this wonderful brick structure has been reduced to just the entry arch. Its function may not have reflected favourably on the colony, housing the guards and their families who stood over the impressed convict labour of the late 19C. Like the convicts, the guard, called Enrolled Pensioner Forces, seem to have been readily forgotten.

Continue north one block on King Street, past **His Majesty's Theatre** (☎ 08 9322 2929; daily tours 10.00–16.00), on the corner of Hay and King Streets. Designed by A. Wolffe and built in 1904, the theatre was the first steel and concrete building in Australia and is billed as Australia's only remaining Edwardian theatre. Locally known as 'the Maj', the theatre is still the city's most important venue for theatre, opera, ballet and musicals.

To the east on Hay Street at its juncture with William Street is **Wesley Church**. Having opened in 1870, the church served a Methodist congregation which had been active since the colony's founding. In fact, about 50 of the earliest farmers and their families were Methodists brought en masse to the colony aboard the *Tranby*, chartered by the Hardey and Clarkson families of Yorkshire and Lincolnshire in 1830. Methodism grew rapidly during the gold rush boom of the 1890s. The design will be recognised as another of Jewell's many creations.

Perth's museums

The **Western Australia Cultural Centre** (☎ 08 9492 6600) is directly behind the railway station from the city, accessible via Barrack Street. It incorporates the **Art Gallery of Western Australia** (☎ 08 9328 7233, open daily 10.00–17.00) on Roe Street, the **Museum** (☎ 08 9328 4411; Sun–Fri 10.30–17.00, Sat 13.00–17.00) on Francis Street and the **State Library** (☎ 08 9427 3111), all between Beaufort Street (Barrack Street to the south) and William Street.

The **Art Gallery of Western Australia** is a modern construction (1979) by Charles Sierakowski. Its collection is eclectic, preferring Australian and contemporary Asian topics. Particularly well represented are works by Robert Juniper (b. 1929), a well-known Perth artist who paints, according to art historian Terry Smith, 'in delicate, sun-drenched colour and in large, decorative forms, his deep affection for the burnt hills of his native country'. The gallery's collection includes one of the finest exhibitions of Aboriginal art in Australia.

The **Western Australian Museum** has grown from a modest Old Gaol's history museum and basement gallery to become a substantial complex of buildings. The main entrance is on Francis Street, and this part of the museum contains Aboriginal archaeology and a 25m-long blue whale skeleton. Hackett Hall houses the museum's changing exhibition space; the Jubilee Building has the natural history section; and the Beaufort Street Building incorporates the Hellenic Gallery. Centred within this rectangle of buildings is the Old Gaol and Roe Street Cottage. The story of the successive functions of these buildings is a study in civic improvement.

The Library and Museum were originally in the **Victoria Jubilee Building** (the library was in the basement, the mammals on the first floor and the birds on the second floor). Although the cornerstone was laid in June 1887, building work was not begun until 1897. Its design was by G.T. Poole's successor as Colonial Architect, J.M. Grainger, Percy Grainger's father. A 'Victorian Byzantine' style structure, its arches and columns are of Rottnest Island sandstone and its foundations and basement are of Cottesloe Sandstone.

The **Gaol** housed the state's art collection for many years before the current gallery building was constructed. R.R. Jewell designed this utilitarian structure which functioned as a gaol and court in 1853 (☎ 08 9328 4411; open Sun–Fri 10.00–17.00, Sat 13.00–17.00). Used for female prisoners, debtors and those awaiting trial, it was only briefly used as a prison before that function was transferred to the Fremantle Gaol. The stone for the building was quarried at Rocky Bay near the mouth of the Swan River and transported by barge to the site. The most handsome elevation is from Beaufort Street, and the design for the entrance can be found in the Royal Engineers' pattern book. In 1895 the gaol's function changed to that of a historical museum. In the 1970s the building was renovated. While it could not be restored to its original form, ceiling heights were returned to those specified by Jewell. The gaol now houses (for some reason) a display of a historical dental surgery and pharmacy, as well as artefacts of Perth's early history.

When nearing retirement, Colonial Architect G.T. Poole was commissioned to design the **Beaufort Street Building** to house the art collection. Although the 1896–97 exterior is far from Poole's best, the Hellenic Gallery's interior features jarrah floors and remarkably good interior light. The library was eventually housed in **Hackett Hall**, built in 1920 and named after John Hackett of the *West Australian* newspaper. When it outgrew the space, it was housed on the northwest corner of the centre, freeing Hackett Hall for special exhibits. The hall is targeted for further renovation. Throughout this tumult, the Old Gaol has remained devoted to the social history of the region.

In addition to this central complex, the museum is responsible for the Fremantle History Museum (a wing in the Fremantle Arts Centre), the Maritime Museum and Boat Shed, and regional museums for Albany, the gold fields, and Geraldton.

West Perth

St George's Terrace at this end turns into Malcolm Street and then becomes Kings Park Road, running along the edge of Kings Park itself. This section of town is called West Perth; from St George's Terrace, take the Purple Clipper train to reach the area.

Just west of the Mitchell Freeway on Harvest Terrace is **Parliament House** (☎ 08 9222 7429; open weekdays 09.00–17.00 when in session), which offers tours. On Havelock Street, one block west of Harvest Terrace, is the **Old Observatory**, constructed in 1897 and at one time the official astronomer's residence. The observatory, which was originally sited on Mount Eliza, was dismantled in the 1960s and the telescope moved to the new observatory at Bickley, southeast of town. This elegant building now serves as headquarters for the Western Australian branch of the National Trust.

Kings Park

The most stunning feature of Perth is this 5 sq km city park, 2km west of the middle of town at the end of St George's Terrace. Fortunately set aside in 1872, the park includes the lovely **Western Australian Botanical Gardens** off FRASER AVENUE, planted with 1700 native species; appropriately, the gardens host the annual Wildflower Show in the spring. Also on Fraser Avenue are an Education Centre (☎ 08 9480 3600), the State War Memorial and Cenotaph, and several other sculptural monuments. An Aboriginal art gallery also includes regular performances and exhibitions. The best way to enjoy the park is either by bicycle, which can be rented at the stand near Fraser's Restaurant on Fraser Avenue, or simply by foot through the many trails.

The **Perth Tram Company** also conducts a one-hour tour of the park and on to the campus of the **University of Western Australia**, which borders the park to the southwest. The campus is especially notable for its beautiful landscaped gardens surrounding the original buildings, which date from the 1920s when the university was founded. The university overlooks Matilda Bay, and is considered by many to be Australia's most beautiful campus setting.

The campus houses the **Berndt Museum of Anthropology** (☎ 08 9380 2854; open Mon and Wed 14.00–16.30; Fri 10.00–14.00), with interesting collections of artefacts from Western Australian Aboriginal groups, as well as material from Melanesia and Southeast Asia; and the **Fortune Theatre** (☎ 08 9380 3838), a replica of Shakespeare's Fortune Theatre in London. Also near the campus on Mounts Bay Road in Crawley are the **Old Swan Brewery Buildings**, built between 1898 and 1918 by leading architect J.J. Talbot Hobbs. Its site was chosen because it was next to a clear spring, regarded by local Aborigines as a sacred site of the sleeping rainbow serpent. (The Swan Brewery still operates from its original headquarters in 25 Baile Road, Canning Vale c 12km south of central Perth; the main brewery has been here since 1857. Tours of the brewery depart Mon and Wed 14.30 and Tues 18.30, ☎ 08 9350 0650.)

Off Mounts Bay Road, travel along Matilda Bay on Hackett Drive to Australia II Drive, so named because it leads to the **Royal Perth Yacht Club**, whence came member Alan Bond to challenge and win the America's Cup in 1983. This unprecedented accomplishment stopped the entire nation, and the celebrations were long and ebullient. Subsequently, Fremantle became the site of the 1987 America's Cup race, the first time the event was held in the Southern hemisphere.

North of Central Perth

Herdsman Lake Settlers Cottage (☎ 08 9321 6088) is about 5km northwest of central Perth via Selby Street. Herdsman Lake is now the headquarters for the **Gould League** (see box), the Australian bird watchers' society named, like the Audubon Society in the USA, after an eminent early ornithologist and artist. The state government built the cottage here in 1931 as part of an agricultural settlement scheme. The National Trust's presentation of the cottage follows the history of the Hatcher family who lived in it for 30 years.

John Gould

John Gould (1804–81) had gained his reputation as a leading ornithologist with the publication in 1831 of his work on birds of the Himalayas, for which his wife Elizabeth (1804–41) had drawn and hand-coloured the plates. The couple travelled to Australia accompanied by their son John Henry (1830–55) in 1838–40 to collect specimens and data which resulted in the magnificent series, *The Birds of Australia* (1840–48); its supplement appeared in 1869. The illustrations, many of them completed by Elizabeth before her untimely death, amounted to 681 hand-coloured lithographs, making them the standard work on Australian birds, many of which were relatively unknown at the time. Later, Gould also produced a volume on Australian mammals, as well as his famous five-volume set, *The Birds of Great Britain* (1862–73). The Gould League was founded in 1909 at the suggestion of Miss Jessie McMichael, a Victorian schoolteacher who wished to emulate the American Audubon Society in its efforts to interest children in bird protection. The league originally promoted Bird Day, to be observed in October; now the efforts of the organisation are extensive, including bird-watching programmes and conservation activities. Gould's illustrations from the Australian series appear in many Australian museums and art galleries, most notably at the National Library in Canberra.

Further to the west around Herdsman Lake off Flynn Pearson Street in Churchlands is the main campus of Edith Cowan University.

Edith Cowan

Edith Cowan (1861–1932) was a much-loved figure in Western Australia, the founder of professional social work in Australia and the first woman member of any parliament in the country. She was born in Geraldton of a prominent pioneer family (her mother was the daughter of Rev. J.B. Wittenoom, for whom the Western Australian town was named and who arrived in the colony in 1829). In 1879 in Perth, Edith married James Cowan, registrar and master of the Supreme Court. When her husband became police magistrate, she learned of the distressing situation faced by many indigent women and children, and devoted the rest of her life to their cause. She was a member of the Children's Court in 1912, and was elected to the Legislative Assembly in 1921. During her term she introduced the groundbreaking Women's Legal Status Act and worked tirelessly for reform of children's rights.

South Perth

The **Old Mill** (☎ 08 9367 5788; open daily 10.00–16.00) can be reached by foot across Narrows Bridge or most pleasantly by ferry from the Barrack Street jetty across the Swan River. This extremely popular historic landmark functioned as a flour mill from 1835 until 1859. Known as Shenton's Mill due to its owner William Kernot Shenton, it was subsequently a residence, wine saloon, poultry farm and eventually a protected site under the National Trust. Its foundation stone was laid by Governor Stirling, and the building now contains important furnishings and artefacts from Perth's early colonial days.

Also on this side of the river, on Labouchere Road (Mill Point Road veers right

The Old Mill, Perth

at Labouchere Road), are the **Zoological Gardens**, that is, **Perth Zoo** (☎ 08 9367 7988; open daily 09.00–17.00). The area for the zoo, situated on the river, was reserved in 1896. The landscaping was carried out by the first director, A. Le Soeuf, with the assistance of Andrew Wilkie, who had worked at the Melbourne Zoo. One intriguing facet of the zoo is that the main water supply for the grounds comes from a deep artesian well, which pumps up water with a surface temperature of 39° C; this makes it possible to house tropical flora and fauna at a constant temperature. The zoo is one of the most popular in Australia; it has recently made concerted efforts to create natural enclosures for animals, and conducts a successful research and breeding programme for endangered animals.

William Thomas Leighton

William Thomas Leighton (1905–90) was the architect responsible for a number of public buildings in Perth and Fremantle, particularly 1930s Art Deco and Art Moderne cinemas. Those still functioning include the **Piccadilly Theatre and Arcade**, 700 Hay Street, which was built for gold-mining entrepreneur Claude de Bernales in 1938 and is probably his best remaining design. The Ambassadors Theatre (1928, refurbished under his supervision 1939) is a good example of his early work. In the late 1930s he also received commissions for the Windsor Theatre on the Stirling Highway in Nedlands and the Cygnet (originally the Como), 16 Preston Street in South Perth. He refurbished a number of theatres, most of which are gone or, like the Princess Theatre (Fremantle), the Hoyts (Newtown) and the Lyric (Bunbury), now have alternative uses.

Some of his public buildings include the Fremantle Port Authority's Passenger Terminal, the Institute of Agriculture Building on the University of Western Australia's campus, and the Devon House in Central Hay Street. The latter two are excellent examples of his use of International Style modern proportions and Art Deco ornament.

Eastern Perth

Tranby House (☎ 08 9272 2630, open Mon–Sat 13.00–17.00, Sun 11.00–13.00, 14.00–17.00) is about 10 minutes' drive 6km east from Perth's city centre, on the next loop up the river in Maylands. Take Lord Street, route 51, which continues as Guildford Road, c 3km; turn right on Peninsula Road and travel c 3km to the National Trust property. **Transperth buses nos 42 and 43** pass nearby, and a Transperth ferry stops at Tranby. Some of the river cruise boats will also stop here. This section of town was largely settled by a group of Wesleyan Methodists who migrated to Australia aboard the brig *Tranby*, arriving in Perth in 1830 after a voyage of 147 days, ten of which were spent ashore at the Cape of Good Hope.

The house was built in 1839 as part of a farm owned by Joseph and Ann Robinson Hardey. Joseph Hardey was an ardent Methodist, acting as a preacher until the Rev. John Smithies arrived and provided a substantial portion of the funds necessary to erect the Methodist church on the corner of William and Hay Streets in downtown Perth in 1870. The house is set in a garden with 100-year-old oak trees and is furnished with original objects brought to the colony by the Hardeys, as well as period furniture from the 1850s.

Fremantle

Only 19km from Perth, the port of **Fremantle** (population 25,000) at the mouth of the Swan River is an architectural gem, with more than 150 buildings classified by the National Trust. Still a thriving port city, its maritime atmosphere makes for continuous activity and variety for visitors. **Tourist information**: Town Hall, St John's Square, High Street; ☎ 08 9430 2346.

To get there by car from Perth, follow Stirling Highway past the Kings Park Botanic Gardens, the University of Western Australia and Peppermint Grove to Fremantle. The **train** to Fremantle follows a route north of the park. Along the way look out for the Claremont Railway Station at Leura Avenue, a two-storey stone building from 1887, designed by George Temple Poole. This stop would also be the place to disembark to reach by train the **Museum of Childhood** (☎ 08 9442 1373; open weekdays 10.00–16.00) at the Claremont campus of Edith Cowan University on Bay Road, about 1km southwest of the station. The museum houses one of Australia's most comprehensive collections of toys and children's educational items. At the southern end of Bay Road, turn left on Victoria Avenue to reach almost immediately the **Claremont Museum** (☎ 08 9386 3352; open Mon–Thurs 10.00–16.00, Sun 13.00–16.00), a delightful local history museum on Freshwater Bay. The building is known as the Freshwater Bay School, and was built in 1862 by convicts and the community of Pensioner Guards. The entire suburb of Claremont is filled with elegant houses and upmarket art galleries and boutiques. Bayview Terrace, c 600m west of Claremont Museum, is one of Perth's most fashionable shopping precincts.

Trains from Perth to Fremantle leave regularly from the central station, and several **buses**, including nos 102–106, leave the City Busport on Wellington Street and stop in Fremantle.

History

Fremantle's first settlers arrived in the winter of 1829. The conditions were severe. No housing had been provided; at the end of the first season, the visiting Miss Friend thought that the town resembled 'a country fair and has a pretty appearance, the pretty white tents looking like booths'. In 1834 the Colony's Advocate-General, George Fletcher Moore, observed that the city had 'a few wooden houses among ragged-looking tents and contrivances for habitation. The colonists are a cheerless, dissatisfied people with gloomy looks, who plod through the sand from hut to hut to drink grog and grumble out their discontent to each other.'

Visiting adventurer Charles von Hügel's description is somewhat less condemnatory: 'A few of the residents, not exactly in Sunday best, let alone in clean clothes, were standing on the bank fishing. Others—it being evening—were weaving their unsteady way through the sand, unmistakably under the influence of the spirits they had consumed. Despite the dirt, their faces all glowed with rude health, and the children splashing about in the water could certainly vie with any European street urchins.'

By the end of the 1840s, however, the town had become a health resort for tourists from India and a trans-shipping point for goods moving up or down river. Land transport to Perth was facilitated in 1866 by the construction of the River Swan bridge to North Fremantle. An interesting, and apocryphal, anecdote relating to the bridge maintains that the first person to cross it was an Irish political prisoner named John Boyle 'Moondyne Joe' O'Reilly, who managed to escape from the Bunbury prison (about 150km south of Perth) on the night before its dedication. He subsequently settled as a newspaperman in Boston, where he organised the escape of six of his fellow Fenian transportees remaining in Western Australia.

As a port, Fremantle has a controversial history. Originally piers stood quite open on the western edge of town, ships standing at anchor and their cargoes lightened ashore often by nimble-fingered thieves. The river offered more than adequate protection from such robbery, but was blocked by sandstone bars. Based on new methods of dredging, Irish engineer Charles Yelverton O'Connor (1843–1902) challenged renowned British engineer John Coode's assertions regarding the feasibility of constructing an inner harbour. Between 1892 and 1900, the new harbour and Victoria Quay were completed. O'Connor was also responsible for the water pipeline from the Darling Range to the eastern gold fields (350 miles) and the extensive enlargement of the state's rail system. Tragically, he succumbed to the pressure of criticism from avaricious landowners hoping to profit from the Coolgardie pipeline and took his own life in 1902. Beyond his engineering vision, he was brilliant at fiscal matters. His water pipeline, for instance, was completed within a year of his death at a cost consistent with that he had estimated, an unprecedented accomplishment in those days.

Much of the city of Fremantle itself was built in the 1880s in a Classical style. The incredible consistency of limestone and the darker window frames suggests that the designs conspire with the elements to make Fremantle a city of light.

A walk around town

This walk begins at the station's car park, makes its way to the Fremantle Museum and Arts Centre (about 10 minutes), then goes past the Gaol and back through the centre to the Round House at Arthurs Head. A free **Tripper Bus** operates on weekends, running in a loop around this tour's area.

The **Railway Station** is situated on Victoria Quay Road, parallel to the inner harbour, with a cluster of late-19C warehouses in a pocket a little to the south and seaward. Rail transport began along the Fremantle–Perth–Guildford route in 1881. The current station opened in 1907. The building is made from Donnybrook sandstone. Immediately in front of it is a watering trough and drinking fountain from 1905, commemorating the loss of Englishman John Taylor's sons Ernest and Peter who died in Western Australia.

You will find Fremantle **Tourist Bureau's Office** (☎ 08 9431 7878) by walking down Market Street, directly in front of the station, and across the mall at the corner of William and Adelaide Streets in the Fremantle Town Hall. From here the **Fremantle Tram** departs on the hour, giving 45-minute tours of the town.

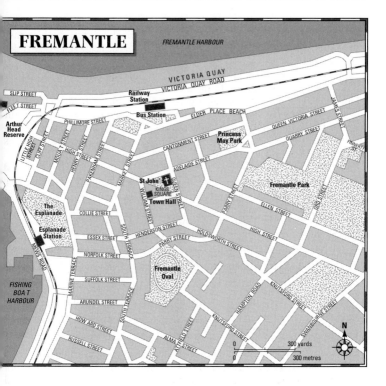

FREMANTLE

FREMANTLE HARBOUR

VICTORIA QUAY
VICTORIA QUAY ROAD

SLIP STREET

Railway
Station

FLEET STREET

PHILLIMORE STREET

Bus Station

ELDER PLACE BEACH

Arthur
Head
Reserve

LITTLE HIGH ST

CLIFF STREET

MOUAT STREET

HENRY STREET

HIGH STREET

PAKENHAM STREET

MARKET STREET

CANTONMENT STREET

Princess
May Park

QUEEN VICTORIA STREET

QUARRY STREET

JAMES STREET

PROPERTY
ST

ADELAIDE STREET

St John's

KINGS
SQUARE

Town Hall

WILLIAM STREET

QUEEN STREET

Fremantle Park

The
Esplanade

COLLIE STREET

SOUTH TERRACE

PARRY STREET

ELLEN STREET

ORD STREET

Esplanade
Station

ESSEX STREET

HENDERSON STREET

HOLDSWORTH STREET

HIGH STREET

MEWS ROAD

NORFOLK STREET

MARINE TERRACE

PARRY STREET

FISHING
BOAT
HARBOUR

SUFFOLK STREET

Fremantle
Oval

ARUNDEL STREET

SOUTH TERRACE

HAMPTON ROAD

KNUTSFORD STREET

KNUTSFORD STREET

SWANBOURNE STREET

HOWARD STREET

RUSSELL STREET

ATTFIELD STREET

ALMA STREET

KNUTSFORD STREET

N

0   300 yards
0   300 metres

Also here, on the square on Adelaide Street, is **St John's** Anglican Church. Designed in London by W. Smith, it was built around 1880, and was originally intended to have a tower and steeple. The floors are jarrah; the bell turret is from 1907. Architect Robin McKellar Campbell mentions that the membership was convinced to build this replacement somewhat to the north of the original, allowing the site for the Town Hall.

The **Town Hall** (beside St John's) has been largely unaltered since its construction in 1885–87. This late Victorian building was designed by Melbourne architects Grainger and D'Ebro and built by E. Keane. A local watchmaker, W. Hooper, imported its clock from England in 1888.

A bit further along Adelaide Street at Parry Street is **Proclamation Tree**, an enormous Moreton Bay fig planted in 1890. From here either walk through the park to Ord Street then left to the Fremantle Museum and Art Centre or continue along Quarry Street past the former Boys' and Princess May Schools. The **Boys' School** is now the Film and Television Institute; its administration is housed in William Leighton's Princess Theatre (see box on Leighton, p 544), left to the north, past the car park, right on Edward Street. Thought to have been designed by Sanford in 1852, the renovations and additions to this Victorian Revival building are sometimes compatible enough to be a challenge to identify. **Princess May School** is currently a Community Education Centre.

Constructed in 1902, on adjacent land set aside for a girls' school in 1894, the design is a conscious attempt to match the Boys' School. This two-storey institutional building offers a vista from its tower. Prior to its dedication, girls attended the adjacent Boys' School.

The **Fremantle Arts Centre and History Museum** (☎ 08 9335 8244/ 9430 7966, open daily 10.00–17.00) is east of the schools, left at the Celtic Cross along Quarry Street to its junction with Ord Street; a short jag leads to the entrance on Finnerty Street. Originally the lunatic asylum contiguous with the gaol, it was designed by Captain Henderson and built by convict labour in the 1860s. After various uses, it was renovated by architect Robin McKellar Campbell and opened to the public as a museum in 1970 and as an art centre in 1972.

The most significant part of the historical collections is the display and description of the many ships of the Dutch East India Company which explored and were wrecked along the Western Australian coast.

The arts centre presents sometimes challenging changing exhibitions of Australian artists. The **Western Australian History Museum** is in the other wing of the centre and includes excellent changing exhibitions depicting the early social history of Fremantle. It was the original home of a visionary and successful publishing house, the Fremantle Arts Centre Press, now independent. As you might expect, the bookstore here is worth the trip itself.

The next stop is the **Fremantle Prison Gates and Museum**. To reach them, cross Ord Street to Fremantle Park. Continue diagonally across the park to Parry Street, follow it to Holdsworth Street, which leads to Fairbairn Street and The Terrace. This a bit of a detour, but the **Gaol Gateway** and **Prison Museum** are both interesting (☎ 08 9430 7177; open daily 10.00–18.00, tours on half-hour from 10.00). Both structures were designed by H. Way and James Manning in a Georgian style uncommon in the colony at that time (1855). The limestone was quarried locally, but the most visible parts were stuccoed shortly after the buildings were erected. The walls, incidentally, are 5m high. The museum was originally the superintendent's residence. The site was used as a maximum security prison from 1855 until 1991, when it became a cultural heritage centre.

Return to Fairbairn Street, take Parry Street around the Fremantle Oval; at Henderson Street are the **Fremantle Markets**, designed by Oldham and Eales and built in the late 1890s. The iron gates are original. The market (☎ 08 9335 2515) has operated continuously since 1897, offering both produce and handicrafts. It is open Friday 09.00–21.00, and weekends 10.00–17.00.

Across South Terrace are the **Technical School** buildings. That on the right dates from 1912. The use of Donnybrook stone for the plinth and facings provides a handsome Art Nouveau style designed by H. Beasley. The other was originally an Infants and Girls School which dates from 1877.

SOUTH TERRACE itself is known as **Cappuccino Strip**, famous for its many outdoor cafes and great coffee.

Leaving the markets, take South Terrace one block east, then left down Collie Street. At Marine Terrace, facing the Esplanade Reserve, is a handsome Victorian corner pub, the **Esplanade Hotel**, dating from 1897. Continuing east along the reserve leads to the Old Court House, the Maritime Museum and the Round House.

The **Maritime Museum** (☎ 08 9431 8444, open daily 10.30–17.00) was built as a commissariat store between 1851 and 1862 using Lieutenant H. Wray's designs. The Colonial Government converted the structure into a Customs House in 1878. It opened as the Maritime Museum in 1977 with displays which include marine archaeology, especially 18C Dutch shipwrecks on the Western Australian coast. The boat shed or **Historic Boats Museum** (☎ 08 9430 4680; open Mon–Fri 10.00–15.00, weekends 11.00–16.00) nearby on the Victoria Quay of the inner harbour immediately north has an extensive display of functional boats, including modern racing yachts. Marine engines operate on Thursday–Sunday afternoons.

The **Old Court House**, across Mouat Street from the Barracks on Marine Terrace, was built in 1883–84 by Harwood and Sons. Like their design for the railway station, it is of stone in a Classical style with semicircular arches around its windows. After a number of civic uses, the building was given to the Salvation Army. More recently, it has been a centre for food distribution and welfare services for the Uniting Church.

The **University of Notre Dame (Australia)** is nearby at 19 Mouat Street, situated neatly in one block. It allows some public access to the interior of several restored limestone warehouses. The university is affiliated with the University of Notre Dame in Indiana, United States, having an active exchange programme with them and organising the curriculum along Catholic university lines—an unusual situation among Australian universities.

From the university, take High Street down to Bathers Bay and Arthur Head. Here is the **Round House** and **Whaler's Tunnel** (☎ 08 9430 7351, open daily 09.00–18.00), dating from 1831 and probably the oldest structure in the state. Rather than round, it has twelve sides. It was designed by Henry W. Reveley, the colony's first engineer, as a prison; it includes the Whalers' Tunnel, cut in 1837 to connect High Street to the beach. The limestone was quarried on site. There is an excellent view of the harbour from the west side of the structure. From here you can easily walk diagonally towards Victoria Quay and the Fremantle Port Authority at Cliff Street (☎ 08 9430 4911; tours weekdays 13.30). The authority's observation tower offers spectacular views out to the Indian Ocean, as well as explanations of the port's still-busy activities.

From the Port Authority return via Cliff Street to High Street. Walking up HIGH STREET through the warehouse and commercial district of Fremantle presents evidence of the area's success following the late-19C gold rush. The **Samson Building**, for example, dates from 1898 and is typical of the Georgian-style architecture at the end of this period. The owners, Lionel Samson Pty Ltd, were granted the lot as spirit merchants in 1829 and have been operating here since that time. The **Samson House** (☎ 08 9430 7966; open Thurs and Sun 13.00–17.00) is located on the corner of Ord and Ellen Streets. It was designed in 1900 by J.J. Talbot Hobbs for Michael Samson, who became Fremantle's mayor. Built of limestone, the house has original furnishings.

One block to the right off High Street at Pakenham Street is Bannister Street, which has at no. 8 an excellent crafts workshop where you can watch crafts being made (and buy them, too).

To return to the railway station, turn left on Market Street walking past the ornate **Post Office**. The first postal service in the colony was carried between Fremantle and Perth by a runner who was paid a wage of about £1 per week.

The service was private until 1835 when John Bateman was appointed post-master. The first stamp in the colony was a black swan design used in 1854; in a few instances, this design was mistakenly inverted, creating one of the most valuable stamps among philatelists. This neo-Romanesque building was erected in 1906.

Rottnest Island

Rottnest Island (☎ 08 9372 9729 or 08 9432 9111) measures 11km long by 4.5km wide. It was in the 19C—like so many other islands around Australia—an horrendous penal colony for Aborigines. It has five salt lakes (Government House Lake and Lake Bagdad being the two largest), a lighthouse, 40km of coastline and a variety of modes of accommodation.

This limestone island was named by Dutch explorer Willem de Vlamingh in 1696 who mistook the **quokka**, a native wallaby on the island which can be quite tame, for large rats. Currently a holiday venue allowing no personal cars, it can be reached by ferry. The trip is 30 minutes from Fremantle, a little over an hour from Perth. Three ferry companies provide the service, *Rottnest Express* (☎ 08 9335 6406), *Boat Talk* (☎ 08 9430 5844) and *Oceanic* (☎ 08 9930 5127). An information post at the jetty provides a number of brochures describing the island. Thompson Bay is the island's main settlement. The beaches here are spectacular. School holidays mean tremendous crowding here, so be mindful of these times, and book accommodation well ahead!

Day trip east of Perth

Travelling across the Perth's Causeway to the Great Eastern Highway (or, alternatively, north on Lord Street to Guildford Highway) leads to Guildford and John Forrest National Park, eventually reaching York. *Westrail* also provides bus connections all the way to York (☎ 08 9326 2222), and many tours to the region can be arranged through Perth's tourist centre on Forrest Place (☎ 08 9483 1111).

About 20km from Perth along route 51, the GREAT EASTERN HIGHWAY, is the small town of **Guildford**, planned in 1830 as the first settlement east of Perth. H.C. Sutherland, the assistant surveyor for the colony, set it at the confluence of the Swan and Helena Rivers as an inland port and market town. From here the **Swan Valley Heritage Trail** begins (see below), a 40km drive along the trail of Captain Stirling's 1827 exploration; follow the signs from Success Hill Reserve, where Stirling's party first found fresh water. In Guildford, the **Garrick Theatre** (1853) was the original Commissariat Store and Headquarters, devoted to storing road building materials and equipment for the convict work parties. Vineyards were established in the surrounding Swan River Valley in the 1860s, making this region today the oldest wine-producing area in Western Australia. The Old Courthouse and Gaol on Meadow Street (☎ 08 9279 1248; open Sun 14.00–17.00), also established in the 1860s, is now a local history museum. On Swan Street is the **Rose & Crown Hotel** (☎ 08 9279 8444), which opened as an inn in 1841; it is the oldest trading hotel in Western Australia. The hotel was in the 1890s an important stop for travellers to the gold fields further east.

To the north of Guildford the **Upper Swan Valley** begins, with its beautiful scenery and its many well-established wineries. 7km north of Guildford via route 52 (or from Bayswater north via route 4) is **Whiteman Park** (☎ 08 9249 2446), one of Perth's most popular bushland parks. With 26 sq km of parkland—six times the size of Kings Park—the park offers a variety of walking and cycling tracks, picnic areas and playgrounds. A tram in the park connects the picnic areas with a craft village, farm machinery museum, old railway displays, and camel and emu rides.

Also north of Guildford on route 52 is the village of **Henley Brook**, situated in picturesque surroundings. Here on Henry Street is All Saints Church (☎ 08 9279 9859), a small rammed-earth building opened for worship in 1841 at the furthest point inland reached by Captain Stirling when he explored the Swan River in 1827. It is the oldest church in Western Australia. Next door to the church is **Henley Park Wines** (☎ 08 9296 4328), one of the older wineries among the many in this region, most of which provide tastings and cellar sales.

A little further east on the Great Eastern Highway is **Midland**; and on Third Avenue and Ford Street is **Woodbridge House** (☎ 08 9274 2432; open Mon, Tues, Thurs and Fri 13.00–16.00, Sun 11.00–17.00; closed July). The house first built on this land was named by Governor James Stirling after his wife's family's home in Surrey. The original house stood

Woodbridge House, Midland

on a high bank overlooking the Swan River. Charles Harper, MP and leading publisher, had the current house built in 1885 by local contractors, the Wright Brothers. A number of pleasant stories date from Harper's time—his billiard room becoming the first neighbourhood school is one anecdote favoured by the volunteer guides of the National Trust. This school eventually became the Guildford Grammar School. Passing from the Harper family in 1921, the property served as the school and then a home for aged women before the National Trust began its stewardship in the late 1960s. The house is furnished in typical late Victorian and early Edwardian fashion.

Midland also holds two popular markets on weekends: the Midland Sunday Markets, at the Crescent car park each Sunday, selling food and speciality goods; and the Midland Military Markets, on Clay Street in Bellevue, c 2km west of Midland. With over 200 stalls and a wildlife sanctuary in the grounds, this market is a favoured weekend excursion (open weekends 09.00–18.00).

North of Midland on the Great Northern Highway is the **Swan Valley**, with its many vineyards and wineries. For tours and maps, check with the **Swan Valley Tourist information centre**, Guildford Village Potters, 22 Meadow Street, Guildford, ☎ 08 9279 9859. The most historic of these wineries is **Houghton Winery** (☎ 08 9274 5100; open daily), Dale Road, Middle Swan (c 5km north of Midland via the Great Northern Highway, near 1/95). The property was acquired in 1833 by T.N. Yule and bought in 1839 by colonial surgeon John Ferguson, who established the vineyards. Ferguson's homestead, built in 1863, is incorporated into the present-day winery grounds, making it one of the prettiest wineries in the state. Houghton's popular white burgundy is known internationally; a museum cellar chronicles the history of Western Australian winemaking, and the beautiful lawns make for great picnicking.

From Middle Swan, continue north c 20km (on Highway 1) to **Walyunga National Park** (☎ 08 9571 1371; open daily 08.00–18.00). Situated along the Darling Escarpment, the park is bisected by the Avon River, which rushes swiftly through a narrow gorge to join the Swan River. The park's steep drop in elevation, from 280m to 30m above sea level, has produced spectacular and rugged scenery. Walking tracks pass through forests of wandoo and marri trees, with magnificent wildflowers in the spring and winter. This escarpment also marks the end of the Swan Valley.

From Midland, continue west on the GREAT EASTERN HIGHWAY (route 94) on the old road to York. At Mahogany Creek (c 11km) is the **Old Mahogany Inn**, believed to be the oldest licensed inn in Western Australia and still in use. The inn dates from 1837, although the building's appearance is largely due to additions in 1847 and 1848. Also en route are the **John Forrest National Park** (☎ 08 9298 8344) and **Kalamunda National Park**, c 12km south of the Great Eastern Highway. Each park has wonderful displays of wildflowers in spring (August to October). John Forest has long been a popular venue for Perth residents; it remains a pleasant and accessible park near the **Mundaring Weir**. The weir was part of C.Y. O'Connor's method of providing water to the gold fields. A museum (☎ 08 9295 2455) in his name has a display describing the project. Kalamunda is a fairly small park, but easily accessible off the Great Eastern Highway on Kalamunda Road. Buses 300 or 302 (via Maida Vale) and 292 or 305 (via Wattle Grove), all from stop no. 43 in St George's Terrace, Perth, make the trip to Kalamunda as well.

Kalamunda National Park is also the starting point for the **Bibbulmun Track**, Western Australia's only long-distance walking trail, and one of the longest, continuously marked trails in the country. It is named for the Bibbulmun people who inhabited this region. It continues 650km from here to Walpole on the south coast. Accommodation in shelters is available along the track. Currently the track is undergoing renovation and extension to 950km. For more information, ☎ 08 9334 0265, or consult the website: www.calm.wd.gov.au

York

Another 60km from Mundaring Weir, 97km from Perth is **York** (population 1950), founded in 1831 on the Avon River, making it the oldest inland city in Western Australia. **Tourist information**: 105 Avon Terrace; ☎ 08 9641 1301. As a wheat-producing region, the York valley has provided the state with agricultural products since its founding. York has a well-known country music festival in July, and a great jazz festival every October. Much of its civic architecture dates from the early 1890s and remains largely unchanged. Earlier structures relate to the jurisprudence in the district.

The **Old Gaol and Courthouse** (☎ 08 9641 2072; open weekdays 11.00–15.00, weekends 10.00–16.00) on Avon Terrace, north of the Great

Southern Highway, present the prison cell block, the stables and trooper's cottage.

To travel to the Yilgarn area's gold fields, prospectors would catch the train on the south coast at Albany, provision themselves in York and continue on foot to the gold fields. This prosperity slackened in 1894 when the train to the Coolgardie and Kalgoorlie mines from Perth passed through Northam, about 30km north of York.

Noteworthy early buildings in York include the Old Gaol of 1838, with cells added in the 1850s. The **Residency Museum** (☎ 08 9641 1340; open Tues–Thurs 13.00–15.00, weekends 13.00–17.00), Brook Street, is a bungalow with verandah and iron roof. It dates from 1843 and was restored by the York Society. The Church of the Holy Trinity (1858 with additions in 1873, 1893, and 1907) replaced the area's first church (1858); St Patrick's (1887), the Roman Catholic church for the area, similarly replaced the original structure (1852). Settler's House, a bed and breakfast with a long verandah and courtyard, was built in 1853 and enlarged in 1877.

The **Castle Hotel** dominates the intersection of York's two primary streets, South and Avon. This brick building with comfortable verandah and balcony is one of the state's oldest hotels. Most of the buildings in this section of town date from the late 19C. **Balladong Farm**, probably the area's first farm and situated at the southern end of town, has buildings dating from the 1850s. Opposite the tourist office on Avon Terrace is the **York Motor Museum** (☎ 08 9641 1288; open daily 09.00–17.00), a truly impressive collection of antique cars. At the end of the Terrace is evidence of the old Sandalwood Yards, a reminder of the proliferation of this aromatic wood throughout Western Australia during colonial days. Appropriately named, the **Sandalwood Press** (☎ 08 9641 1714) is also located in York; on McCartney Street, the press is now the state's only working printing museum, with tours available by appointment.

Southern Western Australia

A 30-minute drive south from Perth on the Western Highway leads to **Pinjarra**; alternatively it can be reached from Fremantle on Highway 1 to Mandurah, then east (it is also accessible by train). In addition to its lovely rose garden, which conveniently blossoms at the opposite end of the year from the wildflower season, south of town on the South West Highway is **Old Blythewood** (☎ 08 9531 1485, open Fri–Tues 10.00–16.00). The great-grandsons of John McLarty, its builder, donated this brick farmhouse from the 1860s, with verandahs and lovely gardens, to the National Trust. In its heyday at the beginning of the 20C, it functioned as an inn for coaches and a post office. In the vicinity are a variety of **waterbird reserves**. A steam railway runs from Pinjarra to nearby **Dwellingup**, which offers great views of the ocean on entering town.

The road south beyond Pinjarra leads to Bunbury and the southwest region of the state. Albany, the holiday resort Esperance, and Kalgoorlie-Boulder are vacation destinations popular among Western Australians. The southwest region is known for agriculture, timbering and excellent surfing around Margaret River. *Westrail* and *South-West Coachlines* (☎ 08 9324 2333) provide a **bus service** to the region, and the **train** runs between Perth and Bunbury.

This region, and east into the heavily timbered sections of the state, was

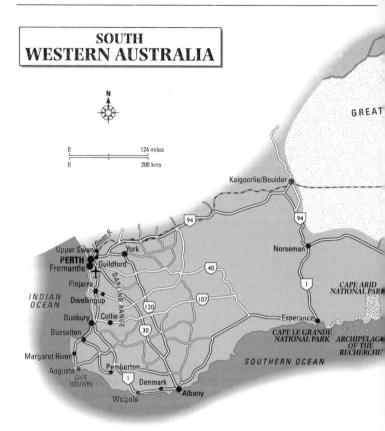

SOUTH WESTERN AUSTRALIA

relatively densely inhabited by Aboriginal groups before white settlement, especially in the summer months, when large bands gathered to 'fire' the country; controlled fires were lit to drive out game and to promote new growth. Archaeological excavation demonstrates that Aborigines lived here from at least 27,000 years ago.

Just north of Bunbury (11km) is **Australind** (population 5694), site of an ill-fated settlement in the 1840s which planned to breed horses for the Indian Army (hence the name). The town is now a popular fishing resort, noted also for the Church of St Nicholas (1842), at 4 x 7m the smallest church in Western Australia.

Bunbury

Only 180km south of Perth, and accessible by train, **Bunbury** (population 26,550) is one of the state's most popular tourist resorts as well as the major industrial port of the region. The French in 1803, aboard the ships *Casuarina* and *Géographe*, explored the area, naming this point Port Leschenault, in honour of the expedition's botanist. With the settlement of the Swan River colony in 1829, favourable reports about the area led to further exploration; in 1836, the

town site was selected, and named after Lieutenant Henry Bunbury, who had made an overland trek from Pinjarra to the district and published the journal of his findings. Today, the town has a nice **regional art gallery** in Wittenoom Street (☎ 08 9721 8616; open weekdays 10.00–16.30, weekends 12.00–16.30), located in a former convent built in the 1860s. **King Cottage Museum** (☎ 08 9721 3929; open daily), on Forrest Avenue, is an 1870s house now run as a historic house by the Bunbury Historical Society. There are some pleasant drives along the harbour and coastline. Indeed, the area's greatest attractions are its stunning white beaches and, at **Koombana Beach**, a 'swimming with the dolphins' opportunity less fraught with tourist hype than the experience at Monkey Mia north of Perth. The beach now has a Discovery Centre (☎ 08 9791 3088; open daily 08.00–17.00 Oct–April, 08.30–16.30 May–Sept), with excellent audio-visual exhibits about the dolphins. **Tourist information**: Old Railway Station, Carmody Street; ☎ 08 9721 7922.

From Bunbury, take the BUSSELL HIGHWAY, route 10, another 100km south to **Margaret River**. The highway travels around Géographe Bay and past **Busselton** (population 10,700), a popular seaside resort, named for the pioneering family of John Bussell, who settled the area in the 1830s. **Tourist information**: Civic Centre Complex, Southern Drive, ☎ 08 9752 1288. About 26km west of Busselton is **Yallingup** on the Indian Ocean, known by surfers for its stupendous waves, but also for its limestone caves, the northernmost of this cave system. A famous story of the region concerns the rescue of shipwreck survivors off the coast here by an Aboriginal stockman Sam Isaacs and Grace Bussell in 1876.

Some 7km northwest is **Ellensbrook** (☎ 08 9757 2911; open weekends and holidays), the wattle-and-daub farmhouse of pioneers Alfred and Ellen Bussell, built in the 1850s. It is now owned by the National Trust. Nearby, about 30 minutes' walk, is **Meekadarribee Falls**, an unusually spiralling waterfall that is worth the view. Ellensbrook Homestead and Meekadarribee Falls are situated within one section of **Leeuwin-Naturaliste National Park** (☎ 08 9752 1677), a wonderful park broken up in segments running along the 120km of coast from Bunker Bay at Cape Naturaliste in the north to Cape Leeuwin near

Augusta in the south. Along with windswept views of this rugged coastline, parts of the park include the Boranup Karri Forest (near Hamelin Bay, c 35km south of Margaret River), an unusual stand of these enormously tall trees (some up to 60m, and most them 100km inland from here). Camping facilities are available in the park, and walking trails for every level of bushwalker are well marked.

To the east of Busselton (c 10km on Layman Road) is **Wonnerup House** (☎ 08 9752 2039; open daily 10.00–16.00), another National Trust property. Built in 1859 by pioneer George Layman, the stone house and many out-buildings contain family memorabilia and colonial artefacts.

The road south from here leads to **Prevelly Park**, a popular surf beach just south of the mouth of the Margaret River. On the Walcliffe Road leading into the town is the Greek **Chapel of St John**, a memorial to the Preveli Monastery in Crete, where Allied soldiers were sheltered during the Second World War.

The town of **Margaret River** (population 1300) is situated on the banks of the Margaret River itself. The region is becoming increasingly well known for its excellent wines, many of which can be sampled at the wineries of Cowaramup, Willyabrup, and at the Leeuwin Estate Winery tasting room. **Tourist information**: Bussell Highway; ☎ 08 9757 2911. Tours to the wineries and other information on the region can be obtained here. On the southwest outskirts of the town is **Eagles Heritage**, Boodjidup Road (☎ 08 9757 2960; open daily 10.00–17.00), a wonderful wildlife centre devoted to the care and rehabilitation of Australian raptors. The centre gives demonstrations of eagle-flying.

21km south of Margaret River is **Mammoth Cave**, one of some 300 limestone caves in the region (five are open to the public). This cave reveals 35,000-year-old fossils and a stunning number of stalactites. At **Lake Cave** (☎ 08 9757 7543), 3.2km south of Mammoth Cave, is the CaveWorks Interpretative Centre, an education complex that describes and explains the area's cave systems. Even more impressive is **Jewel Cave**, 8km north of Augusta, with its delicate 5m long helictites. Less impressive is the most northerly cave, **Yallingup/Ngilgi**.

Augusta

From this point, route 10 continues south to **Augusta** (population 1040), 29km from Margaret River and the state's third-oldest settlement.

History

While Europeans arrived as early as 1830, development was hampered by the massive amount of hardwood timber in the area, which was not easily cleared, and most early settlers moved north to Busselton within 10 years. In the 1880s, a real timber industry was established (the woods were of prized jarrah, karri, and marri), and the district was further opened by the disastrous Group Settlement Scheme of the 1920s, whereby English settlers, lured by promises of land but themselves inexperienced at farming, were brought to Western Australia supposedly to develop the rural industry. Most settlements were completely unproductive, due to haphazard planning and incorrect planting of crops; thousands of settlers were left in dire circumstances, many of them forced to return to England.

Today, most visitors come to Augusta on the way to nearby **Cape Leeuwin**, 9km south of town, the most southwesterly point of Australia, at the juncture of the Indian and Great Southern Oceans. The cape was named after the ship of a Dutch captain sailing from the Cape of Good Hope who sighted the point in 1632. A 34m lighthouse, constructed in 1895, identifies the point; at its top, which can be reached by climbing, you get a tremendous view of this rather bleak and ominous point. In *Bony and the White Savage* (1961), Arthur Upfield describes the cape's jagged rocks and terrifying 'sneaker waves', one of which nearly causes the death of his detective-hero 'Bony'.

Georgina Molloy

Augusta was the first Australian home of a remarkable woman, Georgiana Molloy (1805–43), daughter of a genteel Cumberland family who at 24 married the 48-year-old John 'Handsome Jack' Molloy, an army officer who had been wounded at Waterloo. In 1830, they migrated to Western Australia, settling in Augusta, where Georgiana became fascinated with the botanical wonders of the new land. In 1832, she wrote home to her sister, 'I am sitting in the Verandah surrounded by my little flower garden of British, Cape and Australian flowers pouring forth their odour... The native flowers are exceedingly small but beautiful in colour...' Georgiana became the first to study the colony's native flowers with any seriousness and began to send back to England both seeds and pressed plants. Her letters to English botanist James Lindley provided long and informative descriptions of the region's flora, and as a collector she rivalled the greatest European scientists of the time. In 1839 the Molloys moved to Busselton and established a property called Fair Lawn with an exquisite garden. She often went into the bush, which she described as being in 'the most delightful states of existence,' taking along local Aborigines for guidance and as companions. Georgiana died in childbirth, aged 37, deeply mourned by the scientific community. Her surviving children went on to marry leading figures in Western Australian society. Her story is the basis for many books, including Alexandra Hasluck's *Portrait with Background: a Life of Georgiana Molloy* (1955).

From Augusta, you can travel east via route 10 through timber country to **Nannup** (population 522); here route 10 becomes the Vasse Highway south to **Pemberton** (population 995), another timber town famous for its karri forests and high-quality woodcraft centres. Tourist information: **Karri Visitors centre**, Brockman Street, 08 9776 1133. Here you can also ride the **Pemberton Tramway** (☎ 08 9776 1322), a replica 1907 tram that travels through the impressive karri and marri forests. 3km along the 18km road east from Pemberton to connect with Highway 1, is the **Gloucester Tree**, touted as the world's tallest fire-lookout tree—you can make the 61m climb along a rather harrowing set of steps, after which you receive a certificate for bravery. This tree gives some indication of the magnificence of the karri, the world's third largest after the California sequoia and the Australian mountain ash. Their leaves are two different colours, and their bark changes from orange-yellow to grey-white when old.

The drive along the SOUTH WESTERN HIGHWAY, as route 1 is called here, passes through impressive Tall Timber country with turn-offs to many national parks, all of them awe-inspiring displays of enormous karri forests and spectacular waterfalls. More detailed information about the parks is available on the national park website (www.calm.wa.gov.au) and at the Pemberton or Manjimup tourist offices.

Western Australian writer and socialist Katharine Susannah Prichard set her novel of timber-workers, *Working Bullocks* (1926), in this region. If coming from Perth, you may join the South Western Highway at Bunbury to travel down to the southern coast at Walpole, in which case you will pass through (36km south of Bunbury) **Donnybrook** (population 1635), settled by Irish in 1842 and now known for its apple orchards. **Tourist information:** Old Railway Station, ☎ 08 9731 1720. The railway station in town on Turner Street is the site of the **Boyanup Transport Museum** (☎ 08 9731 5250; open daily) and Old Gold-fields Orchard and Cider Farm (☎ 08 9731 1071), with cider tastings and gold-fossicking opportunities.

The next major spot on the road south is **BRIDGETOWN** (population 2123), 57km from Donnybrook. Bridgetown is the administrative centre of the region, situated on the Blackwood River at the junction of the South Western and Brockman Highways. It is frequently described as 'the prettiest country in the state'. **Tourist information:** Hampton Street, ☎ 08 9761 1740. Also on Hampton Street is **'Bridgedale'** (☎ 08 9761 1508; open Thurs–Mon 10.00–16.00), a National Trust property; it was the first substantial house in the region, built by pastoralist John Blechynden in 1862. Also in the area are the Donnelly Timber Mill Museum at the Donnelly River Settlement 26km south-west of Bridgetown; and the **Geegelup Heritage Trail**, a 52km tourist drive through the Bridgetown–Greenbushes area, highlighting historic buildings and locations. A brochure of the trail is available from the Bridgetown tourist centre.

A further 37km on the South Western Highway brings you to **Manjimup** (population 4353), called 'the Gateway to Tall Timber Country'. **Manjimup Tourist Bureau** is on the corner of Rose and Edwards Street, ☎ 08 9771 1831. The town is the region's commercial centre, and clearly demonstrates the impor-tance of the timber industry here. Most of the walking tracks and picnic spots in the area centre on stands of hundred-year-old trees of karri or jarrah, such as the **King Jarrah Tree**, 4km northeast of Manjimup on Perup Road; it is believed to be 600 years old. Also in town is the Manjimup Regional Timber Park. The tourist centre is open daily and has an impressive visitor's centre high-lighting the history of the timber industry here. (You will not find much about the great controversies and environmental struggles surrounding the destruc-tion of these forests!) A further 15km south on the highway is the junction with Highway 1, which is 16km from Pemberton to the west.

It is 103km from the junction with Highway 1 to **Walpole** on the so-called **'Rainbow Coast'**; the coastline here is a mixture of sheltered inlets and rugged headlands on the Southern Ocean, and has recently become home for retirees and craftspeople, as well as a newly developing wine-growing region.

From Walpole, the highway continues east 120km to Albany, passing through the pleasant town of **Denmark** on the Denmark River. The area is filled with scenic drives, with turn-offs to rocky beaches which are ideal locations for bush-walking and picnics. Between Walpole and Denmark is **Walpole-Nornalup National Park** (☎ 08 9840 1027), 13,354 ha of enormous trees and rushing rivers. Trees include karri, jarrah, and tingle, and the walks through these forests are particularly impressive in the park's Valley of the Giants. Spectacular coastal scenery can also be reached in the park. It is important to note that Denmark is only 414km southeast of Perth, making the district a very accessible holiday destination for most Western Australians, and therefore crowded during school holidays and the summer.

Albany

Albany (population 27,000) is on King George Sound, which was named by British explorer George Vancouver when he passed by in 1791. **Tourist information**: Old Railway Station, Proudlove Parade; ☎ 08 9841 1088.

History

It is this section of the southern coastline which first appeared on early Dutch maps and inspired Jonathan Swift to locate the island of Houyhnhnms in *Gulliver's Travels* (1726) off this mainland. The town itself was the site in 1826 of Major Lockyer's short-lived penal colony. The town's continued existence was due to whaling after the 1840s and as a coaling station for steamers bound for Europe after the 1850s. Until Fremantle became a viable port in the 1890s, Albany was the main Australian port between England and Sydney. It was the staging area for the Australian Light Horse regiment destined for Gallipoli in 1914. Until agricultural improvement in the 1950s and the rise in popularity of wines since the 1980s, much of the area's economy depended upon lumbering the breathtaking karri and jarrah trees that grow here. Conservation efforts, a more rational approach to governmental subsidies for the industry, and the simple scarcity of the stands of trees has seen their off-plantation harvesting begin to wane. The town is now one of the fastest-growing in the state, advertised as a great tourist destination without the tourist traps.

The **southern right whales** still frequent the area between July and September, and can be seen off the coast; tours to view the whales are also available from *Southern Ocean Charters* (☎ 08 9841 7176). Southeast of town, 21km on Frenchman Bay Road, is **Whaleworld** (☎ 08 9844 4021; open daily 09.00–17.00), located in the area's last whaling station, closed only in 1978—a reminder of how recently this barbaric operation was still sanctioned, and why the whale numbers here still need time to increase substantially. The museum includes a grisly film on whale-hunting and processing, as well as remnants of machinery and ships used in whaling operations.

Albany's **tourist bureau** (☎ 08 9841 1088/1 800 644 088), in the old railway station on Proudlove Parade, can provide a walking tour of the city. Just around the corner on STIRLING TERRACE is a Tudor-style **cabmen's shelter** of about 1910, from horse and buggy days, with a 1926 extension built as a women's rest room. Stirling Terrace also includes many fine Victorian-period buildings, including the **Old Gaol** (☎ 08 9841 1401; open daily 10.00–16.15), the surviving buildings of which were erected in 1873. Opposite the gaol in an 1850s building is the **Albany Residency Museum** (08 9841 4844; open Mon–Sat 10.00–17.00, Sun 14.00–17.00), a good historical museum with seafaring artefacts, Aboriginal relics, and displays of flora and fauna. Next to the museum is a full-scale replica of the brig *Amity*, Albany's 'founding ship'.

The town also has several splendid 19C residences in attractive architectural styles. At 6 Cliff Way is **'Hillside'**, built in 1886 for Albert Young Hassell, parliamentarian and delegate to the Constitutional Convention of 1897. The house has two-storey verandahs with cast-iron lacework and Classical Revival details. Even more impressive is **'The Rocks'**, 182–8 Grey Street, overlooking the town and harbour. This large stone house was built in 1884 for Albany's first mayor, William Grylls Knight. During the 1920s, the house served as the summer residence of the Western Australian governor, thus its label as Government House/Cottage. Its lovely verandah and balcony surrounding the building is characteristic of much of Albany's best early architecture.

On York Street, the **Church of St John the Evangelist**, along with its Hall and Rectory, provides a good example of early stone architecture in the area; the church itself, with fine stained-glass windows and wrought-iron screen, was built in 1841–48, while the Hall of local brick was added in 1889.

The view from **Mount Clarence**—something of a scramble by foot starting at Grey Street East or a drive up from the hill's opposite side—overlooks the town and harbour. Also on the mountain is the Desert Mounted Corps Memorial, a bronze monument originally placed at Port Said, Egypt, to commemorate the Australian troops who sailed from Albany in 1914. Another casting of this monument, sculpted by Webb Gilbert, Paul Mountford, and Bertram Mackennal, is also erected on Anzac Parade in Canberra. Here the monument looks out to sea, where the troops would have last seen Australian soil before landing at Gallipoli.

Albany's finest demonstration of its heritage, called the **Old Farm** (☎ 08 9841 3735; open daily 10.00–17.00 July–May), was government resident Richard Spencer's gentlemanly country estate. This spectacularly well-maintained property was repaired in the early 1960s by the National Trust and last renovated in 1889 by then owner architect Francis Bird who also named it. The original function of the property was as a vegetable garden and maize farm, serving the military detachment at King George Sound in 1827. The first government resident was Dr Alexander Collie who built a cottage near the garden in 1831. Sadly, the fittings Spencer brought for the house and its extensions were largely lost to fire in 1870. There is continued debate about whether the structure can be considered the oldest house in Western Australia; it is certainly the finest old structure, sitting in gardens which include plants and trees from Spencer's seeds brought from England.

Northeast of Albany (14km) in Mirambeena Park, Down Road, is **Mount Romance** (☎ 08 9841 7788; open daily 09.00–17.00), described as a 'boutique factory' and perfumery, which uses native plants and emu oil to produce unique herbal products. Traditionally, emu oil has been used for its medicinal properties, especially for arthritis. The factory is a quite fascinating experience, with unique perfumes available.

Directly north of Albany c 40km is **Porongorup National Park** (☎ 08 9841 7133), filled with wooded granite formations believed by geologists to be among the oldest rocks in the world. These peaks, some as high as 600m, have distinctive shapes and consequently descriptive names such as Castle Rock, Sheep's Head, and Devil's Slide. The park has a variety of picnic spots and bushwalking opportunities, from the easily accessible Tree in the Rock, a 5-minute walk from the northern entrance, to rugged all-day climbs of the peaks. Camping in the park is prohibited but reasonable accommodation is available around the northern entrance. This region also has a number of excellent wineries (both red and white wines), and each March the Porongorup Wine Festival is a festive event. Information on Great Southern Wineries tours is available at the tourist offices in nearby Mount Barker or in Albany.

The natural environment around Albany is the real attraction for holiday-makers. On the east side of town, the protected waters of King George Sound offer excellent calm beaches, such as Middleton Beach, 4km east of Albany. Here also is the 4-star **Esplanade Hotel** (☎ 08 9842 1711), including the Extravaganza Gallery, an upmarket collection of arts, crafts, wine and classic cars.

To the southwest of Albany (c 10km) is **Torndirrup National Park** (☎ 08 9841 3333), around Princess Royal Harbour and south to Frenchmans Bay and the Flinders Peninsula. This park includes some of the most scenic landscape along this windswept coast, with awe-inspiring glimpses of the fearsome waves of the Southern Ocean crashing against the granite rocks. Jimmy Newhill's Harbour in the park offers calmer waters, and the entire region is famous for its brilliant displays of wildflowers. Take extra care when walking around the coastal rocks, as accidents are frequent when the waves are high.

Esperance to Norseman

If you have been driving across the Nullarbor from South Australia to Western Australia, you will be overjoyed to reach **Norseman** (population 520); it is the westernmost town on the highway across the Nullarbor Plain. The nearest town to the east of any size is Ceduna, South Australia, 1200km away. Norseman was founded on gold and was named after a horse that pawed the ground here and unearthed the first specimen of ore. The **Jimerlana Pike** nearby is one of the oldest geological features in the world. **Tourist information**: Robert Street, ☎ 08 9039 1071.

Esperance

If you have travelled east from Albany on route 1, the end of the road is **Esperance** (population 11,700), with 480km of fairly boring road between the two points. At Esperance, the road heads north to Norseman and then on to Kalgoorlie-Boulder. While the town's name does indeed sound hopeful, the actual settlement is largely a port and service centre for the agricultural region around it, although the coastal and harbour beaches around the town are spectacular. **Tourist information**: Dempster Street; ☎ 08 9071 2330. *Westrail* provides a regular bus service (currently three times a week) from Kalgoorlie to Esperance.

History

The bay on which the town sits was first discovered by Dutch navigator Peter Nuyts in 1627, although the area was not mapped until 1792, when a French expedition in the ships *L'Esperance* and *La Recherche* entered the area and gave names to the surrounding geographical features. The first permanent settlers arrived in 1863, although explorer Edward John Eyre had passed through this spot on his overland journey from Adelaide in 1841. The town really came into its own during the 1890s gold rush; only in the 1950s did agriculturalists discover that the addition of minerals to the poor soil could transform the area into fertile farmland.

The town has a good **Municipal Museum** (☎ 08 9071 1579; open daily 13.30–16.30), between Dempster Street and the Esplanade, housing remnants of *Skylab*, the US space station launched in 1973 that crashed to earth over Esperance in 1979. Next to the museum is an arts-and-crafts **Museum Village**. On Windich Street is the town's excellent Public Library (☎ 08 9071 0680) with a comprehensive collection of books about Esperance and the surrounding landscape.

From the middle of town begins a 36km SCENIC LOOP ROAD, signposted as Tourist Way 358, which encompasses several interesting vistas, as well as the popular **Pink Lake**, so-called because a salt-tolerant algae actually colours the waters pink. In his poem, 'Cycling in the Lake Country', contemporary poet Les Murray writes about it: 'I reached a final lake/cupped in rough talcum./Soft facepowder bloom made all the hanging country/fairly peach.' The other highlight along the drive is a swim at the idyllic and sheltered Twilight Cove.

Just outside town to the east (56km) is **Cape Le Grand National Park**, extending between 20km and 60km from Esperance and filled with beautiful white-sand beaches and brilliant blue bays. Off the coast is the **Archipelago of the Recherche**, a scattered array of some 100 small islands, many of them home to colonies of seals, feral goats and penguins. Tour cruises of all sorts are available through the Esperance tourist office. Further along this stretch is the less accessible **Cape Arid National Park**, the real starting point of the Great Australian Bight. For information about these and other national parks, contact the National Parks office in Esperance, ☎ 08 9071 3733.

WARNING. If you are travelling off the major roads, please pay attention to your maps. Ask at each juncture along the way about the advisability of your route. Pay attention to distances, road types and provisions (especially water). Let someone know where you are going, what your route is and when you expect to arrive. Let them know when you do arrive. Stay with your vehicle if it breaks down. If you are absolutely certain of how far along the road you have to walk to get help, leave a note describing your direction of travel and the time.

Kalgoorlie-Boulder

From Esperance, Norseman is 204km north. From here it is about two hours north to another, more famous gold-mining region in **Kalgoorlie-Boulder** (population 28,100). **Tourist information**: 250 Hannan Street; ☎ 08 9021 1966. 600km east of Perth, it completes a rectangle of roads in the southern section of the state. The Prospector **train service** from Perth to Kalgoorlie runs 10 times a week, stopping at the main railway station. The India-Pacific train also comes into town twice a week en route to Perth from Adelaide and returning to the eastern states; travellers may break their journey here if they wish to wait until the next train comes in two or three days.

Paddy Hannan, an itinerant prospector, discovered gold in the area in 1893. The resulting town was briefly known as Hannan's Find until residents chose the present name, from the Aboriginal 'galgurlie', referring to a local species of scrub acacia or wild pear. The region is extremely dry; water, transported by the railroad, routinely sold on the gold fields for as much as 2 shillings a gallon. Eventually, a 563km-long pipeline from the Mundaring Weir near Perth was built from designs by engineer C.Y. O'Connor, who also constructed the Fremantle Harbour.

By the time water arrived, the Golden Mile at Boulder was legitimately famous as the world's richest gold-bearing reef. Museums in town depict the gold rush (**Museum of the Gold fields**, next to the British Arms Hotel, Hannan Street; ☎ 08 9021 8533; open daily 10.00–16.30), mining technology and mineralogy (the **School of Mines Museum**; ☎ 08 9088 6110; open weekdays 08.30–12.30, closed school holidays) and a functioning mine (**Hannans North Mine**; ☎ 08 9091 4074; open daily 09.00–17.00 Aug–Dec, Tues, Wed, Fri–Sun, 09.00–16.00 Jan–July). Especially impressive in Kalgoorlie is the Hannan Street precinct, all of which is heritage-listed. Exceptional wealth from the gold mines in the late 1890s saw the erection of many substantial public buildings along this street, all the more imposing when one considers their utter isolation in the dry and flat countryside. These buildings include the **Kalgoorlie Town Hall** on the corner of Hannan and Wilson Streets (open weekdays 09.00–16.30), completed in 1908 by J.W.S. James, with an enormous staircase, chandeliers, and painted pressed metal ceiling. A bronze statue of Paddy Hannan also stands in the hall. At 119–127 Hannan Street is the Kalgoorlie Miner Building, erected in 1900 as the newspaper office and printers of the *Kalgoorlie Miner*, still published here.

Despite the water pipeline not reaching Kalgoorlie-Boulder until 1903, most of the town's architecture dates from the late 1890s. The town of **Boulder**, now twinned officially with its more famous neighbour Kalgoorlie, also has on Burt Street an interesting collection of Victorian buildings. Boulder's Town Hall, on the corner of Burt and Brookman Streets, opened four months after Kalgoorlie's did, with week-long celebrations. Its stage saw performances by Dame Nellie Melba, and still has its original drop curtain by Philip Goatcher, the only one of its kind left. In keeping with its status as a genuine gold-rich boom-town, the many substantial buildings now seem out of proportion to the town's present population, although a certain Las-Vegas-style exuberance still permeates the atmosphere. Citizens remain proud of their peculiar isolation and their rugged lack of sophistication.

The open areas within the town's borders are often marked by grey mine tailing, known locally as 'slimes', and numerous abandoned shafts. Caution is needed when walking away from frequented paths; these shafts are not always posted and are not normally fenced.

Gambling ~ two-up

Two-up, sometimes referred to as Australia's 'national game', is also called *swy*, from the German *zwei*; this term was used extensively until anti-German sentiment set in with the First World War. The game has taken on legendary status in the folklore of Australia. Its significance in Australian life is evident in legions of stories dating from convict times; indeed, it was certainly played by members of the First Fleet. In the classic Australian story, C.J. Dennis's *Songs of a Sentimental Bloke* (1915), and in the 1919 film of the same name, two-up plays a major part: 'Me that 'as done me stretch fer stoushin' Johns,/An' spen's me leisure gittin' on the shick,/An' 'arf me nights down there in Little Lons.,/Wiv Ginger Mick/ Jist 'eadin' 'em, an'doin' in me gilt.' (Translation: I who have been in gaol for fighting with policemen,/ and spent my leisure getting drunk/ and half my nights there in Little Lonsdale Street [where a two-up school was]/with Ginger Mick/just tossing the coins and losing my money.) Dymphna Cusack's novel *Come In, Spinner* (1951) derives its title from a two-up term.

One of the most enthusiastic descriptions, centred on the multitude of slang originating from the game, is given in Sidney J. Baker's excellent book *The Australian Language* (1966), in which he devotes eight pages to the traditions, history, and terminology of the game. The 'rules' are ludicrously simple, at least at first glance: it involves two coins tossed in the air, with bets placed on landing heads or tails. The rituals that have developed around this version of pitch-and-toss, however, are as complex as a ceremonial ritual and say much about traditional Australian attitudes. Indeed, legend has it that during the famed Battle of Gallipoli in the First World War, the Turks refrained from bombing a group of Anzacs playing two-up, since it appeared from all their bowing and stooping that a religious ceremony was taking place. While the game is still considered illegal when played outside casinos, common tradition still dictates that no one can be arrested for playing two-up on Anzac Day.

The game is played in 'schools'; these can be small informal groups or well-organised and long-established clubs. The most famous was Thomas' sor **'Thommos'**'s in Sydney, where the Thomas family ran the school for more than 50 years. Thommos's reputation rested on its scrupulous honesty and supervision, something decidedly lacking in many two-up matches. In a government probe into organised gambling in 1951, the New South Wales police determined that Thommos alone turned over thousands of pounds a night and had 30 permanent employees earning at least £600 a week. Another famous school, and one steeped in outback mythology, is this tin shed in Kalgoorlie. The Western Australian government made the school legal in 1983. Today the game is played, amidst the glamour and glitz of blackjack, craps, and roulette, at the casinos, although some of its cultural ambience seems to have disappeared in such predictable surroundings.

Some 7km to the north of Kalgoorlie is the site of a tin shed that is one of Western Australia's most famous institutions, the state's only (legal) 'school' for **'two-up'**, Australia's most traditional form of gambling (see box, p 563–4). From Menzies Road, follow the signs that say 'two up' to reach this 'casino'; gambling commences every day at 16.30 except on fortnightly pay days.

Coastal route north to the Northern Territory

The coastal highway, no. 1, north from Perth passes through Geraldton, Carnarvon, along the Pilbara to Port Hedland, skirting the Great Sandy Desert to Broome and below the Kimberley region to Kununurra and the Northern Territory. The only unsealed section of Highway 1, which encircles Australia, occurs between Fitzroy Crossing and Halls Creek, in the remote Kimberley region of the state. The other route north is no. 95, the Great Northern Highway, which takes an inland course all the way to Port Hedland, where it connects with Highway 1.

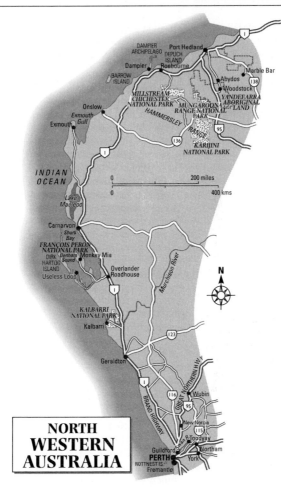

NORTH
**WESTERN
AUSTRALIA**

On the **GREAT NORTHERN HIGHWAY**, 131km north of Perth, is **New Norcia**, an intriguing Benedictine community, established in 1846 by Spanish monk Rosendo Salvado. **Tourist information**: New Norcia Museum and Art Gallery, ☎ 08 9654 8056. Salvado (see also p 538) had been recruited in Italy by Western Australian bishop John Brady to serve as a missionary to the Aboriginal groups in the region. Salvado set about learning the languages of the Yuet and Balardong groups, producing significant early ethnographic studies. These studies have been published as *The Salvado Memoirs* (1851; 1977), expressing sympathetic and well-informed assessments of Aboriginal spirituality and customs. Salvado established the mission here as an efficient farm, and returned to Europe to recruit more monks in the 1850s. In 1867 he became abbot of the monastic community for life.

The remarkable monastic buildings, constructed in a Spanish colonial style unlike others in Australia, are planned axially, with cemetery, pro-cathedral and monastery placed on an east–west axis, and orphanages and school on a north–south axis, roughly in the form of a cross. The most ornate buildings are **St Gertrude's Residence for Girls** and **St Ildephonsus' Residence for Boys**, complete with Moorish minarets.

The monastery is still a functioning one, with a few resident monks; the community offers weekend retreats to the public (☎ 08 9654 8097). The community's tourist office (☎ 08 9654 8020) is in a complex with general store, hotel and post office. Tours depart daily at 11.00 and 13.30 and last about two hours. Also open to the public is an impressive **museum** and **art gallery**, with a substantial collection of religious art including paintings by Spanish and Italian artists, gifts from the Queen of Spain, and Australian art. The monastery's library contains many rare books, including 2000 volumes dated before 1800 and the oldest one from 1508.

Geraldton

Leaving Perth on Highway 1, the first town of any size north of the city is **Geraldton** (population 25,000), some 425km away. **Tourist information**: Bill Sewell Complex, Chapman Road; ☎ 08 9921 399. An agricultural and fishing centre (lobster season is from summer through autumn), the town dates from the 1850s after explorer Lieutenant George Grey praised the area to the authorities in 1841. Author Randolph Stowe described the town as 'clean and tidy and pretty, the iron roofs of the houses small and near, the harbour blue as New Guinea butterflies, the dunes to the south blinding white against the sea' (*The Merry-go-round in the Sea*, 1965). The town has long been a popular holiday destination, aided by its famous climate: an average year-round temperature of 28°C and eight hours of sunshine a day. Long sandy beaches and great splashes of wildflowers in the surrounding countryside add to its popularity with holidaymakers; be sure to book well ahead if travelling here during school or summer holidays.

Nearly all the early descriptions mention displaced Aborigines living on its fringe. The **cathedral**, dedicated to St Francis Xavier, was designed by Monsignor John Cyril Hawes and built between 1916 and 1938. Trained in London, Hawes designed a number of churches and buildings in the diocese. In 1939 he left Australia to become a hermit in the Caribbean. The cathedral is a handsome building of functional appearance largely without exterior ornament. The interior features include an octagonal dome, arches, circular windows and pleasant natural light.

The **Maritime Museum** (☎ 08 9921 5080; open daily 10.00–16.00), on Marine Terrace and one section of two buildings comprising the Geraldton Museum (the other side is artefacts and memorabilia) has displays describing the shipwreck *Batavia*. One of several Dutch East India Company ships wrecked on Australia's east coast during the 17C, her crew were marooned on the Houtman Abrolhos Islands 60km offshore. A party made the trip to Batavia (now Jakarta) in an open boat and sent a rescue ship to the crew's aid. In the intervening three months a mutiny occurred during which more than 120 of the crew were murdered. The leaders of the mutiny were hanged and two of their followers were abandoned on the coast near Geraldton. The islands offshore are accessible by boat or plane, and tours can be arranged through the tourist office; they offer excellent opportunities for snorkelling and diving. Overnight visits are not allowed.

Also in the area, 24km south of Geraldton, is **Greenough** (pronounced 'grenuf') **Village** (☎ 08 926 1084, open daily 09.00–16.00), a National Trust presentation of eleven 1880s buildings, eight of which are furnished from the late 19C. Crossing the Greenough River is the McCartney Road Bridge, built by convict labour in the 1860s.

Natural settings in the vicinity of Geraldton include the Murchison River, which cuts a spectacular and rugged gorge in the **Kalbarri National Park**, some 186,000 ha of interesting geological features. The popular holiday resort of **Kalbarri** sits at the mouth of the river, and is the best place to begin tours of the national park. **Tourist information:** Grey Street; ☎ 08 9937 1104. The area is especially renowned for the more than 500 wildflower species that bloom here each year. Just south of the town at Wittecarra Creek, a cairn marks the spot believed to be where the first white men walked on the Australian mainland: two mutineering sailors exiled from the Dutch ship *Batavia* in 1629.

Back on Highway 1, the road between Geraldton and Carnarvon—all 481km of it—passes through nearly all of the local floral zones. The winter agriculture belt ends in low, scrubby mallee around the Kalbarri National Park. Near the Overlander Roadhouse varieties of daisies form the understorey. Once on the approach to Carnarvon, arid hearty salt and blue bush alternate with acacia. This vegetation continues along the fringe of the Great Sandy Desert.

Shark Bay

From Kalbarri, 228km north is the turn-off at Overlander Roadhouse, for **Shark Bay**, another of Australia's World Heritage-listed sites. Comprised of two peninsulas, this intriguing geographical feature is now a 22,000 sq km national park. The small settlement of **Denham** (population 1100) in the park is considered the westernmost town in Australia and is the main centre for the region. The **Shark Bay Visitor and Travel Centre** is located here on Knight Terrace (☎ 08 9948 1253) and can provide great quantities of tourist information.

As any visitor to Australia will no doubt learn, the great tourist attraction at Shark Bay is **Monkey Mia**, a beach where friendly bottlenose dolphins come voluntarily into the shallows and can be hand-fed and touched by visitors. The **information centre** here is open daily, 08.30–16.30, ☎ 08 9948 1366. While enthusiastic throngs have somewhat overwhelmed the beach in the last few years and are kept under control by harried park rangers, the experience of seeing the dolphins can still be an enjoyable one, if a bit over-advertised (dolphins do this in other less crowded locations along the coast, especially at Bunbury). Visitors should note that Monkey Mia is 850km from Perth and plan their visit accordingly!

The park is also home to some 10,000 dugongs, green turtles, manta rays, whales and many species of sharks. The area also includes ancient rock formations known as stromatolites, built over hundreds of years by blue-green algae. Some of these stromatolites were formed up to three billion years ago, and some at Shark Bay are known to have formed over a period of 1000 years or more. Monkey Mia borders the **François Peron National Park** (☎ 08 9948 1208), proclaimed a national park in 1990 and named for the French naturalist who visited here in 1801 as part of the Baudin voyage. The most striking feature of this 40 million ha park is the clash of brilliant red sand dunes with the bright blue Indian Ocean. Camping areas with limited facilities are available in the park. An old homestead in the middle of the park, built in the late 19C when the land was a sheep station, is accessible; to the north of the site, access is by four-wheel-drive only.

This stretch of coastline also includes **Shell Beach**, 110km of shoreline filled with tiny shells. On the western side of Shark Bay is **Dirk Hartog Island**, where Dutch explorer Dirck Hartog landed in 1616. It was here that he nailed an inscribed plate, later taken by a Dutch visitor and now on display in the Rijksmuseum in Amsterdam. Another Dutch explorer, Willem de Vlamingh, landed in Shark Bay in 1697. This area also had an early pearling industry and a mixed population including Malays and Chinese; today, it is world-famous for its superb fishing.

Carnarvon (population 6600), a further 480km north, sits at the mouth of the Gascoyne River. Known for banana plantations and marine crayfish (harvested April to October), the town dates from the 1880s. Novelist Nene Gare, who lived here after the Second World War, wrote of the town in *Green Gold* (1963): 'The wide main streets were made to take a double team of camels pulling twelve-foot drays shod with big iron wheels. There had to be room for the Afghan drivers to take a round turn, with the result that modern traffic finds itself with parking space in the middle of the road as well as at both sides.' **Tourist information:** Robinson Street; ☎ 08 9941 1146.

Hibiscus and bougainvillea flourish in its tropical climate. The area has excellent fishing and crabbing, good beaches and curious blowholes and one of the continent's best place-names in **Useless Loop**.

The towns on the northeast corner of the state are devoted to marine shipping and deep sea sport fishing around the **Dampier Archipelago**. **Exmouth** (population 3058) is a naval station founded only in 1967, and severely damaged by Cyclone Vance in March 1999; **Onslow**, one of the few towns in Australia bombed in the Second World War, had to be relocated due to cyclones. **Dampier** is a deepwater port loading iron ore. **Roebourne**, the area's oldest town, has a number of stone buildings from the 1880s and 1890s. **Port Hedland** ships handle Australia's highest tonnage, principally iron ore and salt. Of greatest interest at Exmouth and the peninsula is **Cape Range National Park**, 39km west of the town (☎ 08 9949 2808). The **Milyering Visitor Centre** (open daily 10.00–16.00), 52km southwest of Exmouth, is the best place to begin a visit to the park; it has excellent displays and detailed information about the many walking trails and interesting sites in the park, and a particularly enthusiastic staff of rangers. Of special interest in the park, accessible on walking tracks, are **Yardie Creek Gorge**, with bands of fossil-bearing limestone contrasting with the brilliantly aqua blue waters of **Yardie Creek**; and **Charles Knife Canyon**, whose views are frequently described as 'indescribable'.

Adjacent to Cape Range Park is **Ningaloo Marine Park**, on Ningaloo Reef, Western Australia's largest and most accessible coral reef (its extension is from latitude 21°40' to 23°15' and longitude 113°35' to 114°10'—some 250km from North West Cape towards Cape Farquhar). The lagoon formed between the reef and the shore is up to 15m deep with coral and algae colonies supported on a limestone base. Ningaloo is the world's largest coral reef so close to a continental landmass; it offers fantastic snorkelling and fishing possibilities. From

June to November, humpback whales from Antartica travel up this part of the coastline to breed; from March to June, whale sharks descend on the reef to eat coral spawn, providing an unprecedented opportunity to view these enormous creatures. Whale-watching cruises can be arranged through the visitor's centre.

Perhaps more interesting than iron ore shipping, the area has a number of Aboriginal **rock art sites**. The most noteworthy are in the valleys southwest of Dampier, on **Depuch Island**, in the **Millstream Chichester National Park** (☎ 08 9144 4600) about 80km inland to the south from Roeburne, on the **Burrup Peninsula** and directly south of Port Hedland around **Abydos** and **Woodstock**.

The engravings at the **Dampier Art Site** are in valleys southeast of the town. At **Skew Valley** a well-known group of petroglyphs include a crab, two eggs, and an ibis with a snake in its mouth. In **Gumtree** and **Kangaroo valleys** the images are again of animals and were produced by abrading grooves. Within the **Hunter Valley**, the Altar Site has bats, humans and a large boomerang engraved on an outcrop of stone. **Happy Valley** has a variety of motifs, including a Tasmanian Tiger. The associated cultural artefacts have been radio carbon-dated from 2300 to 6600 years ago.

The **Burrup Peninsula**, 17km northeast of Dampier, has a dense concentration of rock art sites also presenting a diversity of motifs and forms. That at about 9km northeast of town has a number of panels on which figures are portrayed climbing and gathering. These were produced by pecking dots into the rock with a sharp stick or other implement.

Visiting rock art sites

Approaching these sites requires some delicacy. Control over them has only recently been ceded to the Western Australian Aboriginal communities. The previous stewards of the sites at the Western Australian Museum implied that they were not open to unescorted visitors. Although some discussion of access has begun in the Aboriginal communities, arrangements for routine interpreted access proceeds slowly. The brief descriptions of the areas around Dampier and Port Hedland may alert tourists to avail themselves of access should the Kariyarra or Martuthunira Aboriginal custodians elect to provide it; check with the tourist offices in Dampier or Port Hedland for the current status of the sites and accessibility policy. The art is said to be on a par with that in the Hawkesbury near Sydney and that in the adjacent Kimberley.

Depuch Island sits 4km offshore between Roebourne and Port Hedland. The exposed basalt surfaces are red-brown or orange; beneath the surface they are a grey-green to yellow. The Ngarluma group call the variously sized figures '*mani*'. Generally pecked, they depict thousands of figures and implements. The male and female figures on the surfaces erected at **Hunters Pool** on the island's northwest are described as impressive. The most recent figures relate to contemporary religion.

Accessible engravings around Port Hedland include some rays, turtles and a whale beside the BHP main gate on Two Mile Ridge.

The **rock art sites** on **Abydos** and **Woodstock stations**, about 150km south of Port Hedland off the Great Northern Highway, are of two sorts. The older (c 17,000 years ago) are usually abraded grooves on the horizontal brown granite boulders. The more recent are pecked and include human, part human and part animal, and a variety of animal representations. Most interesting are mythological figures with long narrow bodies, flexible arms and legs without elbows or knees, muzzled visages and exaggerated genitalia. Anthropologists surmise that the sites are part of women's rituals, in part because, being males, they could get only vague interpretative statements from the people living near the sites. PLEASE CHECK WITH LOCAL ABORIGINAL GROUPS OR THROUGH TOURIST OFFICES BEFORE ATTEMPTING TO VISIT ANY ROCK ART SITES.

Incidentally, **Marble Bar**, 203km southeast of Port Hedland, is popularly known throughout Australia as having the continent's hottest and most inhospitable weather. This spot set a world record in the 1920s with temperatures over 37°C (the old 100° Fahrenheit mark) for 160 consecutive days. Temperatures over 40°C are quite common from October through March, and Marble Bar has reached as high as 50° C. Its wildflowers in late winter, on the other hand, make this town pretty and surprisingly well frequented. The town's name derives from the amazing bar of jasper crossing the Coongan River near town, with patterns resembling marble.

Traditional land holders here are the Martuthunira near Dampier and the Kariyarra near Port Hedland. Stockmen from this group were the first in the **stockmen's strikes** immediately after the Second World War. Aboriginal stockmen, essential for the running of the region's huge sheep stations, were for the most part working under near-slave conditions. When they finally walked off the job, it led to police intervention and harrassment. Eventual support by unionists and others brought some government concessions, but black stockmen never returned to the stations; they became instead leading activists in the 1960s civil rights campaigns. Further, people from this region were instrumental in the outstation movement in which land rights were secured for new settlements on traditional land. An instructive local story recounts that the wife from a sheep station moved with her children to the local Aboriginal camp to avoid the coarse gold miners when they descended upon her husband's station in the 1880s, underlining the complex and contradictory interactions between native and white settlers from the beginning.

About 260km south of Port Hedland and 1375km north of Perth on the Great Northern Highway (route 95) is Munjina Roadhouse at the entrance to **Karijini National Park** (☎ 08 9143 1488), an enormous 650,000 ha reserve ecompassing the central section of the Hamersley Range of the Pilbara region. It is considered a 'must see' for its exquisite gorges, lookouts and waterfalls. It also contains Western Australia's highest peak, Mount Meharry (1245m); with four-wheel drive, one can drive to the peak. Entrance stations are at several points in all directions and an information centre is open in season near Yampire Gorge Road and Joffre Falls Road—both Yampire Gorge and Joffre Falls are worth visiting. As in so many other Western Australian parks, the wildflower display in Karijini in the spring is stunning.

It is advised that tourists, unless quite daring, avoid the odd little asbestos-ridden town of **Wittenoom**, on the northern edge of the park 18km west of Munjina Roadhouse. The town is marked with warning signs at the entrance, but inhabitants stubbornly refuse to leave the town.

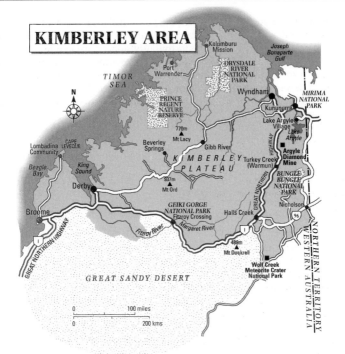

KIMBERLEY AREA

Kimberley region

Across the **Great Sandy Desert** is the **Kimberley region**. Spoken of simply as the Kimberley, this region is a peninsular-shaped plateau of Early Proterozoic sandstone and occasional volcanic rock. Draining generally to the northwest, the area receives about 380mm rainfall in the southeast and up to 1300mm in its northwest, this largely as intermittent storms during December to April. While most tourists have preferred travelling in the north during the dry and sunny period, travellers increasingly recommend the still wet months of April and May. Tides can be substantial (as much as 12m) and frequently trap hapless fishermen off shore. The coastal areas are extremely rugged. Except at estuaries, cliffs rather than beaches are the rule.

The Great Northern Highway, still no. 1, more or less marks the furthest southern extent of the monsoonal rains, though sections of the road may be closed following heavy rains during the season. The cities from east to west include Derby, Fitzroy Crossing, Halls Creek, Wyndham and Kununurra.

Broome

Broome (population 8900) sits as a port on Roebuck Bay, a full 2200km north of Perth off the Great Northern Highway (Highway 95) or 2352km via North West Coastal Highway (route 1). Despite this tremendously distant location, with vast expanses of desert in between here and any centre of population, Broome is frequently voted Australia's favourite holiday destination, a result of its historic ambience and the efforts of English entrepreneur and philanthropist

Alistair McAlpine. In the 1980s McAlpine took the town under his wing to renovate its unique environment; when McAlpine experienced financial difficulties, Broome's development, perhaps fortuitously, stopped just in time to prevent any theme parks or Club-Med-style overkill. There is an international airport, flights arrive from Indonesia as well as from the other Australian states.

Broome stages two important annual festivals: the Shinju Matsuri, the **Festival of the Pearl**, in late August/early September, a week-long celebration of the town's ethnic diversity and history, which includes the crowning of a Pearl Queen; and the **Broome Fringe Arts Festival** in early June, focusing on local arts and culture. Another great event is **Stompen Ground**, presented in even years in late September. Organised by the Broome Musicians Aboriginal Corporation (☎ 08 9192 2550), it is a celebration with music and dance of Aboriginal culture. **Tourist information**: on the corner of Bagot Road and Great Northern Highway; ☎ 08 9192 2222.

History

Broome sits on the land that pirate William Dampier sailed by in 1688; he landed in nearby King Sound, where he made his famous derogatory remarks about this entire western coastline (see p 575). Dampier returned in 1699 as captain of a vessel of the Royal Navy, the *Roebuck*, after which the bay is named. Some material evidence indicates that the Portuguese may also have travelled this far south in the 1500s. No permanent settlement began here until the 1880s, although the Djuelen group of Aborigines were traditional inhabitants, and fishermen from China, Indonesia and Malaysia have plied the waters around Broome for centuries.

Since the 1880s, Broome has been one of the most famous **pearling ports** in the world; it was named after Western Australia's governor in the 1890s, Frederick Broome. Pearling brought 'luggers' and divers from a variety of cultures, as many as 400 in the early 1900s; by 1910, Broome provided 80 per cent of the world's mother-of-pearl shell, the real source of profit for the industry, as long as most fashionable buttons were made from shell. Not surprisingly, Aboriginal trade in mother-of-pearl shell extended well into the interior, as far as Yuendumu and the desert regions of northern South Australia. Usually the shell was incised prior to trade and often the pattern was in-filled with fat and red ochre. The introduction of steel tools to work the shell saw this trade flourish in the early 20C. These shells are still prized, but the decorated shells are rarely produced now.

The town's ethnic mix and its frontier isolation made it for many years a rough-and-ready boom town, a source of imaginative romance for many writers and travellers. Novelist Henrietta Drake-Brockman lived here in the 1920s, and set her first historical romance, *Blue North* (1934), on the pearling grounds around Broome. Even realist writer Katharine Susannah Prichard waxed poetic about the place in *Moon of Desire* (1941): 'Always that rare blue-green of the bay, stretching up to the land, to gloat over ochre and terra-cotta cliffs to the north, and the lost grey-green line of the mangroves about the mouth of the creek.' Prichard's description highlights the most fascinating natural features of the town's location: the bright-blue waters of the bay contrasted against the white beaches, and the tropical trees and flowers of the community's gardens. One other natural characteristic is the extreme tidal range in the bay, which at the equinox twice a year can vary as much as 10m in a 12-hour cycle.

J.M. Harcourt's portrayal of the pearling industry's racial injustices is at the heart of his novel *The Pearlers* (1933); and popular adventure writer Ion Idriess described the pearling trade in his *Forty Fathoms Deep* (1937). Arthur Upfield set one of his best 'Bony' mysteries, *The Widows of Broome* (1950), in the town, which at the end of the Second World War had a population of just 800. Indeed, Upfield chronicles the death of the old-fashioned pearl industry, a situation that nearly ended Broome. Recent pearl cultivation techniques have once again brought the town and pearling some economic stability, as Broome pearls begin to reappear on world markets.

Broome continues to attract writers and artists. Most recently, Broome native Jimmy Chi (b. 1948) produced one of the first Aboriginal musicals, *Bran Nue Dae*, dealing with political and cultural issues facing contemporary Aborigines in Western Australia; the play was first performed in 1990 at the Festival of Perth. Jimmy Chi, of Chinese and Aboriginal background, is a good example of the ethnic diversity characterising the current population of Broome: Chinese, Aborigine, Anglo, and other Asian groups comprise one of Australia's most multicultural communities. This diversity is most cheerfully evident in the remainders of the town's early vernacular architecture: a blend of British colonial timber houses such as the teakwood **Court House** (1889), with verandahs and ventilated rooms; some Asian-style building conventions in the shops in Chinatown; and a few thoroughly idiosyncratic touches, such as the mother-of-pearl chancery in the **'Little White Church'** Anglican church of 1903.

The **Broome Tourist Information Centre** is near the airport, and provides good maps and 'Heritage Trails' tourist guides. An interesting map to acquire is the **Lurujarri Heritage Trail**, prepared as a Bicentennial Project by the town's Aboriginal community to present, as the brochure says, 'the Song Cycle from Minarriny to Yinara'. The trail leads along the Cable Beach coast north for several kilometres from Gantheaume Point (Minyirr is its Aboriginal name). It explains the spiritual significance to the Aboriginal people of the various natural rock formations and geological features.

At **Gantheaume Point**, the outgoing tide reveals giant dinosaur tracks, believed to be 130 million years old. Cement casts of the tracks are displayed near the warning light on the cliff. At the end of **Cable Beach**, at CABLE BEACH ROAD, is the **Broome Crocodile Farm** (☎ 08 9192 1489; open daily 10.00–17.00; shorter hours Nov–March), one of the better examples of these attractions; it was founded by adventurer Malcolm Douglas, famed for his many nature documentaries about Australia. Since Broome is considered the western-most limit for saltwater crocodiles, this is a good place to learn about them.

Back into town on Cable Beach Road, some 3km, at the juncture of Frederick Drive and Port Drive, is the **old cemetery**, most poignant for its many Japanese graves, testament to the dangers of pearl diving. More than 900 divers lost their lives searching for these precious shells, many of them Japanese. Also in the cemetery are sections for Chinese, Muslim, and Aboriginal graves, a fascinating indication of Broome's unique cultural heritage.

The touring trail in town begins appropriately in **Chinatown**, a remnant of the enormous Chinese presence in the pearling industry here. Many of the original buildings have been reconstructed, with 'Oriental' touches even on the telephone booths. At the end of DAMPIER TERRACE are old boat sheds, next to the dilapidated **Streeter's Jetty** which includes an old refurbished pearl 'lugger'. Dampier Terrace also houses some pearl dealers operating in original warehouses, and at the end of the block the old offices of the *Broome News*. Of particular interest in the neighbourhood is **Sun Pictures**, on Carnarvon Street, between Short Street and Napier Terrace (☎ 08 9192 1677). Opened in 1916 as an outdoor cinema, the 'theatre' is the oldest 'picture garden' still in operation, with palm trees swaying in the breeze behind the screen.

On NAPIER TERRACE near Wing's Restaurant is an enormous boab tree and behind it, by the old gaol, a plaque identifies another tree as one planted in 1898 by a policeman when his son was born; the son was killed in the Great War, but the tree lives on. (See Derby, p 575, for more on the boab tree.) **Kimberley Bookshop**, at no. 6 Napier Terrace, is one of the only real bookshops between Perth and Darwin.

The few blocks of HAMERSLEY STREET between Frederick and Mary Streets contain several public buildings, including the lovely teakwood **Court House** of 1889, which originally served as a cable station of the Eastern Extension Telegraph Company, the company responsible for linking Broome by cable with Java. The Court House markets are held here on Saturday mornings. Other buildings here are the post office, the bank, and a civic centre with library and **art gallery**. The latter is in a charming building in Broome vernacular style; it stages excellent local art exhibitions. Around the corner on Weld Street is an odd building notable only because it contains a Wackett Aircraft originally owned by Horrie Miller, founder of what became the Western Australian branch of Ansett Airlines.

At the junction of Hamersley and Carnarvon Streets is **Captain Gregory's House**, not open to the public, but a good example of the luxurious bungalows owned by Broome's leading merchants and seamen in the glory days; Gregory owned the largest pearling enterprise in town. At Bedford Park is one of the old train cars that originally travelled the 2km from Chinatown to Town Beach.

Further along Hamersley Street at Saville Street is the **Broome Historical Society Museum** (☎ 08 9192 2075; open weekdays 10.00–16.00, weekends 10.00–13.00, shorter hours Nov–March), which contains, not surprisingly, an excellent exhibition on pearling and the history of the town.

Also on Saville Street at no. 28 is **Magabala Books**, a thriving publishing house (named after a local type of bush banana) catering for Aboriginal writers of the Kimberley region. The store is a locus for Aboriginal activities in the region.

North of Broome

On Highway 1 east of Broome towards Derby 9.2km opposite the Cape Leveque Road is the turn-off to the 9.6km drive to the **RAOU Broome Bird Observatory** (☎ 08 9193 5600; open daily), on Roebuck Bay. The observatory is on the site of one of the best non-breeding grounds for migrant Arctic waders, as well as over 250 other species of birds. More than 150,000 migratory birds from the Northern hemisphere pass through Roebuck Bay and 800,000 birds use the site annually, making this centre a prime location for birdwatchers of all levels. The observatory is well organised and can offer a variety of tours and camping facilities. It is one of four in Australia; the others are Eyre in Western Australia;

Rotamah Island in Victoria; and Barren Grounds in New South Wales.

Further along Highway 1 and near the Cape Levegue Road, 35km north of Broome, is **Willie Creek Pearl Farm** (☎ 08 9193 6000; open daily), an excellent facility housed in a lovely building, with informative demonstrations of pearl seeding. **Cape Leveque**, the point of which is some 200km north of Broome, is Aboriginal land. Relaxed and casual tours and cabin-style accommodation on the **Lombardina Aboriginal Reserve** can be arranged through Lombardina Tours in Broome (☎ 08 9192 4936) or by phoning Kooljaman Resort, ☎ 08 9192 4970.

Derby

Situated on King Sound 220km northeast of Broome, **Derby** (population 3250) is the administrative centre for the western part of the Kimberley, and the base for many adventurous outback expeditions. Once extremely isolated, recent road improvements have made it accessible enough to support a good tourist industry. Its location on the edge of mirage-producing mud-flats and mangrove swamps made it unsuitable as a port, and contributes to a rather drab appearance. Still, the residents are friendly and, as J.K. Ewers wrote in *With the Sun on My Back* (1953), 'Whoever named Derby after an erstwhile Secretary of State for the Colonies either had no imagination or else conceived it as a prodigious joke...forget about the classic "Darby" and its English pronunciation, for here, ...it's "Derby".' The annual **Boab Festival** in July, named in honour of the town's many boab trees, features a rodeo and a famous mud-football competition, as well as cockroach races. **Tourist information**: 1 Clarendon Street; ☎ 08 9191 1426.

> ### The boab tree
> The boab tree of northern Australia, *Adansonia gregorii*, is also called a baobab, related but distinct from the African tree of that name. A grotesquely shaped tree with an enormous girth out of proportion to its height, it produces edible fruit often called sour gourd. In *The Great Australian Loneliness* (1937), Ernestine Hill called it 'a Caliban of a tree, a grizzled, distorted old goblin—a friendly ogre of the great North-west'.

To the south of Derby (7km) is the famous **Boab Prison Tree**, reputedly used as a cell to hold Aboriginal prisoners. In his *Gifts Upon the Water* (1978), Alec Choate includes the poem 'Prison Tree, Derby', which ends: 'Can it ever remind us/Of the alien heartbeats/That took the place of its heart?/For here was a prison cell./Here Man was a kept shadow...' Also near the Prison Tree is **Myall's Bore**, a huge cattle-trough, 120m long and 4.2m wide, used to water cattle in the old droving days.

The **Pigeon Heritage Trail**, the historic tour through town (brochure available from the tourist office), alludes to the nearby hideout of the Aboriginal outlaw Jandamarra, called Pigeon by the authorities, who was central to the stories of black–white hostilities here in the 1880s. The great adventure writer Ion Idriess relates Pigeon's escapades in his *Outlaws of the Leopolds* (1952), referring to the King Leopold Ranges to the east of Derby. A former police tracker, Pigeon, after killing several officers, went on a three-year spree of mayhem and murder. He was eventually tracked down by fellow trackers and killed in 1897.

The spectacular Devonian **limestone gorges** on the Fitzroy River at **Giekie Gorge** (now a national park, ☎ 08 9191 5121) and on the Margaret River as it cuts through the Leopold Range near **Fitzroy Crossing** (population 1120) are popular attractions.

In addition to the geology, the area is recognised for the freshwater crocodiles, barramundi fish and red river eucalypts; and here you can spot numerous migratory and resident bird species in the lagoons and intertidal marshes around Derby and, particularly, Wyndham. The flora is generally eucalypt forest. The monsoonal forests are noted for deciduous trees which drop their leaves during the hot and arid winter. Among these, the baobab's curiously oval trunk can be used for storing water.

The Kimberley coast was the first area on the western edge of the continent to be charted, on this occasion by the Dutch merchant seaman Dirck Hartog in 1616. Unlike Hartog's, William Dampier's descriptions (1688) were not kept secret. Dampier was also the first to describe Aborigines. He found the people living in the King Sound to be 'the miserablest people in the world'. The Aborigines were equally mistaken, calling him 'Ngaarri' (rather than Dampier's transcription 'Gurri'), the name of a fickle and malevolent spirit being.

Alexander Forrest's 1879 description of the potential of the land for grazing led to early settlement. Noteworthy pastoralists included the Murray Squatting Co., which took nearly 50,000 ha in the east near Beagle Bay (Yeeda Station, 1881), and the Durack family (Ord River, 1885), who reached the western Kimberley area after a two-year-long cattle drive from southwestern Queensland.

The rough hills and steep ravines and gorges of the King Leopold, Napier and Durack Ranges still separate these two areas. The writer Mary Durack spent her early childhood on the family company's stations in the eastern Kimberleys; she returned here with her sister in the 1930s and took charge of Ivanhoe Station. Durack's books, *Kings in Grass Castles* (1959) and *Sons in the Saddle* (1983), commemorate the pioneering families of this region. Her most famous book, *Keep Him My Country* (1955), portrays a typical Kimberley cattle station in the early days.

A short-lived gold rush brought some permanent settlers to **Halls Creek** (population 1265) in the 1880s. The inhospitable dry months and resistance from the Aboriginal population stalled the influx of settlers. After the Second World War an effort was made to encourage settlement around the Lake Argyle irrigation project on the Ord River. Nonetheless, Wyndham's cattle-processing facility closed in 1985. **Tourist information**: Great Northern Highway, ☎ 08 9168 6262; open April–Oct only.

From Halls Creek you have access to the **Bungle Bungle National Park** (also called the Purnululu National Park), c 100km northeast, and the **Wolf Creek Meteorite Crater**, 150km south. The crater is the second largest found, measuring nearly 1km wide and 50m deep. The rock formations of the Bungle Bungle Range in the national park are famed for their tiger-striped rocks and beehive-shaped domes consisting of sandstone formations encased in silica and lichen. Covering almost 320,000 ha, the area conserves 110,000 ha as reserve and the rest is open as national park. Picnic and camping grounds are well established throughout the park, with some amenities; and walking trails lead to the magnificent Cathedral Gorge and Echidna Chasm. Scenic flights over the

Kuril Kuril painting

The Aboriginal community at **Warmun** (also known as Turkey Creek), 163km north of Halls Creek on the Great Northern Highway, have been painting Kuril Kuril (pronounced 'grill grill') paintings since the early 1970s. These are based on the *palga* narrative dance cycle related to Cyclone Tracy. The most famous of these artists, **Rover Thomas** (d. 1998), had a spirit dream from a female relative. She had died while being flown to hospital in Perth. In the dream she revealed to Thomas that she had been over the ocean whirlpool home of a Rainbow Serpent named Juntarkal; Thomas interpreted Cyclone Tracy as this creature, furious that the people had not kept the law. She also gave him a number of songs and dances commemorating her trip from the place of her death to that of her conception near Turkey Creek.

Initially, the Kuril Kuril paintings were for ceremonial use, but secular paintings were made in the early 1980s as a result of public interest in them and the introduction of canvas as a substitute for the wooden boards carried in the *palga* dances. Rover Thomas's fame rests on his broad areas of canvas in natural colour and the striking composition of his canvases. Rightly admired for his colour sense, he said of Mark Rothko upon seeing the New York artist's work, 'That white fella paint like me, but he don't understand black.'

The Warmun artists use a number of conventions from the Central Desert groups (the best known for Aboriginal paintings), but rather than depicting ancestral events, their works are maps of the landscape. They depict where ancestral events happened in order to be appropriate in secular settings. Rover Thomas's *Cyclone Tracy* (1991), on view at the National Gallery in Canberra (see also colour plate section), presents a stark depiction of the cyclone's black path.

Some of the Warmun community's works would be available at Waringarri Aboriginal Arts in Kununurra (☎ 08 9168 2212) and in the reputable dealers' galleries in the major cities.

ranges can be arranged through the tourist offices at Halls Creek or Kununurra. Please keep in mind that this region is rugged territory; BE PREPARED with provisions (water!) and expect rigorous walking and serious camping if you are staying. This park has not been 'touristised'. It is closed from January to April, that is, during 'The Wet'.

The **Mirima (Hidden Valley) National Park**, on Barringtonia Avenue in Kununurra (☎ 08 9168 2000), is referred to locally as 'the mini-Bungles', with similar beehive formations as at Purnululu. Pleasant walking trails and picnic grounds are worth exploring.

Speaking of the area between Halls Creek and Wyndham, Ray Erickson in *West of Centre* (1972) writes: 'The hills, grass-covered and tree-crowned, ranging in shape from long flat-tops to inverted pudding basins, are constantly engaging in form, but it is colour above all which distinguishes them. They bring to its climax the pervasive purple which strongly identifies this region.'

The drive from Kununurra to Wyndham, c 160km, passes through some spectacular gorges. The **Five Rivers Lookout** provides a view west across the region. **Kununurra** (population 4800) is 151km north of Warmun and is the

Central Aboriginal Land

The regional Aboriginal rock paintings centre around **Wandjina spirits**. Involved in the creation myths, these wondrous fertility guardians bring the monsoons and cyclones to ensure regeneration of life. They are in human form with hair that is also the area's large, white cumulonimbus clouds. They can cause lightning to emanate from their feathered headdresses. The Wandjina live the dry months of the year in their self-portrait rock paintings. During The Wet, the local Aboriginal people preserve them by retouching the paintings while the Wandjina are away tending to the rains.

The principal sites of the rock paintings are the **Prince Regent Area**, 250km northeast of Derby, and the **Donkey Ridge Area**, 190km southwest of Wyndham. Sites south of Kalumburu include the **Derre Area**, 125km south-southwest, the **Paten Area**, 40km southeast, and the Carson River Station Area, 23km southeast. Most of these sites can be visited, some requiring permission to travel on Aboriginal land. Check in Derby or Kununurra or Wyndham for more information.

Older paintings are known as **Bradshaw figures** after explorer Joseph Bradshaw who first reported them (1892). These are smaller, averaging about 30cm in height, in red or off-red ochre. Interesting compositions, they depict hunting and dancing scenes and are said to have been done by a bird which could see spirits invisible to humans. These figures seem similar to figures in Arnhem Land paintings. Josephine Flood, conservation officer at the Australian Heritage Commission, surmises that these paintings mark the westernmost extent of an earlier cultural group formerly prevalent across the northern section of the continent. Some of the best known of the Bradshaw figures appear in areas around the Kalumburu Aboriginal community, located on the King Edward River near the northern tip of the Kimberley, 313km from Gibb River at the end of the Derby Road. You will need a permit to visit the community, ☎ 08 9161 4300, fax 08 9161 4331, weekdays 07.00–12.00) and provisions for camping. For more information on accessible rock art in the region, the CALM offices are helpful (Kununurra, ☎ 08 9168 0200), as is their website: www.calm.wa.gov.au

hub of the eastern Kimberley region next to the Ord River Scheme. **Tourist information**: East Kimberley Tourism House, Coolibah Drive, ☎ 08 9168 1177. It is also the centre of Australia's diamond-mining industry (particularly renowned for pink diamonds); the Argyle Diamond Mine, located southwest of town and accessible by tour only (through the tourist office), is the world's largest diamond mine, most of them industrial quality. Also south of Kununurra (72km) is **Lake Argyle**, Australia's largest artificial lake, measuring 980 sq km and containing 10 times as much water as Sydney Harbour. The lake now teems with birdlife and has good spots for swimming and fishing. Also here is the Argyle Homestead Museum (open daily 09.00–16.00), the structure built by pioneer Patsy Duracle in 1894; its original location was flooded when the lake was made, and so it was moved brick by brick to this location.

NOTE. When travelling through the Kimberley region, be sure to follow all precautions and advice for outback travel: carry water, tell the authorities of your whereabouts, and prepared for food and accommodation.

The Northern Territory

The Northern Territory is six times the size of Great Britain and boasts two paved highways. The **Stuart Highway** comes north from South Australia through Alice Springs, gateway to Uluru, and on to Darwin, the capital. The other, which changes name, crosses the north from Western Australia to Katherine, jogs south to about Tennant Creek, then continues to Mount Isa in Queensland.

The northern portion of the Territory is known as the **Top End**. It receives monsoonal rains during 'The Wet' (November to May) and virtually no precipitation from June to October. The area south of Tennant Creek is arid to semi-arid to well south of the border with South Australia.

Temperatures vary greatly across the year and also within a day. In arid regions like Alice Springs, evenings will be quite cool, reaching single digits before dawn in July and August. Midday temperatures during these cooler months routinely reach the high 20°s. Summer temperatures (January and February) are 20° warmer, with highs routinely over 40° C.

From Katherine northwards the dry winter months are somewhat warmer, ranging between the mid-teens to the low 30°s. The monsoons moderate the temperature in the summer, yielding highs in the mid-30°s and lows in the mid-20°s. In short, the desert is hot and the Top End is wet from November through May.

Geologically, the state is the northeast section of the Precambrian Shield. The most recent formations are cretaceous marine deposits in the Simpson Desert in the far southeast, in a basin extending about 200km around Daly Waters in the state's central north, and small plains which lie intermittently along the coast. Paleozoic (mostly Cambrian) rock extends across the centre of the state, forming a tongue which nearly reaches Darwin. Proterozoic material forms a semicircle around these areas, including nearly all of Arnhem Land and the western and southern borders.

The state is virtually surrounded by desert. The Great Sandy, Gibson and Great Victorian Deserts form its west and southwest. The Simpson Desert is the southeast corner. Near its centre is the Tanami Desert.

Other dominant geological features include the Musgrave and Macdonald Ranges and the intervening Amadeus Depression in the southwest, the Barkly Tablelands in the northeast and the spectacular Kakadu and Arnhem Land at the Top End. In addition to these latter areas are the remarkable Uluru and Kata Tjuta monoliths near Alice Springs, Katherine Gorge, and the curious granite boulders south of **Tennant Creek**.

Not unexpectedly, the soil types and flora conform to this geological and climatic pattern. Soil scientists mention extremely soda-filled rock, limited permeability and inherently low fertility. Deep siliceous soils form the Simpson and Tanami Deserts where the hummock grass spinifex prevails. Most of the

Barkly Tablelands are cracking clays which allow some acacia to grow, but mostly sustain tussock grasses. The rest of the state is shallow sand over stone or nearly solid subsoil. The north–south highway actually passes along a corridor of scrub for most of its length.

As one approaches the Top End, increased precipitation allows some increased variety of plant life. Immediately north of Lake Woods the vegetation changes to scrub and by Daly Waters patchy low eucalypts have appeared. Fauna on the windward, western side of the peninsula tends towards eucalypt, that in Arnhem Land tends towards scrub and cypress pine. Within 300km of the coast, larger eucalypts dominate. Those on the coast become a fairly dense forest. There are any number of exceptions to this pattern. A large section of eastern Arnhem Land, for instance, is barely wooded despite having conditions virtually identical to the surrounding areas.

Spinifex

Spinifex is a characteristic tussock grass growing throughout the arid interior of Australia. The term, which literally means 'thorn-maker', most correctly refers to three species of maritime grasses which range widely across Asia and Australasia, but the more popular usage refers to grasses of the genus *Triodia*. Of the 30-odd species of this genus, *T. basedownii* (lobed spinifex), *T. pungens* (spinifex) and *T. irritans* (porcupine grass) are the most noteworthy. The former grows in tussocks 30cm to 1m in circumference and, like most *Triodia*, presents irritating prickles. More mature plants can be recognised by their hollow centre. Its fibrous grass blades can be 2m long. It produces seeds in the spring and these erect oat-like inflorescences are a major food source, fattening range horses.

Spinifex's resinous nature makes them highly inflammable. Aboriginal methods of land care involve burning off the spinifex in late spring. The resin is also used as a hafting glue for their spear and axe heads. Porcupine grass is less a monoculture plant and extends as far south as Victoria among mixed grasses. In fact a number of species are commonly called porcupine grass.

History of exploration

The Territory's arid conditions inclined its history to one of exploration rather than settlement. Like their exploration elsewhere in Australia, the Dutch kept their charts secret. Arnhem Land (the northeastern area of Northern Territory, now Aboriginal Land Trust) is the namesake of the Dutch yacht captained by Willem van Coolsteerdt who visited briefly in 1623. The first substantial exploration, however, was during Tasman's 1644 coastal voyage from Cape York to Western Australia. Failing to find an expeditious route to their Spice Islands, in what is now Indonesia, the Dutch lost interest.

Flinders charted the coast in the Gulf of Carpentaria in 1802–03. Unfortunately, his ship, the *Investigator*, was in such poor condition that he was only able to make a detailed survey of the eastern coast of Arnhem Land. The remainder of the Northern Territory was charted by Australia's second great cartographer, **Phillip Parker King**. King visited the area between Cape Arnhem and Cape Leeuwin in Western Australia during his four-year-long voyage between 1818 and 1822. Curiously, he did miss Port

Darwin. King pressed for the settlement of the Northern Territory.

Exploration by land was similarly late. Explorer **Ludwig Leichhardt** travelled from Brisbane to the Gulf and northeast across Arnhem Land in 1845. He returned to a celebrity's welcome in Sydney after a 14-month absence. A.C. Gregory followed much the same route in reverse. Starting near the Western Australian border in 1855, he proceeded south first until desert conditions forced him to retrace his steps. By mid-1856 he had crossed the Top End, found his ship had not met the expedition as planned, and proceeded to the east coast.

In 1859 J. McDouall Stuart began his efforts to cross the continent from south to north. He required five attempts. The first ended in retreat from aptly named Attack Creek about halfway through the Territory. When the second ended in scrubland 100 miles further north, he wrote, 'The plains and forest are as great a barrier as if there had been an inland sea or a wall built around.' He succeeded in his last effort, reaching the Top End in 1862 after a ten-month slog.

In the early 1870s a number of expeditions crossed to and from the western coast to McDouall Stuart's line. Their reports ended speculation about the hoped-for arable centre, inland sea, or navigable interior rivers. In reality, the looked-for inland sea is an exaggeration of the infrequently filled salt lakes in central South Australia; when filled by greater than average rainfalls, these lakes indeed become luxuriant and are brimming with wildlife.

History of settlement

Early attempts to settle the Territory were futile. The first settlements, Fort Dundas on Melville Island and at Raffles Bay, were meant to provide an alternative to the Dutch ports which imposed heavy duties. Both were abandoned in 1829 due to tropical diseases, hostile local Aborigines and Timor pirates.

Port Essington fared somewhat better. Founded in 1838 in Barrow Bay, it lay so far off the beaten track that visitors could be counted individually. They did include French sailors in a pair of corvettes under Commodore Dumont d'Urville in 1839; Commander J.C. Wickham aboard the *Beagle* that same year; naturalist John Gilbert was stranded there for a time in 1840 after a cyclone damaged his ship; and Ludwig Leichhardt used it as the westernmost point of his exploration in 1845–46. The settlement was abandoned in 1849.

Significantly, the first settlement after South Australia accepted responsibility for the Northern Territory in 1863, a mismanaged mosquito-infested swamp named **Escape Cliffs**, failed as well. Former British army officer Boyle Travers Finniss had established it at the mouth of the Adelaide River. John McKinlay, leader of the search for Burke and Wills, described it prior to its abandonment in 1866, saying, 'A greater sense of waste and desolation is unimaginable. As a seaport and a city this place is worthless.'

By 1859, following the formation of Queensland and Victoria, the map of Australia gave New South Wales administrative responsibility for an awkward area north and west of South Australia. To solve this discontinuity, either Queensland or South Australia had to be given governance of the Northern Territory.

In 1860 it was very nearly named Albert Territory and given to Queensland to administer. Despite A.C. Gregory's expedition across the north in 1855–56, the Queensland government was too busy to bother with the opportunity. South Australian governor Richard MacDonnell became interested largely as a result of McDouall Stuart's reports. For reasons that may have made sense at the time, Queensland's western border was inset about 300km from the South Australian border. Perhaps this three degrees latitude change had something to do with a three-degree addition to South Australia's western border?

The first town destined for success in the Northern Territory was **Palmerston**, eventually called Port Darwin, then Darwin. John Lort Stokesnamed Port Darwin after his former ship mate Charles Darwin during a visit to the area in 1839 aboard the *Beagle*. George Goyder, as South Australian Surveyor-General, had read Stokes's journals and established Palmerston at this location in 1869. It may be unfair to suggest that its success depended upon the Overland Telegraph Line. Suffice it to say, this line necessitated settlements north from South Australia to the Timor Sea.

Construction of the **Overland Telegraph Line** (OTL) deserves description. By 1870 a telegraph service extended across Europe and Asia and Australia desperately needed to establish direct communication. At best, land mail took ten weeks to convey. Proposals to replace the expensive and slow Peninsular and Oriental Steam Navigation Company with a cable terminus at Northwest Cape, Western Australia, or at Normanton on the Queensland coast were flawed by both the extent of undersea cable and the distance from Australia's populated southeast.

The South Australian Parliament loaned £120,000 to the OTL; the British-Australian Telegraph Company agreed that all of the Australian revenues would be paid to the OTL but that the line must be completed in 18 months. Recalling that it took McDouall Stuart ten months, it is hardly a surprise that the telegraph company insisted upon substantial penalties for non-compliance.

Charles Todd (1826–1905) was put in charge of the project. As (Astronomical) Observer and Superintendent of Telegraph for South Australia, he was an enthusiastic proponent of the undertaking. He had already successfully run the line from Adelaide to Sydney. Subsequent to the line to Darwin, he organised one to Eucla at the South Australian border with Western Australia, establishing direct communication with the entire continent. He also outfitted the Western Australian astronomical observatory. Upon Federation, his postal and telegraph service in South Australia was found to be the only one in the country to operate at a profit.

Construction of the telegraph line proceeded along three sections simultaneously. E.M. Bagot contracted for the southern portion through settled country between Port Augusta and the Macumba River near Charlotte Waters. Five government parties working on the central section made a number of discoveries along their way, the most important being reliable water sources for the relay stations. Among these was Alice Springs, named after Todd's wife, Alice Gillam. The settlement's river, usually dry, was also named in honour of Todd himself.

Construction of the northern section, however, was hampered by monsoons. The initial contractors proceeded south as far as Katherine River before the rains prevented supplies coming to them. The government's overseer cancelled the contract just as the wet season ended. By the time he had sailed to Adelaide and returned with six ships full of workers and supplies, the rains had returned. After a visit to the area, Todd put railway engineer R.C. Patterson in charge of the frantic effort to complete the line.

The submarine cable reached Port Darwin from Banjuwangi in Java in late June 1872. South Australia's line, however, had only reached Daly Waters. The 380km gap to Tennant Creek was crossed by pony express for the first message on 23 June 1872. A problem with the undersea cable delayed normal communication until late October. The land line had been completed on 22 August 1872, eight months into the penalty clauses in the original contract.

In our era of radio communication it is difficult to gauge the effect of this first iron line. Even with this telegraphic link to the continent, communication was not instantaneous. Because of the necessary repeater stations, it took two days for a signal to be passed. Among the nine such stations along the OTL, those in the Northern Territory were established as the first continuous presence of European society in the inland regions of the continent. The line itself was a landmark for subsequent surveyors, particularly those from Western Australia. Telegraphic communication between Melbourne and Sydney began in 1858, between Sydney and Adelaide in 1867, and between Adelaide and Perth in 1877.

After the Overland Telegraph Line was established, little of historical note occurred in the Territory until Federation. Chinese labour was used during the 1880s to mine gold, but immigration restrictions imposed at the end of the decade resulted in a decline in this population. Some cattle industry started in the Barkly Tableland, but tick fever and drought reduced the industry.

In 1909, the Commonwealth bought the Northern Territory's development loans and railroads from South Australia. Under federal administration Palmerston was renamed **Darwin**. A census conducted at the time counted 3310 people of non-Aboriginal descent in the Territory. Scottish veterinarian Dr J.A. Gilruth was appointed in 1912 as the first Territorial Administrator. His lack of judgement and fairness provoked a stop-work union meeting at the Vestry meatworks in Darwin at which they voted to boycott the state hotels to protest against the price rise for bottled beer. Following the meeting, hundreds of workers marched on government house where they burnt Gilruth in effigy. The central importance of **beer** in the life of Territorians had already been established.

More ready access to the Territory came in the 1930s. Air travel to Europe began in 1934, necessitating fuelling stops in Darwin or Daly Waters. But the construction of the Alice Springs-to-Darwin section of the Stuart Highway had an even greater effect. Under David D. Smith, the road was constructed largely by manual labour supplied by camel train. When reprimanded for exceeding his budget to straighten and widen sections, his defence was 'Too bloody bad!' His anticipation that war would shortly start and that the improved road would be required proved correct. He was put in charge of its upgrade and sealing in 1943.

Camels

Camels came to Australia as draft animals from the Canary Islands in 1840, but did not become a major import until the 1860s. In 1860, 24 of them arrived from India for use on the Burke and Wills expedition. The first serious camel stud was at Thomas Elder's station at Beltana, South Australia. This station, by the way, was the basis for the multinational firm Elders IXL. Between the 1860s and 1907, imports may have been as many as 12,000 head despite a number of breeding herds in Australia. The camel herdsmen were imported as well. These 'Afghans', as Australians would have the term, came from throughout western Asia, but predominantly from Peshawar in present-day Pakistan.

The caravans supplying stations and settlements beyond the railheads were generally comprised of 40 camels under four handlers. They routinely covered about 40km per day; the camels carried around 500kg each, depending on the breed. They were tremendously important to the exploration and development of vast areas of the inland. As late as 1912, they were used as water-carriers for the building of the Trans-Australian Railway, and were still used as pack animals in the 1930s. As motor transport came to dominate, camels were simply left to run wild in the outback. A current resurgence in interest in camel-raising is due to their relatively unobtrusive effect on semi-arid pasturage.

The Japanese attack on Pearl Harbour caused the evacuation of women and children from Darwin. The first of about 60 bombings of Darwin during the **Second World War** occurred on 19 February 1942. It was the most effective of the war, resulting in 10 ships being sunk in Darwin harbour, 250 individuals killed and 320 injured. During the war nearly half of the town's buildings were damaged. Darwin was the only place in Australia to be repeatedly attacked by the Japanese. It is this period, 1937–43, that author Xavier Herbert treats in his epic novel *Poor Fellow My Country* (1975). Herbert had earlier written *Capricornia* (1938), the name he gave to Northern Australia; here he describes the Territory's history as 'more bloody than that of the others'.

The one great improvement to come out of the war was the sealed roads from the south and the east, and improved communications with the rest of the country. Since the Second World War, the Northern Territory has developed in terms of pastoral and mining industry, although the population still remained small. Darwin came to world attention in 1974, when, on Christmas Day, Cyclone Tracy destroyed most of the town, killing 66 people and leaving thousands homeless. The evacuation of these survivors by Qantas Airlines, with 674 passengers on one flight, still ranks as one of the largest mass air evacuations in history. Within four years, Darwin had been completely rebuilt.

Today, the Territory's greatest industry, and a booming one, is tourism, as it is the gateway to the 'real' Australia: the **Red Centre**, the outback, the beauties of **Kakadu** and **Uluru**. **Alice Springs**' population has grown from a little over 1000 in the 1950s to more than 20,000 entirely as a result of tourism. The benefits of this influx of new people and new ideas have been substantial, although the Territory's limited population still leads to its marginalisation in terms of Australian politics and mainstream affairs—a situation that leads to the sense of transience and difference that is part of the Territory's charm.

Darwin

Darwin (population 80,907) sits on the edge of the Timor Sea in the Northern Territory's coastal northwest. Much of its architectural history has been destroyed by cyclones, most notably those in 1897, 1937 and 1974. This fact, coupled with the city's proximity to Asia, has led to a major attitudinal transformation in the last 20 years. Darwin has become a racial melting pot, with its focus turned towards Asia; in many ways, as a recent article in the Sydney paper stated, Darwin 'has been transformed into a bustling, if small, South-East Asian town'. This may be a bit of an exaggeration, but the ethnic mix of the population certainly substantiates such a claim: the town is home to more than 60 ethnic groups, with mixed marriages quite common and intriguing cultural festivals emphasising these new combinations. The food markets dotted around the city offer the greatest evidence of Darwin's strong Asian flavour. It is important to remember that Timor is only one hour away by plane, and even Malaysia is a shorter distance than Sydney. Many of the city's businesses are owned by Indonesia's leading families, and the Sultan of Brunei owns three large cattle properties nearby. One-quarter of the Territory's small population is Aboriginal, a much higher ratio than anywhere else in Australia.

The image of Territorians as beer-swilling red-necks is becoming increasingly dated; as the Territory's former Chief Minister Shane Stone has said: 'It is the southern cities that have ethnic ghettos; we have one of the most free-flowing racial communities in the world.' With 25 being the average age in the city, Darwin does express a different outlook than the rest of the country: the tropical climate, and the isolated location, do contribute to a feeling at times of transience and 'no worries' inconsequentiality. The atmosphere of Darwin, in its various directions, can best be seen in the city's **Festival of Darwin**, held in August, and including plays, musical performances, art and other activities; and, most famously, in the **Beer Can Regatta**, also in August, with boats made entirely of beer cans.

▉ Practical information

Tourist information. **Northern Territory Government Tourist Bureau**, 31 Smith Street Mall, ☎ 08 8981 6611. Due to the relatively sparse population, a number of functions located in individual cities are coordinated by territorial administration, including **Parks and Wildlife** (☎ 08 8999 5511), **Museums and Art Galleries** (☎ 08 8999 8201), and the **Northern Territory Tourist Commission** (☎ 08 8999 3900 or toll free 1800 621 336). For information on arranging tours of the city, its environs or the national parks and land trusts, contact the **Northern Territory Holiday Centre** (☎ 1800 808 244). The summer rains preclude touring many outlying venues between about November and April.

Airport. All flights to the Territory arrive at Darwin Airport, 12km northwest of the city centre. Airport shuttle buses (☎ 08 8981 5066) take you to your hotel or to the central Transit Centre, 69 Mitchell Street.

As the closest Australian city to Asia, Darwin offers regular flights to Asian destinations, and at prices that are much cheaper than those to the rest of Australia. Check out connections with *Malaysian Airlines* (☎ 13 2627) to Singapore; and *Merpati Nusantaran* (☎ 08 8941 1606) for flights to Bali and Kupang. *Ansett Airlines* (☎ 08 8962 2355) also provides one-way cheap backpacker flights from here to Broome and Kununurra.

Bus. **Interstate buses** also arrive at the Mitchell Street Transit Centre, and involve gruelling journeys. *Greyhound-Pioneer* (☎ 13 2030) provides interstate services, passes, and connecting buses.

The **city bus service** is relatively inexpensive and reasonably convenient, running to the many suburbs of Darwin, and as far as Palmerston and Humpty Doo, 50km out on the Kakadu Road. The bus kiosk is located on Harry Chan Avenue. Information is available on ☎ 08 8924 7666.

Taxi. Service is reasonably priced and readily available. Call *Darwin Radio Taxi*, 15 Finniss Street, Stuart Park (☎ 13-1008; 08 8981 8777).

Boat. Darwin Harbour, twice the size of Sydney Harbour, is worth a cruise. *Mandorah Jet Shuttle* (☎ 08 8981 7600) operates high-speed ferries every day across the harbour to the beach at Mandorah. *Harbour Safaris* (☎ 08 8981 7600) also provides regular services around the harbour and to the seaside resort of Mandova; and *Darwin Duchess Cruises* (☎ 08 8978 5094) leaves Stokes Hill Wharf at 14.00 Wed–Sun for a two-hour cruise.

Useful addresses
Post Office, Cavenagh Street.
Hospital: Royal Darwin, Rocklands Drive, Casuarina, ☎ 08 8922 8888.
Police: Emergency ☎ 000 or 08 8927 8888; Headquarters, Peter McAulay Centre, ☎ 08 8922 3344; City, Mitchell Street, ☎ 08 8999 6666; Federal Police, 21 Lindsay Street, ☎ 08 8981 1044.
Consulates: Indonesia, 18 Harry Chan Avenue, ☎ 08 8941 0048.

The town
Darwin's earliest surviving buildings are the **Fannie Bay Gaol Museum** (1883), several kilometres north on Smith Point Road; the **Victoria Hotel** (1890), Smith Street on the mall; and the old **courthouse** and **police station** (1884) at the end of Smith Street on Esplanade. In fact, these buildings are not as interesting as those designed in the late 1930s by B.C.G. Burnett (see below). **Admiralty House** (open Mon–Sat 10.00–17.00) on the southeast corner of Knuckey Street and Esplanade remains from the 1930s as do some houses on Myilly Point.

Nearly all of the dwellings and most of the commercial and governmental buildings were destroyed when Cyclone Tracy struck on Christmas Day in 1974. Heroic efforts by emergency services prevented widespread tragedy. In the end 49 people died as an immediate result of the storm rather than in its aftermath. The town was rebuilt, another heroic effort, with marked respect for the inevitable cyclones making the architecture somewhat blockish.

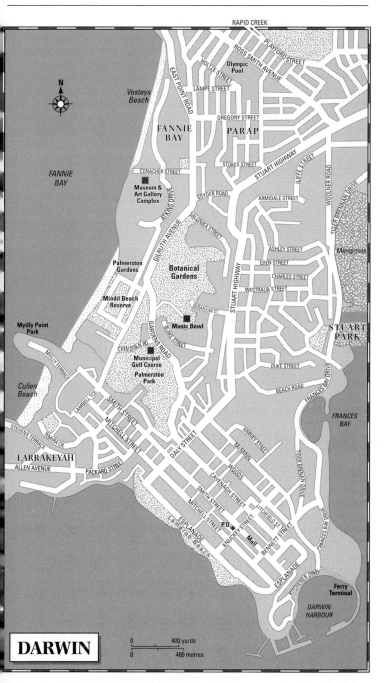

DARWIN

RAPID CREEK

PLAYFORD STREET
ROSS SMITH AVENUE
HOLTZE STREET
Olympic Pool
LAMPE STREET

East Point Road

Vesteys Beach

GREGORY STREET

FANNIE BAY

PARAP

FANNIE BAY

STOKES STREET
STUART HIGHWAY
ILIFFE STREET
WOOLNER ROAD

CONACHER STREET

GOYDER ROAD

ARMIDALE STREET

Museum & Art Gallery Complex

Atkins Drive

Salonika Street

Gilruth Avenue

TIGER BRENNAN DRIVE

Mangroves

Palmerston Gardens

Botanical Gardens

ASHLEY STREET
EDEN STREET
CHARLES STREET
WESTRALIA STREET

Mindil Beach Reserve

GERANIUM ST

Myilly Point Park

Gardens Road

Black Street

Music Bowl

STUART PARK

Cullen Beach

CHIN QUAN RD

Municipal Golf Course
Palmerston Park

DUKE STREET

Myilly Terrace

Lambell Tce

BEACH ROAD

Frances Bay Drive

Stevens Terrace

Temira Cr

SMITH STREET

MITCHELL STREET

DALY STREET

FRANCES BAY

LARRAKEYAH

ALLEN AVENUE

PACKARD STREET

HARVEY STREET

McMINN

WOODS

CAVENAGH STREET

Smith Street

Mitchell Street

Knuckey Street

LITCHFIELD ST

Bennett Street

Tiger Brennan Drive

ESPLANADE

Lameroo Beach

P.O.

Mall

ESPLANADE

KITCHENER DRIVE

Frances Bay Drive

Ferry Terminal

DARWIN HARBOUR

N

| 0 | 400 yards |
| 0 | 400 metres |

House at Myilly Point, Darwin

The city is fairly small and quite flat. Bicycles are readily hired and the bike paths are well maintained. The STUART HIGHWAY enters Darwin proper from the northeast, becoming Daly Street. Wharves and marinas are south and east of the city centre. To the north of Daly Street along EAST POINT ROAD are Palmerston Park, the golf course, Mindil Beach Reserve, the Botanic Gardens and the museum and art gallery. The city centre has a large pedestrian mall with governmental buildings mostly to its south near the harbour. An esplanade skirts the beaches.

The **Botanic Gardens** (☎ 08 8981 1958; open daily 08.30–17.00) are immediately north of the city centre and accessible by car off the Stuart Highway on Geranium Street or by **bus no. 10** to Casuarina or **no. 8** to Palmerston from the city centre to Tucker Hut Inn and left at the next corner. The gardens were started by Maurice Holtze, a German hired in the 1870s to establish a fruit and vegetable plantation. Not surprisingly, Cyclone Tracy ravaged the garden's trees and shrubs, but the tropical collection has since been admirably re-established. The new water fountain and its incredible cubbyhouse in a fallen tree are recommended by visiting children.

The **National Trust**'s office (☎ 08 8981 2848, open daily 10.00–17.00) is in Burnett House at the edge of the Myilly Point historic district immediately south of Mindil Beach. Although Cyclone Tracy destroyed nearly all of the domestic buildings in Darwin, this district's dwellings from the 1930s were largely spared. Beni Carr Glynn Burnett, an architect who had worked for some years in China, came to Darwin in 1937 as the Territory's Principal Architect. He designed the houses on this elevated point to take advantage of the sea breezes. The houses are elevated and have louvres for their casement windows. The internal walls are three-quarters height and have lower louvres as well as openings in the eaves. In addition to the National Trust in Burnett House, another Burnett-designed house on Burnett Place is open as a gallery and cafe.

Mindil Beach Reserve (bus nos 4 or 6) is best visited on Thursday night during the dry season for its elaborate market and food stalls. The al fresco cuisine is unsurpassed and the atmosphere worth the trip itself. Similar food stall markets are found on Saturday morning at the **Parap market** (further north, bus no. 6), on Sunday morning in **Rapid Creek** (a suburb north of the airport which hosts the Mindil market during the Wet, bus no. 4) and in the central **Smith Street mall** every evening except Thursday. On the beach is an interesting bamboo-and-cane sculpture by Hortensia Masero, created for the **Festival of Darwin**, which takes place every August.

The **Museum and Art Gallery** (☎ 08 8999 8201, 08 8899 6573; open week-days 09.00–17.00, weekends 10.00–17.00, free) is in an oceanside park north of Mindil Beach Reserve off East Point Road. It has a remarkably good collection representing regional Aboriginal and Torres Strait Island culture, an ambitious maritime display presenting a number of vessels. The natural history display includes a graphic description of Cyclone Tracy's effects and the national response to the devastation it wreaked. Local pride in the ethnic community is expressed, particularly in a display of a Malaysian *prahu* (a marine houseboat) and a Japanese pearling lugger. The museum also administers the Australian Pearling Exhibition, located directly on the left upon entering the Stokes Hill Wharf. In addition to a video describing pearl oyster farming, its displays feature the early history of pearling in the region.

Day trips from Darwin

The **Darwin Regional Tourism Association** (☎ 08 8945 3386) is in the mall at 33 Smith Street. The **Northern Territory Parks and Wildlife** (☎ 08 8999 5511) maintains a desk here as well. The **Darwin Bushwalking Club** (☎ 08 8985 1484) welcomes visitors and offers advice on walking tracks in Litchfield National Park and Kakadu, among others.

Day trips from Darwin include visits to **Litchfield National Park** (☎ 08 8976 0282, 115km south); flights to **Peppimenarti** (☎ 08 8981 1633), a small cattle-raising outstation community of Kintyirri, an Aboriginal group well known as weavers; and to the Tiwi people (☎ 08 981 5115) on **Melville** and **Bathurst Islands**. Longer tours to Peppimenarti and to Manyallaluk (☎ 08 975 4727, near Katherine Gorge) are available. The Northern Territory Tourist Commission in Darwin (☎ 08 999 3900) has considerable information on these and other organised Aboriginal cultural experiences.

Bathurst and Melville Islands

Tours conducted by the **Tiwi** are the only means of visiting Bathurst and Melville Islands. The traditions on the islands are still quite intact, largely due to the Tiwi's independent character. They had a history of hostility towards the Macassan who came to fish for trepang (sea cucumbers) from Sulawesi, formerly the Celebes, as early as the 17C. Their relations with the British who attempted settlements at Fort Dundas and Raffles Bay were cool as well. Both settlements were abandoned in 1829. In the late 1890s, Joe Cooper and Paddy Cahill hunted buffalo on Melville Island. They were chased off, but Cooper eventually returned to live there for 16 years. Initially, the Catholic Church mission on Bathurst Island received little support, reputedly because the Tiwi were suspicious of priests without wives.

Tiwi Tours (☎ 08 8941 0224) fly from Darwin to Nguiu on Bathurst Island to visit the Catholic mission's buildings and a craft workshop. Then tourists are ferried across the narrow Apsley Strait to Melville Island, the more traditional of the two islands, for a visit to the pukumani burial site. The burials are marked by poles which are painted, carved and erected as part of the final funerary cere-mony in which the spirit of the deceased is released.

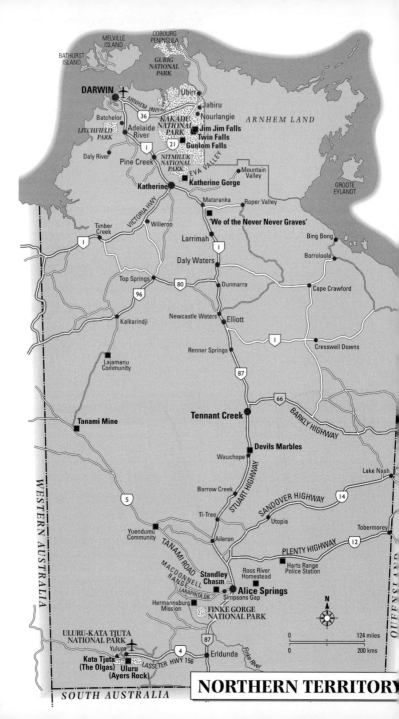

NORTHERN TERRITORY

Litchfield National Park

Litchfield National Park is less than two hours' drive (115km) south of Darwin on the STUART HIGHWAY. Its proximity to Darwin makes it a local favourite, so the park can be somewhat crowded on holiday weekends.

Sandstone cliffs at the edge of a plateau separate the park's two major ecological areas and produce a number of spectacular waterfalls. Atop the plateau is an open eucalypt forest, and there are pockets of rainforest throughout the park. Below the escarpment is a black soil wetlands noted for speargrass of the *Aristida* genus, a tall bright green grass in growth and a pleasant straw colour during the dry season. Florence, Tolmer and Wangi Falls are the most accessible of the park's waterfalls.

Shortly after entering the park from the east, via the town of **Batchelor**, a display and boardwalk present the flood plain and **magnetic termite mounds**. These termites have built above-ground nests as an adaptation to the high water table and flooding during the summer. The wedge shape and north–south orientation of the mounds are to cope with daily temperature changes. At night the insects congregate in the middle of their mound; during the day they move to its cooler eastern side.

Beyond the mounds the road climbs the escarpment at Aida Creek Jump-up. About 6km along is the turn-off to **Florence Falls**. Here a boardwalk suitable for wheelchair access leads to a spectacular lookout. Below, the exuberant rainforest and a swimming hole at the end of the steep path to the cascade's bottom make this an attractive stop. About 9km from Florence Falls is **Tabletop Swamp**, a good wetland for bird watching and a picnic site. A number of the park's sites are along tracks accessible to experienced drivers of all-terrain vehicles. The most notable is arguably the **Lost City**, a jumble of natural sandstone pillars and blocks.

Tolmer Falls, about 14km beyond Florence Falls, has a good boardwalk, providing wheelchair access to its view as well. The cascade and pools immediately around its base are inaccessible to protect a number of bat species nesting here. The most popular site in the park is **Wangi Falls** (pronounced wong guy). These flow strongly year round and cascade into a large pool which is suitable for swimming except during periods of high water.

Kakadu National Park

Kakadu and **Uluru** (see p 600) are World Heritage Sites for their natural setting and association with Australia's Aboriginal traditions. The land rights of the associated Aboriginal communities are recognised in both cases, each area being governed by its traditional owners.

Kakadu National Park (☎ 08 8938 1120) encompasses nearly all of the South Alligator River system, 22,000 sq km in all. Its World Heritage Listing in 1984 came as a result of the second stage of its formation. In 1979, the eastern and central sections of the park were ceded. These had been the Woolwonga and Alligator River wildlife sanctuaries, set aside in 1969 and 1972. Finally, in 1991, the southern sections were listed. Some of this area is being claimed by the Jawoyn people in adjacent Katherine Gorge. Should they be awarded the claim, they will receive financial benefits and representation on the board of management.

History

Captain Philip King was the first European to enter the area. During three voyages between 1818 and 1822 to complete Matthew Flinders' exploration, he travelled up the East and South Alligator Rivers. He named the rivers, mistaking the local crocodiles for alligators. Ludwig Leichhardt crossed the Arnhem Plateau and South Alligator River on his exhausting 14-month-long trip from the Darling Downs in Queensland to Port Essington.

A short-lived gold rush to Pine Creek, immediately southwest of the park, and the first pastoral leases in the area brought some Europeans here in the late 1870s. From the 1890s to the present, feral water buffalo were hunted at first for skins and since the 1950s for sport. These animals are the descendants of those released upon the abandonment of military settlements at Raffles Bay and Port Essington on the Cobourg Peninsula and from Escape Cliffs.

Baldwin Spencer (see box) was the first anthropologist to describe the Aboriginal culture of the area. In a visit to Oenpelli on the Arnhem Land plateau in 1912, he described a nearby rock art site:

The slanting roofs and sides [of the rock shelter] were one mass of native drawings, precisely similar to those done on bark, but here, the rocks had been blackened for long years by the smoke of countless camp fires and the drawings, most of them fishes, had been superimposed on one another, the brighter colours of the more recent ones standing out clearly on the darker background.

Subsequent work by anthropologists N. B. Tindale and, most notably, by Charles P. Mountford in the 1920s and 1930s brought the region's art to the attention of an international community. The 1954 UNESCO World Art Series was possibly the first to disseminate widely Aboriginal images to the world at large.

Uranium was discovered in Kakadu in 1953 and four large deposits were found in the early 1970s. The very real dangers the proposed mines pose was controlled until the recent Liberal government put aside the previous Three Mines policy. Fortunately, the prevailing low price of uranium makes development a legally symbolic gesture rather than a fiscally prudent operation.

Baldwin Spencer

Sir Walter Baldwin Spencer (1860–1929) began his career as a biologist, after graduating from Oxford and being appointed to the professorship of biology in Melbourne in 1886. Spencer's indefatigable curiosity and scholarly energy led him to join the first expedition of Central Australia, under W.A. Horn, in 1894. Here he met the remarkable F.J. Gillen (1855–1912), a government employee who had steeped himself in knowledge of the Central Desert's Aborigines, their language and their customs. Gillen was called 'Oknirrabata', or 'great teacher', by the Aranda tribe. Spencer and Gillen began the first in-depth anthropological study of these tribes, producing in 1899 the ground-breaking *Native Tribes of Central Australia*. Spencer continued his academic duties in Melbourne, while carrying out additional field-work in the Northern Territory in 1901 with Gillen, identifying previously unknown Aboriginal tribes and languages; these studies resulted in the book *The Northern Tribes of Central Australia* (1904). In that same year, Spencer became President of the Board of the University of Melbourne, and in 1911, he was asked by the Commonwealth Government to lead an expedition into the Northern Territory to enquire into conditions of the Aboriginal inhabitants; his report, again with Gillen, was the two-volume *Across Australia* (1911), another pioneering achievement.

In 1912 Spencer became Chief Protector of Aborigines and in that capacity carried out further exploration of unknown tribes and outback regions. Throughout the 1920s, he continued to publish important works on Aboriginal life and customs. In that decade, he turned his attention to the study of the natives of Tierra del Fuego; on an expedition there in 1929, at the age of 69, he died. While much of Spencer's work has certainly received critical revision in subsequent anthropological studies, his initial achievement in identifying Aboriginal material culture, languages, and social customs remain as an extraordinary accomplishment, and established the discipline of anthropology in Australia.

Flora and fauna

The park contains four major landforms: the Koolpinyah plains, the coastal riverine plains, the Arnhem Land plateau and escarpment, and some southern hills.

Extending from Darwin to the Arnhem Land escarpment, the **Koolpinyah Plains** are gently undulating Late Tertiary deposits of heavily weathered Mesozoic sediments. Comprised of gravels, sands and clays, the soils at the surface are relatively infertile, having been leached of minerals and alkali earths. Accumulations of iron and aluminium further reduce the fertility. The proliferation of iron creates the characteristic ironstone found as broken pavements or outcrops at the headwaters of creeks. The associated stands of tall trees are the Darwin stringybark and Darwin woolybutt eucalypts, with an understorey of ironwood and green plum, pandanus palms and extensive and fast-growing tall grasses, the most prevalent being spear grass. The more prevalent lowland forests grow on heavier, less well-drained soil. The eucalypts here are markedly stunted and scattered amid sparse shrub and annual grasses.

This habitat supports a variety of wallaby and wallaroo, as well as nocturnal sugar gliders, brushtail possums and quolls. A variety of skinks are routinely sighted as are sand goannas. The well-known frilly-necked lizard, though present, is elusive. Bird species include lorikeets, yellow-tailed and red-tailed black cockatoos, rainbow bee-eaters and a variety of kingfishers.

In addition to the gentle slope northward to the sea, two other features of these plains are sinkholes forming seasonal or permanent bodies of water and, of course, the five rivers in the park. These flow strongly during the seasonal rains and dry out to a string of billabong wetlands by the end of the dry season in their inland reaches. The most accessible **wetland areas** are Mamukala a few kilometres east of the South Alligator River; Yellow Water and associated billabongs near the Warradjan Cultural Centre; and Ubirr in the northeastern part of the park. Their signal trees are broadleaf and weeping paperbark eucalypts, freshwater mangroves, pandanus and water lilies.

In addition to endemic species, the less commonly seen magpie geese, shining flycatchers and black-necked storks frequent these freshwater wetlands.

The coastal riverine plains tend to be black organic clays associated with tidal or flood plain estuaries on the Magela, Nourlangie and Jim Jim Creeks and the South Alligator River. Most of these areas are flooded four months of the year, some as many as nine months. Like the Kimberley region in northern Western Australia, the tides here are remarkable. The 5- to 6m rises in the spring extend 105km upstream on the South Alligator River. The associated coastal monsoon rainforests are marked by banyan, kapok and milkwood trees.

The geological history of this landform dates from the end of the last ice age. About 14,000 years ago the sea level was some 150m below the present level and the shoreline was more than 300km north. By 6800 years ago, the sea level was more or less as it is currently. During the next 500 years, mangroves developed along the rivers until sedimentation reduced the marine effects upriver and fresh-water swamps and wetlands began to appear. This process continued until quite recently, the Magela flood plain being formed as recently as 1300 years ago.

The **Arnhem Land Plateau and Escarpment** is of quartz sandstone with drops of up to 330m to the adjoining plains. Largely confined to inaccessible areas in the park's southeast, it is more readily viewed at Katherine River Gorge. Soil is absent from large areas of the plateau, sand deposits being interspersed above the Cretaceous bedrock. Eucalypt woodland is interspersed with spinifex grasslands and scrubby heath. Acacia and grevillea blossom in the early dry and throughout the wet season. Associated animal life includes Pamela's and Jewelled velvet geckos, skinks, white-throated grass wrens and chestnut quilled rock pigeons. Both birds are unique to the area. As elsewhere along Australia's coastal regions, the white-bellied sea eagle is an important predator of the smaller marsupials.

The joints, faults and dykes of the Arnhem Land Plateau make the plain act as a major aquifer from which the South Alligator and Mary Rivers spring. The permanent springs in the gorges create monsoon rainforests of evergreen allo-syncarpia. During the dry season these areas are well frequented by bird species. Those largely confined to the park and its immediate surrounds are the rainbow pitta, orange footed scrubfowl and the Torresian imperial pigeon.

Aboriginal history
Archaeological evidence suggests that Aboriginal people came to Kakadu between 40,000 and 60,000 years ago, the latter figure being the more likely. They would have come in the late Pleistocene period from the Indonesian arch-ipelago. Archaeologists debate the circumstances of the earliest arrivals, basi-cally relating fluctuations in sea levels with methods of dating which use radio-carbon and optically stimulated luminescence. If the Aboriginal population crossed during low sea levels around 70,000 years ago, the crossing would have been between 60 and 100km. If rising sea levels had provided impetus to develop watercraft, the most likely date would have been about 60,000 years ago or later across distances not unlike those existing at present.

By 20,000 years ago the Kakadu residents were making sophisticated stone tools including one of humankind's earliest examples of hafted edge-ground axes. From about 8500 to 7000 years ago the sea level rose, forcing the popula-tion off the coastal region onto the Arnhem Land plateau during a period of increased rainfall. The current flood plain developed between 4000 and 1500 years ago. In the last 1000 years the Aboriginal population increased dramati-cally as they became adept at using the resources of this freshwater environ-ment. Immediately prior to European contact, the area now defined as Kakadu Park probably supported 2000 people.

The **rock art** in Kakadu follows a typical sequence for indigenous art in Australia. Large quantities of ochre have been found around rock shelters which date to as early as 20,000 years ago, suggesting that the same people who made the edge-ground axes decorated their walls as well. Images from the immediate post-glacial period of rising sea levels do exist. Chronology of the succeeding styles relate them to the effects of climate on the area's flora and fauna as well as the chemical changes in the pigments and rock surfaces.

George Chaloupka summarises the stylistic changes in Kakadu in the 'Rock Art of the Northern Territory' in *The Inspired Dream* (1988), a catalogue of an exhibition presented at the Queensland Art Gallery in Brisbane. The styles of rock paintings are grouped as pre-estuarine (before 8000 years ago), estuarine (8000 to 1500 years ago), freshwater (since 1500 years ago) and contact (following Macassan and European contact in the last 300 years). The greatest number of pre-estuarine art dates from 20,000 to 8000 years ago. Its earliest images are prints of hands followed by naturalistic depictions of kangaroos and wallabies at about 18,000 years ago. Interesting to palaeontologists, these images include now extinct megafauna (large echidnas and wombats). Later in this period the images present human activities such as men with hunting implements (boomerangs and hooked sticks) and women with digging and fire sticks and stone axes. Initially the style was quite representative and dynamic, but the depictions became increasingly stylised and abstracted. Towards the end of the period human and animal figures become more stylised. By the end of the pre-estuarine period, yam figures and the Rainbow Snake Being occur.

In common with the art of the Kimberley region (see p 577), **yam figures** become increasingly important in art, while human figures become more stylised as the rising sea levels forced the people further south. By about 8000 years ago the **Rainbow Serpent** begins to appear, indicating a new and unifying mythology coming to the area. Currently, the Rainbow Snake is associated with rain and floods in which the serpent rises from the sea and eats people. Fish are also increasingly depicted as the technology changes from hunting to fishing.

The **estuarine period** commenced during the climatic change at the end of the last ice age. Sea levels rose to isolate Australia from Papua New Guinea and Tasmania from the mainland and the current monsoon pattern emerged here in the north.

Once the **x-ray style** of depiction becomes prevalent (about 1500 to 1000 years ago), the freshwater period is fully established. Namarrgon, 'Lightning Man', also appears as the climate of the wet becomes the norm. During this period, the food sources of the Aboriginal population became truly aquatic. These foods were depicted in readily recognisable fashion and include jabirus, waterlilies, magpie geese and a number of fish. The didgeridoo is first depicted at this time.

The style of the rock art remains consistent throughout the freshwater period and into the **contact period**, the depiction of guns, ships and intro-duced animals being the first indication of this current period. Additionally, new colour sources such as Rickett's Blueing, a laundry product, become avail-able for use. Wax from Australian wild bees is used to model small images of animals and humans, which are then painted. These figures are called *kamou korngi* and are occasionally found adhering to the walls of rock art sites. Unlike the impression many people have of indigenous art, the more recent images are not drawn prior to food gathering as a means of ensuring success. Rather they are likely to be part of a religious ritual or undertaken at a moment of idleness.

Aboriginal calendar

While the European calendar divides the year into a dry winter, from May through September, and a wet summer, from November through March, not surprisingly, the Aboriginal people resident in Kakadu and the surrounding region have much finer distinctions for the seasons. The pre-monsoon storm season, **Gunumeleng**, begins in October when the humidity and temperature rises and spectacular thunderstorms begin; fruit trees are bearing at the beginning of this season. **Gudjewg**, the monsoon season, begins in late December and the water apple bears fruit in early January at the beginning of the heavy rains. By the end of the monsoon season about 1300mm of rain will have fallen. One year in ten will bring a cyclone. In February the plains are flooded, though some occasional fine hot spells can be expected. The magpie geese begin laying. The last of the storms begin in March at the onset of **Banggereng**. These come from the southeast and their strong winds knock down the tall seasonal grasses. A cooler, humid season begins in late April, **Yegge**. The green grasshoppers are calling, the yams are ready for harvest and the tourists start arriving in force. At the end of Yegge, in mid-June, it is time to start lighting fires to burn off the ground vegetation. This burn off causes spectacular sunsets. The woollybutt trees blossom at the start of **Wurrgeng**, a relatively cool weather season between mid-June and mid-August. By the start of **Gurrung**, mid-August, when the fruit trees begin blossoming, the weather has become hot and dry. A number of deciduous trees lose their leaves to preserve water. The blossoming of the water apple signals the end of this season.

Kakadu tour

Travel in the park is via the Arnhem Highway crossing west to east and the Kakadu Highway crossing southwest to northeast. The former runs more or less east to west for 247km between Darwin (its junction with the Stuart Highway is 43km south of Darwin) and the park's only town, **Jabiru**. The Kakadu Highway is diagonally southwest, northeast from Pine Creek on the Stuart Highway and the western areas of the Arnhem Land Aboriginal Land Trust. While these roads are sealed and passable in all seasons by two-wheel-drive vehicles, a number of secondary roads leading from them require four-wheel-drive, particularly in the wet season.

Entering the park after a rather uneventful 210km drive across a low eucalypt scrubland from Darwin, the first river crossed is the Wildman River. Shortly thereafter, a track north leads to popular fishing and camping sites at **Two Mile Water Hole** on this river, an 8km trip passable by conventional vehicles in the dry. A further 38km leads to **Four Mile Water Hole**, but this track is only passable by four-wheel-drive vehicles.

The next river crossed is the West Alligator, then its West and East branches. At about 37km into the park a track south leads to camp grounds at **Alligator Billabong** and **Red Lily**, **Bucket** and **Leichhardt Billabongs**. A four-wheel-drive road leads from Alligator Billabong to the Old Darwin Road near **Kunkamoula Billabong**. Even in the dry season, all of these tracks are difficult.

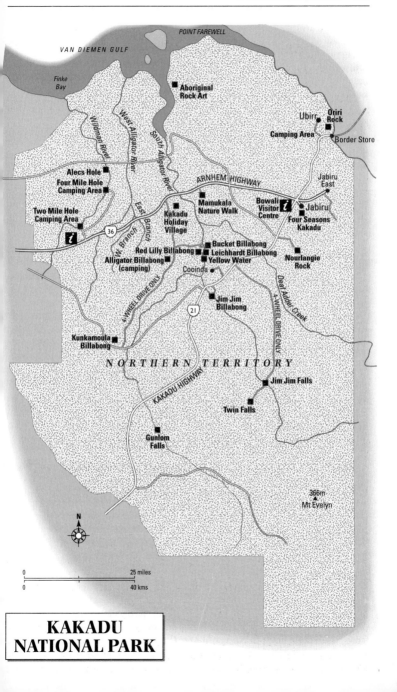

POINT FAREWELL

VAN DIEMEN GULF

Finke
Bay

Wildman River

West Alligator River

South Alligator River

East Br. Branch

N. Branch

Aboriginal
Rock Art

Ubirr
Oriri
Rock
Camping Area
Border Store

Jabiru
East

ARNHEM HIGHWAY

Alecs Hole
Four Mile Hole
Camping Area

Two Mile Hole
Camping Area

36

Mamukala
Nature Walk

Bowali
Visitor
Centre

Jabiru
Four Seasons
Kakadu

Kakadu
Holiday
Village

4-WHEEL DRIVE ONLY

Bucket Billabong
Red Lilly Billabong
Leichhardt Billabong
Alligator Billabong
(camping)
Yellow Water
Cooinda

Nourlangie
Rock

Deaf Adder Creek

4-WHEEL DRIVE ONLY

Jim Jim
Billabong

21

Kunkamoula
Billabong

N O R T H E R N   T E R R I T O R Y

KAKADU HIGHWAY

Jim Jim Falls

Twin Falls

Gunlom
Falls

366m
Mt Evelyn

N

| 0 | | 25 miles |
| 0 | | 40 kms |

KAKADU
NATIONAL PARK

Kakadu Holiday Village (☎ 08 8979 0166) is about 43km into the park, just west of the South Alligator River. About 10km beyond Kakadu Holiday Village a short way south of the highway is a favoured bird-watching area at **Mamukala**. Here a 3km easy walking trail with bird hides and an observation building allows access to the flood plain of the South Alligator River. The wetlands bird species of the park are plentiful here, especially in the dry season.

A second walk, the **Gu-ngarre Monsoon Rainforest Walk**, is somewhat shorter and passes through monsoon rainforest and woodlands. The pamphlet on Aboriginal plant use available from the Bowali Visitor's Centre makes possible plant identification along this easy walk.

The park headquarters and **Bowali Visitor's Centre** (☎ 08 8938 1121) is just beyond Gu-ngarre, 80km into the park at the junction of the Arnhem Highway from Darwin and the Kakadu Highway just west of **Jabiru**, the park's single town. This company town, with an airport, was built to service the adjacent **Ranger Uranium Mine**. In town is an Olympic-sized public swimming pool and a nine-hole golf course. The best published guides to the park are available at the Visitor's Centre. Also available here are schedules for the excellent **walking tours** of the rock art sites at Obiri Rock and Nourlangie Rock and of the areas around the major natural sites.

The **Gagudju Crocodile Hotel Kakadu**, Flinders Street, Jabiru (☎ 08 8979 2800/1 800 808 123, fax 08 8979 2707) is also known simply as the Crocodile Hotel for being shaped like a crocodile (you enter through its mouth). An Aboriginal-owned luxury hotel, its shape is a reference to the myths of the Gagudju people. Like the Crocodile Hotel, the Kakadu Frontier Lodge and Caravan Park (☎ 08 8979 2422) was designed with Gagudju advice which gave rise to its circular shape.

The track north from the park's information centre leads 43km to **Ubirr**, site of some of Australia's finest **rock art**. The art may be seen at the end of an easy 1km walk to **Obiri Rock**. The entire historical range of styles is evident here, including depictions of extinct thylacine (Tasmanian Tiger), stick figure spirits called mabuyu, x-ray-style brush-tailed wallabies and post-contact European figures. The Rainbow Serpent and Namarkan Sisters paintings have particularly interesting mythologies. Following a short, steep track to a lookout provides a view of the East Alligator River flood plain.

Other walks in the area are the **Manngarre Monsoon Rainforest Walk** (about an hour mostly on a boardwalk from the boat ramp downstream from the Border Store) and the **Bardedjilidji Sandstone Walk**. This latter walk is 2.5km long and starts from the car park near the upstream picnic area. It traverses some wetland areas and leads to sandstone formations geologically related to the escarpment.

The **Guluyambi River Trip** (☎ 1 800 089 113), which departs from the boat ramp below the Border Store, lasts about two hours. Aboriginal guides describe their relationship between the land and their culture. The fairly small boats make the trip seem quite personal and the guides are engaging.

Australia's most famous rock art gallery is at **Nourlangie**, 31km from the park's headquarters south off Kakadu Highway. Two galleries are open for view, one at Nourlangie and the other at Nanguluwur. A fairly easy 4km return walk from Nourlangie leads to **Nanguluwur Gallery**, a much less frequented site with significant post-contact images, as well as post-estuarine x-ray-style painting and hand stencils.

The principal site at Nourlangie is the **Anbangbang Rock Shelter**, which is 1.5km from the car park and wheelchair accessible. The mythical figures **Nabulwinjbulwinj**, **Namarrgon** (Lightning Man, an insect-like figure who produces lightning by striking rocks with axes protruding from his head and joints) and **Barrkinj** (Lightning Man's wife) at Anbangbang Rock were repainted in accordance with tradition in 1963–64. The famous realistic painting of a sailing ship with its trailing dinghy is at this site as well.

In addition to walks to the rock art sites, the area has a number of nature walks. **Nawulandja Look-out** is a short track uphill to overlook the Nourlangie Rock. The **Anbangbang Billabong** hosts a picnic area with a 2.5km track around the billabong. The **Barrk Sandstone Bushwalk** is a 12km, 6-hour strenuous walk to the top of Nourlangie Rock. In fact, it is the only long walk along marked trails in the park. Should you wish to take any other independent bushwalks, you are required to inform the rangers at the park headquarters of your itinerary.

Further south on the Kakadu Highway is the turn-off to **Jim Jim Falls**. Although the track leading to the falls requires four-wheel-drive and the short walk to the falls is something of a scramble over and around boulders near the base of the falls, the 215m cascade and swimming hole at their plunder pool are well frequented. Because the flow from the escarpment gradually lessens and even ceases as the dry period proceeds, the area is best visited as soon after the road reopens as possible. Even in the dry period of the year (The Dry), the surrounds and gorge at Jim Jim Falls are worth the effort.

Twin Falls, which can be counted on to flow through The Dry, is 10km further along and something of an adventure to reach. After fording Jim Jim Creek at the camp site (the sandy creek bed can mean the creek is deeper than the depth indicators suggest), follow a short walk from the car park. From here visitors must swim a few hundred meters through a monsoon forest gorge to the falls (an air mattress is a very pleasant means of covering the distance!). A fairly difficult path up the ravine at the right of the falls leads to a lookout from the edge of the escarpment at the top of the falls.

Yellow Water, 50km south of the park headquarters on the Kakadu Highway, is a wetlands near the juncture of Jim Jim Creek and the South Alligator River. The **Warradjan Cultural Centre** is along the way. The building is circular and its shape reminiscent of the pig nose turtle, hence its name. The displays recount creation myths in which the first people, the Nayuhyunggi, established the land and its laws.

At **Yellow Water Billabong** proper, a raised boardwalk leads to a viewing platform. At sunrise and sunset, the wetland birds and sky views are worth braving the mosquitoes (apply insect repellent beforehand!). *Yellow Water Cruises* (☎ 08 8979 0111) take visitors onto the waterways. They are popular and usually require advanced booking, particularly for the dawn cruise. The Gagudju Lodge is in Cooinda, near the Yellow Waters wetland bird spotting area.

The junction of the Old Darwin Road and Kakadu Highway is about 11km from **Cooinda**. The road is passable with conventional vehicles though unsealed and rejoins the Arnhem Highway after 90km through sparse woodlands. The trip from Cooinda to Darwin is about 3 hours' drive via this route.

The park's southern exit eventually leads to **Pine Creek**. Tracks to the south of this road lead to **Maguk Walk** (12km from the highway and about a 90-minute return walk to a pleasant swimming hole at the base of a small, year-round cascade, and **Gunlom Waterfall** (36km from the highway and an hour's return walk to a paperbark-shaded pool below a seasonal waterfall).

Arnhem Land

Adjacent to Kakadu National Park across the East Alligator River is **Arnhem Land** (see also pp 580 and 594). Owned by a number of Aboriginal groups, it is normally closed to independent visitors. Travel must be authorised and requires a permit from the Aboriginal Land Council; for eastern Arnhem Land, contact the **Gove Regional Tourist Association** (☎ 08 8987 1985).

The best way to visit Arnhem Land is as part of a tour group. The **Umorrduk** (☎ 08 8948 1306) have established a safari camp adjacent to the Gummulkbun clan's land. As many as 16 visitors can visit the area, staying in a comfortable bush camp for a day, overnight or longer. The tour is organised around photographing wildlife and visiting rock art sites along the Arnhem escarpment and nearby flood plain. It departs from Darwin.

Cobourg Peninsula

Seven Spirit Wilderness is in **Gurig National Park** (☎ 08 8979 0244) on the Cobourg Peninsula, 200km northeast of Darwin. The park presents a diverse coastal environment—sandy beaches, dunes and grasslands, mangroves and their associated swamps and lagoons, forest. The award-winning **tourist hotel** provides income for the traditional owners of the area and a well-sited wilderness experience for tourists. Access is by light plane or boat from Darwin. The area is only open during winter.

Uluru ~ Ayers Rock

Even more so than elsewhere in Australia, the distances to travel by car in these outback territories are surprising. The Northern Territory border is 1600km north from Adelaide. The road north from the border passes the roadhouse communities of **Kulgera** and **Erldunda** and **Stuart's Well**. The gravel road east from Kulgera follows the GOYDER STOCK ROUTE, crossing the Ghan on the way to Finke, itself a stop on the former Ghan railway line. **Finke** is now an Apatula Aboriginal settlement quite near **Lambert Centre**, the geographical centre of Australia, which is visited as something of a shrine by touring Australians. Erldunda marks the road leading 250km west to Uluru and is said to have the most expensive petrol on the Stuart Highway.

Uluru Kata Tjuta National Park

Situated about 450km south and west of Alice Springs, **Kata Tjuta** (the Olgas), and particularly, **Uluru** (**Ayers Rock**) are major emblems of Australia. Isolated on a dry plain of red soil, they were described by explorer Ernest Giles in 1875, who compared the mounts, saying 'Mount Olga [Kata Tjuta] is more wonderful ... like five or six enormous pink haystacks ... Mount Ayers [Uluru] the more ancient and sublime.'

Geologically, these formations are a sediment of well-weathered Proterozoic material. About 600 million years ago, the southern edge of the surrounding Amadeus Basin began to fracture. A range of mountains was exposed as they were pushed 50km northwards, overriding the basin's edge. Subsequent processes of sedimentation deposited sands which became rock, the material of Uluru, or pebbly conglomerates which became Kata Tjuta. These sedimentary rocks came to the surface as basin movements tilted the sandstone 75 degrees and the conglomerate some 30 degrees. The most recent erosion of these formations left Uluru and Kata Tjuta. A number of caves at the base of Uluru were cut by wave action about 70 million years ago when it stood as an island in an extensive lake. Iron oxide in the fragile sandstone accounts for the subtle red and ochre colours.

The first **European exploration** of the area was undertaken by Ernest Giles in 1872. Although he saw the two formations, he was north of Lake Amadeus and could not cross it. William Gosse and his Afghan camel driver Khamran reached the Uluru in July of 1873 by following Giles's route but skirting the lake on the east. Gosse named it for Henry Ayers, then Premier of South Australia. Giles reached Uluru on his next venture in September of that year. The first scientific collections were made in 1894 when the Horn Expedition visited Central Australia. Baldwin Spencer (see box, p 592), the expedition's zoologist who collected specimens and recorded some of the rock art, subsequently devoted his career to Aboriginal anthropology. The surrounding desert area was set aside as part of the Peterman Aboriginal Reserve in 1920. The first track graded in was from Curtin Springs in 1948.

The area around Uluru and Kata Tjuta was proclaimed Ayers Rock-Mount Olga National Park in 1958. Its name was changed, reverting to the traditional Uluru and Kata Tjuta, and it was recognised by UNESCO as a Biosphere Reserve in 1977. The Pitjantjatjara and Yankuntjatjara people claimed the reserve in 1979 but the Aboriginal Land Commissioner excluded Uluru from the award. Finally, amendments to the Aboriginal Land Rights (NT) Act and the National Parks and Wildlife Act in 1985 granted these people freehold title to the park. The park has been cooperatively managed with great success by an Aboriginal board and the National Parks and Wildlife service since this grant.

Yulara

Yulara (population c 900) functions as the service village for Uluru and Kata Tjuta. Opened in 1984, Yulara's design takes some care to match the structures with their environment. In addition to the only accommodation near the monoliths, the community has a medical centre, police station, service station, modest shopping precinct, and airport providing plane service from Alice Springs, Melbourne and Sydney.

Incidentally, Yulara translates as 'place of the howling dingo'. Its **Visitor Centre** (☎ 08 8956 2240) has displays describing the area's geology, natural and social history and presents a collection of photographs of the region.

A number of tour agencies operate out of Yulara. *Anangu Tours* (☎ 08 9566 2123) is Aboriginal owned and operated, and gives you an excellent chance to speak informally with the area's traditional owners. *Uluru Experience* and *AAT Kings* also have offices here. All the tours are alike in that guided visits to Kata Tjuta and Uluru are interspersed with meals and a sunset viewing.

Uluru stories

The mythology of Uluru involves a number of more or less unrelated totemic events. While they all occurred during the *tjukurapa* creation times and are largely secular in content, the differences in the recorded versions make them difficult to present. Generally, the southern face of Uluru is marked by the battle between the Liru poisonous snakes and the peaceful Kunia carpet pythons. The story of the Mala hare wallabies is seen on the northern and northwestern corner of the rock. The Kandju sand lizard made the Kandju Soak and its immediate surrounds on the western side of Uluru.

Wiyai Kutjara

The monolith itself was built as part of the Wiyai Kutjara story. The two boys made the rock while playing with mud after a rain. At the end of their play, they left Uluru, travelling south to Wiputa in the Musgrave Range, then north to Atila (Mount Connor). Here one of the boys threw his club at a hare wallaby. He missed, but a spring rose where it struck the ground. Refusing to reveal the site of the spring, he nearly caused his brother to die of thirst. The boys fought, eventually ending up on top of Mount Connor where their bodies are preserved as boulders.

Tjati or Lingka

Tjati (the name in Yankuntjatjara for a small, red lizard living on the mulga flats; in Pitjantjatjara the lizard is called *lingka*) travelled past Atila to Uluru. He threw his boomerang, a curved kali stick, which embedded itself into the northeast face of Uluru. Tjati dug a series of bowl-shaped hollows at Walaritja trying to retrieve his weapon. The boomerang itself is the curving edge of one of the holes. In some accounts he failed to retrieve his throwing stick and eventually died in a cave at Kantju. His tools and body are the large boulders on the cave floor.

In other versions, he found his weapon and stayed here for some time. When he moved to the north side of Uluru, he became known as Linga and lived on honey ants. They eventually chased him to the southern side of the rock where he nearly starved. After eating a Kunia python girl, he left for some place south of the Musgrave Range.

Mita and Lungkata

Two crested bell-bird brothers called Panpanpalala were hunting an emu at Wangka Arrkal, south of present-day Mulga Park near the South Australian border. They wounded the bird Kalaya with a spear. It ran north to Uluru and the brothers lost its tracks.

Meanwhile, the blue-tongue lizardmen Mita and Lungkata had come to Uluru from near Mount Liebig to the north via Mount Currie (Mulya Iti). They burnt the country where they walked, showing how to use fire to manage the land.

Reaching Uluru they camped at a cave on the rock's western face overlooking the area around the ranger station. While hunting along the southern part of the rock, they came upon the injured emu which still dragged the spear of Panpanpalala. After they had killed the bird with a stone axe at Kurumpa, to their dishonour they cut it up and started cooking it rather than try to discover who had first speared it.

When the crested bell-bird brothers saw the smoke, they came and asked after the wounded emu. Mita and Lungkata lied, saying they had not found the bird. Shortly thereafter the bell-bird brothers found the emu's tracks and realised what had happened.

Lungkata and Mita picked up as much of the best meat as they could carry and hurried towards their camp, dropping bits as they ran. The lean joints are now the fractured slabs of sandstone immediately to the west of Mutitjulu. They buried the meaty thigh at Kalaya Tjunta on the southeast side of Uluru just north of Ikari.

When the bell-bird brothers caught up with the lizardmen again, they were so angered by the mistreatment that they set fire to the lizardmen's shelter. Mita and Lunkata tried to escape by climbing the rock face at Mita Kampantja, but fell into the fire and were burned to death. The lichen on the rock here is the smoke from the fire and the two half-buried boulders are the remains of the blue-tongued lizards.

In other published versions of the story, Mita and Lungkata are a single, particularly lazy, blue-tongued lizard camping at Miltjan. In another, they offered the crested bell-bird brothers the gristly lean joints, lying about the fleshy thighs buried nearby.

Kurrpanngu attacks the Mala

The Mala hare wallabies travelled south to Uluru from Mawurungu, Warlpiri country near **Yuendumu**, through the Haasts Bluff area. At Katjitilkil on Uluru's northern side they began preparing for men's ceremonies. The men made a decorated *ngaltawata* ceremonial pole and carried it up to the top of Uluru. (Because tourists are brash enough to use this same route to scale Uluru, the local people fear for their spiritual and physical safety.) The ceremonies at Kantju and Warayuki on the northeast corner of Uluru began when they planted the *ngaltawata* there.

The women were careful not to know anything about these ceremonies so they collected and prepared food for the men in the caves around the Mala Walk and at Taputji on the eastern side of the rock. One of their *wana* digging sticks can be seen there in the form of a stone. The old men camped between the women and the ceremonies to protect against accidental intrusion. Their camp is directly opposite **Taputji rock**.

Just as the ceremonies had started, the Wintalka *mulga* seed men had the bell-bird Panpanpanala invite the Mala to come to a ceremony of their own at Kikingkura near the Docker River. More than wanting the Mala to participate, the Wintalka wanted to use down from the Mala's eagle chick to decorate their participants. Of course the Mala could not interrupt their ceremony and found the request to use their eagle chick feathers offensive. They responded curtly. The call of the bell-bird is still 'Pak', meaning 'They can't come; they can't come'.

Their refusal enraged the *mulga* seed men. In their anger they constructed **Kurrpanngu**, an evil magic monster in a form something like a hairless dingo dog, a *mamu*. It moved as a violent wind storm across the sand dunes from the west until it found the Mala track at Muly Iiti (Mount Currie). Then it followed them south to Uluru. The Mala women were dancing at Tjuktjapinya, just to the east of the ceremonial grounds. Their *mawulari* hair skirts were transformed into the pendant cones of rock at Tjukutjapi.

In one recorded version of the story, the women drove him off and he continued around Uluru to Inintitjara to find the Mala men sleeping. For calling a warning to the men, Kurrpanngu turned Lunpa kingfisher woman into a boulder. You can still see Kurrpanngu's paw prints in the rock there.

In another version, when Lunpa saw the monster approach she screamed a warning from her home at Ininti waterhole to the women. In a panic, the women fled south through the men's ceremony at Malawati. This ruined the ceremony. The monster caught a Mala man and ate him. Some of the tracks of the Mala run past the northern edge of the Musgrave Ranges to Ulkiya south of the Mann Ranges, others run past Altjinta near **Mulga Park Homestead**.

Liru Fight Kuniya

The Kuniya pythons came to Uluru from three directions. One group travelled west from Paku-paku and Waltanta near Erldunda. Another came south through Wilpiya past Wilbia Well. The third came north from Yunanpa or Mitchell's Knob. A number of Uluru's physical features date from their occupation. The boulders at Tjukiki Gorge, also known as Miltjan, were once Kuniya women sitting in their camp; the tall slab of rock at the head of the gorge is one of their *coolamon* carrying dishes.

A Kuniya python woman from Waltanta carried her eggs either as a necklace or in a *manguir* grass head pad. Once at Kuniya Piti she dived into the sand, leaving the eggs behind in a ring or she buried them there on the eastern side of Uluru. The Kuniya python woman camped at Taputji where the grooves she made as she left and returned each day can be seen on the north.

Kuniya python woman's young nephew had made enemies of some Liru poisonous snake warriors. They came to Uluru having travelled along the southern edge of the Petermann Ranges to the west from beyond Wangkari (Gills Pinnacle). They saw Kuniya python nephew resting just west of where the tourists now climb Uluru and attacked the Kuniya nephew. The scars left by their spears can be seen at Ayurungu on the southwest face of Uluru. He fought as best he could, but was outnumbered and killed. The two black watercourses there are the bodies of two Liru.

His aunt, Kuniya python woman, was sad and angry about his death. When she travelled underground from Kuiya Piti to Mutitjulu the Liru warriors mocked her. Beside herself, she began a dance which would give her the power to avenge her nephew and her honour. She had so much power she had to pick up handfuls of sand to hold the poisonous power. Where this sand fell, fig trees and spearvine became poisonous and unusable. In fact her ill-will so infected the place that the local people would avoid the area immediately around Mutitjulu.

She had her *wana* digging stick with her and was going to make a grief scar on the forehead of a Liru warrior. Her anger was so strong that she hit him on the head. You can see the face of the Kuniya woman on the eastern face of the gorge. The wounded, a Liru warrior, is on the western side. His eye and head wounds are the vertical cracks on the face of the gorge. His severed nose is plainly seen. The Kuniya who lives at Uluru rock hole stops the water from flowing into Mutitjulu. She will move away if someone shouts 'Kuka! Kuka! Kuka!' which means 'meat, meat, meat!'

The **Uluru-Kata Tjuta National Park Centre** (☎ 08 8956 3138) is 1km from the rock. As well as a display describing Uluru and Anangu art, it houses the **Maruka Arts and Crafts Centre**. This Aboriginal owned enterprise presents dancers and working artists. *Anangu Tours* (☎ 08 9566 2123) also have a booking office here.

A tour of Uluru

The guide on the three-hour walk around Uluru will provide access to and descriptions of cultural sites otherwise closed to inspection as well as relating the mythology of Uluru to its physical features. The walk is easy, but a 20-minute tour from the base of the rock to Mutitjulu is offered as an alternative.

Tourists are inclined to climb up Uluru despite requests from its Aboriginal keepers not to. The climb takes about two hours, is difficult and somewhat dangerous in spots and does not present particularly fulfilling views of the desert surrounds. In short, it is a sweaty waste of time which might otherwise be spent learning something about the mythology and way of life of the Aboriginal people who hold Uluru in trust for the rest of us.

Greg Lenthen, writing in the *Sydney Morning Herald*, gives an insightful description of Uluru-climbing:

> *The Aborigines call those who climb Uluru 'ants'. It's not disrespect; just how the climbers look on Uluru's great back. You're told repeatedly that the traditional owners believe Uluru is sacred and should not be climbed. The chain that climbers use traces the traditional route taken by the ancestral Mala men on their arrival at Uluru. Still the tourists climb. But, according to the Ayers Rock Resort, the proportion of visitors who do is declining. (One would hesitate to say falling. Quite a few do; 29 dead at last count.)*

Parking is at the base of the climb which probably does not further the attempts to dissuade people from making it. The walk around the rock, travelling to the left takes in rock-art sites at **Mala Puta** and **Walaritja** and eventually at **Mitutjulu**. Sacred areas at **Ngaltawata** and **Tjukatjapi** on the north, **Kuniya Piti** on the east and **Pulari** on the south are protected by fences.

Kata Tjuta (the Olgas)

The **Kata Tjuta** is a group of granite and basalt conglomerates initially named the **Olgas** by explorer Ernest Giles in 1872 after Queen Olga of Spain. It lies about 30km west of Uluru. The sacred significance of the rocks to the Anangu is due to their importance to male education and initiation. Being sacred, the site is closed to visitors. Two trails, however, give glimpses of the 36 domes and the chasms between them. Iron oxide in the fragile sandstone accounts for the subtle red and ochre colours.

The **Valley of the Winds trail** is a three-hour, 6km walk requiring a bit of scrambling as it winds through gorges. The curious round pebbles of granite and gneiss are the remains of a Proterozoic (1.2 billion years ago) mountain range which eventually eroded into the Amadeus Basin. It gives excellent views of the domes. A shorter walk leads into **Olga Gorge** along the side of Mount Olga. In fact, the picnic area to the west of the rocks just before the junction of these two trails offers about as good a view as that on the Valley of the Winds trail. The best impression of Kata Tjuta is likely to be at sunset from this vantage point.

Pitjantjatjara Tours (also known as *Desert Tracks*, ☎ 08 8952 8984) offer an in-depth introduction to the traditional life in a small outstation camp near Angatja, a remote area about 100km southwest of Uluru. Here ten tours per year offer a maximum of 20 people each trip the opportunity to learn daily life skills while living with a Pitjantjatjara family. Hunting and gathering, story-telling, artefact manufacture are demonstrated. The basic steps of a traditional dance, the *inma*, are also taught to visitors.

Other trips into this more remote area in the south of the territory are better made as part of a four-wheel drive or camel tour (☎ 08 8956 0925) booked out of Alice Springs. These normally visit **Rainbow Valley** and **Chambers Pillar**. Rainbow Valley is in the easternmost extent of the James Ranges and is known for the subtly attractive sandstone cliffs with characteristic iron oxide colouring. The 50m tall sandstone pillar in Chambers Pillar Historical Reserve was used as a navigational aid for overland travellers prior to the rail line being laid.

The **Henbury Meteorite Conservation Reserve** west of Stuart's Well is about an hour's drive south of Alice Springs on the Stuart Highway. Stuart's Well itself simply marks the junction of Ernest Giles Road and Stuart Highway. The reserve is 16km east and north of the junction on passable unsealed roads. The 12 visually unremarkable craters were made several thousand years ago when a meteor broke into fragments quite near the ground. The largest of the craters is 180m across and 15m deep. It would have been made by a meteor about the size of the average 3-year-old child.

Alice Springs

Almost 300km north from the South Australian border, 450km north of Uluru, and 1480km south of Darwin, **Alice Springs**, known familiarly as 'the Alice' (as in the famous book and film *A Town like Alice* (1956) by Nevil Shute), sits on an alluvial plain near Heavitree Gap cut by the Ross River in the eastern section of the MacDonnell Range. This range runs east and west and rises steeply from an elevation of about 650m. Gorges and gaps cut these dramatic red mountains, providing year round water holes and pools, literally oases. Some remnant plant life is only found here and in well-watered coastal areas of Australia. Two major rivers flow from the MacDonald Range during winter: the Ross and Finke Rivers eventually run dry both in seasonal and geographical terms. In October, the Henley-on-Todd Regatta offers a series of leg-powered bottomless boat races on the 9dry) Todd River.

■ Practical information
Tourist information. The Central Australian Tourism Industry Association visitor's centre (☎ 08 8952 5199, open daily 09.00–16.00) on the corner of Harley Street and Gregory Terrace serves travellers in the southern section of the territory. Parks and Wildlife also has a well-provisioned desk in the centre. Permits to visit Aboriginal lands are available from the Central Land Council (☎ 08 8951 6211) at 31–33 Stuart Highway about 1km north of the city centre.
Airport. The airport is 14km south of town and is served by taxis and a shuttle

serving the hotels. Qantas and Ansett fly to and from the major cities.

Rail. The *Ghan* provides a weekly train service from Adelaide. The station is across the Stuart Highway on George Crescent, a 15-minute walk from the city centre.

Bus. The *Greyhound* (☎ 13 2030) terminal is at Melanka Lodge on Todd Street. *McCafferty's* (☎ 13 1499) is at 91 Gregory Terrace. Local bus service departs from the Yeperenge shopping centre.

Most of Alice Springs (population 25,700) has been rebuilt or renovated since the 1960s. As will be immediately apparent, the town has been completely transformed from a dusty outback centre to a tourist mecca. As writer Bernard Boucher wrote as early as 1979: 'Alice Springs had lost its quaintness as the isolated centre of the Australian wilderness. It was no longer a one-horse town ... International tourism had brought a peculiar sophistication to the place, still small by city standards but beyond the days of being just a cattleman's town. Now the Aborigines sold their boomerangs and nulla-nullas from a glass-fronted craft centre close by the smart shopping arcades ...'

History

Like other towns along the Stuart Highway, Alice Springs was founded as a telegraph station. J. McDouall Stuart's route of exploration was about 50km west of the site. Surveyor William Whitfield Mills and local pastoralist John Ross brought the telegraph line along Ross River, establishing a repeater station at a spring about 7km north into the plain. They named the station for Charles Todd's wife, Alice. The river in town, usually dry, was named after Todd himself.

An associated settlement called Stuart eventually took the station's name, becoming Alice Springs or 'The Alice' in 1933. While some cattle were run in the area early, the population was minimal until the railroad finally reached town in 1929. An extension of this railway to Darwin (a commitment imposed on the federal government when South Australia ceded the Northern Territory) is currently under discussion.

The bitumen road to Darwin was completed during the Second World War and its extension south was paved in the 1980s. Service to the area prior to the rail was by camel train. Commemorating the Afghani camel handlers, the rail service is called the Ghan. An unfounded gold rush in the early 1930s brought a flurry of settlement. Most of the population since the Second World War have lived here to service a mid-winter flow of tourists.

Sites of historical interest in the area are modest structures and include the **Stuart Town Gaol** and **Hartley Street School** in Alice Springs and the **Alice Springs Telegraph Station** and **Hermannsburg Aboriginal Mission** in the vicinity.

The Hartley Street School also houses the local **National Trust Centre** (☎ 08 8952 4516, open Mon–Fri 10.30–14.30). The town's earliest school building dates from 1929. The gaol dates from 1907–08 and functioned until 1938. As the Trust's brochure states, 'The floor plan and fittings reflect the harsh discriminatory treatment of Aborigines during the time of its use.' It is virtually closed in the heat of summer (Dec–Feb), but normally functions between 10.00 and 12.30 weekdays and a half-hour earlier on weekends. An arid zone botanical garden, the **Olive Pink Flora Reserve** (☎ 08 8952 2154 open daily, 10.00–18.00) is across the Todd River from the city's centre. The reserve, named after a prominent early ethnographer of the Aboriginal people in the vicinity, displays shrubs and trees typical in the Alice Springs area. Annie Meyer Hill is an Arrernte sacred site, Tarrarltneme. To the south an east-to-west running ridge can be discerned. One of the first creations of the Caterpillar Spirits, this was where they crossed the Todd River.

Aboriginal art and culture

Maruku Arts and Crafts Centre (☎ 08 8956 2153) at Uluru, and Alice Springs galleries **Papunya Tula Artists**, 78 Todd Street (☎ 08 8952 4731) and **Jukurrpa Artists**, 18 Leichhardt Terrace (☎ 08 8953 1052) offer tourists possibly the best selection of Aboriginal and Torres Strait Islander art and craft outside the communities in which they were produced. All of these venues are owned and run by Aborigines, so proceeds go directly to the Aboriginal communities and artists. Also of interest a little outside the centre of town, on Larapinta Drive, is the **Araluen Centre for Arts and Entertainment** (☎ 08 8952 5022). Here is the **Albert Namatjira Gallery**, with an extensive collection of works by the artist (see box p 610); as well as an important collection of art by contemporary Australian artists and craftspeople. Also in the complex is Alice Springs's **performing arts centre**, which can seat 500. The gem of the complex are the stained glass windows in the foyer, designed by local artist Wenten Rubuntja, and featuring the popular local theme of the Honey Ant Dreaming.

Next door to the Araluen Centre is the **Strehlow Research Centre** (☎ 08 8951 8000; open daily, admission fee), an excellent and serious centre for the study of Aboriginal culture. Carl Strehlow (1871–1922) was a Lutheran missionary at Killalpaninna and Hermannsburg missions who compiled the first extensive linguistic and ethnographic information on the Arrernte and Luritja peoples. Known as Ingkata, or trusted leader, among the Western Desert peoples, Strehlow was entrusted with the most sacred of artefacts by the Arrernte for safekeeping. These items are stored at the centre, and can now only be viewed by initiated male members of the tribe. Accessible displays, however, discuss the life of the Arrernte, as well as examine the work of Strehlow. The centre's building is particularly attractive, including the largest rammed-earth wall in the Southern hemisphere.

Alice's role in modern communication, as one might expect, extends beyond the Overland Telegraph Line. The Reverend John Flynn, founder of the Royal Flying Doctor Service, and Alf Teager experimented with pedal-generated electricity for portable short-wave radio at Flynn's residence, **Adelaide House**. Their experiments and the impact of the Flying Doctor Service and Teager's radio are described (open Mon–Fri 10.00–16.00, Sat 10.00–12.00, small admission fee, tea and biscuits).

The **Old Telegraph Station** itself is 3km by riverside walk from Wills Terrace or 4km north via the highway. Situated on the billabong-like Alice Springs, the buildings were constructed of local rock in 1871–72. It served as the station until 1932 (open daily 08.00–19.00, until 21.00 Oct to April; admission fee).

MacDonnell Ranges

As mentioned in the geological description of the area, the MacDonnell Ranges extend east to west across 400km. Alice Springs is situated more or less in their centre. The ranges are steep ridges in which water courses flowing into the **Simpson Desert** cut ravines and gorges.

West MacDonnell National Park (☎ 08 8951 5210) extends west from Alice Springs to Mount Zeil (1531m above sea level, rising 900m above the surrounding plain). Access is via Larapinta then Namatjira Drives by vehicle or via Larapinta Trail from the Telegraph Station. Maps for either are available from the Parks and Wildlife desk in the Hartley Street visitor's centre and at the visitor's centre at Simpson's Gap.

At **Dr John Flynn's gravesite**, just outside the entrance to the national park, Mount Gillen is visible to the south. Flynn was, of course, the founder of the Royal Flying Dctors' Service and the Australian Inland Mission. 22km west of Alice Springs, an unpaved road leads north to **Simpson's Gap** (open daily 08.00–20.00). The gap was identified by OTL surveyor Gilbert McMinn as an alternative to Stuart's more rugged route 60km further west. The Arrernte people know the gap as Rugutjirpa, home of the Goanna Spirits.

29km west of the Simpson Gap road is **Standley Chasm**. While glimpses of the wildlife make Simpson's Gap best seen in the early morning or late afternoon, the walls of the chasm are renowned for midday displays of reflected light.

Shortly beyond the road to Standley Chasm, the road diverges. Namatjira Drive continues into the western section of the park and Larapinta Drive proceeds as a rough road to Hermannsburg.

To the east of Alice Springs the MacDonnell Ranges extend about 100km. Access to them is via the **Ross River Homestead Road** from the Stuart Highway immediately south of Alice Springs. This scenic drive passes a number of high ridges and eucalypt-lined creeks. **Emily Gap** is 10km from the Stuart Highway. Called Anthwerrke by the Arrernte, it was the birthplace of the Mparntwe Caterpillar Dreaming. The site of petroglyphs related to the Caterpillar Dreaming is south of the Ross River Homestead Road at N'Dhala. Four-wheel-drive is necessary to reach the site. Currently a tourist camp offering a variety of bush activities, **Ross River Homestead** (☎ 08 8956 9711) was originally Love's Creek Station.

Hermannsburg Mission

An interesting day trip to the **Hermannsburg Mission** is reached west of Alice Springs via Larapinta Drive past John Flynn's grave and Simpson's Gap National Park. The latter is popular as a picturesque river of white sand flanked by red and ghost gums. By the way, the Twin Ghost Gums made famous by artist Albert Namatjira's depiction are just before **Standley Chasm** (see above).

Hermannsburg (☎ 08 8956 7402, open daily 09.00–16.00) is about 120km from Alice Springs. Like Killapaninna Mission on the Birdsville Track (see p 645), it was founded by German Lutherans trained at Hermannsburg near Hannover in Germany. This seminary had trained missionaries since 1849 following Ludwig and Theodor Harms's methods. Support for the missions was based in the German communities in South Australia.

Albert Namatjira

Albert Namatjira (1902–59) was born at the Hermannsburg Mission; he was a member of the Arrernte people, and was a fully initiated member of his tribe. At Hermannsburg in the 1930s, he became acquainted with the artist Rex Batterbee, who encouraged him to paint and trained him in Western landscape style and watercolour techniques. He made his first paintings in 1934 and had his first exhibition in Melbourne in 1938, when all of his paintings sold within three days. By the end of the 1940s, Namatjira was one of the best-known Australian artists in the world. The response to his work epitomises the ambivalent attitudes to Aborigines who supposedly assimilated: while the works were recognised for their stylistic maturity, as Western-style landscapes, they were considered by many purists as being inappropriate for an Aboriginal artist's subject matter. Despite his fame, as an Aboriginal in the Northern Territory Namatjira was denied a pastoral lease in 1949, and his attempt to build a house in Alice Springs in 1951 was rejected. While a special act of Federal Parliament upheld a tax office decision that Namatjira should be taxed for income, he was not considered an Australian citizen. In 1953, the artist was awarded the Queen's Coronation Medal, and the next year Namatjira met the Queen in Sydney. In 1957 he and his wife Rubina became the first Aborigines to be given Australian citizenship, although their children were still state wards. As a citizen, Namatjira was able to purchase alcohol, which he shared with his people. This act led to his imprisonment for illegally supplying alcohol to Aborigines; he was held under house arrest for two months. Three months later he died of a heart attack in Alice Springs. Recent reassessment of his work places his paintings within the history and development of Aranda art and stresses his influence on later artists, including his sons Enos, Ewald, Oscar and Kevin, and his grandchildren.

History of Hermannsburg

Hermannsburg was established in 1877 after an arduous 22-month trek from the Barossa Valley in South Australia. In keeping with the Harms's missionary methods, the first permanent building was a school. Doctrinal disputes saw its brief abandonment in 1893 prior to Reverend Carl Strehlow's tenure (see also p 608). Strehlow, bush builder Dave Hart and the local Aranda-speaking people rebuilt the mission between 1894 and the turn of the century.

Again consistent with German methods, the first school presented the gospel in the local Aranda language. Strehlow and his successor, Pastor F.W. Albrecht, consistently sought to provide educational, humanitarian and aesthetic opportunities well advanced of those advocated in Australia at the time. Carl Strehlow and his son T.G.H. (Ted) Strehlow significantly added to the white population's understanding of Aboriginal culture. Like Johann Reuther and Otto Siebert at Killapaniana, the German missionaries were more likely to record and publish the traditions of their community members.

In 1982 the Lutheran Synod returned the land and its buildings to the heredi-tary owners. The Ntaria Council renovated the buildings and opened the mission to visitors in 1988; the region is now called by its original name, Ntaria. The 11 buildings are of whitewashed local stone with sheet metal roofing. They seem curiously German amid the palms and river gums. In addition to the school and church, the mission house is open and functions as a tea room, and an exhibit of Arrernte paintings here features work by Albert Namatjira (see box, p 610) among others.

Finke Gorge National Park

The **Finke Gorge National Park** (☎ 08 8956 7401) is 12km beyond Hermannsburg on a four-wheel-drive track. Tours should be booked in Alice Springs and can be joined at Hermannsburg. Travellers who have come as far as Finke Gorge National Park will probably have already noticed the effect that a small amount of dependable water has in the midst of arid country. Nonetheless, a valley full of cabbage palms (20m tall), cycads, eucalypts and shrubs growing in sandstone along the dry bed of the Finke River is a surprise. The area was, in fact, a rainforest as recently as 10,000 years ago. The porosity of the sandstone makes the vegetation possible.

The Finke River flows beneath the surface most of the time. Some of its numerous soaks are less saline than the river in such circumstances. They were a necessary water resource for the local western Arrernte. Following heavy rainfall, though, the Finke can spread to several kilometres across, eventually flowing into the Macumba River and Lake Eyre.

The cabbage palms, *Livistona mariae*, after which Palm Glen and Palm Valley are named, are found nowhere else. Their nearest relatives are in two small areas on the Fortescue River in Western Australia and near Matoranka, south of Katherine. The cycads were the world's first seed-bearing plants. The seeds are poisonous, but once ground and thoroughly washed, they formed a staple source of starch for Aborigines throughout the Territory and Queensland. Symptoms of cycad toxaemia are occasionally presented to outback doctors still.

The **Glen of Palms** was first described by Ernest Giles in 1872 in notes he made for Ferdinand von Mueller, director of the Melbourne Botanical Gardens. He had been following the Finke River from Chambers Pillar. Dissuaded from exploring further by fires lit by Aborigines, he did not find either Palm Creek or Palm Valley. These areas were named by missionaries from Hermannsburg. The Horn Scientific Expedition to Central Australia spent time here in 1894. Practically speaking, the area was inaccessible until Len Tuit and Jack Cotterill opened the track and established tourist ventures here in the late 1950s.

Of the three trails in the vicinity, the 5km **Mpulungkinya Track** is the most popular. It proceeds through Palm Valley, then up to a track overlooking the valley and back to the car park. **Mpaara Track**, also about 5km long, is more strenuous. It proceeds from the Kalarranga car park, following a trail along the Finke River to Palm Bend and eventually to the rugged Amphitheatre. The shortest walk is c 1.5km and offers fine views of Palm Creek and the Amphitheatre.

Tanami Track

The road west from Alice Springs follows the **Tanami Track**. It is usually passable with a 2-wheel drive vehicle, although care is necessary in areas of blown sand. Because it traverses Aboriginal land, travellers without a permit are required to stay within 50m of the roadway.

WARNING. Ask the police about the road and weather conditions while notifying them of your travel plans. In fact, the road is fairly frequently travelled. The Lonely Planet publication *Outback Australia* mentions that as many as 40 vehicles per day may pass during the cooler dry season of May through August.

The track passes near the Aboriginal community **Yuendumu**, 290km from Alice Springs, where petrol and provisions can be bought. This is also the site of the **Yuendumu Sports and Cultural Festival** (☎ 08 8956 4021) held over the Northern Territory's picnic weekend in early August. This event is the Territory's oldest festival. An eagerly-anticipated gathering, Aboriginal peoples from everywhere compete in a variety of sports and cultural performances. On the weekend, visitors are welcome and no permits are needed. As many as 5000 people come here for the Games weekend.

Yuendumu is also the centre of one of the desert's most public art movements. Just as had happened at nearby **Papunya** in the 1980s, the principal of the Yuendumu school, Terry Davis, suggested in 1983 that the senior men of the community paint the school doors. Seeing the opportunity to express their heritage values and provide a comment on the European values fostered by the school, the doors were painted in a scale and time frame such as that of ceremonial painting. That the artists here were of one language group, the Warlpiri, facilitated the organisation of individuals' art work. The theme of one of the doors described by Wally Caruana in his book *Aboriginal Art* (1993) was the creation story in which the Rain Being, having tired of his work making the current owners of the land, transformed himself into a cloud and travelled north. The painting depicted an encounter with a second Rain Being and the resulting deluge and lightning storm. After painting the school doors, these artists began painting on canvases; one of these works, *Yanjilypiri Jukurrpa (Star Dreaming)* (1985) by Paddy Jupurrurla Nelson, Paddy Japaljarri Sims and Larry Jungarrayi Spencer, is reproduced on the cover of Caruana's book.

Subsequently, painting for sale began here on a commercial scale. Women artists in Yuendumu have had a particularly strong role making painting for the public. They had been decorating traditional implements for sale prior to the middle 1980s, largely due to an interest expressed by anthropologists working in the community. The subsequent collaborative efforts are generally more densely worked than the art the men make. Some of the best-known Yuendumu women artists include Libby Napanangka Walker, Uni Nampijinpa Martin and Dolly Nampijinpa Daniels.

Because of its well-established social organisation, Yuendumu also became the centre for the **Tanami Network**, a pioneering television link-up connected with Darwin and broadcasting Aboriginal news and cultural events. Tanami Network is also connected to Imparja Television in Alice Springs, the Aboriginal-owned and operated satellite television station.

360km further along the Tanami Track is the **Tanami Mine**. A four-wheel-drive only branch of the road leads 230km (about 4 hours) north to **Lajamanu** where Cambrian soils and better water allow eucalypts and some variety of grasses to grow as the road passes through some interesting country to **Kalkarindji** on the Buchanan Highway. The break between spinifex desert and Mitchell grass cattle range occurs nearer Kalkarindji.

About 230km west of Tanami Mine lies the Billiluna community's land near Lake Gregory in Western Australia.

The Aboriginal community at **Lajamanu** are part of the Warlpiri language group; they are closely related to the Yuendumu, having been forcibly settled there in 1947 by the government in order to make way for pastoral and mining interests on their traditional land. Again, the local school provided the impetus for public painting. Their paintings are freer in their compositions than those by the other Warlpiri. Both the Lajamanu and Yuendumu are represented by the Warlukurlangu Artists Association.

North of Alice Springs

North of Alice Springs on the STUART HIGHWAY are roadhouses at **Aileron** and **Ti Tree**. The Anmatjura people have had the Ti Tree lease since 1971; the Aboriginal communities at **Utopia** and **Pmara Jutunta** on the SANDOVER HIGHWAY use Ti Tree as their provisioning station.

Textiles and paintings

Cattle stations since the 1920s, Utopia and the neighbouring Mount Skinner were purchased by the Aboriginal Land Fund in 1976. After some temporary arrangements, the Anmatyerre and Alyawarre were granted ownership in 1979. The women in the community began producing wood-block-printed and tie-dyed fabric, but quickly came to prefer batik. Silk became their preferred fabric because it allowed the most fluid brush and pen strokes. With the support of the Central Australian Aboriginal Media Association, they produced a series of batik designs and sold them in 1988 to the Holmes à Court collection in Western Australia. Exhibited at Tandanya in Adelaide in 1989, the success of this project induced the women to begin painting in acrylic as well. The senior woman of the Utopia Group, Emily Kame Kngwarreye (d. 1998), has subsequently brought international recognition to the region; her unusually powerful paintings, both in 'dot' and 'line' style, have been exhibited around the world, and represented Australia at the 1997 Venice Biennale. Major exhibitions of Emily's work have been mounted by the Art Gallery of New South Wales and the National Gallery of Australia, Canberra.

Along the southern section of the STUART HIGHWAY route, some variety of vegetation and geology occurs until north of Barrow Creek. Much as the desert on the Tanami Track beyond Yuendumu, from Barrow Creek virtually to Newcastle Waters, the flora is hummock grass with occasional acacia bushes. Geologically, the country is from the early Proterozoic remains of the Davenport Range.

At present a rather drab cluster of buildings with an interesting pub and the remains of a Second World War army camp, **Barrow Creek** was the site of an attack by Kaytej men on the telegraph station in 1874. The result was the death of station master James Stapleton and a linesman. In the ensuing two months the South Australian government killed 50 or more Aboriginal people.

Immediately beyond **Wauchope** (c 10km north of Barrow Creek) are the **Devil's Marbles**. These granite boulders were formed by exfoliation. Also known as onion skin weathering, this form of erosion occurs as layers of rock peel away due to expansion and contraction caused by daily warming and cooling of the rock's exterior. These boulders are part of the Davenport Range. While not particularly interesting visually, these mountains have been continuously exposed for 1.8 billion years.

Tennant Creek

Tennant Creek (population 3550) is the largest town between Alice Springs, 530km to the south, and Darwin, 960km to the north. About 10km south of the Overland Telegraph Line repeater station, it has supported gold mines since the 1930s and a copper mine since the 1950s. Locals sometimes maintain that its site is south of the station because a beer wagon broke down here, it being safer to move the town than to move the beer. Among the more interesting sites in town is the **Jurnkurakurr Mural** on the side of the Central Land Council Building. It depicts lightning, fire, the budgerigar, crow and cockatoo and the snake, all symbols of particular importance to the neighbouring Aboriginal people. **Tourist information centre**: on the corner of Paterson and Davidson Streets; ☎ 08 8962 3388. An airport here provides flights with **Airnorth** (☎ 1 800 627 474) to Alice Springs, Darwin, and Katherine; and all long-distance bus services will stop at the Tennant Creek Transit Centre, where tourist information is located.

The **Australian Inland Mission** building is a corrugated iron prefabricated structure from the 1930s. These modular structures were designed by Sidney Williams, an architect and designer who had initially specialised in windmills. His so-called Comet Buildings had steel frames and interchangeable finishings and cladding. They are still encountered in remote areas but are generally small huts rather than buildings like this mission.

History

The indigenous population, the **Warumungu**, call the area Jurnkurakurr. A number of dreaming tracks intersect here and five languages are spoken locally. In a sense, Tennant Creek can stand as an example of the history of Aboriginal/white relations. J. McDouall Stuart reached the area in his first attempt to cross the continent in 1860. The local Aboriginal population resented his intrusion and raided his nearly exhausted party. Stuart named Attack Creek, about 70km north of Tennant Creek, in remembrance of this event. In 1872 the OTL repeater station was established near here.

In 1933 an Aboriginal stockman named Frank discovered a gold nugget south of the repeater station. The town site was surveyed and attracted a number of Aboriginal people from central Australia. The **Aboriginal Inland Mission** established a mission in town in the late 1930s. Among the missionaries were George Cormier and his wife. In 1943 and 1944 the mission opened a ration station and church, but the Northern Territory government decided to move about 200 Aboriginal people 40km north to Phillip Creek. The mission followed.

Inadequate water at Phillip Creek necessitated a second move to Warrabi in 1956. In the 1960s the owner of the Banka Banka pastoral station bought six houses in Tennant Creek for retired Aboriginal employees. When legal restriction on Aboriginal freedom of movement was lifted, also in the mid-1960s, the number of Aboriginal people living in and around Tennant Creek increased.

Living in camps lacking amenities and marked by social problems, these people formed the **Julalikari** ('one big family') Aboriginal Cooperative Council in 1985. Working with the Tennant Creek town council, the cooperative began improving life in the camps. In the late 1980s a language centre to foster the locally spoken languages, a health service and a centre devoted to supporting the re-establishment of traditional lands (the outstation movement) have furthered this initial effort.

Along the way to Daly Waters, roadhouses serve travellers at Renner Springs and Elliott. Further along, the cattle drive watering stop at **Newcastle Waters**, now virtually abandoned, was named by Stuart after the Duke of Newcastle, secretary for the colonies. A.J. Browne of Adelaide contracted Alfred Files to bring stock for the area in the 1880s. In 1886 Newcastle Waters became a stop on the **Murranji stock route** from the eastern Kimberleys to the railhead at Mount Isa in central western Queensland. Scant water along the route prevented its full development until a series of 13 bores were drilled between 1917 and 1924.

The **Junction Hotel** was built in 1932 out of abandoned windmill parts picked up along the stock route. Wet straw cooled the drovers' first few beers; warm beer was their lot once drinking became earnest. The licence was transferred to Elliot in 1962. Road transport had replaced the stock drover. The last overland drive was during the 1988 bicentennial. 1200 donated head of cattle spent four months to make the trip to Longreach, Queensland.

At Newcastle Waters small acacia bushes quite suddenly become dominant then give way to eucalypts. Here the soil geology changes from 1.8 billion years old to Cretaceous formations of a mere 100 million years old. These conditions continue to favour scrubby eucalypts (called Mulga in much the same manner as the scrub in the Murray River corridor is called the Mallee) to a point between Mataranka and Katherine where Palaeozoic geology and eucalypts of medium height mark the approach to the Top End.

The historical marker commemorating the joining of the northern and southern sections of the Overground Telegraph Line stands on the way to the roadhouse at **Dunmarra**. The settlement was named in the 1930s by drover and station owner Noel Healy. It comes from the Aboriginal pronunciation of Dan O'Mara, a linesman who disappeared in the region.

Further north, past the junctions with the Buchanan and Carpentaria Highways, is **Daly Waters**, named after the then governor of South Australia by Stuart on his third and successful attempt to cross the continent. The Daly Waters pub's walls are decorated with just about anything passing travellers have thought to leave. While the building dates from the late 1920s, as a pub it was founded to serve drovers in the 1890s.

Incredible as it may seem, this scattering of houses was the site of Australia's first international airport. Qantas used it as a refuelling stop between Australia and Singapore in the early 1930s Sydney to London route. It served a similar function for bombers during the Second World War.

Larrimah's population, like most of the roadhouse settlements, is less than 50. In the Second World War, the Royal Australian Air Force (RAAF) built Gorrie Airfield about 10km north of town. At its height the population was

6500 people. The Birdum Hotel was moved from the airfield to Larrimah when the field closed and its facilities were sold.

Mataranka is a tourist stop due to its hot springs—16,000 litres per minute at 34°C. Australians also know it as the setting of Jeannie Gunn's pastoral novel, *We of the Never Never* (1908). Indeed, it is this region that is generally accepted as the 'true' location of 'The Never Never' of popular description; Henry Lawson wrote *The Never-Never Land* in 1901, and in 1905, explorer Alexander McDonald, in his accounts of an overland journey, refers to the Central Australian deserts as the Never-Never.

Should you be in the area over the Queen's birthday long weekend in June and have camping gear, try to attend the **Barunga Wugularr Sports and Cultural Festival** (☎ 08 8975 4504). The four-day event attracts Aboriginal people from across the territory for sports, dancing, arts and crafts.

Katherine

At 1200km north of Alice Springs and a mere 337km from Darwin, **Katherine** (population 8809) is at the junction of the Victoria and Stuart Highways. Pronounced locally as 'Kath rhyne', it was named by Stuart on 4 July 1862 after Catherine Chambers, a daughter of James Chambers, one of his patrons. The river is the first permanent water north of the South Australian border. In early 1998, the town flooded to such an extent that abandonment was seriously considered. **Tourist information centre**: on the corner of Stuart Highway and Lindsay Avenue; ☎ 08 8972 2650, open weekdays 09.00–17.00, Sat 09.00–15.00, Sun 09.30–16.00. Parks and wildlife is 1km north on Giles Street (☎ 08 8973 8770, weekdays 09.00–16.00). **Airnorth** (☎ 1800 627 474) flights are daily from Alice Springs and Darwin. *Greyhound Pioneer* (☎ 13 2030) provides a bus service daily on north–south and east–west routes.

Like Alice Springs, Katherine is a railhead and has some interesting aviation-related history. A Gipsy Moth biplane, originally owned by the area's first flying doctor, Clyde Fenton, is on display at the **Katherine Museum** (☎ 08 8072 3945; open Mon–Fri 10.00–16.00 Oct–March) on Gorge Road about 3km from the centre of town. The site of the Overland Telegraph Line station was at nearby Knotts Crossing. One of Australia's best Aboriginal-owned and operated arts and crafts galleries, **Mimi Arts and Crafts** (☎ 08 8971 0361), is on Pearce Street which runs parallel to Murphy Street.

The first attempts to settle the area were pastoral. Alfred and Mary Giles established **Springvale Station** in 1878. While not particularly successful, the station began the cattle industry in the region to the immediate north. Currently Springvale Homestead (☎ 08 8972 1355) is a tourist accommodation on the northern shore of the Katherine River about 3km downstream.

A similar station called **Manyallaluk** (☎ 08 8975 4727) in Eva Valley is now a prize-winning tourism venture operated by the Jawoyn people. Manyallaluk is a Frog Dreaming site on the eastern edge of the 3000 sq km station which the Jawoyn share with people speaking the Mayali, Ngalkbon and Renbarrnga languages. The station is about 100km north of Katherine and transportation to and from Katherine or Darwin (via Litchfield or Kakadu National Park) can be arranged. The activities include demonstrations of traditional skills (collecting, dyeing and weaving baskets), visits to billabongs and bushwalks.

Katherine Gorge and Nitmiluk National Park

The Katherine Gorge area itself is a series of 13 gorges along the Katherine River in **Nitmiluk National Park** (☎ 08 8972 1886), which is about 30km north of Katherine via Giles Street then Gorge Road. The walls of the gorges are not particularly high, but are vertical. Along its more easily accessible stretch the river is about 50m across and the cliffs about the same height. Rapids of varying force separate the gorges. Where the water is too shallow for canoes or air mattresses, trails follow the sides of the river.

The Katherine River's headwaters are in southern Arnhem Land. The river joins and becomes the Daly River before flowing into the Timor Sea 80km south-west of Darwin. The placid flow from April to October makes it hard to imagine it as a raging torrent during The Wet. In fact, the only cruise scheduled during The Wet is contingent upon the river not being too rough.

Signal flora include the salmon gum (so-called due to the colour of its sap), northern ironwood, Darwin woollybutt and an occasional boab tree. In less well-watered areas eucalypt woodlands with acacia and spinifex are the general flora species. Within the gorges one finds mosses, ferns and livingstonia palms, pandanus, silver paperbark and even mangroves. Fauna includes a variety of wallabies, freshwater crocodiles and long-necked tortoises. The birds, particularly around the picnic areas, include friar birds, red winged parrots, black cockatoos, grey bower birds, blue winged kingfishers, and honeyeaters.

The park takes its name from the Jawoyn people's Cicada Dreaming. Its **headquarters and visitor centre** are near the first gorge. In keeping with the wishes of the traditional owners, there is no entry fee. There are charges for cruises (two, four or eight hours long, ☎ 1800 089 103 or 08 8972 1253), the guided tour (2.5 hours long, ☎ 08 8972 1044) and canoe rentals. The cruises can be booked at the Katherine **tourist information centre**. Bush walks range from a short path to the lookout over the first gorge to several days' trek. With the exception of the walk to the lookout, bush walkers are required to register when undertaking a walk and upon its completion. A refundable deposit is required for those making the ten-day round-trip journey to Edith Falls. (The deposit is to ensure that those who register also de-register to preclude unnecessary search and rescue operations.)

Butterfly Gorge walk is about four hours long or 5.5km return. It passes through a pocket of monsoon rainforest on the way to the second gorge. The row butterflies often seen in the ravine descending to the river provide the name. Properly provisioned, a walk to Butterfly Gorge followed by an air mattress descent by river to return to the visitor's centre is about perfect. The walk itself follows black and white markers to match the colours of the butterflies. The first track encountered to the left (north, blue markers) is the **Lookout walk**; the next track to the left is to **Windolf lookout** following yellow markers. The Butterfly Gorge track is the third track to the left and about 3.5km from the information office.

The track to the right at this juncture leads to Lily Ponds. This 7km walk to the third gorge will take six hours there and back. Should camping overnight be desired, a site at **Dunlop Swamp** on the way to Smitts Rock is reputedly a pleasant stay. The visitor's centre (☎ 8972 1886) will have information regarding the availability of camp sites.

Queensland

Queensland comprises the northeastern section of Australia. Most of the settlements are along its eastern coastline, particularly near Brisbane, its capital in the extreme southeast. From Brisbane the **highways** are no. 1, the **Bruce Highway**, which follows the coast northwards and a variously named and numbered highway extending inland to the **Stuart Highway** of the Northern

Territory. Other highways between these two lead from Rockhampton (no. 66 Capricorn Highway) and Townsville (no. 78, Flinders Highway).

Queensland's most praiseworthy geological features include the **Great Barrier Reef** and associated islands, **Cape York Peninsula**, the coastal areas to Brisbane's south (the **Gold Coast**) and north (the **Sunshine Coast**), mountain ranges around **Lamington National Park** and the **Great Artesian Basin** which makes up the interior of the state west of the Great Dividing Range. The **Tropic of Capricorn** passes through the state. The monsoons along the north of the continent fill seasonal rivers flowing into the Gulf of Carpentaria and, under exceptional circumstances, south into Lake Eyre in South Australia.

Towards the interior south from the Gulf of Carpentaria, mangroves line the coast. Monsoon, blue and Mitchell grass eventually yield to hummock grasses and acacia as the conditions become more arid, finally leading to the Simpson Desert's expansive parallel sand dunes. The Cape York Peninsula is about 150km south of Papua New Guinea to which it was attached in the last Ice Age. This land bridge allowed considerable movement of flora and fauna into Australia. Most of the species shared with Papua New Guinea are found on the peninsula. Queensland has the most diverse wildlife of any Australian state: of the 223 Australian mammals, Queensland has 149; of the 683 birds, it has 546, and 251 out of the country's 431 reptiles.

Travelling across the coastal highlands towards the interior of the state, the conditions become increasingly arid. In common with the rest of the northern section of the continent, rain from December through March or April alternates with seasonable hot and dry conditions increasing during the middle of the year. The far southwest of the state is unlikely to receive rain at any time of year, and flooding is often the result when it does rain. Climatic extremes include Australia's hottest day, 53° C, recorded at Cloncurry in January 1889; and the wettest month was recorded in Bellenden Ker near Cairns with nearly 5.4m in February 1979. The state's vast size and climatic diversity is further evidenced in the contrasts of rainfall averages: Tully, on the coast 1500km north of Brisbane, receives an average rainfall of over 4000mm, and in one year received 7900mm; while Birdsville, in the far southwest corner of the state, is lucky to get 150mm a year.

South along the east coast conditions are not dissimilar to those of New South

Wales and Victoria. Highland **rainforests** extend from Cooktown to Townsville. In the southern part of this area and on the interior of the coastal ranges, native forest alternates with cultivated and pasture land. The most productive land is comprised of volcanic soils and includes the Atherton Tablelands south of Cairns, Peak Downs south of Townsville, the Capricornia region west of Rockhampton and Darling Downs west of Brisbane. West of Brisbane from about St George to Cunnamulla and north to Cloncurry, cattle and sheep range in mulga brush land or Mitchell grass. The southwestern corner is interior desert uplands.

The Queensland coast itself faces the **Coral Sea** to the north and the South Pacific Ocean in the south. The modern names of the Sunshine and Gold Coast regions are real estate developers' idioms; the shore in either case is splendid and swimmable nearly all year round except at times of jellyfish invasion. The coastal ranges to the interior are verdant.

The Great Barrier Reef

The **Great Barrier Reef** extends for 2000km from north of Newcastle to the Torres Strait. It is not a single reef, but consists of nearly 3000 individual coral reefs, making it the most complex living coral reef system in the world. It protects numerous island groups, the best known of which are probably the Whitsundays. The predominant **corals** include the fragile staghorn, brain corals in communities as large as 3m across, and solid Porites in even larger communities. Mushroom corals are individuals as large as 25 or 30cm each. Red pipe organ and blue coral are also prevalent.

The reef's structure is based on numerous sea-level changes which have built a foundation slightly more than 100m deep. The **Outer Barrier** follows the continental shelf at the 100 fathom line. At times the shelf drops steeply from the Outer Barrier, reaching 1000 fathoms (555 metres) within 10km. The Pacific rollers and cyclones have broken and assembled reef limestone and beach rock to create the Outer Barrier.

The **Inner Reef** may have crescent-shaped formations of reef due to southeasterly winds, but most are platform reefs which slope back towards the interior sand reefs. It is among these reefs that tourists can fish, snorkel or simply explore tide pools, especially at low tide. Many of the sightseeing boats have glass bottoms and most have well-informed guides. The distance to the reef from the continent varies from 150km in the south to within 75km in its central section at Townsville and 15km off the coast near Cooktown.

Its wildlife is spectacularly abundant. Better-known fish species include **clown fish** (*Amphiprion percula*) which live in the anemones, the beautiful and fiercely territorial **butterfly fish** (Chaetodons), coral trout, manta rays, and whale sharks. The reef is an important breeding area for **sea turtles**. Six of the seven species of these reptiles have been sighted in the reef. The green turtle and loggerhead, flatback and hawksbill all nest predominantly or exclusively in the reef.

Bird species are not particularly prevalent on the reef itself. The associated islands, however, support numerous populations of **terns**, particularly large colonies of the crested tern and sooty tern (breeding on Michaelmas Cay and the Swain Reefs) and breeding populations of the roseate tern, wedge-tailed shearwaters and brown gannets (Raine Island and Swain Reef cays).

Naturalist and poet Judith Wright describes the profusion of species on Lady Elliot Island in the Bunker Group:

White-breasted sea-eagles and frigate birds soared and circled over it, herons fished the shallows and the reef edge, noddies swept over and into the waves, boobies and gannets dived and plunged into passing shoals of fish...Between the terns and the other breeding species, and the mutton-birds underground grumbling and booming in the tunnels, it seemed there could be no more room for wings in the air or nests on the ground.

The island groups associated with the Great Barrier Reef are the **Southern Coastal Islands**, the **Southern Reef Islands**, the **Whitsunday Islands** and the **Tropical North Islands**. A description of a tour north from Brisbane can be followed on p 650.

History

The establishment of Queensland and the selection of **Brisbane** as its capital followed a course familiar in Australian history. The desire to deter a perceived rising crime rate in Britain, hostility between free and convict colonists in Sydney, and insecurity about potential settlements by foreign interests prompted a plan to establish a penal colony somewhere along Australia's northeast coast.

The selection of Moreton Bay as the location of this colony in 1823 and its subsequent selection as the state's capital were largely accidents of weather and tide. Brisbane's current form and appearance is due to its river and the civic aesthetic of its late 19C merchants, developers and benefactors.

The essential dates for the area include when Captain Cook mapped the coastline in 1770. **John Oxley** landed at Red Cliff on Moreton Bay in 1823 and shortly afterwards moved the colony to where Brisbane stands today, selecting what would become the corner of William and Queen Streets for settlement in 1825. His accompanying botanist Allan Cunningham described the inland country, particularly the Darling Downs and Cunningham Gap leading to the Moreton Bay area in 1828.

Squatters Patrick Leslie and his brothers followed Cunningham's overland route to the Darling Downs agricultural area in 1840. New South Wales opened the area for free settlement, beginning land sales upon the end of the penal interests in 1842. Brisbane became the capital of Queensland upon the state's founding in 1859. Gold discoveries in the period from 1861 to 1882 and sugar cane plantations kept the young state prosperous. Severe floods in 1893 prompted prominent citizens to rebuild on higher ground at Hamilton, Ascot and Clayfield. Dr and Miss Mayne donated St Lucia as the permanent site for the University of Queensland in 1926. Long-serving National Party Premier Joh Bjelke-Petersen, the epitome of political corruption Queensland-style, was suspected of fraud and indicted for perjury in 1987 (see p 625). The Great Barrier Reef received World Heritage Protection in 1982.

In greater detail, the history of Queensland begins when the Dutch **Captain Willem Jansz** mapped part of the west coast of Cape York in 1606 as did Jan Carstensz in 1623. Jansz described the region in his journal in the most uncomplimentary terms: 'In our judgement this is the most arid and barren region to be found anywhere on earth; the inhabitants, too, are the most wretched and poorest creatures that I have ever seen.'

More than a century and a half later, **Captain Cook** mapped the coast, making nine landfalls and spending seven weeks repairing his reef-damaged ship at the mouth of the Endeavour River, near present-day Cooktown, at Cape Tribulation. Legend has it that it was here he learned from local Aborigines to call the strange hopping creature 'kangaroo', which probably meant 'I don't know'. Matthew Flinders visited the area in the first decade of the 19C, although he missed the Brisbane River.

Reporting in 1822 to Lord Bathurst, who was then Secretary of State for War and the Colonies, John Thomas Bigge suggested that new **penal colonies** be established at Port Bowen (now Point Clinton south of Townsville), Port Curtis (now Gladstone) and Moreton Bay. Their purpose was to provide more punitive conditions for transported convicts who subsequently offended in New South Wales or Van Diemen's Land and to act as a further deterrent to crime in Britain, as if the threat of transportation to Sydney were not enough.

Simultaneously, Governor Brisbane was trying to cope with the growing conflict between free settlers and former transportees. A penal colony at Moreton Bay was a concession to the free settlers, which did little to lessen free settler animosity towards the emancipists (convicts who had served their time) and their allies in the trades in Sydney. Port Macquarie in New South Wales was founded in 1821 for similar purposes. By the time Parliament enacted enabling legislation in 1824, sufficient numbers of transportees had been assigned to private employers to reduce the number of additional colonies needed to one, that at Moreton Bay.

Lord Bathurst instructed Brisbane to affect Bigge's proposals, and in 1823 surveyor John Oxley (see box, p 622) travelled to the northeast coast to examine his locations. Weather prevented him from visiting Port Bowen; seasonal dry conditions and scant timber led him to discourage settlement at Port Curtis. The Brisbane River and surrounding land suitable for agriculture led Oxley to recommend **Moreton Bay**. He described the Brisbane River as 'by far the largest freshwater river on the east coast of New South Wales'. Red Cliff Peninsula on the northern shore of the river's mouth was a convenient initial settlement and the eventual permanent colony could be located a little further inland.

In 1824 Oxley, commandant Lieutenant Henry Miller, botanist Allan Cunningham, assistant surveyor Robert Hoddle, a handful of 40th Regiment guards, 29 convicts (mostly skilled volunteers) and a few family members established the outpost on Red Cliff. The next year Miller moved the colony to the present-day location of **Brisbane**, above Breakfast Creek.

Immediately, the prospects at Moreton Bay Penal Colony proved too favourable for intractable convicts. In response, Norfolk Island was slated to be reopened and Governor Darling, Brisbane's successor, toughened the regime at Moreton Bay by sending the vicious **Captain Patrick Logan** to be commandant in 1826. He had convicts flogged for misbehaviour, routinely exceeding the regulation 50-lash maximum. Men worked shackled in irons. He had cells for solitary confinement erected and a treadmill installed. Not surprisingly, he had occasion to explain the low productivity of the colony.

During Logan's command, however, the limestone kiln at what would eventually be Ipswich was built, Cunningham described the Darling Downs

John Oxley

John Oxley (c 1785–1828) was born in Yorkshire and named John Joseph William Molesworth Oxley. The *Australian Encyclopedia* reports that when he joined the navy as midshipman in 1799 the interviewing officer impatiently exclaimed, 'Damn it all, plain John Oxley is good enough!'

He first visited Australia in 1802 and returned in 1808 as a commissioned lieutenant and in 1812 as surveyor general. He traced the Lachlan and Macquarie Rivers and reported disparagingly on what became the rich pastoral lands of the Liverpool Plains, maintaining that the country was 'uninhabitable and useless for all purposes of civilised men'. Similarly, his report of the Illawarra stated that he 'saw no place on which even a cabbage might be planted with a prospect of success'. Rather than on these inaccurate assessments, his fame derives from his work furthering the settlement of Brisbane.

Sent north along the coast to select a site for the new penal colony in 1823, he favourably described Moreton Bay and the Brisbane River.

His civic responsibilities were fairly ambitious. He was an early member and officer of the Bible Society, a founding member of the Philosophical Society, on the committees of the Female and Male Orphan Institutions and the Public School Institution, a subscribing member of the Scots and St James churches and briefly a member of the Legislative Council.

Despite having at one time or another owned large tracts of good land and having engaged in a variety of mercantile interests, he died aged only 42 'much embarrassed in his pecuniary circumstances'. The colony's Executive Council recommended special assistance to his widow and children; the British government granted his sons 5000 acres adjoining what is now Bowral in recognition of his services to the colonies.

and a route to them, and several stone buildings were erected in Brisbane itself. Logan was murdered in 1830 while mapping the area around Mount Beppo. The circumstances were never made clear, but it seems likely that his skull was bashed in by convicts accompanying him.

The number of prisoners at the colony increased to 1066 in 1831, then declined as reoffending convicts were increasingly used as road workers in the Sydney region. Calls for the colony to be closed as a penal settlement and opened to **free settlement** continued until 1839 when all but 94 male convicts were removed; those remaining looked after the governmental livestock.

Colonial functions established the course of many of Brisbane's streets. Although only two structures survive from the penal era—the Commissariat Store and the Windmill—paths, now roads, which led from them to the bridge, the gardens and the outlying farms can still be followed. Logan situated the Prisoners' Barracks, a large stone building, perpendicular to the river. The surveyors who laid out **central Brisbane** in 1839 accepted this structural orientation and ran what would become a main thoroughfare, **Queen Street**, past its front. The remainder of the grid and the naming of the streets after British royalty followed shortly thereafter.

Governor Brisbane's initial conception of an area where the intractable convicts from Sydney could be sequestered proved impractical. The area was considered too far from Sydney, an objection which did nothing to deter

squatters eager for new land. In fact, the first substantial number of permanent settlers to the territory crossed inland from Cardwell to the Herbert
River following a track cleared by pioneering pastoralist Walter J. Scott's
party as late as 1864.

The selection of Brisbane as the state's capital was often in jeopardy.
Commandant Logan would have preferred moving the colony up river near
to Oxley Creek to service more easily the Logan River and Tweed districts to
the city's south. Commandant Major Sydney Cotton and his foreman of
works Andrew Petrie ended the discussion to move Brisbane Town entirely
following their survey of the area in 1838. Cotton then set about improving
road transport to facilitate cartage in the area.

For a period in the 1840s **South Brisbane** rivalled Brisbane proper as a
port, particularly after the Hunter River Steam Navigation Company built a
wharf and warehouses there. **Kangaroo Point**, again on the south side,
became a manufacturing centre with ferry access beginning in 1844. By
the 1850s, however, the north side of the river took ascendancy. In addition
to businessmen with commercial interests centred in North Brisbane, the
populist Reverend Dr J.D. Lang sponsored the settlement of **Fortitude
Valley** in 1849. The colony spread west via access to the Darling Downs
and West Moreton through Ipswich and Bremer.

Squatters had moved into southwest Queensland from the New England
district of New South Wales in 1840, two years before the area was formally
opened to free settlement. One Francis Bigge suggested Ipswich be the agricultural service centre with a port on Moreton Bay. Robert Dixon, a
surveyor, pressed for Cleveland as the port. These suggestions were the basis
of Governor Gipps's inspection tour in 1848.

Theoretically, the area around the Moreton Bay colony was not available
for settlement until 1842. Nonetheless, a German missionary community
established itself several miles northwest of Brisbane at Xion Hill (now
Nandah) in 1838, two years before squatters settled in the Darling Downs.

In fact, it was the building of the Customs House in Brisbane in 1855, the
dredging of the Brisbane River and establishment of Queensland as a state
independent of New South Wales in 1859 that finally established Brisbane
as the capital city.

In the first 20 years after its separation from New South Wales the population of Queensland increased from about 28,000 to 211,040. In addition
to some mining and industry in the Ipswich area, the rise of sugar plantations along the coast and grazing land on less fertile land ensured that the
state would be solvent. The discovery of gold in 1867 in Gympie, in 1872
in Charters Towers and in 1882 near Rockhampton did much to spread the
population throughout the state. It kept the state bank afloat and financed
Brisbane's growth in the 1880s and 1890s.

The second period of pastoral settlement followed William Landsborough's description of interior grazing land. He had been sent in 1861 by the
Victorian government to search for the **Burke and Wills expedition**.
Robert Burke was commissioned by the Royal Society of Victoria to find a
route along which the inevitable telegraph line could be laid. Eminently ill
suited to the task, he made it as far as Normanton, virtually within sight of
the Gulf of Carpentaria. The party's retreat ended at the base camp at

Cooper Creek the day after their rearguard who had been waiting for their return had abandoned it.

William Landsborough's rescue party was one of several that established that the semi-arid interior was habitable if harsh. A number of herds of cattle were overlanded to central and northern Queensland in the early 1860s based on these reports. An example of these settlers, John Jardine, who was the first government magistrate in Somerset on the tip of the Cape York Peninsula, sent his sons with a herd of cattle from Rockhampton overland to the Cape York Peninsula in an eventful ten month trek in 1864–65. His son Frank built an empire from cattle-raising and pearl-fishing.

Simultaneously, the agricultural regions along the coast were being settled. Initially, cotton was the major export, but the end of the American Civil War in 1865 opened the market for inexpensive cotton and its transport. Fortunately, the second crop of choice was sugar cane. It became the mainstay of the southern coastal region. Driving through this region is as monotonous as driving through the cornfields of the American Midwest, perhaps more so because the cane is equally dense, equally monotonal and considerably taller. Lengths of road become corridors with no hint of landscape, and certainly no views of the sea.

Slaves were abducted from the South Pacific Islands and sold to cotton and pineapple plantation owners in Queensland between 1863 and Federation in 1901. These people were called **Kanakas** (Hawaiian for 'man'). To assuage the conscience of sensible Australians, the trade in Kanakas was presented as voluntary servitude, something like apprenticeships. The two most despicable of the traders were Ross Lewin, who first offered the 'best and most serviceable natives to be had in the islands at £7 a head', and Dr James Patrick Murray, who kidnapped and murdered about 70 labourers then turned Queen's evidence to escape punishment. Efforts to control the practice failed. The courts used jurisdictional and legal definitions as a way of avoiding convictions or carrying out sentences. The licensing authorities gave little heed to the practices they were authorised to control. In the end, the Pacific Island Labourers Act was passed in 1901 as Australian labourers pressed for the jobs the islanders held and the **White Australia Policy** came to full effect. In all something like 60,000 men were brought to Queensland; about 1600 of those working at the turn of the century stayed. Faith Bandler, an important activist in the Aboriginal rights movement today, has Kanaka heritage. Increased conversions to Christianity in the South Pacific Islands was a consequence of enslavement, repatriation and public concern about the practice of 'Blackbirding', as this trade was known.

In the last quarter of the 19C considerable acrimony existed in the state. When the railroad was laid to Ipswich, the agricultural interests clamoured for similar consideration. Improved roads to the cane fields and stringent requirements of land tenure caused disaffection among the pastoralists. Crown tenants on large properties pressed subsistence squatters from small parcels of better land. Nearly all of the outlying communities were angered by rather than proud of Brisbane's civic building boom. For a period there were calls for the state to be divided into thirds.

Once the alluvial gold had been gleaned, the diggers returned to a tight labour market. Shearers unionised and the Darling Downs Pastoralists'

Association hired non-union workers exclusively in 1889. The maritime workers refused to load wool from Jondaryan woolshed and insisted on other conditions as well. The shearers were returned to the sheds, but the maritime workers lost their award in 1890.

The most serious **shearers' strike** was near Barcaldine in 1891. By the time the matter was controlled, the unions had formed militias and the government had sent 1400 soldiers, armed with machine guns and artillery, to support the pastoralists. In any event, another army of unemployed labourers was more than eager to work at any wage. The **Labor Party**, born of this dispute, actually won the first labor government in the world in 1899 (the decision to spell 'Labor' in American style was a conscious choice of the organisers, to stress their affinity with the more 'progressive' American labour movement). After six days in office, the feuding Liberals and Conservatives resolved their arguments, formed a coalition, and dissolved parliament.

Amid these fractious times, the Whites Only Policy became legitimate. The Kanakas were repatriated or absorbed into the local population. The Chinese living in Australia were virtually expelled. For decades immigrants had to prove language proficiency in a dictation test which could be given in a language as obscure as the testers could manage. This test was only abolished in 1958.

Miraculously, by 1908 the minimum wage had been implemented and was sufficient to support a male worker, his wife and three children. Old age and invalid pensions were being paid. The 40-hour working week was the norm. In 1915 the Labor Party was returned to office on an anti-conscription policy. (It remained in office until 1957 when Labor lost due to internal strife and a coalition between Country and Liberal parties.)

Australia shared the worldwide economic Depression of the early 1930s. Strong wool and ore prices and a surfeit of mutton, wild rabbit and agricultural produce sustained the state. Arguably these factors contributed to Australia's subsistence economy until reconstruction following the Second World War. As Queensland native and author David Malouf frequently asserts in his writings, the arrival of large numbers of American troops in Brisbane during the Second World War caused a significant transformation of the city into a more modern, 'Americanised' place.

The Liberal loss in 1957 brought National Party leader **Joh Bjelke-Petersen** into office for 19 years of self-righteousness and resulting strife and, in the end, corruption. In 1989 the National Party was finally voted out of office when the state returned Labor to government. Since the 1980s, Queensland has been the fastest-growing state in terms of population, as increasing numbers of pensioners and young families have opted for the warm climate of the north. The negative effect of this influx has been the massive high-rise developments from the New South Wales border all the way to Brisbane, turning the Gold Coast into a Miami-Beach-style community. The positive effect has been a breaking up of Queensland's traditional conservativism and 'red neck' image. Brisbane now has more sophisticated cultural institutions and dining experiences, and the rest of the state, with all its lush scenery, is more aware of the needs of visitors from all over the world.

Brisbane
....

Brisbane (population 1,530,000) is situated on the delta of the Brisbane River, which flows as a serpentine path through the city to Moreton Bay. The central business district faces South Brisbane Reach on a northern tongue of the river. The streets are named after British monarchs—the queens running southeast to northwest and the kings perpendicular. The art gallery, performing arts centre and convention centre can be found across Victoria Bridge. Like the city centre, the university is on the northern bank of the river in the next ox-bow inland. 5km to the west, Mount Coot-Tha rises to 250m.

Among the city's most pleasant picnic locations are C.T. White Park, on Kangaroo Point with a view across the Brisbane River to the city centre. It is accessible by ferry and a short walk. Between Woowong and St Lucia, University of Queensland, Kaye's Rocks on Brisbane Street offers good river views of St Lucia and Toowong. Bellbird Grove Picnic Area is in the Enoggera State Forest about 20km west of the city centre following Musgrave and Waterworks Roads.

■ Practical information

Tourist information. The most conveniently located offices are on Queen Street Mall, on the corner of Queen and Albert Streets (☎ 07 3229 5918) and in City Hall (☎ 07 3221 8411) on King George Square. The Tourist Bureau is at 234 Edward Street (☎ 07 3221 6111). National park information is at 160 Ann Street (☎ 07 3227 8185, open weekdays 08.30–17.00). Another information centre is on the second floor in the Transit Centre (☎ 07 3236 2020). They will all act as booking agents for travel, accommodation and venues.

Airport. Brisbane has an international airport, 9km northwest of the centre of town, on Kingsford Smith Drive. Some flights from Europe and America stop here before continuing on to Sydney, so it is possible to book flights specifically to Queensland. Flights between Asia and the Pacific Islands are particularly numerous from this airport, as is evident in the number of Asian and islander airlines headquartered here. Some examples are *Polynesian Airlines*, ☎ 07 3854 2828; *Solomon Airlines*, ☎ 07 3229 7813; and *Garuda*, ☎ 07 3210 0688. Within the state, regional airline services are handled by *Qantas*, ☎ 13 13 13 or *Ansett*, ☎ 13 13 00.

From the airport, a shuttle bus takes passengers into the Transit Centre on Roma Street in the centre of town; it takes about 40 minutes into town. Taxis from the airport will cost at least $15 into the city.

Train. Rail services in Queensland are operated by *Queensland Rail*; the main office is 305 Edward Street, Brisbane, ☎ 07 3235 1323. The rail system runs mostly along the coast, and is slower and more expensive than the bus; some of the trips, however, pass through beautiful scenery that would not be accessible on a coach trip, and others are touted as tourist adventures.

Within Brisbane, the electric **Citytrain** provides good service, although service to the outer suburbs (as far as Caboolture and Beenleigh) is fairly infrequent. Trains depart from Central Station, Ann Street, ☎ 13 12 30.

Bus. Coach travel throughout Queensland is the most popular form of 'public' transportation. The main operators here are *Greyhound Pioneer* (☎ 13 20 30) and *McCafferty's* (☎ 07 3236 3033). All buses arrive at the Transit Centre on Roma Street.

Brisbane is the only place in Queensland with a reasonable local transport system. Bus routes are extensive and tickets, on a zone system, are relatively inexpensive. Information and timetables are available at the Administration Centre, Ann Street, and from *TransInfo* (☎ 13 12 30).

Taxis. *B & W Cabs*, 37 Quay Street, ☎ 07 3238 1000; *Yellow Cabs*, ☎ 07 3391 0191.

Ferries. The ferry service on the Brisbane River is a pleasant and often expeditious means of getting around. Rover tickets, honoured by bus lines as well, route maps and schedules are available at tourist information centres and most newsagents. The main transportation service, *TransInfo* (☎ 13 12 30) will provide information on the ferry service as well as other forms of transportation.

Useful addresses
Consulates. **British Consulate-General**, Level 26, Waterfront Place, 1 Eagle Street; ☎ 07 3236 2575; **New Zealand**, 288 Edward Street; ☎ 07 3221 9933.
Disabled services. For information on facilities, ☎ 07 3225 4416; for *Disabled Persons Service*, ☎ 07 3224 8031.
Hospitals. *Royal Brisbane*, Herston Road, Herston, ☎ 07 3253 8111.
Police. *Emergency*, 000; *Headquarters*, Roma Street, ☎ 07 3364 6464; *Queen Street Mall*, ☎ 07 3220 0752.
Rape Crisis Line. 1 800 24 45 26; 07 3844 4008.

City tour
Some years ago the Royal Australian Institute of Architects, Queensland Chapter, published *A Map Guide to the Architecture of the City* which provides the basis for the following tours. The Brisbane City Council Heritage Unit also publishes pamphlets describing buildings of note in areas of the city. They are available by calling the council on ☎ (07) 3403 8888 or from any of the city's customer service centres—the one in the city centre is at 69 Ann Street.

This walk leads from the Tourist Bureau on Adelaide Street beyond Edward Street at the edge of Anzac Square to the Post Office on Queen Street east to the Brisbane River, then either by ferry across to Kangaroo Point or, continuing on foot, along lower Edward Street. In either case, the walk leads to the Botanic Gardens then proceeds up George Street to the Queen Street Mall.

The **General Post Office** is on Queen Street between Edward and Creek Streets and was built on the site of the female convict factory. The design has a Tuscan colonnade at the street level and Corinthian columns with pilasters above. Stone for the columns and façade was quarried near Helidon and at Albion Heights. The cast-iron balustrades on the upper verandah give the building a pleasant lightness, unconventional in governmental buildings. Details include a hitching post, a clock on the pediment of the northern wing and a crest in the first-floor balustrade. The northern wing was built by John Petrie in 1871–72; the central

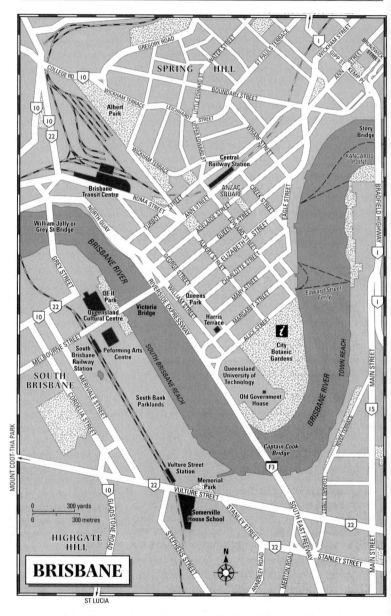

tower and matching southern wing were added in 1877–79. Colonial Architect F.D.G. Stanley designed the southern wing.

Newspaper House (formerly the Colonial Mutual Life Building and currently serviced apartments, adjacent to the General Post Office to the east), designed by Hennessey and Hennessey, is a steel frame construction with a locally manufactured Benedict stone façade. Hennessey and Hennessey designed the CML Building on King Street in Adelaide as well. The sculptural detail on the street and side façades adds style to this 1931 building.

Central to **ANZAC SQUARE**, the **Shrine of Remembrance** (designed by Buchanan and Cowper) commemorates the Boer War. The square is contained by the General Post Office, the Central Railway Station and **St John's Cathedral**. English architect John Pearson designed the cathedral; the Duke of Cornwall (later George V) laid the cornerstone in May 1901. In a Gothic Revival style, a number of slender piers support a high stone-vaulted ceiling; there are rose windows at the transept ends and elegant curved choir stalls.

R.S. Dods designed the associated buildings Webber House (1904–05) and Church House (1910), using steep gabled roofs and brick and stone building materials to match the cathedral. Interesting Art Nouveau ornament makes them visually interesting as well.

The **National Australia Bank**, across Queen Street on the corner of Creek Street, is a good example of the Classical Revival style in Australia. Former Colonial Architect F.D.G. Stanley designed this opulent building with references to Italian Renaissance architectural detail. The bank was awarded the government account in 1879 and became the Queensland National Bank. Many of its branches are of similar, though more modest, style. The bank's interior features fine joinery and fireplaces (the second floor was originally intended to be residential), a massive leaded glass central chamber and coffered ceiling in the entry corridor. Conrad Gargett and Partners restored the bank in 1982; their work on the interior cedar joinery and plasterwork is particularly praiseworthy.

Crossing Queen Street at the apex formed by Eagle Street leads to the **Mooney Memorial Fountain**. It commemorates volunteer fireman James Mooney who lost his life fighting a fire at a Queen Street grocery store in 1877. Using funds from a public appeal, his friends and relatives built a memorial to him at the Toowong Cemetery. Due to the persistent popular notion that the Gothic-style fountain at the head of Queen Street was his memorial, the Brisbane City Council installed a tablet to Mooney here. In fact, this fountain was erected in 1880 at the request of nearby merchants who simply wanted to improve this triangle of land.

Customs House, at the top of Queen Street, is currently the city offices of the University of Queensland. Between 1842, when the Morton Bay Colony was opened for free settlement, and 1848, when the New South Wales government established customs facilities in Brisbane, some debate occurred regarding the location of the colony's principal port. Cleveland, the site favoured by settlers in the Ipswich region, might have become the port had the tide not been out during Governor Gipps's inspection tour. Local lore has it that he and his party were forced to trudge some distance across mud flats to reach that city at low tide. He thought it would make an inadequate port. Establishing Customs House in Brisbane seriously disadvantaged other ports from contention as the capital.

John Petrie built this classical Renaissance building in 1886–89 to designs by Charles McLay who worked in the Colonial Architect's office. Its features include Corinthian columns, a fine copper dome, unusual heraldic shields and fig trees in the grounds. The solidity of this imposing building seemed to Brisbane native David Malouf to counter the transience of the town's other architecture; in his book, *A Spirit of Play* (1998), he says of the Customs House, the Post Office and Parliament House, 'they were the nearest thing we had to something ancient and historical'. Customs House Gallery, on the Riverside, features changing exhibitions by Queensland artists (open daily, 10.00–16.00)..

The **Story Bridge** (visible behind the Customs House) was designed by Dr J.C. Bradfield, who also designed the Sydney Harbour Bridge. Opened in 1940, it is often referred to as Jubilee Bridge in reference to George V's Silver Jubilee. The massive abutments were built of river gravel and coral cement dredged from near the river's mouth. The largest steel cantilevered bridge in Australia, it was built by Evans Deakin and Hornibook Constructions.

Either walk south along the Brisbane River through the Plantation Reserve and along the riverside boardwalk to the Botanic Gardens or ferry across the Brisbane River to Kangaroo Point. Either way is about the same distance.

Kangaroo Point was originally a manufacturing area. In addition to a number of pleasant residences dating from the middle and late 19C are the immigrant hostel **Yungaba** ('land of the sun') and the Story Bridge Hotel.

The return **ferry** from Thornton Street docks near the Alice Street entrance to the Botanic Gardens (see below).

St Stephen's Cathedral, on ELIZABETH STREET beyond Creek Street, an English Gothic Revival structure, is made of local porphyry stone. Designed by Benjamin Backhouse and built between 1863 and 1874, it was meant to replace the original St Stephen's which stands beside it. This earlier church is a fine piece of Gothic Revival architecture designed by A.W. Pugin, the English architect associated with the construction of the London Houses of Parliament. Consecrated in 1850 as part of Sydney's diocese, this is Brisbane's oldest standing church and with the cathedral offers insights into the development of the city's 19C aesthetic aspirations.

The lower EDWARD STREET area contains a number of late 19C warehouses. **Brisbane Community Arts Centre**, Coronation House, was built in 1884. It features five levels and a basement with original ironbark support beams. The State Health Building, on Charlotte Street beyond Edward Street, has kept the Classic Revival façade of the original Brabant and Company import firm.

The busy Greek and Egyptian motifs of **Charlotte House**, adjacent to the State Health Building, were erected in the 1880s for Wallace and Warren, shipping agents. The **Inglis Tea Merchants** have leased part of the building since 1912. James Inglis (1845–1908) made 'Billy Tea' a common-place in Australia. His merchandising tactics included setting 'Banjo' Paterson's poem 'Waltzing Matilda' to music and wrapping it around the tea packet as a promotional gift; this was the method by which the song became so well known throughout Australia (see p 645).

Sydney architects A.L. and C. McCredie designed **Naldham House** as an Indian Colonial, Classic Revival building for the Australasian United Steam Navigation Company in 1889. It is currently a private club on the corner of Mary and Market Streets. Flood levels from 1890, 1893 and 1897 are recorded on the base of the tower.

In contrast to Stanley's design for the Queensland National Bank, the **Harbours and Marine Building** at the corner of Margaret and Edward Streets is a Victorian Classic Revival structure. Erected by John Petrie, this was originally the Port Office with a river bank location in 1878–80. Note the restored *porte cochère* coach drive and cast-iron roof ridging. A reference guide for flood levels, the ground floor was added long after the original two-storeyed section with bays and verandahs.

On the same corner, the **Naval Stores** offers a welcome relief from the Classic Revival pomposity. This building dates from 1900–01. Constructed for the Queensland Marine Defence Force, it is Queen Anne style with a Rococo porch entry, Tuscan columns and an elaborate coat of arms.

The site of the **Botanic Gardens** (☎ 07 3870 8136; open daily 24 hours) was originally an Aboriginal river crossing. Situated below Alice Street from the river to George Street, they were established in 1825 as a Government Garden at the instruction of Governor Thomas Brisbane. The area was extended in 1855 as Grace Botanical Garden. In 1865 it became Queen's Park when Governor George Bowen added the river frontage and former sports fields.

The gardens were the site of the first sugar cane grown in Queensland. John Buhôt made the first sugar in Queensland from the garden's cane, using a lever to extract cane juice and his kitchen stove to boil off the liquid. The first commercial plantation and mill was established by Louis Hope in 1886–65 at Ormiston, about 35km east of Brisbane.

Noteworthy early plantings still evident include the **Bunya Pines**. These were planted in the 1850s by the first Colonial Botanist, Walter Hill. Hill experimented with a number of tropical crops which eventually became central to Queensland agriculture, including pineapple, mangoes and ginger. The avenue of **weeping figs** was planted in the 1870s. The garden's water features, especially the Mangrove Boardwalk along the river, are particularly popular. The garden seeks to provide native and exotic plant species in a traditional park. Volunteers give guided tours at 11.00 and 13.00 Mon–Sat. The new gardens at Mount Coot-tha (see p 636) are devoted to the Queensland natural habitat.

Parliament House (☎ 07 3226 7562) is across GEORGE STREET. Colonial Architect Charles Tiffin designed the building in a French Renaissance style. Its walls are of freestone quarried from the banks of the Brisbane River at Woogaroo. Parliament's first sitting here was on 14 July 1865, but the colonnade was not completed until 1879. The Alice Street wing was built in 1889–91. The *porte cochère* and any number of other original designs were restored in 1981–82 by Conrad Gargett and Partners. The first sitting of Queensland's Parliament was actually at the Military and Convicts Barracks (Queen Street between George and Albert Streets) on 22 May 1860. At the time of Parliament House's erection, the *Guardian* newspaper observed that the legislature would be 'transferred from the forbidding-looking building in Queen Street, with its evil recollections of cells and bolts and chains ... to a hall of assembly befitting the dignity of the legislature'. Guided tours are given daily at 10.30, 14.30, 15.15 and 16.15 when Parliament is not in session.

Unlike most clubs in Australia, entrance to which is simply a matter of signing a register, the **Queensland Club** (diagonally across George Street) is strictly for members and has been since it opened in 1859. This climate-conscious building, again from designs by F.G.D. Stanley, opened in 1884 and features an interesting upper level verandah balustrade, pleasant grounds and high ceilings in the members' common rooms.

The George Street campus of **Queensland University of Technology**, more generally known as QUT, is one of three campuses. Its noteworthy buildings date from the 1970s and include the Community Building, particularly for the brick finishes, and the Music Conservatory, complete in 1974. The Kindler Theatre's design by Blair M. Wilson allowed the first in-the-round staging in Brisbane.

Northwest along George Street to Margaret Street leads to **The Mansions**. Oakden, Addison and Kemp designed these six terrace houses which were built in 1890. They feature considered responses to the climate—the large verandah, recessed main hall and, particularly, the bay windows which extend across the roof line to the attic. A stylish address at the turn of the century, their red brickwork accentuates the Oamaru (New Zealand) limestone. The same firm designed the Albert Street Uniting Church on Ann Street at about the same time. (They used the same contrasting limestone for a similarly striking visual effect.) Note the cats on the parapets at each end.

The **Sciencentre** (☎ 07 3220 0166; open daily 10.00–17.00), up George Street towards Charlotte Street, was originally the Government Printing Office, hence the Printers' Devils as gargoyles atop the parapet. The centre functions as an interactive science and engineering display.

A number of Italian Renaissance-style governmental buildings from the late 19C and early 20C are set around **Queen's Park**. This area was the site of the Moreton Bay penal colony. The Commandant's residence was on the site of the Sciencentre. Across William Street is the **Commissariat Stores**, built in 1829 under the infamous Captain Patrick Logan as a two-storey structure. Convict labour quarried local stone, adzed ironbark for the girders and pit-sawed the yellowwood floorboards. The building is open to the public thanks to the Royal Historical Society Museum (☎ 07 3221 4198; open Tues–Fri 11.00–14.00) and offices located here.

The substantial **Treasury Building** facing Queens Park is an Italian Renaissance-styled structure with elaborate façades and verandahs. It sits on the location of the original Officers' Quarters and Military Barracks. Designed by Colonial Architect J.J. Clark in 1885, it was built in three sections and currently functions as a casino. The former Lands Administration Building directly across the park is the casino's associated hotel. A. Morry designed this well-proportioned building at the turn of the century.

Walking along George Street, past the Queen Street Mall, taking a right turn up Adelaide Street leads to the **City Hall** on King George Square. Except for the tower, the building is a well-proportioned Classical Revival structure designed by Hall and Prentice and built between 1920 and 1930. Its tympanum relief, though difficult to see without field glasses, was designed by Daphne Mayo. The figures in the tympanum are allegories for the cattle and wool industries. The City Hall Art Gallery and Museum (☎ 07 3403 4048; open daily 10.00–17.00) is on the first floor.

The variety of building styles fronting on the Queen Street Mall provide a welcome relief from the imposing governmental district. On the corner of Queen and George Streets is the **Bank of New South Wales** (now the Westpac) which was erected in 1929 to designs by Hall and Devereaux. The sandstone facing on the modern steel-framed structure suggests that the 19C aesthetics of stolid banks lasted well into the 20C. Across Queen Street the Colonial Mutual Life

Assurance Society building, designed by Richard Gailey in 1883, originally had a tower which, like many such towers was removed during the Second World War to be used as shell casings.

Further along is the former **Myer Store**, part of the Myer Centre. Originally constructed in the 1880s as well, it is on the site of the colony's Prisoners' Barracks. The store and neighbouring building were the locus of the mall's refurbishment in 1988. Opposite are the **New York Hotel** which replaced the York in 1929 and the former **Newspaper House** which was erected in 1891 for the Telegraph Newspaper. The parapet atop the Newspaper House and its second level bay windows enliven the façade. The front of the adjoining **Carlton Hotel** features decorative cast-iron verandah railings and balustrades. The upper level's wooden balustrades, added in 1925, were replaced with matching iron during the mall's refurbishment.

In the next block are the **Hoyt's Regent** and **Majesty's Theatres**. The Hoyt's Regent, designed by B. Hollingshead and built in 1928–29, originally seated 3000 viewers. The remaining entrance, foyer and staircase preserve the lavish detail expected of the picture palaces of the era. Her Majesty's Theatre was designed as an opera house in 1888 by Andrea Strombucco. Like the Hoyt's Regent, its lavish Italianate stuccoed exterior reflects the expectations of Victorian era theatre-goers. Whereas the Hoyt's Regent's interior was revamped in 1979, the opera's was renovated in the early 1930s.

South Brisbane

Queensland Cultural Centre

South Brisbane is an easy walk across Victoria Bridge from the city centre. The **Queensland Cultural Centre** (☎ 07 3840 7100) here includes the State Library, the Art Gallery and Museum and the Performing Arts Centre. The **Queensland State Library** (☎ 07 3840 7666; open Mon–Thurs 10.00–20.00, Fri–Sun 10.00–17.00) occasionally has interesting smaller exhibitions but is best known for its collection of materials relating to Queensland's history and society. They present films from their collection Sundays at 14.00. The **Queensland Art Gallery** (☎ 07 3840 7303; open daily 10.00–17.00, except Christmas and Good Friday; free admission and guided tours at 10.00, 13.00 and 14.00; wheelchair access), while concentrating on Australian painters, also has a selection of Aboriginal and European art.

The Art Gallery first opened in 1896, with an exhibition of British and European artworks purchased in London. The collection now includes such important European paintings as Tintoretto's *Resurrection* (c 1552), Sir Henry Raeburn's *Portrait of Major General Alexander Murray MacGregor* (c 1780), Picasso's *La Belle Hollandaise* (1905), and Degas' *Three Dancers* (1888–90). English art is still a focus, including Walter Sickert's 1925 painting of Whistler's studio, and an excellent collection of English porcelain. Australian art is understandably strong, with major works by Tom Roberts, S.T. Gill, Piguenit, and Streeton; Charles Conder's *Quiet beach* (1887) is a particularly good example of the Heidelberg School's Impressionistic phase. Also in the Australian collection is the important Symbolist work by Sydney Long, *The Spirit of the Plains* (1897) and Frederick McCubbin's *Edge of the Forest* (1911). More recent Australian painters' work include those of Hilda Rix Nicholas and Noel Counihan from the

1930s; representative works from the 1960s by Iain Fairweather and Leonard French; and some of John Brack's later paintings (*Procession* from 1979) among the most contemporary pieces. The gallery carries out an ambitious programme of educational activities and lecture series.

The **Queensland Museum** (☎ 07 3840 7555) is contiguous to the art gallery and has the same opening hours. The displays are devoted to natural history and archaeology (notably maritime archaeology), with particular attention being paid to Queensland. The display devoted to aviator Bill Hinkler is particularly moving for the transcript of his final message to his family.

Finally, the **Performing Arts Complex** (☎ 07 3840 7400) was designed by architect Robin Gibson and opened in 1985. Its concert hall features a Klais pipe organ (7089 pipes) as the central architectural feature. While the complex offers an ambitious schedule of performances in both popular and classical genres, during the Brisbane Festival (usually every even-numbered year in August and September) the schedule is particularly busy. Their *Out of the Box* festival is directed at young children, ages three to eight years. The **Queensland Maritime Museum** (☎ 07 3844 5361; open daily 09.30–17.00) is located in a former dry dock at the southern end of the Southbank Parklands. As well as an exhibition devoted to shipwrecks, the museum has a reconstruction of a first-class passenger cabin, a functioning coal-fired steam tug built in Scotland in 1925 and the Second World War frigate *Diamantina*.

About 2km southeast of the cultural centre, on STANLEY STREET between Merton and Annerly Roads, is an interesting block of shops and shop houses which indicate aspects of the late 19C in Brisbane. They serviced the fine houses of **Highgate Hill**, which has been one of Brisbane's 'dress circle' residential areas since the 1920s. On MERTON ROAD, the six two-storey shops called the Phoenix Buildings, were built for mining entrepreneur William Davies in 1889–90.

Further down the street are Hillyard's and Pollock's shops and houses from the 1860s. Those next to the hotel are from around 1903. To the left, at Stanley Street's junction with Vulture Street, is an obvious three-part building, initially a telegraph and post office (left facing), a library (central with turret) and concert hall (behind). To the left on Vulture Street is an Italianate clock tower of archetypal proportions above the **Town Hall**.

The elegance of the area can best be seen in the **Memorial Park** across the street and the **Somerville House School**, which was originally built as William Stephens' mother's residence in 1890. William and his father Thomas were politicians and businessmen supportive of the South Brisbane area.

North Brisbane

Fortitude Valley is about 1km northwest of the business district and centred at Ann Street and Brunswick Street (**bus nos 370, 375, 379** from Ann Street). Formerly a working-class residential area, its multicultural population, ethnic restaurants and cheap rents have attracted a new and younger population. Brisbane's cafe and nightclub scene is centred here. It can still be a bit seedy, so travel accompanied after dark.

Some of the nicest public buildings in Fortitude Valley are a pair of hotels designed by Richard Gailey, the **Empire Hotel**, 339 Brunswick Street at the

The 'Queenslander' house

'Miegunyah' House is one of the more elaborate examples of the distinctive vernacular architectural style referred to now as the 'Queenslander'. At one time, these timber houses, built on stilt-like stumps with ample verandahs and adequate ventilation to reduce heat and humidity, could be found everywhere throughout the state. Many of these delightfully idiosyncratic structures have now fallen victim to 'progress' and the penchant for air-conditioning, and have disappeared. Only in recent years has an active restoration campaign attempted to save these wooden marvels. Authors who grew up in them or with them around remember them nostalgically. Brisbane native David Malouf writes most eloquently of their appropriateness to coastal Queensland's semi-tropical climate in his *12 Edmonstone Street* (1985):

They have about them the improvised air of tree-houses. Airy, open, often with no doors between the rooms, they are on easy terms with breezes, with the thick foliage they break into at window level, with the lives of possums and flying-foxes, that living in them, barefoot for the most part, is like living in a reorganised forest.

As Malouf also notes, 'most people in my youth were ashamed of this local architecture. Timber was a sign of poverty ... it made "bushies" of us'. Termites, of course, were another reason for the Queenslander's lack of favour. Another Queensland writer, Thea Astley, in a 1976 lecture titled 'Being a Queenslander: a form of literary and geographical conceit,' alludes to the insect-infested architecture as a metaphor for the place and its difference from the rest of the country:

Houses perched on stilts like teetering swamp birds held stiff skirts all around, pulled a hat-brim low over the eyes; and with the inroads of white-ants [termites] not only teetered but eventually flew away. And then, we tend to build houses so that we can live underneath them. Perhaps those stilts made southerners think of us as bayside-dwelling Papuans.

Fortunately, Brisbane and other Queensland towns were still too poor in the 1960s heyday of 'urban renewal' to be entirely rebuilt, when Sydney lost so much of its architectural history to progress and brick, so enough of the Queenslanders survive to still get a glimpse of their whimsical and imaginative character. Along with the Brisbane suburbs of Highgate Hill and West End and other inner-city neighbourhoods, Queenslanders of all kinds—from simple one-storey weatherboard houses to extravagant multi-storeyed hotels and public buildings—can be found in abundance in most Queensland towns, especially around Ipswich and Warwick, Rockhampton and Charters Towers.

junction with Ann Street, and the simpler **Prince Consort Hotel**, at the juncture of Brunswick and Wickham Streets. He also designed 'Windermere' on Sutherland Avenue in Ascot which has an elegant verandah forming a pavilion by the front entrance. His design somewhat later for a bank in Normanton, a small town at the tip of the Gulf of Carpenteria, continues his penchant for lighter, timber balustrades and open verandahs.

The Queensland Women's Historical Association maintains **Miegunyah Folk Museum** (☎ 07 3252 2979; open Wed 10.30–15.00, weekends 10.30–16.00), north of Fortitude Valley at 35 Jordan Terrace, Bowen Hills, as a memorial to pioneer women. This fine colonial homestead was built in 1884 by William Perry and features lacy wrought-iron on the verandah and remarkable period furnishings and household accoutrements. Honeycomb brickwork screening covers the underhouse area.

Newstead House (☎ 07 3216 1846; open Mon–Fri 09.30–16.00, Sun 14.00–17.00; bus no. 117), on Breakfast Creek Road about 4km northeast of the city centre, is operated by the Royal Historical Society. The oldest of the existing private homes in the area, it was built in 1846 for Patrick Leslie, an early settler of the Darling Downs. He sold it to his brother-in-law John Wickham, the Police Magistrate and Government Resident at Moreton Bay. Until 1859 the house served as the government house, making it the social centre of the district. It would have been the first house of substance seen from approaching ships. The Bulimba and Hamilton reaches the Brisbane River can be seen from its verandah.

St Lucia ~ south of Brisbane

Queensland University can be reached by bus no. 269. To get there by car, follow Ann Street to North Quay, and Coronation Drive to Sir Fred Schonnel Drive and then on to St Lucia.

The school's first substantial benefactor was grazier and philanthropist Samuel McCaughey who gave £228,000 in 1920. To provide a campus for the school, Dr J.O. Mayne and his sister Miss Mary E. Mayne donated their property at St Lucia for its permanent home. Architects Hennessey, Hennessey and Company designed the original plan of the setting which acknowledged the curve in the Brisbane River and laid out the Great Court. This is a semicircular arrangement of seven buildings (named for the university's founders) faced with Helidon sandstone. The variety of carved figures, historical scenes, coats of arms of other universities, and prominent historical thinkers on the older buildings are the work of John Theodore Muller. The more recent ones are by Rhyl Shepherd. A central figure not depicted is C.B. Christesen who as a student in 1940 founded the literary journal *Meanjin*. The **Anthropology Museum** (☎ 07 3365 2674; open Tues–Thurs 11.00–15.00) and **Antiquities Museums** (☎ 07 3365 1111; open weekdays 09.00–17.00, closed 13.00–14.00 for lunch) in buildings on the Great Court are well worth a visit.

In the vicinity of Brisbane

Beyond the central city are several interesting venues easily accessible by car or public transport. The drive through Forest Park, 12km west of town, is very pleasant.

Mount Coot-tha refers to the area rather than the botanic gardens here and is from the local Aboriginal language, a phrase meaning 'dark honey'. The park is open continuously, but the gardens (☎ 07 3403 2533) are open from 08.00–17.00 (17.30 in the summer). A pleasant arrangement proscribes vehicles in the botanic gardens on the weekends and on holidays. The new botanic gardens and tropical display house, a **planetarium** with observatory, and superb views of the city and bay (particularly at night) can be found a few minutes by car to the west of Brisbane's centre on Milton Road. Bus no. 37A from Ann Street on King George Square stops at both the gardens and the lookout. The Aboriginal Trail presents plants used by the area's Murri people and features tree marking, rock painting and etching and a dance pit.

The planetarium's name honours Sir Thomas Brisbane, Governor of New South Wales from 1821 to 1825. Known as the father of Australian science, he established an observatory at Parramatta and was first president of the Philosophical Society of Australia in his first year as governor. The park is at the end of the Taylor Range, Mount Coot-tha rising to 244m at the lookout and 285m at the summit.

At its base is Brisbane's oldest cemetery, the **Toowong Cemetery**. Initially, it was received with little enthusiasm, being a difficult 7km from the city. At its entrance on Frederick Street is the Temple of Peace, designed and constructed by Richard Ramo for his sons who died in the First World War, his adopted son Fred and the family dog. Bearing several inscriptions defaming war and its effects, several thousand people attended its dedication. Among the other notable funeral monuments is that for the Petrie family, builders and stone masons from the 19C and 20C.

Racial conflict in 19C Brisbane

The Petrie family's interest and respect of Aboriginal people living in their traditional areas (see box, p 638), while not unique, was an exception. During the period immediately after establishment of the Moreton Bay colony, the military administration considered them little more than a nuisance. Guards were posted in the grain fields, but small rewards were given them for the return of escaped convicts. By the late 1830s officials in London and Sydney were pressing for a more active conversionary approach to Aborigines. The Reverend Dr J.D. Lang went so far as to arrange for a small community of Germans to establish itself at Xions Hill (now Nundah) with a missionary purpose. Although it did become a fairly prosperous agricultural community, the Aborigines took virtually no heed of efforts to civilise and convert them.

Once the Brisbane area was opened to free settlers, however, the lot of the local Aborigines worsened considerably. The traditional owners of the land were generally given no access to it and no recompense for it. The poisoning of an Aboriginal community at **Kilcoy Station** on the Darling Downs in 1842 is arguably one of the central illustrations of atrocious greed in the 19C.

The **Cullin-la-ringo Massacre** resulted in 19 white settlers—men, women and children—being killed, the worst such incident in Australian history. More frequently, there is no record of the deaths. Following the slaughter of ten whites in the Dawson Valley in 1857, white settlers spent a full year killing every Aboriginal in the area. Frequently quoted figures estimate that as many as 500 whites and anywhere between 5000 and 15,000 Aborigines died as a result of settlement-related racial conflict.

Andrew Petrie

Andrew Petrie (1798–1872) and his sons John and Thomas (1831–1910) played interesting roles in Queensland's early history. Andrew was recruited as a free migrant by Rev. Dr J.D. Lang, emigrating in 1831 with his family which included three-month-old Thomas. After working in Sydney until 1837 as a civil engineer, he was sent to Moreton Bay as the Clerk of Works. Here he was appointed Engineer of Works and subsequently acted as the builder of most of early Brisbane.

Among the stories associated with Andrew, the rescue of two white men who had lived with the Aborigines for a number of years is most remarkable. James Bracefield (or Bracefell, known as *Wandi*, 'great talker') and James Davis (*Duramboi*, 'kangaroo rat') were retrieved from indigenous life during an exploratory trip up the Mary River. Davis had escaped from Moreton Bay as a lad and lived with local Aborigines for 16 years. Petrie assured both Bracefield and Davis that they would not be punished upon their return to Brisbane. Although Davis could only haltingly remember English, he was able to break into Scottish songs learned in childhood. As he embarked with Petrie and Henry Stuart Russell, members of his community appeared and chanted him farewell. In response he promised to return 'when the moon has come back to you in three months'. In fact, he died in Brisbane 47 years later, having worked as a blacksmith and owned a crockery shop. Both men soon became reticent about their lives in the Aboriginal community, Davis suggesting, 'If you want to know about the blacks, take off your clothes and go and live with them, as I did.'

Andrew's eldest son John took over the family business when his father became blind, acting as a builder and city patron. A cabinet maker by inclination, his buildings are marked by tasteful interior finishes. Among his most prominent buildings are the General Post Office, Customs House and the Harbours and Marine Building.

Andrew's third son Thomas fraternised with Queensland Aborigines, particularly in his youth. As a 14-year-old he was honoured to have accompanied a tribe on a bunya nut (*bon-yi*) feast in the Bunya Range. His capacity to speak some local languages allowed him to intercede during conflicts between settlers and Aborigines and gave him access to unexplored areas of the settlement. His daughter's book *Tom Petrie's Reminiscences of Early Queensland* (1904) presents a detailed account of his early life and settlement on Murrumba, a property on the Pine River.

Day trip east of Brisbane

The traveller interested in rural life can take a day trip west of Brisbane to the verge of the **Darling Downs**. Toowoomba is a leisurely two-hour drive, but you might consider a stop in Ipswich, and given sufficient time, a southern return route through Warwick. Darling Downs was discovered by botanist Allan Cunningham in 1827, four years after his visit to Moreton Bay. The name refers to then governor of New South Wales, Sir Ralph Darling (1775–1858), who was in office at the time of the region's first exploration.

The drive from Brisbane to Ipswich is via the CUNNINGHAM HIGHWAY (the Bradfield Highway, no. 1, south to 15). Toowoomba is west on route 54 (here the Warrego Highway). Warwick is south of Toowoomba on route 42; the return trip to Ipswich can be made via the Cunningham Highway.

Wolston House, Wacol

About 18km along the way at Grindle Road in **Wacol** is a National Trust property called **Wolston House** (☎ 07 3271 1734; open daily 10.00–16.00 except Mon and Fri). Built from local material in 1852, it is a good example of the country residences of the era. William Pettigrew designed and built it for Dr Stephen Simpson, then Commissioner for Crown Lands in Moreton Bay. Before coming to Australia, Simpson studied under Samuel C.F. Hahnemann and wrote the first book on homoeopathy in English.

Ipswich

The area around **Ipswich** (population 73,000) was initially known as Limestone Hills and was the starting point for Cunningham's exploration of the Darling Downs. The limestone was quarried by convicts as early as 1827, the blocks being ferried to Brisbane on the Bremer River in whale boats. Subsequent coal-mining and the arrival of the railroad in 1876 made for a prosperous town.

Drive through the town on Brisbane Street; the **tourist information centre** is on the corner of Brisbane Street and d'Arcy Doyle Street in the **Claremont House** (☎ 07 3281 0555). A walk around the older section of town gives a lesson on the changing styles of civic architecture in the last decades of the 19C. The corner building is the former Bank of Australasia (1879) with the manager's residence behind. Next to the bank is the Town Hall built in 1869. Across Nicholas Street is **St Paul's Anglican Church** built in 1859, but modified in 1886 (aisles and vestry) and 1929 (sanctuary and chapel).

Turning south on Ellenborough, South and Nicholas Streets gives views of the **Ipswich Technical College** and **RSL Memorial Hall**, both designed by George Brockwell Gill. The **CSA Hostel**, a few steps along Limestone Street, is a Colonial Georgian home built in the 1860s for the Campbell family. As well as the Technical College and RSL, Gill designed a private home called **'Arrochar'** in a district of substantial houses just north of the Boys' Grammar School and the City View Hotel on the corner of Brisbane and Roderick Streets. These buildings are much less heavy than most public buildings of the era, and sympathetic to the climate. Among the many other interesting buildings in town, the former Courthouse on East Street (by Charles Tiffin, 1859) and former incinerator (by Walter Burley Griffin, 1936) deserve mention.

Toowoomba

The fertile bottom land where Toowoomba (population 76,000) now stands atop the Great Dividing Range was a stop for travellers and team-drivers. Initially a reedy, grassy swamp, **Toowoomba** (Aboriginal for 'a place to get melons') grew around that function, becoming an important stage stop between Brisbane and the Darling Downs by the time it was formally established in 1860. This history makes its most significant building the **Royal Bull's Head Inn** (☎ 07 4630 1869; open Thurs–Sun 10.00–16.00) on the corner of Brisbane and Drayton Streets. The inn was a stage stop in about 1847 and the present structure dates from 1859. The Lynch family home from 1879 until 1874, its renovation is due to the efforts of the National Trust.

The **Cobb & Co Museum** at 27 Lindsay St (☎ 07 4639 1971; open 09.00–17.00 daily) describes the history of this firm and horse-drawn transport generally. The town has literary and artistic leanings evident in the **Toowoomba Regional Art Gallery**, 531 Ruthven St (☎ 07 4631 6652; open Tues–Sat 10.00–16.00).

Warwick

The area around **Warwick** (population 10,000) was settled in 1841 by Patrick Leslie and his brothers as the Canning Downs Station. Warwick was surveyed and established by Patrick Leslie in 1849, becoming the first town proper in Queensland after Brisbane. The railway line from Ipswich opened in 1871.

Warwick's single most significant event occurred in 1917 when Prime Minister Billy Hughes was pelted with an egg during a speech here. Hughes was defending his attempt to impose conscription during the First World War. He demanded that the local police arrest the man who threw the egg. The policeman refused. Based upon this refusal, Hughes eventually established the Commonwealth Police Force.

Most of the buildings of note in Warwick are constructed of locally quarried sandstone. On Dragon Street, **Pringle Cottage** (☎ 07 4661 2028; open Wed–Fri 10.00–12.00, Sat and Sun 14.00–16.00), now a local museum comprised of several buildings, was built in 1869 by John McCullouck and is reminiscent of Scottish cottages. The massive two-storey **Masonic Hall** (1886) is an example of the architectural taste of late-19C businessmen, with eclectic

---

Jackie Howe

The blue singlet, a sleeveless undershirt, the uniform of the Aussie country worker, is known as a Jacky Howe. The shearer Jackie Howe (1855–1922), along with cricket batsman Don Bradman, are the nearly iconic symbols of early 20C male Australia. Howe was a Warwick native. In 1892 he used hand blades to shear 327 merino ewes in 7 hours 20 minutes. No Luddite, he sheared 337 sheep in 8 hours using machine shears in 1904.

His father had been a well-known circus acrobat and his mother a companion of Catherine Leslie, wife of pastoralist Patrick Leslie. Jackie was taught shearing by a Chinese shearer in the late 1880s. Recognised as a good bloke, the publican Jimmy Ah Foo described him, saying 'Jack Howe champion. Him much first-class man altogether. Quiet man. No dlink much. No dance Highland Fling. No pullee girl around. No lallikin tlicks [larrikin tricks].' He was also an outstanding athlete, particularly excelling at running and jumping. A memorial to Howe stands in a small park on the corner of New England Highway and Jackie How Drive.

classical and Doric elements. The design of the **Court House** (1885–87) and **Town Hall** (1888) derives from similar sources. The **National** (c 1890) and **Criterion** (1917) **Hotels** show more character and sympathy with the climate. Both have pleasant verandahs and the Criterion has a splendid bar and Art Nouveau ornament.

The **Jondaryan Woolshed Complex** (☎ 07 4692 2229; open daily 08.30–17.00), 45km northwest of Toowoomba, presents demonstrations of horse shoeing and shearing. It was non-union labour at Jondaryan that prompted the maritime workers to refuse to handle its wool-clipping in 1890. The maritime workers lost this battle, though the shearers eventually received their wage award. Station owners continue their animosity towards maritime union workers to this day.

Returning to Ipswich from Warwick, the road passes through **Cunningham's Gap**, a remarkable feature due to the steep rise on either side of the road. There are a variety of walks from the car park at the Gap which gives a look at the **Main Range National Park**'s (☎ 07 4666 1133) forest.

West of the loop to Toowoomba and Warwick is pasture and range land on Mesozoic sediments. As the scattered eucalypts become shorter and further apart, the ground cover changes to tussock grass. Highlands of the Dividing Ranges cause some increased rainfall east of the road running north and south through St George.

Southern Queensland

Some 350km west of Toowoomba on the Warrego Highway is **Roma** (population 6100). The first gazetted settlement in Queensland after its separation from New South Wales in 1859, the town was not named for the Italian city, but after the wife of Sir George Bowen, Queensland's first governor. Its great claim to fame is as the site of the trial in 1872 of Harry Redford, alias **Captain Starlight**, one of the most notorious bushrangers. Also at Roma were the beginnings of Queensland's wine-making in 1863, when vine cuttings were brought to the district. Today, Roma is best known as the source of natural gas, with a 450km pipeline running to Brisbane. **Tourist information**: Bowen Street, ☎ 07 4622 3399.

Carnarvon National Park

270km north of Roma is the **Carnarvon National Park** (☎ 07 4984 4505), which has some of the most extensive stencilling art by Aborigines in the country. The largest of the 46 sites recorded in the area are the **Art Gallery** and **Cathedral Cave**. Engraving and stencilling are by far the most common techniques. Entire walls of hands make the most striking stencil, but emu feet, and implements are readily found as well. The engravings are of women's vulvas, human and animal tracks and geometric shapes. Some free-hand drawings are also displayed.

Walking tracks into the gorge proceed from the information centre. The Art Gallery is 5.6km into the gorge and Cathedral Cave is 9.3km in. Expect to spend

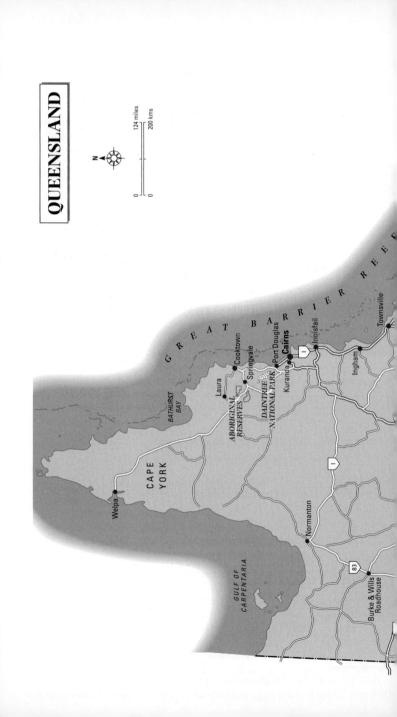

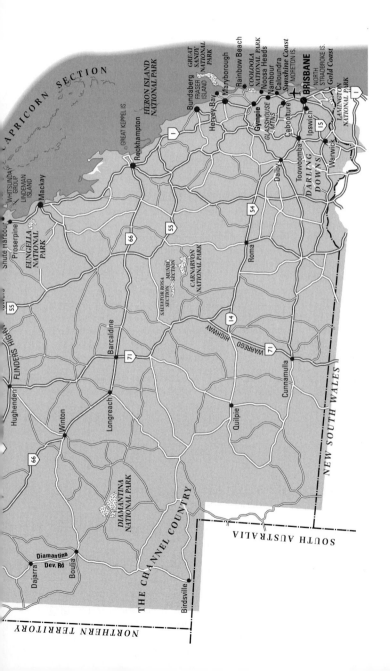

a half-day walking. There are no facilities beyond the information centre, so carry your own water. Recent efforts to protect the area by controlling the number of visitors recommends telephoning or stopping at the National Park information centre, 160 Ann Street, Brisbane, ☎ 07 3227 8185.

Archaeological evidence suggests that Cathedral Cave was only occasionally and recently inhabited, but that considerable tool-making occurred here. Further, a large amount of cycad seed shells were found here. The palm cycad seeds are toxic until thoroughly processed in a manner not dissimilar to that used for acorns by native American groups—grinding, then leeching and fermenting. A relatively recent addition to the diet (4000 years ago), they are currently believed to be associated with large ceremonial events. An ochre mine existed at West Branch Camp 12km away. Visitors can stay in Injune or at the *Oasis Lodge* (☎ 0749 84 4503) at the entrance to the gorge.

The next road inland is the **MITCHELL HIGHWAY** (no. 71) north from Bourke, New South Wales, through Cunnamulla and Charleville to Barcaldine near Longreach. This **Bourke** is the place referred to when one speaks of being 'back o'Bourke', that is, in the middle of nowhere. It marks the cessation of eucalypt and commencement of acacia wattle, called the **mulga**. In fact, north of Charleville and certainly beyond Bardaldine, Mitchell grass becomes the prevalent flora.

Barcaldine is remembered for a shearers' strike here in 1891, which led to the birth of two of Australia's current national political parties, Labor and National (p 625). Although the strike was a failure and the leaders were imprisoned, the effort eventually led to significant changes in industrial relations and labourers' conditions.

Longreach (population 3610) has more noteworthy history than its modest size and remote location would suggest. A range cattle and sheep station district,

Waltzing Matilda

The image of the outback stockman as a defining attribute of the Australian character received its greatest anthem further north on the Diamantina River beyond **Winton**. While staying with the Macpherson family at Dagworth Station, Andrew Bardon 'Banjo' Paterson wrote Australia's most popular national theme, **'Waltzing Matilda'**. He set his poem to a Scottish tune played for him by one of the family's daughters Christina Macpherson. Its first public performance was at the North Gregory Hotel in Winton (burnt down in 1900, 1915 and 1946 and now constructed of brick). Matching sentiment centred on the struggle by itinerant shearers and station workers, the song was an immediate success. It spread rapidly through the outback in the repertoire of the very swagmen it honoured. The music for the ballad in its current form was composed by Marie Cowen, wife of James Inglis. He used it as a promotional wrapping for his Billy Tea, an inexpensive black tea which is still available.

A **Waltzing Matilda Festival** is held in **Winton** in April, and there is a museum and information office on Elderslie Street, ☎ 07 4657 1544. Winton also has the **Royal Theatre Open Air Picture Show**, also on Elderslie Street (☎ 07 4657 1488). Opened in 1918 it is, along with Broome's open-air cinema, the last of its kind in Australia.

it was the home of the **Queensland and Northern Territory Aerial Service** (QANTAS), founded by Flying doctors W. Hudson Fysh and P. J. McGuiness. The hangar in which they had six DH-50 biplanes contracted is still in use at the local airport. The visitor desk at the information centre (☎ 07 4658 3555, on Eagle Street in the centre of town) is a replica of the first Qantas booking office.

Longreach also has the **Stockman's Hall of Fame** (☎ 07 4658 2166; open daily 09.00–17.00 except Christmas; wheelchair access). An important symbol as well as a description of working life in the outback stations, the displays here are largely of text and photographs documenting outback life from the 1860s to the present.

19C author 'Rolf Boldrewood' described a cattle theft by 'Captain Starlight' and accomplices in the area in his book *Robbery Under Arms* (1888). In fact, in 1870 Harry Redford and four associates gathered 1000 head of mixed range cattle and drove them to South Australia, pioneering a 2400km stock route along the meagre Thomson, Cooper and Strzelecki Rivers. Arrested in Adelaide and tried in Roma for the obvious theft of Bowen Downs Station cattle, they were acquitted for their stockman daring-do.

Cloncurry and Mount Isa

Cloncurry and Mount Isa are mining and agricultural communities in Queensland's remote northwest, reached via route 66 from Winton. Silver, lead, copper and zinc are extracted and processed here. Places on tours of both surface and underground mines at **Mount Isa** can be booked at the **tourist office**: Riversleigh Fossils Interpretative Centre, Marian Street, Mount Isa (☎ 07 4749 1555).

Ore from the Mount Isa Mine comes from shafts up to 2km below the surface. The extent of the works may be gauged by the large open-cut mine. Its entire production is used not as a source of ore but as in-fill for shafts being closed.

Cloncurry (population 2300) was the first location of the **Royal Flying Doctor Service**, conceived by Reverend John Flynn and initiated in 1928. Flynn recognised the need for the service during his outback missionary work in the 1910s and '20s. Communication with the service was made possible by Alfred Traeger's development of a pedal-powered wireless radio with a typewriter-style keyboard. The service is free, supported by donations and a variety of fund-raising efforts.

The history of the service is presented at the **John Flynn Place Museum** (☎ 07 4742 1251; open weekdays year round 09.00–16.00 and weekends 09.00–15.00 May–Oct).

Southwest Queensland

The southwest corner of Queensland is known as **Channel Country**. An area of sparse population and uncertain water, it has been a range cattle producing area since the 1870s. **Birdsville**, one of the smaller towns in the region, is the starting point of the **Birdsville Track**, a former stock route, now the start of a cross-country car race. The Birdsville Cup Race Meeting is held on the first weekend in September. As many as 6000 visitors come for the event, an attraction known for the number of light planes flying in for the Friday and Saturday races and semi-professional boxing matches in the evening.

NOTE: Travel in this area qualifies as serious outback travel and requires full preparation, including the supply of your own water, food, and petrol. Motorists must ring the Northern Roads Hotline, ☎ 07 4775 34600 for information before departing down the Birdsville Track. At times flooding will completely shut down the road.

Stock routes

Australia's three most mentioned stock routes are the **Birdsville Track**, the **Canning Stock Route**, the **Murranji Track**. They were used to transport cattle overland to railway lines prior to the introduction of haulage by truck. Until the state governments bore wells along their lengths, cattle losses during the drives were often prohibitively high.

The Birdsville Track opened in the 1880s once the Port Augusta-to-Oodnadatta railway line was completed in South Australia. Cattle mustered in the Channel Country of Queensland were driven about 480km to Marree. They came under tariff as they crossed the border into South Australia near Birdsville, confirming it as the logical starting point of the drive.

The track proceeds south from Birdsville along the Diamantina River. During dry periods, Goyders Lagoon (into which the Diamantina flows) could probably be crossed. Otherwise the longer and sandier outer track would be used. From the bore at Clifton Hills, the track continued south to the bore near Mulka. The final leg of the journey is across the Cooper, Clayton and Frome Rivers to Marree. During wet periods, these crossings are quite dangerous.

The Canning Stock Route in Western Australia proceeds from around Halls Creek in the East Kimberley region nearly 1400km to Wiluna. Surveyor Alfred Canning discovered the route in 1906. The Aboriginal people along the route directed him to their wells. In his second pass through the country, he established dependable water supplies in 52 places. The Aboriginal people across whose land the cattle passed were never happy about this use of their land. A number of incautious drovers were speared while on this route.

The Murranji Stock Route was reputed as the most difficult due to uncertain water at Murranji. Pastoralist Nat Buchanan (1826–1901) pioneered the route in the 1890s, which extended from the Victoria River region of northwestern Northern Territory to Camooweal in western Queensland. It more or less followed what is now the Buchanan Highway, eventually depending on bores every 30km to 50km.

The coastal road south

The Queensland coastal road from the south passes between lush coastal mountains and extensive beaches. A number of interesting islands lie just offshore. Brisbane is about 550km south of the point at which the Great Barrier Reef begins. The tropical north begins south of Townsville and continues up Cape York beyond the extent of readily passible roads.

The **Gold Coast** is the first 42km north from the New South Wales border. Visited by three million people a year, it has been the developers' dream. The beach-front property looks much as you should expect from the advertisements: a bit crowded, a few too many towers, and an occasional building design deserving an award. If you are looking for a Miami Beach-style experience, with excellent beaches, the Gold Coast is the place to come. At all costs avoid the place during the end-of-school holidays, when the area is mobbed by recent graduates (and others).

Fortunately, the area has natural attractions as well. These include Lamington National Park (an extensive temperate rainforest), near perfect surfing waves at Burleigh Heads, and miles of beaches with swells varying from negligible to rough, and all surfing levels in between.

Lamington National Park

Lamington National Park is accessible at either Binna Burrra via Beechmont (10km) or Green Mountains via Canungra (37km). These roads diverge from Nerang on the Pacific Highway. The park is served by ranger stations. The area (☎ 075 544 0634; open daily 13.00–15.30 at Green Mountains and ☎ 07 5533 3584; open daily 08.00–16.00 at Binna Burra) is a subtropical rainforest set on a plateau at 600–1100m high. A Mesozoic lava flow from a caldera centred on Mount Warning, the area is in the Macpherson Range. Ecologically consistent since the supercontinent Gondwana split into continents, the park contains Antarctic beeches related to those in Tasmanian rainforests, though much larger. It is also the home of a rare and curious rootless and leafless precursor to ferns, *Psilotum nudum*. The rainforest flora most readily identified, though, are elkhorn and staghorn ferns, figs and a plethora of orchid species. The birdlife is diverse and includes three bowerbird species, both species of lyre-bird and a variety of kingfishers, lorikeets, cockatoos and fairy wrens. As ever, the mammals are harder to see, but the pademelon wallaby and some of the possums (ringtailed and mountain brushtail) can be seen in the late afternoon, around dawn and, of course, during nightwalks.

Well-marked **walking tracks** and **hiking trails** lead to much frequented as well as secluded areas. The two most recommended starting points are the guest houses at **Binna Burra** (☎ 07 5533 3622) and at **O'Reillys** (☎ 07 5544 0644) on the Green Mountains side of the park. A 14km Border Trail links the two. Both are accessible by car via Canungra or by bus daily from the coast.

Reserved as a park in 1915, Lamington became part of the popular imagination due to a campaign at the time to save the area from loggers, undertaken by R.W. Lahey, at the time a young civil engineer. Its stature grew in the 1940s when personal accounts of experience in natural settings were a popular genre.

In *One Mountain After Another*, Bernard O'Reilly (founding owner of the guesthouse mentioned above) describes his search in 1937 for the crash site of a Stinson aeroplane bound for Sydney with eight aboard. He reports that the surviving passengers first asked after Bradman's cricket score (165 not out). In all it took O'Reilly ten days to find the site and return with a rescue party.

Romeo Lahey and Arthur Groom, early conservationists, established Binna Burra Mountain Lodge in 1933. The name is from a local Aboriginal dialect and translates as 'where the beech trees grow'.

Walks in the park can take anywhere from an hour to half a day and are particularly fulfilling during wildflower blossoming in July and September. At Binna Burra is a 'senses trail', designed for blind people. A **botanical garden** near

O'Reilly's Guest House is an educational treat before walking. O'Reilly's also has rainforest walkways raised far enough off the ground to give a view into the canopy.

Camping hikes can last as long as you like. Dirk Flinthart, author of the irreverent *Coasting: Real Guide to the East Coast of Australia* (1996), praises the four-day caldera rim walk as utterly unforgettable. Less adventurous forays into these coastal mountains would stop at the tea rooms at Tamborine Mountain (North Tamborine and Eagle Heights) or Springbrook Plateau. Roads to either are branches off the road to Lamington National Park out of Nerang.

Brisbane area islands

A number of islands lie offshore from Brisbane. Moreton Island and North Stradbroke Island are both accessible by ferry from Lytton, and Holt Street Wharf in Pinkenba; St Helena Island is reached by private plane charter. Fraser Island is accessible from Hervey (pronounced Harvey) Bay at Mary River Heads, Moon Point and Inskip Point. In addition to fishing, bird-watching and swimming, these islands are favourite four-wheel-drive sand-buggy venues. The Queensland Department of the Environment office in Brisbane (☎ 07 3227 8197) oversees recreational boating and yachting and has information regarding public moorings.

Moreton Island

Moreton Island, 40km from Brisbane, is 38km long and 9km across. Its most prominent physical feature, **Mount Tempest** (280m), is one of the highest stable sand dunes in the world. Except during the Christmas holidays, the island is largely left to the **125-plus bird species** and the lovely beaches. The lighthouse at its northern tip was built in 1857 and still functions. In addition to Aboriginal shell middens, the island boasts freshwater lakes and associated bird life, native scrub and banksias and big-game fishing from its resort hotel at Tangalooma (☎ 07 3268 6333). This hotel operates the daily catamaran between the Holt Street Dock off Kingsford Smith Drive in Eagle Farm and the island. Booking is essential (☎ 07 3268 6333). While four-wheel drive vehicles can be rented at the hotel, vehicular ferries depart from Scarborough (☎ 07 3203 6399), a suburb in Northern Brisbane and from Lytton on the south bank of the Brisbane River near its mouth.

North Stradbroke Island

North Stradbroke Island, like Moreton Island, is a wildlife sanctuary. Ferry and water taxi service is from Cleveland, a suburb at the end of Cleveland Road (highway number 22) from south Brisbane, bus numbers 621 or 622 or by train. Stradbroke Island has a bus service between its three small towns, Dunwich, Point Lookout and Amity Point. A visitor's centre (☎ 07 3409 9555) is near the Dunwich Ferry Terminal. **Dunwich**, 40km long, was originally a quarantine station (1828). A typhoid plague (other authorities identify it as having been cholera) in 1850 is recorded in the local graveyard. A storm in 1896 broke the spit at Jumpinpin which joined the north and south islands. The well-known fishing competition, the **Stradie Classic**, is held in August. As with many other places on the coast in winter, humpback whales can be spotted migrating northward. A number of literary figures frequent North Stradbroke

Island. In a light-hearted poem entitled 'Ocean Beach', John Manifold describes the tourists here in a sense familiar to nearly every vacation spot:

> *Visitors with three weeks' tan*
> *Flaunt it at the raw beginners—*
> *Raw indeed, like uncooked dinners*
> *Pink and oily for the pan.*

Aboriginal poet Oodgeroo Noonuccal (Kath Walker, 1920–93) grew up on the island and lived here near Myora Springs outside Dunwich.

St Helena Island, just 4km from the mainland, was originally planned as a quarantine station as well. It acted as a model prison from 1867 to 1932. Its reputation was largely due to its being more or less self-sufficient. The island was named for an unfortunate Aborigine called Napoleon who was marooned here by keepers at Dunwich gaol. St Helena Island Guided Tours (☎ 07 3260 7944) provides ferry services from Breakfast Creek.

Sunshine Coast

A day trip further north to the Sunshine Coast offers similar opportunities to the Gold Coast. The area extends from Caloundra 96km north of Brisbane to Noosa. The highway (no. 1) passes through a dairy farming area around Caboolture and past the **Glasshouse Mountains**. These curious trachyte volcanic cores rising to 300m were named by Captain Cook. He gave the name either because they reminded him of the reflections off his Yorkshire garden sheds or, as more trustworthy sources suggest, of that region's glass furnaces. **Caboolture** is famous for dairy products, particularly yoghurt. The **Abbey Museum** (open Tues and Thur–Sat, 10.00–16.00) is 7km east towards Bridie Island, on Old Toorbul Road. The museum's collection spent time in a number of cities between London and Australia. It describes itself as devoted to the cultural history of the Mediterranean and Europe, and contains an impressive, if incongruously located, collection of ancient artefacts and weaponry. Near it are two Aboriginal sites, one a tidal fish trap, the other a bora ground. An end-of-year event worthy of note in the area, the **Maleny-Woodford Folk Festival**, held on a property at Woodford, 29km south of Maleny, has an active Aboriginal participation (☎ 07 5476 0700 for information).

The coastal road is accessible from **Nambour**. This superb stretch of coastline is less heavily developed than the Gold Coast. Agriculturally very productive, the area has a thriving Devonshire tea/cottage garden/bed-and-breakfast gentility about it. Queenslanders would not be comfortable in a less structured fantasy strip. The pride of Nambour is the **Giant Pineapple**, a hollow roadside grotesque at the Sunshine Plantation which offers a display describing pineapple cultivation.

Gympie and **Cooloola National Parks** are north of Noosa Heads. Named for a kind of stinging tree, **Gympie** (population 11,200) is a favourite place in Australia because the gold found here in the 1860s saved the state and, perhaps, the national bank. Situated among picturesque hills and sharp ravines, larger hills are visible inland. **Tourist information**: Bruce Highway, Lake Alford; ☎ 07 5482 5444. At the nearby Cooloola National Park (☎ 07 5485 3245) is **Rainbow Beach**, noted for multicoloured sandstone caused by minerals leaching down cliffs. Several walking trails, including the 46km Cooloola Wilderness Trail, depart from the park's visitor's centre. At Inskip Point ferries leave for Fraser Island.

Fraser Island

Fraser Island is about three hours north of Brisbane by car followed by a short ferry ride from River Heads or Hervey Bay. Travel on the island is by four-wheel drive or on foot. Like Moreton Island, it is composed of quartz sand weathered from the Great Dividing Range. At 132km long, it is the world's largest sand island and is World Heritage-listed for that reason. Noteworthy for its slightly acidic dune lakes, its cover ranges from mangroves to temperate rainforests and includes a variety of low open scrub, heath and low eucalypt forests.

> The island is named for Eliza Fraser who was among a group shipwrecked somewhat north of the island in 1836. Making their way to the island and with the help of the Butchulla Aboriginal community, they waited two months for rescue. She alone survived. The story is re-worked by Patrick White in his novel *A Fringe of Leaves* (1977) and by Sidney Nolan in a series of paintings (1947). The Aboriginal people were displaced to missions when the satinay timber cutters came for this wood. Highly resistant to marine borer, this timber lined the Suez Canal.

The coastal road north

While air transport from Brisbane is the quickest means of reaching the **Great Barrier Reef**, there is a coastal road north from Brisbane. Understandably, the associated mainland towns and inland nature areas tend to be slighted in favour of the reef. The trip by land follows in segments. Note that much of the highway passes through endless fields of cane, with few views of the coastline itself. An excellent rail service extends from Brisbane 1680km north to Cairns (☎ 13 2232).

The **Capricornia** section of the southernmost part of the Great Barrier Reef lies off the area between Bundaberg and Rockhampton. Maryborough, Hervey Bay and Bundaberg lie well south of the group.

Maryborough (population 23,000) is known for the gardening in its city parks and well-presented colonial architecture. The 19C bandstand in Queen's Park is a cast-iron fantasy that originally housed a drinking fountain. **Geraghty's Store** on Lennox Street (☎ 07 4121 2250; open daily 10.00–15.00) has a remarkable façade for such a small building. **Maryborough and District Tourist Information Centre**, 30 Ferry Street, ☎ 07 4121 4111. Excellent 'heritage walk' brochures of the town's colonial architecture, including its many 'Queens-lander' buildings, are available here. Poet John Blight described the area based on his perceptions while there as a proprietor of a timber mill in the 1960s.

> *A lazy couch of beach and sun in the morning*
> *make me forget the threat of rocks and warning*
> *beacons on the bay. Comfortable mooring*
> *for little ships and an elderly beachcomber snoring*
> *intermittently between blink and blink of the waves*
> *wash and splash of the waters, until the tide comes in.*

Set on rich basalt soil, **Bundaberg** (population 47,200) is known to every Australian as the home of **Bundaberg Rum**. Another of Australia's icons, 'Bundy' begins as sugar cane molasses and ends as a spirit to rival that distilled in the Caribbean. Tours of the distillery are more or less on the hour and, following a video presentation and tour of some of the facilities, end with an opportunity to sample some of the best of their product. The **tourist information centre** (on the corner of the highway and Bourbong Streets; ☎ 07 4152 2333) can direct you to the distillery on Avenue Street in East Bundaberg.

Rockhampton (population 65,000) first flourished as a result of a gold find 60km upriver at Canoona in 1858. Prosperity followed the discovery of gold and, particularly, copper at Mount Morgan in 1882. A number of historic buildings on the south bank of the Fitzroy River date from the 1880s and 1890s. The commercial buildings along Quay Street show the effect of a tropical climate in the use of verandahs, colonnades and loggias. **Tourist information centre**: Curtis Park, Gladstone Road; ☎ 07 4927 2055. On the Fitzroy River, Rockhampton eventually became the shipping point for the inland pastoral country as far west as Longreach. In fact, the livestock auction Gracemere Sale Yards (☎ 07 4933 1222; open weekdays 08.00–15.00) immediately west of town receives mention as a novel tourist venue. A number of limestone caves are about 20km north of town at Cameroo Caves and Olsen's Capricorn Caves (both open daily from 09.00). The Tropic of Capricorn passes a few kilometres south of town. The town's **Botanical Gardens** (☎ 07 4922 1654) were established in 1869; it has an attractive Japanese garden section.

The Capricornian Group

The accessible islands of the Capricornian Group include Lady Elliot, Lady Musgrave, Heron, Great Keppel and North West Islands. These lie off the coast from Bundaberg to Rockhampton. Overnight accommodation is available on Lady Elliot Island (☎ 07 4153 2485, light plane from Bundaberg and Hervey Bay), Heron Island (☎ 07 4978 1488, catamaran or helicopter daily from Gladstone), Great Keppel Island (light plane from Rockhampton or launch from Rosslyn Bay). Camping permits are available from the Marine Parks Authorities (☎ 07 4936 0511) for Lady Musgrave Island (catamaran from Bundaberg). All of these islands provide world-class diving opportunities for all levels of divers.

Lady Elliot Island is a sand-covered coral cay 80km from Bundaberg at the far southern edge of the reef. Set in 40m deep water, the coral gardens in the ten or more major dive sites contain spectacularly diverse submarine life. From about November to February the shores are nesting sites for green turtles. Rookeries serve up to 56 bird species. The island's resort is spartan but comfortable and accommodates a small number of people.

Lady Musgrave Island is similarly a coral cay with a navigable lagoon and an underwater observatory. Turtles nest here in the summer. The large pisonia trees common to tropical coral-limestone soils provide roosting places for gannets and terns. The extremely sticky fruit of these trees occasionally trap small birds. The two-hour catamaran trip from Bundaberg (daily during summer, Tues, Thurs, Sat and Sun during winter) make this a day-trip venue. A limited number of camping permits are available from the Marine Parks Authority (☎ 07 4972 6055). Day tours depart from Port Bundaberg (☎ 07 4152 9011; Tues, Thurs, Sat and Sun 08.30).

Heron Island's surrounding reef is partly exposed at low tide. Despite being only about 1km across, the island's bird life has a dense palm, pisonia and she-oak forest for refuge. Prevalent species include herons, muttonbirds, noddy terns and sea eagles. Like the other islands in the Capricornian group, the turtles lay their eggs here from October to January; hatchings occur from late December to May. Visits to the island, except by helicopter (☎ 07 4978 1177), require an overnight stay at Heron Island Resort (☎ 13 24 69).

Great Keppel Island has over 30km of white, sandy beaches. The resort here accommodates about 500 people and offers a variety of activities, including organised activities for children during the school holidays. The water here is clear and warm. The beaches even slightly beyond the immediate area of the hotel are not likely to be crowded. Snorkelling at **Monkey Beach**, about 30 minutes' walk south of the resort, is said to be fine. Quantas flies here from Rockhampton. Several ferries depart from Rosslyn Bay Harbour just south of Yeppoon to a number of islands in the Keppel group. Halfway Island has particularly good snorkelling as well.

The Whitsundays

Mackay, Townsville and Ingham are the mainland towns for the Whitsundays and the central section of the reef. **Mackay** is known for sugar-processing and as a coal-shipping port. **Eungella National Park** (☎ 07 4958 4552), a rainforest in the Clarke Range, is 74km inland. Platypuses are frequently seen near Broken River bridge at dawn and dusk.

Queens Hotel, Townsville

Townsville (population 97,000) has an attractive waterfront residential area around Cleveland Bay, the basis for its existence. Its origin was on Castle Hill overlooking Ross Creek. **Tourist information**: Bruce Highway; ☎ 07 4778 3555. The intellectual life of the town is centred on **James Cook University** and the marine sciences carried out at the Great Barrier Reef Marine Park Authority and at the Australian Institute of Marine Science. The **Great Barrier Reef Aquarium**, Flinders Street East (☎ 07 4750 0800; open daily 09.00–17.00) is the largest living coral reef aquarium in the world, and includes excellent underwater displays and shark and turtle feeding sessions. Today Townsville is best known as a military town, as many Australian troops are stationed here.

The Flinders Highway to Mount Isa starts here. Passing along the way the nearby mining community **Charters Towers** and **Ravenswood** (the latter a near ghost town of surprising vitality—two hotels, a cavaran park and free tenting at the showgrounds an easy morning drive from the Whitsundays'

Street scene, Charters Towers

mainland). As elsewhere, fine pastoral land lies further inland beyond the Great Dividing Range at Flinders, Thompson and Diamantina.

Along the coast, an hour to the north, **Ingham** (population 5700) is interesting for its Basque and Italian settlers. Cairns is less than three hours' drive from Townsville along the coast, about six hours with minimum stops inland via Charters Towers.

Another 53km north of Ingham on the Bruce Highway is the tiny town of **Cardwell** (population 1400), the only place on the highway between Brisbane and Cairns that is actually on the coast directly. **Tourist information centre**: Seaview Cafe, ☎ 07 4066 8690. Directly north of Cardwell is **Edmund Kennedy National Park** (☎ 07 4066 8601), one of the parks included in the Wet Tropics World Heritage Area of northern Queensland. It is named for explorer Edmund Kennedy (1818–48), who in 1848, along with his Aboriginal guide Jacky-Jacky and a party of 13, attempted to land near here and make an overland voyage north to Cape York. The mangrove swamps and dense vegetation, as well as the enormous mosquitoes, in the park today give a good indication of why Kennedy's expedition failed (Kennedy was speared to death trying to reach the rescue ship at Cape York; only Jacky-Jacky survived from Kennedy's group and eventually led a rescue party to the two survivors stranded at Pascoe River). The park has beautiful walking tracks and boardwalks into the forests and near the beach at Wreck Creek. Estuarine crocodiles live in the creeks here, so swimming is not allowed. Insect repellent is also essential for any visitor in the park.

Cardwell's greatest attraction is its close proximity to **Hinchinbrook Island**, 5km offshore and accessible by private boat, water taxi or charter boat from Cardwell or Dungeness; check with the tourist information office for details. According to legend, an old sailor remarked about the channel separating the island from the mainland, 'nobody can sail through the Hinchinbrook Channel and not believe in God'; it is indeed paradisaical, with the most complex system of mangroves in Australia. The island is the largest totally protected island national park in the world, over 45,000 ha ranging from mountainous peaks (the highest is Mount Bowen, at 1121m) to waterfall-laden rainforests and virginal beaches.

The park is a bushwalker's dream; the 32km **Thorsborne Trail** follows the coastal side of the island and takes three to five days to complete. The numbers walking this trail at any given time are limited, so bookings are advisable (☎ 07 4776 1700). The **wildlife** here includes wallabies, large cassowaries (*Casuaris* *casuarius*) the brilliant blue Ulysses Butterfly (*Papilio ulysses*), the small Boyd's Forest Dragon (*Gonocephalus boydii*), and the nocturnal Giant Tree Frog (*Litoria infrafrenata*). The Atlas Moth (*Coscinocera hercules*), one of the world's largest moths with a wing span of 25cm, can also be found in the forest canopy. Less welcome sights for campers and bushwalkers are the Giant White-tailed Rat (*Uromys caudimaculatus*), a native species that has an insatiable appetite for all foods brought in by campers; and marine stingers, one of the highly venomous jelly-fish of the northern waters that make swimming here impossible between October and April. Estuarine crocodiles are also in the creeks and mangrove areas, so avoid these waters as well.

Hinchinbrook Island has a small (maximum 50 people), low-key resort in the park itself (☎ 07 4066 8585); some of its accommodation is listed as 'treehouse units'.

Unlike the relatively flat coral cays of the Southern Reef Islands, the **Whitsundays** are continental which gives most of them a mountain peak in their interior. As well as affording remarkable views of the neighbouring islands, this variety of elevation results in a greater variety of wildlife. **Long Island**, for instance, is known for its scrub turkeys and **Lindeman** for its butterflies. Coral reefs fringe most of them, although the Barrier Reef itself is 10 or more kilometres oceanward.

Shute Harbour and the nearby Airlie Beach, Mackay and Prosperine are the starting points for tours. Most of the resort islands are accessible by launch and light plane from Shute Harbour, Hamilton Island and Mackay. The **Queensland National Parks and Wildlife Service Whitsunday District Office** (☎ 07 4921 2399) is between Shute Harbour and Airlie Beach.

Captain Cook sailed though the Whitsunday Passage on 3 July 1770. He remarked that the area was a safe harbour, but the fast-flowing tidal currents (the tide shifts are relatively large, sometimes turning lovely beaches into extensive tidal mud-flats) and brief squalls can be tricky for the inexperienced boatman.

The resort islands of the Whitsundays include **Lindeman, Hamilton, Long Island, South Molle, Hook, Hayman** and **Daydream**. All of these have anchorages, those at Hamilton and Hayman are marinas with full services. There are over 70 uninhabited islands as well. In fact, there is little to be said about these paradisiacal places. They satisfy all the senses in a languorous, tropical fashion. Each has splendid beaches, unexcelled snorkelling and scuba diving. As a group they are a fantasy for amateur sailing.

Hamilton Island was developed by Gold Coast property developer Keith Williams. Controversy surrounded the permission to convert the farming lease to a tourism venue during Joh Bjelke-Petersen's premiership. The resort was completed in 1986 and is currently a publicly held company managed by Holiday Inn. The Hamilton yacht race begins from the island in May.

Innisfail
Innisfail's opera festival in December and **Nerada tea plantation tours** (☎ 07 4064 5177, 28km west of town, daily between 09.00 and 16.30) add to its presence as the point of access to Dunk Island (see below).

A fascinating side trip from Innisfail is to travel west 17km on the small road into the South Johnstone River Valley, through gorgeous rainforest scenery, until you reach **Paronella Park**. The park's address is Japonvale Road (Old Bruce Highway), Mena Creek (☎ 07 4065 3225). As Dirk Flinthart describes it, the park is 'a bizarre monument to one Spaniard's homesickness'. It was built by Jose Paronella, a Catalonian who came to Australia in 1911 as a cane cutter. With his wife, he began to build Paronella Park in 1929; he opened it to the public in 1935, at which time it included a dance hall, a theatre, a tennis court, a tea garden and a children's playground. Paronella, alas, did not understand the area's tropical climate, and many of his concrete buildings were washed away by floods. Since he reinforced them with steel railway tracks, the buildings have now become rusty, and the wooden parts have been eaten away by termites. Consequently, the complex now looks like an old ruin in the middle of the rainforest. The gardens are particularly wonderful, with a 'Tunnel of Love' now filled with little bats leading to a waterfall, and rare rainforest plants that Paronella planted.

Dunk Island was the home of E.J. Banfield author of *The Confessions of a Beach-comber*, between 1897 and 1923. Having suffered something like a mental breakdown after some years' work as a journalist in Townsville, he retired to Dunk and took up natural history. His descriptions were instrumental in familiarising Australians with the beauties of the reef:

> ... *gardens of the sea, nymphs, wherein fancy feigns cool, shy, chaste faces and pliant forms half-revealed among gently swaying robes; a company of porpoise, a herd of dugong; turtle, queer and familiar fish, occasionally the spouting of a great whale, and always the company of swift and graceful birds.*

Today Dunk Island is three-quarters national park and the rest is resort development. Access to the island—the largest of the Family Group—is from Mission Beach, 5km away on the mainland. **Tourist information**: Mission Beach Tourist Information Centre, Porters Promenade, ☎ 07 4068 7099. The resort on the island is a popular but nice one (☎ 07 4068 8199), good for families, and there are still superb rainforests and beaches to enjoy. The island has over 150 species of birds, and most of the brilliant tropical butterflies associated with northern Queensland.

Cairns

Cairns (population 66,000), the next town of substance up the coast, is 1717km north of Brisbane. Writing in 1895, Archibald Meston praised its Trinity Inlet, as well as Port Curtis at Gladstone, as second only to Port Jackson (in Sydney Harbour) as the finest ports in Australia. In fact, Gladstone is a busier port than Sydney, shipping coal and alumina smelted from nearby Weipa's bauxite. As a port, Cairns shipped tin until about 1915. After the Second World War sugar came to prominence, but the real growth here was in tourism after the airport was built 4km north of town in 1984. **Tourist information**: on the corner of Sheridan and Aplin Streets; ☎ 07 4051 3588; Marine Parks Authority ☎ 07 4052 3092.

The boardwalk through a mangrove at the entrance to the airport sets the natural tone of the area. The town is a tourist centre, a backpackers' Mecca and a starting point for explorations of the tropical rainforests around the town. All activities can be booked at the visitor's centre.

Cairns sits on Trinity Inlet, described and named by Captain Cook on Trinity Sunday 1770. Like a number of northern Queensland ports, mineral export started the town in the 1880s, in this case tin from the Atherton Tablelands immediately to the west. Timber, cane and tableland agriculture supported the town prior to tourism.

The palm-lined coast extends north and south of town. Oceanward are **Arlington**, **Moore** and **Sudbury Reefs** and **Green Island National Park** (☎ 07 4052 3096) where visitors can scuba dive, snorkel or simply putter about in a glass-bottomed boat. Trips beyond the reef allow surfing in three metre breakers.

Rivers flowing from the **Atherton Tablelands** provide a chance to white-water raft or canoe. The **Daintree National Park** is an hour north. This is Australia's largest pristine rainforest and some of the world's oldest existing rainforest. Cruises on the Daintree River are in the Wet Tropics World Heritage Area; cruise operators abound between the small township at the edge of the park and the ferry. Ecotourism is saving this area from timber-felling operations. Visitors can even join bird-watching and bird-banding tours in the Daintree (Fine Feather Tours ☎ 07 4516 3493).

The **Tjapukal Aboriginal Dance Theatre** and **Menmuny Museum** present the area's Aboriginal community. The dance theatre (daily hour-long performances at 11.00, 13.30 and, on market days, at 12.15 as well) is in **Kuranda**, 27km northwest of Cairns, a town known for its Wednesday through Sunday craft markets. The most interesting way to get to Kuranda is by steam train. The tracks were laid in 1891 and pass through 15 tunnels. Book at the **Kuranda Scenic Railway** office in the Cairns railway station (☎ 07 4052 6249).

Port Douglas, 75km north of Cairns, is an upmarket, if casual, beach community much redeveloped by Christopher Skase in the 1980s. Skase escaped to Majorca, where he remains in exile from his creditors, perhaps a banking loss but a social gain for Australia. Its allure is from its four-mile (6.5km) beach (no waves or swells, of course, due to the nearby reef). Port Douglas is the kind of well-run and predictably tidy resort where people such as President Clinton stay when they holiday in Australia. **Tourist information**: 23 Macrossan Street, ☎ 07 4099 5599.

Cooktown

Cooktown (population 1300), 350km north of Cairns, is the departure point for touring Cape York. Captain Cook touched land here for repairs after running the *Endeavour* aground on the coral reef in 1770. His description of the kangaroo was written here (see p 621). The only river Cook named was Cooktown's Endeavour River. **Tourist information** is handled now by the Port Douglas centre.

Botanist Alan Cunningham visited the area in 1820, climbing the jungle-clad Mount Coongoon. Cooktown's settlement in 1873 was furthered by a brief gold rush in 1876, but the town's evacuation for fears of Japanese bombing during the Second World War nearly led to its demise. The Aboriginal name Carco surfaced repeatedly in early accounts referring to the harbour. Its **James Cook Historical Museum**, St Helen Street near Furneaux Street (☎ 07 4069 5386; open daily 09.30–16.30), presents a lucid history of the town, including the gold rush, riots against the Chinese during that period and the Aboriginal presence. The museum's building was erected in 1889 as the

The James Cook Historical Museum, Cooktown

Convent of St Mary and became North Queensland's first high school. During the Second World War, the US troops took over the convent as a command post, and the Sisters of Mercy never returned. The National Trust took over in 1969 and have created one of the best local history centres in Australia. The museum includes the original cannon and anchor from Captain Cook's ship *Endeavour*.

Rock art in northern Queensland

80km south of Cooktown is the **Quinkan Rock Art Gallery** on Aboriginal land near Springdale on the road to Lakeland and Laura. The Split Rock and Guguyalangi sites, 12km south of Laura, are the only galleries easily accessible to the public. The earliest examples here are the pecked geometric motifs in the Early Man shelter which date from about 13,000 years ago. Later pecked and engraved images (c 4000 years ago) portray tracks, designs and occasional human figures.

The most impressive works here are the post-contact rock paintings around **Laura River**. These present human figures, horses, and, most impressive, the mythological figures from which the area takes its name. The figures are generally plain solids in red ochre. Human figures and ancestral heroes are in red or yellow ochre or white clay and in-filled with spots, stripes or bars. The spidery figures with pendulous earlobes are Quinkan; the heavier figures, often with legs bent to their sides and branches coming from their heads, are Anurra.

Easiest access to the area generally and the rock art galleries specifically is with the *Trezise Bush Guide Service* (☎ 07 4060 3236) or through the *Quinkan Hotel* (☎ 07 4060 3255) at **Laura**. The hotel hosts an Aboriginal dance festival during the last weekend in June on odd-numbered years. This festival has attracted increasing numbers of participants and spectators recently. For more information, contact the Ang-Gnarra Aboriginal Corporation (☎ 07 4060 3214). Incidentally, the hotel was built in 1887 and features bushlore construction of timber and iron with exposed round posts. Its rooms are air-conditioned.

The rock art of the Mutumui People in the **Bathurst Bay** area of eastern Cape York revolves around the lives of cultural heroes Itjibiya and Almbarrin. Their burial site on Clack Island continues to have ritual significance to Mutumui males. The art on Stanley Island and at Bathurst Head is probably less culturally sensitive. In addition to incidents during the travels of Itjibiya and Almbarrin, the depictions are of butterflies, animals and humans.

Cane toads

Falling into the category of 'it seemed like a good idea at the time', cane toads (*Bufo marinus*) were introduced into Queensland from Central America in 1935 in a failed attempt to control the indigenous Frenchi and Greyback beetles whose grubs were infesting the cultivated sugar cane. While the toads do eat these beetles, they will not eat the grubs simply because they do not dwell on the ground, a fact that seemed to escape the attention of the authorities responsible for introducing the toad to Australia. The mature beetles propagate in cleared cane fields in daylight; the toads avoid sunlight, thus missing the breeding beetles as well as their grubs.

Not only do they prefer to eat just about everything else, but behind each eye they have a sack of poison. Contrary to most defence mechanisms, which give predators a chance to learn to avoid noisome or dangerous prey, any creature which eats these toads dies. When pressed, the glands can even squirt this poison as far as a metre.

Further, the toads are legendary breeders. Males mount long-dead road-killed females, preferring to breed even over food after starvation. The females lay remarkable quantities of eggs in any available water.

In an award-winning documentary written and directed by Mark Lewis entitled *Cane Toads: An Unnatural History* (1989), the toad's role in Queensland's ecology and society receives truly humorous treatment. Despite everything—the folly of the agricultural agents who introduced the pest, the danger the toads present to indigenous and domestic animals, their grotesque sexuality—any number of Queenslanders appreciate their adaptability, intelligence, and even patience when handled as playthings by children. They are reportedly moving south, and have been sighted in Sydney in 1999. Great efforts are being made to prevent their spread into Kakadu National Park, where the toad's impact on the natural environment would be particularly devastating.

Normanton

Situated 2152km northwest of Brisbane and 577km west of Innisfail on the Gulf of Carpentaria, **Normanton** (population 1150) is the major business centre for the gulf. It would not be worth mentioning as a place for visitors to stop except that it is the starting point for the *Gulflander*, the award-winning tourist train that travels between here and Croydon, 153km east of here.

Originally planned to link the river port at Normanton to the cattle stations around Cloncurry, the line was diverted to Croydon when huge gold reefs were discovered in the area in 1891. The route begins at the National Trust-registered Normanton railway station, built in 1891 and ends in Croydon three hours later. Contact Normanton Railway Station, ☎ 07 4745 1391. Both towns have interesting heritage-listed buildings dating from the gold rush times.

Acknowledgements

The favours done for us in the writing of this guide have been modest—neither transport, meals, nor commercial accommodation. When individuals have been supportive, however, their efforts have been thoughtful and energetic. First we need to thank all of Erika's colleagues in the Art History Department of the Australian National University, for moral support as well as practical assistance in the form of supplies, photocopy and fax access, and mailing facilities; Margaret Brown, Departmental Administrator, deserves a special mention for her unstinting patience and encouragement. Dr Paul Duro must also be singled out for his willingness to read several sections. Sylvia Deutsch, Grants Administrator for the Faculty, was tremendously creative and energetic in her attempts to find financial assistance for this project. As for Australian agencies, the greatest assistance was given to us by the National Roads and Motorists Association—the NRMA as it is known far and wide.

Other friends gave us varying degrees of help by allowing us to sleep on their floors, talking to us about Australianness, and offering suggestions on what to include and where to find information: Peter McNeil, Woollahra, NSW; Bruce and Diane Swalwell and family, Castlecrag and Pearl Beach, NSW; Di Lajuan Canberra; Dr Elisabeth Findlay, Townsville, QLD; Dr Dagmar Eichelberger, Melbourne, VIC, now Aachen, Germany; Ian Bulgin and Chantal Chalier, Balmain, NSW; Dr Roger Benjamin and Kate Sands, Parkville, VIC; Dr Greg Brophy, Peppermint Grove, WA; Dr Margaret Maynard, Brisbane, QLD; Dr David McNeill, College of Fine Arts, Sydney.

Pam Frost and Dennis Tongs, Canberra, gave us all kinds of insights into being Australian (and gave us photographs, too). Tony Cristofaro and his rabid band of footy fans at Fyshwick Markets, Canberra, ACT, taught us everything we could possibly hope to learn about Australian Rules Football. Margaret Shaw, Librarian of the National Gallery of Australia, and her wonderful staff deserve praise for many professional and personal services.

Dr John Chappell, former Professor, Division of Archaeology and Natural History, Research School of Pacific and Asian Studies, Australian National University, most graciously agreed to read and improve our geological and natural history sections. Mildred and Colin Campbell of Ballina, NSW, provided pertinent insights regarding Canberra's early history.

Andrew and Deb Bowman of Corryong, VIC, reminded us continually that the intelligent reader can be trusted to understand what we want to say.

Chris Pettman, Senior Travel Consultant for Tourism Tasmania, was most helpful, providing corrections to the section on Tasmania. Dr Joel Dando, itinerant humanist, formerly of Fremantle, WA, helped with information about Perth restaurants. Heather Harper, Heritage Unit, Brisbane City Department of Development and Planning, provided some much-needed records of building in Queensland. Kris Nielsen and Brian Fleming, North Adelaide, SA, had great insider information about their home state of South Australia.

Barry Cundy and Geoff Grey, both of the Australian Institute of Aboriginal and Torres Strait Islander Studies, Canberra, were most helpful on questions about Aboriginal culture (and about Melbourne!).

Virginia and Robin Wallace-Crabbe, Araluen, NSW and Canberra, deserve enormous thanks for sharing literary and cultural knowledge.

Wally Caruana, National Gallery of Australia, gave guidance on access to Aboriginal art.

Robyn Holland, Erika's sister, tracked down errant American phone numbers and the like. Ambassador and Mrs Stephan Toth, formerly Austrian Ambassador to Australia and now in Vienna, were wonderfully supportive and interested in this project.

Finally, our editor Gemma Davies can only be praised for tremendous patience and continuous assurances to us, especially in these final phases of production. Thank you!

Picture acknowledgements

All the photographs in the colour plate sections were provided by the Australian Tourist Commission, with the exception of *Cyclone Tracy* by Rover Thomas, reproduced by kind permission of the executors of the Rover Thomas Estate, and the *Aboriginal Memorial*, kind permission granted by the Ramingining Artists.

The illustrations on pages 2, 60, 61, 212, 371, 419 and 474 have been taken from the *Picturesque Atlas of Australia*.

The black and white photographs in the text are reproduced by permission of the Australian Heritage Commission. The photographers are gratefully acknowledged in the list below:

p 113 The History House, Sydney, by A. Pappas.
p 131 Fort Street School, Sydney, by D. Chapman.
p 139 Queen Victoria Building, Sydney, D. Chapman.
p 156 Ferry Wharf, Balmain, by D. Chapman.
p 165 Elizabeth Farm, Parramatta, Sydney, K. Charlton.
p 192 Detail of iron-work on the bandstand, King Edward Park, Newcastle, by J. Houldsworth.
p 277 Lanyon Homestead, by J. Houldsworth.
p 313 City Baths, Melbourne, by K. Charlton.
p 334 Como House, South Yarra, Melbourne, by P. Wright.
p 351 Corio Villa, Geelong, by P. Wright.
p 363 Burwood House, Portland, by P. Wright.
p 375 Reids Coffess Palace, Ballarat, by p. Wright.
p 434 Ross River Bridge, Tasmania, by Dr W. Nicholls.
p 440 Shotts Umbrella Shop, Launceston, by K. Charlton.
p 480 Elder Hall, Adelaide, by P. Wright.
p 482 Botanic Chambers Hotel, Adelaide, by K. Charlton.
p 492 Haebichs Cottage, Hahndorf, by Dr W. Nicholls.
p 502 Tanunda Museum, by P. Wright.
p 505 Collingrove near Yalumba, by P. Wright.
p 538 Old Court House, Perth, by P. Wright.
p 539 Town Hall, Perth, by P. Wright.
p 544 Old Mill, Perth, by P. Wright.
p 551 Woodbridge House, Midland, by M. Bourke
p 588 House at Myilly Point, Darwin, by Y. Webster.
p 639 Wolston House, Wacol, by M. Bourke.
p 652 Queens Hotel, Townsville, by M. Bourke.
p 653 Charters Towers street scene, by Australian Information Service.
p 657 James Cook Historical Museum, Cooktown, by Dr R. Bruce.

Index